Canada

The Original United States

(By Treaty with Great Britain, 1783)

5)

1810 1812-3 (By Treaty with Spain, 1819)

(Seized from Spain)

Florida

1783-1853

Political Consolidation of Half a Continent

Growth of the United States

A DIPLOMATIC HISTORY
OF THE
AMERICAN PEOPLE

THOMAS A. BAILEY
Stanford University

A Diplomatic History

of the

American People

Ninth Edition

Prentice-Hall, Inc., Englewood Cliffs, New Jersey

Library of Congress Cataloging in Publication Data

BAILEY, THOMAS ANDREW
   A diplomatic history of the American people.

   Includes bibliographies.
   1. United States—Foreign relations.   I. Title.
E183.7.B29 1974   327.73   74-8875
ISBN 0-13-214718-1

PRINTED IN THE UNITED STATES OF AMERICA

10   9   8   7   6   5   4   3

PRENTICE-HALL INTERNATIONAL, INC., *London*
PRENTICE-HALL OF AUSTRALIA, PTY. LTD., *Sydney*
PRENTICE-HALL OF CANADA, LTD., *Toronto*
PRENTICE-HALL OF INDIA PRIVATE LIMITED, *New Delhi*
PRENTICE-HALL OF JAPAN, INC., *Tokyo*

PREFACE TO THE SIXTH EDITION

THE FRIENDLY RECEPTION accorded this book during the past eighteen years has seemed to justify a stem-to-stern overhauling. The original approach and purposes remain the same. The volume is an introductory survey with emphasis on the role of American public opinion, and with de-emphasis on encyclopaedic detail. An effort has been made to write not only a "study book" but a "reading book" as well. There is considerable attention to main currents; to broad interpretations; to significant personalities; and to economic, political, and social developments intertwined with diplomacy. Some contemporary atmosphere has been recreated by numerous brief quotations from original sources. The general framework is still chronological, so that the reader may better follow the tides of public opinion as they rose and fell.

Specific changes in this edition will be of interest. Large sections, whole chapters, and countless paragraphs have been completely rewritten, not only to tighten the style but to incorporate the most recent scholarship. Some episodes that now seem less important have been telescoped; others have been expanded. There is a new introductory chapter on the machinery of diplomacy, and it incorporates some of the observations found in the last chapter of previous editions. The organization remains basically the same—a topical approach within a chronological skeleton—except that for the 1920's and 1930's events are now grouped topically into five chapters to avoid excessive fragmentation. A final new chapter brings events up to date, and a new Epilogue presents some food for thought.

Other changes may be noted. Some of the less striking quoted passages have been eliminated. The footnotes have been reduced in number and size. Informative or anecdotal material previously included in them has, when important enough, been melded with the text above. There are more and—in many cases—newer subheads. The overlong bibliographies, which came to resemble geological strata, have been consolidated and somewhat streamlined in the hope that they will be more useful to the student. All of the maps, including several new ones, have been drawn especially for this edition in an effective modern style. More cartoons have been added, and in many cases fresh substitutes have been found for the tired old standbys. Additional diagrammatic charts have been inserted. The glossary of diplomatic terminology has been slightly enlarged, and a new bibliographical Appendix lists some of the best books on given topics, arranged alphabetically by countries.

v

My enduring indebtedness to about one hundred fellow scholars for reading the original manuscript, or portions of it, has already been expressed, albeit inadequately, in previous editions. This list of academic creditors has swelled with the present edition. For valuable over-all suggestions, my sincere thanks go to Professor Paul H. Clyde, of Duke University; Professor Richard N. Current, of the Women's College, University of North Carolina; Professor Alexander DeConde, of the University of Michigan; President Frank E. Duddy, Jr., of Westminster College and formerly of the United States Naval Academy; Professor W. Stull Holt, of the University of Washington; Professor William W. Jeffries, of the United States Naval Academy; Professor Robert M. Langdon, of the United States Naval Academy; Professor Ernest R. May, of Harvard University; Professor Armin Rappaport, of the University of California; and Professor Arthur P. Whitaker, of the University of Pennsylvania. For criticizing chapters of the manuscript my thanks are also due to Professor Claude A. Buss, of Stanford University; Professor Wayne S. Cole, of Iowa State College; Professor Alexander DeConde, of the University of Michigan; Professor Norman A. Graebner, of the University of Illinois; Professor Robert M. Langdon, of the United States Naval Academy; Professor Bradford Perkins, of the University of California at Los Angeles, Professor Raymond G. O'Connor, of Stanford University; Professor Per Goran Ohlin, of Stanford University; Professor Daniel M. Smith, of the University of Colorado; Professor Ivor D. Spencer, of Kalamazoo College; Professor Graham H. Stuart, of Stanford University; and Professor Wayne S. Vucinich, of Stanford University. The listing of these names does not imply approval or endorsement; it is merely a most inadequate way of expressing my lasting gratitude. I must also record my thanks to Mrs. Celeste C. McKee for invaluable secretarial services.

Some wag has remarked, with obvious exaggeration, that fortunately most diplomats have long noses, for they usually cannot see beyond the ends of them. Every citizen in a democracy like the United States is a diplomat, whether he knows it or not. This book is offered in the hope that at least in some slight degree it may help extend the mental visibility of those citizen-diplomats who read it.

Stanford University, California   THOMAS A. BAILEY

PREFACE TO THE SEVENTH EDITION

I HAVE UNDERTAKEN to do the following: (1) to update all end-chapter bibliographies; (2) to provide an extensive Bibliographical Addendum to accommodate the overflow for which there was no room at the ends of the chapters; (3) to supply a brief analysis of most of the new books and articles; (4) to make all necessary corrections and to change a number of statements that needed revision in the light of more recent scholarship; (5) to prepare two new chapters, with illustrations and maps, covering the events from 1957 through mid-1963; (6) to expand the alphabetically arranged General Bibliography in Appendix E; and (6) to revise and expand the index. Altogether I have made changes of one kind or another, mostly minor, on about 180 of the original plates.

As before, I am deeply indebted to a host of scholars for their published contributions. I am particularly grateful to the following colleagues for a critical reading of all or substantial parts of the new chapters: Dr. Claude A. Buss, Dr. Peter J. Duignan, Dr. Wayne S. Vucinich, all of Stanford University, as well as Dr. Thomas F. McGann, of the University of Texas.

THOMAS A. BAILEY

Stanford University, California

PREFACE TO THE EIGHTH EDITION

THE GENERAL PATTERN of revision follows almost precisely that for the seventh edition. I have kept the overflow bibliographies exceptionally full and informative, and have substantially expanded the General Bibliography in Appendix E. I have added a new chapter on the Johnson Administration and substantially revised the Epilogue. Altogether I have made additional changes of some kind, mostly minor, on about 200 of the original plates.

I am grateful for expert advice to Dr. Claude A. Buss, Dr. John J.

Johnson, and George S. Rentz, all colleagues at Stanford University, and also to two former doctoral students: Dr. Charles A. Lofgren, of Claremont Men's College, and Dr. Raymond G. O'Connor, of Temple University. I am also indebted to several sharp-eyed correspondents for corrections or other suggested improvements, particularly Dr. Allen Bowman, of Marion College, Marion, Indiana. George D. Bullock, an advanced doctoral candidate, rendered superb research assistance.

THOMAS A. BAILEY

Stanford University, California

PREFACE TO THE NINTH EDITION

THE PREPARATION of this new edition has followed the same general guidelines that were used for the seventh and eighth editions. The most obvious new material consists of the added chapter on the Nixon administration and the updated and expanded bibliographies, including the overflow in the appendix. My impulse was to trim and compress the bibliographies in the interests of saving space, but I was urged not to do so by many scholars who have found this feature of the book highly useful. Naturally, I have changed a number of pages in the original text to square with the findings of the most recent objective scholarship.

I am much indebted to the following colleagues in the profession for information, suggestions, or criticism: Barton J. Bernstein, Claude A. Buss, Stephen M. Dobbs, John K. Emmerson, Wilton B. Fowler, Norman A. Graebner, Charles A. Lofgren, Raymond G. O'Connor, George S. Rentz, Paul B. Ryan, Harold W. Thatcher, Lyman P. Van Slyke, and Wayne S. Vucinich.

THOMAS A. BAILEY

Stanford University, California

CONTENTS

MAPS AND CHARTS

A DIPLOMATIC HISTORY
OF THE
AMERICAN PEOPLE

WHEN foreign affairs were ruled by autocracies or oligarchies the danger of war was in sinister purpose. When foreign affairs are ruled by democracies the danger of war will be in mistaken beliefs. The world will be the gainer by the change, for, while there is no human way to prevent a king from having a bad heart, there is a human way to prevent a people from having an erroneous opinion. That way is to furnish the whole people, as a part of their ordinary education, with correct information about their relations to other peoples, about the limitations upon their own rights, about their duties to respect the rights of others, about what has happened and is happening in international affairs, and about the effects upon national life of the things that are done or refused as between nations; so that the people themselves will have the means to test misinformation and appeals to prejudice and passion based upon error.

EX-SECRETARY OF STATE ELIHU ROOT
Foreign Affairs, I, 5 (September, 1922).

CHAPTER

I

Factors, Forces, and Functions

Since the time when Thomas Jefferson insisted upon a "decent respect to the opinions of mankind," public opinion has controlled foreign policy in all democracies.

SECRETARY OF STATE HULL, 1936

TAP-ROOT FOREIGN POLICIES

THE ACID-TONGUED American ambassador in London, George Harvey, was quoted in 1923 as saying that "the national American foreign policy is to have no foreign policy." This sneer has been repeated countless times. What such critics usually mean is that they do not approve of existing policy, or that no ready-made formula exists to deal with an unexpected crisis, such as the sudden seizure of the Suez Canal by Egypt in 1956.

The plain truth is that the United States has always had fundamental foreign policies or objectives, whether farsighted or shortsighted, successful or unsuccessful. A half-dozen or so of them have persisted for well over a century. In some cases these objectives or policies, notably "no-entangling alliances," were pursued with a blind devotion long after the reasons for their existence had passed, and when their continued existence did positive harm. Few, if any, of the great powers can point to such a large body of traditional policy adhered to so tenaciously over so many decades.

In the United States, as in any true democracy, public opinion shapes basic foreign policies. They are not cooked up secretly in the State Department and then sprung overnight on the country. Sprouting from the fertile soil of experience, they represent the needs, interests, and hopes of the people. A partial list of such needs and aspirations would include peace, security, neutrality, justice, freedom, humanitarianism,

1

territorial elbow room, commercial prosperity, and opportunity for investment and trade abroad. Peace, for example, is not a foreign policy but the *objective* of a foreign policy.

Six of the most important traditional or fundamental foreign policies are:

1. *Isolation,* meaning originally, "We'll keep out of Europe's broils." Actually, it broke down into nonintervention, noninvolvement, and no-entangling alliances. Objectives: peace, neutrality, prosperity, security.

2. *Freedom of the seas,* meaning originally, "Hands off our merchant ships." Objectives: prosperity, neutrality, security.

3. *The Monroe Doctrine,* meaning originally, "Europe, you stay out of America." Objectives: peace, security, freedom, prosperity.

4. *Pan-Americanism,* meaning originally, "Let's get together, we republics of the Western Hemisphere." Objectives: prosperity, peace, security, freedom.

5. *The Open Door,* meaning originally, "A fair field for American businessmen in competition with other foreigners abroad, particularly in China." Objectives: prosperity, peace, justice, security, humanitarianism.

6. *The peaceful settlement of disputes,* meaning originally, "Let's negotiate or arbitrate our differences." Objectives: peace, security, justice.

Not all of these fundamental policies were consistently upheld during the 19th Century, but generally they were. In addition, there have been dozens of secondary or tertiary policies that have existed for shorter periods to cope with specific situations. Among them would be disarmament, imperialism, nonrecognition, commercial reciprocity, expatriation, Dollar Diplomacy, Good Neighborism, and containment. Some of these secondary policies are becoming, or have become, fundamental policies.

Much confusion has arisen because the same policy has often been applied in different ways in different parts of the globe. For example, noninvolvement wore three faces in the 19th Century:

1. *Nonintervention in Europe*—where America was too weak to risk entanglement with the great powers.

2. *Intervention in Latin America*—where the United States, particularly in its Caribbean danger zone, was strong enough to twist the arms of weak Latin neighbors and head off possible European intervention.

3. *Co-operation in the Far East*—where the United States collaborated with the major powers in upholding the Open Door, simply because it did not have the strength there to "go it alone."

Thus national self-interest—the very mainspring of all foreign policy—has caused the nation to become involved in contradictions that are otherwise unexplainable.

IMPLEMENTING *VERSUS* TRADITIONAL POLICIES

In the military world, grand strategy must be carried out by detailed tactics; in the diplomatic world, fundamental policy must be carried out by implementing policies. The American people themselves, by expressing their attitudes and desires, decide fundamental policies or objectives. The Executive branch, by framing specific courses of action, provides implementing policies or tactics.

Shortly after World War II, the American people were so deeply alarmed by Soviet aggressions that they overwhelmingly favored a get-tough-with-Russia course. This came to be a fundamental postwar policy. But the people themselves could not devise a specific course of action. This was the responsibility of President Truman, who worked in close collaboration with the State Department, with the leaders of Congress, with military experts, and with other advisers.[1] The net result was the famed Truman Doctrine of 1947, designed to save Greece and Turkey from a Communist take-over.

The American public is like a back-seat driver. It knows in general where it wants to go, and it voices views which in turn lead to fundamental policies or objectives. But the public is not well enough informed to tell the driver—the Executive branch—precisely what roads or turns to take. These must be charted in Washington by implementing policies. And once the specific routes have been chosen, the public should be careful not to joggle the elbow of the driver by ignorant or misguided interference.

If the ordinary American wants to know who shapes fundamental foreign policy, all he has to do is look into a mirror. The story is somewhat different regarding issues of secondary importance. The President and the State Department, with various advisers, are forced to devise policies that they think will square with the basic desires of the electorate. If they fly in the face of popular desires, they run the risk of being thrown out of office at the next election—and this is a risk that few administrations wish to incur.

The classic example is the Spanish-American War of 1898—an unnecessary and trouble-brewing conflict of immense significance. President McKinley did not want war; the State Department did not want war; Big Business did not want war. But the people did—and so violent were their demands that they forced McKinley to give in to them.

---

[1] The National Security Act of 1947, among other things, set up an important advisory board in the National Security Council, consisting now of the President, the Vice-President, the Secretaries of State and Defense, and several other key civilian advisers concerned with foreign and military affairs.

The sovereign voter is ever at the elbows of the policy-makers in Washington. They will sometimes attempt to educate public opinion to a new course, as Woodrow Wilson belatedly tried to do with the League of Nations. They will sometimes try to deceive it into an awareness of what they regard as its best interests, as Franklin Roosevelt attempted to do on the eve of Pearl Harbor. They will occasionally defy it, as Grover Cleveland did in regard to intervention in Cuba—after he had already served most of his two terms. But they defy public opinion only at their peril.

FUNDAMENTAL FACTORS

Peculiar conditions in America, some of them unique, have profoundly influenced the thinking of the citizenry regarding foreign policy. The most significant have been:

1. *Geographical position.* Physical separation from Europe and Asia enabled the United States to pursue, notably in the 19th Century, an isolationist course. The two oceans have been referred to as America's greatest "liquid assets." They were of incalculable importance during the adolescent days of the republic, when the United States was too weak to risk involvement in outside affairs, and when it was forced to play for time and let its birth rate fight its battles for it. Physical separation from warlike Europe in the 19th Century also enabled the American people to escape crushing armaments burdens.

2. *Weak neighbors.* During the national period, though not in the colonial period, America enjoyed the boon of weak neighbors, both north and south. It did not have to fear attacks from them; they had to fear attacks from it. The witty Jules Jusserand, French ambassador in Washington from 1902 to 1925, once quipped that America was blessed among the nations. On the north, she had a weak neighbor; on the south, another weak neighbor; on the east, fish; on the west, fish. This enviable situation enabled the United States to avoid burdensome standing armies in the 19th Century, and to escape being used as a makeweight in an American balance of power manipulated by European imperialists.

3. *Room for expansion.* The American colonists were fortunate in securing a beachhead on the eastern fringe of a virgin continent. When the British sought elbow room, they had to expand overseas—and that was "imperialism." When the Americans sought elbow room, they merely moved west—and that was just normal expansionism. When they brushed aside or killed Mexicans and Indians, they felt that they were merely responding to their "Manifest Destiny." They thus acquired rich and thinly inhabited territories without having to fight long and exhausting wars.

4. *"Hyphenated" Americans.* The United States is a nation of immi-

grants or the descendants of immigrants. Most of the older stock has lost its sentimental ties with the Mother Country, but the newer stock has retained ancient loyalties. When wars, revolutions, and persecutions have convulsed the homeland, Irish-hyphen-Americans, German-hyphen-Americans, Polish-hyphen-Americans, Jewish-hyphen-Americans, and others have brought pressure on the Washington government to shape foreign policy in their interests. The result has been that the United States has often not been able to speak to the outside world with the authority of one voice. When King Saud of Saudi Arabia, whose role in the Suez crisis was of vital concern to Washington, was invited to the United States in 1957, New York refused to give him a royal welcome. Mayor Wagner was quoted as saying that this Moslem potentate was anti-Jewish and anti-Catholic—all of which was a crude appeal to the prejudices of the hyphenated voters.

5. *A mercantile and industrial people.* The United States, with its fine harbors and other priceless advantages, was from the earliest days a maritime nation, vitally interested in freedom of the seas. Late in the 19th Century it became a leading industrial and financial power, with a lively concern for the Open Door for American traders and investors abroad. The relative economic self-sufficiency of the United States naturally strengthened its independence of spirit.

6. *A democracy.* The devotion of the American people to the democratic ideal colored the national psychology, and caused the United States to adopt a hostile, chip-on-the-shoulder attitude toward monarchs and dictators. This same state of mind also led to an active sympathy for liberal movements the world over.

7. *Primacy of domestic affairs.* Sheltered behind two billowing oceans and involved in the back-straining task of conquering a continent, the American people in the 19th Century were generally indifferent to foreign affairs. Circumstances were such that mistakes in diplomacy were not too costly, and one result was a poorly paid foreign service. During the first century-and-a-quarter of the nation's existence, there was only one period when foreign affairs vied with domestic affairs for primary attention—and that was during the upheaval of the French Revolution and the Napoleonic wars. The picture changed sharply after 1914, and especially after 1939, when foreign affairs came to rival or eclipse domestic affairs.

8. *Europe's distresses.* During the 19th Century, the great powers of Europe were not in a position to "gang up" on the United States. Deadlocked in wars or in delicately poised balances of power, they seldom had a completely free hand to interfere with America. On critical occasions they were sometimes forced to make important concessions to the United States in order to purchase an advantage in dealing with a European rival. Europe's distresses thus contributed to many of America's

most spectacular diplomatic successes, and the republic unwisely began to rely upon them as a first line of defense.

MILITARY POLICY—HANDMAIDEN OF FOREIGN POLICY

The intimate relationship between foreign policy and military policy is only dimly recognized, if at all, by the American people. This was painfully true in the 19th Century.

Americans have been habitually unprepared for all of their major wars. A peace-loving people with nonaggressive tendencies is never ready. Dictators like Hitler and Mussolini are always better prepared; they know when they are going to strike. Chronic American unpreparedness has also flowed from a hatred of taxes, a nonmilitary tradition, a distrust of large standing armies, a heavy dependence on ocean barriers, and an overreliance on Europe's distresses to fight America's battles. Finally, there has been an exaggerated belief that America won all of her wars, including the stalemated War of 1812, without any indirect or direct foreign aid.

In the 19th Century, and even somewhat later, the United States relied upon the navy as its first line of defense. The tiny regular army was to be supplemented by militia and volunteers when emergencies arose. The theory was that the navy would beat the enemy off the American coasts, and one unfortunate result of this concept was the burning of Washington in 1814 by the British invaders. Near the close of the century, thanks to the influential writings of Captain A. T. Mahan, a new concept won acceptance. Instead of beating the enemy off its doorstep, the United States would build enough powerful warships to command adjacent seas. Thus the foe could be met some distance from America's shores—or, better yet, he might be deterred from going to war altogether. If the United States had boasted a considerably larger navy in 1812, and a considerably larger army in 1917, both the British and the Germans probably would have avoided a shooting showdown.

The nation's armed forces exist for two basic purposes: (a) to provide national defense (b) to uphold foreign policy. The size of armaments should be proportioned to the scope of the foreign policies that the nation has enunciated and proposes to uphold. Policy without power is impotent. When the United States had only one coast, it needed only a small navy; when it had acquired global responsibilities, it needed immense forces. The authors of a wise foreign policy, like the authors of a wise financial policy, will not take on commitments that cannot be covered in a pinch. Otherwise both may go bankrupt. One basic shortcoming of American policy in the Far East between 1898 and 1941 was that the United States never amassed sufficient strength to defend its Philippine Islands against a determined Japanese attack.

Adequate armed forces also serve as a deterrent. In 1941 the ill-fated Pacific fleet was stationed at Pearl Harbor, primarily to restrain Japan. Alarmists complained then, and critics charged after the disaster, that the ships would have been safer at San Diego, California. They would have been even safer in the Chesapeake Bay, where their deterrent power would have been virtually nil. In short, armed forces are not supposed to exist in a vacuum, but to support the basic aims of national defense and foreign policy.

THE EXECUTIVE AND FOREIGN AFFAIRS

The President of the United States, although designated by the Constitution as commander-in-chief of the armed forces, is not specifically authorized to be director-in-chief of foreign affairs. But he is by implication, and his powers in this capacity have become globe-shaking.

The President is empowered to make treaties, "by and with the advice and consent of the Senate." He may also negotiate Executive agreements, although not specifically authorized to do so by the Constitution, such as the destroyer-base deal with Britain in 1940. These understandings do not require the approval of the Senate: they merely pledge the word of the incumbent Executive. His successors may or may not feel bound by such commitments.

The President may also sever diplomatic relations, as Wilson did in 1917, when he gave orders that the German ambassador in Washington be handed his passports. Such a step is normally the prelude to war.

The President may recognize new governments, as Franklin Roosevelt recognized Russia in 1933 after a delay of sixteen years, and as Harry S. Truman recognized Israel *de facto* in 1948 after a delay of eleven minutes. Conversely, the President may hold a diplomatic club over a foreign regime by refusing to recognize it, as Truman and Eisenhower did over Communist China.

The President is empowered by the Constitution to nominate ambassadors and other important foreign envoys, who in turn must receive Senate confirmation. He may also informally appoint special representatives known as executive agents, who do not require Senate confirmation. Several hundred of these shadowy figures, including President Wilson's self-effacing Colonel House, have served in various capacities at various times.

The President may denounce treaties—that is, give formal notice of their termination. Franklin Roosevelt, acting through the State Department in 1939, terminated the Japanese Treaty of 1911, preparatory to clearing the way for a munitions embargo six months later.

The President ordinarily serves as the mouthpiece of the United States in enunciating foreign policy, as Monroe did in 1823 in connection with the Monroe Doctrine. He may also send direct appeals to the heads of foreign states, as Franklin Roosevelt did when he appealed to Hitler and Mussolini in 1938, in a dramatic effort to avert World War II.

The President is also commander-in-chief of the armed forces, which must go where he orders them. He may provoke a war, as Polk did in 1846, when he sent troops into an area in Texas claimed by Mexico. He may wage a war, as Truman did in 1950, when he ordered the armed forces into Korea. But he cannot formally declare war; only Congress can. Yet Congress sometimes finds itself compelled to rubber-stamp warlike situations created by the Executive, who, over the years, has landed troops more than one hundred times on foreign soil without Congressional authorization.

All these powers are enormous, and they call for wide knowledge and experience. But unfortunately, the President has ordinarily had little or no direct contact with foreign affairs before entering the White House. (See Appendix C). As the head of a great political party, he is primarily concerned with domestic affairs—civil rights, inflation, housing—and only secondarily with foreign affairs. A great banking chain would risk failure if it handed over its management to an ex-lawyer or an ex-general, but the American people will enthusiastically elevate an inexperienced man to their highest office. They are quite willing to entrust their public affairs to rank amateurs whom they would not think of entrusting with their private affairs.

Fortunately, the President has usually revealed executive capacity in other fields, and he can adjust to his new duties fairly well. He can also turn to an unlimited number of experienced advisers. But the disquieting fact remains that the public normally entrusts the handling of diplomatic dynamite to men who are not professional handlers of dynamite.

THE SECRETARY OF STATE

The principal agency for conducting foreign affairs is the Department of State, with the Secretary of State at its head. Like his chief the President, the Secretary has traditionally been completely innocent of experience in foreign affairs before coming to the headship of the foreign office. (See Appendix D). Sometimes he has received his high post as a reward for outstanding service to the party, as was partly true of Daniel Webster; sometimes the Secretaryship has been a "consolation prize" for men who failed to attain the White House, as was notably true of James G. Blaine and William J. Bryan. But since 1944 there has been less of a tendency to appoint dominant political figures as Secretary of State.

The extent to which the Secretary of State is in the driver's seat usually depends on the temperament of the Chief Executive. Strong Presidents tend to dominate their associates. This was notably true of President

Wilson, who hammered out many documents on his own typewriter, and then sent them out over the signature of Secretary Lansing, whom Wilson regarded as a kind of "administrative assistant."

The inexperience and short tenure of the Secretary of State have been largely offset by the presence of an able and permanent career staff within the Department of State. William Hunter, who entered the Department in 1829, served for fifty-seven years, eventually becoming Second Assistant Secretary of State. His remarkable career overlapped that of Alvey A. Adee, who came in 1878, rose to the rank of Second Assistant Secretary, and died in 1924, after serving for forty-seven consecutive years. Deaf, retiring, unmarried, Adee would install a cot in his office when the pressure of work became intense. For some thirty years, scarcely a written communication went out from the Department that he had not passed upon or drafted with his facile red-inked pen. From 1829 to 1924, a period of nearly one hundred years, either Hunter or Adee was at hand as walking encyclopaedias of precedent, international law, and diplomatic procedure. The green politicians in the Secretary's seat were well served.

Yet the handicap of inexperience has been less serious than might be supposed. The Secretary of State has ordinarily been a man of unusual ability, often one who has made his mark in law or politics. The same talents that enabled him to attain eminence in one walk of life have often enabled him to adjust successfully to another. An outstanding domestic lawyer can, with a minimum of difficulty, acquire the rudiments of international law. Furthermore, crises have often brought experience to the fore: big events tend to call forth big men. During the critical years of the French Revolution and the Napoleonic Wars, either the Secretaries of State or the Presidents or both were old hands at diplomacy. When the menacing war clouds passed in Europe and Jacksonian democracy dawned, America could once more afford to run the risks of inexperience in high office.

DIPLOMATIC AGENTS ABROAD

The Department of State has expanded phenomenally, like a growing boy constantly bursting his breeches. In 1789 it had six employees; by the 1970's, about 40,000. It has endured repeated reorganizations, and the scope of its activities has widened incredibly, even to include propaganda functions. But its underlying purpose remains the same—to provide the machinery for carrying out the foreign policy of the United States.

Until 1924 the agents of the State Department abroad fell into two categories. The first were the diplomatic officers, who were stationed at embassies or legations in foreign capitals. The second were the consular officers, who were stationed at consulates in important seaports or other commercial centers. There they discharged various duties, including the processing of immigration forms and sending home the clothing of dead seamen. The diplomatic officers, with a degree of snobbery, tended to look down their noses at the lowly consular officers. A gratifying change for the better came with the Rogers Act of 1924, which merged the diplomatic and consular services and formally ended the second-class status of consuls.

The highest ranking officer in the American diplomatic service used to be a minister, whose place of business is called a legation.[2] But in 1893, in recognition of the growing prestige of the United States, Congress created the higher rank of ambassador. His place of business is called an embassy. The United States missions in foreign capitals are now served by ambassadors rather than ministers; the lower rank for this purpose was abandoned in the 1960's.

A primary duty of the American diplomat abroad, say in Moscow, is to gather data that will help the officials in Washington to formulate an effective policy regarding the Soviet Union. As a kind of licensed spy, he sends home information in the form of dispatches, either by wire or by diplomatic pouch. The diplomat must thus be a crack reporter—the eyes, ears, and nose of his government. He must report fully and honestly what he discovers, and make his recommendations fearlessly. This explains why he should mingle freely with the people, and why he is handicapped if he cannot speak their language. Yet Americans have long been notoriously deficient as linguists, especially the political appointees. Some years ago an ambassador who was sent to a South American country reputedly knew only two words of Spanish—"si, si."

Entertainment is an important duty of the American diplomat, just as it is of a traveling salesman. The more people the ambassador ingratiates himself with, the better he can do his job. Many an important bit of information is dropped over the fourth cocktail, and a well-dined Foreign Secretary may prove to be in a more amiable mood the next day than one who is not. Cynics have defined a diplomat as an "honest man sent to lie abroad for his country." He might perhaps better be defined as a man sent abroad "to dine for his country," sometimes on stewed cat. Many a diplomat, cursed with the occupational disease of dyspepsia, has regretted that he had only one stomach to give for his country.

Yet the American people, although admittedly a nation of salesmen, take a cheese-paring approach to foreign-service expense accounts. The public does not expect an admiral to provide the oil for his fleet, but it expects the ambassador to provide diplomatic oil for his embassy. A number of small and poor nations, some of them depending on economic aid from Washington, actually outshine the ambassador of the rich United States in the social whirl of foreign capitals.

[2] For a glossary of similar diplomatic terms, see Appendix A.

GOVERNMENTS SPEAKING TO GOVERNMENTS

A prime duty of the American diplomat is to carry out orders that have been cabled or mailed to him in the form of "instructions" from Washington. Just as the military man must obey orders, so the diplomat must obey orders. A cardinal sin of the diplomat in the field is to violate instructions, as Robert R. Livingston and James Monroe reluctantly did in 1803, when they arranged for the bargain-basement purchase of Louisiana in Paris. But this was before the days of the cable, which has greatly simplified the task of the diplomat. Now he can report immediately to the State Department, and receive new instructions in the light of changed conditions.

The government in Washington may conduct diplomatic negotiations in several ways. The most common method is for the Secretary of State, for example, to send instructions to the American ambassador in Paris, who in turn communicates them to the French Foreign Minister. Another method is for the President or the Secretary of State to deal directly, for example, with the Japanese ambassador in Washington, and he in turn receives instructions from Tokyo, as Ambassador Nomura did in 1941 on the eve of Pearl Harbor. Such written exchanges in Washington are known as "notes." Another method, increasingly common, is for the President or the Secretary of State to meet personally with his opposite number, as Franklin Roosevelt dramatically did with Winston Churchill on a warship off Newfoundland at the time of framing the Atlantic Charter in 1941.

Regrettably, there is no intercontinental loud-speaker through which one people may communicate directly with another. President Wilson at Paris appealed directly to the Italians in 1919, but his voice was not the voice of a united nation. Diplomatic intercourse must be undertaken through regularly constituted officials. Even where attempts have been made to propagandize the Communists by short-wave radio, noisy "jamming" has often choked off the message. If the American people could speak directly to the Russian people, without official propaganda stifling their voices, the outlook for amity would be immensely improved.

STARVING THE FOREIGN SERVICE

The American foreign service in the 19th Century was traditionally ill-chosen, ill-trained, ill-paid, ill-housed, ill-co-ordinated, and under-manned. Enheartening strides forward have come in recent decades, but historically this dismal picture remains correct.

The shameful neglect of the foreign service is not difficult to explain. During most of the 19th Century, and even later, foreign affairs did not seem vital. The people were preoccupied or indifferent, and many red-blooded democrats regarded the whole "striped-pants brigade" as an expensive and unnecessary carry-over from effete monarchies. The feeling was not uncommon that if diplomatic negotiations were necessary, the other nation could send over its own stuffed shirts.

The frugal habits of a poor and struggling republic have clung to a rich and mighty power. The American people, who are willing to spend billions for the Department of Defense, are reluctant to spend the pennies that would spell the difference between an outstanding foreign service and one that is constantly pinched. The Department of State is the Department of Peace. The right man in the right place at the right time may prevent a war that will cost more in a few minutes than the entire foreign service costs in a year. If the American people were fully alive to the immense importance of the diplomatic arm, they would insist that Congress provide it with the necessary financial sinews. As it is, American diplomats have been paid poorly in money and richly in abuse when things go wrong. The anti-Communist witch hunt in the 1950's, for example, shattered the morale of the State Department, and almost ruined its recruitment program. Many a bright young man reluctantly suppressed his love for the foreign service and turned to the law or some other less hazardous calling.

Until belated improvements in recent years, the American legation or embassy in a foreign country often lacked dignity in appearance or location. Congress, responding to the penny-pinching demands of the electorate, was unwilling to provide adequate quarters, although two score or more ornate embassies could have been built for the price of a modern warship. American envoys were forced to rent buildings for limited periods, often in undesirable parts of a capital, sometimes, as in Paris, above a grocery store or, as in Rome, above a wineshop—with attendant flies and odors. Ambassador Page, on coming to London in 1913, found the quarters of his predecessor "a cheap hole."

A lack of permanent location for the legation or embassy was still another handicap. The constant change of locale, keeping pace with differing pocketbooks and political overturns in Washington, hampered the conduct of business. By contrast, relatively poor nations have long had permanent embassies on Massachusetts Avenue in Washington. Many an American envoy has had to spend much of his time legation-hunting, and then renovate his new quarters out of his own pocket, as millionaire Henry White did in Paris to the tune of $35,000. A famous English caricature showed a London policeman approaching the house-hunting American ambassador, Joseph Choate, as the latter wearily clung to a lamppost one dismal night. When the officer requested him to move on home, he replied, "Home! home! I have no home. I am the American ambassador."

PLAYBOYS, PLUTOCRATS, AND POLITICIANS

Conditions were much worse before World War I than they are today. Scores of top-flight men were forced to decline foreign appointments— men like President C. W. Eliot of Harvard—simply because they did not have enough supplementary income or could not afford to sacrifice their life savings. The supreme irony was that the American democracy was often represented abroad by a snobbish plutocracy. Many of these "cooky-pushers" and "tea gladiators" were playboy sons of aristocratic families, educated at Harvard, Yale, and Princeton, and inclined to regard the foreign service as their own private club.

Politics also polluted the foreign service, and still does to some extent. Some men have been sent abroad to get them out of the country, notably Secretary of War Simon Cameron, whom President Lincoln shipped off to Russia in 1862 when odorous scandals began to develop in the War Department. Rich politicians, some of whom have cleverly contributed to the campaign coffers of both parties, have long been given high preference for important posts. A wealthy Democrat, James J. Van Alen, donated some $50,000 to Cleveland's campaign chest in 1892. Having thus "bought" an office, he was appointed minister to Italy but did not serve. One unhappy result of having purely political appointees was a disconcerting turnover in the foreign service. The brilliant Jules Jusserand served France in Washington for twenty-three consecutive years; during the same period there were nine different American ambassadors in Paris.

The appointment of political hacks or wealthy amateurs to high diplomatic office sometimes brought disgrace to the service. Most of the appointees were inexperienced, many were inept, some were uncouth, and a few were drunkards. John Randolph, when presented to the Russian Czar, is supposed to have blurted out, "Howaya, Emperor? How's the Madam?" The absence of diplomatic finesse, together with ignorance of protocol, often led to a bluntness and brusqueness that caused American techniques to be branded as "shirt-sleeve diplomacy." A low point in rough-and-readyism was reached when an American envoy in a Caribbean republic officially received callers in a flaming red-flannel undershirt.

Even today, with the emphasis on salaried career men, a substantial minority of America's diplomatic appointments could be classed as political. Incredibly enough, this haphazard system of selecting representatives has turned out better than one might expect. Many of the appointees have been men who have made fortunes in business or law, and their ability has been so marked that they often adapted themselves to their new duties surprisingly well. They also have had the advantage of a permanent staff of counselors or secretaries at the legation or embassy. Even the highly professionalized diplomatic services of Europe have sent some incredible blunderers to America's shores. In the early days of the republic a French minister in Washington, who habitually beat his wife, employed a fife player to drown out her piteous cries. But the "you're another" shortcomings of others should not be used to gloss over American deficiencies. Ideally, as Ambassador Page remarked in 1913, "We'd train the most capable male babies we have from the cradle."

PROGRESS WITH THE BRAKES ON

Enheartening changes for the better have come in recent decades. The Rogers Act of 1924 introduced the merit system by providing for a career service based on competitive examinations, written and oral. The Porter Foreign Service Buildings Act of 1926 launched a large-scale and long-overdue program of construction. The Foreign Service Act of 1946, among other improvements, substantially increased salaries and expense accounts ("representation allowances"). All these reforms, in the view of one leading expert, were sufficient to provide the United States with a foreign service "as good as any in the world." [3] As of 1956, about two-thirds of the heads of missions in foreign capitals were professionals. Most of them could live and entertain with reasonable dignity on their salaries and expense allowances. Congress, at long last, was grudgingly prepared to recognize the wisdom of the Japanese schoolboy: "Poverty are no disgrace for Methodist Minister, but for Foreign Minister it are a crime."

Yet there are still glaring inequalities. At some of the ambassadorial posts the American envoy must have private income with which to supplement governmental funds. The traditional social obligations at London, for example, have been such as to require additional out-of-pocket sums amounting to about three times the ambassador's salary and allowances. This meant that only a favored plutocracy could represent America's classless democracy at the major capitals, as is still the case to some extent. The first question that the President had to ask about a prospective appointee did not relate to his ability or experience but to his private wealth—whether inherited, married, or made. "It's a damned mean outfit, your American government," a Britisher remarked to Ambassador Walter H. Page in 1914.

THE SENATE AND FOREIGN AFFAIRS

Congress has come to play an increasingly vital role in foreign affairs, and of the two houses the Senate is by far the more important. The

[3] H. M. Wriston, *Diplomacy in a Democracy* (New York, 1956), p. 43.

President should keep in intimate contact with its leaders, including those of both parties, if he wishes to pursue a genuine bipartisan foreign policy. The most coveted chairmanship in the Senate has traditionally been that of the Committee on Foreign Relations. Some of the men who have held this post—figures like Charles Sumner and Henry Cabot Lodge—have exercised such great power that they have been referred to as "the second Secretary of State." The rule of "seniority"—perhaps "senility" in some cases—has sometimes brought to this key position Senators of limited vision but unlimited vocal power. Some, like Sumner, have acted as though their thunderous epithets could not be heard beyond the three-mile line.

The Senate enjoys varied powers in the field of foreign relations. It confirms—occasionally rejects—Presidential nominations to diplomatic posts, in this case by a simple majority vote. It passes Senate resolutions, in some cases on irrelevant subjects like independence for Ireland, in others, on relevant subjects, such as advising the President in 1948 that it would support a regional security pact (ultimately the North Atlantic Treaty Organization). It can launch investigations, notably the tragically misleading Nye Committee investigation in the 1930's of the international munitions scandal. It *approves* treaties by a two-thirds vote, and then sends them to the President for ratification and exchange of ratifications with the other power or powers. The Senate cannot *ratify* treaties; only the President can.

Criticisms of the Senate's role regarding treaties have been numerous and bitter. First of all, the accusation is that the two-thirds affirmative vote has resulted in chronic obstruction, notably in the rejection of the all-important Treaty of Versailles in 1919–1920. Second, the Senate is a political body, and it may try to embarrass the President by a partisan manhandling of a treaty, as the Republicans did in 1888 when they rejected the fisheries pact with England. Third, the Senate is unduly jealous of its prerogatives, as when it took deep offense at President Wilson's snubbing in 1918–1919. Fourth, the Senators, who are elected for six years, are notoriously less responsive to public opinion than are the two-year members of the House. This was conspicuously true in the 1920's and 1930's, when the Senate shelved the World Court in spite of strong popular sentiment.

The two-thirds rule, in particular, has come under repeated fire. A one-third-plus-one minority may veto a treaty, and in a democracy, where the majority rules, such a procedure seems undemocratic. The two-thirds rule, moreover, leads to subterfuge, if not downright dishonesty. When the President needs speedy action and does not want to risk rejection, he often by-passes the Senate by concluding an Executive agreement. Although such a pact does not require Senate approval, it has the force of a treaty while it lasts, as was true of the famous destroyer-base deal of

1940. The Senate, ever jealous of its prerogatives, has attempted in recent years, through the proposed Bricker amendment to the Constitution, to curb Executive agreements and treaties.

The American method of approving treaties has rarely been copied by other nations. It encourages delay and deadlock. There is some truth in the witticism that "the President proposes, the Senate disposes, and the country dozes."

IN DEFENSE OF THE SENATE

Arguments in behalf of the two-thirds rule are not lacking. The Senate, in going over treaties with a fine-toothed comb, is merely discharging its constitutional duty, and the President has no legal right to bind the Senators in advance, as Wilson did in connection with the Treaty of Versailles. Moreover, most treaties run the Senatorial gauntlet without undue delay, even though the Caribbean Isle of Pines Treaty, owing to opposition from the sugar interests, took twenty-one years!

The supposed villainy of the Senate in vetoing treaties by wielding the two-thirds rule has been much overplayed. From 1789 to 1934, only 15 of the 928 treaties presented to the Senate were rejected. Yet these figures are somewhat misleading. More than a hundred have been amended or have had reservations added. A few treaties have been so drastically altered by the Senate that the other nation, notably England in connection with the Hay-Pauncefote Treaty of 1900, refused to go through with ratification. Some have been filed in the White House wastebasket after Senatorial mutilation, as was the fate of President Taft's arbitration treaties in 1912.

But the figures on fatalities in the Senate do not take into account the large number of treaties that were never born because of the menacing two-thirds rule. For example, a treaty of alliance with Great Britain in 1900 to uphold the Open Door in the Far East would probably have been to the advantage of the United States, but the Britain-haters and devotees of the anti-alliance tradition were too vocal. "For God's sake," Secretary John Hay reported Senators as saying to him, "don't let it appear we have any understanding with England."

On the other hand, additional arguments can be presented in defense of the Senate. The Committee on Foreign Relations contains able lawyers, who are competent to give treaties a microscopic scrutiny. Treaties, like matrimony, are serious business, and are not to be entered into lightly. Some of them have no time limit, and they cannot be repealed by Congress, except at the risk of an international scandal. The Senators, in truth, have sometimes saved the administration serious embarrassment. In refusing to approve a treaty for a nonfortified Panama Canal, the Senate in 1900 was right, and Secretary Hay was wrong—despite his spoiled-child reaction. Finally, the one-third veto, like the filibuster, is designed to protect the minority rights of the states, notably those of the South, against the "tyranny of the majority."

The two-thirds rule, which can be changed only by constitutional amendment, will no doubt continue for a long time to come. Like monogamy, it is not completely satisfactory, but, like monogamy, it has won general if somewhat grudging acquiescence. A simple majority vote in the Senate seems like an insufficient safeguard; a simple majority vote in both Houses of Congress, as on a pork-barrel bill, also seems inadequate. A majority vote in both houses *of the total membership,* whether present or not, would have some merit, and would have the advantage of bringing the House of Representatives more intimately into the making of foreign policy.

THE PARTNERSHIP OF THE HOUSE

The House is already playing a role of increasing consequence, particularly since the distinction between domestic and foreign legislation is largely breaking down. Bills involving immigration, tariffs, and other "domestic" problems have far-reaching foreign implications, and the House has to approve or reject such measures. Like the Senate, it may also pass general resolutions on any subject, relevant or irrelevant, and it may undertake investigations of foreign policy. It may also collaborate with the Senate in passing a war resolution or in annexing territory by a simple joint resolution, as in the case of Texas and Hawaii. Most important of all, the House shares with the Senate control of the purse strings, and may slash the budget of the Department of State. If it refuses to vote the appropriations required by a treaty, as it almost has done on occasion, the pact falls to the ground. In the years after 1945, when the United States embarked upon a multibillion dollar foreign-aid program, the whole Congress was brought into the picture as never before.

Thus the House, the Senate, the President, the State Department, the National Security Council, the foreign service, the economic and military advisers, and above all the public are involved in the making of foreign policy. Water can rise no higher than its source, and American foreign policy can rise no higher than the intelligence, knowledge, experience, and vision of those who make it.

SELECTED BIBLIOGRAPHY

(See also the Bibliographical Appendix, at the end of this book)

On basic factors and conditions see T. A. Bailey, *The Man in the Street: The Impact of American Public Opinion on Foreign Policy* (New York,

1948); Gabriel Almond, *The American People and Foreign Policy* (New York, 1950); Dexter Perkins, *The American Approach to Foreign Policy* (Cambridge, Mass., 1952); Dexter Perkins, *The Evolution of American Foreign Policy* (New York, 1948); H. J. Morgenthau, *In Defense of the National Interest* (New York, 1951); R. E. Osgood, *Ideals and Self-Interest in America's Foreign Relations* (Chicago, 1953); W. Y. Elliott, *et al.*, *United States Foreign Policy: Its Organization and Control* (New York, 1952).

On the machinery of diplomacy, see E. S. Corwin, *The President's Control of Foreign Relations* (Princeton, 1917); G. H. Stuart, *The Department of State* (New York, 1949); G. H. Stuart, *American Diplomatic and Consular Practice* (2d ed., New York, 1952); J. M. Mathews, *American Foreign Relations* (rev. ed., New York, 1938); H. M. Wriston, *Diplomacy in a Democracy* (New York, 1956); Elmer Plischke, *Conduct of American Diplomacy* (New York, 1950); J. L. McCamy, *The Administration of American Foreign Affairs* (New York, 1950); R. C. Snyder and E. S. Furniss, Jr., *American Foreign Policy* (New York, 1954); P. W. Buck and Martin B. Travis, Jr., eds., *Control of Foreign Relations in Modern Nations* (New York, 1957); H. M. Wriston, *Executive Agents in American Foreign Relations* (Baltimore, 1929); Wallace McClure, *International Executive Agreements* (New York, 1941).

On the role of Congress, consult R. A. Dahl, *Congress and Foreign Policy* (New York, 1950); G. L. Grassmuck, *Sectional Biases in Congress on Foreign Policy* (Baltimore, 1951); E. E. Dennison, *The Senate Foreign Relations Committee* (Stanford University, 1942); A. C. F. Westphal, *The House Committee on Foreign Affairs* (New York, 1942); D. F. Fleming, *The Treaty Veto of the American Senate* (New York, 1930); R. J. Dangerfield, *In Defense of the Senate* (Norman, Okla., 1933); W. S. Holt, *Treaties Defeated by the Senate* (Baltimore, 1933); C. V. Crabb, Jr., *Bipartisan Foreign Policy: Myth or Reality?* (Evanston, Ill., 1957).

7TH ED. REFS. Dexter Perkins, *The American Approach to Foreign Policy* (rev. ed., Cambridge, Mass., 1962) is a thorough revision of a classic. D. A. Graber, *Crisis Diplomacy: A History of U.S. Intervention Policies and Practices* (Washington, 1959) regards intervention as a useful traditional policy. J. A. Logan, Jr., *No Transfer: An American Security Principle* (New Haven, 1961) accepts "no transfer" as an historic policy. W. F. Ilchman, *Professional Diplomacy in the United States, 1779–1939: A Study in Administrative History* (Chicago, 1961) is a solidly documented monograph. William Barnes and J. H. Morgan, *The Foreign Service of the United States: Origins, Development, and Functions* (Washington, 1961) is a broadly conceived account by two foreign service officers. See also C. W. Thayer, *Diplomat* (New York, 1959). International law involving the United States is treated in P. E. Corbett, *Law in Diplomacy* (Princeton, 1959) and Henry Reiff, *The United States and the Treaty Law of the Sea* (Minneapolis, 1959).

For additional new titles see the overflow in the BIBLIOGRAPHICAL ADDENDUM, p. 977 and also the headings listed alphabetically in the GENERAL BIBLIOGRAPHY, p. 968, particularly under Ambassadors, Open Door, Good Neighbor, Intervention, Military, Monroe Doctrine, Navy, No-Transfer, Pan Americanism, and Secretary of State.

8TH AND 9TH ED. REFS. See BIBLIOGRAPHICAL ADDENDUM, p. 977.

2

The Colonial Backdrop

*America has been long enough involved in the wars
of Europe. She has been a football between contending nations from the beginning. . . .*

JOHN ADAMS, 1782

PRENATAL IMPRESSIONS

A DIPLOMATIC HISTORY of the United States can officially begin with
July, 1776, when the Continental Congress declared the thirteen rebellious colonies an independent nation. But to take this date as a starting point would be like writing a biography of George Washington and
completely ignoring all the events of his life before he reached the age of
twenty-one.

One must never forget that a total of 169 years elapsed from the
planting of Jamestown, Virginia, to the declaring of independence—a
period equal in length to that from 1776 to 1945. The experiences of the
English colonists during this troubled century-and-a-half not only determined the nature of the new republic, but left an unmistakable im-
print upon its basic foreign policies. One is reminded of the old-wives'
tale that if a pregnant woman is frightened by a bear, she will give birth
to a baby with bearish features and traits.

A detailed scrutiny of colonial backgrounds is not within the scope of
this book. But a brief examination of certain prenatal influences during
these formative years will contribute to a richer understanding of
American diplomacy during the national period.

At the outset one must remember that the early English settlers in the
New World were not Americans at all—at least from an international
point of view—but Europeans transplanted to American soil. Their personal fortunes came second; those of England's empire first. Several of
the colonies were actually founded partially or primarily for purposes of
imperial defense. The best example is Georgia, which was planted as a
buffer to protect the Carolinas from the Spaniards and the Indians

America, in brief, was but the farthest fringe of Europe—an offshoot from, an appendage to, the mother continent.

The second-class status of the American settlers is nowhere better underscored than by the early intercolonial clashes. Whenever trade rivalries, dynastic ambitions, or other schemings plunged England and Spain into war, Spaniards would massacre Englishmen along the southern frontier. Whenever France and England tangled, the war whoop of French-led Indians would split the night air along the northern frontier. The colonials were not supposed to reason why; they were but to do and die as the advance agents of empire.

A PAWN ON THE EUROPEAN CHESSBOARD

The English colonials did not fully appreciate their disagreeable role. When war broke out in Europe, they were forced to raise money and armies and to shoulder, albeit somewhat grudgingly, a share of the burden. But their achievements, though considerable, bore little relation to the terms of peace. In general, America was but a side show. The main tent was in Europe, and what happened there largely determined the final outcome.

The classic example is the fate of the supposedly impregnable French fortress of Louisbourg, which, located on Cape Breton Island, had long been a thorn in the flesh of New England. By incredibly good luck the English colonists managed to capture it in 1745. But in Europe the war ended in a virtual stalemate, and Louisbourg was restored to France when Madras (India) was restored to Britain. The English colonials naturally viewed with acute dissatisfaction the tossing away of the fruits of victory and the re-establishment of the old menace. But their protests were wasted words.

Until the middle of the 18th Century, the English colonies in America were to a considerable degree pawns on the European chessboard. Their interests, though not wholly ignored by London, were definitely subordinated to those of the Empire as a whole. Ignorance went hand-in-hand with indifference. The Duke of Newcastle discussed Cape Breton for a decade without knowing that it was an island, while George III was probably not the only Briton to confuse the Mississippi River with the Ganges River in India.

But what is true of the early intercolonial conflicts certainly is not true of the last one. When the first of these struggles broke out in 1689 as King William's War, a majority of the colonists probably had no real desire to fight France. There were no acute centers of friction vitally affecting the welfare of large numbers of English settlers. The same is also true, though to a lesser extent, of Queen Anne's War (1702–1713). But thereafter the advance guard of the British Empire in North America began to trickle over the Appalachian Mountain barrier into territory claimed by France. The subsequent rivalries of buckskinned squatters, land speculators, and fur traders became increasingly intense. By 1713, armed conflict had broken out or was about to break out in eight different places in the Western Hemisphere.[1] Following King George's War (1744–1748), the English colonists apparently realized that the continent was not big enough for both themselves and the French. Regardless of European issues, the colonials were ready to fight.

The last of the four great Anglo-French wars—the French and Indian War—erupted in the wilds of the Ohio Valley, in May, 1754. It was the only one of the series that started in America, and it was actually fought there for two years before it widened into the Seven Years' War in Europe (1756–1763). But in a sense the French and Indian War was not a colonial conflict. By that time the English settlers had attained their majority—or were about to attain it. They were on the eve of becoming independent Americans.

THE ILLUSION OF ISOLATION

The English colonists were finally willing to fight for their own interests—and they did. There is also evidence that they were becoming fed up with being used as cats'-paws for European purposes. Thomas Paine, in his sensationally effective pamphlet *Common Sense* (1776), appealed to this sentiment:

> . . . Any submission to, or dependence on, Great Britain, tends directly to involve this Continent in European wars and quarrels, and set us at variance with nations who would otherwise seek our friendship, and against whom we have neither anger nor complaint. As Europe is our market for trade, we ought to form no partial connection with any part of it. *It is the true interest of America to steer clear of European contentions*, which she never can do, while, by her dependence on Britain, she is made the makeweight in the scale of British politics.[2] [Italics inserted]

The yearning to be isolated from the broils of Europe does much to explain early American foreign policy. In searching for its roots, one must bore deeply into colonial thinking and experience. The truth is that even before the colonists sailed from Europe they had become isolationists in spirit. They left the countries of their birth because they had not been able to get along there—whether spiritually, socially, politically, or economically. Many of them emigrated because they were

[1] See M. H. Savelle, "Diplomatic Preliminaries of the Seven Years' War in America," *Canadian Hist. Rev.*, XX (1939), 17.
[2] M. D. Conway, ed., *The Writings of Thomas Paine* (New York, 1906), I, 88–89.

weary of the periodic upheavals in Europe, as was notably true of the Rhineland Germans. The Swedish invaders had so thoroughly devastated their fair land in the Thirty Years' War (1618–1648) that more than three hundred years later a common German saying was, "Oh, something the Swedes left behind."

The voyage across the Atlantic usually lasted from one to three months, and often involved such incredible hardships as to take a heavy toll of human life. One traveler testified:

> . . . There is on board these ships terrible misery, stench, fumes, horror, vomiting, many kinds of sea-sickness, fever, dysentery, headache, heat, constipation, boils, scurvy, cancer, mouth-rot, and the like. . . . Add to this want of provisions, hunger, thirst, frost, heat, dampness, anxiety, want, afflictions and lamentations, together with other troubles, as c.v. the lice abound so frightfully, especially on sick people, that they can be scraped off the body. . . . We were compelled to eat the ship's biscuit which had been spoiled long ago; though in a whole biscuit there was scarcely a piece the size of a dollar that had not been full of red worms and spiders' nests.[3]

These prolonged nightmares had two inevitable results. The colonists realized keenly that they were separated from Europe in space and time. And those who staggered ashore alive did not return except for compelling reasons. They began to develop a typically American way of living and thinking—a transformation that further widened the gulf between them and Europe. A noted Massachusetts clergyman, Increase Mather, declared in 1677 with obvious exaggeration: "There never was a generation that did so perfectly shake off the dust of Babylon, *both as to*

---

[3] Gottlieb Mittelberger, *Journey to Pennsylvania* (Philadelphia, 1898), pp. 21–22, 24 (trans. from German by C. T. Eben).

ecclesiastical and *civil constitution,* as the first generation of Christians that came into this land for the gospel's sake." [4]

But only geographically, and in part psychologically, were the American colonists isolated from Europe. A thousand different cords—cords of race, kinship, language, literature, religion, custom, tradition, law, gov-

ernment, finance, trade—bound them to the Mother Country. Even though these pioneers of empire desired to hack out their own destiny without interference, they were repeatedly sucked into wars of Europe's making. Between 1689 and 1815 England and France fought each other seven times—about 60 years of warfare in a period of 126 years. Four of these wars, as already noted, were waged while the Americans were still colonials. Even today the tourist may visit the dungeons at Nantes, in France, and find carved on the walls the names of Massachusetts fishermen who had been captured during the intercolonial wars. There could hardly be a more forceful reminder that America was then a part of Europe.

Lumping together both the colonial and national periods, one finds that between 1688 and 1945 there were nine general European wars which involved a struggle for dominant sea power. The American people were involved in every one of them, whether they wanted to be or not. The conclusion is inescapable that America has never been, and certainly now can never be, completely isolated from Europe. A mere listing of the long series of tragic conflicts presents a vivid picture of the seeming inevitability of involvement.

[4] Quoted in J. W. Thornton, *The Pulpit of the American Revolution* (2nd ed., Boston, 1876), p. xviii.

THE NINE WORLD WARS

In Europe	*In America*
1688–1697 War of League of Augsburg	King William's War, 1689–1697
1701–1713 War of Spanish Succession	Queen Anne's War, 1702–1713
1740–1748 War of Austrian Succession	King George's War, 1744–1748
1756–1763 Seven Years' War	French and Indian War, 1754–1763
1778–1783 War of the American Revolution	American Revolution, 1775–1783
1793–1802 Wars of the French Revolution	Undeclared French War, 1798–1800
1803–1815 Napoleonic Wars	War of 1812, 1812–1814
1914–1918 World War I	World War I, 1917–1918
1939–1945 World War II	World War II, 1941–1945

FOREIGN POLICY IN EMBRYO

The policy of isolation—or more correctly the desire to be isolated—was not the only one to have its germs in the colonial era. The principle of the two hemispheres, which is the core of the Monroe Doctrine, may also be traced back to these precarious years.[5] The American settlers gradually came to realize that the New World had a set of interests peculiarly apart from that of the Old World, and they sought to secure recognition of this basic truth. Why should they disrupt profitable trade, butcher their neighbors and be butchered by them, simply because of a European clash in which they had no direct stake?

Similarly, there were faint foreshadowings of other fundamental policies in the colonial era. Among them one must include nonintervention in the wars of others, freedom of the seas, freedom of trade (the Open Door), and the peaceful settlement of international disputes. The incidents illustrating the emergence of these principles are so widely scattered that the scholar could hardly hazard many sweeping generalizations. But this much is crystal clear. Colonial experience convinced the Founding Fathers that the new nation must, at all costs, stay on its own side of the water and keep its skirts clear of foreign entanglements.

Geography contributed powerfully to a policy of noninvolvement. A billowing ocean moat three thousand miles wide separated but did not completely isolate the American people from Europe. The brilliant young Alexander Hamilton pointed out in 1787, in Number 8 of the *Federalist Papers*, that England did not have to maintain a large standing army because the English Channel separated her from Europe. How much better situated, he noted, was the United States. His point was well taken, for geographical separation—not isolation—made possible the partial success of a policy of nonentanglement during most of the 19th Century.

[5] See M. H. Savelle, "Colonial Origins of American Diplomatic Principles," *Pacific Hist. Rev.*, III (1934), 334–350.

SELECTED BIBLIOGRAPHY

A useful survey appears in S. F. Bemis, *The Diplomacy of the American Revolution* (New York, 1935). Detailed studies on special aspects are T. C. Pease, ed., *Anglo-French Boundary Disputes in the West, 1749–1763* (Springfield, Ill., 1936); Max Savelle, *Diplomatic History of the Canadian Boundary, 1749–1763* (New Haven, 1940); and J. F. Rippy and Angie Debo, "The Historical Background of the American Policy of Isolation," *Smith College Studies in History*, IX (1924), 71–165. Max Savelle has two suggestive shorter studies, "The American Balance of Power and European Diplomacy, 1713–78," in R. B. Morris, ed., *The Era of the American Revolution* (New York, 1939), pp. 140–169; and "The Appearance of an American Attitude toward External Affairs, 1750–1775," *Amer. Hist. Rev.*, LII (1947), 655–666. Consult also Felix Gilbert, "The English Background of American Isolationism in the Eighteenth Century," *William and Mary Quar.*, I (3d Ser.) [1944], 138–160; A. K. Weinberg, "The Historical Meaning of the American Doctrine of Isolation," *Amer. Pol. Sci. Rev.*, XXXIV (1940), 539–547; F. G. Davenport, "America and European Diplomacy to 1648," Amer. Hist. Assn., *Annual Report, 1915*, 153–161. A classic account is C. W. Alvord, *The Mississippi Valley in British Politics* (2 vols., Cleveland, 1917).

See footnotes of this chapter and Oscar Handlin, *et al.*, *Harvard Guide to American History* (Cambridge, Mass., 1954), Chs. 7–10.

7TH ED. REFS. General backgrounds are handled perceptively in R. W. Van Alstyne, *The Rising American Empire* (New York, 1960). Felix Gilbert, in *To the Farewell Address: Ideas of Early American Foreign Policy* (Princeton, 1961) develops the origins of United States foreign policy, with attention to British and Continental roots. T. R. Reese, "Georgia in Anglo-Spanish Diplomacy, 1736–1739," *William and Mary Quar.*, Ser. 3, vol. XV (1958), pp. 168–190 notes that the Florida-Georgia boundary dispute was one of the secondary causes of the Anglo-Spanish war that erupted in 1739. J. M. Sosin, "Louisburg and the Peace of Aix-la-Chapelle, 1748," *ibid.*, XIV (1957), pp. 516–535 reveals that Louisburg was not given up for Madras (India), as supposed, but for the evacuation by France of (Dutch) Flanders. J. C. Rule, "The Old Regime in America: A Review of Recent Interpretations of France in America," *William and Mary Quar.*, Ser. 3, vol. XIX (1962), 575–600 assesses in depth a large body of literature and calls for more studies designed to present a "balanced history of New France to replace the romantic portrait by Francis Parkman."

8TH ED. REFS. Max Savelle has crowned a lifetime of labor with his magisterial *The Origins of American Diplomacy: The International History of Angloamerica, 1492–1763* (New York, 1967). As the first full-length treatment of the subject, it fleshes out some of his earlier contributions, and stresses the developments of such concepts as isolation, the two spheres, freedom of the seas, "free ships, free goods," contraband and non-contraband lists, continuous voyage, the open door, and the balance of power. See especially Chapters XII and XX.

Savelle summarizes many of his conclusions in Ray A. Billington, ed., *The Reinterpretation of Early American History: Essays in Honor of John Edwin Pomfret* (San Marino, Calif., 1966), pp. 201–231, under the title, "The International Approach to Early Anglo-American History, 1492–1763."

9TH ED. REFS. L. S. Kaplan, *Colonies into Nation: American Diplomacy, 1763–1801* (New York, 1972) is an excellent detailed survey.

3

The Diplomacy of the French Alliance, 1775-1778

> *Every nation in Europe wishes to see Britain humbled, having all in their turns been offended by her insolence. . . .*
>
> BENJAMIN FRANKLIN, 1777

THE BREAK WITH BRITAIN

GREAT BRITAIN emerged from the Seven Years' War (1756–1763) the mightiest nation in the world. Her fleets whitened the seas and her many-tentacled empire sprawled over two hemispheres. But with overweening power went an arrogance that aroused hatred among the peoples of Europe. Horace Walpole, the English author, described his contemporaries in England as "born with Roman insolence" and behaving with "more haughtiness than an Asiatic monarch." He, himself, threatened to burn his Greek and Latin books—"those histories of little people."

No nation felt the humiliation of defeat by the British more keenly than France. Forsaken by allies and humbled on the battlefield, she had lost a vast empire, including all her possessions on the mainland of North America. Formerly arbiter of the destinies of Europe, she now saw her ministers walk at the heels of those of Britain in every chancellery on the Continent. Count de Vergennes, French Minister of Foreign Affairs, wrote bitterly in 1776: "England is the natural enemy of France; and she is a greedy enemy, ambitious, unjust and treacherous: the unalterable and cherished object of her policy is, if not the destruction of France, at least her degradation and ruin."[1]

To the dispirited French there was but one bright spot in the picture. The English colonies in America had huddled close to the wings of the

[1] Henri Doniol, *Histoire de la Participation de la France à l'Etablissement des Etats-Unis d'Amérique* (Paris, 1886), I, 244 (Reflections of Vergennes, early in 1776).

Mother Country while Canada was in the hands of France. But now that the French hawk was removed, the colonials might wander afield—perhaps even shake off imperial control. Encouraged by this prospect, the Paris government sent secret observers to America to report on developments and, if possible, to stir up trouble. When the British Parliament passed the ill-advised stamp tax in 1765, and the English colonists cried out in protest, the hoped-for break seemed near. But the obnoxious law was repealed the next year, and the French ministers began to lose hope.

The wound was torn open again in 1773, when Parliament enacted the trouble-brewing Tea Act. This measure provoked the destructive Boston Tea Party, which in turn brought punishment from London in the form of the so-called Intolerable Acts of 1774. The outraged colonials resisted, and blood finally reddened the greensward at Lexington, Massachusetts, on April 19, 1775.

But the great majority of Americans still hoped for reconciliation and for a reform of abuses. France, on the other hand, was interested in the destruction, not the reformation, of the British Empire. Until the colonials were prepared to make the final break, the French could offer no open aid.

British bungling continued, and on July 2, 1776, the Continental Congress declared the colonies independent. Two days later it adopted Jefferson's immortal draft of the Declaration of Independence. This official severance of relations with the Mother Country was a diplomatic stroke of major significance. It made possible foreign alliances, toward which colonial sentiment was now veering. It also served notice on the European powers that the cheapest and most effective way to wreak vengeance on Britain was to aid the struggling Americans in their attempt to break up her empire. "The colonies," wrote Catherine II of Russia hopefully and prophetically, "have told England good-bye forever."

MILITIA DIPLOMATS AND MILITIA DIPLOMACY

The foreign affairs of the United States during the Revolution fell under the direction of Congress—not of the unborn Department of State. As early as November, 1775, more than seven months before the Declaration of Independence, a secret committee of correspondence was appointed by Congress to maintain foreign contacts. It commissioned Arthur Lee, an erratic Virginian then residing in London as commercial agent for Massachusetts, as its confidential correspondent. Then, on March 3, 1776, still four months before independence was declared, Congress decided to send one of its members, Silas Deane, as a "commercial" agent to France.

Deane was instructed to secure financial and military assistance, and to sound out Paris on the possibilities of an alliance. Fearful of British spies, he adopted the name "Jones," wrote his letters in invisible ink, and vowed that in the presence of English-speaking people he would use only the French language. This led Foreign Minister Vergennes to jibe: "He must be the most silent man in France, for I defy him to say six consecutive words in French." Although Deane appears to have been in some degree both disloyal and dishonest, he did useful work in fitting out privateers and in securing arms for the struggling colonies. Perhaps his most valuable contribution was in helping to create the machinery for later military assistance from France.

Silas Deane was but the first of a procession of envoys sent abroad by Congress. Uninvited and unwanted, they were generally rebuffed, except in France, where they were either secretly or informally welcomed. This hesitancy is not difficult to explain. The official reception of diplomatic representatives is regarded as a formal recognition of the country from which they come; and the premature recognition of revolting colonies is generally considered just grounds for declaring war. The nations of Europe all feared Britain's might, and none of them wanted to incur her wrath by welcoming the American agents. Frederick the Great of Prussia, whose attitude was typical, instructed his ministers not to treat with the American envoy but *"mit Complimenten abweisen"* (put him off with compliments).

These pioneer American agents labored under other difficulties. Most of them, like Deane, were totally without experience in the wiles of European diplomacy. But John Adams, who was one of them, did not feel that this lack was a serious handicap. "Wise men know," he wrote, "that militia sometimes gain victories over regular troops even by departing from the rules." But Adams was unduly optimistic. Some of the "militia diplomats"—that is, those without diplomatic experience—were as ineffective as the blundering militiamen at home. Arthur Lee, for example, employed as clerks at least six British spies, who must have penetrated his assumed name, "Mary Johnston."

Yet these were not the only handicaps that vexed America's militia diplomats. Two full months were required, even under the most favorable conditions, for written instructions from Congress to reach Europe. Approximately one-third of the American diplomatic correspondence failed to reach its destination. Some of it was seized by the swarming British cruisers; much of it was thrown overboard to avoid capture. At a time when the Continental Congress had twelve paid agents in Europe, eleven months once passed without a word from any of them. The secret codes, in which the correspondence was conducted, occasionally were lost or changed without notification. Letters, when they did come through, arrived in formidable batches. And occasionally instructions dated, for example, December 30, would be received weeks before those dated November 30. John Adams summarized these difficulties in a classic statement:

> Ambassadors in Europe can send expresses [messages] to their courts and give and receive intelligence in a few days with the utmost certainty. In such cases there is no room for mistake, misunderstanding, or surprise, but in our case it is very different. We are at an immense distance. Dispatches are liable to foul play and vessels are subject to accidents. New scenes open, and the time presses, various nations are in suspense, and necessity forces us to act.[2]

This complaint does much to explain some of the obstacles confronting American diplomats before the Atlantic cable was successfully laid in 1866.

BEAUMARCHAIS' MOST COMPLEX PLOT

Looming large in Franco-American diplomacy from 1775 to 1778 was the work of Pierre Augustin Caron de Beaumarchais. The early years of this remarkable Frenchman were spent as an inventor and watchmaker, in which capacity he constructed a watch small enough for the ring finger of Madame de Pompadour, famous mistress of Louis XV. Later he distinguished himself as a courtier, a master of intrigue, and finally as a playwright-poet-politician. He is best remembered as the author of two of the most popular comedies of his day, *The Barber of Seville* and *The Marriage of Figaro*.

Beaumarchais early became interested in the events agitating America. Visiting London in 1775 he met the militia diplomat Arthur Lee, who discussed plans for assisting the rebellious Americans against Britain. The Frenchman soon became enamored of the colonial cause, and threw himself into it with almost fanatical zeal. He further stimulated the interest of Foreign Minister Vergennes, who had already been watching developments in America with a calculating eye. Through him—and even directly—Beaumarchais bombarded the French king with his passionately worded arguments for assistance.

The youthful Louis XVI, although somewhat thick-headed, showed little enthusiasm for these impassioned pleas. He knew full well that Britain would probably—and properly—declare war if France should provide open aid to the struggling colonies. But the king and his ministers finally decided that they could inflict the maximum damage on England, with the minimum of expense and risk to themselves, by encouraging the American rebels with secret shipments of needed munitions, money, and supplies. This crucial decision was made on May 2, 1776, two months before Congress declared the colonies independent

---

[2] Francis Wharton, ed., *The Revolutionary Diplomatic Correspondence of the United States* (Washington, 1880), VI, 52.

and before a single American agent had set foot on French soil. France could not afford to let the fire go out for want of fuel.

Thus a fictitious private concern, Roderique Hortalez et Compagnie, was organized in France to send military supplies to America. With Beaumarchais as its founder and guiding genius, and with the French and Spanish governments as its silent partners and financial backers, this bogus firm shipped immense quantities of all kinds of stores. Many of these contributions, in fact, were taken from the king's own arsenals and bore his monogram. Agricultural America, with its critical lack of military equipment, simply could not have carried on without this aid. Ninety per cent of the powder used by the colonials during the first two and one half years of the war came from Europe. Most of it was supplied by Hortalez et Compagnie, which at one time was operating fourteen ships. Beaumarchais, skilled playwright though he was, never conceived a more successful plot.

Nor did French aid end here. The Paris authorities, though officially issuing proclamations to the contrary, secretly permitted American privateers to fit out in their ports and prey upon England's commerce. The British diplomatic representative in France was well aware of these activities, but his repeated protests were wasted words. When his complaints became too pressing, Vergennes would order American privateers seized. Later, he would secretly compensate the owners for their losses and allow their vessels to escape. Had Britain not wished to avoid war with France at this time, she could have found abundant cause for hostilities in this flouting of neutrality.

A FUR CAP AMONG POWDERED HEADS

Not until September 26, 1776, nearly three months after the Declaration of Independence, did Congress appoint an official commission to France. It consisted of Arthur Lee and Silas Deane, both of whom were already abroad, and, most important of all, Benjamin Franklin. The famous Philadelphian, then seventy years of age, had grave doubts as to his usefulness. "I am old and good for nothing," he remarked humbly, "but as the store-keepers say of their remnants of cloth, I am but a fag end, and you may have me for what you please to give." America, in truth, gave little and received much, for the next seven years were destined to be among the most noteworthy of Franklin's remarkable career.

The mistake has often been made of regarding Franklin as a "militia diplomat." The United States has never sent abroad a man better qualified by training, character, and temperament for the task at hand. For more than a decade Franklin had served in the quasi-diplomatic capacity of colonial agent in London, and he was already hailed throughout Europe as the most distinguished man America had yet produced. His writings had been translated into the Continental languages, and his spectacular experiments with electricity had captivated the science-loving French.

The venerable American, after braving a rebel's noose and a wintry sea, landed on French soil in December, 1776. Master psychologist and showman that he was, Franklin discarded his conventional wig and substituted a fur cap.

> Figure me in your mind [he reported] as jolly as formerly, and as strong and hearty, only a few years older; very plainly dressed, wearing my thin gray straight hair, that peeps out under my only coiffure, a fine fur cap, which comes down my forehead almost to my spectacles. Think how this must appear among the powdered heads of Paris! [3]

Stripped of borrowed hair and attired in the simple costume of "an American agriculturist," Franklin took the bored Paris society by storm. His patriarchal appearance, his unpretentious manner, his benevolent countenance, and his agreeable eccentricity all appealed to the Gallic mind. To the French, he was the embodiment of the ideals of Rousseau and the personification of the American cause. Even Voltaire spoke quite unconsciously of Washington's army as "Franklin's troops." The adoring French compared Franklin with Tell, Socrates, even Jesus; and he grew weary of sitting for his portrait. His face appeared everywhere on rings, medals, medallions, watches, bracelets, and snuff boxes. The French ladies, among whom Franklin was a great favorite, did him the honor to adopt the high *"coiffure à la Franklin"* in imitation of his cap. No social affair was a success without him. So great were the crowds that followed and pressed about him in the streets that the curious even paid money for vantage points from which to see him pass.

Without this background one cannot understand the amazing success of Franklin's diplomacy. Taking full advantage of his popularity, he published a number of newspaper articles and pamphlets to discredit the British. The most famous of his propaganda efforts was the forged letter which purported to prove that the British were buying bales of American scalps (including those of women and children) from the Indians.

FRENCH FEARS OF REUNION

Franklin's wiles alone were not sufficient to enlist France on the side of the embattled colonies. The complexion of the American war changed radically when, on October 17, 1777, General Burgoyne, commanding the British invaders from Canada, surrendered his entire force to the Americans at Saratoga, New York. In a diplomatic rather than in a military sense this blow to Britain's arms must be regarded as one of the

---

[3] John Bigelow, ed., *The Life of Benjamin Franklin* (3rd ed., Philadelphia, 1893), II, 380.

decisive battles of world history. The American envoys in Paris wrote home that the news had apparently caused as much joy in France "as if it had been a victory of their own troops over their own enemies." No one was more elated than the playwright Beaumarchais, who, in his haste to get to the king with the glad tidings, was injured in a carriage wreck.

After Saratoga the diplomatic wheels began to turn rapidly. The disaster impressed upon London the necessity of making concessions to the rebels and ending the war. Franklin, in Paris, played his cards with consummate skill. On the one hand, he entered into negotiations with the principal British agent; on the other, he hinted to the French that unless they could offer something better, the Americans might have to accept Britain's terms. Foreign Minister Vergennes immediately bestirred himself. To him reconciliation would be a catastrope. As he pointed out to his colleagues, it would end the heaven-sent opportunity to ruin Britain and restore French prestige on the Continent.

But revenge was not the only argument that Vergennes used with his fellow ministers and the king. He appealed to cupidity—the possibility of winning the lush American trade—and he appealed to fear. If Britain should reconcile her colonies, he argued, what was to prevent her from turning against the French West Indies? These sugar-rich islands, which were France's most profitable colonial possessions, would provide compensation for the cost of the American rebellion. In addition, Vergennes noted, the trend of events indicated that war between Britain and France was inevitable within a few years anyhow. Was it not far better to fight England when she had her hands full with the rebellious Americans than to wait until the reunited British Empire could marshal its entire strength? This appeal to fear, which Franklin also cleverly exploited, appears to have done more than anything else to bring the reluctant king and his ministers to the edge of the precipice.

SPANISH PROCRASTINATION

But France was not free to move as she chose. She was bound by the Family Compact, negotiated in 1761, to act in close concert with Spain in decisions involving war. Besides, France needed the Spanish navy if she hoped to assemble a fleet more formidable than England's.

Unfortunately for Vergennes' plans, Spain showed no enthusiasm for the proposed war. To be sure, she hated Britain with a burning bitterness, for no other nation had done more to reduce her from her former proud position to a secondary role in the family of nations. The rock of Gibraltar, which England had wrested from her in 1704, was a galling reminder of her impotence. Although she was attracted by the prospect of a war for restitution and revenge, she was repelled by the specter of an independent and powerful American republic. Such a new state might reach over the Alleghenies into the Mississippi Valley and grasp territory that Spain wanted for herself. Even worse, it might eventually seize Spain's colonies in the New World.

BRITAIN FALLS UPON EVIL DAYS

An American is cutting off the horn of the cow representing British commerce; the Dutchman is milking the cow; the Spaniard and the Frenchman stand by for their share of milk; the British officers, with their warship beached, are dallying in Philadelphia; the British lion is indifferent to these indignities, while the Englishman wrings his hands and the dog shows his contempt.

A French print, *Library of Congress*

The bogeyman that cast the longest shadow over the Spanish Court was rebellion. Charles III could not forget that he had the largest and most vulnerable colonial empire in the New World. If he openly assisted the American rebels, the British might in turn encourage his own subjects to revolt against the Spanish crown. If rebellion and republicanism were successful in the English colonies, these twin plagues might easily spread to the Spanish dominions—as indeed they did. The few secret contributions from Charles III to the American cause were apparently made in the vain hope that both the colonies and the mother country would bleed themselves white, and thus render his own possessions more secure.

The dilly-dallying of the Spanish Court drove Vergennes to the verge of distraction. He did his best to quiet Spain's fears, while dangling before her eyes the prospect of reconquering from Britain the Floridas,

Gibraltar, and Minorca, and of securing a large slice of trans-Allegheny America. But still the Spanish Court wavered. Fearful that if he delayed any longer Britain would conciliate her colonies, Vergennes decided to plunge into the war alone. Spain might be persuaded to join France later.[4]

THE RACE FOR EMPIRE

The rebellious Americans were reluctant to enter into an alliance with France, their hereditary foe. Moreover, they retained unpleasant memories of their earlier involvements with the alliances and broils of Europe. But Congress, faced with the necessity of obtaining help, eventually modified its instructions so as to permit its agents in Paris to make binding treaties. The diplomatic marriage of the two nations was finally arranged on February 6, 1778, when Franklin, Deane, and Lee signed two epochal pacts, one of commerce and one of alliance.

The Treaty of Amity and Commerce generously granted valuable privileges to American shippers. It was closely patterned after the famous "Plan of 1776," which Congress had drawn up as a model for its diplomatic agents in Europe. In the interests of the weaker mercantile nations, including the United States, the French Treaty of Commerce provided for a whittling down of contraband lists—that is, lists of war materials that neutral ships could not carry without risking seizure by belligerent cruisers. The pact also stipulated that noncontraband enemy goods should be immune from capture when being transported on neutral vessels ("free ships, free goods"). In addition, the Franco-American Treaty of Commerce contained a most-favored-nation-clause—that is, both signatories agreed that if they subsequently granted commercial favors to other nations, those same favors would immediately be made available to each other.

The formal signing of this Treaty of Amity and Commerce, in 1778, constituted an official recognition of the United States by France. Britain was expected to retaliate with a declaration of war. When she did, as she did, the second and more important treaty—that of alliance—would become effective.

The Franco-American Treaty of Alliance contained three highly significant provisions. First, both nations pledged themselves to fight until American independence was "formally or tacitly assured." Second, neither France nor the United States would conclude a "truce or peace" with Britain without the "formal consent of the other first obtained." Third, each of the two nations guaranteed the possessions of the other in America "mutually from the present time and *forever* against all other powers." [Italics inserted]

[4] S. F. Bemis, *The Diplomacy of the American Revolution* (New York, 1935), p. 60.

Meanwhile the British Prime Minister, Lord North, had been devising schemes to salvage the Empire. On December 10, 1777, he announced to a startled Parliament that after the Christmas holidays he would move to consider concessions to the rebellious colonies. Early the next year he introduced his conciliation bills, which offered virtual home rule to the Americans. On March 9, 1778, Parliament approved these measures.

"The two greatest countries in Europe," remarked the historian Edward Gibbon, then a member of Parliament, "were fairly running a race for the favor of America." The French terms were received with rejoicing in the United States, despite the tenacity of the isolationist tradition. As fate would have it, they arrived just in time to stop the movement toward reconciliation that had followed the receipt of advance copies of Lord North's conciliation bills. France held out to the Americans everything that the British were prepared to concede—and one thing more, independence. So the colonials, having tasted the sweets of freedom, cast in their lot with France. With the acceptance of the French treaties and the breakdown of conciliation, France and Britain inevitably clashed, in June, 1778.

MISMATED YOKEFELLOWS

France, in her haste to forestall Britain's terms, promised much and received little. She dealt with the Americans on a plane of equality, as if with a powerful and long-established nation. She even went so far as to bind herself by the Treaty of Alliance not to retain French-founded Canada or any of Britain's other mainland possessions in North America. She abandoned secret aid, which had proved cheap and effective, and gave the colonials, at a ruinous cost to herself, that overt assistance without which they probably could not have won their independence when they did.

With the wisdom of hindsight, one can now see the folly of the French officials in plunging blindly into this struggle. Their reasons for doing so may have seemed convincing to them, but here one witnesses the incredible spectacle of monarchy openly courting, and winning, both bankruptcy and revolution—in behalf of a republic. Turgot, the great French Minister of Finance, had warned bluntly that war would mean ruin. But the thick-witted Louis XVI turned a deaf ear to these calculations—and dismissed him. The King was told that his valets, clad in royal livery, were openly begging in the streets. "I believe it," he blandly replied, "they are paid nothing."

But the inconsistencies do not stop with France. Many critics were amazed at the eagerness with which the United States grasped the Gallic hand, drenched though it was with the blood of American settlers. In four successive wars, extending over three-quarters of a century, Indians led by Frenchmen had ravaged the Anglo-American frontier. Yet scarcely had the war whoop died away and the scalping knife become dry when the Americans found themselves arrayed beside their former archenemy against the nation that had given them birth. As one English commentator later said, "When our house is burning, we do not inquire too curiously into the moral antecedents of those who hand the water-buckets." [5]

In America, the British pamphleteers, as well as the Loyalist supporters of George III, did their best to undo the alliance by resurrecting the Gallic peril. They insisted that this was the old story of the wooden horse over again, and that when the French came they would exact a heavy price for their help—perhaps American territory and sovereignty. In Protestant New England, where the Pope was distrusted, great stress was laid upon the Catholicism of the French. And Loyalist newspapers made much of the expected arrival of ships laden with tons of holy water, crucifixes, hair shirts, and other so-called "trappings of popery."

The French representatives in America, alive to their peril, launched a counterattack of propaganda. They even employed the potent pen of Thomas Paine, at a salary of $1000 a year, to create sentiment favorable to France and the alliance. But such efforts were probably unnecessary. Water buckets and carriers of water buckets were too desperately needed.

FRENCH SENTIMENT OR SELF-INTEREST?

Now that the French alliance was consummated, Louis XVI did the handsome thing by sending over a full-fledged minister, Conrad Alexandre Gérard. Flattered by such attention, Congress engaged in a wordy debate over the etiquette of receiving this Old World dignitary. The Loyalists hid their fear in the derisive tune of "Yankee Doodle":

> From Lewis [Louis XVI], Monsieur Gerard came,
> To Congress in this town, sir.
> They bowed to him, and he to them
> And then they all sat down, sir.[6]

But the patriots, who remembered that Americans had long been regarded as lackeys by the British, rejoiced to see the day when they were treated as equals by the greatest power on the continent of Europe.

The silly myth has often been repeated that France entered the war primarily because of her love for the United States—a myth that Vergennes deliberately encouraged. It is true that there was a considerable

---

[5] H. E. Egerton, *The Causes and Character of the American Revolution* (Oxford, 1923), p. 127.

[6] *Rivington's Gazette*, Oct. 3, 1778, quoted in C. H. Van Tyne, *The Loyalists in the American Revolution* (New York, 1902), p. 153.

body of French liberals and intellectuals, including Rousseau and Voltaire, who were fired with enthusiasm for the cause of liberty and for the American experiment in republicanism. It is also true that the struggle of the colonials touched the imagination of the more romantic and chivalrous elements in France, especially in the cities and notably Lafayette. It is likewise true that the American cause was popular at the French Court and in the inner circles of French society. The wily Franklin had done his work well. Even the frivolous queen, Marie Antoinette, inquired eagerly about "our good Americans," "our dear republicans." But it is not correct to say that the illiterate and ignorant French masses were on fire for America, and that they forced their government into the war. Such statements grossly exaggerate sentiment for the colonies and clothe the absolutist French monarchy with the responsiveness of a popular regime.

The documents do not reveal that the hard-headed Vergennes and his calculating fellow ministers were swayed to any appreciable extent by sentiment. France came to the aid of the Americans because the men in charge of her government concluded—whether wisely or not—that it was to her advantage to do so. A desire for revenge and restitution, to say nothing of cupidity and fear, dictated her course. France's distresses made possible America's diplomatic success.

SELECTED BIBLIOGRAPHY

The outstanding monograph on the subject is S. F. Bemis' scholarly *The Diplomacy of the American Revolution* (New York, 1935), which largely supplants E. S. Corwin's *French Policy and the American Alliance of 1778* (Princeton, 1916). The story is told in briefer compass in the early chapters of A. B. Darling, *Our Rising Empire, 1763–1803* (New Haven, 1940). The best life of Franklin is Carl Van Doren's *Benjamin Franklin* (New York, 1938), while his diplomacy is fully analyzed in Gerald Stourzh, *Benjamin Franklin and American Foreign Policy* (Chicago, 1954). The most recent treatment of clandestine French aid is Helen Augur, *The Secret War of Independence* (New York, 1955). See also J. J. Meng, ed., *Dispatches and Instructions of Conrad Alexandre Gérard, 1778–1780* (Baltimore, 1939).

Useful articles are C. H. Van Tyne, "Influences which Determined the French Government To Make the Treaty with America, 1778," *Amer. Hist. Rev.*, XXI (1916), 528–541; C. H. Van Tyne, "French Aid before the Alliance of 1778," *ibid.*, XXXI (1925), 20–40; P. L. Haworth, "Frederick the Great and the American Revolution," *ibid.*, IX (1904), 460–478; J. J. Meng, "A Footnote to Secret Aid in the American Revolution," *ibid.*, XLIII (1938), 791–795.

See footnotes of this chapter; *Harvard Guide*, Ch. 10; and S. F. Bemis and G. G. Griffin, eds., *Guide to the Diplomatic History of the United States, 1775–1921* (Washington, 1935), pp. 1–25.

7TH, 8TH, AND 9TH ED. REFS. See BIBLIOGRAPHICAL ADDENDUM, p. 978.

~~~~~~~~~~ *4* ~~~~~~~~~~

The Diplomacy of Peace
with Britain, 1778-1783

You will notice that the English buy the peace more than they make it.

VERGENNES, 1782

SPAIN: LUKEWARM PARTNER

THE SPANISH COURT was deeply offended by France's decision to plunge into war against Britain without first securing the consent of Madrid. Charles III, whose injured pride would not permit him to move hastily, knew that the French were in urgent need of his navy, and that he was in an excellent position to drive a hard bargain. In the end, and only after costly delays, Vergennes succeeded in satisfying Spanish honor. Spain and France formally came to terms at Aranjuez, on April 12, 1779, more than a year after the signing of the Franco-American alliance.

The provisions of the secret convention of Aranjuez were not noteworthy, except for one bothersome article. Charles III, who desired above all else to attach Gibraltar once more to Spanish soil, forced France to agree to fight until Britain yielded the defiant fortress. As the French had already bound the United States not to make a separate peace, the Aranjuez agreement "chained" the Americans, without their knowing it, to the rock of Gibraltar.

Spain's belated entrance into the war as an ally of France did not mean that she was an ally of the United States. The Madrid government not only harbored unfriendly sentiments toward the new republic, but flatly refused to recognize its independence. Yet Congress, in the hope of persuading Spain to lend money and enter into an alliance, decided to send an envoy to the Spanish Court. The man chosen was John Jay, thirty-four year old scion of a distinguished New York family, and one of the ablest statesmen of his day.

Jay's mission was one long purgatory. He was never officially received during the two-and-one-half years of his sojourn in Spain. His mail was secretly opened and read; his letters to the foreign minister lay unanswered; he was put off with the most transparent excuses. The frigidity of the Spanish Court was determined with almost thermometric precision by the successes or failures of American arms. Jay reported that the news of the loss of Charleston to the British had an effect "as visible the next day as that of a bad night's frost on young leaves." In desperation, Congress instructed him to offer an abandonment of American claims to navigate the Mississippi River in exchange for recognition and an alliance. Fortunately for the future expansion of the United States, the Spanish government was unwilling to come to terms on this basis.

As if all these vexations were not enough, Jay became involved in serious financial embarrassments. His salary failed; his meager funds gave out; his attempts to wring money from the unsympathetic Madrid Court met with scant success. The Spanish Foreign Minister, disgusted with the American envoy's constant begging, wrote of him: "His two chief points were: Spain, recognize our independence; Spain, give us more money." Jay finally did succeed in borrowing a small sum, and he did encourage the Spaniards to keep up their half-hearted assistance to the colonials. But beyond this his mission did little more than create in him a profound distrust of European courts and European diplomacy.[1]

BRITAIN AT BAY

Before the end of 1779 Britain was fighting with her back to the wall. For the first time since 1690 her naval supremacy in the English Channel was jeopardized, and she was faced with the grim prospect of invasion.

The opportunity had come at last for the weaker maritime nations of Europe to rise up and assert their rights—rights which, in their eyes, the Mistress of the Seas had for generations haughtily ignored or flagrantly abused. Catherine II of Russia, secretly encouraged by Vergennes of France, took the lead in organizing the Baltic countries into the Armed Neutrality of 1780. This group of small-navy nations, seeking to improve their position in time of war and weaken the preponderant sea power of Britain, ringingly enunciated certain advanced rules of international law.

The list thus published was impressive. It lashed out against "paper blockades"—that is, a blockade to be binding must be effectively enforced. It declared for a more liberal interpretation of contraband of war—that is, less confiscation of neutral goods regarded as war materials by the belligerents. It proclaimed the principle "free ships, free goods"—that is, immunity of noncontraband enemy goods being carried on neutral

[1] For the Spanish mission see Frank Monaghan, *John Jay* (New York, 1935), pp. 125–183.

ships. Interestingly enough, a number of these principles could be found in the memorable American "Plan of 1776," which had formed a basis for the Franco-American commercial treaty of 1778.

Almost all the neutral trading nations of Europe joined the Armed Neutrality, for they were eager to humble the British "tyrant of the seas." The roster included Russia, Prussia, Denmark, Norway, Sweden, the Holy Roman Empire, Portugal, and the Two Sicilies. These countries did not declare war, but they assumed an unfriendly, even menacing attitude, and thus rendered Britain's position more precarious.

BRITAIN AGAINST THE WORLD

Britain and Allies		*Enemy or Unfriendly Powers*
Great Britain		United States, 1775–1783
Some Loyalists and Indians	Belligerents	France, 1778–1783
(Total population on Britain's side: c. 8,000,000)	(Total population: c. 17,500,000)	Spain, 1779–1783
		Holland, 1780–1783
		Ireland (restive)
	Members of the Armed Neutrality (with dates of joining)	Russia, 1780
		Denmark–Norway, 1780
		Sweden, 1780
		Holy Roman Empire, 1781
		Prussia, 1782
		Portugal, 1782
		Two Sicilies, 1783 (after peace signed)

One must not fall into the error of overestimating the influence of the Armed Neutrality as a military or naval force. John Adams sneered at it as a "sublime bubble," while Catherine II herself contemptuously referred to her brain child as the "Armed Nullity." Yet the Armed Neutrality was a promising beginning toward clarifying and making more tolerable the position of neutral shippers. These precious principles eventually took root, and many of them were at last formally recognized by the great powers in the Declaration of Paris of 1856. But of more immediate importance was the fact that the Armed Neutrality discouraged the British and inspirited their enemies. Virtually the entire trading world was now arrayed against Great Britain.

The energetic and money-wise Dutch had meantime been taking advantage of England's misfortunes to wrest from their rival a rich carrying trade. They had also developed profitable new markets, notably with the American rebels by way of the hitherto obscure Dutch island of St. Eustatius. This Caribbean rock, only six miles long and three miles wide, quickly became the halfway house for an enormous volume of European trade with the United States. Much of it was in contraband of war. During one thirteen-month period of the Revolution, a total of

3182 ships touched at St. Eustatius, including many of those sent out by the bogus French Hortalez et Compagnie.

This scandalous situation in the Caribbean, combined with a bustling Dutch trade with France in naval supplies, finally became intolerable to Britain. In December, 1780, she found a pretext for declaring war on the Netherlands. Admiral Rodney, in command of a powerful British squadron, promptly descended upon St. Eustatius and captured it, together with 130 ships. The spoils of war, so he boasted to his wife, were "rich beyond comprehension." But he dallied so long with the plunder that an enemy fleet, under the French Admiral de Grasse, was able to slip away from the West Indies. It joined with a Franco-American army at Yorktown, Virginia, to force the surrender of a powerful British force on October 19, 1781, in one of the most decisive battles of the war.

MILITIA DIPLOMACY IN THE NETHERLANDS

The rupture between England and the Netherlands presented America with a new opportunity. Congress hoped that the Dutch, who were the bankers of Europe, might be induced to make a commercial treaty and grant desperately needed loans.

John Adams, who had been lingering in Paris, was accordingly sent to the Netherlands in the summer of 1780. Although a man of first-rate ability, Adams was pompous, egotistical, and conspicuously lacking in tact. His departure greatly improved the atmosphere in Paris. He was jealous of the aged Franklin, whose harmless dalliance with the French ladies seemed disgraceful to Adams, and he had quarreled bitterly with Vergennes. On one occasion Adams flatly informed the French Foreign Minister: "The United States of America are a great and powerful people, whatever European statesmen may think of them." [2]

Adams' mission to the Netherlands lasted nearly two years. Although coldly received at first, he applied himself to his task with patience, resourcefulness, and a surprising amount of tact. But he encountered the utmost difficulty in persuading the canny Dutch bankers to lend money. On one occasion he reported, "I can represent my situation in this affair of a loan, by no other figure than that of a man in the midst of the ocean negotiating for his life among a school of sharks."

Despite personal shortcomings, Adams played his cards cleverly. Aided by the growing embarrassments of Britain, he finally delivered what he immodestly described as "the greatest blow that has been struck in the American cause, and the most decisive." First of all, he secured from the Netherlands, in April 1782, a formal recognition of American independence. Soon afterward he made the final arrangements

[2] C. F. Adams, ed., *The Works of John Adams* (Boston, 1852), VII, 588 (Adams to Livingston, May 16, 1782).

for a life-giving loan—the beginning of financial assistance that averted complete bankruptcy in the United States. Finally, on October 8, 1782, he concluded a treaty of amity and commerce, the second that the young republic had succeeded in negotiating.

Adams returned to Paris in an exultant mood. He confided to his private journal: "The compliment of '*Monsieur, vous êtes le Washington de la négociation*' [you are the Washington of negotiation] was repeated to me by more than one person. . . . A few of these compliments would kill Franklin if they should come to his ears." [3]

BRITAIN'S OPENING MOVES

Setbacks to British arms had meanwhile been stirring up a political tempest in England. The disaster at Yorktown finally led to the resignation of Lord North, the Tory Prime Minister, whose ministry was succeeded, in March, 1782, by that of the Whig Marquis of Rockingham.

THE HORSE "AMERICA" THROWING HIS MASTER

The rider is Lord North, British Prime Minister, wielding a whip of swords.
Note the Frenchman in the background.
A British cartoon, 1779, *New York Public Library*

Public opinion in England, never enthusiastic about the war in America, was becoming increasingly vocal in demanding a cessation of hostilities with the colonies.

[3] Francis Wharton, ed., *The Revolutionary Diplomatic Correspondence of the United States* (Washington, 1889), I, 510.

Lord Shelburne, who then had charge of colonial affairs, took the initial plunge in April, 1782. He sent to Paris a retired Scottish trader, Richard Oswald, with instructions to enter into conversations with Franklin. From the standpoint of experience and temperament, Oswald was fully as much a militia diplomat as Silas Deane. His chief qualifications seem to have been an acquaintanceship with Franklin and some first-hand knowledge of the colonies, derived in part from the slave trade. With remarkable candor Oswald admitted to Franklin that Britain had become "foolishly involved in four wars," and that her financial condition was such that peace was "absolutely necessary."

The shrewd American at once perceived that here was a man after his own heart. Among other things Franklin suggested to Oswald that Britain cede Canada to the United States in order to salve the bitterness created by the war and to prevent future friction—a startling scheme indeed when one considers the costly American failure to conquer Canada in 1775. The British emissary nevertheless was attracted by the idea, and he promised to present it to the Ministry upon his return to London. "We parted exceedingly good friends," wrote Franklin.

Upon returning to London, Oswald found the picture confused. He urged Franklin's proposal with considerable warmth, and encountered serious objection only from Foreign Secretary Fox. The latter felt that the negotiations were within his province rather than within that of the Colonial Office, headed by his rival Lord Shelburne.

The Cabinet finally decided to send to Paris an additional negotiator, who would represent Fox in all matters relating to a general peace. Oswald was to continue the negotiations for a settlement with the Americans. The upshot was that the two men, representing different and conflicting interests, worked at cross-purposes. The employment of such inexperienced and mediocre agents is in part explained by the fact that they were instructed to report their every movement to London. "We can consider ourselves," one of them wrote, "as little more than pens in the hands of the government at home. . . ."

JAY FIGHTS FIRE WITH FIRE

Franklin now had the negotiations well in hand. But since he was suffering from various diseases of old age, he felt the need of help. John Adams was busy in the Netherlands, so Franklin instructed John Jay, who was still lingering impotently in Spain, to come on to Paris. When Jay shook the dust of Spain from his boots, he did not shake the deep prejudice he had developed against the Spaniards, and also against the French, who in his opinion were partly responsible for his woes. After a long encounter with "bad roads, fleas, and bugs," he arrived at Paris in June, 1782, in a highly suspicious frame of mind.

By now the diplomatic chessboard was immensely complicated. The combined Spanish and French forces were making furious but futile efforts to capture the rock of Gibraltar. And the longer the fortress resisted the more insistent Spain became. Vergennes, who was disturbed by his ill success in delivering Gibraltar, felt under strong obligations to support the demands of Spain for the area between the Appalachian Mountains and the Mississippi River—a region which the Americans regarded as marked out for them by Providence.

Vergennes, to be sure, desired an independent United States, but he privately favored a weakly independent United States confined east of the Appalachians. He was like the farmer who wanted a horse strong enough to plough but not strong enough to kick back at its master. A weak United States could be made to serve French interests in America; a powerful United States might prove headstrong.

Jay's distrust was further aroused by certain highly suspicious circumstances. First of all, Vergennes' secretary, Joseph Rayneval, made the informal proposal to Jay that in the interests of Spain the United States coop itself up east of the Appalachians. The American envoy naturally surmised—and correctly so—that this was also the view of Vergennes. A short time later Jay learned that Rayneval had secretly left Paris for London, the enemy's capital, after having taken elaborate precautions to conceal his destination. This incident, coming on the heels of a number of suspicious maneuvers, convinced Jay that Vergennes was about to sacrifice American interests and, through under-the-table negotiations with Britain, limit the United States to the area east of the Appalachians.

Thoroughly alarmed, Jay decided to take vigorous action. He first communicated his fears to Franklin, who was inclined to make light of them. Then rather than supinely see his country's interests betrayed, Jay determined, without consulting his aging associate, to forestall the apparent treachery of the French by opening separate negotiations with the British. On September 11, 1782, therefore, he dispatched a special emissary to London. Lord Shelburne, who had become Prime Minister on July 2, was delighted with the prospect of driving a wedge between the allies, and he took full advantage of the opening.

The undercover negotiations in Paris now moved rapidly to a climax. John Adams, arriving fresh from his Dutch triumphs, heartily approved of what Jay had done. He was delighted to note that "no wrestler was ever so completely thrown upon his back as the Count de Vergennes." The enfeebled Franklin protested mildly against separate action. But finding himself outvoted by his younger and more zealous colleagues, and realizing that the best results could be obtained only by harmonious action, he acquiesced in their course. His rather weak protests were probably for the sake of appearances, for there were earlier instances in the negotiations when Franklin had definitely foreshadowed Jay's independent course. Finally, after protracted interchanges with the British agent Oswald, the three American commissioners signed the *preliminary* treaty of peace with Great Britain, November 30, 1782.

THE ETHICS OF A SEPARATE PEACE

The secret maneuvering of the American envoys was highly questionable. First, it did violence to the French Alliance of 1778, which stipulated that "Neither of the two Parties shall conclude either Truce or Peace with Great Britain, without the formal consent of the other first obtained." Second, Congress had specifically instructed its diplomatic agents to enter into the "most candid and confidential" relations with their French allies, and to undertake no steps in the negotiations for peace without their "knowledge and concurrence." How then can Jay's action be explained, much less justified?

First of all, an Atlantic cable lay in the future. The ambassador of today describes by cablegram the changing scene, and promptly receives new instructions to meet new emergencies. Jay could have written home, but months would have elapsed before a reply could have been received —and delay might have proved disastrous.

Jay, moreover, distrusted Congress. He knew that Vergennes, acting through the French minister in Philadelphia, had influenced that body with undue pressures. These included, scholars now know, bribery. By such tactics Vergennes had brought about a reshuffling of the American peace commission in Paris more to his liking, and had caused it to be instructed to take no steps without French permission. Vergennes would have saved valuable time and roundabout effort if, instead of communicating with Philadelphia, he had handed the rewritten orders directly to the American commissioners. John Adams fully shared John Jay's feelings regarding these "tainted" instructions:

> Congress surrendered their own sovereignty into the hands of a French minister. Blush! blush! ye guilty records! blush and perish! It is glory to have broken such infamous orders. Infamous, I say, for so they will be to all posterity. How can such a stain be washed out? Can we cast a veil over it and forget it? [4]

The documents now available reveal that Jay's suspicions of Vergennes, who himself was negotiating separately, were far from groundless. The French Foreign Minister may not have been deliberately betraying the Americans, but he evidently was carrying water on both shoulders. He was attempting to discharge his obligations to Spain at the

---

[4] *Works of John Adams*, III, 359 (diary entry, Feb. 18, 1783). Some thirty years later Gouverneur Morris declared, "Jay, what a set of d——d scoundrels we had in that second Congress." "Yes," replied Jay, "that we had. . . ." George Pellew, *John Jay* (Boston, 1890), p. 157.

expense of the United States, while keeping the young republic so weak that it would remain in French leading strings. Indeed, some critics have argued that Vergennes' double-dealing released the Americans from any moral obligation to adhere strictly to the terms of the alliance. Certainly, from the viewpoint of American interests, Jay would have been censurable if he had not acted as he did. By pursuing an independent course, he probably secured more advantageous terms than otherwise would have been possible.

As for the French alliance, Jay and his colleagues did not, strictly speaking, make a separate peace. They merely negotiated and signed *preliminary* articles, which were specifically not to take effect until France had come to terms with England. But since the Americans were clearly going to accept Britain's generous concessions, separate peace or no separate peace, the French were forced to go along with them or risk a costly rupture with their ally.

VERGENNES APPEARS VEXED

What was the attitude of Vergennes during these critical weeks? With a small army of spies at his command, he must have known what the American commissioners were up to, yet he was silent. The day before the Americans signed the preliminary articles, they actually notified Vergennes of their intentions, and if he had been violently opposed to separate action, he could have lodged a strong protest then and there.

The official French silence is not difficult to explain. Despite desperate efforts, France was finding it impossible to deliver Gibraltar to Spain, and Vergennes was faced with the intolerable prospect of fighting indefinitely to discharge his obligations. America's threatened defection, which would obviously strengthen Britain, would put pressure on Spain to make peace and accept something less than Gibraltar. The independent action of Jay and his colleagues, in brief, actually helped Vergennes out of a bad hole. Contrary to the traditional tale, he seems to have been more pleased than angered, for he complimented the Americans on the excellence of their terms.

But Vergennes naturally felt some little resentment at the failure of the American envoys to consult with him in advance. After delaying an unaccountable two weeks, he sent a note of remonstrance to Franklin that was not nearly so vigorous as might have been expected. The mildness of his protest, combined with his delay in sending it, indicates that he was writing primarily for the sake of form, and probably with the additional purpose of making the shamefaced Americans more subservient to French influence. His rebuke to Franklin read in part:

> I am at a loss, sir, to explain your conduct and that of your colleagues on this occasion. You have concluded your preliminary articles without any com-

munication between us. . . . You are about to hold out a certain hope of peace to America without even informing yourself on the state of the negociation on our part.

You are wise and discreet, sir; you perfectly understand what is due to propriety; you have all your life performed your duties. I pray you to consider how you propose to fulfill those which are due to the King? [5]

Franklin, facile penman and master diplomatist, was called upon by his colleagues to make the necessary explanations and apologies. The venerable philosopher truthfully pointed out in his reply to Vergennes that the Americans had not really made a separate peace at all; they had merely agreed upon the *preliminary* articles of peace. He admitted, however, that in failing to consult with the French Foreign Office they had been guilty of neglecting a point of *bienséance* (propriety), but not from "want of respect to the King, whom we all love and honor." Franklin hoped that this unhappy incident would cause no break between the allies, for if this should occur all their common expenditure of blood and treasure would probably be for naught. Then came the cleverest touch of all, which may have caused Vergennes to smile at the craftsmanship of a fellow artist: *"The English, I just now learn, flatter themselves they have already divided us. I hope this little misunderstanding will therefore be kept a secret, and that they will find themselves totally mistaken."* [6] [Italics Franklin's]

In the same letter, and with amazing self-assurance, Franklin suggested the desirability of a further loan. Incredible though it may seem, the semibankrupt French government, which the Americans had just offended, advanced another 6 million livres. It could not afford, as Franklin slyly pointed out, to let the already costly fire die out for lack of fuel.

THE AMERICAN BIRTH CERTIFICATE

The final Anglo-American treaty, signed on September 3, 1783, with the full permission of France, was virtually the same as the preliminary draft. Great Britain not only recognized the independence of the United States but granted astonishingly liberal boundaries. The new republic was to stretch magnificently westward to the Mississippi, with the northern limits roughly what they are now. The southern boundary was to be the frontier of Spanish East and West Florida, even though the Americans had made no real effort to conquer the vast area south of the Ohio River. As for the region north of the river, it is true that a venturesome Virginian, George Rogers Clark, had seized the British posts in the southwestern part, and had established military control over a considerable

---

[5] Wharton, *Revolutionary Diplomatic Correspondence*, VI, 140.
[6] *Ibid.*, 144 (Franklin to Vergennes, Dec. 17, 1782).

portion of the entire area. But scholars still dispute whether this conquest was fully known to the Paris negotiators, and whether it had any real bearing on the final yielding of the territory.[7]

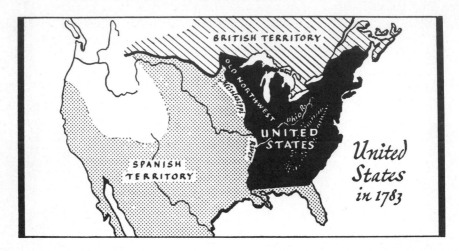

The third article of the treaty related to the North Atlantic fisheries, chiefly the Grand Banks of Newfoundland. The British negotiators contended that these on-shore privileges should be reserved for the loyal parts of the Empire, chiefly the Canadians, and denied to the Americans, who had broken away from the Empire. But this priceless and self-perpetuating codfish lode—"the gold mines of New England"—was highly regarded by. the New Englanders. Doughty John Adams, one of them, battled valiantly for New England's interests at the peace table. He argued that the fisheries had been wrested from France twenty years before, partly by the efforts of the Americans, and that even though the thirteen colonies were receiving a divorce from the British Empire, they should be permitted joint custody of the fish.

Adams carried the day through his persistence and eloquence, despite the lukewarmness of Jay and Franklin. He secured for his countrymen all the privileges of fishing that were enjoyed by British subjects, though certain restrictions were placed on drying and curing. But the British did succeed in inserting ambiguities in the treaty, notably where they substituted the "liberty" to fish for the "right" to fish. The foundations were thus laid for a controversy that bobbed up repeatedly in British-American relations for well over a century.

[7] Professor S. F. Bemis (*The Diplomacy of the American Revolution* [New York, 1935], p. 219 n.) finds no evidence that Clark's conquest played an important part in the negotiations. The opposite view is fully presented by J. A. James, *Oliver Pollock* (New York, 1937), pp. 242–248.

DEBTORS AND LOYALISTS

The fourth article of the treaty concerned the debts that a number of Americans, notably Virginia planters, had owed British merchants when the Revolution erupted. Many of these hard-pressed colonials had hoped that independence would result in a cancellation of prewar liabilities— an attitude that caused the Loyalists to sneer, "Liberty or debt." But the anxious British creditors, not wishing to lose approximately £5 million, insisted upon writing safeguards into the treaty. After prolonged wrangling, during which Adams burst out that he had "no notion of cheating anybody," the negotiators finally agreed that British merchants should "meet with no lawful impediment" in seeking to recover their bona fide debts. This article was influential in enlisting the support of the powerful British commercial class on the side of what was otherwise an unpopular pact.

The portions of the treaty that dealt with the Loyalists in America, Articles V and VI, had almost wrecked the negotiations. Tens of thousands of these luckless souls, having remained loyal to George III, had suffered confiscations, personal abuse, and finally exile. Some 80,000 of them had been driven from the United States. The London government naturally felt that it would be guilty of the basest ingratitude if it failed to secure restitution and compensation for those faithful subjects who had lost their all in support of the crown. But so savage had been the warfare between the Loyalists and their neighbors that the American negotiators would listen to no scheme for welcoming them back. Even the benign Franklin burst out: "Your ministers require that we should receive again into our bosom those who have been our bitterest enemies, and restore their properties who have destroyed ours; and this while the wounds they have given us are still bleeding!" [8]

At length, and only after heated discussions, a half-baked solution emerged. The negotiators agreed that all persecutions should cease, and that Congress would "earnestly recommend" to the states that they restore property taken from the Loyalists. But in view of the inflamed passions in America, the peace commissioners, British as well as American, must have foreseen that the recommendation would be ignored. These hollow words were necessary to save the face of the British government. Without them, peace probably could not have been made—at least, not at that time. The luckless Loyalists, like the unhappy Canadian fishermen, were thus sacrificed on the altar of Britain's imperial necessities.

[8] Wharton, *Revolutionary Diplomatic Correspondence*, VI, 80 (Franklin to Oswald, Nov. 26, 1782).

LORD SHELBURNE'S LONG VISION

The treaty with the United States, one must not forget, was but a part of the general settlement that England made with her four official enemies, including the Netherlands. The preliminary articles of peace that had been drawn up with Spain, France, and the United States were all signed as definitive treaties on September 3, 1783. On the whole, and considering the odds against her, Britain emerged from these settlements with a remarkably whole skin. The one exception was the American pact, which was so generous to the colonials that the preliminary draft evoked an outburst of condemnation in England.

The feeling was general that the American treaty was a dishonorable surrender, which spelled the end of Britain's greatness. One Englishman wrote an open letter to Lord Shelburne urging him not to "submit to such a disgraceful ruin as American independence" until the "Tower of London be taken sword in hand." The provisions regarding the Loyalists were denounced with bitterness by those who regarded the evasive arrangements as a base subterfuge. Lord North, now a member of the opposition, cried in Parliament: "Never was the honour of a nation so grossly abused as in the desertion of those men [Loyalists]. . . . Nothing can excuse our not having insisted on a stipulation in their favour. . . ." [9] Under the storm of criticism the ministry of Lord Shelburne fell, leaving that of his successor to conclude the final peace.

In America, public opinion was not altogether enthusiastic about the treaty. Considerable grumbling was heard about the kid-gloved treatment of the Loyalists, about the failure of the American negotiators to co-operate wholeheartedly with the French, and about the absence of a provision guaranteeing a reopening of trade with the British West Indies. But the great majority of Americans seem to have been pleased with the settlement, and especially with the success of their "militia diplomats" in outwitting their European adversaries.

Judging solely from the treaty, the United States had ground the Mother Country into the dust. But this was far from being the true picture. Large, well-equipped British armies still held strategic points in America, and if England had not been war-weary and pinned down elsewhere by her European foes, she might have crushed the crumbling colonial armies. The highly advantageous terms of the treaty bore so little relation to the military situation in America as to prompt Vergennes' classic exclamation: "You will notice that the English buy the peace more than they make it. Their concessions, in fact, as much as to the boundaries as to the fisheries and the loyalists, exceed all that I should have thought possible." [10]

[9] *Parliamentary History of England*, XXIII, 453 (Feb. 17, 1783).
[10] Wharton, *Revolutionary Diplomatic Correspondence*, VI, 107.

How can one account for England's unexpected generosity? In the first place, Prime Minister Shelburne had long been kindly disposed toward the colonials. He was eager to close the bloody chasm and avert future friction, particularly over the inevitable westward expansion of the American republic. He likewise desired to establish profitable commercial relationships, to wean the United States away from French postwar influence, and perhaps to lure the Americans into a loose tie with the British Empire. Yet one should not forget that Lord Shelburne, despite his sympathy for America, was a Briton, stanchly upholding the interests of his country. The Americans were forced to fight with skill and persistence for every important concession they won.

Finally, the attractive British terms must be considered in the light of the European conflagration. At the time when Jay opened separate negotiations, Britain was in desperate straits. Here was a golden opportunity for her to improve her position by seducing America from the ranks of the enemy. The colonials could not conceivably have received such generous terms if Britain had not been at war with three European powers. Europe's international distresses, as was often true during these formative years, spelled America's diplomatic successes. Without them the alliance would never have been made; without them independence could hardly have been won; without them the Americans would never have secured such highly advantageous terms of peace.

SELECTED BIBLIOGRAPHY

The most comprehensive single volume is S. F. Bemis' scholarly *The Diplomacy of the American Revolution* (New York, 1935). A much briefer survey is A. B. Darling, *Our Rising Empire, 1763–1803* (New Haven, 1940). On Franklin, consult Carl Van Doren, *Benjamin Franklin* (New York, 1938), and Gerald Stourzh, *Benjamin Franklin and American Foreign Policy* (Chicago, 1954); on Adams, Gilbert Chinard, *Honest John Adams* (Boston, 1933); on Jay, Frank Monaghan, *John Jay* (New York, 1935). See also P. C. Phillips, *The West in the Diplomacy of the American Revolution* (Urbana, Ill., 1913); T. P. Abernethy, *Western Lands and the American Revolution* (New York, 1937); N. V. Russell, *The British Régime in Michigan and the Old Northwest, 1760–1796* (Northfield, Minn., 1939); Friedrich Edler, *The Dutch Republic and the American Revolution* (Baltimore, 1911); J. B. Scott, ed., *The Armed Neutralities of 1780 and 1800* (New York, 1918).

Useful articles are J. F. Jameson, "St. Eustatius in the American Revolution," *Amer. Hist. Rev.*, VIII (1903), 683–708; Eunice Wead, "British Public Opinion of the Peace with America, 1782," *ibid.*, XXXIV (1929), 513–531; S. F. Bemis, "The Rayneval Memoranda of 1782," *Proceedings of the American Antiquarian Society*, XLVII (1937), 15–92.

See also footnotes of this chapter; Bemis and Griffin, *Guide*, pp. 3–48; *Harvard Guide*, Ch. 10.

7TH, 8TH, AND 9TH ED. REFS. See BIBLIOGRAPHICAL ADDENDUM, p. 979.

5

Foreign Affairs under the Articles of Confederation

I am uneasy and apprehensive; more so than during the war.

JOHN JAY, 1786

A DEMOCRATIC BLACK SHEEP

WHEN PRESIDENT LINCOLN declared at Gettysburg that the Founding Fathers had "brought forth a new nation" in 1776, his patriotic zeal outran his historical accuracy. He might better have said that those Fathers had brought forth a litter of small nations. The United States, during the six troubled years after independence was won in 1783, consisted of thirteen separate entities, each going its own way under a weak constitution called the Articles of Confederation. "United" seemed at times merely an ironical adjective. The truth was that only with alarming difficulty could Congress assemble a quorum to approve the treaty with England ending the war. With apathy and bankruptcy threatening the central government at home, the *dis*-United States of America could not—and in fact did not—command respect abroad.

Most Europeans did not bother their heads about the new infant in the family of nations, or, if they did, their opinions were colored by ignorance. Envoys representing the United States abroad had to go to considerable pains to explain that Americans were white and that they did not adorn themselves like savages. As Captain Snow testified in 1788: "I, sir, since the war, have had commerce with six different nations of the globe . . . and . . . I find this country held in the same light, by foreign nations, as a well-behaved negro is in a gentleman's family." [1]

But such indifference was not shared by the monarchs of Europe. If

---

[1] Jonathan Elliot, ed., *The Debates in the Several State Conventions on the Adoption of the Federal Constitution* (2nd ed., Philadelphia, 1891), II, 34 (Jan. 17, 1788).

the huge American experiment in democracy should succeed, the rulers of France and Spain would have created a veritable Frankenstein's monster. Oppressed subjects, pointing to the promised land of liberty and self-government, might well demand the same blessings for themselves. The ruling classes of the Old World were anxious, therefore, that the dangerous American experiment should fail. As an oasis of democracy in a Sahara of absolutism, the new republic offended them by merely existing. This hostile attitude continued to be a stumbling block in the relations between America and Europe far into the 19th Century.

But jealousy was not the only motive present. The crowned heads of Europe also cast greedy eyes upon the United States, and waited like vultures for the seemingly inevitable breakup. When that came, they could gobble up the most desirable pieces. Or, failing a complete collapse, the powers might use the impotent republic as a makeweight in their schemes for territorial conquest.

REBUFFING THE REBELS

Once the shooting had stopped, many Americans expected "sweet reconciliation" with the motherland. More than that, they were counting on a restoration of commercial privileges and other imperial advantages. But England was slow to forget that the Americans had unfurled the flag of rebellion; that they had joined hands with foreign allies; that they had almost wrecked the British Empire; and that they had brutally expelled tens of thousands of His Majesty's most loyal subjects. Now forsaking the role of rebels for that of suppliants, these same Americans were expecting the fatted calf of forgiveness. This was asking too much of human nature.

In 1785 John Adams was sent to England as the first minister of the United States. The London *Public Advertiser* was scandalized:

> An Ambassador from America! Good Heavens what a sound!—The Gazette surely never announced anything so extraordinary before. . . . This will be such a phenomenon in the Corps Diplomatique that 'tis hard to say which can excite indignation most, the insolence of those who appoint the Character, or the meanness of those who receive it.[2]

Adams soon discovered that the "popular pulse seems to beat high against America." Both he and Jefferson, who visited England about the same time, found ample evidence of a malicious campaign to poison British public opinion against the United States.

Adams, like other diplomats, was presented to George III, and made his three bows. The erstwhile rebel, who had been on the King's list for hanging, comported himself well and delivered a surprisingly tactful

---

[2] Quoted in Gilbert Chinard, *Honest John Adams* (Boston, 1933), p. 195.

speech. His Majesty, not to be outdone, replied in kind. The noteworthy feature of this incident is not that both principals made gracious remarks, but that any American minister should have been received so soon after the close of hostilities.

Adams' three years at the Court of St. James's, despite this auspicious start, were galling. He was treated with a "dry decency and cold civility which appears to have been the premeditated plan from the beginning." He would be frozen out of conferences with dead silence, and he found it impossible to obtain an answer "from the ministry to any one demand, proposal, or inquiry." "In short, sir," he complained to John Jay late in 1785, "I am likely to be as insignificant here as you can imagine."

Even more annoying was England's refusal to return the compliment and accredit a minister to the United States. The British Foreign Secretary rather cruelly suggested that if he sent one representative, he would have to send thirteen. But America, though so weak as to be contemptible, was too important to be ignored. London took pains to keep a sharp eye on developments through unofficial observers and officially appointed consuls.

THE BITTER FRUITS OF INDEPENDENCE

One of the most exasperating controversies to vex Anglo-American relations during these years arose over commerce. Before the rebellion most of the colonial trade had naturally been with the Mother Country, and when hostilities came to a close American commerce just as naturally sought the old and familiar channels. But in the absence of a formal commercial treaty granting reciprocal privileges, the London government was in a position to ruin American shippers by imposing arbitrary restrictions overnight.

With this sword hanging over their heads, American merchants threatened to extort a satisfactory pact from England by resorting to retaliatory legislation. But the British laughed in their faces. It was painfully clear, as events proved, that the thirteen sovereign states could not unite on any such program. Lord Sheffield, whose best-selling pamphlet opposing commercial concessions to the United States profoundly influenced his countrymen, drew unflattering comparisons with the more numerous and even more disunited German principalities: "It will not be an easy matter to bring the American states to act as a nation. They are not to be feared as such by us. . . . We might as well dread the effects of combinations among the German as among the American states. . . ." [3]

England had no desire to negotiate a commercial treaty, especially with

[3] Quoted in S. F. Bemis, ed., *The American Secretaries of State and Their Diplomacy* (New York, 1927), I, 223–224.

a government too weak to force the thirteen constituent states to observe it. And why should the British tie their hands with such a pact when, without one, they were reaping all the advantages they desired? Americans were again buying English goods, partly because British merchants were willing to extend long-term credits, and partly because of lifelong associations and habits. By 1789 England's trade with America was actually greater than it had been before the war—a classic case of getting the milk without having to support the cow.

THE RECONCILIATION BETWEEN BRITANNIA AND HER
DAUGHTER AMERICA

America (represented by a red Indian) is invited to buss
(kiss) her mother. A liberal view.

Detail from a British cartoon, *New York Public Library*

The Americans, on the other hand, were learning the disagreeable lesson that they could not eat their cake and have it too. Now that they had shaken off the duties and responsibilities of the British connection, they were confidently expecting to continue the privileges and profits that had formerly been theirs. They particularly hungered for the once-lucrative trade with the British West Indies.

The British naturally chose to treat the United States as the foreign nation it had so ardently desired to become. Specifically, they sought to strengthen the Empire by reserving its benefits for those colonies, such as Canada, that had remained loyal. Certain English liberals, notably Lord Shelburne, argued that in the long run England would profit most by making concessions to the Americans and by building up their good will. But powerful and selfish mercantile interests thwarted all effective moves in this direction. The Americans, as past masters of smuggling, did succeed in developing an illicit trade of considerable volume with the British colonies, notably the West Indies. But the whole situation was charged with resentment and ill will.

TREATY VIOLATIONS AND COUNTERVIOLATIONS

Another serious roadblock in Anglo-American relations was the so-called "peace" Treaty of 1783. This document belied its name, for nearly all of its major provisions led to many years of bitter wrangling. One reason that London repeatedly gave for its unwillingness to negotiate a commercial treaty was the failure of America to honor the treaty that had ended the war.

The peace of 1783 had solemnly stipulated that British creditors, who claimed an estimated £2 million to £5 million, should meet with "no lawful impediment" in attempting to collect what was owed them. The spineless Congress did what it could to execute this article, but state legislators and state courts openly flouted the plain provisions of the treaty.

Public opinion in Virginia was particularly strong against payment. Everywhere George Mason heard men say, "If we are now to pay the debts due to British merchants, what have we been fighting for all this while?" Responding to such pressures, the Virginia legislature enacted laws designed to prevent the collection of debts. One victim of such legislation disdainfully remarked, with more truth than tact, that some of the members were voting to retain the very shirts on their backs. Brought before that august body, he was forced to kneel and apologize. As he arose he dusted off his knees and muttered, with evident double meaning, "Upon my word, a domned dirty house it is indeed!"

More widely and flagrantly violated was the article in the Treaty of 1783 regarding the Loyalists. It provided that the persecution of these unfortunates should cease, and that Congress should *recommend* to the states the restoration of confiscated Loyalist property. The second part of this obligation was quickly discharged, for the recommendation to the states was duly made—and widely disregarded. But the first part of the obligation was deliberately violated. Seven years of Loyalist-Patriot fighting—including burnings, killings, and incitings to Indian massacres—had aroused a fearsome amount of ill will. In May, 1783, the Massachusetts *Chronicle* reflected a common sentiment:

As Hannibal swore never to be at peace with the Romans, so let every Whig [Patriot] swear . . . by the shades of departed friends who have fallen in battle, by the ghosts of those of our brethren who have been destroyed on board of prison-ships and in loathsome dungeons, never to be at peace with those fiends . . . whose thefts, murders, and treasons have filled the cup of woe. . . .[4]

Most Loyalists were not personally molested after the war, but many suffered from discriminatory state legislation and a few from physical abuse—all in flagrant violation of the treaty.

ANGLO-AMERICAN FRONTIER FRICTION

The Americans, for their part, had good reason to accuse the British of having violated the treaty. In spite of clear stipulations to the contrary, departing British armies had carried away some 3000 Negro slaves, whose owners now demanded indemnification. Far more irksome

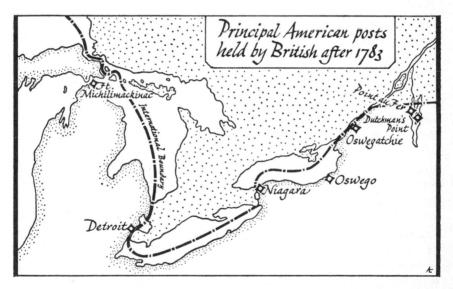

Principal American posts held by British after 1783

was the refusal of the British to turn over to the Americans a long chain of military and trading posts, stretching from Lake Champlain to Lake Superior within the river-and-lake boundary of the United States. Yet the treaty had provided for evacuation "with all convenient speed." The Canadians, who felt that their interests had been grossly neglected in regard to the fisheries and boundaries, insisted that relinquishment of the posts would dislocate their profitable fur trade and antagonize their

[4] Quoted in J. B. McMaster, *A History of the People of the United States* (New York, 1893), I, 116.

Indian wards. They therefore sought to have the British occupation continued, preferably until such time as they could satisfactorily withdraw their property and reorganize their business.

London was impressed by the arguments of the Canadians for hanging on to the posts. Not only was there the fur trade but there were the Indians, who had proved to be England's only allies in the recent world conflict. Their territory and other interests had been bartered away during the haste at the Paris peace table, and, unless properly pacified, they might turn against their British custodians in a bloody uprising. More than that, sparsely populated Canada needed allies in holding back the pushful and procreative American pioneers. And the paint bedaubed redmen were the only possible allies in this part of the world.

A prolonged overstay by the Redcoats at the American posts seemed imperative if the Indian tomahawks were to be lined up properly. Accordingly, on April 8, 1784, the Secretary of State for Home Affairs in London ordered the posts to be held. Ironically enough, this order was issued the day before George III officially proclaimed ratification of the treaty of peace and solemnly enjoined his subjects to observe it.

The saying is that a man often has two reasons for what he does—the real one and a good one. When the British decided to retain the posts in the interests of the Canadian fur traders and their red allies, they sought a plausible pretext to give to the world. They were not long in finding one. The Americans, as already noted, were not faithfully carrying out the terms of the treaty regarding debts and Loyalists. So the British, alleging prior violations, tightened the deadlock when they announced that they would hold the posts until the American debts were paid.

As time wore on John Jay, Secretary for Foreign Affairs of the Continental Congress, began to develop considerable sympathy for the British point of view regarding the posts. He was frank to confess that there had not been a single day since the ratification of the treaty when it had "not been violated . . . by one or other of the states." With inexcusable indiscretion he revealed these opinions to the British consul at New York, who in turn relayed them to London. The British could hardly be expected to hasten their evacuation of the posts when they knew that Secretary Jay was privately acknowledging the strength of their case.

The explosive problem of the posts was complicated by another danger spot on the northern frontier. Vermont, then a semi-independent entity, had not been admitted to the United States because of boundary disputes with neighboring states. The people of this backwoods area were vitally in need of the St. Lawrence River outlet to the sea, and a considerable number of them, led by the energetic Ethan Allen and his two brothers, were showing a lively interest in British flirtations designed to promote reunion with the mother country. No one could then tell whether Vermont would throw herself into the arms of Great Britain or the United States.

SPANISH SCHEMINGS

Relations with Spain were no less embittered than those with England. The Madrid Court had never been sympathetic toward the rebel republic, and it felt even more hostile when the United States in 1783 snatched the vast trans-Appalachian region from its grasping hand. The unfriendly atmosphere was further thickened by the development of a boundary dispute and, more ominously, by friction over the navigation of the Mississippi River.

The definitive Treaty of 1783 with Britain had stipulated that the southwestern boundary of the United States should begin where the 31st parallel intersects the Mississippi River. Yet when West Florida had been in British hands from 1763 to 1783, its northern boundary had not been the 31st parallel but the line cutting across the mouth of the Yazoo River, more than one hundred miles farther north. Spain therefore refused to be bound by the line of the 31st parallel, and in addition claimed the area to the Ohio and Tennessee rivers, largely by virtue of successful military operations against the British in the recent war.

An immense portion of the Old Southwest thus became involved in a twelve-year dispute between the Spaniards and the Americans. Within that region, which the United States claimed as its own, the Spanish flag waved over Natchez and other posts, just as the British flag waved over American soil in the North. To strengthen her position, Spain played a deep game of intrigue with the powerful Indian tribes of the Southwest. She also provided them with firearms for murderous forays against the American settlers, just as the British in the North were tightening their hold on the posts by similar tactics. This common policy enabled Spain and England, through their forts and the influence that radiated from them to the Indians, to exercise virtual control over more than one half of the territorial domain of the United States.

Even more ominous was the dispute with Spain over the free navigation of the Mississippi. By 1785 some 50,000 adventuresome pioneers had trickled over the Alleghenies and had spilled out onto the rich lands of what are now Tennessee and Kentucky. The cost of transporting their bulky agricultural produce over the mountains was prohibitively high. But nature had placed at their very doors a huge waterway, the Mississippi River, which could carry their grain and other products inexpensively to ocean-going ships. The mouth of this stream, unhappily, was in the hands of jealous and hostile Spaniards, who were determined to protect their own possessions from conquest by closing the river and damming up the American West. Such a catastrophe the frontiersmen would not tolerate.

The controversy came to a boil in 1784, when Spain announced that henceforth the Mississippi outlet would be closed to American shipping. This reversal of policy was dramatically brought to the attention of "the men of the western waters" when an enterprising trader ventured down the river, only to have his entire cargo seized by the Spaniards at Natchez. Permitted to return to the American settlements, he arrived with a tale of woe that lost nothing in its repeated telling to groups of indignant frontiersmen. These fierce spirits, unwilling to endure economic strangulation, threatened to settle the dispute with their rifles. Agents of Great Britain circulated throughout the western settlements, glibly telling sympathetic listeners of the possibility of a British protectorate George Washington, after a journey of 680 miles through the back country, reported in 1784: "The western settlers (I speak now from my own observation) stand as it were upon a pivot. The touch of a feather would turn them any way." [5]

THE JAY-GARDOQUI DEAL

Commercial difficulties with Spain added fuel to the flames of discontent. The Spaniards had partially relaxed their iron-clad trade monopoly during the recent war with England, and the United States had tasted the sweets of that trade. When hostilities ended, these conces-

[5] W. C. Ford, ed., *Writings of George Washington* (New York, 1891), X, 408.

sions were abruptly withdrawn, to the acute distress of American shippers. With the United States government facing bankruptcy, and with the Spanish trade capable of providing a large quantity of gold and silver money, a satisfactory commercial treaty with Spain seemed urgently necessary. Against this background one must consider the wearisome negotiations of 1785–1786 at New York, then the nation's capital, between Secretary Jay and the Spanish envoy, Don Diego de Gardoqui.

The smooth Gardoqui, having learned of Jay's vanity and his deep attachment to Mrs. Jay, undertook through lavish entertainment and other expenditures to curry favor with his American hosts. He "loaned" one member of Congress a total of $5000. When he learned that General Washington desired some Spanish jackasses for breeding mules at Mount Vernon, he so informed his government. His superiors had anticipated his request by sending a handsome animal to the general, who appreciatively named it "Royal Gift." Gardoqui meanwhile continued his attentions to Mrs. Jay, whose beauty and charm made the Spanish diplomat's task by no means a disagreeable one. "Notwithstanding my age," he wrote, "I am acting the gallant and accompanying Madame to the official entertainments and dances, because she likes it and I will do everything which appeals to me for the King's best interest." [6] To judge from some of his official reports, Gardoqui danced his way through the negotiation— one of the few instances of terpsichorean diplomacy in American annals.

Gardoqui had received positive instructions from Madrid that the free navigation of the Mississippi was not to be yielded to the Americans. Jay had received equally positive instructions from Congress that no treaty was to be concluded which did not guarantee this right. After months of nerve-racking negotiation, agreement seemed impossible. If, however, the Americans were willing to give way on the Mississippi issue, Spain was prepared to make important trade concessions. American merchants on the Atlantic seaboard could see no valid reason why such a prize should be denied them, particularly if it meant sacrificing the interests of a horde of uncouth backwoodsmen.

Responding to the clamor of Eastern merchants, Jay now began to change his views. After all, the West was not populous, and no great hardship would befall the United States if the right to navigate the Mississippi was yielded for a decade or two. With regard to the immediate future, a commercial agreement with Spain probably would offset by a considerable margin the economic loss resulting from a closure of the river. Finally, there was no other way to secure the treaty which languishing American commerce needed.

Overborne by such arguments, Jay at length surrendered. On August 3, 1786, he urged Congress to change his instructions so as to permit the United States to "forbear" the right to navigate the Mississippi for twenty-five or thirty years in return for a commercial treaty with Spain.

[6] Quoted in S. F. Bemis, *Pinckney's Treaty* (Baltimore, 1926), p. 84.

After a heated debate, in which the Southern states with Western interests violently protested, Jay's request was finally granted, on August 29, 1786, by a close vote of seven states to five. But since the approval of nine states would be necessary before the treaty could be ratified, further negotiations proved futile.

THE REVOLT OF THE WEST

When the hair-triggered men across the mountains learned that the Eastern merchants were proposing to sacrifice them for the sake of more trade, they arose in an outburst of anger. The Virginia orator, Patrick Henry, whose interests were identified with theirs, declared that he "would rather part with the confederation than relinquish the navigation of the Mississippi." There was wild talk in the West of an alliance with England, or even with Spain, or of making a descent upon New Orleans, rifle in hand. One of these inquiet spirits vented his indignation:

> The [proposed] commercial treaty with Spain is considered to be cruel, oppressive and unjust. The prohibition of the navigation of the Mississippi has astonished the whole western country. To sell us and make us vassals to the merciless Spaniards is a grievance not to be borne. Should we tamely submit to such manacles we should be unworthy the name of Americans, and a scandal to the annals of its history.[7]

In the face of this storm of protest the Jay-Gardoqui negotiations collapsed, leaving the deadlock exactly where it had been, except that it was now complicated by a deep-seated distrust of the West for the East. Just a few months later, the ratification of the federal Constitution of 1787 was almost defeated by Southerners with Western interests. They concluded, not illogically, that the group which had backed the abortive Jay Treaty could not be trusted to draw up a new framework of government. The constitutional provision that a two-thirds vote of the Senate be required for the approval of treaties apparently reflected the suspicions engendered among many Southerners and Westerners by the Jay-Gardoqui negotiation. They felt—or at least some of them did—that they needed at least a one-third veto voice to protect themselves against the selfishness of the East.

The United States could afford to be patient as long as the West was scantily populated, and as long as New Orleans and Florida were in Spanish hands. With its multiplying millions, the republic was growing stronger each year; Spain, already fallen upon evil days, was growing progressively weaker. A diplomatic crisis or a general war in Europe would, as Thomas Jefferson counseled from Paris, enable the United States to press its claims with vigor and success.

For nearly ten years after the collapse of the Jay-Gardoqui negotiations, Spain made no serious effort to conclude a commercial treaty with

[7] *Secret Journals of Congress,* IV, 315.

the United States. She found that the employment of Indian allies, as well as the use of gold among American leaders in the West, provided a reasonable degree of security. She was also able to pacify the West to some extent when, in 1788, she granted the right to navigate the Mississippi, subject to the payment of stipulated duties. But on the whole the American people were content with the strategy of delay.

THE FRENCH ALLY COOLS OFF

Unfriendly treatment might have been expected by Americans from both Britain and Spain, but what of France, the beloved ally of Revolution days? Actually, relations were not a great deal better. Following the strategy outlined by Vergennes, the Paris government continued its underhanded policy of trying to keep the United States a weak and subservient satellite. A feeble America would be much more dependent on the benevolent protection of France, and much less likely to embark on an ambitious foreign policy that would conflict with Gallic interests. As a consequence, the French viewed with little satisfaction the movement to establish a stronger central government under the new federal Constitution.

But France did make some slight concessions. She granted American shippers the right to trade with a few ports of her West Indies, though only in small ships and for a limited number of commodities. This sop was admittedly far from satisfactory, but it was liberality itself when compared with the policy of Spain and Britain. France had so little confidence in American courts that in 1788 she negotiated a consular convention, by the terms of which French consuls in the United States could try certain cases involving Frenchmen. Similar privileges, to be sure, were granted American consuls in France, but this whole arrangement suggests that type of extraterritorial jurisdiction which the United States later insisted upon in its dealings with backward Asiatic countries.

During the most anxious years of the Confederation period Thomas Jefferson, *"connaisseur en révolutions,"* was the United States minister to France. He later remembered that the position "was an excellent school of humility":

> On being presented to any one as the minister of America, the commonplace question used in such cases was *"c'est vous, Monsieur, qui remplace le Docteur Franklin?"* "it is you, Sir, who replace Doctor Franklin?" I generally answered, "no one can replace him, Sir: I am only his successor." [8]

Jefferson was unduly modest. He developed a strong liking for the French, for whose revolution he acted as godfather, and they in turn found him a patron after their own hearts.

[8] A. A. Lipscomb, ed., *The Writings of Thomas Jefferson* (Monticello ed., Washington, 1904), VIII, 130.

Yet at best Jefferson's position was uncomfortable, largely because of the American debt of 35 million livres, for which he was "daily dunned." The rumor even spread in diplomatic circles that France might take a part of Rhode Island as payment. "We are," Jefferson wrote despairingly from Paris, "the lowest and most obscure of the whole diplomatic tribe." But the government of France probably preferred a United States too weak to pay its debts to one that might take the bit in its teeth and break away from French influence. The debts themselves were a trifling sum when compared with the enormous costs of winning America's independence, and the Paris regime was determined to cash in on these expenditures by using the United States to promote French schemes in the New World.

BARBARY BLACKMAIL

The feebleness of America under the Articles of Confederation was nowhere more glaringly revealed than in dealings with the Barbary pirates. The rulers of the petty North African states—Morocco, Algiers, Tripoli, and Tunis—loosed upon the commerce of the Mediterranean as ruffianly a lot of cutthroats as history can offer. They not only enslaved their captives for ransom but collected large sums of protection money from those nations that could afford to make payments. Piracy was a profitable national industry.

Why should the nations of Europe, with their powerful navies, have tolerated these piratical nests? Perhaps the basic reason was that in the long run the payment of blackmail seemed to be the cheapest, surest, and least troublesome way of handling the problem. Even big-navy Great Britain chose the easier way out and paid tribute, as a result of which the American colonials had developed a thriving Mediterranean trade.

With the winning of independence the United States lost its British shield, although some Yankee shippers were clever enough to carry forged British passes. The Barbary pirates fell upon unprotected American ships, enslaved the crews, forced up insurance rates, and virtually drove the Stars and Stripes from the Mediterranean Sea. The United States was too poor to pay blackmail; too weak to offer effective resistance. England naturally rejoiced at the crippling of a formidable shipping rival. Perhaps the chief reason why she did not use her navy to wipe out the pirates was that the commerce of the Mediterranean was thus reserved for those nations, like herself, wealthy enough to pay protection money.

The commercial picture in the Mediterranean continued dark during Confederation days. By a stroke of good fortune, the United States in 1787 concluded a reasonably satisfactory treaty with Morocco, at the bargain price of less than $10,000. But there remained the swarm of marauders at Algiers, Tripoli, and Tunis. Secretary Jay viewed this degrading situation with a curious satisfaction. If the Barbary corsairs would only cause deep enough humiliation, the American people might be shamed into strengthening their national government to meet foreign peril. When Jay heard of a reported declaration of war against the United States by Algiers, he was pleased. "This war," he wrote, "does not strike me as a great evil. The more we are ill-treated abroad the more we shall unite and consolidate at home."

Jay's hope was fulfilled in 1788–1789 when the United States, dropping the toothless Articles of Confederation, adopted the present federal Constitution. A shameful weakness in foreign affairs must be given a high rank among the forces that aroused American public opinion to support this change. In an indirect sense, the brutal Dey of Algiers was a Founding Father of the Constitution. The mercantile men in America also helped lead the drive for a stronger central government, for they could see no other way to wrest commercial treaties from reluctant powers. In an indirect sense, the illiberal Lord Sheffield was likewise a Founding Father. Thus the open hostility of foreign nations, combined with the narrow trade policies of Britain and other powers, helped transform the disunited states of America from thirteen squabbling sovereignties into one nation.

SELECTED BIBLIOGRAPHY

A brief survey appears in A. B. Darling, *Our Rising Empire, 1763–1803* (New Haven, 1940); the broader setting in Merrill Jensen, *The New Nation: A History of the United States during the Confederation, 1781–1789* (New York, 1950). New light on the northern posts is shed by A. L. Burt, *The United States, Great Britain, and British North America* (New Haven, 1940), which corrects in part S. F. Bemis' older standard monograph, *Jay's Treaty* (New York, 1923). See also Frank Monaghan, *John Jay* (New York, 1935). Useful monographs are S. F. Bemis, *Pinckney's Treaty* (Baltimore, 1926); A. P. Whitaker, *The Spanish-American Frontier, 1783–1795* (Boston, 1927); and R. W. Irwin, *The Diplomatic Relations of the United States with the Barbary Powers, 1776–1816* (Chapel Hill, N.C., 1931).

See footnotes of this chapter; Bemis and Griffin, *Guide*, pp. 49–67, 156–161; *Harvard Guide*, Ch. 10.

7TH, 8TH, AND 9TH ED. REFS. See BIBLIOGRAPHICAL ADDENDUM, p. 980.

CHAPTER

6

Embroilments with Britain
1789-1795

*You cannot imagine what horror some persons are
in, lest peace [with England] should continue.*
JOHN ADAMS, April 19, 1794

THE NEW FEDERAL ROOF

THE NEW CONSTITUTION, unlike the discarded Articles of Confederation, clothed the national government with sufficient power to deal boldly and vigorously with both domestic and foreign affairs. But monarchical Europe, with its hereditary distrust of republicanism, was frankly skeptical. The future alone could tell whether General Washington, who was inaugurated President at New York City on April 30, 1789, would be able to breathe life into the parchment entrusted to him.

The Cabinet was chosen with care. Washington selected as his Secretary of the Treasury the brilliant young Alexander Hamilton, who, by a series of daring financial manuevers, revived the corpse of American credit. The new Department of State, which succeeded the old Department of Foreign Affairs under the Confederation, was entrusted to Thomas Jefferson, then United States minister to France. The appointment was a logical one, for the distinguished Virginian was well qualified by intellectual background and practical experience for the duties of Secretary of State. His chief task, as it turned out, was to create precedent and to lay the foundation stones upon which others were to achieve fame.

Jefferson, unhappily, was handicapped by friction with Hamilton, who regarded himself as a kind of prime minister and who repeatedly thrust his fingers into his colleague's business. Hamilton was a deep-dyed conservative and, although first of all an American, a warm admirer of English institutions. Jefferson, his complete opposite, was a strong liberal who, though passionately attached to his own country, admired

66

the civilization of France. He cherished little love for the English—those "rich, proud, hectoring, swearing, squibbling, carnivorous animals who lived on the other side of the Channel."

Partly as a result of such deep-seated differences two political parties crystallized during Washington's first administration: the Federalists, led by Hamilton, and the Democratic-Republicans or Republicans,[1] led by Jefferson. Both groups were basically American, but the Federalists believed that the interests of America would be best served by closer relations with England rather than with France. The Jeffersonian Republicans, on the other hand, favored closer relations with France rather than with England.

EVOLUTION OF MAJOR PARTIES

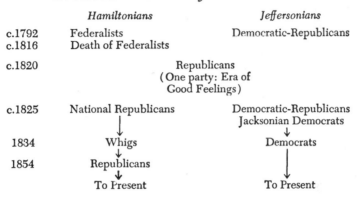

	Hamiltonians	*Jeffersonians*
c.1792	Federalists	Democratic-Republicans
c.1816	Death of Federalists	
c.1820		Republicans (One party: Era of Good Feelings)
c.1825	National Republicans ↓	Democratic-Republicans Jacksonian Democrats ↓
1834	Whigs ↓	Democrats
1854	Republicans ↓ To Present	↓ To Present

Hamilton was so anxious to preserve friendly intercourse with the motherland that he kept in close touch with the British officials in America, supplying them with highly confidential information. When, for example, Jefferson lodged a powerful 17,000-word protest against Britain's violation of the Treaty of 1783, Hamilton took a grossly improper step. He inaccurately informed His Majesty's minister in Philadelphia that the American note was not to be taken seriously, primarily because it did not represent the views of the administration. The force of Jefferson's protest was consequently weakened.

NOOTKA AND NEUTRALITY

The first diplomatic crisis to bedevil the new government came from an unexpected and almost unheard-of quarter. In the summer of 1789 the Spanish authorities seized several British trading ships that had ventured into Nootka Sound, a small inlet on the western coast of Van-

---

[1] Not to be confused with the present-day Republican Party, which emerged in 1854.

couver Island over which Spain claimed jurisdiction. When the news finally reached England, the nation rocked with excitement and the government feverishly prepared for war. This was not merely a question of the ownership of a few trading ships or squalid huts: the outposts of two great colonial empires had clashed in the Pacific Northwest.

It was widely assumed that in the event of war the British in Canada would strike at Spain's New Orleans, Florida, and Louisiana. If they asked permission to send troops across American soil to win their objectives, the United States would be placed in an awkward position. Acquiescence might mean war with Spain; refusal might mean war with Britain. Confronted with this fateful dilemma, President Washington sought the advice of his official family. As might be expected, opinions varied widely, with the pro-British Hamilton urging that permission be granted.

Fortunately for the United States, the British were not forced to make the anticipated request. Spain turned desperately to her former ally, France, who was now in the throes of the French Revolution and unable to lend a hand. Since war was hopeless, the only alternative was submission. Spain reluctantly swallowed the British demands and, in the Convention of 1790, receded from her former position, leaving Nootka as the high-water mark of her sprawling empire.[2]

From the standpoint of the United States, certain highly beneficial results flowed from the unhappy Nootka incident. This early Cabinet discussion of neutrality—that is, aloofness from the wars of Europe—helped clarify thinking regarding the policy of noninvolvement that finally developed in 1793. The prospect of hostilities following the Nootka dispute, moreover, opened British eyes to the importance of the United States—a revelation that elicited greater respect. London officialdom even perceived that the Americans might go so far as to seize their own northern trading posts, which the British still occupied, when the Mother Country was at grips with an adversary elsewhere.

Nor did the obvious strength of the new government under the Constitution fail to impress London. Congress was now in a position to enact retaliatory commercial legislation against England; indeed, such a measure had already made considerable headway in the House of Representatives. The United States was Britain's best overseas customer, and the London officials quickly perceived that American tariff discrimination would deal their commerce a staggering blow.

The Foreign Office now realized that it could no longer rely on the reports of consuls and unofficial observers. Hence, in 1791, seven years after the ratification of the peace treaty, London sent a minister plenipotentiary to Philadelphia, the new temporary capital, in the person of

[2] See W. R. Manning, "The Nootka Sound Controversy," Amer. Hist. Assn., *Annual Report, 1904*, pp. 279–478.

George Hammond. The youthful envoy, who proceeded to fall in love with a local belle, was not the ablest man who could have been chosen. But the significant fact is that Great Britain now considered the United States of sufficient weight to justify the presence of a full-fledged diplomatic representative.

THE FRENCH REVOLUTION

World-shaking events had meanwhile been erupting in Europe. On July 14, 1789, a little more than ten weeks after Washington's inauguration, the Parisian masses rose and stormed the Bastille, dreaded prison-fortress and symbol of tyranny. The American people, many of whom felt that their own example had inspired the French to revolt, greeted the news with a tidal wave of rejoicing that was called the "Bastille fever" and the "love-frenzy for France." The names of streets in the United States that even suggested monarchy were properly rechristened. In Boston, for example, Royal Exchange Alley became Equality Lane. Exclusive, therefore nondemocratic, societies fell into disrepute, including the infant scholarship fraternity, Phi Beta Kappa. Titles such as "Judge" or even "Mister" suggested social gradations; hence in American republican circles Mr. and Mrs. Smith became "Citizen" Smith and "Citizeness" Smith, as in France.

The French Revolution entered upon a bloodier phase in 1792, when the monarchs of Europe, aided by the exiled nobles, began to invade France for the purpose of restoring the yoke to the peasants. When the citizen army of France finally managed to hurl back the foe, American enthusiasm broke its dikes. Frenzied crowds sang French songs and danced joyously in the streets. Through the haze of thirty years William Wirt could look back and write:

> Even at this moment my blood runs cold, my breast swells, my temples throb, and I find myself catching my breath, when I recall the ecstasy with which I used to join in that glorious apostrophe to Liberty in the Marseilles Hymn. . . . And then the glorious, magnificent triumph of the arms of France. . . . O, how we used to . . . weep and to sing and pray over these more than human exertions and victories! [3]

But centuries of pent-up emotion were not to be unloosed in France without frightful consequences. The revolution took an ugly turn when the guillotine was erected and aristocratic heads began to roll into executioners' baskets. In January, 1793, Louis XVI, who had helped the Americans win their independence, bowed his neck to the bloody knife. Several months later the frivolous queen, Marie Antoinette, suffered a similar fate. The Reign of Terror, with its symbolic crash of the guillotine, was well under way.

[3] J. P. Kennedy, *Memoirs of the Life of William Wirt* (Philadelphia, 1856), II, 108.

In America, the arch-Jeffersonians rejoiced at the royal executions, although conservative Jeffersonians were distressed. The Pittsburgh *Gazette* gloated brutally, "Louis Capet has lost his caput." William Cobbett, a prominent journalist, testified:

> Never was the memory of any man so cruelly insulted as that of this mild and humane monarch. He was guillotined in effigy, in the capital of the Union [Philadelphia], twenty or thirty times every day, during one whole winter and part of the summer. Men, women and children flocked to the tragical exhibition, and not a single paragraph appeared in the papers to shame them from it.[4]

The tragic excesses of the French Revolution completely alienated the conservatives in America, especially the Hamiltonian Federalists. To them the new regime was merely the substitution of the tyranny of the unwashed masses for the tyranny of their legitimate rulers. It seemed to spell the end of religion, private property, and all that Americans held most dear. The fear was commonly expressed that this "moral influenza," more to be dreaded than a "thousand yellow fevers," might even spread to the United States.

THE PRO-FRENCH FUROR

On February 1, 1793, eleven days after the execution of Louis XVI, France declared war on Great Britain. Thus began a titanic conflict that was fated to last almost uninterruptedly for twenty-two years and to suck the United States into its vortex. The Federalists looked upon Britain as the world's last hope. But the pro-French faction, composed mostly of Jeffersonian Republicans, regarded the issue as that of 1776 over again. To them the tyrannical George III was once more using Redcoats to suppress human liberties, this time at the expense of America's ally, France. Although many pro-French sympathizers in the United States were not pleased with the gory by-products of the revolution, they felt that the sacrifice of a few thousand aristocratic necks was a cheap price to pay for toppling despotism. Jefferson, who believed that a nation could not be transferred "from despotism to liberty in a feather bed," lapsed into characteristic extravagance:

> The liberty of the whole earth was depending on the issue of the contest, and was ever such a prize won with so little innocent blood? My own affections have been deeply wounded by some of the martyrs to this cause, but rather than it should have failed I would have seen half the earth desolated; were there but an Adam and an Eve left in every country, and left free, it would be better than as it now is.[5]

[4] William Cobbett, *History of the American Jacobins* (Philadelphia, 1796), pp. 26–27.
[5] A. A. Lipscomb, ed., *Writings of Thomas Jefferson* (Monticello ed., Washington, 1904), IX, 10 (Jefferson to Short, Jan. 3, 1793).

The Jeffersonian Republicans, who were generally sympathetic with the French, thus found themselves arrayed in a hostile camp against the Federalists, who were branded "British bootlickers." Political passions, aroused by both domestic and foreign affairs, ran incredibly high. In every walk of life, including business and religion, men were divided into Federalist and Republican groups, some of whom drank in separate taverns.

THE CONTRAST

A comparison between French and American Liberty.

From C. C. Coffin, *Building a Nation*, 1882, after sketches in an old Philadelphia pamphlet

This was the age of personal journalism, and editors vied with one another in devising vile epithets. The Jeffersonian-Republicans were called "a despicable mobocracy," "Gallic Jackals," "lying dogs," "stinking caitiffs," "tools of baboons," "frog-eating, man-eating, blood-drinking cannibals." The most venomous of the Federalist editors, William Cobbett, let fly the following blast at his Jeffersonian adversaries: "I say, beware, ye under-strapping cut-throats who walk in rags and sleep amidst filth and vermin; for if once the halter gets around your flea-bitten necks, howling and confessing will come too late." [6] The Jeffersonian editors were fully capable of replying in kind.

BRITAIN'S RED ALLIES

With passions at fever heat many of the Federalists demanded intervention in the war on the side of Britain, while many of the Jeffersonians

[6] *Porcupine's Gazette*, quoted in Charles Warren, *Jacobin and Junto* (Cambridge, Mass., 1931), p. 90.

clamored for intervention on the side of France. But President Washington steered a more level-headed course, and in circumstances which will be described in the next chapter, issued his memorable Proclamation of Neutrality on April 22, 1793. But proclaiming neutrality did not guarantee neutrality, for a number of incendiary developments brought Britain and America to the very brink of war.

The most galling of all American grievances was Britain's continued retention of the northern posts. The Union Jack still flapped over these tiny forts ten full years after England had solemnly promised to give them up. Canadian fur traders were making off with rich profits that belonged to the Americans, while the British authorities showed no intention whatever of withdrawing. Not only had they taken additional new steps to strengthen their hold, but the commander of the fort at Niagara even refused to permit Americans to view their own Niagara Falls.

A problem intimately related to the posts, and perhaps even more inflammatory, was that of the Indians. The British perceived that they could maintain their grip on the fur trade more securely if they extended their influence to the surrounding tribes. A primary goal of London's frontier policy during these years was not only to curry favor with the Indians but to unite them in a buffer state against the steadily advancing American pioneers. England would thus protect three areas: the source of the fur trade, the posts themselves, and Canada itself. British agents glibly encouraged the Indians to believe that the cession of the trans-Appalachian region to the Americans was but a temporary arrangement, and that in a few years George III, the "Great White Father with a Red Coat," would return. In pursuance of this policy, England kept the Indians in a state of dependence, providing them with "firewater," blankets, muskets, ammunition, war paint, and even scalping knives. As has been well said, "The hand that sells the whiskey rules the tomahawk."

From 1783 to 1794 the butchering of American pioneers was a frequent tragedy on the Ohio frontier, as well as on the Spanish-controlled southern frontier. The very arms used by the northern red men bore fresh British trademarks, and many Americans believed that these murderous forays were deliberately incited or directed by His Majesty's officers at the American posts. There can be little doubt that the liberal disbursement of firearms and firewater to the Indians, together with assurances of a return of British authority, bore a close relation to the numerous scalping forays.

Anglo-American tension became markedly worse early in 1794. First of all, Lord Dorchester, Governor-General of Canada, committed the serious indiscretion of making a warlike speech to a delegation of Indians hostile to the United States. He openly encouraged them to believe that England and America would be at each others' throats within a year, thus affording them an opportunity to recover their lands from the "long knives." Two months later the British had the effrontery to penetrate American territory and establish a fort at the rapids of the Maumee River, some sixty miles southwest of Detroit.

THE SPECTER OF WAR WITH ENGLAND

As if the controversies over the posts and the Indians were not troublesome enough, London suddenly proclaimed a policy that struck brutally at American merchant shipping. In time of peace, trade with the French Islands of the Caribbean had been reserved for French shippers, but the French authorities, fearing starvation by British warships, had now thrown open these ports to Yankee merchantmen. London was determined to halt this profitable traffic in foodstuffs by invoking its arbitrary Rule of 1756—that is, commerce not open in time of peace shall not legally be thrown open to neutrals in time of war.

Like a thunderclap came two British decrees. The first was the Order in Council of June 8, 1793, which authorized the seizure and pre-emptive purchase of all neutral [*i.e.*, American] cargoes of foodstuffs bound for the ports of France or ports under French control. Second—and more menacing—was the Order in Council of November 6, 1793. It provided for the detention of all ships carrying the produce of a French colony or supplies for the use of such a colony. French private property on neutral American vessels would thus be confiscated, contrary to the American "Plan of 1776," which avowed the principle that "free ships make free goods."

Hard-boiled British naval officers proceeded to carry out these new orders with ruthlessness and dispatch. They speedily seized about 300 American vessels, mostly in the West Indies, and threw many of their crews into foul jails or forcibly impressed them into the British navy. American shipping, which had experienced a life-giving boom since the beginning of Anglo-French hostilities, was partially paralyzed.

The news of these confiscations, coming at the height of ill feeling over the Indians and the posts, produced an outraged cry in America for war against George III, that "prince of land and sea-robbers." With patriotic songs on their lips, thousands of citizens volunteered to erect fortifications. Even Alexander Hamilton, who regarded Britain's conduct as "atrocious," advised President Washington to prepare for hostilities while continuing negotiations. An infuriated mob in Charleston tore down the statue of Lord Chatham (William Pitt) which had been appreciatively erected a quarter of a century before. When John Hodgkinson, the popular actor, appeared on a New York stage in the uniform of a British officer, as the role required, he was greeted with a storm of derision which subsided only when he stepped forward and explained that he was playing the part of a coward and a bully. The governor of Upper Canada asserted on August 6, 1794: "I hold war to be inevitable. . . ."

ON THE BRINK OF FINANCIAL SUICIDE

An aroused Congress cleared for action. On March 26, 1794, it struck back at the British Orders in Council by imposing a thirty-day embargo, later extended by one month, on all shipping in American harbors bound for foreign ports. This restriction was nominally impartial, for it applied to France as well as to England. Shortly thereafter the Jeffersonian Republicans in Congress, riding the wave of anti-British hysteria, threw their support behind legislation to suspend all intercourse with Great Britain in British products. Although their object was to force a repeal of the odious Orders in Council, the hard-pressed Mother Country was in no mood to yield to the commercial hatchet.

Many Federalists feared that anti-British discrimination would lead to war, and that war would lead to disaster—perhaps national suicide. The fate of the new central government hinged on the success of Hamilton's ambitious financial structure, which in turn derived about three-fourths of its revenue from customs duties on imports. Some 90 per cent of America's imports came from England. If these well-springs of revenue had been dried up by retaliation or war, the whole Hamiltonian edifice probably would have collapsed. In this event the federal government possibly would have fallen to pieces, and Alexander Hamilton might have gone down in history not as the greatest Secretary of the Treasury but the last.

Hamilton and his Federalist following, who stoutly opposed discriminatory measures against England, held several strong cards. In the first place, the French, angered because the Americans were permitting the British to search United States vessels laden with provisions for France, were retaliating by seizing Yankee ships carrying supplies to England. These confiscations rapidly mounted into the hundreds, and incidentally involved the brutal treatment of American crews. Secondly, London modified its odious Orders in Council early in 1794, thus allowing the United States to enjoy for the time a thriving trade with the British West Indies. Finally, Britain arranged to pay for many of the confiscated American cargoes—a conciliatory gesture which could not be expected from France.

Logically, if the Americans were going to resort to stern measures, they should have taken them against both France and Great Britain. In some respects Britain's offenses on the high seas were actually less galling than those of France. But the pro-British Federalists rallied and, after a bitter struggle in Congress, were able to block the legislative slap at Britain. At the same time they temporarily quieted the Jeffersonian Republicans by backing a proposal to send a special envoy to London.

JOHN JAY'S THANKLESS MISSION

Alexander Hamilton was at first proposed for the delicate English mission, but he had made himself so offensive to the Jeffersonians as to be an impossible choice. John Jay, then Chief Justice of the Supreme Court and a seasoned diplomat, was selected instead. Like Hamilton, he was a staunch Federalist and a strong admirer of England—a circumstance that made him highly acceptable to the British officials and aristocrats. Indeed, they knew both their man and the vulnerable joints in his armor, for they had been secretly forewarned by an agent who had earlier known Jay:

> [Jay] has good sense and much information; has great appearance of coolness; and is a patient hearer with a good memory. He argues closely, but is long-winded and self-opinioned. He can bear any opposition to what he advocates provided regard is shown to his ability. He may be attached by good treatment but will be unforgiving if he thinks himself neglected. . . . He certainly has good sense and judgement. . . . But almost every man has a weak and assailable quarter, and Mr. Jay's weak side is *Mr. Jay*.[7]

The British-hating Jeffersonians were outraged by the choice of so notorious an England-lover. They feared that the man who had earlier tried to sell out the West to Gardoqui, the Spanish envoy in 1786, would sell out the entire country to Britain. Jay's nomination was finally confirmed by the Senate on April 19, 1794, but only after a three-day debate in which partisan feelings ran high. John Adams, the Vice-President and presiding officer, noted that the "prospect of peace" threw some persons "into distress." Jay, who foresaw the possible consequences to his "personal popularity," accepted with reluctance. As he far-sightedly remarked, "no man could frame a treaty with Great Britain without making himself unpopular and odious."

Upon arriving in London, Jay was cordially embraced by English society. The anti-British following of Jefferson immediately raised the cry that the American envoy had sold out for foreign gold. In due season Jay was presented to the Queen. She graciously extended her hand to the American who, after the fashion of the day, bowed and kissed it. When the news of this incident reached the United States, one rabid Jeffersonian exclaimed that Jay had "prostrated at the feet of her majesty the sovereignty of the people," and that "he richly deserved to have his lips blistered to the bone." Another jeered: "Hear the voice of truth, hear and believe! John Jay, ah! the arch traitor—scize him, drown him, burn

[7] Frank Monaghan, *John Jay* (New York, 1935), p. 372.

him, flay him alive! Men of America, he betrayed you with a kiss!"[8] At
all events, the John Jay who was wined, dined, and flattered by the
British nobility was clearly not the vigilant, suspicious John Jay who had
acted independently at Paris in 1782.

BRITAIN'S HARD BARGAIN

Much was expected of Jay. First of all, he was instructed to adjust the
differences, chiefly over the northern posts, that had arisen over the
Treaty of 1783. He was also to secure compensation for British seizures
under the recent Orders in Council; to arrange for an opening of the
British West Indian trade that had been officially closed since the Revolution; and, if possible, to negotiate the long-deferred commercial treaty.
Although Jay was allowed certain discretionary powers because of his
distance from home, he was specifically instructed to sign no pact contrary to America's treaty engagements with France.

Jay did not hold a strong hand, but he did have a few trump cards.
The British realized that the United States had been goaded to the verge
of war; and they did not want war. It would disrupt their valuable flow
of supplies from America and divert strength from the real enemy, France.
London therefore reprimanded Lord Dorchester for his indiscreet speech
to the Indians and his aggressions on American soil southwest of Detroit.
The British also took steps to soften their objectionable Orders in Council.
But rather than abandon entirely their high-handed maritime practices
and jeopardize their chances of beating France to her knees, they probably would have accepted war. In these circumstances it was difficult, if
not impossible, to extort sweeping concessions.

Jay held but one ace—and a poor one at that. A new and weaker
Armed Neutrality, including only Sweden and Denmark, was being
formed to resist Britain's arbitrary maritime practices. The British officials,
although not fearing it, preferred not to have America join it. Unknown
to them, the Washington administration had already discussed the issue
and adopted the policy of steering clear of European quarrels. Yet Hamilton, in his desperate efforts to preserve both the peace and his financial
edifice, committed the serious indiscretion of informing the British minister in Philadelphia, George Hammond, that the United States would
in no circumstances join the new Armed Neutrality. Hammond promptly
relayed this important information to London. Thus the only ace that Jay
might have played was trumped with the card that Hamilton had furnished the British. The unpopular pact that Jay finally signed on November 19, 1794, has sometimes been called Hamilton's Treaty, on the highly

[8] *Oracle of the Day*, Nov. 25, 1795 [1794?], quoted in J. B. McMaster, *A History of
the People of the United States* (New York, 1885), II, 213 n.

questionable assumption that the British could have been bluffed by the abortive Armed Neutrality.

JOHN JAY'S TREATY

The new pact was a curious one. The only immediate concession of any real value that Jay won was a promise by the British to surrender the posts that they had already promised to surrender in the Treaty of 1783. But this time they got out. Other matters of controversy, including the Northeastern (Maine) boundary, pre-Revolutionary debts, and compensation for the recent maritime seizures, were all referred to mixed arbitral commissions.[9]

The clauses regarding arbitration were doubly significant. In the first place, although international arbitration was not then unknown, the impetus it received from Jay's Treaty was so strong that modern arbitration is generally dated from the ratification of this pact. Secondly, since the United States was then relatively weak but growing rapidly, the Americans were the gainers by postponing the final decision of pending questions.

But Jay's Treaty was perhaps most noteworthy for its silences. Nothing was said about the slaves whom the British had carried off; nothing about tampering with the Indians. Jay not only failed to wring concessions from the British regarding such questions as seizures of ships, but he actually yielded some ground. Contrary at least to the spirit of America's treaty engagements with France, he agreed in effect that American foodstuffs bound for French ports might, in certain circumstances, be seized if paid for, and that French property on American ships might be confiscated by the British. In short, "free ships" did not make "free goods."

The Jay Treaty, for all its shortcomings, was the long-coveted commercial treaty with England. It was surprisingly generous in opening trade with the British Isles on a most-favored-nation basis,[10] and in making available the British East Indian trade. But as regards the West Indies, direct American commerce was limited to vessels with a carrying capacity of not more than seventy tons. In return for this niggardly con-

[9] In 1798 the mixed commission appointed for that purpose established the identity of the St. Croix River, the principal issue in the Northeastern boundary dispute. But the problem was not finally settled until later. The arbitration of the debt question failed; and the dispute was finally adjusted in the Treaty of 1802, by which Great Britain accepted £600,000. In 1804 a mixed commission awarded the United States $11,650,000 for damages to American shipping resulting from the Orders in Council. On the other hand, the United States was assessed $143,428.14 for its derelictions as a neutral in favor of France.

[10] That is, Britain would grant to the United States such commercial privileges as she granted to other nations.

cession, Jay bound the United States not to export certain tropical staples, such as sugar and cotton, in American ships. As fate would have it, the year previous to the negotiation of the treaty, Eli Whitney had invented the cotton gin, and the restriction on tropical products, if adhered to, might have blighted the budding cotton industry of the South. Yet, distasteful though these arrangements were to Americans, no other negotiator probably could have secured substantially more.

THE DAMNATION OF JOHN JAY

When Jay's Treaty reached America, the Senators were shocked by its terms. Fearful of stirring up a popular outcry, they voted to keep its provisions secret during the forthcoming debate behind closed doors. The necessary two-thirds majority seemed unobtainable. But after a heated discussion, and with the restrictive article on West Indian trade completely suspended, the Senate voted its reluctant approval by the closest possible of margins, 20 to 10.

The terms by now had leaked out to the people and stirred up a frightening uproar. America was in no mood to bend the knee to Britain. For one thing, the new federal government had recently demonstrated its power by crushing, with an impressive show of force, the Whiskey Rebellion in Western Pennsylvania. For another, "Mad Anthony" Wayne, the Revolutionary hero, had chastised the British-armed Indians in the Northwest, on August 20, 1794, at the battle of Fallen Timbers. The bodies of several white Canadian volunteers had been found on the field of combat, thereby underscoring charges of British tampering with the redskins.

Seldom has a conscientious public servant been so viciously maligned as Jay. Public meetings passed condemnatory resolutions, flags were lowered to half-mast, and hangmen officially burned copies of the treaty. Jay was guillotined in effigy, and scores of villages were lighted at night by burning effigies of "that damned arch-traitor, Sir John Jay." He was represented in effigy as holding a pair of scales, the treaty on one side and a bag of gold on the other, with the placard, "Come up to my price, and I will sell you my country." On one fence were chalked these words: "Damn John Jay! Damn every one that won't damn John Jay!! damn every one that won't put lights in his windows and sit up all night damning John Jay!!! [11] The British minister in Philadelphia was openly insulted by jeering crowds, and when Hamilton attempted to speak in New York, he was stoned from the platform, bleeding at the mouth.

Popular pressures speedily converged on President Washington, who was in a position to kill the treaty by not carrying through the final stages

[11] John Jay, *Mr. Jay's Second Letter on Dawson's Introduction to the Federalist* (New York, 1864), p. 19.

of ratification. The United States was fortunate indeed that in the midst of this uproar a man of his stature stood at the helm. His heart must have sunk as he read the treaty, but at this point he could not have sent Jay back to London to negotiate a better one. The choice seemed to be either this pact or war. With the country disunited, Indians on the war-path, Spain on the southwestern frontier, and Hamilton's delicate financial structure faced with ruin, hostilities might have spelled national disaster. Washington instinctively recoiled from war. One of his cardinal policies was to avoid armed conflict at all costs while the United States was still disorganized and disunited. If the nation could only consolidate its strength and wait for its natural increase of population, it would one day be powerful enough to command respect. Time and pioneer fecundity were fighting America's battles for her.

JAY'S TREATY: THE PRICE OF PEACE

As time wore on the Federalists, who had been badly shaken by the impassioned outcry of the Jeffersonian Republicans, recovered their composure. Hamilton entered the fray with his persuasive pen. An increasing number of sensible citizens, Federalists and Republicans alike, concluded that the treaty could not be nearly so bad as partisan spokesmen had represented.

After prolonged deliberation, Washington decided to carry through the ratification of the treaty. This was one of the most courageous decisions of a decision-filled life. But the extreme Jeffersonians were provoked to a renewed outburst, which included John Randolph's celebrated toast, "Damn George Washington!" Even Jefferson so far forgot himself as to write privately, "Curse on his virtues; they have undone the country." He likewise placed Washington in the company of those "who have had their heads shorn by the harlot England."

Washington's decision was not only courageous but wise. Jay's Treaty, unsatisfactory though it was, postponed war with Britain for eighteen years and enabled adolescent America to establish its footing. The pact was the price that the Hamiltonians were willing to pay for peace, financial stability, continuing prosperity, and the salvation of the new government. Perhaps the most significant feature of the agreement was not that Britain drove a hard bargain, but that only eleven years after granting independence she consented to meet the United States on terms of equality and sign a treaty of any description. The British officials probably would not have consented to go even this far if they had not needed all their sinews for the exhausting war with France.

The pro-French group in America held one final card. If they could muster enough votes in the House of Representatives to defeat the appropriation necessary for carrying the treaty into effect, they would yet be able to undo Jay's handiwork. Jefferson voiced a general Republican sentiment in a private letter:

> I join with you in thinking the treaty an execrable thing. . . . I trust the popular branch of our Legislature [the House] will disapprove of it, and thus rid us of this infamous act, which is really nothing more than a treaty of alliance between England and the Anglomen of this country, against the Legislature and people of the United States.[12]

The outcome in the House hung in doubt during a savage, two-month debate. Behind the scenes the French minister lobbied to persuade individual members to vote down the appropriation bill, while the British minister used his influence to secure its passage. There was much wild talk that if the House failed to do its duty the Union would dissolve. At a critical moment the ailing Fisher Ames, premier orator of the Federalist party, took the floor. He stigmatized the uproar of the Jeffersonian Republicans as opposition not to the Jay Treaty but to any treaty with Britain. In solemn tones, which grew stronger as he summoned all his physical resources for this supreme effort, he proclaimed that the Union would collapse and that war would break out should the pact fail. Then "the wounds yet unhealed" would "be torn open again; the war whoop shall waken the sleep of the cradle." "I can fancy that I listen to the yells of savage vengeance and the shrieks of torture; already they seem to sigh in the western wind; already they mingle with every echo from the mountains."[13] Impressed—perhaps moved—by this superlative oratorical effort, the House passed the necessary appropriation on April 30, 1796, by the narrow margin of three votes.

FRUITS OF EUROPE'S DISTRESSES

Jay's Treaty in some respects proved to be more important for its by-products than for its provisions. For one thing, the Indians of the Northwest, chastised by "Mad Anthony" Wayne and deserted by their red-coated friends in London, were forced to come to terms with the "pale-faces." By the Treaty of Greenville, concluded in 1795, they yielded a spacious virgin tract in the Ohio Valley to white settlement.

Vastly more important was the impact of Jay's Treaty on the Spanish Court. In 1795 turncoat Spain withdrew from the European War, and the next year allied herself with France, her former enemy, against England, her former ally. If this bold move should lead to war with Britain, as it eventually did, Spain would do well to placate the Americans. She would thus lessen the number of her enemies, and at the same time shield her semidefenseless flank against the aroused Western

---

[12] *Writings of Thomas Jefferson* (Monticello ed.), IX, 314 (Jefferson to Edward Rutledge, Nov. 30, 1795).

[13] Seth Ames, ed., *Works of Fisher Ames* (Boston, 1854), II, 66.

frontiersmen. The full wisdom of such a policy dawned upon the Spanish ministers when they heard of the Jay negotiations, which seemed to foreshadow an alliance between England and America.

The Madrid government therefore made haste to conclude a memorable treaty with Thomas Pinckney, the American envoy, on October 27, 1795. It conceded to the United States virtually everything that Spain had bitterly resisted for the past twelve years. Specifically, the United States secured free navigation of the Mississippi River, with the priceless right during a period of three years to deposit goods at New Orleans for transshipment. This privilege was to be renewed either at New Orleans or at some equivalent place. Spain not only agreed to restrain the Indians on America's southwestern frontier, but to push the boundary of West Florida down to the 31st parallel, which was precisely what the Americans had claimed since 1783. In view of these sweeping Spanish concessions, the Pinckney Treaty proved as popular in America as the Jay Treaty had been unpopular. The Senate approved it, on March 3, 1796, by a rousing unanimous vote.

The Pinckney Treaty, although not removing all sources of friction with Spain, was of such far-reaching significance as alone to justify the Jay Treaty. It temporarily quieted the discontent of American frontiersmen by opening the Mississippi River and by curbing the Indian menace. The national government thus struck a body blow at Spanish intrigue in the Southwest, removed the threat of Western disunion, and kindled a new sense of loyalty in the West. The concessions made by Spain marked a backward step in her policy of maintaining a buffer against the long-rifled frontiersmen, and did much to pave the way for the later expansion of the United States into the Mississippi Valley. Finally, the Pinckney Treaty eliminated the necessity of America's becoming involved in European intrigues to secure those concessions that the Spaniards now freely granted.

The over-all diplomatic gains for the United States in 1795–1796 were breathtaking. Seven years earlier, when George Washington had taken office, Britain and Spain had exercised control over the greater part of America's trans-Appalachian territory. Now, by virtue of the Jay and Pinckney Treaties, the United States had freed its own soil from foreign domination.

The happy results could be traced to several sources. First, there was the mounting pressure of the expansive Westerner on the frontiers of Spain in the Southwest and of Britain in the Northwest. There was also Washington's "patient and persuasive" diplomacy, which had so skillfully employed the strategy of delay—of waiting instead of warring. Finally, there were Europe's distresses. If Britain had not been involved in a death struggle with France, it is improbable that she would have concluded Jay's Treaty. If Spain had not been threatened by war with

Britain, she almost certainly would not have yielded Pinckney's Treaty in 1795. Europe's distresses thus contributed significantly to America's successes, not only in achieving independence but also in redeeming American territory from the clutch of foreign control.

SELECTED BIBLIOGRAPHY

A useful survey is A. B. Darling, *Our Rising Empire, 1763–1803* (New Haven, 1940). The standard monograph is S. F. Bemis, *Jay's Treaty* (New York, 1923), which is modified somewhat by A. L. Burt, *The United States, Great Britain, and British North America* (New Haven, 1940). The most recent scholarship on the aftermath of Jay's Treaty is Bradford Perkins, *The First Rapprochement; England and the United States, 1795–1805* (Philadelphia, 1955). See also S. F. Bemis, *Pinckney's Treaty* (Baltimore, 1926) and A. P. Whitaker, *The Spanish-American Frontier: 1783–1795* (Boston, 1927). For public reactions consult C. D. Hazen, *Contemporary American Opinion of the French Revolution* (Baltimore, 1897). See also N. V. Russell, *The British Régime in Michigan and the Old Northwest, 1760–1796* (Northfield, Minn., 1939); Bernard Mayo, ed., *Instructions to the British Ministers to the United States, 1791–1812* (Washington, 1941).

Valuable articles are Bradford Perkins, "Lord Hawkesbury and the Jay-Grenville Negotiations," *Miss. Valley Hist. Rev.*, XL (1953), 291–304; Joseph Charles, "The Jay Treaty: The Origins of the American Party System," *William and Mary Quar.*, XII, 3rd ser. (1955), 581–630; A. H. Bowman, "Jefferson, Hamilton and American Foreign Policy," *Pol. Sci. Quar.*, LXXI (1956), 18–41; Alice B. Keith," Relaxations in the British Restrictions on the American Trade with the British West Indies, 1783–1802," *Jour. of Mod. Hist.*, XX (1948), 1–18.

See footnotes of this chapter; Bemis and Griffin, *Guide*, Ch. IV; *Harvard Guide*, Ch. 11.

7TH ED. REFS. J. C. Miller's *The Federalist Era, 1789–1801* (New York, 1960), discusses Jay's Treaty. His *Alexander Hamilton: Portrait in Paradox* (New York, 1959) concludes that Hamilton's collusion with Hammond did not hamstring Jay. S. F. Bemis' *Jay's Treaty* (New Haven, 1962) is a careful revision of a classic, as is his revision of *Pinckney's Treaty* (New Haven, 1962). J. A. Carroll and M. W. Ashworth, *George Washington: First in Peace* (New York, 1957) has a Washington-oriented account of the British crisis. Contemporary foes of the Jay treaty appear in D. L. Sterling, "A Federalist Opposes the Jay Treaty: The Letters of Samuel Bayard," *William and Mary Quar.*, Ser. 3, vol. XVIII (1961), pp. 408–424; E. F. Kramer, ed., "Senator Pierce Butler's Notes of the Debates on Jay's Treaty," *South Carolina Hist. Mag.*, LXII (1961), pp. 1–9; G. S. McCowan, Jr., "Chief Justice John Rutledge and the Jay Treaty," *ibid.*, pp. 10–23. J. A. Logan, Jr., *No Transfer* (New Haven, 1961) sees in the Nootka Sound controversy, involving British designs on Spanish territory, the catalyst of the no-transfer policy. British complicity is revealed in Reginald Horsman, "The British Indian Department and the Resistance to General Anthony Wayne, 1793–1795," *Miss. Valley Hist. Rev.*, XLIX (1962), 269–290.

8TH AND 9TH ED. REFS. See BIBLIOGRAPHICAL ADDENDUM, p. 981.

7

Friction with France
1789-1800

*The nation which indulges toward another an ha-
bitual hatred or an habitual fondness is in some
degree a slave.*
WASHINGTON'S FAREWELL ADDRESS, 1796

THE ALLIANCE BECOMES AN ENTANGLEMENT

As LONG As THE WARS of the French Revolution were confined to
the continent of Europe, the United States was able to avoid serious
international friction. But the picture became dangerously clouded when,
on February 1, 1793, France declared war on England. A cry rose from
thousands of Jeffersonian Republicans that America should rush to the
assistance of the nation that had helped her in the hour of need. The
common foe—so it appeared—was Great Britain, that ancient enemy and
oppressor of human liberty, that arrogant power which seemed to be
making every effort to strangle the United States in the cradle, "Americans, be just!" proclaimed the *New York Journal.* "Remember . . . who
stood between you and the clanking chains of British ministerial despotism."

President Washington now found himself in an agonizing predicament.
His fixed policy was to avoid hostilities at all hazards while the nation
was still unstable. Yet by the Alliance of 1778 the United States was
bound "forever" to assist France in the defense of her West Indies. Unless America flagrantly disregarded her now distasteful obligations, she
could scarcely avoid the very calamity that the Hamiltonians were seeking to avert—war with England.

At this critical hour Washington turned to his Cabinet for advice as
to whether the pacts with France should now be considered binding.
Hamilton, who had no love for the French or the French alliance, argued
that the treaties were not in full force because they contemplated only

a defensive war and because they had been negotiated with the French monarchy under Louis XVI—and both the monarchy and Louis XVI were dead. Jefferson, though by no means desiring war with England in behalf of France, insisted that simple honesty should prevail:

> . . . The treaties between the United States and France, were not treaties between the United States and Louis Capet [Louis XVI], but between the two nations of America and France; and the nations remaining in existence, though both of them have since changed their forms of government, the treaties are not annulled by these changes.[1]

As it turned out, France did not call upon the United States to defend her West Indies. The Washington administration, therefore, was not compelled to take an official stand on the applicability of the Alliance of 1778. The course pursued by the Paris officials was not dictated by solicitude for the United States but by purely selfish motives. If the Americans had possessed a strong naval and military force, France would almost certainly have insisted that they live up to their treaty obligations. But since the United States had no considerable navy and since the Americans, as neutrals, were able to ship food to both France and her hungry West Indian colonies, the expected demand was never made. America could be far more useful as a friendly feeder than as an ineffective fighter.

Washington also asked his advisers if, in their opinion, he should receive a diplomatic envoy from the newly created French republic. This was an important decision, for the reception of such a person would mean official recognition of his government. Jefferson, applying the "consent-of-the-governed" philosophy of his own Declaration of Independence, had already outlined in classic form a recognition policy for the United States.

> We certainly cannot deny to other nations that principle whereon our government is founded, that every nation has a right to govern itself internally under what forms it pleases, and to change these forms at its own will; and externally to transact business with other nations through whatever organ it chooses, whether that be a King, Convention, Assembly, Committee, President, or whatever it be. The only thing essential is, the will of the nation.[2]

This policy—in effect a corollary of the Declaration of Independence—was adopted by President Washington and was consistently followed by all his successors, with minor departures, until the time of Woodrow Wilson.

Jefferson unquestionably did his most memorable work as Secretary of State in laying the bases for the American policies of recognition and neutrality. Although his personal sympathies were with France in her

[1] A. A. Lipscomb, ed., *Writings of Thomas Jefferson* (Monticello ed., Washington, 1904), III, 227–228 (April 28, 1793).
[2] *Ibid.*, IX, 7–8 (Jefferson to Pinckney, Dec. 30, 1792).

struggle with England, his official correspondence with the British and French ministers never betrayed the interests of the United States. As the French representative in America reported:

> Mr. Jefferson likes us because he detests England; he seeks to draw near to us because he fears us less than Great Britain; but tomorrow he might change his opinion about us if Great Britain should cease to inspire his fear. Although Jefferson is the friend of liberty and science, although he is an admirer of the efforts we have made to cast off our shackles . . . Jefferson, I say, is an American, and as such, he cannot sincerely be our friend. An American is the born enemy of all the peoples of Europe.[3]

NASCENT NEUTRALITY AND CITIZEN GENÊT

During these months of unbridled political passions, the danger was ever present that some irresponsible persons might plunge the country into war. Washington therefore discussed with his advisers the desirability of issuing a pronouncement that would cool the ardor of the more bellicose spirits. Every member of the Cabinet strongly favored a policy of nonbelligerency, but there was not unanimous agreement on the manner of announcing it.

After considerable argument the document now known as Washington's Neutrality Proclamation was given to the world on April 22, 1793. Though its purpose was unmistakable, the declaration did not, curiously enough, contain the word "neutrality." It merely stated that the conduct of the United States should be "friendly and impartial toward the belligerent powers," and that American citizens found guilty of illegally assisting the warring nations would be prosecuted. Congress provided the appropriate teeth when it passed the Neutrality Act of 1794. The Neutrality Proclamation itself was a notable document in the evolution of American policy, primarily because it helped set the ship of state on a course away from Old World embroilments.

But the proclamation came as a bitter pill to the great mass of ardent Jeffersonians who were expecting active intervention on behalf of France. They denounced government "by proclamation" and showered upon Washington's head a storm of abuse that sorely tried his spirit. But in the end saner counsels prevailed, and most Americans accepted the proclamation as a wise and necessary measure.

The neutrality policy of Washington was given its severest test by the conduct of the first minister from the new French republic, Citizen Edmond Genêt. Although only thirty years of age, Genêt had behind him a remarkable record of intellectual achievement and diplomatic experience. Unfortunately, he lacked balance and sound judgment. Aflame with

---

[3] Amer. Hist. Assn., *Annual Report*, 1903, II, 983 (Adet to Minister of Foreign Relations, Dec. 31, 1796).

enthusiasm for the ideals of the French Revolution, impulsive, passionate, and hotheaded, he was at times all sail and no anchor.

Genêt reached Charleston, South Carolina, early in 1793. There he was greeted with a wild enthusiasm that would have turned the head of a less excitable man. Although he could not act officially until he had presented his credentials in Philadelphia, he was so carried away by the huzzas of the masses as to engage immediately in questionable activities. In disregard of American neutrality, he sent out French privateers that returned with British prizes, some of them taken within the three-mile limit. He also opened negotiations with a number of American frontier leaders, notably the disgruntled George Rogers Clark, with a view to attacking Spanish territory in Florida and Louisiana. (It will be remembered that from 1793 to 1795 Spain was fighting against France on the side of England.)

Genêt might have proceeded to Philadelphia by any one of three routes: by sea, by land up the coast, or by land through the back country. Whether by accident or design, he chose the back-country route—the one that best lent itself to his purposes. The people in this region were small farmers who favored the democratic, pro-French, Jeffersonian Republican party and opposed the aristocratic, pro-British, Hamiltonian Federalist party. As a consequence, Genêt's leisurely journey through the back country quickly turned into one long ovation. The trip, which might have been made in less than a week, was dragged out over twenty-eight days, to the accompaniment of salvos of artillery, fraternal embraces, and frenzied cheering. One wag remarked that the Americans burned more powder in celebrating French liberty than was consumed in achieving it.

GENÊT'S INDISCRETIONS

The streets of the Quaker City throbbed with fanatical crowds as Genêt was welcomed to the nation's capital. At a banquet ($4 a plate) the impetuous diplomat thrilled the diners by singing a French fighting song. Throughout the city wild toasts were drunk to the guillotine, and showers of fiery poems descended upon the youthful minister. As one contemporary later exclaimed:

> . . . Can it ever be forgotten, what a racket was made with the citizen Genêt? The most enthusiastic homage was too cold to welcome his arrival; and his being the first minister of the infant republic . . . was dwelt upon, as a most endearing circumstance. What hugging and tugging! What addressing and caressing! What mountebanking and chanting! with liberty-caps, and the other wretched trumpery of *sans culotte* foolery! [4]

[4] A. Graydon, *Memoirs of a Life Chiefly Passed in Pennsylvania* (Harrisburg, 1811), p. 335.

Shortly before arriving in Philadelphia, Genêt learned of Washington's Neutrality Proclamation. He was profoundly shocked, though not completely disillusioned. His roaring reception had convinced him that the American public overwhelmingly favored intervention against England on the side of France, and he did not believe that the proclamation correctly represented the popular will. Many pro-French editors agreed with him.

In due season the annoyed Genêt presented himself to Washington. He may have expected the President to kiss him resoundingly on both cheeks, after the French fashion, and call him "Citizen." But Washington, always dignified and never effusive, was deeply displeased by Genêt's demagoguery and by the premature assumption of his ministerial functions. The President's few remarks were therefore frostily formal—a reception that seemed all the more chilling when contrasted with the warmth of the populace. The impulsive Frenchman left in anger, convinced that "this old man" was not what history painted him and that he was an enemy of liberty. Attributing the President's frigidity to jealousy of his own popular reception, Genêt went so far as to report, "old Washington envies me my success."

The continued acclaim of the masses only strengthened Genêt in his conviction that President Washington was not faithfully interpreting the public will. Crowds of Francophiles damned the President for his coolness toward the French alliance, and accused him of seeking a crown and of trying to pass himself off as an honest man. Genêt admitted that one of these published attacks was the work of his own private secretary. Maddened Francophiles even went so far as to print woodcuts of George Washington being guillotined. In later years John Adams, Vice-President in 1793, reminisced to Thomas Jefferson:

> You certainly never felt the terrorism excited by Genêt, in 1793, when ten thousand people in the streets of Philadelphia, day after day, threatened to drag Washington out of his house, and effect a revolution in the government, or compel it to declare war in favor of the French revolution and against England.[5]

Adams went on to report the belief held in some quarters that nothing but the terrible epidemic of yellow fever, which broke out in Philadelphia at this time, "could have saved the United States from a fatal revolution of government."

In the midst of all this uproar, Washington remained cool and unperturbed, determined not to be swayed from sound policy by the clamor of a rabble aroused by foreign agents. The British poet of later years, Rudyard Kipling, is believed to have been moved to write his inspirational poem, "If," by the General's levelheadedness in this crisis.

[5] C. F. Adams, ed., *Works of John Adams* (Boston, 1856), X, 47.

THE UNDOING OF GENET

The fiery Frenchman continued to be the storm center of American politics from the time of his arrival in Philadelphia until his departure. He fitted out fourteen privateers, which swarmed from American ports and brought back, under the very nose of the national government, over eighty prizes, some of them taken within American waters.

These ventures appear to have been flagrant violations of American neutrality, but offenders were promptly freed by pro-French juries. Public opinion was stronger than law. The British minister lodged strongly worded protests against this unneutral activity, and Secretary Jefferson made the appropriate representations to Genêt. The latter indignantly accused the American Secretary of State of hunting up legalistic excuses "in the dusty tomes of Vattel and Grotius." "I thank God," the French emissary exulted, "I have forgot what these hired jurisprudists have written."

The protests of Genêt became more shrill and his conduct more arrogant. Jefferson obtained from him what appeared to be a promise that a British vessel, *Little Sarah,* which the French had recently captured, would not be sent to sea as a privateer. Yet a few hours later she slipped down the Delaware River to begin a career of destruction. Washington and Jefferson were both furious. Such defiance of the government was even turning pro-French enthusiasts against the French minister. Jefferson, who perceived that Genêt was proving to be a Jonah, wrote to Madison in alarm, "he will sink the Republican interest if they do not abandon him."

Genêt finally overreached himself. In a moment of fuming anger he threatened to appeal over the head of the cold and unresponsive government to the sovereign masses. President Washington, oppressed by the heat of fetid, disease-ridden Philadelphia, exploded:

> Is the minister of the French Republic to set the acts of this government at defiance *with impunity?* And then threaten the executive with an appeal to the people? What must the world think of such conduct, and of the government of the United States in submitting to it? [6]

Excited throngs of Francophiles might vilify Washington, but when the issue was squarely drawn between him and a foreign diplomat, sanity returned with a rush. The Federalists gleefully spread broadcast the news of Genêt's indiscretion, and their most caustic spokesman, William Cobbett, branded the Jeffersonian Republicans as "bastard offspring of Genêt, spawned in hell, to which they will presently return." Everywhere French sympathizers were hushed and shamed, except for a few who attempted to condone Genêt's offenses.

[6] W. C. Ford, ed., *Writings of George Washington* (New York, 1891), XII, 302.

Washington's Cabinet met and unanimously agreed to demand the recall of Genêt. A new faction had come into power in France, and they were eager to cut off the diplomatic career as well as the head of the ill-starred envoy. But Washington, wisely declining to make a martyr of a fallen idol, refused to send the Frenchman home to an almost certain death. The discredited Genêt—Hamilton called him "a burned-out comet"—ultimately retired to New York, where hand in hand with the daughter of Governor Clinton, he faced the altar instead of the guillotine.

THE HUMILIATION OF MONROE

While Genêt was making himself objectionable, the able United States minister to France, Gouverneur Morris, was committing equally serious indiscretions. Morris was an arch-conservative so openly hostile to the French Revolution that he had offered his house as an asylum to many a refugee from the guillotine. He even drafted and promoted a plan for the escape of Louis XVI, who, in turn, made him the custodian of several hundred thousand livres to be used as bribe money. When the United States demanded the recall of Genêt, the Paris government insisted that Morris be withdrawn.

James Monroe, the successor of Morris, sympathized with the French Revolution so ardently that he should never have been chosen. He was officially received in Paris before the entire Convention, where, amid cries of *"Vive la République!"* he made a flaming speech. The French spokesman, carried away by the frenzied cheering, thereupon administered the fraternal kiss to Monroe on both cheeks. Such conduct was all the more indiscreet because Washington had already proclaimed a policy of neutrality. Yet here was the official representative of the United States, by word and deed, virtually ranging his nation on the side of France in the war against Britain. With the delicate Jay negotiations then under way in London, the conduct of Monroe placed the United States in an embarrassing, not to say perilous, position.

The pro-French excesses of Monroe merely served to hasten his own downfall. The Paris officials were hoping for the failure of Jay's mission, for they wanted Great Britain to become involved in a war with the United States. Monroe, inadequately informed by the State Department as to Jay's instructions, gave emphatic assurances that nothing was to be feared from the London negotiations. When the terms of Jay's treaty were finally divulged, the anger of the French was deepened by this unwitting deception. Although Monroe had achieved considerable success in dealing with the French seizures of American ships, he was now thoroughly discredited.

The text of Jay's Treaty in itself proved annoying enough to the Paris officials. It was not, to be sure, technically in conflict with previous commitments made by the United States to France. But it did violate the spirit of the Commercial Treaty of 1778, for it conceded that American ships sailing for France with foodstuffs might be confiscated by British cruisers if the cargoes were paid for. In the eyes of the French, the Americans had turned their backs on their old benefactor, France, and were virtually allying themselves with their old enemy, England.

Monroe, in desperation, floundered even deeper into the diplomatic quicksands. He assured the French that the Jay Treaty would never be ratified, but again he proved to be a false prophet. On July 2, 1796, some four months after the pact had been officially proclaimed, the Paris government issued a decree announcing that it would treat neutrals as they permitted England to treat them. In other words, French seizures of American merchantmen would be renewed. Now frantic, Monroe promised that the Federalist regime of Washington and Adams would be overthrown by the voters in the election of 1796, and that Jay's shameful surrender to Britain would be annuled. His protestations were finally cut short, on August 22, 1796, by a peremptory recall by the United States.

WASHINGTON'S FAREWELL TO THE NATION

A weary Washington was now prepared to bow out. He had planned to retire at the end of his first term, in 1793, but friends persuaded him that the critical state of foreign affairs demanded a continuance of his strong hand at the helm. Now, with the Jay and Pinckney Treaties negotiated, he felt that he could conscientiously lay down his burdens. He therefore prepared his famed Farewell Address with extreme care, and instead of presenting it as a public speech, gave it to one of his favorite newspapers as a special "scoop," on September 17, 1796.

Washington wrote his Farewell Address in collaboration with several of his intimate advisers, notably Hamilton, who contributed the incisive style. His immediate object was to announce that he would not be a candidate for a third term. But to this declaration he saw fit to add some sage advice, particularly regarding involvement in the broils and intrigues of Europe.

The memory of recent and current French intrigues was painfully fresh. Both Vergennes and Genêt, it will be recalled, had attempted to use the United States as a pawn in French schemes. The successor of Genêt, Joseph Fauchet, had sought by every means at his command to block the ratification of Jay's Treaty. His successor, Pierre Adet, through subsidies to the press and through Jeffersonian Republican societies, had aroused the people against the pact and had labored with the House of Representatives to defeat the necessary appropriation. Failing in this, he had attempted to bring about the defeat of Washington for re-election in

1796, and the elevation of the pro-French Thomas Jefferson to the Presidency—a scheme that was blocked by Washington's withdrawal. Following Washington's Farewell Address, Adet continued to labor unsuccessfully, through a public appeal and otherwise, for the defeat of the presumably pro-British John Adams, the Federalist candidate, and the election of the presumably pro-French Thomas Jefferson, the Republican candidate.

With such outrageous foreign intermeddling specifically in mind, Washington issued an earnest warning in his Farewell Address to the American people. He especially deplored the growth of a violent partisan spirit that inflamed the people with fierce likes or dislikes for foreign countriès.

> . . . Nothing is more essential than that permanent, inveterate antipathies against particular nations and passionate attachments for others should be excluded, and that in place of them just and amicable feelings toward all should be cultivated. The nation which indulges toward another an habitual hatred or an habitual fondness is in some degree a slave. . . . Against the insidious wiles of foreign influence (I conjure you to believe me, fellow-citizens) the jealousy of a free people ought to be *constantly* awake. . . .[7] [Italics inserted]

Washington then turned to formal entanglements. With the disputes caused by the "forever" French alliance clearly in mind, he solemnly asserted: "It is our true policy to steer clear of *permanent* alliances with any portion of the foreign world. . . . [But] we may safely trust to temporary alliances for extraordinary emergencies." [Italics inserted] [8] Washington, in other words, was giving specific advice to a youthful and disunited nation in the year 1796—advice that had been dictated by recent and bitter experience. He was thinking of the existing permanent alliance with France, and probably had no intention of charting a specific course which the United States would have to follow for all time. He did not say —as he was later made to say—"No alliances, with any nation, at any time, for any purpose." The policy of noninvolvement—not isolation—that he recommended was not so much aloofness from the affairs of Europe as the exclusion of European agents and intrigue from the affairs of the United States. The American people might then enjoy, for the first time as a nation, the blessings of complete independence, and not be a tail to the French kite. The course that Washington advocated so chimed in with America's isolationist instincts, reaching back deep into colonial times, that it was bound to be a major, if misunderstood, foundation stone of future American foreign policy.

[7] J. D. Richardson, ed., *Messages and Papers of the Presidents* (Washington, 1896), I, 221, 222.
[8] *Ibid.*, I, 223.

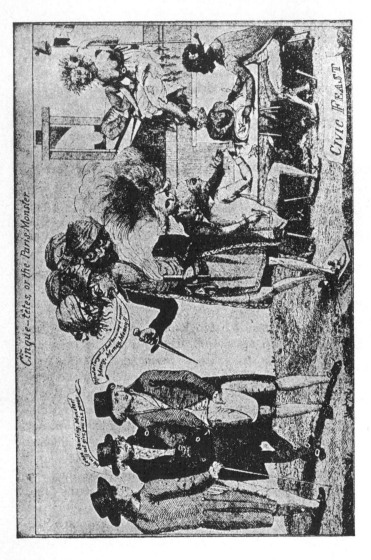

CINQUE-TÊTES, OR THE PARIS MONSTER

A rare American print (1799) showing the five-headed French Directory demanding money of the Americans. The dagger and flaming torch, the Jacobin sitting at a "Civic Feast" of frogs with a Negro and the devil, and the terrible Goddess of Liberty guarding the guillotine, all reflect a Federalist bias.

From Volume 1 of *A History of American Graphic Humor*, by William Murrell

THE TRICKERY OF TALLEYRAND

French anger at the alleged duplicity of Jay's Treaty had meanwhile continued to vent itself in the seizure of American merchant ships and the manhandling of their crews. Secretary of State Pickering reported, in June, 1797, that 316 vessels flying the Stars and Stripes had fallen prey to French cruisers since July, 1796. There was not, in fact, much to choose between British and French violations of American rights. The conduct of both nations would have justified war, if the United States had been looking for war.

In a final effort to patch up differences, Washington sent to France a distinguished South Carolina Federalist, Charles C. Pinckney, who could be counted on to avoid Monroe's pro-French excesses. The corrupt, five-headed French Directory, then in power, flatly refused to accord him official status. It threatened him with arrest if he did not get a permit, and gave point to its insolence by tendering a grand farewell reception to Monroe. With well-justified indignation, Pinckney left for the Netherlands, and the diplomatic rupture between France and America was complete.

Federalist John Adams, who became President early in 1797, despite French wirepulling, was determined to turn the other cheek. In the hope of averting a disastrous war, he dispatched a commission of three men to France. It consisted of the rejected Federalist envoy, Charles C. Pinckney; Elbridge Gerry, a prominent Massachusetts Republican; and John Marshall, a Virginia Federalist who was destined to be Chief Justice of the Supreme Court.

The American trio, upon reaching Paris in October, 1797, found the atmosphere discouraging. After exasperating delays, they were finally approached by three mysterious personages, obviously puppets of Talleyrand, the astute and unscrupulous French Minister of Foreign Relations. The three go-betweens were accompanied by the inevitable beautiful woman, without whom no European diplomatic intrigue was complete, and who, incidentally, made a highly favorable impression on John Marshall.

The French agents announced that before official negotiations could proceed, the French Directory would have to receive an apology for certain allusions to France in President Adams' recent message to Congress. In addition, the Americans were to pay a bribe of 1.2 million livres, and make a loan of 32 million florins, which, in the circumstances, would be largely or wholly a gift. Taken aback, the American envoys did not give a satisfactory answer. Their official report is revealing:

M.X. [a French agent] again returned to the subject of money: Said he, gentlemen, you do not speak to the point: it is money: it is expected that you will offer money. We said that we had spoken to that point very explicitly: We had given an answer. No, said he, you have not: what is your answer? We replied, it is no; no; not a sixpence.[9]

The three American diplomats were not so naïve as one might think. They could not have been greatly shocked by the mention of money, for bribes, as well as petticoats, were accepted tools of 18th Century diplomacy. But they rejected the barefaced French proposals because they had no instructions to pay such a large sum, and because a substantial loan to France at the time would have been a breach of neutrality which might have involved the United States in war with England. Even if otherwise unobjectionable, the terms demanded were excessive for mere recognition of the three Americans.

Pinckney and Marshall, convinced that further negotiations were hopeless, left France in disgust. The wily Talleyrand, who did not want war with the United States and who saw the wisdom of protracting negotiations, persuaded the allegedly pro-French Gerry to stay on. After more fruitless interchanges, the lingering Gerry was summarily recalled by his own government.

UNDECLARED FIGHTING WITH FRANCE

When the news of Talleyrand's insolence reached America early in. 1798, the lusty young republic was aroused as probably never before. The excitement increased when President Adams laid the dispatches from the American envoys before Congress, anonymously designating the French go-betweens as X, Y, and Z. Ten thousand copies of these documents were promptly distributed at public expense, and American resentment was quickly lashed into a fury of indignation. War preparations were rushed, and even the peaceful Quakers favored fighting. The slogan, "Millions for defense but not one cent for tribute," was on countless tongues.[10] Resolutions, addresses, public meetings, patriotic poetry, songs, and banquets contributed to the crescendo of patriotic fervor. When John Marshall returned from France to New York City, he received an ovation such as had been given to no other American, except Washington. Countless thousands of husky throats bawled the words of "Adams and Liberty" and "Washington and the Constitution." The few bold Francophiles who tried to sing "*Ça Ira*" or the "*Marseillaise*" were quickly hissed down.

Under the inspiration of the hour Joseph Hopkinson wrote his stirring song, "Hail Columbia," which was set to the tune of the popular "Presi-

---

[9] *American State Papers, Foreign Relations*, II, 161 (Oct. 27, 1797).

[10] This slogan was erroneously attributed to Pinckney. Throughout his life he denied its authorship, yet when he died it was inscribed on a tablet to his memory in his native city, Charleston.

dent's March." It was introduced to a Philadelphia audience by an actor in full sailor dress. This patriotic song spread like a rushing torrent, and probably did more than anything else to express the new national consciousness. The masses of the republic were no longer pro-French or pro-British—but pro-American.

Responding to the popular clamor, Congress took a hand. In May and July of 1798 it authorized the capture of French armed ships, but not merchantmen, as would have been the case in a full-fledged war. On June 13, 1798, commercial intercourse with France was suspended. Eight days later President Adams informed Congress in a ringing message: "I will never send another minister to France without assurances that he will be received, respected, and honored as the representative of a great, free, powerful, and independent nation." [11] On July 7, 1798, Congress declared the two treaties of 1778 with France void on the grounds that they had already been violated by the French government.

The undeclared war with France, which lasted two-and-one-half years, was fortunately confined to the sea. The tiny but efficient United States Navy, supplemented by privately owned warships, captured more than eighty armed French ships, principally privateers operating in West Indian waters against American merchantmen. George Washington was summoned from retirement to command the army of 10,000 men that was being raised. These military preparations, together with several brilliant naval successes, further aroused patriotic enthusiasm. Seafaring men sang lustily:

> Now let each jolly tar, with one heart and one voice
> Drink a can of good grog to the man of our choice;
> Under John, the State pilot, and George's command,
> There's a fig for the French and the sly Talleyrand.[12]

The aging Washington, though nominally in command of the army, stipulated that Alexander Hamilton be entrusted with active command. The young financier, a frustrated military genius, was eager for a full-dress war with France, as were many of his fellow Federalists. In co-operation with the navy of his beloved England, he would bring laurels to himself and his party by despoiling Spain of New Orleans, Florida, Mexico, and perhaps points south. Spain, it will be remembered, had forsaken England in 1796 and allied herself with France.

The British were delighted with the turn affairs had taken, and the presence of a common foe brought England and America closer together than they were to be for many a year. There was, in fact, much talk of an alliance. The Duke of Gloucester actually proposed lending the Americans a number of warships. Although nothing came of this suggestion,

[11] Richardson, *Messages and Papers of the Presidents,* I, 266 (June 21, 1798).
[12] J. B. McMaster, *A History of the People of the United States* (New York, 1896), II, 406 n.

the British did provide the United States with a considerable quantity of arms, and shared their naval signals so that American and British ships could recognize one another. The pro-British party in America was everywhere in the ascendant, while the pro-French Republicans were disgraced. Many of them went so far as to join enthusiastically in the war preparations against France.

ADAMS PUTS COUNTRY ABOVE PARTY

President John Adams, who had led the nation to the brink of war by publishing the inflammatory XYZ dispatches, now recoiled from the prospect. He managed to keep a level head in spite of the dizzy heights of popularity to which his administration had suddenly been elevated. Like George Washington and many other statesmen of his generation, he now realized that a major war had to be avoided at all costs. Yet the Federalists, who had elected him to office, were eagerly making preparations for a Franco-American conflict, which, unlike a clash with England, would presumably not disrupt revenue and destroy Hamilton's financial system. In clamoring for hostilities with France, the Federalists were discrediting their Republican opponents and strengthening their hold on the national administration. Adams probably suspected that he would dig his own political grave if he averted the war the Hamiltonians so ardently desired. In this event, the inflated popularity of the Federalists might well collapse, and he himself might not be re-elected in 1800.

Yet Adams perceived that France wanted to avoid a full-dress war with the Americans. If she had desired one, she would have responded to American attacks on her ships with large-scale offensive operations. Talleyrand himself was fearful that limited hostilities might widen into unlimited hostilities. In such an event, France would further jeopardize her commerce and colonies, ruin her plans for reviving the French empire in Louisiana, and add one more foe to the ranks of her enemies. Talleyrand therefore instructed the French consul-general in Philadelphia to issue propaganda to counteract the anti-French hysteria. He also let it be known, particularly through the American minister in the Netherlands, William Vans Murray, that he would respectfully receive a new American diplomatic representative.

Talleyrand likewise conveyed this conciliatory information to a peace-loving Quaker, the Pennsylvanian George Logan, who had made a special trip to France at his own expense in an effort to patch up the undeclared war. Logan was much criticized by Federalists for his intermeddling, and Congress rewarded him by passing the so-called Logan Act of 1799, which in modified form is still on the books. It forbids a private citizen to engage in unauthorized negotiations with foreign governments regarding issues in dispute with the United States.

When President Adams learned of Talleyrand's receptive mood, he decided upon a spectacularly courageous course. Without consulting his Cabinet on this particular issue, he boldly sent to the Senate, on February 18, 1799, the nomination of William Vans Murray, then in the Netherlands, as minister to France. The Federalist leaders in the Senate, at first thunderstruck, burst into a fury of indignation. If Murray went to France, there might be no war—no further discrediting of the Jeffersonian Republican party, no conquest of New Orleans and Florida. War-bent Federalists heatedly pleaded with Adams, but to no avail. The only concession that he would make was to expand the single nomination into a commission of three. The Federalists were finally forced to accept this compromise or incur the odium of deliberately rejecting the peace.

On the issue of peace or war, Adams appears to have had a majority of the people with him, Jeffersonian Republicans and reasonable Federalists alike. In spite of the anger and obstructive tactics of certain Federalist leaders, he again displayed his courage by bluntly ordering the three commissioners, who had been delaying their departure, to proceed at once to France.

By the time the American commission arrived, in March, 1800, the hard-pressed French armies, beset by an Allied coalition, were in a better posture. The brilliant young Napoleon Bonaparte, who was now first consul, crushed the Austrians in June. But even with his improved position, he had no desire to fight America, force her into an alliance with England, and at the same time ruin his plans for taking over Louisiana. France's distress was still such as to contribute to an American diplomatic success.

A DIVORCE FROM THE FRENCH MISALLIANCE

The Franco-American negotiations in Paris rapidly became deadlocked. The United States presented two major demands. First, that France pay approximately $20 million for the recent seizures of American merchant shipping, and second, that France consent to a mutual abrogation of the two treaties of 1778, notably the vexatious alliance, that Congress had already formally ended. The French flatly refused to pay anything if they had to give up the treaties, for these conferred special military and commercial benefits on them.

The log jam was finally broken after seven months of wearisome discussion. By the convention signed on September 30, 1800, France agreed, as subsequent amendments were worked out on both sides, to cancel the vexatious treaties if the United States would drop its bothersome financial claims.[13] This horse-trading arrangement meant, of course, that

[13] For the intricacies of the subsequent amendments, see E. Wilson Lyon, "The Franco-American Convention of 1800," *Jour. of Mod. Hist.*, XII (1940), 329–333.

the United States government would have to assume the claims of its own citizens. In effect, America consented to pay $20 million in alimony in order to secure a divorce from the twenty-two-year-old French marriage of (in) convenience, as represented by the Alliance of 1778. This was the price—and perhaps a cheap price—that had to be paid to get rid of the only formal treaty of alliance to which the United States was a party for nearly a century-and-a-half. The troubled history of the French pact does much to explain why the American people developed so violent an allergy to overseas entanglements.

Other indirect benefits flowed from the Convention of 1800, which was also a substitute commercial treaty less favorable to the French. Much to the disappointment of the embattled British, it restored peace with France at a time when peace was imperative for the development of the United States. More than that, it cleared the way for the incalculably significant purchase of Louisiana in 1803. If Adams had insisted upon full-blown hostilities with France in 1800, it is inconceivable that Napoleon Bonaparte, three years later, would have sold this vast windfall to the United States. In a real sense, President John Adams was the forgotten purchaser of Louisiana.

But Adams, the bubble of his popularity pricked by peace, was shabbily rewarded for his far-sighted and courageous efforts. The country, though generally grateful for peace, had bestirred itself mightily for war, and was now left with a frustrating, all-dressed-up-but-no-place-to-go feeling. Although Adams was a candidate for re-election in 1800, he was defeated, as he had feared, by the Jeffersonian Republicans. His now-split Federalists never regained control of the national administration, and he was never again elected to federal office. But he had no lasting regrets as to his conduct during the French crisis. In his declining years he wrote:

> . . . I will defend my missions to France, as long as I have an eye to direct my hand, or a finger to hold my pen. They were the most disinterested and meritorious actions of my life. I reflect upon them with so much satisfaction, that I desire no other inscription over my gravestone than: "Here lies John Adams, who took upon himself the responsibility of the peace with France in the year 1800." [14]

The conservative Federalist party of Washington and Adams, whatever its shortcomings in dealing with domestic affairs, had done well in foreign affairs. When it laid down the reins of authority in 1801, there were no menacing clouds on the horizon. It had established as the polestar of American diplomacy the policies of peace, neutrality, noninterference, and nonintervention. Thanks to Europe's distresses, it had persuaded Britain and Spain to make treaties that adjusted existing grievances. Thanks also to Europe's distresses, it had negotiated the

[14] *Works of John Adams,* X, 113 (Adams to Lloyd, Jan. 1815).

Convention of 1800 with France, by which the United States honorably terminated its entangling alliance and shook off the last diplomatic shackle binding it to Europe. Another chapter in American diplomatic history had come to a gratifying close.

SELECTED BIBLIOGRAPHY

A useful survey is A. B. Darling, *Our Rising Empire, 1763–1803* (New Haven, 1940). The best biography is Gilbert Chinard, *Honest John Adams* (Boston, 1933). On neutrality, consult C. M. Thomas, *American Neutrality in 1793* (New York, 1931). American reactions are well portrayed in C. D. Hazen, *Contemporary American Opinion of the French Revolution* (Baltimore, 1897). British backgrounds are set forth in Bradford Perkins, *The First Rapprochement; England and the United States, 1795–1805* (Philadelphia, 1955). See also G. W. Allen, *Our Naval War with France* (Boston, 1909). The standard biography is F. B. Tolles, *George Logan of Philadelphia* (New York, 1953).

Important articles are S. F. Bemis, "Washington's Farewell Address: A Foreign Policy of Independence," *Amer. Hist. Rev.*, XXXIX (1934), 250–268; E. W. Lyon, "The Directory and the United States," *ibid.*, XLIII (1938), 514–532; Alexander DeConde, "Washington's Farewell, the French Alliance, and the Election of 1796," *Miss. Valley Hist. Rev.*, XLIII (1957), 641–658. Dr. DeConde has additional articles on the diplomacy of William Vans Murray in the *Huntington Library Quar.*, XV (1952), 185–194, 297–304, and in the *Maryland Hist. Magazine*, XLVIII (1953), 1–26. Two older articles by J. A. James are still useful: "French Diplomacy and American Politics, 1794–1795," *Amer. Hist. Assn., Annual Report, 1911*, I, 153–163, and "French Opinion as a Factor in Preventing War between France and the United States, 1795–1800," *Amer. Hist. Rev.*, XXX (1924), 44–55. See also B. W. Bond, Jr., *The Monroe Mission to France, 1794–1796* (Baltimore, 1907).

See footnotes of this chapter; Bemis and Griffin, *Guide*, Ch. IV; and *Harvard Guide*, Ch. 11.

7TH ED. REFS. See new references at end of preceding chapter. J. C. Miller, *The Federalist Era, 1789–1801* (New York, 1960) is a readable survey; it notes that Adams, at first ardent for war in 1798, cooled off when he recognized Hamilton's ambitions. The same author's *Alexander Hamilton: Portrait in Paradox* (New York, 1959) treats fully Hamilton's dreams of a war of conquest. Dumas Malone, *Jefferson and the Ordeal of Liberty* (Boston, 1962) finds Jefferson's final year as Secretary the most trying thus far of his public life. Page Smith, *John Adams* (New York, 1962), Vol. II concludes that when the President decided to patch up the quarrel with France, he acted on principle, even though he assumed that his decision would meet with popular approval. But he knew that he would alienate the Hamiltonian Federalists, who could manipulate the Electoral College to his disadvantage. Alexander DeConde's *Entangling Alliance* (Durham, N.C., 1958) stresses the interaction of politics and diplomacy, and concludes that the Farewell Address was a campaign document aimed at the pro-French opposition. For other works see BIBLIOGRAPHICAL ADDENDUM, p. 982.

8TH AND 9TH ED. REFS. See BIBLIOGRAPHICAL ADDENDUM, p. 983.

8

Jefferson and the Louisiana Purchase, 1801-1803

The cession of Louisiana [to America] is an excellent thing for France. It is like selling us a Ship after she is surrounded by a British Fleet; it puts into safe-keeping what she could not keep herself, for England could take Louisiana in the first moment of war without the loss of a man.
GEORGE CABOT, July 1, 1803

CHASTISING THE BARBARY CUTTHROATS

THE ELECTORAL UPHEAVAL of 1800, which threw the Federalists out of power, swept Thomas Jefferson into the Presidential chair in March, 1801. The distinguished Virginian speedily found that the theories developed in his closet did not fit the harsh realities of world politics. As if some evil genius were pursuing him, he was forced to reverse most of the major policies he had championed while head of the opposition party.

In analyzing Jeffersonian concepts, one must first remember that Jefferson, though fundamentally an American, had warmly favored the French as against the British. Second, he was strongly opposed to European involvements, and in his inaugural address issued a solemn warning against "entangling alliances"—a phrase to which he, not Washington, gave currency. Third, he had pledged himself to a policy of economy and reduction of the national debt. Fourth, as leader of the agrarian party, he detested costly frigates, which he regarded as the tools of Federalist manufacturers and shippers. In fact, he urged that these vessels be laid up on the Potomac River. Fifth, he was a vigorous opponent of war, though not, strictly speaking, a pacifist. "Peace," he declared, "is our passion." Finally, he advocated a strict or narrow construction of the Constitution, and he had upbraided the Federalists for strengthening the central government at the expense of the states by a broad or loose construction.

The continued outrages of the Barbary pirates speedily compelled Jefferson to undertake an agonizing reassessment of his theoretical pacifism. Both President Washington and President Adams had been forced to humiliate themselves by purchasing treaties with three of these North African states—Algiers, Tripoli, and Tunis—and by sending to them tens of thousands of dollars in "protection" money ("presents"). Ironically enough, at almost the very time when the American people were shouting themselves hoarse with the slogan, "Millions for defense but not one cent for tribute," an American ship arrived at Algiers with twenty-six barrels of blackmail dollars. The depths of degradation were reached in October, 1800, when the Dey of Algiers forced a United States man-of-war, most inappropriately named the *George Washington,* to haul down the flag of the proud young republic, replace it with that of Algiers, and sail to Constantinople bearing an ambassador and presents to the Sultan. When Captain Bainbridge vainly protested, the Dey replied: "You pay me tribute, by which you become my slaves. I have, therefore, a right to order you as I may think proper." [1]

Shortly after the peace-loving Jefferson was sworn in, the showdown came. The Pasha of Tripoli, feeling neglected in the apportionment of tribute, declared war on the United States, in May, 1801, by cutting down the flagstaff at the American consulate. Three of Jefferson's most precious principles were immediately involved. He was pledged to economy—and a clash with Tripoli would be costly; he disliked the navy; and he detested war. But his concern for the honor of the flag and the safety of American seamen, reinforced by a vivid memory of Barbary brutality, induced Jefferson to forsake the quill for the sword. He adopted the bold and in the long run the less expensive course of sending warships to Mediterranean waters. In 1805, after hair-raising exploits, the United States succeeded in extorting from Tripoli a favorable treaty, which, however, required the payment of $60,000 to ransom American prisoners still enchained.

The War of 1812 delayed a thorough chastisement of the remaining North African corsairs. But at the close of hostilities the United States dictated a satisfactory treaty with Algiers, in 1816, at the cannon's mouth. This piratical state, and later both Tunis and Tripoli, were forced—for a change—to pay out money for losses to American shipping. Jefferson's vigorous action thus inaugurated a policy that freed American commerce in the Mediterranean, aroused patriotic fervor at home, and awakened a new respect among foreigners for the United States. The man of peace, by facing up to harsh realities, thus reaped a rich harvest with the sword.

[1] G. W. Allen, *Our Navy and the Barbary Corsairs* (Boston, 1905), p. 77.

NAPOLEONIC DESIGNS ON LOUISIANA

The anxieties of the American people had meanwhile turned to a more pressing problem nearer home—the fate of Louisiana. This magnificent expanse of territory had been ceded by the French to Spain in 1762 as compensation for her losses to Britain in the Seven Years' War. Yet no true Frenchman could ever forget that Louisiana, which immortalized the name of Louis XIV, had once belonged to France. Beginning about 1792, the French officials began to lay plans and enter into intrigues for regaining their lost colony. Napoleon Bonaparte, like Talleyrand and others, became fascinated by this vision. Once in power, he proceeded to act with his usual energy and ruthlessness.

The tradition is that the masterful Bonaparte put the screws on the Spanish King and forced him to disgorge Louisiana. The fact is that the trans-Mississippi wilderness was so heavy a liability to the Spaniards that they had been eager to dispose of it since 1795. First, and most oppressive, the administration and defense of the colony cost the Spanish treasury an annual deficit. Second, the sprawling territory, defended by flimsy ramparts and a few rusty guns, was a standing invitation to an invader. It was liable to fall at the outbreak of hostilities with the United States, France, or Great Britain. Finally, Spain valued Louisiana chiefly as a buffer to protect her more valuable lands to the south against the possessive American frontiersmen. She was weary of holding them back, and apprehensive over the prospect of becoming involved in war. But if France could be persuaded to take over Louisiana, she would have to shoulder the burden of keeping the aggressive Westerner in check— at no cost to Spain. As Talleyrand promised:

> Let the Court of Madrid cede these districts to France, and from that moment the power of America is bounded by the limit which it may suit the interests and the tranquillity of France and Spain to assign her. The French Republic . . . will be a wall of brass forever impenetrable to the combined efforts of England and America.[2]

The terms of the transfer from Spain to France were finally hammered out. Napoleon offered to give the son-in-law of the Spanish King the North Italian kingdom of Tuscany, or an equivalent, in exchange for all Louisiana. Well might Charles IV of Spain think that he was getting a splendid bargain in trading his trans-Mississippi wilderness, with some 50,000 multicolored inhabitants, for a million civilized white subjects on the banks of the Arno. The preliminary arrangements were concluded at San Ildefonso, Spain, on October 1, 1800, the day after the American

[2] Henry Adams, *History of the United States of America during the Administrations of Jefferson and Madison* (New York, 1889), I, 357.

envoys signed at Paris the Convention of 1800 with France. Exactly one year later Napoleon concluded the Preliminary Peace of Amiens with Britain, thereby bringing to a temporary end seven long years of fighting. He was making sure, among other things, that neither a war with America nor one with England would interfere with his ambitious adventure in empire building.

But over two years elapsed before Charles IV of Spain signed the order to deliver Louisiana to France. He had begun to suspect, with good reason, that Bonaparte was not going to carry through the exchange of Tuscany in good faith. To quiet his suspicions, the French minister to Spain was instructed to give a written pledge that under no conditions would France ever transfer Louisiana to a third power. Somewhat reassured by this promise, but still reluctant, Charles IV yielded to the peremptory demands of Napoleon and, on October 15, 1802, signed the fateful order.

THE RISING OF THE WEST

During 1801 and 1802 rumors of the momentous Louisiana transaction drifted into the United States without causing undue alarm. But Jefferson was uneasy. At this time his friend, Pierre Samuel du Pont de Nemours, the distinguished French physiocrat, was about to return to France after a three-year sojourn in the United States, and Jefferson made unofficial use of him to lay before the French authorities his arguments against acquiring Louisiana.

The full seriousness of the situation was not brought home to the American people until October, 1802. The Spanish authorities at New Orleans, annoyed by American smugglers and acting under orders from Madrid, arbitrarily suspended the right of deposit without naming another place, as required by the Pinckney Treaty of 1795. Although freedom of navigation as such was not affected, the Mississippi flatboatmen, who were now handling a large quantity of agricultural produce, would find it highly inconvenient not to land cargoes while waiting for ocean-going ships.

The ominous tidings from New Orleans rolled slowly up the great river and penetrated the valleys. The Westerners, whose wartime prosperity had recently been depressed by the Peace of Amiens between England and France, gave vent to a prolonged cry of anger. The loss of the right of deposit was in itself bad enough. But many people assumed that the order had been dictated by Napoleon, and that the river would be completely closed when he took over Louisiana. There was wild talk of secession and of direct action. "The Kentuckymen," reported one American, "have often wished for an opportunity of sacking New Orleans, and the day may not be far distant." A bellicose Westerner wrote, "I am certain that I could raise 500 men in and have them Ready in one week if permesion [*sic*] was only gave." [3]

The demoralized Federalists, now the "outs," were overjoyed at the prospect of strong measures against their old foe, France. Here was a rare opportunity for them to pose as protectors of the West, whose interests they had hitherto opposed, and with the aid of Western votes ride once more into popularity and power. The Jefferson administration was confronted with a perplexing dilemma. Unless it took prompt and effective steps to quiet the hair-triggered Westerners, they might disrupt the Union. And if Jefferson resorted to strong measures, he might provoke a foreign war, which in turn might bring disaster.

The Westerners, to whom the sudden conversion of the Federalists did not ring true, fortunately showed unexpected moderation. They were preponderantly Jeffersonian Republicans, and hence were willing to give their President a fair chance to see what he could do by diplomacy. In addition, even without the right of deposit the Spanish authorities were allowing produce to flow freely down the Mississippi. They had taken away enough to infuriate the Westerners, but had left enough to keep them from fighting. Finally, in spite of loud boasting, "the men of the Western waters" perceived that a war with both France and Spain was not to be undertaken lightly. One Kentuckian faced realities:

> . . . I am affraid the united States are too Weake to attempt any thing by force, therefore I Suppose some other means must be used. I fear we Shall be insulted by other nations and not have it in our Power even to make an attempt to Repell the Insult. No Army No Nevy and worst of all an Empty Treasury.[4]

A PRO-FRENCH JEFFERSON BECOMES PRO-BRITISH

Jefferson, though mildly optimistic outwardly, was by this time genuinely concerned. The crisis, he wrote privately, was "the most important the United States have ever met since their independence." He was content to have senile Spain as a neighbor, because he had long believed that the Americans could take what they wanted when they needed it. But if Louisiana fell into the clutches of France, the greatest military power in Europe, the future would be dark—and probably bloody.

Again the realist triumphed over the theorist. Confronted with the necessities of the moment, Jefferson—the France-lover, the Britain-hater, the pacifist, and the isolationist—abandoned four of his most sacred principles. "We stand completely corrected of the error," he declared,

[3] A. P. Whitaker, *The Mississippi Question 1795–1803* (New York, 1934), p. 222.
[4] *Ibid.*, p. 228.

"that either the Government or the nation of France has any remains of friendship for us." As he wrote to Minister Livingston in Paris:

> There is on the globe one single spot, the possessor of which is our natural and habitual enemy. It is New Orleans. . . . The day that France takes possession of New Orleans, fixes the sentence which is to restrain her [the French Nation] forever within her low-water mark. . . . From that moment, we must marry ourselves to the British fleet and nation.[5]

This astonishing statement is indicative of Jefferson's anxiety. Here was a statesman, whose advice against "entangling alliances" was still ringing through the nation, proposing an entanglement with his old enemy, England, to fight, if need be, his old friend, France—a France that had forsaken republicanism for dictatorship. His words were matched by deeds. Without fanfare, he embarked upon vigorous military measures in the Mississippi Valley in preparation for that day when the French might take over Louisiana.[6] Congress, reflecting the temper of the country, later authorized him to call upon the state governors for 80,000 militiamen.

But Jefferson's most immediate problem was to quiet the home front. The Federalists might ride into power on the Louisiana issue—and Federalist control in Washington was about as distasteful to the Jeffersonian Republicans as French control in New Orleans. Moreover, if negotiations with France were to have any prospect of success, the Westerners had to be kept quiet, and above all restrained from making a rash descent upon New Orleans.

Jefferson meanwhile was pulling wires quietly behind the scenes. He openly consorted with the British *chargé* in Washington, as if to announce that French policy was throwing America into the arms of France's enemy. In addition, he cleverly used the outbursts of the Westerners to play upon the fears of the French and Spanish diplomatic representatives in the United States. His methods soon brought results. The Spanish government, proceeding with unaccustomed haste, restored the right of deposit at New Orleans, although the United States was not officially informed of this about-face until April 19, 1803. Meanwhile something spectacular had to be done to placate the West.

Jefferson came up with the happy thought of sending James Monroe to France as a special envoy to assist Robert Livingston, the regular minister. The nomination received Senate confirmation on January 12, 1803. Livingston, however, needed no assistance. He had been presenting the disadvantages of Louisiana to the French officials with such zeal that one of them offered to give him a certificate as the most persistent

[5] A. A. Lipscomb, ed., *Writings of Thomas Jefferson* (Monticello ed., Washington, 1904), X, 312–315 (Jefferson to Livingston, April 18, 1802).

[6] See Mary P. Adams, "Jefferson's Reaction to the Treaty of San Ildefonso," *Jour. of Southern Hist.*, XXI (1955), 173–188.

negotiator he had ever met. But Monroe possessed the confidence of the West to an unusual degree. He owned large holdings of land there, and of all the men then prominent in public life he had most conspicuously identified himself with the interests of the Westerners. The Monroe mission, in its primary object of calming the West, was a success before Monroe even left America.

The chances that a special envoy could accomplish anything by negotiation were poor; only extraordinarily good luck would help Monroe. Yet he and Livingston were instructed to offer as much as 50 million livres (about $10 million) for New Orleans and West Florida—an area thought to be included in Louisiana. If France proposed to close the Mississippi entirely to American commerce, or seemed "to meditate hostilities," the two envoys were to enter upon negotiations for an alliance with England. "On the event of this mission," Jefferson reminded them, "depend the future destinies of this Republic."

THE DOMINICAN DEATH TRAP

Napoleon had meanwhile been taking vigorous preliminary measures to occupy Louisiana. His first task was to wrest the French colony of Santo Domingo from control of the revolted Negro slaves. This enormously productive sugar island, France's prize overseas possession, was heavily dependent upon the United States for foodstuffs, lumber, and other necessities. One of Napoleon's principal motives for securing Louisiana was to provide a granary within the French empire for the more important Caribbean sugar islands, notably Santo Domingo, which he intended to make both the capital and key of his New World domain.

Napoleon was free to occupy Santo Domingo after the preliminary Peace of Amiens, signed October 1, 1801, for it removed the menace of the British navy. He dispatched to the revolted colony an army of veterans, under the command of his brother-in-law, the able Leclerc. The leadership of the maddened Dominican slaves had fallen to a gifted, full-blooded Negro named Toussaint L'Ouverture, whose career afforded some striking parallels to that of Napoleon. Toussaint was aware of these similarities, for he prided himself on being the "Bonaparte of the Antilles." The real Bonaparte, who feared that the apings of this "miserable Negro" would make him the laughing stock of all Europe, ordered his men to make short work of these "gilded Africans."

Napoleon planned to occupy Louisiana next. For this purpose, he was assembling a powerful army under General Victor in Holland, and he instructed it upon arrival to take up the strongest possible position and engage in intrigues with the Indians. If France's military might had entrenched itself in Louisiana, it probably could not have been dislodged by any force that the United States alone was then capable of raising.

As fate would have it, Victor's fleet was icebound in Holland during the crucial months of January and February, 1803, and then was delayed by storms.

The French reconquest of Santo Domingo went well—at first. Toussaint's resistance collapsed in less than three months. He was treacherously seized, taken to France, and imprisoned in a chilly cell, there to cough his life away. But the fury of the ex-slaves swept away 17,000 Frenchmen, disrupted Napoleon's plans, and delayed complete conquest until the deadly scourge of yellow fever descended. Five hundred thousand Negroes, heartened by this unexpected ally and maddened by the news that Napoleon planned to enchain them once more, arose again with an almost unparalleled fanaticism. "These men may be killed," General Leclerc reported, "but will not surrender. They laugh at death;— and it is the same with the women." [7] In one group of 176 Negro prisoners, 173 strangled themselves.

Decimated by bullets and disease, one French army after another melted away. "The rebellion grows," lamented Leclerc, "the disease continues." Over 4000 Frenchmen died of yellow fever in the month of September, 1802. Desperate, Leclerc reported that he could never subdue Santo Domingo without 12,000 acclimated troops, and he estimated that 70,000 Frenchmen would have to die before that many would be immune from the scourge. He recommended extreme methods:

> We must destroy all the mountain negroes, men and women, sparing only children under twelve years of age. We must destroy half the negroes of the plains, and not allow in the colony a single man who has worn an epaulette. Without these measures the colony will never be at peace, and every year, especially deadly ones like this, you will have a civil war on your hands which will jeopardize the future. [8]

Less than a month after writing this letter Leclerc himself died of yellow fever.

BONAPARTE FORESTALLS THE BRITISH

Bonaparte, though outwardly calm, was by now inwardly frantic. Some fifty thousand men had already been sacrificed in the fiery furnace of Santo Domingo. Fifty thousand more men and an enormous sum of money would have to be thrown into the pestilential island before it could be subdued. Even with such a force Napoleon might fail. If he did succeed, he would lose anyhow—for the island would be ruined. While in this state of mind Napoleon received the news of Leclerc's death—a blow that staggered him. A few days later, during a private conversation

[7] T. L. Stoddard, *The French Revolution in San Domingo* (Boston, 1914), p. 335 (Leclerc to Bonaparte, Aug. 6, 1802).
[8] *Ibid.*, p. 342 (Oct. 7, 1802).

on another subject, he suddenly burst out, "Damn sugar, damn coffee, damn colonies!" With his prestige suffering badly at home and abroad, he could not afford to go on with this mad venture and risk another setback. Since he was forced to abandon Santo Domingo, what need had he for the granary—Louisiana?

The fate of Louisiana was intimately bound up with the crisis in Europe. The Peace of Amiens with England was only a between-acts truce. The old sources of friction still rankled and hostilities were bound to erupt again within a few months. Napoleon was tired of the role of beneficent shopkeeper; his destiny lay in war. A few glorious campaigns, and the French people would forget all about his failure in Santo Domingo. Besides, he could not hold Louisiana against the naval power of the British, who, he had recently learned, were raising a powerful force to seize New Orleans. He would be far wiser to sell the vast area to the Americans for a substantial sum than to let it fall into the jaws of the British lion.

What else prompted Napoleon? Money, although important to a war-bent dictator, was hardly the compelling consideration. Spain almost certainly would have been willing to outbid Jefferson for Louisiana. Nor did the cynical Napoleon act, as sometimes alleged, out of regard for "traditional" French "affection" for America. His supposed words— "We have helped them to be free, now let us help them to be great"— simply do not ring true. Aside from forestalling the British fleet, he apparently had in mind keeping the United States from being driven into British arms, and at the same time averting future wars with the boundary-bursting young nation. More than this, Napoleon had in view beefing up the American republic so that it would thwart the expansion of England in the New World, compete with her merchant marine, and, as he far-sightedly put it, "sooner or later humble her pride." [9]

BUYING AN EMPIRE TO GET A CITY

With General Leclerc dead in Santo Domingo and General Victor delayed by storms in Holland, Bonaparte acted with typical unexpected-ness and dispatch. On April 11, 1803, he summoned his finance minister and, with a magnificent gesture, announced:

Irresolution and deliberation are no longer in season. I renounce Louisiana. It is not only New Orleans that I will cede, it is the whole colony without any reservation. I know the price of what I abandon. . . . I renounce it with the greatest regret. To attempt obstinately to retain it would be folly.

[9] The British were immensely relieved to see Napoleon quit his foothold in North America. Private English bankers were permitted to float the necessary bonds, even though by this time Britain and France were again at war. See Bradford Perkins, "England and the Louisiana Question," *Huntington Library Quar.*, XVIII (1955), 279–295.

I direct you to negotiate this affair. . . . Do not even await the arrival of Mr. Monroe: have an interview this very day with Mr. Livingston. . . .[10]

Livingston had meanwhile redoubled his efforts in Paris to persuade France to sell New Orleans and West Florida. He was spurred on by the knowledge that Monroe was on his way, and by a desire to avoid sharing the glory of the negotiation with another man. On April 11, 1803, the day of Napoleon's orders, Talleyrand most unexpectedly asked Livingston what the United States would give for all Louisiana. Scarcely able to believe his ears (he was deaf anyhow), Livingston replied that the wishes of the United States extended only to New Orleans and the area to the east. But the issue was now out on the table.

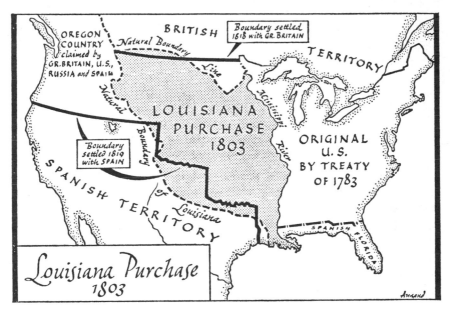

The next day, on April 12, 1803, Monroe reached Paris and joined Livingston in the negotiations. For a nerve-racking week the two envoys haggled over the price—while an empire hung in the balance. Finally, the American representatives bound the United States to pay approximately $15 million in money and claims for all Louisiana. In so doing they knew perfectly well they were violating their instructions. Authorized to pay as much as $10 million for New Orleans and as much *east* of the Mississippi as they could obtain, they had agreed to give $15 million for New Orleans and a trackless expanse that lay entirely *west* of the river.

The violation of instructions could easily be justified in those cableless days. Monroe and Livingston were far from home, and the opportunity

[10] Marquis de Barbé-Marbois, *History of Louisiana* (Phila., 1830), pp. 274–275.

called for immediate action. Napoleon would sell all or none, and unless the Americans took all they would not obtain the needed window on the gulf. They therefore felt justified in exceeding their instructions, while counting on the good sense of Jefferson and the American people to uphold them. After setting his name to the treaty of cession, Livingston solemnly declared:

> We have lived long, but this is the noblest work of our whole lives. . . . From this day the United States take their place among the powers of the first rank. . . . The instruments which we have just signed will cause no tears to be shed: they prepare ages of happiness for innumerable generations of human creatures.[11]

What had the two American envoys actually bought? Did the purchase embrace Texas or West Florida? Livingston approached the slippery Talleyrand, who knew perfectly well what Napoleon conceived the boundaries to be. He reported:

> I [Livingston] asked the minister [Talleyrand] what were the east bounds of the territory ceded to us? He said he did not know; we must take it as they had received it. I asked him how Spain meant to give them possession? He said . . . I do not know. Then you mean that we shall construe it our own way? I can give you no direction; you have made a noble bargain for yourselves, and I suppose you will make the most of it.[12]

The United States did make the most of it—as the subsequent history of the Floridas and Texas will attest. Meanwhile the exact northern, western, and southeastern boundaries were undetermined. The only undisputed limits were the shifting Mississippi River on the east and the Gulf of Mexico on the south. But the American negotiators did know that they had bought the western half of the world's most valuable river valley, sprawling between the Rockies and the Mississippi, and bounded somewhere on the north by British North America.

Why all the evasiveness and downright untruthfulness on the part of Talleyrand? The answer is that Napoleon was playing the crafty old game of divide and conquer. He hoped that boundary disputes would embroil Spain and the United States, and that he could play one antagonist off against the other to his own advantage. "If an obscurity did not already exist," he cynically remarked, "it would perhaps be good policy to put one there." His fondest dreams in this regard were abundantly realized. The two decades that followed were enlivened by much bickering and quarreling, notably with Spain over West Florida, with Spain over Texas and the Southwest, and with England over the vast northern reaches of the Louisiana territory.

---

[11] Barbé-Marbois, *ibid.*, pp. 310–311.
[12] *American State Papers, Foreign Relations,* II, 561 (Livingston to Madison, May 20, 1803).

ELASTIC CONSCIENCES MAKE ELASTIC CONSTITUTIONS

The news of the purchase caused unrestrained joy in the West, where speeches, toasts, and monster celebrations were the order of the day. One heard little else but talk of "America's Extension of Empire" and "The Immortal Jefferson."

But Jefferson was not happy over the astonishing turn of affairs. Having set out to buy a relatively small area at the mouth of the Mississippi, he now had well-nigh half a continent on his hands. Nor was this all. For over ten years he had been preaching strict construction and precise deference to constitutional niceties. But what article of his beloved Constitution stipulated that the federal government might buy, and then incorporate in the Union, a partially inhabited wilderness as large as the Union itself?

With much anguish of spirit, Jefferson perspired over the legalistic problem. The only alternative seemed to be a constitutional amendment. But months of precious time, perhaps years, would be wasted by such a clumsy procedure. Livingston and Monroe were meanwhile urging Jefferson to make haste, for they well knew that the capricious Napoleon might suddenly decide to sell the territory to a more appreciative buyer. The only sensible solution seemed to be to accept the purchase, and then hope that a later constitutional amendment would legalize the transaction,[13] or that the American people would merely acquiesce. Jefferson himself privately admitted that the transfer was "an act beyond the constitution," but he trusted that Congress would overlook "metaphysical subtleties." He thus compromised with conscience in a private letter:

> It is the case of a guardian, investing the money of his ward in purchasing an important adjacent territory; and saying to him when of age, I did this for your good; I pretend to no right to bind you: you may disavow me, and I must get out of the scrape as I can: I thought it my duty to risk myself for you.[14]

The Federalists, in turn, found themselves in an inconsistent position. Just a few months before they had been advocating a seizure of New Orleans for the sake of the abused Westerner—a course that might have meant a disastrous war with both France and Spain. Now that Jefferson had succeeded in purchasing the coveted outlet at a bargain price and without shedding a drop of blood, the Federalists raised a chorus of criticism. They argued heatedly that the Jeffersonian Republicans were

[13] Twenty-five years later, in *American Insurance Company* v. *Cantner,* the Supreme Court, dominated by Federalist John Marshall, indirectly upheld the purchase under the war- and treaty-making clauses of the Constitution.

[14] *Writings of Thomas Jefferson* (Monticello ed.), X, 411 (Jefferson to Breckinridge, August 12, 1803).

"tearing the constitution to tatters." They insisted that the title to Louisiana was illegal and immoral. They railed against paying such an enormous price for a worthless desert that was too vast to be governed. They condemned Jefferson, who had pledged the administration to rigid economy, for having wasted a sum which, if piled in silver dollars, would make a stack three miles high or would fill 866 wagons. Most of all, the Federalists feared that in due time a group of agricultural states would be formed from the new territory, thus unhinging the political balance and causing the industrial and commercial East to be outvoted by "wild men" in Congress. There were even threats of secession. Senator White of Delaware solemnly averred that the Louisiana purchase would be "the greatest curse that could at present befall us. . . ."

But the common sense of the American people ultimately prevailed. Even a Federalist like Alexander Hamilton, who could hardly object to Jefferson's sudden conversion to Hamiltonian loose construction, gave the purchase his qualified blessing. The Senate approved the treaty of cession, together with the accompanying two conventions covering financial arrangements, on October 20, 1803, by a vote of 24 to 7. The Senators could not fail to heed the public ground swell for Louisiana, especially in the West. They were quite capable of overlooking "metaphysical subtleties" when face to face with what was perhaps the greatest real-estate bargain in history—828,000 square miles of imperial domain at approximately 3 cents an acre.

RECEIVERS OF STOLEN GOODS

There was disquieting truth in the Federalist charge that the title to Louisiana was faulty. First of all, Napoleon had obtained the territory from Spain on the condition that he deliver Tuscany to the son-in-law of Charles IV. Bonaparte never completely fulfilled this promise, though solemnly bound to return Louisiana if he failed to do so. In addition, Charles IV had secured from Napoleon a written pledge that Louisiana would never be handed over to a third nation. Bonaparte flagrantly and cynically broke this promise.

Louisiana, in fact, was not Napoleon's to sell. It was still occupied by Spanish troops, and not until seven months after the signing of the treaties did France take formal possession. In short, Bonaparte had sold the United States only a scrap of paper. Small wonder that he could gloat: "Sixty millions of francs for an occupation that will not perhaps last a day!" Moreover, the French constitution, which was still on the books, provided that the Executive could not dispose of the nation's territory without the consent of the legislative Chambers.

Fortunately for the United States, Napoleon had decided to put himself above constitutional encumbrances and carry through what he called his "Louisianacide." But few true Frenchmen ever completely forgave him for shattering these dreams of empire. Two of his brothers rushed to him in his bath, and argued against the transfer so heatedly that he finally terminated the scene by splashing water over them. But the problem of Napoleon's authority was one that concerned France, not America.

All things considered, the title to Louisiana was highly questionable. Professor Edward Channing of Harvard University even went so far as to conclude in 1906 that the Americans had acted as "the accomplices of the greatest highwayman of modern history. . . ." This judgment is harsh, but there is much about the transfer that suggests the purchase of property known to have been stolen, or at least obtained under false pretenses.

In view of all this irregularity, why should the American people have accepted Louisiana? The question is all the more pointed when one notes their repeated claims to moral superiority over Europe, and the high value that they placed upon clear titles as a result of their frontier experience. The answer is that the need for Louisiana was so pressing, and its acquisition by peaceful or bloody means so inevitable, that America would have been foolish to be finicky about the title. There seemed to be a "higher law" than mere titles, and the United States was willing to take a chance when the stakes were so large. Besides, for many generations the Americans had regarded the Spaniard as grasping, bloody, perfidious. They were inclined to feel that if Napoleon had betrayed his confederate, the treacherous don had merely got what he richly deserved.

The outraged Madrid government, as was to be expected, protested vigorously to both France and the United States against Napoleon's betrayal. Jefferson's position was that the transaction involved only Paris. Yet the prospect of a refusal by Spain to carry out her part of the transaction stirred up another furor in the West. One Kentuckian reported that "Nothing but war is the topick of the day," while old General Russell exclaimed, "Our Western Country [is] all on fire!" [15] But Spain was not so foolhardy as to back up her protests with force. There was little point in risking a war with both the United States and France, particularly over a liability that the Spaniards were well rid of.

The formal transfer ceremonies took place in due season. The Spanish governor of Louisiana, on November 30, 1803, handed to the French representative a silver platter containing the keys to the public buildings of New Orleans. This change of ownership occurred more than a year after it had been authorized by the Spanish king, and seven months after the signing of the purchase treaties in Paris by Livingston and Monroe. The official French occupation of Louisiana actually lasted only twenty

[15] Bernard Mayo, *Henry Clay; Spokesman of the New West* (Boston, 1937), p. 141.

days. Then, on December 20, 1803, at New Orleans, the blue, white, and red of the descending French tricolor met the red, white and blue of the ascending Stars and Stripes. A cheer burst forth from the handful of Americans gathered in the square—and Louisiana belonged to the United States.

THE LOUISIANA WINDFALL

Who deserves the credit for this bloodless bargain? Livingston, and to some extent, Monroe, did yeoman work on the diplomatic front, yet Napoleon's decision to sell apparently had little relation to their overtures. Jefferson deserves slight direct credit. The brutal truth is that Napoleon, for purely realistic reasons, dumped the vast domain into his lap. An embarrassed Jefferson squirmed, but he found it less embarrassing to keep the windfall than to brush it off.

John Adams and Toussaint L'Ouverture, in whose honor statues should be erected in appropriate spots, are the forgotten purchasers. Adams courageously brought about peace with France in 1800, and without peace Napoleon almost certainly would not have transferred the territory to the United States. Toussaint L'Ouverture, in the interests of his own race, delayed the conquest of Santo Domingo to the point where Napoleon was willing to abandon the whole project.

Regardless of who deserves the credit, the results of the purchase were so far-reaching as to defy analysis. At one stroke, the republic laid additional foundations for a mighty world power. Specifically, the acquisition of this vast area, a magnificent storehouse of natural resources, meant that the American people had doubled their original endowment, and that they would have almost limitless room for expansion. Without Louisiana in their possession, they would have been unable to carry the Stars and Stripes on into Texas, California, Oregon, and the Pacific. The purchase also set the precedent for acquiring foreign territory and peoples by treaty.

Jefferson's map-changing achievement, moreover, gave a new vitality to the budding spirit of national unity. It further reduced the Federalists to "sectional impotence." The Westerners, in particular, felt a new confidence in their central government. The removal of the mouth of the Mississippi from the reach of foreign faithlessness ended Western intrigue, and enabled the federal government to pursue its chosen policy of noninvolvement without having to embark upon wars with France or alliances with Britain.

America was fortunate among the nations. Once more the rivalries and distresses of Europe had worked to her advantage. From them she won her independence; from them she derived greatness. Maddened Negroes, yellow fever, international jealousies, Napoleonic caprice, and even icebound ports and fierce storms were all on her side. Perhaps the new republic had a noble destiny to fulfill.

SELECTED BIBLIOGRAPHY

The story is briefly told in A. B. Darling, *Our Rising Empire, 1763–1803* (New Haven, 1940). The Western side of the Louisiana purchase is developed in A. P. Whitaker, *The Mississippi Question, 1795–1803* (New York, 1934), while the European side is developed in E. W. Lyon, *Louisiana in French Diplomacy, 1759–1804* (Norman, Oklahoma, 1934). The view of the State Department appears in Irving Brant, *James Madison: Secretary of State, 1800–1809* (Indianapolis, 1953). Bradford Perkins, in *The First Rapprochement; England and the United States, 1795–1805* (Philadelphia, 1955), sheds new light on British backgrounds. See also C. C. Tansill, *The United States and Santo Domingo, 1798–1873* (Baltimore, 1938) and R. W. Logan, *The Diplomatic Relations of the United States with Haiti, 1776–1891* (Chapel Hill, N.C., 1941). The complicated tale is unfolded in R. W. Irwin, *The Diplomatic Relations of the United States with the Barbary Powers, 1776–1816* (Chapel Hill, N.C., 1931). See also L. B. Wright and J. H. Macleod, *The First Americans in North Africa: William Eaton's Struggle for a Vigorous Policy against the Barbary Pirates, 1799–1805* (Princeton, 1945). A valuable article is P. C. Brooks, "Spain's Farewell to Louisiana, 1803–1821," *Miss. Valley Hist. Rev.*, XXVII (1940), 29–42.

See footnotes of this chapter; Bemis and Griffin, *Guide*, pp. 113–125; 156–161; *Harvard Guide*, Ch. 12.

7TH ED. REFS. George Dangerfield's well written *Chancellor Robert R. Livingston of New York, 1746–1813* (New York, 1960) builds up Livingston's role in the Louisiana Purchase. He was persistent and he may have planted the idea in Napoleon's mind by pushing for the area above the Arkansas River; he also stressed the danger of throwing America into Britain's arms. S. G. Brown, ed., *The Autobiography of James Monroe* (Syracuse, 1959) reveals that Monroe modestly did not claim undue credit for the Purchase. But Monroe does observe that his arrival, with full powers and with a rank superior to Livingston's, was followed by Napoleon's shift of position. Monroe played an important role in getting a "down payment" on the Purchase. J. A. Logan, Jr., *No Transfer* (New Haven, 1961) concludes that Hamilton's dreams of conquering Louisiana in 1799, followed by Jefferson's purchase designed to exclude Britain and France, strengthened the principle of no-transfer of territory in the Americas from one European power to another. H. C. Bailey and B. C. Weber, "A British Reaction to the Treaty of San Ildefonso," *William and Mary Quar.*, Ser. 3, vol. XVII (1960), pp. 242–246 points out that the British Parliament approved the Peace of Amiens without knowing of the retrocession of Louisiana in the Treaty of San Ildefonso (1800); otherwise, fearing the French menace to Canada, they might have rejected it. Joel Larus, "Pell-Mell Along the Potomac," *ibid.*, pp. 349–357 notes that Jefferson's highly informal (pell-mell) receptions offended the British Minister Merry, who was nevertheless instructed by London to conform.

9TH ED. REFS. See BIBLIOGRAPHICAL ADDENDUM, p. 984.

9

Jefferson and Neutral Woes
1803-1809

*The winds and seas are Britain's wide domain,
And not a sail, but by permission, spreads.*
MOTTO OF BRITISH NAVAL REGISTER

BOOM DAYS FOR NEUTRAL SHIPPING

NAPOLEON REOPENED hostilities with England on May 18, 1803, scarcely two weeks after he had signed away his Louisiana liability. The titanic upheaval that ensued did not subside until twelve years later, when Bonaparte was safely marooned on the distant island of St. Helena. Thus the war that had erupted in 1793 lasted—except for the nineteen-month Amiens breathing spell—almost continuously for twenty-two years.

The conflict was of crucial importance to the New World. It kept Europe from casting greedy eyes on American possessions, and in the end left her so exhausted that the United States could face westward without fear. The American people owe a debt to Bonaparte for having shaken Europe so violently that Louisiana fell into their hands, and for having given them ten years in which to consolidate their gains. Although the United States was eventually sucked into the European whirlpool, every year of delay gave to the poorly defended yet rapidly growing republic the greatest of all boons—time.

From 1803 to 1812 the United States was the most important neutral carrier, notably of foodstuffs. The death struggles of Europe enabled American shippers to exploit markets hitherto closed to them, and to demand abnormally high prices for their cargoes. Such rewards led to a boom in shipping, which the caustic John Randolph of Virginia referred to as "this mushroom, this fungus of war." The American people were quite willing to work both sides of the street—to enjoy unrestricted trade with all nations and interference from none.

116

Incredibly enough, for over two years after the renewal of hostilities the battling British and French refrained from drastic interference with American commerce. But this was merely the calm before the storm. British shippers watched with ill-concealed jealousy the enrichment of a competing merchant marine and the loss of once-profitable markets. And since much of America's newly won trade strengthened France, Britain's arch-enemy, many Englishmen looked upon the Yankees as little better than accomplices of Bonaparte.

BRITANNIA RULES THE WAVES

The American colonies of France and Spain proved to be a perennial sore spot. In time of peace, these two nations restricted direct trade to and from their Caribbean outposts to their own vessels. But when the British navy swept enemy shipping from the seas, France and Spain were both forced to throw open their West Indian ports to the United States. Otherwise their colonials might have been starved into submission. Britain thereupon invoked her hoary and arbitrary Rule of 1756— trade not open in time of peace could not legally be thrown open in time of war. But this restriction did not apply to commerce in American ships between the Caribbean colonies and the mainland of the United States. A considerable amount of trade had flowed through these channels before the war.

The Yankee skipper, long notorious as a resourceful fellow, quickly took advantage of this loophole by using the subterfuge known as the "broken voyage." He would, for example, carry his cargo of sugar from the French West Indian island of Martinique to Savannah, Georgia. There he would pay duties on it and perhaps land it for a short time, thus Americanizing the toothsome product. Then he would reload it, often on the same ship, and receive back all or most of the money that he had paid in duties. His vessel would then sail merrily on its way to a European port under French control.

The British courts at first tolerated this round-about trade, notably in the case of the *Polly* (1800), an American ship carrying Cuban sugar to Spain by way of Massachusetts. But British shippers became increasingly critical. Of what advantage was it, they complained, to sweep enemy merchantmen from the seas if the dollar-chasing Yankees stepped in and took over this trade by underhanded means?

British indignation was quieted in the spring of 1805, when the Lords Commissioners of Appeals handed down their celebrated decision in the case of the *Essex*. This vessel had been carrying a cargo from Spain to Spanish Cuba by way of Salem, Massachusetts. The tribunal now held that payment of duties in America could no longer be accepted as evidence of good faith. Instead, shippers were asked to furnish further proof that they did not intend to evade the Rule of 1756 by what amounted to a "continuous voyage" between Spain and her colony. Unhappily, convincing evidence of this nature was almost impossible to obtain.

In the wake of the *Essex* ruling, British cruisers seized scores of American merchantmen. A storm of protest arose from the commercial centers of the United States; mass meetings were held, and indignant memorials poured in on Congress. "Never will neutrals be perfectly safe," insisted the Salem *Register*, "till free goods make free ships or till England loses two or three great naval battles."

Nor did England's offenses stop here. In looking for evidence of "continuous voyage," British men-of-war hovered off American ports in such numbers as to establish a virtual blockade. Here they exercised the undoubted right of a belligerent to search neutral merchantmen, both to establish their identity and to ascertain the nature of the cargo. Upon evidence of irregularity, or mere suspicion of it, American vessels were seized and sent to far-away Halifax, Nova Scotia, where, according to John Adams, the code of the Admiralty Court was "Rule, Britannia!" If the ships were not actually confiscated, they encountered delay that was often ruinously costly.

Visit and search were annoying at best, but the British officers, who had nothing but contempt for their "money-grubbing" cousins, discharged their disagreeable duties in a maddening manner. Basil Hall, then a young midshipman stationed off New York on His Majesty's ship *Leander*, was not surprised to find the name of his vessel cursed by the people of that city twenty years later. The British were sometimes careless when they fired a solid shot across the bow of the American merchantmen as a signal to heave to. Hall described a distressing incident that occurred in April, 1806:

> A casual shot from the *Leander* hit an unfortunate sloop's main-boom; and the broken spar striking the mate, John Pierce by name, killed him instantly. The sloop sailed on to New York, where the mangled body, raised on a platform, was paraded through the streets, in order to augment the vehement indignation, already at a high pitch, against the English.[1]

"BRITISH MANSTEALERS"

The most infuriating of all American grievances against England was the impressment of seamen. The United States had already suffered considerably from this practice during the wars of the French Revolution, but when hostilities were renewed in 1803, and the British navy was in desperate need of sailors, tensions mounted dangerously.

Impressment was a crude form of conscription or "selective service."

[1] Basil Hall, *Fragments of Voyages and Travels* (First series, London, 1840), I, 47.

Men would not ordinarily enlist in the British navy, even in time of crisis. The pay was poor, the food wretched, the quarters vile, and the discipline brutal—often taught to the tune of the savage cat-o'-nine tails. The naval authorities therefore sent out press gangs, on land or sea, to seize able-bodied subjects and forcibly enlist them. Whatever the legal basis of impressment, it had been employed by England for over four hundred years; and if long and undisputed usage established legality, impressment was legal.

The British themselves set limits to this harsh practice. They did not claim the right to exercise it on foreign soil or against American citizens— only British subjects. If an American citizen was impressed, London insisted that because of his physical similarity to an Englishman he had been seized by mistake. If his American birth could be established, his release might be obtained, though often not until after several years of confinement in Britain's "floating hells."

The United States, with its large population of immigrants, reacted violently to certain aspects of impressment. English press gangs, carrying clubs and stretchers, would obviously not invade the streets of New York City and there lay hold of either British or American sailors. This was United States territory, and angry mobs would release the victims. But on the high seas, where Britain reigned supreme, press gangs dragged so-called British subjects from the decks of American merchantmen with complete impunity. The Washington government argued that the American flag transformed into American territory the deck beneath it, and that the crew, whatever its nationality, was not subject to impressment. But Britons like Lord Harrowby replied that this "pretension" to floating territory was "too extravagant to require any serious refutation." More blunt was the report of a British naval commander in 1797: "It is my duty to keep my Ship manned, and I will do so wherever I find men that speak the same language with me." [2]

British officers, especially if short-handed, frequently violated their own rules when stopping American ships. The process of determining a seaman's nationality was always arbitrary, frequently capricious, and never judicial. The press gang, exercising the belligerent right of visit and search, would line up the crew of a merchantman. If a sailor pronounced "peas" as "paise," he was an Irishman and hence a British subject. If he talked through his nose, he probably was a Yankee. If no one who even remotely resembled a British subject was found, the boarding party would often make convenient mistakes. The officer in command, performing the triple function of judge, jury, and jailer, would pick out a likely-looking hand and claim him as a fellow Englishman. The luckless seaman was forthwith dragged off; if so ill-advised as to

[2] Quoted in Bernard Mayo, *Henry Clay: Spokesman of the New West* (Boston, 1937), p. 39.

resist, he was struck down and dragged off. In this way Swedes, Danes, and Portuguese, all of whom could not possibly be mistaken for Englishmen, were snatched from the decks of American ships and condemned to nautical slavery.

The American people were injured, both directly and indirectly, by this inhumane practice. All told, British press gangs claimed perhaps 8,000 to 10,000 bona fide American citizens, many of whom were killed in action or died from maltreatment. The victims often left behind dependents who suffered extreme hardship. The searched merchantman was frequently delayed, with loss of wind, tide, and sometimes markets, and on occasion the vessel was left so shorthanded that it sank in the next storm with all on board. Little wonder that the British press gangs were regarded as murderers.

ONCE AN ENGLISHMAN ALWAYS AN ENGLISHMAN

The same wretched conditions in the British navy that discouraged enlistments and made impressment necessary caused desertion to flourish. Lord Nelson reported that 42,000 sailors had jumped ship during the war ending in 1801. British warships were frequently left so short of hands that they could not sail, or, if they did, they occasionally sank. If England was not to yield naval supremacy to Napoleon, she would have to find men by fair means or foul.

The Americans, unfortunately for their case against "sailor snatching," openly connived at desertion. Their prospering merchant marine was urgently in need of sailors, and in a position to offer alluring bounties, better working conditions, and seductively higher wages. "Dollars for shillings" was the current saying. Every British warship that touched at American ports during the years of the Napoleonic wars was in danger of losing some men. In 1804 twelve ships of the Royal Navy were detained at Norfolk, Virginia, because of deserters, some of whom paraded the streets cursing their officers and thumbing noses at them. Such episodes do much to explain why British press gangs made "mistakes" at the expense of the Americans on the high seas.

Naturalization or "protection" papers could be legally secured in America by a British deserter within a few months. They could be fraudulently obtained overnight from agencies that sold them for as low as $1 each. One woman engaged in this illicit business had constructed a man-sized cradle; if haled into court, she could swear that she had known the men "from their cradles." One is not surprised to learn that when deserters produced such naturalization documents, the press gangs laughed in their faces. Even if the certificate had been secured legally, the British would have ignored it. They did not believe that a man could change his nationality like a shirt, and until 1870 they clung to the doctrine of indelible or indefeasible allegiance. If a man was born an Englishman, he was always an Englishman—and his king could call upon him for needed service in time of peril.

Britain needed men in order to make war; America needed men in order to make money. The British Ministry would have been swept from office if it had dared to give up, at the demand of the Yankee, a practice already sanctified by usage long before the American colonies were founded. England would fight before she would yield—and she did.

THE ABORTIVE MONROE-PINKNEY PACT

With the controversy over impressment and ship seizures fast approaching a breaking point, and with the commercial benefits of Jay's Treaty about to expire, President Jefferson took an extraordinary step. He sent to London a distinguished Maryland lawyer, William Pinkney, who was to associate himself with the regular minister, James Monroe. The two envoys were authorized to settle all matters in dispute between America and England, including a resumption of "broken voyages" and the payment of indemnity for recent maritime seizures. Pinkney and Monroe were also specifically instructed not to sign a treaty which did not contain a renunciation of the alleged right to impress sailors from American vessels on the high seas.[3]

The British officials were prepared to make some concessions, particularly in regard to the enemy West Indian trade. They were prompted by a realization that America's temper was reaching the boiling point, as evidenced by a recent retaliatory act passed by Congress in 1806 prohibiting the importation of certain English goods. But the British public, which was angered because the Yankee had been "stealing" both commerce and seamen, would tolerate no surrender to the demands on impressment. The Foreign Office did offer to give an informal pledge that an earnest effort would be made to avoid molesting bona-fide American seamen, but it refused to include such a statement in a formal agreement. When Monroe and Pinkney realized that they had run into a stone wall, they disregarded their instructions, and wry-facedly signed a treaty on December 31, 1806. Perhaps the most important British concession was that American ships might trade between French colonies and certain French ports, provided that the voyage was interrupted at a United States port.

President Jefferson, dissatisfied with the handiwork of his negotiators, flatly refused to submit their pact to the Senate. Instead, he requested

---

[3] See Anthony Steel, "Impressment in the Monroe-Pinkney Negotiation, 1806–1807," *Amer. Hist. Rev.*, LVII (1952), 352–369.

them to reopen negotiations in conformity with their original instructions. If Jefferson had been willing to accept a half loaf on impressment, some of his later difficulties might have been avoided.

BLOCKADES AND COUNTERBLOCKADES

The world conflict had meanwhile entered upon a new phase. Lord Nelson's crushing victory at Trafalgar over the combined French and Spanish fleets, on October 21, 1805, ended British fears of invasion. So complete was England's naval ascendancy that her frigates ceased gun practice. But scarcely more than a month later Napoleon overwhelmed the combined Russian and Austrian forces at Austerlitz—the Battle of the Three Emperors. If Britain was the tyrant of the sea, Bonaparte was the despot of the land.

With neither side able to come to grips with the other, like the tiger and the shark, each was driven to indirect blows. England, for her part, established a naval blockade against ports under French control. By a system of fees and licenses, she was able to curb neutral trade, including American, and at the same time derive a substantial revenue from it. Napoleon, in retaliation, proclaimed a "paper" blockade against the British Isles. By closing the European ports under his domination to English goods, he established his sweeping Continental System. He reasoned that this stoppage of trade would cause British factories to close, bread lines to form, riots to develop, revolution to break out. And once-proud Britain would be forced to accept the conqueror's terms.

England fired the first broadside in the war of paper edicts, which followed one another in an ever louder succession.[4] On May 16, 1806, London proclaimed a blockade of the European coast from the Elbe River, in Germany, to the fortified town of Brest, in France. Six months later Napoleon struck back with his Berlin Decree. Although the remnants of his navy were partially bottled up, he declared the British Isles to be in a state of blockade. When the system of mutual strangulation was well established, any American ship that attempted to trade with England, or even allowed itself to be searched by British cruisers, was liable to seizure by French privateers. And any American vessel that attempted to trade with ports under Napoleon's control, without first having paid tribute to England and having received her permission, was liable to capture by British frigates. The Yankee skippers, like their predestined Calvinist ancestors, were damned if they did, damned if they did not.

[4] The principal orders and decrees of 1806 and 1807 were as follows: The British Order in Council of May 16, 1806; Napoleon's Berlin decree, Nov. 21, 1806; the British Orders in Council of Jan. 7, 1807 and Nov. 11, 1807; Napoleon's Milan decree of Dec. 17, 1807.

THE *CHESAPEAKE* OUTRAGE

In America, public excitement over the war of paper bullets was temporarily eclipsed by a spectacular revival of the impressment-desertion controversy. In February, 1807, a boat's crew escaped to the Virginia shore from a British man-of-war, and four of the fugitives subsequently enlisted on an American frigate, the *Chesapeake*. When the news reached Halifax, Nova Scotia, the hot-headed British commander, Vice-Admiral Berkeley, issued an order requiring his subordinates to retrieve the deserters from the American vessel. This drastic action was taken on Berkeley's own responsibility, for London did not claim the right to impress seamen from a neutral man-of-war—only from merchantmen. Warships might shoot back.

The *Chesapeake* set sail from Norfolk, Virginia, for Mediterranean waters, on June 22, 1807. When about ten miles off the coast, she was hailed by His Majesty's frigate, the *Leopard*. The American commander, Commodore Barron, thinking that he was about to be asked to carry dispatches to Europe, permitted her to approach without summoning his men to their proper quarters and without having the loggerheads heated red-hot for firing guns. When the British commander requested permission to search the *Chesapeake*, the astonished Barron quite properly refused. The *Leopard* thereupon fired three point-blank broadsides into the defenseless *Chesapeake*, killing three men and wounding eighteen. After an American officer had brought up a live coal from the galley and had fired one gun in honor of the flag, the *Chesapeake* surrendered. A British searching party then boarded the frigate and removed the four deserters.

This disgraceful affair was not so much a case of impressment as the recovery of specific deserters. Three of the four men seized were Americans—two Negroes and one white—and had allegedly been impressed into the Royal Navy, but apparently had volunteered. The fourth seaman, who was dragged out of a coalhole, was undeniably a British subject and a deserter. He was tried by a court martial at Halifax and hanged from the yardarm of his own ship. The three Americans received less severe punishment.

When the bloody hulk that was the *Chesapeake* limped back to Norfolk with a tale of humiliation, a wave of indignation swept over all America. English officers on shore leave fled to their ships; infuriated mobs destroyed the water casks of the British fleet; the governor of Virginia called out the militia to maintain order. "But one feeling pervades the nation," wrote Joseph Nicholson. "All distinctions of [Hamiltonian] federalism and [Jeffersonian] democracy are vanished. The people are ready to submit to any deprivation. . . ." [5] The West, with its fighting breed of men and its high ideals of national honor, vibrated with anger. "On my Conscience and Faith and Honor I hope that war will take place," wrote a friend of Andrew Jackson. Jackson himself, referring to the sensational Burr trial at Richmond, cried, "Millions to persecute an American; not a cent to resist England!" Even in faraway Boston toastmakers were crying, "Let us whet the sword! Let us bend the bow!"

Not since the XYZ days of 1798 had the American people been more united on an issue. "Never since the battle of Lexington," wrote President Jefferson, "have I seen this country in such a state of exasperation as at present, and even that did not produce such unanimity." [6] "I had only to open my hand," he further said, "and let havoc loose."

JEFFERSON BENDS THE BOW TOO FAR

Supported by an outraged public sentiment, Jefferson took vigorous— but not too vigorous—steps. He issued a proclamation ordering all British warships out of American waters. He summoned Congress into special session, although setting the date far enough ahead to permit popular passions to cool. He knew perfectly well that he could lead the United States—a united United States—into war. But with peace his "passion" he was determined to avoid hostilities and, by capitalizing on the blunder of the British, wring concessions from them.

British reactions varied. The "Rule Britannia" press, angered by Jefferson's reprisals against His Majesty's warships, applauded the *Leopard*'s treatment of the "cowardly Yankees." British officials, fearing that the incident might result in an invasion of Canada, encouraged the Northwest Indians to resist the westward-pushing Americans—a policy that helped bring on the War of 1812. But the Foreign Office, recognizing that the *Leopard* had been in the wrong, disavowed the act. Moreover, despite the protests of the merchant class, London recalled Admiral Berkeley, who was further "punished" by being promoted to a new and more important command off the Portuguese coast.

But Jefferson made the mistake of pushing the embattled British too far—of trying to settle both "the old and the new" at one stroke. He insisted on using the *Chesapeake* indignity as a lever, and on coupling a demand for reparation with one for a complete abandonment of impressment. England was prepared to make amends for her unwarranted attack on the American frigate, but she was convinced that impressment was essential for her national existence. Jefferson consequently drove the

[5] Henry Adams, *The Life of Albert Gallatin* (Philadelphia, 1880), p. 360 (to Gallatin, July 14, 1807).

[6] A. A. Lipscomb, ed., *Writings of Thomas Jefferson* (Monticello ed., Washington, 1904), XI, 274 (Jefferson to Du Pont de Nemours, July 14, 1807).

British from a defensive to an offensive position. The *Chesapeake* outrage, which could have been quickly atoned for, became so hopelessly involved with other issues as to develop into a five-year running sore. The war spirit evaporated; the republic hit the depths of national degradation; and the disgusted French minister in Washington could report that the United States was "disposed to suffer every kind of humiliation, provided it can satisfy . . . its sordid avarice. . . ." [7]

THE EMBARGO BLUDGEON

Jefferson, despite maddening provocations, was still firmly committed to peace at almost any price. Time, if it could be purchased, was on the side of the adolescent but rapidly growing republic. With the nation doubling its population about every twenty years, and quadrupling its energy, it would be in a strong position if it could only postpone a showdown with "the starved and rickety paupers and dwarfs of English workshops." Time, Jefferson sagely concluded, was "the most precious of all things to us."

With continued submission unthinkable and war ruinous, the nation would have to find some halfway measure. Jefferson had long toyed with the idea of economic coercion as a substitute for arms, and here was a heaven-sent opportunity to carry out his pet scheme. The warring nations, particularly England, were heavily dependent upon the United States for foodstuffs and other commodities. If America refused to ship anything at all to Europe, Jefferson concluded, both Britain and France would be forced to come around, hat in hand, and agree to end their high-handed practices.

Jefferson succeeded in forcing a hastily drawn Embargo Act through Congress in December, 1807, but only in the teeth of vehement opposition from Federalist New England. The South and West stood faithfully behind their President. Bolstered by supplementary legislation, the embargo virtually prohibited the export of any goods from the United States, by sea or by land. But coastwise trade was permitted, provided that the proper bond was posted.

Stagnation slowly laid its clammy hand on much of America's economic life. Ships rotted at their moorings; forests of bare masts sprang up in many harbors; grass grew on once bustling wharves; soup kitchens opened their doors; bankruptcies, suicides, and crimes increased. From New England, where the Yankee had long wrested his livelihood from the sea, a cry arose against the "Virginia lordlings" in Washington who were sacrificing American shipping to their own ends. What the merchant wanted most of all was to be let alone. In spite of confiscations and loud

[7] Quoted in Henry Adams, *History of the United States of America during the Administrations of Jefferson and Madison* (New York, 1890), IV, 141.

talk about national honor, he was making money. If one cargo out of three reached its destination safely, he could still show a profit. And the greater the risk, the greater the profit. But the embargo destroyed the very trade it was designed to protect. It was, so the New England Federalists insisted, like "cutting one's throat to cure the nosebleed."

THE BREAKDOWN OF THE EMBARGO

Opposition in New England to the self-crucifying embargo breathed new life into dying Federalism. A New Hampshire poet vented his indignation in song:

> Our ships all in motion,
> Once whiten'd the ocean
> > They sail'd and return'd with a Cargo;
> Now doom'd to decay
> > They are fallen a prey,
> To Jefferson, worms, and EMBARGO.

OGRABME [EMBARGO], OR, THE AMERICAN SNAPPING-TURTLE

New York Historical Society

The letters of the word "embargo" were transposed to read "o-grab-me," "go-bar-em," and "mob-rage," the last of which was declared to be the inevitable outcome of this infamous policy. One irate New Englander wrote Jefferson a letter beginning, "You Infernal Villain": "How much longer are you going to keep this damned Embargo on to starve us poor people [.] one of my children has already starved to death of which I [am] ashamed and declared that it died of apoplexy. . . . I am a Federalist." [9]

Different sections reacted differently. New England was the most vocal in its condemnation, although it gleaned considerable profit from illicit trade and from transfering capital to manufacturing. But the South and West, though even harder hit by the loss of export markets for their farm produce, complained the least. The West, which had been suffering from a depression attributed to British blockade measures, welcomed economic coercion as a weapon for extorting redress.[10] Moreover, the embargo was an administration measure—and Jefferson's stronghold was in the South. Hence loyal Republicans, in the South and elsewhere, made light of the country's sufferings. One Jerseyman defended the embargo in doggerel:

> Should Hessian fly our wheat destroy
>   Or granaries crawl with weevil,
> *The Embargo's* curst in language worst,
>   As source of all the evil.
>
>   . . .
>
> Do vermin bold on trees lay hold,
>   And make their limbs quite bare go,
> 'Tis ten to one the mischief done
>   Is saddled on *the Embargo*.[11]

Collapse was inevitable. From the days of the colonial navigation acts, respect for unpopular laws has never been an American virtue. The citizenry have demonstrated time and again that when public opinion runs overwhelmingly counter to a law, that law will be disregarded. The embargo was flagrantly violated, in spite of iron-toothed enforcing acts passed by Congress. An illicit trade of immense proportions gradually sprang up in New England. It was particularly heavy across the Canadian border, and especially on Lake Champlain, where huge produce-laden rafts, manned by scores of armed men, openly defied the revenue officers and the state militia. Law and order had almost completely broken down.

THE CONSEQUENCES OF COERCION

But what was the impact of the embargo on the warring powers, against whom it was directed? Perhaps the first noticeable result was an increased bitterness among the British ruling class for America. In the

[9] L. M. Sears, *Jefferson and the Embargo* (Durham, N.C., 1927), p. 103.
[10] G. R. Taylor, "Agrarian Discontent in the Mississippi Valley preceding the War of 1812," *Jour. of Pol. Economy*, XXXIX (1931), 471 ff.
[11] *Boston Independent Chronicle*, Oct. 27, 1808, 1:3.

summer of 1808, at a grand dinner in London, Sir Francis Baring proposed as one of the regular toasts the health of the President of the United States. Instantly his voice was drowned in a chorus of hisses and protests. Britain was in a mood to endure acute hardship before she would bend her knee to the Yankee.

In certain other areas the embargo backfired badly. Canadian smugglers reaped a lush harvest, while British shippers joyfully took over the carrying trade abandoned by their Yankee rivals. Unemployed American seamen were faced with the alternative of starving or finding jobs elsewhere. Hundreds of Yankee sailors, as well as British subjects or deserters, were thus driven into Britain's merchant marine or navy—with an incidental easing of impressment. One unemployed seaman met another on the streets of Hartford, Connecticut:

> "Holla! messmate, where are you bound!
> Bound to Halifax by the pipers, which way are you steering?
> By the powers of Moll Kelly, I am steering the same course, for there's no standing this *dambargo* any longer." [12]

On the other hand, the stoppage of American foodstuffs and other supplies did cause real distress in some parts of the British Empire, notably in the West Indies and Newfoundland. A number of English textile factories dependent upon American cotton were forced to close down, while their owners urgently petitioned the government for a repeal of the Orders in Council that had driven the Americans to the embargo. Thousands of unemployed factory workers faced pauperism and starvation. The alarming shortage of grain even caused the English authorities to curtail the manufacture of alcoholic liquor.

Why, then, did Jefferson's embargo fail to force concessions? First of all, the classes hardest hit in England were unable to vote and could bring the least pressure to bear on the government. In addition, the proud Briton, who resented the commercial restrictions of the United States, steeled himself to endure much before capitulating. Moreover, the crops of 1808 were so unexpectedly good as to render the British Isles less dependent than usual upon American foodstuffs. Finally, the stay-at-home Americans abdicated much commerce to British shippers, who were edging into the Spanish-American trade, first on an illegal basis and then as a result of the Latin-American revolutions.

As for Napoleon, the United States was playing his game. Unable to blockade Britain himself, he was delighted to see the distress caused in England by the embargo, and he rejoiced over the widening rift between Britain and America. No wonder the French minister in Washington could say, "the Emperor applauds the embargo." Bonaparte even pretended to help the United States enforce it. By the Bayonne Decree of April

---

[12] *Connecticut Courant*, Jan. 13, 1808, 3:3.

17, 1808, he ordered the seizure of all American ships in French harbors on the pretext that, with the embargo still in force, they must be disguised British craft. Within a year Napoleon confiscated American vessels and cargoes to the value of $10 million.

THE EMBARGO: A SUCCESSFUL FAILURE

By the end of 1808 the impatience of the American people over the embargo was fast approaching a breaking point. Threats of secession were heard on every hand. Even Dr. George Logan, the peace-loving Quaker who had inspired the Logan Act, denounced the administration for "dastardly attacking the humble cottage" instead "of meeting in an open & honorable conflict the armed battalions of our enemy." The *Washington Federalist* demanded to know "how much longer we are to pant under the pestiferous breath of this poisonous dragon." And a circular issued at Newburyport, Massachusetts, exhorted "every man who holds the name of America dear" to "stretch forth his hands and put this accursed thing, this *Embargo* from him."

Even Jefferson, who admitted privately that the embargo experiment was three times more costly than war, confessed failure. In later years he declared, "I felt the foundation of the government shaken under my feet by the New England townships." The only alternatives to repeal of the embargo were seemingly disunion and civil strife. On March 1, 1809, three days before Jefferson handed over the reins to President Madison, a rebellious Congress repealed the unpopular measure. It substituted the Nonintercourse Act, which legalized American commerce with all ports of the world, except those under British and French control. America was still committed to the economic hatchet.

Why did the embargo, Jefferson's most daring act of statesmanship, collapse so dismally? Abroad, bumper crops and other unexpected developments conspired against him. At home, conditions were such that the experiment could not be given a fair trial. Avarice and disloyalty weakened the pinch of the embargo, while public sentiment demanded a premature repeal.

But did the embargo fail? It unexpectedly drove capital and labor into manufacturing, thus laying the real foundation stones of America's industrial might and lessening her dependence on Europe. The embargo also relieved impressment and in other ways helped postpone war. Although Jefferson's unpopular experiment was admittedly an economic boomerang, it gave the United States more of that greatest of all boons— time. Finally, as will be noted, the cumulative effect of economic coercion contributed to the repeal of the odious Orders in Council in 1812. The supreme irony is that in the end Jefferson's policy triumphed, but the republic was not patient enough to reap the fruit of its sacrifices.

SELECTED BIBLIOGRAPHY

General backgrounds are challengingly set forth in A. L. Burt, *The United States, Great Britain, and British North America* (New Haven, 1940). On maritime matters see A. T. Mahan's classic *Sea Power in its Relations to the War of 1812* (Boston, 1905). Recent scholarship on British restrictions appears in Bradford Perkins, *The First Rapprochement; England and the United States, 1795–1805* (Philadelphia, 1955). See also Irving Brant, *James Madison: Secretary of State, 1800–1809* (Indianapolis, 1953). On their respective subjects consult J. F. Zimmerman, *Impressment of American Seamen* (New York, 1925); L. M. Sears, *Jefferson and the Embargo* (Durham, N.C., 1927); E. F. Heckscher, *The Continental System* (Oxford, 1922); I-Mien Tsiang, *The Question of Expatriation in America Prior to 1907* (Baltimore, 1942). See also Bradford Perkins, "Sir William Scott and the *Essex*," *William and Mary Quar.*, XIII (1956), 169–183; L. S. Kaplan, "Jefferson, the Napoleonic Wars, and the Balance of Power," *ibid.*, XIV (1957), 196–217. Canning appears in a more favorable light in Bradford Perkins, "George Canning, Great Britain, and the United States, 1807–1809," *Amer. Hist. Rev.*, LXIII (1957), 1–22.

See footnotes of this chapter; Bemis and Griffin, *Guide*, pp. 137–147; *Harvard Guide*, Ch. 12.

7TH ED. REFS. The most widely researched recent book on the period is Bradford Perkins, *Prologue to War: England and the United States, 1805–1812* (Berkeley, Calif., 1961). The focus is on maritime grievances growing out of the European convulsion, and the author is highly critical of Jefferson's low intrigues. The embargo policy, which betrayed weakness and lack of vision, had dual purposes: coercive (against the belligerents) and protective (for American shipping). That it preserved the peace is "not proved." Less exhaustive on the European backgrounds but also focused on them is Reginald Horsman, *The Causes of the War of 1812* (Philadelphia, 1962). Like Perkins, Horsman notes that the embargo was weakened by the newly opened Spanish and Spanish-American markets. The British government applauded the embargo; self-crucifying, it would hurt the United States more than it would hurt the British, and it would also pinch Napoleon. Both Perkins and Horsman stress the concern of Britain for her export markets rather than imports from the United States. L. S. Kaplan, "Jefferson's Foreign Policy and Napoleon's Idéologues," *William and Mary Quar.*, Ser. 3, vol. XIX (1962), 344–359 observes that although Jefferson's own ideas closely paralleled those of the French intelligentsia (*idéologues*), he arrived at his pro-French slant in foreign policy, notably the embargo, without undue influence from them. L. S. Kaplan, "Jefferson, the Napoleonic Wars, and the Balance of Power," *ibid.*, XIV (1957), 196–217 concludes that Jefferson, while distrusting both Britain and France, favored France because she did not control the seas. His embargo was actually designed to help France, though advertized as impartial. He applauded the declaration of war in 1812, and was glad that news of British concessions had not arrived in time to avert it. He had avoided war at the time of the *Chesapeake* affair because he thought the embargo, which would not hurt France, a better weapon.

8TH AND 9TH ED. REFS. See BIBLIOGRAPHICAL ADDENDUM, p. 984.

10

Blundering into War with Britain, 1809-1812

> *May the Twelfth Congress no longer tamely submit to British outrages, but wrest from her every foot of possession she holds in North America.*
> TOAST REPORTED IN PITTSBURGH MERCURY, January 11, 1812

ERSKINE'S OFFSIDE PLAY

JAMES MADISON, scholarly and somewhat irresolute, took the Presidential oath on March 4, 1809, while the European conflagration was roaring with increased fury. "Little Jemmy," as he was dubbed by opponents, inherited not only Jefferson's crown but his policy of economic coercion. The Nonintercourse Act of 1809, a watered-down version of the embargo, forbade any commerce with Britain and France until American rights were respected.

The British minister in Washington, David M. Erskine, had married an American wife and, unlike most of his predecessors, felt sympathetic toward the United States. The inflexible George Canning, then Foreign Secretary, instructed him to secure from the Madison administration a series of categorical avowals and disavowals regarding the commercial questions in dispute. Erskine was desperately eager to secure an agreement. Instead of reading his instructions to the Secretary of State, as he was authorized to do, he outlined them in such a way as to gloss over their disagreeable features.

The subsequent negotiations proceeded smoothly, and in April, 1809, the over-anxious Erskine signed a fateful pact. It bound Britain to withdraw her Orders in Council, so far as they touched the United States, in return for a lifting of nonintercourse against England and an enforcement of it against France. But Erskine violated his instructions by not first securing certain additional concessions from the Americans, including the right to seize Yankee ships violating nonintercourse with France.

President Madison now proceeded to make the first in a series of tragic blunders. He unwisely assumed that the Erskine agreement would be speedily embraced in London, and he issued a proclamation, effective June 10, 1809, withdrawing nonintercourse with Britain. "Great and glorious news!" proclaimed a broadside "extra" of the *New Hampshire Patriot*. "Our Differences with Great Britain Amicably Settled." Hundreds of American vessels rushed to sea, heavily laden with those raw materials and foodstuffs which Britain sorely needed and which, incidentally, did much to wipe out the hard-won fruits of Jefferson's embargo. For a few brief weeks Madison and his colleagues lived in a fool's paradise.

Then came the disheartening news that Canning had flatly disavowed the agreement and had recalled Erskine for having violated his instructions. America was infuriated. "The late conduct of the British ministry," declared the *Washington National Intelligencer*, "has capped the climax of atrocity toward this country." Even pro-British Federalists were aroused, and one of them exclaimed that England could not expect to "crop off our noses" while we "remain content because our heads are spared." The crestfallen Madison, everywhere branded the dupe of Canning, was forced to restore nonintercourse with Britain, on August 9, 1809. Having thrown himself eagerly into the arms of the Mother Country, he had been violently hurled back.

Canning's repudiation of the Erskine agreement marked the parting of the ways for London and Washington. With relations restored to their former instability, America tended more and more to gravitate toward the strangling embrace of Bonaparte. This unnatural partnership ultimately begot war.

THE INSOLENCE OF "COPENHAGEN" JACKSON

Canning now decided to replace the conciliatory Erskine with a man of sterner stuff. He selected an overbearing Briton, Francis James Jackson, who had presented the ultimatum which preceded the brutal confiscation of the Danish fleet at Copenhagen in 1807. The choice of so infamous an emissary was regarded in the United States as nothing short of an insult. The American newspapers published numerous invitations to tar and feather "Copenhagen" Jackson, and meetings were later held which passed resolutions "to resist all attempts to 'Copenhagen' us."

Jackson reached America in September, 1809, and his first impressions only increased his irritability. He regarded President Madison as a "plain and rather mean-looking man," and his wife, the incomparable Dolley, as "fat and forty, but not fair." To him, the Americans were "all alike," except that some few were "less knaves than others." The "mob" was "by many degrees more blackguard and ferocious than the mob in other countries." After Jackson had spent some time examining the correspondence in the British legation, he concluded that it was "charity" to call Erskine a "fool," and that with respect to the American notes "Every third word was a declaration of war."

With the British emissary in this mood, negotiations proceeded bumpily. They were brought to a climax when Jackson insisted on implying that the State Department had known that Erskine was violating his instructions when the ill-starred agreement was concluded. Following this charge of bad faith, the Secretary of State refused to receive any further communications from the overbearing Briton. As Jackson became more and more insolent, he received a number of letters threatening personal violence, including horsewhipping. One irate Kentuckian ran afoul of his state's profanity law when he shouted: "God damn Mr. Jackson;—the President ought to . . . have kicked him from town to town until he is kicked out of the country. God damn him!" [1]

Jackson was plainly doing more harm than good, yet he lingered on during the year for which he had been paid. The London Foreign Office, refusing to disapprove its representative's conduct, did not send a successor until nearly two years after his dismissal. Instead, the legation in Washington was left with a *chargé d'affaires*. The whole incident, coming so close upon the heels of the Erskine blunder, further widened the diplomatic breach.

Relations with Napoleon had meanwhile drifted from bad to abominable. Jefferson's embargo, though amounting to a partial blockade of the British Isles, had also pinched France to some extent. Napoleon was none too happy with the substitute Nonintercourse Act, which was aimed at him as well as Britain. In retaliation, he issued the notorious Rambouillet Decree of March 23, 1810, under which scores of American ships in French ports were confiscated. The protests from Washington were so many words in the wind.

NAPOLEON HOODWINKS MADISON

With the Nonintercourse Act due to expire after about one year, Congress passed an ingenious substitute, on May 1, 1810, called Macon's Bill No. 2. It officially permitted commerce with both England and France. But it also provided that if France repealed her offensive decrees, the United States would renew nonimportation against England. And if England repealed her obnoxious Orders in Council, the United States would renew nonimportation against France. In either case, a three-month period of grace was given the nonrepealing nation to repeal, and

[1] Bernard Mayo, *Henry Clay: Spokesman of the New West* (Boston, 1937), p. 325.

in either case the United States could export to but not import from the nonrepealing nation.

The mischievous Macon's Bill, which could be justified only by a desperate desire to keep out of war, created a situation made to order for Bonaparte. On August 5, 1810, he had his Foreign Minister, Duc de Cadore, send an ambiguous letter to the American minister in Paris. Although ostensibly announcing the immediate repeal of the French decrees, it included a nullifying "string." England would either have to revoke her Orders in Council or the Americans would have to "cause their rights to be respected" by establishing complete nonintercourse against her, both as to exports and imports. These, of course, were impossible conditions, for Britain was mistress of the seas, and the United States was but a second-rate power.

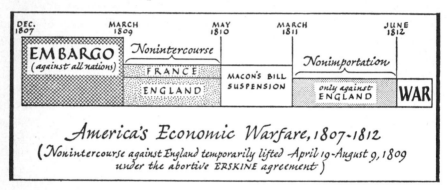

America's Economic Warfare, 1807-1812
(*Nonintercourse against England temporarily lifted April 19-August 9, 1809 under the abortive ERSKINE agreement*)

The fateful Cadore letter was worded so cleverly as to commit France to nothing, while dangling before Madison the hope that a promise had been made. Eager to compensate for the Erskine blunder, he issued a fateful proclamation, on November 2, 1810. It declared in effect that nonimportation would be imposed on Britain if the latter did not withdraw her Orders within three months. This announcement was unduly hasty, for Madison was bound by the terms of Macon's Bill not to take such a step until he had convincing proof that the French decrees had been repealed. Napoleon, in fact, had accompanied his presumed pledge with no evidence whatever of good faith, as Madison was painfully aware. On the very date of the Cadore letter, August 5, 1810, Bonaparte ordered the sale of a number of confiscated American ships. Furthermore, every mail to the United States indicated that the French decrees were still in effect, and that American merchantmen were being seized and scuttled.

The British stood firm. They naturally refused to repeal their Orders in Council, for any fool could see that Napoleon had not revoked his decrees. They felt a new bitterness against the United States for having been so willing to turn against them at the behest of Bonaparte. This feeling was not improved when Congress passed a new measure, on March 2,

1811, which, in accord with Macon's Bill, officially renewed nonimportation against Great Britain.

REDRESS AND RED MEN

A new British minister, Augustus Foster, landed in the United States in the summer of 1811. Although not authorized to make substantial concessions regarding other disputes, he was instructed to offer formal reparation for the still-festering *Chesapeake* affair. To his astonishment, he found interest in the four-year-old outrage almost completely eclipsed by enthusiasm for invading Canada, and by excitement over the *Little Belt* incident.

On May 16, 1811, several weeks before Foster's arrival, a forty-four-gun American frigate, the *President,* had hailed in the gathering darkness the twenty-gun British corvette, *Little Belt.* Someone fired a shot, and in the ensuing engagement His Majesty's ship was almost knocked out of the water, suffering a loss of thirty-two killed and wounded. The *Little Belt* was about as severely mauled as the *Chesapeake* had been, and suffered the loss of three killed for every one killed on the *Chesapeake.* The ensuing protests from London were vigorous, but to this day no one has proved which ship opened fire.

The regrettable *Chesapeake* and *Little Belt* incidents were in principle poles apart, yet undiscerning American opinion now regarded the account with England as squared. Had not the *President* exacted three eyes and three teeth for every eye and tooth lost on the *Chesapeake?* A writer in the *Philadelphia Aurora* rejoiced that the proud Briton had got another taste of 1776, when with "our hay forks, pitch forks and grubbing hoes . . . we knocked down his teeth and scowered his blackhell throat." Minister Foster did atone in some measure for the *Chesapeake* assault by arranging to return two of the three Americans to her decks—one had died in captivity—and by offering appropriate financial compensation to the victims and their families. But such medicine as he had to offer came too late to heal the wound. "Presented at *such a time*," scoffed the *Baltimore Whig,* "[it] is like restoring a hair after fracturing the skull." [2]

Bloodshed on the high seas had meanwhile been partially eclipsed by butchery on the Northwest frontier. For many years countless Americans, West and East, had believed that the British officials in Canada were egging their red allies upon the American pioneers, and paying a bounty —allegedly $6 apiece—for the scalps of men, women, and children. The scalping forays were no doubt inspired primarily by the encroachments of the whites upon the red man's lands. But the general attitude of the British officers, together with their liberal exchange of firearms and "firewater" for furs, encouraged the Indians to fight back. Yet the

[2] Quoted in Mayo, *Clay,* p. 388.

"hair-buying" charge, whether true or not, was widely accepted, and it had an inflammatory effect on the American mind.

About a thousand advancing American troops, led by General William Henry Harrison, clashed with the Indians at Tippecanoe, on November 7, 1811, near the Wabash River in present Indiana. The so-called white victory was hardly decisive, but the red attackers were beaten off, leaving behind newly marked British arms. The American casualties numbered more than sixty killed and one hundred wounded.

The West reacted angrily. A typical voice was that of Andrew Jackson, who cried, "The blood of our murdered heroes must be revenged." *"The War on the Wabash is purely British,"* proclaimed the *Lexington Reporter.* "The British scalping knife has filled many habitations both in this state as well as in the Indiana Territory with widows and orphans." From the West to the East spread the impassioned cry, "Look to the Wabash, look to the impressed seamen!" [3]

THE SEALESS WEST DEMANDS A FREE SEA

The fight-thirsty Twelfth Congress convened on November 4, 1811, three days before the hollow victory at Tippecanoe. The recent elections had swept out almost half of the old membership of the House, with many of the casualties being "submission men." Conspicuous among the new faces were a group of ultranationalists, called the "War Hawks"— hotheads like Henry Clay of Kentucky and Felix Grundy of Tennessee. Most of these "pepperpot politicians" hailed from the lower South and the West, from the new states or the frontier regions of the old ones. Their leaders were all comparatively young men, some in their late twenties and early thirties, who were determined to "pull John Bull by the nose" and end "putrescent peace." John Randolph acidly referred to these young "buckskin statesmen" as "the boys," while Josiah Quincy dubbed them "young Politicians, their pinfeathers not yet grown. . . ."

The western War Hawks, though lacking a majority in the House, succeeded in elevating to the Speakership their magnetic leader, the thirty-four-year-old Henry Clay. He forthwith proceeded to pack the important committees with fellow "Coonskin Congressmen," and otherwise to prepare for hostilities. Why was the land-locked West so determined to force a war with Britain on the sea-fronting East?

The youthful, vigorous Westerners bitterly resented British impressment, even though few of them were ever impressed. The explanation seems to be that personal rights meant more to the Westerner, who was generally footloose and often in debt, than they did to the Easterner, who was conservative and property-loving. The brutal seizure of a free-born

[3] Quoted in *ibid.,* p. 398.

American and his "enslavement" in Britain's navy, with an excellent chance of being killed, was an intolerable outrage to the men beyond the mountains. Their code called for a quick resort to arms to avenge an indignity against one's person. To them, an offense against an individual American was an offense against all Americans.

The Westerners also felt that the patriotism of the East had become deadened by moneymaking—what Clay branded as the "low groveling parsimony of the counting room." The Eastern seaboard, particularly New England, was still closely bound by cultural and commercial ties to Old England, while the West was American to the core and eager to avenge insults to the flag. As Henry Clay declaimed: "No man in the nation wants peace more than I; but I prefer the troubled ocean of war, demanded by the honor and independence of the country, with all its calamities and desolation, to the tranquil and putrescent pool of ignominious peace." [4]

The Westerner, although not a seafarer, likewise resented Britain's other restrictions on a free sea. But the profit-conscious Eastern shipper, who handled most of the nation's seaborne trade, acquiesced in these restrictions. If he sailed only one cargo in three between the reefs of Orders in Council and the shoals of French decrees, he would probably make a handsome haul. Then why should the Westerner become aroused if he had no personal stake?

The solution of the riddle is that the Westerner did have a personal stake in a free sea. If he owned no ships to sail the oceans, he raised agricultural produce to put into those ships. In fact, ever since 1808 he had been suffering from a serious depression, and he blamed his economic distress largely on the British Orders in Council that ruined his overseas markets and dammed up his surplus.[5] He also suspected that England was deliberately attempting to crush out American economic life so that her own would benefit. The West had at first supported the embargo and nonintercourse in the hope of extorting concessions, but such devices had proved unavailing. A Fourth of July (1811) toast at Frankfort, Kentucky, reflected the new spirit: "Embargoes, nonintercourse, and negotiations, are but illy calculated to secure our rights. . . . Let us now try old Roman policy, and maintain them with the sword." [6] The patience of countless Americans, not Westerners alone, had evidently worn thin, and many of the more red-blooded citizens were determined to resort to extreme measures.

[4] *Annals of Congress*, 11 Cong., 1 sess., I, 579 (Feb. 22, 1810).
[5] This thesis is fully developed in G. R. Taylor, "Agrarian Discontent in the Mississippi Valley Preceding the War of 1812," *Jour. of Pol. Economy*, XXXIX (1931), 497; see also his "Prices in the Mississippi Valley Preceding the War of 1812," *Jour. of Econ. and Business Hist.*, III (1930), 148–163.
[6] Quoted in Taylor, "Agrarian Discontent," p. 497.

THE CANADIAN MIRAGE

The War Hawks, despite all their fiery talk about a free sea, early fixed their sights on Britain's colony, Canada. If they were going to punish the Mother Country for her "insolence" on the ocean and elsewhere, how could they do so without a navy? The answer lay in their vast and snowclad northern neighbor. Here was an eminently desirable, poorly defended territory, which could presumably be seized by the American frontiersmen with the ease of falling off a log. Clay boasted that the Kentucky militia could capture the rich prize by themselves; just "a mere matter of marching," wrote Jefferson smugly.

But Western eyes were focused on Canada for another reason, perhaps the most burning of all.[7] England was supplying the murderous Northwest Indians with firearms and other supplies. If the savages were ever to be pacified, the United States would have to seize Canada and wipe out their base—at least in the opinion of many Westerners. Representative Felix Grundy, three of whose brothers had been butchered by the red men, exclaimed in a fiery speech: "We shall drive the British from our Continent—they will no longer have an opportunity of intriguing with our Indian neighbors, and setting on the ruthless savage to tomahawk our women and children." [8]

Canada possessed still other allurements. With her immense expanse under the Stars and Stripes, the United States would control the rich fur trade with the Indians, as well as the coveted St. Lawrence outlet to the sea. Future generations of pioneers would have a marvelously fertile and richly wooded domain into which to expand. Furthermore, liberty-loving Americans would realize their dream of banishing the British Union Jack and substituting for it the banner of freedom. The cynical Congressman John Randolph of Virginia heard the War Hawks cry "On to Canada!" so often that he was seriously misled, for he concluded that the West was merely concealing its land lust behind the shield of American rights. Sneering at all this talk about the Canadian "tit-bit," he asserted:

> Agrarian cupidity, not maritime right, urges the war. Ever since the report of the Committee . . . we have heard but one word—like the whip-poor-will, but one eternal monotonous tone—Canada! Canada! Canada! Not a syllable about Halifax [Nova Scotia], which unquestionably should be our great object in a war for maritime security.[9]

[7] J. W. Pratt, "Western Aims in the War of 1812," *Miss. Valley Hist. Rev.*, XII (1925), 36–50, holds that it was a desire to remove the Indian menace rather than a lust for land that actuated the Westerner, thus refuting the thesis of L. M. Hacker, "Western Land Hunger and the War of 1812," in *ibid.*, X (1924), 365–395.

[8] *Annals of Congress*, 12 Cong., 1 sess., I, 426 (Dec. 9, 1811).

[9] *Ibid.*, 12 Cong., 1 sess., I, 533 (Dec. 16, 1811).

A war for Canada would also facilitate the seizure of Florida, which still remained in the senile grip of Spain, now Britain's ally. The acquisition of this area would not only end Indian forays but round out the "natural boundary" of the United States. Thus while the Northern War Hawks clamored for Canada, the Southern War Hawks clamored for Florida. "Florida and Canada" ran a Kentucky toast—"A fee simple in the one, a mortgage upon the other." Josiah Quincy, a Federalist foe of war, thus jeeringly summarized the argument of the Southern War Hawks: "We want West Florida. Our Western brethren will have West Florida. By G—— we will take West Florida. By G—— it is in the title deed." [10] The seizure of West Florida late in 1810, under circumstances to be described later, merely whetted Western appetites for all Florida.

The catchword "Manifest Destiny" had not come into use, yet red-blooded Americans displayed all the symptoms of its spirit. The more men talked about the ridiculously easy conquest of Canada—a mere "frontiersmen's frolic"—the more inflamed became their imaginations. Congressman Harper of New Hampshire declaimed: "To me, sir, it appears that the Author of Nature has marked our limits in the south, by the Gulf of Mexico; and on the north by the regions of eternal frost." [11]

CONGRESS TAKES THE PLUNGE

By the spring of 1812 the clamor for hostilities, chiefly in the western areas and the Jeffersonian Republican states south of Pennsylvania, had become almost irresistible. In March, 1812, the populace was further aroused by the publication of certain damaging letters, written by the English agent John Henry. They revealed that the British were deeply involved in intrigues with the Federalist leaders of New England. In April, Congress passed an act establishing a ninety-day embargo as a curtain-raiser for hostilities. And on June 1, President Madison, who together with his Cabinet was hardly less determined to fight than the War Hawks, sent his memorable war message to Congress.

Madison's summation of the nation's grievances is highly revealing. He gave first place to impressment, which he branded a "crying enormity." Second place went to the infuriating British practice of venturing into American territorial waters, and there engaging in unlawful seizures and other acts which sometimes "wantonly spilt American blood." Third place went to the Orders in Council, which established paper blockades or "mock blockades," and which had grievously injured American exports. Last place went to the renewal of Indian warfare, which was supposedly encouraged by British agents, and which had brought "shocking" barbarities that spared "neither age nor sex."

[10] Quincy to Sullivan, Dec. 21, 1810, quoted in Mayo, *Clay*, p. 365.
[11] *Annals of Congress*, 12 Cong., 1 sess., I, 657 (Jan. 4, 1812).

With the President's inflammatory message before it, the House of Representatives rolled up its sleeves. Under the driving leadership of the War Hawks, it promptly passed a war resolution, on June 4, 1812, by the comfortable margin of 79 to 49. The affirmative vote came not only from frontier New England and the trans-Appalachian West—the nest of the War Hawks—but also from the Jeffersonian states, ranging from Pennsylvania through Georgia. Even though the strongest sentiment for hostilities welled up from the frontier and the states of the South, the declaration of war would never have passed the House without anti-Federalist votes from the seacoast states, notably Pennsylvania and Massachusetts.

WAR VOTE IN HOUSE OF REPRESENTATIVES
1812
(SHOWING WESTERN AND SOUTHWESTERN WAR SENTIMENT)

		For War	Against War
N.H.	Frontier New England	3	2
Vt.		3	1
Mass.	Maritime and Federalist New England;	6	8
R.I.	Mass. includes frontier Maine	0	2
Conn.		0	7
N.Y.		3	11
N.J.	Commercial and Federalist Middle States	2	4
Del.		0	1
Penn.	Jeffersonian Middle States	16	2
Md.		6	3
Va.		14	5
N.C.	Jeffersonian Southern States	6	3
S.C.		8	0
Ga.		3	0
Ohio	The trans-Allegheny West—Nest of the	1	0
Ky.	War Hawks	5	0
Tenn.		3	0
		79	**49**

In the Senate, where the Federalists and conservative Easterners were more strongly entrenched, action was slower. During the two weeks of heated debate, attempts were made to retreat from outright war; to substitute for it the use of privateers against both France and England; and then to authorize privateers against Britain alone. Not until June 17, 1812, did the war resolution pass the Senate by the dangerously narrow margin of 19 to 13. A change of four votes would have reversed the result.

THE WEST PRESENTS THE EAST WITH A WAR

A careful analysis of the vote in both houses reveals that the so-called war for neutral rights had curious backing. The declaration was generally supported by the agrarian states of the West, Southwest, and South, together with certain agricultural centers elsewhere. It was generally opposed by the maritime sections of New England, and by the commercial centers of the Middle Atlantic states. All these seacoast states, incidentally, were vulnerable to British blockade, bombardment, and invasion. The *Columbian Centinel* of Boston complained bitterly about "wild backwoodsmen" who had never seen "the ocean but on a map, or conceived the taste of it except from a salt lick."

> We, whose soil was the hotbed and whose ships were the nursery of Sailors, are insulted with the hypocrisy of a devotedness to Sailors' rights, and the arrogance of a pretended skill in maritime jurisprudence, by those whose country furnishes no navigation beyond the size of a ferryboat or an Indian canoe.[12]

The charge has repeatedly been hurled at the Westerners that they merely wrapped their greed for Canada in the American flag and orated loudly but insincerely about neutral rights. Critics have made much of the fact that early in 1812 the Western members of Congress voted down a proposal to expand the navy, while the maritime states, though opposing war, voted for it. A partial explanation seems to be that both the anti-navy Jeffersonian Republicans and the War Hawks logically concluded that they had an excellent chance to thrash the British in Canada; none at all on the high seas. Canada, in fact, was regarded by some Americans as a potential hostage: it could be used to force Britain to return areas captured by her on the seacoast of the United States. Actually—and for reasons already discussed—the men of the West and South, a few of them from seaport areas, appear to have been sincerely concerned about neutral rights. The presence of Canada, which was both a menace and a lure, not only added to the vigor of their cry but probably tipped the scales in favor of hostilities. Without Canada, there could hardly have been a War of 1812.

BONAPARTE OR BRITAIN?

Why did America fight England rather than Napoleon? Certainly his conduct had been just as provocative—possibly more so. While the British had been arrogant and highhanded, he had been treacherous and double-dealing. "His Majesty loves the Americans," lied the infamous Cadore letter. Yet during the years from 1803 to 1812 Bonaparte had confiscated 558 American vessels. In the same period the British had seized a comparably large number, totaling 917. Napoleon's ships had in fact been guilty of about every outrage that America could lay at the door of England, although not on so large a scale or so close to home.

---

[12] Jan. 13, 1813, quoted in Allan Nevins, ed., *American Press Opinion* (Boston, 1928), p. 53.

French press gangs even impressed a few American sailors, but because Bonaparte had little need for seamen, this practice did not become an intolerable grievance.

Even worse in some respects than British impressment was Napoleon's imprisonment of the crews of confiscated ships. The *New York Evening Post* reminded its readers that American sailors had been "robbed and

INTERCOURSE OR IMPARTIAL DEALING

A cartoon by "Peter Pencil" (1809) shows Jefferson being victimized by both England and France.

Houghton Library, Harvard

manacled . . . and marched without shoes to their feet or clothing to their backs in the most inclement weather some hundreds of miles into the interior of France; lashed along the highway like slaves, treated with every possible indignity, and then immured in the infernal dungeons of Arras or Verdun." [13]

The Federalists heatedly accused the Jeffersonian Republicans of excessive favoritism to France. President Madison, who carried on the pro-

[13] *New York Evening Post,* July 12, 1809, 2:4.

French tradition, unprotestingly suffered insults from France that he probably would not have tolerated from Britain. One Massachusetts poet declared:

> If England look askance, we boil with rage;
> And blood, blood only, can the wound assuage;
> Yet, whipt, robbed, kicked, and spit upon by France,
> We treat her with the greater complaisance.[14]

The United States had ample reasons, if it had been looking for them, to fight both France and Britain. "The Devil himself," asserted Nathaniel Macon, "could not tell which government, England or France, is the most wicked." Consistency indeed would have dictated war with both offenders. This was the argument of the ever-logical Calhoun, but Jefferson properly regarded as fantastic the proposal "to fight two enemies at a time rather than to take them in succession." Clay believed that after silencing "the insolence of British cannon . . . we can then speak to the hushed batteries of French aggression." President Madison himself gave serious thought to recommending a declaration of war on both belligerents, but in the end decided against such folly. A proposal to include France in the declaration of hostilities against Britain lost in the Senate by the surprisingly narrow vote of 18 to 14.

Why, then, did the United States choose as it did? First of all, England's offenses took place nearer home. An American sailor imprisoned by Bonaparte in faraway France excited much less popular indignation than one seized by British press gangs off New York harbor. And impressment, above all things, was humiliating to the American people. Secondly, England's operations resulted in the violation of territorial waters and the actual killing of United States citizens, notably in the case of the *Chesapeake.*

Nor did the indictment against Britain end here. France had helped America win independence; England was the ancient foe. France was not tampering with the Indians of Canada; England was. Besides, the Americans were in no position to fight Napoleon. Lacking a strong navy, they could not cross the seas to attack him. On the other hand, as *Niles' Weekly Register* pointed out, Britain was "tangible in her tenderest points." Lush English commerce would fall an easy prey to swift American privateers. And Canada, a tempting domain indeed. would be quickly overrun by Kentucky militiamen. Small wonder that Congress overlooked French insults and declared war on England.

STUMBLING INTO THE ABYSS

Hostilities might have been averted if a series of mischances had not conspired to defeat the diplomats. In November, 1810, the aged George

[14] E. B. White, *American Opinion of France* (New York, 1927), p. 12.

III went completely insane. Several precious months were consumed in establishing the regency, while American affairs drifted. By May, 1812, mounting pressure from the British manufacturing and mercantile groups foreshadowed a repeal of the odious Orders in Council. American non-intercourse had produced unemployment, hunger, the pawning of furniture, and giant petitions to Parliament from distressed workers. The appeal from Birmingham alone contained 20,000 names on a sheet of parchment 150 feet long. Yet before the Ministry could act to repeal the Orders in Council, more delay and confusion developed when Prime Minister Perceval was assassinated by a madman.

Not until June 16, 1812, could Lord Castlereagh, then Foreign Secretary, announce in the House of Commons that the Orders in Council would be immediately suspended. Formal repeal came seven days later. British shippers, joyfully confident that this overdue concession would result in a repeal of American nonimportation, prepared to dump their surplus stocks on America. Yet two days after Lord Castlereagh's momentous announcement, Congress declared war. Had there been a trans-Atlantic cable to convey the glad tidings to America, the Senate probably would have mustered the necessary four votes to defeat the War Hawks.

During these fateful prewar weeks, the United States regrettably had no first-class representative in London. The able William Pinkney, who had endured five years of evasion and delay, finally quit his post in February, 1811, leaving behind a less able *chargé d'affaires.* If Pinkney had been on the ground, he might have foreseen the imminent repeal of the Orders in Council. Certainly he would have been able to report that England, suffering from acute economic distress as a result of America's restrictions, did not want to add another foe to the ranks of her enemies.

By a fateful coincidence, America plunged into the conflict at such a time as to be a virtual ally of the dreaded Bonaparte. The Madison administration was counting on him to pin down British strength in Europe and thus clear the path for the invasion of Canada. During the ensuing months Napoleon's victories were greeted in Madisonian circles with joy; his defeats with gloom. The reactions of the New England Federalists were precisely the opposite.

In Federalist eyes, America was fighting against her true long-range interests. As the leading champion of constitutional government in the New World, she should have been waging war on the greatest despot of the age, Napoleon, at the side of England, the surviving champion of constitutional government in the Old World. The British, in a sense, were fighting America's battle. This explains why New England Federalists could prayerfully drink Pickering's famous toast: "The world's last hope —Britain's fast-anchored isle." Yet at the very moment when the fate of constitutionalism was trembling in the balance, when Napoleon was launching his mighty invasion of Russia with 500,000 men, when England was nerving herself for the last desperate struggle, the United States knifed the Mother Country in the back and threw what strength it had on the side of despotism. Britain's extremity seemed to be America's opportunity.

The War of 1812 was a rash departure from the judicious policy of Washington, Adams, and Jefferson—of playing for time and letting America's booming birthrate and Europe's recurrent distresses fight the nation's battles. The grievances of the United States were perhaps less acute in 1812 than they had been at any time since 1807, and a discerning observer should have foreseen that the European upheaval was about to subside. With the end of the war American complaints, including the infuriating practice of impressment, were bound to disappear. But the republic was suffering from such a long accumulation of injuries that, when the War Hawks gained control, national honor unsheathed the sword.

SELECTED BIBLIOGRAPHY

The most challenging brief account is perhaps A. L. Burt, *The United States, Great Britain, and British North America* (New Haven, 1940), which corrects in some degree the overstress on the West in J. W. Pratt's earlier important monograph, *Expansionists of 1812* (New York, 1925). A penetrating analysis is W. H. Goodman, "The Origins of the War of 1812: A Survey of Changing Interpretations," *Miss. Valley Hist. Rev.*, XXVIII (1941), 171–186. Important new data on the economic stake of the War Hawks in a free sea are found in G. R. Taylor, "Agrarian Discontent in the Mississippi Valley preceding the War of 1812," *Jour. of Pol. Economy*, XXXIX (1931), 471–505; Margaret K. Latimir, "South Carolina—a Protagonist of the War of 1812," *Amer. Hist. Rev.*, LXI (1956), 914–929; J. S. Pancake, "The 'Invisibles': A Chapter in the Opposition to President Madison," *Jour. of Southern Hist.*, XXI (1955), 17–37. See also Abbot Smith, "Mr. Madison's War: An Unsuccessful Experiment in the Conduct of National Policy," *Pol. Sci. Quar.*, LVII (1942), 229–246; Bradford Perkins, "George Canning, Great Britain, and the United States, 1807–1809," *Amer. Hist. Rev.*, LXIII (1957), 1–22.

See footnotes of this chapter; Bemis and Griffin, *Guide*, pp. 137–147; *Harvard Guide*, Ch. 12.

7TH ED. REFS. The four most important new books are Bradford Perkins, *Prologue to War: England and the United States, 1805–1812* (Berkeley, Calif., 1961); Reginald Horsman, *The Causes of the War of 1812* (Philadelphia, 1962); and Irving Brant, *James Madison: The President, 1809–1812* (Indianapolis, 1956) and *James Madison: Commander in Chief, 1812–1836* (Indianapolis, 1961). For an evaluation of these four volumes and other titles, consult BIBLIOGRAPHICAL ADDENDUM, p. 985; Perkins and Horsman are also considered at the end of the previous chapter.

8TH AND 9TH ED. REFS. See BIBLIOGRAPHICAL ADDENDUM, p. 986.

The Truce of Ghent
and After, 1812-1818

> *Ghent, the city of Peace; may the gates of the temple of Janus, here closed, not be opened again for a century.*
> TOAST OF JOHN QUINCY ADAMS, January 5, 1815

THE WAR OF AMERICA THE UNREADY

THE UNITED STATES in 1812 was wretchedly unprepared for war. The army and navy were inadequate; the people were disunited. Federalist New England, which regarded Napoleon as anti-Christ and hostilities with Britain as immoral, almost solidly opposed what it branded "Mr. Madison's war." "Is there a Federalist, a patriot, in America," *cried* the *Boston Gazette,* "who conceives it his duty to shed his blood for Bonaparte, for Madison or Jefferson, and that Host of Ruffians in Congress who have set their faces against the United States for years . . . ?"[1] Such words were matched by deeds. New England defiantly withheld her militia from service, sold large quantities of provisions to the British invaders, and in other ways sabotaged the American cause.

The disappointing results of the war should, therefore, come as no surprise. The Canadians, many of them descended from the Loyalists earlier expelled from the United States, rose to defend their homes and firesides. In 1812, and again in 1813, the overconfident and bungling American armies were hurled back from their "mere marching" into Canada. By 1814, with Napoleon temporarily crushed, the United States was desperately defending its own territory. At the end of the shooting the British controlled an immense territory in the northwestern Great Lakes area, substantial tracts along the northern frontier, and the eastern half

---

[1] *Boston Gazette,* quoted in F. A. Updyke, *The Diplomacy of the War of 1812* (Baltimore, 1915), p. 134 (no date given).

of Maine. The inhabitants of Maine dwelling east of the Penobscot River took the oath of allegiance to their old sovereign, George III, without undue protest.

On the sea, the swift American sloops and the oversized frigates won a dozen single-ship naval duels, losing only two. But these exhilarating victories had no appreciable bearing on the outcome of the war. When hostilities ended, the British still had over 800 ships in the Royal Navy, while the American fleet had been reduced from sixteen men-of-war to about three. Much more significant were the hundreds of pestiferous American privateers. These speedy craft even ventured into the English Channel, where they succeeded in bringing the war painfully home to British merchants and shippers.

THE CZAR BEARS AN OLIVE BRANCH

Diplomatic machinery, at least in modern times, ordinarily grinds to a halt when war breaks out. The armies clash on the field of battle, and one of the antagonists is beaten to his knees. Then the diplomats gather about the green-baize peace table to discuss terms. The War of 1812 was unusual in that negotiations for peace started almost as soon as the conflict began, and they continued to the signing of the treaty. In fact, the demands of the negotiators were strengthened or tempered by the news constantly flowing in from the fighting front.

Abortive negotiations actually began on June 26, 1812, a week after the declaration of war. Secretary Monroe instructed the American *chargé* in London to negotiate for a cessation of hostilities, provided that England would renounce impressment. At the same time London made overtures to Washington. Both attempts collapsed because the British were unwilling to yield their ancient practice of impressment, and because the Americans, having keyed themselves up for war, were reluctant to abandon their objectives. Whatever the causes of the hostilities, the United States clearly persisted in continuing them largely because of impressment. The bitterness of American sentiment on this subject may be gauged by a statement appearing in *Niles' Weekly Register: Accursed be the American government, and every individual of it, who . . . shall agree to make peace with Great Britain, until ample provision shall be made for our impressed seamen, and security shall be given for the prevention of such abominable outrages in future.*[2]

Several months after this premature diplomatic sparring, Alexander I of Russia proposed, in September, 1812, to mediate between the United States and his ally, Great Britain. Napoleon had marched into his domain at the head of a mighty army and had just captured Moscow. The Czar naturally wished to see the American war ended. It was not only diverting

[2] *Niles' Weekly Register*, II, 119 (April 18, 1812).

Britain's strength from the common effort against Bonaparte, but it was cutting off much-desired Russian trade with the United States.

American prospects were rapidly dimming when Secretary Monroe received the Russian proposal of mediation. The attempted invasions of Canada had backfired disastrously, and America would be lucky to escape with a whole skin. By this time also, the whole face of the European situation was changing. Napoleon's frost-bitten army had been

BRUIN BECOME MEDIATOR

The Russian Bear mediates between John Bull and America. Actually, Russia rather than England took the initiative.

New York Historical Society

wiped out during the awful retreat from Moscow, and the crestfallen conqueror was back in France frantically raising a new force. If his resistance collapsed, America would have to face the wrath of Britain alone.

President Madison therefore embraced the Russian proposal with open arms when it was officially presented, on March 8, 1813. Without even waiting to learn if London had accepted, he appointed two special envoys, Albert Gallatin and James Bayard. They were instructed to join John Quincy Adams, United States minister to Russia, in negotiations with Great Britain. Gallatin and Bayard together set sail for the Russian capital, St. Petersburg, in May, 1813.

At almost the same time the British Foreign Secretary, Lord Castlereagh, reluctantly informed the Czar that Britain could not accept mediation. His chief excuse was that the questions in dispute with the United States involved "principles of the internal government of the British nation [impressment]." The Foreign Office was plainly not going to permit the Czar to have a voice in the peace settlement, for the maritime grievances of small-navy Russia against big-navy Britain were strikingly similar to those of small-navy America.

But in a curious way the Russian attempt at mediation started the diplomatic wheels moving. The British Foreign Office, wishing to mollify the Czar and prevent the American conflict from becoming entangled with the European settlement, proposed to the United States, in November, 1813, that the two nations enter into direct negotiations for peace. President Madison promptly accepted this proposition, and shortly thereafter sent Henry Clay and Jonathan Russell to join the three envoys already selected. The quaint Flemish town of Ghent, then garrisoned by British troops, was chosen as the meeting place.

THE GALAXY AT GHENT

The American peace commission, as finally constituted, consisted of five men: John Quincy Adams, Henry Clay, Albert Gallatin, James A. Bayard, and Jonathan Russell. Russell was not a man of unusual attainments, but the other four were among the ablest Americans of their generation. The quintet in fact contained too many prima donnas for its own good. If there had been less ability, there would have been more harmony.

John Quincy Adams, already an experienced diplomat, was nominal head of the group. But no one deferred to him. In self-righteousness, chilling reserve, and strength of character he was a replica of his distinguished father, John Adams. Like him, he found his colleagues frivolous. His diary is most revealing:

> I dined again at the table-d'hôte, at one. The other gentlemen dined together, at four. They sit after dinner and drink bad wine and smoke cigars, which neither suits my habits nor my health, and absorbs time which I cannot spare. I find it impossible, even with the most rigorous economy of time, to do half the writing that I ought.[3]

Adams' background and ability were nevertheless of real value to the commission.

Quite in contrast was Henry Clay—warm, impulsive, magnetic. He brought with him a reputation for dueling, horse racing, and gambling that was highly irritating to Adams. "Just before rising," Adams recorded (he rose habitually at five o'clock), "I heard Mr. Clay's company retiring from his chamber. I had left him . . . at cards. They parted as I was

---

³ C. F. Adams, ed., *Memoirs of John Quincy Adams* (Philadelphia, 1874), II, 656.

about to rise."⁴ Despite such dissipation of energy, Clay's buoyancy and optimism shed a ray of light in the hour of darkest despair; his shrewdness and persuasive powers proved invaluable; and his mastery of the Western game of brag (resembling poker) enabled him to sense when the British were bluffing.

In happy combination of personality and ability, the tactful and urbane Albert Gallatin was the best qualified negotiator of the group. His Swiss birth and foreign training, while not dampening his patriotism, had endowed him with a breadth of view lacking in his somewhat provincial colleagues. His most trying and useful work at Ghent was in keeping the peace among the argumentative Americans, rather than negotiating peace with the embattled British.

James A. Bayard, a prominent Federalist from Delaware, was an able representative of one of the most distinguished families in American history. Like Gallatin, he brought to these heated deliberations a pacifying evenness of temper. He was, in fact, the only member of the commission not cordially disliked by one or more of the others. Adams was unpopular with all four.

BRITAIN PRESENTS A CONQUEROR'S TERMS

It seemed as though the five Americans had been endowed with a surplus of talent so as to compensate for the lack of it on the other side of the table. To Ghent the British Foreign Office sent a group of such inexperienced mediocrities as to cause Gallatin to suspect that London had no serious intention of making peace. The head of the British commission was Lord Gambier, whose elevation to the peerage had come as a result of his rather discreditable part in the brutal bombardment of Copenhagen. Next was Henry Goulburn, an aggressive young undersecretary, of the "Copenhagen" Jackson type. Finally, there was one William Adams, a doctor of civil law and a learned academician who was presumably appointed for his legal knowledge. As historian Henry Adams devastatingly remarks, he "was an unknown man, and remained one." None of the three had ever had the slightest experience in diplomacy.

Why were these three nonentities chosen? First of all, they were intended to be mere transmitting clerks for the Foreign Office. Men of intelligence and spirit might have balked at surrendering all initiative to their superiors. Furthermore, from a military point of view Britain held the high cards, and the Ministry may have concluded that able negotiators were unnecessary. Finally, London was then making preparations for the historic Congress at Vienna, where the map of Europe was to be unscrambled. Vienna was the main tent; Ghent was a side show. And where the stakes were high Lord Castlereagh sent no underlings,

⁴ *Ibid.*, III, 32 (Sept. 7, 1814).

able or mediocre. He went to Vienna himself and took the Duke of Wellington with him.

The five high-strung Americans had gathered at Ghent by early July, 1814, but the Foreign Office kept them waiting in suspense for a full month. Napoleon was now exiled on the Mediterranean isle of Elba, and a formidable force of Wellington's veterans had embarked for American shores. It was obviously to the advantage of England to make no terms until she had learned of the confidently expected victories.

The three British commissioners finally arrived in Ghent, and on August 8, 1814, negotiations got under way. The State Department had instructed its five envoys to insist on the abandonment of impressment, the cessation of illegal blockades, and satisfaction regarding other neutral rights in dispute. But the British, who straightway assumed the offensive, presented demands that fairly took away the breath of the Americans. For one thing, the United States must never thereafter maintain either fortifications or armed ships on the Great Lakes. The British felt that such a precaution was an essential safeguard against another invasion of Canada. The Canadians were also to be shielded by the transfer of a large tract reaching to the Mississippi River west of Lake Superior, by another area in northern New York, and by still another in northeastern Maine.

Most stunning of all, the British demanded the creation of an enormous Indian buffer state south of the Great Lakes. Embracing all or large parts of five present-day states—Ohio, Indiana, Illinois, Michigan, and Wisconsin—this area would safeguard Britain's quasi-independent red allies, who in turn would further protect Canada and the fur trade against Yankee encroachment. The British commissioners, in accordance with their instructions, made the Indian buffer state a *sine qua non* (indispensable condition) of peace. Certain other proposals were of less significance.[5]

DEADLOCK AT GHENT

So unthinkable were the British demands that the Americans at Ghent rejected them at once without even referring to Washington for authorization. The five envoys, with the possible exception of poker-playing Clay, were convinced that England was not prepared to make a satisfactory peace. They were so sure their response would end the discussions that they gave notice to their landlord and began to pack their baggage. The elder Gallatin reported:

[5] For British designs in the West, see C. M. Gates, "The West in American Diplomacy, 1812–1815," *Miss. Valley Hist. Rev.*, XXVI (1940), 499–510, and J. W. Pratt, "Fur Trade Strategy and the American Left Flank in the War of 1812," *Amer. Hist. Rev.*, XL (1935), 246–273.

Our negotiations may be considered as at an end. Some official notes may yet pass, but the nature of the demands of the British . . . is such that there can be no doubt of a speedy rupture of our conferences, and that we will have no peace. Great Britain wants war in order to cripple us. . . . I do not expect to be longer than three weeks in Europe.[6]

But the Ministry in London was not willing to break off negotiations. It realized that its commissioners had presented their demands so forcibly as to enable the Americans to place upon England the onus of fighting merely for conquest and for the enlargement of Canada—objectives that the groaning British taxpayer would not tolerate. The results of employing such inferior agents became unpleasantly apparent to the Foreign Office, which sternly rebuked Goulburn for his clumsiness. The Ministry preferred to keep the discussions alive until the news of expected victories arrived from America. If the British won their anticipated triumphs, they would be in a position to dictate, not negotiate. Meanwhile the American envoys would be kept busy. Goulburn, who understood this game, observed that "as long as we answer their notes, I believe that they will be ready to give us replies."

When the crushing British demands reached America, President Madison cleverly resorted to a bit of "shirt-sleeve" or "house-top" diplomacy. He went so far as to publish the correspondence that had been interchanged, much to the annoyance of London. But the stratagem worked. A wave of indignation swept over America—even up into the New England Federalist country. The *United States Gazette,* a Federalist newspaper published in Philadelphia, cried: "England now turns upon us in the fullness of her wrath and power. No alternative is left us but to resist with energy or submit with disgrace. As the latter is not possible to Americans, we must prepare our minds for an extremely long, arduous, and sanguinary war."[7] Legislative bodies vied with one another in passing defiant resolutions. In Newark, New Jersey, 1000 men volunteered for work on the city's defenses, marching forth with flags and music and wearing labels bearing the slogan, "DON'T GIVE UP THE SOIL!"

The British were not slow to recognize the danger signals. Their success thus far against the United States had been largely due to disunion and apathy. Now the Americans might, if pushed far enough into the corner, unite and call forth their latent energies. Worse yet, the war might even become unpopular in England. The upshot was that the Ministry decided to abandon its ultimatum for exclusive control of the Great Lakes and for the establishment of an Indian buffer state. Instead, it proposed a relatively innocuous provision regarding the rights of the Indians on United States territory. With the clearing away of these obstacles, the first faint prospects of a treaty began to appear.

[6] Henry Adams, *The Life of Albert Gallatin* (Philadelphia, 1880), p. 524.
[7] *United States Gazette,* Oct. 19, 1814, quoted in Updyke, *Diplomacy of the War of 1812,* p. 280.

THE IRON DUKE DECLINES

A new crisis developed at Ghent early in October, 1814, when news arrived that a British army had captured Washington and burned the government buildings. Word was shortly expected of further victories by Wellington's veterans in northern New York and at New Orleans.

The opportunity for which Downing Street had been waiting was now at hand. The British commissioners at Ghent were instructed to demand that peace be made on the basis of *uti possidetis,* that is, actual occupation or possession of territory. This would give England the Fort Michili-mackinac area, Fort Niagara (with a surrounding strip of territory), and roughly half of present-day Maine. This last-named cession would insure the British an overland road from their naval base at Halifax to their fortress at Quebec, which was marooned several months each year by the ice-locked St. Lawrence River. The American envoys, who regarded these terms as intolerable, again prepared to pack their baggage and leave for home.

Suddenly the complexion of the negotiations changed radically. The electrifying news reached Ghent of Macdonough's decisive victory for the American cause on Lake Champlain, with the consequent hurling back of the invading army of some 10,000 Redcoats. The American negotiators, greatly enheartened, flatly refused to treat on any other basis than *status quo ante bellum* (territorial status as it existed before the war).

The British were now neatly impaled on the horns of a dilemma. They either had to back down from their demands or redouble their efforts to conquer a peace. In desperation the Ministry turned to the redoubtable Duke of Wellington, hero of the war with France, and offered him the command in Canada. To this chestnut-extricating invitation the "Iron Duke" replied that he could not promise much success without control of the Great Lakes. As the British then had little hope of gaining such superiority, this answer was equivalent to advising an abandonment of the projected invasion of the United States. Wellington went on to add some disagreeable truths:

> I confess that I think you have no right, from the state of the war, to demand any concession of territory from America. . . . You have not been able to carry it into the enemy's territory. . . . You can get no territory; indeed, the state of your military operations, however creditable, does not entitle you to demand any; and you only afford the Americans a popular and creditable ground . . . to avoid to make peace.[8]

With such advice from the foremost military authority in England, the Ministry had no choice but to abandon its demands for *uti possidetis.*

[8] Adams, *Gallatin,* pp. 538–539 (Wellington to Castlereagh, Nov. 9, 1814).

COMPROMISE AND CONCESSION

The United States had meanwhile grudgingly yielded ground. Secretary Monroe had originally instructed the five American negotiators to insist upon an abandonment of impressment as a *sine qua non* of peace; otherwise "the United States have appealed to arms in vain." But the stubbornness of the British, combined with the cessation of impressment after Napoleon's collapse, induced the Madison administration to modify its demands in June, 1814. In the light of these new instructions, which arrived on the first day of the conference at Ghent, the American commissioners consented to complete silence on impressment and other disputes involving a free sea.

Still other friction points provided fuel for controversy, including the Newfoundland fisheries. London insisted, not illogically, that the privileges granted the Americans in the Treaty of 1783 should not be renewed without an equivalent concession. The British coupled this surprise move with a demand that they be granted a renewal of the privilege of navigating the Mississippi from its source to its mouth. The questions thus raised were explosive. To New England the fisheries were so important that the governor of Massachusetts would have preferred to yield a considerable amount of territory rather than lose the fishing privileges.

New England fortunately had on the ground, as in 1782 at Paris, a stout champion of codfish in the person of an Adams. In his fight for the fisheries, John Quincy Adams was forced to contend not only with the British but with his own colleagues, notably Henry Clay. The dashing Kentuckian, now a frustrated War Hawk, exploded when Adams proposed to grant the right to navigate the West's Mississippi in return for the privilege of fishing. "The navigation principle," Clay declaimed, "is much too important to concede for the mere liberty of drying fish on a desert." Clay finally worked himself up to the point where he favored continuing war for three years longer. Months of close contact in stuffy lodgings had played havoc with nerves, and the elder Gallatin was hard pressed to prevent his colleagues from flying at one anothers' throats.

Gallatin's urbanity and skill finally triumphed. To him goes the chief credit for persuading the British to omit all reference to the fisheries and the Mississippi, and to reserve such thorny problems for future discussion. These concessions cleared away the last serious obstacles, and the formal signing of the pact took place on Christmas Eve, December 24, 1814.

THE GAINS OF GHENT

The most significant comment that can be made about the Treaty of Ghent is that it restored peace. Ironically enough, it made no mention whatever of the neutral rights, especially impressment, for which America had presumably gone to war. This omission was not proof, as often alleged, of the insincerity of the War Hawks; rather it was proof that the United States had not beaten Britain. The Napoleonic upheaval had subsided, and there was little point in America's continuing hostilities to force England to surrender in principle abuses which she had already abandoned in practice. In brief, the treaty was an armistice or a truce— a truce of exhaustion rather than of persuasion. Both sides simply agreed to stop fighting and restore the *status quo ante bellum*. Of great importance for the future, however, were those clauses that provided for mixed arbitral commissions to adjust boundary disputes along the northern frontier.[9]

The question logically arises why Britain, after having won the upper hand on land and sea, was willing to grant such favorable terms. Aside from the factors previously mentioned, the British Ministry, already staggering under a heavy debt, was finding the American conflict more costly than anticipated. The taxpayers had no stomach for continuing the highly unpopular property tax for a war of conquest in the interests of Canada. One Tory remarked that if the party in power "had not put an end to the war, the war would have put an end to their Ministry." Agricultural distress in England, moreover, had become acute, and the powerful merchant class was complaining bitterly of American privateers.

But the argument that probably weighed most heavily with the London Ministry was the European powder keg. France was seething with discontent, ready to rally to the banner of Napoleon should he return from Elba (as he soon did). The astute Talleyrand, now unwittingly helping America, had cleverly driven a wedge between the late allies over the division of spoils. Britain was highly suspicious of the designs of her ally, Russia, on Poland. In the face of an imminent blow-up in Europe, the British wanted to cut loose from what Lord Castlereagh called "the millstone of an American war." Once more Europe's necessities were operating to America's advantage—perhaps to her salvation.

THE LION LICKS HIS WOUNDS

The Treaty of Ghent was greeted with mixed emotions in England. The British had viewed the attack on the rear by their "treacherous" offspring with an anger that was equalled only by their contempt. The Yankees, they felt, were degenerate Englishmen. "Despicable in the cabinet, ridiculous in the field!" growled one newspaper. "Is Great

---

[9] The questions at issue were the ownership of certain islands in Passamaquoddy Bay and the Bay of Fundy; the boundary of the United States from the source of the River St. Croix to the St. Lawrence; and the boundary along the middle of the Great Lakes to the northwestern point of the Lake of the Woods.

Britain to be driven from the proud eminence," sneered the *London Evening Star*, ". . . by a piece of striped bunting flying at the mast-heads of a few *fir-built frigates,* manned by *a handful of bastards and outlaws.*" [10] Disillusionment in naval duels merely added to Britain's wrath. The *Globe* expressed a general sentiment when it declared that the Yankee should be "confoundedly well flogged." The *London Times* exploded:

> They [the Americans] are struck to the heart with terror for their impending punishment,—and oh! may no false liberality, no mistaken lenity, no weak and cowardly policy interpose to save them from the blow! Strike, Chastise the savages; for such they are. . . . With Madison and his perjured set, no treaty can be made; for no oath can bind them.[11]

When the Treaty of Ghent reached London, the journals that had voiced these sentiments used gall-mixed ink. They felt, with some justification, that Britain had thrown away at the peace table whatever she had gained on the battlefield. The *London Times* was sure that the result would merely invite the scorn of other nations. Similar dissatisfaction was also expressed on the floor of Parliament, where the British peace commissioners were roughly handled for their "gross mismanagement."

Yet the war-weary English masses, hungry and tax-burdened, welcomed the dove of peace. They were joined by the merchants and manufacturers, who rejoiced at the end of Yankee privateering and at the opportunity to dump the contents of their bulging warehouses upon the American market. Within a few weeks even the hate-America diehards were silenced. The news of Andrew Jackson's smashing victory at New Orleans showed that there were worse things than peace, while the Corn Riots and Napoleon's dramatic return from Elba diverted public attention elsewhere. The ministers were left free, says Henry Adams, "to redeem at Waterloo the failures they had experienced in America."

A POPULAR PEACE

While the Treaty of Ghent was being slowly borne homeward by stormy winds, America tasted the bitter dregs of despair. There was a widespread fear that the peace negotiations had collapsed. The British veterans were expected to rout General Andrew Jackson's motley collection of militiamen, creoles, and pirates at New Orleans, and perhaps detach the entire Southwest. Disgruntled Federalists were talking openly of disunion in their convention at Hartford, Connecticut, and many gloomy citizens were freely predicting the disruption of the republic.

Then, early in February, 1815, came news of Jackson's devastating

[10] *Niles' Weekly Register*, III, 271 (Dec. 26, 1812).
[11] *London Times*, May 24, 1814, 3:3–4.

victory over superior British forces. The flagging American spirit bounded to extravagant heights of rejoicing, as streets were littered with printed circulars bearing poems of praise. A week or so later came word of the Treaty of Ghent. *Niles' Weekly Register* rejoiced:

GLORIOUS NEWS!

[New] *Orleans saved and peace concluded.*
"The star spangled banner in triumph shall wave
O'er the land of the free and the home of the brave!"

. . . .

Who would not be an American? Long live the republic!
All hail! last asylum of oppressed humanity! [12]

The triumph at New Orleans ended hostilities on a deceptive note, for the battle had been fought two weeks *after* the signing of the treaty. But the arrival of the news of both events so close together led the unthinking to believe that the United States, having beaten the British into submission, had extorted a victor's terms. One contemporary rejoiced that "in the fullness of our glory we grant peace to a worsted enemy." The Madison administration was quite happy to hide its blunders behind the smoke of General Jackson's glorious victory, and to permit the legend to take root that the United States had won the War of 1812 because it had whipped the British in the last battle.

Without even waiting to read the treaty, the populace burst into wild demonstrations of joy. There were a few sour notes from merchants who had on hand stocks of high-priced goods, and from smugglers near the Canadian border whose profitable game was at an end. But most people were delighted to know that peace had come, whatever its terms. Holidays were proclaimed; pupils were dismissed from school; militiamen paraded; bells were rung; guns were fired; and cheering, shouting, and drinking citizens embraced one another on the streets.

With the seas now open to commerce even the New Englanders rejoiced, although they had good reason to fear that they had lost both territory and the right to fish in Canadian waters. When they read the actual terms of peace, their joy was unrestrained. So certain were they to lose something that a return to the *status quo ante bellum* was regarded as a handsome victory. The slogan of the hour became "Not one inch of territory ceded or lost"—in glaring contrast with the earlier "On to Canada!"

The harassed Madison administration, to whom the treaty had come as a "reprieve from doom," promptly submitted it to the Senate. The next day, and by a unanimous vote, that body gave its enthusiastic approval. The Treaty of Ghent certainly was the most popular peace pact with a major power ever concluded by the United States.

[12] *Niles' Weekly Register*, VII, 385 (Feb. 18, 1815).

THE RUSH-BAGOT DISARMAMENT AGREEMENT

The Canadians read the terms of peace with both disappointment and apprehension. They had fought bravely against heavy odds to repel the Yankee invader, and they felt that they should have been rewarded with exclusive control of their own fisheries, together with such territorial cessions as would erect maximum safeguards against future invasion. When the war came to an end both the Americans and the Canadians had substantial naval forces on the Great Lakes, and the British were planning to build enough additional warships to guarantee supremacy over their grasping offspring.

The stage was set for either disaster or disarmament. Reviving an earlier scheme, the State Department instructed Minister J. Q. Adams in London to propose to Lord Castlereagh mutual disarmament on the Great Lakes. The London officials were finally persuaded to take a chance. For one thing, the superior local resources of the United States put the British at a heavy disadvantage in an arms race; for another, costly warships on the interior lakes would be useless to the Royal Navy on the high seas. The Canadians, on the other hand, viewed possible disarmament with apprehension, for they did not want to be left naked in the face of their powerful and rapacious neighbor. But once more the interests of the overseas colony were sacrificed on the altar of Britain's imperial necessities.

The final negotiation of the Rush-Bagot disarmament agreement of 1817 was transferred to Washington, where the able Charles Bagot represented Britain. He disliked Americans, but spurred on by the prospect of a European promotion and acting under explicit instructions from Castlereagh, he concealed his feelings and flattered the Yankees. At one of President Madison's receptions he was heard to murmur— quite in contrast with "Copenhagen" Jackson—"Mrs. Madison looks every inch a Queen." It was not difficult for a man of his tact and ability to succeed where others had failed. An exchange of notes between him and the Acting Secretary of State, late in April, 1817, constituted the Rush-Bagot executive agreement for mutual disarmament on the Lakes. The next year the Senate formally approved the pact, thus giving it the status of a treaty.

The Rush-Bagot agreement, though a landmark in disarmament and a salve to Anglo-American discord, has been widely misunderstood. It did not provide for complete or immediate disarmament on the Great Lakes. Small armed craft for revenue-regulation could still be maintained by both sides, and for many years thereafter the two rivals kept their dismantled warships and naval stations on a moth-ball basis. The pact was subjected to repeated strains, but during World War II, when Canada and the United States were allies or virtual allies against Hitler, it was modified to permit naval construction, naval training, and other activities.

The Rush-Bagot agreement of 1817 had no direct bearing on land armaments. Not until 1871, when the Treaty of Washington cleared the diplomatic skies, did the Canadians feel sufficiently secure to permit their border fortifications to fall into decay. Thus by tacit agreement disarmament on the Lakes was finally extended to the land, and the myth of the "unguarded frontier" became a reality.[13]

THE AIR-CLEARING CONVENTION OF 1818

The much underrated Convention of 1818, negotiated in London by Albert Gallatin and Richard Rush, likewise took care of some unfinished business that had been swept under the rug at Ghent. Britain argued that the recent war had ended the fishing "liberties" granted by the peace Treaty of 1783, and British cruisers had been stirring up much anger by seizing American fishing craft. The Convention of 1818 granted

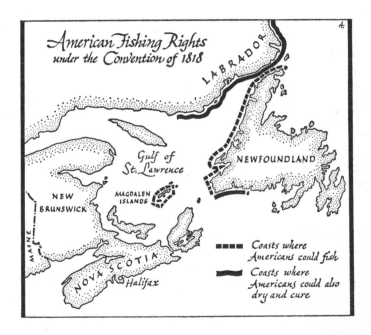

the Yankees the "liberty" to fish "forever" along specific stretches of the coasts of Newfoundland and Labrador, and to cure fish along less extensive parts of the coast as long as these areas remained unsettled. When such places should become inhabited, other arrangements would

[13] C. P. Stacey, "The Myth of the Unguarded Frontier, 1815–1871," *Amer. Hist. Rev.*, LVI (1950), 1–18.

be made. Thus the New England fisherfolk could continue to catch cod and other fish on a profitable basis.

The Convention of 1818 likewise adjusted the ill-defined northern boundary of the Louisiana purchase. Henceforth it was to begin with the Lake of the Woods, and then run westward along the forty-ninth parallel to the "Stony [Rocky] Mountains." Since no agreement could

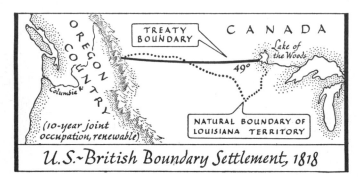

U. S.-British Boundary Settlement, 1818

then be reached on running the boundary on through the Oregon territory, the negotiators decided to leave the question hanging fire. For a period of ten years, subject to renewal, the Oregon country should be "free and open" to both Britons and Americans—an arrangement that came to be popularly known as "joint occupation."

A FRUSTRATING BUT FINAL PEACE

One often hears that neither the War of 1812 nor the Peace of Ghent settled anything. This is far from the truth. The Indians of the Northwest, abandoned by the British at the peace table and beaten by the Americans on the battlefield, ceased to be either a menace or a source of friction. The four joint commissions set up by the treaty proved to be landmarks in the amicable adjustment of international disputes. Other controversies, such as impressment, were entirely ignored. Growing rapidly and awkwardly, America could ask for nothing better than to postpone the final adjustment of such issues until a day when she would be great and powerful. A century later every unsettled dispute of 1814 had either dropped into oblivion or had been settled by mutual accommodation.

The fiery furnace of war also brought forth a new nation. New England disloyalty hung its head in the face of the tremendous triumph at New Orleans. America's humiliating defeats faded from mind, while her glorious victories were celebrated in verse and song. The republic sensed as never before its unlimited potentialities and its future greatness. Men began to perceive increasingly that America's destiny lay in the West—not on the ocean.

If America did not win a formal admission of her rights, she did gain a grudging respect from British statesmen and warriors. The hot breath of American broadsides spoke a language that could not be misunderstood. Gone were the sneers about Yankee cowardice and degeneracy, for American "fir-built frigates" had proved themselves. The words of Michael Scott, a well-known British writer, are a remarkable tribute to what he called "those damned Yankees":

> I don't like Americans; I never did, and never shall like them. . . . I have no wish to eat with them, drink with them, deal with, or consort with them in any way; but let me tell the whole truth, *nor fight* with them, were it not for the laurels to be acquired, by overcoming an enemy so brave, determined, and alert, and every way so worthy of one's steel, as they have always proved.[14]

Never again was the United States to be treated by Britain and France as other than a sovereign nation. In this sense the War of 1812 may properly be called the "second war for American independence."

Unhappily, the conflict left bruised and rancorous feelings on both sides of the Atlantic. The British might grudgingly entertain more respect for America's fighting prowess, but they could not forget the stab in the back while they were struggling for their lives and liberties against Napoleon. Canadian distrust of the United States was likewise increased many fold. The unconcealed greed of the Yankees aroused a new resentment, and largely explains why the peaceful infiltration and annexation of Canada, which previously had some prospect of success, were now doomed to failure.

In the United States, the embers of 1776 were stirred anew. When Congress faced the problem of rebuilding the burned-out buildings in Washington, one member proposed to encircle the ruins of the Capitol with an iron railing and place thereon an inscription: "Americans! This is the effect of British barbarism! Let us swear eternal hatred to England!" Fortunately, this spiteful proposal was not accepted, but anti-British bitterness remained.[15]

Whatever its shortcomings, the Treaty of Ghent was not a victor's peace. It imposed no rankling conditions that made inevitable another war to undo them. Therein lay the secret of its longevity. Yet, given the sheaf of unsolved problems and the burning animosity on both sides, few

---

[14] *Blackwood's Magazine*, XXXII, 146 (Aug., 1832).

[15] Stratford Canning, British minister in Washington, wrote to his sister in 1822: ". . . I know two young ladies who can play 'God Save the King' on the harp, and who do occasionally play on the condition prescribed by their papa, of playing 'Yankee Doodle' immediately afterwards!" Beckles Willson, *Friendly Relations* (Boston, 1934), p. 121.

men of that generation could have believed that the two nations would celebrate in 1914 and 1915, as they did, the one hundredth anniversary of unbroken peace.

SELECTED BIBLIOGRAPHY

The most recent scholarship is ably presented in A. L. Burt, *The United States, Great Britain, and British North America* (New Haven, 1940). F. A. Updyke, *The Diplomacy of the War of 1812* (Baltimore, 1915) is the most detailed study on the diplomatic side. See also the older classical account, A. T. Mahan, *Sea Power in Its Relations to the War of 1812* (Boston, 1905), and particularly Henry Adams, *History of the United States during the Administrations of Jefferson and Madison* (New York, 1891), vol. IX. The best biographical studies are S. F. Bemis, *John Quincy Adams and the Foundations of American Foreign Policy* (New York, 1949) and J. H. Powell, *Richard Rush, Republican Diplomat, 1780–1859* (Philadelphia, 1942). Solid outlines appear in J. M. Callahan, *American Foreign Policy in Canadian Relations* (New York, 1937).

See footnotes of this chapter; Bemis and Griffin, *Guide,* pp. 147–155, 277–280; *Harvard Guide,* Chs. 12, 13.

7TH ED. REFS. Irving Brant, *James Madison: Commander in Chief, 1812–1836* (Indianapolis, 1961) is a strong pro-Madison effort to depict the President as an energetic and successful war leader. Ignoring the loss of the navy, Brant leaves the impression that the United States "won" the war—a view shared by many relieved contemporaries but less by the Federalists, who tended to criticize the peace treaty. To some extent they had weakened the negotiators. F. L. Engelman, *The Peace of Christmas Eve* (New York, 1962) is a popularized account which gives much credit to the stubbornness and skill of the American negotiators. The Americans "did not really *win* the war; the British withdrew from it" (p. 301), partly because of Macdonough's victory but more because of troubled affairs in London, Paris, and Vienna. Raymond Walters, Jr., *Albert Gallatin: Jeffersonian Financier and Diplomat* (New York, 1957), now the standard biography, builds up Gallatin to his rightful place, to some extent at the expense of the British negotiators. Frank Ewing, *America's Forgotten Statesman: Albert Gallatin* (New York, 1959), is laudatory and sketchy, and leans too heavily on James Gallatin's diary, which was exposed as a hoax in Raymond Walters, Jr., "The James Gallatin Diary: A Fraud?" *Amer. Hist. Rev.,* LXII (1957), 878–885. W. D. Jones, "A British View of the War of 1812 and the Peace Negotiations," *Miss. Valley Hist. Rev.,* XLV (1958), 481–487 focuses on British negotiator Goulburn, who regarded the war as one of unprovoked aggression for Canada. J. I. Shulim, "The United States Views Russia in the Napoleonic Age," *Proceedings of the American Philosophical Society,* CII (1958), 148–159 shows how public reactions shifted as Russia's conduct seemed to support or undermine American objectives.

8TH AND 9TH ED. REFS. See BIBLIOGRAPHICAL ADDENDUM, p. 987.

CHAPTER

~~~~~~~~~~~~~~~~~~~ 12 ~~~~~~~~~~~~~~~~~~~

Acquiring the Floridas
1803-1821

[Florida] will just as naturally come into our posses-
sion as the waters of the Mississippi seek the sea;
and any thing done to obstruct the operation will
be as useless, in the end, as an attempt to arrest and
turn back the course of that mighty stream.
NILES' WEEKLY REGISTER, May 29, 1819

A POLITICAL AND GEOGRAPHICAL ABSURDITY

THE PEACE OF GHENT marked a dramatic turning point in American diplomatic history. Hitherto the fate of the young republic had been intimately involved with hostilities abroad; the United States had been a kind of tail to the European kite. But after Napoleon's collapse at Waterloo in 1815—one of the red letter dates in American history— Americans no longer scanned the horizon anxiously for every approaching sail. In September, 1815, the *Washington National Intelligencer* could complain that subscriptions had fallen off because of a belief that European affairs no longer mattered. "They pay no more attention to us and our business," wrote the disgusted Russian *chargé* in Washington, "than if we were so many Chinamen." [1]

The ending of the Napoleonic nightmare thus left the American people free to work out their own destiny with a minimum of foreign meddling. Responding to the robust new sense of nationalism engendered by the War of 1812, they turned their backs confidently on the Old World, and concentrated on the task of felling trees and Indians and of rounding out their natural boundaries.

From the earliest days of the republic, American statesmen had noted the paramount importance of Florida. Like a giant pistol, with the peninsula serving as the butt and West Florida the barrel, it pointed

[1] W. P. Cresson, *Diplomatic Portraits* (Boston, 1923), p. 334.

163

directly at the mouth of the all-important Mississippi River. At the time of the Louisiana Purchase crisis in 1803 President Jefferson had vainly sought to buy West Florida, and the acquisition of the vast area in the Mississippi Valley merely whetted the appetite of the American public for more.

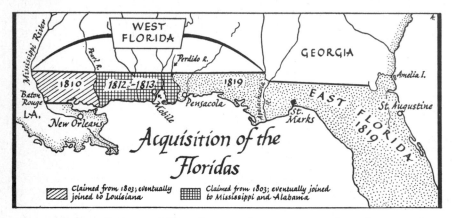

But the broad acres of Florida were by no means the sole attraction. The huge peninsula, thrust deeply into the Gulf of Mexico, possessed vital strategic value, offering as it did a constant threat to shipping between New Orleans and the Atlantic seaboard. In addition, most of the navigable rivers of the present states of Alabama and Mississippi flowed through East and West Florida while seeking the Gulf. Control of the mouths of these streams by the Spanish officials created a number of vexatious bottlenecks that were reminiscent, on a smaller scale, of the old New Orleans problem.

JEFFERSON'S FLORIDA FINAGLING

During the Louisiana negotiations in Paris, Livingston and Monroe had fruitlessly tried to buy West Florida, as instructed. They knew perfectly well they had failed to do so when they signed the purchase treaty. Yet Livingston, after studying the historical backgrounds, wishfully contended that the Louisiana territory embraced that portion of West Florida between the Mississippi and the Perdido Rivers. President Jefferson eagerly adopted this view, and later in 1803 expressed his secret intentions:

> We have some claims . . . to go eastwardly [into West Florida] . . . . These claims will be a subject of negotiation with Spain, and if, as soon as she is at war, we push them strongly with one hand, holding out a price in the other, we shall certainly obtain the Floridas, and all in good time.[2]

[2] A. A. Lipscomb, ed., *Writings of Thomas Jefferson* (Monticello ed., Washington, 1904), X, 408.

Jefferson at first tried the quiet channels of diplomacy, but they netted him nothing. He next sounded a surprising blast in his annual message of December, 1805, when he referred in a bellicose tone to relations with Spain and hinted at the necessity of raising 300,000 soldiers for defense and offense. His obvious purpose, of course, was to frighten the Spaniards into yielding West Florida. He then confidentially asked Congress for a secret appropriation of $2 million to be used in facilitating the negotiation. The fiery John Randolph of Virginia denounced this scheme as a barefaced attempt to bribe Napoleon into forcing Spain to cede Florida. Whatever the truth of such an accusation, Jefferson did enter into negotiations with Bonaparte, who liked nothing better than to use the Florida bait to lure the American President on.

In the end, Jefferson's highly questionable tactics brought him no nearer his goal. He exposed his gullibility to Napoleon; aroused the distrust of Spain; and further embittered the British, who resented his intrigues with the French despot. Yet Jefferson kept his eyes steadfastly on the prize. On the eve of retiring from the Presidency he was heard to say, "We must have the Floridas and Cuba."

INFILTRATING WEST FLORIDA

West Florida was rapidly becoming ripe for the plucking. As early as June, 1810, President Madison was prepared to connive at a separatist movement in that area, where a group of hardy American settlers had been chafing under Spain's corrupt rule. The outbreak of revolutions in Latin America provided a spark. In September, 1810, these "inquiet spirits," encouraged if not actively assisted by the Washington government, arose in revolt and captured the Spanish fort at Baton Rouge. The Bourbon banner was torn down and dragged through the village dust, later to be replaced by that of the "Republic of West Florida"—a blue woolen flag with a lone silver star. Having proclaimed its independence, the infant republic, like lone-star Texas of a later day, knocked at the door of the United States.

Madison moved rapidly to harvest the West Florida fruit. On October 27, 1810, he issued a proclamation extending American jurisdiction to the Perdido River, although he actually occupied only the smaller area to the Pearl River. Madison justified this grab on the grounds that the territory had rightfully belonged to the United States since the purchase of Louisiana. But his conscience must have troubled him, for he went so far as to falsify the dates of certain important documents, evidently with an eye to deceiving posterity. John Quincy Adams, then United States minister to Russia, undertook to explain, somewhat shamefacedly, how his country had acquired its neighbor's territory. The Czar bowed and, obviously referring to Napoleon's reshaping of the map of Europe, remarked pleasantly, "Everyone always grows a little in this world." [3]

The other powers were less tolerant. Madrid made heated but altogether fruitless protests to the State Department against the devious doings in West Florida. Europe's distresses again operated to America's advantage, for Spain was too heavily involved in her desperate war with Napoleon to welcome fighting in America. England was likewise alarmed by this new evidence of Yankee greed, and her minister in Washington protested against the occupation of West Florida as "contrary to every principle of public justice, faith, and national honor." But Britain, like Spain, was too deeply enmeshed in the Napoleonic war to provoke hostilities with the United States over this issue. The British, however, did not forget. The *London Times*, while urging unrelenting war upon America in 1814, insisted that "Mr. Madison's dirty, swindling manoeuvres in respect to Louisiana and the Floridas remain to be punished."

NIBBLING AT EAST FLORIDA

President Madison was not content to rest upon his West Florida laurels—if they may be called that. His direct if dubious methods had been so simple and effective as to recommend the employment of similar tactics in East Florida. The tool that came to hand was one George Mathews, an almost illiterate former governor of Georgia, who, despite his seventy-two years, was more distinguished for energy and patriotism than for deliberation and discretion.

The colorful Mathews was secretly encouraged by the Washington authorities to collaborate with American "insurgents" in East Florida, after the manner of the Baton Rouge uprising. With the aid of American gunboats, some two hundred insurgents captured the smugglers' paradise of Fernandina, on Amelia Island, a short distance from the Georgia border, and proclaimed independence. Mathews then took over, in the name of the United States, and with regular troops occupied other spots. By this time the Madison administration was thoroughly embarrassed. Mathews was disavowed when he reached the gates of Spain's St. Augustine early in June, 1812, and the captured Spanish territory was reluctantly relinquished. Bitterly disappointed at his repudiation by the Washington authorities, Mathews swore that he would "be dam'd if he did not blow them all up." Fortunately for them, he suddenly died.

A few days later America embarked on the War of 1812 with England, and an avowed objective of the Southern War Hawks was Spanish Florida, held by an ally of Britain. Although Congress had formally annexed all of West Florida between the Pearl and Perdido Rivers to

[3] "On s'agrandit toujours un peu, dans ce monde." C. F. Adams, ed., *Memoirs of John Quincy Adams* (Philadelphia, 1874), II, 261.

Mississippi territory by act of May 14, 1812, the Mobile area was still occupied by Spanish troops. This eyesore was summarily removed when, in April, 1813, General James Wilkinson effected a bloodless conquest of Mobile. The irony is that after all the loud boasting by the War Hawks about taking Canada, the Mobile region was the only permanent territorial gain of the War of 1812. The United States again profited by Spain's distress at home and in her revolted colonies.

RECOGNITION OF THE SPANISH REPUBLICS

By 1816 the cession of East Florida to the United States seemed inevitable. The remaining step was the negotiating of terms—a responsibility that fell to the able and experienced Secretary of State, John Quincy Adams. Recognizing the importance of defining the vague western limits of the Louisiana purchase, he drew up, in January, 1818, a detailed proposal for including boundaries, claims, and the cession of Florida in one package. But his task was immensely complicated by the question of recognizing the newly born republics of Latin America.

When the South-American revolutions had broken out in 1809 and 1810, the people of the United States were flattered to think that Latin America was emulating their example. They instinctively favored the cause of democracy as against despotism. At a public dinner in Nashville, Tennessee, the twenty-second toast was enthusiastically received: *"The patriots of South America:* palsied be the arm that would wrest from them the standard of liberty for which they have so nobly struggled. Six cheers." [4] Interest in the United States was further stimulated by stories of Spanish atrocities, especially those describing the Inquisition.

Sympathy for the Spanish-American insurgents was so strong that Congress, in 1818, felt obliged to pass a new and comprehensive Neutrality Act. Yet filibustering expeditions continued to sail from the United States with but scant restraint from the authorities. Several American ports, notoriously New Orleans and Baltimore, became bases for privateers supporting the rebels. Secretary Adams noted with disgust that the federal officers in Baltimore, some of whom had become involved in privateering, were "all fanatics of the South-American cause."

A loud demand for recognizing the new Latin-American republics arose from sympathizers in the United States. These ardent spirits found a mouthpiece in Henry Clay, who was perhaps the most eloquent orator of his generation. His efforts attracted wide attention in the press and undoubtedly swayed a considerable body of public opinion. The gallant Kentuckian warmly defended the sheltering of insurgent privateers, and,

James Parton, *Life of Andrew Jackson* (Boston, 1860), II, 575, quoting the *Nashville Whig.*

partly for political reasons, condemned the Monroe administration for its cautious if correct policy. His enthusiasm led to some remarkable oratorical flights on the floor of the House:

> Within this vast region we behold the most sublime and interesting objects of creation; the loftiest mountains, the most majestic rivers in the world; the richest mines of the precious metals, and the choicest productions of the earth. We behold there a spectacle still more interesting and sublime —the glorious spectacle of eighteen millions of people, struggling to burst their chains and to be free.[5]

The dilemma that confronted Secretary Adams was one of the most perplexing of his career. If the United States waited too long before recognizing the new republics, it would incur their ill will—and probably a corresponding loss of trade to British rivals. If, on the other hand, the Washington government acted too hastily, Spain would be fully justified in declaring war. And a clash with Spain could mean that all the European monarchs unfriendly to democracy might come to her aid. Finally— and this was a point of deep concern to Adams—premature recognition would so deeply offend Madrid as probably to ruin all chances of securing East Florida by friendly negotiation.

The Monroe administration therefore had to walk warily, and suppress whatever sympathy it may have harbored for the revolutionists. The hard-headed Secretary Adams was ideally equipped for such a role. Never one to let sentiment blind him to duty, he frowned upon the popular enthusiasm for the revolutions and repelled the advances of the South-American agents with a coldness that bordered on frigidity. He also made a significant contribution to American policy when he declared that recognition should be deferred until the chances of recovery by the mother country were "utterly desperate." As Spain's chances were by no means hopeless, the administration, supported by many influential newspapers, threw its weight against a recognition resolution then before the House. Amid great excitement, which resulted in some of the sick members being carried into the chamber to vote, the resolution was defeated, on March 30, 1818, by a count of 45 yeas to 115 nays.

JACKSON'S FLORIDA FORAY

For some months Secretary Adams had been discussing Florida with Luis de Onís, the Spanish minister in Washington. The negotiations were proceeding rather favorably when a sensational episode threatened to sever relations completely.

Spain had been forced to weaken her grip on East Florida, as

---

[5] Calvin Colton, ed., *The Works of Henry Clay* (Federal ed., New York, 1904), VI, 140 (March 24, 1818). This speech, translated into Spanish, was read at the heads of the revolutionary regiments, which greeted it with applause.

previously noted, by withdrawing troops to fight the South-American insurgents. Amelia Island, an outpost near the Georgia border which had slipped away from Spanish control, became such an intolerable nest of pirates that an expedition authorized by the Washington officials seized the islet in 1817. Far more irritating were the Indians of Florida. Joined by runaway Negroes, white renegades, and others, they periodically sallied across the international line to pillage, burn, and murder. The harboring of such a villainous lot of outcasts under the Spanish flag was a clear violation of the good-neighbor pledge embodied in the Pinckney Treaty of 1795, but Spain was admittedly powerless to control or restrain these cutthroats.

Late in 1817 Andrew Jackson, hero of New Orleans and idol of the Southwest, was commissioned by the Monroe administration to chastise the Indians. His instructions were broad, but he was empowered to pursue the red men across the Spanish boundary, if necessary. He was, however, to respect all posts under the Bourbon flag. Jackson later insisted that President Monroe sent additional instructions authorizing a seizure of the Spanish towns. This Monroe denied. In any event the peppery hero of New Orleans apparently thought that he had the official blessing of the administration.

General Jackson, who hated both the Spaniard and the red man with all the venom of a Westerner, burst into Florida in hot pursuit of the Indians. He seized the military post of St. Marks, in April, 1818, and replaced the Spanish flag with the Stars and Stripes. Two British subjects, Alexander Arbuthnot and Robert Ambrister, had the misfortune to fall into Jackson's clutches. Charged with inciting the Indians against the whites, they were speedily tried by a court martial and put to death. The overzealous Jackson reported to the Secretary of War without expressions of regret:

> I hope the execution of these two unprincipled villains will prove an awful example to the world, and convince the Government of Great Britain, as well as her subjects, that certain, though slow retribution awaits those unchristian wretches who, by false promises, delude and excite an Indian tribe to all the horrid deeds of savage war.[6]

Nor did Jackson halt here. Learning that Indians were being sheltered at Pensacola, he made a forced march westward and captured the town. Thus in a few weeks he chastised the Indians, seized every important post in Florida except St. Augustine, confiscated the royal archives, deposed the Spanish governor and named an American in his place, executed two British subjects, and declared in force "the revenue laws of the United States." He later expressed regret that he did not hang the Spanish governor.

[6] *American State Papers, Military Affairs*, I, 702.

"OLD HICKORY" RIDES OUT THE STORM

The news that the "ruffian" Jackson had "murdered" two British subjects on Spanish soil led to an explosion of wrath in England. "We can hardly believe," one London journal remarked, "that any thing so offensive to public decorum could be admitted, *even in America!*" The press seethed with demands for disavowal, apology, and reparation. One foreign envoy in London told the United States minister, Richard Rush, that "*we have had nothing of late so exciting; it smacks of war.*" Rush's own words are graphic:

> Out-of-doors, excitement seemed to rise higher and higher. Stocks experienced a slight fall. The newspapers kept up their fire . . . [giving] vent to angry declamation. They fiercely denounced the Government of the United States. Tyrant, ruffian, murderer, were among the epithets applied to their commanding general. He was exhibited in placards through the streets. The journals, without distinction of party, united in these attacks.[7]

For a few critical days Downing Street was in grave danger of being forced to demand redress—even at the risk of war. But Lord Castlereagh concluded, after an examination of the evidence, that Ambrister and Arbuthnot had been involved in "practices of such a description as to have deprived them of any claim on their own government for interference." As a result, London neither demanded redress nor supported the outraged protests of Spain. The friendly Lord Castlereagh later told Minister Rush that war might have broken out "if the Ministry had but held up a finger." This statement was perhaps an exaggeration, but the crisis was ticklish enough to cause many anxious moments.

Apparently unmoved by the international uproar, Jackson returned to Tennessee amid the huzzas of the masses—more than ever the hero of the West. Two-fisted Americans wasted little sympathy on Ambrister and Arbuthnot; in Western eyes these conspirators were entitled to no more mercy than a sheep-killing dog. "Among the people of the west," observed *Niles' Weekly Register,* "his [Jackson's] popularity is unbounded—old and young speak of him with rapture, and at his call, 50,000 of the most efficient warriors on this continent, would rise, armed, and ready for any enemy." [8] At public dinners given in honor of the unrepentant warrior, patriotic toasts were greeted with tumultuous applause. In American eyes he had not only put the fear of God into the treacherous Spaniards and Indians, but he had hurled defiance into the teeth of the arrogant Britons. Tammany Hall in New York passed a rousing resolution:

[7] Richard Rush, *A Residence at the Court of London* (London, 1833), p. 412 (Jan. 15, 1819).
[8] *Niles' Weekly Register,* XIV, 399 (Aug. 8, 1818).

. . . Resolved . . . That the conduct of General Jackson . . . was justified by the law of nations, and the laws of war, and the immutable principles of retaliation and self-defence; and we highly approve of the manly spirit of the American general, who promptly punished the offenders and culprits against humanity and the rights of his country, and taught foreign emissaries that the United States was not to be outraged by spies, traitors, and lawless adventurers.[9]

But in Congress, where Jackson had vengeful political enemies like Henry Clay, the Florida escapade was viewed more critically. A Senate committee launched a probe. Some of its members began to carry pistols after Jackson, raving "like a madman," allegedly threatened to cut off the ears of any who reported against him. After a twenty-seven day debate in Congress, during which the galleries were "crowded to suffocation" and cuspidors were overturned in the aisles, the four resolutions condemning Jackson were defeated by comfortable margins. The news caused a slight fall of stocks in England, where newspapers renewed their denunciation of the "ruffian" Jackson. But the American people endorsed the judgment of Congress by tendering "Old Hickory" a series of rousing ovations. The one in Philadelphia lasted four days; the one in New York five, and included the keys of the city in a golden box.

LONE-WOLF ADAMS TAKES THE OFFENSIVE

The entire Cabinet, with one exception, agreed with President Monroe that Jackson had committed an unauthorized and unwarranted act. But "Old Hickory" found an unexpected champion in Secretary of State Adams, who, despite strong personal feelings against the General, held out for an aggressive course in dealing with Spain. His arguments prompted the administration to abandon any thought of disciplining Jackson—a decision that was made less difficult by the obvious popularity of the Florida invasion among the masses. President Monroe was a clever enough politician to see the folly of tangling with the temperamental Jackson on an issue which could not fail to weaken the administration politically. Monroe therefore steered a prudent middle course. He smoothed Spain's ruffled feathers by returning the captured posts; he tactfully avoided a collision with Jackson by shunning punitive measures. He even offered to falsify certain official documents so that the invasion of Florida would appear in a more favorable light.

In this atmosphere Secretary Adams, reacting to the demands of Madrid for indemnity and punishment, drew up a memorable reply based on self-defense. Spain, he insisted, could not restrain her Indians; hence the United States would. Adams must have felt a bit uneasy when he penned this dictum, for he admitted that there were no citations in

[9] *Ibid.*, XVI, 30 (March 6, 1819).

international law to support him. "It is," he declared, "engraved in adamant on the common sense of mankind." Describing in lurid detail the butcheries by the Indians, he defended the execution of the British trouble makers. Jackson, he averred, would have been fully justified in hanging them both without even the formality of a trial.

Adams then took the offensive. Far from apologizing, he accused the Spanish officials of having encouraged and sheltered the Indians. With breath-taking audacity he demanded the punishment of the culpable officers and an indemnity for the heavy expenses incurred in pursuing the Indians. If, ran Adams' thinly veiled threat, the disorders were not quelled, the United States would have to do the same thing again, and in this case "another unconditional restoration . . . must not be expected." In stressing the self-confessed inability of the Spanish officials to control the Indians, Adams met the issue head on:

> . . . Spain must immediately make her election [choice], either to place a force in Florida adequate at once to the protection of her territory, and to the fulfilment of her engagements, or cede to the United States a province, of which she retains nothing but the nominal possession, but which is, in fact, a derelict, open to the occupancy of every enemy, civilized or savage, of the United States, and serving no other earthly purpose than as a post of annoyance to them.[10]

In short, control or cede. And since Spain had already admitted her inability to control, the only alternative was to cede.

Adams' eloquent reply, which comprises twenty-nine pages of his published works, was enthusiastically received throughout the country. It reflected the rising spirit of American nationalism, and helped dispel any lingering doubts as to the legality of the Florida invasion. But it contained passages in which Adams, who was writing largely for "home consumption," stood on untenable ground. His statement was not a judicial presentation of the facts; it was a devastating brief for the defense.

SPAIN BOWS TO THE INEVITABLE

In Washington the Adams-Onís negotiations for Florida, which had been rudely interrupted by the Jacksonian invasion, were now renewed. Incredibly enough, the bull-in-the-china-shop tactics of Jackson actually facilitated the work of the diplomats. The slow-moving Spanish Court now saw clearly the handwriting on the wall. Laboring under domestic difficulties, lacking effective support from Britain, and hoping for a freer hand to crush the South-American rebels, Madrid perceived that Florida would inevitably fall to the grasping Yankee. The course of wisdom would be to dispose of the territory gracefully and for a consideration, while

---

[10] *American State Papers, Foreign Relations*, V, 542 (Adams to Erving, Nov. 28, 1818).

there was yet time, rather than lose it after a bloody, costly, and humiliating war. Spain's distresses, at home and in Latin America, again paved the path for another brilliant American diplomatic success.

After protracted negotiations, the memorable Adams-Onís treaty was signed in Washington, on February 22, 1819. By its terms the United States acquired East Florida, a validation of its seizure of West Florida, and a definition of the jagged western boundary of the Louisiana Purchase. The new line began at the mouth of the Sabine River, zigzagged northwesterly to the 42nd parallel—the present northern boundary of California—and then ran due west to the Pacific Ocean. Spain also formally deeded over to the United States its vague claims to the Oregon Country.

In exchange for these sweeping concessions, Adams surrendered America's shadowy claim to Texas growing out of the Louisiana Purchase. Each government renounced the damage claims of its nationals against the other, while the United States agreed to assume the claims of its own citizens against Spain to the tune of $5 million. These had stemmed principally from Franco-Spanish seizures of American shipping in the undeclared war of 1798–1800, and from Spain's withdrawal of the right of deposit at New Orleans in 1802. The United States therefore did not purchase Florida for $5 million, as is commonly stated. The Spaniards never saw the money. In essence, Spain ceded Florida and her vague toehold in Oregon in exchange for the tenuous American title to Texas and the renunciation of $5 million in claims.

CASTILIAN PROCRASTINATION

The subsequent history of the Adams-Onís pact was troubled. The Senate approved the treaty unanimously only two days after the signing, while the country warmly ratified its judgment. But the pact now met with an agonizing delay in Spain. The feet-dragging tactics of the Madrid regime could be partially accounted for by the Revolution of 1820 at home, and by personal intrigues over huge land grants in Florida. Perhaps most important of all was Spain's fear that once Florida was safely in the possession of the United States, Washington would promptly recognize the rebellious Latin-American republics. But Secretary Adams, faithful to his earlier policy, sternly resisted all pressures to extort a nonrecognition pledge. The longer Spain withheld ratification, the more worried the administration became, and President Monroe seriously considered a forcible occupation of Florida.[11] But fortunately he decided upon a policy of patience, and Madrid finally yielded.

The Senate was required to approve the treaty again, for the six

[11] S. F. Bemis, ed., *The American Secretaries of State and Their Diplomacy* (New York, 1928) IV, 29–30, 33.

month time limit stipulated in the document had expired. Meanwhile considerable opposition had developed, notably in the West, over the alleged surrender of Texas. Henry Clay, who was not unmindful of politics, denounced the base betrayal, while the *Louisiana Advertiser* declared that Texas was "worth ten Floridas." Finally, on February 19, 1821, the Senate again approved the treaty, this time with four dissenting votes.

In fairness to Adams, one must say that he fought resolutely for the interests of his country. He strongly favored retaining Texas, and the documents now reveal that he probably could have obtained the huge area to the Colorado River (about half of present Texas) if his colleagues had not overruled him. But practical politics, combined with the fearsome slavery issue, decreed against holding out for Texas. The South—even Andrew Jackson—had few qualms about sacrificing the West if, by so doing, the nation could acquire Florida. In fact, there probably would have been no treaty at all if the United States had not yielded its claims to at least a substantial portion of Texas. The Spanish minister had to have something to show for his concessions. During a give-and-take-negotiation in time of peace, one nation cannot expect all "take" and no "give."

FULFILLING A PHYSIOGRAPHIC DESTINY

On March 8, 1822, more than a full year after the formal exchange of treaty ratifications with Madrid, President Monroe sent a message to Congress recommending recognition of the Latin-American republics. He pointed out, in accordance with the "utterly desperate" formula of Adams, that Spain's chances of reconquest were "most remote." In less than two months Congress overwhelmingly approved the President's request by voting $100,000 to establish the appropriate diplomatic missions, and the necessary steps were then taken to welcome the new republics into the family of nations. Spain's aggrieved protests received scant consideration in Washington.

Recognition of the Latin-American republics, so soon after the acquisition of Florida, has been branded an act of bad faith. But the Monroe administration had given no pledge, tacit or formal, not to recognize; and it waited more than a year before acting. Moreover, subsequent events fully justified Monroe's belief that Spain was incapable of winning back her wayward colonies. It is perhaps unfortunate that all aspects of the Florida transfer are not so defensible as this one.

The Adams-Onís Treaty, even though it surrendered Texas, was of incalculable value to the West. The republic could now present a strong claim to a corridor to the Pacific north of the 42nd parallel. Great Britain, to be sure, also claimed the Oregon country, to which she had admitted the United States to joint occupation by the Convention of 1818. But the snarl was simplified by the elimination of all but two rivals. Although the United States inherited Spain's claims, they were not unduly emphasized in the subsequent diplomatic controversy with London. Yet the westward-moving American pioneers tended to avoid Spanish California, which was a foreign land, and settle in Oregon, to which the United States had now established a double-barrelled claim. As will become evident later, the presence of thousands of American settlers in the Oregon country played a dominant role in the final diplomatic settlement.

Of more immediate significance was the acquisition of Florida. The hornet's nest of lawless raiders was removed; constant bickerings with Spain ceased. The rivers of Mississippi and Alabama thenceforth ran unvexed to the Gulf; the southeastern corner of the United States was filled out; and the rapid development of the Cotton Kingdom was facilitated. Finally, an area of enormous strategic value fell into the hands of the United States.

Despite the inevitability of Florida's fate, the negotiation had its ugly aspects. Spain, to be sure, was shuffling, dilatory, and irresponsible; but the United States was rough, highhanded, and arrogant. Some writers have cited the acquisition of Florida as a case of international bullying. Others have called it Manifest Destiny—the falling of ripe fruit. Perhaps it was the manifest determination of the American people to achieve their physiographic destiny, coupled with the manifest weakness of Spain. The normal and inexorable push of the American pioneers was not to be denied. It was Spain's misfortune, as it was later Mexico's, to be in their way.

SELECTED BIBLIOGRAPHY

The backgrounds are briefly surveyed in S. F. Bemis, *The Latin American Policy of the United States* (New York, 1943). Detailed monographs bearing on the Florida negotiation are A. P. Whitaker, *The United States and the Independence of Latin America, 1800–1830* (Baltimore, 1941); C. C. Griffin, *The United States and the Disruption of the Spanish Empire, 1810–1822* (New York, 1937); P. C. Brooks, *Diplomacy and the Borderlands: The Adams-Onís Treaty of 1819* (Berkeley, Calif., 1939). See also Harry Bernstein, *Origins of Inter-American Interest, 1700–1812* (Philadelphia, 1945). Older standard treatments are I. J. Cox, *The West Florida Controversy, 1798–1813* (Baltimore, 1918) and H. B. Fuller, *The Purchase of Florida* (Cleveland, 1906). The role of Secretary Adams is ably described in S. F. Bemis, *John Quincy Adams and the Foundations of American Foreign Policy* (New York, 1949), while Jackson's Florida adventure is related with zest in Marquis James, *Andrew Jackson, The Border Captain* (Indianapolis, 1933).

Useful articles are W. S. Robertson, "The United States and Spain in 1822," *Amer. Hist. Rev.*, XX (1915), 781–800; R. K. Wyllys, "The East Florida Revolution of 1812–1814," *Hispanic Amer. Hist. Rev.*, IX (1929), 415–445; W. S. Robertson, "Recognition of the Hispanic American Nations by the United

States," *ibid.*, I (1918), 239–269; J. J. Johnson, "Early Relations of the United States with Chile," *Pacific Hist. Rev.*, XIII (1944), 260–270; W. L. Neumann, "United States Aid to the Chilean Wars of Independence," *Hispanic Amer. Hist. Rev.*, XXVII (1947), 204–219.

See footnotes of this chapter; Bemis and Griffin, *Guide*, pp. 125–130, 162–189; and *Harvard Guide*, Ch. 13.

7TH ED. REFS. J. A. Logan, Jr., *No Transfer* (New Haven, 1961), Ch. 4 ("The 'Madison Doctrine' of 1811") explores Jefferson's interest in securing the Floridas and Cuba to keep them out of British hands in pursuance of the no-transfer principle. In 1811 Congress authorized Madison, in a memorable resolution, to take Florida east of the Perdido River to prevent its transfer to another European power. The same no-transfer resolution was later applied to the rest of East Florida, which was believed to be threatened by a British coup. L. S. Kaplan, "Jefferson, the Napoleonic Wars, and the Balance of Power," *William and Mary Quar.*, Ser. 3, vol. XIV (1957), 196–217 deals with Jefferson's abortive scheme to secure the Floridas through Napoleon as a reward for the embargo.

8TH ED. REFS. Bradford Perkins, *Castlereagh and Adams: England and the United States, 1812–1823* (Berkeley, Calif., 1964), shows that Castlereagh not only soft-pedaled the Jackson foray but pressured Spain, despite his preference for Spanish occupancy, to carry through the ratification of the Florida Treaty.

George Dangerfield, *The Awakening of American Nationalism, 1815–1828* (New York, 1965), has a chapter presenting the story of the Adams-Onís Treaty of 1819 and its antecedents in the larger context of the so-called Era of Good Feelings.

E. B. Billingsley, *In Defense of Neutral Rights: The United States Navy and the Wars of Independence in Chile and Peru* (Chapel Hill, 1967), notes that American officers, despite natural sympathies for the revolutionists, generally upheld American rights to commerce, particularly in opposition to paper blockades. The revolutionists were often resentful.

Maury Baker, "The Spanish War Scare of 1816," *Mid-America*, XLV (1963), 67–78, shows that serious tensions between Spain and the U.S. over such matters as the Georgia-Florida border and the attack on an American ship helped prepare the ground for the so-called Florida Treaty of 1819.

9TH ED. REFS. C. L. Egan, "The United States, France, and West Florida, 1803–1807," *Fla. Hist. Quar.*, XLVII (1969), 227–52, details Jefferson's blundering and futile efforts to secure West Florida from Spain by negotiation.

13

America and the Monroe Doctrine, 1815-1825

The American continents . . . are henceforth not to be considered as subjects for future colonization by any European powers.

PRESIDENT MONROE, 1823

MAKING THE WORLD SAFE FOR DESPOTISM

THE LONG-EXILED MONARCHS of Europe, once they had been restored to the thrones overturned by Napoleon, banded together to stamp out the dangerous democratic embers kindled by the French Revolution. In 1815 the Czar of Russia, Alexander I, devised a visionary pact known as the Holy Alliance, which he persuaded most of the sovereigns of Continental Europe to accept. This mystical union was not, properly speaking, used by these monarchs to carry out their reactionary policies. The effective military combination was the Quadruple Alliance, formed in 1815 and containing Russia, Austria, Prussia, and England. It was followed in 1818 by the Quintuple Alliance, to which France, now restored to her monarchical ways, was admitted. To avoid confusion, the term Holy Alliance will be used here, as contemporaries used it, to refer to the concert of European powers.

The fears of the re-throned despots were by no means groundless. In 1820 and 1821 a veritable rash of revolutions broke out in Spain, Portugal, Naples, and Greece. The alarmed monarchs hastened to launch repressive measures, and in 1821 Austria crushed the Italian uprisings with ferocity and dispatch. In the spring of 1823 a French army invaded Spain, and by October succeeded in restoring the depraved and vengeful Ferdinand VII to his throne. The powers then discussed plans for summoning a Paris congress which, it was rumored, would send a powerful Franco-Spanish force to the Americas to crush the new crop of republics.

Great Britain viewed with increasing dissatisfaction the savage sup pression of the rebellions in Italy and Spain, and gradually parted company with her European allies. Not only were there liberal stirrings in England, but the Ministry was alarmed by the shift in the balance of power that would result from French influence in Spain. Vastly more important were the lucrative markets of South America, once closed by Spanish monopoly, but now opened by the revolutionists to English merchants. A restoration of Spanish despotism would undoubtedly mean an abrupt cessation of this trade. The powerful British commercial groups, their appetites already whetted, were determined at all costs to prevent such a misfortune.

MONARCHY MENACES THE AMERICAS

The American people were by no means indifferent witnesses of these fateful events. At first the Holy Alliance seems to have caused little anxiety, though as early as 1816 the editor of *Niles' Weekly Register* (Baltimore) declared that it was only a mask "to blind the misguided multitude." But by mid-1821, after the powers had mopped up in Italy, America was thoroughly aroused. The Russian minister refused to attend a Fourth of July banquet because, as he reported, "some one would be sure to attack the Holy Alliance." "The Holy Alliance and the Devil," ran a contemporary American toast: "May the friends of liberty check their career, and compel them to dissolve partnership." [1]

Many apprehensive Americans began to entertain wider fears. They suspected that the forces of reaction, after having trampled on the last vestiges of liberty in Europe, would next turn to the Spanish-American republics. But would the despots be content to stop there? Why not, while they were at it, wipe out the original hotbed of democracy, which had propagated so many of their recent woes? Even if these powers did not attack America directly, they might secure Spanish-American territory and erect powerful monarchical establishments dangerously near the vitals of the United States. In the spring of 1823 the rumor was current that France would receive Cuba as a reward for assisting Spain to regain her wayward dominions.

Anxiety over the schemes of the European powers quickly spread to Washington. On November 13, 1823, following a gloomy Cabinet meeting, Secretary of State John Q. Adams wrote that Secretary of War John C. Calhoun was "perfectly moonstruck" by the success of the French invasion of Spain. As for President Monroe,

> I [Adams] find him . . . alarmed, far beyond anything that I could have
> conceived possible, with the fear that the Holy Alliance [European powers]
> are about to restore immediately all South America to Spain. Calhoun stimu-
> lates the panic, and the news that Cadiz [Spain] has surrendered to the

[1] *National Intelligencer*, June 2, 1821, 3:1 (Toast at New Haven).

French has so affected the President that he appeared entirely to despair of the cause of South America.[2]

Even Secretary Adams, who was less inclined to take an alarmist view than his colleagues, wrote, as late as November 25, 1823, that the challenge of the Alliance "is, and has been, to me a fearful question."

THE SOUTHWARD PUSH OF THE RUSSIAN BEAR

Czarist Russia also darkened the diplomatic picture on the northwest coast of North America. Late in the 18th Century and early in the 19th,

The West and Northwest 1819 ~ 1824

[2] C. F. Adams, ed., *Memoirs of John Quincy Adams* (Philadelphia, 1875), VI, 185.

adventuresome Russian traders had not only established posts in what is now Alaska but had pushed down into Spanish California. In 1812 they constructed rough-hewn Fort Ross, north of San Francisco and near the mouth of the present Russian River. At the same time American fur traders—"Boston men"—had been sailing along the Alaskan coast, where they had debauched the Indians with alcohol.

Annoyed by these foreign intrusions, the Czar issued an imperial ukase, in September, 1821, warning foreign vessels not to come within one hundred Italian miles of the coast of Russian America (Alaska) north of the 51st parallel. This edict was not only an indefensible assertion of sovereignty over the high seas, but it seemed to indicate that Russia was prepared to push the southern boundary of what is now Alaska deep into the Oregon country—an area which both Great Britain and the United States then claimed jointly.

The Russian ukase, surprisingly enough, did not cause widespread alarm in the United States. The Pacific Northwest was far away; plenty of land remained nearer home; the few American traders thus affected were not important; and the real Russian menace seemed to lie in the Czar's leadership of the Holy Alliance. The editor of *Niles' Weekly Register*, though ultimately expressing some concern, remarked somewhat casually that "even if the emperor of Russia should make good his claim to the 51st degree, we *guess* that there will be a region of the country large enough left for us." [3] A rhymester, writing some months later in the same journal, was inclined to poke fun at the Czar's ukase:

> Old Neptune one morning was seen on the rocks,
> Shedding tears by the pailful, and tearing his locks;
> He cried, a *Land Lubber* has stole, on this day,
> Full four thousand miles of my ocean away;
> He swallows the *earth*, (he exclaimed with emotion),
> And then, to quench appetite, *slap* goes the *ocean;*
> Brother Jove must look out for his skies, let me tell ye,
> Or the Russian will bury them all in his belly. [4]

American public opinion may have been apathetic, but the Washington authorities could not let the Russian challenge stand. The United States, as well as Great Britain, lodged vigorous protests. Secretary Adams' blunt warning to the Russian minister in Washington was pregnant with meaning:

> I told him specially that we should contest the right of Russia to *any* territorial establishment on this continent, and that we should assume distinctly the principle that the American continents are no longer subjects for *any* new European colonial establishments. [5]

[3] *Niles' Weekly Register*, XXI, 279 (Dec. 29, 1821).
[4] *Ibid.*, XXIV, 146 (May 10, 1823).
[5] C. F. Adams, *Memoirs*, VI, 163 (July 17, 1823).

One finds here, almost word for word, the noncolonization principle that emerged in the Monroe Doctrine some four months later.

CANNING'S FLATTERING PROPOSITION

George Canning—a brilliant orator and caustic wit—brought a new outlook to the British Ministry when, in September, 1822, he became Foreign Secretary. A wily and gifted diplomatist, he was said to have been unable to drink a cup of tea without a stratagem. In August, 1823, he proposed to Richard Rush, United States Minister in London, that America join with Britain in a manifesto designed to prevent possible intervention by the European powers in the New World. The clever Briton was evidently planning a stroke in Spain's colonies that would regain the prestige that he had lost by his inability to prevent the French invasion of Spain's homeland. Later, after President Monroe had stolen his thunder, he extravagantly boasted, "I called the New World into existence to redress the balance of the Old." He thus claimed to have saved Spanish America, though not Spain, from despotism.

Even though the Monroe administration had for several years been seeking an understanding with London to safeguard the new Latin-American republics, Rush was without instructions to accept what amounted to an informal alliance with the Mother Country. But in line with previous American overtures, he hinted that the British proposal might prove acceptable if Canning would consent to recognize the Spanish-American republics—a step that powerful conservative forces in England were blocking. Upon Canning's unwillingness to rise to the bait, Rush referred the momentous issue home.

President Monroe's first reaction was rather favorable, but before making so crucial a decision, he consulted his two predecessors in the White House. The seventy-two-year old Madison and the eighty-year-old Jefferson, both of whom had once been anti-British, forthwith advised cooperation with Britain. Madison even went so far as also to urge a declaration in favor of Greek freedom.

Two years earlier, in 1821, the Greeks had revolted against Turkish tyranny. The enthusiasm for their cause which speedily sprang up in America had numerous roots. The Greeks were imitating America's revolutionary blow for liberty; they were challenging the despotic policies of the Holy Alliance; they were Christians battling against Moslem infidels; and they were the "classical creditors" of Western Civilization. The so-called "Greek fever" was further heightened by atrocity stories: the Turks reputedly collected bushels of Greek ears. Pro-Greek enthusiasm also took the form of sermons, orations, balls, mass meetings, poems, resolutions in Congress, and the solicitation of funds. Yale college students alone contributed $500.

ADAMS GOES IT ALONE

The cool-headed Secretary of State Adams was not swayed by the Greek fever or the pro-British advice of the two ex-Presidents. Intensely nationalistic and individualistic, he viewed with deep suspicion Britons bearing gifts. No blind isolationist, he was not so much opposed to associating with Britain as he was to associating under conditions in which Canning would assume the leadership and England would get the credit in Latin America, commercially and otherwise. "It would be more candid," Adams insisted in Cabinet meeting, "as well as more dignified, to avow our principles explicitly to Russia and France, than to come in as a cock-boat in the wake of the British man-of-war." [6]

Ever vigilant, Adams had other grounds for misgivings. Lurking in the Canning scheme was the suggestion that neither the United States nor Great Britain would seize any part of Spanish America. Such a pledge would tie the hands of the American people should they ever want, as they ultimately did, Texas, California, and Cuba. Canning, who was particularly nervous about the fate of Cuba, appears to have had in mind erecting a barrier against the southward surge of the Yankees. But Secretary Adams, who feared a self-denying trap, expressed his opposition forcibly and convincingly in a Cabinet meeting.

Adams also reasoned that the danger of armed intervention in Latin America by one or more of the European powers was not imminent. Although some dispute continues among historians as to a real peril, none of the powers of the Quadruple Alliance had apparently worked out a definite policy of intervention. Adams, to be sure, did not have the secret documents before him, but his ability to piece together isolated bits and make a shrewd deduction is a tribute to his statesmanship. The United States was not prepared to fight, but neither, he suspected, were the Allied powers. They did not have enough at stake. The astute Adams could therefore scoff at Calhoun's fears of intervention when he said, ". . . I no more believe that the Holy Allies will restore the Spanish dominion upon the American continent than that the Chimborazo [Ecuadorian peak 20,702 feet high] will sink beneath the ocean." [7]

Adams likewise surmised—also without full knowledge—that even if the European powers attempted to intervene, the all-powerful British navy would prevent them. The new Spanish-American markets simply had to be kept open. So whatever the Washington government did or failed to do, there would presumably be no intervention. Sheltered behind Britain's "stout wooden walls," President Monroe could safely blow a "republican blast" of defiance at all Europe. Again the discords of the

[6] C. F. Adams, *Memoirs*, VI, 179 (Nov. 7, 1823).
[7] *Ibid.*, VI, 186 (Nov. 15, 1823).

European powers—their diplomatic distresses—made possible a red-letter success in American foreign policy.

A CLOSED SEASON ON COLONIZATION

Once Adams had carried the day for his lone-wolf course, he had to grapple with the problem of how to proclaim it to the world. His suggestion that the new policy be communicated to the European foreign offices through sharp diplomatic notes did not find favor. Instead, President Monroe hit upon the scheme of launching his pronouncement as a part of his regular message to Congress. He evidently did not regard this step as a rejection of Canning's overture, but as a stop-gap warning to the Allied powers while the State Department continued its efforts to work out an acceptable joint manifesto with London.[8]

Monroe laid the first draft of his memorable message before his Cabinet on November 21, 1823. It was bold, even defiant, in tone. Adams immediately expressed alarm, particularly over the proposal to champion the Greek revolutionists. "The ground that I wish to take," he explained the next day, "is that of earnest remonstrance against the interference of the European powers by force with South America, but to disclaim all interference on our part with Europe; to make an American cause, and adhere inflexibly to that." [9]

Monroe was at first reluctant to accept Adams' clear-cut concept of the two hemispheres. But he finally concluded that meddlesome interference in the affairs of Europe would weaken his hand. He therefore changed his stirring declaration in behalf of the Greeks to a pious wish for their success, and watered down his proposed reproof of France for invading Spain.

The now famous Monroe Doctrine was embedded in the President's regular annual message to Congress, on December 2, 1823. It consisted of two widely separated passages, comprising about two printed pages out of a total of thirteen. After some preliminary remarks, Monroe alluded to the negotiations with Russia over the Northwest coast:

> In the discussion . . . the occasion has been judged proper for asserting . . . that the American continents, by the free and independent condition which they have assumed and maintain, are henceforth not to be considered as subjects for future colonization by any European powers.[10]

Monroe thus enunciated, rather incidentally, the highly significant non-colonization principle. His failure to make more of it was probably a

[8] See G. W. McGee, "The Monroe Doctrine—A Stopgap Measure," *Miss. Valley Hist. Rev.*, XXXVIII (1951), 233–250.

[9] Adams, *Memoirs*, VI, 197–198 (Nov. 22, 1823).

[10] J. D. Richardson, ed., *Messages and Papers of the Presidents* (Washington, 1896), II, 209 (Dec. 2, 1823).

result of his knowledge that the so-called Russian menace in the Northwest was not threatening, and that negotiations were proceeding smoothly regarding the Czar's ukase of 1821.

MONROE LECTURES THE POWERS

The remainder of the Monroe Doctrine appeared after an interval of seven pages which the President devoted principally to domestic affairs. The most striking passages were inspired by the rumored intervention in America of the so-called Holy Alliance.

> The political [monarchical] system of the allied powers is essentially different . . . from that of America. . . . We owe it, therefore, to candor and to the amicable relations existing between the United States and those powers to declare that we should consider any attempt on their part to extend their system to any portion of this hemisphere as dangerous to our peace and safety.[11]

Monroe then served notice:

> With the existing colonies or dependencies of any European power we have not interfered [Florida?] and shall not interfere. But with the Governments who have declared their independence . . . we could not view any interposition for the purpose of oppressing them, or controlling in any other manner their destiny, by any European power in any other light than as the manifestation of an unfriendly disposition toward the United States.[12]

Monroe concluded with a ringing restatement of the doctrine of the two hemispheres. "Our policy in regard to Europe," he said, "which was adopted at an early stage of the wars which have so long agitated that quarter of the globe, nevertheless remains the same, which is, not to interfere in the internal concerns of any of its powers. . . ."[13] In short, the United States would refrain from intervention in embroilments like the Greek war for independence. In return for this hollow act of self-denial, Europe would be expected to keep its hands off the Latin-American wars for independence.

Monroe's basic ideas, grounded as they were on security and self-defense, were neither novel nor original. A possible exception would be the implication, here officially voiced for the first time, that the United States would fight to defend the Spanish-American republics. But this commitment in turn was inspired by self-defense. The essential ideas of the Monroe Doctrine go back deep into the colonial period, and they had been repeatedly foreshadowed, if not definitely formulated, by George Washington, John Adams, Thomas Jefferson and other Founding Fathers. Monroe, so to speak, merely codified existing ideas like those of

[11] *Ibid.*, p. 218.
[12] *Ibid.*
[13] *Ibid.*, pp. 218–219.

the two hemispheres, no transfer of territory, nonintervention, and non-entanglement. The President was ably assisted by John Quincy Adams, who contributed so much to the formulation of the Doctrine, especially the noncolonization dictum, that he has often been referred to as its real author. Actually, the credit should be about equally divided between the two men.

THE COMMENDATION OF MONROE

The American people on the whole responded favorably to Monroe's manifesto. The commercial world was especially gratified by this assurance that the Spanish-American markets would not be slammed shut. More than that, the doctrine was intoxicating to the national spirit. The upstart young republic, the strongest independent power in America, had hurled defiance into the teeth of a despotic Europe. Nothing could better illustrate the rising tide of nationalism. Speaking from a capital burned by the British invader only nine years before, and backed by only a tiny army and navy, the American government was proclaiming its ability to repulse the European allies should they challenge Monroe's pretensions. "If the Holy Alliance [Quadruple Alliance] attempt to control the destinies of South America," remarked the *Boston Centinel*, "they will find not only a [British] lion, but an [American] eagle in the way." [14]

The American press, which had feared European intervention, teemed with self-confident, exulting words of praise. The *Eastern Argus* (Portland, Maine) observed that Monroe's message "has been received throughout the country with a warm and universal burst of applause." One Congressman remarked that the new doctrine was "as wise as it was magnanimous." At least two state legislatures passed commendatory resolutions. Perhaps the most trustworthy general observation was that of the British *chargé* in Washington:

> The President's message . . . seems to have been received with acclamation throughout the United States. . . . The explicit and manly tone . . . has evidently found in every bosom a chord which vibrates in strict unison with the sentiments so conveyed. They have been echoed from one end of the Union to the other. It would, indeed, be difficult, in a country composed of elements so various . . . to find more perfect unanimity than has been displayed on every side. . . .[15]

But the United States, preoccupied with internal problems, was probably not so enthusiastic or unanimous as described. Here and there a dissenting voice was raised. One member of Congress found the pronouncement "rash and inconsiderate"; another "an unauthorized, un-

[14] Quoted in E. B. White, *American Opinion of France* (New York, 1927), p. 76.
[15] C. K. Webster, ed., *Britain and the Independence of Latin America, 1812-1830* (London, 1938), II, 508.

meaning, and empty menace, well calculated to excite the angry passions and embroil us with foreign nations." The *Richmond Enquirer* wanted evidence of a real danger of intervention, while a writer in the *Boston Advertiser* demanded: "Is there anything in the Constitution which makes our Government the Guarantors of the Liberties of the World? of the Wahabees? the Peruvians? the Chilese? the Mexicans or Colombians?" [16] But such criticisms were generally drowned in the widespread chorus of approval.

STEALING A MARCH ON CANNING

Public opinion in England at first reacted favorably to the "bold" American message, for Englishmen were quite content to let Monroe help pull their South-American chestnuts out of the fire. An immediate rise in Spanish-American securities reflected British appreciation of American support. The influential *London Times* applauded the "resolute policy" of the United States, and interpreted the new doctrine to mean that intervention in the Americas by the Holy Alliance would be "*a just cause of war.*" "With what satisfaction," continued the *Times*, ". . . must we receive the tidings, when they announce the intended prosecution of a policy so directly British!" [17] Britons apparently did not realize, at least at the time, that the noncolonization clause was as applicable to England as to Russia.

But Canning labored under no illusions. Annoyed because the United States had stolen his thunder and was currying favor with the Latin Americans, he perceived that the noncolonization principle could be invoked against his own country as well as against Continental Europe. The Monroe administration may indeed have had Britain's alleged designs on Cuba specifically in mind.

The attitude of Canning toward the Monroe Doctrine was based partly on his positive knowledge that the European allies would make no hostile movement. After waiting briefly for something to come of his overtures to Rush, he had taken matters into his own hands. He was confident that the French army would be used in the event of intervention, as it had been in Spain, and that Russia would not embark upon such an enterprise alone. Canning therefore brought strong pressure to bear upon Prince de Polignac, the French Ambassador in London. As a consequence, the latter signed a memorandum, on October 9, 1823, formally disclaiming any intention on the part of France to invade Spanish America. Thus, nearly two months *before* Monroe's famous message to

[16] Quoted in Dexter Perkins, *The Monroe Doctrine, 1823–1826* (Cambridge, 1927), p. 146.
[17] *London Times*, Jan. 6, 1824, 2:4.

Congress, the British Foreign Office, without Monroe's knowledge, removed the most serious remaining threat to Latin-American liberties.

Canning was not at all secretive about his intervention. Weeks before Monroe's message reached Europe, the substance of the Polignac memorandum was known in Austria, Russia, and France, and even by Minister Rush. In March, 1824, Canning published this document. He wanted the world to know that the might of Britain's fleet, and not the bombast of President Monroe, had given the death blow to any possible schemes of the European allies.

THE INDIGNATION OF THE DESPOTS

In Continental Europe the aristocrats, who viewed the Monroe message with mingled annoyance and contempt, gave vent to such epithets as "haughty," "arrogant," "blustering," and "monstrous." The principle of "America for the Americans" came as a shock to nations which for centuries had looked upon the Western Hemisphere as their own private hunting grounds. If the monarchs had been prepared to intervene, their first reaction probably would have been to do so just to put the upstart Yankee in his place.

In Austria, a ringleader of reaction, Chancellor Metternich denounced the "indecent declarations" of Monroe, while his colleague, the councilor of state, was startled by the presumption of "that new transatlantic colossus." The French minister of foreign affairs spoke jeeringly of the gulf between American pretensions and American naval power, and *L'Étoile* (Paris) responded tartly:

> Mr. Monroe, who is not a sovereign has assumed in his message the tone of a powerful monarch, whose armies and fleets are ready to march at the first signal. . . . Mr. Monroe is the temporary President of a Republic situated on the east coast of North America. This republic is bounded on the south by the possessions of the King of Spain, and on the north by those of the King of England. Its independence was only recognized forty years ago; by what right then would the two Americas today be under its immediate sway from Hudson's Bay to Cape Horn? [18]

The Russian government, though annoyed, could not have been greatly surprised by the Monroe Doctrine. During the preceding weeks Secretary Adams had presented even sharper warnings to the Russian minister in Washington. But the Czar was not frightened by the Yankee blast. Of all the European monarchs he most warmly sympathized with Spain's aspirations for the recovery of her lost domains; and with France eliminated by the Polignac pledge, he was the one most likely to embark upon an intervention. Early in 1824 he appears to have given some thought to

[18] *L'Étoile*, Jan. 4, 1824, quoted in Perkins, *Monroe Doctrine, 1823–1826*, p. 30.

doing so. But, lacking assistance from the other powers, he soon abandoned any such plans. The British navy could not be laughed aside.

In 1824, four and a half months after the birth of the Monroe Doctrine, Secretary Adams negotiated a treaty by which Russia agreed to retreat up the Northwest coast from 51° to 54° 40′—the present southernmost tip of Alaska. This withdrawal, reinforced by an Anglo-Russian treaty the next year, neatly solved the problem raised by the ukase of 1821. Some observers have concluded that the Czar, alarmed by Monroe's blunt warning, was browbeaten into this surrender. But scholars now know that even before Monroe posted his no-trespassing sign, the Russian regime, preoccupied at home and gorged with territory in Asia, had decided to pull in its horns on the American coast. The terms that the Czar granted to the United States, despite the annoying message of Monroe, merely represented a predetermined policy.

THE DISILLUSIONMENT OF LATIN AMERICA

The American people are prone to believe that the infant republics to the south were duly grateful for their rescue from the European allies by chivalrous Uncle Sam. Present knowledge of popular reactions in Spanish America is fragmentary, but in some quarters the message was greeted with rejoicing, in others with indifference, and in still others with dissatisfaction—on the whole with no more than tepid enthusiasm. Simón Bolívar, the George Washington of the recent revolutions, apparently did not regard Monroe's pronouncement as of world-shaking importance.

The United States in any event did not elbow aside its arch rival, Great Britain, as the moral and commercial leader of South America. Shortly after Monroe sent his message to Congress, the Polignac memorandum was published throughout Spanish America. The newly hatched republics speedily recognized that they had been saved from the European powers not by the paper shield of Monroe but by the oaken fleets of Britain. The leaders of Latin America also perceived that the new Monrovian policy was essentially selfish. The United States had naturally been thinking first of its own safety, and only secondarily of its neighbors.

Three of the new Latin-American republics applied to Washington for assistance, while two others, Colombia and Brazil, interpreted Monroe's message as an invitation to form an alliance against European aggression. But Secretary Adams, restrained by the traditional policy of nonentanglement, did not grasp the hands so eagerly outstretched below the border. He made it clear that the United States would not act unless there was a general European intervention and unless the British navy stood athwart the invaders. Monroe had, in short, created false hopes that he was forced to disappoint. All this did nothing to diminish the role of the British navy or to transform the cautious Yankee into a dashing Sir Galahad.

MYTHS ABOUT THE MONROE DOCTRINE

What came to be known as the Monroe Doctrine was not law, national or international, although repeated attempts were made in Congress to legalize it. It was merely a simple, unilateral, Presidential statement of foreign policy. Adams even spoke of it as a "lecture" to the powers. It did not commit subsequent administrations to any definite course. As Lord Clarendon politely remarked in the 1850's, "The Monroe Doctrine is merely the dictum of its distinguished author." He might have added, no less pointedly, that it was no stronger than the power of the United States to eject the trespasser—no bigger than America's armed forces.

The new dogma did not even need a distinguishing name. It might just as well have been called the Long-Range Self-Defense Doctrine— for that is essentially what it was. Monroe warned the European allies to keep out of Latin America, and Russia to forego further colonization, primarily because he felt that their presence would be dangerous to the peace and safety of the United States. If, at a later date, the powers should again menace the Americas, all that the State Department had to do was to base its protests on self-defense, without having to drag in Monroe's name. Yet Monroe gave definite form, as well as a global emphasis, to a fundamental foreign policy. When his successors later had to invoke the Doctrine, it carried greater weight with the American people because it had an "aura of antiquity" and because it was associated with a big name.

One question remains unanswered: Did the Monroe Doctrine prevent the dismemberment of Latin America? Even if one grants that the European allies had no concrete plans for coming, they could easily have worked them out in later months. Were they frightened away by the wide publicity given to the Monroe Doctrine? One common answer is to point to the fact that there is now vastly less European territory in the Americas than in 1823, whereas European land-grabbers after 1823 absorbed nearly all of Africa and much of Asia.

This geographical comparison must be used with caution. With the passage of time the larger republics of Latin America, protected in part by distance, were capable of putting up a stiff resistance. The European powers, moreover, established profitable commercial and financial relationships with Latin America without the need of physical conquest. Finally, during most of the 19th Century the European imperialists were too deeply preoccupied with difficulties and designs elsewhere, including the easier and richer pickings of Asia and Africa, to give much thought to

Latin America. By the time all desirable holdings had been staked out on other continents, the United States was much too powerful to be pushed aside.

The Monroe Doctrine, when first enunciated, commanded relatively little attention at home and even less respect abroad. It was not even generally known as the *Monroe* Doctrine until the 1850's. Yet by mid-century the powers were aware that such a policy existed, and that it was backed by a sturdy and growing United States. It is possible—though by no means provable—that there would be somewhat more European territory in the Americas today if the Monroe Doctrine, or some similar doctrine, had not been proclaimed. It became an increasingly potent stick behind the door.

SELECTED BIBLIOGRAPHY

Brief backgrounds appear in S. F. Bemis, *The Latin American Policy of the United States* (New York, 1943) and Dexter Perkins, *A History of the Monroe Doctrine* (Boston, 1955). The standard monograph is Dexter Perkins, *The Monroe Doctrine, 1823–1826* (Cambridge, Mass., 1927), which is somewhat modified by A. P. Whitaker, *The United States and the Independence of Latin America, 1800–1830* (Baltimore, 1941). See also S. F. Bemis, *John Quincy Adams and the Foundations of American Foreign Policy* (New York, 1949) and J. H. Powell, *Richard Rush, Republican Diplomat, 1780–1859* (Philadelphia, 1942). Special studies of consequence are J. F. Rippy, *Rivalry of the United States and Great Britain over Latin-America, 1808–1830* (Baltimore, 1929); M. A. Cline, *American Attitude toward the Greek War of Independence, 1821–1828* (Atlanta, 1930); E. H. Tatum, Jr., *The United States and Europe, 1815–1823* (Berkeley, Calif., 1936); C. A. Manning, *Russian Influence on Early America* (New York, 1953).

Helpful articles are W. C. Ford, "John Quincy Adams and the Monroe Doctrine," *Amer. Hist. Rev.,* VII (1902), 676–696; VIII (1902), 28–52; T. R. Schellenberg, "Jeffersonian Origins of the Monroe Doctrine," *Hispanic Amer. Hist. Rev.,* XIV (1934), 1–32; W. S. Robertson, "The Monroe Doctrine Abroad in 1823–1824," *Amer. Pol. Sci. Rev.,* VI (1912), 546–563; W. S. Robertson, "South America and the Monroe Doctrine, 1824–28," *Pol. Sci. Quar.,* XXX (1915), 82–105; Laura Bornholdt, "The Abbé de Pradt and the Monroe Doctrine," *Hispanic Amer. Hist. Rev.,* XXIV (1944), 201–221; T. B. Davis, Jr., "Carlos De Alvear and James Monroe: New Light on the Origin of the Monroe Doctrine," *ibid.,* XXIII (1943), 632–649; A. G. Mazour, "The Russian-American and Anglo-Russian Conventions, 1824–1825: An Interpretation," *Pacific Hist. Rev.,* XIV (1945), 303–310.

See footnotes of this chapter; Bemis and Griffin, *Guide,* pp. 189–198; and *Harvard Guide,* Ch. 13.

7TH ED. REFS. For J. A. Logan, Jr., *No Transfer* (New Haven, 1961) and other references, see BIBLIOGRAPHICAL ADDENDUM, p. 988.

8TH AND 9TH ED. REFS. See BIBLIOGRAPHICAL ADDENDUM, p. 989.

14

The Awkward Age of Diplomacy, 1825-1840

There has, indeed, rarely been a period in the history of civilized man in which the general condition of the Christian nations has been marked so extensively by peace and prosperity.
PRESIDENT JOHN QUINCY ADAMS, 1825

DIPLOMACY TAKES A BACK SEAT

THE CHRONICLE OF American foreign affairs from 1825 to 1840 is not thickly studded with striking developments. During no other period of similar length prior to 1872 does the student of diplomacy find so little of significance to record. Of the numerous explanations that may be offered, two seem basic. First, the energy of the American people was being absorbed by breath-taking internal expansion; and second, the European cockpit was so quiet as to threaten no serious involvements.

The decreasing emphasis on foreign relations called for a different type of Chief Executive. With the exception of George Washington, who had successfully held a number of quasidiplomatic posts, every one of the first six Presidents had served as an envoy to a foreign court, or as a Secretary of State, or as both. But beginning in 1829 with Andrew Jackson, the American people elevated to their highest office a succession of men who, though directors-in-chief of foreign affairs, were almost totally without experience in foreign affairs. (See Appendix C).

John Quincy Adams, the last of the seasoned diplomats to become President, entered the White House on March 4, 1825. Unhappily, he did not enjoy the success, in either the foreign or domestic theater, that his brilliant diplomatic record promised. After narrowly defeating Andrew Jackson for the Presidency, he had floundered into hot water by selecting the glamorous Henry Clay as his Secretary of State—an office then regarded as the natural steppingstone to the White House. For nearly four long years the embittered Jacksonites denounced this appointment as a "corrupt bargain"—or a scheme by which Clay had allegedly thrown his support to Adams in order to rob Jackson of the Presidency.

Abroad, Adams ran afoul of Foreign Secretary Canning. The embittered Briton could not forget Adams' lone-wolf course at the time of the Monroe Doctrine, nor could he overlook America's challenge to British influence in Latin America. Canning's hand was greatly strengthened when, late in 1824, his government belatedly recognized the Spanish-American republics. "The deed is done," he gloated, "the nail is driven, Spanish America is free; and if we do not mismanage our affairs badly, *she is English.*" Canning did not mismanage. Alert for British markets and worried about Yankee political domination, he thwarted Adams at nearly every turn. It is not surprising that when Canning died in 1827, the crusty New Englander could note the event in his diary with satisfaction.

THE TRAGICOMIC CONGRESS AT PANAMA

The flamboyant Simón Bolívar, liberator of northern South America, took the lead in 1825 in summoning a Pan-American Congress at Panama. He evidently envisioned a kind of Latin-American league of nations which would repulse any attempts by Spain at reconquest and otherwise serve the common interests of the recently freed republics. The disproportionately powerful United States was not on the original guest list but finally secured an invitation. Secretary Clay, a passionate pioneer for the Pan-American ideal, persuaded President Adams to accept. Adams then sought, unwisely and unnecessarily, Senatorial approval of his two appointees and a Congressional appropriation for their expenses.

The immediate aftermath was a stormy debate. Much of the opposition came from the Jackson men, who, smarting from the so-called Adams-Clay "corrupt bargain," left no stones unturned in their efforts to harass the administration. The acid-tongued John Randolph of Virginia became involved in a bloodless duel with Henry Clay when he sneered at the Adams-Clay combination as a "coalition . . . between the Puritan and the blackleg."

But political sniping aside, there were serious objections to participation at Panama. Prominent in the eyes of isolationist gentry was the danger of foreign entrapments. Many high-spirited Southerners also objected to the Panama Conference, primarily because they feared that Negro slavery might be discussed. The press in the north, on the other hand, was almost unanimous in favoring the Congress, for it believed that cooperation was necessary to protect American commercial interests against British competitors.

After a four-month debate in the House, Congress finally gave its grudging consent to the Panama appropriation. One of the delegates died of fever en route; the other, waiting for the unhealthful season to end, delayed his departure so long that the conference adjourned before he could start. The numerous foes of Adams rejoiced. The luckless President, after having aroused all this partisan furor, had come away empty-handed.

Meanwhile, on June 22, 1826, the Panama Congress had convened with its wagon hitched to a star. One delegate rose to ludicrous heights:

> An entire world is about to witness our labours. . . . Our names are about to be written either in immortal praise or in eternal opprobrium. Let us raise ourselves above a thousand millions of inhabitants, and may a noble pride inspire us, likening us to God himself on that day, when He gave the first laws to the Universe.[1]

Such sky-reaching pretensions were equaled only by the abysmal failure of the Congress. None of its recommendations was ever adopted; none of its projected meetings was ever held. Yet the roots of the Pan-American ideal, which was later to assume major significance, were definitely planted.

Some critics have seen in this seriocomic episode a tragic failure by the United States to seize the leadership of the American republic and alter the course of history. Such an interpretation seems unduly optimistic. Even if the two delegates had arrived in time, they could have accomplished little. And that little would have been undermined by Canning, who had a British agent at Panama, scheming to put the United States in a bad light and to bolster Britain's influence in Latin America.

ADAMS FUMBLES THE WEST INDIAN ISSUE

The once-flourishing commerce with Britain's West Indies, closed since the Americans broke loose from the Empire, again became a burning issue during Adams' administration. The British had permitted a restricted trade during the Napoleonic wars, owing to a shortage of foodstuffs, but when peace returned these concessions were withdrawn. Throughout the succeeding decade American diplomats repeatedly tried to win back these privileges. In 1817 Lord Castlereagh, who was rather kindly disposed to the United States, did offer a limited trade with the British West Indies. But the American Congress, hoping to extort more, passed retaliatory legislation, beginning in 1818. These two-edged retaliatory laws, which incidentally hurt certain producers in the United States, did annoy the British carrying trade and the West Indian planta-

[1] Quoted in H. W. V. Temperley, "The Later American Policy of George Canning," *Amer. Hist. Rev.*, XI (1906), 786; see also F. L. Reinhold, "New Research on the First Pan-American Congress Held at Panama in 1826," *Hispanic Amer. Hist. Rev.*, XVIII (1938), 342–363.

tions. In 1822 Parliament gave way to the extent of opening certain ports in the West Indies, but under such restricted conditions that the diplomatic controversy remained a running sore.

President Adams, able and experienced, inherited the West Indian tangle in March, 1825. Some four months later Parliament passed another act opening trade, but still under distasteful restrictions. Instead of promptly accepting this half loaf, Adams dallied a year, and then sent the veteran Albert Gallatin to London to win more favorable terms. The President's view was that access to the West Indian ports should be demanded as a right and not requested as a privilege.

Irked by Adams' stiff attitude, London had meanwhile withdrawn its offer completely. *Bell's Weekly Messenger,* a British publication, hoped that the Cabinet would reply with "contemptuous defiance" to the threats of the Americans "to bully us out of a policy which has been one of the main pillars of the navigation system." Canning needed no urging. He had already told Minister Gallatin in blistering terms that what Britain did with her own colonial trade was her own business.

Adams was denounced in America for having bungled an opportunity to elbow his way into the West Indian trade. The *Richmond Enquirer* employed caustic adjectives in describing "the clumsy and mischievous manner, in which the benefits of the Colonial Trade" had "been lost by the Administration." The failure of Adams' "diplomatised Administration" was, in fact, one of the most vulnerable joints in the New Englander's armor during the noisy Adams-Jackson Presidential campaign of 1828.[2]

JACKSON'S WEST INDIAN TRADE TRIUMPH

War-hero Andrew Jackson, beau ideal of the recently enfranchised masses, took over the Presidential reins in 1829. Many citizens feared that the hot-tempered general—"Old Hickory"—would speedily upset the diplomatic apple cart. Nine years earlier, when President Monroe had proposed sending him as minister to Russia, Jefferson had burst out, "Good God, he would breed you a quarrel before he had been there a month!"

In handling the West Indian dispute, surprisingly enough, Jackson curbed his violent anti-British prejudices. He requested the coveted commerce as a privilege rather than demanding it as a right. Britain was pleased by this unexpected moderation, and eventually consented to a compromise in 1830. By its terms direct trade with the West Indies was thrown open to the United States, subject to such duties as the London government chose to levy. But the trade was open, and quickly rose to $2,225,000 in one year.

[2] F. L. Benns, *The American Struggle for the British West India Carrying-Trade, 1815–1830* (Bloomington, Ind., 1923), p. 160.

American merchants and shippers rejoiced, while admirers of Jackson were elated. The *United States' Telegraph* (Washington), a supporter of the general, printed "extras" proclaiming "Honor to the President of the people's choice," and announcing that the trade which had been lost "by the blundering diplomacy of the coalition [Adams] administration" had been restored "by the upright, able, and honest administration of Andrew Jackson." ·But more than one critic, pointing to the required import duties, complained that the alleged victory was a barren one. "A few more such *bargains*," growled a Baltimore editor, "and we may lay our shipping up in dry dock."

Devotees of "Old Hickory" attributed his triumph to direct and soldierly methods, but the truth is that international events played into his hands. The stiff-necked Canning had died in 1827, and Lord Aberdeen, his successor, proved much more agreeable. As a result of unforeseen economic changes, Britain's faith in her ancient navigation laws was definitely weakening, while the demands of the British West Indies themselves for American foodstuffs and lumber played an influential role. Jackson had the good fortune to inherit the thorny West Indian problem just at the time when Britain's economic distress made possible America's diplomatic success.

THE FRENCH CLAIMS FUROR

The peppery Jackson ran much truer to form in his handling of claims against France—claims that had grown out of the wholesale seizure of American merchant ships, chiefly those confiscated under the Napoleonic decrees after 1805. The State Department's demands for compensation were finally rewarded in 1831, when the French formally agreed to pay 25 million francs in six annual installments. In March, 1833, when the first payment fell due, the Secretary of the Treasury drew a draft which the French finance minister refused to honor because the French Chambers had not appropriated the necessary funds. The attitude of the Chambers became more serious when, in April, 1834, it flatly refused to vote the first payment.

By this time Jackson was thoroughly aroused. "I know them French," he was reported to have shouted. "They won't pay unless they're made to." He decided to end all this shilly-shallying by laying the whole dispute before Congress in his annual message of December, 1834. In it he declared that if the overdue payments were not voted at the next session of the Chambers, Congress should authorize the federal government to "seize" French property.[3]

[3] Henry A. Wise records that when Jackson's advisers surreptitiously attempted to soften the wording, the President shouted, "That, sir, is not my language; it has been changed, and I will have no other expression of my own meaning than my own

A HICKORY APOLOGY

"Old Hickory," egged on by Neptune, with warships in the background, threatens King Louis Philippe of France, whose crown is about to fall off, while a group of French frogs condemn the insulting American.

New York Historical Society

Jackson's defiance caused a thrill of warlike excitement, as Democrats acclaimed the fighting words of their fighting hero. But the Whigs, especially those who faced commercial losses from war, condemned the message as "bad taste," "injudicious," "coarse and offensive," and "legalized piracy." Securities fell and marine insurance companies refused to assume risks resulting from a war with France. Jackson's Senatorial foes, led by the vengeful Henry Clay, pointed to this wild outburst as one more example of the general's unfitness for the Presidency.

The country on the whole seems to have responded favorably to "Old Hickory's" two-fisted tactics, even though the Whig opposition in the Senate helped to block defense measures. The Whig *National Gazette,* an opposition newspaper, sided with the President, declaring, "We have negotiated enough,—more than enough: we are indisputably in the right . . . and the French government in the wrong. . . . The American people will, we doubt not, ratify this sentence of the Message." [4]

JACKSON BROWBEATS THE FRENCH

Young America may have applauded Jackson's bluntness, but French sensibilities were rasped. The French minister in Washington demanded his passports and left the legation in the hands of a *chargé.* The French Chambers, stung to the quick, passed the belated appropriation, but with the proviso that the money was not to be paid until the language of the President's message was satisfactorily explained.

The very suggestion of an apology merely served to arouse Jackson further. He may not have roared, as reported, "Apologize! I'd see the whole race roasting in hell first." But the Hero of New Orleans was no man to eat his words. "France will get no apology," cried the powerful *Washington Globe,* "nothing bearing even the remotest resemblance to one." Throughout the nation excitement ran high. The slogans of the hour were: "Hurrah for Jackson!" "No explanations!" and "No apologies!"

The crisis steadily worsened to the point of a complete diplomatic rupture. In November, 1835, the United States closed its legation in Paris, and two months later, the French *chargé* in Washington, Alphonse Pageot, returned to France. Having married the daughter of one of Jackson's bosom friends, he took with him his wife and an infant son bearing the proud name of Andrew Jackson Pageot.

Both nations had now worked themselves into a dangerous corner. Neither could back down without an intolerable sacrifice of national pride. The United States bustled with vigorous naval preparations, while the Paris government dispatched a special squadron to its West Indies.

words." The confidential proofreader reported that he did not know what sulphurous profanity was until this incident occurred. H. A. Wise, *Seven Decades of the Union* (Philadelphia, 1881), p. 146.

 [4] Quoted in E. B. White, *American Opinion of France* (New York, 1927), p. 99.

Faced with this explosive prospect, Jackson attempted to make explanations without apologies in his annual message of December, 1835. But he hastened to add:

> The honor of my country shall never be stained by an apology from me for the statement of truth and the performance of duty; nor can I give any explanation of my official acts except such as is due to integrity and justice and consistent with the principles on which our institutions have been framed.[5]

When 1836 dawned, the tempers of both the Americans and the French had cooled perceptibly. Both nations were now willing to make concessions, provided that they could do so without loss of face. The deadlock was finally broken, in January, 1836, by the friendly mediation of the British. They did not want to see their ally, France, waste her strength in a fruitless war with the United States. Again Europe's distresses were operating to America's advantage. The French found that their wounded honor had been salved by rereading Jackson's "explanatory" messages, and both disputants were able gracefully to abandon their high ground. France arranged to pay the money—and Monsieur Alphonse Pageot returned to Washington with Madame Pageot and little Andrew Jackson Pageot.

Probably at no time during the uproar was war really imminent. The dispute was basically too trivial. Yet where proud peoples are involved, inflamed national honor is a dangerous combustible. At one stage Ex-President John Quincy Adams expressed the opinion that "if the two countries be saved from war, it seems as if it could only be by a special interposition of Providence."[6] Similar fears were voiced in London and Paris. But too much weight must not be given to the excited observations of contemporaries.

The excitable warrior in the White House, it seems, was unduly provocative. He did not fully realize that if the French ministry yielded too quickly on the unpopular American claims, it would be overthrown. But his tactless techniques did have the virtue of getting the money. By arousing the support of a once apathetic public opinion, he eliminated a dispute that might ultimately have caused a violent rupture. At the same time, he inspired a new respect in European capitals for the vigor of the hitherto scorned United States.

CANADA IN CONVULSION

General Jackson hand-picked as his successor Martin Van Buren, the dapper "Little Magician" from New York, who has been called a "first-

[5] J. D. Richardson, ed., *Messages and Papers of the Presidents* (Washington, 1896), III, 157, 160 (Dec. 7, 1835).
[6] See C. K. Webster, "British Mediation between France and the United States, 1834–36," *Eng. Hist. Rev.*, XLII (1927), 58–78.

class second-rate man." Before his first year in office had ended, Van Buren was bedeviled by problems arising from a rebellion in Canada engineered by a small minority of malcontents.

Many red-blooded Americans, notably in the northern states, applauded what they falsely regarded as an attempt by the Canadian people to cast off the British yoke. Hostile to monarchy anywhere, Americans flattered themselves by regarding this uprising as a second chapter of their own glorious War of Independence. Along the northern frontier, moreover, dwelt a vocal New England Puritan element which felt a powerful missionary impulse to carry the blessings of republicanism to its "benighted" Canadian neighbor.[7] But sympathy in the United States was commingled with selfishness. If, with America's help, the Canadians should succeed in winning their independence, what would be more logical than a union of the two English-speaking peoples under the Stars and Stripes?

British troops and the Canadian militia were able to crush the tiny rebel forces without serious difficulty. But south of the border the still-glowing embers of Anglophobia were fanned to a flame by sympathy for the underdog, by the failure of the insurrectionists, and by exaggerated reports of the punishment meted out to them In addition, the Panic of 1837 had thrown a large number of Americans out of work, particularly on the northern waterfront, and these tough-fisted characters were both irresponsible and desperate. Many of them, lured by promises of land ranging from 160 to 320 acres, flocked noisily to the rebel banner.

On the American side of the border the Canadian sympathizers were so numerous, and the federal officials so few, that the Washington government was unable to preserve strict neutrality. Singing the "*Marseillaise*," American citizens openly enlisted in the rebel ranks on United States soil, while mobs emptied several American arsenals and turned over their contents to the insurrectionists. The defeated William L. Mackenzie, leader of the rebellion in Upper Canada, found refuge in Buffalo, where, from his headquarters at the Eagle Tavern, he flung the insurgent banner to the breeze.

With American help, Mackenzie managed to re-establish himself on Navy Island, a small dot of land on the Canadian side of the Niagara River, a short distance above the thundering falls. A small American steamer, the *Caroline*, was engaged to carry supplies from the New York shore to the rebel rendezvous. The British were naturally angered by this unneutral assistance. On the night of December 29, 1837, a British volunteer party rowed across to the New York side, overpowered the men on board the *Caroline*, set fire to the vessel, turned it adrift, and let it sink a short distance above the falls. The Canadian loyalists and British

---

[7] W. P. Shortridge, "The Canadian-American Frontier during the Rebellion of 1837–1838," *Canadian Hist. Rev.*, VII (1926), 16.

patriots roundly applauded this daring act, while the officer responsible for it was knighted.

THE *CAROLINE* CRISIS

The *Caroline* had undeniably been engaged in unneutral activity. But the seriousness of her offense was softened by the fact that she had made only three trips to Navy Island, all on the afternoon of the day on which she was destroyed. Yet the British took the law into their own hands without even protesting to the American authorities, and without giving them an opportunity to act. Such hasty conduct would have been more defensible if the *Caroline* had been doing, or was about to do, substantial damage to the British cause. But the rebellion had already been crushed, and the steamer had carried only a negligible amount of material to the insurgents.

The destruction of an American ship in American waters by a British force, with the killing of at least one American and the wounding of others, set the border ablaze. Lurid American propaganda pictures showed the burning *Caroline*, laden with shrieking souls, plunging over the Niagara Falls. The draped body of Amos Durfee, the one known victim, was put on public display in Buffalo, and his funeral was widely advertised by coffin-shaped placards. "In recording this horrid tragedy," asserted the *Rochester Democrat*, "we dare not give utterance to our feelings; but we must say that if this outrage be not speedily avenged— not by simpering diplomacy—BUT BY BLOOD our national honor deserves the indignity it has received." [8] The British, in thus arousing a dangerous spirit of retaliation on the American side, harmed their own cause far more than a dozen *Carolines* could have done.

President Van Buren responded with a vigorous proclamation on January 5, 1838. He called upon American citizens to observe their own neutrality laws, and he summoned those who had joined the rebel banner—many had done so in anger over the *Caroline* affair—to return home. He energetically followed up this proclamation by sending General Winfield Scott to the border on a mediatory mission, and by requesting the governors of New York and Vermont to call their militia into service.

Some of the most influential Eastern newspapers, though resenting the *Caroline* raid, advised caution. The farther one traveled from the border the less condemnation one found of the British outrage. The *New York Evening Star*, the *New York Commercial Advertiser*, and the *Boston Times* told their excited countrymen bluntly that the Americans themselves were largely to blame for the explosive situation. As the *Boston*

[8] Quoted in Alastair Watt, "The Case of Alexander McLeod," *Canadian Hist. Rev.*, XII (1931), 162.

Times pointedly remarked, "It makes a vast deal of difference whose bull it was that gored the ox."

The diplomats meanwhile had unlimbered their pens. In Washington, the Secretary of State protested strongly against this "extraordinary outrage." The British minister refused to be drawn into the argument, and quite properly referred the complaint to London. But his private observations to Downing Street reveal that the "international derelict" argument, which Adams had used to justify Jackson's Florida invasion, could be turned against the United States.

Curiously enough, the *Caroline* incident aroused little interest in England, and there was only one brief reference to it in Parliament. The opinion was even voiced in certain quarters that the Mother Country would do well to cut loose completely from its Canadian liability. But the British officials continued to believe that they had acted in necessary self-defense, and they put off the demands of the United States for reparation and apology. Yet delay was probably all for the best. It gave passions an opportunity to cool and enabled both nations to weather the *Caroline* crisis without unsheathing the sword.

VIOLATIONS AND COUNTERVIOLATIONS OF NEUTRALITY

Electric tension along the border was temporarily eased by the almost complete stamping out of the Canadian rebellion early in 1838. But throughout the ensuing months a number of incendiary incidents occurred, notably the destruction of a Canadian vessel, the *Sir Robert Peel,* while plying within American jurisdiction on the St. Lawrence River. A party of disguised Americans, operating on the principle of a steamboat for a steamboat, boarded, looted, and burned the Canadian vessel, in May, 1838. To the half-dressed passengers whom they set ashore, they yelled, "Remember the *Caroline.*" [9]

Nervous excitement was further stimulated during the summer of 1838 by the organizing of Hunters' Lodges along the American side of the border from Vermont to Michigan. Their membership embraced thousands of men, with estimates running from 15,000 to 200,000. Their announced purpose was "to emancipate the British Colonies from British Thraldom." A part of their elaborate oath read: ". . . I promise, until death, that I will attack, combat, and help to destroy . . . every power, or authority, of Royal origin, upon this continent; and especially never to rest till all tyrants of Britain cease to have any dominion or footing

[9] Several weeks later the well-known British novelist, Captain Marryat, who was then visiting Canada, gave a toast complimentary to the men who had destroyed the *Caroline.* The excited people of Lewistown, New York, held a town meeting and resolved to burn all of Marryat's books that could be found. This was done with appropriate ceremony. Allan Nevins, ed., *The Diary of Philip Hone, 1828–1851* (New York, 1936), p. 323 (May 5, 1838).

whatever in North America. . . . So help me God." [10] Owing to the increasing vigilance of the federal authorities, this organization was necessarily secret, with a fantastic hierarchy of degrees and an elaborate system of secret signs, grips, badges, and passwords. In September, 1838, it elected officers for the future Canadian republic, consoling the former captain of the *Caroline* with the title of Admiral of Lake Erie.

The Hunters, who expected the Canadians to greet them as deliverers, drew up a number of schemes for invasion. General Winfield Scott, a giant of a man and a gifted pacificator, did yeoman work in traveling up and down eight hundred miles of the border and using his personal influence to sooth inflamed feelings. Despite his generally successful efforts, several armed bands invaded Canada in November ("Battle of the Windmill") and December of 1838. They were easily dispersed, and a number of prisoners were shipped off to a British penal colony south of Australia. From then on the influence of the Hunters, although still considerable, quickly waned. By early 1839 the Washington officials could congratulate themselves on having the situation well in hand.

THE AFTERMATH OF THE CANADIAN UPRISING

President Van Buren has been condemned, chiefly by Canadians, for having permitted all this unneutral activity. But when one considers the many miles of border, the inflammation of the populace, the fewness of federal officials, and the inadequacy of the American neutrality laws, the administration deserves some credit for a sincere attempt to meet its international obligations.

Aside from the precautions already noted, Van Buren directed a vigorous prosecution of those citizens who had violated the neutrality laws. The highly popular "General" Rensselaer Van Rensselaer, one of the American ringleaders, was convicted by an American jury and sentenced to a year's imprisonment. Van Buren finally yielded to the pressure of 300,000 petitioners and issued a pardon, but he waited until after the Presidential election of 1840. There can be no doubt that the conscientious discharge of his duties hurt him politically. The influence of Canadian sympathizers, particularly of the Hunters, whose cry was "Woe to Martin Van Buren," contributed to his repudiation at the polls.

Britain and America were closer to the brink during these turbulent 1830's than is generally realized. Any one of a number of incidents might have provoked a war—had the two nations been looking for war. But neither had a fundamental grievance, and neither wanted a fight. What is more, London realized that Washington was making a determined

[10] Charles Lindsey, *Life and Times of William Lyon Mackenzie* (Toronto, 1862), II, 199.

attempt to restrain its overzealous citizens. Probably a clash did not come because a will to keep the peace was present on both sides.

SELECTED BIBLIOGRAPHY

A survey treatment of the period is in S. F. Bemis, ed., *The American Secretaries of State and their Diplomacy* (New York, 1928), IV, 115–343. Two background volumes are indispensable: S. F. Bemis' *John Quincy Adams and the Foundations of American Foreign Policy* (New York, 1949) and *John Quincy Adams and the Union* (New York, 1956). On the Panama Congress, consult A. P. Whitaker, *The United States and the Independence of Latin America, 1800–1830* (Baltimore, 1941); J. F. Rippy, *Rivalry of the United States and Great Britain over Latin America, 1808–1830* (Baltimore, 1929); and J. B. Lockey, *Pan-Americanism: Its Beginnings* (New York, 1920). On French claims, consult R. A. McLemore, *Franco-American Diplomatic Relations: 1816–1836* (University, La., 1941) and Marquis James, *Andrew Jackson; Portrait of a President* (Indianapolis, 1937). The best work on the Canadian rebellion is A. B. Corey, *The Crisis of 1830–1842 in Canadian-American Relations* (New Haven, 1941).

Consult also O. E. Tiffany, "The Relations of the United States to the Canadian Rebellion of 1837–1838," *Buffalo Hist. Soc. Pubs.*, VIII (1905), 1–147, and C. P. Stacey, ed., "A Private Report of General Winfield Scott on the Border Situation in 1839," *Canadian Hist. Rev.*, XXI (1940), 407–414.

See footnotes of this chapter; Bemis and Griffin, *Guide*, 238–240; and *Harvard Guide*, Chs. 13–16.

7TH ED. REFS. Henry Blumenthal, *A Reappraisal of Franco-American Relations, 1830–1871* (Chapel Hill, N.C., 1959) explores in depth the "myth of the uninterrupted historical friendship" between the two countries. There was, however, considerable popular attachment in both France and America. During these decades Paris repeatedly tried to thwart American expansion, at times fearing a union of the United States and Britain against France. The large two-way trade (cotton and silk) helped keep the peace. At the time of the Jackson-claims crisis France was concerned about the Near Eastern problem and the possibility of an American lodgment in Africa if war should come. J. A. Logan, Jr., *No Transfer* (New Haven, 1961) discusses the abortive Panama Congress of 1826, and notes that the United States would not favor the transfer (by seizure) of Cuba to Mexico or Colombia, even though they were New World nations. J. L. Mecham, *The United States and Inter-American Security, 1889–1960* (Austin, Tex., 1961) deals briefly with the Panama Congress. The future President appears as a successful minister in Moscow, negotiating the commercial treaty of 1832, in P. S. Klein, *President James Buchanan: A Biography* (University Park, Pa., 1962). Knowing that his mail was being opened, he deliberately inserted complimentary references to the Tsar. J. J. Lerski, *A Polish Chapter in Jacksonian America: The United States and the Polish Exiles of 1831* (Madison, Wis., 1958) handles the Tsar's bitter reaction to criticism in the American press at the time he crushed the Polish rebellion of 1830. The secret pro-revolutionary machinations are revealed in Oscar A. Kinchen, *The Rise and Fall of the Patriot Hunters* (New York, 1956).

9TH ED. REFS. See BIBLIOGRAPHICAL ADDENDUM, p. 989.

15

Britain and the Webster-Ashburton Treaty

The portraits of Webster and Ashburton that hang on the walls of the State Department at Washington commemorate two negotiators whose happy co-operation solved a problem the solution of which might, in the hands of lesser men, have been remitted to the sword.

JAMES BRYCE, 1914

ANGLOPHOBIA FESTERS

ILL FEELING between America and Britain neared the breaking point in the early 1840's. At bottom were the embers of 1776 and 1812, which Americans had patriotically kept alive. When the Englishman Captain Hall inspected a Boston school in 1827, a small boy was called upon to "speak" for the visitor's pleasure. The youth launched into a "furious philippic" against British tyranny. Three years later a keen-witted French traveler, Alexis de Tocqueville, concluded that he could not conceive of a hatred more poisonous than that which the American people felt for the Mother Country.

The atmosphere worsened when the Americans began to borrow large sums of money from England to finance their ambitious schemes for internal improvements. The debtor rarely cherishes a love for the coupon-clipping creditor, especially where the borrowings involve, as they did by 1839, approximately $150 million. It is not strange that during these years, and for many years to come, the phrase, "bloated British bond-holder," rolled from many an American tongue.

The lordly British, for their part, had little love for rebellious offspring whose most conspicuous traits were regarded as arrogance, swagger, patriotic conceit, and a hemispheric appetite for neighboring territory. Ever present among Britons was the jealous fear that a successful American democracy might prove an incendiary example to the inarticulate masses of England.

Another fruitful source of irritation was the absence of a copyright law in the United States to protect British writers against the flagrant borrowing of their literary product. This thievery became so intolerable that in 1836 fifty-six English authors petitioned Congress for copyright legislation, but in vain. Little wonder that the members of this influential literary guild dipped their pens in acid when writing of the United States.

Tens of thousands of sturdy Britons were lured off to America during these troubled years by the promise of a more satisfying life—"three meat meals a day," they could report. The English upper classes, unwilling to lose their underpaid factory workers, naturally tried to discourage immigration by painting America in the blackest possible hues.

The disastrous Panic of 1837 merely added fuel to the flames. It prompted more than a half-dozen American states and one territory to default on their interest payments, or openly to repudiate their obligations. The British investing public, touched on its sensitive pocket nerve, poured the vials of its wrath upon this "nation of swindlers." The London *Punch* referred to the eagle as an "unclean bird" of "the vulture tribe" which was "extremely fatal to the large species of goose called the Creditor. . . ."[1] The Reverend Sydney Smith wrote to the *London Morning Chronicle:*

> I never meet a Pennsylvanian [Pennsylvania had defaulted] at a London dinner without feeling a disposition to seize and divide him. . . . How such a man can set himself down at an English table without feeling that he owes two or three pounds to every man in the company, I am at a loss to concede; he has no more right to eat with honest men than a leper has to eat with clean men. . . .[2]

THE WAR OF WORDS WITH BRITAIN

Additional venom was provided by a steady stream of British travelers to the United States, notably in the 1830's and 1840's. They looked down their noses at the rustic scene so critically as to implant the suspicion that they were poison-pen artists hired by the British government and factory owners to frighten away emigrants.

These trans-Atlantic visitors were struck with the dirt, discomfort, and crudity of American life (pigs ran wild in the streets of New York). They lamented the general ignorance, shiftlessness, and corrupt speech— "nasal jargon." They bemoaned the money grubbing and food bolting— "gobble, gulp and go is the order of the day." They were appalled by the

[1] *Punch*, X, 238 (1846).
[2] Quoted in R. C. McGrane, *Foreign Bondholders and American State Debts* (New York, 1935), p. 59.

quarrelsomeness, godlessness, and boastfulness—"lick all creation." They were shocked by the prevalence of tobacco chewing—"the salivary propensity"—as well as by the noisy, undiscriminating and inaccurate "cataract" of juice. They were scandalized by religious revival meetings, gambling, drunkenness, fisticuffs, dueling, corruption, cattle rustling, lynching, slave-beating, and gouging—the gouging out of an opponent's eyes in free-for-all fighting. The general theme of these self-appointed critics was that America had only to be seen to be despised. The Niagara Falls were about the only sight that failed to disappoint them.

The best known of the British travelers was the beloved Charles Dickens, whose host of American admirers gave him a rousing reception in 1842. But the author of *Pickwick Papers*, smarting from the absence of a copyright law and from heavy losses in his American investments, did not view the United States through rose-colored spectacles. Although he made some pleasant observations in his *American Notes* (1842), he also described in photographic detail a number of disagreeable realities. When the Americans learned how the famous author had repaid their hospitality, they were immensely angered. "If the scamp," growled a New York merchant, Philip Hone, "had no regard for his own character, he ought to have had for ours, who made fools of ourselves to do him honor." [3] In England, the caustic Carlyle wrote gleefully that "all Yankee-doodle-dom blazed up like one universal soda bottle."

The influential British quarterlies gave a prominent place to reviews of these travel books, and their all-wise reviewers improved upon the barbs of eyewitnesses. Even when an occasional favorable feature of American life was discovered, it was treated with infuriating condescension. Sneering references were made to America's cultural advance, to the "miasma of democracy," to the "tyranny of the majority," and to the degenerate "bipeds" and "mammals" who inhabited the United States. To some of the reviewers these convict-descended Yankees were an "anarchic, godless, brutal crew," who spent their time cutting razor strops from the backs of still-living Indians. Particularly offensive to the South were the savage criticisms of slavery and the slave trade; Jefferson was even outrageously accused of selling his own ill-begotten Negro offspring under the hammer. Nothing short of maddening were the confident predictions that in time all Americans would be of mixed color.

Patriotic journals in the United States naturally sprang to the defense of their native land, and the third war with England—the "War of the Quarterlies"—was on. Fortunately, only paper broadsides were fired. The strongest American reply was to point to deficiencies in British society, including cockney English, political corruption, prize fighting, class servility, and exploitation of "wage slaves," including women and

[3] Allan Nevins, ed., *The Diary of Philip Hone* (New York, 1936), p. 673 (Oct. 12, 1843).

children. A common language may draw nations together, but in this case it was a barrier because the people of each country were able to read the offensive remarks written in the other. Ill feeling reached a dangerous peak.

One of the most potent factors working for peace was the economic interdependence of the two nations. Violent though the warmongers became on both sides, sensible men perceived that hostilities would result in disastrous commercial dislocations. The Americans were England's best customers, buying approximately 15 per cent of her total exports. The British were heavily dependent upon the United States for raw materials. Most important of all, they consumed about 50 per cent of the South's cotton crop, without which the spindles of the vital textile centers would be stilled. Each nation was thus tied to the other with threads of cotton. But even so, the diplomats could afford to make few false steps.

THE MAINE BOUNDARY IMBROGLIO

As if the dangerous incidents growing out of the Canadian rebellion of 1837 were not enough, the perennial Maine boundary dispute flared up again in 1838. Unable to reconcile the terminology of the Treaty of 1783 with realities, Great Britain and the United States had agreed in

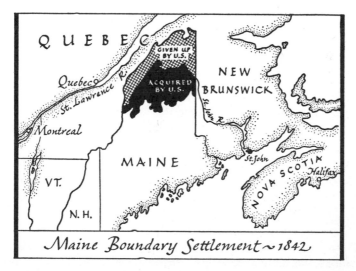

Maine Boundary Settlement ~ 1842

1827 to submit the questions at issue to the King of the Netherlands. In 1831 the royal arbitrator, finding it impossible to render a judicial decision on the basis of the evidence then available, decided upon a compromise. In the light of the ultimate settlement, the United States would have been acreage ahead if it had accepted this solution. But the people of Maine, who had expected to get much more than was awarded them, protested vehemently against the proposed loss of territory. In June, 1832, the United States Senate, responding to the outcry from Maine, refused by a vote of 21 to 20 to accept the award. The principal objection raised was that the King had made a political rather than a judicial decision.

As the year 1838 approached, England betrayed increasing interest in the disputed region. During the Canadian insurrection of 1837, as well as during the War of 1812, British troop movements had been seriously hampered by the annual freezing of the St. Lawrence River. A military road from St. John and Halifax to Quebec and Montreal seemed to be imperatively necessary. But unhappily for the cause of peace, the most practicable route ran through that part of the Maine bulge, north of the St. John River, which was claimed by the Americans.

A crisis came when, in February, 1839, a party of Canadian lumber-jacks began operations on the Aroostook River, within the disputed area. Warned to depart, they seized the American agent and stood their ground. Heavy-fisted American lumbermen moved into the no-man's land singing lustily:

> Britannia shall not rule the Maine,
> Nor shall she rule the water;
> They've sung that song full long enough,
> Much longer than they oughter.[4]

Hostilities impended as Maine called out her militia and New Brunswick did likewise. Troops nervously faced each other across a stream only thirty yards wide. The Nova Scotia legislature, amid singing of "God Save the Queen," voted war credits. The fever spread to Washington, where Congress appropriated $10 million and authorized the President to summon 50,000 volunteers. Even the mild-mannered Senator Buchanan of Pennsylvania, later President, was in a surprisingly bellicose mood:

> . . . If war must come, it will find the country unanimous. On the part of Great Britain, it will be a war of pure aggression, waged, during the pendency of peaceful negotiations. . . . In such an event, the only alternative is war or national dishonor; and between these two, what American can hesitate?[5]

The "Aroostook War" fortunately proved bloodless. President Van Buren sent to the danger zone his trusted pacificator, General Winfield Scott, who, in March, 1839, succeeded in arranging a truce during which neither side was to abandon its claims. But this dispute was potentially too explosive to be allowed to drift along indefinitely.

[4] J. T. Faris, *The Romance of the Boundaries* (New York, 1926), p. 4.
[5] *Cong. Globe,* 25 Cong., 3 sess., p. 239 (March 2, 1839).

THE STRANGE CASE OF ALEXANDER McLEOD

By the beginning of 1840 the tension in Anglo-American relations had greatly eased. Popular excitement growing out of the Canadian insurrection had largely died down. But the fat was once more thrown into the fire in November, 1840. Alexander McLeod, an unpopular Canadian deputy sheriff accused of participation in the *Caroline* raid, was arrested in New York state and imprisoned on charges of murder and arson.[6]

Great was the indignation of the British government when it learned of the arrest. The Foreign Office, now headed by the spirited Lord Palmerston, made vigorous representations to Washington. It argued that the party which had attacked the "pirates" on the *Caroline* was a regular military expedition, and that the participants, even assuming that the prisoner had been among them, could not properly be held for murder. The immediate release of McLeod was "formally demanded," and the most serious consequences were threatened should the United States refuse this request.

But Palmerston had not reckoned on the peculiarities of the American federal system. The state of New York had sole jurisdiction over the prisoner, and Washington was powerless to intervene. The federal authorities did, however, bring strong pressure to bear on New York to release McLeod, or transfer his case to a federal court. But feeling over the *Caroline* and other incidents was still too bitter to permit leniency. One member of the New York legislature insisted that "there was not power enough—there was not gold enough in Great Britain to take this man's body out of the county of Niagara, until he shall have gone through the form of a trial."[7] The state of New York therefore stood defiantly on its legal rights and went ahead with the trial.

Feeling ran dangerously high in Britain. Public opinion could not believe that in a dispute concerning foreign affairs the Washington government was not sovereign. Widely echoed was the cry of the *London Times* that McLeod must be surrendered if alive, avenged if dead. The British dockyards became ominously active. The stock market sagged. Lord Palmerston, greatly disturbed by what he regarded as an impending "judicial murder," wrote bluntly to the British minister in Washington: "McLeod's execution would produce war, war immediate and frightful in its character, because it would be a war of retaliation and vengeance."[8]

---

[6] The traditional story that McLeod boasted of his exploit while under the influence of liquor is refuted by Alastair Watt, "The Case of Alexander McLeod," *Canadian Hist. Rev.*, XII (1931), 165–167. He probably was confused with his brother, who did take part in the raid.

[7] Albany *Argus*, April 19, 1841, quoted in *Niles' Weekly Register*, LX, 135 (May 1, 1841).

[8] H. L. Bulwer and Evelyn Ashley, *The Life of Henry John Temple, Viscount Palmerston* (London, 1874), III, 49 (Palmerston to Fox, Feb. 9, 1841).

In Canada, the *Montreal Courier* hurled defiance: ". . . If war must come, let it come at once, for it is very evident unless we settle all our disputes now, it will only be putting off the evil day to a period when we may not be so well prepared to deal with our wilful and headstrong neighbors." [9]

Meanwhile McLeod, with lawyers provided by the Canadian government, went before a Utica jury. The town was full of strangers, and there was even some talk of lynching. Daniel Webster, now Secretary of State, took precautions to protect the prisoner, writing, ". . . It becomes us to take all possible care that no personal violence be used on McLeod. If a mob should kill him, War w'd be inevitable, in ten days. Of this there is no doubt." [10] Fortunately, the trial went ahead in an orderly fashion. Fortunately, also, the prosecution brought a weak and inconsistent case against McLeod, who stoutly maintained that he was five or six miles distant at the time of the raid. His alibi must have been convincing, for an American jury took only twenty minutes to return a verdict of not guilty, on October 12, 1841.

The conclusion is not warranted that McLeod's conviction would necessarily have resulted in war. London was determined to take extreme measures only in the event of his execution, not his conviction. Had the defendant been found guilty, he could have used the remaining legal expedients. As a last resort, Governor Seward of New York probably would have pardoned him—at least, so he confidentially informed Secretary Webster.

Spurred by the McLeod affair, Congress proceeded to plug this legal loophole before disaster struck. The law of 1842 provided that persons accused of crimes committed under the orders of a foreign government were to be tried in the federal courts. But there still remained abundant opportunities for the states to embroil the federal government in their treatment of aliens.[11]

LORD ASHBURTON'S SPECIAL MISSION

Even with the removal of the Canadian rebellion and the McLeod affair as active irritants, the outlook by the end of 1841 was still inauspicious. The smoldering Maine dispute might flare up again at any time; the rankling *Caroline* raid remained unatoned for. The call from the West for the sole occupation of Oregon, then held jointly with the British, was becoming more insistent.

Friction over the African slave trade was likewise generating heat. The

---

[9] *Niles' Weekly Register*, LX, 368 (Aug. 7, 1841).

[10] J. W. McIntyre, ed., *The Writings and Speeches of Daniel Webster* (National ed., Boston, 1903), XVI, 344 (Webster to Tyler, July, 1841).

[11] See the Italian Mafia affair of 1891 (p. 414) and the Japanese incidents of 1906 and 1913 (pp. 521, 547).

British, in an effort to halt this odious traffic, were attempting to establish a right to search American merchant ships in time of peace—a privilege they had hitherto claimed only in time of war. This new departure brought back bitter memories of the pre-1812 days, and proved deeply offensive to patriotic Americans.[12] The people of the South, already sensitive on the issue of the slave trade, were further aroused by an incident that occurred in November, 1841. The officers on board the *Creole*, an American ship sailing from Hampton Roads to New Orleans, were overpowered by their cargo of slaves, and one white passenger was killed. The Negroes then sought refuge in the British Bahamas. Despite the insistent demands of the owners and the outcries of Southerners generally, the British officials refused to turn the ex-slaves over to the American authorities. The actual murderers, however, were held for their crime.

The London government now decided upon unusual measures to patch up differences with America. The shift of policy was made possible when, in September, 1841, the aggressive Lord Palmerston yielded the Foreign Office to the conciliatory Lord Aberdeen. Realizing that the American tangle needed the attention of a special envoy, Aberdeen made the happy choice of Lord Ashburton. This gracious and tactful Briton, though not a professional diplomat, was distinguished in both the political and the financial world. He had visited extensively in America, where he had met the woman he later married, a wealthy Philadelphia socialite. And his numerous social and commercial connections with the United States had caused him to appreciate the desirability of cultivating cordial relations with the Americans—a course which he had conspicuously urged for many years.

The American people, on the whole, were gratified by Lord Ashburton's appointment. The sending of a special mission was in itself proof of a desire to settle outstanding disputes, while the selection of so notable and sympathetic an envoy gave promise of a lasting adjustment. As Philip Hone, a prominent New York Whig, remarked:

> This is an unusual piece of condescension on the part of our haughty elder sister. It will make Brother Jonathan feel his importance, and the devil is in it if it does not put him in a good humor. Besides the gracious nature of the act itself, the choice of the messenger of peace may be considered highly complimentary.[13]

The political auguries in America were now quite favorable. The overturn in England, which had brought Lord Aberdeen to the Foreign Office, was preceded by a Whig triumph in the United States, which had

---

[12] H. G. Soulsby, *The Right of Search and the Slave Trade in Anglo-American Relations, 1814–1862* (Baltimore, 1933), pp. 51 ff.

[13] Bayard Tuckerman, ed., *The Diary of Philip Hone* (New York, 1910), II, 110 (Jan. 24, 1842).

brought General Harrison to the Presidency and Daniel Webster to the Department of State. The new President died only a month after taking office, and Vice-President Tyler, a stiff-backed individualist, launched out on such an independent course on internal issues that he was read out of the Whig party and branded a Benedict Arnold.[14] The entire Cabinet, with the exception of Webster, resigned in protest. But the Secretary of State, then in the midst of delicate dealings with Great Britain, stayed on through two trying years.

Daniel Webster was admirably fitted by taste and talent for negotiating the pending disputes with Great Britain. Three years earlier he had visited England, where he met many of the leading British statesmen, including Lord Ashburton. His obvious intellectual power, his massive head, his masterful glance, and his distinguished bearing made a vivid impression. Sydney Smith, a merciless critic of the United States, is credited with the witticism that Webster "was a living lie, because no man on earth could be so great as he looked." Everywhere in England, the American visitor was lionized, and it is not strange that he should have returned home in a mood of sweet reasonableness toward Britain.

CARTOGRAPHICAL CONFUSION

Webster realized at the outset that he could not possibly accomplish in a few weeks of negotiation what a small army of diplomats, historians, geographers, cartographers, and surveyors had failed to do in fifty-nine years. Lord Ashburton agreed with him. Accordingly, the two men decided to sweep aside the mass of accumulated data and attempt to draw a compromise line. Without this decision there would probably have been no treaty—or at least not an acceptable one.

Lord Ashburton then proposed that the two negotiators step down out of the Olympian atmosphere which usually surrounds diplomatic negotiations, and arrive at an understanding through informal discussions rather than through a formal interchange of notes. Webster acquiesced. The result was that no minutes were kept, and the few official documents that the diplomats did exchange were largely agreed upon in advance. This arrangement undoubtedly facilitated the negotiations, although it frustrated later historians.

The boundary controversy was immensely complicated by a curious local problem. Maine until 1820 had been a part of Massachusetts, and both states had vested interests in the disputed area. Both were vehemently opposed to any concessions until fortune placed in Webster's

---

[14] At a dinner given in New York City to Lord Ashburton, a toast to the President was announced. No one stood except the British guest and his suite. When the health of the Queen was proposed, the assemblage arose and gave three cheers. C. M. Fuess, *Daniel Webster* (Boston, 1930), II, 117–118.

hand a timely and potent lever. The year before the negotiations began, Jared Sparks, a prominent American historian, had discovered a map in the French archives on which the northeastern (Maine) boundary of the United States was marked with a red line. There was some reason to believe that it had been sketched by Franklin in 1782 to indicate the frontier agreed upon by the peace commissioners. If so, the map could be used to buttress British claims to all of the Maine territory in dispute. Sparks made a copy of the map for Webster, who had himself picked up another of more dubious origin, which also strengthened the British case.

This evidence was secretly revealed to the proper Maine authorities, who at once perceived that if the settlement were further delayed, the British might learn of the maps and use them with disastrous effect. After considerable difficulty, both Maine and Massachusetts agreed in principle to accept a compromise line, and their representatives, seven all told, arrived in Washington in June, 1842, there to help hammer out details.

DIPLOMATIC HORSE TRADING

As the negotiations dragged on, the stubbornness of the state commissioners, to whom Webster was constantly forced to defer, almost unnerved Lord Ashburton. No longer young and nearly prostrated by the Turkish-bath heat of a Washington summer, he found it increasingly difficult to understand why he should be involved in a four-way negotiation. Nor could he comprehend why a presumably sovereign government had to get permission from two of its subordinate states before dealing with a matter concerning foreign affairs. As he perspiringly but good-naturedly complained to Webster:

> I contrive to crawl about in these heats by day and pass my nights in a sleepless fever. In short, I shall positively not outlive this affair, if it is to be much prolonged. I had hoped that these gentlemen from the northeast [Maine and Massachusetts] would be equally averse to this roasting. Could you not press them to come to the point, and say whether we can or cannot agree? I do not see why I should be kept waiting while Maine and Massachusetts settle their accounts with the General Government. . . . Pray save me from these profound politicians, for my nerves will not stand so much cunning wisdom.[15]

Even Webster, who was usually optimistic, became discouraged.

At last the commissioners from Maine and Massachusetts protestingly consented to a specific compromise boundary line. But they yielded only after they had been offered a number of inducements, including the payment of $150,000 to each of the two states by Washington. The puzzled

[15] G. T. Curtis, *Life of Daniel Webster* (5th ed., New York, 1889), II, 113 n. (July 1, 1842).

Ashburton objected to inserting such purely domestic stipulations into a formal treaty between two sovereign nations. Logic was on his side— but not practical politics. Webster eventually persuaded the noble Briton to acquiesce by explaining to him that such a provision was necessary to secure the votes of the Senators from Maine and Massachusetts when the treaty came before the Senate.

The boundary line as finally run through Maine permitted Canada to retain some 5000 of the 12,000 square miles of territory in dispute. The British thus secured their coveted route for a military road. To make this partition more palatable, Lord Ashburton granted free navigation of the St. John River to Maine farmers and lumbermen, conceded the major portion of the American claim to approximately 200 square miles of land near the head of the Connecticut River, and arranged for a minor terri- torial adjustment in New York state along the 45th parallel. The con-

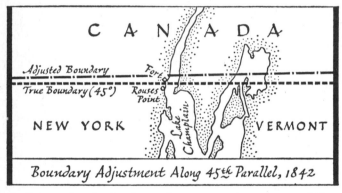

Boundary Adjustment Along 45th Parallel, 1842

troversy in this region had arisen when a recent resurvey of the northern frontier revealed that Fort Montgomery ("Fort Blunder"), which the Americans were building at Rouses Point at the head of Lake Champlain, was actually located on Canadian soil about half a mile north of the true line. Lord Ashburton agreed to let the old boundary stand. The United States thus secured a valuable strategic site, as well as a narrow strip of territory along the northern extremities of New York and Vermont.

Much farther to the west, Lord Ashburton made a valuable and often-overlooked concession to the United States. Between Lake Superior and the Lake of the Woods lay a disputed area, which was an unsettled legacy from the peace table at Ghent. In balancing off American against British claims, Lord Ashburton yielded to Webster some 6500 square miles. Unknown to the negotiators, this area contained a large part of the magnificent iron-ore deposits of Minnesota, which, later in the century, were to become one of the foundation stones of America's industrial might. In losing 5000 square miles of pine forest in Maine, while gaining 6500 square miles of priceless ore-bearing land, Webster drove an in-finitely better bargain than he or anyone else then realized.

THE STARS AND STRIPES SAFEGUARD SLAVERS

A controversy that came near wrecking the Webster-Ashburton negotiations involved the slave trade. The British, who had already abolished slavery in their colonies, were attempting to crush the inhumane African trade in "black ivory." But the greatest obstacle that they encountered was the American flag. Britain, when a belligerent, had a perfect right to search neutral merchantmen on the high seas, but in time of peace she had no such right, unless it was specifically granted to her by treaty. A number of nations had already given her permission to search suspected slavers flying their flags. But the United States, hypersensitive over a possible abuse of maritime rights, flatly refused to become a party to any such agreement. The American flag thus protected every slaver bold enough to raise it, and in some cases shielded vessels so filthy that they could actually be smelled before they were sighted coming over the horizon.

The perpetuating of the scandalous slave traffic by the unco-operativeness of the United States made for bad feeling on both sides. The British, who were forced to concede that there was no *right of search* in time of peace, attempted to establish the *right to visit* a suspected ship in order to determine its true status. But Washington insisted that there was no essential difference between the two concepts, and Lord Ashburton privately agreed.

The so-called right to visit in time of peace, many Americans feared, would inevitably become a wedge for the odious right of search and the interruption of American trade. If a British boarding officer could legally scrutinize the papers of a merchantman to determine its nationality, he would find it an easy next step to examine the cargo, and perhaps impress a few American seamen. ". . . It is not African slavery, the United States wish to encourage," wrote Minister Cass, in France. "It is . . . American slavery, the slavery of American sailors, they seek to prevent." [16] Many Southerners also feared that England, flushed by a successful attack on the slave trade, might next turn her guns on American domestic slavery.

After tedious discussions, Webster and Ashburton finally agreed to compromise on the slavery dispute. Each nation bound itself to keep a squadron, comprising a total armament of no fewer than eighty guns, on the African coast. Each would enforce its own laws against the slave trade on those merchantmen flying its flag, and both would act together when the necessity arose. Unhappily, this joint-cruising scheme did not work out satisfactorily, owing largely to the remissness of the United States in maintaining a proper police force. But the solution did relieve some of

[16] *Niles' Weekly Register*, LXII, 54 (March 26, 1842).

the current tensions. Not until 1862, twenty years later and following the secession of the slave-holding South from the Union, was the United States willing to conclude a treaty with England providing for the mutual right to search suspected slavers in time of peace. By that time slavery was doomed in the United States, and was on its way out in the rest of the Americas.

HALF-LOAF SOLUTIONS

Webster and Ashburton also took up the subject of extradition—that is, the mutual return of fugitive criminals. The recent epidemic of disorders along the northern border had been a painful reminder that the inadequate extradition provisions of Jay's Treaty had long since expired. The negotiators finally agreed to include seven extraditable offenses of a nonpolitical nature in the Webster-Ashburton Treaty. Other crimes, including embezzlement, were not to be added until many years later—a loophole which explains why "Gone to Canada" subsequently told the story of many an absconding bank clerk.

Webster and Ashburton, aside from the formal articles of the treaty, made commendable headway in dealing with pending controversies through exchanges of notes. The thorny question of the *Creole,* whose mutinous slaves had been liberated in the British Bahamas, nearly wrecked the entire negotiation.[17] Although Ashburton had come without instructions on this controversy, Webster persuaded him to go so far as to promise that the governors of British colonies would be ordered to avoid "officious interference" with American vessels driven by accident or by violence into their ports. With these assurances, which did something to quiet Southern fears, Webster was content to let the explosive issue drop. Eleven years later, in 1853, the Anglo-American Mixed Claims Commission awarded the United States $110,330 for the slave property lost.

As for the *Caroline* affair, Webster was unable to obtain complete satisfaction. The best he could do was to induce Lord Ashburton, after lengthy arguments, to express "regret" that the incident "should have disturbed the harmony" subsisting between Great Britain and America. The Briton added: "Looking back to what passed at this distance of time, what is, perhaps, most to be regretted is, that some explanation and apology for this occurrence was not immediately made. . . ."[18] A careful examination of this statement will reveal that Lord Ashburton did not apologize. But he did use the word "apology." The resourceful Web-

---

[17] W. D. Jones, "The Influence of Slavery on the Webster-Ashburton Negotiations," *Jour. of Southern Hist.,* XXII (1956), 48–58.

[18] *Webster's Writings* (National ed.), XI, 300 (Ashburton to Webster, July 28, 1842).

ster, in a reply obviously written for home consumption, indicated that his diplomatic adversary had gone further than he really had.

Secretary Webster likewise attempted to wring from Great Britain concessions on the long-dormant but vividly remembered practice of impressment. Lord Ashburton, who again revealed the willingness of the nonprofessional diplomat to discuss problems on which he had no instructions, lent a sympathetic ear. But Foreign Secretary Aberdeen insisted upon upholding the full letter of British rights. Nothing came of the interchange, except to remind the British of American sensitiveness and the Americans of British obduracy.

As for the rapidly heating Oregon dispute, both negotiators were content to sweep it under the rug. Lord Ashburton was instructed to offer the line of the Columbia River, but this was completely unacceptable to the United States. Actually, neither negotiator was as much concerned about the thorny question as he should have been. Webster was never deeply interested in the Pacific Northwest, while Ashburton doubted whether the Americans would "for many years to come make any considerable lodgement on the Pacific." Both diplomats seemed to fear that an attempt to grapple earnestly with the Oregon problem would endanger the rest of the negotiation.[19]

A SOLEMN BAMBOOZLEMENT?

Webster again made effective use of the magical Sparks map when the treaty came before the Senate. But several of the members refused to be browbeaten. Senator James Buchanan of Pennsylvania lamented that on three sides Maine was now left "naked and exposed to the attacks of our domineering and insatiable neighbor." Senator Thomas Hart Benton of Missouri, who spoke for many Western expansionists, branded the treaty a "solemn bamboozlement." Despite these outbursts, the pact was approved on August 20, 1842, only eleven days after it was signed, by a vote of 39 to 9. The news of the final ratification of the treaty by the British was greeted with salvos of artillery in New York, Brooklyn, and Jersey City, while the members of the New York Chamber of Commerce waited on Webster in a body to express their appreciation.

The chief centers of dissatisfaction in the United States were naturally Massachusetts and Maine. Loyal Maine men, especially in the eastern part of the state, regarded the treaty as a weak-kneed surrender. But certain factors combined to create an acquiescent sentiment. Among them were the "equivalents" offered by Washington, including cash payments. The New Englanders were also influenced by Webster's clever

[19] Frederick Merk, "The Oregon Question in the Webster-Ashburton Negotiations," *Miss. Valley Hist. Rev.*, XLIII (1956), 379–404.

employment of special agents,[20] and by a sense of obligation to the rest of the United States. Four years later Webster could assert with much truth that there were not fifty respectable persons in Maine who wanted to see the treaty abrogated.

THE ASHBURTON BALANCE SHEET

The Webster-Ashburton Treaty, as is inevitably true of compromises, was not completely satisfactory to either party. The Canadians assailed it because they felt, as in 1783 and 1814, that they had been sacrificed on the altar of Anglo-American amity. In England, where the settlement was greeted with considerable relief, the opposition press was highly critical of the concessions to the Yankee. The outspoken Palmerston, now out of power, launched a sensational attack in the newspapers and in Parliament against what he branded the "Ashburton capitulation." In the heat of argument he went so far as to accuse the British negotiator of having fallen under the influence of his American wife.

The opposition attacks rose to new heights when the existence of the Sparks map became known in England. Palmerston condemned Webster for his duplicity in having withheld an important piece of evidence, while at the same time professing a desire to arrive at a fair compromise. Actually, Webster's two maps were of doubtful authenticity, and he was not ethically bound to hurt his nation's case, as Ashburton conceded, by presenting questionable evidence that might have blocked any settlement.

The confusion in the so-called "Battle of the Maps" thickened when another turned up in England—one that strongly supported the American claim to the entire area in dispute. What is more, its authenticity seemed more clearly established than that of Sparks. Thus each party to the negotiation had secretly held its opponent's high card. The exhuming of the British map had somewhat the same pacifying effect on the opposition in England as the Sparks map had produced on the two American states and the Senate.

But it is unfair to speak of the Treaty of 1842 as a "capitulation" by either Webster or Ashburton. Neither negotiator capitulated; each compromised. The territorial phases of the settlement represented a balancing of claims. It is true that the cartographical evidence as to the authenticity of the British map proves that the Americans were entitled to the entire area north of Maine that Great Britain received. Neither negotiator knew this, and neither is to be blamed for not having acted on the basis of yet undisclosed evidence.

If the United States had insisted upon its full claims, there probably

---

[20] R. N. Current, "Webster's Propaganda and the Ashburton Treaty," *ibid.*, XXXIV (1947), 187–200.

would have been no treaty, and possibly there would have been war. The 5000 square miles of forested land surrendered in Maine, though desirable, were of no vital value to a sprawling United States, and, as fate ordained, this area was far less valuable than the 6500 square miles gained west of Lake Superior. If the loss of the Maine territory was the price of peace, as it may well have been, the price was not too high— though perhaps not all staunch Maine men would agree with this judgment.

FAIR ROSAMOND, OR THE ASHBURTON TREATY

The Yankee, portrayed as a slave-driving Indian, presents
Britannia with two horrible choices.
London Punch, 1842

The Webster-Ashburton Treaty had a wider significance than the adjustment of a series of current controversies. It resulted in a general clearing away of the poisonous atmosphere that had besmogged Anglo-American relations, and it facilitated the amicable settlement of other controversies that arose in the 1840's and 1850's. This happy result was possible because the two diplomats approached their common task, not in the spirit of shysters attempting to overreach each other, but in the spirit of judges seeking an equitable solution.

SELECTED BIBLIOGRAPHY

The best monograph is A. B. Corey, *The Crisis of 1830–1842 in Canadian-American Relations* (New Haven, 1941). On the "War of the Quarterlies," consult Max Berger, *The British Traveller in America, 1836–1860* (New York, 1943), and the earlier volume by Jane Mesick, *The English Traveller in America, 1785–1835* (New York, 1922). See the sketch of Webster in S. F. Bemis, ed., *American Secretaries of State and their Diplomacy* (New York, 1928), V, 3–53, and C. M. Fuess, *Daniel Webster* (2 vols., Boston, 1930). President Tyler's important role is discussed in O. P. Chitwood, *John Tyler: Champion of the Old South* (New York, 1939). On the "Battle of the Maps" and Oregon, see S. F. Bemis, *John Quincy Adams and the Foundations of American Foreign Policy* (New York, 1949).

Useful articles are Thomas Le Duc, "The Maine Frontier and the Northeastern Boundary Controversy," *Amer. Hist. Rev.*, LIII (1947), 30–41; W. D. Jones, "Lord Ashburton and the Maine Boundary Negotiations," *Miss. Valley Hist. Rev.*, XL (1953), 477–490; David Lowenthal, "The Maine Press and the Aroostook War," *Canadian Hist. Rev.*, XXXII (1951), 315–336; E. D. Adams, "Lord Ashburton and the Treaty of Washington," *Amer. Hist. Rev.*, XVII (1912), 764–782; E. D. Adams, "The British Traveler in America," *Pol. Sci. Quar.*, XXIX (1914), 244–264.

See footnotes of this chapter; Bemis and Griffin, *Guide,* pp. 280–288; and *Harvard Guide,* Ch. 16.

7TH ED. REFS. W. D. Jones, *Lord Aberdeen and the Americas* (Athens, Ga., 1958) shows that Aberdeen regarded much of Maine as a "Pine Swamp" and was eager to accept almost any terms that would not sacrifice the defense of Canada and would keep Parliament under control. Ashburton employed bribes and Aberdeen encouraged him to do so, so anxious was he to avert war. W. D. Jones, "The Influence of Slavery on the Webster-Ashburton Negotiations," *Jour. of Southern Hist.*, XXII (1956), 48–58 explains how Ashburton's desire to allay all ill feeling foundered on problems arising from slavery. R. J. Zorn, "Criminal Extradition Menaces the Canadian Haven for Fugitive Slaves, 1841–1861," *Canadian Hist. Rev.*, XXXVIII (1957), 284–294 notes that Article X of the Webster-Ashburton Treaty provided for the extradition of criminals, but the British government, under pressure from its own abolitionists, refused to permit the extradition of fugitive slaves, even when they had committed murder in effecting their escape. O. A. Kinchen, *The Rise and Fall of the Patriot Hunters* (New York, 1956) details the activities of the Hunters' Lodges during and after the Canadian insurrection of 1837. M. F. Brightfield, "America and the Americans, 1840–1860, as Depicted in English Novels of the Period," *American Literature*, XXXI (1959), 309–324 examines 2000 novels and categorizes such stereotypes as crudity, bumptiousness, and dishonesty.

8TH ED. REFS. Thomas LeDuc, "The Webster-Ashburton Treaty and the Minnesota Iron Ranges," *Jour. of Amer. Hist.*, LI (1964), 476–481, reveals that neither negotiator knew of iron ore in this area when Webster secured 6,500 square miles of its soil.

9TH ED. REFS. See BIBLIOGRAPHICAL ADDENDUM, p. 989.

16

The Oregon Dispute and Its Settlement

The Rocky mountains are mere molehills. Our destiny is onward.
CONGRESSMAN ROBERT WINTHROP, 1845

OREGON—OUTPOST OF EMPIRES

THE OREGON COUNTRY, as it had come to be called by the 1840's, was a magnificent expanse of territory embracing some half million square miles. It lay west of the Rockies and north of the 42nd Parallel, to which Spain had withdrawn following the so-called Florida (Adams-Onís) Treaty of 1819. The northern limit was the line of 54° 40', to which Russia had retreated as a result of the treaties of 1824 and 1825 with America and Britain. Translated into present-day terms, Oregon included approximately half of British Columbia, all of the states of Washington, Oregon, and Idaho, and substantial portions of Montana and Wyoming.

With Spain and Russia out of the picture, the ownership of Oregon narrowed down to Britain and the United States. The British did not press a claim to the entire area, but looked forward to an equitable division with the Americans. Britain's case was based primarily on the Nootka Convention with Spain in 1790; on the explorations of Cook, Vancouver, and Mackenzie; and on the establishment of fur-trading posts in the Oregon country. The American claims were supported by the principles of contiguity and continuity; by the Adams-Onís Treaty of 1819, which relinquished Spain's rights in Oregon to the United States; by the explorations of Captain Gray, who in 1792 penetrated the majestic river that bears the name of his ship *Columbia;* and by the famed Lewis and Clark overland expedition of 1804–1806. Finally, in 1811 the Americans had established a fur-trading post at Astoria, near the mouth of the Columbia. Although forced to sell out to their British rivals when the

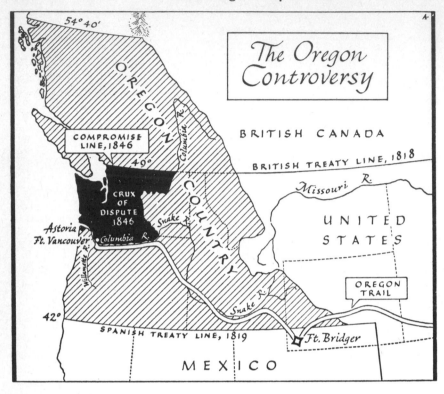

War of 1812 broke out, they regained this foothold in 1818, under the mutual-restoration provision of the Treaty of Ghent.

Obviously, neither Britain nor America had a clear legal title to the whole region in dispute. With regard to discovery and exploration, as well as to Spanish treaty rights, the claims of each nation more or less offset those of the other. But with regard to actual occupation there was little ground for dispute. By 1821 the powerful Hudson's Bay Company, a monopolistic British organization, had become commercially and politically dominant in the Oregon country.

THE OREGON FEVER

With American settlers destined to push to the Pacific, time was on the side of a fast-growing United States, and the postponement of a final division of Oregon seemed like sound strategy. In the Treaty of 1818 with Britain, the Americans refused to divide Oregon by the Columbia River. They accepted instead a ten-year agreement, under which each power had free access to the whole territory without prejudice to the claims of the other. In 1827 both parties were content to extend the so-called joint-occupation arrangement indefinitely, subject to abrogation by either on one year's notice.

Until 1840, and even later, there was a surprising amount of indifference in the United States as to the ultimate fate of Oregon. In 1825 the voluble Senator Benton of Missouri hoped that the Rocky Mountains might be the "everlasting boundary" of the republic. Even as late as 1843 Senator McDuffie of South Carolina could condemn the Oregon country: "I would not for that purpose [agricultural] give a pinch of snuff for the whole territory. I wish to God we did not own it. I wish it was an impassable barrier to secure us against the intrusion of others. . . . I thank God for his mercy in placing the Rocky Mountains there." [1] On the other hand, a few far-sighted souls were thinking of Oregon as a future vestibule to the commerce of the Orient.

By 1841 there were perhaps not more than five hundred scattered American traders, trappers, and settlers in all the Oregon country. Conspicuous among this small band were Catholic and Protestant missionaries, notably Marcus Whitman, who was finally butchered by the Indians whom he came to save. There were also a few propagandists for Oregon, men like Hall J. Kelley, who spread glowing reports of the marvelously fertile soil among people "back East."

Beginning with 1842 an increasingly large number of immigrants, victims of the so-called "Oregon fever," began to darken the Oregon Trail across the plains. Some were suffering from hard times following the Panic of 1837; some were restless adventurers; some wanted to enlarge the territorial domain of the United States by creating a new haven for the oppressed and underprivileged; some longed to snatch the rich prize of Oregon from the ancient enemy, England. But the great magnet was the fertile meadowland of the lush Willamette Valley. By 1845 the editor of the *Independence* (Missouri) *Expositor* could record with bubbling enthusiasm:

> Even while we write, we see a long train of wagons coming through our busy streets; they are hailed with shouts of welcome by their fellow voyagers, and, to judged [sic] from the pleased expression on every face, it "all goes merry as a marriage bell." . . . But they are past, and now comes team after team, each drawn by six or eight stout oxen, and such drivers! positively sons of Anak! not one of them less than six feet two in his stockings. Whoo ha! Go it boys! We're in a perfect *Oregon fever.*[2]

In this same year (1845) some 3000 immigrants made the long trek bringing the total number of Americans south of the Columbia River to approximately 5000, as compared with perhaps 700 British to the north of the river. But as yet there could be neither regular government nor valid title to the land.

[1] *Cong. Globe,* 27 Cong., 3 sess., p. 200 (Jan. 25, 1843).
[2] *Niles' Weekly Register,* LXVIII, 203 (May 31, 1845).

THE IMPENDING CRISIS

As early as 1841 the controversy over Oregon was clearly nearing a climax. In that year a bill was introduced in Congress providing for the erection of forts along the route to Oregon, and for the granting of generous acreage to each American settler there. The peppery Palmerston, flaring up in the House of Commons, declared that if the measure passed "it would be a declaration of war." But Senator John C. Calhoun was opposed to forcing the issue. He favored instead a policy of "wise and masterly inactivity," while the foot-loose and fecund frontiersman solved the problem. This was also the view of Representative Kennedy of Indiana:

> Our people are spreading out with the aid of the American multiplication table. Go to the West and see a young man with his mate of eighteen; after the lapse of thirty years, visit him again, and instead of two, you will find twenty-two. That is what I call the American multiplication table.[3]

The Oregon bill, though approved by the Senate and favored by rousing mass meetings in the Middle West, was fortunately defeated in the House early in 1843.

In 1842, as already noted, Webster and Ashburton had finally agreed to avoid the Oregon issue for fear of jeopardizing more pressing settlements. Surprisingly enough, Secretary Webster and President Tyler had proposed to yield the area north of the Columbia River, in return for British support in acquiring California from Mexico. Rumors of this proposed "surrender," coming close on the heels of the Maine "surrender," aroused the people of the West. They held numerous indignation meetings, known as "Oregon conventions," to reassert America's claim to the line of 54° 40'. The climax came in July, 1843, when the Cincinnati convention, consisting of 120 delegates from six states, issued a ringing Oregon manifesto. Senator Benton, speaking in the Senate, insisted that the dispute be settled by the pioneers:

> Let the emigrants go on; and carry their rifles. We want thirty thousand rifles in the valley of the Oregon; they will make all quiet there. . . . Thirty thousand rifles on Oregon will annihilate the Hudson's Bay Company, drive them off our continent, quiet their Indians, and protect the American interests. . . .[4]

By 1844 the deadlock over Oregon could be summarized in these words. England had repeatedly offered to compromise on the line of the Columbia. This meant that she tacitly conceded the claim of the United States to that part of Oregon which lay south of the river—the region of

[3] *Cong. Globe,* 29 Cong., 1 sess., p. 180 (Jan. 10, 1846).
[4] *Ibid.,* 28 Cong., 1 sess., p. 678 (June 3, 1844).

the fertile Willamette Valley, where nearly all the American immigrants had settled. Three times, and during two different administrations, the United States had offered to compromise on the 49th Parallel, which is the present international boundary. Thus Washington virtually acknowledged the claim of Britain to the entire area north of that line. In short, by 1845 the only region in serious dispute was the rough triangle between the Columbia River and the 49th Parallel, or approximately the northwest two-thirds of the present state of Washington. The controversy, if reduced to these terms and left to the diplomats, might have been quietly solved. But, as fate decreed, it was tossed into the noisy arena of Presidential politics.

EXPANSIONISM IN THE CAMPAIGN OF 1844

The Whigs nominated the ever-popular Henry Clay as their standard bearer in 1844. The deadlocked Democrats compromised on James K. Polk, the first "dark horse" Presidential candidate in American history. The Whig jeer, "Who is James K. Polk?" was unfair. Though a "dark horse," Polk lacked neither ability nor a program. Industrious, experienced, tenacious, and purposeful, he was an expansionist who knew what he wanted—and he got it.

The Democratic convention was remarkable not only for its candidate but also for its platform. This document screamed defiance at John Bull when it resolved:

> That our title to the whole of the Territory of Oregon is clear and unquestionable; that no portion of the same ought to be ceded to England or any other power, and that the re-occupation of Oregon and the re-annexation of Texas at the earliest practicable period are great American measures, which this Convention recommends to the cordial support of the Democracy of the Union.[5]

In the light of this extravagant claim, one should note that few, if any, responsible Americans had ever maintained that the United States had a clear title to the "whole" of Oregon up to 54° 40'. One should further observe that the Texas and Oregon questions were tied together—Siamese twins as it were—in the same plank. The explanation is simple. The Southern wing of the Democratic party demanded Texas, which was an attractive field for slavery expansion. The Northern wing demanded Oregon, which was a prospective area for free-soil. The platform represented a compromise.

The issues of expansion gave free rein to the imagination of young America, although the more prosaic tariff question proved to be important in the campaign. Tens of thousands of lusty throats raised such cries

[5] K. H. Porter, ed., *National Party Platforms* (New York, 1924), p. 6.

as "The re-annexation of Texas and the re-occupation of Oregon." The spirit of the times was reflected in a stump speech reproduced in a New Orleans newspaper:

> Whar, I say *whar* is the individual who would give the first foot, the first outside shadow of a foot of the great Oregon? There aint no such individual. Talk about treaty occupations to a country over which the great American eagle has flown! . . . Some people talk as though they were affeerd of England. . . . Hav'nt we licked her twice, and can't we lick her again? Lick her! yes; jest as easy as a bar can slip down a fresh peeled saplin.[6]

"Manifest Destiny," the name given in the 1840's and 1850's to an upsurge of emotion that resembled a lay religion, reached its crest in the Presidential campaign of 1844. Countless citizens ardently believed that the Almighty in His infinite wisdom had "manifestly" "destined" the vigorous and procreative American people to spread their ennobling republican institutions from Panama to the North Pole, and perhaps over all South America as well. This imperialistic crusade was to be a regenerative one, for it would bring superior democratic institutions and purer blood to backward peoples. But it was not necessarily to be achieved by force. The general intoxication led men to boast of "the Universal Yankee nation," and "an ocean-bound republic"—to cause the eagle to scream and the buffalo to bellow. One impassioned spellbinder caught the spirit at the New Jersey Democratic State Convention of 1844:

> Land enough—land enough! Make way, I say, for the young American Buffalo—he has not yet got land enough; he wants more land as his cool shelter in summer—he wants more land for his beautiful pasture grounds. I tell you, we will give him Oregon for his summer shade, and the region of Texas as his winter pasture. (Applause.) Like all of his race, he wants salt, too. Well, he shall have the use of two oceans—the mighty Pacific and turbulent Atlantic shall be his. . . . He shall not stop his career until he slakes his thirst in the frozen ocean (Cheers.) [7]

It is clear that Manifest Destiny lent zest to the election of 1844, but this is about all that is clear. On the burning Texas issue, certainly the most important one in the campaign, Henry Clay tried to carry water on both shoulders, and thus placate both the slavery and antislavery elements. But such political acrobatics aroused widespread distrust and helped engineer his defeat. The election hinged on the state of New York, which gave its votes and victory to Polk by a narrow margin. Yet in view of the closeness of the contest and the multitude of domestic issues—notably the tariff, slavery, currency—the Democratic Party did not receive a clear mandate to annex either Oregon or Texas. The British, nevertheless, were sufficiently disturbed by the rising temper of the

[6] Quoted in *Niles' Weekly Register*, LXVI, 114 (April 20, 1844).
[7] *Young Hickory Banner*, October 15, 1845, quoted in A. K. Weinberg, *Manifest Destiny* (Baltimore, 1935), p. 119.

American people to propose arbitration of the Oregon question. Their offer was declined by Secretary of State Calhoun, on January 21, 1845.

BRITAIN REFUSES TO BE BULLIED

Polk may not have received a mandate from the country to take Oregon, but he was certainly bound by the Democratic platform to assert America's claims to the entire territory. Nor was he one to flinch from his responsibilities. In his forceful inaugural address, on March 4, 1845, he declared that it was his

> duty to assert and maintain by all constitutional means the right of the United States to that portion of our territory which lies beyond the Rocky Mountains. Our title to the [whole?] country of the Oregon is "clear and unquestionable," and already are our people preparing to perfect that title by occupying it with their wives and children.[8]

Polk thereupon recommended that the protection of American laws be extended over American citizens who had ventured into this far country.

Polk's inaugural pronouncement caused no great splash in an America which had been shouting "All of Oregon or none" for several months past. But in England, where Presidential messages were regarded as formal state papers rather than manifestoes of republicanism, Polk's declaration was regarded as a defiant challenge. It was one thing to proclaim extravagant pretensions in a political platform; it was another to announce them to the world with the solemnity of an inaugural address. This latest "Yankee bluster" was looked upon as an attempt to bully Britain out of her rights, and the British press bristled up in instant denunciation. "It is the *manner,* not the matter in dispute, that is offensive," declared one journal.

Jingoism had its day on both sides of the Atlantic. There were ominous reports of British naval preparations. The powerful *London Times* asserted that "the territory of Oregon will never be wrested from the British Crown, to which it belongs, but by WAR." Foreign Secretary Aberdeen, though disposed to be conciliatory and to regard Polk's address as a declaration for political effect, solemnly asserted in the House of Lords: ". . . We possess rights which, in our opinion, are clear and unquestionable; and, by the blessing of God, and with your support, those rights we are fully prepared to maintain." [9]

During succeeding weeks the general theme of the British press was that Oregon possessed little value, but that the "blustering attitude" of Polk should be resented. Only one important journal appears to have

[8] J. D. Richardson, *Messages and Papers of the Presidents* (Washington, 1897), IV, 381.
[9] *Hansard,* LXXIX, 124 (April 4, 1845).

believed that war with the United States would be "productive of good." The *London Times* opined that democracies found it necessary to resort to "grotesque exhibitions" of "overbearing recklessness toward foreign nations" in order to flatter the vanity of the masses, but that if Polk intended his bombast for more than home consumption, "he may rely on having before him a career of no ordinary toil, agitation, and peril."

In America, the attitude of the more extreme journals was no less determined. The *Albany Argus* insisted that "there is not the remotest possibility that our people will ever consent to surrender an acre." The *Washington Madisonian* declared:

> We calmly, cooly, and dispassionately, say to Old England, that Oregon is our property; we own it, and we shall take possession of it. We ask not whether it is valueless or otherwise; be it a sterile rock, a barren desert of pathless sand, where no green spot blesses the aching eye, no bubbling fountain cools the parched lips,—*Oregon is ours*, and we will keep it, at the price, if need be, of every drop of the nation's blood.[10]

But from the ranks of the opposition Whig party, and from conservatives in general, came less lurid expressions. The editor of *Niles' Weekly Register* asserted that war over Oregon would be one of "the most reckless and insane exhibitions that the civilized world has ever witnessed."

LOOKING THE LION IN THE EYE

President Polk, as already noted, was to some extent committed by the offers of his predecessors. Before taking a more extreme position, he decided to make one final effort at negotiation. On July 12, 1845, Secretary of State Buchanan informed the British minister in Washington, Richard Pakenham, that the United States was prepared to divide the Oregon country at the 49th Parallel. This was the fourth time that the American government had formally made such a proposition, although the three previous offers had also conceded free navigation of the Columbia to Great Britain. Pakenham should have referred this proposal, upon which hung peace or war, to London. But instead of doing so, he committed a major diplomatic blunder by flatly rejecting it on his own responsibility.

Polk now realized that tactically his position was strong. He had so far retreated from his campaign pledges as to propose the 49th Parallel— a compromise that had been bluntly refused. He now felt justified in withdrawing his offer completely, reasserting America's claim to the entire area, and insisting that "if we do have war it will not be our fault." Although Pakenham's indiscretion was promptly disavowed by the Foreign Office, and although the chastened minister made two offers of arbitration during the ensuing weeks, Polk obdurately maintained that it was

[10] *Niles' Weekly Register*, LXVIII, 184 (May 24, 1845).

Britain's turn to make some substantial concession. He recorded in his diary a conversation with a timid Congressman:

> I remarked to him that the only way to treat John Bull was to look him straight in the eye; that I considered a bold & firm course on our part the pacific one; that if Congress faultered [*sic*] or hesitated in their course, John Bull would immediately become arrogant and more grasping in his demands. . . .[11]

Polk's annual message to Congress, of December, 1845, was thoroughly in accord with this uncompromising attitude. He reviewed the history of the Oregon dispute at some length, and then declared that the United States was now prepared to maintain its claim to the *whole* of Oregon. As an essential first step in this direction, he recommended giving Britain the one year's notice necessary for ending joint occupation. Meanwhile, the "patriotic pioneers" venturing into Oregon should be accorded such protection, including fortified stockades en route, as was consistent with existing treaty obligations. Polk concluded by laying down a virtual ultimatum:

> At the end of the year's notice, should Congress think it proper to make provision for giving that notice, we shall have reached a period when the national rights in Oregon must either be abandoned or firmly maintained. That they can not be abandoned without a sacrifice of both national honor and interest is too clear to admit of doubt.[12]

Nor did Polk stop here. Leaving the question of Oregon, he proceeded directly to a strong reaffirmation of the long-dormant principles of the Monroe Doctrine. He declared unequivocally that "no future European colony or dominion shall with our consent be planted or established in any part of the North American continent." Although he did not refer specifically to Oregon, the inference was unmistakable. He also had in mind checking what he suspected were British designs upon California.

Polk's surprising reference to the Monroe Doctrine was largely eclipsed by his bolder assertions regarding America's title to Oregon. Yet this resurrection of the almost forgotten principles of 1823 was one of the most significant steps in the development of the Doctrine. Henceforth it took on a new and enlarged stature.

POLITICS IN THE OREGON PICTURE

Polk's resounding message to Congress met with a generally favorable response, except for the opposition Whig party and sober men generally. One Congressman from Maine praised the President for his firm stand,

[11] M. M. Quaife, ed., *The Diary of James K. Polk* (Chicago, 1910), I, 155 (Jan. 4, 1846).
[12] Richardson, *Messages and Papers of the Presidents*, IV, 397 (Dec. 2, 1845).

and added, with a slap at Daniel Webster, "We want no more half-English half-American secretaries to barter away any other portion of our territory." Senator Hannegan of Indiana proposed as a toast for a Philadelphia banquet: "Oregon—every foot or not an inch." Shortly thereafter he delivered a masterpiece of spread-eagleism against yielding 54° 40':

> History, speaking from the sepulchre of the sainted dead, forbids it. The shades of Washington, of Adams, of Henry, and of their immortal compeers, forbid it. The still small voice of Camden and Concord forbids it. The holy blood that fell in torrents in the parched fields of Monmouth, and Camden, and the Brandywine, forbids it. . . . In the name of the past, in the name of the unborn millions whose proud fortune it will be to direct the destinies of free America—I protest here, in the face of Heaven and all men, against any dismemberment of our territory—the surrender of our principle—the sacrifice of our honor! . . . Come weal or wo, come peace or war, here I hope to stand.[13]

The wordy debate in Congress over the termination of joint occupation in Oregon continued throughout four months. Sectionalism and politics alike proved to be formidable obstacles to concerted action. The South had already acquired Texas, and its enthusiasm for America's claims to Oregon had largely evaporated. Representative Toombs of Georgia, a Whig at odds with the Democratic President, privately declared that "Mr. Polk never dreamed of any other war than a war upon the Whigs." The resolution empowering the President to terminate joint occupation finally passed Congress, and was signed on April 27, 1846.

BRITAIN BACKS DOWN

Following Polk's ringing annual message, one American editor remarked that "either England or the United States must back out of Oregon, or fight for it." This seems to have been the interpretation in Britain, for the rising war fever brought increased preparations for hostilities. Even the amiable Foreign Secretary Aberdeen told the American minister in London that the British had to consider "the possibility of a rupture with the United States."

Fortunately for peace, the domestic uproar in England acted as something of a brake on the warmongers. The nation was then being torn asunder by agitation for and against the repeal of the corn laws—that is, the tariff on grain to protect British agriculture. The potato shortage in Ireland, foreshadowing the terrible famine of 1846 and 1847, was already causing some distress. Finally, British manufacturers were heavily dependent upon America for a consuming market, and almost completely so for a supply of raw cotton.

[13] *Cong. Globe,* 29 Cong., 1 sess., p. 374 (Feb. 16, 1846).

Public sentiment in England was in a mood to favor concessions, provided that they could be made gracefully. A writer in the *Edinburgh Review* reflected a common belief when he declared that Oregon was "a

"WHAT? YOU YOUNG YANKEE-NOODLE, STRIKE YOUR
OWN FATHER?"

A British conception of the Yankee at the time of the Oregon boundary dispute. Note the belligerent attitude, unkempt hair, cigar, and slave driver's whip.

London Punch, 1846

costly, unprofitable encumbrance." Even the crestfallen Minister Pakenham, in Washington, confided to Secretary of State Buchanan with surprising frankness that "the British government would be glad to get clear of the question on almost any terms; that they did not care if the arbitrator should award the whole territory to us [United States]." [14] On the other hand, President Polk, despite the pugnacity of his annual message, was

[14] J. S. Reeves, *American Diplomacy under Tyler and Polk* (Baltimore, 1907), p. 260.

letting it be known through diplomatic channels that he would submit any reasonable proposal to the Senate.

Yet Foreign Secretary Aberdeen, despite his sincere desire for peace, found his path a thorny one. It was blocked by a need for consistency, by national honor, and by the bitterness of the opposition Whig Party. The outspoken Palmerston, a leading English Whig who had denounced the "Ashburton capitulation" in the Maine negotiation, was attacking the policy of the Tory Ministry as "resistance at home and . . . concession abroad." Obviously nothing could be done while the Whigs were keeping up their furious verbal bombardment.

At this critical juncture there occurred a political development of prime significance. In December, 1845, the Tory Ministry of Sir Robert Peel resigned. Lord John Russell, leader of the Whig opposition, was asked by Queen Victoria to form a new Ministry, but to his great humiliation found it impossible to do so. A major reason was that Palmerston's saber-rattling utterances had undermined confidence in his Whig Party. In February, 1846, therefore, Russell gave the Peel Ministry definite assurances that his followers would observe a truce while the Oregon question was being settled. With Palmerston thus muzzled, the Foreign Office under Aberdeen could seriously contemplate concession to the United States.[15]

Lord Aberdeen had meanwhile quietly begun a campaign of propaganda designed to prepare the British mind for a surrender of the Columbia River triangle. His chief instruments were leading journals and newspapers, notably the influential *London Times*. Through these mouthpieces he undertook to show that the Oregon country south of the 49th Parallel was not of vital value to Great Britain. Fortunately, the monopolistic Hudson's Bay Company had made itself unpopular in England by profiteering in furs. Fortunately, also, this was an era when the antiexpansionist "little Englanders" were vocal. The recent disorders in Canada were fresh in mind, and there was little desire to wage a war for additional territory. Moreover, British business was recovering from the economic collapse of 1837–1841, and war with America would undoubtedly produce another serious setback.[16] Finally, peace societies on both sides of the Atlantic were demanding a pacific settlement.

THE AMERICAN MULTIPLICATION TABLE WINS

It has sometimes been said that the 5000 American immigrants in Oregon guided the hand that wrote the final settlement. This is an over-

[15] Frederick Merk, "British Party Politics and the Oregon Treaty," *Amer. Hist. Rev.*, XXXVII (1932), 667–672.

[16] Frederick Merk, "British Government Propaganda and the Oregon Treaty," *ibid.*, XL (1934), 38–62.

simplification. If possession had decided the issue, the United States would have obtained no territory north of the Columbia, because there were only eight or so Americans in that whole region in 1846.[17]

But the American pioneers in the Willamette Valley did exert considerable indirect influence upon the final settlement. Some of them were "border ruffians," skilled in the use of the bowie knife and "revolving pistol." Just across the Columbia River was Fort Vancouver, a depository for the stores of that hated British monopoly, the Hudson's Bay Company. Perhaps the Americans would one day descend upon the outpost and despoil it. Faced with this menace, and also with the "trapping out" of its fur resources, the Hudson's Bay Company began, in 1845, to move its main depot from Fort Vancouver on the Columbia River to Vancouver Island. Although this shift had been decided upon several years earlier, the threat of the aggressive Americans probably hastened the initial steps.

The news of this transfer came as a godsend to the harassed Foreign Secretary Aberdeen. Until then the members of his own Cabinet had steadfastly maintained that the Columbia was the St. Lawrence of the West—an indispensable artery for the western provinces. But if the Hudson's Bay Company, which knew the country best and had the most vital stake in it, could voluntarily withdraw, the British public could hardly regard a surrender of the Columbia triangle as a serious national loss.

DUMPING OREGON ON THE SENATE

With the atmosphere now highly favorable to compromise, Downing Street prepared to move. At this point the news came to England that Washington had given courteous notice of the termination of joint occupation. Aberdeen, choosing to regard this step as a reopening of the negotiation by Polk, drew up a compromise offer of the 49th Parallel. The proposal was formally presented to Secretary Buchanan by Minister Pakenham on June 6, 1846.

Three days earlier Polk had received advance information of the British proposal, and he was "certain" that it ought to be rejected. Unpalatable to his extreme nationalism was the guarantee of free navigation of the Columbia River to the Hudson's Bay Company. But a majority of the Cabinet were strongly of the opinion that the proposed treaty, before either signed or rejected, should be referred to the Senate for *previous* advice—a most unusual procedure. If this should be done, the responsibility for accepting or rejecting the compromise would fall squarely

[17] Frederick Merk, "The Oregon Pioneers and the Boundary," *Amer. Hist. Rev.,* XXIX (1924), 683.

upon that body, and not upon the administration. Polk, apparently with some reluctance, consented.

The Senate moved with dispatch, and wisely so, for in two weeks the conciliatory Ministry of Sir Robert Peel had fallen. On June 12, 1846, after only two days of discussion, the Senators advised Polk, by a vote of 38 to 12, to accept the British proposal without change. On June 15 the treaty was formally signed as drafted, and three days later approved by the Senate, 41 to 14. The negative vote of the "fifty-four forties" is surprising, particularly since the United States was then deep in the war with Mexico. Most of the opposition came from the states of what is now the Middle West, where the feeling was strong that Polk had cravenly betrayed their interests. Senator Hannegan of Indiana and Senator Allen of Ohio delivered memorable tirades against the administration. Allen was so outraged that he resigned in protest his chairmanship of the Senate Committee on Foreign Relations.

Except for the diehards in the West, the country approved the peaceful settlement of the war-fraught question. The feeling of relief was especially strong in the commercial East. It was also shared by the South, which by this time had shepherded Texas safely into the slaveholding fold.

DID POLK CAPITULATE?

On the basis of what the London Foreign Office had repeatedly insisted upon, and on the basis of actual occupation, the Oregon settlement was a "capitulation" by England. The great triangle north of the Columbia was the price that Lord Aberdeen was willing to pay for peace, just as the Maine salient was the price that Webster was willing to pay for peace.

Polk has been branded a braggart who sounded his horn for 54° 40′, and then beat a cowering retreat. Senator Benton scoffed: "And this is the end of that great line! all gone—vanished—evaporated into thin air— and the place where it was, not to be found. Oh! mountain that was delivered of a mouse, thy name shall henceforth be fifty-four forty!" [18] The probabilities are that Polk was bluffing, for during these critical months he took no active steps to prepare for war with England.

But Polk was not so inconsistent as the final result would indicate. Committed by his predecessors, he at first offered a compromise. When it was disdainfully rejected, he returned to 54° 40′ and outwardly stayed there to the end, although privately holding the door ajar for compromise. The final settlement was ostensibly not his, but the Senate's. He might

[18] *Cong. Globe*, 29 Cong., 1 sess., pp. 852–853 (May 22, 1846).

not have given way to this extent if war with Mexico had not already broken out on the Rio Grande, and if the British had not undertaken menacing naval preparations. Senator Benton taunted Polk: ". . . Why not march up to 'Fifty-four Forty' as courageously as we march upon the Rio Grande? Because Great Britain is powerful, and Mexico is weak. . . ." [19]

The nation had given Polk no clear mandate to fight for *all* of Oregon. The Whig Party was certainly opposed to war for such an objective. Even within Polk's own Democratic following the Southern and moderate wings were content to accept the 49th Parallel. If the President had gone to war over 54° 40', he would have had a divided nation on his hands— perhaps a mutinous one. He would have been guilty of criminal folly if he had persisted in his extreme demands at the cost of war, especially when reactions in the press 'and Congress revealed that a majority of his own party would not support him in such a course. So Polk, though outwardly and technically still consistent, did the expedient thing. The result was that he got neither 54° 40' nor a fight, but something better: an advantageous settlement without spilling a drop of blood.

SELECTED BIBLIOGRAPHY

A useful survey appears in S. F. Bemis, ed., *The American Secretaries of State and their Diplomacy* (New York, 1928), V, 245–264. The role of the pioneers is stressed in M. C. Jacobs, *Winning Oregon* (Caldwell, Ida., 1938). The ablest scholarship on the subject has been provided by Frederick Merk, three of whose articles appear in the footnotes of this chapter. See also his *Albert Gallatin and the Oregon Problem* (Cambridge, 1950); "The Ghost River Caledonia in the Oregon Negotiation of 1818," *Amer. Hist. Rev.*, LV (1950), 530–551; "The Oregon Question in the Webster-Ashburton Negotiations," *Miss. Valley Hist. Rev.*, XLIII (1956), 379–404; "The Genesis of the Oregon Question," *Miss. Valley Hist. Rev.*, XXXVI (1950), 583–612; "The British Corn Crisis of 1845–46 and the Oregon Treaty," *Agricultural Hist.*, VIII (1934), 95–123. The standard work on the subject is A. K. Weinberg, *Manifest Destiny* (Baltimore, 1935).

See also the following articles: N. A. Graebner, "Maritime Factors in the Oregon Compromise, *Pacific Hist. Rev.*, XX (1951), 331–345; N. A. Graebner, "Polk, Politics, and Oregon," East Tenn. Hist. Soc. *Pubs.*, No. 24 (1952), 11–25; J. W. Pratt, "The Origin of 'Manifest Destiny,'" *Amer. Hist. Rev.*,

[19] T. H. Benton, *Thirty Years' View* (New York, 1856), II, 610. For Polk's lack of naval preparations see Harold and Margaret Sprout, *The Rise of American Naval Power*, 1776–1918 (Princeton, 1939), pp. 129–130. For evidence that British naval activity cooled Polk see J. W. Pratt, "James K. Polk and John Bull," *Canadian Hist. Rev.*, XXIV (1943), 341–349, and W. D. Jones and J. C. Vinson, " British Preparedness and the Oregon Settlement," *Pacific Hist. Rev.*, XXII (1953), 353–364. For evidence that French naval power cooled Britain, see J. S. Galbraith, "France as a Factor in the Oregon Negotiations," *Pacific Northwest Quar.*, XLIV (1953), 69–73.

XXXII (1927), 795–798; and Joseph Schafer, "The British Attitude toward the Oregon Question, 1815–1846," *ibid.*, XVI (1911), 273–299; E. A. Miles, "'Fifty-four Forty or Fight'—An American Political Legend," *Miss. Valley Hist. Rev.*, XLIV (1957), 291–309.

See footnotes of this chapter; Bemis and Griffin, *Guide,* pp. 289–330; *Harvard Guide,* Ch. 16.

7TH ED. REFS. The broad backgrounds of the Oregon question are set forth in R. A. Billington, *The Far Western Frontier, 1830–1860* (New York, 1956). A provocative new work, Frederick Merk's *Manifest Destiny and Mission in American History* (New York, 1963), argues that popular support for Manifest Destiny has been greatly exaggerated and that the mission to promote American idealism was more representative of the nation's real self. Various aspects of relevant problems are touched upon lightly in R. W. Van Alstyne, *The Rising American Empire* (New York, 1960); in Raymond Walters, Jr., *Albert Gallatin: Jeffersonian Financier and Diplomat* (New York, 1957); and in Henry Blumenthal, *A Reappraisal of Franco-American Relations, 1830–1871* (Chapel Hill, N.C., 1959), which discusses France's "premature neutrality." P. S. Klein, *President James Buchanan* (University Park, Pa., 1962), notes that Buchanan regarded himself as superior to Polk in international affairs. He not only opposed Polk annoyingly in working out a compromise on Oregon but got credit in England for the treaty. J. O. McCabe, "Arbitration and the Oregon Question," *Canadian Hist. Rev.*, XLI (1960), 308–327 concludes that the British offered arbitration because the "pine swamps" of Oregon meant little to them if they could emerge with honor; the Americans refused arbitration because they were unwilling to risk losing a part of their legitimate Pacific frontage. W. D. Jones, *Lord Aberdeen and the Americas* (Athens, Ga., 1958) believes that the dispute narrowed down not to the triangle formed by the Columbia but to Vancouver Island, the navigation of the Columbia, and other issues. The British feared American privateers even as far away as Singapore. The author thinks that Dr. Merk's earlier emphasis on the influence of British party politics is a "slur" upon Aberdeen, who thought little of Oregon and was pushed unnecessarily by Polk. N. A. Graebner, "Politics and the Oregon Compromise," *Pacific Northwest Quar.*, LII (1961), 7–14 observes that since diplomacy had reduced the dispute to the Columbia triangle, the heated political debate in Congress among Whigs, Democrats, and abolitionists confused the issue needlessly. J. H. Franklin, "The Southern Expansionists of 1846," *Jour. of Southern Hist.*, XXV (1959), 323–338 reveals that while most Southern Congressmen cooled off on Oregon after Texas was secured, a group of about twenty war-hawk Congressmen from the South clamored for all of Oregon in the national interest. These were Manifest-Destiny Americans, not narrow sectionalists.

8TH ED. REFS. See BIBLIOGRAPHICAL ADDENDUM, p. 989.

The Annexation of Texas

> *Man and woman were not more formed for union,*
> *by the hand of God, than Texas and the United*
> *States are formed for union by the hand of nature.*
> DOLLAR GLOBE, August 29, 1844

THE ATTEMPTED "RE-ANNEXATION" OF TEXAS

SECRETARY ADAMS, who had been loath to surrender Texas in the Spanish Treaty of 1819, resented the charge that he had disregarded the interests of the West. Upon becoming President in 1825, he undertook to purchase the vast region southwest of the Sabine River. Secretary of State Clay naïvely pointed out to the Mexicans, among other arguments, that if Texas were ceded to the United States, the capital of Mexico would then be situated nearer the center of Mexico. But the proud Mexicans did not care to sell, and nothing came of these feelers or of those that were renewed in 1827.

President Jackson, hoping to succeed where Adams had failed, reopened negotiations for Texas in August, 1829. Unfortunately for his plans, the United States minister to Mexico during these years was the unscrupulous and blundering Anthony Butler. Learning that $500,000 "judiciously applied" would secure Texas, Butler recommended to Jackson the employment of bribe money. On the back of one of these surprising proposals the doughty general wrote, "A. Butler. What a scamp." Yet Jackson, whose conduct in the affair was censurable, did not recall the "scamp" for over a year. By this time the Mexican government had become so outraged by his intrigues that it handed him his passports.

The tactless American offers to buy Texas were regarded in Mexico as studied insults; their repetition merely aroused deep suspicion. No Mexican government dared to sell. To do so would be to sign its own death warrant. So the fertile and sparsely populated expanse of Texas remained in the hands of a people who were not able to develop or protect it, and who were too proud to dispose of it. The stage was set for trouble.

THE AMERICANIZATION OF TEXAS

The plains of Texas lacked people, but the Spanish authorities in Mexico showed a fatal lack of discrimination when, in 1821, they arranged to grant a huge tract of land to an enterprising Missourian named Moses Austin. The understanding was that he would settle three hundred American families on it. Shortly thereafter he died, and the actual colonization was begun the next year by his son Stephen. The successful revolution in Mexico against Spanish rule gave the Mexicans an excellent opportunity to cancel the contract, but with the same fatal blindness as their predecessors, they legalized the arrangements. This was but the beginning of a series of grants that were to divert many westward-moving Americans into Texas.

Antislavery agitators in the United States later raised the cry of conspiracy. They charged that the American pioneers who pushed into Texas were parties to a gigantic and sinister plot to add new slave states to the Union. One suspicious circumstance was the fact that the great majority of these settlers came from the Southwest. But historians have found no convincing evidence of a slave-state conspiracy, and they have concluded that the exodus was but the normal and relentless course of the westward movement. This being the case, no one should have been surprised when most of the immigrants who entered Texas came from the states nearest that area. The explanation was proximity rather than conspiracy.

The westward-movement theory is further bolstered by the motives that brought the frontiersmen to Texas. On the one hand, there was the propulsion of acute economic distress produced by the Panic of 1819; on the other, the magnet of fertile, cheap, and easily accessible agricultural lands. The United States still boasted of huge unsettled areas, but the soil was generally inferior and the price was $1.25 an acre cash—at a time when there was little cash. Across the southwestern border much better land was available for about one-tenth that price or less. The *Missouri Advocate* declared in 1825 that the emigration to Texas was explained by the difference between a republic that "gives first-rate land gratis and a republic which will not sell inferior land for what it is worth." [1]

By 1835, fourteen years after the fateful Austin grant, there were about 30,000 white settlers in Texas. Most of them were hard-working, God-fearing Americans, sincerely desirous of improving their lot. But a considerable sprinkling were men who had left their country for their

[1] E. C. Barker, *Mexico and Texas, 1821–1835* (Dallas, Texas, 1928), p. 18.

country's good—frequently only a few jumps ahead of the sheriff. (G.T.T. became current slang for "Gone to Texas.") One Savannah newspaper, referring to the Australian convict colony, dubbed Texas the "Botany Bay" of the United States, while a Mexican journal branded the Texans "a horde of infamous bandits." Notable among the aggressive type were Sam Houston, who settled down and developed remarkable powers of leadership, and James Bowie, reputed inventor of the murderous eighteen-inch knife that came to be known as a "genuine Arkansas toothpick." These were not men to bow their necks to what they called a "greaser yoke."

Friction rapidly developed between the Mexicans and the Americans. The newcomers, who were required to be Roman Catholics and to become Mexican citizens, were overwhelmingly Protestants who thought of themselves as Americans dwelling in a foreign land. Offensive reminders were the convict soldiers, tariffs on goods from the United States, and belated attempts to shut the immigration floodgates. Especially worrisome was the precarious status of Negro slavery, without which the Texans could not hope to attain wealth. Finally, dictator Santa Anna attempted to establish a strongly centralized government in Mexico, at the expense of what the Texans regarded as their rights under the Mexican constitution of 1824. In 1835 the men of Texas rose in revolt.

THE TRIUMPH OF THE LONE STAR REPUBLIC

Led by General Santa Anna, an overwhelming Mexican force swarmed into Texas. At the Alamo, in San Antonio, approximately two hundred Texans held off some five thousand Mexicans for twelve days. Then, on March 6, 1836, the Americans perished to a man, including Davy Crockett, surrounded by heaps of their dead foes. Three weeks later a Texan force under James Fannin, numbering about four hundred recent volunteers from the United States, surrendered at Goliad, and over three hundred of the men were massacred in cold blood.

With the victorious Mexicans crying, "Exterminate to the Sabine!" the lone star was in danger of flickering out. Scores of panic-stricken Texan families were stampeding toward the American border. Seemingly all that Santa Anna had to do was to reach out and crush Sam Houston's disorganized force, and the rebellion would be over. But at San Jacinto, on April 21, 1836, the tiny Texan army turned furiously upon its over-confident pursuers, many of whom were enjoying their afternoon *siestas*, and with cries of "Remember the Alamo," "Remember Goliad," and "Death to Santa Anna," routed the Mexican force.[2]

The cowering Santa Anna, disguised in the uniform of a common soldier, was found hiding in the tall grass near the battlefield. Sam

[2] W. H. Callcott, *Santa Anna* (Norman, Okla., 1936), p. 136.

Houston realized that he was worth more to Texas alive than dead, so with difficulty he persuaded his followers not to take vengeance into their own hands. On May 14, 1836, the quaking dictator, obviously under duress, agreed to sign two treaties. By their terms the fighting was to cease, Mexican troops were to leave Texas, preparations were to be made for a peace commission, and Texas was "not to extend beyond the Rio Grande." The provisions of the two treaties were vague and contradictory, and the slippery Santa Anna declared, when liberated, that he had not legally bound his nation to accept anything. He was, of course, supported in this interpretation by the Mexican government.

BLOOD IS THICKER THAN NEUTRALITY

The American people viewed with intense interest the dramatic events at the Alamo and at Goliad. Always quick to espouse the cause of freedom, they sympathized all the more keenly with the Texans because most of them were Americans—fathers, brothers, uncles, cousins, sweethearts of those left behind. "Bone of our bone, and flesh of our flesh," one Congressman put it. The widely repeated stories of Mexican atrocities, exaggerated in the telling, aroused intense feeling in the United States. The Chief Justice of the Tennessee Supreme Court testified:

> The savage barbarities of murdering Fanning [*sic*] and his core [at Goliad], *after a Capitulation,* has so enraged the people of this Country, that they were raising men openly to fight St. Anna. . . . The men under 35, *and all the women,* are for having St. Anna shot, and the *Texas Eagle* planted on his capitol.[3]

Enthusiastic mass meetings on behalf of Texas were held in the larger cities throughout the United States, even in Boston, a stronghold of abolitionism. Large sums of money were subscribed and companies of volunteers were raised as far north as New York, Pittsburgh and Cincinnati. From distant Maine two men wrote that they would "fite or dye" for Texas, provided that their expenses were paid to the scene of hostilities.

But American support was not prompted solely by love of liberty. The revolutionary Texan government held out to volunteers the promise of land grants, which, in view of the mistaken belief that the "cowardly" Mexicans could not fight, were extremely tempting. On one occasion when a battalion of American volunteers was passing through an Alabama town under the banner "Texas and Liberty," a local wit in the crowd cried out that the words ought to be changed to "Texas, Liberty, and Land." The economic motive was unquestionably present.

What was the Washington government doing in the meantime? It was attempting to enforce, albeit lukewarmly, the inadequate neutrality law of 1818. But public sentiment was so overwhelmingly in favor of the

[3] J. H. Smith, *The Annexation of Texas* (New York, 1911), p. 32.

Texans that if this statute had been drafted by the angels, it would have been ineffective. Some of the federal officials were so sympathetic with the Texan cause as to connive at open violations of the law. And even if Washington had brought to trial considerable numbers of offenders, no jury would have convicted them.

But all this does not mean that the United States was absolved of all responsibility for flagrant unneutrality. Civilized governments are under moral obligation to have adequate neutrality laws and to enforce them. As the Texas revolution probably would not have succeeded without American support, Mexico had a genuine grievance against the United States. A case in point was General Gaines' detachment of United States troops, which had crossed the Texan border, ostensibly to control the Indians but actually, from the Mexican point of view, to give aid and comfort to the Texans. Yet this movement, the Americans were prepared to argue, had no demonstrable effect on the outcome of the revolution.

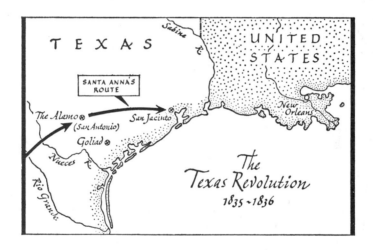

The Texas Revolution 1835-1836

SNUBBING THE BUCKSKIN REPUBLIC

With independence achieved, although not recognized by Mexico, the Texans proposed to place their vast and unprotected country beneath the familiar folds of the Stars and Stripes. The chief obstacle to annexation was the explosive slavery question. The abolitionists in the United States were already proclaiming that the revolution had been a plot by the slave aristocracy, and that the Texans were a gang of land speculators, horse thieves, and desperadoes. The *Salem* (Mass.) *Observer* asserted in 1842 that the United States had territory enough, "bad morals enough, and public debt enough, and slavery enough, without adding thereunto by such a union." In the same year William Lloyd Garrison, abolitionist editor of *The Liberator*, wrote with a gall-dipped pen:

Texas is the rendezvous of absconding villainy, desperate adventure, and lawless ruffianism—the ark of safety to swindlers, gamblers, robbers, and rogues of every size and degree. Its distinguishing characteristic is unmitigated depravity. Nothing homogeneous is found among its population, except a disposition to extend and perpetuate the most frightful form of servitude the world has ever known, and to add crime to crime.[4]

President Jackson perceived that the annexation of Texas might split the Democratic Party so badly as to make impossible the choice of Martin Van Buren as his successor. Worse still, it might disrupt the Union and goad Mexico into war. Although both houses of Congress passed resolutions favoring the recognition of Texas, Jackson advised caution. Not until the last day of his administration, nearly a year after the victory at San Jacinto and several months after Van Buren had been safely elected, did he recognize the independence of Texas. Whatever his motives, his action can hardly be described as unduly hasty.

Following recognition, the Lone Star Republic formally offered itself for annexation. But President Van Buren, already bedeviled by the Panic of 1837, had as little desire as Jackson to espouse the Texan quarrel with Mexico, or to arouse further the ominous question of slavery. The South, hoping to carve Texas into five or so slave states, enthusiastically backed annexation. But the North, speaking through resolutions passed by eight legislatures and petitions bearing some 600,000 signatures, deluged Congress with protests. In the face of this popular uprising, the proposal of annexation was somewhat frigidly rejected. For several years thereafter the American people showed little interest in Texas. They seemed to proceed on the comforting assumption that they could scoop up the infant republic whenever they were of a mind to do so.

THE BRITISH BOGEYMAN

Weary of being snubbed by the United States, the Texans tried another tack. In October, 1838, they formally withdrew their offer of annexation, and during the next six years launched out on an independent course beset with grave uncertainty and danger.

The anarchy-ridden Mexican government, blindly refusing to admit that Texas was independent, continually threatened invasion. Twice in 1842 Mexican bands sallied across the Rio Grande and fled with their booty—an unpleasant foretaste of what might be more formidable things to come. Texas had a population of perhaps 70,000; Mexico, 7,000,000. The threat of imminent chastisement from so large and vengeful a neighbor was demoralizing. The cost of maintaining an army, a navy, and a government was annually plunging the nation deeper into debt.

Spurned by Washington and unwilling to return to Mexican rule, the

---

[4] *The Liberator,* Oct. 14, 1842, 3:2.

Texans were forced to make their position more secure. Accordingly, they sent agents to Europe to work for a recognition of their independence, to negotiate treaties of commerce, and to borrow money for financing their government and developing their economy.

The Texan envoy was welcomed with open arms by the British, who recognized many advantages in an independent Texas. The already lusty United States, whose expansion England had watched with jealous alarm, would be robbed of an imperial domain. Texas—stretching, as its leaders planned, to the Pacific—would interpose a barrier against the southward expansion of the Americans. It would likewise safeguard Britain's possessions in the Caribbean and serve as a makeweight in the hemispheric balance of power against the Yankee. Brother could be turned against brother, in the hoary game of divide and conquer, while Britain would be left free to challenge the Monroe Doctrine and expand her vast empire.

The British also saw important economic advantages in an independent Texas. For one thing, it would relieve the English textile industry of its dangerous dependence upon the cotton supply of the South—a supply that might be cut off by embargo or war. An independent Texas, moreover, would sell its cotton to England and in return buy British manufactured goods. These would be carried in British ships, and presumably would enter Texan ports duty free. This lowering of trade barriers in turn would probably arouse the jealousy of the tariff-burdened Southern states, which would increase their clamor for removing the highly protective tariffs that were so offensive to British manufacturers and shipping interests.

The English abolitionists, who were a force to be reckoned with, likewise favored an independent Texas. They cherished the hope that the Lone Star Republic might be persuaded, either through gold or through a guarantee of independence, to liberate its Negro slaves. Having gained this outpost, the British abolitionists could then begin a flank attack on the citadel of slavery in the United States—a prospect most unpalatable to the Southerners. The *Washington Madisonian* burst out:

> If Great Britain . . . entertains a design . . . to interfere in any manner with the slaves of the Southern States, but a few weeks we fancy . . . will suffice to rouse the whole American People to arms like one vast nest of hornets. The great Western States . . . would pour their noble sons down the Mississippi Valley by MILLIONS.[5]

France, for her part, was no less attracted than England by some of the arguments for supporting an independent Texas. Both Paris and London formally recognized the new republic, and proceeded to conclude treaties of amity and commerce with it.

[5] *Washington Madisonian,* June 24, 1843, quoted in Smith, *Annexation of Texas,* p. 115.

POLITICS AND SLAVERY IN THE TEXAS ISSUE

Presidents Jackson and Van Buren had both shied away from the Texas question as one charged with too much political dynamite. But the unpopular President Tyler—a man without a party—was in a different position. He had everything to gain and nothing to lose by annexing Texas. Perhaps this impressive achievement would enable him to be elected in 1844 in his own right—at least, this is what his enemies accused him of conspiring to do.

The Texans had no desire to receive another rebuff at the hands of the United States. But they were assured by the Washington authorities that a two-thirds vote for an annexation treaty would undoubtedly be obtained in the Senate. On the strength of these promises, the Texans swallowed their pride and again knocked at the portals of the United States. President Sam Houston warned the aged Andrew Jackson:

> Now, my venerated friend, you will perceive that Texas is presented to the United States as a bride adorned for her espousals; but if, in the confident hope of the Union, she should be rejected, her mortification would be indescribable. She has been sought by the United States, and this is the third time she has consented. Were she now to be spurned . . . she would seek some other friend. . . .[6]

Unfortunately for Tyler's schemes, Secretary of State Upshur was killed in February, 1844, when a giant cannon on the warship *Princeton* exploded. This tragic accident not only interrupted the rather promising annexation negotiations that he had initiated but brought to the Secretaryship of State a leading Southerner, John C. Calhoun. Resentful of English abolitionist schemes in Texas, the fiery South Carolinian addressed to the British minister in Washington a vigorous defense of Negro slavery. Calhoun attempted to prove that bondage was beneficial to both master and slave by pointing to the alleged increase in deafness, blindness, and mental disorders among the ex-slaves. This indiscreet outburst, when made public, merely served to hurt the cause of annexation by further antagonizing the abolitionists and free-soil advocates in the North.

The Texas treaty was not submitted to the Senate until late in April, 1844, just on the eve of the Polk-Clay Presidential campaign. Oregon and Texas, as already noted, were leading issues, and annexation, which was bitterly opposed by the antislavery forces, became a political football. When the final vote was taken in the Senate on June 8, 1844, the treaty of the "renegade" President and his proslavery Secretary was overwhelmed by a vote of 35 to 16. Tyler was right when he predicted a two-

---

[6] *House Ex. Doc.*, 28 Cong., 1 sess., no. 271, p. 110 (Houston to Jackson, Feb. 16, 1844).

thirds majority—but the majority was on the other side. Philip Hone reflected a common Northern Whig viewpoint when he rejoiced:

> Mr. Tyler's infamous treaty, by which he hoped to rob Mexico of her province of Texas, against the consent of the people of the United States, to promote his political ends with the Southern States, at the risk of plunging the country into an unjust and discreditable war, and to force the country to assume thereby the enormous debts of a set of vagabond adventurers, has received its quietus in the Senate. . . .[7]

During the ensuing Presidential contest between the Democratic Polk and the Whig Clay, the Southerners whipped up much enthusiasm for Texas. They were determined not to be robbed of this potential gain for slavery. "Texas or disunion" shouted the "fire-eaters," while the abolitionists threatened disunion if annexation were consummated. The enfeebled Andrew Jackson observed that one might just as well "attempt to turn the courrent [sic] of the Mississippi" as to keep the Democratic Party from Texas. If other evidence were lacking as to the deadly earnestness of the South, the words of Calhoun would be convincing:

> I regard annexation to be a vital question. If lost now, it will be forever lost; and, if that, the South will be lost. . . . It is the all absorbing question, stronger even than the presidential. It is, indeed, under circumstances, the most important question, both for the South and the Union, ever agitated since the adoption of the Constitution.[8]

At a critical moment Clay attempted to straddle on the Texas issue. The purposeful Polk, who left no doubts as to his intention to take both Texas and Oregon, emerged victorious. But the campaign was so confused and the margin of victory so narrow that he can hardly be said to have received a mandate on anything, much less the annexation of Texas.

ANNEXATION BY JOINT RESOLUTION

The Texas issue was complicated by the lame-duck interlude, which lasted from November, 1844, when Polk was elected, to the following March. The discredited President Tyler still desired the honor of bringing the Lone Star Republic into the Union. His zeal was encouraged by the erroneous belief, shared by many Southerners, that the recent election had been a clear-cut mandate to annex Texas. But if Tyler waited until Polk took office, the British might succeed in snatching the rich prize. The Texan leaders cleverly took advantage of this situation by alternately playing on the fears of England and America. To the British, they hinted that annexation would be difficult to avoid; to the Americans, that ac-

---

[7] Allan Nevins, ed., *The Diary of Philip Hone, 1828–1851* (New York, 1936), p. 706.

[8] Amer. Hist. Assn., *Annual Report, 1899*, II, 585–586 (Calhoun to Mrs. T. G. Clemson, May 10, 1844).

ceptance of British-guaranteed independence was imminent. At one stage of the negotiations, Dr. Anson Jones, Texan secretary of state, slyly remarked: "I will have to give them [the United States] another *scare*. One or two doses of *English* calomel and *French* quinine will have to be administered, and the case will be pretty well out of danger." [9]

It was obviously impossible to overcome the hostile two-thirds majority in the Senate and push through another treaty. But a joint resolution, although never used to acquire foreign territory before, would require only a simple majority in both houses of Congress. So an annexation resolution passed the House of Representatives, on January 25, 1845, by a vote of 120 to 98, and the Senate on February 27, 1845, by a vote of 27 to 25. On March 1, 1845, with only three days left in office, President Tyler signed the fateful measure.

Yet annexation by joint resolution encountered last-ditch opposition. Many Whigs joined with free-soilers and abolitionists to insist that the Constitution was now a "dead-letter." "The Annexation of Texas," wrote John Jay, a descendant of the negotiator of Jay's Treaty, ". . . is a clear, deliberate, fraudulent, wicked, and irremediable violation of the Constitution. The real object of the annexation is the protection of slavery." [10] The abolitionist *Liberator* of William Lloyd Garrison proclaimed "Diabolism Triumphant" and predicted the "Overthrow of the government and Dissolution of the Union."

BRITISH STRATAGEMS

Downing Street had meanwhile been busy. In May, 1844, during the early stages of the Presidential election, Foreign Secretary Aberdeen made his first serious effort to establish a satellite in Texas. He proposed that England, France, Mexico, Texas, and the United States join in a "diplomatic act" guaranteeing the independence and the boundaries of the Lone Star Republic. But the British minister in Washington, Richard Pakenham, warned the Foreign Office to move with the utmost caution. Should Clay be elected President, as seemed likely, annexation by the United States would presumably be thwarted anyhow. On the other hand, if the news leaked out that England was about to intervene in Texas, the American people would probably rise up in their wrath and elect Polk, the expansionist.

Lord Aberdeen, who was faced also with the unwillingness of the French government to guarantee the independence of Texas, decided to postpone action until after the election. The results of the canvass revealed that to tamper with Texas was to play with fire. Aberdeen there-

---

[9] Anson Jones, *Memoranda and Official Correspondence Relating to the Republic of Texas* (New York, 1859), pp. 335–336 (Jones' memorandum of April 4, 1844).
[10] *Niles' Weekly Register,* LXVIII, 89 (April 12, 1845).

upon temporarily dropped his schemes for guaranteed Texan independence.

Late in January, 1845, London began its second serious attempt to bolster Texas. The chief theater of diplomatic activity shifted to Mexico. In May, 1845, a special British emissary finally persuaded the slow-moving Mexican Cabinet to agree to recognize the independence of Texas—with the understanding that the Lone Star Republic was to bind itself not to join any other power. But the United States Congress had meanwhile passed its joint resolution of annexation, and the Texans were more attracted by the American than the Mexican offer. Fortunately for the peace of the Americas, Aberdeen's schemes died aborning.[11]

Three snags ruined British plans. The first was France, which, though favorable to an independent Texas, was unwilling to offend the United States by supporting any pact of joint guarantee. The second snag was Mexico. Incapable of facing disagreeable realities, the Mexican government dallied with the British proposals until the time for decisive action had passed. The disgusted Aberdeen remarked to the Mexican minister in London, "You always do everything too late."

The final snag—and the most important one—was Texas herself. If Mexico had been willing to recognize the Lone Star Republic earlier, the Texans, cherishing transcontinental aspirations, might have spurned a union with the United States. But continuing Mexican hostility merely drove them nearer the American fold. When Mexico City finally made its belated concession, Texas preferred to join the United States rather than continue as a weak republic propped up by the bayonets of foreign powers.

In the summer of 1845 the Texans summoned a convention to choose between annexation to the United States and the Mexican offer of guaranteed independence. The delegates voted almost unanimously to merge their Lone Star with "the constellation of the stars and stripes." Yet this one-sided vote did not reflect considerable support for an independent course, particularly among the personally ambitious Texan officials. The president of Texas appeared to be lukewarm toward annexation, while his secretary of state was twice burned in effigy for toying with the British proposal.

EXCISING AN INTERNATIONAL CANCER

The Texan revolution came about naturally, and largely as a result of Mexican short-sightedness, not to say blindness. The American people, as already noted, rendered unneutral assistance—assistance which their government technically should have prevented.

[11] See E. D. Adams, *British Interests and Activities in Texas, 1838–1846* (Baltimore, 1910).

But the annexation of an independent Texas was a far different story. The United States put off the willing bride for nine long years—surely a decent wait between the beginning of the courtship and the consummation of the marriage. At the time of annexation, Texas had been formally recognized not only by the United States but by Great Britain, France, and the Kingdom of the Netherlands as well. Mexico, moreover, was clearly incapable of recovering her lost territory. In spite of all her boastful talk about crushing Texas, she had not made a single serious effort to do so. And the longer she waited the stronger the Lone Star Republic became. As early as 1840 Lord Palmerston remarked that any hope of recovery was "visionary," while Lord Ashburton observed that Texas was more likely to overrun Mexico than the reverse.

An independent Texas, from the standpoint of the United States, was a kind of international cancer. Serious border friction would inevitably arise over such problems as smuggled goods and fugitive slaves. An aggressive rival republic to the south, supported by British and French bayonets, would stand athwart the irresistible expansive power of the United States—a situation that savored of burned gunpowder. Finally, some alarmists feared that the Southern states would gravitate toward Texas and dismember the Union by forming a new confederacy of the South. "Let us take it [Texas] now," warned old General Jackson, "and lock the door against future danger."

Whatever may be said of the unneutral conduct of the United States during the Texan revolution, President Tyler's course was honorable. He was faced with a condition, not a theory—and that condition was not of his making. Texas had pursued an independent course for nine years, and she was free to dispose of herself as she chose. Mexico, unable to reconquer Texas and unwilling to see her go, was now cast in the role of Aesop's dog in the manger. As President Tyler informed Congress in April, 1844, no "civilized government on earth" would reject the free offer of a vast domain so "rich and fertile," so important for "national greatness and wealth," and so necessary to "peace and safety." The pages of history have yet to reveal a nation which, in similar circumstances, would have denied itself this priceless boon.

SELECTED BIBLIOGRAPHY

The older standard monograph on the subject, J. H. Smith's *The Annexation of Texas* (New York, 1911), is still well worth reading. The story is told more briefly in Stanley Siegel, *A Political History of the Texas Republic, 1836–1845* (Austin, 1956) and J. W. Schmitz, *Texan Statecraft, 1836–1845* (San Antonio, Texas, 1941). Purely diplomatic matters are surveyed in S. F. Bemis, ed., *American Secretaries of State and their Diplomacy* (New York, 1928), Vol. V and J. M. Callahan, *American Foreign Policy in Mexican Relations* (New York, 1932). On the revolution itself see W. C. Binkley, *The Texas Revolution* (Baton

Rouge, La., 1952). President Tyler's role in annexation is set forth in O. P. Chitwood, *John Tyler: Champion of the Old South* (New York, 1939). See also E. D. Adams, *British Interests and Activities in Texas, 1838–1846* (Baltimore, 1910). An important documentary collection is W. C. Binkley, ed., *Official Correspondence of the Texas Revolution, 1835–1836* (2 vols., New York, 1936). Consult also Donald Day and H. H. Ullom, *The Autobiography of Sam Houston* (Norman, Okla., 1954) and Llerena Friend, *Sam Houston: The Great Designer* (Austin, Texas, 1954).

See footnotes of this chapter; Bemis and Griffin, *Guide,* pp. 248–264; *Harvard Guide,* Ch. 16.

7TH ED. REFS. The problem of Texas is broadly considered against the background of Manifest Destiny in R. A. Billington, *The Far Western Frontier, 1830–1860* (New York, 1956). Special aspects are treated briefly in R. W. Van Alstyne, *The Rising American Empire* (New York, 1960) and in Henry Blumenthal, *A Reappraisal of Franco-American Relations, 1830–1871* (Chapel Hill, N.C., 1959), which downgrades France's alleged willingness to fight for an independent Texas. W. D. Jones, *Lord Aberdeen and the Americas* (Athens, Ga., 1958) concludes that the advantages of an independent Texas, in Foreign Secretary Aberdeen's mind, were much less important than driving a wedge between the United States and France and cementing an *entente cordiale* with the latter for pursuing larger projects (p. 35). Though willing to risk war for his policies, Aberdeen much preferred not to have war. J. C. McElhannon, "Relations between Imperial Mexico and the United States, 1821–1823," in T. E. Cotner and C. E. Castañeda, eds., *Essays in Mexican History* (Austin, Tex., 1958), pp. 127–141 demonstrates that the United States, which abhorred monarchy, revealed hostility toward this transitional imperial regime, and made it clear that Texas was in jeopardy unless properly colonized and defended by Mexico. C. H. Hall, "Abel P. Upshur and the Navy as an Instrument of Foreign Policy," *Virginia Mag. of Hist. and Biog.,* LXIX (1961), 290–299 observes that Upshur was active in strengthening the navy and displaying it in support of expansionist policies regarding Texas and California; evidently his oral presentation to Commodore Jones encouraged the latter to seize Monterey in 1842.

8TH AND 9TH ED. REFS. See BIBLIOGRAPHICAL ADDENDUM, p. 990.

18

War and Peace with Mexico

Destiny beckons us to hold and civilize Mexico.
SECRETARY OF STATE BUCHANAN, 1846

EXPANDED BOUNDARIES AND DEFAULTED DEBTS

MEXICO HAD LONG threatened war if the United States should annex Texas. Accordingly, on March 6, 1845, a few days after Congress passed the fateful annexation resolution, the Mexican minister in Washington lodged a formal protest and demanded his passports. Several months later the United States representative in Mexico City was forced to return home, and all diplomatic intercourse between the two nations ended.

The rupture of relations made war more certain, because it made more difficult an adjustment of a boundary dispute involving Texas. During the long generations of Spanish and Mexican rule, the southwestern limits of Texas had generally been recognized as the Nueces River. Yet the Texans, relying upon the treaties extorted from Santa Anna under duress and upon an arbitrary act of their own Congress, insisted upon the Rio Grande. Technically, from the point of view of Mexico, there was no boundary dispute at all. The Mexicans could not work up much interest over the question as to whether the Nueces or the Rio Grande was the southwestern border of Texas; in their eyes the whole area was still Mexican anyhow. But the Texans were now under the Stars and Stripes, and President Polk felt obligated by a promise to protect them in the area that they claimed as their own.

The boundary issue was complicated by monetary claims, largely for damages, against the Mexican government. As a result of chronic anarchy in Mexico, much American property had been destroyed and a number of Americans had been killed. In 1835, to cite a flagrant case, twenty-two

American citizens were accused of complicity in a revolution and executed without trial. President Jackson declared in a special message to Congress, in February, 1837, that the nature of these outrages and the unwillingness of the Mexican government to offer satisfactory redress "would justify in the eyes of all nations immediate war."

The Mexican government, faced with the mailed fist, gave way. It finally agreed, in 1839, to submit a substantial part of the disputed claims to a mixed commission, which ultimately awarded $2,026,000 to American claimants. As might have been expected from a revolution-ridden

debtor, the stipulated payments rapidly fell into arrears. But this default, one should note, was not outright repudiation; Mexico merely confessed an inability to pay.

The United States was hardly in a position to press its claims at bayonet point. Following the Panic of 1837, about eight states had defaulted on their obligations to British creditors, or had repudiated them outright—much larger sums, in fact, than were involved with Mexico. Nor could Washington claim discriminatory treatment. London and Paris had also presented lengthy bills to the bankrupt Mexican government, with similarly unsatisfactory results. In 1838 the French lost patience, and in the so-called "Pastry War" forced a settlement at the cannon's mouth. This incident enabled General Santa Anna heroically to lose a leg at Vera Cruz and to regain the prestige that he had lost at San Jacinto.

The debtor powers, including the United States, might well have shown more forbearance. They seemed to be unaware that Mexico had been plunged into the cold water of independence without any training in self-government, unlike the English colonials with their long tradition of the town meeting. Even so, the American government under the Articles of Confederation had fallen into impotence and bankruptcy. Mexico naturally felt that in the circumstances the other nations of the world were demanding too high a standard of accountability, particularly since Mexican citizens, no less than foreigners, were suffering from the current disorders.

CALIFORNIA—A POTENTIAL TEXAS

With the Oregon dispute nearing a settlement, and America's Pacific frontage taking shape, Polk became increasingly concerned about the fate of California. This vast and thinly populated region, with its sleepy settlements basking in the sun, was another potential Texas. Its nominal connection with the distant and chaotic Mexican government was tenuous in the extreme. Hundreds of stiff-backed Americans, many of whom had "left their consciences at Cape Horn," were drifting into California and revealing their contempt for the easy-going Mexican authorities. A successful separatist movement seemed almost inevitable within a few years.

At an early date the roving eye of the Yankee had looked upon the fair land of California and found it good. In 1835 President Jackson directed his Secretary of State to offer $500,000 for San Francisco Bay and the area to the north, but this overture proved fruitless. In 1842, during the Webster-Ashburton negotiations, President Tyler favored a project for settling the Oregon dispute on the line of the Columbia River, provided that Britain would bring pressure to bear on Mexico to sell northern California to the United States. The cash payment was to be used to reimburse British and American creditors. But nothing came of this scheme.[1]

American interest in California was further betrayed by an incident that occurred on October 20, 1842. A United States naval officer in Pacific waters, Commodore Jones, had received information which led him to believe that war had broken out with Mexico. Hoping to forestall what appeared to be the suspicious movements of British warships, he appeared before Monterey (the capital of California), forced the Mexican authorities to surrender the fort, raised the Stars and Stripes, and issued a high-flown proclamation of annexation. The next day he was embarrassed to discover that there was no war, and that Mexican-United

[1] See M. C. Jacobs, *Winning Oregon* (Caldwell, Idaho, 1938), pp. 130–135.

States relations were normal—that is, strained almost to the breaking point. Although the red-faced Jones lowered the flag and made what amends he could for his precipitancy, he was temporarily relieved of his command. The State Department forthwith tendered the necessary apologies to the Mexican government, which was deeply disturbed by this latest revelation of Yankee rapacity.

FOREIGN AGENTS IN CALIFORNIA

Commodore Jones' suspicions of Britain were not, however, without some foundation. Already there was a sprinkling of British subjects in California, and they were making no bones about their preference for the Union Jack. The activities of energetic British agents, and to a less extent those of France, provided further stimulus to American misgivings. There can be no doubt that these British representatives, both in Mexico and California, were enthusiastically involved in plans to promote annexation to Great Britain, to say nothing of schemes to defeat the ambitions of the United States.

The London government, as distinguished from its agents, took a different view. For various reasons, including preoccupation with Texas, Downing Street was not actively interested in securing California. Lord Aberdeen therefore sent categorical instructions to his agents advising them to be "entirely passive" in their conduct. Although he made it clear that he did not wish California to go the way of Texas, he made it no less clear that Britain would not fight to thwart the grasping Yankees.

Such progress as the British agents in California were able to make was partly offset by the zeal of Thomas O. Larkin, who became United States consul at Monterey in 1844. This energetic New Englander, who had reached California by sea twelve years earlier, had established himself as a prosperous merchant, and he had greatly whetted American appetites for the region by his articles in the newspapers of Boston and New York. On October 17, 1845, Polk appointed him a confidential agent, with instructions to counteract foreign influence, stimulate separatist tendencies, and encourage annexation to the United States.

It is not surprising that the American public should have expressed considerable alarm over presumed British and French schemings. As the *New York Courier* put it: "This idea that England is desirous to possess herself of the Californias seems as great a bugbear with the American people as the designs of Russia on India are with the English." [2] Polk shared this alarm, for, as earlier noted, his resurrection of the Monroe Doctrine in 1845 was partly aimed at Britain's alleged designs on California. Although his fears were exaggerated, he can hardly be blamed for having drawn the obvious inference from the activities of British

[2] *Niles' Weekly Register*, LXIII, 337 (Jan. 28, 1843).

agents, particularly after Britain's determined bid for Texas. He probably would not have been so eager to precipitate a showdown with Mexico had there not existed a hornet's nest in California that seemed to imperil the United States. Again supposition proved to be stronger than the truth.

THE LAST-CHANCE MISSION OF JOHN SLIDELL

Polk was determined to make one more serious effort to reopen diplomatic relations with Mexico before precipitating a crisis. He therefore inquired through the American consul at Mexico City if a new envoy would be received. The Mexican foreign minister replied, on October 15, 1845, that "although the Mexican nation is deeply injured by the United States . . . my government is disposed to receive the *commissioner* of the United States who may come to this capital with full powers . . . to settle the present dispute in a peaceful, reasonable, and honorable manner. . . ." [3] [Italics inserted]

Upon receipt of these assurances, Polk appointed John Slidell of Louisiana as the American emissary. Although the Mexican government had agreed to receive only a *commissioner* and to treat only the Texas boundary difficulty, Washington disregarded these arrangements and made Slidell a full-fledged minister plenipotentiary, empowered to discuss (1) claims (2) California, and (3) the Texas boundary.

With the penniless Mexican government unable to pay its obligations in cash, Polk was willing to accept land instead. He believed that the claim of Texas to the Rio Grande from the mouth of that river to El Paso was incontestable. But he did acknowledge that there was a difference of opinion as to the location of the western boundary of Texas, north to the 42nd Parallel. Slidell was therefore authorized to assume the claims of the United States against Mexico, provided that Mexico would consent to the Rio Grande as the western boundary of Texas.

Slidell carried with him several alternate proposals. He was instructed to secure, if possible, all New Mexico for an additional $5 million. Although his most pressing objectives were to adjust the claims and the boundary, he was to offer a maximum of $25 million, in addition to assuming the American claims, for California and the intervening area. "Money would be no object," wrote Secretary Buchanan in concluding Slidell's instructions, "when compared with the value of the acquisition." But one should note that at this stage of the game Polk, as an absolute minimum, was willing to exchange American claims for a settlement of the Texan boundary. He was not prepared to serve an ultimatum for California; this area might yet be acquired by processes of internal revolution, in the manner of Texas.

[3] *Senate Doc.*, 29 Cong., 1 sess., no. 337, p. 12 (Peña y Peña to Black, Oct. 15, 1845).

SLIDELL'S FAILURE

The news of Slidell's proposed mission quickly leaked out, despite all efforts to keep it secret. Mexican public opinion was instantly aroused by the very suggestion of negotiating with the nation that had made off with Texas. Even before Slidell's appointment, a Mexican newspaper had burst out:

> This vile [Mexican] government has been and is in correspondence with the [American] usurpers. The Yankee [agent] . . . has departed for the North to say to his government to send a commissioner to make with our government an ignominious treaty on the basis of the surrender of Texas and we know not what other part of the republic.[4]

No sooner had Slidell appeared in Mexico City, on December 6, 1845, than printed circulars outlining his objectives were scattered broadcast throughout the city. The government was accused of a treasonable attempt to dismember the country. The Herrera administration, already tottering, would obviously have been thrown out of power if it had attempted to consider Slidell's "insulting" proposals. It therefore refused to negotiate with the American envoy, primarily on the technically defensible grounds that it had agreed to receive a commissioner, not a minister plenipotentiary, to discuss the Texas boundary difficulty.

The snubbing of Slidell marked a parting of the ways. The fast-slipping Herrera government was promptly overthrown by a military faction, which charged the regime with "seeking to avoid a necessary and glorious war" and incurring an "ignominious loss of national dignity." Polk next instructed Slidell to open negotiations with the new government, but the American envoy met with no better success. His proposals were not rejected; he simply was not given an opportunity to present them. "Be assured," he advised Polk, "that nothing is to be done with these people until they shall have been chastised."

With the door now slammed shut on any kind of peaceful adjustment, Polk proceeded to force a showdown. Until then he had not attempted to occupy with armed forces the expansive no-man's land between the Rio Grande and the Nueces, although he had stationed General Zachary Taylor at Corpus Christi, just southwest of the Nueces. The Mexicans tolerated this nominal invasion. But on January 13, 1846, the day after learning of Slidell's rejection, Polk issued the fateful order that provocatively sent General Taylor all the way to the Rio Grande. Although the Mexican commander warned Taylor to retire beyond the Nueces, the American general took up a position threatening the Mexican town of Matamoros, near the mouth of the Rio Grande. He also built a fort there,

---

[4] Quoted in J. S. Reeves, *American Diplomacy under Tyler and Polk* (Baltimore, 1907), p. 284.

and instituted a blockade of the river. Some authorities regard this last step as an act of war.

AMERICAN BLOOD ON AMERICAN (?) SOIL

On May 9, 1846, the day after Slidell's return to Washington, Polk discussed the Mexican crisis at length with his Cabinet. He asserted that there were ample grounds for sending a war message to Congress—referring, of course, to unpaid claims, the Slidell rejection, and other grievances.

> I told them [Polk recorded] that I thought I ought to make such a message [to Congress] by tuesday next, that the country was excited and impatient on the subject, and if I failed to do so I would not be doing my duty. I then propounded the distinct question to the Cabinet and took their opinions individually, whether I should make a message to Congress on Tuesday, and whether in that message I should recommend a declaration of War against Mexico.[5]

Secretary of the Navy Bancroft demurred, but added that if the Mexicans were to commit an act of aggression, he would favor immediate hostilities. Secretary of State Buchanan stated that he was prepared to vote for war, but that he would feel better satisfied if the Mexican forces first attacked the Americans. The Cabinet finally agreed that a draft message should be prepared and submitted to it for discussion at its next meeting.

Then occurred one of the strangest coincidences in history. That very evening dispatches arrived from General Taylor relating how the Mexicans had crossed the Rio Grande, on April 25, 1846, and had killed or wounded sixteen of his men. Polk would no longer have to urge a declaration of war on the rather hollow basis of unpaid claims and the Slidell rejection. The misgivings of the more sensitive members of the Cabinet would be quieted, the public conscience would be salved, and the country would presumably rally behind the President. Polk, a staunch Christian, regretted having to break the Sabbath by working on his war message, but he eased his conscience by interrupting his labors long enough to go to church.

The war message, submitted to Congress on May 11, 1846, was an extraordinary document. It outlined at length the twenty years of accumulated grievances against Mexico, stressing the events leading up to the rejection of Slidell "upon the most frivolous pretexts." Two passages near the end were not completely candid:

> The cup of forbearance had been exhausted even before the recent information from the frontier. . . . But now, after reiterated menaces, Mexico has passed the boundary of the United States, has invaded our territory and

[5] M. M. Quaife, ed., *The Diary of James K. Polk* (Chicago, 1910), I, 384 (May 9, 1846).

shed American blood upon the American soil. She has proclaimed that hostilities have commenced, and that the two nations are now at war.

Continuing, Polk made this significant observation:

As war exists, and, notwithstanding all our efforts to avoid it, exists by the act of Mexico herself, we are called upon by every consideration of duty and patriotism to vindicate with decision the honor, the rights, and the interests of our country.[6]

Polk then urged Congress to recognize the existence of war and to take steps to wage it vigorously. Two days later the legislators formally declared war, empowered the President to use the army and navy, and appropriated $10 million for military purposes.

The prompt and overwhelming vote in Congress for war—174 to 14 in the House and 40 to 2 in the Senate—is deceptive. Aroused by the loss of American lives, all sections and all parties at first enthusiastically endorsed the conflict. Popular slogans were "Ho for the Halls of the Montezumas!" and "Mexico or Death!" But gradually considerable sentiment developed against fighting "Jimmy Polk's War," especially among the opposition Whig party and the antislavery men. One abolitionist Congressman denounced the conflict as "unholy, unrighteous, and damnable." The distinguished Whig orator, Senator Corwin of Ohio, declared in a memorable speech that if he were a Mexican he would say to the Americans, "Have you not room in your own country to bury your dead men? If you come into mine, we will greet you with bloody hands; and welcome you to hospitable graves." [7]

Abraham Lincoln, who entered the House as a Whig some months after the war began, joined the dissenters. Through his famous "spot resolutions," which caused him to be dubbed the "spotty Lincoln," he demanded to know the precise "spot" on American soil where the shooting had begun. Certainly Polk would have been much nearer the truth if he had said that "American blood has been shed on soil in dispute between the United States and Mexico"—soil to which Mexico perhaps had a better technical claim than the United States.

DID POLK PROVOKE WAR?

The Whigs, branding Polk a liar, challenged his allegation that he had put forth "considerable efforts" to avoid war. If so, they asked, why had he sent troops deep into the disputed territory, within a provocatively short distance of a large body of Mexican troops? And why, scholars have later queried, does the President's diary contain several references to the anticipated clash between Taylor's force and the Mexicans? War

[6] J. D. Richardson, *Messages and Papers of the Presidents* (Washington, 1897), IV, 442.
[7] *Cong. Globe*, 29 Cong., 2 sess., appendix, p. 217 (Feb. 11, 1847).

probably would have erupted in any event, for Polk was evidently determined to force it after Slidell's rejection. Yet if General Taylor had not been sent to the Rio Grande, the conflict would not have broken out when it did or where it did.

The most plausible explanation of the President's course—assuming that he did not want to provoke war—is that he had obligated himself to protect the Texans. Occupation of the disputed area was in this sense a defensive step, even though it removed a deep buffer. But if the disorganized Mexicans had failed to make a serious effort to invade Texas during the nine years when it was weakly defended, they probably would not have attempted to do so when it was under the formidable wing of the United States. As events turned out, the action of Polk gave the Mexicans a good excuse to start what they regarded as a defensive war by repelling an invader. Curiously enough, each nation could seriously claim that it had been invaded by the other.

The Whigs also charged that Polk, having failed by every other wile to win California, deliberately provoked war in order to despoil his neighbor. In this way, they alleged, he would be able to gratify his ambition and rescue the territory from the British. But it seems clear that Polk did not really want war—provided that he could get California without it. It is equally clear that he did not lean over backward to avoid hostilities when the news came to him that Slidell's attempts at purchase had failed. For him patience and forbearance had ceased to be virtues. Probably he welcomed war. He would have been a little less than human if, in the circumstances, he had not.

BELLICOSITY ON BOTH SIDES

Diplomacy broke down in 1846 because the will to preserve peace was not present on either side. During the summer and autumn of 1845, some months before Taylor's border skirmish, the United States was giving every evidence of a bellicose spirit. "Nine-tenths of our people," asserted the *New York Morning News,* "would rather have a little fighting than not." "LET US GO TO WAR," bluntly began an editorial in the *New York Journal of Commerce.* The *Richmond Enquirer* was confident that the American people favored "a full and thorough chastisement of Mexican arrogance and folly." On March 16, 1846, the *New Orleans Commercial Bulletin* declared:

> The United States have borne more insult, abuse, insolence and injury, from Mexico, than one nation ever before endured from another. . . . [T]hey are now left no alternative but to extort by arms the respect and justice which Mexico refuses to any treatment less harsh.[8]

[8] Quoted in J. H. Smith, *The War with Mexico* (New York, 1919), I, 121.

From all indications the Mexicans were even more eager to fight the hated "Yanquis" than the Yankees were to fight them. But Mexico had been verbally reconquering Texas for nine years, and due allowance must be made for braggadocio. On paper the Mexican army, heavily overstaffed with generals, was about five times larger than that of the United States. One Mexican officer boasted that his cavalry could break the American infantry squares with the lasso. There was even wild talk of bursting into Louisiana, arming the slaves, and arousing the Indians against "the Bullies of the North." With the blundering attempt of the Yankees to invade Canada in mind, the Mexicans did not think that the Americans either could or would fight—an impression that was confirmed by Polk's repeated attempts to buy a peace. To the Mexicans, the United States was a nation of "money-grubbers" and dollar worshipers; the Yankee was an impossible braggart; and the Southern slaveholder was a "degenerate portion of the English race."

Mexico was counting to some extent, though apparently not heavily, on an outbreak of war between Britain and the United States over the Oregon dispute. The London government did what little it could to restrain the Mexicans, but English public opinion encouraged them in their delusions. The *London Times* expressed a common contempt for the United States when it declared that "The invasion and conquest of a vast region by a State which is without an army and without credit, is a novelty in the history of nations. . . ." [9] And the weekly *Britannia* insisted that America as "an aggressive power is one of the weakest in the world . . . fit for nothing but to fight Indians."

CONQUERING A PEACE

Despite the bloodshed on the Rio Grande, there was still an outside chance that Polk would be able to buy what he wanted without having to prosecute a full-fledged war. The most promising approach involved General Santa Anna, who was then exiled in Cuba. In February, 1846, Polk learned through an intermediary that if the deposed dictator were allowed to return to Mexico, he would make peace with the United States and promptly sell the desired territory. Orders were therefore issued to let Santa Anna pass through the American blockading squadrons. But when the slippery Mexican leader reached his native land, he used his remarkable talents to arouse his countrymen against the invader. The crestfallen Polk was farther than ever from a purchased peace.

There was nothing left now but to fight it out. General Zachary Taylor pushed across the Rio Grande and drove deep into the northern reaches of Mexico. There he managed to win several victories, notably at Buena

* *London Times*, April 15, 1845, 5:4.

Vista in 1847, where he defeated Santa Anna despite heavy numerical odds.

Polk had meanwhile matured his basic plan. He would seize what he had tried to purchase, hold it in pawn, and then force the Mexicans to come to terms—to "conquer a peace" was his own curious phrase. Pursuant to this scheme, General Kearny marched overland from Fort Leavenworth, captured Santa Fé, and then pushed on to California. There American naval forces, co-operating with the dashing explorer, Captain John C. Frémont, had already brought most of the area under control. Considerable mystery still enshrouds the doings of this young army officer, but it was a strange coincidence—if indeed a coincidence—that when war broke out he should have been in California with several dozen well-armed men, and in serious conflict with the Mexican authorities.

Polk now had what he wanted—California and the intervening territory—but the Mexicans had not had enough of fighting. The only way to bring them to their knees was to strike a smashing blow at the very vitals of their country and capture their capital. General Winfield Scott was placed in command of this key expedition, and after seizing the seaport

Major Campaigns of the Mexican War

city of Vera Cruz, in March, 1847, he undertook the mountainous march toward Mexico City in the face of formidable obstacles.

Then occurred one of the most bizarre incidents in American diplomatic annals. Polk decided to send along with the invading army an executive agent, who would be empowered to conclude peace whenever the moment seemed to be favorable. The President preferred Secretary of State Buchanan; but months might elapse before the Mexicans would consent to negotiate, and a prominent member of the Cabinet could not be spared.[10] Polk finally appointed the Chief Clerk of the State Department, Nicholas Trist, a man of modest attainments and reputation. His selection would cause no jealousy among the leaders of the Democratic Party, and if negotiations did not go well he could be recalled— a course that would be more awkward in the case of a prominent man.

THE STRANGE SAGA OF NICHOLAS TRIST

General Scott had meanwhile been fighting his way toward Mexico City against serious odds. His nerves were already frayed when Polk's perambulatory plenipotentiary put in an appearance. Scott sent a heated letter to the newly arrived envoy, for he misunderstood Trist's instructions and feared that civilian interference with military operations would jeopardize his already perilous position. Trist, who was an overfluid penman, replied in a caustic thirty-page note. The rather childish quarrel was patched up when General Scott sent a jar of guava jelly to his epistolary adversary, who had become ill.

Having buried the hatchet, Scott and Trist entered upon tortuous negotiations designed to bribe Santa Anna, at a cost of $10,000, into making a peace. The double-dealing conspirator pocketed the money, and used the ensuing armistice to bolster his defenses. With the breakdown of bribery and the renewal of hostilities, Scott captured Mexico City, on September 14, 1847, after heavy fighting. Formal Mexican resistance thereupon ended.

Polk was meanwhile becoming increasingly annoyed by Trist's bunglings, and by the awkwardness of waging war with a pen in one hand and a sword in the other. A satisfactory treaty seemed beyond reach, and the presence of the American envoy was thought to betray undue eagerness on the part of the United States to end the fighting. Early in October, 1847, therefore, the State Department sent an instruction advising Trist of his summary recall.

But Trist embarked instead upon a surprising course. Shortly before receiving notice of his recall, he had opened negotiations with the moderate Mexican faction that had recently come into power. This group, whose foothold was shaky, was evidently the only one with which a

[10] Polk, *Diary*, II, 466–467.

reasonable treaty could be made. In fact, the moderate Mexican leaders urged Trist to continue with the negotiations despite his instructions from Washington. Trist realized that if he did not take advantage of this opening, anarchy might result, and with it the possibility of prolonged guerrilla warfare or the conquest of all Mexico. Either eventuality would be fraught with peril. Communication with Washington was so slow, and the advantages of striking while the iron was hot were so obvious, that Trist decided to disregard his instructions and do what seemed best for his country.

This decision involved considerable courage. If things went wrong, Trist could expect little mercy from the angered Polk, whom he was now openly defying. But having made up his mind, Trist sent the President a remarkable sixty-five page letter explaining why he was remaining. Polk was furious at the conduct of this "impudent and unqualified scoundrel." "I have never in my life," he noted in his diary, "felt so indignant. . . ." [11]

AN UNAUTHORIZED TREATY BY A DISAVOWED AGENT

After prolonged negotiations, Trist signed the terms of peace at Guadalupe Hidalgo, near Mexico City, on February 2, 1848. The treaty ceded New Mexico and California outright to the United States, and confirmed the American title to Texas as far as the Rio Grande. This vast region, including Texas, was approximately one-half of Mexico. In return, the United States agreed to pay $15 million and assume the claims of its own citizens to the extent of $3.25 million. Since Polk regarded the territory as an indemnity exacted from Mexico for having provoked the war, and since Slidell had been authorized to pay $25 million for approximately the same area, one is surprised to find the victor granting so much money to the vanquished. Some writers have said that the consciences of the Americans troubled them; others, that this was "rather characteristic of American generosity and fair play." In any event, the Mexican President was able to save face by referring to the $15 million as an indemnity wrested from the Yankee.

Polk was vastly annoyed when the treaty negotiated by his disavowed agent arrived posthaste from Mexico. But there were compelling reasons for accepting it as it stood. First of all, Trist had generally conformed to his original instructions. Moreover, if Polk should now repudiate a treaty made on the terms that he had authorized in April, 1847, the irate Whigs and anti-slavery agitators might get out of hand.

The growth of opposition to the war was particularly ominous. As early as May, 1846, the *Boston Atlas* had declared, "It would be a sad and woeful joy, but a joy nevertheless, to hear that the hordes under

[11] Polk, *Diary*, III, 201 (Jan. 15, 1848).

Scott and Taylor were, *every man of them, swept into the next world.*" [12]
Following the elections of 1846, the Whigs had enjoyed a majority in
the House of Representatives, and in January, 1848, that body resolved,
85 to 81, that the war had been "unnecessarily and unconstitutionally begun by the President of the United States." The danger loomed that
the Whig House might block further appropriations for the armies in
the field. Had this happened, the United States probably would not have
acquired as much as Trist had managed to gain, and the Democratic
Party would have run an increased risk of repudiation during the forthcoming Presidential election.

Polk therefore grimly submitted the treaty to the Senate, urging that
it be approved despite "the exceptional conduct of Mr. Trist." The country wanted peace, and further delay might render a satisfactory peace impossible. So, on March 10, 1848, the Senate registered the stamp of its
approval, with minor amendments, by a vote of 38 to 14. The ardent
Whig, Philip Hone, complained that the peace "negotiated by an unauthorized agent, with an unacknowledged government, submitted by
an accidental President, to a dissatisfied Senate, has, notwithstanding
these objections in form, been confirmed. . . ." [13]

THE ALL-MEXICO MOVEMENT

The ratification of the Trist Treaty must be viewed in the light of
Manifest Destiny—"the great American disease"—which was rampant
in the 1840's. Early in 1846 William H. Seward testified that "The popular
passion for territorial aggrandizement is irresistible." Under the spell of
the Mexican War, Senator Dickinson of New York offered this toast at a
Jackson Day dinner: "A more perfect Union, embracing the Whole of
the North American continent." Several years later one editor prophesied
that before the end of the century "every sea that laves the shores of
North America will mirror the stars and stripes." [14]

The exhilarating American victories over the Mexicans had stimulated
an already voracious appetite for territory, and had led to a mounting
demand for annexing all of Mexico. Sheer greed for land was curiously
commingled with idealism. The idea took root that the "universal Yankee
nation" had a mandate from Providence to embark upon a "civilizing

[12] Quoted in Smith, *War with Mexico*, II, 281.
[13] Bayard Tuckerman, ed., *The Diary of Philip Hone, 1828–1851* (New York, 1910),
II, 347 (March 13, 1848).
[14] John Fiske records a toast allegedly proposed by an American citizen during the
Civil War at a Paris banquet: "I give you the United States—bounded on the north
by the Aurora Borealis, on the south by the precession of the equinoxes, on the east
by the primeval chaos, and on the west by the Day of Judgement!" John Fiske,
American Political Ideas (New York, 1885), p. 102.

mission" and rescue its neighbor from anarchy. The *New York Evening Post* declared:

> Now we ask, whether any man can coolly contemplate the idea of recalling our troops from the territory we at present occupy . . . and . . . resign this beautiful country to the custody of the ignorant cowards and profligate ruffians who have ruled it for the last twenty-five years? Why, humanity cries out against it. Civilization and christianity protests against this reflux of the tide of barbarism and anarchy.[15]

The movement for all Mexico, though poorly organized, was beginning to gather strong momentum when the Trist Treaty arrived in Washington. Polk did not favor this extreme demand because it would mean more fighting, with highly uncertain political and military results. One

The Mexican eagle before the war   The Mexican eagle after the war

PLUCKED

Yankee bumptiousness in the 1840's.
Yankee Doodle, 1847

of the reasons why he accepted the treaty, in spite of his annoyance, was a desire to spike the guns of the extremists. He was supported by leading

[15] Quoted in *Niles' Weekly Register,* LXXIII, 334 (Jan. 22, 1848). The standard monograph is J. D. P. Fuller, *The Movement for the Acquisition of All Mexico, 1846–1848* (Baltimore, 1936).

Southerners like Calhoun, who perceived that the arid Mexican territory was unlikely to prove fertile slave soil, and that bending the bow too far would dangerously provoke the free-soil North. One of the strangest things about this strange episode is that the treaty was condemned by some who wanted no territory at all, and by some who wanted all Mexico.

The submission of the Trist treaty to the Senate before the extremists had time to organize effectively was one of the chief factors in stopping the all-Mexico boom. The discredited Trist, by courageously violating his instructions, probably saved the United States from prolonged guerrilla warfare and the staggering problems that would have arisen from trying to absorb the more densely settled portions of Mexico. But Trist got scant thanks. While he sank into obscurity and poverty, the government refused to pay his salary and expenses for the period following his recall. Not until twenty-two years later did Congress vote Trist the unpaid $13,647, and President Grant made him postmaster at the hamlet of Alexandria, Virginia.

THE GADSDEN AFTERGULP

The Treaty of Guadalupe Hidalgo by no means ended friction between the United States and Mexico. Serious disputes arose over Indian raids and the exact location of the southwestern boundary. The problem was complicated by the immense increase of population in California, following the gold discovery of 1848, and by the increasing necessity of constructing a transcontinental railroad.

The most feasible southern railway route lay through the area south of the Gila River, which was undeniably Mexican territory. On the recommendation of Jefferson Davis, Secretary of War in the expansionist Pierce administration, a prominent Southern railroad man, James Gadsden, was chosen minister to Mexico in May, 1853. A primary object of his mission was to purchase the important right of way.[16]

Fortune smiled upon the American negotiator. By another turn of the wheel of chance, Santa Anna was again in power, and as usual in need of money. On December 30, 1853, Gadsden concluded a treaty by which Mexico agreed to sell the huge area now comprising the southern portions of Arizona and New Mexico. The pact not only insured the coveted railroad route, now used by the Southern Pacific line, but released the United States from its obligation under the Treaty of Guadalupe Hidalgo for damages inflicted by its Indians raiding into Mexico.

The Gadsden Treaty received rough treatment in the Senate. It became a football not only for railroad speculators but also for antislavery agitators, who were alarmed by recent Southern expansion. The aged Senator

[16] See P. N. Garber, *The Gadsden Treaty* (Philadelphia, 1923).

Benton condemned the land included in the Gadsden purchase as so "desolate" and "God-forsaken" that "Kit" Carson, the famous scout, had reported that "a wolf could not make a living upon it." The treaty was finally approved with numerous amendments, but not until the purchase price had been reduced from $15 million to $10 million and the boundary line had been shortsightedly changed in such a way as to exclude a window on the Gulf of California.

The Gadsden Purchase thus rounded out the enormous territorial gains of the United States before the Civil War. With a clear title to both Oregon and Texas, and with the Mexican cession and the Gadsden Purchase newly acquired, the republic had increased its previous domain by about two-thirds. The United States was now a two-ocean nation. One can fairly criticize Polk's methods, but one can hardly fail to be impressed by the results.

SELECTED BIBLIOGRAPHY

A brief but vigorous defense of Polk appears in S. F. Bemis, *The Latin American Policy of the United States* (New York, 1943). The older detailed standard work, also pro-Polk, is J. H. Smith, *The War with Mexico* (2 vols., New York, 1919). For a full-length study consult E. I. McCormac, *James K. Polk: A Political Biography* (Berkeley, Calif., 1922). See also J. M. Callahan, *American Foreign Policy in Mexican Relations* (New York, 1932) and J. F. Rippy, *The United States and Mexico* (rev. ed., New York, 1931). N. A. Graebner's path-breaking study, *Empire on the Pacific* (New York, 1955), finds Polk the expansionist in advance of Manifest Destiny. This book includes a highly useful Bibliographical Essay. See also A. P. Nasatir, *French Activities in California* (Stanford, Calif., 1945).

Helpful articles are E. D. Adams, "English Interest in the Annexation of California," *Amer. Hist. Rev.*, XIV (1909), 744–763; L. M. Sears, "Nicholas P. Trist: A Diplomat with Ideals," *Miss. Valley Hist. Rev.*, XI (1924), 85–98; George Tays, "Frémont Had No Secret Instructions," *Pacific Hist. Rev.*, IX (1940), 157–171; and three contributions by N. A. Graebner, "American Interest in California, 1845," *Pacific Hist. Rev.*, XXII (1953), 13–27; "Party Politics and the Trist Mission," *Jour. of Southern Hist.*, XIX (1953), 137–156; "James K. Polk's Wartime Expansionist Policy," East Tenn. Hist. Soc. *Pubs.*, No. 23 (1951), 32–45.

See footnotes of this chapter; Bemis and Griffin, *Guide*, pp. 265–274; *Harvard Guide*, Chs. 16–17.

7TH ED. REFS. See reference at the end of the previous chapter and the. extended list in the BIBLIOGRAPHICAL ADDENDUM, p. 991.

8TH AND 9TH ED. REFS. See BIBLIOGRAPHICAL ADDENDUM, p. 991.

19

The Ferment of the Fifties

> *These Yankees are most disagreeable Fellows to have to do with about any American Question; They are on the Spot, strong, deeply interested in the matter, totally unscrupulous and dishonest and determined somehow or other to carry their Point. . . .*
> LORD PALMERSTON, 1857

THE YANKEE COMES OF AGE

TEXAS, OREGON, and the Mexican cession territory—an imperial domain —had fallen into the outstretched hands of the United States within the span of three years. One would think that the American people, confronted with the task of settling such an enormous area, would be content. But not so. Senator Mallory of Florida declared that it was "no more possible for this country to pause in its career than it is for the free and untrammeled eagle to cease to soar." If the slavery issue had not appeared as an apple of discord, the American people could hardly have failed to grasp more.

The swift and relatively easy victories of the Mexican War caused the United States to rise to the full height of its "exulting manhood." One British journal quoted an American as boasting, "Your little isle, sir, would make a pretty addition to this fine country!" The rulers of the Old World, particularly of Britain, were not pleased with these latest exhibitions of bumptiousness or with Yankee rapacity in Mexico. But they could not fail to be impressed by the uninterrupted triumphs of American arms. Early in 1847 the United States minister in London reported that "they do not love us; but they are compelled to respect us." In America, Philip Hone noted in his diary:

> They [the British] may occasionally abuse us as an arrogant people. . . .
> But the language of contempt is heard no more. . . . Brother Jonathan . . .

is growing to be a "big boy," and must be treated with a little more respect. . . . The Yankees may be ignorant of the most approved method of using the knife and fork; but it cannot be denied that they are competent to make a good use of the sword and musket. They eat fast, but they go ahead wonderfully; they use some queer expressions, but in defence of their rights they are apt to talk much to the purpose.[1]

The heightened nationalism of the American people was strikingly illustrated by an increased contempt for the "effete monarchies" of Europe and their "trappings." In 1853 Secretary of State Marcy, a professional politician from New York who had never set foot in Europe, issued his famous "Dress Circular." Convinced that the gold braid and ostrich feathers of European diplomatic livery were out of harmony with American democracy, he encouraged diplomats of the United States ordinarily to appear "in the simple dress of an American citizen"—that is, the conventional black evening clothes. With considerable misgivings Minister James Buchanan, in London, donned his black coat. To avoid the embarrassment of being confused with the servants, who were similarly attired, he fastened a dress sword to his side. The *London Chronicle*, irked by this latest evidence of Yankee conceit, printed an editorial on "American puppyism" which was directed at " 'the gentleman in the black coat' from Yankee-land." [2] It seems clear that this "war on knee breeches," though roundly applauded in America, did nothing to increase respect for the United States or win converts to democracy. Subsequent generations of American diplomats were given greater latitude in donning the traditional garb and joining the "peacock parade."

DEMAGOGIC DIPLOMACY

The revolutionary outbursts of 1848 in Europe, even more than those of 1830, acted as a powerful stimulus to the heady new spirit of American nationalism. The traditional friendliness of the United States to the cause of liberty in other lands was intensified by the presence of tens of thousands of recently arrived Irish and German immigrants. Most of them had poured in during the 1840's and many of them had but recently cringed under the lash of despotism. A considerable group of enthusiasts in the United States inaugurated the "Young America" movement, which had as one of its goals active intervention against the despotisms of Europe.[3]

[1] Allan Nevins, ed., *The Diary of Philip Hone* (New York, 1936), pp. 869–870 (Feb. 5, 1848).
[2] In Berlin, the British ambassador accosted the American minister, George Bancroft, and asked in the presence of many listeners why the representatives of the United States appeared at court "all dressed in black, like so many undertakers." Bancroft retorted that "we could not be more appropriately dressed than we are—at European courts, where what we represent is the Burial of Monarchy." M. A. DeWolfe Howe, *The Life and Letters of George Bancroft* (New York, 1908), II, 174.
[3] See M. E. Curti, "Young America," *Amer. Hist. Rev.*, XXXII (1926), 34–55.

THE LAND OF LIBERTY

Recommended to the Consideration of "Brother Jonathan"

British satire: the leering, cigar-smoking, unprincipled Yankee, guarding his almighty dollar and his title to Oregon and Texas, with elevated feet, unkempt hair, slave driver's whip, repeating pistol, and liquor glass. Note slave trading, slave beating, and slave lynching; also references to repudiation, dueling, fighting with knives in Congress, and erecting gallows and pillaging churches in Mexico.

London Punch, 1847

IRISH AND GERMAN IMMIGRATION BY DECADE

Years	Irish	German	All Others	Grand Total
1820–1830				151,824
1831–1840	207,381	152,454	239,290	599,125
1841–1850	780,719	434,626	497,906	1,713,251
1851–1860	914,119	951,667	732,428	2,598,214
1861–1870	435,778	787,468	1,091,578	2,314,824
1871–1880	436,871	718,182	1,657,138	2,812,191
1881–1890	655,482	1,452,970	3,138,161	5,246,613
1891–1900	388,416	505,152	2,793,996	3,687,564

Americans reacted with bitterness when the Hungarian revolution, headed by the dynamic Louis Kossuth, was ruthlessly crushed by Austria, with help of troops sent in by the Russian Czar. Congressman Sweetster of Ohio cried out:

> If I was authorized to speak for the whole American people, and had the voice of ARTICULATE THUNDER, I would tell the despotic Governments of Europe that henceforth in contests for liberty . . . there must be no such interference as there has been in the past. . . . I will pledge that portion of the people of my State that I am authorized to represent, that they will, when the time comes, protest against the interference of Russia in another contest in Hungary for liberty.[4]

In June, 1849, while the Hungarian revolution was still running its ill-starred course, the Whig administration of President Taylor issued special instructions to A. Dudley Mann, an American diplomat then in Europe. He was to proceed to Hungary and hold out to the revolutionary government assurances of recognition, if such a step seemed warranted. As fate would have it, the revolt quickly collapsed and Mann did not reach Hungary. But the Austrian government instructed its *chargé* in Washington, Chevalier Hülsemann, to lodge a vigorous protest against this meddling in the affairs of a friendly nation.

To Daniel Webster, again Secretary of State under the new Whig administration, the Hülsemann note presented both an opportunity and a challenge. He was distressed by the internal controversy over slavery, and by the increasing threats of secession. He therefore decided to "write a paper which should touch the national pride, and make a man feel *sheepish* and look *silly* who should speak of disunion." He also deemed it desirable "to speak out, and tell the people of Europe who and what we are, and awaken them to a just sense of the unparalleled growth of this country." Accordingly, his reply to Hülsemann contained this high-flown passage:

> The power of this republic at the present moment is spread over a region one of the richest and most fertile on the globe, and of an extent in com-

[4] *Cong. Globe*, 32 Cong., 1 sess., p. 177 (Jan. 3, 1852).

parison with which the possessions of the house of Hapsburg [Austria] are but as a patch on the earth's surface.[5]

Webster did not mistake the public temper, for his rebuke to Hülsemann aroused instant enthusiasm in the ranks of both parties.

Three years later, in 1853, the Koszta affair provided another opportunity for stump-speech diplomacy. Martin Koszta was a Hungarian revolutionist who had fled to the United States, where he had declared his intention of becoming an American citizen. He was later seized within Turkish jurisdiction by an Austrian naval officer, who in turn was forced to release his captive by an American warship.[6] To the subsequent protest in Washington of Hülsemann, William L. Marcy, now Secretary of State, returned a ringing reply which, however, had a tenable legal basis. There was reason to believe that Marcy desired the Democratic Presidential nomination, and that he was appealing to the large immigrant vote. At all events, the country applauded wildly. But one Vienna newspaper snarled, "We must get out of the way of the Yankee, who is half a buccaneer, and half a backwoodsman, and no gentleman at all."

THE KOSSUTH CRAZE

The exiled Hungarian leader Louis Kossuth, after various misadventures and with American assistance, arrived in New York on December 5, 1851. The "illustrious" Magyar, who was a gifted orator and a magnetic personality, received a tumultuous welcome. In New York one burst of cheering, so it was reported, lasted without interruption for fifteen minutes. Henry W. Longfellow, the famed poet, remarked that the people had gone *"clean* daft." No foreign visitor since Lafayette's triumphal tour had ever received such an ovation. With the ghost of slavery temporarily laid by the crucial Compromise of 1850, the nation was free to outdo itself.

Diplomatically, the Kossuth incident was brought to a head by Secretary Webster. The leonine orator, speaking at a Washington banquet in the Hungarian's honor and possibly overstimulated by champagne, asserted:

> We shall rejoice to see our American model upon the Lower Danube and on the mountains of Hungary. . . . I limit my aspirations for Hungary, for the present, to that single and simple point,—Hungarian independence, Hungarian self-government, Hungarian control of Hungarian destinies.[7]

[5] *Senate Ex. Docs.,* 31 Cong., 2 sess., no. 9, p. 7 (Webster to Hülsemann, Dec. 21, 1850).

[6] See Andor Klay, *Daring Diplomacy: The Case of the First American Ultimatum* (Minneapolis, 1957).

[7] J. W. McIntyre, ed., *The Writings and Speeches of Daniel Webster* (National ed., Boston, 1903), XIII, 461, 426 (Jan. 7, 1852).

Webster may have been motivated by a desire to repeat the smashing success of his Hülsemann note. Such, at least, was the interpretation of Hülsemann, who regarded the new Websterian outburst as a thinly disguised bid for the Presidential nomination. As the *New York Herald* remarked, the Kossuth excitement was "a first-rate piece, as good as a queen, in the political game of chess." The Austrian government was so deeply offended by the uproarious welcome extended to its most notorious rebel, and by the blatant indiscretion of the American Secretary of State, that it instructed its representative to have no further dealings with Webster. Relations remained strained until the great orator died in October, 1852.

The Kossuth infatuation had meantime been running its course. Hungarian history, music, dances, and wine became popular. Kossuth clubs were organized. Immense crowds turned out and shed tears while the eloquent Magyar addressed them in flawless English. Ladies impulsively contributed rings and necklaces to the Hungarian cause. Some money was raised, but most of it, to Kossuth's disgust, was frittered away on parades and banquets. The traditional policy of the republic, sanctified by the Founding Fathers, restrained the United States from active interference in Hungary. The South, moreover, could not support intervention in Europe on behalf of liberalism lest it provide sanction for European intervention in the South on behalf of abolitionism.

When it became evident that intervention was what Kossuth wanted, the enthusiasm for him evaporated with a suddenness proportionate to its extravagance. The magnetic Magyar, alias Alexander Smith, finally sailed from America a sadder and wiser man. But he left behind him Kossuth beards, Kossuth hats, Kossuth overcoats, Kossuth cigars, the Kossuth grippe, and Kossuth County, Iowa.

ISTHMIAN INVOLVEMENTS

From the days of Balboa, men's minds had toyed with the idea of severing North and South America by an artificial waterway. The American people had revealed some early interest in such a dream, but not until near the middle of the century did they begin to show a lively concern about the Isthmus. The reasons are crystal clear. In the 1840's the United States received its share of Oregon, and acquired from the Mexicans a vast frontage on the Pacific Ocean. Nine days before the signing of the treaty with Mexico, gold was discovered in California—an event that touched off one of the most explosive population movements of history. Control of water communication with distant American territory on the Pacific Coast rapidly became a question of pressing importance to the United States.

American needs were partly met by a foothold at the Isthmus of Panama, then held by the republic of New Granada (later Colombia). In December, 1846, the United States minister in Bogotá signed a treaty which proved to be of unforeseen significance. New Granada, which feared that Great Britain or some other imperialistic power might seize the Isthmus of Panama, granted the United States important transit rights in that region. In return, Washington bound itself to maintain the "perfect neutrality" of the route so that "free transit of traffic might not be interrupted." This right-of-way was of incalculable value to American commerce, but the Senate was so suspicious of possible entanglements that it did not approve the pact until June 3, 1848, a year-and-a-half later. The treaty paved the way for the Panama railway line, completed in 1855 by Americans as the first transcontinental railroad—forty-eight miles long.

Mounting interest in the Isthmus also involved a novel invocation of the Monroe Doctrine. In 1848, when the rumor spread that the local rulers of the Mexican peninsula of Yucatan were about to offer their land to Britain, President Polk swung into action. In a resolute message to Congress, on April 29, 1848, he proclaimed that the United States would not permit such a transfer, even *with the consent* of the inhabitants. This so-called Polk Corollary of the Monroe Doctrine went a step further than the original dictum, which had envisaged intervention or acquisition *without the consent* of the inhabitants.

Nor did American concern for this general area end here. The Gadsden Purchase Treaty of 1853 included an article guaranteeing to the United States certain transit rights on the projected railroad across the Isthmus of Tehuantepec, the narrow waist of Mexico.

The British, already alarmed by the outcome of the Mexican War, viewed the southward push of the American eagle with grave misgivings. For one thing, they had an important territorial stake in the Caribbean, including Jamaica, Belize (British Honduras), and other colonies. For another, they were jealously guarding their position as the number one mercantile power, and they would go to extreme lengths before they would permit the Yankee to secure a stranglehold on the Isthmus—one of the commercial nerve centers of the globe.

A canal across Nicaragua was then regarded as the most feasible Isthmian waterway, with its Atlantic terminus the San Juan River. Near the mouth of this navigable stream lived a tribe of savages known as the Mosquito Indians, over whom England had long claimed a protectorate. In 1848 the British authorities seized San Juan, renamed Greytown, at the entrance of the San Juan River. Their ostensible reason was to protect their dusky ward, "His Mosquito Majesty," against the Nicaraguans.

On the Pacific side the British had a weather eye cocked, particularly

at the Gulf of Fonseca, which commanded the prospective western termini of the proposed canal. In October, 1849, a British naval officer boldly entered that body of water and seized Tigre Island. The London authorities promptly disavowed the rash act, but American public opinion was alarmed by this evidence of aggression, as well as by the iron-handed occupation of Greytown. Secretary of State Clayton wrote that a "collision will become inevitable if great prudence is not exercised on both sides."

THE CLAYTON-BULWER HAIRSPLITTING

The London Foreign Office fortunately revealed a willingness to enter into negotiations. Late in 1849 it sent to Washington an able new minister, Henry Lytton Bulwer, brother of the famous author of *The Last Days of Pompeii*. His discussions with Secretary Clayton had scarcely begun when it became painfully evident that neither Britain nor America would consent to the sole control of a canal route by the other. Nor did England, with the aggressive Palmerston again Foreign Secretary, show the slightest desire to relinquish her elastic Mosquito protectorate.

But Secretary Clayton held a few high cards. Zealous American agents in Central America had recently concluded several transit treaties, which conveyed to the United States exclusive canal-route privileges. Although these pacts had not yet been laid before the Senate, Clayton could threaten to submit them if Britain refused to come to terms. Moreover, several of the Central American republics, including Nicaragua, had become so apprehensive of British designs that they were looking to the United States for protection. As Clayton bluntly informed Bulwer:

> There is not one of these five Central American states that would not annex themselves to us tomorrow, if they could, and if it is any secret worth knowing you are welcome to it—*Some of them have offered and asked to be annexed to the United States already.* [Italics in original.] [8]

After prolonged diplomatic fencing, the famous Clayton-Bulwer Treaty was signed on April 19, 1850. By its terms both parties agreed to co-operate in facilitating the construction of an Isthmian canal; both bound themselves never to fortify or exercise exclusive control over it. As regards clashing territorial ambitions in Central America, the pact was less clear. London was dead set against relinquishing the Mosquito Coast, and had no intention whatever of abandoning British Honduras. Secretary Clayton knew all this, yet he could not make specific concessions on these points for fear of arousing a partisan clamor from the Britain-haters in America. Both negotiators therefore deliberately consented to the use of ambiguous language to conceal their official differences; otherwise, a treaty probably could not have been concluded.

The much-disputed Article I of the Clayton-Bulwer Treaty provided that neither party was to "occupy" or "colonize" or exercise "dominion" over "any part of Central America." When Bulwer consented not "to occupy" any part of Central America, he understood that Britain was not "to occupy" anything *further.* Clayton, on the other hand, hoped to make the provision retroactive. As the *London Times* not inaptly remarked, the negotiation was a struggle "for generalship in the use of terms."

AN IGNOBLE SURRENDER OR A DIPLOMATIC COUP?

The Clayton-Bulwer Treaty was approved by the Senate, after only a brief debate, by a vote of 42 to 11. This surprisingly speedy action is not difficult to account for. For one thing, the Senators had been consulted during the negotiations; for another, they were able to read their own meaning into the ambiguous language of the document. Before the final

[8] S. F. Bemis, ed., *American Secretaries of State and their Diplomacy* (New York, 1928), VI, 57.

ratification, Clayton and Bulwer exchanged confidential notes which attempted to clarify their interpretations of what the treaty was really intended to accomplish. Clayton resorted to these under-the-table tactics primarily because he feared that the Senate would throw out the entire pact if the reservations were made public. At best, such stratagems were a questionable way of circumventing the regularly constituted treaty-making authority.

Whatever unclarity may exist about the negotiations, it is clear that the Clayton-Bulwer Treaty was the most persistently unpopular pact ever concluded by the United States. Former Secretary of State James Buchanan, a member of the opposition Democratic Party, wrote that Bulwer deserved a "British peerage." Senator Stephen Douglas, also a Democrat, condemned the agreement as "truckling to Great Britain." Specifically, opponents of the treaty declared that it was a self-denying pledge which would thwart the southward expansion of the American people. There was much truth in this assertion, for the United States formally bound itself not to acquire any of Central America.

Critics also charged that the Clayton-Bulwer Treaty violated the Monroe Doctrine by permitting Britain to keep the territory she had already illegally seized in Central America. On this point there is much difference of opinion. But it is evident that the treaty, by placing a barrier in the path of British aggression in Central America, actually strengthened the Monroe Doctrine. In a sense, the agreement marked the first important acceptance by a foreign power of the principles underlying Monroe's noncolonization clause.

Much more can be said in defense of the Clayton-Bulwer Treaty. The United States, at no great cost to itself, averted serious difficulties with Britain, possibly war. The pact also marked the high tide of British expansion in Central America. It was undeniably unpopular, but its unpopularity grew largely out of the fact that it was a compromise. The United States abandoned its schemes for a canal under exclusive American control; Britain did likewise. But without compromise and concession there would have been no agreement.

In later years, when the United States had become a major power and had outgrown the treaty, the complaints about having been bamboozled by slippery British diplomats were redoubled. So it seemed in 1900. But in 1850 the picture was radically different. America was still only a second-rate power, torn by a violent slavery controversy. Yet she persuaded the number-one naval power to treat with her on a plane of equality. She also succeeded in halting British expansion in Central America, as well as a formidable attempt to secure a death grip on the Isthmian route. Considering the times, the Clayton-Bulwer Treaty was something of a triumph for American diplomacy.

THE CENTRAL AMERICAN COCKPIT

The decade from 1850 to 1860 was one of misunderstanding and bickering over the Clayton-Bulwer Treaty. Whatever may have been American desires, the British showed little inclination to relinquish the Mosquito protectorate. They not only refused to abandon the Honduran Bay Islands, but they made these bits of territory a crown colony in 1852. This "colony-snatching" was widely regarded in America as a deliberate evasion of a treaty obligation and a provocative violation of the Monroe Doctrine.

The explosive possibilities of the Mosquito controversy were dramatically illustrated at Greytown, in July, 1854. Mob outbursts there included an attack upon a United States diplomatic official, whose face was cut by a broken bottle. An American naval officer, backed by frowning guns, demanded reparation. When it was not forthcoming, he literally blew the town off the map. No lives were lost, but the property of foreigners was destroyed, including that of Britons and Frenchmen.

President Pierce, in his annual message to Congress, defended the iron-handed act of the American commander. But the London government, already disturbed by the aggressive policy of the United States toward Cuba, was greatly angered. Even the ordinarily unruffled Lord Clarendon, then Foreign Secretary, showed extreme displeasure when discussing the incident with the United States minister. The First Lord of the Admiralty declared, "We are fast 'drifting' into a war with the U. States. . . ."[9]

The London authorities, after vainly attempting to secure a disavowal of the bombardment, ceased to push their grievance. They took the position that British subjects must seek redress from the Nicaraguan government, which had tolerated such disorders. This moderate course was no doubt prompted in part by a realization that American public opinion was far from unanimous in supporting the brutal bombardment. Moreover, the blood-draining Crimean War had broken out several months earlier, and Britain had her hands full without a fight with the Yankees over the somewhat ridiculous Mosquito protectorate. Even at this late date Europe's distresses were helping to safeguard the United States.

The already vexed situation in Central America was further complicated by the filibustering activities of William Walker, an adventuresome Tennessean who became known as the "grey-eyed man of destiny." A shy individual weighing scarcely one hundred pounds, he led an unsuccessful foray into Lower California in 1853. He followed it with three expeditions into Central America, in 1855, 1857, and 1860.

[9] R. W. Van Alstyne, ed., "Anglo-American Relations, 1853–1857," *Amer. Hist. Rev.*, XLII (1937), 497 (Graham to Clarendon, Oct. 24, 1854).

With the aid of a motley group of American adventurers and disaffected Central Americans, Walker finally established himself as dictator of Nicaragua, from 1855 to 1857. His complex plans apparently embraced the formation of a Central American federation with himself at the head. But among American free-soilers he was regarded, though mistakenly, as being merely a front for the pro-slavery expansionists of the South. Such an interpretation gained greater plausibility when the Democrats, who were well entrenched in the South, expressed approval in their 1856 platform of Walker's efforts "to regenerate" Nicaragua.

The British naturally regarded this prince of filibusterers as "the advance guard of Manifest Destiny." Specifically, they accused him of secretly attempting to secure territory for the United States in Central America, in plain violation of the letter and the spirit of the Clayton-Bulwer Treaty. This conclusion did not seem unreasonable in view of the ineffective efforts being made by Washington to enforce its antifilibustering laws in the face of profilibustering public opinion. But fortunately for relations between the two English-speaking nations, Walker's ambitious plans were finally ruined by disease, bad liquor, treachery, the opposition of Cornelius Vanderbilt's transit company, and British and French hostility. The "grey-eyed man of destiny" crumpled before a Honduran firing squad in 1860.

CODFISH SEASONED WITH CHAMPAGNE

Trouble bobbed up in another quarter in the 1850's, when the Canadians sought to delimit the limited fishing privileges granted to Americans by the Convention of 1818. Among other things, they attempted to prevent the Yankees from hovering within three miles of the coast and from purchasing bait and supplies in British colonial ports. As soon as the local authorities undertook to uphold these new restrictions by seizing American fishing craft, the hardy New Englanders flared up in instant resentment. They found an able advocate in Daniel Webster, a fellow New Englander, who publicly demanded that his sea-going countrymen be protected, " 'hook and line, and bob and sinker.' " By July, 1853, fishing vessels were being armed for any possible contingency. President Pierce sent a fleet to the troubled waters with ominous orders to prevent, forcibly if necessary, interference with the rights of the United States.

The possibilities of an armed clash were freely discussed on both sides. Senator Davis of Massachusetts asserted that "if Great Britain wants a war, undoubtedly she can have it." But across the Atlantic the *London Spectator* thought it nothing short of a "crime" that the "right of catching fishes in the Bay of Fundy" should have brought "two powerful nations linked by closest ties of kindred, sympathy and interest" to the verge of war. The *London Punch*, forsaking the usual role of lampooning its transatlantic kinsmen, observed:

> Perish all the cod and mackerel in the Ocean—fine eating as they are—
> before we go to war with Brother JONATHAN for a cause as scaly as any
> fish can be that have no scales. We can't think of quarrelling with JONA-
> THAN about fish at a time when our general enemy [Russia ?] is plot-
> ting everywhere to reduce us, in a greater measure than we like, to a fish
> diet. . . .[10]

The quarrel over the fisheries was intimately bound up with the internal crisis in Canada. The repeal of the preferential British corn laws in 1846, combined with the high American tariff and other handicaps, had brought much distress. A small but vocal minority of the Canadian people agitated, particularly in 1849, for union with their great neighbor. Had it not been for the hostility of Southern slaveholders to Northern expansion, the United States undoubtedly would have shown a much more lively interest in the possibilities of annexation.

But Britain had her hands too full with the tangled European skein to permit the fisheries dispute to drift to a bloody conclusion. Downing Street finally decided to make an extraordinary effort by sending to America a special mission, headed by Lord Elgin, a hard-headed but genial Scot famous for his racy anecdotes and brilliant repartee. The British delegation arrived in Washington a day or so before the passing of the fateful Kansas-Nebraska Bill of 1854. The South, which felt that it had racked up a hard-won gain for slavery, was in a mood to placate the North by approving a treaty with Canada. The Americans wanted fishing privileges; the Canadians wanted to batter down the Yankee tariff walls. The stage was set for bargaining.

Wise in the ways of men, Lord Elgin recognized the value of social amenities as a lubricant for diplomatic wheels. His brilliant young secretary, Laurence Oliphant, has left some vivid if exaggerated passages describing the fortnight of wining and dining that accompanied the negotiations. One is struck with his frequent mention of the champagne which "irrigated" the table.

> It was the height of the season when we were at Washington, and our
> arrival imparted a new impetus to the festivities, and gave rise to the taunt,
> after the treaty was concluded . . . that "it had been floated through on
> champagne." Without altogether admitting this, there can be no doubt that,
> in the hands of a skilful diplomatist, that beverage is not without its value.[11]

The kind of diplomacy that the British employed was cynically described by Oliphant as "chaffing Yankees and slapping them on the back." "If you

[10] *Punch*, XXIII, 88 (Aug. 21, 1852).

[11] Laurence Oliphant, *Episodes in a Life of Adventure* (4th ed., Edinburgh, 1887), pp. 46–47.

have got to deal with hogs," he queried, "what are you to do?" This remark was most unfair to Secretary Marcy, who conducted the negotiations with genuine skill and who won most of the concessions.

RELUCTANT CANADIAN RECIPROCITY

The resulting Reciprocity Treaty of 1854, the first of its kind entered into by the United States, was signed on June 5. By its terms the Americans were granted much more generous fishing privileges than those guaranteed by the Convention of 1818. Specifically, they were permitted to fish virtually without restriction along the shores of Canada, New Brunswick, Nova Scotia, Prince Edward's Island, and a number of smaller islands. In return, and of much less importance, British subjects were permitted to fish southward for about a thousand miles along the American coast. Of much greater concern to the Canadians were the reciprocity provisions. The treaty stipulated that a long list of commodities, chiefly farm products, should be reciprocally admitted by both Canada and the United States without duties.

Ratification of the pact by the United States was assured. The North approved reciprocity because it seemed like a long step toward the annexation of Canada; the South approved reciprocity because it seemed likely to relieve Canada's economic distress and quiet Canadian demands for union with the Yankees. With the two major sections backing the treaty for precisely opposite reasons, it slid through the Senate with little opposition. Lest there be any slip, the State Department employed an able lobbyist, Israel D. Andrews, who later claimed that he spent $118,000 on members of Congress and others.

The provincial legislatures of what is now Canada were required to pass the needed legislation before the treaty could become effective. The State Department, anticipating trouble in this quarter, had employed Andrews during the winter of 1853–1854 to smooth the way in the Maritime Provinces. Using American and Canadian governmental funds, the clever agent spent over $90,000 for newspaper articles, entertainment, and various kinds of bribery. He paid $840 to one New Brunswick legislator who had been "adverse to a surrender of the fisheries," but who, after the "disbursement," became an ardent supporter of the treaty. However questionable these tactics may be, the reciprocity pact removed the most serious sources of Canadian-American friction, and inaugurated a new era of commercial prosperity.

THE CRAMPTON AND WALKER COMPLICATIONS

When the Crimean War erupted in 1854, the British were shocked by the lack of sympathy for them in the United States. The hereditary anti-

British feeling, reinforced by the presence of tens of thousands of Irish immigrants, caused many Americans to conclude that in any war between Britain and a foreign power, the foreign power must be in the right. There was also much sentiment in America for Russia because of the curiously friendly relations that had long existed between the giant despotism of the East and the giant democracy of the West. The Russian minister in Washington actually received a communication from three hundred Kentucky riflemen who asked to be sent to the Crimea. But the feeling of the American people on the whole was probably more anti-British than pro-Russian.

British bungling and stubborn Russian resistance caused an alarming drain on the manpower of the United Kingdom. The ghastly "charge of the light brigade" in the Crimea—an episode soon immortalized by the British poet Tennyson—brought home with crushing force the seriousness of the problem. To fill decimated ranks, Her Majesty's government turned to foreign lands. The British minister in Washington, John Crampton, was instructed to take discreet steps to enlist volunteers. Soon a trickle of prospective recruits was being directed to Halifax, in conformity, Crampton insisted, with the strict letter of the inadequate American neutrality law of 1818.[12] But public opinion in the United States reacted so violently against this unneutral activity that Secretary Marcy protested vigorously to Crampton. When remonstrances proved ineffective, Marcy demanded his recall, but the Foreign Office refused to consent to such hasty action. Crampton was then abruptly dismissed, on May 28, 1856, together with three British consuls implicated with him.

Two weeks before sending Crampton home, President Pierce, overriding Secretary Marcy, shamelessly extended recognition to the bayonet-supported government of William Walker in Nicaragua. Both the Walker and Crampton incidents should be interpreted in the light of current politics. The Democratic national nominating convention assembled in Cincinnati only four days after Crampton's dismissal, and the news of his fate was promptly telegraphed to the assembled delegates. This move becomes more understandable when one remembers that Pierce was an active candidate for renomination; that the great body of Irish-Americans, to say nothing of other Anglophobes, was enrolled in the ranks of the Democratic Party; and that these England-hating expatriates enjoyed the protesting roars of the British lion when his tail was given a twist. One should also note that the Democrats, whose aggressive slavery policy was under fire, were eager to divert attention to Crampton and Central America on the eve of an election.

The British were angered by the inhospitable treatment accorded their diplomats and consular representatives. Nor was the atmosphere im-

[12] R. W. Van Alstyne, "John F. Crampton, Conspirator or Dupe?" *Amer. Hist. Rev.*, XLI (1936), 495.

proved by Pierce's recognition of Walker's Nicaragua regime, and by the apparent determination of the United States to violate the Clayton-Bulwer Treaty by annexing Nicaragua. English newspapers bristled with ugly talk of war. The American minister in London, George M. Dallas, confidently expected the axe to fall on his neck in retaliation for the Crampton dismissal:

> If *The Times* and the *Post* are reliable *organs,* I shall probably quit England soon, *never* to return. . . . It will not surprise me if I should turn out to be the last Minister from the United States to the British Court, and that will certainly be fame if it be not honour.[13]

The saner counsels of the British shipping and manufacturing interests, as well as of other moderates, fortunately prevailed. The *London Morning Star* attacked the *Times* for its recklessness of tone and for "hurling insults across the Atlantic with as little thought as a schoolboy." The Crampton controversy, moreover, involved nothing fundamental; and, as the American minister in London observed, Southern cotton, upon which English spindles were critically dependent, was "pretty good bail for the peaceful behavior of this country." Enough blood had been spilled during the recent war with Russia.

JOHN BULL AND COUSIN JONATHAN

Secretary Marcy's firm handling of the Central American and Crampton episodes had its effect in London. The possibilities of a frightful conflict, particularly over such relatively minor issues, opened the eyes of the British public to a situation that had been allowed to drift dangerously. Opposition to the Yankee had merely stimulated his aggressiveness and jeopardized the peace. Was it wise to risk a war with the United States, whose trade amounted to more than that with all of the other American republics combined? Besides, if the Yankee should absorb all of North America to the Isthmus, would not his presence bring stability to this revolution-torn region and make for an improvement of British trade? In June, 1856, the powerful *London Times* could "look with great resignation and even pleasure" to the day when the United States would extend to the Isthmus of Panama. In February, 1856, Minister Buchanan could report from London that there "has been a marked and favourable change of feeling here within the last month towards the United States. I am now made something of a lion wherever I go. . . ."[14] Even the *London Punch,* pleading that the fault-finding of British travelers be bygones, quipped:

---

[13] Beckles Willson, *America's Ambassadors to England* (London, 1928), p. 298.
[14] G. T. Curtis, *Life of James Buchanan* (New York, 1883), II, 167.

Say is it your intent to wallop
Us on account of Mrs. TROLLOPE?
Or are we by you to be smitten
By something DICKENS may have written? [15]

The gratifying improvement in Anglo-American relations during the late 1850's, though hampered by the impact of the Panic of 1857 on British investments, had many roots. Among them should be mentioned an increased literary fellowship which resulted from the acceptance in England of hitherto scorned American writers, including Longfellow. There was also the temporarily successful laying in 1858 of the Atlantic cable, which led to a highly publicized exchange of felicitations between Queen Victoria and President Buchanan. Finally, there was the relative decline of the American merchant marine, notably the foam-cleaving clipper, whose formidable challenge for ascendancy had alarmed British competitors.

A NEW DAY IN ANGLO-AMERICAN RELATIONS

Early in 1858 British officers stationed in West Indian waters began a systematic search of American merchantmen suspected of being slavers. They even went so far as to fire at several United States vessels that refused to show their colors.[16] This revival of the odious right of search caused American indignation to mount dangerously, and Washington rushed warships to the Gulf of Mexico with orders to resist illegal practices. When Secretary of State Cass lodged a ringing protest, the British Foreign Secretary wrote a memorable reply, dated June 8, 1858, in which he formally disclaimed any pretension to a right of search in time of peace. The ease with which this dangerous reef was cleared provided further proof of London's desire to preserve the recently achieved cordiality.

Under the mellowing influence of the new Anglo-American accord, the Central American snarl was gradually untangled. British public opinion seems to have favored a settlement, provided that it could be secured honorably. But, as a writer in *Blackwood's* put it, Britain "cannot consent to be bullied out of her rights." The Foreign Office revealed its willingness to abandon the Bay Islands and the Mosquito protectorate when Lord Clarendon signed a convention with George M. Dallas, the American minister in London, in October, 1856. The Senate approved the agreement with amendments, but when these proved unacceptable to Downing Street, the so-called Dallas-Clarendon Convention was dropped. Henceforth Britain bided her time waiting for a favorable opening.

---

[15] *Punch*, XXX, 258 (June 28, 1856).
[16] R. W. Van Alstyne, "The British Right of Search and the African Slave Trade," *Jour. of Mod. Hist.*, II (1930), 39.

The immediate Isthmian controversies between England and America were settled indirectly, when London concluded separate treaties with the interested Central American republics. By the pact of 1859 with Honduras, the British recognized that the Bay Islands belonged to that republic; by the pact of 1860 with Nicaragua, the British relinquished their claims to the Mosquito territory. In his annual message of December, 1860, on the eve of the Civil War, President Buchanan could report that these two treaties had resulted "in a final settlement entirely satisfactory to this Government." Time, patient diplomacy, and fortuitous developments had won a series of diplomatic successes for the United States, including a victory for the Monroe Doctrine.

SELECTED BIBLIOGRAPHY

A useful survey is S. F. Bemis, ed., *The American Secretaries of State and their Diplomacy* (New York, 1928), Vol. V. On Austrian affairs, consult M. E. Curti, "Austria and the United States, 1848–1852," *Smith College Studies in History,* XI (1926), no. 3. See also J. G. Gazley, *American Opinion of German Unification, 1848–1871* (New York, 1926), and A. J. May, *Contemporary American Opinion of the Mid-Century Revolutions in Central Europe* (Philadelphia, 1927). The standard monograph is M. W. Williams, *Anglo-American Isthmian Diplomacy, 1815–1915* (Washington, 1916). See also Dexter Perkins, *The Monroe Doctrine, 1826–1867* (Baltimore, 1933), for the bearing of the Doctrine on the Isthmus. The classic work on Walker is W. O. Scroggs, *Filibusters and Financiers* (New York, 1916). The most recent study of Canadian reciprocity is L. B. Shippee, *Canadian-American Relations, 1849–1874* (New Haven, 1939). The present writer is indebted to Ivor D. Spencer for an opportunity to read his book manuscript "The Victor and the Spoils: A Life of William L. Marcy."

Useful articles are E. N. Curtis, "American Opinion of the French Nineteenth-Century Revolutions," *Amer. Hist. Rev.,* XXIX (1924), 249–270; J. W. Oliver, "Louis Kossuth's Appeal to the Middle West—1852," *Miss. Valley Hist. Rev.,* XIV (1928), 481–495; F. A. Golder, "Russian-American Relations during the Crimean War," *Amer. Hist. Rev.,* XXXI (1926), 462–476; R. W. Van Alstyne, "The Central American Policy of Lord Palmerston, 1846–1848," *Hispanic Amer. Hist. Rev.,* XVI (1936), 339–359; R. W. Van Alstyne, "British Diplomacy and the Clayton-Bulwer Treaty, 1850–60," *Jour. of Mod. Hist.,* XI (1939), 149–183.

See footnotes of this chapter; Bemis and Griffin, *Guide,* pp. 203 ff.; and *Harvard Guide,* Ch. XVII.

7TH ED. REFS. The manuscript mentioned above has been published as I. D. Spencer, *The Victor and the Spoils: A Life of William L. Marcy* (Providence, R.I., 1959), and presents interesting details on aspects of Marcy's tenure as Secretary of State. For additional references see BIBLIOGRAPHICAL ADDENDUM, p. 992.

8TH AND 9TH ED. REFS. See BIBLIOGRAPHICAL ADDENDUM, p. 993.

America and Cuba
to 1860

> [America is bounded on the] East by sunrise, West
> by sunset, North by the Arctic Expedition, and South
> as far as we darn please.
>
> PHILADELPHIA PUBLIC LEDGER, July 8, 1853

CUBA: A KEY TO THE CONTINENT

THE UPHEAVAL of the Spanish-American revolutions resulted in the complete banishment of Spain from the American continents. From her once vast empire, she was able to salvage only two insular remnants, Puerto Rico and Cuba. The latter, known as "The Ever Faithful Isle" (*Isla Siempre Leal*), was by far the more fertile and valuable. Flowing with sugar and molasses, it fully justifies such titles as "The Pearl of the Antilles" and "The World's Sugar Bowl."

Cuba, moreover, enjoys a unique strategic position. Located at the crossroads of the Caribbean trade routes, it is wedged like a giant Havana cigar into the mouth of the Gulf of Mexico in such a way as to dominate the only two entrances to that body of water. A powerful and unfriendly nation could have transformed the island into a veritable Gibraltar. The United States has thus had reason to fear a jeopardizing of its Isthmian routes, a bottling up of its Gulf ports, and a virtual closing of the mouth of the Mississippi.

All things considered, one of the miracles of the 19th Century was the failure of Cuba to fall into the basket of Manifest Destiny. Not only is the island strategically priceless, but it is geographically almost a part of the United States. And the American people, partly under the spur of the slavery men, were expanding during the 1840's and 1850's with seemingly irresistible energy. The spotlight of Manifest Destiny was bound to fall on the Pearl of the Antilles.

INCREASING COVETOUSNESS FOR CUBA

At an early date American statesmen, notably Jefferson, were keenly aware of the importance of Cuba to the United States. Their solicitude was stimulated by the Louisiana Purchase and by the threatened break-up of Spain's colonial empire. Late in 1808, following disquieting rumors, Jefferson's Cabinet put itself on record as strongly opposing the acquisition of the island by Britain or France. Thus was foreshadowed the no-transfer principle of the Monroe Doctrine.

As the century lengthened, reports were periodically revived of Britain's presumed designs on Cuba. This speculation was stimulated in 1823 by the movements of a British fleet in Caribbean waters, and, as already noted, may have had some bearing on the enunciation of the Monroe Doctrine. In April, 1823, Secretary of State Adams sent to the Madrid legation a memorable instruction in which he asserted that "the annexation of Cuba to our federal republic will be indispensable to the continuance and integrity of the Union itself." He concluded:

> . . . There are laws of political, as well as of physical gravitation; and if an apple, severed by the tempest from its native tree, cannot choose but fall to the ground, Cuba, forcibly disjoined from its own unnatural connexion with Spain, and incapable of self-support, can gravitate only towards the North American Union, which, by the same law of nature, cannot cast her off from its bosom.[1]

In 1825 alleged French designs on Cuba, as reflected by the unexplained presence of a powerful fleet, evoked strong protests from both London and Washington. Foreign Secretary Canning went so far as to propose that America, France, and Britain enter into a three-way guarantee of the island to Spain. But for various reasons both Paris and Washington refused to be inveigled into such an entrapment. The United States, however, was not averse to a lone-hand guarantee, and in 1840 it assured Madrid that it was fully prepared to help defend Cuba against aggression "from whatever quarter."

As far as international rivalries were concerned, there was one basic reason why neither America, France nor Britain acquired Cuba during the decades before the Civil War. Each of these powers was so jealous of the others that no two of them would permit the third to despoil senile Spain. The *London Courier,* referring to a similar situation in Europe, pointedly remarked in 1825 that Cuba was a transatlantic Turkey, "kept from falling only by the struggles of those who contend for the right of catching her in her descent."[2] Spain was indeed the "sick man" of

---

[1] *House Ex. Docs.,* 32 Cong., 1 sess., no. 121, p. 7 (Adams to Nelson, April 28, 1823).

[2] Quoted in J. M. Callahan, *Cuba and International Relations* (Baltimore, 1899), p. 140.

America, and this very weakness proved at times to be a source of strength.

Thus, even before the Monroe Doctrine was launched, the United States had developed a clear-cut policy toward Cuba. First and foremost, the island should never be allowed to pass into the hands of a European nation other than Spain. Secondly, by implication, Cuba would one day be gathered beneath the protective wings of the American eagle. As a determined patriot told the British consul at Philadelphia in 1851: "When we Yankees have once set our *souls* upon a thing, we always have it. Not England, France, and Spain, united, can prevent Cuba from one day becoming ours." [3]

THE OBSTACLE OF SPANISH PRIDE

Until the Mexican War the attitude of the United States toward Cuba was defensive and protective. Thereafter this passive policy was dropped in favor of an acquisitive one. From New Orleans, *De Bow's Review* trumpeted the spirit of the times:

> The North Americans *will* spread out far beyond their present bounds. They *will* encroach again and again upon their neighbors. New territories *will* be planted, declare their independence, and be annexed! We have New Mexico and California! We *will* have old Mexico and Cuba! The isthmus cannot arrest—nor even the Saint Lawrence!! Time has all of this in her womb. [4]

There were special reasons for the covetous concern of the United States after 1848. Havana was a natural port of call for ships engaged in trade with newly acquired California and Oregon. With that strategic harbor in the hands of an unfriendly nation, American commerce could be hampered by vexatious regulations. Cuba was also in a position to command the vital Isthmian routes, in which a deepening interest had developed since the unearthing of gold in California.

But the most important stimulant to the growing appetite for Cuba was the slavery issue. As a result of the Mexican War, the South had secured disappointingly little territory into which its "peculiar institution" could expand. If the voting preponderance of the North in Congress was to be checked, the South would have to find new areas for its Negroes. Cuba, which already had a large slave population and which presumably could be carved into two or more slave states, was by far the most desirable territory for such a purpose. And apparently it was the most readily available.

There was still another aspect to slavery in Cuba. If Spain should retain the rich island and free the slaves, an inflammatory example to the

---

[3] Quoted in L. A. White, "The United States in the 1850's as seen by British Consuls," *Miss. Valley Hist. Rev.*, XIX (1933), 528.

[4] *De Bow's Review*, VI, 9 (July, 1848).

Negroes of the South would be created off the back door of the United States. Perhaps there would be a repetition of the Negro butcheries in Haiti; the establishment of a black government; the "Africanization" of Cuba. In the eyes of many Southerners, annexation would avert all these calamities.

The purposeful Polk, ever-willing servant of Manifest Destiny, in 1848 confidentially authorized the United States minister to Spain, Romulus M. Saunders, to open negotiations for the purchase of Cuba. If necessary, he was to offer as much as $100 million. When news of the proposition leaked out, Spanish public opinion reacted so violently that the Ministry dared not dispose of the island at any price. The blundering overtures of Saunders were soundly rebuffed, and a Spanish spokesman declared that "sooner than see the island transferred to any power, they [Spain] would prefer seeing it sunk in the ocean." This untimely maneuver not only increased the suspicions of the Spaniards, but strengthened them in their determination to hang on.

THE FILIBUSTERER REPLACES THE NEGOTIATOR

With Cuba so desirable and Spain so obdurate, adventuresome Americans turned naturally to filibustering expeditions as a means of shaking the tree of Manifest Destiny. A daring leader appeared in the person of General Narciso López, a Venezuelan adventurer who had recently been involved in an uprising in Cuba and who believed that the disaffected elements there would welcome a deliverer. He planned to land with a considerable force, summon the Cubans to raise the banner of freedom, wrest the island from Spanish dominion, and then presumably offer it to the United States. Fortunately for these schemes, the spirit of expansion was abroad in the land, particularly in the South. As John A. Quitman, one of the most ardent Southern expansionists, insisted:

> Our destiny is intertwined with that of Cuba. If slave institutions perish there they will perish here. Thus interested, we must act. Our government, already distracted with the slavery question, can not or will not act. We must do it as individuals.[5]

Other circumstances favored López. Hundreds of restless veterans of the Mexican War were eager to carry out the dictates of Manifest Destiny, while thwarting the presumed designs of Britain on Cuba. Some of these adventurers regarded themselves as torch bearers of liberty, which had been brutally snuffed out in the recent European revolutions. But probably many more of them were seduced by promises of rewards, including confiscated sugar plantations. American speculators, who had bought up

[5] J. F. H. Claiborne, *Life and Correspondence of John A. Quitman* (New York, 1860), II, 208 (Quitman to Reed, Aug. 24, 1854).

Cuban bonds at from 3 to 20 cents on the dollar, could scarcely restrain their enthusiasm for Cuban liberty.

Failure dogged López's heels. His first expedition, that of 1849, was prevented from leaving New York by the vigilance of the federal authorities. López thereupon organized another expedition, and slipped out of New Orleans with about 700 men. Many of them, indiscreetly reflecting American zeal for the European revolutions of 1848, wore red shirts and thereby increased the risk of detection from passing steamers. The motley force landed on Cuban shores in May, 1850. But when the inhabitants, who were represented as panting for liberty, failed to rise and greet their deliverers, López was forced to flee to the United States. He arrived in Key West just a few minutes ahead of a pursuing Spanish warship. Arrested at Savannah for having violated the neutrality laws, he was released for lack of evidence, and was greeted as a conquering hero. López and other leaders were also indicted at New Orleans, but public opinion was so sympathetic that three successive juries disagreed. Prosecutions in New York and Ohio met with similar failures.

FILIBUSTERING FIZZLES OUT

Still undaunted, López laid plans for his third and last descent upon Cuba with about 500 men, mostly Americans. He offered the command of the expedition successively to Jefferson Davis and Robert E. Lee, both of whom were interested but not sufficiently so to risk their necks. In August, 1851, López stole out of New Orleans with the connivance of the collector of the port. His tiny army, after landing in Cuba, was crushed by Spanish troops. López and fifty of his followers were speedily executed, and more than one hundred of the remaining prisoners were condemned to penal servitude. The severity of the punishment was doubtless designed to discourage these annual descents upon the island. In fact, a number of eager Americans in New Orleans were awaiting only the news of López's success before rushing on to his assistance.

When the news of the mass execution of "the gallant fifty-one" reached New Orleans, hotbed of filibusterism, the indignation of the populace rose to fever heat. Many of the ill-fated adventurers were from the "best families" of the South, and their kinsfolk and friends were outraged. A Spanish newspaper in New Orleans was so ill-advised as to gloat over the executions. A mob thereupon wrecked the press, destroyed other property belonging to Spaniards, sacked the Spanish consulate, defaced portraits of the Queen and of the Captain-General of Cuba, and tore to bits a Spanish flag.

Violence flared up elsewhere, notably in Key West, Florida, where sympathy for the filibusterers was red hot. Mass meetings were held in cities as far north as Cincinnati and Pittsburgh. Even in Philadelphia, where there had been strong opposition to López, the reports of Spanish ruthlessness produced a revulsion of sentiment.[6]

In Spain, where a mob was barely restrained from sacking the American legation in retaliation, there was wild talk of war. The Spanish minister in Washington demanded redress and reparation. The Whigs, less aggressively expansionist than the Democrats, were now in power, and fortunately Secretary Webster did not employ the same rabble-rousing tactics that he had earlier used against Hülsemann over Hungary. Although pointing to certain extenuating circumstances, Webster gallantly acknowledged the wrong and promised the necessary apologies.

This unexpectedly soft answer helped turn away the wrath of the Spaniards. Early in 1852 the Spanish minister in Washington announced that the Queen, as an act of grace, had pardoned the American survivors of the López expedition. Gratified by this concession, Congress in turn voted $25,000 as compensation for the damage done to Spanish property by the New Orleans mob.

AMERICA AVOIDS A SELF-DENYING TRAP

In 1849, when López attempted his first expedition, difficulties with Great Britain in Central America were coming to a boil. Cuban filibusterism merely added new combustibles. The *London Spectator* referred with disgust to the "arrogance" of the "Model Republic," and to the motives of the "loafers" and "vagabonds" who made up the filibustering expeditions. A British fleet was ordered to Cuban waters to co-operate with the French in defending the island. The British minister in Washington was instructed to explain that this precaution was being taken in the most friendly spirit—a protestation which, of course, the American people did not believe. López's failure at least had the merit of preventing serious international complications.

Anxieties aroused by López's activities led to another three-power proposition. At the instigation of Madrid, the British and French governments proposed, on April 23, 1852, that the United States join with them in a pact by which Cuba would be guaranteed to Spain. Secretary Webster favored the plan. But after he died and the American people had apparently shown themselves favorable to expansion in the November elections, President Fillmore would have none of the self-denying scheme.

To Secretary Edward Everett, Webster's successor, fell the task of explaining to Madrid why the United States could not tie its hands by such a tripartite pact. Among other things, Everett referred to the time-honored policy of no entanglements, and declared that no American government "could stand a day" if it bound itself in no circumstances to

[6] R. G. Caldwell, *The López Expeditions to Cuba, 1848–1851* (Princeton, 1915), pp. 65–66.

acquire the island. He even suggested, with considerable force, that if Cuba lay off the mouth of the Thames River in England, Great Britain would not be proposing such an arrangement.

THE AMERICAN ROVER-GENERAL WOT TRIED TO STEAL A CUBA

The British chortle over Yankee ejection.
London Punch, 1850

THE EXCESSES OF SOULÉ

After a four-year Whig interlude, the expansionist Democratic Party returned to power in 1853. The amiable President Pierce, strongly under Southern influence, was expected to launch a determined campaign for Cuba. But enthusiasm for the Pearl of the Antilles was by no means confined to the South. In Albany, New York, for example, enthusiastic Demo-

crats drank to such toasts as: "Cuba and the Sandwich [Hawaiian] Isles
—may they soon be added to the galaxy of States"; "The fruits of the
late Democratic victory—Pierce and Cuba"; and "May the Queen of the
Antilles be added to our glorious Confederacy under the prosperous administration of Pierce."

The pliable President Pierce chimed in with these enthusiasms for
Cuba. Responding to popular pressures, and quite willing to divert attention from the slavery controversy by a spirited foreign policy, he proclaimed in his inaugural address:

> . . . The policy of my Administration will not be controlled by any timid
> forebodings of evil from expansion. Indeed . . . our attitude as a nation
> and our position on the globe render the acquisition of *certain possessions
> not within our jurisdiction* [Cuba] eminently important for our protection,
> if not in the future essential for preservation of the rights of commerce and
> the peace of the world.[7] [Italics inserted]

With Cuba the focal point of America's foreign policy, the post of
United States minister to Spain took on unusual significance. For this
critical position Pierce chose the hotheaded Pierre Soulé, United States
Senator from Louisiana, a naturalized American who had been exiled from
France for his unrestrained republicanism. He had commended himself
to the Pierce administration by his notorious enthusiasm for seizing Cuba,
and for this reason alone his appointment was little short of an insult to
Spain.

The beginnings of the new mission were singularly inauspicious. On
the eve of sailing, Soulé made an indiscreet pro-annexationist speech to a
group of Cuban sympathizers in New York. The attitude of Soulé's diplomatic colleagues in Madrid was unfriendly. Several of them, notably the
French ambassador, the Marquis de Turgot, had allegedly sought to have
this middle-class French expatriate rejected. During a ball given by
Turgot, one of the guests made an offensive remark about Madame
Soulé's low-cut gown. The upshot was that the American envoy challenged
the French ambassador to a duel on the far-fetched grounds that the
alleged insult had occurred at the latter's home. In the resulting encounter Soulé had the satisfaction of shooting his adversary in the thigh
and laming him for life. The *New York Herald* lamented, "We wanted an
ambassador there, we have sent a matador."

The notoriety growing out of all these incidents caused the American
minister to be ostracized socially, and his usefulness was so sharply restricted that he should have been promptly recalled. Although the antics
of Soulé—that "damned little Frenchman"—met with considerable cen-
sure in the press of the United States, the more patriotic journals were
inclined to condone his conduct. The *Boston Post* hoped that "the ex-

[7] J. D. Richardson, *Messages and Papers of the Presidents* (Washington, 1897), V,
198–199 (March 4, 1853).

hibition of a little American grit may do these lacqueys of despotism some good." The Detroit *Free Press* exulted that "they are beginning to find out on the other side that Americans are considerable pumpkins, all right." [8]

THE *BLACK WARRIOR* EMBROILMENT

The Spanish officials in Cuba, partly as a result of the López expeditions, developed a bitterness toward the United States that was reflected in the enforcement of shipping regulations. A long series of vexatious incidents culminated in the seizure, on February 28, 1854, of the *Black Warrior*, an American steamer engaged in coastwise trade between New York and Mobile, Alabama. The charge was that she did not have a proper manifest of her cargo, although this technicality had been ignored during the thirty-odd times the vessel had previously touched at Havana.[9]

A wave of indignation, heightened by resentment over the outcome of the López expeditions, swept the United States. Although the country was convulsed by the Kansas-Nebraska debate, the tone of the press was unmistakably warlike. The *Washington Union*, organ of the Pierce administration, declared that the time had come when Spain must be met in Cuba with "the purse in one hand and the sword in the other." The *New York Herald* was no less belligerent:

> If the administration have any heart left, if there be among them one spark of American spirit, let them take up this matter in the tone which befits the gravity of the case, and the chronic character of the Cuban disease. No ambassadors, or diplomatic notes are needed. Let them simply fit out, in a week at farthest, three or four war steamers, and dispatch them to Cuba, with peremptory orders to obtain satisfaction for the injury done to the Black Warrior.[10]

The news of the *Black Warrior* incident came as a godsend to the impetuous Soulé. Here was an opportunity to lay down the law to the high-spirited Spaniard, goad him into war, and rob him of his Caribbean pearl. First presenting an offensively worded note, Soulé next delivered an ultimatum in which he demanded an indemnity of $300,000, the dismissal of all persons responsible for the *Black Warrior* seizure, and a reply within forty-eight hours. On all points except the demand for an indemnity, Soulé had impetuously exceeded his instructions from Secretary of State Marcy.

The center of the negotiations now shifted to Washington. The Spanish

[8] A. A. Ettinger, *The Mission to Spain of Pierre Soulé, 1853–1855* (New Haven, 1932), pp. 237–238.

[9] H. L. Janes, "The Black Warrior Affair," *Amer. Hist. Rev.*, XII (1907), 281.

[10] *New York Herald*, March 9, 1854, 4:4.

foreign minister, shrewdly suspecting that Soulé had violated his instructions, presented to Secretary Marcy such an able and tactful defense
of Spain's position as to make a deep impression on Pierce's Cabinet.
Rather than bicker with the overbearing Soulé, the Madrid authorities
dealt directly with the American owners of the *Black Warrior.* Months
before the affair had ceased to be a diplomatic problem, the vessel was
again plying its usual course in the usual way, except that it was receiving
unusual deference from the Spanish officials at Havana. The owners, who
received $53,000 in damages, were satisfied, even if Soulé was not.
Secretary Marcy, one should note, went out of his way to keep this indemnity at a minimum figure.

THE STILLBORN OSTEND MANIFESTO

The bloody Crimean War, in ordinary circumstances, would have provided enough distress in Europe to enable the United States to seize
Cuba. The London and Paris governments, though sympathizing with
Spain in the *Black Warrior* crisis, were in no position to intervene. But
Spain found one powerful and unexpected ally in America—Negro slavery. The Pierce administration had aroused so much antagonism in the
North by its efforts to ram the Kansas-Nebraska bill through Congress
that it simply did not dare take a second forward step in behalf of
slavery by provoking war for Cuba. Had it done so, it would have had a
tragically disunited nation on its hands. As the *New York Courier and
Enquirer* declared:

> Does the sane man live who believes that if Cuba was tendered us tomorrow
> . . . that this people would consent to receive and annex her? . . . There
> was a time when the North would have consented to annex Cuba, but the
> Nebraska wrong has forever rendered annexation impossible.[11]

For once, the United States could not take advantage of Europe's
distresses because of its own distresses.

The Pierce administration, though restrained by the black hand of
slavery from seizing Cuba, did take advantage of the *Black Warrior*
crisis to reopen negotiations for purchasing the island. Secretary Marcy's
remarkable instructions to Soulé, dated April 3, 1854, outlined the course
of action. If Spain should prove unwilling to accept a reasonable sum,
even a maximum of $130 million, "you will then direct your efforts to the
next most desirable object which is *to detach* that island from the
Spanish dominion and from all dependence on any European power." [12]
The succeeding passage indicates that what Marcy had in mind by

[11] Quoted in J. F. Rhodes, *History of the United States* (New York, 1896), II, 33 n.
[12] S. F. Bemis, ed., *The American Secretaries of State and their Diplomacy* (New
York, 1928), VI, 193 (Marcy to Soulé, April 3, 1854). Italics inserted.

"detach" was to assist Cuba to become independent, whereupon she would become eligible for annexation to the United States.

Secretary Marcy next suggested that Soulé arrange a conference with James Buchanan, United States minister in London, and John Y. Mason, minister in Paris. The three envoys were to exchange opinions and report their conclusions in a dispatch to Marcy. The ministerial trio finally met at Ostend, Belgium, in October, 1854. The European press, suspecting that the secret conference boded no good, indulged in wild speculation as to the fate of Cuba. The *London Morning Advertiser,* which feared for both Cuba and Hawaii, remarked, "Jonathan's legs are getting so long that he requires more room." Apparently desiring greater privacy, the three ministers left Ostend after three days for Aix-la-Chapelle, in Rhenish Prussia, where they concluded their work six days later, on October 18, 1854.

The recommendations of the three diplomats were embodied in a memorable dispatch, subsequently known as the "Ostend Manifesto." It was really the work of Soulé, though Buchanan tempered and wrote it. After recommending that an immediate effort be made to purchase Cuba for a price not to exceed $120 million, the American envoys then considered what should be done if Spain refused to sell. If this happened, and if her continued presence in Cuba should be regarded as dangerous to the United States:

> . . . Then, by every law, human and divine, we shall be justified in wresting it from Spain if we possess the power; and this upon the very same principle [referring to "Africanization"] that would justify an individual in tearing down the burning house of his neighbor if there were no other means of preventing the flames from destroying his own home.
>
> Under such circumstances we ought neither to count the cost nor regard the odds which Spain might enlist against us.[13]

In short, first undertake peaceful negotiations with Spain; then, *if the danger seemed great enough,* direct action.

The term Ostend Manifesto is a misnomer. In the first place, the document was not signed at Ostend but at Aix-la-Chapelle; in the second place, it was not a manifesto. A manifesto is ordinarily a public declaration of policy, and the misuse of the word in this connection has given rise to the mistaken conception that the document was presented to Spain as an ultimatum. On the contrary, the so-called Ostend Manifesto was a confidential dispatch, drawn up in deep secrecy and sent by a special messenger to the State Department. Neither Washington nor Madrid took official diplomatic notice of it, although public opinion at home and abroad certainly did.

[13] *House Ex. Docs.,* 33 Cong., 2 sess., no. 93, pp. 129, 131.

SOULE BECOMES THE SCAPEGOAT

The thinly disguised plottings of the three ministers at Ostend and Aix-la-Chapelle excited much hostile comment in Europe and elsewhere. Observing that the naïve Americans did not even bother to hatch their mischief in secret, the *London Times* gibed, "The diplomacy of the United States is certainly a very singular profession." Even before the official copy of the Ostend dispatch reached Secretary Marcy, the American press was publishing garbled versions of the Manifesto, while the antislavery and anti-Democratic newspapers were attacking the administration and its "Democratic minions."

Secretary Marcy was probably startled when, in November, 1854, he received the formal report of the three ministers. After prolonged discussions in the Cabinet, he framed a reply to Soulé, in which he politely but firmly rejected the suggestions of his agents. This repudiation becomes more understandable when one notes that the Democratic Party had suffered severe losses in the recent Congressional elections, partly, it appears, as a result of the administration's grasping Cuban policy. Soulé, though directed to continue negotiations for peaceful purchase, was so humiliated by his repudiation and so discredited by his increased notoriety that he resigned.

The outburst of criticism against the administration continued in the United States, much of it directed at "that French fop, Soulé." Even as confirmed a Democrat as Senator Cass of Michigan condemned the attempt to "steal" Cuba and asserted, "Such a case of rapacity will, I trust, never stain our annals." The public demand for an authentic copy of the Manifesto became so great that Congress published the relevant papers in March, 1855. Immediately the opposition press redoubled its uproar. The *New York Evening Post,* jeering at "The Three Wise Men of Ostend," branded the dispatch as "weak in its reasonings and atrocious in its recommendations." The *New York Tribune* condemned this "manifesto of brigands," which could be paraphrased: "If Spain will not sell us Cuba, we must steal it in order to preserve our national existence."

For nearly seventy-five years historians assumed that nothing essential had been omitted from the published documents. But in 1928 a scholar revealed that several important passages had been deleted, notably the one containing the famous "to detach" clause.[14] When these missing sections are supplied, a flood of light illuminates the formerly incomprehensible aspects of the Ostend affair.

On April 3, 1854, as already noted, Secretary Marcy directed Soulé to offer as much as $130 million for Cuba, and then, if unsuccessful, to take steps *"to detach"* the island from Spain. Surprising though it may seem,

---

[14] H. B. Learned, in Bemis, *American Secretaries of State,* VI, 214.

the essential portions of the Ostend Manifesto were not badly out of harmony with these rather ambiguous instructions. The three ministers had proposed that the United States offer $120 million for the island, and then, if need be, to "*wrest*" it from Spain. "To *wrest*" is certainly not a far cry from "to *detach*," even though Secretary Marcy probably had in mind a negotiated independence for Cuba. The excitable Soulé can perhaps be forgiven for having misread his instructions. But the Ostend Manifesto had aroused so much partisan opposition that the Pierce administration could not afford to blacken itself by revealing that Marcy's ambiguity was in part responsible for the damaging document. Soulé, whose appointment Marcy had opposed in the first place, was thus to some extent made the scapegoat for the sins of his superiors.

MANACLED MANIFEST DESTINY

Even before the distracted President Pierce left the White House, his blundering domestic and foreign policy had ruined whatever chance there may have been of securing Cuba. But the Southern annexationists, not realizing that they had slain their prospects of annexing the island on the altar of the Kansas-Nebraska Act, refused to give up hope. They elevated to the Presidency the complaisant James Buchanan, who had commended himself to the favorable attention of the Southern Democrats by his co-authorship of the Ostend Manifesto.

Buchanan fared no better than Pierce in his efforts to acquire Cuba. Two days after he took office in 1857, the Supreme Court handed down its momentous Dred Scott decision, which intensified the slavery struggle and further foreshadowed the impending sectional clash. Yet Buchanan, blind to the fact that Cuba was lost, still cherished a lively hope of securing the island, or perhaps he was just placating the South. In three of his four annual messages he vainly urged upon Congress the desirability of purchasing this Antillean jewel—recommendations which did nothing to quiet the suspicions of Spain.

Gradually Cuba began to fade into the background. An increasing amount of commerce that formerly had gone through the Gulf was now carried by railroads and canals. The Republicans in Congress wanted to pass the Homestead Act so as to open up Western lands to white settlers; the Southern Democrats desired Cuba so as to open up slave lands to slave owners. Neither side would gratify the aspirations of the other. With passions as inflamed as they were, the North probably would not have permitted the acceptance of Cuba if it had come as a voluntary gift from Spain. Yet as late as 1860 the two platforms of the divided Democratic Party declared for Cuba.

Then came such diversions as the terrible Civil War, oppressive problems of reconstruction, and amazing internal expansion. Slave territory was no longer needed: America already had territory enough and ex-slaves enough. The long-projected transcontinental railroad was com-pleted in 1869, thereby binding California with hoops of iron to the rest of the Union. The pressure for an Isthmian canal decreased, and the agitation for annexing Cuba declined. But, with the fateful Spanish-American War of 1898 still in the future, the troubled island had yet to play its most important role in American diplomacy.

SELECTED BIBLIOGRAPHY

An excellent survey appears in S. F. Bemis, ed., *The American Secretaries of State and their Diplomacy* (New York, 1928), VI, 183–216. The most detailed account is A. A. Ettinger, *The Mission to Spain of Pierre Soulé, 1853–1855* (New Haven, 1932), while Basil Rauch, *American Interest in Cuba: 1848–1855* (New York, 1948) is broader in coverage. See also R. F. Nichols, *Franklin Pierce* (rev. ed., Philadelphia, 1938). The most satisfactory monograph is R. G. Caldwell, *The López Expeditions to Cuba, 1848–1851* (Princeton, 1915). See also G. B. Henderson, "Southern Designs on Cuba, 1854–1857, and Some European Opinions," *Jour. of Southern Hist.*, V (1939), 371–385; C. S. Urban, "The Abortive Quitman Filibustering Expedition, 1853–1855," *Jour. of Miss. History*, XVIII (1956), 175–196; and C. S. Urban, "The Africanization of Cuba Scare, 1853–1855," *Hispanic Amer. Hist. Rev.*, XXXVII (1957), 29–45. The present writer has been privileged to read Ivor D. Spencer's book manu-script, "The Victor and the Spoils: A Life of William L. Marcy."

See footnotes of this chapter; Bemis and Griffin, *Guide*, pp. 302–308; and *Harvard Guide*, Ch. 17.

7TH ED. REFS. The manuscript listed above is now published as I. D. Spen-cer, *The Victor and the Spoils: A Life of William L. Marcy* (Providence, R.I., 1959), and effectively presents the case for the Secretary in the Ostend Mani-festo affair. J. A. Logan, Jr., *No Transfer* (New Haven, 1961) details America's inflexible unwillingness to see Cuba in other European hands, notably British or French. Henry Blumenthal, *A Reappraisal of Franco-American Relations, 1830–1871* (Chapel Hill, N.C., 1959) discusses French efforts to keep Cuba out of the hands of both Britain and America. P. S. Foner, *A History of Cuba and Its Relations with the United States* (New York, 1962), Vol. I (1492–1845) describes America's growing impatience with the "ripening-fruit" policy, especially after prospective Africanization under British auspices. P. S. Klein, *President James Buchanan* (University Park, Pa., 1962) notes that Buchanan strongly opposed the conference at Ostend as unnecessary; he helped tone down the final dispatch, which was not a direct threat in its final wording. B. D. Gooch, "Belgium and the Prospective Sale of Cuba in 1837," *Hispanic Amer. Hist. Rev.*, XXXIX (1959), 413–427 reveals that Cuba was for sale, and that Belgium's interest was chilled by London, which thought Cuba too much for Belgium to handle.

8TH AND 9TH ED. REFS. See BIBLIOGRAPHICAL ADDENDUM, p. 994.

CHAPTER

~~~~~~~~~~~~~~~~ 2 I ~~~~~~~~~~~~~~~

The Dawn of
Asiatic Interests

*Who does not see, then, that . . . the Pacific Ocean,
its shores, its islands, and the vast regions beyond,
will become the chief theatre of events in the world's
great hereafter?*

SENATOR SEWARD, 1852

TRADE PRECEDES THE DIPLOMAT

WHILE THE UNITED STATES was absorbed with the dramatic happenings
of the 1840's and 1850's, quieter but hardly less significant events were
taking place on the other side of the globe. The American people, to be
sure, were only secondarily interested in the Orient, but they were
nevertheless interested.

In 1784, the year after independence was won, a tiny merchantman, the
Empress of China, slipped quietly out of New York harbor on a 13,000
mile voyage to Canton, China. Its cargo consisted of assorted goods, but
chiefly a weed called ginseng which was highly prized by the elderly
Chinese gentlemen as a supposed cure for impotence. Fifteen months
later the vessel created a sensation when it returned with its hold full of
strange-smelling products, including tea. The reported profits, some
twenty-five per cent, were not remarkably high in view of the risks. But
other merchants were tempted to follow suit—sometimes recovering their
entire investment in one voyage—and a lucrative new avenue of commerce was opened.

The Old China trade grew so rapidly that in 1801 alone thirty-four
American vessels reached Canton, the only port open to foreigners. This
newly found commerce, although crippled by the Jeffersonian embargo
and the War of 1812, expanded profitably during the 1830's and 1840's.
From 1850 to 1855—the heyday of the graceful clipper ship—American
carrying trade with China reached a new high point.

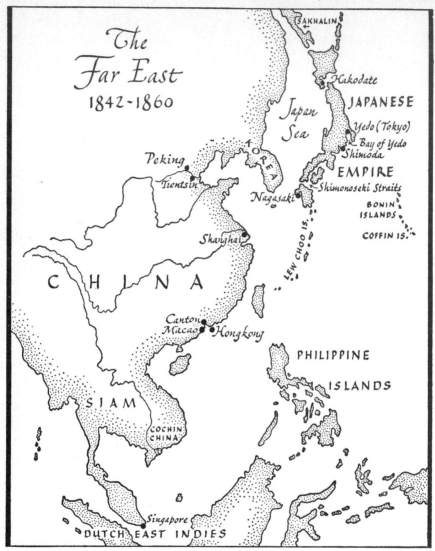

The Far East 1842-1860

Only two aspects of this fascinating story need be mentioned here. The demand at Canton for sea-otter pelts lured venturesome "Boston men" to the Pacific Northwest, and consequently did something to build up in the United States a public demand for the retention of Oregon. The China trade also helped the Americans to gain a solid foothold in the Hawaiian Islands, then known as the Sandwich Islands after the Earl of Sandwich. This glamorous archipelago was not only used as a provisioning station for the Northwest fur traders on their way to China, but it also provided an important supply of fragrant sandalwood, which the Chinese prized for wood carvings, boxes, and other articles.

Unfortunately for outsiders, the Chinese had long held that China—the Middle Kingdom—was *the* great nation and the only truly civilized one. All other nations, like barbarians on the outer edges, were regarded as inferior "foreign devils." If representatives of a foreign power were brought before the Emperor (Son of Heaven), they were forced, as were the Chinese themselves, to prostrate themselves before him in the kowtow.

China, being largely self-sufficient, was not eager to carry on trade with the outside world. Yet as a special concession, a restricted group of foreigners was permitted to engage in commercial enterprises at the single port of Canton, in South China. Here a few Occidental merchants lived rather precariously at their places of business (factories), while suffering indignities which included occasional stonings. Foreign hucksters who had forsaken the tombs of their ancestors for mere profit were held in especially low esteem. In an official Chinese customs report one finds this entry: "The barbarian Marks [a merchant] residing in the English devil factory; . . . the barbarian Just, residing in the French devil factory." [1]

EDMUND ROBERTS—PIONEER NEGOTIATOR

A lively public interest in the Far East was slow to develop in the United States. Not until 1831 was the word "China" mentioned in a public Presidential message or paper, and not until 1852 was reference made to Japan. Not until the early 1830's, when the murder of an American crew in Sumatra (Dutch East Indies) excited indignation, did the United States attempt to establish formal diplomatic relations with a Far Eastern nation.

Edmund Roberts, a sea captain of considerable mercantile experience, was sent out as a special agent in 1832, with instructions to draw up commercial treaties with Cochin China (Indochina), Siam, Muscat (on the Arabian Sea), and later with Japan. China was not included on the list, apparently because the nervous American merchants at Canton wished to let sleeping dragons lie. The diplomatic mission evidently was not considered to be of primary importance. Roberts was listed as "secretary to the commander" of the sloop of war, at a salary of $1500 a year, and was forced to sleep on the gun deck with the crew a part of the way.

Roberts met with varied success. In Cochin China he got nowhere, partly because he refused to submit to the degrading kowtow. But he did show resourcefulness when, discovering that he had to have titles, he reeled off the names of the counties in his native New Hampshire. In Siam and Muscat he concluded treaties in 1833 that were designed to free American trade from annoying restrictions. He finally decided not

[1] J. W. Foster, *American Diplomacy in the Orient* (Boston, 1903), p. 44.

to go on to Japan and attempt to open negotiations, partly because he was without funds to buy appropriate presents, and partly because he felt that his expedition was too small to impress the Japanese. He thereupon came back to the United States with his two treaties, which were duly approved by the Senate. Upon returning to the Orient to open negotiations with Japan, he died of the plague in 1836. Edmund Roberts was a pioneer—and a worthy one—in America's Far Eastern diplomacy.

INCREASED CONCERN FOR CHINA

In 1839 Britain and China clashed in the opening stages of the so-called Opium War. To the Chinese, the primary cause of the conflict was the determination of the British to force trade in opium upon the Celestial Empire. To foreigners, the primary issue was the effort to gain treatment as equals by the arrogant and haughty Chinese mandarins. The British rapidly demonstrated Western superiority over the spears and ancient muskets of their foes. By the Treaty of Nanking, concluded in 1842, the victor forced China to cede outright the key island of Hongkong (near Canton), and to throw open five Chinese ports to unrestricted residence and travel by Britons.[2]

The Opium War seems to have aroused the first widespread interest among Americans in the land which produced their tea and silk. The 1840's in the United States were an era of Britain-hating, and the American people were angered by what they regarded as John Bull's atrocious attempt to force opium on the heathen Chinese. But John Quincy Adams, braving "the strong current of popular opinion," delivered before the Massachusetts Historical Society a lengthy address, in which he justified Britain's course. The rugged New Englander recorded: "The excitement of public opinion and feeling by the delivery of this lecture far exceeds any expectation that I had formed. . . ."[3] The editor of the *North American Review* refused to publish his manuscript.

The sympathy for China evoked by the Opium War brought to a head in the United States a quiet educational process that had been going on over a period of years. The interest of American commercial groups, particularly those in the trading centers of New England and the Middle Atlantic states, has already been noted. Farther south, cotton growers were beginning to take notice of "China's illimitable markets" and the prospect of clothing several hundred million Chinese. In 1830 the first American missionaries had arrived in China, and reports from them,

---

[2] See J. K. Fairbank, *Trade and Diplomacy on the China Coast: The Opening of the Treaty Ports, 1842–1854* (Cambridge, 1953).

[3] C. F. Adams, ed., *Memoirs of John Quincy Adams* (Philadelphia, 1876), XI, 31 (Dec. 3, 1841).

together with financial support of their work, attracted widespread attention. The displaying of a Chinese girl with the traditional bound feet in a New York theater, as well as the opening of an excellent Chinese museum in Philadelphia in 1839, contributed to public impressions of the Middle Kingdom.

In 1842, at the conclusion of the Opium War, an American squadron appeared in Chinese waters under the command of the able and tactful Lawrence Kearny. Shortly after the British signed the Treaty of Nanking, he requested of the Chinese authorities that American merchants be put on the same footing as those "of the nation most favored." In short, Americans should enjoy all the commercial privileges that had just been extorted by the British. The next year, 1843, the Chinese government threw open the five new treaty ports on equal terms to all foreign nations, thus laying one of the foundation stones of the later Open-Door policy. The probable influence of Kearny's intercession is still in dispute, but the Chinese were evidently prepared to extend most-favored-nation treatment to all foreigners as a means of watering down British privileges and staving off future quarrels.

The fateful developments in China were watched with growing interest in the United States, where fears were expressed that American traders would suffer discrimination. The merchants of Boston, who were especially worried, urged with increasing vigor that a diplomatic representative be sent to China. Congress finally voted $40,000 for a special mission, although some members felt that its trifling importance did not warrant so large an expenditure. One Congressman from South Carolina was hopeful that the Chinese could be persuaded to chew American tobacco rather than Asiatic opium.

THE CUSHING MISSION

In 1843 Caleb Cushing, a handsome scholar-politician, was appointed the first American commissioner to China, pursuant to the recent vote of Congress. Among other attainments, he was a remarkable linguist and a profound student. When the publishers of a well-known dictionary sent a copy to him, he found over 5000 errors among the geographical names alone. He had, in fact, already become interested in the China trade, and he had acquired a storehouse of information about the Celestial Empire.

The Cushing mission sailed in July, 1843. It consisted of four warships laden with specimens of Western scientific wonders and other gifts, including a pair of six-shooters, a telescope, and a set of the *Encyclopedia Americana.* Cushing carried instructions which stated that his primary object was to secure for the United States those commercial privileges that had recently been won by British arms. The somewhat childish letter that he bore from President Tyler to the Son of Heaven reflected the "lick-all-creation-spirit" of the era, as well as the language customarily used in addressing Indian chiefs:

> I hope your health is good. China is a Great Empire, extending over a great part of the World. The Chinese are numerous. You have millions and millions of subjects. The Twenty-six United States are as large as China, though our People are not so numerous. The rising Sun looks upon the great mountains and great rivers of China. When he sets, he looks upon rivers and mountains equally large, in the United States. Our territories extend from one great ocean to the other. . . .[4]

The arrival of the Cushing expedition at Macao, southern China, in February, 1844, created a sensation. The Chinese had already granted most-favored-nation privileges to foreign countries, and they were not eager to make another treaty. Cushing therefore decided to combine the iron hand with the velvet glove. Backed by the obvious power of his fleet, he declared that not to receive envoys was considered, among Western nations, "an act of national insult and a just cause for war"— and the recently humbled Chinese wanted no war. He threatened to take the unheard-of step of going to Peking and there dealing directly with the Son of Heaven. The silk-gowned Chinese underlings were shocked by such boldness. After weeks of delay, the Emperor finally condescended to dispatch an envoy to southern China to treat with Cushing. The ensuing negotiations were hampered by several untoward incidents, including a mob demonstration against a weather vane which Cushing had brought and which was allegedly causing widespread sickness. At length the negotiators came to an understanding and signed the famed Treaty of Wanghia in the village of that name, near Macao, on July 3, 1844.

Cushing's success was noteworthy, even though his achievements in securing commercial privileges already won have been exaggerated. He did succeed in putting the concessions recently granted to foreigners on a formal treaty basis, and in formally securing a most-favored-nation clause. In addition, he took advantage of Chinese inexperience to secure a clear statement of extraterritoriality. This was the right of American citizens accused of crimes in China, other than certain trade infractions, to be tried before an American consular official. Foreigners feared the caprice of Chinese justice, which sometimes involved torture to extract confessions. Juridically speaking, extraterritoriality meant in effect that a bit of American territory had been transferred overseas to China.

Extraterritoriality, which was to curse China's relations with the West for generations to come, was not a new concept. The British and the Portuguese in the Celestial Empire already enjoyed to a limited extent

[4] Hunter Miller, ed., *Treaties and other International Acts of the United States of America* (Washington, 1934), IV, 661.

what amounted to the same privilege. From the standpoint of the United States, the issue had first been brought dramatically to the fore in 1821, in the famous Terranova case. An Italian crewman on an American ship had caused the drowning, accidentally it seems, of a Chinese woman peddling fruit. After a farcical trial, the seaman was strangled to death by the local authorities. Cushing's great contribution was in regularizing and formalizing the protective privilege of extraterritoriality as far as Americans were concerned.

MERCHANTS AND MISSIONARIES

In the decade following the Cushing treaty of 1844 commerce between the United States and China boomed.[5] The famed American clipper ship showed its rivals a streak of foam, and transported the new tea crop so swiftly as to wrest shipments to the London market from British vessels. Missionaries from the United States, now assured of a foothold under the Cushing treaty, came to China in increasing numbers, and extended their spiritual vineyards into the interior. These earnest soul-savers, though regarded as incomprehensible nuisances by most Chinese, contributed immensely to the awakening of American interest in the Celestial Empire. Throughout the forty years after 1847 books written by missionaries, though reflecting a pro-Christian bias, were the most reliable sources of information about the Far East generally circulated in the United States.

Unhappily, China did not carry out all the stipulations of the Cushing Treaty, and American citizens, as well as other "foreign devils," suffered repeated indignities. The empire was so sprawling that the central government, even if it had earnestly desired to do so, could not have fully safeguarded foreign treaty rights in the semiautonomous provinces.

Internal disorder was enormously aggravated by the bloodiest civil war in history, the Taiping Rebellion, which lasted from 1850 to 1864 and took an estimated toll of 20,000,000 lives. The leader of the Taiping rebels against the existing Manchu dynasty in Peking was a presumed convert to Christianity, and American public opinion was inclined to favor his cause. But American agents in China generally came to throw their support behind the existing regime—a standard practice for a half century or more. The basic reason was that if China broke up, the European powers would probably partition her, with consequent jeopardy to equality of trade (the Open Door). The United States was interested in commerce, not colonies, and Washington did what it could by peaceful means to restrain the predatory powers.

[5] On this subject see the exhaustive monograph of Eldon Griffin, *Clippers and Consuls: American Consular and Commercial Relations with Eastern Asia, 1845–1860* (Ann Arbor, Mich., 1938).

JACKAL DIPLOMACY IN CHINA

Britain and France, their hands freed by the end of the Crimean War in 1856, finally decided on two-fisted measures. They were particularly aroused by the seizure of a British ship and the murder of a French Catholic missionary. London and Paris both demanded of China an honoring of existing treaties, reparations for losses of life and limb, and expanded trade concessions.

America, though invited to join in coercive measures, declined. She was then distracted by the slavery controversy, and joint action with the European powers ran counter to her tradition of nonentanglement. But Washington declared that it believed the purposes of the allies to be "just and expedient." Thus the United States, like the jungle jackal, was in the profitable position of avoiding the trouble and expense of fighting, while being in a position to reap advantages secured by the efforts of others.

Joint British and French forces, after administering a sound beating to the ill-prepared Chinese, extorted new treaties at Tientsin, in June, 1858. The victors won the right to maintain diplomatic representation at Peking, as well as additional trade privileges, including the opening of some ten new treaty ports. A few days before the French and British pacts were signed, the American minister negotiated a new treaty at Tientsin. One of its chief features was a new and more sweeping most-favored-nation clause, which gave the United States substantially all the advantages that France and Britain had wrested after costly naval operations.[6]

Fresh hostilities broke out in June, 1859, when the British attempted to force their way up the Pei-ho River to exchange ratifications of their treaties at Peking. The British were badly worsted, and the American naval officer, Josiah Tattnall, ignoring the plain requirements of neutrality and allegedly muttering "blood is thicker than water," went to their rescue. The discomfited European allies then collected a powerful force, captured Peking, destroyed the priceless summer palace of the Emperor, and wrested new concessions in the Convention of Peking (1860). These additional commercial advantages also accrued to the United States under the beneficent operation of the most-favored-nation clause. The Washington government was quite content to let someone else shake the Chinese tree while it gathered the apples.

ANSON BURLINGAME—TWO-WAY DIPLOMAT

The most noteworthy feature of Chinese-American relations during the decade after 1858 was the work of Anson Burlingame, United States

[6] Tyler Dennett, *Americans in Eastern Asia* (New York, 1922), p. 314.

minister in Peking for six years. Burlingame was a Massachusetts Congressman of magnetic charm who, in 1861, was rewarded for his oratorical contributions to Lincoln in the recent Presidential campaign by being appointed minister to China. Here he encountered a perplexing situation. The Chinese government, ever the despair of its friends, found itself powerless to carry out the recent onerous treaties because of the semi-autonomous status of the provinces. Yet the foreign merchants were clamoring for rights which, in some cases, went even beyond the generous treaty stipulations.

Burlingame, though a newcomer among the diplomats in Peking, quickly emerged as their leader. He proved notably successful in persuading them to co-operate in withstanding the extreme demands of the foreign merchants, on the one hand, and in adopting a more tolerant attitude toward the harassed Chinese government, on the other. This conciliatory course may have forestalled a crisis that could have led to the partition of China by the European powers. Burlingame's conduct naturally won the confidence of the Chinese government, which showed its appreciation by issuing orders not to succor the Confederate warship *Alabama*. On a return visit to the United States in 1865–1866, the personable minister made remarkable progress, through speeches and conferences, in enlisting sympathy for China among influential Americans.

Burlingame had long urged upon the Chinese officials the wisdom of coming down off their high horses and sending diplomatic representatives abroad. In 1867, when he was about to resign as minister, the Peking government asked him to represent China on a mission to the principal powers. Its object was to correct misapprehensions abroad, and to persuade the interested nations not to demand more than China could reasonably be expected to concede when the time should come for treaty revision. The selection of Burlingame to head the mission was highly complimentary to him, particularly since he did not know the Chinese language.[7] In 1868 a picturesque party, numbering more than thirty, came to the United States and attracted wide attention. Everywhere the Oriental dignitaries were wined, dined, and greeted by cheering crowds. Burlingame, who was a superb showman, took advantage of these opportunities to burst into oratory and paint China's condition in much more roseate colors than strict truth would permit.

The most visible fruit of the mission was a pact, signed in Washington and known generally as the Burlingame Treaty of 1868. It consisted of an addendum to the Tientsin Treaty of 1858, and related to consuls, commerce, residence, travel, and kindred items. It could more properly be

[7] See Knight Biggerstaff, "The Official Chinese Attitude toward the Burlingame Mission," *Amer. Hist. Rev.*, XLI (1936), 694; see also F. W. Williams, *Anson Burlingame and the First Chinese Mission to Foreign Powers* (New York, 1912), pp. 153–155.

called the Seward Treaty, for Secretary of State Seward, who showed more interest in the Far East than any other Secretary since Webster, seems to have desired it more than Burlingame. At that time Chinese coolies were much in demand for Western railroad construction, and Seward, who was a "cheap-labor" man, wrote into the convention a guarantee to the Chinese of unrestricted immigration to the United States. Interestingly enough, California applauded the arrangement at the time, although it was soon to repent.

Burlingame went on to Europe, where he achieved considerable success in a half-dozen or so capitals. Tragedy finally struck when he died of pneumonia in Russia. He was the ablest representative of the United States in China since Cushing, and one of the most notable products of American "militia diplomacy."

JAPAN—A HERMIT EMPIRE

If Britain took the lead in blowing China open, America took the lead in forcing Japan open. The inhabitants of these picture-book islands, like those of China, wanted little traffic with the Occidentals. It is true that from 1550 to 1620 the Japanese had welcomed the Western world. But the excessive zeal of missionaries, together with the sharp practices of traders, had caused them to slam their gates and pursue a rigid policy of both exclusion and seclusion. The Dutch, who had proved the least offensive of the Europeans, were granted a slight concession. For over two centuries they, as well as the Chinese, were allowed a severely restricted trade at the single port of Nagasaki. Through this tiny wicket in the gate flowed virtually all of Japan's intercourse with the outside world.

During the first half of the 19th Century the United States, as well as the European powers, made repeated but futile efforts to induce Japan to emerge from her isolationist cocoon. The problem, hitherto approached only half-heartedly, took on a new aspect in the 1850's. Shipwrecked sailors, chiefly from America's whaling fleet, were customarily treated in Japan as felons. Some alleged that they had been required to trample and spit upon the Christian cross. Others testified that their companions had died as a result of having been shut up in small cages or exposed in stocks to the elements and public ridicule.

Commerce also entered the picture. Uncharted Japanese waters lay in the path of the most direct route from San Francisco to Shanghai, and the expansion of steam navigation called for the establishment of coaling stations in Japan. In addition, certain farsighted American businessmen were already looking hungrily upon the Land of the Rising Sun as a prospective market. As early as 1852, *De Bow's Review,* an influential

New Orleans journal, optimistically predicted an annual trade with Japan amounting to $200 million.

The Washington government, prodded by petitions to Congress and other pressures, decided upon a determined effort to pry Japan open. In January, 1852, the command of a formidable expedition was entrusted to Commodore Matthew C. Perry, a younger brother of the hero of Lake Erie in 1813 and a distinguished officer in his own right. The ensuing preparations excited comment both in America and Europe. While a few optimists expressed hope for success, there was a general note of skepticism. The *London Sun* looked forward to the result with as much interest as if a balloon were "to soar off to one of the planets under the direction of some experienced aeronaut." The Washington correspondent of the *Philadelphia Public Ledger* dismissed the expedition as a "romantic notion," while his colleague on the *Baltimore Sun* scoffed that it would sail about the same time as an "aerial ship."

COMMODORE PERRY AND HIS BLACK SHIPS

After various adventures Perry entered the beautiful Bay of Yedo (later called Tokyo) with four men-of-war, on July 8, 1853. The Japanese, who had never before seen steamers, stood agape. As the American flagship, belching black smoke, moved steadily up the bay in the teeth of a strong wind, the people were struck with consternation. A curiously prophetic folk song came to mind as they made haste to defend themselves:

> Thro' a black night of cloud and rain,
>   The Black Ship plies her way—
> An alien thing of evil mien—
>   Across the waters gray.[8]

The American expedition, despite its warlike appearance, was under strict orders not to use force except in self-defense or to resent an insult. Deciding to outdo the Orientals in ceremony, Perry haughtily secluded himself and refused to deal with any but the highest officials. When he was ordered to proceed to Nagasaki, he refused to go on the grounds that he was charged with delivering a friendly letter from the President of the United States to the Emperor of Japan. He added menacingly that, if rebuffed, he would consider his country insulted and would not "hold himself accountable for the consequences." This mixture of firmness, dignity, and tact at length induced the Japanese to receive his documents. Perry realized that the answer would require mature deliberation. He therefore sailed away at the end of ten days, after pointedly hinting that he would return in the spring with a much more powerful squadron.

[8] Inazo Nitobe, *The Intercourse between the United States and Japan* (Baltimore, 1891), p. 1.

Internal conditions in Japan were such that Perry could hardly have timed his visit more strategically. The nation was ripe for change, for the feudal system was breaking down, and a power-hungry commercial and urban class was rising rapidly. Ever since the early 17th Century the shogunate, which represented the military elements, had exercised actual sovereignty in Japan, though in theory subordinate to the Emperor. The Shogun, now faced with an answer to Perry, took the unprecedented step of referring the issue to the feudal barons and also to the Emperor himself.

The more progressive leaders of Japan, who were surprisingly well informed about the outside world, favored opening negotiations with Perry. With the object lesson of China's humiliation in the Opium War before them, they were well aware of the power of Western arms. In particular, they perceived the wisdom of adopting modern weapons to combat aggressive foreigners like the Russians, whose vessels had been entering Japanese waters with increasing frequency. After prolonged debate, the views of these far-visioned Japanese leaders undermined the official inclination for continued isolation. This result was doubtless hastened by the appearance of a four-ship Russian squadron off Nagasaki, in August, 1853, a month after Perry had arrived.

PRYING OPEN THE PORTALS OF JAPAN

In February, 1854, Perry again sailed into the Bay of Yedo, this time with seven rather than four men-of-war. The negotiations, which proceeded smoothly, were facilitated by a number of curious presents that the Americans had brought. These included various kinds of liquors, which were thirstily imbibed, and a miniature steam locomotive, which delighted the ingenious Japanese and impressed them with the progress of Western nations. A high point in the festivities was a banquet on board the American flagship, at which the Japanese consumed mounds of food and drank gallons of alcoholic beverages. Perry's official chronicler recorded:

> It was now sunset, and the Japanese prepared to depart with quite as much wine in them as they could well bear. The jovial Matsusaki threw his arms about the Commodore's neck, crushing, in his tipsy embrace, a pair of new epaulettes, and repeating, in Japanese, with maudlin affection, these words, as interpreted into English: "Nippon and America, all the same heart." [9]

Amid such scenes the famous treaty between Japan and the United States was signed, on March 31, 1854.

The Perry pact was in some ways a disappointment, particularly when

[9] F. L. Hawks, *Narrative of the Expedition of an American Squadron to the China Seas and Japan* (New York, 1856), I, 438.

one considers the costly display of pomp and force. On the surface, it was little more than an agreement governing shipwrecked sailors—a "wood and water treaty." Only two ports, Shimoda and Hakodate, both of them relatively inaccessible, were thrown open to American trade, and no adequate arrangement was made for coaling stations. Commercially, Perry had just got his toe in the door—he had not opened it. There was, to be sure, a most-favored-nation clause, but no extraterritorial arrangement. From a narrow point of view, Perry had won no great diplomatic triumph, and the Japanese negotiators had held their ground remarkably well.

But it is not fair to judge the Perry treaty under a microscope. The seemingly meager concessions were revolutionary when one considers the former Japanese policy of isolation. Perry was pursuing a far-sighted course. He was looking to the future and preparing the ground for the sweeping commercial treaty that came later. He was satisfied to drive the entering wedge and to make the next move relatively easy for the Japanese. In achieving his aims, he fired no shot, as he might well have done, and left little or no rancor. His statesmanlike diplomacy not only won the respect of the Japanese but laid the foundations of the famous "historic friendship." [10]

The reopening of Japan was unquestionably a red-letter day in world history. If the Land of the Rising Sun had continued its exclusion-seclusion policy, it might soon have been dismembered by Russia, for the scattered islands were far more vulnerable to naval attack than the sprawling Chinese Empire. Japan was opened not because Perry forced it open but because the Shogun's advisers were convinced of the wisdom of taking this step. As an American humorist of a later generation, Finley Peter Dunne (Mr. Dooley), put it, "Whin we rapped on the dure, we didn't go in, they come out."

Few Americans, if any, grasped the true significance of what had happened. Certainly the event attracted little attention. It is true that New York City presented Perry with a set of silver plate, and that the merchants of Boston had a medal struck off in his honor. But President Pierce gave the opening of Japan, undertaken by a rival Whig administration, only two sentences in his twenty-one page annual message to Congress. The *North American Review* wondered why the Walker filibustering operations into Mexico "should have awakened more display of interest among the people" than "one of the most honorable triumphs of our age." Perry's exploit was deserving of more acclaim than it received.

---

[10] Perry is far better known in Japan than in the United States. The Japanese erected an imposing monument in his honor on the shores of the Bay of Yedo, and dedicated it with appropriate ceremony on July 14, 1901, the forty-eighth anniversary of Perry's first landing.

HARRIS KEEPS THE GATES AJAR

The Washington government, in accordance with its interpretation of the Perry treaty, appointed a consul general at isolated Shimoda, in August, 1855. The man chosen was Townsend Harris, a New York merchant with considerable experience in the Far East who had suffered such heavy financial reverses as to be an active applicant for the position.

The Japanese gave Harris no red-carpet treatment. They interpreted the Perry treaty to mean that a consul was to be appointed only by mutual consent; and since they did not want one at this time, they put Harris off with obstruction, evasion, and downright prevarication. The only Occidental with whom he came in contact was his secretary. He did not see an American ship for fourteen months, and he was without communication from the State Department for eighteen months.[11] As if unfamiliar food and the annoyances of rats and cockroaches were not bad enough, the Japanese regarded the earthquakes, typhoons, and cholera which followed his coming as evidences of divine disapproval of the Perry treaty. A nondrinker and a bachelor, Harris found some solace, according to tradition, in the charms of a beautiful Japanese mistress.

Harris' patience and tact, which finally won the respect of the Japanese, resulted in commendable progress. The Perry agreement had opened scarcely more than a crack in the door, and the chief task of the newly appointed American consul was to negotiate a comprehensive commercial treaty. A promising step forward came in 1857, when he managed to conclude a convention which secured additional concessions, notably regarding trade, residence, currency, and extraterritoriality. Harris finally secured an audience with the Shogun, and the Japanese were astonished to see him, as he wrote home, "look the awful 'Tycoon' in the face, speak plainly to him, hear his reply—and all this without any trepidation, or any 'quivering of the muscles of the side.'"[12] During the following months Harris emphasized the disinterestedness of the United States, while making a strong point of the greed and strength of the European powers. He argued persuasively that the Japanese would be wise if they yielded voluntarily to America those concessions that the other nations ultimately would extort by force. The beating that the joint British-French forces were then giving China lent force to his pleas.

Harris' persistent diplomacy, combined with friendliness and helpfulness, at length bore fruit in a path-breaking commercial treaty, signed on

[11] See M. E. Cosenza, ed., *The Complete Journal of Townsend Harris* (New York, 1930).

[12] *Living Age*, LX, 570 (Feb. 26, 1859). Harris to a friend, July 3, 1858.

July 29, 1858. Additional Japanese ports were thrown open; more favorable trade and residential rights were granted; reciprocal diplomatic representation was provided for; and a species of extraterritoriality for Americans was established. The pact of 1858 was in fact so well drawn that it served as a treaty model and a foundation stone of Japan's foreign relations until near the end of the century.

THE WESTERNIZATION OF JAPAN

The Harris treaty of 1858 made provision for a Japanese mission to journey to America and exchange ratifications. A party of envoys and their retinue, totaling more than seventy persons, were transported on an American man-of-war early in 1860. Congress appropriated $50,000 for the entertainment of the wide-eyed visitors, who for seven weeks were whirled past the wonders of America, both mechanical and natural. They were feted by the cities of the Atlantic seaboard, and honored by a great parade up Broadway. The American people were fascinated by the gentlemanly behavior and quick intelligence of the Japanese, and another barrier of ignorance was partially beaten down. Another colorful mission came in 1872, and likewise attracted wide attention.

The overnight transformation of Japan from an isolated feudal state to a full-fledged member of the family of nations naturally resulted in severe internal disturbances. Powerful opponents of the new policy united in opposition to the Shogun, who was blamed for forsaking isolation. During the ensuing disorders a number of foreigners, including the secretary of the American legation, were killed. But Harris, who had been elevated to the rank of minister resident, stuck to his post until 1862 and, though shattered in health, labored manfully to preserve the gains already made. Few, if any, American diplomats have ever done better work in the face of extreme personal hardship. Perry, the opener, has received the plaudits. Harris, the pioneer, is well-nigh forgotten, except by the Japanese, who in 1927 erected an impressive monument to his memory near Shimoda.

The United States, though torn by the Civil War, did not lose sight of Japan, as the curious intervention at Shimonoseki in 1864 bears witness. The episode is all the more remarkable because it represents a strange departure from America's traditional policy of avoiding entanglements with other powers. One of the independent-minded Japanese feudal lords, whose cannon commanded the Straits of Shimonoseki, began to fire upon "barbarian" (foreign) ships. The Shogun was not strong enough to rap his knuckles, so the aggrieved powers themselves organized a joint punitive expedition. The United States was invited to join, but was able to spare only one hastily improvised warship. The highhanded feudal lord was severely mauled, and the Japanese government, in the Convention of 1864, agreed to pay an indemnity of $3 million.[13]

The Shimonoseki affair taught the antiforeign elements in Japan a harsh lesson. They now perceived that the only wise course was to unite under the Emperor and to adopt Western ways—to fight the "foreign devils" with their own fire, so to speak. The subsequent centralization of authority contributed powerfully to the rapid Westernization of Japan. In 1894, on the eve of their surprising victory over China, the Japanese managed to secure a general revision of existing treaties. They thus freed their nation from a number of inequities that had been imposed upon it, and further established themselves as an emerging world power. One can reasonably conclude that modern Japan was largely a child of American diplomacy, even though one must recognize the secondary role of other powers, notably Great Britain.

ISOLATION BECOMES CO-OPERATION

Korea, the Hermit Kingdom loosely attached to China, had long fallen prey to disorders which, unhappily, involved the murder of Westerners. An attempt by the United States in 1871 to open diplomatic relations and secure protection for missionaries came to a tragic end. An American squadron of five ships, after being fired upon, destroyed three Korean forts and killed several hundred Koreans. Eleven years later, in 1882, the conciliatory Commodore Shufeldt, U.S.N., persuaded the Koreans to sign a pioneer pact, their first with any Western power. It made provision, among other concessions, for American trade, residence, and most-favored-nation treatment under treaties to be granted to other nations. The opening of Korea, though far less important than that of Japan, nevertheless was a significant step in projecting the Hermit Kingdom into the fateful international arena.

The taproot of American policy in the Far East during the 19th Century was plainly the most-favored-nation treatment—a precursor, as will be noted, of the Open Door. Its logical corollary, as developed later, was that the Asiatic nations, notably China, should be made strong enough not only to keep the door open but also to be their own door-keepers. The United States likewise worked for peace in the Orient, since war-making and land-grabbing were disturbing to both trading and soul-saving. One must remember that the American missionaries, and those church members at home supporting their work, were numerous enough and influential enough to make their wants known in Washington.

---

[13] The share of the United States, $785,000, was grossly disproportionate to the loss sustained, and in 1883 Congress voted to return this sum to Japan. This gesture paid ample dividends in good will, and the Japanese expended the money on the breakwater in Yokohama harbor. P. J. Treat, *Diplomatic Relations between the United States and Japan, 1853–1895* (Stanford, Calif., 1932), II, 545–559.

During the 19th Century the United States steadfastly refused to acquire naval stations in Asiatic waters, and secured no territory until 1898, when the Philippine Islands came as a perplexing gift from heaven. The ambitious designs of Commodore Perry are a case in point. Before returning from his memorable trip of 1853–1854 to Japan, he drew up a wood-and-water treaty with the Lew Chŏo (Ryukyu) Islands, several hundred miles southwest of Japan, and established a temporary base at their principal island of Okinawa. He also purchased a coaling depot at Port Lloyd, some five hundred miles southeast of Japan in the Bonin Islands; took formal possession of Bailey Island in the same group; and recommended a protectorate over Formosa. All these activities, except the Lew Choo treaty, were much too advanced for Washington, which promptly reversed Perry's policies.

The United States, in pursuing its objectives in the Far East, was forced to rely not upon force but upon international law and treaty commitments. One basic reason was that it had a weak navy at home, and no naval bases in the Far East. This general avoidance of "gunboat diplomacy" placed the United States in a much more favorable position than the more aggressive powers. But the Americans, while generally fighting shy of co-operative military or naval demonstrations, were not backward about claiming, under their magic most-favored-nation clauses, whatever advantages other countries might garner. A latter-day writer has branded this practice "hitch-hiking imperialism." Yet one should note that foreign nations also benefited, under similar most-favored-nation guarantees, from the treaties concluded by the United States, notably those with Japan and Korea.

During the mid-century years and even later, the United States generally pursued a policy of co-operation with the European powers in maintaining Asiatic trade privileges. Curiously enough, Washington thus maintained a double standard: isolation and nonentanglement toward Europe; co-operation and entanglement toward the Far East. But in the last quarter of the 19th Century, when interest in foreign affairs was at low ebb, the United States had little occasion to assert itself in Asia. The stage was thus set for Secretary of State John Hay to play his dramatic if somewhat ineffective lone hand in proclaiming the Open Door.

SELECTED BIBLIOGRAPHY

The best general survey is F. R. Dulles, *China and America: The Story of their Relations since 1784* (Princeton, 1946). Much more detailed is the older treatment, Tyler Dennett, *Americans in Eastern Asia* (New York, 1922). See also K. S. Latourette, *The History of Early Relations between the United States and China, 1784–1844* (New Haven, 1917) and F. R. Dulles, *The Old China Trade* (Boston, 1930). A convenient compilation is P. H. Clyde, ed., *United States Policy toward China: Diplomatic and Public Documents, 1838–1939*

(Durham, N.C., 1940). Most revealing is Earl Swisher's *China's Management of the American Barbarians* (New Haven, 1953). The best biography on the subject is C. M. Fuess, *The Life of Caleb Cushing* (2 vols., New York, 1923).

On the opening of Japan consult Arthur Walworth, *Black Ships off Japan: The Story of Commodore Perry's Expedition* (New York, 1946); also F. R. Dulles, *America in the Pacific* (Boston, 1932). The most exhaustive documentary study is P. J. Treat, *Diplomatic Relations between the United States and Japan, 1853–1895* (2 vols., Stanford, Calif., 1932). On Townsend Harris see Carl Crow, *He Opened the Door of Japan* (New York, 1939).

On Korea consult G. McCune and J. A. Harrison, eds., *Korean-American Relations: Documents pertaining to the Far Eastern Diplomacy of the United States, Vol. I* [1833–1886], (Berkeley, Calif., 1951).

Helpful articles are P. C. Kuo, "Caleb Cushing and the Treaty of Wanghia, 1844," *Jour. of Mod. Hist.*, V (1933), 34–54; T. F. Tsiang, "The Extension of Equal Commercial Privileges to Other Nations than the British after the Treaty of Nanking," *Chinese Social and Pol. Sci. Rev.*, XV (1931), 422–44; Chitoshi Yanaga, "The First Japanese Embassy to the United States [1860]," *Pacific Hist. Rev.*, IX (1940), 113–138; W. L. Neumann, "Religion, Morality, and Freedom: The Ideological Background of the Perry Expedition," *ibid.*, XXIII (1954), 247–257.

See footnotes of this chapter; Bemis and Griffin, *Guide*, pp. 469–489; *Harvard Guide*, Ch. 17.

7TH ED. REFS. L H. Battistini, *The Rise of American Influence in Asia and the Pacific* (East Lansing, Mich., 1960) is an account for the general reader based primarily on secondaries. P. A. Varg, *Missionaries, Chinese, and Diplomats: The American Protestant Missionary Movement in China, 1890–1952* (Princeton, 1958) describes how the missionaries got their foothold in China, especially after clauses for religious toleration were inserted in the treaties of the 1850's. G. A. Lensen, *The Russian Push toward Japan: Russo-Japanese Relations, 1697–1875* (Princeton, 1959) reveals that Russia's repeated but half-hearted attempts to open Japan clearly helped "soften up" the Japanese for the opening that came with Perry. Boleslaw Szczesniak, ed., *The Opening of Japan: Diary of George H. Preble* (Norman, Okla., 1962) is a revealing diary by one of Perry's officers. M. C. Vernon, "The Dutch and the Opening of Japan by the United States," *Pacific Hist. Rev.*, XXVIII (1959), 39–48 notes that the Dutch officially agreed to co-operate, though not favoring strong measures by Perry. But other elements in Holland were unhappy about the expedition because the Americans might succeed where the Dutch had failed for two centuries. Leonard Gordon, "Early American Relations with Formosa, 1849–1870," *The Historian*, XIX (1957), 262–289 discusses initial contacts, whether strategic, commercial, or humanitarian (shipwrecked sailors). W. L. Neumann, "Determinism, Destiny, and Myth in the American Image of China," in G. L. Anderson, ed., *Issues and Conflicts* (Lawrence, Kans., 1959) suggests that much of America's early policy regarding China was based on self-deception, including the idea that the Chinese regarded Americans as purer than other foreigners.

8TH AND 9TH ED. REFS. See BIBLIOGRAPHICAL ADDENDUM, p. 994.

22

The Early Crises of the Civil War

The Confederates . . . are fighting for independence. . . . But with the Northerners all is different. They are not content with their own! They are fighting to coerce others. . . .
                    LONDON TIMES, September 13, 1862

SEWARD: SECRETARY OR PREMIER?

THE ELECTION OF Abraham Lincoln to the Presidency, in November, 1860, triggered the secession of seven Southern states. Four others teetered in the balance, pending the outbreak of hostilities. Grave doubts developed in the North as to the ability of the untried prairie politician, now elevated to the White House, to handle the crisis.

Before the recent Presidential election, the outstanding figure in the Republican Party had plainly been Senator William H. Seward, not Abraham Lincoln. But Seward had made too many speeches and too many enemies, and he had been passed by in favor of a less conspicuous candidate. Lincoln was therefore compelled by custom and courtesy to offer his defeated rival the Secretaryship of State, the highest office within the gift of the President. Seward accepted this consolation prize after some hesitation, confiding to his wife that his "distracted country" could not spare him in the hour of crisis. He felt that his mission was to grasp the helm while the inept Lincoln, a countrified politician whom the wheel of chance had placed over him, occupied the role of figurehead.

Seward, like a few otherwise sane Americans, believed that a rousing foreign war would cause the seven seceded states to rally around the Stars and Stripes and thus re-cement the Union. On All Fool's Day, 1861, appropriately enough, he submitted to Lincoln a memorandum in which he recommended a "wrap-the-world-in-fire" policy:

I would demand explanations from Spain and France, categorically, at once. [Spain, with French support, had just reacquired Santo Domingo.]

I would seek explanations from Great Britain and Russia, and send agents into Canada, Mexico, and Central America, to rouse a vigorous continental spirit of independence on this continent against European intervention.

And, if satisfactory explanations are not received from Spain and France, Would convene Congress and declare war against them.[1]

Lincoln's response was firmly but tactfully to pigeonhole Seward's preposterous suggestions, and to forgive him his temporary delusion.

Unfortunately for the cause of the North, Seward was profoundly distrusted in London. In 1860, and probably in jest, he had told the visiting Duke of Newcastle that if he became Secretary of State, he would find it his "duty to insult England" and that he intended "to do so." The story went the rounds in Britain, where many people believed, whether correctly or not, that Seward had not been joking. Minister Charles Francis Adams wrote from London that the Secretary was regarded as "an ogre fully resolved to eat all Englishmen raw."

Nor did Seward's inexperience in foreign affairs and his known attachment to the "foreign-war panacea" inspire confidence at Downing Street. Several of his early instructions to the American minister in London were belligerently worded, and if they had not been toned down in delivery, grave consequences might easily have followed. Henry Adams, son of Minister Adams, wrote that if Seward's "crazy dispatch" of May 21, 1861, had been obeyed "literally," war would have resulted "in five minutes." Yet Seward settled down after these early indiscretions, and finally came to be rated as one of America's more effective Secretaries of State. Like Lincoln, he grew with experience.

Seward's initial blunders were partially offset by the presence in London of Charles Francis Adams, one of the ablest diplomats in American history. Lacking none of the ability of his father and grandfather (John Quincy Adams and John Adams), Charles Francis Adams possessed two gifts in which they had been painfully deficient: exquisite balance of mind and the ability to get along pleasantly with his fellow men. Educated at an English boarding school, cultured, intelligent, well bred, and reserved, he had much in common with the English ruling class, intellectually and socially. And, unlike Seward, he enjoyed the respect and confidence of the London government.

BRITISH OPINION AND THE SLAVERY ISSUE

The long-predicted shooting war finally flared forth on April 12, 1861, when the South Carolinians, fearing the arrival of Northern reinforce-

[1] J. G. Nicolay and John Hay, *Abraham Lincoln: A History* (New York, 1890), III, 446.

ments, opened fire on Fort Sumter. Lincoln promptly issued a call for troops, and four additional Southern states parted company with the Union.

At the outset it was evident that London would be the focal point of United States diplomacy during the conflict. France, of course, was highly important. But Napoleon III, though sympathetic with the South, was unwilling to interfere without the backing of the British fleet. If England had intervened on behalf of the Confederacy the North in all probability would have retaliated with a declaration of war. Powerful British ironclads would then have broken the blockade, and perhaps would have bombarded Northern cities. In the general melee, the South would doubtless have made good its attempt to achieve independence. The overshadowing diplomatic problem confronting Lincoln, therefore, was to keep England neutral. The British were thus caught in the center of a tug of war, with the Confederacy pulling them toward intervention and the North pulling them toward nonintervention.

When the Civil War erupted, relations between Britain and America were probably more friendly than they had been at any time since the undeclared Franco-American War of 1798–1800. With the Isthmian controversy just settled, no serious dispute divided the two peoples. As a special mark of friendship, the Prince of Wales had made a twenty-nine day tour of America in 1860. He escaped from crushing crowds, balls, and torchlight processions long enough to sleep in the White House and plant a tree at the tomb of Washington.

When secession first began, press opinion in England was rather favorable to the cause of the North. Editors generally assumed, whether correctly or not, that the struggle was one for the freeing of the slave— a goal for which the British had long been agitating. But during the first year-and-a-half of the war Lincoln was powerless to capitalize on this strong moral issue. The crucial border states of Maryland, Kentucky, and Missouri, in all of which slavery still existed, would be driven into the arms of the Confederacy if the administration should proclaim that it was waging war to free the Negroes. Lincoln was thus forced to declare on various occasions that the North was not fighting to unshackle the slaves but to preserve the Union. The British naturally came to take his word at its face value.

INDEPENDENCE *VERSUS* EMPIRE

To many outsiders, the moral cause of the underdog South was definitely stronger than that of the North. Self-determination for a minority group had a more universal appeal than mere union. Many Britishers felt that the issue of freedom related not to the Negro but to the freedom of the South from the domination of the North. Many antislaveryites in

England, though prepared to applaud an emancipation proclamation, were not willing to support the ideal of union—that is, oneness or bigness or imperialism. A number of English liberals, failing to see that Lincoln's hands were tied on the slavery issue, regarded his efforts to pin one section to the other with bayonets as positively immoral. A comparison of peculiar relish to Englishmen suggested itself to the *London Times:*

> . . . The contest is really for empire on the side of the North, and for independence on that of the South, and in this respect we recognize an exact analogy between the North and the Government of George III., and the South and the Thirteen Revolted Provinces. These opinions may be wrong, but they are the general opinions of the English nation. . . .[2]

The great majority of English journals were therefore unfriendly to the North, particularly during the first half of the war. Consistently unsympathetic were the lofty *London Times* and the pungent London *Punch.* Both journals mirrored the prejudices of the privileged classes and exercised immense influence, not only in England but on the Continent as well. *Punch* persistently caricatured Lincoln as a boor, a sharper, a braggart, a poltroon, and even as the Devil. Aroused by these attacks, the American press, notably the *New York Herald,* replied savagely in kind. Once more ill feeling began to mount dangerously in a vicious circle.

Northerners were angered by the failure of the British, after all these years of condemning slavery, to look beneath the surface and perceive that the success of the Union spelled the doom of slavery. What the North wanted was warm sympathy, not cold neutrality. The lament of James Russell Lowell reflected widespread resentment:

> We know we've got a cause, John,
>   Thet's honest, just, an' true;
> We thought 't would win applause, John,
>   Ef nowheres else, from you.[3]

ARISTOCRACY APPLAUDS SECESSION

British unfriendliness toward the North during the Civil War was concentrated in the upper classes. Socially, the landed aristocracy of Britain presented a close affinity to the plantation aristocracy of the South. To the cultured Englishman, the Southerner was more a "gentleman" than the noisy, boastful, and "vulgar" Yankee. When the correspondent of the *London Times* saw Jefferson Davis, President of the Confederacy, he recorded, "Wonderful to relate, he does not chew [tobacco], and is neat and clean looking, with hair trimmed, and boots brushed." [4]

---

[2] *London Times,* Nov. 7, 1861, 6:3.
[3] James Russell Lowell, *Poems* (Boston, 1891), II, 296.
[4] W. H. Russell, *My Diary North and South* (London, 1863), I, 250 (May 9, 1861).

The British aristocrats, to an even greater degree, detested the anarchy of "demon democracy" and "democratic degeneracy." They had long expected the collapse of the ungainly American government, supported, so they believed, by a "gibbering mob" derived from the "scum of Europe." Now they were witnessing the end of the "detestable" democratic experiment.[5] The caustic historian Carlyle wrote that America was but a "smoky chimney which had taken fire." Another British commentator snarled, "The republic had rotted into Empire and the gangrene had burst." *Blackwood's* was especially vicious in assailing Lincoln—that "obscure and commonplace man" who was now the "imbecile executive" of America. It sneered:

> Every four years the constitution is in travail . . . and the latest result is —Mr. Abraham Lincoln. The great achievement in self-government of this vaunted democracy, which we have been so loudly and arrogantly called on to admire, is, to drag from his proper obscurity an ex-rail-splitter and country attorney, and to place what it calls its liberties at his august disposal. . . . It would have been impossible for him, or any of his Cabinet, to have emerged, under British institutions, from the mediocrity to which nature had condemned them, and from which pure democracy alone was capable of rescuing them.[6]

British contempt for American institutions was to some extent a cloak for fear. Should the North triumph, the disfranchised masses of England would clamor louder than ever for democracy. In fact, the eventual success of the Union was a powerful argument advanced in behalf of the great Reform Bill of 1867. To discredit democracy abroad was to discredit it at home; and one can hardly be surprised at the satisfaction expressed by British aristocrats over the apparent dissolution of the United States.

BRITAIN'S STAKE IN DISUNION

There were additional reasons for the disapproving attitude of the English ruling classes. In their eyes the United States was a formidable commercial competitor, an ominously growing rival, and a potential menace to Canada and other valuable British possessions in the Western Hemisphere. The *London Morning Post* felt that if the North triumphed "Democracy will be more arrogant, more aggressive, more levelling and vulgarizing, if that be possible, than . . . ever . . . before." After a series of Northern defeats, the *London Times* reported that "people are

---

[5] The distinguished English historian, Edward A. Freeman, published in 1863 the first volume of a work entitled: *History of Federal Government, from the Foundation of the Achaian League to the Disruption of the United States.* The second volume never appeared; Freeman's history, not the Union, was disrupted.

[6] *Blackwood's Magazine*, XCI, 121 (Jan. 1862).

breathing more freely, and talking more lightly of the United States, than they have done any time these thirty years." [7]

The fragmentation of the United States, whatever its form of government, seemed clearly to the advantage of the British rulers. If the South should triumph, there would be at least two rival republics where only one had grown before, and England would no longer have to fear a unified and aggressive democracy. The London *Economist* concluded that instead of one nation "showing an encroaching and somewhat bullying front to the rest of the world, we shall have *two*, showing something of the same front to each other." Each would be "occupied with its immediate neighbour, and therefore less inclined to pick quarrels with more distant nations." [8] Europe could then extend the principle of the balance of power to a "Balkanized" Western Hemisphere, and play the ancient game of divide and conquer by egging one republic against the other. The truth is that the Civil War presented the European powers with their best opportunity, since the days of the Holy Alliance, to reassert their influence in the New World.

Economic factors likewise influenced the British ruling groups. Early in 1861 Congress passed the Morrill Tariff, which, though only moderately protective, paved the way for the high Civil War tariffs. The British, who were then on a free-trade basis, regarded the new measure as a deliberate blow at their manufactured goods and carrying trade. On the other hand, the Confederacy, as primarily an agricultural area, would certainly establish a low tariff or none at all. The British exporters would then be able to compete on a more profitable basis with their Yankee rivals.

Cotton also entered the picture. Britain's textile industry—the very heart of its industrial life—drew approximately 80 per cent of its fiber from the South. An independent Confederacy would ship its cotton to England, and then receive in exchange British manufactured goods. Thus Britain would have a cotton supply free from the control of the aggressive Yankee, and in addition would enjoy an enlarged free-trade market and an expanded carrying trade. The aging Palmerston, now Prime Minister, could scarcely have compressed more meat into fewer words when he growled, "We do not like slavery, but we want cotton, and we dislike very much your Morrill tariff."

BRITISH NONINTERVENTIONISTS

Powerful forces in England, on the other hand, were tugging toward nonintervention. Lincoln was upholding law, order, and legitimate rule; and Britain, with her sprawling colonial empire, would be ill advised

---

[7] *London Times,* August 15, 1862, 6:2.
[8] *London Economist,* XIX, 58 (Jan. 19, 1861).

to give open encouragement to rebellion. Many educated Englishmen, furthermore, were indifferent to the struggle and genuinely desirous of remaining neutral. A more positive force was an influential group of liberals, including Richard Cobden and John Bright, who had early concluded that this was a war involving slavery and perhaps the fate of democracy. These leaders labored valiantly to keep Great Britain out of the quarrel.

British economic interests also opposed intervention. Shippers realized that their business would be damaged by Yankee privateers if England and America clashed. The longer the Civil War lasted the greater the inroads the Confederate commerce destroyers would make on the American merchant marine—Britain's most active competitor. English merchants were likewise reaping huge wartime profits by supplying the needs of the North, and to some extent those of the South. "Neutrality forever" might well have been their watchword.

Possibly the most potent single force in keeping the London government neutral was the English laboring class. Upon this group Harriet Beecher Stowe's famous novel, *Uncle Tom's Cabin,* had made a profound impression. Countless British workers logically concluded that the war in America was one in which he had a genuine stake. If the North won and the slaves were liberated, free labor would be exalted; if the South triumphed, free labor would be debased. The dead hand of Uncle Tom, wielded by British laborers—perhaps a majority—thus exercised a restraining influence on the London regime.

The English masses tended to regard the North, to which many of their fellows had emigrated, as the haven of free labor and democracy. They realized that if the Union won, their own chances of securing the ballot would be greatly improved. On the other hand, as John Bright put it, "There would be a wild shriek of Freedom to startle the world if that republic was overthrown." The battle for democracy in England was indeed being fought on the battlefields of America.

Downing Street probably knew that the English workingmen would never willingly consent to intervention in behalf of slavery. Although the aristocracy, with its powerful press, generally favored the South, the attitude of the masses could not be ignored. If they could not cast the ballot, they could at least hurl the brick.

THE MISTRESS OF THE SEA UPHOLDS A FREE SEA

On April 19, 1861, a week after the firing on Fort Sumter, Lincoln proclaimed a maritime blockade of seven seceded states. By this act, later extended, he elevated the struggle from a domestic insurrection into a full-fledged war. The patrol of some 3500 miles of coastline was never completely effective, but, as finally established, it was sufficiently tight to be hazardous for ordinary shipping. Yet whatever its degree of effectiveness, the maritime powers recognized the blockade as binding—and recognition was the acid test.

Surprisingly enough, London did not insist that the Northerners maintain impossibly high blockading standards, and it carefully instructed British naval officers in American waters to observe a rigid neutrality. Such solicitude did not spring from sympathy for the North, but rather from a desire to establish a precedent that might later be used to good advantage. As the *London Times* asserted, "a blockade is by far the most formidable weapon of offense we possess. Surely we ought not to be overready to blunt its edge or injure its temper?" [9] Britain's acquiescence in the Union's blockading practices thus conferred an immense advantage upon the Union cause.

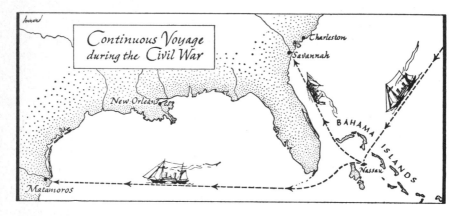

In enforcing its leaky blockade, the North employed the highly useful doctrine of continuous voyage which the British had earlier invoked against the United States during the Napoleonic wars. For example, the British port of Nassau, strategically located in the Bahama Islands, suddenly began to receive from England enormous quantities of contraband, including firearms, cartridges, Confederate insignia, and other materials of war. One did not need to be a private detective to conclude that the scantily populated islands could not begin to use all these stores, and that the ultimate destination, either directly or after transfer to blockade runners, was the South. On the theory that such shipments really involved a "continuous voyage," designed to break the blockade, Union cruisers captured on the high seas in 1862, among others, the British-owned *Bermuda*, bound for Bermuda, and the British-owned *Springbok*, bound for Nassau. The United States also seized British cargoes of non-contraband on the high seas if suspicious circumstances indicated that

---

[9] *London Times*, Feb. 24, 1862, quoted in J. P. Baxter, 3rd, "The British Government and Neutral Rights, 1861–1865," *Amer. Hist. Rev.*, XXXIV (1928), p. 12.

the cargoes were to be run by a water route—not a land route—into the Confederacy.

The Mexican town of Matamoros, across the mouth of the Rio Grande from Texas, fed large amounts of supplies into the Confederacy by a land route. In 1863 the British-owned steamer *Peterhoff* was captured by a Union cruiser near the Danish West Indies on the ground that, though destined for this Mexican port, it was attempting to run the blockade by what amounted to a continuous voyage. But the Supreme Court held that while the contraband in the cargo was seizable, the noncontraband was not, because it was destined from an unblockaded port (Matamoros) for the Confederacy by overland transportation.

The British government generally acquiesced in all these interpretations, though objecting vigorously on occasion to some of the high-handed methods used in carrying them out. When World War I came in 1914, England effectively used the doctrine of continuous voyage against the United States in achieving the economic strangulation of Germany. The British, in playing the unusual role of neutral carrier during the Civil War while the Yankees played the unaccustomed role of dominant sea power, were taking the long view.

LONDON'S PREMATURE (?) PROCLAMATION

The question of recognizing the Confederacy as a belligerent greatly perplexed the London government, which, despite the pro-Southern sympathies of the aristocracy, genuinely desired to remain neutral. The problem became more complicated when, on May 4, 1861, unofficial news reached England of Lincoln's blockade proclamation. Two days later London announced that it would issue a proclamation of neutrality, that is, recognize the belligerent status of the Confederacy. From a purely technical point of view, such a step was imperative. A Union blockade had been instituted, and British shippers must be warned of its existence, lest they be seized by Union cruisers.

Lincoln, from the outset, had attempted to maintain the legal fiction that the war was merely a domestic disturbance, and that it would soon be brought under control. The recognition of the Confederates as belligerents by London upset his plans. He failed to realize that he, himself, had already recognized the belligerency of the Confederacy, for a proclamation of blockade is not ordinarily issued unless a state of war exists.

The British declaration of neutrality had the effect of placing the infant and partially organized Confederacy on the same footing as the mature and long-established United States. It gave the Southerners license to send forth privateers and commerce destroyers, as well as to float loans abroad. It boosted their morale and stiffened their resistance. It encouraged them to believe that a formal recognition of their independence would soon follow. And it set an example that was ultimately followed by the other powers of the world.

Downing Street knew that Minister Adams was en route to England, yet it issued the proclamation on the very day that he arrived. Americans naturally concluded that the British had acted hastily in order to forestall Washington's protests. In view of all these circumstances, the North was deeply provoked, and it came to regard the recognition of belligerency as the first conspicuously unfriendly act on the part of England.

Yet, on balance, the British proclamation probably operated more to the advantage than to the disadvantage of the Northerners. First, it formally recognized and consequently strengthened the blockade. Secondly, the time of its issuance proved to be highly favorable to the Union. If the British had waited until two months later, when the disgraceful rout at Bull Run tarnished Northern arms, they probably would have recognized the independence rather than the belligerency of the Confederacy—a step that would have been much worse from the standpoint of the North.

The British officials, thinking that they had acted correctly, were astonished at the bitterness aroused in the North. During the ensuing months they moved with caution, at times leaning over backward in an effort to avoid giving further offense. By July, 1861, Minister Adams, who until then had not dared to engage quarters for more than a month at a time, took a house for a year. The twenty-three year old Henry Adams, who was then serving as his father's secretary at the Court of St. James's, noted:

> The English . . . thought that . . . their Proclamation was just the thing to keep them straight with both sides, and when it turned out otherwise they did their best to correct their mistake. . . . Now that England has eaten her humble-pie for what was, I must say, a natural mistake from her point of view, I cannot imagine why we should keep on sarsing her.[10]

PRIVATEERING AT BAY

Whether consciously or not, London made partial amends for its recognition of Confederate belligerency. On June 1, 1861, it issued a proclamation forbidding the armed ships of either belligerent to bring their prizes into British ports. This decree worked no real hardship on the Union, because the Southerners had no merchant marine vulnerable to Yankee privateers. But the British restriction resulted in the death blow to Confederate privateers, which, cut off by the Union blockade, had counted on bringing their prizes into British ports.

In the first weeks of the conflict, privateering became briefly a diplomatic problem. At the end of the recent Crimean War in 1856, the major

[10] W. C. Ford, ed., *A Cycle of Adams Letters, 1861–1865* (Boston, 1920), I, 16–17.

European powers had adopted the memorable Declaration of Paris. It attempted to abolish both privateering and blockades inadequately enforced—that is, "paper blockades." It likewise forbade the seizure at sea of noncontraband enemy goods on neutral ships—that is, "free ships, free goods." Finally, it interdicted the seizure at sea of noncontraband neutral goods on board an enemy merchantman—that is, "free goods always free."

The United States, which had long championed the last three of these principles, was loath to give up privateering—the seagoing militia of the small-navy nation. But it expressed a willingness to accept all four propositions, provided that the powers would agree to the immunity of all noncontraband enemy property at sea, even on enemy ships. This condition proved unacceptable to the other nations. When the Civil War broke out, Secretary Seward made a belated but unsuccessful effort to ratify the Declaration of Paris in the hope of averting privateering by the Confederates. This attempt to change the rules after the game had started not only proved unsuccessful, but further aroused British suspicions of Seward's slipperiness.

THE *TRENT* HYSTERIA

During the hundred days after the firing on Fort Sumter, British opinion was not conspicuously unfriendly to the Union. Then, on July 21, 1861, came the disillusioning rout at Bull Run, where the "uniformed civilians" of the North fled the battlefield in scenes of utter confusion.

Bull Run unquestionably produced a revulsion of feeling in England. The aristocratic press sneered at the "wretched" and "gibbering" mobs of "Irish and German mercenaries"—"scum" who had been "drugged with whiskey" and then enlisted. But even among the more reasonable Englishmen the conviction spread that the Confederacy was too strong to be overthrown. The pro-Union Cobden did not believe that the North and the South would "ever lie in the same bed again." And as a prolongation of the conflict would presumably result only in more senseless slaughter, a growing body of Britons argued that, in the interests of humanity, an uncontested divorce ought to be granted.

Such was the troubled atmosphere late in 1861, when the *Trent* crisis burst like a thunderclap. The Confederate government, dissatisfied with the earlier efforts of its commissioners in Europe to secure recognition, decided to send abroad two of its ablest statesmen, James M. Mason and John Slidell. After running the blockade the two men reached Havana, where they boarded a British mail steamer, the *Trent*. The overzealous Captain Wilkes, of the Union warship *San Jacinto*, acting wholly without orders from Washington, lay in wait for the *Trent* north of Cuba. When she appeared on November 8, 1861, he brought her to a stop by firing two shots across her bow, and then sent a party of men on board. Mason, Slidell, and their two secretaries were removed after a show of force, but the *Trent* was allowed to continue unmolested on her way. The whole episode was a startling reminder of pre-1812 days, when British

LOOK OUT FOR SQUALLS

JACK BULL: "You do what's right, my son, or I'll blow you
out of the water."

Britain's strong stand on the *Trent* against the swaggering,
sharp-nosed, cigar-smoking Yankee.
London Punch, 1861

boarding parties had arbitrarily removed men from American merchant-men without judicial processes.

News of the *Trent* affair touched off a delirium of rejoicing in the North that can be understood only in the light of current conditions. For many months the Northerners had been on edge, confidently awaiting news of victory but repeatedly receiving only reports of defeat. Captain Wilkes' bold stroke, which was the first considerable Union success of the war, instantly produced a hysterical reaction.[11] Few men in the South were more cordially hated in the North than Mason and Slidell. The fear was widespread that if they reached Europe, foreign intervention and the breaking of the blockade were virtually assured. Many Union men also felt that by giving Britain a dose of her own quarter-deck medicine they were getting revenge for old impressment wrongs, to say nothing of new wrongs like the recognition of Confederate belligerency. The governor of Massachusetts publicly expressed satisfaction that the captain of the *San Jacinto* had "fired his shot across the bows of the ship that bore the British lion at its head."

Captain Wilkes became the hero of the hour. He was wined, dined, serenaded, and promoted. The Secretary of the Navy wrote him a letter expressing his "emphatic approval"; the House of Representatives passed an official vote of thanks. But President Lincoln, who was concerned about having to fight more than one war at a time, remarked prophetically that Mason and Slidell might yet "prove to be white elephants."

When the news of the seizures reached England, a veritable "typhoon of fury" swept the country. Anger mounted when the ill-founded story spread that the British captain, stepping between Yankee bayonets and the undefended breast of Slidell's daughter, had cried, "Back, you damned cowardly poltroons!" The "Rule Britannia" group, assuming that the seizure had been authorized, rose up in arms over the "ruffianly outrage" offered the flag by the "impudent pirate" Wilkes. His "swagger and ferocity" made him, asserted the London *Mercury*, "an ideal Yankee." The British widely assumed that Seward was trying to provoke his foreign war, and they forthwith began feverish military and naval preparations in England and Canada. Henry Adams wrote ominously from London, "This nation means to make war. Do not doubt it." Eleven thousand crack redcoats embarked for Canada, with two of the departing transports being serenaded by a volunteer band playing, "I Wish I Was in Dixie."[12] Britain had been hit below the water line—and it hurt.

SATAN REPROVES A SINNER

The time element was crucial in the *Trent* affair. Three days after the news arrived in England, the Foreign Office dispatched an ultimatum to Washington demanding a release of the prisoners and a suitable

[11] See C. F. Adams, Jr., "The Trent Affair," *Mass. Hist. Soc. Procs.*, XLV, 37 (Nov., 1911).

[12] An amusing anticlimax developed when a British troopship, unable to enter the ice-bound St Lawrence, put into Portland, Maine. Seward graciously granted permission for the troops to cross Maine. Frederic Bancroft, *The Life of William H. Seward* (New York, 1900), II, 245.

apology for the affront to the Union Jack. Several days later word reached London of the wild rejoicing in America, and public indignation mounted to an even higher pitch. Fortunately for the Union, the newly laid Atlantic cable had gone dead. If the British had known at once of Northern jubilation, they probably would have presented their demands in terms so vigorous as to make war the only honorable alternative. Even so, the ultimatum as originally drafted was couched in such strong language that Prince Albert, though suffering from the illness that was to claim his life three weeks later, successfully urged that it be toned down.

The absence of cable communication likewise had a sobering effect on the United States. The British legation in Washington did not receive the London ultimatum until more than a month after news of the *Trent* affair had reached the United States. American enthusiasm had meanwhile cooled markedly, and the Lincoln administration was left on the horns of a cruel dilemma. If it released the prisoners, the popular outcry might undermine the government. If it did not, war would undoubtedly ensue —and war would insure the independence of the Confederacy and the breakup of the Union.

International law, moreover, seemed to be on the side of the British. A strong case could have been made out for Captain Wilkes if he had brought the *Trent* before an American prize court for adjudication. But this he failed to do. Thus the United States found itself in the unfamiliar position of denying the very doctrines for which it had presumably fought Britain in 1812. Young Henry Adams expostulated to his brother:

> Good God, what's got into you all? What do you mean by deserting now the great principles of our fathers, by returning to the vomit of that dog Great Britain? What do you mean by asserting now principles against which every Adams yet has protested and resisted? [13]

After a prolonged debate, Lincoln's Cabinet reached the painful decision to release the prisoners. To Secretary Seward fell the task of preparing a lengthy note, dated December 26, 1861, making official explanations. He conceded that Captain Wilkes had made a grave error in not seizing the *Trent*, and that consequently the prisoners would have to be freed. Then, with an eye to placating American public opinion, Seward expressed satisfaction that Britain had finally accepted the principles for which America had fought in 1812. This adroit sweetening of the pill, which seemingly put England on the defensive, caused the release of the captives to be more palatable to the Northerners. But Seward's stump-speech reply revealed that his familiarity with American psychology was sounder than his knowledge of international law.

[13] Ford, *Cycle of Adams Letters,* I, 83 (Henry Adams to Charles Francis Adams, Jr., Dec. 13, 1861).

THE *TRENT* AFTERTASTE

The *Trent* affair left a most unfortunate legacy in the North. Many Americans were angered because Britain had adopted so pugnacious a tone against a practice that she herself had long employed. Many more resented what appeared to be a bullying attempt to take advantage of Northern internal misfortunes. As James Russell Lowell protested with bitterness:

> It don't seem hardly right, John,
> When both my hands was full,
> To stump me to a fight, John—
> Your cousin, tu, John Bull! [14]

Representative Lovejoy of Illinois, who "literally wept tears of vexation" at the outcome, expressed a not uncommon sentiment when he proclaimed in Congress:

> . . . I hate the British government. I have never shared in the traditional hostility of many of my countrymen against England. But I now here publicly avow and record my inextinguishable hatred of that Government. I mean to cherish it while I live, and to bequeath it as a legacy to my children when I die. And if I am alive when war with England comes, as sooner or later it must, for we shall never forget this humiliation, and if I can carry a musket in that war I will carry it.[15]

The British people, the great majority of whom did not want war, were relieved by the peaceful solution of the controversy. As sober afterthoughts, they realized that Ireland was a smouldering volcano; that the prosecution of an overseas war would be immensely difficult; that Canada was vulnerable to the swarming Northern armies; and that Britain's merchant marine would be riddled by Yankee privateers. Finally, the English laboring classes, still under the spell of *Uncle Tom's Cabin*, had no desire to fight their own kinsmen as allies of a Southern Confederacy resting on slavery.

The *Trent* outburst, by serving as an emotional outlet, probably improved feeling for the North in England. Seward's clever note did not inspire confidence among British statesmen, yet he had been given his opportunity to fight and had avoided it. Thus passed the first great diplomatic crisis of the war, and Minister Adams confided to his London diary: "I am to remain in this purgatory a while longer."

[14] Lowell, *Poems,* II, 266.
[15] *Cong. Globe,* 37 Cong., 2 sess., p. 333 (Jan. 14, 1862). One of Minister Adams' sons wrote to his father: "I at least would care to impress but one thing on a son of mine, and that should be an inveterate, undying, immortal hatred of Great Britain." C. F. Adams, Jr., "The Trent Affair," *loc. cit.,* p. 68.

SELECTED BIBLIOGRAPHY

The diplomacy of the Civil War is treated briefly in S. F. Bemis, ed., *The American Secretaries of State and their Diplomacy* (New York, 1925), VII, 3–70. Two indispensable monographs are E. D. Adams, *Great Britain and the American Civil War* (2 vols., London, 1925) and F. L. Owsley, *King Cotton Diplomacy* (Chicago, 1931), which deals with the Confederates. Public opinion abroad is treated in D. Jordan and E. J. Pratt, *Europe and the American Civil War* (Boston, 1931). On Lincoln, see J. G. Randall, *Lincoln the President* (2 vols., New York, 1945) and Jay Monaghan, *Diplomat in Carpet Slippers* (Indianapolis, 1945). Intimate glimpses of the London legation appear in S. A. Wallace and F. E. Gillespie, eds., *The Journal of Benjamin Moran, 1857–1865* (2 vols., Chicago, 1949). On the *Trent* affair, see Thomas Harris, *The Trent Affair* (Indianapolis, 1896); W. W. Jeffries, "The Civil War Career of Charles Wilkes," *Jour. of Southern Hist.,* XI (1945), 324–348; V. H. Cohen, "Charles Sumner and the *Trent* Affair," *Jour. of Southern Hist.,* XXII (1956), 205–219. See also W. D. Jones, "The British Conservatives and the American Civil War," *Amer. Hist. Rev.,* LVIII (1953), 527–543; F. L. Owsley, "America and the Freedom of the Seas, 1861–65," in Avery Craven, ed., *Essays in Honor of William E. Dodd* (Chicago, 1935), pp. 194–256; J. P. Baxter, 3rd, "Some British Opinions as to Neutral Rights, 1861 to 1865," *Amer. Jour. Internat. Law,* XXIII (1929), 517–537; A. M. McDiarmid, "American Civil War Precedents: Their Nature, Application, and Extension," *ibid.,* XXXIV (1940), 220–237.

See footnotes of this chapter; Bemis and Griffin, *Guide,* Ch. XIII; *Harvard Guide,* Ch. 18.

7TH ED. REFS. M. B. Duberman, *Charles Francis Adams, 1807–1886* (Boston, 1961) demonstrates anew that Adams, though reserved and resenting British arrogance, got along well with Foreign Secretary Russell. Britain had to issue her neutrality proclamation so as not to get involved in difficulties over privateering. France was hurt by the cotton famine almost from the outset, and hence was more impatient for action. The prior opinion of the crown lawyers allegedly supporting a *Trent*-like seizure has been misinterpreted. Henry Blumenthal, *A Reappraisal of Franco-American Relations, 1830–1871* (Chapel Hill, N.C., 1959) has a sketchy account. Mercier, the French minister in Washington, was definitely pro-South. Much to the gratitude of the British, but unsolicited by them, Paris urged Washington to comply with British demands at the time of the *Trent* crisis. A detailed treatment of this episode is L. M. Case, "La France et l'affaire du 'Trent,'" *Revue Historique,* CCXXVI (1961), 57–86, which shows that the French note supporting Britain's position was influential in persuading Washington to retreat. N. B. Ferris, "The Prince Consort, 'The Times,' and the 'Trent' Affair," *Civil War History,* VI (1960), 152–156 suggests that Prince Albert's memorandum, which resulted in a softening of the government's ultimatum, was indebted in ideas and language to views already published by the London *Times.* As the only leading journal to do so, it counseled moderation. See also references at end of next chapter.

8TH AND 9TH ED. REFS. See BIBLIOGRAPHICAL ADDENDUM, p. 995.

23

The Collapse of King Cotton Diplomacy

> *No, sir, you dare not make war on cotton. No power on earth dares make war upon it. Cotton is king.*
> SENATOR HAMMOND OF SOUTH CAROLINA, 1858

THE KING COTTON COMPLEX

WHEN THE CIVIL WAR broke out, about one fifth of the population of England earned its livelihood, directly or indirectly, from the manufacture of cotton products. About 80 per cent of the fiber that supported this huge establishment came from the South. If the American supply should suddenly be cut off, the most important industry in England would be paralyzed, and the economic life of the British Isles would suffer a crippling blow. In March, 1861, before the war had actually begun, *Punch* confessed:

> Though with the North we sympathise,
> It must not be forgotten
> That with the South we've stronger ties,
> Which are composed of cotton. . . .[1]

The potential coercive power of "King Cotton" fascinated countless Southerners. They confidently believed that if the North should establish a strangling blockade, the English textile workers would be thrown out of work, and starving mobs would literally force the British government to intervene in the South. "The cards are in our hands!" gloated the *Charleston Mercury* seven weeks after the firing on Fort Sumter, "and we intend to play them out to the bankruptcy of every cotton factory in Great Britain and France or the acknowledgment of our independence." [2]

---

[1] *Punch*, XL, 134 (March 30, 1861).
[2] *Charleston Mercury*, June 4, 1861, quoted in F. L. Owsley, *King Cotton Diplomacy* (Chicago, 1931), pp. 25–26.

The Southerners also perceived that the tighter the blockade, the greater the pinch in England. They, themselves, restricted cotton production and burned some 2,500,000 bales in order to cause a more acute shortage abroad.

WHY KING COTTON WAS DETHRONED

On paper, King Cotton seemed to have a flawless case. Why, then, did he fail? The basic answer is that when war erupted there was a 50-percent oversupply of raw cotton in England, primarily because the South had already shipped most of its bumper crop of 1860. The surplus also extended to the manufactured product, and when the Civil War began the factory owners were being forced to shut down completely or operate on a part-time basis. The Union blockade of the South actually came as a temporary godsend to the British cotton manufacturers. It increased the value of their huge stocks of raw material, in some cases five- or six-fold. It also gave them an opportunity to dispose of their manufactured goods, then a drug on the market, at three or four times their normal price.

Other unforeseen developments combined to de-scepter King Cotton. During the course of the war some 1,500,000 bales of cotton were run out through the blockade—about three-fourths of a normal year's export to England. New sources of supply were developed in India and particularly in Egypt. As the war progressed and Northern armies penetrated the South, the Washington regime made strenuous efforts to secure cotton and ship it to England. When the real pinch came in 1863, the North was committed to an antislavery crusade, as well as a war for the Union, and any imminent danger of British intervention had passed.

King Cotton also met an unexpected adversary in King Corn. During the Civil War years, crop shortages at home forced the British to turn elsewhere for a grain supply. They found a profitable solution of this problem in exchanging huge quantities of their munitions for Yankee "corn," as they generally called American cereals, the most important of which was wheat. Secretary Seward and other Northern propagandists harped on the theme that if England went to war on behalf of cotton, which she could not eat, she would be deprived of a grain supply, which she had to eat. As a versifier in the *American Continental Monthly* exulted:

Wave the stars and stripes high o'er us,
  Let every freeman sing,

         • • •

Old King Cotton's dead and buried: brave young Corn is King.[3]

  [3] August, 1862, quoted in Edward Channing, *History of the United States* (New York, 1925), VI, 340.

Certain scholars have cast doubt on the "King Wheat" theory. They point out that although England needed grain, she could, if necessary, have secured it in Europe at a somewhat higher price. But many uninformed Englishmen *thought* that they were fatally dependent upon American foodstuffs. This impression, even though erroneous, no doubt helped to strengthen the policy of neutrality being pursued by Downing Street.

King Cotton encountered another powerful rival in war profiteering. In England, the iron, munitions, and shipbuilding industries were booming; British shippers were wresting sea-borne trade from their Yankee rivals; cotton speculators, who had cornered all available fiber, hoped that the war would go on for years; and the languishing linen and woolen factories, with competition from cotton lessened, were enjoying unexpected activity. So great was the general prosperity that, even with several hundred thousand cotton workers thrown out of jobs, the total number of unemployed in England during the war was about normal. The spectacle of Great Britain waxing fat at the expense of the United States aroused much ill will in America. An anonymous Northerner wrote a bitter parody on "God Save the King":

> God save me, great John Bull!
> Long keep my pockets full!
>   God save John Bull.
> Ever victorious,
> Haughty, vainglorious,
> Snobbish, censorious,
>   God save John Bull.[4]

BUNDLES FOR BRITAIN

Despite the generally roseate economic picture in the British Isles, a vast amount of misery was concentrated in the cotton manufacturing centers. By December, 1862, over 400,000 operatives were unemployed or working only part time. Slender stores of savings had melted away; virtuous daughters were being driven into prostitution. The question arises why the textile workers did not get out of hand and force the government to recognize the Confederacy and break the blockade.

The submerged classes of England, first of all, had no vote and little voice. Accustomed to scanty fare, they were docile and generally uncomplaining. Many of them had been led to believe that they were suffering in the interests of democracy and free white labor. This impression was assiduously cultivated by Northern propagandists, notably by the visiting clergyman Henry Ward Beecher. But one finds it difficult to believe that the English workers would have quietly starved to death simply because they sympathized with the abstract ideals of the North—

[4] *Harper's Weekly*, V, 723 (Nov. 16, 1861).

that conscience was stronger than cotton. The famishing operatives appear to have been held in line largely because private and public charity relieved the worst of their suffering.

Discerning Northerners were aware of the explosive situation in the textile industry. A number of them collected money and sent several shiploads of food to England. These donations, as well as the larger ones dispensed by the local authorities, were received with gratitude. The unemployed cotton workers sang:

> Our mules and looms have now ceased work, the Yankees are the cause.
> But we will let them fight it out and stand by English laws;
> No recognizing shall take place, until the war is o'er;
> Our wants are now attended to, we cannot ask for more.[5]

ENGLAND ON THE EVE OF INTERVENTION

The spirit of victory pervaded the North in the first half of 1862. Union armies were generally successful, and the ironclad *Monitor* halted the destructive career of the Confederate ironclad *Merrimack*. The British had already made path-breaking progress in building armored ships, but the Royal Navy was not so sure now of its ability to cope with Yankees on the sea. Then came a staggering setback to Confederate hopes, in April, 1862, when the Union forces captured New Orleans, the largest city and chief seaport of the South—an achievement that sobered Southern sympathizers abroad. Dismay gave way to anger when General Butler, the occupying commander, decreed that all Southern women insulting his men should be locked up in jail as prostitutes. This scandalous "woman order" stirred up a tempest in England, but it quickly passed away under the skillful ministrations of Charles Francis Adams.

The North confidently expected additional military successes from young General George B. McClellan, who was fashioning and polishing the formidable Army of the Potomac. But the utter failure of his Peninsular campaign against Richmond completely changed the outlook. "There is an all but unanimous belief," wrote the friendly Richard Cobden from England to Charles Sumner, "that you *cannot* subject the South to the Union."

Diplomatically, the most critical period of the war came in September and October of 1862, following a crushing Northern defeat at the Second Battle of Bull Run. An increasing number of Englishmen felt that this bloody and senseless strife would probably be inconclusive anyhow, and that in the interests of humanity it ought to be halted. Accordingly, on September 14, 1862, Prime Minister Palmerston, noting that the Northerners "had got a very complete smashing," wrote to Earl Russell at the

[5] E. D. Adams, *Great Britain and the American Civil War* (London, 1925), II, 17 n.

Foreign Office. He proposed that Britain and France join hands in proposing to the Washington government an arrangement "on the basis of a separation." In his reply three days later, Russell favored such a plan of mediation and suggested that "in case of failure, we ought ourselves to recognize the Southern States as an independent State." But on September 23, 1862, Palmerston, having learned of the Confederate drive under General Robert E. Lee into Maryland, wrote to Russell in a more cautious vein:

> It is evident that a great conflict is taking place to the northwest of Washington, and its issue must have a great effect on the state of affairs. If the Federals [Unionists] sustain a great defeat, they may be at once ready for mediation, and the iron should be struck while it is hot. If, on the other hand, they should have the best of it, we may wait awhile and see what may follow. . . .[6]

The decision was thus left to the gods of war.

THE ANTIETAM PIVOTAL POINT

The chilling news reached England, by the end of September, 1862, that Lee's invasion had been halted at Antietam Creek, Maryland. The hard-fought battle revealed that the North was stronger than had been supposed. Interest in intervention waned so rapidly that by late October, 1862, only two members of the British Cabinet supported it. Although hardly more than a draw, Antietam was, diplomatically speaking, one of the decisive battles of the world. The South was probably never so near success as on the eve of that desperate encounter.

Other setbacks contributed to the thwarting of intervention. Notable among them was the conduct of William E. Gladstone, Chancellor of the Exchequer, the third member of the British Cabinet in importance and allegedly its most strongly pro-Southern member. On October 7, 1862, Gladstone delivered a sensational speech at Newcastle, where he went so far as to assert, amid loud cheers and cries of "Hear, hear!":

> . . . There is no doubt that Jefferson Davis [President of the Confederacy] and other leaders of the South have made an army; they are making, it appears, a navy; and they have made what is more than either—they have made a nation. (Loud cheers.) . . . We may anticipate with certainty the success of the Southern States so far as regards their separation from the North. (Hear, hear.) [7]

The British Cabinet, as already noted, was not prepared to intervene following the disturbing news from Antietam. But for Gladstone publicly to recognize the Confederate "nation" left the impression that he was speaking for the government, and that official recognition and interven-

---

[6] Spencer Walpole, *Life of Lord John Russell* (London, 1891), II, 362.
[7] *London Times*, Oct. 9, 1862, 7:6; 8:1. He later disclaimed pro-Southernism.

tion would soon follow. The prospect of breaking the blockade not only caused cotton prices in Britain to fall but produced panic in the business world. Gladstone's indiscretion also caused the pro-Northern group in England to cry out in protest, thus revealing to the Cabinet that intervention would encounter formidable opposition. In the end, the pro-South speech appears to have boomeranged to the advantage of the North.

The decisive reason why Britain did not formally propose mediation probably was the conviction that such a step, vigorously pushed, would mean war. A conflict with the North, particularly after the display of strength at Antietam, was even less inviting than at the time of the *Trent* affair. Russell and Palmerston were both old enough to retain vivid memories of Yankee privateering. Neutrality had on the whole proved highly profitable to the British, and since the South probably would win its independence anyhow, why become embroiled with the United States and possibly lose Canada?

NAPOLEONIC INTERVENTIONISM

The London Cabinet, in its discussions of mediation, had correctly assumed that Napoleon III would co-operate with Britain. From first to last the slippery French Emperor was more than willing to go along. As early as October, 1861, after previous hints of mediation, he had approached London with plans for a joint breaking of the blockade. Periodically he renewed this suggestion. But Britain was the barrier that stood between the South and success.

The reasons for Napoleon's schemings are not far to seek. Jealous of the growing might of the United States, he was evidently eager to establish an American balance of power by dividing the powerful republic. More immediately important was the fact that he had just undertaken to establish a French puppet empire in Mexico. A permanent division of the United States into North and South, with possible Southern support as a reward for his intervention, would insure the success of his Mexican gamble. On the other hand, a victory for the North would jeopardize his ambitious scheme.

Nor was Napoleon III far out of line with French public opinion in his sympathy for the South. Some French textile factories suffered acutely from the cotton famine, as did many other industries dependent on Southern patronage. Except for the first months of the war, French opinion seems to have favored mediation either alone or in the company of other powers, provided that actual hostilities were avoided.[8]

Late in October, 1862, after London had been cooled off by Antietam,

[8] L. M. Case, ed., *French Opinion on the United States and Mexico, 1860–1867* (New York, 1936), pp. 257–258.

Napoleon proposed three-power intervention with England and Russia to secure a six-month armistice in America. This proposition was all the more plausible because it was cloaked in a humanitarian guise. London rejected the offer, while St. Petersburg responded with frigidity. Napoleon did not have the nerve to risk war by a go-it-alone policy, even though his powerful navy possessed considerable iron-clad strength. Thus ended the last serious attempt at joint diplomatic intervention.

Shortly after the ghastly Northern defeat at Fredericksburg, in January, 1863, the persistent Napoleon offered mediation directly to Washington. Seward firmly but politely rebuffed his overture. Congress registered its disapproval by overwhelmingly passing a resolution which declared that attempted mediation, or any other form of intermeddling, would be regarded as an unfriendly act. Napoleon III continued to play a devious game, but this was his last noteworthy attempt at outright intervention.

THE UNION STANDS AGAINST SLAVERY

As the war ground on, Lincoln became increasingly aware of the inconsistency of smiting the slave-holding South with his right hand while upholding slavery in the border states with his left. He longed for the day when the domestic front would permit some decisive action regarding slavery. In July, 1862, following an apathetic reaction in the border states to his plans for a compensated freeing of the Negroes, he summoned a memorable meeting of his Cabinet and read the draft of an emancipation proclamation.

Lincoln's proposal met with general favor in the Cabinet, but Secretary Seward questioned the wisdom of publishing the document at precisely that moment. The North had just suffered a series of defeats, and such a Proclamation, Seward pointed out, would look like an attempt to incite a servile war as a last desperate expedient—"our last shriek, on the retreat." Lincoln, who was struck with the force of this observation, pigeon-holed the statement until such time as a victory should crown Northern arms.

The so-called victory came at Antietam, on September 17, 1862. Lincoln was prompt to seize upon this indecisive success as the springboard from which to launch his preliminary Emancipation Proclamation, dated September 23, 1862. It announced that on January 1, 1863, all slaves would be "forever free." But Negroes in the loyal border states and in certain reconquered areas were not to be affected.

The immediate response to this momentous announcement was disappointing to Lincoln. The South regarded the Proclamation as an inhuman attempt to stir up the "hellish passions of servile insurrection," and girded itself for a more desperate resistance. The Northern abolitionists, bitterly disappointed, demanded a more drastic measure, while the border states feared that they were facing the imminent loss of their valuable slave property. Resentment was reflected at the polls, where the administration suffered heavy losses in the crucial Congressional elections of 1862.

ABE LINCOLN'S LAST CARD, OR ROUGE-ET-NOIR

A British view of Lincoln's Emancipation Proclamation. Note the satisfied expression of President Jefferson Davis and the Negro face on the ace of spades.
London Punch, 1862

In Europe, the preliminary Proclamation did little at first to strengthen the Union cause. Pro-Southern sympathizers cried that this gesture was a public confession that the North had come to the end of its tether. Emancipation, they declared, was a fiendish attempt to conquer the South by a stroke of the pen, now that arms had failed. Pointing to the fact that the proclamation was a war measure designed to free only Confederate slaves, the *London Spectator* scoffed:

> The Government liberates the enemy's slaves as it would the enemy's cattle, simply to weaken them in the coming conflict. . . . The principle asserted is not that a human being cannot justly own another, but that he cannot own him unless he is loyal to the United States.[9]

[9] *London Spectator,* XXXV, 1125 (Oct. 11, 1862).

Blackwood's Magazine spoke of emancipation as a "monstrous, reckless, devilish" "project," and declared that rather than lose the South "the North would league itself with Beelzebub, and seek to make a hell of half a continent."

A PROCLAMATION WITHOUT EMANCIPATION

Undeterred by criticisms at home and abroad, Lincoln went ahead and issued the final Proclamation on January 1, 1863. His action required courage, following as it did reverses at the ballot box and the bloody repulse at the battle of Fredericksburg. Even so, his Proclamation was largely illusory. It was merely a Presidential pronouncement of dubious constitutionality, designed chiefly as a war measure. Legend to the contrary, Lincoln's pen did not strike the shackles from 3,500,000 slaves. Where he could presumably free the Negroes—that is, in the border states—he refused to do so. Where he could not—that is, in the Confederate states—he tried to. In short, where he *could*, he would not, and where he *would*, he could not. But only the wilfully blind could deny that Lincoln's pronouncement foreshadowed the doom of slavery.

In England, the news of the final Proclamation caused a fresh outburst of indignation among anti-Union critics. They had earlier condemned Lincoln because he would not proclaim a crusade against slavery; now they were irked because he did. But the evident determination of the North to wipe out the black curse greatly encouraged the antislavery elements in England. They had at first doubted the sincerity of the preliminary edict, or had been slow to grasp its implications. But now they revealed their delight in various ways, including rousing mass meetings. Referring to one of these demonstrations early in 1863, Henry Adams related:

> As for enthusiasm, my friend Tom Brown of Rugby schooldays, who was one of the speakers, had to stop repeatedly and beg the people not to cheer so much. Every allusion to the South was followed by groaning, hisses and howls, and the enthusiasm for Lincoln and for everything connected with the North was immense. The effect of such a display will be very great. . . .[10]

The distinguished English clergyman, C. H. Spurgeon, prayed before a congregation of many thousands: "God bless and strengthen the North! Give victory to their arms. . . ." The audience responded with a mighty "amen."

The Emancipation Proclamation was clearly a cardinal stroke in Northern diplomacy. It robbed the South of much of its moral cause, while elevating the conflict to a holy crusade against human bondage. It helped nerve the British workingmen to withstand the famine; it gave them an

[10] W. C. Ford, ed., *A Cycle of Adams Letters, 1861–1865* (Boston, 1920), I, 251.

opportunity to demonstrate anew that the masses in England would be loath to stand behind their government in intervention. As Henry Adams reported from London: "The Emancipation Proclamation has done more for us here than all our former victories and all our diplomacy. It is creating an almost convulsive reaction in our favor all over this country." [11]

THE SOUTH BUILDS A NAVY—IN ENGLAND

The next diplomatic crisis grew out of Confederate commerce destroyers. Southern privateering had failed because, handicapped by the peculiar conditions of the war, it could not be pursued with profit. But government-owned commerce destroyers could be used with devastating effect.

The Confederacy, which lacked adequate shipbuilding facilities, naturally turned to the shipyards of England. The British Foreign Enlistment Act of 1819 was designed to prevent the construction of warships for belligerents, but the strict letter of the law could be evaded by not actually arming the vessels in Great Britain. The *Florida* and *Alabama*, for example, sailed from England unarmed, and each received its cannon at a distant island rendezvous. Hence, as far as the shipbuilders and the law were concerned, these craft were not warships at all. But the building of such vessels appears to have been inconsistent with true neutrality and with the spirit of Britain's own statutes.

All told, Confederate commerce destroyers constructed in England burned, sank, or otherwise incapacitated about 250 Yankee ships. American merchant shipping was thus badly riddled. Most of the damage was done by three famous raiders, the *Florida*, the *Shenandoah*, and the *Alabama*, which alone accounted for over sixty victims.

The *Alabama*, built by the Laird Brothers near Liverpool, was launched in May, 1862. Everyone assumed, including the workingmen, that she was being constructed for the Confederacy, and her sides were actually pierced for cannon. Minister Adams collected a mass of affidavits as to her true character and presented them to the proper authorities. But the British officials, some of whom were pro-Southern, feared an outcry in Parliament if the suspicious vessel were seized without full warrant. Outward appearances were damning, but on purely technical grounds the courts would probably decide against the government, which would then be embarrassed by having to pay heavy damages.

The conspirators constructing the *Alabama*, now suspecting that detention was imminent, made ready for her escape. On July 29, 1862, the vessel slipped down the river, ostensibly on a trial run, with a party of

[11] W. C. Ford, ed., *A Cycle of Adams Letters, 1861–1865* (Boston, 1920), I, 243 (Henry Adams to C. F. Adams, Jr., Jan. 23, 1863).

sight-seers on board. When she reached the sea, the visitors were sent back on a tug. The *Alabama* then continued to the Azores, islands under Portuguese jurisdiction, where she received her equipment and crew from two other vessels that arrived from England. She then proceeded to light the skies from Europe to the Far East with the burning hulks of Yankee merchantmen.

The *Alabama* had flown the coop scarcely a moment too soon. The evidence supporting her detention had lain untouched for five critical days on the desk of the Queen's advocate, who had suddenly gone insane. The documents were finally retrieved, London officialdom sprang to life, and orders were telegraphed to hold the *Alabama*—but the ship had left. Many Northerners felt that Her Majesty's government should have made determined efforts to pursue the vessel, which did not leave British waters until some thirty-one hours later. Yet no credible evidence has come to light proving that the Ministry actually connived at her escape to sea.

Adams continued to harass Downing Street with a monotonous list of sinkings and burnings, and with rapidly mounting bills for damages. Under such needling the British began to see that they had created a two-edged precedent that might one day be used against them with terrible effect, perhaps by a foe without a navy (Ireland?) or without even a seacoast (Switzerland?).

A grim hint came in March, 1863, when Congress passed a bill authorizing the President to commission Northern privateers. As there were no Southern merchantmen upon which such raiders might prey, was the North preparing this weapon for use against Britain? The next month the British minister in Washington reported:

> I think the state of things here, as far as peace with us is concerned, more alarming than it has been since the *Trent* affair. . . . I would rather the quarrel came, if come it must, upon some better ground for us than the question of the ships fitted out for the Confederates.[12]

Assailed by doubts, the British authorities decided to cast caution to the winds. In April, 1863, they issued orders to seize the *Alexandra*, another warship being built for the Confederates. In the subsequent court proceedings the government was unable to produce convincing evidence and, to the accompaniment of applause from the crowded courtroom, was assessed costs and damages. Yet the trial involved such long delays that the vessel, when finally released, arrived in American waters too late to be of use to the Confederacy. The North at last had the satisfaction of knowing that London was actively upholding the spirit, as well as the letter, of its neutrality policy. Such a realization softened some of the bitterness.

[12] Lord Newton, *Lord Lyons* (London, 1913), I, 101 (Lyons to Russell, April 23, 1863).

THE LAIRD RAMS CRISIS

Much more menacing than the commerce destroyers, from a military point of view, were the Laird rams. These were powerful ironclad steam warships which the Confederacy had arranged to have built by the same firm that had constructed the *Alabama*. They were obviously designed to break the blockade. Equipped with powerful wrought-iron "piercers" or rams, these floating fortresses could have smashed the wooden ships of the Union blockading squadron like egg shells. Then, with their powerful nine-inch rifled guns, they could have laid the Northern seaport cities under tribute and caused the North to scream for mercy. In short, if the rams had reached America, the South would probably have won its independence, and the North, already angry over the *Alabama* affair, would almost certainly have gone to war with Britain. The imminent departure of these vessels precipitated the last major diplomatic crisis of the conflict.

Downing Street was deeply troubled by the rams. Even though the legal papers showed that they were being built for private purchasers, everyone knew that they were destined for the Confederacy. If the government tried to seize them, it would be liable to a costly damage suit. If it permitted them to sail, it might provoke the United States into a declaration of war—a United States that had just triumphed spectacularly at Gettysburg and Vicksburg. At length, and as a matter of expediency rather than legality, Foreign Secretary Russell privately issued an order on September 3, 1863, that the rams be held. When the news was finally published, Confederate bonds sank fourteen points—and Confederate hopes even lower. The tangle was at last unsnarled when the British government bought the rams for the Royal Navy at a figure considerably in excess of the contract price. Everyone was satisfied—except the Confederates and Confederate sympathizers.[13]

As the sailing date for the rams approached, Minister Adams increased his pressure on the Foreign Office. Fearing that the decision had been reached for their release, he sent a memorable note to Lord Russell on September 5, 1863: "I trust I need not express how profound is my regret at the conclusion to which her Majesty's Government have arrived. . . . It would be superfluous in me to point out to your Lordship that this is war. . . ."[14] This stern warning suggested that either Britain would be making war on the Union, or the Union would declare war. Actually,

---

[13] In 1867 Charles F. Adams attended the great naval review at Portsmouth, where one of the two Laird rams, already obsolete, was pointed out to him. He wrote that "as I looked on the little mean thing, I could not help a doubt whether she was really worthy of all the anxiety she had cost us." C. F. Adams, *Charles Francis Adams* (Boston, 1900), p. 316.

[14] See E. D. Adams, *Great Britain and the American Civil War*, II, 141–144.

Adams' famous "superfluous" note was really superfluous, for two days earlier Russell had secretly issued the order to detain the rams. When the American minister's correspondence was published shortly there-after, it left the unfortunate impression that Adams had bullied the British into yielding.

The last hope of the Confederates for blockade-breaking warships was France. Napoleon III, quite in contrast with the British government, actively connived with the Confederate agents. In April and June, 1863, contracts were signed for four ships of the *Alabama* type, allegedly for service in China waters, plus two powerful rams. Napoleon III, not wish-ing to be publicly involved, gave his approval to the transaction on the condition that the true destination of the vessels be kept confidential. But the secret finally leaked out, and in June, 1864, the builders received official orders to sell all these ships and provide proof of a genuine transaction. One of the rams, though sold to Denmark, finally reached American waters, but too late in the war to be a menace.

THE LOST CAUSE

Southern hopes, already blighted by the rams detention and by defeats on the battlefield, were further dimmed by Europe's distresses. The Mother Continent became much less interested in the American Civil War as war threatened to convulse Europe. In the autumn of 1863 Britain and France almost clashed with Russia over the Czar's rebellious Poles. Austria and Prussia were preparing to pounce upon Denmark and detach Schleswig-Holstein, as they soon did. Henry Adams wrote gleefully in November, 1863:

> . . . Nothing has caused us more gentle slumbers since the seizure of the iron-clads than the delicious state of tangle Europe has now arrived at. Nothing but panic in every direction and the strongest combination of cross-purposes you can conceive. The King of Denmark has just died with a clearly perverse purpose of increasing the confusion, and any day may see a Danish war. Russia expects war and France acts as though it were unavoidable. Meanwhile England hulks about and makes faces at all the other nations. Our affairs are quite in the back-ground, thank the Lord.[15]

But the South died hard. In November, 1864, the Union commander, General Sherman, began his devastating march through Georgia to the sea. The *London Times* criticized "the wild and desperate effort of an out-manoeuvred General" to extricate himself from an untenable situa-tion. Lincoln's triumphant re-election that same month, combined with General Grant's elephantine progress toward Richmond and Sherman's swath east and northward, further opened British eyes. The South played

[15] Ford, *Cycle of Adams Letters*, II, 103 (Henry Adams to C. F. Adams, Jr., Novem-ber 20, 1863).

its final card when it made desperate, last-minute efforts to secure assistance from Britain and France by promising the abolition of slavery. But these overtures came to nothing.

Rumors of the end drifted across the Atlantic to England, only to cause panic among cotton speculators and other profiteers. With delicate irony Charles Francis Adams described the effect of one of these false reports:

> The consternation was extraordinary. The public funds fell. . . . You would have thought that a great calamity had befallen the good people of England. . . . Happily for the distressed nerves of our friends, the next day brought them a little relief. A steamer had come with . . . later news. It was not so bad as they had feared. . . . There would be no peace. Hurrah. The papers of this morning are all congratulating the public that the war will go on indefinitely.[16]

Then came the news of Lee's surrender, closely followed by that of Lincoln's assassination. As if conscience-stricken for its years of defamation, even the pro-Southern press of England outdid itself in writing tributes to the fallen President. Lincoln was now proudly claimed as a fellow Anglo-Saxon. The London *Punch*, which had distinguished itself for coarse caricatures of Lincoln, published a remarkable poem from the once-acid Tom Taylor:

> Yes, he had lived to shame me from my sneer,
> To lame my pencil, and confute my pen—
> To make me own this hind of princes peer,
> This rail-splitter a true-born king of men.[17]

Charles Francis Adams' great work was now done. Probably no other diplomatic representative of the United States had ever had to endure, at least for so protracted a period, critical official responsibility combined with tense excitement and a hostile atmosphere. And rarely did his foot slip. No Northern general on the military front rendered more useful service than this frock-coated warrior on the diplomatic front.

SELECTED BIBLIOGRAPHY

Consult the references in the preceding Bibliography, particularly the books by E. D. Adams and F. L. Owsley. The work of a key Union diplomat in France is described in Margaret Clapp, *Forgotten First Citizen: John Bigelow* (Boston, 1947). See also W. R. West, *Contemporary French Opinion on the American Civil War* (Baltimore, 1924). Lincoln's diplomacy is analyzed in J. G. Randall, *Lincoln, the President: Midstream* (New York, 1952) and J. G. Randall and R. N. Current, *Lincoln, the President: Last Full Measure* (New York, 1955).

Useful articles are J. H. Park, "The English Workingmen and the American Civil War," *Pol. Sci. Quar.*, XXXIX (1924), 432–437; L. M. Sears, "A Confederate Diplomat [Slidell] at the Court of Napoleon III," *Amer. Hist. Rev.*, XXVI (1931), 255–281; M. P. Claussen, "Peace Factors in Anglo-American

---

[16] Ford, *Cycle of Adams Letters,* II, 256–257 (C. F. Adams to his son, Feb. 17, 1865).
[17] *Punch,* XLVIII, 182 (May 6, 1865).

Relations, 1861–1863," *Miss. Valley Hist. Rev.*, XXVI (1940), 511–522; D. H. Maynard, "Union Efforts to Prevent the Escape of the *Alabama*," *Miss. Valley Hist. Rev.*, XLI (1954), 41–60 and the same author's "Plotting the Escape of the *Alabama*," *Jour. of Southern Hist.*, XX (1954), 197–209. See also M. B. Hamer, "Luring Canadian Soldiers into Union Lines during the War between the States," *Canadian Hist. Rev.*, XXVII (1946), 150–162.

See footnotes of this chapter; Bemis and Griffin, *Guide*, pp. 340–349; and *Harvard Guide*, Ch. 18.

7TH ED. REFS. F. L. Owsley's standard *King Cotton Diplomacy* (Chicago, 1959), now appears in this second edition as revised by Harriet C. Owsley. M. B. Duberman, *Charles Francis Adams* (Boston, 1961) shows that this able minister was hampered by Seward's numerous agents and by Seward's practice of publishing Adams' correspondence prematurely. Russell and Palmerston were both friendly and unfriendly to the North at various times, but Palmerston's enthusiasm for intervention cooled off after Antietam; Russell and Gladstone still clung to the idea for a while. Britain developed other sources of cotton, and by 1863 British commercial interests felt that they had about as much to lose as to gain by opening Confederate ports. Henry Blumenthal, *A Reappraisal of Franco-American Relations* (Chapel Hill, N.C., 1959) concludes that Napoleon succeeded only in irritating both North and South; his ministers restrained him by arguing that war with the United States would weaken him in Europe. Except for the Antietam crisis, Napoleon took the lead in most interventionist attempts; one reason why the British held back was their distrust growing out of his deception in connection with Mexico. French economy was hit by the Civil War, but Seward sent Archbishop John Hughes to France, where he was effective as a propagandist. For R. W. Winks, *Canada and the United States: The Civil War Years* (Baltimore, 1960) see new references for Chapter 26. W. D. Jones, *The Confederate Rams at Birkenhead* (Tuscaloosa, Ala., 1961) argues, contrary to many earlier writers, that the London government was not gravely concerned about the departure of the rams, and that their escape "would not have brought Britain into the fight." The author concedes that there is considerable but less weighty evidence to support the opposite view. For Prussia during the Civil War see H. M. Adams, *Prussian-American Relations, 1775–1871* (Cleveland, 1960), as discussed herein at the end of Chapter 24. Harriet C. Owsley, "Henry Shelton Sanford and Federal Surveillance Abroad, 1861–1865," *Miss. Valley Hist. Rev.*, XLVIII (1961), 211–228 deals with a Federal agent who did important work in England and France in thwarting Confederate plans for building warships and running the blockade. D. H. Maynard, "The Forbes-Aspinwall Mission," *ibid.*, XLV (1958), 67–89 describes the activities of two Northern agents sent to England to buy up Confederate ironclads and raiders; they failed in their main objective but invigorated Federal espionage and established valuable contacts with British leaders. J. O. Baylen and W. W. White, "A. Dudley Mann's Mission in Europe, 1863–1864," *Va. Mag. of Hist. and Biog.*, LXIX (1961), 324–328 discusses Mann's efforts to improve Confederate credit and secure recognition. For additional articles, see BIBLIOGRAPHICAL ADDENDUM, p. 996.

8TH AND 9TH ED. REFS. See BIBLIOGRAPHICAL ADDENDUM, p. 997.

24

Napoleon III and Mexico

What a lot of cannon-shots it will take to set up an emperor in Mexico, and what a lot to maintain him there.
PRINCE METTERNICH, AUSTRIAN MINISTER TO FRANCE, 1861

IMPOTENT MONROEISM

THE CIVIL WAR on the whole caused Latin America to draw closer to the United States, and did something to offset the anti-Yankeeism engendered by the Mexican War and the Southern-inspired filibustering expeditions of the 1850's. The sympathies of Latin Americans generally went out to the North. As republicans, they were anxious for the success of the great democratic experiment; as humanitarians, they were themselves in the throes of abolishing slavery; as nationalists, they were opposed to foreign intervention in the affairs of their hemisphere. A powerful and reunited United States could brandish the Monroe Doctrine more fearsomely at the land-grabbers of Europe.

Behind the smoke screen of the Civil War two European nations, Spain and France, undertook to challenge the vitality and validity of the Monroe Doctrine. The first important test came in the revolution-rent Dominican Republic, which, officially at least, asked for re-annexation to Spain. The mother country accepted this unique invitation, and in May, 1861, incorporated the prodigal daughter in the Spanish empire.

Secretary Seward was not caught napping. A month earlier, in a note to the Spanish minister in Washington, he had flatly challenged Spain's right to take back Santo Domingo. The Spanish Foreign Office did not even bother to reply. The American envoy in Madrid next made strong remonstrances to the effect that Spain was violating the basic principles of the Monroe Doctrine. (Monroe had made no reference to the reincorporation of colonies with the consent of the colonials.) In reply, the Spanish foreign minister stalwartly stood his ground, and did not bother to allude to the Monroe Doctrine. Seward emerged from this verbal duel with his fingers burned, and no doubt with the realization that the magic memory of Monroe commanded less respect in the foreign offices of Europe than on the public platforms of America.

The oppressive measures of the Spaniards soon drove the Dominicans to a bloody and costly revolt, to which were added the ravages of their ancient ally, yellow fever. Disease and the desperate courage of the islanders ultimately succeeded where Seward's paper protests and the dead hand of Monroe had failed. In 1865, with a victorious Union crushing the South, the Spaniards voluntarily withdrew, thus removing the necessity of vindicating Monroeism by force. But there remained a second and far more serious challenge to the Monroe Doctrine—that from the French in Mexico.

PREPARING A PUPPET EMPIRE

Relations between the United States and Mexico had continued to be troubled during the 1850's. Chronic disturbances resulted in heavy loss of both American and European life and property. Disorders finally became so intolerable that in December, 1859, President Buchanan urged Congress to authorize him to send a military force into Mexico for the purpose "of obtaining indemnity for the past and security for the future." The Buchanan administration also made several unsuccessful proposals to the Mexican government for the purchase of spacious areas in northern Mexico, particularly Lower California. In 1859 Washington did succeed in negotiating a treaty which secured a perpetual right of way across the narrow Isthmus of Tehuantepec. But the Senate voted down the pact during the internal excitement preceding the outbreak of the Civil War.[1] The aggressive policy of Buchanan aroused fear in Europe that the Yankees were bent on absorbing Mexico, and helped crystallize the schemes of those imperialists who were themselves planning armed intervention.

The crisis finally came to a boil in the bankrupt Mexican republic when its Congress passed a law, in July, 1861, suspending the payments on the government's foreign obligations for two years. An anguished outcry arose from British investors, whose stake in Mexico was the largest, as well as from those of Spain and France. But the legitimate demands of creditors must not be confused with one enormously inflated claim, which the unscrupulous Napoleon III backed in the interests of his half brother. At length, in October, 1861, representatives of Britain, France, and Spain

[1] H. L. Wilson, "President Buchanan's Proposed Intervention in Mexico," *Amer. Hist. Rev.*, V (1900), 696.

signed the trouble-brewing Convention of London, which provided for a
joint military expedition to collect the debts in default. This tripartite
agreement contained the self-denying proviso, which was soon scrapped,
that none of the signatory nations would attempt to secure for itself any
"peculiar advantage."

Napoleon tipped his hand shortly after a Spanish force captured Vera
Cruz, in December, 1861. The British and Spaniards soon withdrew in
disgust from the joint enterprise, leaving a clear field to the imperialistic
plotter. Signs multiplied that Napoleon was planning, not to collect debts,
but to overthrow the republican government of Mexico, set up a satellite
regime, and enthrone a European puppet prince. Overtures had actually
been made to Maximilian of Austria some three weeks *before* the Convention of London, in which Napoleon had solemnly disclaimed any
"peculiar advantage."

What were the probable motives of the French emperor? He apparently hoped to curry favor with the strong Catholic elements at home,
which he had alienated, by rescuing the Catholic Church in Mexico from
the attacks of the anticlericals. Responding also to the urgings of Mexican monarchists, he was evidently planning to erect a Latin, Catholic
monarchy in Mexico as a dike against the expansionist waves of the
Anglo-Saxon, Protestant republic to the north. Perhaps most important
of all was the fact that a resurrection of France's colonial empire, which
even the great Napoleon I had failed to achieve, would win applause from
the glory-loving French masses.

The time for launching this bold venture could hardly have been
better chosen. The Yankees, torn apart by the Civil War, were in no position to invoke the Monroe Doctrine. Napoleon also recognized that his
foothold in Mexico would be strengthened if the United States were permanently sundered. This knowledge largely explains his sympathy for
the South, and why he toyed with the idea of exchanging recognition of
the Confederacy for permission to enchain Mexico.

MAXIMILIAN ON A PHANTOM THRONE

The French conquest of Mexico proceeded with vigor. President
Juárez, a remarkable full-blooded Indian, led the Mexican patriots in a
stubborn resistance, but his opposition was ultimately reduced to guerrilla bands. The French invaders finally occupied Mexico City in June,
1863. A hand-picked Assembly of Notables, consisting almost entirely of
clericals and fawning Mexican reactionaries, then met and voted to offer
the throne to Ferdinand Maximilian of Austria, a younger brother of
the Emperor Francis Joseph.

Maximilian had been willing for some little time. He was a handsome,
fair-haired, and extremely likable young man of thirty-one, with artistic

tastes and a somewhat modest intellectual endowment. Unhappily, he was without serious occupation, and an aimless existence—even in a magnificent palace overlooking the blue Adriatic—grew boresome. His bride, the young, beautiful, and extravagant Carlotta, daughter of the King of the Belgians, was extremely ambitious for her Hapsburg husband. She herself was passionately eager to become an empress—a desire that had little chance of being gratified except in Mexico.

A delegation of Mexican monarchists formally offered the synthetic new crown to Maximilian in October, 1863. The invitation presumably was based upon the vote of the people, although one prominent British diplomat remarked that the plebiscite had been held in places that "were possibly inhabited by two Indians and a monkey." Maximilian, knowing that the French armies had pacified little more than the area from the sea to the capital, replied that he would not accept the invitation unless it was confirmed by the will of the entire nation. If the ill-starred young Hapsburg had adhered to his initial decision, his career probably would not have had such an abrupt and tragic ending. But like many another wishful thinker under the spurs of an ambitious wife, Maximilian listened to the false assurances of self-seekers, disregarded the advice of influential members of the royal family, and even ignored the words of Carlotta's exiled and worldly-wise grandmother, former Queen of France, who reputedly said, "They will murder you." [2] In April, 1864, six months after receiving the original invitation, and without any convincing plebiscite having been taken in the meantime, Maximilian permitted himself to believe what he wanted to believe and accepted the call. On the same day he signed the Convention of Miramar, by which France, in return for heavy financial guarantees, bound herself to lend him military support until 1867.

SEWARD'S SOFT ANSWERS

The United States, though convulsed by Civil War, had been viewing with concern the dramatic events unfolding in Mexico. Napoleon had been an unpopular figure in America since 1852, when he had broken faith with the French Republic and established himself as Emperor. At that time the three epithets most commonly used to describe him were "murderer," "perjurer," and "traitor." The *New York Tribune* called him a "perjured villain," a "knave," and a "bankrupt profligate living in open adultery." The American press reported with glee a story to the effect that during a triumphal tour Napoleon was to pass under an arch from which hung a crown with the placard, "He well deserves it!" Before his arrival the wind blew away the crown, leaving only a dangling rope and "He well deserves it."

[2] E. C. Corti, *Maximilian and Charlotte of Mexico* (New York, 1928), I, 332.

Preoccupation with the Civil War, as well as ignorance of Napoleon's true designs, caused the American public to show surprisingly little anxiety during the early months of the Mexican venture. Several newspapers went so far as to suggest that a thrashing might do unruly Mexico some good. During 1861 and 1862 little was said in Congress about the French invasion, and the Mexican minister in Washington met with real difficulty in keeping alive an interest in his country's plight.

As the fortunes of the North grew brighter and the objectives of France clearer, public opinion in the United States revealed increasing impatience. Shortly before the crown was formally offered to Maximilian, Senator Sumner of Massachusetts delivered a smashing speech in New York in which he paid his respects to Napoleon: "Trampler upon the Republic in France, trampler upon the Republic in Mexico, it remains to be seen if the French Emperor can prevail as trampler upon this Republic." The *New York Herald* sounded a bold note:

> As for Mexico, we will, at the close of the rebellion, if the French have not left there before, send fifty thousand Northern and fifty thousand Southern troops, forming together a grand army to drive the invaders into the Gulf. That is the way we shall tolerate a French monarchy in Mexico.[3]

Amid the rising tide of public resentment, Secretary Seward steered a steady course. He realized that his hands were tied by the Civil War, and that if he pushed France too vigorously he might force her into a military alliance with the South. He therefore adopted the sound strategy of reasserting America's traditional antipathy to intervention by foreign powers, and of reserving for the future the right to act. In brief, he did little more than put his position on record so that the Monroe Doctrine would not go by default. In response to a plea from the United States Consul General at Paris for more vigorous action, Seward answered:

> I think . . . that, with our land and naval forces in Louisiana retreating before the rebels instead of marching toward Mexico, this is not the most suitable time we could choose for offering idle menaces to the Emperor of France. We have compromised nothing, surrendered nothing, and I do not propose to surrender anything. But why should we gasconade about Mexico when we are in a struggle for our own life.[4]

Early in 1864 Congress, traditional weathercock of public opinion, began to veer sharply toward a two-fisted course. On April 4, a week before Maximilian accepted his gilded throne, the House of Representatives passed a resolution by the resounding vote of 109 to 0:

> . . . The Congress of the United States are unwilling by silence to leave the nations of the world under the impression that they are indifferent spectators of the deplorable events now transpiring in the republic of

[3] *New York Herald*, Jan. 21, 1864, 4:4.
[4] Frederic Bancroft, *The Life of William H. Seward* (New York, 1900), II, 430 (Seward to Bigelow, May 21, 1864).

Mexico, and that they therefore think fit to declare that it does not accord with the policy of the United States to acknowledge any monarchial Government erected on the ruins of any republican Government in America under the auspices of any European Power.[5]

The House resolution was naturally rasping to French sensibilities. When the United States minister in Paris, William L. Dayton, hastened to the Foreign Office, he was greeted with these ominous words, "Do you bring us peace or bring us war?" American diplomacy administered soothing syrup by pointing out that a resolution passed by a branch of the Congress could not properly speak for the administration, and that no departure from existing policy regarding Mexico was contemplated. When this explanation was published in the United States, much criticism was leveled at "Seward's apology." The public mood was hardening dangerously.

STORM WARNING'S FOR NAPOLEON

As the North pushed the war to a victorious conclusion, public opinion began to increase its demands that the French be expelled. Napoleon had definitely bet on the wrong horse in sympathizing with the Confederacy. His position was further undermined when Maximilian ill-advisedly gave some support to the South during the closing months of the war. Andrew Johnson, recently nominated for the Vice-Presidency, declared in a speech at Nashville:

> The day of reckoning is approaching. It will not be long before the Rebellion is put down. . . . And then we will attend to this Mexican affair, and say to Louis Napoleon, "You cannot found a monarchy on this Continent." (Great applause.) An expedition into Mexico would be a sort of recreation to the brave soldiers who are now fighting the battles of the Union, and the French concern would be quickly wiped out.[6]

At war's end the victorious North had over 900,000 men under arms, and some of their officers could scarcely be restrained from attempting to eject Maximilian, bag and baggage. Notable among these was General Grant, who ordered General Sheridan with about 50,000 troops to the Texas border. He likewise took steps to send General Schofield to Mexico, there to organize an army of unemployed Confederate and Union veterans.

Secretary Seward removed the danger in this quarter by persuading Schofield to undertake a diplomatic mission to France instead. According to the recollections of the General, "Mr. Seward's explanation and instructions to me, after several long conversations on this subject, were

[5] *Cong. Globe*, 38 Cong., 1 sess., p. 1408.
[6] Dexter Perkins, *The Monroe Doctrine, 1826–1867* (Baltimore, 1933), p. 471 n. (June 10, 1864).

summed up in the words: 'I want you to get your legs under Napoleon's mahogany and tell him he must get out of Mexico.'" [7] There can be no doubt that the secrecy-enshrouded presence of a leading Northern general in France caused much uneasiness and probably further impressed upon Napoleon the wisdom of pulling out of Mexico.

By this time Seward held most of the high cards, and he could now speak with a bluntness that hitherto would have been dangerous. "It is clear," declared the *New York Herald*, "that our foreign relations need to be taken up in a new and vigorous spirit, and our despatches to France to be written in quite another than the sweetened water style that now flavors them through and through." [8] The *New York Evening Post* feared that "trifling will drift us into war." "Let Mr. Seward tell Napoleon to get out of Mexico," it insisted. "That is all we need." In commenting on this statement the Washington correspondent of the *London Times* reported:

> That these words express the feeling of the American people is absolutely certain. . . . The people, I repeat, would rather go to war with France than see her remain in Mexico. . . . They would, of course, much prefer that France withdraw peaceably; but if she will not do that they mean to make her go. That is their own language, used at every public meeting, and at every dinner table, and in every paper, from Maine to California. [9]

SEWARD TURNS ON THE HEAT

Seward realized that the French were a proud and sensitive people. Unless he played his hand with the utmost caution, he might drive them into a corner from which the only honorable escape would be war. His policy therefore was to push Napoleon gently with one hand, while courteously showing him the door with the other.

Not until well into 1865 did anything suggesting a threat creep into Seward's communications with Paris. In September, 1865, they revealed an unmistakable note of veiled hostility. Two months later his tone was positively shrill. When John Bigelow, the new American minister in Paris, read this last instruction to the French Foreign Minister, the latter replied that "he derived neither pleasure nor satisfaction from its contents." Then came Seward's peremptory demand of February 12, 1866: ". . . We shall be gratified," he declared, "when the Emperor shall give to us . . . definitive information of the time when French military operations may be expected to cease in Mexico." [10] Stripped of diplomatic verbiage, these were strong words. On April 5, 1866, the official organ of the Paris government made public a decision that had been reached several months be-

---

[7] J. M. Schofield, *Forty-Six Years in the Army* (New York, 1897), p. 385.

[8] *New York Herald*, Jan. 28, 1866, 4:4.

[9] *London Times*, Nov. 18, 1865, 9:5.

[10] *House Ex. Doc.*, 39 Cong., 1 sess., no. 93, p. 34 (Seward to Montholon, Feb. 12, 1866).

fore: the Emperor would withdraw the French troops from Mexico over a period of nineteen months.

This news of withdrawal, though pleasing to the United States, was followed by a new threat. When word reached America that 4000 Austrian volunteers might sail for Mexico to rescue their countryman, Maximilian, Seward took even more vigorous action. He instructed the United States minister in Vienna to protest, and then to demand his passports if the soldiers were allowed to go. Austria, already faced with serious complications in Europe, was forced to eat humble pie. Seward promptly communicated the relevant correspondence to Congress, probably with a view to strengthening President Johnson, who was then in hot water with the legislative branch.

NAPOLEON TAKES FRENCH LEAVE

Historians are by no means agreed on what motives caused Napoleon to cut loose from Maximilian, or precisely how much weight ought to be attached to the motives that were clearly present. Yet certain facts stand out.

First of all, French public opinion, which had never favored the mad enterprise, was becoming increasingly hostile. Exactly what impact the masses had on Napoleon, who as a dictator was not immediately responsive to popular pressures, is difficult to ascertain.[11] But as a usurper of the throne, he must have seen that he could not safely defy the wishes of the people indefinitely.

The second indisputable fact is that the Mexican venture was expensive. By the end of 1865 the armed expedition ostensibly designed to collect some 40 million francs had already cost 274,698,000 francs—an almost intolerable burden to the thrifty French taxpayers. Napoleon could not have been altogether indifferent to this aspect of the problem.

A third factor that the French could not ignore was the guerrilla war that President Juárez doggedly sustained. This resistance added enormously to the cost of the expedition, raised serious doubts as to the possibility of ever subduing the Mexicans, and probably did more than any other one development to open Napoleon's eyes. If the United States had refrained from bringing any kind of pressure to bear upon France, the Maximilian house of cards probably would have collapsed in time of its own weight.

Two probable motives are not so clearly established. It used to be taken for granted that a major element in the French withdrawal was the unfriendly attitude of Prussia, and Napoleon's desire to withdraw his

---

[11] F. E. Lally, *French Opposition to the Mexican Policy of the Second Empire* (Baltimore, 1931), p. 147, concludes that French domestic opposition had no important bearing on the withdrawal policy.

armies from Mexico for the home front. If true, this would be another
prime example of Europe's distress contributing to America's advantage.
But later scholarship indicates that the French Emperor was not particularly concerned about the European situation when he made the

LETTING HIM SLIDE

NAPOLEON (To MAXIMILIAN of Mexico): "I am really very
sorry, but I must let go, or you might pull me over!"
London Fun, 1866

decision to withdraw from Mexico.[12] On the other hand, his solicitude
probably was greater than the rather fragmentary contemporary documents reveal.

Many red-blooded Americans have long assumed that Napoleon with-

[12] See Perkins, *The Monroe Doctrine, 1826–1867,* pp. 515–518. The author takes
exception to the earlier findings of C.A. Duniway, "Reasons for the Withdrawal of
the French from Mexico," Amer. Hist. Assn., *Annual Report,* 1902, 1, 323.

drew because he feared the powerful armies of the United States. But the republic, already wearied by one war, was in no position to welcome a conflict with a first-class foreign power. At least, this is what the Secretary of the Navy and the Secretary of the Treasury testified in Cabinet meeting. Yet the obvious military might of the United States, combined with the immense difficulties in waging a war overseas, could scarcely have failed to impress the French Emperor.

With the withdrawal of Napoleon's steel and gold in the spring of 1867, the deluded Austrian "archdupe" was left to shift for himself. His flimsy empire tottered to its fall. The beautiful Carlotta returned to France to plead with Napoleon that he fulfill his solemn written pledge of military support. But the dissolute and calloused schemer was not one to be turned from his selfish course by the tears of a woman, albeit a physically attractive one. Carlotta then took her case to the Pope, who of course could do nothing. The unfortunate woman's reason then fled. She lived on in insane impotence for sixty interminable years until 1927, when she died at the age of eighty-seven—a tragic reminder of a shattered dream.

Maximilian was urged by his well-wishers to desert the sinking ship while there was yet time. But the ill-fated young man, torn by pride and a sense of duty, insisted that every drop of his blood was now Mexican and that he would stay. He soon fell into the clutches of the Juaristas, who condemned him to death. Several European governments made strong efforts to save him, and they were even joined by Secretary Seward. But Juárez was determined to make an object lesson of this usurper for the benefit of other ambitious young noblemen. On June 19, 1867, Maximilian fell gallantly, if stupidly, before a firing squad. The *Portland* (Maine) *Transcript* not inaptly observed, "If anybody deserves to be shot it is Louis Napoleon. He is the chief criminal in this great national crime." [13]

A MATURING MONROE DOCTRINE

Maximilian's empire was at once the most serious and the most insolent challenge ever flung into the teeth of the Monroe Doctrine. It involved not only the forcible subjection of a neighboring republic by an unfriendly European power, but the substitution of a monarchial form of government as a barrier against the United States. Maximilian even dreamed of extending his control as far south as Brazil.

Yet in this first acid test of the Monroe Doctrine, Secretary Seward never officially referred to it by name. His disillusioning experience with Spain in Santo Domingo had demonstrated that the Doctrine was un-

---

[13] Quoted in J. G. Gazley, *American Opinion of German Unification, 1848–1871* (New York, 1926), p. 308.

popular in Europe. He may even have concluded that an insistence upon it in Mexico might so provoke the powers that they would recognize the Confederacy—and possibly intervene on behalf of the South.

The basic reason why Seward did not invoke the Monroe Doctrine probably was that he did not need to. The French invasion of Mexico threatened America's national security, and on the basis of self-defense Washington was fully justified in asking the French to depart. Although the Monroe Doctrine was not mentioned by name, its principles were implicit in the diplomatic discussion—and Seward never surrendered them. In Europe, as newspaper and parliamentary discussion reveals, informed people understood perfectly well that the Maximilian affair was a direct challenge to the doctrine of Monroe.

When the Civil War crashed to an end, and a mightier United States emerged from the ashes to demand the evacuation of Mexico, European respect for the Yankee and his pretentious doctrine was increased. *Harper's Weekly* gave expression to a not uncommon feeling:

> The United States Government has now furnished Europe with an argument which every government understands. It has proved itself, by the most tremendous test, to be practically invincible. We are not surprised, therefore, to hear of the sudden and amazed respect for us which has suddenly arisen in the most hostile foreign circles.[14]

With the Civil War, the Monroe Doctrine came of age. In the 1830's it had been ignored, if not forgotten; in the 1840's it had been reasserted without commanding much respect; and in the 1850's it had come to be rather generally accepted by the Democratic Party. But in the 1860's, embraced by the Republican administration of Lincoln, it attained the dignity of a national heritage. Respected at home and acknowledged abroad, it was never again to be challenged so baldly and frontally. If Monroe enunciated the Doctrine and Polk, a Democrat, resurrected it, Seward, a Republican, vindicated it.

THE MAXIMILIAN AFTERMATH

The Mexicans, on the whole, were pleased by Seward's handling of Napoleon III. The United States, of course, had been thinking primarily of itself, and only secondarily of its neighbor. But the intervention of Washington did do something to wipe out the bitterness resulting from the Mexican War, and when Seward visited Mexico in 1869 he was hospitably received.

With France, the story was reversed. The Maximilian affair produced a definite chilliness in the somewhat hollow Franco-American friendship —hollow because from 1794 to 1867 the Paris government was probably as unfriendly to the United States as that of any other major power. For

[14] *Harper's Weekly*, IX, 418 (July 8, 1865).

a number of years after Maximilian's execution, the newspapers of France expressed much resentment toward the United States. The Americans, for their part, continued their hostility toward Napoleon, although feeling much less bitterness toward the French people. The latter, it was believed, had been misled by the untrustworthy dictator.

Napoleon had few well-wishers in America when the Franco-Prussian War broke out in 1870. The Germans were fighting in part for national unity, as the North had been. Nor could Northerners forget that while the French had been lending money to the Confederates and intervening in Mexico, the Germans had been buying generous amounts of United States bonds. In addition, tens of thousands of German-born soldiers, mostly volunteers, had served in the armies of the North. "I side with the Prussians," wrote authoress Louisa M. Alcott, "for they sympathized with us in our war. Hooray for old Pruss!"

The Franco-Prussian War ended with the overthrow of Napoleon, and with the erection of a new republic on the ruins of empire. Much of America's old sentiment for France returned, and the era closed with the semimythical Franco-American friendship still enjoying real vitality.

SELECTED BIBLIOGRAPHY

The best detailed work on the diplomacy of the Maximilian adventure is Dexter Perkins, *The Monroe Doctrine, 1826–1867* (Baltimore, 1933). Brief accounts appear in J. F. Rippy, *The United States and Mexico* (rev. ed., New York, 1931) and J. M. Callahan, *American Foreign Policy in Mexican Relations* (New York, 1932). The key consular official in France is ably treated in Margaret Clapp, *Forgotten First Citizen: John Bigelow* (Boston, 1947). See also F. L. Owsley, *King Cotton Diplomacy* (Chicago, 1931); L. M. Case, ed., *French Opinion on the United States and Mexico, 1860–1867* (New York, 1936); and W. R. West, *Contemporary French Opinion on the American Civil War* (Baltimore, 1924). Valuable public opinion studies are E. B. White, *American Opinion of France* (New York, 1927); J. G. Gazley, *American Opinion of German Unification, 1848–1871* (New York, 1926); C. E. Schieber, *The Transformation of American Sentiment toward Germany, 1870–1914* (Boston, 1923); H. W. Casper, *American Attitudes toward the Rise of Napoleon III* (Washington, 1947). See also Sister Claire Lynch, *Diplomatic Mission of John Lothrop Motley to Austria, 1861–1867* (Washington, 1944).

Useful articles are W. S. Robertson, "The Tripartite Treaty of London," *Hispanic Amer. Hist. Rev.*, XX (1940), 167–189; R. W. Frazer, "Maximilian's Propaganda Activities in the United States, 1865–1866," *ibid.*, XXIV (1944), 4–29; K. A. Hanna, "The Roles of the South in French Intervention in Mexico," *Jour. of Southern Hist.*, XX (1954), 3–21; R. B. McCornack, "James Watson Webb and French Withdrawal from Mexico," *Hispanic Amer. Hist. Rev.*, XXXI (1951), 274–286; N. L. Ferris, "The Relations of the United States with South America during the Civil War," *ibid.*, XXI (1941), 51–78.

See footnotes of this chapter; Bemis and Griffin, *Guide*, pp. 349–359; *Harvard Guide*, Chs. 18–19.

7TH, 8TH, AND 9TH ED. REFS. See BIBLIOGRAPHICAL ADDENDUM, p. 998.

CHAPTER

~~~~~~~~~~~~~~~~~~~~ *25* ~~~~~~~~~~~~~~~~~

The Caribbean and Alaska
1865-1867

*Our population is destined to roll its resistless waves
to the icy barriers of the north, and to encounter
oriental civilization on the shores of the Pacific.*
WILLIAM H. SEWARD, 1846

SEWARD'S SEARCH FOR CARIBBEAN BARGAINS

THE BLOOD-DRAINING Civil War brought a twilight to the heyday of
American expansion. Yet, as fate would have it, Secretary Seward, who
remained in the State Department from 1861 to 1869, had shown himself
to be an expansionist of hemispheric appetite. The war started the month
after he took office, and he reluctantly concluded that a union fighting
for its existence could not expand. But with the close of the conflict his old
dreams returned. In June, 1867, he declared in a Boston speech:

> Give me only this assurance, that there never be an unlawful resistance by
> an armed force to the . . . United States, and give me fifty, forty, thirty
> more years of life, and I will engage to give you the possession of the Amer-
> ican continent and the control of the world.[1]

The revival of Seward's expansionist urge was perhaps not solely the
product of a fevered imagination. President Johnson, who had come from
the Vice-Presidency to the White House upon Lincoln's death in 1865,
had incurred the wrath of many bitter Northerners by not reconstructing
the South with lash and rope. Secretary Seward, who was being condemned for remaining in the Cabinet, probably felt that he could improve his own political standing and strengthen the administration by
a spectacular program of expansion.

Recent experiences with Confederate blockade runners had emphasized
the desirability of having naval and coaling stations in the Caribbean.

[1] V. J. Farrar, *The Annexation of Russian America to the United States* (Washington,
1937), p. 113.

Seward proved to be a willing realtor. As soon as the Maximilian intrusion seemed to be nearing an end, he suddenly left for the Caribbean on a cruise "for his health." After studying the prospects at first hand, he entered into negotiations for at least a base—or seriously contemplated doing so—with Spain, Sweden, Haiti, the Dominican Republic, and Denmark. Only two of these overtures are worthy of mention.

The Caribbean in the 1860's and 1870's

The spacious Bay of Samaná, in the Dominican Republic, seemed ideally suited to Seward's purposes. The rulers of this wretched country, harassed by revolution and bankruptcy, tried to transfer the harbor, and then the entire island, to the United States. But Congress frowned upon the scheme, and early in 1869 the House twice overwhelmed resolutions looking for closer ties. "It may be convenient to have a naval station in the West Indies," declared *Harper's Weekly;* "but is it wise to buy it by adding to our population nearly a million of creoles and West Indian negroes, and by the assumption of nobody knows what debts and liabilities?" [2]

SPURNING THE DANISH WEST INDIES

More noteworthy was Seward's attempt to buy the Danish West Indies (Virgin Islands), which boasted an excellent naval-base harbor on St. Thomas. There was also some fear that they might be transferred to Austria or Prussia, with a consequent violation of the Monroe Doctrine. Early in 1865 Seward approached the Danish minister in Washington, and the ensuing dickering continued for more than two years. When the news leaked out that the United States was proposing to offer several million dollars for these insular crumbs, a storm of ridicule burst upon the administration.

The Danish Treaty, which was formally signed in October, 1867, provided for a cession of two of the Virgin Islands for $7,500,000, subject to a favorable vote by the inhabitants. But hardly was the ink dry

[2] *Harper's Weekly,* XIII, 130 (Feb. 27, 1869). The standard monograph is C. C. Tansill, *The United States and Santo Domingo, 1798–1873* (Baltimore, 1938).

when the islets were ravaged by an earthquake, a hurricane, and a tidal wave. A good many Americans heartily agreed with the *New York Tribune* that "our proposed foothold in the West Indies is likely to be a shaky one." Bret Harte jibed:

> Till one morn, when Mr. Seward
> Cast his weather eye to leeward,
> There was not an inch of dry land
> Left to mark his recent island.[3]

Aside from these natural cataclysms and partisan sniping at President Johnson, there were solid reasons for opposition to the Danish Treaty. The United States was deeply preoccupied with postwar reconstruction and with developing the Great West. The navy, which was being allowed to drift into shameful decay, had little use for its old bases, much less for new ones in the Caribbean. In November, 1867, the House of Representatives resolved, by a vote of 93 to 43, that it was "under no obligation to vote money to pay for any such purchase unless there is greater present necessity for the same than now exists." The *New York Nation* agreed that "If the national future be in peril at all, it is not for want of territory but from excess of it. . . ."[4] Deaf to the siren call of Manifest Destiny, the American people had come to "value dollars more and dominion less."

In spite of these storm warnings, the Danish government formally ratified the treaty. The inhabitants of the islands voted overwhelmingly to come under the powerful and prosperous wings of the American eagle. But the pact sickened in the United States Senate. The Danish minister in Washington, fearful that his government would not unload these defenseless islands after all, went so far as to employ American lobbyists and publicists to create favorable sentiment. But his efforts were unavailing. America simply was not in an expansive mood.

The Danish treaty was still gathering dust in a Senatorial pigeonhole when Ulysses S. Grant became President, in March, 1869. The hero of Appomattox, who had quarreled with the Johnson administration, contemptuously brushed aside the Danish Treaty as a "scheme of Seward's." The pact was thereupon left to die quietly in the Senate. The government of Denmark, to which the first overtures had been made, was gravely affronted; and there was a good deal of criticism, both at home and abroad, of America's breach of faith. But this accusation was far-fetched. No President, in negotiating treaties, can bind either his successor or the Senate.

Ironically enough, the only semitropical outposts of any importance

---

[3] *The Poetical Works of Bret Harte* (Boston, 1912), p. 44. The standard monograph is C. C. Tansill, *The Purchase of the Danish West Indies* (Baltimore, 1932). See also H. Koht, "The Origin of Seward's Plan to Purchase the Danish West Indies," *Amer. Hist. Rev.*, L (1945), 762–767.

[4] *New York Nation*, VI, 5 (Jan. 2, 1868).

acquired during Seward's term as Secretary of State were the Midway Islands. These tiny flyspecks of land, one thousand miles northwest of Hawaii, were occupied by an American naval officer in August, 1867. Completely frustrated were Seward's designs on Hawaii, Cuba, Puerto Rico, Sweden's St. Bartholomew's Island (West Indies), Canada, Greenland, Iceland, and, if one may believe his enemies, a part of China.

RUSSIA AND AMERICA: STRANGE BEDFELLOWS

Seward's one great triumph as an expansionist came with his purchase of Alaska, then known as Russian America. This dramatic story can be understood only when viewed in the light of the international situation.

Almost from the beginning, American feeling toward Russia had been generally friendly, except at the time of the Czar's ukase of 1821 regarding the Northwest Coast and his ruthless suppression of the Polish rebellion in 1830 and the Hungarian uprising in 1849. This traditional Russo-American cordiality was puzzling, for what kinship could the most advanced democracy of the New World find with the most absolute despotism of the Old—"an absolutism tempered by assassination"?

Certain points of similarity immediately suggest themselves. Both countries were huge, self-sufficing areas. Both were energetic and expanding nations. Both, as huge melting pots, had the common task of fusing many different races. Both had almost simultaneously freed millions of subject peoples—slaves in America, serfs in Russia. Both had been faced during the Civil War years with the task of suppressing insurrection. In 1863 the London *Punch* had Lincoln say to Czar Alexander II:

> Imperial son of Nicholas the Great,
> We air in the same fix, I calculate,
> You with your Poles, with Southern rebels I,
> Who spurn my rule and my revenge defy.[5]

In 1866, the year after the Civil War ended, Oliver Wendell Holmes reflected this fraternal spirit in his "America to Russia."

> Though watery deserts hold apart
> The worlds of East and West,
> Still beats the selfsame human heart
> In each proud Nation's breast.[6]

Other factors are more basic to an understanding of this curious friendship. Wide physical separation, combined with a common isolationist spirit, had resulted in an almost complete absence of friction points. "The two peoples," the Czar remarked pleasantly in 1866, "have no injuries to remember." On the other hand, the overweening seapower of Britain

---

[5] *Punch*, XLV, 169 (Oct. 24, 1863).
[6] *The Complete Poetical Works of Oliver Wendell Holmes* (Boston, 1923), p. 198.

had proved highly offensive to both nations. From an early date the Czar's government had deliberately undertaken to cultivate the United States in the hope of building up a New World naval rival that would curb England's power and pride. There is nothing quite like a common enemy to bring incompatible peoples together.

THE RUSSIAN FLEET MYTH

The seeming friendliness of Russia was spectacularly underscored during the Civil War. In the bleak autumn of 1863, when the outcome of the fighting still hung in doubt and foreign intervention still seemed possible, two Russian fleets unexpectedly dropped anchor in American harbors, one at New York, the other at San Francisco. Many gullible Americans, though by no means all, jumped to the conclusion that these warships—about six in each fleet—had been sent to strengthen the United States in its efforts to prevent British and French interference. Even though the fleets were small and to a considerable extent antiquated and unseaworthy, the visiting Russians were almost hysterically overwhelmed with entertainment. The name of the Czar was extolled, and new life was infused into the cause of the North. The entire nation echoed the prayer, "God bless the Russians."

American gratitude continued to express itself in various forms. The year after the close of the Civil War, the Czar narrowly escaped assassination at the hands of a fanatic. Congress passed a resolution of felicitation, which the Assistant Secretary of the Navy carried to Russia on a United States warship. In 1871 the Grand Duke Alexis, son of the Czar, visited America. He was received with extravagant rejoicing, and was even taken out to Nebraska to shoot buffalo. Oliver Wendell Holmes wrote his memorable "Welcome to the Grand Duke Alexis," which was sung to the Russian national air by the children of the public schools:

> Bleak are our shores with the blasts of December,
> Fettered and chill is the rivulet's flow;
> Throbbing and warm are the hearts that remember
> Who was our friend when the world was our foe.[7]

Unaffected by popular enthusiasms, a considerable number of clearheaded or cynical Americans *guessed* that something ulterior lay behind the visits of the fleets. But not until about a half century later did the official Russian archives yield their secret.[8] In 1863 a general European

---

[7] *The Complete Poetical Works of Oliver Wendell Holmes* (Boston, 1923), p. 199.

[8] F. A. Golder, "The Russian Fleet and the Civil War," *Amer. Hist. Rev.*, XX (1915), 802–803. Professor Golder, who secured access to the Russian documents, was the first American scholar to demolish the fleet legend. See also T. A. Bailey, "The Russian Fleet Myth Reexamined," *Miss. Valley Hist. Rev.*, XXXVIII (1951), 81–90.

war over Poland seemed imminent, with England and France arrayed against Russia. Should hostilities erupt, the Russian vessels would probably be bottled up in the Baltic or in the Far East by the vastly more powerful British navy. But each Russian warship might become a veritable *Alabama* if the craft could be transferred to strategically located neutral ports before the outbreak of war. A friendly United States was ideally situated for this purpose. The American assumption that the coming of the fleets was primarily a gesture of friendship was based upon a misapprehension. But whatever its foundation, the illusion existed and played an important part in paving the way for the purchase of Alaska. Myths are often more potent than facts in the making of history.

ALASKA—A FROZEN ASSET

Even before 1867 the Czar's government had come to regard Alaska (Russian America) as a potentially valuable but immediately unprofitable colonial stepchild. The Russian American Company, which administered this chill region, had ravaged its fur resources and was facing bankruptcy. The Russian officials, unwilling to shoulder the burdens of the Company, remembered that several years earlier certain American spokesmen had shown a mild interest in buying Alaska. Perhaps the Czar, by capitalizing on the friendship generated by the visit of the fleets, could unload this bothersome liability on the Americans for a substantial sum.

Other anxieties hastened the sale. The Russians fully realized that in the quite probable event of another war with their archenemy England, nothing could prevent all Alaska from falling an easy prey to the British navy. A transfer of the territory to the Americans would forestall this loss, while striking a blow at Britain's ambitions in the Pacific. Alaska, moreover, was breeding trouble with the United States. The monopolistic tactics of the Russian American Company were causing increasing friction with American traders and thus jeopardizing a valuable friendship, at a time when the Czar needed friends. He was so deeply involved in Asia and in Europe that he wanted his hands free to press for his objectives there. Once again Europe's distresses were coming to America's aid.

Alaska itself, which the Russians knew to contain some gold deposits, might yet be seized by American expansionists. The propulsive power of Manifest Destiny or an overnight gold rush might enable the Americans to acquire the territory, in a manner unpleasantly reminiscent of West Florida and Texas. A momentary scare had already been caused by a rumor that the prolific Mormon following of Brigham Young was planning to settle in Alaska and overrun it. Caution suggested selling while the selling was good, even though the price obtained did not, in Russian eyes, come anywhere near the potential value of the territory.

The Czar's minister to the United States, Édouard de Stoeckl, was much too clever to approach Seward directly with his proposition. He let it be known through one of the Secretary's friends that Russia might be coaxed into selling Alaska. Seward, who had long dreamed of extending American boundaries to the Arctic, eagerly rose to the bait and made the first overtures, in March, 1867. After considerable haggling, the price finally agreed upon was $7.2 million, or $2.2 million more than the minimum price set by the Russian minister's superiors. With Congress about to adjourn, Seward had Stoeckl send an outline of the proposed treaty to St. Petersburg over the newly laid and expensive Atlantic cable.

On the evening of March 29, 1867, Stoeckl called at Seward's home in Washington. He brought the welcome news that the Czar had given his consent to the transaction, and suggested that the treaty be concluded the next day at the State Department. The eager Seward pushed away the card table:

> "Why wait till tomorrow, Mr. Stoeckl? Let us make the treaty tonight!"
> "But your Department is closed. You have no clerks, and my secretaries are scattered about the town."
> "Never mind that," responded Seward. "If you can muster your legation together, before midnight you will find me awaiting you at the Department, which will be open and ready for business." [9]

At four o'clock on the morning of March 30, 1867, the treaty was put into final form and signed.

"SEWARD'S POLAR BEAR GARDEN"

Only an expansionist with Seward's undiscriminating appetite could have seriously considered buying Alaska. Americans today probably know more about Antarctica than their countrymen then knew about Russian America. Senator Sumner, later a stalwart champion of the treaty, admitted that only Greenland and Central Africa were less well known.

When the American people heard of the transaction—"a dark deed done in the night"—they could scarcely believe their ears. Surprise and ignorance immediately combined in an outburst of derision, and for a time the treaty was in danger of being hooted out of court. It was "an egregious blunder," a "bad bargain," palmed off on "the silly administration" by the "shrewd Russians." Alaska, the land "of short rations and long twilights," was "a barren, worthless, God-forsaken region," "a hyperborean solitude" consisting of nothing but "walrus-covered icebergs." It was "Walrussia," "Johnson's Polar Bear Garden," "Polario," "Frigidia," "a national icehouse," "Seward's Icebox." The *New York Herald* ran this

[9] F.W. Seward, *Reminiscences of a War-Time Statesman and Diplomat, 1830–1915* (New York, 1916), p. 362.

filler: "HOW TO MAKE BOTH ENDS MEET—Buy Patagonia, Mr. Seward." The same newspaper published a satirical advertisement:

CASH! CASH! CASH!—Cash paid for cast off territory. Best price given for old colonies, North or South. Any impoverished monarchs retiring from the colonization business may find a good purchaser by addressing W.H.S. [Seward], Post Office, Washington, D.C.[10]

The prospects of ratification appeared so dim that Senator Sumner advised Stoeckl to withdraw the treaty and avoid the inevitable rebuff to America's good friend, Russia. But Seward did not lose heart. He realized that the most vociferous opposition came from those who were most ignorant of Alaska's resources, and he concluded that a vigorous campaign of education might save the treaty. He therefore handed over to the press a number of letters that had come to his office from influential men who favored the transaction. When he discovered that the opposition was voicing the same objections that the Federalists had used against the acquisition of Louisiana, he sent a clerk to New York to copy passages from the newspapers of 1803, and these in turn were printed by the daily press of 1867.[11] So successful was Seward in marshaling public opinion behind the treaty that charges of bribery were brought against him. But he later testified that he had spent only $500 in his "campaign of education." The truth appears to be that the people were eager for information about their new windfall, and that the press was willing to publish without charge much of what Seward provided.

SEWARD, SUMNER, AND THE SENATE

The Senate was yet to be heard from, and there Seward was hated for his loyalty to President Johnson. Some of the Senators even went to Stoeckl and explained that they were going to vote against the treaty simply because the Secretary was behind it. But the resourceful Seward called certain Senators to his office one by one, and there made confidants of them. One member later confessed that Seward did "a good deal of hustling" on behalf of the treaty. The Washington correspondent of the *New York Herald* graphically described what was happening:

Secretary Seward has another diplomatic symposium at his elegant establishment to-night, at which Mr. Sumner is present, with numerous other Senatorial luminaries. Madame Rumor again associates Russian-American icebergs and refrigerated champagne; and, putting this and that together, makes Mr. Seward's dinner bear in some way on the proposed slice of hyperborean territory.[12]

[10] *New York Herald*, April 12, 1867, 6.5.
[11] T. A. Bailey, "Why the United States Purchased Alaska," *Pacific Hist. Rev.*, III (1934), 43–44.
[12] *New York Herald*, April 9, 1867, 3:1.

PREPARING FOR THE HEATED TERM

King Andy and his man Billy lay in a good stock of Russian ice in order to cool down the Congressional inquiry.

Seward (*left*) and Johnson (*right*), facing impeachment, represented as buying Alaska so as to appease Congress.
Leslie's Illustrated News, 1867

Of crucial importance was the support of Charles Sumner. As chairman of the powerful Senate Committee on Foreign Relations, and as one of the most forceful orators in the country, he was in a position to make or break the treaty. At first he was unenthusiastic about Alaska, but once converted, he threw himself into the cause with irresistible vigor. After a short period of intensive study, and with only one sheet of notes before him, he made a brilliant three-hour speech in support of the purchase. He emphasized the vast natural resources of Alaska, as well as the commercial advantages that would accrue to the Pacific Coast from its acquisition. He also pointed to the gain for democratic institutions that would come from the banishment of Russian monarchy from North America, and he noted that in acquiring Alaska the United States would not only steal a march on Britain but put the seal upon its friendship with Russia. Yet he warned against "indiscriminate and costly annexation." The Senate, deeply impressed by Sumner's tremendous effort, approved the purchase that same day, April 9, 1867, by a vote of 37 to 2.

ALASKA CLEARS THE HOUSE HURDLE

But the other branch of Congress had its hatchet sharpened. Many members were indignant because Seward had bound them to pay the sum of $7,200,000, without so much as saying "by your leave." The question again arose as to whether, in such instances, the House of Representatives was also a part of the treaty-making power. The members delayed coming to grips with the question until after the United States had formally taken possession of Alaska. Then they were confronted with an accomplished fact. If they refused to vote the money, they would affront Russia and at the same time humiliate the United States by hauling down "Old Glory."

Numerous members of the House voiced varied complaints, although they seemed to be more concerned about their injured dignity than anything else. They were particularly disturbed by the presumed worthlessness of Alaska. Representative Washburn of Wisconsin suggested that Seward could have purchased a much superior white elephant in Siam or Bombay "for one hundredth part of the money" and "with not a ten thousandth part of the expense incurred in keeping the animal in proper condition." Others objected that there was no point in provoking Britain unnecessarily, because in due time the United States would get Alaska for nothing when Canada was annexed. Representative Cullom of Illinois introduced the ever-recurring fruit metaphor: "I believe that we are destined to own and control the whole western continent from Baffin's bay to the Caribbean sea. But, sir, we need not be in a hurry. When the fruit is ripe it will fall into our hands." [13]

Opponents of Alaska in the House also made much of the argument that America was establishing the dangerous precedent of acquiring noncontiguous territory. One of the Representatives spoke feelingly in behalf of a compact country; he objected to one so large that he could love only "half of it at a time." Others feared that this purchase would pave the way for further indiscriminate annexation. There was no telling what Seward would do next if he was able to acquire Alaska.[14]

Despite this barrage of criticism, Congressional supporters of the purchase stood their ground. They stressed Russian friendship, as well as the economic, commercial, and strategic potentialities of Alaska. They argued that if the United States did not take the territory Britain would, and that sound policy pointed to the wisdom of snatching this choice morsel from the lion's jaws. Other Congressmen asserted that with

[13] *Cong. Globe*, 40 Cong., 2 sess., appendix, p. 474 (July 10, 1868).
[14] The *New York Herald* emphasized this possibility in fictitious advertisements. "THE MILK IN THE COCOANUT.—We can get it with the Feejee Islands. Having commenced the purchase of outside countries, we can go on. We have icebergs, but we want cocoanuts." April 12, 1867, 6:2.

Alaska on the north and the United States on the south, British Columbia (and with it all Canada) would be caught in the jaws of a vise and forced into a union with America. "Canada will fall into our lap like a ripe apple," declared Representative Mungen. The *New York World* expressed the same thought more delicately: ". . . A gap in our possessions on the Pacific Coast will always be an eyesore to the nation, whose sense of symmetry will be offended by the ragged look of the map." [15]

Some of the Representatives, despite the general apathy toward expansion at the time, insisted that the acquisition of Alaska was but inevitable Manifest Destiny. Outside Congress a few newspapers echoed these sentiments. The *New York Herald* spoke of carrying out "the fiat of inevitable destiny, which, in time, must give us the whole of the North American continent." The *Sacramento Union* reflected the prevailing spirit in an editorial entitled "We Approach the Pole":

> There once floated about the world of humor a definition of the boundaries of the United States, which ran as follows: On the north by the aurora borealis, on the east by the Atlantic, on the west by the Pacific, and on the south by manifest destiny. Despite the smack of Yankee exaggeration in this, we are getting along. Our flag has advanced to the northern verge of the continent—the auroral land fringed by the ice of the Arctic Sea.[16]

THE ACCEPTANCE OF "SEWARD'S ICEBOX"

The prolonged debates in the House drove Stoeckl almost to distraction. Much of the obstruction came from members who were backing an enormously inflated claim against Russia growing out of the alleged purchase of American arms during the Crimean War. In desperation, Stoeckl undertook to give heavy subsidies to the press and to employ high-priced lobbyists. One received $30,000. All else having failed, Stoeckl suggested to his superiors that they offer Alaska to the United States as a gift, and thus shame the Americans into paying the money. The Czar promptly vetoed this suggestion: he feared that the Yankees might accept it.

As a last resort, the Russians employed bribery. The evidence is not clear as to which Congressmen accepted Stoeckl's gold, but the Russian documents indicate that some of them did.[17] Finally, on July 14, 1868, the debate in the House ended and the appropriation passed, 113 to 43. Stoeckl then requested that he be allowed to go somewhere where he might "breathe for a while a purer atmosphere than that of Washington." He ignored his own contribution to its pollution.

[15] *New York World*, April 1, 1867, 4:2.
[16] *Sacramento Union*, April 1, 1867, 2:2.
[17] F. A. Golder, "The Purchase of Alaska," *Amer. Hist. Rev.*, XXV (1920), p. 424. See also W. A. Dunning, "Paying for Alaska, *Pol. Sci. Quar.*, XXVII (1912), 386; and R. H. Luthin, "The Sale of Alaska," *Slavonic Review*, XVI (1937), 171.

But Russian good will, far more than Russian gold, influenced the final result. The backers of the purchase repeatedly stated that since America had solicited Alaska from her friend Russia, Congress could not honorably throw the frigid territory back into the Czar's face. Many felt with Senator Cameron of Pennsylvania that the purchase was "an act of recompense to a tried friend."

Yet the influence of Russian friendship, powerful though it was, probably would not have prevailed had not the American people come to realize that the territory was potentially valuable. Seward's campaign of education was effectively conducted, and an examination of contemporary newspapers reveals that as knowledge of the new territory spread, enthusiasm for it increased correspondingly. The members of the House could not mistake or fail to heed the ground swell of approval. Fundamentally, the American people accepted Seward's treaty because of the feeling that Alaska was probably worth the money. Yankee love for a bargain and a highly developed speculative instinct were not to be denied. Bret Harte caught the spirit:

> 'T ain't so very mean a trade,
> When the land is all surveyed.
> There's a right smart chance for fur-chase
> All along this recent purchase,
> And, unless the stories fail,
> Every fish from cod to whale;
> Rocks, too; mebbe quartz; let's see,—
> 'T would be strange if there should be,—
> Seems I've heered such stories told:
> Eh!—why, bless us,—yes, it's gold! [18]

Harte was right; Alaska did "pan out." Few there are today who, on economic grounds at least, will accuse Seward of folly in having bought this enormous domain—larger than the Mexican Cession without Texas—for $1\frac{19}{20}$ cents an acre. The magnificent natural resources of Alaska, including fabulous deposits of gold, have paid for the territory many times over.

In recent years various spokesmen in the Soviet Union, thinking in part of the strategic proximity of Alaska, have argued that the Czar was duped and that the American title is invalid. But the United States is not likely to move out at this late date. The American people would rather have their bombers stationed in northern Alaska than Soviet bombers perched on the southern tip of the Alaskan panhandle.

SELECTED BIBLIOGRAPHY

Russian-American relations are outlined in T. A. Bailey, *America Faces Russia* (Ithaca, N.Y., 1950) and F. R. Dulles, *The Road to Teheran* (Prince-

[18] Harte, *Poetical Works*, p. 42.

ton, 1944). The purchase of Alaska is described briefly in F. R. Dulles, *America in the Pacific* (Boston, 1932). The fullest account is V. J. Farrar, *The Annexation of Russian America to the United States* (Washington, 1937). See also Virginia H. Reid, *The Purchase of Alaska: Contemporary Opinion* (Long Beach, Calif., 1940) and J. M. Callahan, *The Alaska Purchase and Americo-Canadian Relations* (Morgantown, W. Va., 1908). Especially valuable is F. A. Golder, "The Purchase of Alaska," *Amer. Hist. Rev.*, XXV (1920), 411–425. Lincoln is brought into the story in A. A. Woldman, *Lincoln and the Russians* (Cleveland, 1952). On the Polish insurrection consult H. E. Blinn, "Seward and the Polish Rebellion of 1863," *Amer. Hist. Rev.*, XLV (1940), 828–833, and A. P. Coleman and M. M. Coleman, *The Polish Insurrection of 1863 in the Light of New York Editorial Opinion* (Williamsport, Pa., 1934).

Useful articles are Hunter Miller, "Russian Opinion on the Cession of Alaska," *Amer. Hist. Rev.*, XLVIII (1943), 521–531; D. M. Dozer, "Anti-Expansionism during the Johnson Administration," *Pacific Hist. Rev.*, XII (1943), 253–275; A. G. Mazour, "The Prelude to Russia's Departure from America," *Pacific Hist. Rev.*, X (1941), 311–319.

See footnotes of this chapter; Bemis and Griffin, *Guide*, pp. 360–369; *Harvard Guide*, Chs. 18–19.

7TH ED. REFS. D. L. Smiley, *Lion of White Hall: The Life of Cassius M. Clay* (Madison, Wis., 1962) deals with the mission of a bowie-knife diplomat to St. Petersburg; Russia was determined to be friendly despite the crudities of this egregious misfit. Clay's claim to credit for the Alaska purchase is without foundation, although he did have a few dealings with business interests that desired the purchase. Alexandre Tarsaïdzé, *Czars and Presidents* (New York, 1958) is the work of a Russian emigré turned amateur historian. Tracing Russian-American relations to 1917 through personalities and colorful details, he nostalgically attempts to prove that the traditional friendship was more genuine than appears to have been the case. The Civil War chapters, including the fleet visits, are among the more interesting. Popularized versions of the fleet visits and the Alaska purchase, derived from a series of articles in *The American Heritage* magazine and edited by Oliver Jensen, appear in *America and Russia: A Century and a Half of Dramatic Encounters* (New York, 1962). E. W. Ellsworth, "Sea Birds of Muscovy in Massachusetts," *New England Quar.*, XXXIII (1960), 3–18 examines newspaper reactions to the visit of the Russian fleet at Boston; the editors showed much enthusiasm for the visitors but little for the rumored alliance. Charles Vevier, "The Collins Overland Line and American Continentalism," *Pacific Hist. Rev.*, XXVIII (1959), 237–253 reveals that the dealings with Russia over the abortive telegraph line helped to stimulate and facilitate the purchase of Alaska. M. B. Sherwood, "George Davidson and the Acquisition of Alaska," *ibid.*, 141–154 discloses that the investigative report of this government scientist had some influence in swinging the House appropriation, although it was quoted by both sides. R. E. Welch, Jr., "American Public Opinion and the Purchase of Russian America," *American Slavic and East European Rev.*, XVII (1958), 481–494 finds forty-eight newspapers on the whole favorable to the transaction.

8TH AND 9TH ED. REFS. See BIBLIOGRAPHICAL ADDENDUM, p. 999.

26

Great Britain and the Grant Era, 1865-1877

If the Americans don't embroil us [England] in war before long it will not be their fault. What with their swagger and bombast, what with their claims for indemnification, what with Ireland and Fenianism, and what with Canada, I have strong apprehensions.
CHARLES DICKENS, 1865

CANADA AND THE CIVIL WAR

WHEN THE CIVIL WAR began, free-soil Canada sympathized strongly with the antislavery North. Even the children, as they played North and South with wooden guns, experienced difficulty in persuading enough of their playmates to represent the Confederates. But much of the rancor aroused in the United States by Britain's conduct was directed at nearby but unoffending Canada. As violent American denunciations led to bitter Canadian recriminations, the fat was once more in the fire.

Ill feeling reached the breaking point when plain-clothes Confederate agents, despite the vigilance of Canadian authorities, began to use Canada as a base for annoying raids into the United States. The most serious of these was directed at St. Albans, Vermont, in October, 1864, at which time three banks were looted and one citizen was killed. Nervous tension on the frontier caused Secretary Seward to give London the formal six-months' notice of intention to terminate the Rush-Bagot disarmament agreement of 1817 for the Great Lakes. Fortunately, the border quieted down, and Seward rescinded his action in March, 1865.[1]

The Canadian Reciprocity Treaty of 1854 fared less well. Partly as a result of bitterness engendered by the war, and partly as a result of American jealousy of Canadian prosperity under the pact, Washington

---

[1] See J. M. Callahan, *The Neutrality of the American Lakes and Anglo-American Relations* (Baltimore, 1898), pp. 136–167.

gave formal notice of abrogation, in March, 1865, effective twelve months later.

When the Civil War ended the Northerners, flushed with victory, boasted of pouring into Canada and taking it over as part payment for the wrongs suffered at the hands of lordly Britain. A Northern marching song, set to the tune of "Yankee Doodle," ran:

> Secession first he would put down
> Wholly and forever,
> And afterwards from Britain's crown
> He Canada would sever.[2]

Perspiring American orators spoke passionately of the boundaries that "God Almighty had established, reaching to the Aurora Borealis on the north." In July, 1866, a bill was introduced in the House, though not passed, making provision for the admission of Canada into the Union.

CANADIAN UNION—BY-PRODUCT OF YANKEE GREED

For a brief time there was hope that the object of America's desires would fall into her arms without resort to cave-man tactics. The spirit of disunion was rife in Canada, especially in faraway British Columbia, where, in 1869–1870, over one hundred residents petitioned the United States for annexation. The British minister in Washington and other influential Englishmen were declaring that if Canada chose to join the United States peaceably, the Mother Country would raise no serious objections. But Britain would fight before she would permit the loosely united colony to be wrested from her.

A unified Canada, curiously enough, was largely a by-product of Yankee covetousness. The necessity of uniting against a vengeful neighbor was a potent argument in bringing about the passage in London of the British North American Act, effective July 1, 1867, under which the Dominion of Canada came into being. But unity was not what the United States wanted. In disunity lay annexation. The House of Representatives went so far as to pass a resolution, on March 27, 1867, deploring the formation of the Dominion of Canada as a violation of American principles [Monroe Doctrine] and as a step toward strengthening monarchy. Actually, the British had purposely used the word "Dominion" instead of "Kingdom" for fear of waving a red flag at the Yankee bull.

Gradually the American people came to accept the new order in Canada. The British Columbia annexation movement, perhaps the only one that ever had any real chance of success, died away. It was blighted by American apathy, by the inclusion of the province in the Dominion, and by the completion of the Canadian Pacific Railway in 1885. The sledge

[2] Quoted in H. L. Keenleyside, *Canada and the United States* (New York, 1929), p. 139.

hammer that drove the last spike cracked the knuckles on the feebly outstretched hand of American Manifest Destiny.

FENIAN FORAYS

British-American relations were further embroiled during these years after the Civil War by the Fenians—a secret Irish brotherhood, organized in the 1850's, whose prime objective was the independence of Ireland. Using the United States as a base, these Irish-Americans planned first to conquer Canada, and perhaps involve America and Britain in a war that would result in liberating the Emerald Isle.

The Fenians, many of whom had served in Northern armies during the Civil War, made no bones about their intentions. One of their wartime marching songs ran:

> We are the Fenian Brotherhood, skilled in the art of war,
> And we're going to fight for Ireland, the land that we adore.
> Many battles we have won along with the boys in blue,
> And we'll go and capture Canada, for we've nothing else to do.[3]

After the South fell, the Fenians held balls, picnics, and conventions in the United States, and finally organized an Irish "Republic."

After much drill and parade, and much excitement and alarm, Fenian "armies" gathered on the northern frontier. The first serious push came in May and June of 1866, when a few hundred Irishmen crossed the Niagara River, only to flee after a lucky initial success known as "the Battle of Limestone Ridge." But the faithful kept up the agitation. The next Fenian incursion of any consequence came four years later, in May, 1870, when the nondescript force of "General" John O'Neill was completely dispersed after a United States marshal had arrested the leader. The belatedly energetic action of the American officials won the commendation of the British minister in Washington, and the condemnation of so-called "professional Irishmen" everywhere.

The Canadians, who had been put to unwelcome expense in repelling these invasions, were more angered than alarmed. They did not fully appreciate the plight of the Washington authorities, who, confronted with the potent Irish vote and a public sympathetic with Fenian aspirations, were unable to live up fully to their international obligations. The harboring of Irish armies in the United States not only wet-blanketed annexation sentiment in Canada, but further stimulated a swelling surge of Canadian nationalism.

Yet the Fenians, in a curious way, made a significant contribution to the betterment of British-American relations. During these troubled postwar years much indignation was aroused in the United States when American Fenians, upon returning to Ireland, were jailed for inciting

[3] *Ibid.*, pp. 146–147

revolt. Some of the ensuing diplomatic disputes between London and Washington grew out of the difficulty of distinguishing between a naturalized American citizen born in Ireland and an American citizen of Irish descent born in the United States. The British, in the Treaty of 1870, finally recognized the right of naturalization, and thus abandoned the hoary principle, so trouble-brewing in the years before 1812, "Once an Englishman, always an Englishman." [4]

THE ABORTIVE *ALABAMA* SETTLEMENT

At the end of the Civil War, public opinion in the North was poisonously aroused against Britain. The bitterest of all memories was that of the "British pirates"—that is, the Confederate commerce destroyers constructed in England, notably the *Alabama*, the *Florida*, and the *Shenandoah*. Though officered by Southerners, these three craft were British-built, largely British manned, and (except the *Florida*) never saw a Confederate port.

The *Alabama* had been the most destructive, but the *Shenandoah* was not soon forgotten. In a flagrant breach of neutrality, the British in Australia had permitted her to be dry-docked, to make repairs, to take on supplies, and to enroll forty-two crew members ("stowaways"). She then proceeded to ravage the Pacific whaling fleet, and she continued her destruction even *after* unofficial word had come of the Confederate collapse. But the *Alabama* symbolized all these raiders, and after she was destroyed off the French coast by a Union cruiser in 1864, a picture of the sinking that sold well in the North carried the inscription: "Built of English oak, in an English yard, armed with English guns, manned by an English crew, and sunk in the English channel." [5]

The British, now worried about the two-edged precedents they had created, viewed the reunited United States after Appomattox with apprehension. ". . . The sunken *Alabama*," noted a writer in the *Fortnightly Review*, "leaves a brood of her kind to be hatched out by the heat of the next English war. . . ." The nightmare began to take on reality when, in 1866, the House of Representatives unanimously voted to modify the Neutrality Act of 1818 so as to permit Americans to sell vessels to belligerents. Although this measure never passed the Senate, it was an unmistakable invitation to other nations to attack Britain's rich and vulnerable merchant marine with American ships. Many Irishmen hoped to see the day when American-built *Alabamas* would be ravaging English shipping under the flag of an Irish republic.

[4] See R. L. Morrow, "The Negotiation of the Anglo-American Treaty of 1870," *Amer. Hist. Rev.*, XXXIX (1934), 663–681; also I-Mieng Tsiang, *The Question of Expatriation in America Prior to 1907* (Baltimore, 1942).

[5] R. G. Albion and J. B. Pope, *Sea Lanes in Wartime* (New York, 1942), p. 172.

The prospect of settling the *Alabama* claims brightened in June, 1866, when a change of ministry ousted Earl Russell from the Foreign Office and ushered in a series of more conciliatory successors. Secretary Seward, who was eager to revitalize the discredited Johnson administration, hastened to take advantage of the opening. Unfortunately, he could no longer work through the able Charles Francis Adams, who had resigned. His successor, the windy and convivial Reverdy Johnson of Maryland, attempted to woo the British with speeches that were so gushing as to elicit amused comments even in England. His worst blunder was in cordially shaking the hand of John Laird, the Scottish-born and still unrepentant builder of the *Alabama*. When the news reached America, red-blooded Northerners demanded the instant recall of "Junketing Reverdy Johnson." *Harper's Weekly* published a cartoon with these words:

> And here's a hand my trusty Laird
> And gie's a hand o' thine,
> And we'll tak a right gude willie-waught [drink]
> For auld lang syne.[6]

The negotiations that followed these ill-omened preliminaries resulted in the Johnson-Clarendon Convention, which was signed in January, 1869. It made provision for the arbitration of individual claims *on both sides* since 1853—"both batches on an equality." There was not a word of regret about the *Alabama;* there was not a single reference to the indirect damages caused by British-built, British-manned, and British-succored commerce destroyers.

The American people, from the outset, seem to have been hostile to the treaty. It might have been accepted with amendments in 1865, when the nation was war-weary, but not in 1869. Americans were in the grip of extravagant ideas; sane men were talking seriously of taking over Canada in part payment for the *Alabama* claims. The Senate, moreover, did not appreciate the hasty efforts of the unpopular Johnson administration to patch up the controversy. On April 13, 1869, as everyone expected, the treaty was struck down by a vote of 54 to 1.

THE SPEECH THAT SHOOK TWO HEMISPHERES

The defeat of the treaty was so certain that no oratorical floral offerings were needed. But the egotistical Senator Charles Sumner charged into the arena, on April 13, 1869, with a smashing indictment of Britain. He claimed first of all that England owed the United States $15 million for the actual damages to American ships caused by the *Alabama*. But there were

---

[6] *Harper's Weekly,* XII, 810 (Dec. 19, 1868). For a defense of Johnson see B. C. Steiner, *The Life of Reverdy Johnson* (Baltimore, 1914), pp. 236 ff.

also "national" losses, such as the transfer of registry to neutral flags and the increase of insurance rates. This item alone would total $110 million. In addition, Britain's moral and material support to the Confederacy, the Senator argued, had prolonged the war by two years—a four-year conflict that had cost $4 billion.

With unaccustomed moderation, Sumner did not bluntly conclude that Britain owed the United States a total of $2.125 billion. He merely remarked, "Everybody can make the calculation." Nor did he say that since England could not pay this enormous sum in cash, America would accept Canada instead. But this idea was so prevalent that the inference was unmistakable.

Sumner's sensational speech was widely reproduced and avidly read. James Russell Lowell probably was not far from the mark when he said that it "expressed the feeling of the country very truly." The *New York Nation* found that it "set about all Americans swinging their hats for eight or nine days. . . ." But thoughtful men feared that this intemperate outburst would put another stumbling block in the way of settlement. Henry Adams, then in Washington, had grave doubts as to Sumner's sanity.

In England, disgust was mingled with indignation. The British had extended what they regarded as a friendly hand in the Johnson-Clarendon Convention. It had been rudely rebuffed. Then, like a slap in the face, the most influential member of the Senate had made these preposterous demands, apparently with the full approval of his colleagues. A British correspondent of the *New York Tribune,* realizing that Sumner's figures were a war indemnity without a war, wrote that "England will fight rather than even negotiate on any such basis." The *London Spectator* declared that "it is war that speeches like those of Mr. Sumner would force on us." United States bonds dropped 5 per cent. Many months would have to pass before Great Britain would again consent to negotiate the *Alabama* claims.

A WARRIOR IN THE WHITE HOUSE

On March 4, 1869, five weeks before the rejection of the Johnson-Clarendon Convention, General Ulysses S. Grant was sworn in as President. This narrow and bewildered military hero, suddenly elevated from a seat in the saddle to one in the White House, proved to be a pathetic and naïve misfit. By a happy accident he chose as his Secretary of State Hamilton Fish, a wealthy and socially prominent New Yorker, who had been a one-term Congressman, governor, and Senator. Although Fish was totally without diplomatic experience, he was a student of international affairs and enjoyed the breadth which can come from broad social background and extensive travel. Lacking the brilliance of Seward, he nevertheless brought to the floundering Grant administration a soundness of judgment that was desperately needed.

The foreign service under Grant sank scandalously low, even though some of his major appointments were good. His first Secretary of State, E. B. Washburne, was appointed to that post for ten days as a reward for personal favors. He thus enjoyed greater prestige when he later arrived in France as United States minister. A nephew of Congressman "Beast" Butler was made consul general in Egypt, where he disgraced his country by drunkenness, brawling, a shooting affray, and the purchase of dancing girls. General Sickles, who had lost a leg at Gettysburg, became minister to Spain, where as the "Yankee King" he reputedly formed an adulterous relationship with the former Spanish Queen in Paris. Such were the fruits of rewarding friends or supporters by appointing them or their favorites to the diplomatic service.

The key post of minister to England was awarded to a high-spirited historian, John Lothrop Motley, whose candidacy had been vigorously championed by his close friend, Senator Sumner. Grant made the appointment with reluctance. He had little in common with the intellectual Motley, and he did not like men who parted their hair in the middle.[7] With both Grant and Fish inexperienced in foreign affairs, Sumner, veteran chairman of the Senate Committee on Foreign Relations, looked upon himself as the director—perhaps the dictator—of the administration's foreign policy. Motley shared this view. The retired Charles Francis Adams acidly but correctly observed that the historian evidently expected to represent two powers abroad: Mr. Sumner and the United States government.

Tension reached a climax when Motley, in flat violation of Secretary Fish's instructions, represented Sumner's views on the *Alabama* claims to the British government. Grant, whose military mind regarded disobedience of orders as unpardonable, declared, "Motley must be dismissed at once." Fish remonstrated, for he feared that a quarrel with Sumner at this point would further discredit the administration and complicate a settlement with Britain. The upshot was that Fish gave Motley a tactful verbal spanking, and transferred the negotiations from London to Washington.

THE CUBAN BELLIGERENCY CRAZE

Smoking Cuba had meanwhile claimed the spotlight. The rebellion against Spain, which had erupted in 1868, was being fought out with savagery on both sides. The American people, with their proliberty and antimonarchy traditions, were deeply concerned. Cuban exiles in the United States formed *juntas* which disseminated propaganda, held mass meetings, offered bribes of bonds to the press and to Congressmen, and

[7] W. B. Hesseltine, *Ulysses S. Grant, Politician* (New York, 1935), p. 141.

organized filibustering expeditions. Such unneutral activity naturally angered the Spanish government. The danger of a clash mounted when American property was destroyed in Cuba, and when American citizens, mostly naturalized and of Cuban birth, were arbitrarily imprisoned or summarily shot. Press, pulpit, and platform demanded intervention, or at least a recognition of belligerency.

But picking a fight with Spain was not to be undertaken lightly. Level-headed Americans could not ignore the still-complicated problems of reconstruction, the huge debt, the worm-eaten navy, and the tiny army. Secretary Fish also realized that war with Spain would weaken his hand elsewhere, and postpone, if not prevent, a final settlement of the *Alabama* claims controversy with Britain.

Many Americans, including President Grant, believed that the United States owed at least a recognition of belligerency to the struggling Cuban insurgents, even though war probably would have followed such a species of interference. The insurgent Cuban government consisted of hardly more than some fugitive leaders under palm trees, and Spain was in a resentful mood. Yet in August, 1869, Grant wrote Secretary Fish a letter instructing him to issue a proclamation, which he had already signed, recognizing the belligerent status of the Cuban rebels. Fish, who no doubt remembered the uproar in the North when London had recognized the belligerency of the Confederacy, quietly pigeonholed the explosive document. The President, momentarily distracted by pressing financial difficulties, forgot about his blunder.

The Cuban belligerency agitation, which would not die, came to a head in Congress in the early summer of 1870. Secretary Fish, with threats of resignation, persuaded the reluctant Grant to send a special appeal to Congress urging strict noninterference. The message was heartily applauded by the more conservative newspapers, and made a strong impression on the House. Yet the belligerency resolution was reported favorably and, after a bitter debate, was voted down, on June 16, 1870, by the not too comfortable margin of 101 to 88 votes. The timely Grant-Fish message probably spiked the resolution and possibly averted war over Cuba.

THE *VIRGINIUS* OUTRAGE

For about three more years the Cuban insurrection continued to run its destructive course without precipitating a new major crisis. A long series of disagreeable incidents involving American citizens and property finally culminated in an explosion of public opinion when, in October, 1873, the *Virginius* broke into the headlines. This vessel, which was owned by Cubans, had for several years notoriously been running arms and supplies into the gore-soaked island. While sailing under papers obtained by fraud, while illegally flying the American flag, and while carrying some munitions and a party of revolutionists, she was captured on the high seas by a Spanish warship.

The passengers and crew were brought to Santiago, Cuba, where, after hasty and secret courts martial, fifty-three of them were summarily shot as pirates. Among the victims were a number of Americans and Englishmen. Probably more would have perished had not Captain Lorraine, of the British warship *Niobe,* arrived in haste and trained his guns on the city. He was later presented with a service of plate by the grateful citizens of New York, while appreciative Nevada miners sent him a fourteen-pound silver brick.

The *Virginius* outrage evoked an outburst of righteous anger that had no parallel since the firing on Fort Sumter. Even granting the improper activity of the *Virginius,* the indiscriminate massacre of those on board seemed unwarranted. Indignation meetings were held from Boston to New Orleans. The Cuban propaganda *juntas* in the United States, now sensing intervention and liberation, played up the incident. Dana's lurid *New York Sun* beat the tom-toms of war. Anger likewise rocked Spain, where a frenzied mob threatened to destroy the American legation in Madrid.

Fortunately, the dove of peace was not completely frightened away. For one thing, the dubious character of the *Virginius* had a sobering effect. The horrors of the Civil War were fresh, and the United States had no burning desire to annex Cuba. Internal problems were still absorbing American energy, while the Panic of 1873 had struck with paralyzing force the month before. The Civil War navy was now a collection of "antiquated and rotting ships," which, testified one officer, a single "modern war-vessel" could probably have destroyed without "serious damage to herself." Even so, the country was in such an ugly mood that a single false step might have precipitated war.

Diplomacy now ran its troubled course. Secretary Fish dispatched to Spain a virtual ultimatum, in which he demanded an apology and redress within twelve days. Naval and military preparations were frantically rushed. But when Fish learned the questionable nature of the *Virginius,* and realized that the wobbling Madrid government could not be pushed too fast or too far, he moderated his demands. After anxious days, Fish worked out an amicable adjustment with the able Spanish minister in Washington, and Spain eventually paid an indemnity of $80,000 to the families of the executed Americans. Less satisfactory was the treatment of the brutal officer responsible for the massacre. He was removed from his command and further "punished" by being promoted to a higher rank. The best that can be said about the whole unhappy episode is that war with Spain over the Cuban crisis was averted—that is, for a quarter of a century.

THE SANTO DOMINGO DEBACLE

The disorders in Cuba by no means eclipsed the strenuous efforts of Grant to annex the Caribbean republic of Santo Domingo. The president of this bankrupt and revolution-rent country was willing to cede his domain to the United States, provided that the latter would shoulder the public debt. This plan was enthusiastically championed by an unsavory group of American speculators and promoters. It also found favor with the navy men, who, still seeking Caribbean bases, were eager to secure the splendid Bay of Samaná. The gullible Grant was easily persuaded to fall in line, and he ardently embraced the annexation project—or rather it embraced him. It became an obsession.[8]

Secretary Fish, although not enthusiastic about the Santo Domingo scheme, acquiesced. He perceived that Grant, if wrapped up in it, would be more likely to keep his clumsy hands out of the delicate negotiations involving Cuba and the *Alabama* claims. Late in 1869 the Dominican annexation treaty was completed in proper form.

But the American people responded coldly to the whole idea. Involved as they were in the exploitation of the Great West, they were not expansionist-minded, particularly after the unwanted purchase of Alaska two years before. Moreover, the current difficulties in the South over adjusting the freed Negro to his new status were definitely curbing any appetite for the annexation of insular outposts that were thickly inhabited by alien peoples.

Grant, in his enthusiasm for the Dominican project, went to see Charles Sumner, chairman of the Senate Foreign Relations Committee. After a conversation in which the President muddle-headedly addressed the Senator as "chairman of the Judiciary Committee," Grant went away thinking, apparently with some justification, that Sumner had pledged his support to the project. But the Senator, after a careful study had uncovered grave irregularities, turned violently against it. In spite of the President's immense personal and political power, the final vote on annexation, taken in June, 1870, was 28 to 28, far short of the necessary two-thirds.

The treaty was now dead but the quarrel was not. Deeply angered by Sumner's apparent treachery, Grant promptly demanded the scholarly scalp of the Senator's friend, Motley. The unhappy historian was summarily removed from his London post. The dogged hero of Appomattox kept up the fight for Santo Domingo with all the weapons at his command, while the embittered Sumner attacked the President's questionable methods in spectacular speeches. In private, the Senator would roar "like

[8] See C. C. Tansill, *The United States and Santo Domingo, 1798–1873* (Baltimore, 1938).

the bull of Bashan" and condemn Grant as "a colossus of ignorance." The general, when told that Sumner did not believe in the Bible, snapped, "No, he did not write it." Grant even shook his fist as he passed the Senator's residence, and ominously hinted that if he were not President there would be a challenge to a duel. The war hero got in the final crushing blow when he arranged to have Sumner deposed from the cherished chairmanship of the Senate Committee on Foreign Relations.

The disgraceful quarrel over Santo Domingo actually cleared the path for a pact with England. Sumner and Motley, both obstructionists, were rendered relatively harmless.[9] Grant, who had once favored the Senator's extreme demands for indirect damages, changed his views and became more friendly to a reasonable settlement with London.

ANGLO-AMERICAN DIPLOMACY

Negotiations for a settlement with England of the so-called *Alabama* claims had meanwhile been further complicated by two additional disputes. First, there was the ever-dangerous North Atlantic fisheries controversy. Following America's abrupt abrogation of the Reciprocity Treaty of 1854, certain privileges extended to Yankee fishermen had ended, and a bitter quarrel soon developed over American rights. Secondly, there were periodic flare-ups over the Northwest water boundary, which involved ownership of the small but strategically located San Juan Islands, southeast of Vancouver Island. The outbreak of the Civil War had eclipsed the so-called "Pig War," during which British and American armed forces almost came to blows when an American settler shot a British-owned pig.[10]

Informal conversations designed to bring about a general settlement with Britain were informally launched in Washington during the summer of 1869. London's eagerness for an adjustment mounted with the rising international tension that finally flared forth in the Franco-Prussian War of 1870–1871. The attitude of Russia was most disturbing to the British, who feared that in the event of an Anglo-Russian war dozens of Russian-owned *Alabamas* might be built in American ports for the ravaging of Britain's commerce. With England in a chastened mood, and evidently willing to arbitrate outstanding differences, arrangements were

[9] Motley's successor in London was General Schenck, who had befriended Grant while in Congress. He became the lion of the hour when he introduced draw poker to London high society. His downfall came when he permitted his name to be used to influence wealthy Britons to invest in bogus Western mining stock.

[10] See J. W. Long, Jr., "The Origin and Development of the San Juan Island Boundary Controversy," *Pacific Northwest Quar.*, XLIII (1952), 187–213. See also Hunter Miller, *San Juan Archipelago: Study of the Joint Occupation of San Juan Island* (Bellows Falls, 1943); and *Northwest Water Boundary: Report of the Experts Summoned by the German Emperor* . . . (Seattle, 1942).

concluded early in 1871 for a joint commission of ten to draw up a general treaty.

The historic meetings of the Joint High Commission were held in Washington from February to May of 1871. The five Americans, on the whole able men, were headed by Secretary Fish. The five British representatives, a truly distinguished group, included the Canadian Prime Minister, Sir John A. MacDonald, who vigorously championed Dominion interests. A surprising spirit of cordiality prevailed on both sides, particularly in view of the recent bitterness. Nor were social

The Northwest
Water Boundary Settlement
1872
▬▬▪▬▪▬ *U.S. claim and final award, 1872*
▬▬▬▬▬ *British claim*
■ *San Juan Islands in dispute*

lubricants neglected. Diversions included a spring fox hunt in Virginia, and a round of balls and receptions, during which both sides entertained lavishly.

BRITAIN EATS HUMBLE PIE

The Treaty of Washington, a lengthy document consisting of forty-three articles, was comprehensive in scope. The prickly San Juan boundary dispute was referred to the German Emperor as arbitrator. The perennial fisheries controversy took more time than any other—seventeen sessions, as compared with ten for the *Alabama* claims. The final articles gave Yankee fishermen much more extensive privileges than the Convention of 1818. In return, British subjects were permitted to fish along the coast of the United States as far south as the 39th Parallel—approximately the latitude of Delaware Bay. In view of the Canadian complaint that this was not a fair exchange, arrangements were made for another commission to award an appropriate cash equivalent to that nation making the greater sacrifice. The Canadians perceived that the Mother Country was eager to erase the damaging *Alabama* precedent, and they were consequently angered by the alleged sacrifice of their fishing interests to the Yankees.

More noteworthy was the disposition of the so-called *Alabama* claims. The Treaty of Washington provided for an arbitral commission of five members, to be appointed respectively by the rulers of Great Britain, the United States, Italy, the Swiss Confederation, and Brazil. The British inserted in the treaty a frank expression of regret for the escape of the *Alabama*—an unusual if not unique international apology. They further agreed to a set of rules, defining neutral obligations, which were to guide the arbitrators in their decision. A neutral government, the treaty declared, must exercise "due diligence" to prevent the building, arming, equipping, or succoring of ships designed to make war on a nation with which it was at peace.

These new ground rules, which went beyond generally accepted international law, were effectively designed to safeguard Britain in any future war. They amounted, in fact, to a virtual surrender of the British case and to the reduction of the arbitral tribunal to a mere fact-finding body.

The press of the United States was generally enthusiastic about the Treaty of Washington. The *New York World* was but one of a number of newspapers to make the happy discovery that "nearly all of the concessions were made on the British side." But there was some dissatisfaction among New England fishermen, and among those expansionists who clamored for the annexation of Canada. After some partisan wrangling, the Senate consented to ratification, on May 24, 1871, by a vote of 50 to 12.

DEADLOCK AT GENEVA

The arbitral tribunal that gathered in Switzerland by the quiet waters of Lake Geneva, as provided by the Treaty of Washington, was on the whole a distinguished body. President Grant chose the judicious Charles Francis Adams; Queen Victoria selected the Lord Chief Justice of England, Sir Alexander Cockburn. Cockburn was an excitable Briton of French ancestry who antagonized his colleagues by his supercilious manner and who, when angry, pounded the table so hard as to knock stationery onto the floor. The Swiss, Brazilian, and Italian members were men of varying legal ability.

The Geneva Tribunal was almost shipwrecked before it could be fairly launched. When it convened in mid-December, 1871, to receive the printed argument, the American lawyer exploded a verbal torpedo by unexpectedly reviving Sumner's indirect claims. Not only did he include the entire cost of the war since the Battle of Gettysburg—a period of about two years—but he added interest charges at 7 per cent. The ordinarily cautious Secretary Fish had daringly authorized the inclusion of indirect damages, for if they were ignored Congress might refuse to carry

A STILL BIGGER CLAIMANT

Politically-minded Yankee cleverly inflates *Alabama* claims with air-producing bellows.
London Punch, 1872

out the treaty. There was also some point in disposing of this troublesome issue once and for all.

Indirect damages had not been mentioned in the Treaty of Washington, presumably because their specific renunciation would have aroused the Senate. The British therefore assumed that the whole dispute had been dropped by mutual agreement. The unexpected revival of these "monstrous" claims consequently led to a furious outcry in England, and to the accusation that the British had been victimized by a dishonorable Yankee trick. According to the calculations of Prime Minister Gladstone, Britain might be assessed a sum totaling the enormous figure of $8 billion, as compared with the $1 billion that Germany had recently extorted from conquered France. *Punch* expressed a not uncommon sentiment:

> Very likely 'twere cheaper at once to risk fight
> Than to venture a ruinous payment,
> Which would serve but to arm the unquenchable spite
> Of the cunning, unscrupulous claimant.
> For we fools having paid those 'cute Yankees in full
> An indemnity heavy as France's,
> A fresh quarrel they'd pick, and to war with *John Bull*,
> Go supplied by himself with finances.[11]

The demand from angered Britons that the Geneva arbitration be abandoned snowballed to such proportions that the Ministry was in danger of being overthrown—and with it the Treaty of Washington.

An ominous undertone of war talk on both sides spurred friends of peace to exert themselves. Prayers were offered in English churches beseeching divine interposition. The influential editor of the *New York Nation* wrote: "We might find ourselves in war with England to-morrow without more than a dozen men among us being able to say exactly what caused it, or whether it might not have been avoided." [12] The prospect of hostilities caused panicky European investors to unload their American securities on a collapsing market. The crisis was actually costing the United States each day far more in dollars and cents than it could reasonably expect from the Geneva Tribunal. In the face of such pressures, the American press began to veer around and urge moderation.

But with neither side willing to give enough ground, peace hung by a hair. On May 3, 1872, Minister Schenck, in London, came home and threw down his hat. "It is all over. This is the end of the treaty." "Very well, sir," replied his young secretary, "we shall fight Great Britain, and, thank God, we are ready for it!" [13]

THE BRITISH-AMERICAN BALANCE SHEET

The Geneva Tribunal was saved—and with it perhaps the Treaty of Washington and peace as well—by a somewhat irregular procedure. Charles Francis Adams managed to persuade his colleagues on the Tribunal to rule out the indirect claims, although that question was not then before them for adjudication. On June 19, 1872, therefore, the arbitrators took matters into their own hands and rendered an "extra-

[11] *London Punch*, LXII, 55 (Feb. 10, 1872).
[12] *New York Nation*, XIV, 181 (March 21, 1872).
[13] F. W. Hackett, *Reminiscences of the Geneva Tribunal of Arbitration, 1872* (Boston, 1911), p. 202 n.

judicial" decision. They declared, in effect, that if they were competent to decide on the indirect claims, they would find them insupportable in law. Washington acquiesced, for Fish had made his gesture to public opinion and precedent, and the deliberations continued.

The final decision was handed down on September 14, 1872. The Tribunal found that Britain had violated the prescribed rules of "due diligence" agreed upon in the Treaty of Washington in connection with the *Alabama*, the *Florida*, and the *Shenandoah*, and awarded the United States the sum of $15.5 million. Applause burst forth from the hushed audience, and outside the hall salvos of artillery heralded the victory for peace. But the apoplectic Cockburn filed a violent and voluminous dissenting opinion, and departed unceremoniously from the room.

Fortunately, the British people showed a greater degree of sportsmanship, although they were not overjoyed by the decision. The general feeling among them seems to have been that England was lucky to have come out of the affair as well as she did. ". . . We simply wanted," declared the *London Times*, "the judgment of five men of sense and honor; we have obtained it, and we cheerfully abide by it." [14] The British officials subsequently hung the canceled draft for $15.5 million on a wall of the Foreign Office, as a warning to future ministries to be more careful.

But what of the other three arbitrations provided for by the Treaty of Washington?

In October, 1872, the German Emperor upheld in full the contention of the United States regarding the San Juan Islands. Thus Grant could proudly declare, on the eve of his campaign for re-election, that not only had the *Alabama* claims been settled but that for the first time in the history of the republic there was no boundary dispute with Britain.

The commission of three established to consider the general claims on both sides, specifically those growing out of the Civil War, met in Washington from September, 1871 to September, 1873. Britain was awarded the sum of $1,929,819, most of which represented damages to her shipping from illegal Union blockade practices. All American claims were disallowed.

After a delay of several years, a fisheries commission of three men met at Halifax, in June, 1877. Five months later it awarded Britain $5.5 million as compensation for yielding fishing privileges at Washington in 1871. Many Americans felt that the award was unfair and the amount excessive, and the United States commissioner, like Cockburn at Geneva, refused to sign the judgment. But the assessment was belatedly paid.

The final result of the awards under the Treaty of Washington was that the United States received $15.5 million from England, and paid to her $7,429,819. The net was only about $8 million. There was naturally considerable resentment in America that the *Alabama* award should have

[14] *London Times*, Sept. 18, 1872, 7:2.

been thus whittled down, but on balance the results were all for the best.

The Treaty of Washington thus provided one of the most striking triumphs for arbitral methods that the world had yet witnessed. It set up four significant arbitrations, three of them major. It was one of those periodic air-clearings that dispelled every serious cloud darkening Anglo-American relations. It was not only Fish's greatest diplomatic success, but it was also probably the most substantial accomplishment during the eight long years of Grant. It proved to be an oasis of foreign achievement in a desert of domestic scandal.

CUBA AND THE CURTAIN FOR GRANTISM

From 1874 to 1877, the closing years of the Grant era, diplomacy was largely routine. The energy of the country was absorbed by Indian fighting, railroad building, westward expansion, and the acceleration of the Industrial Revolution. The interest of the people was distracted by inflation agitation, race riots, election campaigns, centennial celebrations, the Reverend Henry Ward Beecher adultery trial, and political scandals in Washington—to mention only a few headlines.

But there were certain diplomatic vexations of at least secondary importance. Disorders along the Mexican border resulted in the usual demands for intervention, which Grant successfully resisted. Bickerings arose with Britain over the execution of the Treaty of Washington. The Cuban insurrection, dragging to its bloody and inconclusive close, was always a potential combustible. In the latter part of 1875 the interventionists renewed their pressure on Grant. But Secretary Fish succeeded in preserving a hands-off policy and in persuading the President to take another strong stand against interference in his annual message to Congress.

Fish took an important step when, in November, 1875, he proposed that the six principal European powers bring diplomatic pressure upon Spain to end the war in Cuba. But this famous dispatch (No. 266), which was unfairly criticized in the United States as a departure from the Monroe Doctrine, came to nothing. Europe gave it a chilly reception, and Spain countered with enough concessions to take the edge off the American proposal.

Hamilton Fish could lay down the Secretaryship of State in 1877 knowing that, even with the burden of Grant on his back, he had made no irreparable blunders. He had avoided some that the President had seemed bent on making; he had averted possible war with Britain and Spain; and he had either settled or arranged for the settlement of every pressing diplomatic problem. If by their fruits Secretaries of State are known, the long-suffering and prudent Fish deserves a high place among them.

SELECTED BIBLIOGRAPHY

A survey of these years appears in S. F. Bemis, ed., *The American Secretaries of State and their Diplomacy* (New York, 1928), VII, 125–214. The most revealing single book on the Secretary of State for this period is Allan Nevins, *Hamilton Fish* (New York, 1936). Relations with Britain and Canada are treated in L. B. Shippee, *Canadian-American Relations, 1849–1874* (New Haven, 1939); Goldwin Smith, *The Treaty of Washington, 1871* (Ithaca, N.Y., 1941); F. W. Howay, W. N. Sage, and H. F. Angus, *British Columbia and the United States* (Toronto, 1942); and H. G. MacDonald, *Canadian Public Opinion on the American Civil War* (New York, 1926). The standard work is William D'Arcy, *The Fenian Movement in the United States: 1858–1886* (Washington, 1947); see also F. E. Gibson, *The Attitudes of the New York Irish toward State and National Affairs, 1848–1892* (New York, 1951). The best book on the subject is C. C. Tansill, *The United States and Santo Domingo, 1798–1873* (Baltimore, 1938). See also W. M. Armstrong, *E. L. Godkin and American Foreign Policy, 1865–1900* (New York, 1957).

Useful articles are H. A. Davis, "The Fenian Raid on New Brunswick," *Canadian Hist. Rev.*, XXXVI (1955), 316–334; A. C. Gluek, Jr., "The Riel Rebellion and Canadian-American Relations," *ibid.*, pp. 199–221; D. F. Warner, "Drang Nach Norden: The United States and the Riel Rebellion," *Miss. Valley Hist. Rev.*, XXXIX (1953), 693–712.

See footnotes of this chapter; Bemis and Griffin, *Guide,* 397–415; *Harvard Guide,* Chs. 19, 23.

7TH ED. REFS. R. W. Winks, *Canada and the United States: The Civil War Years* (Baltimore, 1960) notes that there was little pro-North sentiment in Canada, especially after Lincoln proclaimed union to be the war aim and after the *Trent* affair. The Canadians greatly feared annexation; they were anti-North rather than pro-South. The Southerners aroused anger by violating Canadian soil. D. F. Warner, *The Idea of Continental Union: Agitation for the Annexation of Canada to the United States, 1849–1893* (Lexington, Ky., 1960) reveals that particularly after confederation in 1867, economic dislocations and states rights spurred serious pro-annexation agitation (never that of a majority) in Nova Scotia, New Brunswick, Quebec, Manitoba, and British Columbia. Many of these people wanted to come in under the Yankee tariff tent. The British granted confederation more to keep Canada out of the United States than Canada within the Empire; ultimate Canadian independence was regarded as inevitable. The United States never seriously supported annexation; politicians who raised the issue were seeking votes, not Canada. M. B. Duberman, *Charles Francis Adams* (Boston, 1961) points out that while Adams was heavily praised at home and abroad for breaking the Geneva deadlock, he must share the credit in some measure with other men. For further references see BIBLIOGRAPHICAL ADDENDUM, p. 1000.

8TH AND 9TH ED. REFS. See BIBLIOGRAPHICAL ADDENDUM, p. 1,000.

27

Diplomacy a Football
of Politics, 1877-1889

We have separated ourselves so completely from the affairs of other people that it is difficult to realize how large a place they occupied when the government was founded.

HENRY CABOT LODGE, 1889

THE DIPLOMATS MARK TIME

THE AMERICAN PEOPLE in the 19th Century were normally far more interested in their own domestic affairs than in foreign affairs. This absorption was strikingly evident during the two decades following the *Virginius* flareup of 1873. There was, to be sure, some quietly growing interest in the economic infiltration of Latin America, in the profitable expansion of interoceanic trade routes, in increased access to foreign markets, in the multipower Congo Conference of 1884 regarding Africa, in the acquisition of far-flung coaling stations, and, as will be noted, in securing a tropical foothold in Samoa and Hawaii. But in general the rank and file of the American people were so little concerned with diplomacy that the *New York Sun* could declare in 1889:

> . . . The diplomatic service has outgrown its usefulness. . . . It is a costly humbug and sham. It is a nurse of snobs. It spoils a few Americans every year, and does no good to anybody. Instead of making ambassadors, Congress should wipe out the whole service.[1]

Three years later the *New York Herald,* insisting that the trans-Atlantic cable had made diplomats unnecessary, cried, "Abolish our foreign Ministers! Recall our farcical diplomats."

How can all this indifference be explained? First of all, the running sores in Anglo-American relations had been salved by the Treaty of

---

[1] Quoted in *Public Opinion,* VI, 367 (Feb. 9, 1889).

Washington. The remaining danger spot, Cuba, was temporarily removed when the Spanish government, with the iron fist and a honeyed tongue, quieted the insurrection. Elsewhere in the world there were no major wars threatening embroilment.

The one black spot in the picture was troubled Ireland, where disorders reached a high point in the 1880's. The outraged Irish voter in the United States demanded stern treatment of England—and frequently his desires were gratified. In 1886, for example, the Senate refused to include dynamiters in an extradition treaty with London, because Irishmen who had attempted to blow up British buildings might be returned from America to stand trial for their crimes.

Internal developments in America were all-absorbing. For one thing, the energies of the people were being poured into an amazing industrial transformation. The finishing stages of the centuries-long task of conquering and taming half a continent were also demanding attention. Politics continued to be the great indoor-outdoor sport—and these were the years of unusually close and colorful Presidential elections.

The worm-eaten condition of the navy reflected the almost incredible indifference to the outside world. The whole decrepit fleet reminded Admiral Porter, in the 1870's, of the dragons that the Chinese painted on their forts to frighten away the enemy. Not until 1883, and in the face of much apathy and opposition, did Congress appropriate funds for four modern steel ships—the beginning of the New Navy that was to cover itself with glory in the Spanish War of 1898.

Diplomatic inexperience, not surprisingly, continued in high places. From 1877 to 1893, the five Presidents and the five Secretaries of State, with one exception, were all rank amateurs. The Secretaries without exception were appointed primarily for political reasons. Sharp reversals of policy occurred when Democrats ousted Republicans; sharp shifts of policy even occurred within the same administration.

MEXICAN MARAUDERS AND CHINESE COOLIES

Disorders along the Mexican border during the late 1870's continued to be destructive of American life and property. In June, 1877, the Secretary of War issued an order authorizing American troops to pursue raiders across the boundary line. The Mexican government, which resented this move as an invasion of its sovereignty, issued counter orders to repel any such incursion by force. The Mexican press clamored for war, while in the United States the foes of President Hayes, who had succeeded Grant earlier that year, condemned the administration for having taken so belligerent a course. But with the American public generally indifferent, the crisis passed. The harsh hand of dictator Porfirio Díaz finally restored stability, and Washington withdrew the objectionable order for invasion in February, 1880. Actually, in the decade following 1875, United States troops crossed the border into Mexico more than twenty times.

Far more alarming than the incursions of Mexican bandits was the influx of Chinese coolies from the teeming cities of the Orient. "John Chinaman," who was docile and industrious, had at first been welcomed on the Pacific Coast as a laborer. But as he and his brothers continued to pour in, they began to cause increasing concern over the so-called "yellow peril." By 1880, the Chinese totaled 75,000 in California, or 9 per cent of the total population.

The most heated objection to the Chinese was an economic one. Able to live in a hovel, they could undercut the white man and undermine his standard of living. The fundamental objection to the Orientals was not that they were inefficient but that they were too efficient. They had, jeered the *New York Nation,* "disgusting habits of thrift, industry, and self-denial. . . ." In a catch-as-catch-can contest, the beef-eater had no chance against the rice-eater. The present thousands were regarded as a menace; the prospective millions as a calamity. Alarmed Californians rallied against "the moon-eyed menace" in song:

> Oust the pagans, far and near,
> From your fields and homes so dear,
> Falter not, your duty's clear;
> They or you must go.[2]

The Chinese, almost from the beginning, were subjected to discrimination and some physical abuse, just as white "foreign devils" had been in China. Conditions worsened sharply in the early 1870's, when hard times drove to the Golden State a throng of economic derelicts. San Francisco overflowed with malcontents and thugs, many of whom vented their wrath on the defenseless and thrifty Chinese. Hoodlums, young and old, dumped the Chinaman's freshly ironed laundry into the mire. They set dogs upon him, stoned and kicked him, set fire to his house, and put his priceless pigtail "under the scissors." ("Chasing pigtails" was a favorite sport of adolescent rowdies.) In the courts, where he was classed with the Indians, he did not have a "Chinaman's chance." He invariably came out on the short end—not infrequently on the rope's end. Sometimes he was murdered outright. Bret Harte's obituary to Wan Lee is a classic: "Dead, my reverend friends, dead. Stoned to death in the streets of San Francisco, in the year of grace 1869 by a mob of half-grown boys and Christian school children." [3]

The idol of the San Francisco hoodlums was Denis Kearney, an Irish-born and recently naturalized agitator of great power and volubility.

[2] Quoted in E. P. Oberholtzer, *A History of the United States* (New York, 1931), IV, 278.
[3] L. L. Hazard, *The Frontier in American Literature* (New York, 1927), p. 197.

Exhibiting four feet of noosed hemp, he yelled to his wild "sand lot" following, "The Chinese must go!" Or, as some of his Irish adherents shouted, "Immeriky fur Immerikans, bejabers." A Kearney manifesto read:

> . . . We declare that the Chinaman must leave our shores. We declare that white men, and women, and boys, and girls, cannot live as the people of the great republic should and compete with the single Chinese coolie in the labor market. We declare that we cannot hope to drive the Chinaman away by working cheaper than he does. None but an enemy would expect it of us; none but an idiot could hope for success; none but a degraded coward and slave would make the effort. To an American, death is preferable to life on a par with the Chinaman.[4]

The Kearneyite agitation, which came to a head in the summer of 1877, resulted in boycotts of Oriental labor, and in the open murdering of some of the hapless Chinese.

THE CLOSED DOOR FOR CHINA

Congressmen from the Pacific Coast, responding to the cry of their constituents for legislation to exclude the Chinese, encountered strong opposition. Most of it came from idealistic missionaries, hard-headed employers, steamship companies transporting coolies, and railroad lines needing cheap labor. The East, which was generally indifferent to the problem, often assumed a "holier than thou" attitude infuriating to the Californians. The *San Francisco Argonaut* snarled:

> Let a colony of these Asiatic brethren, with souls to save, camp down beside Boston Common, with their filthy habits, their criminal practices, and their nasty vices, and how long would it be before Beacon Hill would sniff the polluted atmosphere, and all the overgodly of New England would send up their prayers for relief.[5]

The big stumbling block in the path of Chinese exclusion was the Burlingame Treaty of 1868, which formally guaranteed to the Chinese the right of unrestricted entry. Despite this solemn compact, Congress took the bit in its teeth and passed a law in 1879 forbidding any ship to import more than fifteen Chinese on any one trip. President Hayes, a man of sterling honesty, found that the law amounted to virtual exclusion, so he vetoed it. His action was greeted with condemnation in the West, where flags were hung at half-staff and "Missey" Hayes was burned in effigy. But the Eastern newspapers found the message "wise and manly." It had, said the *New York Tribune*, "saved the character of the country from humiliation among the family of nations."

---

[4] E. C. Sandmeyer, *The Anti-Chinese Movement in California* (Urbana, Ill., 1939), p. 65.

[5] *San Francisco Argonaut*, II, 5 (Jan. 19, 1878).

The only honorable way to bring about Chinese exclusion was to revise the Burlingame pact. A special commission of three Americans journeyed to Peking, and there negotiated the Treaty of 1880. It gave the United States the right to "regulate, limit or suspend," but not "absolutely prohibit," the immigration of Chinese laborers.

"HERE'S A PRETTY MESS!" (IN WYOMING)

CHINESE SATIRICAL DIPLOMATIST: "There's no doubt of the United States being at the head of enlightened nations!"
Nast in *Harper's Weekly*, 1885

Congress again swung into action. After another heated battle, it passed a bill in 1882 *suspending* immigration from China for twenty years. President Arthur, now Chief Executive, vetoed the measure as an "unreasonable" restriction rather than a *suspension* as provided for by the treaty. Many Eastern editors praised Arthur, but the West again blazed with indignation. Flags were hung at half-mast in San Francisco, and merchants draped their stores in black. At the same time, labor organizations in the larger Eastern cities upheld the demands of their Western brethren by parades and mass meetings.

Congress finally reconsidered its action and passed the Act of 1882, which suspended Chinese immigration for only ten years. President Arthur reluctantly approved the bill, and the West rejoiced over this temporary relief. The Act of 1882, later renewed and strengthened, was epochal. It marked a radical departure from America's policy of maintaining a haven for the oppressed and underprivileged of every race and clime. American missionaries were embarrassed to explain to a Chinese why he could go to the white man's heaven, but not to the white man's country. *Puck* suggested as an answer, "There's no labor vote in heaven."

But the exclusion law of 1882 did not stop anti-Chinese outbursts in America. Continued agitation was much too profitable for the self-seeking demogogue and the salaried labor organizer. Ill feeling came to a boil at Rock Springs, Wyoming, in the late summer of 1885, when foreign-born whites attacked some five hundred docile Chinese coal miners, massacring twenty-eight in cold blood and wounding fifteen others. Riots hardly less serious flared forth elsewhere in the West.

The distant Peking government was naturally outraged. But since China was too weak to wage war against the United States, angered Chinese patriots had to content themselves with talk of boycott and other reprisals. The Peking Foreign Office, accustomed as it was to receive prompt demands for indemnity following outbursts against "foreign devils," made vigorous representations to Washington. But here it encountered the frustrating gap in federal jurisdiction: the United States government had no authority over purely state disorders. In 1887 Congress, braving the displeasure of organized labor and the Pacific Coast, voted an indemnity of $147,000 as a matter of comity and not of right.

THE AMERICAN COASTLINE REACHES PANAMA

Another headache came to the Hayes administration in 1879 with the imminent prospect of a foreign-owned interoceanic canal. A French company, headed by the aging but dynamic Fedinand de Lesseps, builder of the Suez Canal, began to activate plans for severing the two continents at Panama. The American people, who had long dreamed of accomplishing this feat themselves, were disturbed by the threat of French control over this commercial nerve center. Even though the company itself was a private one, the Paris government might later be forced to intervene for the protection of so huge an outlay of capital. The coup by which the British government in 1875 had won control of the Suez Canal was in itself a pointed object lesson.

President Hayes took vigorous action in March, 1880, when he sent a message to the Senate. He declared that the proposed canal would be "virtually a part of the coast line of the United States," and that "the policy of this country is a canal under American control." The press on the whole applauded Hayes' pronouncement, which amounted to a ringing reaffirmation of the Monroe Doctrine. Within the year both houses of Congress formally protested against a canal built by foreign capital or controlled by foreign regulations.

Two weeks before Hayes' bombshell message, de Lesseps, still enthusiastic in spite of his seventy-five years, arrived in the United States. Primarily a promoter, he directed his attention chiefly to quieting American public opinion and raising funds. He toured the country as far west as San Francisco, and everywhere his magnetic personality and global reputation attracted favorable attention. In New York he gave a grand banquet at Delmonico's to 600 influential people. He also created an American advisory board, and made Secretary of the Navy Thompson its head at an annual salary of $25,000. Thompson was forced to resign after accepting this position, but the connection of so prominent a figure with the enterprise tended to give it an American character, which is precisely what the clever de Lesseps intended. More than $1,500,000 was judiciously spent on editors, politicians, bankers, lobbyists, and allegedly on Congressmen, in an effort to create a favorable sentiment or at least acquiescence. So much money was poured out that the *New York Nation* later raised embarrassing questions:

> Are we never to know how much it cost to draw the fangs of the Monroe Doctrine during those critical years, or who were the men superintending the operation? Such dentistry not only comes high, but also requires great skill, and the public is entitled to know who the expert operators were.[6]

But the backstage efforts of de Lesseps should not be overplayed. The American people refused to become unduly concerned, partly because they were preoccupied with internal problems, and partly because many citizens assumed that the task was too formidable for de Lesseps. After about two-fifths of the canal had been excavated in the 1880's, the whole enterprise crashed in scandalous ruin—a victim of incompetence, extravagance, corruption, disease, heat, and jungles.

BLAINE BADGERS THE BRITISH

The Republicans were continued in office when, in 1881, the amiable James A. Garfield succeeded Hayes as President. The outstanding figure in the party was James G. Blaine, the imperious "Plumed Knight" from Maine, who, like Seward in 1860, had been passed over in favor of a less vulnerable Presidential candidate. His appointment to the post of Secretary of State was a foregone conclusion, and in these circumstances

[6] *New York Nation*, LVI, 170 (March 9, 1893).

he could hardly be blamed for regarding himself as the "premier" of the administration.

The impetuous Blaine, although blessed with persuasive magnetism, a quick mind, and a lively imagination, was wholly without diplomatic experience. He was likewise without formal training in the law, whether domestic or international. His profession, aside from politics, had been journalism; and the terse style and dogmatic assertiveness of the editor were poor training for suave diplomatic correspondence. Long years of service in Congress had developed oratorical brilliance and unbending partisanship rather than appreciation of an adversary's point of view— a prime essential in diplomacy. He was accustomed to bask in the limelight and play to the galleries, perhaps not realizing that the best diplomats are those who work the most quietly. His energy, thwarted ambition, and devoted following all foreshadowed an aggressive or "spirited" foreign policy.

One of the earliest vexations to confront Blaine grew out of the illstarred enterprise of de Lesseps at Panama. The American people were beginning to appreciate the desirability of constructing the proposed Isthmian waterway themselves. Yet they would be foolish indeed to sink an enormous sum of money into it unless they could own it outright and fortify it against a possible enemy. But the Clayton-Bulwer Treaty with Britain, which still remained on the books, raised a forbidding hand. Painfully conscious of this diplomatic barrier, the House of Representatives, in the closing days of the Hayes administration, formally resolved that the President take immediate steps to abrogate the objectionable pact.

Secretary Blaine, responding to the mounting public pressure, entered upon a diplomatic interchange with London in an effort to induce the Foreign Office to soften the treaty. He argued, with characteristic vigor, that it had been negotiated thirty years earlier under exceptional circumstances that no longer existed. It offended the spirit of the Monroe Doctrine, he continued, and weakened "our rightful and long-established claim to priority on the American continent." [7] The conclusion was that the United States should build and fortify the canal itself.

Blaine's vigorous thrusts were not difficult to parry. The British Foreign Secretary, Lord Granville, not only punctured his arguments but stood squarely on the treaty. Critics of "Jingo Jim" Blaine accused him of having made an obvious and futile play to the grandstand. Although Blaine did advance some rather naïve and extravagant Americanisms, he did not go so far as to suggest an outright abrogation of the treaty. In expressing with eloquence and forthrightness the views of a growing body of Americans, he even evoked praise from some of his bitterest foes.

It is now clear that mere notes, no matter by whom drafted, could not

[7] *Foreign Relations, 1881*, p. 555 (Nov. 19, 1881).

have extorted the necessary concessions from London at that time. But Blaine caused the British to give serious thought to the problem, and helped to prepare their minds for the inevitable retreat. In 1884, three years later, the *London Daily Telegraph* declared that a wise England would not oppose the United States "over the long-forgotten Clayton-Bulwer Treaty, to which few Englishmen attach very great importance." [8] Blaine, though dead, won a belated diplomatic victory in 1901, when the British, faced with changed circumstances, yielded essentially what he had contended for when they accepted the new Hay-Pauncefote Treaty.

BLAINE'S LATIN-AMERICAN BLUNDERINGS

The spirited Secretary's interest in lands south of the Rio Grande was not confined to the Isthmus. Like Henry Clay, whom he deeply admired, Blaine had an abiding passion for Latin America as a whole. His ideal was to persuade these hemispheric neighbors to accept a kind of "elder sister" relationship. But basically his policy seems to have been influenced by economic rather than idealistic motives. As a big-business Republican, Blaine was grieved to note that his country's adverse balance of trade with Latin America amounted annually to something over $100 million. The explanation was that these republics, though shipping huge quantities of raw materials to the United States, bought the bulk of their manufactured goods from Europe. Blaine's aim was to elbow aside foreign competitors by forming closer commercial ties south of the border. And since economic relationships could not flourish amid whistling bullets, Washington would use its good offices to terminate wars in Latin America.

Blaine's impulsive ventures as an "honest broker" were ill appreciated. Finding that an ugly boundary dispute between Mexico and Guatemala might flare into war, he pressed arbitration upon the larger republic, while revealing considerable sympathy for the underdog. Mexico, after first politely declining these good offices, indignantly rejected them. The upshot was that Blaine neither protected Guatemala nor earned the good will of Mexico. Two other republics, Costa Rica and Colombia, voluntarily arranged to lay their boundary dispute before European arbiters. Blaine's emphatic objections to their referring so purely an American matter to Europeans, without first consulting Washington, resulted in a further harvest of ill will.

A far more serious crisis grew out of the War of the Pacific, which was waged from 1879 to 1884 between Chile on the one side and Peru and Bolivia on the other. Chile, the final victor, was demanding the valuable nitrate beds of Peru as her share of the booty. Blaine, in the interests of

[8] Quoted in *New York Nation*, XL, 5 (Jan. 1, 1885).

peace and stability, opposed territorial cessions in the Americas. But he ran into an impossible situation, partly because Chile had the upper hand, and partly because the American people were clearly unwilling to back his policy with force. Nor can one say that Blaine handled this hornets' nest with conspicuous skill. His nervous temperament was out of tune with the slower Latin tempo. The ministers through whom he had to work, moreover, were unfortunate selections. The United States envoy in Chile strongly espoused the cause of the Chileans, while quarreling bitterly with his colleague in Peru, who as vigorously championed the Peruvians. The upshot of Blaine's well-meaning meddling was that he not only incurred the lasting ill will of Chile, but supplied his political enemies with more ammunition.

Shortly after Blaine left the State Department, a House committee probed charges that his intervention in Chile had been prompted by an improper financial stake in a scheme to exploit the guano and nitrate beds of Peru. This "smear campaign" was stimulated by Blaine's continuing Presidential ambitions, and also by his questionable reputation for honesty. Nothing was proved against him personally, although critics condemned "guano statesmanship" and his efforts "to put the guano beds in his pocket."

One of Blaine's last acts before leaving the Department bore testimony to his hemispheric vision, and also to a desire to divert attention in the grand manner from his diplomatic muddlings. In pursuance of his policy of promoting peace (and commerce) in Latin America, he urged the calling of an International American Conference to consider methods of preventing war. The basic idea, of course, dated back at least to Henry Clay, and since then had received considerable support in Latin America itself. Blaine finally secured the lukewarm assent of President Arthur, who had succeeded the assassinated Garfield late in 1881, and promptly issued invitations to the Latin-American republics. Three weeks later, finding himself increasingly out of harmony with the new President's faction of the Republican Party, Blaine felt obliged to resign. The abrupt termination of his "premiership" at the end of ten months, rather than the anticipated eight years, was one of the deepest disappointments of a life overflowing with frustration.

THE REPUBLICANS REVERSE THEMSELVES

Blaine's successor—and in many ways his opposite—was Frederick Frelinghuysen, a conservative corporation lawyer of Dutch extraction. His policy was in general the traditional one of daily drifting and negativism—of not looking for trouble but settling difficulties when they arose. Some one said, a bit unkindly, that he regarded the American eagle as a mere hen—past middle age.

Frelinghuysen abruptly cancelled Blaine's invitations, some of which had already been cordially accepted, to the International American Conference. The reasons advanced publicly for this rather rude withdrawal were not satisfying to those enlightened souls who were working for closer co-operation with Latin America. The truth is that the new regime in the State Department, shocked by evidences of scandal-tinged "guano statesmanship" and other irregularities, concluded that cancellation would avert serious embarrassments.[9] The Blaine men naturally emitted a pained outcry against this unmannerly reversal, while a considerable number of citizens continued half-hearted agitation for a conference. But the average American could not be bothered.

The cautious Secretary Frelinghuysen was not consistent in his stay-at-home policy. A feeble start was made toward co-operation with other nations in 1884, when the United States participated in the Third International Conference of the Red Cross and in the Berlin Conference regarding the African Congo. These two conclaves were a beginning that found the nation represented in a total of twenty-eight foreign bodies within the next three decades. The newspapers of 1884 gave vent to the usual groans about forsaking traditions and becoming ensnared in dangerous entrapments, and although these fears were grossly exaggerated, developments in Nicaragua gave cause for anxiety.

In the Isthmian region, Frelinghuysen operated differently from Blaine. The latter, as already noted, had made a spirited but unsuccessful effort to induce Britain to modify the Clayton-Bulwer Treaty. But the ordinarily prudent Frelinghuysen, without even attempting to secure a release from this commitment, negotiated an extraordinary pact with Nicaragua in 1884. It provided for joint United States-Nicaraguan ownership of an Isthmian canal, and further stipulated that the United States, under a permanent alliance, was to protect the territory of Nicaragua against outside aggression.

The publication of the Frelinghuysen-Zavala Treaty caused a sensation. America was not only flouting her treaty with the British in a cavalier fashion, but was forsaking the no-alliance tradition and committing herself to inevitable embroilments over Nicaragua's boundaries. The pact was still before the Senate, lacking five votes of approval, when a change of administration spelled its doom.

CLEVELAND AND THE FISHERIES FUROR

Granite-willed Grover Cleveland, the first Democratic President since the Civil War, had mushroomed from the mayoralty of Buffalo to the Presidency of the United States in four short years. His interests were

---

[9] See R. H. Bastert, "Diplomatic Reversal: Frelinghuysen's Opposition to Blaine's Pan-American Policy in 1882," *Miss. Valley Hist. Rev.*, XLII (1956), 653–671.

narrow and his mental visibility was low. He had, in fact, never been to Washington before he went there to be inaugurated President. But he brought to the administration of foreign affairs a rough-hewn honesty and a deep-seated opposition to imperialism, protectorates, and other foreign entanglements.

Cleveland quickly showed his mettle in disposing of the unratified Frelinghuysen-Zavala pact with Nicaragua. After due study, he concluded that it was not consistent with the nation's obligation to England under the Clayton-Bulwer Treaty, and that in addition it would involve the United States dangerously in Central America. In March, 1885, therefore, he killed the treaty by resorting to the rather unusual step of withdrawing it from the Senate.

Cleveland proved to be much less successful in his efforts to avoid friction with Britain over the Canadian fisheries. The United States, having found the relevant provisions of the Treaty of Washington unsatisfactory, gave notice of their termination, effective July 1, 1885. The Canadians, irked by this action, fell back upon an illiberal interpretation of the ancient Treaty of 1818, and their cruisers began to arrest American fishing schooners for alleged violations of the regulations. Much ill feeling was generated, especially in New England, by these disagreeable incidents. Henry Cabot Lodge, a young Congressman from the fishing state of Massachusetts, declaimed, ". . . Whenever the American flag on an American fishing smack is touched by a foreigner, the great American heart is touched." [10]

Popular excitement mounted early in 1887, when the House passed a bill authorizing the President to retaliate against the Canadians by debarring their ships and goods from American ports. Red-blooded citizens talked freely of an armed clash. The *Detroit News* boasted:

> When the next war closes, there should be but one flag floating from the Rio Grande to the pole. The Canadian provinces will make elegant States in the Union. It will be better for them and better for us.
>> We do not want to fight,
>> But, by jingo, if we do,
>> We'll scoop in all the fishing grounds
>> And the whole Dominion, too.[11]

But the *Nashville American* (Democrat) viewed the problem from a more southerly latitude: ". . . We are very certain that the people of this part of the country are not impatient to undergo the miseries and privations of another war all for the sake of a few hundred Yankee fishermen and a few stinking codfish." [12] Cleveland finally signed the retalia-

[10] *New York Nation*, XLIV, 417 (May 19, 1887).
[11] *Public Opinion*, II, 346 (Feb. 5, 1887).
[12] *Ibid.*, p. 345 (Feb. 5, 1887).

tion bill in March, 1887, but he had no intention of enforcing it. He merely planned to use it as a club for extorting concessions.

THE FISHERIES PACT A POLITICAL WHIPPING BOY

Continued friction over the fisheries finally led to the meeting of an Anglo-American joint commission in Washington, in November, 1887. The three British representatives were headed by the distinguished Joseph Chamberlain; the three Americans by Secretary of State Bayard. For a time the negotiations seemed doomed to failure, but timely concessions from Canada, together with the personal charm of Chamberlain and the brilliant social life of the British legation, contributed to a meeting of minds. The Bayard-Chamberlain pact, signed in February, 1888, was a compromise. It yielded substantial advantages to each party and gave promise of ending, for a time at least, the century-old squabble over the fisheries.

But the treaty encountered hopeless odds in the Senate. The Republicans, who controlled that body by a paper-thin margin, were acutely conscious of the impending Presidential election. One of them let the cat out of the bag when he said, "We cannot allow the Democrats to take credit for settling so important a dispute." Other members, with the Irish vote in view, wanted to make President Cleveland appear to be surrendering American interests to the grasping British. Accordingly, the Senate voted to suspend the then-customary rule of secrecy so that the Republican speeches against the treaty might echo forth to the entire country.

The Senators made full use of their sounding board. Hoar of Massachusetts declared that when General Grant was in the White House "no petty British officer hauled it [Old Glory] down from an American masthead." Senator Riddleberger of Virginia cried that the administration "is pro-English from the President to the last Cabinet officer." Senator Teller agreed with his colleague that America would never be a free nation until she had whipped England "a third time," and no less irrelevantly reminded his hearers that British cruelties had "put a million and a quarter of Irish people in the grave. . . ." The Republican press, also conscious of the Hibernian vote, insisted that Bayard and Cleveland had been "duped." The *New York Tribune* was sure that the fisheries treaty was "the most barren and dishonorable compact ever made by an American Secretary of State with a foreign power." [13] On August 21, 1888, the Republican Senators killed the pact by a vote of 27 yeas to 30 nays.

The rejection did not prove disastrous because a working arrangement, already in effect, was continued. But Cleveland felt that since the Repub-

[13] *Public Opinion*, V, 428 (Aug. 25, 1888).

lican Senate was not willing to accept a treaty of mutual concessions, the next logical step was to propose a policy so drastic as to embarrass even Republican Britain-baiters. On August 23, 1888, therefore, he sent a sensational message to Congress, nominally aimed at Canada, but really at the Senate. It recommended in emphatic terms that Congress clothe the Executive with retaliatory power to suspend the transportation of all bonded goods across the Canadian border.

Cleveland was deluged with a snowstorm of telegrams from a host of Irish-Americans and other Anglophobes, who roundly applauded this slap at Britain. "God bless you for your devotion to old Erin," telegraphed one. The Democratic *New York World* was pleased to note that "The Republican fishers for votes were hard hit by the President's unexpected message." [14] So the event proved. The Republicans, fearing business losses and unwilling to face the logic of their partisan rejection of the treaty, refused to heed Cleveland's recommendation for a partial trade stoppage. The dispute was now thrust into the noisy arena of the Presidential election.

THE "SACKING" OF SACKVILLE-WEST

The Presidential campaign of 1888, in which the Democrat Grover Cleveland ran against the Republican Benjamin Harrison, aroused an appalling amount of Anglophobia. Cleveland had courageously made tariff reduction—not free trade—the paramount issue. Britain was then the leading free-trade nation, and the Republicans, who had waxed fat on the high protective tariff, cried that Cleveland had been bribed by English gold. Republican propaganda portrayed Cleveland under the British flag, Harrison under the American. One campaign document printed the statement, falsely attributed to the *London Times,* "The only time England can use an Irishman is when he emigrates to America and votes for free trade." Popular slogans were:

"Protection to American Labor, No Free Trade for us."
"America for the Americans—No Free Trade."
"American Wages for American Workingmen."
"Cleveland Runs Well in England." [15]

So explosive was the political atmosphere that when the visiting British diplomat, Joseph Chamberlain, became engaged to the daughter of Cleveland's Secretary of War, the secret was carefully guarded until after the election.

Cleveland's abandonment of the rejected fisheries treaty, followed by his stern message regarding trade reprisals against Canada, left con-

[14] *Public Opinion,* V, 445 (Sept. 1, 1888).
[15] Oberholtzer, *History of the United States,* V, 47.

siderable doubt as to where he actually stood. A California resident by the name of George Osgoodby, who represented himself as a naturalized citizen of English birth and who signed his name Murchison, undertook to find out. He wrote to the British minister in Washington, Sir Lionel Sackville-West, and inquired confidentially about Cleveland's real views of England. The somewhat stupid envoy, disregarding the rule that diplomats must never interfere in domestic disputes, replied that Cleveland, despite his vigorous message, was at heart friendly to the Mother Country. In short, a vote for Cleveland was a vote for England.

Osgoodby timidly held the explosive letter for twenty-eight days, and then reluctantly turned it over to the Republican Los Angeles *Times,* which published it on the eve of the election. The Republicans were jubilant, the Democrats crestfallen. Van loads of the letter were scattered broadcast. One New York newspaper published a full-page facsimile with the provocative headlines: "THE BRITISH LION'S PAW THRUST INTO AMERICAN POLITICS TO HELP CLEVELAND." "Bounce him," cried the *New York World.*

Cleveland waited a day, but Sackville-West's excuses were weak, and he made matters worse by talking indiscreetly to reporters. The Democratic National Committee telegraphed that the Irish vote "is slipping out of our hands because of diplomatic shilly-shallying." The British Foreign Secretary, Lord Salisbury, who was greatly annoyed by this cheap electioneering trick, refused to throw his minister to the wolves without a dignified investigation of the affair. But the election was only a few days off, and Cleveland felt compelled to dismiss "the damned Englishman." The Republican *New York Tribune* gloatingly published a jingle in which Cleveland addressed John Bull:

> Believe me that I made him go
> For nothing that he wrote,
> But just because, as well you know,
> I feared the Irish vote! [16]

Sackville-West may or may not have cost Cleveland the election, but there can be no doubt that he further embittered Anglo-American relations. The British press, as well as the Foreign Office, was angered by the indecent haste with which Sackville-West had been bundled out of the United States. Lord Salisbury indicated his displeasure by refusing to fill the vacancy until Cleveland had left office several months later. This unfortunate incident further highlights the fact that during these years foreign affairs were of secondary importance, and that friendly relations with a great foreign power were a subordinate consideration when compared with possible political advantage.

[16] *New York Tribune,* Nov. 4, 1888, 7:2.

SELECTED BIBLIOGRAPHY

The main outlines are given in S. F. Bemis, ed., *The American Secretaries of State and their Diplomacy* (New York, 1928), VII, VIII. Hayes' Secretary of State is presented in Brainerd Dyer, *The Public Career of William M. Evarts* (Berkeley, Calif., 1933) and C. L. Barrows, *William M. Evarts* (Chapel Hill, N.C., 1941). See also M. R. Coolidge, *Chinese Immigration* (New York, 1909). The best monograph on the subject is Alice F. Tyler, *The Foreign Policy of James G. Blaine* (Minneapolis, 1927); see also D. S. Muzzey, *James G. Blaine* (New York, 1935) and Herbert Millington, *American Diplomacy and the War of the Pacific* (New York, 1948). The only full-length biography is G. F. Howe, *Chester A. Arthur* (New York, 1934). The most detailed treatment of the Cleveland era is found in C. C. Tansill, *The Foreign Policy of Thomas F. Bayard, 1885–1897* (New York, 1940), and the same author's *Canadian-American Relations, 1875–1911* (New Haven, 1943). See also G. R. Dulebohn, *Principles of Foreign Policy under the Cleveland Administrations* (Philadelphia, 1941), Allan Nevins, *Grover Cleveland* (New York, 1934), and F. E. Gibson, *The Attitudes of the New York Irish toward State and National Affairs, 1848–1892* (New York, 1951).

Useful articles are J. A. Karlin, "Anti-Chinese Outbreaks in Seattle, 1885–1886," *Pacific Northwest Quar.*, XXXIX (1948), 103–130, and the same author's "The Anti-Chinese Outbreak in Tacoma, 1885," *Pacific Hist. Rev.*, XXIII (1954), 271–283.

See footnotes of this chapter; Bemis and Griffin, *Guide*, pp. 384 ff.; *Harvard Guide*, Ch. 23.

7TH ED. REFS. The most important book on this era is now D. M. Pletcher, *The Awkward Years: American Foreign Relations under Garfield and Arthur* (Columbia, Mo., 1961). The author concludes that the nascent but abortive expansionism of the period, though largely concerned with secondary issues (Congo Conference, etc.), provided an important bridge between Reconstruction diplomacy and end-century imperialism. Politics (Blaine, the campaign of 1884), economics (tariffs, pork restrictions), public opinion, hyphenism (Irish dynamiters), and navalism (New Navy) are interwoven with the conventional strands of diplomacy to produce a picture of frustration growing out of efforts to lead the still-isolationist United States in a short cut to the next decade. The proposed foreign policies failed "because too many Americans thought them dangerous, extravagant, and unnecessary . . ." (p. 354). Reversals by succeeding administrations, Blaine's bunglings in Latin America, the aftermath of the War of the Pacific, and the abortive ventures in isthmian diplomacy are treated with exceptional fulness. W. M. Armstrong, *E. L. Godkin and American Foreign Policy, 1865–1900* (New York, 1957) shows the choleric *Nation* editor attacking Blaine's handling of the Chilean problem, the Clayton-Bulwer Treaty, and the Irish terrorists in Britain. For further references, including articles on Blaine's Latin-American policy, the Sackville-West affair, and Chinese in California, see BIBLIOGRAPHICAL ADDENDUM, p. 1,001.

8TH AND 9TH ED. REFS. See BIBLIOGRAPHICAL ADDENDUM, p. 1,001.

28

Blaine and Spirited Diplomacy, 1889-1893

PAN-AMERICANISM ON THE POTOMAC

WHEN PRESIDENT HARRISON reached the White House in 1889, he was obliged to find a place for "Jingo Jim" Blaine, who continued to be the dominant figure in the Republican party. The new Chief Executive, not relishing the prospect of being overshadowed by his theatrical subordinate, reluctantly made Blaine Secretary of State. This step, though considered inevitable, aroused deep misgivings. Many nervous citizens feared that Blaine's thwarted ambition, together with a proneness to take "the hated foreigner by the beard," would inevitably plunge the country into war. Such charges had been aired four years earlier, when Blaine had run for the Presidency, and the Irish Land League in Boston had declared that if he were elected "Ireland would be free in thirty days."

By a remarkable coincidence, Blaine returned to Washington just in time to play host to the First International American Conference (Pan-American Conference), for which he had prematurely issued invitations eight years earlier. During this intervening period the concept had met with increased popular approval, and in May, 1888, Congress, seizing the initiative, had authorized President Cleveland to call a conference. Secretary Bayard thereupon formally invited the nations of Latin America to send delegates to Washington, for the purpose of discussing problems of common interest, principally questions of peace, trade, and communication.

Early in October, 1889, representatives of the Latin-American states—seventeen ultimately sent delegates—assembled in Washington. They listened to a high-flown address of welcome by Blaine, who extended a cordial invitation to tour the industrial areas of the United States as guests of the nation. The object of the trip was to impress upon the visitors the size and wealth of the giant republic, presumably as a step toward weaning them away from their European commercial connections.

The bewildered delegates were whisked on a special train through forty-one cities. They viewed giant factories and other mechanical marvels, listened to speeches and brass bands, and witnessed various displays, including the firing of a natural gas well. One may doubt whether the sightseers, a number of whom knew the United States already, got much out of the trip except fatigue, and possibly, as the *London Spectator* suggested, a wholesome respect for a people "so fearfully energetic that it considers a journey of six thousand miles by rail an entertainment." [1] At all events, the junket did serve to popularize the Pan-American idea in the United States.

The Conference, reassembling on November 18, 1889, buckled down to serious work. Blaine, though not officially representing the United States, presided with his customary brilliance, and used his influence to support two objectives which were dear to his heart. First, he planned to unite the United States and Latin America in a customs union, in which tariff barriers would be beaten down and the flow of trade to Europe curtailed. This scheme met with many expressions of sympathy but was finally voted down as impracticable. Instead, the Conference favored separate reciprocity treaties.

Blaine next advocated the erection of machinery for the arbitration of international disputes. Although he took the floor and spoke passionately for his proposal, it likewise lost by a wide margin. Mutual jealousies, and particularly distrust of a dominating United States, did their ugly work. Nor were the European nations, deeply concerned about their trade, indifferent to the Conference. They took energetic steps, especially in those Latin-American countries where their economic stake was large, to create a backfire of opposition to the better understanding that was being promoted in Washington.

INCIPIENT PAN-AMERICANISM

Despite the blare of trumpets, the First International American Conference could point to only one tangible achievement—the creation of the agency that came to be called the Pan-American Union. This organization was designed as a clearing house for spreading information among the constituent American republics, as well as for encouraging co-operation among them. The millionaire steelman Andrew Carnegie, who

[1] *Spectator,* LXIII, 664 (Nov. 16, 1889); see also A. C. Wilgus, "James G. Blaine and the Pan-American Movement," *Hispanic Amer. Hist. Rev.,* V (1922), 662–708.

had been an official American delegate to the first conference, donated the money in 1907 for the construction of the beautiful building in Washington that now houses the Pan-American Union.

The scanty fruits of the first conference in 1889 evoked considerable criticism from antiadministration Democratic newspapers. They accused the high-tariff Republican Party of hypocrisy in posing, without result, as the champion of low tariffs. The *Philadelphia Record* declared that the Conference would leave little of value, "unless it be the brass tablet which is to commemorate the event."

Every organization has to have a beginning, no matter how feeble, and the Conference of 1889 was the first in a long list of increasingly important Pan-American conferences. It helped transform Pan-Americanism from a phrase to a fact. One may also note that the friendly reception given the Latin-American delegates probably did something to dispel their fears of the Colossus of the North. Furthermore, reciprocal tariff reductions by treaty, which the Conference found more palatable than a customs union, received a strong stimulus.

Secretary Blaine, with characteristic zeal, moved in on reciprocity. Perceiving the difficulty of negotiating individual treaties with each Latin-American republic, he urged Congress to give him blanket authorization to make the necessary arrangements. But the high-tariff Harrison administration was suspicious of attempts to lower trade barriers, and the McKinley Tariff bill of 1890 was so unsatisfactory to Blaine that he appeared before the Senate committee to plead for reciprocity. Carried away by the force of his arguments, he brought his fist down on the table, only to crush the stovepipe hat that he had carelessly laid there. "Blaine Smashes His Hat On the McKinley Bill," ran the sensational headlines.

In a vigorous speech delivered in Maine, Blaine next appealed to the great court of public opinion. He received a gratifying response, especially in the West, which wanted more foreign markets. But the "Old Guard" Republicans were adamant, and the best that Blaine could secure was an arm-twisting type of reciprocity. For example, important raw materials from Latin America, notably sugar, were placed on the free list. But the President was authorized to proclaim retaliatory duties against those republics that did not reciprocate this generosity. With such a threat held over them, a half-dozen Latin-American nations, as well as several European countries, entered into reciprocity agreements. But the Democrats, after returning to power in 1893, soon reversed this policy, to the accompaniment of bitter foreign outcries. Thus one cannot say with certainty what the result of the reciprocity pacts would have been had they been continued over a longer period. But the foundations were thus laid for the reciprocal trade agreements treaties which, in the 1930's, did so much to improve relations with Latin America.

THE SLAUGHTER OF THE SEALS

Reciprocity with Latin America revived agitation for reciprocity with Canada. The Canadians still lamented the spiteful termination by Washington, in 1866, of the Reciprocity Treaty of 1854. During the late 1880's and early 1890's there was much discussion, on both sides of the border, about reciprocity, tariffs, commercial unions, and even outright annexation. But the burning diplomatic problem came to involve the fur seals.[2]

With the purchase of Alaska the United States had acquired the Pribilof Islands, in the Bering Sea, on which a magnificent herd of some four million seals had their home. These sleek animals are polygamous, and as most of the males are not necessary for the propagation of the herd, Washington leased the privilege of killing "bachelors" to a private company. All went reasonably well until the caprice of feminine fashion brought about such a demand for sealskin coats and muffs as to increase the value of the skins many fold. The new price scale made profitable the practice of pelagic sealing, that is, the killing of the animal while it was swimming or floating in the open sea.

The American government could exercise complete jurisdiction over the seals on the Pribilof Islands and within national waters, but no farther. Pelagic sealers—most of them Canadians—stationed their schooners outside the three-mile limit and shot or harpooned the furry creatures as they came to and from the breeding grounds. Swimming females cannot be distinguished from males, and the death of a female ordinarily meant the loss of a nursing pup on land, and an unborn pup in the seal. Thus white milk mingled with red blood and Caesarian-born seals on the slippery decks of the sealers. About half of the animals shot in the water were not recovered, and consequently every skin obtained in the open sea represented the death of approximately four seals.

As the value of the fur rose, the number of pelagic schooners multiplied; and as they increased the herd decreased, with a consequent further rise in prices. The whole brutal process threatened the seals with extermination. There was even serious talk in the United States, then and later, of butchering the entire herd on a mercy-killing basis.

FIGHTING AGAINST A FREE SEA

In 1886 United States revenue cutters began to seize Canadian pelagic schooners outside the three-mile limit. Drastic measures like these could be justified only on the contention that the Bering Sea was a *mare clausum*

[2] See C. C. Tansill, *Canadian-American Relations, 1875–1911* (New Haven, 1943), Ch. X.

(a closed sea), as much under American jurisdiction, in regard to the seals, as the Chesapeake Bay. The Canadians naturally flared up at this unlawful interference with their lawful though disagreeable business, and the British minister in Washington lodged indignant protests. An aroused

ARBITRATION

THE SEAL: "Belay, you two Johnnies!—Avast quarrelling!
Give me a 'close-time,' and leave the 'sea' an open question."

A seal pleads for peace and a closed season on sealing.
London Punch, 1891

Congress, influenced partly by the seal lobby, formally authorized the President, in March, 1889, to seize vessels encroaching on American rights in the Bering Sea. Strangely enough the United States, traditional defender of a free sea, was now cast in the opposite role.

When Blaine became Secretary of State for the second time, the two contestants had unsheathed their swords. Feeling bound by both Congressional statute and public opinion, "the Plumed Knight" entered upon a lengthy diplomatic duel with London early in 1890. In his first note, he argued forcefully that the United States, while not contending that the Bering Sea was a *mare clausum*, held that pelagic sealing was so destructive as to be *contra bonos mores* (against good public morals). "The law of the sea," he insisted, "is not lawlessness." He also declared that the United States had acquired a prescriptive right to fence off that part of the Bering Sea which contained the seals, primarily because the Canadians had not attempted to poach there until recent years. Here one sees Blaine the journalist and orator:

> Whence did the ships of Canada derive the right to do in 1886 that which they had refrained from doing for more than ninety years? Upon what grounds did Her Majesty's Government defend in the year 1886 a course of conduct in the Behring Sea which she had carefully avoided ever since the discovery of that sea? By what reasoning did Her Majesty's Government conclude that an act may be committed with impunity against the rights of the United States which had never been attempted against the same rights when held by the Russian Empire? [3]

"One step beyond that which Her Majesty's Government has taken in this controversy," Blaine declared with startling directness, "and piracy finds its justification."

Unhurriedly and urbanely, Lord Salisbury, the British Foreign Secretary, replied to Blaine's nervous notes. The noble Briton stood squarely on the unassailable ground that, except for piracy or under mutual agreement, no nation in time of peace can properly seize the ships of another nation on the high seas. The Canadians were engaged in a legitimate if unpleasant industry, and they were entitled to protection until it was made illegal. In his next note Salisbury delivered a virtual ultimatum: ". . . Her Britannic Majesty's Government must hold the Government of the United States responsible for the consequences that may ensue from acts which are contrary to the established principles of international law." [4]

SETTLING THE SEALING DISPUTE

Mounting tension over the seals stimulated the inevitable war talk, particularly after British warships were rumored to be gathering in the North Pacific. The *Sioux City Journal* insisted that "the thing to do" was to "shoot *any* British ship which is in those waters." The *Detroit News* concluded that "British dominion on the North American continent should be given an end at as early a date as possible." But such jingoistic utterances were the exception rather than the rule. The *New York Sun*

---

[3] *Foreign Relations*, 1890, p. 368 (Blaine to Pauncefote, Jan. 22, 1890).
[4] *Ibid.*, p. 436 (Pauncefote to Blaine, June 14, 1890).

sneered at the attempt to police the "open ocean in the interests of good morals and pup seals," while the *Spokane Falls Review* was confident that "The United States and Great Britain are not going to fight over a few greasy, ill-smelling sealskins." [5]

The lengthy diplomatic interchange culminated in the signing of an arbitration treaty in Washington, in February, 1892. A mixed tribunal of seven members met at Paris in 1893, and there rendered a decision adverse to the American case on every one of the five major counts. The United States was ultimately assessed $473,151 in damages for the unwarranted seizures of Canadian schooners. The tribunal also made an

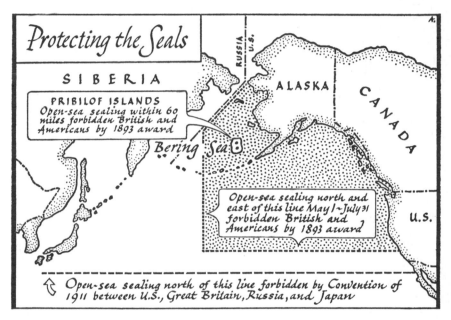

Protecting the Seals

SIBERIA

PRIBILOF ISLANDS
Open-sea sealing within 60 miles forbidden British and Americans by 1893 award

Bering Sea

RUSSIA · U.S.

ALASKA

CANADA

Open-sea sealing north and east of this line May 1–July 31 forbidden British and Americans by 1893 award

U.S.

Open-sea sealing north of this line forbidden by Convention of 1911 between U.S., Great Britain, Russia, and Japan

effort to protect the seals by certain illusory restrictions on pelagic sealing, and these may have slowed up the process of extermination. About the best that can be said of the Paris Award is that it was a victory for arbitration and the pacific settlement of disputes—not for the seals.

The complete overthrow of the American case caused Blaine's numerous enemies to brand him a bombastic bungler. The *New York Nation* rejoiced that the tribunal had declared his history "to be fiction, his geography pure fancy, and his international law a mere whim. . . ." [6] But all this is hardly fair. Blaine did not start the controversy—the Cleveland administration did. He did not pass the law directing the seizures—Congress did. He did not wish to tangle with Britain on this issue—American public opinion did. Like a prosecuting attorney charged

[5] *Public Opinion*, IX, 383 (Aug. 2, 1890).
[6] *New York Nation*, LVII, 113 (Aug. 17, 1893).

with making the best of a bad case, he advanced what arguments he could in behalf of a good moral cause. Incidentally, his setback at Paris further soured American hotheads on arbitration.

LYNCHING ITALIANS IN NEW ORLEANS

The United States became involved in its first major diplomatic controversy with Italy in 1891. Large numbers of Italian subjects from Sicily, many of them with criminal backgrounds and some of them stiletto-wielding members of the Mafia Black Hand Society, had congregated in New Orleans. There they carried on their vendettas, chiefly against fellow Sicilians. An enterprising chief of police, who was ferreting out the wrongdoers, was himself foully murdered. A number of Italian suspects were brought to trial, but none could be convicted. Bribery was allegedly clogging the wheels of justice.

The people of New Orleans now decided to take the law into their own hands in frontier fashion. In March, 1891, a mob of several thousand, openly led by the most respectable citizenry, advanced on the jail derisively shouting, "Who killa da Chief?" Eleven cowering Italians, who had either been acquitted or were being held as suspects, were brutally killed. The *New York Herald* reported that Judge Lynch had taken "the hateful ruler Mafia by the throat" in a "Mardi Gras of mob violence." [7] From the colonies of Italians living elsewhere in the United States came threats of bloody retaliation; and only with difficulty did the authorities of New York City prevent serious disorders.

The outraged Italian government forthwith demanded indemnity for the victims and punishment for their assailants. Blaine tried patiently to explain the embarrassing gap in federalism—that in such cases the state alone had jurisdiction. But Baron Fava, the Italian minister in Washington, could not comprehend this contradiction. In response to his protests, Blaine burst out with characteristic journalistic directness:

> I do not recognize the right of any government to tell the United States what it should do. We have never received orders from any foreign power and we will not begin now. . . . It is a matter of total indifference to me what persons in Italy may think of our institutions. I cannot change them, still less violate them.[8]

In Italy the masses vented their wrath in heated meetings and in indignities to Americans. The shaky Italian ministry felt called upon to make some face-saving gesture, and finding Blaine powerless to do anything, it abruptly withdrew Baron Fava from Washington, on March 31, 1891. The United States instructed its minister in Rome to come home on

[7] *New York Herald*, March 15, 1891, 17:1.
[8] *Ibid.*, May 22, 1891, 3:3.

leave of absence. But diplomatic relations were not severed; each nation left its legation in the hands of a *chargé d'affaires*.

Inflamed feelings, particularly in Italy, led to much discussion of war. In armored ships the Italian fleet outnumbered the American nineteen to one, and on paper these vessels could have devastated America's coastal cities. But Italy was financially unable to sustain a prolonged war with the United States, and she had everything to lose and nothing to gain by hostilities.

In the United States, where mob violence was still common, the flare-up over a lynching caused little real alarm. *Harper's Weekly* declared that if Italians did not like the protection extended by American laws, they were at liberty to go home. The *Atlanta Journal* jokingly hoped that Italy, as rumored, was sending a warship to New Orleans. "We are," it said, "too much in need of a navy to let a thing like that escape." The *Salt Lake Herald* was contemptuous:

> The Italian press may rage and fume, and Italian officials may threaten, but they can do nothing. They are absolutely powerless. The nation is weak in every respect, and financially is almost bankrupt. It has a magnificent navy for which it owes, and has a large army for which it has absolutely no use. The idea of making war upon the United States, the greatest power on earth, is so ridiculous as to be laughable.[9]

Tempers on both sides of the Atlantic fortunately cooled; and the Rome government felt somewhat better when it discovered that only three of the eleven victims were unnaturalized Italian subjects. No foreign nation could properly object to natural-born Americans lynching naturalized Americans. The incident was officially closed when Washington, as a friendly act, paid $25,000 to Italy from the emergency fund of the State Department. Incidentally, the whole episode did much to increase agitation for restricting immigration from southern and eastern Europe.

THE CHILEAN CRISIS

The elongated republic of Chile had not welcomed the return of Blaine to the State Department. It could not forget his "guano statesmanship" in 1881, and his evident determination, at the end of the war with Peru and Bolivia, to snatch away the fruits of victory. Tension became more taut when Blaine appointed an able Irish refugee, Patrick Egan, as United States minister to Chile. The Democrats condemned Egan, who had recently become naturalized, as a "Blaine Irishman" and "an escaped jailbird" of the Irish "dynamite school." At all events, his presence proved highly offensive to the influential British colony in Chile.

In 1891 civil war erupted in Chile when the Congressionalists revolted against the president, who was attempting to seize dictatorial power. A

[9] *Public Opinion*, X, 588 (March 28, 1891).

rebel steamer, the *Itata*, with a cargo of arms, was detained at San Diego, California, by the United States authorities, who feared possible complications. The crew suddenly overpowered the American guard, and shortly thereafter set sail for Chile. A United States cruiser took up the chase; a Congressionalist cruiser rushed to defend the *Itata*. Word was momentarily expected of a clash. But the fugitive ship reached Chile, where the rebels reluctantly surrendered it to the United States. It was finally freed by the American courts as improperly detained.

By this time the Congressionalist rebels had triumphed, and they were naturally slow to forget the *Itata* affair. Nor could they forgive ex-refugee Patrick Egan, who, with commendable humanitarianism but arguable legalism, had given asylum in the United States legation to a number of prominent Chileans fleeing the vengeance of the victors.

With feeling still bitter, Captain Schley, of the U.S.S. *Baltimore*, ill-advisedly gave shore leave to about 120 unarmed men at Valparaiso. On the afternoon of October 16, 1891, a riot started in the True Blue saloon when a Chilean allegedly spat in the face of an American. In the brawl that resulted two United States sailors were killed (one receiving eighteen bayonet and knife wounds), seventeen were injured, and some of the remainder were beaten and imprisoned. The local police reportedly helped the mob of Chilean rioters attack the Americans.

Public sentiment in the United States reacted angrily. Many citizens felt that this affair was no mere lynching of Italians or Chinese but an insult to the uniform and flag of the United States Navy. Captain Schley declared that the men were well behaved and not drunk—at least not when he had last seen them. But Captain "Fighting Bob" Evans, who arrived in Valparaiso harbor on the U.S.S. *Yorktown* eager, as he put it, "to fill hell with garlic," thought Schley's argument irrelevant:

> His men were probably drunk on shore, properly drunk; they went ashore, many of them, for the purpose of getting drunk; which they did on Chilean rum paid for with good United States money. When in this condition they were more entitled to protection than if they had been sober.[10]

THE CAPITULATION OF CHILE

Days dragged by without an apology or even an expression of regret from Chile. The Acting Secretary of State (Blaine was then ill) sent a sharp note complaining of the delay in acknowledging responsibility. The Chilean Foreign Minister dallied, failed to make an acceptable apology, and vaguely asserted that justice would ultimately prevail.

President (General) Harrison, who had worn the American uniform worthily, was much more aroused than the "spirited" Blaine, who had not worn it at all. In his annual message to Congress, Harrison expressed

[10] R. D. Evans, *A Sailor's Log* (New York, 1901), pp. 259–260.

the hope that the current investigation would bring full satisfaction. But he ended on an ominous note: "If these just expectations should be disappointed or further needless delay intervene, I will by a special message bring this matter again to the attention of Congress for such action as may be necessary." [11] The Chilean Foreign Minister, angered by the President's statement, committed the inexcusable indiscretion of scattering broadcast a note of rebuttal in which he attacked Harrison's good faith and truthfulness.

War feeling now ran dangerously high in both countries, particularly in the United States, which had experienced no jingoistic outburst since the *Virginius* affair nearly twenty years earlier. Fight-thirsty young Theodore Roosevelt was on fire to lead a cavalry charge against the Chileans. A Kentucky Congressman declared that a million men would respond to a call to arms. The navy yards, both in the United States and Chile, worked overtime. The body of one of the murdered seamen lay for a time in state in Independence Hall, Philadelphia—an honor previously accorded only Abraham Lincoln and Henry Clay.

The warlike Chileans, rendered overconfident by their victories over weak neighbors, boasted of what their navy would do. It was in fact definitely superior in torpedo boats, and for a time panic struck the vulnerable Pacific Coast of the United States. But Chile had a population of only three million, and was further handicapped by the hostility of neighboring Peru and Argentina. The ultimate advantage was so certain to lie with the United States, with its population of sixty-three million, that war would have been suicidal for Chile and not altogether honorable for the Colossus of the North.

The State Department had meanwhile been keeping the wires humming. On January 21, 1892, Blaine sent to Chile an ultimatum drafted by President Harrison:

> I am now, however, directed by the President to say that if the offensive parts of the dispatch of the 11th of December are not at once withdrawn, and a suitable apology offered, with the same publicity that was given to the offensive expressions, he will have no other course open to him except to terminate diplomatic relations with the Government of Chile.[12]

The new Chilean Foreign Minister bowed to the inevitable and submitted an apology which left nothing to be desired. But while the note was being decoded, Harrison sent a special message to Congress, on January 25, 1892, in which he outlined the affair at great length and submitted the relevant papers for "the grave and patriotic consideration" of Congress "and for such action as may be deemed appropriate." This virtual invitation to declare war, at a time when Chile's capitulation was

[11] J. D. Richardson, ed., *Messages and Papers of the Presidents* (Washington, 1898), IX, 186.
[12] *House Ex. Docs.*, 52 Cong., 1 sess., I, 308.

hourly expected, brought down a storm of criticism on Harrison's head. The Democratic press openly accused the President of angling for re-election, and of planning to precipitate hostilities so that he could sweep to victory with the slogan "don't swap horses in the middle of the stream." But whatever Harrison's motives, the apology ended the crisis. The government of Chile ultimately paid $75,000 to the injured men and to the families of the deceased.

In handling the Chilean crisis, Blaine has been accused of excessive severity in his demands upon a weak sister republic—of using a sledge hammer to crush a butterfly. The *New York Herald,* referring to the current heavyweight boxing champion, declared that the Secretary was trying to be the "John L. Sullivan of diplomacy." But scholars now know that Blaine actually restrained Harrison. The Secretary of State was too thoroughly wrapped up in the ideal of Pan-Americanism to go much beyond what seemed to be the plain requirements of the case. Yet the Chileans could not forgive the United States for having forced them to crawl. This distressing episode unfortunately did much to erase the few happy results of the first Pan-American Conference.

FRICTION WITH THE FATHERLAND

Other vexatious problems claimed Blaine's attention. The Samoan controversy with Germany, which brought both nations to the brink of war, will be discussed in the next chapter. Elsewhere in the Pacific a mounting interest in the Hawaiian islands foreshadowed American an-nexation. During his first abbreviated term as Secretary, Blaine had laid down a policy aimed at the ultimate acquisition of this insular paradise. During his second term he arranged for the appointment of the ardent annexationist John L. Stevens, a journalist friend, as minister to Honolulu. The schemings of this overanxious envoy will also be described in the next chapter.

Changing relationships with Germany in the 1880's and 1890's likewise brought knotty problems to Blaine's doorstep. The two nations were drifting apart, despite the racial tie of hundreds of thousands of German immigrants, and despite memories of Prussian sympathy for the North during the Civil War. Both countries were emerging as great powers at about the same time, and as newcomers both lacked the suave manners of old-timers like Britain and France. Both were developing into naval rivals. Both were becoming commercial competitors, for each under-went heavy industrialization at about the same time. The trade-mark "Made in Germany," came to be more feared abroad than German battleships.

One unhappy result of this keen economic competition was that both the Americans and the Germans sought to safeguard themselves against a flood of exports from each other. The United States resorted to the highly protective tariff, which trod heavily on the toes of German manu-facturers. Germany, to say nothing of the other west European nations, fought back against the "American Peril" with restrictions on fruit, meat, and other commodities. "Buffalo Bill" Cody's Wild West Show actually had some difficulty in getting its buffalo into Germany because of regula-tions against importing American cattle.

The lowly American pig threatened to uproot completely all amity remaining between Germany and the United States. The Germans, among others, placed embargoes on American pork products, allegedly because they were diseased, but basically because they were competitive. This insult to American swine brought a storm of protest from farmers, as well as pressure on Congress and the State Department. After some ten years of wrangling, the hog emerged victorious when provision was made for adequate export inspection in the United States. Blaine, who quietly handled the final negotiations in 1891, received some credit for the satis-factory outcome.[13]

Protection for pigs was paralleled by belated protection for penmen. In March, 1891, Congress finally passed a law making possible an inter-national copyright, under certain conditions, for both American and foreign writers. A long-rankling grievance of British authors since before the days of Charles Dickens was thus happily removed.

THE PASSING OF THE PLUMED KNIGHT

Secretary Blaine abruptly resigned his office, in June, 1892, on the eve of the Republican National Convention. His erratic behavior gave added currency to the rather improbable rumor that he was again a candidate for the Presidency. In any event, Harrison received the Republican nomi-nation, Cleveland the Democratic. Cleveland's triumph that November evoked rejoicing in Latin America, especially in Chile, where the names of *Baltimore*, Blaine, and Harrison were disagreeable reminders of a strong-arm foreign policy.

Blaine's second term as Secretary of State was actually less spirited than his first—the obvious reason being that he had less spirit. The Plumed Knight's plume drooped a bit. Older, disappointed, ill, and work-ing under a jealous chief, he did not take the diplomatic offensive, but dealt almost solely with inherited problems or isolated incidents as they arose. And in handling the New Orleans and *Baltimore* crises, as well as the Samoan affair, he displayed far less vigor than might have been expected.

Whatever may be said against Blaine, he was gifted with energy and

[13] See L. L. Snyder, "The American-German Pork Dispute, 1879–1891," *Jour. of Mod. Hist.*, XVII (1945), 16–28.

imagination. He was more actively interested in a constructive and far-visioned foreign policy than any of his predecessors or successors between William H. Seward and John Hay. More than any other statesman of his generation, he focused attention on foreign affairs at a time when interest was at low ebb, and in doing so probably contributed to the imperialistic upsurge at the end of the century.

Yet Blaine, despite all the commotion he caused, could point to few immediate achievements. The explanation is that he laid foundations upon which others built. His Hawaiian and Isthmian policies found fruition under Presidents McKinley and Theodore Roosevelt; his seal-preservation policy under President Taft; his reciprocal-trade policy, in part, under President Franklin D. Roosevelt and Secretary Hull. By common consent Blaine's chief claim to fame lies in his advocacy of closer commercial and cultural contacts with Latin America, and in his encouragement of the pacific settlement of disputes. Every succeeding Pan-American Conference has been a monument to his foresight and zeal.

SELECTED BIBLIOGRAPHY

A sketch of Blaine appears in S. F. Bemis, ed., *The American Secretaries of State and their Diplomacy* (New York, 1928), VIII, 109–184. The best single monograph is Alice F. Tyler, *The Foreign Policy of James G. Blaine* (Minneapolis, 1927); see also D. S. Muzzey, *James G. Blaine* (New York, 1935). On the Chilean affair consult H. C. Evans, Jr., *Chile and Its Relations with the United States* (Durham, N.C., 1927) and W. R. Sherman, *The Diplomatic and Commercial Relations of the United States and Chile, 1820–1914* (Boston, 1926). Further details may be found in A. T. Volwiler, *The Correspondence between Benjamin Harrison and James G. Blaine, 1882–1893* (Philadelphia, 1940), and A. T. Volwiler, "Harrison, Blaine, and American Foreign Policy, 1889–1893," Amer. Philosophical Soc. Procs., LXXIX (1938), 637–648. On German-American relations see Otto zu Stolberg-Wernigerode, *Germany and the United States of America during the Era of Bismarck* (Reading, Pa., 1937), and Alfred Vagts, *Deutschland und die Vereinigten Staaten in der Weltpolitik* (New York, 1935), I, Chs. I–VII.

Revealing articles are Osgood Hardy, "The *Itata* Incident," *Hispanic Amer. Hist. Rev.,* V (1922), 195–226, and his "Was Patrick Egan a 'Blundering Minister'?" *ibid.,* VIII (1928), 65–81. On the Mafia affair, consult J. A. Karlin, "The Italo-American incident of 1891 and the Road to Reunion," *Jour. of Southern Hist.,* VIII (1942), 242–246, and the same author's "The Indemnification of Aliens Injured by Mob Violence," *Southwestern Soc. Sci. Quar.,* XXV (1945), 235–246.

See footnotes of this chapter; Bemis and Griffin, *Guide,* pp. 453 ff.; *Harvard Guide,* Ch. 23.

7TH, 8TH, AND 9TH ED. REFS. See BIBLIOGRAPHICAL ADDENDUM, p. 1,002.

CHAPTER

29

Samoa and Hawaii:
An Imperialistic Preview

*We need Hawaii just as much and a good deal more
than we did California. It is manifest destiny.*
PRESIDENT MCKINLEY, 1898

THE REBIRTH OF MANIFEST DESTINY

As THE CENTURY neared its sunset, the United States became involved in
serious friction over the ownership of two tiny island chains—Samoa and
Hawaii—lost in the vastnesses of the Pacific. Why should the American
people, with their pressing domestic problems and their huge continental
domain, have become so deeply aroused over these distant insular flyspecks?· What had happened to their traditional policies of staying at
home and keeping their noses out of foreign entanglements?

The roots of the budding spirit of imperialism are to be found in many
places. The Darwinian theory, as popularly interpreted by men like
John Fiske in the 1880's and 1890's, helped to prepare the American
mind for the comfortable belief that the world belonged to the nations
that were strong and fit—like the United States. The "spirited" foreign
policy of Blaine caused many an American to experience a pleasant
tingling that may have been the rising sap of imperialism. During these
years the distinguished American writer Captain A. T. Mahan, the high
priest of navalism, began to preach the gospel that naval power and
world power are Siamese twins. The American people glimpsed faintly
the destiny they were to fulfill; and the new steel navy, started in 1883,
was rushed to completion.

The demand for more and bigger battleships had its counterpart in
the growing agitation for an Isthmian canal to increase the mobility of
the navy in protecting both coasts. A man-made waterway also meant that
outlying islands, like Cuba, the Danish West Indies, and Hawaii, would

have to be annexed to guard its approaches. The fact that the world was growing smaller was dramatically impressed upon the American people when, in 1889–1890, the crack New York reporter Nellie Bly dashed around it in an unprecedented seventy-two days, six hours, eleven minutes, and fourteen seconds.

America was clearly on the march. By 1890 post-Civil War reconstruction had virtually been completed, and the last desirable free land was fast disappearing. During these same years the country experienced a marvelous increase in its industrial production, and American manufacturers were looking for foreign markets to absorb their swelling surpluses. Discerning observers could see that outlets would have to be found for the Vesuvian energy and expansive power of an America that needed "elbow room." "The subjugation of a continent," remarked the *Overland Monthly,* "was sufficient to keep the American people busy at home for a century. . . . But now that the continent is subdued, we are looking for fresh worlds to conquer. . . ." [1]

Everywhere in the United States there were evidences of a growing national consciousness. American history was introduced into the lower schools; scores of patriotic societies sprouted up; genealogists pored over musty documents; respect for the flag was taught in the classrooms; and the propriety of displaying the national colors in comic opera aroused serious debate. In 1893 Congress created the rank of ambassador: that of a lowly minister would no longer do. All signs indicated that America was turning her eyes outward. She was restless, tired of a drab and colorless life, bored by such prosaic issues as the tariff and currency, eager for new thrills—and a stage commensurate with her bursting power.

SAMOA: PAWN OF THE PACIFIC

The Samoan archipelago, with its splendid harbor of Pago Pago on the island of Tutuila, commands important ocean lanes in the South Pacific. As early as 1838 the United States government, responding to pressure from the whaling interests, sent a scientific expedition to the area. But not until after the Civil War did the American people begin to show a real interest in the island paradise. The pursuit of the Confederate commerce raider *Shenandoah* had demonstrated the wisdom of having a coaling station in these waters. Furthermore, the completion of the transcontinental railroad in 1869 stimulated trade with New Zealand and Australia, and focused attention on the Samoan way station.

Various attempts by the United States to secure a foothold in Samoa by treaty finally achieved fruition in 1878. A six-foot-four highborn Samoan, Le Mamea, came to Washington, where he made a striking impression. Negotiations with the "tattooed Prince" resulted in the treaty

[1] *Overland Monthly,* XXXI (1898), 177–178.

of 1878, a cornerstone of America's Samoan policy. It provided that in return for the rights to a coaling station at Pago Pago, the United States would employ its good offices to adjust any differences that should arise between Samoa and a foreign power. This arrangement was not a protectorate, and as a consequence the Senate registered the stamp of its approval. The *New York Times* rejoiced at obtaining these advantages without an equivalent entanglement. But Washington was now formally bound to support the weak native government against foreign powers—a course fraught with unforeseen perils.

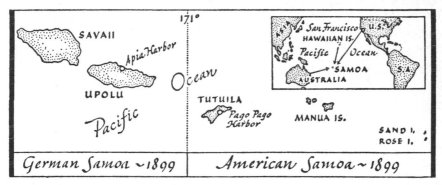

The year following the negotiation of the pact of 1878 Great Britain and Germany both secured treaty rights in Samoa. The Germans, who were latecomers in the scramble for colonies and who found most of the desirable areas already scooped up, were obviously eager to pick up these insular crumbs. The consular agents of Germany, Great Britain, and the United States were, in these circumstances, highly suspicious of the annexationist designs of one another. With the nearest cable in distant New Zealand, each consul was forced to act on his own responsibility—and the resulting schemes wrought havoc with frayed nerves. The English author Robert Louis Stevenson, who reached Samoa in 1889 seeking relief from tuberculosis, reported one politician as saying, "I never saw so good a place as this Apia; you can be in a new conspiracy every day." [2]

The tiny islands fairly seethed with the intrigues of landgrabbers, concessionaires, naval officers, commercial agents, and consuls. The natives were bullied and browbeaten, and brother was set upon brother in the blood and turmoil of civil war. Nervous consuls hoisted the flags of their governments, only to be disavowed by the home office. By the summer of 1887 the tension had become so unendurable that Secretary of State Bayard called the British and German ministers in Washington into a conference. The German representative urged that the power commercially dominant in Samoa be allowed to control the islands—and this

---

[2] R. L. Stevenson, *A Footnote to History* (New York, 1895), p. 26.

meant the Fatherland. He was supported by his British colleague, for Britain had secured equivalents elsewhere from Germany. But the United States stood firm for the preservation of Samoan autonomy, and the conference broke up without agreement.

The unseemly scramble now became more frantic. The Germans, after pressing demands upon the Samoan "king" for alleged wrongs, solemnly declared war upon him. The unhappy Polynesian potentate was finally deported, but the natives took to the jungle in revolt against the German-manipulated puppet. In December, 1888, a party of German sailors was ambushed with humiliating losses, whereupon the Germans shelled the native villages and declared martial law. A fleet of one British, three German, and three American warships gathered in crowded Apia harbor, where the nervous seamen glared at one another over loaded guns.

NATURE INTERVENES AT APIA

By this time the American public had become genuinely aroused over the events in distant Samoa. Reports of the trampling on "Old Glory," of the destruction of American property, and of the jeopardizing of American interests gave the hotheads their inning. There was a serious discussion of war with Germany over the cocoanut kingdom. The *New York World* rattled the saber vigorously:

> The American hog has been discriminated against in Germany and the German hog in Samoa must not be permitted to uproot the rights of Americans there. Our Government has wisely ordered two more war vessels to reinforce the . . . cruisers now in Samoan waters. Perhaps the presence of this small fleet will have the effect of cooling the hostile officers of the German gunboats.[3]

Congress promptly passed an appropriation of $500,000 for the protection of American lives and property in Samoa, and another $100,000 for the development of Pago Pago harbor.

With feeling in the United States already inflamed by the pork controversy and other German restrictions, the Samoan crisis took on a dangerous aspect. But Prince Bismarck, the Iron Chancellor, had no desire to antagonize the United States, whose friendship he valued. He therefore promised a renewal of the negotiations fruitlessly begun at Washington. On March 14, 1889, President Harrison appointed three delegates to attend a conference in Berlin, where representatives of the three great powers were to assemble in an attempt to untangle the Samoan snarl.

---

[3] Quoted in *Public Opinion*, VI, 322 (Jan. 26, 1889). On the other hand, journals like the *New York Nation* condemned this "wild goose chase" as "sheer jingoism and meddlesomeness in other people's affairs." XLVIII, 84 (Jan. 31, 1889).

The American and German ships were still glowering at one another in Apia harbor. Although the atmosphere was somewhat relieved by the approaching Berlin Conference, the tension was still explosive. Then, on March 16, 1889, a terrific hurricane descended upon the poorly protected harbor. All three American and all three German warships were wrecked, sunk, or driven upon the beach with heavy loss of life. The British *Calliope* headed out to sea with straining boilers, and as she crept to safety a cheer arose from the Americans on the doomed *Trenton*. It was returned with a will. This dramatic instance of good sportsmanship was probably not without influence in helping to usher in the new era of Anglo-American friendship that was fast approaching. As a Canadian poet, Charles Roberts, wrote:

> The memory of those cheers
> Shall thrill in English ears
> Where'er this English blood and speech extend.[4]

THE THREE-HEADED SAMOAN PROTECTORATE

The Berlin Conference convened on April 29, 1889, with the atmosphere definitely improved by the Apia disaster. Contrary to expectations, the imperious Prince Bismarck was in a conciliatory mood. Even American jingoes were sobered. The *New York World* adopted a solemn tone:

> Men and nations must bow before the decrees of nature. . . . Surely the awful devastation wrought in the habor of Apia makes our recent quarrel with Germany appear petty and unnatural. Can it not be confidently predicted that the bonds which now join us to Germany as together we mourn the fate of those who perished in their duty will make the coming diplomatic conference at Berlin a council of friends, not a quarrel of restless rivals.[5]

Secretary Blaine, practitioner of a "spirited" foreign policy, was expected to adopt a strong tone in dealing with Bismarck. The unfriendly *New York Nation* predicted that his dispatches would be like the rumble "of distant but fast approaching thunder." But such was not the case. Blaine revealed a conciliatory disposition and, despite a widely repeated tale, did not lay down the law to the supposedly irritable Bismarck.

The final partition of the islands could better have been made then at Berlin than ten years later. But America was not ripe for tropical annexations, and Blaine blocked any possible division by his insistence on the preservation of native autonomy. The only acceptable solution seemed to be a three-power protectorate over Samoa, with the restored native dynasty nominally ruling from the royal hut. Germany and Great Britain were not altogether pleased with this arrangement, but, on June 14, 1889, they formally agreed to it.

---

[4] B. E. Stevenson, ed., *Poems of American History* (Boston, 1908), p. 598.
[5] Quoted in *Public Opinion*, VI, 571–572 (April 6, 1889).

At home, the pro-administration Republican newspapers were sure that Blaine had won a signal triumph; the Democrats were no less sure that he had bent the knee to Bismarck. "It is," growled the *St. Paul Globe,* "the squarest back-down in the history of diplomacy. . . ." [6] A number of influential American journals, notably the *New York Herald* and the *New York Evening Post,* were greatly disturbed by this apparent reversal

"HONEST FRIENDSHIP WITH ALL NATIONS, ENTANGLING
ALLIANCES WITH NONE."
THOMAS JEFFERSON

The American, German, and British entanglement in Samoa.
New York World, 1899

of the historic policy of nonentanglement. But many people, including Blaine, regarded the Samoan condominium as merely a temporary departure. Even so, there was something remarkable about the determination of the United States, ten years before the Spanish-American war, to go to the very brink of hostilities with Germany rather than yield negligible commercial and questionable strategic advantages in faraway Samoa. The muted clamor for the distant island chain may well have been the overture to imperialism.

[6] See *Public Opinion,* VIII, 403–404 (Feb. 1, 1890).

SLICING UP SAMOA

The three-power protectorate proved inherently unworkable. It was the old story of too many cooks—and jealous-ones at that. Yet the arrangement did produce, temporarily at least, a somewhat better feeling among the three nations involved. The well-being of the natives was, of course, a secondary consideration. But inevitable rivalries among the powers and the Samoans again turned the islands into a battlefield. Jealousy, intrigue, and murder once more became the order of the day. Disagreeable incidents involving the United States and Germany again agitated the American press. The *Pittsburgh Dispatch*, for example, emphatically declared that "If there should ever be a popular vote whether the money of the people of the United States should be expended in bulldozing the Samoans . . . the people would record a very emphatic negative." [7]

As fate would have it, Grover Cleveland, enemy of expansion, became President again in 1893. In successive messages to Congress he used the Samoan entanglement to illustrate the folly of departing from the wise policy of the Fathers. He even invited Congress to take steps to terminate the existing arrangement. His Secretary of State, who was no less hostile, drew up a strong indictment:

> Soberly surveying the history of our relations with Samoa, we well may inquire what we have gained by our departure from our established policy beyond the expenses, the responsibilities, and the entanglements that have so far been its only fruits. . . . The general act of Berlin . . . has utterly failed to correct, if indeed it has not aggravated, the very evils which it was designed to prevent.[8]

But the Spanish War of 1898 wrought a profound change in the American mind. With the Philippines, Hawaii, Guam, and Puerto Rico recently acquired, Samoa seemed but a logical complement to the far-flung American empire. Late in 1899, therefore, the Samoan archipelago was divided between Germany and the United States, with Britain gaining compensations elsewhere. Germany was happy to make off with the two largest islands. America secured the remainder, including Tutuila, with its harbor of Pago Pago, on which she had kept an unwavering eye since Grant's day. The embarrassing protectorate was terminated; the decades of squabbling were ended. The division was approved by the Senate without serious difficulty, although a violent anti-imperialist, Senator Pettigrew of South Dakota, shouted: "We blot out, then, a sovereign nation, a people with whom we have treaty obligations, and divide the spoils." But the American public, already overburdened with troublesome island populations, paid little attention to these minor pickings.

[7] *Literary Digest,* IX, 95 (May 26, 1894).
[8] *Foreign Relations, 1894,* appendix, I, 513 (May 9, 1894).

THE AMERICANIZATION OF HAWAII

Much more natural than the squabbling in Samoa was the infiltration of Hawaii. The first Americans to reach this tiny Polynesian kingdom were Pacific traders, and they found the idyllic islands an indispensable halfway house for refreshment and supplies. They were followed in 1820 by the first band of New England missionaries, who established a remarkable influence over the natives. These earnest soul-savers came to do good, and did well—or rather their sons did.

After the fishers of souls came American fishers of whales, and, throughout the four decades preceding the Civil War, they made the archipelago both a base and a rendezvous. During the heyday of whaling, hundreds of rollicking seamen could be found ashore enjoying the languorous delights of living and loving in Hawaii. By 1842 five-sixths of all ships calling at this mid-Pacific paradise flew the Stars and Stripes, and American cultural influence had become so widespread that there was much about Honolulu to suggest a typical New England town.

But other nations were not indifferent to the strategic advantages of Hawaii. British influence, in particular, was also strong. In 1842, following evidences of Britain's designs, Washington declared that while the United States had no intention of acquiring the islands, it could not view with equanimity the annexation of Hawaii by a foreign power. This policy, a virtual extension of the Monroe Doctrine to Hawaii, was reaffirmed on several other occasions by succeeding Secretaries of State. In 1843 an overzealous British naval officer attempted to seize Hawaii, but he was promptly disavowed and restitution was made. Yet the American public was alarmed, and the British minister wrote home from Washington that the "newspapers, with very few exceptions, are filled . . . with vehemently abusive articles against Great Britain." The acting Secretary of State declared that "we might even feel justified, consistently with our own principles, in interfering by force to prevent its [Hawaii's] falling into the hands of one of the great powers of Europe." [9]

In the 1850's, after America had acquired a Pacific frontage, and after the French had temporarily seized Honolulu, a genuine flurry for acquiring Hawaii developed in the United States. Annexation proposals were debated in Congress and in the press, amid wild rumors that filibusters were about to descend on Hawaii, as they were descending on Cuba. In 1854, the expansionist Pierce administration, with Marcy as Secretary of State, negotiated a treaty of annexation with the Hawaiian kingdom. But the pact proved to be unsatisfactory to the Senate, largely because of the article making provision for immediate statehood. This joker had appar-

[9] *Sen. Ex. Docs.*, 52 Cong., 2 sess., no. 77, p. 109 (Legaré to Everett, June 13, 1843).

ently been inserted through the influence of those in Hawaii who were anxious to defeat annexation.

With annexation thus stymied, a commercial reciprocity treaty seemed to be the most satisfactory substitute. Secretary Marcy concluded such a pact in 1855. But the Senate failed to approve it, partly because of strenuous opposition from the sugar-producing state of Louisiana. Another reciprocity treaty, negotiated under Seward in 1867, was defeated largely because certain Senators were determined to accept no substitute for outright annexation.

The champions of reciprocity finally triumphed in 1875, when a sweeping treaty was concluded by Secretary Fish which whittled down tariff barriers on both sides. The miniature kingdom bound itself to make no territorial concessions to any other powers, and in return was permitted to ship sugar and other products to the United States duty free. So profitable was this arrangement that the sickly sugar industry of Hawaii experienced a boom, and the economic life of the islands became so deeply enmeshed with that of America as to make political union virtually inevitable. This goal, in fact, was what many advocates of the treaty had in mind.

The reciprocity treaty, though bitterly opposed by American sugar and rice growers, was renewed in 1884. But the pact was not formally approved until 1887, when the Senate amended it so as to secure an exclusive right to use the priceless Pearl River Harbor as a naval station. Slowly and inexorably Hawaii was being drawn into the American orbit.

THE CONSPIRACY AGAINST "QUEEN LIL"

As the century neared its end, a small group of prosperous Americans had come to control about two-thirds of the total taxable real estate of Hawaii. Many of these men, though the sons of missionaries, were more interested in sugar than in souls. They had flourished until 1890, when the United States Congress put sugar on the free list and provided a bounty of 2 cents a pound for American producers. The Hawaiian product, no longer benefiting from the same privileges as that of America, suffered a crippling blow. Annexation was clearly the only sure safeguard against such discrimination.

This obvious economic motive has led to "sugar conspiracy" charges, and to the accusation that the revolution of 1893 was "of sugar, by sugar, and for sugar." The *New York Herald* repeatedly used as an editorial filler the italicized inquiry: *Is Spreckels & Co.* [a leading Hawaiian producer] *the little nigger in the fence of the sugar islands?"* But a number of Hawaiian cane planters, including Spreckels himself, were opposed to annexation because they feared that the contract-labor laws of the United States would cut off the Oriental labor supply. The German-born

Spreckels growled, "In der sthreets of Honolulu vill grow der grass, schust mark my voords." [10]

But there can be no doubt that a larger economic motive was present. The decadent native dynasty was extravagant, corrupt, capricious. The whites would be much more certain to retain their valuable property, as well as their lives and liberties, if the islands were annexed and white supremacy was guaranteed.

The tension increased in 1891, when Queen Liliuokalani ascended the tottering Hawaiian throne. She vehemently resented the liberal constitution of 1887, which the white élite, though outnumbered, had imposed upon her weak-kneed brother. Adopting the rallying cry of "Hawaii for the Hawaiians," Liliuokalani attempted, on January 14, 1893, to promulgate a new and autocratic constitution by royal edict.

The white leaders, fearing for their position and property, had already organized a revolution. As the great majority of them were Americans or of American ancestry, they appealed for support to John L. Stevens, the notoriously annexationist United States minister in Honolulu. On January 16, 1893, Stevens responded to their entreaties when he arranged to land more than 150 armed men from the U.S.S. *Boston,* then in Honolulu harbor, for the presumed purpose of protecting American life and property. Curiously enough, most of these troops were not stationed near American property at all, but in that part of Honolulu where their presence would intimidate the Queen.

Stevens moved speedily on other fronts. On January 17, 1893, the day after the uprising, he hastily accorded recognition to the revolutionary regime, although unauthorized to do so. There was a gross inconsistency in his action, for only a few hours earlier the revolutionists had been so shaky as to cry for assistance. The Queen, overawed by the American troops and the obvious complicity of the United States, yielded her authority under protest. Less than two weeks later, on February 1, 1893, the enthusiastic Stevens proclaimed Hawaii a protectorate, hoisted the American flag, and advised the State Department: "The Hawaiian pear is now fully ripe, and this is the golden hour for the United States to pluck it. If annexation does not take place promptly . . . these people, by their necessities, might be forced towards becoming a British colony. . . ." [11]

THE RUSH-ORDER TREATY

Three days after the landing of the American troops, a "Hawaiian" commission was hurrying to Washington to lay the islands at the feet of

[10] W. A. Russ, Jr., "The Role of Sugar in Hawaiian Annexation," *Pacific Hist. Rev.,* XII (1943), p. 345.

[11] *Foreign Relations, 1894,* appendix II, p. 402 (Stevens to Foster, Feb. 1, 1893).

the United States. Not surprisingly, this group of "Hawaiians" consisted of four Americans and one Englishman. Their arrival came as no shock to the Harrison administration. Secretary of State Foster had not only allowed Stevens' pro-annexationist ardor to go unchecked, but, expecting a blowup, had been quietly preparing the public for annexation. Negotiations proceeded smoothly. In mid-February, 1893, less than one month after Queen Liliuokalani's downfall, a hastily drawn, hastily signed, and hastily submitted treaty of annexation was before the Senate for approval. The pact had the rather lukewarm support of President Harrison.

The American public forthwith found itself involved in its first major debate on the fateful issue of imperialism. A popular jingle swept the country:

> . . . Liliuokalani
> Give us your little brown hannie!

From a large section of the press—chiefly big-navy, expansionist, and Republican—came a demand for plucking the ripe pear. Strategic, commercial, and humanitarian arguments all pointed to the desirability of annexation. Besides, if the United States did not take the islands, the British or Japanese, who were both actively interested, might scoop them up and use them to America's disadvantage. The *New York Independent* changed Stevens' fruit but not his figure of speech: "The ripe apple falls into our hands, and we would be very foolish if we should throw it away." "The popular verdict is clear, unequivocal, and practically unanimous," cried the expansionist *New York Tribune*. "Hawaii is welcome."

But the voices of doubters, chiefly Democrats, spoiled the symphony. There were aspects of this unsavory affair, they declared, especially the "sugar-baron" angle, that required a thorough airing. Why not give the deposed Queen her day in court? Why all the haste to depart from the time-tested policy of isolation, and embark upon the uncharted sea of imperialistic troubles? Could Hawaii, with its mixed population, ever become a state? There was food for thought in Roger Camerden's "Warily Brothers":

> "Shall we take Hawaii in, sirs?" that's the question of the day.
> Would the speedy annexation of that dusky country pay?
> Would the revenues from sugar and from smuggled opium
> Counteract the heavy burdens that with them are sure to come? [12]

When the annexation pact was rushed to the Senate, only about two weeks of Harrison's Republican administration remained. The treaty still had not been acted upon when the Democrats under Grover Cleveland, an archfoe of imperialism, returned to the White House in March, 1893.

[12] *Harper's Weekly*, XXXVII, 299 (Apr. 1, 1893).

CLEVELAND CHECKMATES MANIFEST DESTINY

A man less courageous than Cleveland would have closed his eyes to the grave irregularities of the Hawaii affair. But the President was "a slave of conscience." His exacting standards of public honor led him to suspect, with good reason, that Queen Liliuokalani had been wronged. He especially wanted to discover whether the disease-riddled natives, to whom the islands had originally belonged, favored annexation.

Cleveland moved energetically. On March 9, 1893, he sent to the Senate a curt, five-line message, in which he resorted to the unusual step of withdrawing the treaty for examination. He next appointed a special commissioner, ex-Congressman James H. Blount, whom he clothed with "paramount" authority to make an investigation. Upon arriving in Hawaii, "Paramount" Blount hustled the American troops back to their ship and ordered the Stars and Stripes to be hauled down. The *New York Commercial Advertiser* could endure no more:

> In ordering "Old Glory" pulled down at Honolulu President Cleveland turned back the hands on the dial of civilization. Native rule, ignorant, naked, heathen, is re-established; and the dream of an American republic at the cross-roads of the Pacific—a dream which Seward and Marcy and Blaine indulged, and the fulfillment of which the more enlightened of our 65,-000,000 people awaited with glad anticipation, has been shattered by Grover Cleveland, the Buffalo lilliputian! [13]

During his stay in Hawaii, "Paramount" Blount conducted an investigation of undoubted thoroughness but disputed impartiality. As an ex-Confederate cavalry colonel from Georgia, he may have been a little startled when the Royal Hawaiian Band, thinking to do him honor, played the Yankee song, "Marching through Georgia." He finally reported to Cleveland that Stevens had improperly interfered with the revolution, and that a strong majority of the voters, including the dwindling natives, emphatically opposed annexation.

Two basic conclusions grew out of Blount's facts. First, the uprising in Hawaii would have failed without American assistance, and second, it probably would not have been launched without Stevens' prior assurances of support. The evidence was in fact so damning as measurably to dampen the annexation craze in America. The *New York Times* concluded that a conspiracy had been exposed, which, "if not repudiated by this nation, would sully the honor and blacken the fair name of the United States."

To Cleveland the only possible course was to make honorable amends for the grave wrong that had been done Queen Liliuokalani, and put the fallen pear back on the tree. He instructed the new American min-

[13] *New York Commercial Advertiser,* April 14, 1893, 4:3.

ister in Honolulu to secure pledges from the deposed Queen that, if restored to her throne, she would deal leniently with the white conspirators. Her dusky highness, with the calm fury of a woman scorned, at first replied that she would have their heads and their property. But the white oligarchy, whose tiny army was in complete control, steadfastly refused to yield to what one mainland paper called a "fat squaw."

The storm of criticism in America redoubled in fury, greatly augmented as it was by the church-missionary people. The Massachusetts Republican platform of 1894 proclaimed: "No barbarous Queen beheading men in Hawaii." Mutterings rose even from Cleveland's Democratic camp. The color-conscious *Atlanta Constitution*, which opposed reinstatement of the Queen, reminded the President that the "Democratic party has not been in the habit of restoring monarchies anywhere."

Cleveland's motives, in a day of international land-grabbing, were honorable to himself and his country. But he could enthrone the deposed Polynesian potentate only by using superior force—and the American public would never have sanctioned the slaying of fellow Americans in Hawaii to restore despotism. Cleveland finally decided to dump the entire snarl on the doorstep of Congress. His lengthy message, which reviewed the controversial affair, roundly condemned the policy of his predecessor. Congress responded, after impassioned and partisan debate, by passing two resolutions of non-interference. There the annexation issue rested until the advent of a President less troubled by conscience and better able to read the signs of the times.

THE NEW TREATY STALEMATE

From 1894 to 1898 the partially Americanized republic of Hawaii waited outside the gate. The Honolulu government, stressing "Mongolization" of the islands by the Japanese, propagandized actively in the United States for annexation. But this goal could not be achieved until Cleveland left the White House. The new Republican administration of President McKinley was favorable to annexation, and a substitute treaty was signed on June 16, 1897.

Unexpected opposition to annexation came from the Japanese, who had recently whipped China and were feeling their new strength in the Pacific. The presence of some 25,000 remarkably reproductive Nipponese in Hawaii—about one-fourth of the total population—had evidently led the Tokyo officials to hope that the islands would one day belong to Japan. The seventy-four year old Secretary of State Sherman, now extremely forgetful, had apparently assured the Japanese minister in Washington that no annexation treaty was in prospect. Evidently stung by this innocent deception and by sharp disappointment, Tokyo lodged a vigorous protest against the acquisition of the islands. It based its case primarily on the grounds that the transfer would disturb the *status quo* in the Pacific and jeopardize the Japanese in Hawaii. The State Department, in parrying these arguments, replied that annexation was but the logical culmination of seventy years' association.[14]

The Hawaiian treaty was blocked in the Senate by determined Democrats, despite the overtime use of the Japanese bogey. Cleveland's former Secretary of State, Richard Olney, wrote exultingly that the annexation project was "in the soup," while the *New York Nation* declared that it was "dead beyond the hope of resurrection."

CONSUMMATION—NOT CHANGE

As if Providence were on the side of Manifest Destiny, Commodore Dewey's breathtaking victory over the Spaniards at Manila, on May 1, 1898, brought an electric change. Hawaii would be useful, not to say indispensable, in sending supplies and reinforcements to the Americans in the Philippines. "Bridge the Pacific," cried the *Philadelphia Press*. The need for haste seemed so obvious that agitation for a joint resolution of annexation, which would require only a simple majority vote, gathered momentum in Congress.

The advocates of annexation argued that America needed to acquire the islands in order to aid Dewey. This assumption was false because the Honolulu government, hoping to create annexation sentiment, was giving the Americans every kind of assistance in open violation of neutrality. Yet the feeling was general that in no circumstances should the heroic Dewey be "let down." The argument was also advanced, in Congress and out, that since the United States had allowed Hawaii to compromise its neutrality, there was no honorable alternative but to bind the islands to America in the holy bonds of annexation.

Champions of a powerful navy also took a leading part in the discussion. Men like Captain Mahan dusted off the old argument—and it was a strong one—that the United States needed Hawaii as a first line of defense to ward off future attacks on the mainland. The point was also made that if the islands should fall into the hands of a hostile foreign power, say Japan, they could be used as a base to menace the Pacific coast of the United States. This argument had been used before, but the fear recently aroused on the Atlantic seaboard by the operations of the Spanish fleet gave it a new force.

Finally, there were the unabashed advocates of territorial and commercial expansion, in Congress and out. Representative Gibson cried:

> Manifest Destiny says, "Take them in." The American people say, "Take them." Obedient to the voice of the people, I shall cast my vote to take

[14] T. A. Bailey, "Japan's Protest against the Annexation of Hawaii," *Jour. of Mod. Hist.*, III (1931), 46–61.

them in; and tomorrow this House of Representatives will by a good round majority say, "Take them in." [Applause.] [15]

War hysteria and the new imperialism were not to be denied. "The jingo bacillus," declared one Congressman, "is indefatigable in its work." The joint resolution passed Congress by large majorities and was signed on July 7, 1898. President McKinley sagely remarked, "Annexation is not change; it is consummation." It was indeed a consummation of the work of American missionaries, traders, whalers, sugar planters, big-navyites, and imperialists. The time had finally come when the American people concluded that an independent Hawaii, like Texas of an earlier day, was both an anachronism and a danger.

SELECTED BIBLIOGRAPHY

Samoa and Hawaii are treated engagingly and briefly in F. R. Dulles, *America in the Pacific* (Boston, 1932). The most exhaustive monograph on Samoa is G. H. Ryden, *The Foreign Policy of the United States in Relation to Samoa* (New Haven, 1933). See also C. C. Tansill, *The Foreign Policy of Thomas F. Bayard, 1885–1897* (New York, 1940), on both Samoa and Hawaii; Sylvia Masterman, *The Origins of International Rivalry in Samoa, 1845–1884* (Stanford University, Calif., 1934); Alice F. Tyler, *The Foreign Policy of James G. Blaine* (Minneapolis, 1927); and Otto zu Stolberg-Wernigerode, *Germany and the United States of America during the Era of Bismarck* (Reading, Pa., 1937).

On Hawaii, perhaps the most useful brief study is J. W. Pratt, *Expansionists of 1898* (Baltimore, 1936). See also H. W. Bradley, *The American Frontier in Hawaii: The Pioneers, 1789–1843* (Stanford University, Calif., 1942); R. S. Kuykendall, *The Hawaiian Kingdom, 1778–1854* (Honolulu, 1938), and the same author's *The Hawaiian Kingdom, 1854–1874* (Honolulu, 1953); S. K. Stevens, *American Expansion in Hawaii, 1842–1898* (Harrisburg, Pa., 1945); Theodore Morgan, *Hawaii: A Century of Economic Change, 1778–1876* (Cambridge, Mass., 1948); G. R. Dulebohn, *Principles of Foreign Policy under the Cleveland Administrations* (Philadelphia, 1941); Allan Nevins, *Grover Cleveland* (New York, 1934).

Useful articles are D. M. Dozer, "The Opposition to Hawaiian Reciprocity, 1876–1888," *Pacific Hist. Rev.*, XIV (1945), 157–183; W. A. Russ, Jr., "Hawaiian Labor and Immigration Problems before Annexation," *Jour. of Mod. Hist.*, XV (1943), 207–222; R. D. Weigle, "Sugar and the Hawaiian Revolution," *Pacific Hist. Rev.*, XVI (1947), 41–58; A. F. Rolle, "California Filibustering and the Hawaiian Kingdom," *ibid.*, XIX (1950), 251–263; J. C. Appel, "American Labor and the Annexation of Hawaii: A Study in Logic and Economic Interest," *ibid.*, XXIII (1954), 1–18.

See footnotes of this chapter; Bemis and Griffin, *Guide*, pp. 372–383; *Harvard Guide*, Ch. 23.

7TH, 8TH, AND 9TH ED. REFS. See BIBLIOGRAPHICAL ADDENDUM, p. 1,004.

---

[15] *Cong. Record*, 55 Cong., 2 sess., appendix, p. 549 (June 14, 1898). See also T. A. Bailey, "The United States and Hawaii during the Spanish-American War," *Amer. Hist. Rev.*, XXXVI (1931), 552-560.

Anglo-American Tensions and the Venezuela Crisis

*In English eyes the United States was then [1895]
so completely a negligible quantity that it was believed only words the equivalent of blows would
be really effective.*

RICHARD OLNEY, 1912

THE ANATOMY OF ANGLOPHOBIA

DURING THE LATE 1880's and early 1890's Anglophobia was still a powerful emotional force in American political life. The old embers of hatred were being constantly stirred by anti-British textbooks, by patriotic juvenile fiction, and by Fourth of July "orators of the day," who annually and perspiringly berated King George III. Thomas Marshall, later Vice-President from Indiana, remembered how small boys chanted on Independence Day:

> Fee, fi, fo, fum,
> I smell the blood of an Englishman;
> Dead or alive, I'll have some.
> Fee, fi, fo, fum.[1]

Hundreds of thousands of Americans firmly believed that big-navy Britain was an arrogant land-grabber; that she was striving to monopolize the world's commerce; that she was a hardfisted creditor who held the republic's financial destinies in her grasp; and that she was flooding America with gold in an effort to bribe the United States into forsaking tariff protection. This last accusation was persistently hammered home by high-tariff Republicans against the tariff-for-revenue Democrats.

Whatever the truth of such charges, no one could deny that during these years John Bull was the leading champion of the gold standard.

---

[1] *Recollections of Thomas R. Marshall* (Indianapolis, 1925), p. 125.

This was the period when millions of the despairing masses of America were turning to free silver as a cure for their economic ills, and they bitterly resented the policy of the supercilious and monocled British. Senator Chandler of New Hampshire was reportedly advocating "a war with England, with or without cause, in the interests of silver." William H. Harvey's "Coin's Financial School," the most effective free-silver pamphlet of the period, declared that war with England would be the most "popular" and "just war ever waged by man."

Immigrants from Ireland, nursing long-lived grievances, contributed their share to the festering ill will. From 1876 to the close of the century the Presidential elections were all close; and the Irish, who were congested in pivotal Eastern cities like New York and Boston, had to be cultivated. In the campaign of 1896, for example, the Republicans solicited Irish support for their candidate with a pamphlet entitled, "How McKinley is hated in England." Legislative bodies, as well as the national nominating conventions of both parties, repeatedly came out in favor of Irish independence—as if that were legitimate business of the United States. Even the State Department was not above catering to the Irish vote by giving the Lion's tail a vigorous twist on the eve of Presidential elections. Fortunately, the British statesmen were not wholly ignorant of this low type of electioneering, and they braced themselves for it.

THE ANCIENT GRUDGE GROWS WEAKER

Happily, certain ties were beginning to bind the British and American people closer together. The increasing democratization of England was bringing about a stronger feeling of kinship. The assassination of President Garfield, in 1881, shocked the British and elicited from them expressions of good will pleasing to America. In the same year the centennial of the British surrender at Yorktown was celebrated with a commendable display of good sportsmanship. The long and respected reign of Queen Victoria, who had many admirers in the United States, also made for a happier feeling. Educated Americans held the writers of Victorian England in high esteem, and when in 1888 James Bryce published his penetrating classic, *The American Commonwealth*, the American people were gratified to find that a Britisher could appreciate their good qualities. For their part, the English authors were delighted when, in 1891, Congress belatedly passed the law making possible an international copyright.

Other signs of the times were favorable to amity. The defeat in 1896 of the Democratic candidate for the Presidency, William Jennings Bryan, whose free silver heresy had caused widespread alarm among British investors, contributed substantially to a better understanding. The great increase in trans-Atlantic travel, in part a result of improvements in steam navigation, led to important Anglo-American friendships. Many of these were developed among key literary figures—what the humorist Artemus Ward called the *"Atlantic Monthly* fellers"—with a consequent warming of the handclasp across the sea. Nor should one fail to note that another strong bond was the high respect that members of the American bar entertained for British legal principles.

THE BRITISH-VENEZUELA BOUNDARY EMBROILMENT

Such was the general atmosphere in 1893, when Grover Cleveland became President for the second time. The attention of Washington had already been drawn to a boundary dispute between British Guiana and Venezuela. The area in question had considerable strategic value, partic-

ularly to the Venezuelans, for it guarded the mouth of the Orinoco, their most important river. As far back as 1840 the British government had commissioned Sir Robert Schomburgk to ascertain the true boundary. Although he made a careful survey, the Venezuelans refused to accept his line, and the dispute dragged on without prospect of settlement.[2]

But the British were not greatly bothered by the dispute. They had territory the world over; the jungle-matted area meant much less to them than to Venezuela; and they were powerful enough to force an adjustment in their own good time. But on several different occasions, they did offer to settle on the Schomburgk line, with one additional concession: they would yield Point Barima, which commanded the Orinoco. The Venezuelans, who extravagantly hoped for much more, spurned this overture. The British thereupon withdrew their offer. The Foreign Office seems to have lost interest in concession after the discovery of new gold deposits in the disputed area.

[2] P. R. Fossum, "The Anglo-Venezuelan Boundary Controversy," *Hispanic Amer. Hist. Rev.*, VIII (1928), 299–329.

Throughout these years Venezuela repeatedly insisted on arbitration. But as her claims were grossly inflated, and as arbiters are sometimes inclined to split the difference, Downing Street declined the offer. London was unwilling to expose some 40,000 British subjects, who were enjoying the stability of Anglo-Saxon institutions, to the hazard of Venezuelan misrule. Hence England, though unwilling to yield any of the area she had long held, roughly east of the Schomburgk line, was prepared to arbitrate her considerable claims west of that line. In 1887 the disgruntled Venezuelans abruptly suspended diplomatic relations with London— a rash act that made a peaceful adjustment with Great Britain all the more difficult.

Venezuela was probably strengthened in her defiant attitude because she could be sure of the sympathetic support of the United States in any clash with Britain. The Venezuelan minister in Washington repeatedly presented his case to the American authorities in such a way as to leave the impression that England was the wanton aggressor, while his nation was wholly without guile. He invoked the name of the "immortal Monroe," and strongly urged the United States to use its good offices to bring about arbitration. The preoccupied British, on the other hand, failed to present their case as actively in Washington.

The State Department, responding to the proddings of the Venezuelan minister, repeatedly brought to Britain's attention the desirability of an amicable settlement. In 1887 it formally suggested arbitration. But London, for the reasons indicated, declined America's good offices. The issue remained suspended in mid-air.

CLEVELAND PREPARES TO BEARD THE LION

President Cleveland gradually began to develop a keen interest in the Venezuela quarrel. He had no reason to love England, especially after the Sackville-West incident, which may have cost him re-election in 1888. The Venezuela question looked to him like just another case of "hoggish" land-grabbing at the expense of a weak nation. His sympathies naturally went out to the underdog, as Queen Liliuokalani could attest, and he was annoyed because Downing Street refused to respond with cordiality to America's overtures.

The boundary dispute entered upon a new phase when the Venezuelan government employed as its propagandist William L. Scruggs, a former minister to Venezuela under the Harrison regime. Scruggs prepared a clever pamphlet, entitled "British Aggressions in Venezuela, or the Monroe Doctrine on Trial," which he began to distribute in the autumn of 1894. This booklet, which quickly ran through four editions and was sold on newsstands, fell into the hands of editors, governors, Congressmen, and other leaders of opinion. Scruggs also sought out his Congressman, who introduced a resolution urging arbitration of the dispute. Early in

1895 this declaration was adopted unanimously by both houses of Congress.

A new complication arose in April, 1895, in connection with Nicaragua. The British, seeking to collect damages growing out of recent disorders, forcibly occupied the port of Corinto and seized the custom house. Although the local government promptly agreed to pay reparations and the British force was withdrawn, all this activity was too close to the proposed Isthmian waterway for comfort. Amid clamor in the American press that the Monroe Doctrine "is a scarecrow that scares no one but the feeble minded," two state legislative bodies condemned Cleveland for his lack of patriotic spirit. This outburst of criticism, coming so soon after the hauling down of Old Glory in Hawaii, may have helped prod him into more energetic measures elsewhere.

The Cleveland administration could hardly fail to note the mounting chorus of protest against Britain's course regarding Venezuela. Editorials and articles were crying for action. Young Senator Henry Cabot Lodge of Massachusetts, a Republican and a leading Anglophobe, was writing for the *North American Review:*

> If Great Britain is to be permitted to occupy the ports of Nicaragua and, still worse, take the territory of Venezuela, there is nothing to prevent her taking the whole of Venezuela or any other South American state. If Great Britain can do this with impunity, France and Germany will do it also. . . . The supremacy of the Monroe Doctrine should be established and at once —peaceably if we can, forcibly if we must.[3]

It is quite evident that if Cleveland did not give the Lion's tail a good old-fashioned twist, and get credit for it, the jingoes—including Republicans—might do so themselves and take credit for it.

OLNEY REWRITES MONROE'S DOCTRINE

Secretary of State Olney, an obstinate and unbending Boston barrister, was descended from a stern line of New England Puritans. He had made his mark as an aggressive railroad attorney, and this experience had not been the best training for conducting delicate diplomatic correspondence. The defiant note that he drafted regarding Venezuela impressed Cleveland favorably, though the latter "softened" the "verbiage" here and there.

The main theme of Olney's bombshell, which went to London under date of July 20, 1895, was that Britain was violating the Monroe Doctrine. This ancient dictum, Olney held, meant that any European [British] interference in the affairs of the New World [Venezuela] would be regarded as an unfriendly act. The American people were vitally interested

[3] *North American Review*, CLX, 658 (June, 1895).

in the Venezuela boundary dispute because they could not permit any flouting or weakening of the Doctrine that had served them so well. Downing Street was asked, therefore, to declare categorically whether it would or would not submit the dispute to arbitration.

To suggest that the United States could insist on the arbitration of any New World dispute growing out of European interference was certainly enough to make Monroe writhe in his grave. Olney would have been on firmer ground, but not too firm ground, if he had regarded the alleged attempt of the British to push their boundary into Venezuela as a violation of Monroe's noncolonization dictum. If the bellicose Secretary had stated this argument concisely and temperately, in language appropriate for diplomatic intercourse, the British could hardly have taken serious offense.

But the note was neither temperate nor concise. The tone was swaggering, even belligerent. Olney denied that he was passing judgment on the merits of the case, but he had obviously drawn his data from Venezuelan sources. There were glaring inaccuracies in his impeachment of Britain's conduct, and in his historical analysis of Monroe's views. In a startling outburst, Olney stated that as a result of the operations of the Monroe Doctrine:

> To-day the United States is practically sovereign on this continent, and its fiat is law upon the subjects to which it confines its interposition. Why? It is not . . . because wisdom and justice and equity are the invariable characteristics of the dealings of the United States. It is because, in addition to all other grounds, its infinite resources combined with its isolated position render it master of the situation and practically invulnerable as against any or all other powers.[4]

Hereafter, Olney no doubt thought, England would sit up and listen respectfully when the United States suggested arbitration.

SALISBURY'S BORED ANSWER

Cleveland, who later dubbed Olney's note a "twenty-inch gun" blast, was confident that the British would be startled into a prompt reply. Olney had in fact concluded by expressing the hope that an answer would be forthcoming before Congress met in December. But Downing Street was maddeningly deliberate. The American press seethed with rumors; the *New York Herald* ran big headlines about a ninety-day ultimatum to Britain. Still there was no answer when Congress met. The Chaplain of the House, reflecting the belligerent mood of the members, prayed: "Heavenly Father, let peace reign throughout our borders. Yet may we be quick to resent anything like an insult to this our nation."[5] When

---

[4] *Foreign Relations, 1895*, I, 558 (Olney to Bayard, July 20, 1895).
[5] *Cong. Record*, 54 Cong., 1 sess., p. 26 (Dec. 3, 1895).

the British reply was at length forthcoming, after an interval of four months, Cleveland's patience had worn thin.

Why the delay? First of all the American note was 10,000 words long, and raised issues that required careful study. Lord Salisbury's government was not only fully occupied at home, but was confronted with pressing problems abroad, notably in the Near East. The amiable and somewhat pro-British Thomas Bayard, United States Ambassador in London, failed to impress upon Lord Salisbury the seriousness of the American mood. Finally, the British had come to expect a "tail-twister" on the eve of a Presidential election, and they probably thought that they were dealing with another "Jingo Jim" Blaine.

Lord Salisbury, one of the most distinguished statesmen of the century, was fully as inflexible as Olney and Cleveland. The essence of his reply, embodied in two notes dated November 26, 1895, was that the seventy-two year old Monroe Doctrine was not applicable to modern conditions, that it was not recognized as international law, and that it was not relevant to a boundary controversy. Salisbury insisted:

> The disputed frontier of Venezuela has nothing to do with any of the questions dealt with by President Monroe. It is not a question of the colonization by a European Power of any portion of America. It is not a question of the imposition upon the communities of South America of any system of government devised in Europe. It is simply the determination of the frontier of a British possession which belonged to the Throne of England long before the Republic of Venezuela came into existence.[6]

Great Britain could not, Salisbury concluded, accept Olney's proposal that the issue be referred to arbitration. In short, it was none of America's "damned business," as many Englishmen felt.

Whatever the legal merits of Salisbury's argument—and on the whole he had a strong case—there can be no doubt that he erred in underestimating the devotion of the American people to the Monroe Doctrine. Nor was the tone of his reply such as to pour oil on the waters. There was about it a note of "civil indifference with just a touch of boredom." The noble lord corrected the obvious historical errors in Olney's composition much as a learned professor would pick to pieces a college freshman's theme. The British answer, moreover, had a disquieting tone of finality. Olney had asked England if she would arbitrate. She had replied flatly, "No."

Salisbury seems to have committed a serious diplomatic error when he failed to keep the door open by making some kind of counterproposal, or even by inviting further discussion. As it was, Olney and Cleveland were left in a highly embarrassing position. They either had to admit that they had thrust their noses into somebody else's business or else plunge straight ahead.

[6] *Foreign Relations, 1895*, I, 564–565 (Salisbury to Pauncefote. Nov. 26, 1895).

A JINGOISTIC DEBAUCH

When Cleveland read the Salisbury response he felt, according to an intimate friend, "mad clear through." He sat up all night redrafting a message which the ruffled Olney had already outlined. On December 17, 1895, the President sent this smashing pronouncement to Congress.

Cleveland took sharp issue with Salisbury's interpretation of the Monroe Doctrine. He especially deplored the rebuff of his friendly attempt to end this dispute—a dispute that might eventuate in war and jeopardize the peace of the American people. Thus far, he added, the Washington government had not undertaken to pass upon the merits of the controversy; but the time had now come when it must determine where the line should be drawn. Cleveland therefore urged Congress to pass an appropriation for the expenses of an investigating commission. When the report was completed, the United States "must resist by every means in its power" any attempt by Britain to exercise jurisdiction over territory that "we have determined of right belongs to Venezuela." Cleveland concluded by asserting that he was "fully alive to the responsibility incurred, and keenly realize[d] all the consequences that may follow." In brief, he was soberly recommending that the United States run the boundary line itself, and, if necessary, fight to maintain it.[7]

Cleveland's two-fisted message swept Congress off its feet. The House cheered these fighting words to the echo, while the ordinarily sedate Senate burst into applause. Members of both parties, including some bitter critics of Cleveland, were unstinting in their praise. Congress promptly, enthusiastically, and unanimously appropriated $100,000 for the expenses of the boundary commission.

War seemed possible, even probable. Many patriots thought it desirable. Senator Stewart, from the silver state of Nevada, insisted that "war would be a good thing," even if the United States lost, "for it would rid the country of the English bank rule." Other members of Congress argued that hostilities would submerge the economic and social discontent of the country. Yet few stopped to realize that the nation had negligible coast defenses, and that Britain, though heavily involved elsewhere, had thirty-two vessels of the battleship class to five for America. Curiously enough, Cleveland undertook no vigorous military or naval preparations—a circumstance that suggested a bluff on his part.

A wave of jingoism swept over the entire country. Public men in all walks of life applauded. Twenty-six of twenty-eight governors who were approached promised their support. Civil War veterans offered their services. The Irish National Alliance pledged 100,000 volunteers. The virile young Theodore Roosevelt hoped that if there was a "muss," he

[7] *Ibid.*, I, 545 (Dec. 17, 1895).

might "have a hand in it myself." "Personally," he wrote, "I rather hope that the fight will come soon. The clamor of the peace faction has convinced me that this country needs a war." [8] The *New York Sun* carried the headline, "WAR IF NECESSARY."

HANDS ACROSS THE SEA

Fortunately, the voices of moderation were not completely drowned by the wild outburst, which began to subside after about three days. The clergy, in particular, exercised a strong restraining hand. The Reverend Dr. Millington, of Newark, believed that "all South America is not worth a drop of blood," while a convocation of Baptist ministers declared that the United States might better go to war to save the Armenians from the Turks. Peace societies on both sides of the Atlantic also labored manfully. Students of international law, like John Bassett Moore, found America's position untenable, while intellectuals, like Edwin L. Godkin, editor of the *New York Nation*, condemned Cleveland's stand.

Financial interests also acted as a powerful brake on jingoism. The sensation created by Cleveland's message caused American securities to tumble in value approximately a half billion dollars. The New York Chamber of Commerce passed resolutions deploring the "war craze." Other financial leaders, whom the red-blooded Theodore Roosevelt condemned as "patriots of the ticker," voiced similar views.

Perhaps the individual who did the most to quiet the uproar was Joseph Pulitzer, enterprising editor of the *New York World*. His journal insisted:

> There is no menace in the boundary line, it is not our frontier, it is none of our business. To make it such without cause, and to raise the spectre of war over a false sentiment and a false conception is something more than a grave blunder. If persisted in, it will be a colossal crime.[9]

Pulitzer cabled a number of prominent Englishmen, including the Prince of Wales, the Duke of York, and William E. Gladstone, seeking their views on the crisis. The replies were uniformly conciliatory and expressive of warm friendship for America, and consequently their publication had a steadying effect on public opinion.

The British, a vast majority of whom had never heard of the Venezuela dispute before, either had to back down or fight. And why should they humiliate themselves by backing down when their navy was in a position

---

[8] *Selections from the Correspondence of Theodore Roosevelt and Henry Cabot Lodge, 1884–1918* (New York, 1925), I, 204–205 (Roosevelt to Lodge, Dec. 27, 1895). Roosevelt also wrote: "Let the fight come if it must; I don't care whether our sea coast cities are bombarded or not; we would take Canada." *Ibid.*, I, 200 (Roosevelt to Lodge, Dec. 20, 1895).

[9] *New York World*, Dec. 21, 1895, quoted in J. E. Wisan, *The Cuban Crisis as Reflected in the New York Press, 1895–1898* (New York, 1934), p. 23 n.

to lay waste the coastal cities of the United States? The jingoes, the fire-eaters, and the "Rule Britannia" class—who fortunately did not constitute a majority—were all for flogging the insolent Yankee. One irate Tory declared that "no dog of a Republican can open its mouth to bark without our good leave. . . ."

The main reason why war did not result probably was that the great mass of the British people did not want to fight. They regarded as "unthinkable" a war with the United States over a few thousand square miles of mosquito-infested jungle land.[10] Protestations of esteem for America were heard at every hand. A total of 354 members of the House of Commons signed a memorial urging arbitration of all future disputes. Thirteen hundred British authors sent an appeal to America urging a peaceful settlement. Eight hundred English workingmen adopted a resolution beseeching their government to arbitrate the quarrel, for "a war between England and the United States of America would be a crime against the laws of God and man; and would cause unspeakable misery to the peoples of both countries."[11]

BRITAIN BENDS THE KNEE

England's position, though strong, was not without serious weaknesses. As usual, Canada was vulnerable to invasion, and the British merchant marine was vulnerable to Yankee privateers. Furthermore, Britain's flank, in the event of war with the United States, would be turned to Europe. And there she had no allies and few friends. The rapid rise of a united and powerful Germany had already begun to cause real anxiety.

By a striking coincidence, British attention was diverted by Germany at this very time. Britain was having serious trouble with the Dutch-descended Boers of South Africa, and an impulsive Englishman by the name of Dr. Jameson led an unauthorized raiding party against them. The Boers forced the expedition to surrender, and on January 3, 1896, the Kaiser sent a telegram to President Kruger, the Boer leader, congratulating him on having repelled the invader "without appealing to the help of friendly powers [i.e., Germany]. . . ."[12]

This uncalled-for slap caused the British to rise in furious resentment. "Yankee Doodle" was cheered in London music halls, while "Die Wacht am Rhein" was hissed. Although the Anglo-American crisis appears to have passed its peak when the Kaiser blundered in, the telegram to Kruger definitely blunted British anger toward America. It also reminded

[10] Jennie A. Sloan, "Anglo-American Relations and the Venezuelan Boundary Dispute," *Hispanic Amer. Hist. Rev.*, XVIII (1938), 495–496.

[11] Bayard to Olney, Dec. 31, 1895 (enclosure), Department of State, *Despatches, Great Britain*, CLXXXI (National Archives).

[12] W. L. Langer, *The Diplomacy of Imperialism, 1890–1902* (New York, 1935), I, 237.

Britain that Germany lay on her flank, and made concession to the United States more palatable. Europe's discords were still operating to America's advantage.

The months of wearisome negotiation that followed the Kruger telegram finally produced a settlement. The British, now revealing a conciliatory disposition, co-operated commendably in providing the Amer-

PEACE PUDDING

BROTHER JONATHAN: "What do you think of it, Johnnie?"
BROTHER JOHN BULL: "Well, it's better than your beastly *humble pie* anyhow!"

The British prefer arbitration to humiliation.
London Punch, 1896

ican boundary commission with data. As a result of the good offices of the United States, representatives of Venezuela and Britain signed a treaty in February, 1897, although not until Secretary Olney, with a fine show of impartiality, had twisted the arms of the Venezuelans. The new pact provided for the submission of the dispute to an arbitral board, but significantly exempted from arbitration those areas that had been held by either party over a fifty-year period. Britain, from the very first, had steadfastly refused to expose her subjects east of the Schomburgk line to an arbitral body, and even in apparent defeat she won her main contention.

The decision of the arbiters was not handed down until October, 1899, two and a half years later, when public interest had largely flickered out. The settlement generally followed the Schomburgk line, with two important exceptions. First, Venezuela secured a considerable area at the southern end; secondly, and much more significant, she obtained control of the mouth of the Orinoco. This whole arrangement, curiously enough, was not badly out of line with what Britain had several times offered the Venezuelans. Such was the diplomatic victory that Cleveland won after skating perilously close to the abyss of war.

CALM AFTER THE VENEZUELA SQUALL

Frock-coat diplomacy finds little to commend in the unorthodox Cleveland-Olney technique. It was crude, blustering, bellicose. It involved an extreme interpretation of the Monroe Doctrine, and seemed far afield from any direct concern of the United States. It gave a costly shock to the nation's wobbly financial structure. It further accelerated a rising jingoistic spirit. Curiously enough, the anti-imperialistic Cleveland may unintentionally have been one of the real fathers of American imperialism. Finally, the top-dog pretensions of the United States in the New World aroused a vast amount of ill will in Continental Europe, especially Germany, and did much to determine the hostile attitude of these powers during the Spanish-American War.

Yet substantial gains were chalked up. The Venezuelan danger spot, which might have involved the United States if the two disputants had gone to war, was at long last erased. The prestige of the United States was enormously enhanced when the British lion slunk away with "his much-twisted tail between his legs." Perhaps this incident—not the Spanish-American War—should date the recognition of America as a great power. Finally, the outcome immeasurably strengthened the Monroe Doctrine. "Never again," exulted the *Chicago Journal*, "will a European nation put forth claims to American territory without consulting the government of the United States." [13]

In Latin America, the books showed both profit and loss. The weaker republics generally applauded the protective position of the United States; the stronger ones resented the pretensions of Cleveland and Olney to hemispheric overlordship. Venezuela, which had at first welcomed Yankee intervention, reacted angrily after being forced into a settlement that on the whole favored England. Yet when Cleveland died in 1908, many Latin-American flags were lowered to half staff.

[13] *Public Opinion*, XXI, 647 (Nov. 19, 1890).

The most encouraging result of the Venezuela flare-up was the vast improvement in Anglo-American relations. The Americans were pleased when John Bull knuckled under to Cleveland. The British, astonished by the outburst of Anglophobia, were impressed with the necessity of cultivating friendly relations. The Kaiser's blundering telegram spotlighted the inadequacy of Britain's policy of "splendid isolation," and the desirability of seeking friends, if not allies. So the protracted period of America's "twisting the lion's tail" was followed by one of England's "patting the eagle's head." British statesmen now went out of their way to cultivate America. The path was thus smoothed for the highly important understanding between Great Britain and the United States at the end of the century.

THE SENATE REBUFFS ARBITRATION

The Venezuela dispute, though stimulating militarism and navalism, gave strong impetus to the peaceful settlement of disputes. Many right-thinking people on both sides perceived that if machinery for such purposes had existed, Britain and America would not have slithered so close to the edge of war. The upshot was the negotiation by Secretary Olney, in January, 1897, of a general arbitration treaty with Britain.[14]

President McKinley, who inherited the pact, threw his weight behind it, as did a large body of opinion throughout the country. Most of the enthusiasm was spontaneous, but some of it was deliberately cultivated by propagandists for peace and arbitration. Senatorial desks groaned with hundreds of petitions, letters, and telegrams from church congresses, bar associations, universities, women's groups, and businessmen's organizations—all the "best people." The *Omaha World-Herald* waxed ecstatic when it declared that the treaty was "one of the grandest triumphs of humanity." Only a relatively few newspapers raised dissenting voices, and they were joined by a considerable number of Irish clubs and societies. Voices at mass meetings cried in a thick brogue, "Hurrah for war!" and "To Hell with England!"

The Senate, unswayed by this upsurge of popular sentiment, and critical of hand-tieing arbitration pacts, went methodically about its business. First, it disemboweled the treaty by attaching a series of amendments which would exempt certain questions from arbitration, and which would require a two-thirds vote of the Senate before submitting any other dispute. Then, after draining so much of the life out of the pact that it was scarcely an arbitration treaty at all, the Senate showed its mettle by rejecting the "miserable remnant" in May, 1897, by a count of 43 to 26. A change of three votes would have insured the necessary two-thirds.

[14] See N. M. Blake, "The Olney-Pauncefote Treaty of 1897," *Amer. Hist. Rev.*, L (1945), 228–243; also W. S. Holt, *Treaties Defeated by the Senate* (Baltimore, 1933).

A curious mixture of motives influenced the final decision. The Senate, ever jealous of its prerogatives, would not allow vital questions affecting foreign policy to slip out of its hands into those of an arbitral board. Deep-rooted Anglophobia, which had resisted the recent blandishments of the British, played a conspicuous part. The heated Bryan-McKinley Presidential campaign of 1896, with free silver the leading issue, had aroused animosities, and the silverites had condemned lordly Britain as the bulwark of the gold standard. A considerable number of the Senators who voted against the treaty were, quite understandably, silver men.

Finally, the Irish, who hoped to snatch their independence from the fiery furnace of an Anglo-American war, were not friendly to arbitration. Many of them feared that an arbitration treaty would be the forerunner of an alliance, and on the day of the final vote two Irish nationalists, one a member of the British Parliament, were working hard in the Senate lobby to defeat the pact. The *Boston Pilot* boasted:

> Had Irish-Americanism anything to do with the failure of the English arbitration treaty? We trust so, and believe so. We should be very much ashamed of our fellow citizens of Irish blood if they had not done their utmost to baffle the attempt to place this republic before the world as a mere colony of Great Britain.[15]

The rejection of the treaty came as a blow to peace lovers, even though the debate did much to popularize arbitration. The stubbornness of the Senate again revealed how a strongly entrenched minority can successfully defy an articulate public opinion. Yet the outcome did not materially dampen the newly found British friendliness for America. The United States was potentially too useful to let a little thing like the Senate stand in the way. On the eve of the Spanish-American War, Britain, alone of the European powers, was ready to cheer America down the slippery path of imperialism.

SELECTED BIBLIOGRAPHY

A sketch of Olney appears in S. F. Bemis, ed., *The American Secretaries of State and their Diplomacy* (New York, 1928), VIII, 273–325. Detailed treatments of the Venezuela dispute may be found in Dexter Perkins, *The Monroe Doctrine, 1867–1907* (Baltimore, 1937); C. C. Tansill, *The Foreign Policy of Thomas F. Bayard, 1885–1897* (New York, 1940); A. L. P. Dennis, *Adventures in American Diplomacy, 1896–1906* (New York, 1928). See also Allan Nevins, *Grover Cleveland* (New York, 1934) and G. R. Dulebohn, *Principles of Foreign Policy under the Cleveland Administrations* (Philadelphia, 1941). A useful survey is F. R. Dulles, *The Imperial Years* (New York, 1956). Helpful articles are W. S. Robertson, "Hispanic American Appreciations of the Monroe Doctrine," *Hispanic Amer. Hist. Rev.*, III (1920), 1–16; J. F. Rippy, "Some Contemporary Mexican Reactions to Cleveland's Venezuelan

---

[15] *Literary Digest*, XV, 140 (May 29, 1897).

Message," *Pol. Sci. Quar.*, XXXIX (1924), 280–292; N. M. Blake, "Background of Cleveland's Venezuelan Policy," *Amer. Hist. Rev.*, XLVII (1942), 259–277; T. C. Smith, "Secretary Olney's Real Credit in the Venezuela Affair," Mass. Hist. Soc. *Procs.*, LXV (1933), 112–147; G. B. Young, "Intervention under the Monroe Doctrine: the Olney Corollary," *Pol. Sci. Quar.*, LVII (1942), 247–280; Otto Schoenrich, "The Venezuela-British Guiana Boundary Dispute," *Amer. Jour. of Internat. Law*, XLIII (1949), 523–530; C. J. Child, "The Venezuela-British Guiana Boundary Arbitration of 1899," *ibid.*, XLIV (1950), 682–693; W. C. Dennis, "The Venezuela-British Guiana Boundary Arbitration of 1899," *ibid.*, pp. 720–727.

See footnotes of this chapter; Bemis and Griffin, *Guide*, pp. 429–436; *Harvard Guide*, Ch. 23.

7TH ED. REFS. E. R. May, *Imperial Democracy* (New York, 1961) considers the Hawaii annexation agitation and the popular concern over Armenian massacres as a prelude to the Venezuela outburst. Previous to this time Britain had slighted the Americans as a factor in the balance of power; now, because of her heavy naval commitments elsewhere, she was not in a strong position to meet the American Navy or to defend Canada. "In effect, Cleveland and Olney startled England and the United States into one another's arms" (p. 267). A. E. Campbell, *Great Britain and the United States, 1895–1903* (London, 1960) deals with the Venezuela crisis from the British point of view; Britain made almost all the concessions, "and all the important ones" (p. 27). The British navy, though much larger, was spread too thin to meet the United States effectively. F. P. Summers, ed., *The Cabinet Diary of William L. Wilson, 1896–1897* (Chapel Hill, N.C., 1957) reveals that, in the opinion of the Postmaster General, Cleveland's Venezuelan vigor had helped the Democratic party politically, and that Olney had won a great victory in the negotiations. Water LaFeber, "United States Depression Diplomacy and the Brazilian Revolution, 1893–1894," *Hispanic Amer. Hist. Rev.*, XL (1960), 107–118 argues that the depression-cursed Cleveland administration feared that the insurgents, under British influence, might terminate the favorable commercial treaty. Washington therefore broke the back of the uprising by sending in superior naval forces. Walter LaFeber, "The Background of Cleveland's Venezuelan Policy: A Reinterpretation," *Amer. Hist. Rev.*, LXVI (1961), 947–967 sees Cleveland acting, not in response to his own bellicosity or to jingo pressures, but to protect American strategic and economic interests in a depression year. Walter LaFeber, "The American Business Community and Cleveland's Venezuelan Message," *Business History Review*, XXXIV (1960), 393–402 contends that only a minority of the business and financial world, chiefly in New York, condemned the message. The author calls for a re-examination of the thesis that big business opposed the Spanish War and imperialism.

8TH ED. REFS. See BIBLIOGRAPHICAL ADDENDUM, p. 1,006.

The Coming of the War with Spain, 1895-1898

We are all jingoes now; and the head jingo is the Hon. William McKinley, the trusted and honored Chief Executive of the nation's will.
NEW YORK SUN, April 20, 1898

SMOKE-CLOUDED CUBA

As THE 19TH CENTURY neared its sunset, the American people were showing unmistakable signs of a desire for a larger stage. The Samoan and Hawaiian adventures revealed a rising spirit of imperialism, while the Venezuela outburst further inflamed fevered imaginations. The republic had fought no real war since 1865, no foreign war since 1848. A younger generation was coming on—a generation tired of hearing about the deeds of its sires and uninitiated in the horrors of battle. By 1897 the country was definitely recovering from the Panic of 1893 and from the Venezuela scare, and prosperity was going to its head. Expand or explode is a fundamental law—and America, bursting with power, was prepared to follow its dictates, especially where commercial profits beckoned.

Cuba proved to be the spark that set off the powder magazine. The "Ever-Faithful Isle," long restive under Spanish misrule, was already ripe for revolt when it received an additional slap from the outside. The American tariff of 1894, by placing relatively high duties on sugar, visited the island with economic prostration. Early in 1895, the unhappy Cubans unfurled the flag of rebellion.

The insurgents, who were hardly less ruthless than the Spaniards, deliberately adopted a "scorched earth" policy—that is, devastating the island so mercilessly that Spain would be glad to pull out. The Americans who had invested about $50 million in Cuba were caught in the middle. The *insurrectos* put the torch to Yankee property in the hope that the

United States would be forced to intervene, or spared it when the owners paid the necessary protection money. This species of blackmail was, in fact, one of the principal methods of financing the revolt.[1] Bands of insurgents also resorted to such desperate expedients as dynamiting passenger trains. But Cuban propaganda, disseminated by refugees in New York and elsewhere, glossed over the seamy side of the rebel cause and painted the Spanish "butchers" in the blackest possible hues. Horrified America, traditionally friendly to liberty, democracy, and the banishment of monarchy from the Americas, thrilled to the cry, *Cuba Libre!*

The Cuban revolutionists capitalized on American sympathy by using the United States as a base for gun-running expeditions. The vigilance of the federal authorities prevented about two-thirds of these ventures from reaching their destinations. But the Spaniards did not appreciate Washington's semisuccessful efforts, and charged, with considerable truth, that only assistance from the United States kept the revolt alive.

THE CUBAN BELLIGERENCY CRAZE

Clouds of smoke from charred cane fields continued to roll over the island. In desperation, Madrid decided upon more energetic measures, and it sent General Weyler to Cuba early in 1896. After surveying the debris, he concluded that the uprising could never be suppressed while the countryside teemed with civilians who secretly aided the rebels. He therefore ordered the populace to be kenneled in barbed-wire reconcentration camps. In the absence of proper hygienic precautions, the unfortunate victims, chiefly women and children, died by the tens of thousands. The American people, outraged by the inhumanity of reconcentration, began to demand with increasing vigor that this nuisance off their very doors be abated. The logical first step seemed to be official recognition of the shadowy Cuban government. But President Cleveland, who referred privately to the "rascally Cubans," set his face against the mounting clamor.

Congress took the bull by the horns early in 1896, when it overwhelmingly passed a resolution favoring recognition of Cuban belligerency. The accompanying debates were so intemperate as to touch off anti-American riots in Spain. In Barcelona a mob of 15,000, shouting "down with the American pig killers," stoned the United States consulate and tore up the American flag. There were counterdemonstrations in America by Princeton University students and Leadville miners, while the Youngstown Chamber of Commerce voted to boycott the Spanish onion. But flinty Grover Cleveland, who regarded the belligerency reso-

---

[1] J. T. Adams remembers that a large sugar estate in which he was interested paid bribes running as high as $10,000. J. T. Adams, *The Epic of America* (Boston, 1931), p. 335.

lution as an attempt to embarrass the Democrats on the eve of a Presidential election, refused to budge. Resenting Congressional interference with the Executive's conduct of foreign affairs, he privately remarked that if Congress should declare war on Spain he, as commander-in-chief, would not mobilize the army.

During the ensuing months, popular enthusiasm for Cuba waned considerably. Behind the scenes Secretary Olney fruitlessly proposed mediation to Spain, while Madrid unsuccessfully attempted to head off possible American intervention by joint-power action. The heated Bryan-McKinley campaign of 1896, during which free silver was the overshadowing issue, temporarily diverted attention from a free Cuba. The month following the election, Cleveland bluntly informed Spain, in his annual message to Congress, that intervention was inevitable if the struggle should continue to degenerate into "senseless slaughter." Three months later he left office, and although the jingo press branded him an "ally of Spain" and as one who would deserve the "damnation of history," he showed genuine courage in withstanding the clamor of the crowd.

YELLOW JOURNALISM AND THE JINGOES

While the revolution in Cuba was running its gory course, a hardly less significant revolution was occurring in American journalism. Late in 1895, wealthy young William Randolph Hearst purchased a staid but fast-failing newspaper, the *New York Journal.* He straightway entered upon a contest for circulation with Joseph Pulitzer's *New York World,* which hitherto had been regarded as the last word in sensationalism. By lurid style, reckless liberties with the truth, imaginative illustrations, screeching headlines, and other devices, Hearst was remarkably successful in his efforts to out-Pulitzer Pulitzer.[2] He "snooped, scooped, and stooped to conquer."

The Cuban conflagration was a godsend to the yellow journals. They burst out in "typographical paroxysms" when disagreeable incidents arose from the attempts of the Spanish authorities to suppress gun-running expeditions. The searching of three Cuban women on a ship flying American colors was reported in Hearst's *Journal* under the headlines, "Does Our Flag Protect Women?" Although the search in this case was conducted by female attendants, the accompanying illustration showed three heavy-handed Spanish officials completely disrobing a comely female in her cabin. The yellow press also stressed the destruction of American property in Cuba, while ignoring the fact that much of the

[2] Notable among the artists that Hearst employed was Frederic Remington, whom he sent to Cuba to draw pictures. Upon arriving the artist allegedly telegraphed: "Everything is quiet. There is no trouble here. There will be no war." Hearst, so the story goes, replied, "You furnish the pictures and I'll furnish the war." J. K. Winkler, *W. R. Hearst* (New York, 1928), p. 144.

damage was done by *insurrectos*. Hearst and Pulitzer also sprang to the defense of imprisoned American citizens, most of whom were naturalized Cubans with embarrassing Spanish names. One of them, a prominent dentist, died in prison after incredibly brutal treatment.

Hearst's *Journal* was not content to get "scoops"; it proceeded to manufacture them. It aroused enormous interest, chiefly among American women, in an imprisoned Cuban girl, Evangelina Cisneros. Although the young woman had evidently been implicated in the revolt, the *Journal* declared that her only crime had been to defend her virtue against the lust of a brutal Spanish officer. With interest in the case at fever heat, a Hearst reporter, acting under orders, spirited Señorita Cisneros from her cell and smuggled her into the United States. The *Journal* gloated in banner headlines, "AN AMERICAN NEWSPAPER ACCOMPLISHES AT A SINGLE STROKE WHAT THE RED TAPE OF DIPLOMACY FAILED UTTERLY TO BRING ABOUT IN MANY MONTHS." [3] The Bishop of London cabled congratulations, while the Governor of Missouri suggested that the *Journal* send down five hundred of its reporters and free the entire island.

The yellow press displayed its greatest inventive genius in reporting atrocity stories. "Butcher" Weyler was called "Wolf" Weyler, a "human hyena," a "mad dog." His men, it was alleged, massacred prisoners or threw them to the sharks; dragged the sick from their cots, shot them, and fed their bodies to the dogs. The *Journal* solemnly asserted:

> It is not only Weyler the soldier . . . but Weyler the brute, the devastator of haciendas, the destroyer of families, and the outrager of women. . . . Pitiless, cold, an exterminator of men. . . . There is nothing to prevent his carnal, animal brain from running riot with itself in inventing tortures and infamies of bloody debauchery.[4]

A correspondent for Pulitzer's *World* reported:

> Blood on the roadsides, blood in the fields, blood on the doorsteps, blood, blood, blood! The old, the young, the weak, the crippled—all are butchered without mercy. . . . Is there no nation wise enough, brave enough, and strong enough to restore peace in this bloodsmitten land? [5]

Conditions in Cuba were undeniably horrible, but many of these atrocity stories, as is almost invariably the case, were grossly exaggerated. Yet the American people were avid for such tales. By 1898 each of the rival "Czars of sensation" was selling over 800,000 newspapers a day; and after Dewey's naval victory at Manila, Hearst's *Journal* shot up to the 1,500,000 mark. Nor was the influence of the yellow press felt only

[3] *New York Journal*, Oct. 10, 1897, p. 1.
[4] *Ibid.*, Feb. 23, 1896, 27:1, 2, 3.
[5] *New York World*, May 17, 1896, 1:8, 2:1.

in New York. A crop of lesser imitators sprang up over the country, using the methods and buying the stories of Hearst and Pulitzer. Many of the old-line newspapers continued their conservative ways, but they paled beside the screaming headlines and journalistic demagoguery of the rival "savants of the sewer."

UNWANTED GUESTS: THE *MAINE* AND DE LÔME

The yellow press, despite its most lurid efforts, was not completely successful in keeping Cuba in the public eye. The rousing free-silver campaign of 1896, together with massacres in Armenia by the Turks, created a diversionary smoke screen. The Republicans returned to power in March, 1897, when the amiable William McKinley took the Presidential oath. In Cuba, the energetic measures of "Butcher" Weyler were producing results, and as the year wore on news from the ravaged island was fast fading from the front page.

A sharp change for the better came late in 1897, when a liberal Spanish ministry assumed power. It recalled Weyler, modified the reconcentration methods, released all American citizens from prison, and granted the Cubans a species of autonomy. But the insurgents spurned the new concessions, while the Spanish sympathizers (loyalists) in Havana flared up in a riot of protest, in January, 1898, amid cries of "Death to Autonomy" and *"Viva Weyler!"* The American press was disturbed by the danger to American lives, and the *Journal* proclaimed, "NEXT TO WAR WITH SPAIN."

The loyalist riots pointed up the desirability of dispatching a battleship to Havana, where it could provide some protection to American lives and property. Although the American consul general reported that ships were not then necessary, the second-class battleship *Maine* was ordered to Cuba, in January, 1898, on a "friendly" visit. Aside from its protective mission, the vessel would presumably impress the Spaniards with the willingness of Washington to take energetic action. Neither the Spanish government nor the loyalists in Cuba were pleased by this gesture. Mark Hanna, President McKinley's mentor, remarked that it was like "waving a match in an oil well for fun."

While the *Maine* lay peacefully at anchor in Havana harbor, a front-page scandal broke. Dupuy de Lôme, Spanish minister in Washington, had written an indiscreet private letter to a friend. Purloined from the mails by a Cuban sympathizer, it had fallen into the hands of Hearst, who, on February 9, 1898, emblazoned it in his *Journal*. The letter not only revealed bad faith in de Lôme's dealings with the United States on pending commercial problems but included a highly offensive analysis of McKinley's recent message to Congress:

Besides the ingrained and inevitable bluntness (*groseria*) with which is repeated all that the press and public opinion in Spain have said about Weyler, it once more shows what McKinley is, weak and a bidder for the admiration of the crowd, besides being a would-be politician (*politicastro*) who tries to leave a door open behind himself while keeping on good terms with the jingoes of his party.[6]

Hearst's "scoop" of the de Lôme letter was the most sensational of the year. Even conservative newspapers agreed that the minister's usefulness was at an end. The *New York Mail and Express* exclaimed: "The necessary preliminaries to his departure cannot be too speedy to satisfy public opinion. . . . Señor de Lôme—the door stands open!"[7] Officially, the incident was closed when Madrid accepted his resignation before the demand for his recall could be presented, but the American public, already inflamed, was slow to forget.

THE MYSTERY OF THE *MAINE*

The de Lôme indiscretion had hardly ceased furnishing a rash of headlines when a supersensation broke—the greatest news story since the assassination of President Garfield in 1881. On February 15, 1898, a terrific explosion sank the *Maine* in Havana harbor with a loss of over 250 officers and men.

It is to the credit of the American people that on the whole they were inclined to suspend judgment, as the captain of the *Maine* urged, pending an official inquiry. This fact is all the more remarkable when one considers the surcharged atmosphere. "A great nation," insisted the *Kansas City Star*, "can afford to take time to be perfectly just."

The yellow journals nevertheless stepped up their production of "war extras." Hearst's headlines blared: "THE WARSHIP MAINE WAS SPLIT IN TWO BY AN ENEMY'S SECRET INFERNAL MACHINE"; "THE WHOLE COUNTRY THRILLS WITH WAR FEVER"; "THE MAINE WAS DESTROYED BY TREACHERY." Three days after the disaster Hearst's *Journal* insisted, "Intervention is a plain and imperative duty."

The exhortations of the sensational press provided additional fuel for jingoism. In Buffalo, three mass meetings urged a declaration of war on Spain. Lehigh University students held daily drills and paraded under the banner, "To Hell with Spain." The Reverend Thomas Dixon elicited cheers from his Christian following when he sermonized against "hesitation, delay, diplomacy and idle talk." The pugnacious Assistant Secretary of the Navy, Theodore Roosevelt, wrote privately: ". . . I would give anything if President McKinley would order the fleet to Havana tomor-

[6] J. B. Moore, *A Digest of International Law* (Washington, 1906), VI, 176.
[7] Feb. 9, 1898, quoted in J. E. Wisan, *The Cuban Crisis as Reflected in the New York Press, 1895–1898* (New York, 1934), p. 383.

row. . . . The *Maine* was sunk by an act of dirty treachery on the part of the Spaniards. . . ."[8]

Responding to the wave of "hearsteria" sweeping the country, Congress, on March 9, 1898, unanimously voted $50 million for war preparations. This gesture, together with other military and naval activities, steeled the Cubans in their determination to hold on and implanted doubts in the Spanish mind as to the sincerity of America's peace professions. Spain, reported the United States minister at Madrid, was "simply stunned."

Oratorical fireworks were now added to the existing combustibles. On March 17, 1898, Senator Proctor of Vermont delivered a sensationally effective speech on Cuba, to which he had gone on a private tour of inspection. His description of several hundred thousand *reconcentrados* was appalling.

> Torn from their homes, with foul earth, foul air, foul water, and foul food or none, what wonder that one-half have died and that one-quarter of the living are so diseased that they cannot be saved? . . . Little children are still walking about with arms and chest terribly emaciated, eyes swollen, and abdomen bloated to three times the natural size. . . . I was told by one of our consuls that they have been found dead about the markets in the morning, where they had crawled, hoping to get some stray bits of food from the early hucksters. . . .[9]

Here was the first-hand report of a respected Senator, and it had a profound effect upon many sober citizens who hitherto had discounted the rantings of the gutter journalists.

SPAIN FOUND GUILTY

The roaring flames received new fuel, on March 28, 1898, with the publication of the official report on the *Maine*. The American Court of Inquiry, consisting of scarcely impartial United States naval officers, concluded that the vessel had been destroyed by a submarine mine. The report made no attempt to fix responsibility. Granting that there had been a mine, it might have been touched off accidentally; it might have been exploded by the Cubans to bring America to their aid; it might have been employed by irresponsible Spanish subalterns or loyalists. The least rational explanation of all is that the Madrid government, which was desperately trying to avert war, had deliberately destroyed the vessel. Nor can one rule out entirely the possibility of an internal explosion: accidents of this kind have occurred on warships with distressing frequency.

But the lid was now off. To the unthinking American masses an external explosion meant only one thing: Spain had treacherously blown

[8] Roosevelt to Diblee, Feb. 16, 1898, Roosevelt Papers, Library of Congress.
[9] *Cong. Record*, 55 Cong., 2 sess., p. 2917.

up the ship in an act, cried Senator Allen, of "wholesale murder." Restraint and suspended judgment were thrown to the winds. The slogan of the hour became:

Remember the *Maine!*
To hell with Spain!

The *New York World* branded the explosion as "an act of war" and demanded, "Are we waiting to be smitten on the other cheek?" It further declared:

Regardless of the question of Cuban independence . . . the DESTRUCTION OF THE MAINE BY FOUL PLAY should be the occasion of ordering our fleet to Havana and *demanding proper amends within forty-eight hours under threat of bombardment.* If Spain will not punish her miscreants, we must punish Spain.[10]

The *Journal* reported the hanging of McKinley in effigy in Durango, Colorado, together with the burning of the Spanish flag by students in Omaha and by a mob in Chicago. "Give Congress a chance to know what the people think," cried Hearst's mouthpiece.

To this day no one knows how the *Maine* was blown up, yet her destruction, quite illogically, was by far the most important single precipitant of war with Spain. Nothing could have brought home to the American republic more forcibly the disordered conditions in Cuba and the proposed solution that the island be freed. The American people no longer reasoned—they felt. Ominously, the Spanish press bristled with insults aimed at the "Yankee pigs," and the masses, ignorant of the odds they faced, seemed athirst for war.

VICTORY ON THE DIPLOMATIC FRONT

The most important single damper on the war spirit during these hectic weeks was the business world. Even though American investors had sunk some $50 million into the turbulent island, and even though annual American trade with Cuba normally ran to about $100 million, the businessmen thus involved were inclined to favor not war but some kind of intervention that would bring an end to the war. Other business interests, more in the eastern centers than in the interior, tended to oppose an armed clash. They feared that hostilities would retard returning prosperity, dislocate the economic structure, produce inflation, and unleash Spanish warships on their shipping.

But the cold-blooded attitude of some shopkeepers was infuriating to the warmongers. "We will have this war for the freedom of Cuba," shouted Theodore Roosevelt, as he shook his fist at Senator Mark Hanna

[10] *New York World,* April 1, 1898, 6:2.

of Ohio, the prototype of big business in politics, "in spite of the timidity of the commercial interests." [11]

President McKinley, a hater of war and a willing servant of the big-business interests, made a determined effort to settle the Cuban problem through the quiet channels of diplomacy. After weeks of wearisome negotiation, the State Department instructed Minister Woodford in Madrid, on March 27, 1898, to ascertain if Spain would consent to the following terms: (1) the granting of an armistice to the insurgents until October 1; (2) immediate revocation of the *reconcentrado* order. Although not an ultimatum, these concessions represented what Washington evidently regarded as the minimum essentials for keeping the peace. A third proposal, envisaging eventual United States mediation (and possible independence) was put in a less imperative category.

The Madrid ministry was in a precarious position. If it yielded too much, it would face revolution at home; if too little, war with the United States abroad. As usual, it shilly-shallied. It proposed submission of the *Maine* question to arbitration, and it agreed to grant an armistice to the Cubans—but only if they would ask for it. This they obviously would not do. Minister Woodford, somewhat discouraged, cabled from Madrid:

> I am told confidentially that the offer of armistice by the Spanish Government would cause revolution here. . . . The ministry have gone as far as they dare go to-day. I believe the ministry are ready to go as far and as fast as they can and still save the dynasty here in Spain. They know that Cuba is lost. Public opinion in Spain has moved steadily toward peace No Spanish ministry would have dared to do one month ago what this ministry has proposed to-day.[12]

Three days later, on April 3, 1898, a rift appeared in the clouds. Woodford learned that the Spanish ministry, responding to the intercession of the Pope, was preparing to grant an armistice. He promptly cabled to McKinley:

> I know that the Queen and her present ministry sincerely desire peace and that the Spanish people desire peace, and if you can still give me time and reasonable liberty of action I will get for you the peace you desire so much and for which you have labored so hard.[13]

Within the next week Spain bent the knee to the two basic American demands. First, the Governor General of Cuba was instructed to revoke reconcentration throughout Cuba. Second, on April 9 came word that the commander of the army was directed to grant an armistice "*for such length of time as he may think prudent* to prepare and facilitate the peace

---

[11] H. F. Pringle, *Theodore Roosevelt* (New York, 1931), p. 179.
[12] *Foreign Relations, 1898*, p. 727 (Woodford to McKinley, March 31, 1898).
[13] *Ibid.*, p. 732 (April 3, 1898).

earnestly desired by all." [14] The passage here italicized constituted a "string," which Spain might have found convenient to pull. But these two concessions were probably as much as Spanish public opinion would have permitted.[15] The armistice was in effect a rejection of McKinley's terms: a true armistice presupposed acceptance by the other side, and this the Cuban insurgents would not grant. Spanish honor would never yield independence without war; yet McKinley and public opinion demanded independence. A proud Spain had made humiliating concessions to a meddling third power, but these were not enough.

PUBLIC PRESSURES ON THE PRESIDENT

The issue now lay in the hands of McKinley. A kindly man who had seen enough bloodshed in the Civil War, he recoiled from the prospect of hostilities. Yet his humanitarian impulses led him to deplore the butchery in Cuba and earnestly desire to have it end. Not until after his death was the fact revealed that he had anonymously contributed $5000 to the sufferers. Spain, moreover, had pursued such a shifty course that he had little faith in her promises, or in her ability to carry them out even if they were sincerely made. It takes two to make an armistice as well as a quarrel; and since the Cuban insurgents had flatly announced that they would not accept the Spanish terms, the war would still go its bloody way.

Even so, the result might well have been different if diplomacy could have been conducted in a vacuum. Madrid was obviously attempting to cut loose from Cuba just as fast as Spanish opinion would permit. But the tidal wave of war sentiment in America, especially after the *Maine* report, would not wait. Within the President's own Republican party a group of young jingoes was making a commotion out of all proportion to its numbers. "McKinley," the bellicose Theodore Roosevelt is reported to have shouted, "has no more backbone than a chocolate eclair!"

The cry for blood was not confined to a few bellicose groups. Following the official report on the *Maine*, the masses were on fire for war. Ex-Confederates, ex-bandits, and Sioux Indians were among those who volunteered for services. Even some religious leaders prayed for hostilities. One Presbyterian journal declared: "And if it be the will of Almighty God, that by war the last trace of this inhumanity of man to man shall be swept away from this Western hemisphere, let it come!" [16]

McKinley, an astute politician, was not blind to political realities. If he tried to thwart the popular will, he would jeopardize, perhaps ruin, his chances of re-election in 1900. The silver-tongued Bryan, his prospective opponent, was already arousing tremendous enthusiasm by his speeches

[14] *Ibid.*, p. 746 (Woodford to Day, April 9, 1898). Italics inserted.
[15] *Ibid.*, p. 747 (Woodford to McKinley, April 10, 1898).
[16] Quoted in J. W. Pratt, *Expansionists of 1898* (Baltimore, 1936), p. 285.

for an independent Cuba. To a staunch party man and gold-standard advocate like McKinley, few things could have been more calamitous than to have the Democratic Party sweep to victory in 1900 with "Free Cuba" and "Free Silver" emblazoned on its banners. Better a foreign war than an internal upheaval; better that Spain should be ejected from Cuba than the Republicans be ejected from Washington.

ANOTHER OLD WOMAN TRIES TO SWEEP BACK THE SEA

Public opinion for war overwhelms McKinley.
Davenport in the *New York Journal*, 1898

Lashed by the yellow press, Congress responded to the clamor of the masses. One Maine Representative declared that every Congressman "had two or three newspapers in his district—most of them printed in red ink . . . and shouting for blood." The Republicans feared that if they did not give the country the war it wanted, they would be unseated by the Democrats in the approaching fall elections. If the hysteria became too great, the Democratic minority in Congress, combining with the more militant Republicans, might even pass a war resolution over the head of the President. Such a blow would be ruinous to his prestige. One bellicose Senator reportedly shouted to the Assistant Secretary of State, "Day, by ——, don't your President know where the war-declaring power is lodged? Tell him by ——, that if he doesn't do something, Congress will exercise the power." [17]

McKINLEY CAPITULATES

Confronted by this tremendous pressure, McKinley made a momentous decision. On April 11, 1898, only two days *after* Spain's partial capitulation, he sent a war message to Congress in which he asked for authority to use the army and navy to end hostilities in Cuba. First of all, he emphasized the urgent need of abating a nuisance which cried to heaven off America's very doors. Second, he stressed the obligation to protect American property and trade. Finally, he pointed to the necessity of ending a disturbance which was a constant menace to the peace of the United States.

Convincing though these arguments may have been to the American people, they find scant support among international lawyers. Humanitarian grounds were perhaps the strongest, but for one nation to set itself up as the sole judge of another, especially a nation that had maltreated its own Indians, was a grave responsibility. Intervention on moral grounds would have been more defensible if undertaken in co-operation with other powers.

McKinley's memorable message had been drafted several days before the eleventh-hour Spanish capitulation arrived. So, near the end of a formidable indictment written on the assumption that concessions had not been made, the President added one sentence in which he stated that concessions had been made. He hoped that Congress—a war-mad Congress—would give them "just and careful attention. . . ."

McKinley has been condemned for not having laid more emphasis upon the belated Spanish surrender. But even assuming that it would have brought a speedy end to the conflict in Cuba, one should note that the press knew of the armistice offer and spurned it as just another attempt at delay. "When Gabriel blows his horn," declared one Pittsburgh journal, "you will still hear Spain asking for a little more time in which to pacify Cuba." [18] On the day that McKinley submitted his message to Congress, the *New York World* cried: "Stop the nonsense! Stop the trifling, let us have peace even at the muzzle of our guns." [19]

CONGRESS TAKES COMMAND

With the hysterical Congress clamoring for war, McKinley's request for authority to use warlike measures needed no urging. During the debates

[17] C. S. Olcott, *The Life of William McKinley* (Boston, 1916), II, 28.
[18] *Literary Digest*, March 26, 1898, p. 368.
[19] *New York World*, April 11, 1898, 6:2.

passions ran incredibly high. The *London Times* correspondent thus reported the scene on the floor of the House:

> Men fought; "Liar," "Scoundrel," and other epithets were bandied to and fro; there were half-a-dozen personal collisions; books were thrown; members rushed up and down the aisles like madmen, exchanging hot words, with clenched fists and set teeth; excitement was at fever heat. Not for years has such a scene occurred.[20]

Groups of Congressmen in the lobbies sang "The Battle Hymn of the Republic," "Dixie," and "Hang General Weyler to a Sour Apple Tree As We Go Marching On."

Finally, on April 19, 1898, Congress passed a fateful joint resolution in four parts that was equivalent to a declaration of war. It (1) declared Cuba free; (2) demanded the withdrawal of Spain; (3) directed the President to use armed force to achieve these ends; and (4) disclaimed any intention on the part of the United States to annex Cuba. This last stipulation, the so-called Teller Amendment, was approved without dissent. It was supported by the sugar interests, who did not want Cuba inside the tariff wall, but vastly more important were the Congressmen who felt that the nation was embarking upon a holy crusade. Cried the *New York Sun:*

> No annexation talk, so far as Cuba is concerned! If the United States government undertakes this high enterprise, there must be no taint of ulterior self-interest in its motives.
> For human lives and the liberty of human beings, for Cuba Libre; not for an extension of United States territory! [21]

By an act of Congress, approved by the Presidential pen on April 25, 1898, war was declared to have existed since April 21.

The genial McKinley was an ear-to-the-ground politician, rather than a dynamic leader; a servant rather than a moulder of public opinion. But he was a stronger man than Theodore Roosevelt gave him credit for being; it took backbone to stay out of war, not to get into it. He had labored long and earnestly for peace. His nerves were so frayed at the critical period that he was forced to resort to sleeping powders. Even today there is no adequate appreciation of the tremendous pressure to which he was being subjected by Congress and the public. And why, he doubtless reasoned, should he continue to hold out when further negotiation would merely prolong the bloodshed in Cuba? Perhaps he was right in concluding that the Gordian knot could be cut only with the sword.

It is futile to argue that the stiff-spined Grover Cleveland would have kept the country out of war. By the spring of 1898 the pressure of herd hysteria had become so overwhelming that it could not have been stemmed by any ordinary mortal. The American people, whipped to a

---

[20] *London Times,* April 14, 1898, 3:1.
[21] *New York Sun,* March 25, 1898, 6:2.

white heat by the yellow press, were determined to have their war to free Cuba—and they got it. McKinley was determined to free Cuba, and war seemed to be the only solution. His views coincided with those of an inflamed and fight-thirsty public opinion.

SELECTED BIBLIOGRAPHY

A brief account appears in S. F. Bemis, ed., *The American Secretaries of State and their Diplomacy* (New York, 1929), IX, 41–95. The causes of the war are provocatively discussed in J. W. Pratt, *Expansionists of 1898* (Baltimore, 1936). On public opinion consult J. E. Wisan, *The Cuban Crisis as Reflected in the New York Press, 1895–1898* (New York, 1934), M. M. Wilkerson, *Public Opinion and the Spanish-American War* (Baton Rouge, La., 1932), and Walter Millis, *The Martial Spirit* (Boston, 1931). On diplomacy see F. E. Chadwick, *The Relations of the United States and Spain: Diplomacy* (New York, 1909), and Orestes Ferrara, *The Last Spanish War* (New York, 1937). See also W. H. Callcott, *The Caribbean Policy of the United States, 1890–1920* (Baltimore, 1942) and E. J. Benton, *International Law and Diplomacy of the Spanish-American War* (Baltimore, 1908). A helpful survey is F. R. Dulles, *The Imperial Years* (New York, 1956).

Revealing articles are G. W. Auxier, "Middle Western Newspapers and the Spanish-American War, 1895–1898," *Miss. Valley Hist. Rev.*, XXVI (1940), 523–534, and his "The Propaganda Activities of the Cuban *Junta* in Precipitating the Spanish American War, 1895–1898," *Hispanic Amer. Hist. Rev.*, XIX (1939), 286–305; also J. C. Appel, "The Unionization of Florida Cigarmakers and the Coming of the War with Spain," *ibid.*, XXXVI (1956), 38–49.

See footnotes of this chapter; Bemis and Griffin, *Guide*, pp. 510–523; *Harvard Guide*, Ch. 23.

7TH ED. REFS. E. R. May, *Imperial Democracy* (New York, 1961) is a significant work based on multiarchival research. The author rather surprisingly concludes that the United States, despite its obvious strength, could not be regarded as a great power before 1898 because it was not so regarded by the others. He concludes that McKinley's final "demands"—although it is not clear that they were ever presented, much less as "demands"—included the additional one that Spain should grant Cuba independence "if the President deemed it necessary (p. 154)." Continental Europe (except Russia) was unfriendly to America, yet, one should note, America was strong enough to stare down all of the six great powers when they attempted mediation. A. E. Campbell, *Great Britain and the United States, 1895–1903* (London, 1960) thinks that war was inevitable after the *Maine* sinking, but that Washington pressed the Spaniards too hard. A second attempt at joint mediation was spiked by the British Ambassador in Washington. Margaret Leech, *In the Days of McKinley* (New York, 1959), deals gently with the kindly McKinley but adds little new. F. P. Summers, ed., *The Cabinet Diary of William L. Wilson, 1896–1897* (Chapel Hill, N.C., 1957) has some interesting passages on Cleveland's resentment against the Republicans who were playing politics with the Cuban belligerency issue. Nancy L. O'Connor, "The Spanish-American War: A Re-Evaluation of Its Causes," *Science and Society*, XXII (1958), 129–143 challenges the Pratt thesis and concludes that the theory of American business opposition to the war "is subject to considerable revision." W. A. Swanberg, *Citizen Hearst* (New York, 1961) has a colorful treatment of yellow journalism.

8TH AND 9TH ED. REFS. See BIBLIOGRAPHICAL ADDENDUM, p. 1,007.

32

America as a Great Power
1898-1900

> O Dewey at Manila
>   That fateful first of May,
> When you sank the Spanish squadron
>   In almost bloodless fray,
> And gave your name to deathless fame;
>   O glorious Dewey, say,
> Why didn't you weigh anchor
>   And softly sail away?
>
> BOSTON TRANSCRIPT, 1899

ENGLAND REDISCOVERS AMERICA

GREAT BRITAIN, alone among the Old World powers, was conspicuously friendly to the United States during the crisis with Spain. The might of an ominously rising Germany, to say nothing of other European alarms, had awakened British statesmen to the necessity of finding allies. And powerful young America, formerly a poor relative, was decidedly worth cultivating. In March, 1898, Alfred Austin, the poet laureate of England, addressed the people of the United States on behalf of his own:

> Yes, this is the Voice on the bluff March gale,
> "We severed have been too long:
> But now we have done with a worn-out tale,
> The tale of an ancient wrong,
> And our friendship shall last long as Love doth last, and be stronger than
>   Death is strong." [1]

The declaration of war on Spain was greeted in England with a colorful display of the Stars and Stripes, and an enthusiastic crowd gathered before the American embassy to cheer. No one could doubt where British

---

[1] *London Times,* March 29, 1898, 8:3.

sympathies lay, even though the London government preserved an official neutrality.

British bidding for American support reached a climax when, early in the conflict, Colonial Secretary Joseph Chamberlain declared in a public speech: ". . . I even go so far as to say that, terrible as war may be, even war itself would be cheaply purchased if in a great and noble cause the Stars and Stripes and the Union Jack should wave together [loud and prolonged cheers] over an Anglo-Saxon alliance." [2] Although an Anglo-American League was founded in London, and an Anglo-American Committee was organized in New York, the idea of an alliance never got beyond mere dalliance. The United States, while pleased with British applause, saw no need for a foreign entanglement. Even if there had been such a need, the dead hand of George Washington, to say nothing of the live hands of American Anglophobes, would have raised insuperable barriers. The *Detroit Tribune* expressed a not uncommon thought: "It might have been better if Great Britain's friendship for the United States were less intense and had been stretched over a longer period of time." [3]

THE MONARCHS HANG TOGETHER

The Continental European powers, quite in contrast with Britain, were virtually unanimous in their disapproval of what seemed to them a war of unprovoked aggression against Spain. They were motivated by dynastic sympathies, by concern for investments in Spain and Cuba, by distrust of American democracy, and by solicitude for the preservation of monarchy.

At the forefront of the unfriendly European powers, at least in the American mind, stood Germany. Relations with her had not been pleasant since the pork and Samoan controversies, and American opinion had reacted unfavorably against the brazen German seizure of Kiaochow, China, in November, 1897. For their part, the Germans bitterly resented the Monroe Doctrine, which Bismarck had branded "a species of arrogance peculiarly American." It was the chief obstacle that stood in the way of Germany's seizing and colonizing large areas in poorly defended South America. As for the Spanish-American War, the Germans did not relish the prospect of Uncle Sam's strengthening both himself and the Monroe Doctrine by elbowing Spain out of the Western Hemisphere, and then appropriating her possessions.

Germany, France, and Austria-Hungary appear to have favored effective mediation or intervention to prevent Spanish-American hostilities. But none of them was willing to bell the cat by assuming responsibility

[2] *London Times*, May 14, 1898, 12:3.
[3] *Literary Digest*, Dec. 10, 1898, p. 686.

for leading such a movement.[4] The United States was now too formidable
to be lightly offended, while the potent British navy, as in the days of
Monroe, could not be laughed aside.

DOCTRINE AND PRACTICE

DAME EUROPA (*coldly*): "To whom do I owe the pleasure
of this intrusion?"
UNCLE S.: "Ma'am—my name is Uncle Sam!"
DAME EUROPA: "Any relation of the late Colonel Monroe?"

Europe regards America's intervention in Spain's Cuban
affairs as a violation of the Monroe Doctrine.
London Punch, 1898

Confronted with such obstacles, the European nations were forced to
proceed gingerly. The climax of their interventionist efforts came early
in April, 1898, following a last-minute appeal by Spain. Austria-Hungary,
acting under pressure from her ally, Germany, led in preparing a joint

[4] L. B. Shippee, "Germany and the Spanish-American War," *Amer. Hist. Rev.,*
XXX (1925), 756.

remonstrance which was signed by representatives of the six Great Powers, including England, and presented to President McKinley. The British ambassador, Sir Julian Pauncefote, had been instructed by London to make sure that the note would be inoffensive to the United States. There is some reason to believe that he submitted an advance draft of the statement to the State Department, which suggested alterations that were finally adopted. Under these conditions both the joint note and McKinley's reply were models of propriety. The affair was aptly summarized by one newspaper:

> Said the Six Ambassadors: "We hope for humanity's sake you will not go to war."
> Said Mr. McKinley in reply: "We hope if we do go to war, you will understand that it is for humanity's sake."
> And the incident was closed.[5]

A "SPLENDID LITTLE WAR"

The Spanish-American War, though short, provided more than its quota of thrills. Assistant Secretary of the Navy Theodore Roosevelt, a frustrated fighter, was one of the relatively few men in Washington who knew that there were Philippine Islands and that Spain owned them. He therefore used his influence to have a Civil War fighting man, George Dewey, placed in command of the American Asiatic squadron at Hong Kong. Then, when his chief was away, Roosevelt cabled Dewey orders to hold himself in readiness to attack the Spaniards in the Philippines. McKinley himself approved the final directive to strike. Attacking the faraway Philippines was an odd way to free Cuba, but in warfare an elementary rule is to hit the enemy wherever he is vulnerable.

Dewey moved energetically as soon as war was declared. Undeterred by reports of mines, he sailed boldly into Manila harbor and blew out of the water the collection of antiquated craft that passed for the Spanish fleet. Europe was impressed; Britain was proud; America was electrified. Hearst's mouthpiece gloated as it heralded the victory, "How Do You Like the *Journal's* War?" Thus the first blow for Cuban freedom was struck on the other side of the world.

A small and ill-equipped American army finally blundered into Cuba. Lieutenant-Colonel Theodore Roosevelt, who had resigned from the Navy Department, hogged the headlines by his spectacular antics as second in command of the volunteer "Rough Riders." The Spanish fleet, which had scurried into the harbor of Santiago, Cuba, ran out to save the honor of Spain, and was completely destroyed. In the closing days of the war American troops hastily occupied the island of Puerto Rico, lest the shooting stop before all the imperial plums were plucked.

[5] *New York World*, April 8, 1898, 6:3.

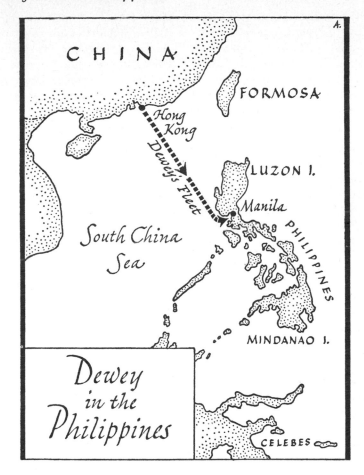

CHINA

FORMOSA

Hong
Kong

Dewey's Fleet

LUZON I.

Manila

*South China
Sea*

PHILIPPINES

MINDANAO I.

*Dewey
in the
Philippines*

CELEBES

GERMAN BLUNDERINGS IN THE PHILIPPINES

Queer things had meanwhile been happening in Manila Bay. Although Dewey had destroyed the Spanish fleet, he was forced to wait for troop reinforcements from the United States before he could capture the city. During these anxious weeks several of the powers dispatched warships to the Philippines for the purpose of protecting the interests of their nationals. The financial stake of Germany in the islands ranked far below that of Britain, but the Germans gradually assembled five men-of-war at Manila, as compared with two for the British. The German squadron was not only the most powerful neutral force there, but it was considerably stronger than Dewey's.

Such an act of discourtesy aroused suspicions in America that the German warships were there to support the Kaiser's designs on the Philippines. The documents now available reveal that this surmise was correct. Germany had no desire to provoke a war with Uncle Sam or challenge his pretensions. But having entered the game of grab late, she was eager to pick up whatever crumbs might fall from the world's banquet table. Berlin believed that if America chose to abandon the Philippines, in whole or in part, the presence of a strong fleet at Manila would buttress German claims to the islands.

Dewey was vastly annoyed by the German fleet. Its commander, Vice-Admiral von Diederichs, disagreed with his interpretation of international law, and failed to observe punctiliously the American blockade regulations. Following a series of unpleasant incidents, Dewey heatedly informed von Diederichs that "if Germany wants war, all right, we are ready." The tension was finally relieved, but the yellow journals in the United States further inflamed German-American relations with their lurid reports. The *New York Times* declared:

> We may not care particularly about taking the Philippines, but we can assure our European friends that we are not going to be dictated to as to the manner in which we shall dispose of them or any part of them. Expansion is a new idea with us. The defense of our rights is an old habit.[6]

In glaring contrast with the Germans, the British commander at Manila, Captain Chichester, was conspicuously friendly to the Americans. On August 13, 1898, the day that Manila fell, he quietly moved his ships so as better to observe the effect of the American naval bombardment. This maneuver chanced to bring him between the German fleet and that of the United States. The legend subsequently took root that Chichester had saved Dewey by scaring off the Germans, who allegedly were about to attack the Americans on the flank. This part of the tale is a fabrication, but its wide currency further high-lighted German antipathy and British sympathy during the Spanish-American War.

PEACE PRELIMINARIES AT PARIS

By this time the honor of the badly beaten Spaniards was more than satisfied. On August 12, 1898, the French ambassador in Washington, acting on behalf of Spain, signed a protocol that ended hostilities and roughly outlined the terms of peace. First of all, Spain agreed to relinquish Cuba. Second, she consented to cede Puerto Rico and an island in the Ladrones (Marianas), ultimately Guam, to the United States. Finally, she would permit the Americans to occupy and hold "the city, bay, and harbor of Manila, pending the conclusion of a treaty of peace which shall determine the control, disposition and government of the

---

[6] *Literary Digest,* XVII, 92 (July 23, 1898). For the entire episode see T. A. Bailey, "Dewey and the Germans at Manila Bay," *Amer. Hist. Rev.,* XLV (1939), 59–81.

Philippines.[7] This last clause was left purposely vague because the United States did not then know what it wanted to do with the islands.

The five-man commission, which was to hammer out the final peace terms at Paris, was chosen by the astute McKinley with care. It consisted mainly of Republicans, expansionists, and Senators. Three prominent members of the Senate were selected, obviously in an effort by the President to win support for the pact in advance. There was much criticism in the press of the impropriety of appointing men, who, in the end, would have to approve their own handiwork.

The fateful negotiations were launched in Paris, on October 1, 1898. At the outset, a protracted controversy over the Cuban question consumed nearly a month. The United States insisted on freeing the island, in accord with the self-denying Teller amendment; the Spaniards insisted on turning it over to the United States. The joker was that annexation would involve annexing a debt of some $400 million which had been incurred by the Spanish authorities in Cuba, largely in an attempt to crush the *insurrectos*. The Americans flatly rejected any such "bargain."

The commissioners then turned to the even thornier question of the Philippines. The instructions from McKinley, though vague, alluded to the commercial advantages of the group, and concluded that the United States could not accept less than Luzon, the largest island and the site of Manila, the principal seaport. The truth is that McKinley, traditionally portrayed as flabby and indecisive, had already decided upon an expansionist course, and was merely waiting for public opinion to catch up with him. The hoary story[8] that he did not know within 2,000 miles where the "darned islands" were at the time he ordered Dewey to attack Manila must go into the trash bin of discredited myths.

During the period when American public opinion was most ill-informed, there was much sentiment for giving the Filipinos their immediate independence. Dewey reported that the natives were more intelligent and more capable of self-government than the Cubans. But as evidence began to pile up as to the economic and strategic value of the archipelago, the natives seemed much less capable of governing themselves. As the *St. Louis Post-Dispatch* later sneered, "The Filipino is treacherous and deceitful. Besides, we want his country."

DOLLARS, DUTY, AND DESTINY

Businessmen, hitherto partly blind to their commercial opportunities, now found their eyes jarred wide open by Dewey's booming guns. The imperialistic powers were carving up China like a ripe melon, and American merchants were beginning to fear that they might be shut out of this

[7] *Foreign Relations, 1898*, p. 29.
[8] H. H. Kohlsaat, *From McKinley to Harding* (New York, 1923), p. 68.

potentially vast market. As a kind of offset, the United States could well acquire Manila, which would provide a vestibule—a veritable Hong Kong—to the trade of Eastern Asia. A powerful naval base in the Philippines, moreover, would protect American interests and increase American prestige. Trade experts were now pointing out, with an alert eye for the dollar, that half the people of the earth lived within reaching distance of the Philippines. Senator Mark Hanna, the bosom friend of McKinley, boldly declared, "If it is commercialism to want the possession of a strategic point giving the American people an opportunity to maintain a foothold in the markets of that great Eastern country [China], for God's sake let us have commercialism." [9]

The United States might have given the Filipinos their immediate independence, but there were weighty objections to a scuttle-and-run policy. The half-naked and half-civilized natives were woefully unprepared for self-government, and anarchy probably would have resulted. Chaos almost certainly would have brought intervention by one or more of the major powers. In the general free-for-all, Germany might have made off with the islands, and American opinion had been bitterly aroused against her by the strange doings in Manila Bay. Worse yet, the imperialistic nations might come to blows over the booty, thus precipitating a world war into which the United States could easily be drawn. The Japanese, who had a strong stake in the peace of Asia, much preferred the United States to any outside occupant of the Philippines, except themselves. [10]

There were also powerful moral arguments. The United States could pull out and let the islands revert to Spain, whose misrule, now that her power had been shattered, would be worse than before. But this prospect was intolerable to the American people, who had recently thrown themselves into a tremendous sentimental and humanitarian crusade to free Cuba. Many Americans concluded that the problem was of their own making, and that they had a moral obligation not to wash their hands of all responsibility for the backward Filipinos, particularly after having destroyed their Spanish guardians.

Finally, the church element in the United States welcomed the "little brown brother" as one to whom the gospel should be carried. The Roman Catholic missionaries had already enjoyed unusual success in the Philippines, but to Protestants this was not enough. "Manila stretches out her torn and bleeding hands," cried one clergyman, "and we must clasp them and accept our work of redemption, not as a piece of political ambition, but as a mission we have from God." [11] A White House visitor found

[9] Quoted in F. R. Dulles, *America in the Pacific* (Boston, 1932), pp. 227–228.

[10] J. K. Eyre, Jr., "Japan and the American Annexation of the Philippines," *Pacific Hist. Rev.*, XI (1942), 55–71.

[11] *New York Herald*, Aug. 22, 1898, 6:3.

Mrs. McKinley, who presumably influenced her Methodist husband, deeply concerned about "converting the Igorrotes."

McKINLEY HEEDS THE VOICE OF DESTINY

The evolution of McKinley's thought is fascinating. At first, he seems to have been thinking only of a coaling station in the Philippines. Then, as already noted, he reached the point where he instructed the commissioners in Paris to take at least the island of Luzon. But if the United States annexed only one island, the other powers might seize the rest. Germany, Japan, and Britain had all shown a lively interest, and if one or more of them had moved in, they would have weakened the American holdings strategically. It was not possible, as the *New York World* pithily put it, to take "the juice of the orange without the rind and pulp." Of course, some kind of joint protectorate might be devised, but such a scheme had brewed only trouble in Samoa. To McKinley there seemed to be no acceptable middle ground between taking all and taking none— and either alternative presented a devil's dilemma.

In these circumstances, and in response to an old habit, McKinley's ear sought the ground. While on his way to and from the Omaha Exposition, in October, 1898, he let fall a number of glittering generalities at convenient rail stops. References to "duty," "destiny," and "Dewey" brought enthusiastic responses, and he could hardly escape the conclusion that the American people welcomed far-flung dependencies.

Nor did McKinley lack other means of plumbing public opinion. As Senator Lodge had noted in June, 1898, "The Republican Conventions are all declaring that where the flag once goes up it must never come down." The *Literary Digest* had published, during September, 1898, the results of a poll of 192 newspaper editors, the overwhelming majority of whom favored outright annexation or naval bases.

As a last resort, McKinley turned to prayer. He, himself, later confessed to a group of his Methodist brethren, as one present recalled.

> The truth is I didn't want the Philippines and when they came to us as a gift from the gods, I did not know what to do about them. . . . I sought counsel from all sides—Democrats as well as Republicans—but got little help. I thought first we would take only Manila; then Luzon; then other islands, perhaps, also. I walked the floor of the White House night after night until midnight; and I am not ashamed to tell you, gentlemen, that I went down on my knees and prayed Almighty God for light and guidance more than one night.

The President's patience was finally rewarded.

> And one night late it came to me this way—I don't know how it was, but it came: (1) that we could not give them back to Spain—that would be cowardly and dishonorable; (2) that we could not turn them over to

France or Germany—our commercial rivals in the Orient—that would be bad business and discreditable; (3) that we could not leave them to themselves—they were unfit for self-government—and they would soon have anarchy and misrule over there worse than Spain's was; and (4) that there was nothing left for us to do but to take them all, and to educate the Filipinos, and uplift and civilize and Christianize them, and by God's grace do the very best we could by them, as our fellow-men for whom Christ also died. And then I went to bed, and went to sleep and slept soundly.[12]

It is possible that McKinley heard the voice of the people rather than the voice of God, for his statement has most of the earmarks of imperialism. A latter-day historian has slyly paraphrased his general attitude to read, "God directs us; perhaps it will pay." At all events, when the Paris commissioners cabled for specific instructions, on October 25, 1898, McKinley replied that since the only alternatives were all or none, the United States would have to take all.

The Spanish commissioners fought strenuously to salvage the Philippines, and their position was not so weak as one might think. By a quirk of fate, the American troops had captured Manila a few hours *after* the signing of the protocol that officially ended hostilities. The United States could hardly claim the islands by right of conquest, although under the terms of the protocol the American commissioners could negotiate for them. The McKinley administration was anxious to avoid further delay, and recognizing that its case was not airtight, it finally offered $20 million, about three times the price of Alaska, to sweeten the pill. Spain, not knowing when she was well off, reluctantly accepted this solution—her last great haul from the treasure chests of the New World.

The terms of the treaty, signed on December 10, 1898, provided no surprises. Spain relinquished her sovereignty over Cuba, and ceded the Philippines, Puerto Rico, and Guam outright to the United States. Guam had been captured by an American expedition en route to the Philippines early in the war. (The Spanish authorities there, having no cable, were unaware of hostilities and at first mistook American gun fire for a salute.) [13] As for Puerto Rico, McKinley believed, with Cuban troubles fresh in mind, that the complete banishment of Spain from the Americas was necessary for permanent peace. Representative McDowell believed, less delicately, that "these murderous, treacherous, bull-fighting hyenas should be made to get off the Western Hemisphere. . . ." Such were America's imperialistic gains from a war that destroyed Spanish imperialism. Such were the curious fruits of a conflict begun with the highest motives but ending with the light-hearted assumption of responsibilities that were to prove increasingly burdensome.

[12] *Christian Advocate* (New York), Jan. 22, 1903. A dubious witness.
[13] See L. W. Walker, "Guam's Seizure by the United States in 1898," *Pacific Hist. Rev.*, XIV (1945), 1–12.

TRADITIONALISM CLASHES WITH IMPERIALISM

The debate over the Spanish treaty, in Congress and out, was one of the most heated in American history. The anti-imperialists, who opposed overseas expansion, argued that hitherto the United States had acquired no territory which could not be Americanized and erected into states. Yet the Philippines, to say nothing of Puerto Rico, were remote and densely populated by peoples of alien race and language. Senator Pettigrew of South Dakota declared, with no little truth, that bananas and self-government could not grow on the same section of land.

Opponents of annexation also made much of America's inconsistency in entering a war to free the Cubans, and then winding up some 8000 miles away trying to rivet shackles on 7 million protesting people. The annexation of populations against their will violated the Declaration of Independence, as well as the spirit of the Constitution. Tyranny abroad, the argument continued, would beget tyranny at home. Furthermore, a land-surfeited United States did not need more land, least of all expensive colonial dependencies. And by meddling in the Far East the United States could not consistently forbid the other powers to meddle in the Americas. "The Monroe Doctrine is gone!" cried Senator Hoar of Massachusetts.

Foes of overseas expansion likewise insisted that the time-honored policy of the Fathers had served the nation well. As long as America stayed at home and minded her own business, she could easily defend her shores without burdensome armaments. But if she plunged into the Far Eastern vortex, she would have to maintain a costly, two-ocean navy to protect her colonies. Just as poorly protected Canada was a hostage for the good behavior of Britain, so would the poorly protected Philippines be a hostage given to the Far Eastern powers for the good behavior of the United States. The islands would be, as annexationist Theodore Roosevelt himself reluctantly came to admit, a veritable "heel of Achilles."

The expansionists, for their part, advanced the familiar arguments about economic and strategic advantages; about national honor and responsibility; about destiny and the cowardice of "hauling down the flag." A fiery young imperialist orator, Albert J. Beveridge, cried that only those should have self-government "who are capable of self-government!" He passionately met the argument of geographical remoteness:

> The ocean does not separate us from the lands of our duty and desire—the ocean joins us, a river never to be dredged, a canal never to be repaired. [Applause]. Steam joins us, electricity joins us—the very elements are in league with our destiny. [Continued applause and cheers.] Cuba not contiguous? Porto Rico not contiguous? The Philippines not contiguous?

Our navy will make them contiguous! [he thundered, as the thousands shouted their delight].[14]

Some of the imperialists wrapped their selfish motives in humanitarian phrases; others sincerely believed that America had a sacred duty to extend an uplifting hand to the benighted "brown brother." Misery loves company, and England, on whose imperialistic headaches the sun never set, cheered the Americans on. She had investments in the Philippines, as well as an enormous economic stake in the Far East, and she desired America's support for a policy of equal commercial opportunity (the Open Door). And of course the Americans could not disappoint Britain, which had stood by them so nobly when Continental Europe had bared its monarchial teeth.

Rudyard Kipling, a minor prophet and major poet of British imperialism, appealed to America's sense of obligation with his "White Man's Burden":

> Take up the White Man's burden—
> Ye dare not stoop to less—
> Nor call too loud on Freedom
> To cloke your weariness.[15]

The poem caught the mood of the hour in America, and "became hackneyed in a day." But the *Omaha World-Herald* kept its head better than most of its contemporaries when it remarked, "In other words, Mr. Kipling would have Uncle Sam take up John Bull's burden."

THE SENATE VOTES FOR PEACE (AND IMPERIALISM)

The Spanish treaty encountered last-ditch opposition in the Senate. The Democrats, though expansionists under Jefferson and Polk, were now nonexpansionists, if for no better reason than that the Republicans were in power. But William Jennings Bryan, titular leader of the Democratic Party, came to Washington and, although a leading anti-imperialist, urged his followers in the Senate to vote for the treaty. The United States could then officially end the war, take over the Philippines, and grant the Filipinos their independence.[16] Two assumptions, both of them highly questionable, followed Bryan's switch: first, that as a potential Presidential candidate in 1900 he was seeking to tar the Republicans with imperialism, and second, that his influence clearly turned the tide.[17] At any rate, enough Democrats supported the treaty to secure its ap-

---

[14] C. G. Bowers, *Beveridge and the Progressive Era* (New York, 1932), pp. 75–76.
[15] *McClure's Magazine*, XII, 291 (Feb., 1899).
[16] M. E. Curti, "Bryan and World Peace," *Smith College Studies in History*, XVI, nos. 3–4 (1931), p. 122.
[17] Highly revealing on these points is P. E. Coletta, "Bryan, McKinley, and the Treaty of Paris," *Pacific Hist. Rev.*, XXVI (1957), pp. 131–146.

proval, on February 6, 1899, by a count of 57 to 27, or one more than the necessary two-thirds. The three Senators who had helped draft it at Paris all voted "yea."

But the action of the Senate was not a fair test of sentiment in that body or throughout the country. In order to reject the Philippines, the Senators would have had to reject the treaty. This course would have resulted in repudiating the President, unsettling business, and adding to the international uncertainties. On the clear-cut issue of retaining the Philippine islands, the imperialists almost certainly would have failed to obtain a two-thirds majority.

McKinley has been savagely condemned for his decision to take the Philippines. But statesmanship is the science of alternatives, and leaders all too often have to choose, not between the good and the bad, but between the bad and the less bad. McKinley was forced to decide among several possible courses, all of which presented grave difficulties. He chose the one that he and his advisers, and probably a majority of the people, thought the least undesirable. From the standpoint of the United States, the misfortune was perhaps not so much the decision to annex the islands as the unfortunate set of circumstances that seemed to make annexation necessary.

The most serious avoidable mistake made during this period was probably the failure to quiet the fears of the Filipinos. They had been encouraged to believe—whether with proper authority or not—that they would be given their independence, and they had assisted materially in the capture of Manila. But when they perceived that they were merely going to exchange Spanish for American overlords, they arose in revolt on February 4, 1899. In annexing an empire, the United States annexed a war.

This unfortunate outbreak might have been avoided if Congress had flatly declared, in January, 1899, that it would give the Filipinos their independence as soon as order was restored. A resolution to this effect was postponed until after the insurrection began; then, in the form of an amendment, it was defeated by the narrowest possible margin. Whatever the motives, Congress was unwilling to make a self-denying pledge, as it had earlier done for Cuba during the heat of a humanitarian crusade.

WATER CURES AND REBELLIOUS BOERS

The American flag had been fired upon by Filipinos, and the insurrection had to be crushed. The United States sent some 70,000 men to the Philippines, an army about four times as large as that which had invaded Cuba. The Filipino insurgents used primitive methods of warfare, and inevitably dragged the American soldiers down to their level. The republic was rocked by scandalous reports that United States troops were butchering prisoners or torturing them with "water cures." The maddening guerrilla tactics of the natives caused the Americans to feel some measure of sympathy for "Butcher" Weyler, and to do him the honor of adopting a form of reconcentration. The *New York World* in 1899 wrote a discouraged reply to Rudyard Kipling:

> We've taken up the white man's burden
> Of ebony and brown;
> Now will you kindly tell us, Rudyard,
> How we may put it down? [18]

Not until after two years of inglorious jungle warfare was the heart taken out of the insurrection by the capture of its leader, Emilio Aguinaldo.

The British had meanwhile been encountering even more humiliating reverses at the hands of their Dutch-descended Boers in South Africa. Considerable agitation developed in the United States, much of it in a rich Irish brogue, for aid to the rebels in the Boer War (1899–1902). But Washington, with the pro-British John Hay as Secretary of State, pursued such a rigidly hands-off policy as to help the British and harm the Boers. If the South-African uprising had come five years earlier, the American people would have shown a much stronger pro-Boer sentiment. But they could not overlook British friendliness during the Spanish War, nor the existence of a comparable insurrection in the Philippines.[19]

THE SPURIOUS MANDATE OF 1900

The thorny issue of the Philippines was finally tossed into the Presidential campaign of 1900. The Democrats nominated Bryan for the second time, and declared in their platform that imperialism was both the "burning" and the "paramount" issue. The Republicans renominated William McKinley for the Presidency, and drafted Colonel Theodore Roosevelt, the popular war hero, for the Vice-Presidency. The ex-Rough Rider protestingly consented to run for an office that had hitherto been regarded as the graveyard of political hopes. The Republicans vigorously denied that imperialism was the "paramount" issue, and charged that the burning question was the threat to full-dinner-pail prosperity from the free-silver heresies of Bryan.

A multitude of voters were distressed by what they regarded as a devil's choice: the wishy-washy McKinley and the wooly-witted Bryan. One voter wrote to Grover Cleveland, "It is a choice between evils, and I am going to shut my eyes, hold my nose, vote, go home and disinfect myself." [20] Many citizens refused to become alarmed about imperialism

[18] Quoted in T. A. Bailey, *The Man in the Street* (New York, 1948), p. 275.
[19] See J. H. Ferguson, *American Diplomacy and the Boer War* (Philadelphia, 1939).
[20] J. S. Morton to Cleveland, Nov. 2, 1900, Cleveland Papers, Library of Congress.

because they felt that the United States was already committed to retaining the Philippines for an indefinite period. Others who disliked McKinley's expansionism believed that the menace of Bryan's free-silverism was more fearsome and should be disposed of first.

The Republicans won a sweeping victory in the election of 1900, and straightway announced that the President's Philippine policy had been endorsed. But the issues were so numerous and so confusing that if the results were a mandate on anything, they were not a clear-cut mandate on imperialism. Prosperity rather than McKinley won. If the out-and-out question of approving the annexation of the Philippines had been presented to the voters, as it never was, they might well have decided to turn the islands loose after a reasonable time.

COMMERCIAL OPPORTUNITY IN CHINA IMPERILLED

The United States, now a Far Eastern power with the Philippines on its hands, became increasingly concerned over the dramatic events on the Asiatic mainland. After China had betrayed her weakness in the Sino-Japanese War of 1894–1895, the imperialistic European powers descended upon her "living carcass" and extorted long-term leaseholds and valuable economic spheres of influence. American merchants viewed this vivisection with alarm. Although their trade with China was relatively small— about 2 per cent of the nation's total—it was growing with promising rapidity. Interested Americans especially feared that the intruding powers would erect prohibitively high tariff barriers, to say nothing of other restrictions within the areas under their control.

The British, who had by far the largest foreign trade stake in China, were even more worried. Twice in 1898–1899 they proposed to Washington a co-operative arrangement to insure equal commercial opportunity in China—that is, the Open Door. Both times the scheme was spurned as inconsistent with the traditional nonentanglement policy of the United States.

Outside the British Foreign Office a number of non-official Englishmen were championing the Open Door. Notable among them was Lord Charles Beresford, a recent visitor to the Far East, whose book, *The Breakup of China* (1899), had made something of a splash. He further popularized the concept of the Open Door by a series of speeches in the United States. The idea of equal commercial opportunity began to meet with increasing favor, especially with American mercantile and missionary groups. The pressures on the State Department finally became so strong that some kind of official gesture became imperative.

See also T. A. Bailey, "Was the Election of 1900 a Mandate on Imperialism?" *Miss. Valley Hist. Rev.*, XXIV (1937), 43–52; F. H. Harrington, "The Anti-Imperialist Movement in the United States, 1898–1900," *ibid.*, XXII (1935), 211–230.

Two private individuals were also actively at work behind the scenes. The first was A. E. Hippisley, a British subject employed in China, and a persistent advocate of the Open Door in the interests of both England and China. While in the United States on leave of absence, he had a number of conversations with his old American friend, W. W. Rockhill, who had seen diplomatic service in China, and who was then the valued private adviser of Secretary of State John Hay on Far Eastern policy. Hippisley, like other Britishers, was eager to have Washington rather than London take the lead in espousing the Open Door, for the Anglophobes in America would have protested bitterly against any such proposal from the Mother Country.

In the late summer of 1899, Hippisley and Rockhill, working with President McKinley and Secretary Hay, threshed out a memorandum which finally became official American policy. By indirection, though not by official intervention, the British thus succeeded in committing the United States to a course favorable to their Chinese interests.

THE OPEN DOOR: FACT AND FANCY

In a dramatic move, on September 6, 1899, Secretary Hay sent the first of his Open Door notes to Berlin, London, and St. Petersburg. Shortly thereafter he included Tokyo, Rome, and Paris. The foreign offices in these capitals were requested to provide assurances regarding the points summarized below:

1. *Within its sphere of interest or leasehold in China,* no power would interfere with any treaty port or any vested interest.
2. The Chinese treaty tariff would be applicable within such spheres of interest, and the duties were to be collected by the Chinese government.
3. *Within its sphere* no power would discriminate in favor of its own nationals in the matter of harbor dues and railroad charges.

Each nation was urged not only to subscribe to these principles but to use its influence to secure acceptance by the others.[21]

Secretary Hay's appeal at once placed the powers in an awkward position. It was like asking all persons in a room who did not have thieving designs to stand up. Replies were at length forthcoming from all of the nations addressed, but each response contained some qualification. The one exception was Italy, which had no sphere of influence in China and which had recently failed in an effort to get one. Most of the governments declared that their acceptance was contingent upon unqualified approval by the others. Russia's response was in effect an evasive declination, which meant that the other powers giving qualified answers were released from their commitment. But Hay, rather than press Russia for a categorical answer (he later secured verbal acquiescence) and run the

---

[21] The correspondence appears in *Foreign Relations*, 1899, pp. 128–142.

risk of a blunt refusal, resorted to Yankee bluff. On March 20, 1900, he proclaimed that the assent of *all* the powers was "final and definitive." Hay's Open Door was thus born with a catch in it.

There has been a vast amount of misunderstanding about the Open Door. In popular phrase it meant equal commercial opportunity in China —a policy as old as America's Far Eastern trade. But the concept, as defined by Hay in 1899, was actually much narrower than is commonly supposed. He did not insist upon the territorial integrity of China. He even assumed that the "sphering out" of the helpless empire would continue, and he omitted all reference to mining and railroad concessions and to capital investment. His Open Door applied to only the relatively small foreign leaseholds and spheres of influence, and even within them it did not guarantee equality of treatment. Vested interests were to be left undisturbed, and this meant that within the German sphere, for example, the Germans would have an advantage.

What, then, was the original Open Door of John Hay? It was merely a dramatic statement of his policy, based primarily upon commercial rather than unselfish motives. The Open Door was designed basically for America's trade rather than China's rights. It did not become legally binding upon the powers, in part because they did not all accept it unconditionally. As far as America was concerned, it was a pious hope rather than a stern international reality.

WIDENING THE THRESHOLD OF THE OPEN DOOR

The Hay notes of 1899 were but academic exercises when compared with the sensational happenings of 1900. A group of fanatical Chinese, called "Boxers" in the Western world, rose up against the "foreign devils," crying "sha!" "sha!" (kill, kill!). After widespread murder and pillaging, a group of whites, including members of the foreign legations, were besieged in Peking and cut off from the outside. Hay refused to give up hope for their safety, and at length succeeded in establishing telegraphic contact with the American minister, who pleaded for speedy relief. The 18,000-man international rescue expedition pressed forward, and in August, 1900 rescued the besieged legations. The United States, despite its hoary nonentanglement policy, contributed some 2500 troops to the British-French-German-Russian-Japanese enterprise. Such were some of the first fruits of having soldiers near at hand in the Philippines.

Secretary Hay strongly suspected, with good reason, that the imperialistic powers would take advantage of the chaos to unhinge the Open Door. As a consequence, he undertook by skillful diplomacy to localize the uprising so that there would be less excuse for invading and perhaps dismembering the rest of China. His most notable effort was a circular note to the powers, dated July 3, 1900. It proclaimed that the "policy of the Government of the United States is to seek a solution" which may "preserve Chinese *territorial and administrative entity*," and "safeguard for the world the principle of equal and impartial trade with all parts of the Chinese Empire." [22]

Hay thus launched an important corollary of his original Open Door notes of September, 1899. He had then applied his policy only to commercial activity, and only within foreign leaseholds and spheres of interest. Now he went a giant stride farther and declared that the United States stood for the *territorial integrity* of all China, and for commercial equality in *"all parts"* of the Chinese Empire. Unlike the original notes, the circular of July 3, 1900, did not call for an answer. Hay had learned his lesson; this time he merely proclaimed America's policy. Yet the powers, suspicious of one another's greed, found it to their advantage to pay lip service to the expanded doctrine.

The victorious and vindictive powers, seeking to collect damages for the Boxer disorders, presented a bill of a third of a billion dollars to the prostrate Chinese government. If Hay had not used his influence for moderation, the sum probably would have been larger, and might have involved territorial cessions as well. America's share was nearly $25 million, but when it proved to be too large, Washington authorized the remission of some $18 million in 1908 and 1924. This generous act paid rich dividends in good will, for the Chinese government used the remitted Boxer fund to educate selected students in the United States.

HAY'S IMPOTENT PEN

The spectacular strokes of John Hay on behalf of the Open Door won for him world-wide acclaim. "Splendid work, splendid diplomacy," gloated the *Philadelphia Inquirer*. But as time wore on discerning observers could perceive that the Open Door was more a phrase than a fact. John Hay, to say nothing of the European powers, realized that the American people did not have a vital enough stake in China to fight for commercial equality. There seemed little point in going to war over some 2 per cent of their foreign trade. And even if the United States had wanted to fight, it did not have sufficient strength in the Far East to do so effectively.

If a prostrate China was saved at this time, the saving was not done by Hay's brilliant pen. The powers were so strong and so suspicious of one another that no one of them was in a position to challenge the Open Door—and the other powers. Doubting one another's integrity, they resigned themselves to acquiescing in China's territorial integrity.

The United States itself proved to be a poor exemplar of the Open Door. A closed door was set up for the Philippines just as soon as American tariffs could be put into effect. Secretly, and incredibly, the United

[22] The correspondence appears in *Foreign Relations*, 1899, p. 299.

States even tried to enter the territorial scramble in China, as the published documents revealed many years later. In November, 1900, at the instance of the Navy Department, Hay undertook to secure from Peking a naval base and territorial concessions at Samsah Bay, in southern China. The Japanese, who had prior claims there, thwarted this surprising move. Gently, and somewhat ironically, they reminded Hay of his recently announced guardianship of China's territorial integrity.[23]

The Open Door might have been made reasonably effective if the British and the Americans, at the turn of the 20th Century, had entered into a firm alliance to uphold commercial opportunity in Eastern Asia. As at the time of the Monroe Doctrine in 1823, their interests ran parallel. But as in 1823, the no-alliance tradition, buttressed by Anglophobia, was too strong to permit such a union, even in the interests of self-interest.

DISCARDING OLD TRADITIONS

The United States, as a weight in international affairs, was a *World* Power from the day of its official birth in 1776. It became a *Great* Power even before the outbreak of the Spanish-American War, which is commonly regarded as its coming-out party. In a little over two years, the new major power established a protectorate over Cuba, annexed Hawaii, secured a definitive title to American Samoa, and acquired Puerto Rico, the Philippines, Guam, and Wake. This last-named islet, a stepping stone to the Philippines, was formally occupied by the commander of the U.S.S. *Bennington* in January, 1899.

Another striking illustration of the new-found willingness of America to forsake isolationist traditions came in 1899, with official participation in the First International Peace Conference at The Hague, in the Netherlands. Called by the Czar of Russia with much fanfare, this twenty-six nation conclave had as its primary objectives the reduction of armaments, a recodification of the laws of war, and the erection of machinery for the peaceful settlement of international disputes.

The suspicious powers could reach no agreement regarding disarmament, and their most important achievement was the establishment of the Permanent Court of Arbitration at The Hague. To this tribunal the nations of the world, on a purely voluntary basis, might submit their differences.[24] American church groups and peace societies generated much enthusiasm for the Hague Conference, but most people were rather indifferent. Elated by recent victories over Spain and hungry for victories over the Filipinos, the masses revealed only lukewarm enthusiasm for beating swords into ploughshares.

[23] See *ibid.*, *1915*, pp. 114–115; P. J. Treat, *Diplomatic Relations between the United States and Japan, 1895–1905* (Stanford University, Calif., 1938), pp. 109–112.
[24] See F. W. Holls, *The Peace Conference at The Hague* (New York, 1900).

At all events, the United States was perhaps fortunate during these transitional years in having a man of John Hay's stature in the State Department. He boldly assumed leadership of the United States as a major power; he revealed unusual qualities of courage and imagination; and he probably accomplished as much in the Far East as was possible without either an entangling alliance or a show of force. Mobilizing public opinion, he helped formulate and publicize an Open Door which his successors were committed to hold ajar. At the same time, he brought a high moral flavor to the conduct of American foreign affairs. His China policy was materialism with strong overtones of evangelism. Finally, he aroused a new interest at home in diplomacy, which Americans had hitherto regarded as a "foreign luxury" or the "deleterious appendage" of effete monarchies.

SELECTED BIBLIOGRAPHY

Helpful introductions are S. F. Bemis, ed., *The American Secretaries of State and their Diplomacy* (New York, 1928), IX, 89–151 and F. R. Dulles, *America's Rise to World Power* (New York, 1955). On the British-American *rapprochement* see C. S. Campbell, Jr., *Anglo-American Understanding, 1898–1903* (Baltimore, 1957); B. A. Reuter, *Anglo-American Relations during the Spanish-American War* (New York, 1924); L. M. Gelber, *The Rise of Anglo-American Friendship* (London, 1938); R. H. Heindel, *The American Impact on Great Britain, 1898–1914* (Philadelphia, 1940); A. L. P. Dennis, *Adventures in American Diplomacy, 1896–1906* (New York, 1928); and N. M. Blake, "England and the United States, 1897–1899," in D. E. Lee and G. E. McReynolds, eds., *Essays in History and International Relations in Honor of George Hubbard Blakeslee* (Worcester, Mass., 1949).

On German friction and the Philippine annexation consult C. E. Schieber, *The Transformation of American Sentiment Toward Germany, 1870–1914* (Boston, 1923); J. F. Rippy, *Latin America in World Politics* (3rd ed., New York, 1938); F. E. Chadwick, *The Relations of the United States and Spain: The Spanish-American War* (New York, 1911). For American opinion on annexation the most valuable monograph is J. W. Pratt, *Expansionists of 1898* (Baltimore, 1936). See also E. S. Pomeroy, *Pacific Outpost: American Strategy in Guam and Micronesia* (Stanford University, Calif., 1951).

For the Far East and the Open Door see A. W. Griswold, *The Far Eastern Policy of the United States* (New York, 1938); Tyler Dennett, *John Hay* (New York, 1933); P. A. Varg, *Open Door Diplomat: The Life of W. W. Rockhill* (Urbana, Ill., 1952); C. S. Campbell, Jr., *Special Business Interest and the Open Door Policy* (New Haven, 1951); E. H. Zabriskie, *American-Russian Rivalry in the Far East, 1895–1914* (Philadelphia, 1946); and Pauline Tompkins, *American-Russian Relations in the Far East* (New York, 1949).

Useful articles are W. E. Leuchtenburg, "Progressivism and Imperialism: The Progressive Movement and American Foreign Policy, 1898–1916," *Miss. Valley Hist. Rev.*, XXXIX (1952), 483–504; J. K. Eyre, Jr., "Russia and the American Acquisition of the Philippines," *ibid.*, XXVIII (1942), 539–562; S. W. Livermore, "American Naval-Base Policy in the Far East, 1850–1914," *Pacific Hist. Rev.*, XIII (1944), 113–135; P. E. Quinn, "The Diplomatic

Struggle for the Carolines, 1898," *ibid.*, XIV (1945), 290–302; F. H. Harrington, "Literary Aspects of American Anti-Imperialism, 1898–1902," *New England Quar.*, X (1937), 650–667.

See footnotes of this chapter and the preceding chapter; Bemis and Griffin, *Guide*, pp. 489–491, 523–530; *Harvard Guide*, Ch. 23.

7TH ED. REFS. See references at end of previous chapter. E. R. May, *Imperial Democracy* (New York, 1961), a work of importance, notes that McKinley was advised as early as September, 1897, of the proposed strike at the Philippines; the Secretary of the Navy twice discussed with him the orders for Dewey; and McKinley approved the final directive sent to Dewey, April 24 (p. 244). While the war was in progress, Britain, Japan, and Germany all expressed an interest in having the islands if America did not want them. In making his final decision McKinley was influenced overwhelmingly by domestic public opinion, and little by other considerations. Frederick Merk, *Manifest Destiny and Mission in American History* (New York, 1963) regards the new overseas Manifest Destiny as the antithesis of the continental Manifest Destiny of the 1840's. W. R. Braisted, *The United States Navy in the Pacific, 1897–1909* (Austin, Tex., 1958) reveals that Lieutenant W. W. Kimball in the Navy Department, not Roosevelt, originated the plan of attacking the Philippines. Germany pushed hard during the war for America not to interfere with her expansionist plans in the Pacific; Ambassador White in Berlin was twice reproved by the State Department for indicating that Germany might have the Philippines. The U.S. Navy, though suspicious of Germany and Russia, co-operated belatedly in the Boxer joint action, and helped prevent the partition of China. The author deals in detail with the interest of the Navy in securing a base at Samsah, in the Chusans, and in Korea, especially Korea. P. A. Varg, *Missionaries, Chinese, and Diplomats: The American Protestant Missionary Movement in China, 1890–1952* (Princeton, 1958) shows the relation of antimissionary feeling to the Boxer outburst. C. D. Davis, *The United States and the First Hague Peace Conference* (Ithaca, N.Y., 1962) contends that the powers, including the United States, were hypocritical in facing up to the disarmament issue; the American delegates, in entering a reservation for the Monroe Doctrine, weakened the Permament Court of Arbitration which they had promoted. T. A. Bailey, "America's Emergence as a World Power: The Myth and the Verity," *Pacific Hist. Rev.*, XXX (1961), 1–16 concludes that the United States, in the sense of affecting the world balance, became a world power from its declaration of independence; a great power, some years before 1898. C. C. Shelby, "Mexico and the Spanish-American War: Some Contemporary Expressions of Opinion," in T. E. Cotner and C. E. Castañeda, eds., *Essays in Mexican History* (Austin, Tex., 1958), pp. 209–228 shows that Mexico, though sympathetic with Mother Spain, was strictly neutral: involvement might mean invasion, and Mexico's economy was too much bound up with that of the United States. The Yankee victory was a "shock and a warning." The Colossus seemed more than ever a colossus. H. H. Quint, "American Socialists and the Spanish-American War," *Amer. Quar.*, X (1958), 131–141 demonstrates that this negligible group, though opposing capitalistic wars, were divided by humanitarianism and hysteria in 1898, but they united against imperialism. For additional references on overseas expansionism, see BIBLIOGRAPHICAL ADDENDUM, p. 1008.

8TH AND 9TH ED. REFS. See BIBLIOGRAPHICAL ADDENDUM, p. 1,009.

CHAPTER

33

Canal Zone Diplomacy
1900-1921

I took the Canal Zone and let Congress debate. . . .
THEODORE ROOSEVELT, 1911

CANAL CONCESSIONS FROM LONDON

PUBLIC INTEREST in an Isthmian canal was revived by the stirring events of the Spanish War. The United States emerged from that conflict not only a Caribbean but a Pacific power. A man-cut waterway seemed imperatively necessary if the American people were to take full advantage of their new trade opportunities in the Pacific, and at the same time unfetter their fleet for two-ocean operations.

The recent hostilities had, in fact, provided a dramatic object lesson in naval needs. The United States battleship *Oregon,* ordered from Puget Sound to Cuban waters, had been forced to make a breakneck voyage around South America—three times the distance that would have been necessary had there been a canal—while all America breathlessly pushed her along.

The chief initial obstacle to building the canal was diplomatic rather than physical. As long as the Clayton-Bulwer Treaty with Britain remained on the books, the United States could not honorably construct an Isthmian waterway and maintain exclusive control over it. The changing temper of Congress was revealed in January, 1900, with the introduction of a bill that provided for the construction of a Nicaraguan Canal in defiance of the treaty. There was a good chance that the proposal would pass, for, as Secretary of State Hay reported, some of the Senators were saying, "dishonor be damned."

The London officials, already involved in the Boer War and faced with an unfriendly Europe, decided that rather than risk the newly won

Anglo-American friendship they would make appropriate concessions. Accordingly, in February, 1900, Lord Pauncefote, the popular British ambassador in Washington, concluded a treaty with Secretary Hay. It provided that the United States could construct, own, and neutralize an Isthmian waterway, but under no conditions fortify it.

At first—but only at first—the treaty was rather favorably received in the United States. It was a definite improvement on the Clayton-Bulwer encumbrance, and it was in keeping with the traditional policy of a neu-tralized canal. But 1900 was a Presidential election year, and the Demo-cratic platform blasted the pact as a base surrender to Britain. The Irish-Americans, who deplored the recent friendliness with the Mother Country, added their voices to the outcry. They were joined by the Ger-man-Americans, who had been greatly aroused by the killing of their fellow Teutons in the Boer War. These "hyphenated Americans" were the "idiots," wrote John Hay, who yelled that he was not an American be-cause he did not say, " 'To Hell with the Queen,' at every breath."

The most serious objection to the Hay-Pauncefote Treaty was the non-fortification clause. This meant that America's enemies could use the pro-posed canal against her or, if they possessed a superior force, seize it for their own. "It would have been a magnet whenever a war broke out," cried Hearst's *New York Journal-American*, which was joined by many other alarmist newspapers. "Another of the administration's 'great diplo-matic victories,' " jeered the *Detroit News*, "has been won—by the British government." [1]

BRITAIN BOWS OUT OF THE ISTHMUS

The Senate, bending to the storm of protests against the Hay-Paunce-fote Treaty, undertook to provide for fortifying the proposed canal. But the Senatorial amendments were so sweeping and so definitely to Amer-ica's advantage that the London government, supported by resentment in the English press, refused to accept them. The entire negotiation fell to the ground in March, 1901.

Secretary Hay, fresh from his Open Door triumphs, did not take kindly to this setback. Destined for a life of ease and endowed with brilliant gifts, he made little effort to conceal his contempt for the Senators, and they reciprocated by manhandling some of his treaties. Chronic ill-health increased his irritability. Humiliated by the failure of the Hay-Pauncefote treaty, he tendered his resignation but was finally persuaded to remain. Although conceding that the pact was not perfect, he felt that on a give-and-take basis the arrangement was a fair one. He lamented:

> I long ago made up my mind that no treaty . . . that gave room for a difference of opinion could ever pass the Senate. When I sent in the Canal

[1] *Public Opinion*, XXVIII, 199 (Feb. 15, 1900).

Convention I felt sure that no one out of a mad house could fail to see that the advantages were all on our side. But I underrated the power of ignorance and spite, acting upon cowardice.[2]

Hay also complained that "there will always be 34% of the Senate on the blackguard side of every question." He likewise asserted that "A treaty entering the Senate is like a bull going into the arena: no one can say just how or when the final blow will fall—but one thing is certain—it will never leave the arena alive."[3] All this was most unfair—and a reflection of Hay's pique. The brutal fact is that, considering America's interests, the Senate was right and Hay was wrong on the fortification issue. This still-born treaty is one of the examples most frequently cited in support of the much criticized two-thirds rule.

The months following the collapse of the Hay-Pauncefote negotiations were fraught with uncertainty. There was much loose talk in the United States of abrogating the Clayton-Bulwer shackle outright, or of going to war to end Britain's thwarting of America's destiny. All this was profoundly disturbing to the British. America was powerful; her friendship was valuable; the Boer War was exhausting; and relations with Germany were deteriorating. Why not, concluded the British, do the graceful thing and permit their offspring to build the canal? The waterway would greatly increase the mobility and hence the power of the American navy, while enabling the United States to guarantee the *status quo* in the Western Hemisphere against Britain's rivals, notably Germany. Even at this late date the distresses of Europe were operating to America's advantage.

Downing Street went the whole way, in November, 1901, when it concluded the second Hay-Pauncefote Treaty. By the terms of this pact the Clayton-Bulwer agreement was specifically superseded, and the United States was given a free hand to build, control, and *fortify* the proposed canal. The last point was tacitly understood. Not content with relinquishing to America the key to a maritime empire, without exacting an equivalent, Britain reduced her West Indian fleet and garrisons during the next few years. Thus she not only recognized the supremacy of the Americans in the Caribbean, but inferentially assigned them the role of watchdog of the Western Hemisphere.

RIVAL ROUTES

The Rough-riding Theodore Roosevelt became President in September, 1901, after McKinley's assassination. Not relishing the satiric title "His Accidency," he set out to prove that he was entitled to be President "in

[2] A. L. P. Dennis, *Adventures in American Diplomacy, 1896–1906* (New York, 1928), p. 168.
[3] W. R. Thayer, *The Life and Letters of John Hay* (Boston, 1915), II, 393.

his own right." Nothing, he believed, would more impress the American people than starting the much-talked-about canal—"making the dirt fly." More kinds of dirt finally flew than he anticipated.

With the Clayton-Bulwer Treaty now cleared away, the next step was to choose between the Panama and the Nicaraguan routes. The New Panama Canal Company, successor to the defunct de Lesseps organization, was asking the exorbitant sum of $109 million for its holdings. The fate of the Nicaraguan route depended largely on the report of the Walker Commission, a group of engineers appointed by President Mc-Kinley. In November, 1901, this body recommended the Nicaraguan route, largely on the basis of lower cost. Panicky, the French canal company dropped its price to $40 million, a saving of $69 million that tipped the scales in favor of Panama. President Roosevelt, who hitherto seems to have favored Nicaragua, now persuaded the Walker Commission to vote for a Panama canal.

But the French company was not yet out of the woods. In January, 1902, nine days before the Walker Commission reversed itself, the House of Representatives voted in favor of a Nicaraguan waterway, 308 to 2. Thoroughly alarmed, the French company swung into action with its high-powered and high-priced lobbyists. Conspicuous among these was a prominent New York attorney, William N. Cromwell, who had recently contributed a reported $60,000 to the Republican campaign chest in order to prevent the party from going on record in 1900 in favor of the Nicaraguan route. He allegedly charged his contribution to the French company, and later presented a bill for $800,000 for his services.

The company was also well served by a remarkable Frenchman, Philippe Bunau-Varilla, former chief engineer of the original organization and a large stockholder of the new concern. In the interests of his fellow investors he came to America and zealously made contacts with the "right people," including John Hay, Mark Hanna, and Theodore Roosevelt. He attempted to disparage the Nicaraguan route by raising the bogey of volcanic activity, but his efforts did not meet with much success until May, 1902, when Mont Pelée, on the West Indian island of Martinique, suddenly blew its top and wiped out a town of 30,000 people. A few days later a Nicaraguan volcano became active—the very mountain that was engraved on the postage stamps of the republic. Bunau-Varilla hastened to the stamp dealers of Washington.

> I was lucky enough [he later wrote] to find there ninety stamps, that is, one for every Senator, showing a beautiful volcano belching forth in magnificent eruption. . . .
> I hastened to paste my precious postage stamps on sheets of paper. . . . Below the stamps were written the following words, which told the whole story: "An official witness of the volcanic activity of Nicaragua." [4]

[4] Philippe Bunau-Varilla, *Panama: the Creation, Destruction, and Resurrection* (New York, 1914), p. 247.

Bunau-Varilla then took steps to place one of these stamps in the hands of each Senator.

Such astute lobbying presumably had some influence in the Senate, where the Panama adherents rallied in force. They were led by Mark Hanna, who, as chairman of the Republican National Committee, was doubtless grateful for Cromwell's $60,000 contribution. After extended debate, the Senate drastically changed the House-approved Nicaraguan bill so as to provide for a *Panama* canal. The amended measure, which the House accepted, became law on June 28, 1902. Under it the President was to secure a right of way at Panama from Colombia, but if he failed to do so "within a reasonable time and upon reasonable terms," he was required to negotiate with Nicaragua.

ROADBLOCK IN BOGOTÁ

The way was now clear for an agreement with Colombia to obtain the Panama route. Secretary Hay, by threatening to turn to Nicaragua and by using other high-pressure methods, finally succeeded in extorting a treaty from the Colombian *chargé* in Washington, Tomás Herrán. The latter signed with serious misgivings on January 22, 1903. Three days later a telegram came from Bogotá instructing him not to sign and to await new instructions. But the die was cast, and the Senate approved the pact on March 17, 1903, after a brief and bitter flare-up from the last-ditch Nicaragua enthusiasts. By the terms of the Hay-Herrán Treaty the United States was to obtain rights to a canal zone six miles wide for a cash payment of $10 million and an annual payment of $250,000, beginning in nine years. The leasehold was renewable in perpetuity.

But the treaty, so highly favorable to the United States, struck an unexpected snag in Colombia. Patriotic Colombians objected to the financial terms, to the undoubted impingement upon the nation's sovereignty, and to the unconstitutionality of disposing of Colombian territory in perpetuity. The weakening dictator of Colombia, José Marroquín, was then in his eighties and beset by domestic factions. He presumably could have brought about ratification of the Hay-Herrán Treaty by executive decree, even though such action was unconstitutional. But so strong was popular opposition to the pact that he decided to summon congress, which he had dispensed with for several years. The Colombian Senate, although favoring a renewal of the negotiations, voted unanimously against ratification, on August 12, 1903.

A major motive for Colombia's surprising action was a natural desire for more money. Indeed, the regime in Bogotá expressed a willingness to accept an additional $15 million. The simple facts are that the Colombians owned the canal strip, that it was one of their most valuable assets, and that they were at liberty to demand the price they wanted. The best chance for more money lay in securing a substantial slice of the $40 million that the United States was prepared to pay the French stockholders for their rights. But by the terms of the Hay-Herrán Treaty Colombia was forbidden to deal with the company. That privilege, thanks largely to the foresight of Cromwell and Bunau-Varilla, was specifically reserved to the United States.

There was one other possible approach for Colombia. The French concession would expire in October, 1904, even though it had been extended by President Marroquín to 1910 without the consent of the Colombian congress. His decree probably could be set aside. Upon the expiration of the French rights, Colombia could dispose of the physical assets of the company to the United States for the coveted $40 million. The Colombians obviously had everything to gain by marking time for about a year.

The impatient Roosevelt, who ardently desired the Republican nomination in 1904, had meanwhile become well-nigh apoplectic. In various utterances, chiefly private, he denounced the "corrupt pithecoid community" of Colombians as "inefficient bandits," "foolish and homicidal corruptionists," "contemptible little creatures," "jack rabbits," and "cat rabbits." He declared that the situation was "exactly as if a road agent had tried to hold up a man," and he insisted that the "cut throats" and "blackmailers of Bogotá" should not be permitted "permanently to bar one of the future highways of civilization." He went so far as to draft a message, which fortunately he did not send to Congress, suggesting that the canal strip be taken by force. Behind the scenes, Secretary Hay cabled a virtual ultimatum, which the Colombians resented as barefaced duress.

The savage epithets of Roosevelt were hardly fair. Even assuming that the congress at Bogotá was wholly corrupt, one must concede that the motives which cause one sovereign state to reject a treaty are not a proper concern of any other state. Hay asserted that the Colombians were honor-bound to ratify a treaty that had been approved by their agent, but his arguments would be more convincing if the Department of State had not brought such great pressure on Herrán to sign. No one knew better than Hay, whose recent experiences with the Pauncefote Treaty were fresh in mind, that the United States Senate frequently delayed or rejected treaties signed by American representatives. And no one knew better than Hay that such action had often been prompted by partisan or other unworthy motives.

PANAMANIAN PLOTTINGS

The press of the United States, like Roosevelt and Hay, was sorely displeased by Colombia's conduct. Editorial columns teemed with such phrases as the "thieves of Bogotá," "brigand Senators," and "organized rapacity." Some journals favored turning to the Nicaraguan route; others advocated seizure of the Panama canal strip under the "right" of international eminent domain. Still others urged that Panama be encouraged to secede so that the United States could make terms with her. "What other world power," queried the *New York Commercial Advertiser*, "has ever hesitated to use force under similar circumstances?" But the *Literary Digest* found that more newspapers favored the Nicaraguan route than advocated connivance at revolt.[5]

The political pot had meanwhile come to a boil in Panama. This department had once been an independent entity but had voluntarily joined Colombia, only to have its rights usurped by a Colombian dictator in the 1880's. The Panamanians had shown their discontent with the rule of Bogotá by numerous uprisings—fifty-three in fifty-seven years, according to Roosevelt's count. Now came the rejection of the Hay-Herrán Treaty, from which the people of Panama had expected juicy commercial benefits. Disappointment rapidly gave way to anxiety when the Panamanians realized that Roosevelt might turn to Nicaragua, as contemplated by act of Congress. Plainly the situation was ripe for revolt—another Isthmian revolt.

The conspirators hatched their plot both in Panama and in the United States. A center of revolutionary activity was Room 1162 of the Hotel Waldorf-Astoria, in New York City, and here the bustling Bunau-Varilla worked out many of the necessary details and raised funds for bribery. The revolutionists were finally able to muster a "patriot" army at Panama City consisting largely of 500 "bought" Colombian troops and members of the local fire department. Obviously, this tiny force would prove most inadequate unless assurances could be obtained as to the attitude of the Roosevelt administration toward the Treaty of 1846 with Colombia (New Granada).

By the terms of this yellowing document the United States had bound itself to maintain the "perfect neutrality" of the Isthmus, so that "free transit" might not be interrupted. When drawn up, the pact was designed to prevent some outside power, particularly Britain, from seizing Panama. Colombia certainly would never have approved it if she had suspected that it would one day be invoked against herself. During the numerous revolutionary outbursts in Panama prior to 1903, the United States on seven different occasions had landed troops to protect "free transit." In each instance these forces had been used only with the approval or consent of the Colombian authorities. Only once had such intervention interfered with the Colombian troops, and then the Washington government had expressed regret for its error. The precedent for noninterference was thus plainly established.

[5] *Literary Digest*, XXVII, 416 (Oct. 3, 1903).

A REPUBLIC IS BORN—WITH CAESARIAN MIDWIFERY

The crucial question was: What would now be the attitude of Washington in the event of another insurrection? Would the United States fly in the face of its own precedents and, by a tortured interpretation of the Treaty of 1846, keep the Isthmus open by refusing to permit Colombian troops to land and crush the revolt? Bunau-Varilla conferred with key figures in Washington, notably Hay and Roosevelt, and although the President seems to have made no commitment, the vehemence of his remarks caused Bunau-Varilla to conclude that a Panama revolution would not be permitted to fail. Apparently acting on "inside information," the astute Frenchman cabled his fellow conspirators that a warship, the U.S.S. *Nashville*, would reach Colón (Panama), on November 2, 1903. It arrived on schedule. The faint-hearted revolutionists, encouraged by this visual evidence that the United States would support them, went ahead with their plans. Bunau-Varilla later asserted that he was able to predict the movements of the American ships by reading notices of their sailing in the newspapers. Roosevelt, who indignantly denied that he had conspired with the scheming Frenchman, later declared:

> He is a very able fellow, and it was his business to find out what he thought our Government would do. I have no doubt that he was able to make a very accurate guess, and to advise his people accordingly. In fact, he would have been a very dull man had he been unable to make such a guess.[6]

On November 3, 1903, the day after the arrival of the U.S.S. *Nashville*, the patriot "army" of Panama revolted. The American naval forces, acting under orders, kept the Isthmus clear by preventing the Colombian troops from moving, and thus insured the success of the uprising. Only a bystander and a donkey were killed. The next day, November 4, the infant republic proclaimed itself a member of the family of nations. A little more than an hour after receiving the news, Roosevelt authorized *de facto* recognition, which was granted on November 6, only three days after the revolution. This action was so precipitate as to lend additional color to the charge that the White House had connived at the outbreak. Nor can one ignore the fact that in the weeks after the revolution American naval forces stood guard at Panama City, thus forcing the advancing Colombian troops to bog down in the surrounding jungles.

Whatever the truth, several facts stand out like lighthouses. Roosevelt was glad that the revolution had succeeded, and he made little effort to conceal his joy. Furthermore, he and his advisers knew a good deal about the conspiracy in Panama, more, in fact, than they were willing to admit.

[6] J. B. Bishop, *Theodore Roosevelt and His Time* (New York, 1920), I, 296 (Roosevelt to Bigelow, Jan. 6, 1904).

Finally, the general attitude of the administration was such as to give the plotters precisely that kind of encouragement that they needed before risking their lives and fortunes.

REACTIONS TO ROUGH-RIDERISM

The bustling Bunau-Varilla now managed to have himself, though a French citizen, represent the infant republic of Panama in Washington. On November 18, 1903, only fifteen days after the uprising, he signed the

THE NEWS REACHES BOGOTÁ

A determined Roosevelt makes the dirt fly.
Rogers in *New York Herald*, c. 1903, courtesy *New York Sun*, Inc.

Hay-Bunau-Varilla pact, which he had induced his nominal superiors in Panama to approve unseen. Like the defunct Hay-Herrán Treaty, it provided for a payment of $10 million down and $250,000 a year. But it also widened the zone from six to ten miles and granted the United States extraordinary sovereign rights.

The terms of the Hay-Bunau-Varilla Treaty were so advantageous as to make Panama virtually a military outpost of the great northern republic—to the increasing discontent of Panamanians. As Hay rushed the treaty to ratification, he knew that two bona-fide citizens of Panama were on their way to help Bunau-Varilla. (They arrived six hours late.) But the concessions made to the United States were so favorable as to place a premium on hasty action. On February 23, 1904, the United States Senate, after another bitter flurry of opposition, approved the treaty by a vote of 66 to 14.

Roosevelt's "cowboy diplomacy" stirred up a vast amount of criticism in his own country, especially among liberals and partisan Democrats. The press heatedly referred to a "cooked-up republic," "piracy," "scandal, disgrace, and dishonor," and "indecent haste." The *Springfield Republican* branded the incident as one of the "most discreditable in our history." The *New York American* would "rather forego forever the advantage of an inter-ocean waterway than gain one by such means as this." "Even the buccaneers who sailed the Spanish Main," lamented the *New York Nation,* "would have found it too much for them."

There were also critics abroad. From Europe, where the seizure of territory from weak neighbors was an old story, came condemnation of Roosevelt's course. One English journal declared that "the United States has shaken the confidence of the civilized world in her honesty." The *Glasgow Herald* found that "Expediency has been stronger than morality."

In Latin America, surprisingly enough, there was no universal outburst of indignation. One explanation is that Roosevelt's role at that time was not fully appreciated. Some Latin Americans, notably those with a commercial stake in the speedy completion of the canal, were inclined to condemn Colombia, congratulate Panama, and condone the United States. But important elements in Latin America castigated Roosevelt's buccaneering tactics, and they seemingly grew more vocal with the passing of time.[7]

The Rough Rider's methods nevertheless commanded substantial support at home, especially among fellow Republicans. His diplomacy at least had the virtue—perhaps the only virtue—of getting results. The *Literary Digest* analyzed the views of some seventy American newspaper editors and found that fifty-three favored the *coup* and seventeen criticized it. The *Hartford Times* expressed a rather common sentiment when it remarked that Colombia's plight was "entirely her own fault," while the *Atlanta Journal* found that she was "needlessly obstructing the world's commerce." *Public Opinion* thus summarized sentiment:

> . . . No one can deny that the majority opinion of the country approves the course of the administration, little as this course can be justified on moral grounds. . . . The sum of public opinion in this matter being simply that we want an isthmian canal above all things, and that the government has taken the surest means of attaining this object.[8]

[7] John Patterson, "Latin-American Reactions to the Panama Revolution of 1903," *Hispanic Amer. Hist. Rev.,* XXIV (1944), 342–351.
[8] *Public Opinion,* XXXV, 643 (Nov. 19, 1903).

A MANDATE (?) FROM CIVILIZATION

The brunt of the defense was borne by Roosevelt, whose zeal outran his candor. He declared that "every action" of his administration in the affair had been "carried out in accordance with the highest, finest, and nicest standards of public and governmental ethics." He insisted that intervention had been necessary for a proper discharge of the treaty obligation to guard the Isthmus, as well as to protect American lives and property. In his annual message to Congress he put his action on a much broader basis:

> . . . I confidently maintain that the recognition of the Republic of Panama was an act justified by the interests of collective civilization. If ever a Government could be said to have received a mandate from civilization . . . the United States holds that position with regard to the interoceanic canal.[9]

If one assumes that Roosevelt did have a "mandate from civilization," certain bothersome questions arise. Would not the interests of "civilization" have been about as well served by a Nicaraguan waterway? Nicaragua was already an independent state: no revolution was needed. Nicaragua was eager to come to an agreement with the United States, and had already revealed a willingness to do so on more advantageous terms than were obtainable from Colombia. The Isthmian Canal Commission had twice endorsed the feasibility of the Nicaraguan route, which, though longer, was about a day nearer the United States. Its estimated cost was greater, but the ultimate expenditures on the Panama Canal far exceeded estimates. Whatever the expense of construction, a Nicaraguan waterway would cost little or nothing in ill will. The President was required by law to adopt this route after a "reasonable time," and he, himself, was beginning to have misgivings as to whether or not a "reasonable time" had elapsed. "Damn the law!" he allegedly shouted in private, "I want the canal built."

Roosevelt's desperate determination to "make the dirt fly" was a key factor in the controversy. But what was the pressing need for haste, aside from Presidential politics and the Rough Rider's stubborn pride? The canal had remained uncut for many centuries. In the long view, a few years one way or another would make little difference. By the very terms of the original Hay-Herrán Treaty, provision was made for delays totaling thirty-six years. Roosevelt presumably could have waited one year, whereupon the concession of the French company could have been made to expire. Colombia would then have obtained the $40 million, and the United States would have secured the canal.

But the impetuous Rough Rider could tolerate no postponement. Congress would meet in December, and the press had already begun to

[9] *Foreign Relations, 1903,* p. 275.

clamor for the Nicaraguan alternative. If the President wanted a canal at Panama, he would be wise to present Congress with an accomplished fact, and this is precisely what he did.

As time wore on, Roosevelt became more belligerent and less discreet in his self-justification. His advisers made out a legalistic case based on the Treaty of 1846, but Roosevelt could not be bothered. Speaking at Berkeley, California, in 1911, he made this unfortunate but characteristic boast:

> I am interested in the Panama Canal because I started it. If I had followed traditional, conservative methods I would have submitted a dignified State paper of probably 200 pages to Congress and the debates on it would have been going on yet; but I took the Canal Zone and let Congress debate; and while the debate goes on the Canal does also.[10]

Roosevelt's two-fisted methods probably hastened the construction of the canal by perhaps a year or two. For this slight gain he gave a sharp setback to the peaceful settlement of international disputes, created a damaging precedent for aggressor-minded nations, aroused the distrust of many Latin Americans, and grievously offended a weak sister republic. The severing of the Isthmus severed Colombia's friendship.

BALM FOR BOGOTA

The Colombians repeatedly proposed that their grievance be submitted to arbitration. But the United States, though traditionally a champion of arbitral methods, flatly refused. Roosevelt would consent to no such confession of wrongdoing while he was President. Under Taft, his political creature and successor, several attempts were made to placate Colombia. But they all ended in failure.

The Democratic administration of Woodrow Wilson, taking office in 1913, was much more willing to do penance for the sins of the Republican Roosevelt. In 1914 it signed a treaty with Colombia in which the United States expressed "sincere regret" for the unfortunate Panama affair, and agreed to pay $25 million as pecuniary balm—"canalimony," one wit called it. But Roosevelt, who regarded such a payment as "blackmail," was determined that no such acknowledgment of guilt should be made. His view now was that Colombia had wronged the United States by not allowing "herself to be benefited." Roosevelt's friends in the Senate, notably Henry Cabot Lodge, sprang to his defense, and the Democratic treaty was shelved.

A revival of the agitation to indemnify mutilated Colombia came in 1921. Harding, a Republican, was President; the restless Rough Rider was safely in his grave. The seven-year old draft of a treaty was amended so as to eliminate "sincere regret" but to keep the $25 million. This large

[10] *New York Times*, March 25, 1911, 10:3.

a sum was in itself an eloquent apology. Lodge now supported the pact on the grounds that it would improve commercial relations, and that Roosevelt would favor it if he were alive. This latter assumption may be seriously doubted.

Certain critics pointed out that there was more to the indemnity move than met the eye. Petroleum, now an essential ingredient in world power, had been discovered in Colombia. The Bogotá government was naturally disposed to deny concessions to Yankees, while granting them to the British and other rivals. The payment of $25 million would presumably grease the ways for a treaty under which the United States could secure its share of "black gold." As oil gushed from the soil of Colombia, tears of remorse gushed from the eyes of American oil men.

Some of the Senators accused the Republican majority of having reversed itself. Johnson of California, himself a nominal Republican, was unable to understand how "blackmail for 17 years had ripened now into honest obligation." Senator Watson of Georgia suspected that "an oil proposition" had been "pipe-lined into this treaty," and that the United States was going to pay "an indirect subsidy to the oil interests." Other Senators stoutly maintained that the payment of "conscience money" was an admission of guilt. But such arguments proved unavailing in the face of a Senatorial machine well lubricated with Colombian oil. The treaty slipped through on April 20, 1921, by a vote of 69 to 19.

Perhaps the saddest aspect of this whole unsavory episode is that if the $25 million finally paid to Colombia had been offered in 1903, a vast amount of unpleasantness almost certainly would have been avoided.

SELECTED BIBLIOGRAPHY

See references at the end of the previous chapter for Anglo-American relations and the Hay-Pauncefote Treaty. Interesting biographical introductions are H. F. Pringle, *Theodore Roosevelt* (New York, 1931) and Tyler Dennett, *John Hay* (New York, 1933). See also *Theodore Roosevelt: An Autobiography* (New York, 1922) and A. L. P. Dennis, *Adventures in American Diplomacy, 1896–1906* (New York, 1928). Perhaps the most complete monograph on the Panama affair is D. C. Miner, *The Fight for the Panama Route* (New York, 1940). Recent scholarship appears in C. S. Campbell, Jr., *Anglo-American Understanding, 1898–1903* (Baltimore, 1957). See also H. C. Hill, *Roosevelt and the Caribbean* (Chicago, 1927); E. T. Parks, *Colombia and the United States, 1765–1934* (Durham, N.C., 1935); J. F. Rippy, *The Capitalists and Colombia* (New York, 1931); W. D. McCain, *The United States and the Republic of Panama* (Durham, N.C., 1937); W. H. Callcott, *The Caribbean Policy of the United States, 1890–1920* (Baltimore, 1942); M. P. DuVal, *Cadiz to Cathay* (Stanford University, Calif., 1940); Gerstle Mack, *The Land Divided* (New York, 1944); and N. J. Padelford, *The Panama Canal in Peace and War* (New York, 1942).

See Bemis and Griffin, *Guide,* pp. 423–428, 554–564.

7TH, 8TH, AND 9TH ED. REFS. See BIBLIOGRAPHICAL ADDENDUM, p. 1,012.

34

Big-Stick Diplomacy
1901-1909

I have always been fond of the West African proverb:
"Speak softly and carry a big stick, you will go far."
THEODORE ROOSEVELT, 1900

CUBAN COMPLEXITIES

WHEN THE SPANISH-AMERICAN WAR ended, prostrate Cuba presented McKinley with perplexities hardly less vexatious than those that had existed before the conflict. Many expansionists in the United States were convinced that the easiest solution was to annex the long-coveted island outright. But there stood the self-denying Teller Amendment, by which Congress, in an outburst of idealism, had spurned the prize. Even so, there were imperialists who were prepared to give a shyster-like twist to the pledge. They argued that the promise had been made in ignorance of actual conditions, and that the unexpected outcome of the war had released the United States from its obligation.

The temptation to annex Cuba was finally thrust aside. For one thing, the frustrating Philippine insurrection had a dampening effect; for another, the Democratic opposition kept nagging the Republicans to honor the Teller Amendment. But obviously the anarchic island of Cuba could not be launched on the international sea without moorings. A major power —Germany was especially feared during these years—might secure a foothold there and jeopardize not only the Isthmian lifeline but the very shores of the United States.

The problem was neatly solved by making Cuba a quasi-protectorate of the United States under the Platt Amendment to the army appropriation bill of 1901. Later that year, the Cubans, responding to strong pressure from Washington, incorporated this restriction in their constitution, and two years later they embodied it in a treaty with the United States. In summary form the principal provisions of the Platt Amendment were:

1. Cuba was not to make a treaty impairing her independence or to permit a foreign power [*e.g.*, Germany] to secure lodgement in or control over the island.
2. Cuba pledged herself not to incur an indebtedness beyond her means. [It might result in foreign intervention.]
3. The United States was at liberty to intervene for the purpose of preserving order and maintaining Cuban independence.
4. Cuba would agree to an American-sponsored sanitation program. [Aimed largely at yellow fever.]
5. Cuba agreed to sell or lease to the United States sites for naval and coaling stations. [Guantánamo became the principal base.]

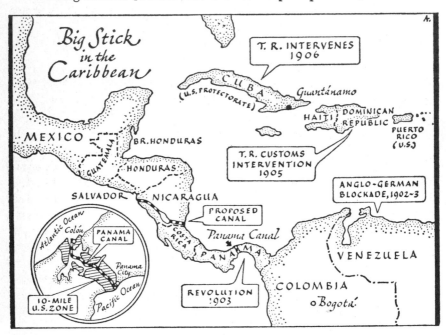

The temptation to remain in Cuba was great, but in 1902 President Roosevelt surprised the imperialistic world by withdrawing. During the ensuing years recurrent disorders revived annexationist hopes in the United States. "It is manifest destiny," declared the *Indianapolis News,* "for a nation to own the islands which border its shores." But Roosevelt, who for once did not welcome an opportunity to brandish the Big Stick, wrote in 1906:

> Just at the moment I am so angry with that infernal little Cuban republic that I would like to wipe its people off the face of the earth. All that we wanted from them was that they would behave themselves and be prosperous and happy so that we would not have to interfere. And now, lo and behold, they have started an utterly unjustifiable and pointless revolution and may get things into such a snarl that we have no alternative save to intervene—which will at once convince the suspicious idiots in South America that we do wish to interfere after all, and perhaps have some land-hunger.[1]

[1] Roosevelt to White, Sept. 13, 1906, Roosevelt Papers, Library of Congress.

Late in 1906, at the invitation of the bedeviled Cuban President, United States troops were landed to restore order. "Necessity," as one New York journal remarked, "is the mother of in(ter)vention."

The alarms of 1906 re-aroused American imperialists. "What a pity," remarked a Southern newspaper, "we did not keep Cuba and let the Philippines find another owner." But public opinion in the United States responded favorably when the American troops were withdrawn in 1909, following the restoration of order. As before, the imperialistic world was puzzled. As before, the Cubans were left with only a limited sovereignty, but in these circumstances the alternative was perhaps no sovereignty at all.

THE KAISER AND CASTRO

American suspicions of Germany continued to mount, as the Platt Amendment attests, with the unfolding of the new century. Rumors were rife that the Kaiser was scheming to pick up naval bases near the projected Isthmian canal, and in other ways to challenge the Monroe Doctrine.

A revival of interest in buying the Danish West Indies was sparked largely by fear that Germany might acquire them. In 1902 Washington concluded a treaty of annexation with Denmark, only to have it rejected by the Danish Parliament. The conviction deepened in American quarters, both official and unofficial, that German pressure had thwarted ratification. But the secret documents that have subsequently been examined do not lend positive support to this view.[2]

The fiercely mustached and saber-rattling Kaiser, whom the American press regarded as a dangerously ambitious and theatrical blunderer, personified distrust of Germany. One contemporary wrote:

> Kaiser, Kaiser, shining bright,
> You have given us a fright!
> With your belts and straps and sashes,
> And your skyward-turned mustaches!
> And that frown so deadly fierce,
> And those awful eyes that pierce
> Through the very hearts of those
> Whom ill fate has made your foes.
>
> . . . .
>
> Kaiser, Kaiser, Man of War,
> What a funny joke you are. [3]

Keenly aware of the disfavor into which he and the Fatherland had fallen, he launched a campaign to curry favor with the American people. He caused a medal to be conferred on Roosevelt, which, John Hay

[2] C. C. Tansill, *The Purchase of the Danish West Indies* (Baltimore, 1932), pp. 452–453.
[3] *Harper's Weekly*, XLVII, 475 (March 21, 1903).

sneered, was worth about 35 cents and of dubious artistic merit. He not only ordered a yacht to be built in the United States but asked Roosevelt's daughter, Alice, to christen it. He also sent Prince Henry to the United States on a good will mission, and presented a bronze statue of Frederick the Great. The *Washington Star* suggested that, as a counter-compliment, the Kaiser be given a statue of James Monroe.

Whatever ground Germany may have gained by this clumsy courtship was thrown away in Venezuela, which was then under the domination of an unscrupulous dictator, Cipriano Castro. This unhappy land was cursed with almost perpetual civil war, and the disorders had proved ruinous to foreign investors, particularly the British and the Germans. Although the powers of Europe were sorely tempted to intervene, they were hesitant to challenge the now redoubtable Monroe Doctrine.

But Roosevelt did not regard mere intervention as a violation of Monroe's principles, provided that no acquisition of territory was involved. He felt that irresponsible Latin-American nations, crying "Monroe Doctrine," should not attempt to hide behind the protective petticoats of the United States. "If any South-American country misbehaves toward any European country," he wrote privately in 1901, "let the European country spank it." The official attitude of Washington certainly offered no deterrent to those powers that wished to "spank" Castro.[4]

Castro, himself, was plainly courting chastisement. In 1901 Germany proposed arbitration of her claims by the Hague Court, but the arrogant dictator turned a deaf ear. Then the British, whose financial stake was five times larger than that of the Germans, showed considerable interest in a joint collection at the cannon's mouth. Berlin, reassured by the acquiescent attitude of Roosevelt, was of a like mind.

The crisis came to a head in December, 1902, when Britain and Germany, later joined by Italy, instituted a "pacific blockade" of Venezuela. The allies seized several Venezuelan gunboats, and the Germans sank two. These iron-fisted measures brought Castro to his knees, and he hastened to accept the arbitration he had once spurned. On December 12 Washington transmitted his proposal to the powers concerned, and within a week both London and Berlin had accepted limited arbitration in principle. But the blockade continued for two months, pending the signing of a protocol by Venezuela. To all outward appearances, Washington was not involved in this diplomatic crisis at all: it merely acted as the messenger boy.

The Venezuela claims were finally settled by The Hague Court in 1904, with Latin America showing surprisingly little official interest. A significant exception was the declaration which Luis M. Drago, Argentine Minister of Foreign Affairs, sent to Washington late in 1902. Arguing that foreign investors took their chances when they invested abroad, he

[4] Dexter Perkins, *The Monroe Doctrine, 1867–1907* (Baltimore, 1937), p. 333.

maintained that the use of armed forces to collect public debts was not justified. A modified form of the so-called Drago Doctrine, supported by the United States, was adopted by the Second Hague Conference in 1907.

PUBLIC OPINION OUTPERFORMS THE BIG STICK

The Venezuelan intervention of 1902 had a dramatic sequel. Thirteen years later, when Roosevelt was violently aroused by Germany's role in World War I, he made public a cloak-and-dagger version of the whole affair. He related how he summoned the German ambassador, laid down a ringing ultimatum, backed it up with a threat to send Admiral Dewey's entire fleet to Venezuela, and forced the Kaiser to arbitrate.

Historians were prompt to point to certain contradictions in Roosevelt's lurid tale, and to the absence of substantial documentary proof. Some doubters even went so far as to conclude that he had fabricated the story out of whole cloth while under the spell of anti-German hate. But several of his private letters reveal that he had the main outlines of his version clearly in mind several years before World War I broke out and while he was still in the White House. It is conceivable that he may have exerted some behind-the-scenes pressure on the Kaiser, although not in the sensational fashion that he later described.[5]

But Roosevelt did not need the Big Stick to bring an end to the Venezuela intervention. Other forces, even more potent, were at work. For one thing, public opinion in the United States was far less tolerant of the Venezuelan blockade than the State Department. Germany was already tainted, and her mailed-fist tactics aroused much additional distrust. "There is a tendency under this administration," declared William Jennings Bryan, "to allow the Monroe Doctrine to acquire a mothballish flavor." "Monroe rhymes with go," pointedly remarked one Chicago newspaper. A writer in the *Minneapolis Tribune* rejoiced that Admiral Dewey, with a menacing fleet, was in Puerto Rican waters:

> Yankee Dewey's near La Guayra,
> Yankee Dewey Dandy.
> Maybe just as well to have our
> Yankee Dewey Handy.[6]

In January, 1903, the Germans bombarded Fort San Carlos, in Venezuela, and incidentally destroyed the village. American indignation was strongly aroused by this incident, and the press generally referred to it as an "outrageous" and "wantonly reckless act"—"a tactless exhibition of vindictiveness and brutality." The *New York Times* stated bluntly: "Worse international manners than Germany has exhibited from the be-

[5] See H. K. Beale, *Theodore Roosevelt and the Rise of America to World Power* (Baltimore, 1956), pp. 395 ff., for the most recent scholarship.
[6] *Review of Reviews*, XXVII, 15 (Jan., 1903).

ginning of this wretched Venezuela business have rarely come under the observation of civilized men." [7] In the face of this outburst the German Emperor, who still had illusions of winning American friendship, revealed a willingness to end the intervention as quickly as possible.

The London government was fully aware of the flare-up in the American press, and sensitive to the even more stinging criticisms in English journals. British editors were demanding to know why the Foreign Office had ever become involved in this stupid business. Perhaps the intervention was a plot on the part of the Kaiser to destroy the newly achieved Anglo-American friendship. The poet Kipling, referring to the Germans as "the Goth and the shameless Hun," wrote:

> 'Neath all the flags of all mankind
>   That use upon the seas,
> Was there no other fleet to find
>   That ye strike hands with these? [8]

In the face of all this uproar, the British Ministry welcomed escape through the peaceful paths of arbitration.

The Monroe Doctrine emerged from the second Venezuela episode, as from the first, with new laurels. The State Department did not specifically invoke the hoary dictum, but the powers went out of their way, before intervening, to make sure that their action was not objectionable to Washington. Such studied deference to the Monroe Doctrine had not been standard practice during the preceding century.

ROOSEVELT'S PERVERSION OF MONROE'S DOCTRINE

America's sensitiveness to possible foreign lodgement near her Isthmian viscera was revealed not only in Cuba, the Danish West Indies, and Venezuela, but also in Santo Domingo. By 1904 the Dominican Republic, after an orgy of murder and civil war, was confessedly bankrupt. The fear prevailed that the four principal European nations with investments there might attempt forcible collection of debts, as they had done in Venezuela. Germany had already taken naval soundings in the Caribbean, and had otherwise betrayed a disquieting interest. If foreign forces came to collect debts, they might stay. If they stayed, they would not only violate the Monroe Doctrine but jeopardize America's Isthmian life line. The United States might then have a full-fledged war on its hands.

Roosevelt realized that the "insurrectionary habit" of these "wretched republics" imposed certain obligations on Washington. The European creditors themselves had not been backward about pointing out this fact. In short, Roosevelt concluded, if he would not permit the foreign powers to collect by force, he had a "moral mandate" to intervene and compel

---

[7] *New York Times,* Jan. 23, 1903, 8:1.
[8] *London Times,* Dec. 22, 1902, 9:5.

the reluctant republics to pay their bills. In his annual message to Congress of December, 1904, he outlined what has come to be known as the "Roosevelt Corollary" of the Monroe Doctrine:

> Chronic wrongdoing . . . may in America, as elsewhere, ultimately require intervention by some civilized nation, and in the Western Hemisphere the adherence of the United States to the Monroe Doctrine may force the United States, however reluctantly, in flagrant cases of such wrongdoing or impotence, to the exercise of an international police power.[9]

In brief, the Monroe Doctrine, which was originally designed to prevent intervention by the European powers, would be used to justify intervention by the United States. The Roosevelt Corollary, in a sense, was a completely new policy, but the President was clever enough to see that it would gain readier acceptance if attached to an old dogma bearing an honored name.

THE BIG STICK IN THE CARIBBEAN SEA

Rogers in *New York Herald, c.* 1905, courtesy *New York Sun,* Inc.

The next step was to secure control of the revenue-producing customs houses of the Dominican Republic. After a show of force by the United States, the island government rather resignedly invited the Yankee big brother to step in. The result was a fateful agreement, concluded early in

[9] *Cong. Record,* 58 Cong., 3 sess., p. 19.

1905. By its terms the United States would take over the customs collecting, retain 45 per cent of the receipts for Dominican expenses, and allocate 55 per cent for the outstanding indebtedness.

But the United States Senate proved balky, and in the end adjourned without approving the Dominican pact. Roosevelt, who had scant respect for the "angleworm" Senators, went ahead and drew up a temporary Executive agreement which accomplished the same ends. The opposition Democrats denounced the arrangement as illegal, unconstitutional, and tyrannical, but it was continued in operation for twenty-eight months. Finally, in February, 1907, the Senate approved a new treaty which incorporated, with some modifications, the substance of the original agreement of 1905.

DOMINION OVER DOMINICAN PALMS

A new era now dawned for Santo Domingo. With the sticky fingers of grafting politicos tied, customs receipts increased, debts decreased, and revolutions declined. The lush plum of the customs houses was now out of reach. Thus Uncle Sam became an international policeman and bill collector, administering spankings to his small nephews, and benevolently doling out spending money.

Reactions varied. Red-blooded citizens in the United States generally approved the application of the Roosevelt Corollary to Santo Domingo. But this was Republican doctrine, and some angry protests arose from the Democratic camp. The *St. Louis Globe-Democrat* aptly summarized the new attitude toward European creditors, "You mind your business, and we'll mind yours." The poet Wallace Irwin poked fun at the new interventionism:

> Here's a bumper to the doctrine of Monroe, roe, roe,
>   And the neighbors whom we cannot let alone;
> Through the thirst for diagnosis we're inserting our proboscis
>   Into everybody's business but our own.[10]

Continental Europe, though welcoming the prospect of debt repayment, revealed the customary hostility to the pretensions of the Yankee. The emphasis had shifted from "Hands Off" for Europe to "Hands On" for the United States. But the British, especially the bondholders, generally applauded Roosevelt's "preventive intervention," and even regretted that it did not go further.

The republics of Latin America, contrary to what one might have expected, showed remarkably little concern *at the time*. Not until later years, when the Roosevelt Corollary was used to justify wholesale landings of marines in the Caribbean, did Latin Americans express violent

[10] From "Monroe Doctrinings," in Wallace Irwin's *Random Rhymes and Odd Numbers* (The Macmillan Co., copyright 1906). By permission of author.

dissatisfaction. Valuing sovereignty higher than solvency, they came to regard the Monroe Doctrine, not as a protective shield, but as a cloak behind which Uncle Sam could strangle them. Yet instead of cursing the unoffending Monroe, they might more appropriately have cursed the offending Roosevelt.

THE ALASKA BOUNDARY CONTROVERSY

The Rooseveltian Big Stick was not confined to the Caribbean, but cast its shadow in more northerly latitudes. In 1896 gold had been discovered in Canada's Klondike region, and the inrushing miners soon found that the best water approaches to the diggings lay through the Alaskan panhandle of the United States. The Canadians thereupon re-read the rather ambiguous Anglo-Russian Treaty of 1825, and came up with a startling claim. They contended that the boundary line, which extended about thirty miles inland from the ocean, should not follow the snake-like

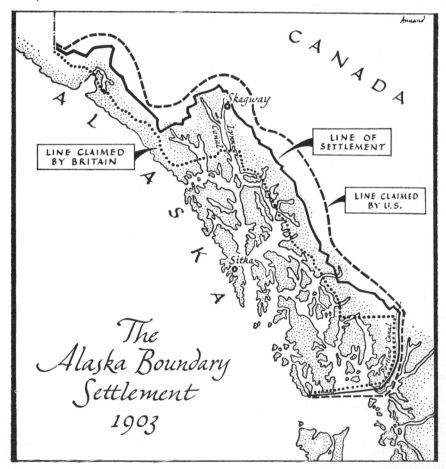

The Alaska Boundary Settlement 1903

windings of the coastline, as commonly supposed, but should run in a straight line. This meant that the heads of the deep inlets would remain in Canadian hands, and with a consequent chopping up of the Alaska panhandle. Whatever the technicalities of the dispute, the negotiators of the Anglo-Russian Treaty of 1825 had clearly intended that the territory in this region should remain contiguous.

The Canadians, who had less to lose than the United States, showed a willingness to arbitrate their claim. But Secretary Hay, realizing that arbitrators are tempted to split the difference, resolutely rejected such a course. In 1899 he finally succeeded in arranging a *modus vivendi* or temporary settlement, without prejudice to the claims of either party. This agreement, though not popular in the United States, permitted passions to cool and enabled President McKinley to avoid a showdown.

Theodore Roosevelt, after coming to the White House, became increasingly convinced that the Canadian case was a trumped-up one. He unbosomed himself to Secretary Hay:

> I think that the Canadian contention is an outrage pure and simple. I do not regard the Canadians as having any more right to the land in question than they have to Maine or than we have to New Brunswick. The fact that they have set up such an outrageous and indefensible claim and in consequence are likely to be in hot water with their constituents when they back down, does not seem to me to give us any excuse for paying them in money or territory. To pay them anything where they are entitled to nothing would in a case like this come dangerously near blackmail.[11]

By the middle of 1902, the Alaska boundary controversy was again heating up. Grave apprehensions were felt that the tough-fisted miners might get out of hand, particularly if rich gold deposits should be discovered in the disputed area. Roosevelt ordered more troops into Alaska to prevent a serious disturbance, and not primarily, as has been supposed, to threaten the British. High Canadian officials, regretful that they had ever stirred up the issue, were revealing a disposition to make concessions. They were backed by certain British leaders, who feared that this dispute, complicated by the inept Anglo-German blockade of Venezuela, might shatter the recently won American friendship.

In this more favorable atmosphere, Secretary Hay succeeded in negotiating the Convention of 1903 with the British. It provided that "six impartial jurists of repute" were to meet in London, and there by a majority vote decide the disputed Alaska boundary. Three members of the tribunal were to be chosen by the President of the United States and three by His Britannic Majesty. The treaty met with considerable opposition in the Senate, particularly from representatives of the Pacific North-

[11] Roosevelt to Hay, July 10, 1902, Roosevelt Papers, Library of Congress. See also T. A. Bailey, "Theodore Roosevelt and the Alaska Boundary Settlement," *Canadian Hist. Rev.*, XVIII (1937), 123–130.

west. They feared that if the "right men" were not selected the United States might lose, but if the "right men" were chosen, the United States could get no worse than a tie. Senator Lodge went to Roosevelt, according to his own story, and obtained in advance the names of the jurists who were to be appointed. The Senate then gave its approval.

BROWBEATING THE BRITISH ON ALASKA

The three "impartial jurists of repute" selected by Roosevelt were a strangely assorted lot: Secretary of War Elihu Root, who accepted under protest; ex-Senator George Turner of Washington; and Senator Lodge of Massachusetts. Root was an outstanding lawyer, although not a "jurist," and his intimate connection with the administration raised grave doubts as to his "impartiality." Ex-Senator Turner had no "repute" as a "jurist," and in view of the financial interest of his state in the decision he was not regarded as "impartial."

Senator Lodge was the most incredible choice of all. He had no standing as a "jurist," what "repute" he enjoyed had come from writing and politics, and he was certainly not "impartial." He had not only publicly scoffed at the Canadian claims in Alaska, but he was probably the leading Britain-baiter of his generation. Amid the outburst of derisive laughter that greeted Roosevelt's appointments, the *Brooklyn Eagle* quipped that the chances of the Canadians were about equal to the possibility of a blizzard "in Hades."

The remainder of the tribunal created less controversy. The British King chose Lord Alverstone, Lord Chief Justice of England, and two prominent Canadians, only one of whom could claim previous judicial experience. The Canadians were outraged by Roosevelt's selections, for they had assumed that the three American jurists would be taken from a high tribunal like the Supreme Court. The British were deeply embarrassed, but rather than precipitate a crisis in Anglo-American relations, they decided to go through with the arrangements. The result could not be a true arbitration, because the deciding vote was not in the hands of disinterested or neutral parties.

The six-man tribunal met in London late in 1903. With the two Canadian members determined to uphold the Canadian claims, the avoidance of a deadlock rested squarely on Lord Alverstone. Roosevelt swung privately into action with his trusty Big Stick. In letters and conversations he declared with vehemence that if the tribunal did not decide properly, he would occupy the disputed area with troops and run the line the way he thought it should go. This, of course, meant war. Roosevelt's bellicose views, as he intended, were relayed to high British officials, who almost certainly communicated them to Lord Alverstone. The Canadians, on their side, brought pressure to bear on the British

Lord Chief Justice, some of them going as far as to threaten secession.

The final decision of the Alaska tribunal proved highly favorable to the United States. The American contention regarding the windings of the coastline was strong, and the "jurists" sustained it by a vote of four to two. Lord Alverstone here parted company with his two Canadian colleagues. But the United States received a somewhat narrower strip than it had claimed, owing largely to the stubbornness of Lord Alverstone. The Canadians netted a consolation prize of two rather inconsequential islands in the Portland Canal, and this solution seems to have been a compromise rather than a legal settlement.[12]

The Canadians angrily charged that Lord Alverstone had been swayed by political pressures, but the distinguished Briton insisted that his decision was purely "judicial." This assertion may be doubted. Whether or not he was influenced by Roosevelt's private threats, the documents now reveal that he privately agreed, during the first week of the deliberations, to vote for the basic American claim.[13]

American newspapers greeted the sweeping victory with jubilation. Some of them thought that it foreshadowed the ultimate annexation of Canada; others rejoiced that a "dynamite charge" in Anglo-American relations had been removed. The Canadians, on the other hand, were acutely unhappy. Their anger was directed in part against the Yankee, and in part against the Mother Country, which they felt had again sacrificed them on the altar of Anglo-American amity. Natural though this reaction was, the peaceful acceptance of the award removed a serious source of international discord. Roosevelt's methods, however questionable, were thus sanctified by success.

POLITICS, POGROMS, AND PERDICARIS

Theodore Roosevelt was a master politician, and his administration overlooked few opportunities to use diplomacy as a handmaiden of politics. In 1902, following vicious persecutions of the Jews in Romania, an outcry arose from Jewish citizens in the United States for intervention. Secretary Hay was aware that the mistreatment of Jews in Romania was basically Romania's affair, just as the mistreatment of Negroes in Alabama was basically America's affair. But he dispatched a vigorous protest on the grounds that these persecutions drove destitute refugees to the United States. This note, designed partly for political purposes, seems to have helped the Republicans in the Congressional elections of

---

[12] Hay wrote jubilantly: "We agree that the Boundary shall be by the North Channel instead of the South, which gives them those two little Islands—worth nothing to us. That is all poor Canada gets by the decision, and I do not wonder they are furious but as Will Thomson used to say 'Serves 'em right, if they can't take a joke.'" Tyler Dennett, *John Hay* (New York, 1933), p. 362.

[13] J. A. Garraty, *Henry Cabot Lodge* (New York, 1953), p. 251.

1902. Hay wrote privately ". . . The Hebrews—poor dears! all over the country think we are bully boys. . . ." [14]

The next year, 1903, witnessed a frightful pogrom involving the Russian Jews at Kishinev; about fifty were murdered and five hundred injured. Scores of mass meetings in the United States demanded that the State Department use its influence to stop these outrages. Washington could not properly intervene in the domestic affairs of Russia, but Secretary Hay made known to the Czar the contents of a petition bearing thousands of protesting signatures. Unhappily, frightful outbursts of a similar nature continued in Russia during the next few years.

A more spectacular type of intervention came in brigand-ridden Morocco, an independent North African sultanate, in the summer of 1904. Ion Perdicaris, a Greek subject who presumably held American naturalization papers, was seized by one of the native chieftains, named Raisuli. United States warships were promptly rushed to Moroccan waters. The Republican National Convention was then meeting in Chicago, and Roosevelt, who was about to be nominated "in his own right," was displeased with the apathy of the delegates. Although arrangements had already been made for the release of Perdicaris, the President consulted Secretary Hay, who, on June 22, 1904, dispatched a ringing telegram to the American consul general at Tangier, Morocco. It insisted that the United States must have "Perdicaris alive or Raisuli dead." When this stirring ultimatum was read to the Chicago convention, it elicited the anticipated cheers for Roosevelt, its presumed author. "It is curious," wrote Hay, "how a concise impropriety hits the public."

The most "curious" parts of this impropriety were not then made known. The unpublished part of the telegram warned the consul general not to use force without specific instructions. Two weeks before the cablegram was dispatched, evidence had come to the State Department that Perdicaris might be a Greek subject rather than an American citizen. The documents were then sent on to Roosevelt, who airily brushed them aside. After the brandishing of the Big Stick in Morocco, his prestige as a world leader would be damaged by such an admission. Some time later the record was set straight when the State Department ruled that Perdicaris had been an American citizen all along. [15]

THE BIG STICK IN MOROCCO

The Perdicaris affair was but a curtain-raiser for a major international crisis in Morocco in 1905, when smouldering friction between Germany and France burst into flames. The French, as aggressive imperialists, were

[14] Dennett, *John Hay,* p. 397.
[15] See H. E. Davis, "The Citizenship of Jon [sic] Perdicaris," *Jour. of Mod. Hist.,* XIII (1941), 517–520.

attempting to secure political and economic control in this area, which was about as weakly independent as China. The Germans, who were traditional enemies of the French, resented what appeared to be an effort to slam shut the Open Door on the fingers of their merchants. The time seemed opportune for Germany to make her move, for Russia, France's ally, was deeply mired down in the Russo-Japanese War. The upshot was that the Kaiser, responding to pressure from his advisers, made a trip to Morocco, where, in March, 1905, he delivered a defiant, saber-rattling speech.

The long-predicted European war seemed near at hand. The French were alarmed, as were the British, who only the year before had formed an epochal accord with them. The tension finally became so acute that the Kaiser sought the support of Roosevelt in calling an international conference. The ex-Rough Rider was reluctant to get involved, for he privately admitted that America had no direct concern of any significance in sun-baked Morocco. But perceiving that the crisis, if allowed to drift, might lead to the bloody abyss, he finally consented to bring pressure to bear on Britain and France. The French, who were confronted with the formidable German army, responded to Roosevelt's good offices, on June 30, 1905, and agreed to attend a multipower conference at Algeciras, a small seaport town in southern Spain near Gibraltar.

When the Algeciras Conference assembled, in January, 1906, the United States, strange to relate, had two official representatives present. How could Roosevelt justify this untraditional involvement in the affairs of Europe and Africa? For one thing, the United States had long enjoyed treaty relations with Morocco, which was in danger of being partitioned. For another, although American trade with Morocco was negligible, the Open Door principle was at stake, and if it was weakened in North Africa it might be correspondingly weakened in China. Furthermore, Roosevelt was anxious to prevent the Germans from gaining a foothold in Northwest Africa, from which they could menace the United States. Finally, and most important, if the crisis erupted into a world war, the United States might be sucked into it.

THE FRUITS OF ALGECIRAS

The Algeciras Conference resulted in a definite setback for Germany. A majority of the votes was against her, and she was confronted by a determined Anglo-French Entente. The only alternatives were to yield or fight, and Germany was not quite ready to fight. Roosevelt, who was inclined to be pro-French, did exercise a strong influence on the final settlement, yet he exaggerated somewhat when he wrote privately, ". . . You will notice that while I was most suave and pleasant with the

Emperor [Kaiser], yet when it became necessary at the end I stood him on his head with great decision. . . .[16]

The pressures of the international situation, perhaps as much as the Big Stick, played a dominant role. The tactful and conciliatory Henry White, senior American delegate, used them to advantage in composing the differences of the two conflicting groups. The resulting Convention of Algeciras, which was signed on April 7, 1906, upheld the territory and sovereignty of the native sultan, guaranteed the Open Door for Germany and the other powers, but left Spain and France in a privileged position with the native police force.

The United States Senate, a stronghold of traditionalism, was disturbed by the Algeciras Convention. After considerable debate, during which the Democrats put up a bitter fight, the necessary approval was reluctantly forthcoming. But the Senators were careful to tack on the safeguarding reservation that this step was taken "without purpose to depart from the traditional American foreign policy. . . ." [17]

The American press, rejoicing over the humiliation of the Kaiser, on the whole applauded the outcome of Algeciras. Yet Roosevelt's numerous critics were less happy. Pointing to the remoteness of Morocco and the tiny American commercial stake there, they condemned the administration for departing from the time-honored policy of nonentanglement. They also charged that Roosevelt's interference in the Old World weakened the Monroe Doctrine in the New World. But in a sense the ex-Rough Rider added another corollary to the Monroe Doctrine—that is, intervention in Europe was justified to prevent Europe's wars from engulfing the United States. However reasonable such a dictum may have been in the light of the changing power picture, Roosevelt's involvement in Morocco marked the sharpest departure from traditional isolationism that the republic was to experience before the outbreak of World War I in 1914.

SELECTED BIBLIOGRAPHY

On most phases of Roosevelt's foreign policy the outstanding monograph is H. K. Beale, *Theodore Roosevelt and the Rise of America to World Power* (Baltimore, 1956). See also H. F. Pringle, *Theodore Roosevelt* (New York, 1931); A. L. P. Dennis, *Adventures in American Diplomacy* (New York, 1928); and N. M. Blake, "Ambassadors at the Court of Theodore Roosevelt," *Miss. Valley Hist. Rev.*, XLII (1955), 179–206.

On the Venezuela episode see also Dexter Perkins, *The Monroe Doctrine, 1867–1907* (Baltimore, 1937); C. S. Campbell, Jr., *Anglo-American Under-*

---

[16] Royal Cortissoz, *The Life of Whitelaw Reid* (New York, 1921), II, 332; Howard K. Beale, in *Theodore Roosevelt and the Rise of America to World Power*, pp. 388–389, argues strongly that some scholars have underrated Roosevelt's role.

[17] W. M. Malloy, *Treaties*, II, 2183.

standing, 1898–1903 (Baltimore, 1957); H. C. Hill, *Roosevelt and the Caribbean* (Chicago, 1937); J. F. Rippy, *Latin America in World Politics* (rev.
ed., New York, 1938); S. W. Livermore, "Theodore Roosevelt, the American
Navy, and the Venezuelan Crisis of 1902–1903," *Amer. Hist. Rev.*, LI (1946),
452–471.

On Cuba and Santo Domingo consult R. H. Fitzgibbon, *Cuba and the
United States, 1900–1935* (Menasha, Wis., 1935); D. A. Lockmiller, *Magoon
in Cuba* (Chapel Hill, N.C., 1938); W. H. Callcott, *The Caribbean Policy of
the United States, 1890–1920* (Baltimore, 1942); J. F. Rippy, *The Caribbean
Danger Zone* (New York, 1940); J. F. Rippy, "The Initiation of the Customs
Receivership in the Dominican Republic," *Hispanic Amer. Hist. Rev.*, XVII
(1937), 419–457; J. F. Rippy, "The British Bondholders and the Roosevelt
Corollary of the Monroe Doctrine," *Pol. Sci. Quar.*, XLIX (1934), 198; J. F.
Rippy, "Antecedents of the Roosevelt Corollary of the Monroe Doctrine,"
Pacific Hist. Rev., IX (1940), 267–279.

On the Alaska boundary see C. C. Tansill, *Canadian-American Relations,
1875–1911* (New Haven, 1943); J. A. Garraty, *Henry Cabot Lodge* (New
York, 1953); C. S. Campbell, Jr., *Anglo-American Understanding, 1898–1903*
(Baltimore, 1957); and J. A. Garraty, "Henry Cabot Lodge and the Alaskan
Boundary Tribunal," *New England Quar.*, XXIV (1951), 469–494. On
Algeciras consult Allan Nevins, *Henry White* (New York, 1930).

See footnotes of this chapter; Bemis and Griffin, *Guide*, 577–581, 436–440,
415–420, 581–583, 389; *Harvard Guide*, Ch. 26.

7TH ED. REFS. See general titles by Mowry, Harbaugh, and Wagenknecht,
listed p. 930. A. E. Campbell, *Great Britain and the United States, 1895–
1903* (London, 1960) points out that the Alaska boundary settlement did not
greatly interest British opinion. Lord Alverstone regarded himself more as an
arbiter between two opposing factions than an independent jurist; the American case was not so overwhelmingly strong as Hay's writings would suggest.
D. C. M. Platt, "The Allied Coercion of Venezuela, 1902–03: A Reassessment," *Inter-American Economic Affairs*, XV (1962), 3–28, shows that the
intervention had ample precedent in international law; that it was more concerned with redressing injuries to life and property than with collecting debts;
and that the British did not take the lead in starting coercive intervention. A
simple inquiry from Lord Lansdowne has been misinterpreted as a proposal
for intervention; the scheme was "entirely German." R. E. Minger, "William H.
Taft and the United States Intervention in Cuba in 1906," *Hispanic Amer.
Hist. Rev.*, XLI (1961), 75–89 notes that the intervention, largely designed
to protect a United States investment of $150 million, was undertaken with
extreme reluctance by T.R.; Taft concluded that neither the masses nor the
ruling classes were capable of self-government. T. P. Wright, Jr., "United
States Electoral Intervention in Cuba," *Inter-American Economic Affairs*, XIII
(1959), 50–71 deals with the interventions of 1906–1909 and 1917–1922, and
concludes that "the impartial support of free elections in countries where democracy has not already been firmly planted is to no avail."

8TH AND 9TH ED. REFS. See BIBLIOGRAPHICAL ADDENDUM, p. 1,013.

Theodore Roosevelt and the Far East

I never take a step in foreign policy unless I am assured that I shall be able eventually to carry out my will by force.

THEODORE ROOSEVELT, 1905

THE FAR EAST IN FERMENT

As THE NEW CENTURY DAWNED, a diplomatic revolution was brewing in the Far East. Russian imperialism was the catalyst. The British feared Czarist designs on China, as well as on India and the Middle East. The Japanese feared Czarist designs on China's Manchuria and on the nominally independent Hermit Kingdom of Korea. Both of these rich areas, especially Korea, were strategic daggers pointed at the heart of Japan. Both of them were regarded by the Japanese as natural and legitimate areas for their own commercial and territorial expansion.

The upshot was the Anglo-Japanese Alliance—concluded in 1902, widened in 1905, and tightened in 1911. If either Japan or Britain should become involved in a war in defense of its Far Eastern interests, the other was bound to remain neutral unless its partner was attacked by an outside power. In the latter contingency, both allies would fight side by side.[1]

The Alliance proved to be a tower of strength to both parties. Japan could now be reasonably sure of not being "ganged-up" on by the European powers, as she had been in 1895, at the end of the Sino-Japanese War. Britain could pull her naval strength out of the Far East, leaving her Nipponese partner as the policeman, and concentrate her fleets in European waters against the rising might of Germany. The United

---

[1] In 1905 Britain's India was specifically included. By the renewal of 1911, neither power was to remain neutral but come at once to the aid of its partner.

States, for its part, could voice no serious objections to these new arrangements: Britain and Japan alike professed to be upholding the Open Door.

Manchuria proved to be the combustible that blew open the Far Eastern powder magazine. In 1900, following the Boxer outburst, Russia had thrown troops into Manchuria, presumably to protect Russian lives and railroad interests. Despite repeated and insincere promises to withdraw, the Russians were still there in 1904. The trans-Siberian Railroad

was nearing completion, and Russia was obviously stalling until the last spike was driven, whereupon large quantities of military supplies could be shipped with relative ease. The Japanese, realizing that time was ticking out, broke diplomatic relations on February 6, 1904. Two days later, without a declaration of war, they launched a damaging sneak attack on the Russian fleet at Port Arthur, Manchuria.

JAPAN PLAYS AMERICA'S GAME

American sympathies immediately went out to the Japanese, even though Russia and Japan were both traditional friends of the United States. The Japanese were not only protégés and underdogs, but they appeared to be upholding the Open Door. And to all outward appearances they had been bullied into fighting by the aggressive Russian Bear. The surprise attack at Port Arthur was widely applauded by American editors, who praised the clever little Japanese for having caught the stupid and overconfident Slav with his guard down. Ex-secretary Root wrote admiringly, "Was not the way the Japs began the fight bully?" [2] All this makes curious reading in the light of the later Japanese assault at Pearl Harbor in 1941.

The Russians, who had counted on American sympathy, were deeply angered. As a Christian people comprising the largest and most populous white nation, they were shocked when the Americans loudly expressed their preference for the non-Christian yellow men of Japan. But by this time the traditional American attachment for Russia had largely gone down the drain. Naked imperialism in Asia, the banishment of political dissenters to Siberian prisons, the Russification of Finland, and the merciless pogroms directed against defenseless Jews had all chilled American friendship. In fact, Jewish-American bankers were happy to lend large sums to the Tokyo government.

President Roosevelt shared the warm sympathies of the American people for underdog Japan. While regarding the Czar as "a preposterous little creature," he feared that the Russians were scheming to bang shut the Open Door in Manchuria. If the Nipponese could stop them, he reasoned, the United States would benefit. "Japan," he wrote smugly and somewhat shortsightedly, "is playing our game." He went so far, according to his own questionable tale, as to warn France and Germany to keep hands off, lest they find an embattled America aligned with the Japanese.[3]

Both before and during the Russo-Japanese hostilities, Secretary Hay labored manfully to preserve the Open Door principle in Manchuria, as well as in all the sprawling territory of China. The responses of the neutral powers to his appeals were encouraging, but the attitude of the Russians was most disquieting. As far as the Open Door was concerned, China was the mat. The land war between Russia and Japan, curiously enough, was fought entirely on the soil of China's Manchuria.

THE PEACEMAKERS OF PORTSMOUTH

The clever Japanese, left to themselves, won an astonishing succession of triumphs on both land and sea. Yet they drew so heavily on their man power and financial resources that, even in victory, they were near col-

---

[2] H. K. Beale, *Theodore Roosevelt and the Rise of America to World Power* (Baltimore, 1956), p. 268; also W. B. Thorson, "Pacific Northwest Opinion on the Russo-Japanese War of 1904–1905," *Pacific Northwest Quar.*, XXXV (1944), 305–322.
[3] Tyler Dennett, *Roosevelt and the Russo-Japanese War* (Garden City, N.Y., 1925), p. 2; for doubts, see Beale, *op.cit.*, p. 154.

lapse. If the Russians had been able to prolong their resistance, they might have worn down their foe and emerged victorious. But by the summer of 1905 they had lost the will to fight. Revolution was flaring up in Russia. The Moroccan crisis with Germany was coming to a head. And France, fearful of a showdown with the Kaiser, was urging her Russian ally to halt the struggle with Japan before she fruitlessly bled herself white.

In the spring of 1905 the Japanese, running dangerously short of men and yen, secretly invited Roosevelt to act as mediator. The Rough Rider was not enthusiastic about taking on this thankless task, but he finally concluded that the best interests of the United States would be served by bringing the bloody conflict to an end. He was especially anxious to preserve the balance of power in the Far East between Russia and Japan. If either nation should become dominant—and he particularly distrusted Russia—the Open Door would be in grave jeopardy. But before consenting to serve as peacemaker, he sought and secured from Tokyo reasonably satisfactory assurances that the Open Door would be preserved in Manchuria. Russia would make no commitments.

After the Russians had shown considerable balkiness, Roosevelt managed to bring delegates from the two warring powers to a conference near Portsmouth, New Hampshire, in August, 1905. The Japanese demanded, among other spoils, the Siberian island of Sakhalin, and, above all, a huge monetary indemnity of $600 million or more, to cover the cost of the war. But the Russian government, suspecting the desperate straits of its adversary, stubbornly refused to consent to either major demand. Roosevelt thereupon addressed an extraordinary appeal to the Czar for concessions, and urged the Kaiser to bring pressure to bear on his fellow monarch. At the same time, the Rough Rider impartially warned the Japanese delegates against persisting in their unwarranted demand for money.

American opinion meanwhile had begun to lose its enthusiasm for "underdog" Japan. The change was sparked partly by Japanese cockiness and partly by clever Russian propaganda, which portrayed the Oriental enemy as grasping, imperialistic, and blood-thirsty. Although American majority opinion evidently did not become pro-Russian, the Japanese saw the handwriting on the wall.[4] They finally responded to Roosevelt's elbow-twisting when they suddenly abandoned their claim for an indemnity, and settled for the southern half of Sakhalin Island rather than all of it.

The Japanese were undeniably the victors, although they might not have been without Roosevelt's vigorous mediation. Not only had they established themselves as the dominant power in the Far East, but they

[4] W. B. Thorson, "American Public Opinion and the Portsmouth Peace Conference," *Amer. Hist. Rev.*, LIII (1948), 439–464.

had emerged with considerable territorial gains. In Korea, they had greatly strengthened their foothold. In Manchuria, they had wrested from Russia the Liaotung leasehold, the South Manchuria Railway, and the economic privileges attached to these two concessions.

Predictably, Roosevelt's mediation won few friends in Russia and little gratitude in Japan. Many Russians fatuously believed that in one more campaign they could whip the little Nipponese "monkeys," as they were contemptuously called. The tax-burdened Japanese masses, who had been counting heavily on the cushion of an indemnity, turned angrily against both the United States and their own leaders. Riots against the government resulted in incidental damage to several American churches.

Yet Roosevelt's reputation as a world leader was tremendously enhanced both at home and in Europe by his strenuous adventure in peacemaking. The next year—1906—this fight-loving ex-Rough Rider, in one of the strangest ironies of history, was awarded the Nobel Peace Prize for his efforts. But the path of the honest umpire is difficult, and few can deny that the Portsmouth Conference did much to undermine the ancient friendship between America and Japan, and further becloud Russian-American relations.

Roosevelt's critics have charged that if he had not meddled, Japan would have collapsed and Russia would have become the chief sponsor of the Open Door. Subsequent events proved that neither a dominant Japan nor a dominant Russia was a satisfactory guardian of the portals. In 1905, and later, there was much to be said for Roosevelt's concept of the balance of power or, perhaps better, balanced antagonisms.

THE CLOSED DOOR IN KOREA

One interesting by-product of the Russo-Japanese War was a secret understanding with Japan. The resounding Nipponese victories had aroused considerable uneasiness in America regarding the Philippines. In July, 1905, the portly Secretary of War Taft, then on a mission to Manila, stopped off in Tokyo and drew up with Prime Minister Katsura a remarkable "agreed memorandum." Katsura disavowed any aggressive designs on the Philippines; Taft approved Japan's "suzerainty" over Korea. This informal understanding received the warm approval of Roosevelt, who four months earlier had privately informed Tokyo of his decision to abandon Korea. He concluded that since he could not prevent Japan's expansion, the next best step was to recognize the inevitable and further secure her goodwill.

Washington carried out its part of the bargain regarding Korea with unusual promptitude. In November, 1905, the Japanese ambassador advised Secretary of State Root that henceforth Tokyo would control the foreign affairs of Korea. The very next day Root informed him that the American legation had been closed, and that henceforth the United States would deal directly with Japan regarding Korea. Twenty-five years later Root was still convinced that his course had been the proper one:

> Many people are still angry because we did not keep Japan from taking Korea. There was nothing we could do except fight Japan; Congress wouldn't have declared war and the people would have turned out the Congress that had. All we might have done was to make threats which we could not carry out.[5]

The Japanese were grateful for the prompt and generous recognition of their special position in Korea. The resulting good will did something to water down the bitterness resulting from Portsmouth. But on the debit side of the ledger one must note that Roosevelt's realistic course marked a backward step in upholding the Open Door in the Far East.

THE "YELLOW PERIL" AGAIN

Aside from ill feeling over the Portsmouth Treaty, the Russo-Japanese War affected America's relations with Japan in other unfavorable ways. In Manchuria the Japanese, despite their prewar pledges, were attempting to consolidate their improved economic position at the expense of the Open Door. Responding to the pleas of American merchants, the State Department protested but was forced to settle for hollow-sounding assurances. The Big Stick could not cast a formidable shadow some 8,000 miles from home.

Fear also began to becloud the picture. The fanatical display of military prowess by Japan in the recent war caused many Americans to fear that the Philippine Islands, to say nothing of possessions nearer home, were none too safe. The Japanese seemed to be getting too big for their kimonos. As Mr. Dooley put it: "A few years ago I didn't think anny more about a Jap thin about anny other man that'd been kept in th' oven too long. They were all alike to me. But to-day, whiniver I see wan I turn pale an' take off me hat an' make a low bow.[6]

The most disturbing by-product of the Russo-Japanese War was the rising tide of immigration from Japan to the Pacific Coast of the United States. By 1906 about a thousand Japanese a month were pouring in. This influx should not have been surprising, for war begets a restless spirit, and many ex-soldiers were reluctant to return to their rice paddies and shoulder heavy tax burdens. To them, California was the land of milk and honey.

But the people of the Golden State remembered their earlier experi-

[5] P. C. Jessup, *Elihu Root* (New York, 1938), II, 62 (Root to Jessup, Sept. 5, 1930).

[6] F. P. Dunne, *Mr. Dooley Says* (New York, 1910), p. 200.

ences with the Chinese "yellow peril." They were determined not to be outbred and overrun by a race whose standard of living, in their judgment, was so low as to jeopardize that of the white laborers. This natural anxiety was inflamed by the recent Japanese military victories, and by the incendiary appeals of America's yellow press. The Washington government, preoccupied with problems nearer at home, was unwilling to halt the inflow of Japanese, so the Californians themselves seized the bull by the horns.

THE JAPANESE SCHOOL-BOY CRISIS

The San Francisco Board of Education burst into the headlines in October, 1906, when it passed an order requiring all Oriental pupils to attend a public school specially set aside for them. The principal excuse given for this action was that the Japanese children—a negligible ninety-three—were crowding the whites out of the schools. The basic reason was a determination to express dissatisfaction with the influx of so much cheap coolie labor. Some of the "boys" were actually young men, twenty-one years or so old.

The Japanese at home, ordinarily sensitive to any suggestion of racial inferiority, flared up. Having recently demonstrated their military superiority over mighty Russia, they were in no mood to laugh off what they regarded as a studied insult. One reputable newspaper expressed an extreme view:

> Stand up, Japanese nation! Our countrymen have been HUMILIATED on the other side of the Pacific. Our poor boys and girls have been expelled from the public schools by the rascals of the United States, cruel and merciless like demons. . . . Why do we not insist on sending [war] ships? [7]

But most of the Japanese journals, particularly after the first shock, showed commendable restraint.

The California segregation incident was but another spectacular instance of the embarrassing blind spot in federalism. The Washington authorities had no jurisdiction whatever over the public schools of San Francisco. All that the federal government could legally do was to institute a test case, with the objective of reinstating the Japanese pupils. But court action would take time, and public opinion in Japan had to be mollified.

The controversy might have become critical if Roosevelt had not stepped into the breach. In various ways he showed that the Washington authorities were not responsible for the action of the school board, and that he did not approve of it. But he was plainly worried. Writing privately he complained, "I am being horribly bothered about the Japanese

[7] *Mainichi Shimbun*, Oct. 22, 1906, quoted in T. A. Bailey, *Theodore Roosevelt and the Japanese-American Crises* (Stanford University, 1934), p. 50.

business. The infernal fools in California . . . insult the Japanese reck-
lessly and in the event of war it will be the nation as a whole which will
pay the consequences." [8]

BIG-STICKING THE SAN FRANCISCANS

The Rough Riding President, unable to budge the San Franciscans,
resorted to the verbal Big Stick in his annual message to Congress. He
not only branded the school order a "wicked absurdity" but hinted at
strong measures. The Japanese were naturally pleased, but Roosevelt's

UP TO HIS OLD TRICKS

An Eastern criticism of California's penchant for stirring up
trouble with Japan, revealed again in 1913 at the time of
the alien land dispute.
Macauley in *New York World*, 1913

violent words stirred up a hornet's nest in California and elsewhere on
the Pacific Coast. "Our feeling is not against Japan," snarled the *San
Francisco Chronicle*, "but against an unpatriotic President who unites
with aliens to break down the civilization of his own countrymen." [9]

[8] Roosevelt to Kermit Roosevelt, Oct. 27, 1906, Roosevelt Papers, Library of
Congress.
[9] *San Francisco Chronicle*, Dec. 10, 1906, 5:2.

The Eastern press of the United States, fearing that California's bull-headedness would precipitate war, generally supported Roosevelt. The *Cleveland Plain Dealer* was but one of a number of journals which regretted that the headstrong state was beyond reach of federal chastisement. The *San Francisco Chronicle* was disgusted at this lack of support:

> There is an astonishing disposition shown by Eastern editors to crawl on their bellies when discussing the Japanese question. Is it really a fact that the prowess displayed by the little brown men in their recent war with Russia has so frightened them that they feel compelled to ask whether American polity must be governed by fear of the consequences of the wrath of foreigners? [10]

The uproar in California convinced Roosevelt that his brandishing of the Big Stick would not unsnarl the tangle: he would have to resort to finesse. He finally concluded that the anti-Japanese attitude of the San Franciscans was proper, but that "its manifestations are often exceedingly improper." In pursuance of his more delicate tactics, he invited the entire school board of San Francisco to travel across the continent at government expense to discuss the controversy with him.

A party of eight men left San Francisco for Washington in February, 1907. They were headed by Mayor Schmitz, a former bassoon player then under indictment for graft. When this little group of small-time politicians fell under the influence of the Big Stick, surrender was inevitable. The San Francisco delegation finally agreed to permit Japanese children of a proper age and preparation to enroll in the appropriate grades with whites. In return, Roosevelt promised the Californians what they most desired—an end to the Japanese inpouring.

The President carried out his part of the bargain, chiefly through the famed Gentlemen's Agreement of 1907–1908, effective 1908. This Executive arrangement was not embodied in any one document, but in a series of diplomatic notes by which the Tokyo government voluntarily bound itself to issue no more passports to coolies coming directly to the mainland of the United States.[11] The San Francisco Board of Education, for its part, rescinded the objectionable school order, and the tension was eased.

Under the Gentlemen's Agreement, Japanese immigration to the United States dwindled to a trickle. A few students, travelers, and others continued to come. Japanese coolies might still go to the Hawaiian islands, but they were prohibited by act of Congress from emigrating to the mainland. Until 1920 the Tokyo government issued passports to women—"picture brides"—who had married *in absentia* Japanese laborers already resident in the United States. But the Japanese officials, by controlling emigration at the source, not only saved face but stopped many illegal entrants by way of Canada and Mexico.

[10] *Ibid.*, Nov. 7, 1906, 6:1.
[11] See summary in *Foreign Relations*, 1924, II, 370–371.

THE GLOBAL FEAT OF THE BATTLESHIP FLEET

Roosevelt, who was afraid of being considered afraid, concluded that the Japanese interpreted his friendly attitude toward them as evidence of fear. He confided to a friend:

> I am exceedingly anxious to impress upon the Japanese that I have nothing but the friendliest possible intentions toward them, but I am none the less anxious that they should realize that I am not afraid of them and that the United States will no more submit to bullying than it will bully.[12]

The United States then had the second largest navy in the world, while that of Japan ranked fifth. To remind the Japanese of this disagreeable fact, and to convince them he was prepared for any emergency, Roosevelt adopted the spectacular plan of sending the entire American battleship fleet around the world. This gesture was perhaps not so much a threat at Japan as a demonstration for the benefit of Japan. It was also for the benefit of Congress, because favorable publicity for the navy might result in more generous naval appropriations.

The original announcement, made in July, 1907, was that the fleet would move only from Atlantic waters to San Francisco on a "practice cruise." But few intelligent observers failed to discern that this flourish of the Big Stick was intimately associated with Roosevelt's Japanese policy. Pained protests arose from the Eastern states, which objected to stripping the Atlantic seaboard of its defenses, and which feared that the fleet might be destroyed by storms or by Japanese treachery. The chairman of the Senate Committee on Naval Affairs informed the President that the money would not be appropriated for this mad venture. But Roosevelt, his fighting blood aroused, replied that he had sufficient funds on hand to send the fleet to the Pacific coast, and that it could stay there if Congress did not want to bring it back. That ended the argument.

The announcement of the fleet cruise had the effect of causing the jingo press of the United States, including the Hearst sheets, to whip up a first-class war scare. The real "yellow peril" of this period was not the Japanese but the yellow journals, which Secretary Root branded "leprous vampires." Despite this agitation, Roosevelt managed to keep a remarkably even keel. He wrote to Senator Lodge:

> I shall continue to do everything I can by politeness and consideration to the Japs to offset the worse than criminal stupidity of the San Francisco mob, the San Francisco press, and such papers as the New York *Herald*. I do not believe we shall have war; but it is no fault of the yellow press if we do not have it. The Japanese seem to have about the same proportion of prize jingo fools that we have.[13]

[12] Allan Nevins, *Henry White* (New York, 1930), pp. 292–293 (Roosevelt to White, July 30, 1907).
[13] *Selections from the Correspondence of Theodore Roosevelt and Henry Cabot Lodge* (New York, 1925), II, 275 (Roosevelt to Lodge, July 10, 1907).

The fleet sailed from Hampton Roads, in December, 1907, for what its commander predicted might be a "feast, a frolic, or a fight." The sixteen smoke-belching battleships aroused wild rejoicing at various South-American ports, and left behind an unmistakable trail of good will. The entire fleet arrived without a serious mishap at Magdalena Bay, Lower California, two days ahead of schedule and ready for battle.

Roosevelt could now announce that the battleships would continue on around the world. The Australians and Japanese, among others, thereupon invited the Americans to visit their lands, and the invitations were accepted. Australia, which was seeking allies to support its Oriental-exclusion policy, greeted the battleships with open arms. The fleet then steamed on to Japan, despite widely voiced fears of a sneak attack. But the Japanese people, as if to spike rumors of their unfriendliness, welcomed the Americans with an unparalleled exuberance that effectively dispelled the war clouds. So painstaking had been the preparations that thousands of Japanese children lined the roads singing the "Star-Spangled Banner" in English. The press of the United States was gratified by this reception, though Hearst's jingoistic *New York American* sneered that "the size of the fleet affected the cordiality."

After sailing on through the Mediterranean, the battleships reached home in February, 1909, just in time to usher out the Roosevelt "reign" in a blaze of glory. The American people were delighted with the success of this unprecedented achievement, and even former critics of Roosevelt were warm in their praise. The voyage contributed markedly to the prestige and outer-world mindedness of America, while proving to be a spectacular step in her coming of age. Roosevelt himself later concluded, presumably not overlooking his Algeciras intervention and the Portsmouth Conference, that sending the battleships around the world was "the most important service that I rendered to peace. . . ." In truth, the Big Stick had taken on some of the attributes of an olive branch. On the other hand—and ominously—the cruise of the fleet stimulated navalism in Japan and elsewhere.[14]

THE ROOT-TAKAHIRA AIR-CLEARING

One striking proof of the mellower atmosphere that followed the fleet cruise was the signing of an important agreement with Japan. More than a year earlier Ambassador Aoki, the Japanese envoy in Washington, alarmed by the mounting tension between the two countries, had approached Roosevelt. He proposed that Japan and America agree mutually to respect (1) the *status quo* in the Pacific and (2) the territorial integrity of China and the Open Door there. But Aoki, who had made

[14] Beale, *op.cit.*, p. 332.

this conciliatory overture without instructions, was soon recalled for his boldness.

A year later, in 1908, following the air-clearing visit of the fleet, Tokyo instructed its ambassador in Washington, Takahira, to reopen negotiations. He was to take the same general position for which Aoki had earlier been reprimanded. After full discussions, Secretary of State Root came to an understanding with Takahira, on November 30, 1908, with an exchange of notes. Briefly, the Root-Takahira Executive agreement provided that both powers were:

1. To subscribe to the policy of maintaining the status quo in the Pacific area.
2. To respect each other's territorial possessions in that region [*e.g.*, Philippines, Hawaii, Formosa].
3. To uphold the Open Door in China.
4. To support by pacific means the "independence and integrity of China. . . ." [15]

The Root-Takahira Agreement was greeted with favor in Europe, for it dovetailed with treaties that several of the powers had recently concluded with Japan. But the Chinese lost much face when they learned that the accord had been concluded without consulting them. Certain observers feared that the agreement would further isolate China diplomatically, weaken her Open Door, and undermine her efforts to prevent encroachments by the foreign powers.

The American press welcomed the Root-Takahira Agreement with considerable acclaim. The United States, which had no designs on the Open Door or on Japanese territory, had secured from Tokyo a pledge to respect both the Open Door and the Philippines. The Nipponese had been suspected of having predatory designs on both.

Japan, for her part, did not come away empty-handed, for America's recognition of the status quo in the Pacific meant a recognition of Japan's economic ascendancy in Manchuria. To this extent, as in the acceptance of Japanese ascendancy in Korea, Roosevelt's policy had undermined Hay's original Open Door. To the very end, the Rough Rider was a realist who sought to extort concessions in exchange for accepting what he did not have the military strength to prevent.

NEW POWER ALIGNMENTS

Theodore Roosevelt, who was widely traveled, easily ranks as the most internationally-minded President of his generation. He understood the role of the United States in the world of power politics more clearly than any of his predecessors and most of his successors. He caused the nation to acquire something of a taste for the grand manner, as the cruise of the

[15] *Foreign Relations, 1908*, pp. 511–512. See also T. A. Bailey, "The Root-Takahira Agreement of 1908," *Pacific Hist. Rev.*, IX (1940), 19–35.

fleet indicates. He did more than any previous President to swing the United States out of its purely continental orbit, as the Algeciras Conference attests. He regarded the republic as no longer isolated but a working member of the family of nations.

It was perhaps fortunate for the United States that a leader of Roosevelt's capacity was in the White House during an era of ominously changing power relationships. During the few short years between 1898 and 1904, England was feeling her isolation, Germany was on the make, Russia was gravely weakened, and America and Japan were both recognized as major powers.

The new and fateful relationship between the United States and Japan was there for all to see. The days had passed when America, with maternal pride, could pat her bright little protégé on the head and show him off. Within the span of six years both nations had stepped with a bang onto the world stage. The United States left its continental bastion to become an insular power in the Philippines; Japan left its insular stronghold to become a continental power in China and Korea. Both nations came increasingly into conflict as they pulled and shoved at the Open Door, the one seeking to open it, the other to close it. Suspicion and jealousy, not unmingled with fear of Japan's newly exhibited military might, were bound to be the bitter fruits of this changed status. Such was the unfortunate price that both America and Japan had to pay for becoming major powers.

A WARRIOR TURNED PEACEMAKER

Roosevelt was much more keenly interested in the machinery of war than in the machinery of peace. Despite his dramatic role at Algeciras and Portsmouth, and despite his adjustment of relations with Japan, he was essentially an apostle of Mars. His close friend and successor, William H. Taft, wrote in 1911 that "he believes in war and wishes to be a Napoleon and to die on the battlefield." [16] The truth is that Roosevelt was not genuinely devoted to arbitration—the Alaska boundary settlement was a pseudo-arbitration—and he accepted lukewarmly the abortive arbitration treaties negotiated by Secretary Hay in 1905 only because public opinion demanded them.

Roosevelt's attitude toward the Second Hague Peace Conference of 1907 was typical. The Czar formally summoned it, but the Rough Rider had initiated it, largely because the American public clamored for it following the bloody Russo-Japanese War. Roosevelt privately confessed that he was too much disturbed by difficulties with the Japanese to give proper attention to The Hague Conference. The results, on the whole,

[16] Henry Pringle, *The Life and Times of William Howard Taft* (New York, 1939), II, 748.

were even more disappointing than those of the first parley in 1899. Of the fourteen agreements drawn up, twelve involved the regulation of war, rather than its prevention. Yet the conclave did mark an important milestone on the long road toward co-operative efforts for peace.

Responsibility undoubtedly sobered the ordinarily bellicose Roosevelt. He had a glorious opportunity to whip up a war with Japan, but went to extraordinary lengths to prevent it. Despite his frustrated Napoleonic ambitions, he is far better known for his efforts at peacemaking than at warmaking. And, what is more, he deserved this acclaim.

SELECTED BIBLIOGRAPHY

The most recent scholarship is found in H. K. Beale, *Theodore Roosevelt and the Rise of America to World Power* (Baltimore, 1956). General accounts appear in H. F. Pringle, *Theodore Roosevelt* (New York, 1931); A. W. Griswold, *The Far Eastern Policy of the United States* (New York, 1938); and T. A. Bailey, *America Faces Russia* (Ithaca, 1950). Older studies are Tyler Dennett, *Roosevelt and the Russo-Japanese War* (Garden City, N.Y., 1925) and T. A. Bailey, *Theodore Roosevelt and the Japanese-American Crises* (Stanford University, Calif., 1934), which treats the school incident and the fleet cruise. See also Eleanor Tupper and G. E. McReynolds, *Japan in American Public Opinion* (New York, 1937); A. L. P. Dennis, *Adventures in American Diplomacy, 1896–1906* (New York, 1928); O. J. Clinard, *Japan's Influence on American Naval Power, 1897–1917* (Berkeley, Calif., 1947); P. J. Treat, *Diplomatic Relations between the United States and Japan, 1895–1905* (Stanford University, Calif., 1938); F. H. Harrington, *God, Mammon, and the Japanese: Dr. Horace N. Allen and Korean-American Relations, 1884–1905* (Madison, 1944).

Helpful articles are R. L. Buell, "The Development of the Anti-Japanese Agitation in the United States," *Pol. Sci. Quar.,* XXXVII (1922), 605–638; XXXVIII (1923), 57–81; R. K. Godwin, "Russia and the Portsmouth Peace Conference," *Amer. Slavic and East European Rev.,* IX (1950), 279–291; E. R. May, "The Far Eastern Policy of the United States in the Period of the Russo-Japanese War: A Russian View," *Amer. Hist. Rev.,* LXII, 345–351.

See footnotes of this chapter; Bemis and Griffin, *Guide,* pp. 491–494, 500–506; *Harvard Guide,* Ch. 26.

7TH ED. REFS. See the general accounts by Mowry, Harbaugh, and Wagenknecht listed in the BIBLIOGRAPHICAL ADDENDUM, p. 1,014. W. R. Braisted, *The United States Navy in the Pacific, 1897–1909* (Austin, Tex., 1958) skilfully ties in diplomacy with naval policy and concludes that America, with a more powerful navy, was less secure in 1909 than in 1897, owing to the rise of other powers, notably Germany and Japan. Unable to stretch the navy over two oceans, the policy makers drew closer to England, concentrated the fleet in the Atlantic to watch Germany, and prepared to retreat to Pearl Harbor in the event of war with Japan. Armin Rappaport, *The Navy League of the United States* (Detroit, 1962) reveals that this pressure group, though striving for a bigger navy, was generally ineffectual and vastly overrated. For additional references see BIBLIOGRAPHICAL ADDENDUM, p. 1,014.

8TH AND 9TH ED. REFS. See BIBLIOGRAPHICAL ADDENDUM, p. 1,015.

Taft and
Dollar Diplomacy

*The diplomacy of the present administration . . . .
has been characterized as substituting dollars for
bullets. It is one that appeals alike to idealistic humanitarian sentiments, to the dictates of sound policy
and strategy, and to legitimate commercial aims.*
PRESIDENT TAFT, December 3, 1912

THE DOLLAR BOLSTERS DIPLOMACY

THE AMIABLE WILLIAM H. TAFT, upon whose portly frame Roosevelt cast
his mantle, possessed a strong judicial temperament. He wanted to be,
as he ultimately became, a justice of the Supreme Court. But the force
of circumstances first caused him to "serve time" in the White House.
Temperamentally unfitted to be a dynamic leader like Roosevelt, he knew
that he would not be able to beat the drum, herd emperors, and settle
the destinies of continents with one grand flourish. "Our ways," he remarked, "are different." So the Big Stick gathered cobwebs, and many
red-blooded Americans lamented that they had not inherited a President
of Rooseveltian proportions.

The somewhat timid Taft was no precedent-breaker, and hardly a
precedent-maker. In glaring contrast with Roosevelt's intervention at
Algeciras, he pursued a strict hands-off policy during the second Morocco
crisis of 1911, which followed the sending of the German warship
Panther to Agadir to protect German interests. During the Italo-Turkish
War of 1911 and the First Balkan War of 1912, Taft, as an ardent lover
of peace, favored mediation but not meddling.

Unlike Roosevelt, Taft did not attempt to be his own Secretary of
State. He chose Philander C. Knox, an able corporation lawyer thoroughly
sympathetic with big business. The new Secretary, a forceful figure with
a peppery temper, dominated the Cabinet and regarded himself as a kind

of prime minister. As befitted his corporation background, he favored a
"spirited foreign commercial policy," and reorganized the State Department so as to further this objective. His slogan might well have been,
"Every diplomat a salesman." All this squared with the fact that the
United States, which had for more than a decade been the foremost industrial power, now had mounting surpluses of goods and capital to
export.

Taft quickly embraced the view that the United States should take its
rightful place as a major power in the commercial and financial world,
just as it recently had in the political and military world. His preoccupation with investments abroad caused his policy to be branded, somewhat unfairly, as "Dollar Diplomacy." The Almighty Dollar came to
supplant the Big Stick.

In a narrow sense, Dollar Diplomacy was nothing new. The use of
foreign policy to protect and promote American commercial interests
dates from the earliest years of the republic, when the State Department
strove to reopen trade with the British West Indies. But the Taft-Knox
regime made a major point of emphasizing the "traveling salesman" concept: Washington would actively encourage and support American
bankers and industrialists in securing new opportunities for profit in foreign lands. Economic imperialism has been defined as the use of power
to sustain investments against the will of an exploited people; Dollar
Diplomacy was designed to prosper both the exploited people and American investors.

Taft and Knox added still another theme when they stressed not so
much the protection of the dollar already invested abroad as the employment of the dollar to promote national policies. Economic penetration of
foreign lands is often the foot in the door for political domination. The
European imperialists, who long ago had learned this lesson, were pursuing a policy of "pound-sterling diplomacy," "franc diplomacy," "mark
diplomacy," and "ruble diplomacy." Taft and Knox aspired to have the
dollar become an active handmaiden of American foreign policy. They
would encourage the bankers to pump their money into sensitive areas,
notably the Caribbean and China, where it would forestall or displace
foreign capital. The dollar would thus lessen the necessity of later having
to employ bullets to uphold the foreign policy of the United States.
Secretary Knox struck a curiously modern note when he declared in 1911:

> If the American dollar can aid suffering humanity and lift the burden of
> financial difficulty from States with which we live on terms of intimate
> intercourse and earnest friendship, and replace insecurity and devastation
> by stability and peaceful self-development, all I can say is that it would
> be hard to find better employment.[1]

[1] S. F. Bemis, ed., *American Secretaries of State and their Diplomacy* (New York,
1929), IX, 327–328.

PUMPING DOLLARS INTO CHINA

American bankers, for various reasons, at first showed a strong reluctance to risk their money in capital-hungry China. This cautious attitude distressed Willard Straight, a dynamic and far-visioned official who, although only in his twenties, served as United States consul general at Mukden (Manchuria) from 1906 to 1908. He viewed with mounting apprehension the economic penetration of Manchuria and other parts of China by the Japanese, and concluded that the United States lacked influence in the Far East largely because of the small amount of money that Americans had invested in that area. He ardently believed that if his country was to play a decisive role in preserving the integrity of China and upholding the Open Door, American bankers would have to be induced to invest large sums there, particularly in Manchuria. He worked hand-in-glove with the famed railway promoter, E. H. Harriman, whose grandiose plans for a round-the-world transportation system envisioned the construction of a key railroad link through Manchuria.

Straight returned to the State Department as Acting Chief of the Division of Far Eastern Affairs (1908–1909), and in that capacity exercised a strong influence upon the views of the new Taft administration. Knox soon adopted the policy, with regard to China, of forcing "American capital by diplomatic pressure into a region of the world where it would not go of its own accord."

The first "dollar pumping" venture involved the Hukuang Railway project, which a consortium of British, French, and German bankers was proposing to build in central and southern China. Under the proddings of the State Department, an American banking group was formed, and Secretary Knox insisted that it be allowed to join the original consortium. When the British objected to these self-invited members, Washington strove to prevent the Chinese from signing the contract until American demands were met. President Taft went so far as to send a personal appeal to the Chinese Prince Regent:

> I have resorted to this somewhat unusually direct communication with Your Imperial Highness, because of the high importance that I attach to the successful result of our present negotiations. I have an intense personal interest in making the use of American capital in the development of China an instrument for the promotion of the welfare of China. . . .[2]

After further difficulties and delay, the American banking group was grudgingly admitted to the consortium. The final papers were signed in May, 1911. But the American capitalists showed only a fitful interest in their new responsibilities. Little railroad building was achieved, and little

---

[2] *Foreign Relations, 1909,* p. 178 (July 15, 1909).

was done to preserve the integrity of China, but a great deal was done to embitter the foreign powers. Willard Straight, who had resigned from the State Department to act as agent for the American group, privately confessed that "the mere mention of Hukuang is like a red rag to a bull to these European Foreign Offices!" [3] As will be noted later, President Wilson's strong disapproval gave the bankers a good excuse in 1913 to pull out of this trouble-brewing enterprise.

KNOX'S MANCHURIAN MUDDLING

The aggressive Japanese and Russians had by 1907 divided China's Manchuria into southern and northern economic spheres of influence. The Russians enjoyed a dominant position in Northern Manchuria, with their key Chinese Eastern Railway, while the Japanese were firmly entrenched in southern Manchuria, with their vital South Manchuria Railway. Knox feared, with good reason, that the increasing influence of these two outside powers boded ill for the integrity of China and the sanctity of the Open Door. He therefore cast about for a scheme that would enable him to use American dollars to block this ominous penetration.

Knox finally evolved his surprising Manchurian Railroad proposal, which he communicated to the interested powers late in 1909. Its essence was that American and European banking groups would lend the Chinese government a huge sum of money. China, in turn, would use the funds thus advanced to regain full control of Manchuria by buying the railroads. Knox privately confessed that he was attempting to "smoke Japan out" from her dominant position.

The Japanese, who had established themselves in Manchuria by their bloody sacrifices in the Russo-Japanese War, were irritated by this thinly veiled attempt to jockey them out of their sphere of influence. Russia saw eye to eye with Japan, and these two powers, which recently had been at each other's throats, were driven toward each other's arms. Both sent to Washington blunt refusals, which were couched in such similar terms as to betray close collaboration. If Knox had only taken the elementary precaution of sounding out St. Petersburg and Tokyo in advance, he almost certainly would not have made his blundering proposal.

The fruits of Knox's abortive Manchurian scheme were almost wholly bitter. He weakened the integrity of China, instead of strengthening it, by driving Japan and Russia closer together. He not only offended the Japanese by his inept approach but apparently reversed Roosevelt's policy under the Root-Takahira Agreement of 1908—an agreement which had recognized Japan's special position in Manchuria. He angered the American banking group, which felt that he had been unduly hasty. In fact, he had to plead with these so-called "wicked" capitalists to continue their

[3] Herbert Croly, *Willard Straight* (New York, 1924), p. 392.

support of Washington. Finally, the unpleasant interchange with Japan stirred up a war scare in America's jingo journals, and this in turn led to agitation for more battleships. The warmongers finally cooled down, but not until the clergy, the peace organizations, and the conservative press had thrown their influence on the side of moderation.

Knox's Far Eastern policy has been branded as one of "bluff and back down." His naïve, lone-hand tactics were foredoomed to failure. The United States, acting alone, did not have the naval or military force to halt either the Japanese or the Russians in the Far East. Even if it had boasted a formidable army, public opinion would not have tolerated a war over faraway economic interests that were of such relatively slight importance. Roosevelt, who had recognized for a consideration what he could not prevent in Korea, was vexed by Taft's ineptness. In a letter to his amiable successor he laid down the law:

> I utterly disbelieve in the policy of bluff, in national and international no less than in private affairs, or in any violation of the old frontier maxim, "Never draw unless you mean to shoot." I do not believe in our taking any position anywhere unless we can make good; and as regards Manchuria. if the Japanese choose to follow a course of conduct to which we are adverse, we cannot stop it unless we are prepared to go to war, and a successful war about Manchuria would require a fleet as good as that of England, plus an army as good as that of Germany.[4]

DOLLAR DIPLOMACY BECOMES LIFE-LINE DIPLOMACY

The Taft-Knox tactics proved most successful, superficially at least, in Latin America. The dollar-minded administration exerted high-pressure salesmanship on certain Latin-American governments to buy battleships from private American yards. More warships would enable the southern republics to uphold the Monroe Doctrine, while keeping the American armor-plate industry going in preparation for a national emergency. Argentina bought two warships, but considerable unpleasantness resulted when Washington, fearing that naval secrets would be revealed, applied pressure to prevent their resale elsewhere. The American builders pocketed their profits, but on the debit side one must chalk up considerable ill will and a further stimulus to the world-wide naval race.[5]

Vastly more important than "battleship" diplomacy was the more conventional type of dollar diplomacy, involving primarily the Caribbean area. The imminent completion of the Panama Canal, the jugular vein of American sea power, greatly increased the sensitivity of the United States in this region. Disorders in the bankrupt "banana republics" of

---

[4] Tyler Dennett, *Roosevelt and the Russo-Japanese War* (Garden City, N.Y., 1925), p. 320 (letter of December 22, 1910).

[5] S. W. Livermore, "Battleship Diplomacy in South America: 1905–1925," *Jour. of Mod. Hist.*, XVI (Mar., 1944), 31–48.

Central America which had formerly been ignored could no longer be tolerated. Chaos might result in foreign intervention, with a consequent threat to the Panama waterway. Secretary Knox stated his position baldly in a New York speech:

> The logic of political geography and of strategy, and now our tremendous national interest created by the Panama Canal, make the safety, the peace, and the prosperity of Central America and the zone of the Caribbean of paramount interest to the Government of the United States. Thus the malady of revolutions and financial collapse is most acute precisely in the region where it is most dangerous to us. It is here that we seek to apply a remedy.[6]

Confronted by these dangers, Taft cheerfully accepted the wider implications of the Roosevelt Corollary of the Monroe Doctrine. As Washington would not willingly permit European nations to intervene on behalf of their investments, the United States had some moral obligation to preserve order. In addition, foreign holdings could be squeezed out of the critical Caribbean areas by putting pressure on the Latin-American governments. At the same time, American capital could be pumped in by holding out inducements to Wall Street, as well as assurances of protection.

Taft's policy resulted in a vigorous attempt to push America's financial empire deep into the Caribbean. In 1909, for example, the State Department became deeply concerned over the difficulties that Honduras was having with British bondholders, and it made energetic efforts to interest Wall Street bankers in refinancing Honduran indebtedness. But the treaty that Knox drew up with Honduras to achieve these ends was spurned by the Senate of the United States. Negotiating with Guatemala likewise proved fruitless.

Haiti presented similar problems. In 1910 Knox, who was anxious to pump American capital into the Haitian National Bank, requested several New York bankers to meet with him in Washington. The upshot was that four American houses invested heavily in the Haitian institution. Taft believed that American capital used in this way not only helped to protect the Canal Zone, but benefited the Latin-American countries by bringing them peace and stability. And if all went well, the Wall Street bankers would pocket their profits.

THE FINANCIAL BIG STICK IN NICARAGUA

Dollar diplomacy appeared in perhaps its most unlovely light in Nicaragua. Here Knox had something of a personal stake, by reason of his previous connection with American mining interests. The investments of United States citizens in Nicaragua were small, when compared with

[6] *Foreign Relations, 1912,* p. 1092 (Jan. 19, 1912).

those in certain other Caribbean republics, but here lay the alternate canal route, which Washington could not permit to fall under foreign control. Unhappily for good relations, Nicaragua suffered from the iron rule of a notorious trouble-maker, José Zelaya. His attitude was summed up in his alleged sneer: "I ridicule the United States, laugh at Germany, spit on England."

The inevitable anti-Zelaya revolution, which was partly fomented by American firms, burst in 1909. During the ensuing fighting, two United States citizens serving with the insurgents were summarily executed. Secretary Knox forthwith drafted a harsh note which condemned the Zelaya regime, expressed sympathy for the revolutionists, and notified the Nicaraguan *chargé* in Washington that he was dismissed. The drastic nature of this communication excited much adverse comment, both abroad and at home. The *New York Nation* remarked that Knox "attacks diplomatic problems of the first rank as easily as he would discharge a refractory window-cleaner in the State Department." [7]

The Knox plan for dealing with the Nicaragua and other storm centers of the Caribbean was simple. First, the troubled government was to be stabilized by reorganizing its finances. This reform would avert foreign intervention. Second, the customs houses were to be removed from the reach of the greedy revolutionists. This precaution would eliminate a major incentive to armed uprisings. In pursuance of such a policy, the Washington officials refused to recognize the new Nicaraguan government until it had arranged for a large loan from American bankers with which to refund the debt that it owed the British. When the United States minister discovered that a strong majority of the Nicaraguan voters opposed such a step, he urged upon the State Department "the advisability of stationing permanently, at least until the loan has been put through, a war vessel at Corinto." [8] A warship soon appeared, and the proper ratification of the transaction followed.

Secretary Knox continued to push ahead with his plans for financial control. Late in 1911, with the approval of the New York bankers and the Nicaraguan government, Colonel C. D. Ham, an Iowa journalist who had been in the Philippine customs service, became collector general of the customs. The next year, during widespread disorders, some 2500 United States marines were landed to protect American life and property. The main body of troops was withdrawn later in 1912, but a legation guard lingered until 1925.

Knox realized that his policy of forcibly enlarging the economic orbit of the United States was highly unpopular in Latin America. Early in 1912 he made a good-will tour through most of the republics touching

[7] *New York Nation*, XC, 27 (Jan. 13, 1910).
[8] *Foreign Relations, 1911*, pp. 661–662 (Northcott to Secretary of State, May 25, 1911).

the Caribbean. "I beg to assure you," he proclaimed in one speech, "and I am sure that what I say meets with the approval of the people and President of the United States, that my Government does not covet an inch of territory south of the Rio Grande." [9] But these fine words were strangely inconsistent with economic imperialism, financial receiverships, and armed intervention.

THE SALVATION OF THE SEALS

Less controversial were Taft's successful efforts to end the destruction of the Alaskan seal herd. Secretary Blaine's attempt to halt open-sea (pelagic) sealing had met with failure in the 1890's, primarily because the powers concerned would not consent to an international agreement abridging their rights on the high seas. By 1910 the once-magnificent herd had dwindled from some 4,000,000 to about 100,000 sleek creatures. Certain naturalists, foreseeing imminent extermination, were urging that the remainder be slaughtered outright on a mercy-killing basis.

International agreement was the only possible solution. But the Japanese and Canadian pelagic sealers, who owned a fleet of schooners, did not want to be deprived of their disagreeable but legal business. On the other hand, if pelagic sealing continued there would soon be no business to be deprived of. After months of patient diplomacy, a conference convened in Washington in the summer of 1911, with representatives present from each of the four great powers bordering the North Pacific—Russia, Japan, Britain, and the United States. When the conference became deadlocked, Taft resorted to the unusual step of appealing directly to the Mikado. The result was a moderation of Japanese demands and complete agreement on a kind of international game law.

The North Pacific Sealing Convention of 1911 required each of the four signatory powers to prevent its nationals from engaging in pelagic sealing. To compensate them for having to abandon this profitable industry, the pact provided that Washington would annually pay to Japan and Britain (for Canada) a stipulated percentage of the proceeds from the strictly regulated land kill. [10] (See map, p. 413.)

Under the new protective regulations the herd on the Pribilof Islands increased from 100,000 to well over a million by 1932. But the Japanese complained that the seals were making heavy inroads on their vital fish supply, and in 1940 gave notice of terminating the agreement, effective the next year. During the thirty years that it lasted the pact not only removed a dangerous source of friction but provided an outstanding example of international co-operation. In the 1940's both Canada and

[9] Bemis, *American Secretaries of State*, IX, 339.
[10] T. A. Bailey, "The North Pacific Sealing Convention of 1911," *Pacific Hist. Rev.*, IV (1935), 1–14.

the United States agreed to continue their ban on pelagic sealing, and by 1948 the seal herd had increased to over 3,600,000, or approximately its original size.

FINISHING THE FISHING CONTROVERSY

As the new century lengthened, the perennial Canadian fisheries controversy began to bob up again with increasing persistence. The shores of Newfoundland were now more thickly settled by local fishermen, and they resented more than ever the incursions of New Englanders, who still claimed privileges under the ancient treaty of 1818. The parliament of Newfoundland therefore passed annoying regulations, such as forbidding fishing on Sunday, which caused the Yankees serious hardship. An angry protest arose from the "seagoing voters" of Massachusetts.

Secretary of State Root, before taking over his official duties in 1905, had made a journey to Newfoundland, where he developed a sympathetic understanding of the problem. A clash between the two embattled groups of fishermen was averted by temporary regulations. Finally, after painstaking negotiations, the United States and Britain concluded a convention, in January, 1909, under which the disputed issues were to be submitted to The Hague Court. The signing of this pact was one of Secretary Root's last official acts before leaving the Roosevelt Cabinet.

The scene now shifted to The Hague, in the Netherlands, to which Root journeyed as an American counsel before the arbitral tribunal. The decision, handed down in 1910, was in the nature of a compromise. New England fishermen were henceforth to be protected against unreasonable local regulations, but the Newfoundlanders were generally sustained in their claims to local jurisdiction. Root was satisfied that the United States had obtained about all that it could have reasonably expected.

The memorable Hague award of 1910, with certain modifications, received confirmation in the Anglo-American Convention of 1912. The key feature of this settlement was the setting up of a permanent body to adjust disputes as they arose, with a consequent removal of long-festering grievances. Root was largely responsible for this epochal settlement, but the final steps were carried through under the Taft administration and hence redounded to its credit. Thus was a happy ending written to the most persistently vexatious dispute in American diplomatic history.

Another greatly underrated achievement of Root as Secretary of State was the signing early in 1909 of the Boundary Waters Treaty with Britain. It established a permanent joint commission to settle disputes, which mostly involved problems of irrigation and navigation growing out of the rivers and lakes along the Canadian-American boundary. In a quiet way the Commission nipped in the bud a number of potentially serious disputes.

THE CANADIAN RECIPROCITY FIASCO

Relations with Canada, though definitely improved by the sealing and fisheries settlements, were badly rasped in another quarter. The Canadians, with fond memories of their prosperity under the abrogated Reciprocity Treaty of 1854, continued their agitation for such a pact. When the United States Congress rebuffed them in 1909 by passing another highly protective tariff, they began to talk seriously of retaliation.

The Taft administration, which had been under heavy fire at home for its reactionary tariff policy, now began to move rapidly. In January, 1911, it concluded a sweeping reciprocity agreement with Canada. Numerous commodities, principally foodstuffs, were to be admitted to each country free of duty or with reduced duties.

The agreement with Canada was not a treaty but an arrangement subject to confirmation by simple majorities in both branches of Congress. The House placed the stamp of its approval on the pact without undue delay. But the Senate, swayed by the outcry of outraged American fishermen, lumbermen, and grain growers, adjourned without taking action. President Taft, ordinarily easy going, was now in a fighting mood. Eager to crown his floundering administration with a triumph in foreign affairs, he called Congress in special session and applied the party whip and spur. The sizzling heat of a Washington summer, combined with the votes of low-tariff Democrats, finally forced the measure through in July, 1911.

But indiscreet supporters of reciprocity, in Congress and out, left the impression that the measure was but an insidious step toward the annexation of Canada. Speaker of the House Champ Clark asserted, for example: "I am for it, because I hope to see the day when the American flag will float over every square foot of the British-North American possessions clear to the North Pole." [11] The *Philadelphia North American* dryly remarked, "Canadian mothers now frighten their children by telling them Champ Clark is coming." President Taft himself was so indiscreet as to inform Congress that the Canadian people were coming "to the parting of the ways"—meaning, of course, the economic ways.

Publisher W. R. Hearst, who was eager to secure cheap wood pulp for his chain of newspapers, enthusiastically supported reciprocity. He even shipped large numbers of his sensational sheets into Canada, where they made many votes—for the other side. Taft was so ill-advised as to express his "high appreciation" to the unpopular Mr. Hearst in helping "spread the gospel of reciprocity."

The issue was finally thrown into the noisy amphitheater of the Canadian general election of 1911. Canadian interests insisted that their land

[11] *Cong. Record*, 61 Cong., 3 sess., p. 2520 (Feb. 14, 1911).

would become "the backyard and lumber camp of New England." Raising the cry, "No truck or trade with the Yankees," they appealed to Canadian nationalism and a lurking distrust of Uncle Sam. "I do not understand," proclaimed the British poet Rudyard Kipling, "how nine million people can enter into such arrangements with ninety million strangers . . . and at the same time preserve their national integrity. It is her own soul that Canada risks today." [12] Thousands of Canadians thronged to the polls convinced that the choice lay between "the Union Jack and Old Glory," and that the fate of the British Empire and the future of Canada hinged on their resolutely rejecting the gilded trap known as American reciprocity.

LOOKING OUR WAY

Canada regards reciprocity as foreshadowing annexation.
Toronto News, 1911

The election resulted in a sweeping victory for the Conservative or anti-reciprocity party. The newly elected majority in Parliament voted down reciprocity, and the friendly hand which Taft had extended at the urgent invitation of the Canadians was sharply rebuffed. The whole incident further discredited the Taft administration, embittered Canadian-American relations, tore open old wounds, and gave the death blow to whatever lingering sentiments for annexation may have persisted in Canada. The *Columbus Dispatch* remarked philosophically, "Uncle Sam's summer flirtation is ended. But there are other summers and other girls."

[12] H. L. Keenleyside, *Canada and the United States* (New York, 1929), p. 319. The Canadian campaign is fully presented in L. E. Ellis, *Reciprocity 1911* (New Haven, 1939).

SENATOR LODGE STRETCHES MONROE'S DOCTRINE

President Taft's troubles with Congress did not end with Canadian reciprocity. The Senate took the bit in its teeth on several occasions, notably in connection with Magdalena Bay, a magnificent body of landlocked water in Lower California.

Magdalena Bay had long been an object of peculiar concern to the United States because of its potentialities as a naval base. In the hands of a powerful foreign nation it would seriously menace the Panama Canal and California, as well as the lines of communication between these two vital points. In 1911 the news leaked out that a Japanese company was negotiating with a syndicate in the United States to purchase a huge tract of land in the vicinity of Magdalena Bay. A momentary flurry of excitement, led by the anti-Japanese Hearst newspapers, swept over the country. But when the State Department frowned upon the transaction, the Japanese company dropped the whole project.

Henry Cabot Lodge, the influential Senator from Massachusetts, took advantage of this opening to introduce a resolution in the Senate. It declared that the United States disapproved of the transfer of strategic spots in the Americas to non-American private companies which might be acting as agents for a foreign power. President Taft and the State Department both regarded the resolution as unnecessary and provocative, but it was approved in August, 1912, by a vote of 51 to 4. This declaration was generally regarded as a corollary of the Monroe Doctrine, because it extended the principles of 1823 to an Asiatic power and to a foreign company, as distinguished from a government. Japan, of course, was not mentioned by name, but the intent was perfectly clear.

The Lodge Corollary has been commonly dismissed as unimportant because it was simply a pronouncement of the Senate. Yet the record shows that the State Department accepted the corollary and invoked it at least four times since 1912, in each case to discourage Americans from disposing of their holdings in Mexico to Japanese.[13] The Lodge resolution, although probably unnecessary, not only remained as a warning sign to foreign nations but illustrated strikingly the expansive powers of the Monroe Doctrine.

FIGHTING FOR ARBITRATION

Taft managed to get into much hotter water with the Senate over the peaceful settlement of international disputes. In 1905 the Senators had leveled their fire at a series of general arbitration treaties negotiated by

[13] T. A. Bailey, "The Lodge Corollary to the Monroe Doctrine," *Pol. Sci. Quar.*, XLVIII (1933), 235–236. See also E. K. Chamberlin, "The Japanese Scare at Magdalena Bay," *Pacific Hist. Rev.*, XXIV (1955), 345–359.

Secretary Hay, and had finally amended them so as to make a two-thirds vote of the Senate necessary for every specific arbitration. The Roosevelt administration had thereupon let the emasculated pacts expire.

Secretary Root, an eminent international lawyer and a devoted friend of arbitration, reasoned that a weak pact was better than no pact. The instruments that he drew up excepted all disputes affecting the "vital interests, the independence, or the honor of the two contracting states"— which could mean every possible dispute. If any controversy cleared these hurdles, it could be referred to arbitration only if the Senate approved a special treaty to that effect by a two-thirds vote. Twenty-five of these Root arbitration pacts were signed during 1908 and 1909, in the closing months of the Roosevelt regime.

President Taft, a conservative lawyer who favored peace and order, was eager to secure much more sweeping arbitration treaties than those obtained by Root. He arranged for the signing of general pacts with both Britain and France in August, 1911. Designed as models, these went beyond the Root treaties by providing for the arbitration of all "justiciable" questions, not even excepting "vital interests" and "national honor." Although the Senators were privileged to vote on each individual arbitration arrangement, they turned against the Taft pacts under the leadership of Senator Lodge, who had little sympathy for the "mushy philanthropists." The Senate clearly was suffering from partisanship, wounded dignity, and jealousy of its treaty-making prerogatives.

Taft, now thoroughly aroused against the "emotionalists or neurotics," went before the country in a vigorous speaking tour. He declared that the Spanish-American war was unnecessary, and this statement angered Theodore Roosevelt, whose special war it had been. The ex-Rough Rider struck back at the arbitration treaties in a vigorous magazine article. Yet there can be little doubt that the public was strongly behind Taft. The *Baltimore Sun* was but one of many newspapers to say that rejection of the agreements would be an "international misfortune." [14] The Senate nonetheless stubbornly applied itself to the task of watering down the treaties. It exempted from arbitration about every question of importance that any other nation would want to arbitrate, including state debts, the Monroe Doctrine, and Oriental immigration. Then, on March 7, 1912, it consented to ratification of what was left by a vote of 76 to 3.

The treaties were so thoroughly mutilated that Taft did not go through with ratification, remarking resignedly, "We shall have to begin all over again." He hoped, to use his own words, that "the Senators might change their minds, or that the people might change the Senate; instead of which they changed me." [15]

[14] *Current Literature*, LI, 354 (Oct. 1911); also W. S. Holt, *Treaties Defeated by the Senate* (Baltimore, 1933), pp. 230–231.

[15] Henry Pringle, *The Life and Times of William Howard Taft* (New York, 1939), II, 755.

DIPLOMATIC FRUSTRATION

Relations with Russia, already strained by the wholesale massacres of Jews, were further embittered during the closing days of the Taft administration.

Refugee Russian Jews, after becoming naturalized American citizens, were being denied permission by Russia to return to their native land. The Czar's government, which discriminated against its own Jews, naturally could see no wrong in its policy. But a tidal wave of opinion welled up in the United States against this blow at freedom of religion and the American flag.

The ancient commercial treaty of 1832 with Russia, under which American citizens were presumably guaranteed nondiscriminatory treatment, was involved. In December, 1911, the House of Representatives, by a thumping vote of 301 to 1, passed a resolution declaring the pact abrogated. But President Taft, who deplored this offensively worded way of handling a delicate diplomatic problem, forestalled drastic action by quietly giving notice of the termination of the treaty, effective a year later. This slap at Russia, while doing American Jews no good and American businessmen positive harm, did serve to relieve public resentment at home.[16]

Taft's foreign policy thus ended on a note of futility and frustration. Certain unfinished business, to be discussed in the next chapter, was left on the doorstep of the incoming Wilson administration, notably the Mexican revolution, the Nicaragua canal-option treaty, the Panama canal tolls issue, and dollar diplomacy. As for Taft's more immediate problems, the Manchurian Railroad proposal was rejected, Canadian reciprocity was spurned, the Lodge Corollary of the Monroe Doctrine was passed by the Senate in the teeth of White House disapproval, the arbitration treaties were amended to death and an abrogation of the Russian treaty was forced upon the administration. About the only solid achievements that Taft could claim in the field of foreign affairs were the preservation of the seal herd and the final settlement of the Canadian fisheries controversy.

SELECTED BIBLIOGRAPHY

A survey of Knox appears in S. F. Bemis, ed., *American Secretaries of State and their Diplomacy* (New York, 1929), IX. The most exhaustive life of Taft is H. F. Pringle, *The Life and Times of William Howard Taft* (2 vols., New York, 1939). On aspects of the Far East, consult A. W. Griswold, *The Far Eastern Policy of the United States* (New York, 1938); Charles Vevier, *The United States and China, 1906–1913* (New Brunswick, N.J., 1955); J. G.

[16] See T. A. Bailey, *America Faces Russia* (Ithaca, N. Y., 1950), Ch. XVIII.

Reid, *The Manchu Abdication and the Powers, 1908–1912* (Berkeley, Calif., 1935). On Latin America, see S. F. Bemis, *The Latin American Policy of the United States* (New York, 1943); B. H. Williams, *Economic Foreign Policy of the United States* (New York, 1929); D. G. Munro, *The Five Republics of Central America* (New York, 1918); C. L. Jones, *The Caribbean Since 1900* (New York, 1936); W. H. Callcott, *The Caribbean Policy of the United States, 1890–1920* (Baltimore, 1942). On Canada, consult C. C. Tansill, *Canadian-American Relations, 1875–1911* (New Haven, 1943). Useful biographical accounts are Herbert Croly, *Willard Straight* (New York, 1924) and P. C. Jessup, *Elihu Root* (2 vols., New York, 1938).

Helpful articles are W. G. Swartz, "The Proposed Canadian-American Reciprocity Agreement of 1911," *Jour. Econ. and Business Hist.*, III (1930), 118–147; W. C. Askew and J. F. Rippy, "The United States and Europe's Strife, 1908–1913," *Jour. of Politics*, IV (1942), 68–79; A. O. Gibbons, "Sir George Gibbons and the Boundary Waters Treaty of 1909," *Canadian Hist. Rev.*, XXXIV (1953), 124–138.

See footnotes of this chapter; Bemis and Griffin, *Guide*, pp. 445 ff.; *Harvard Guide*, Ch. 26.

7TH ED. REFS. J. A. DeNovo, "A Railroad for Turkey: The Chester Project, 1908–1913," *Business Hist. Rev.*, XXXIII (1959), 300–329 describes how the Taft administration, without political motives and solely to back the dollar, unsuccessfully supported Admiral Chester's ambitious railroad scheme. Naomi W. Cohen, "Ambassador Straus in Turkey, 1909–1910: A Note on Dollar Diplomacy," *Miss. Valley Hist. Rev.*, XLV (1959), 632–642 points out that this old-time nonentanglement diplomat objected to serving as an advance commercial agent for the dollar, notably in the Chester railroad project. D. G. Munro, "Dollar Diplomacy in Nicaragua, 1909–1913," *Hispanic Amer. Hist. Rev.*, XXXVIII (1958), 209–234 demonstrates that here Washington's primary objectives were political; the New York bankers deserve praise for continuing their financial help when the investment could not be justified on a profit basis. T. P. Wright, Jr., "Honduras: A Case Study of United States Support of Free Elections in Central America," *ibid.*, XL (1960), 212–223 demonstrates that Washington's concern for free elections led to diplomatic pressure and the landing of marines, all of which unwittingly protected American economic interests. The policy of upholding free elections failed because "the prerequisites for democracy were missing." E. J. Berbusse, "Neutrality-Diplomacy of the United States and Mexico, 1910–1911," *The Americas,* XII (1956), 265–283 concludes that Washington, influenced to some extent by public opinion, interpreted existing neutrality statutes with strong sympathy for the Madero insurgents. L. L. Blaisdell, "Henry Lane Wilson and the Overthrow of Madero," *Southwestern Soc. Sci. Quar.*, XLIII (1962), 126–135 is a solidly documented study which shows that this meddling U.S. Ambassador connived at the ascent of Huerta, who in turn murdered Madero. The conclusion is that President Wilson's nonrecognition of Huerta grew in part out of a sense of guilt that the United States should have become so deeply involved in this unsavory affair.

8TH AND 9TH ED. REFS. See BIBLIOGRAPHICAL ADDENDUM, p. 1,016.

37

Wilson and the "New" Diplomacy, 1913-1917

It is a very perilous thing to determine the foreign policy of a nation in the terms of material interest.
WOODROW WILSON, 1913

GRAPE-JUICE DIPLOMACY

THE REPUBLICAN DYNASTY, which had been entrenched in the White House since 1897, was broken in 1913, after the Roosevelt-Taft feud had split the party wide open in the election of 1912. The new Democratic President, ex-Governor Woodrow Wilson of New Jersey, was a comparative newcomer in politics. Three years earlier he had resigned under fire from the presidency of Princeton University; now, as if by a miracle, he was President of the United States. This "professor in politics," although well equipped to grapple with pressing domestic problems, had devoted little study to foreign policy. Yet, ironically enough, diplomatic difficulties were destined to overshadow all others during much of his troubled administration.

William Jennings Bryan was the uncrowned king of the Democratic Party, and Wilson, though distrustful of his intellectual capacity, was forced to offer him the Secretaryship of State. Wilson probably felt, as Mr. Dooley quipped, that the silver-voiced orator would cause less trouble "in his bosom than on his back." But in all fairness one must note that Bryan proved to be loyal, co-operative, and self-effacing. He was a better-than-expected Secretary of State, and he managed to keep his head, particularly during the European War, when some of his more highly esteemed colleagues were losing theirs.

The appointment of Bryan, whose name had long been connected with the free-silver heresy, aroused savage criticism, particularly among conservative Republicans. The brickbats increased when the new Secretary, a lifelong prohibitionist, announced that he would not serve alcoholic beverages at official functions. He thus inaugurated an era of aridity which led some of the diplomatic dignitaries to fortify themselves in advance—in some cases too strongly. The opposition press indulged in unholy laughter at the expense of "grape-juice diplomacy."

Republican newspapers renewed their blasts when they learned that Bryan felt obliged to supplement his salary by continuing his Chautauqua lectures on peace, prohibition, and kindred subjects—"grape-juice guff" and "peace piffle." [1] An even noisier storm broke when word leaked out about his unabashed but not unique spoilsmongering. Bryan had run for the Presidency three times, and he now felt that he could discharge many of his political debts by parceling out diplomatic offices. In a letter to the American receiver-general of Dominican customs he asked for information as to "what positions you have at your disposal with which to reward deserving Democrats." The publication of this indiscretion promptly elicited hypocritical outbursts from "resolute Republicans."

BRYAN'S "COOLING-OFF" TREATIES

In making diplomatic decisions of major importance, Wilson acted as his own Secretary of State. But he gave Bryan a free hand in drawing up his so-called peace treaties, thirty of which were signed and twenty-two put into effect. The great orator, who had thrilled countless audiences with his speech, "The Prince of Peace," threw himself into this task with all the enthusiasm of a life-long pacifist. The series of pacts that he negotiated during 1913 and 1914 were, strictly speaking, conciliation rather than arbitration treaties. They provided that every otherwise insoluble dispute, not even excluding questions of national honor, should be submitted to international commissions for investigation. The nations involved agreed not to go to war until a recommendation was forthcoming, ordinarily within a year. They could then accept or reject the findings. But by that time overheated tempers normally would have cooled, and world opinion would have been marshaled on the side of peace. The *Brooklyn Eagle* saw in the plan a new version of the juvenile admonition, "when angry count fifty, when very angry count a hundred."

Bryan showed genuine skill in dealing with the headstrong Senate. But the taint of free silver, grape juice, and Chautauqua lectures caused the "wait-a-year" pacts to be greeted with more than ordinary skepticism. Many editors believed that the treaties could do no harm and might do some good, and this attitude accounted for much amused contempt. The *Memphis Commercial-Appeal*, for example, gibed that the completion of

[1] Many felt that the dignity of the government was lowered when published notices showed Bryan's address sandwiched between acts by Tyrolese yodlers and Neapolitan troubadours. One cartoon had Bryan being congratulated after a performance by the strong man: ". . . Old pal, youse got a swell act. Youse is killin' 'em dead out in front." *Literary Digest,* XLVII, 514 (Sept. 27, 1913).

treaties with Switzerland, Denmark, and Uruguay takes "a great load off our minds. The thought of war with them was terrible."[2] A few newspapers thought the treaties positively vicious because they lacked teeth. But a stronger type of pact probably would have met with the usual Senatorial roadblock.

These earnest efforts at peacemaking have been generally underrated, partly because of Bryan's association with them and partly because the outbreak of World War I converted treaties into "scraps of paper." Yet the existence of one of these pacts with Britain, together with the absence of one with Germany, had some bearing on the chain of events that brought America into the war on the side of the Allies. Furthermore, Secretary Bryan's work was reflected in the peace machinery set up at the close of World War I. To the end of his days Bryan regarded the "cooling-off" pacts as his most notable contribution to the nation, and his official portrait in the Department of State shows him with a copy of one of them in his hand.

DOLLAR DIPLOMACY DENOUNCED

The loose ends of Taft's Dollar Diplomacy lay on the steps of the White House, and President Wilson, an outspoken foe of bankers and trusts, had already put himself emphatically on record as opposed to such iniquities. Turning to Latin America first, he made public a spectacular statement of policy on March 11, 1913, only a week after taking office. Condemning disorders to the south, he then lashed out at Dollar Diplomacy by proclaiming that he was not interested in supporting any "special group or interests." Instead of communicating this stinging declaration through the regular channels of the State Department, he resorted to the irregular procedure of giving it directly to the newspapers. This hasty move, though suggestive of "shirt-sleeve diplomacy," appears to have met with generally favorable comment in the press. The friendly *New York World,* a Democratic supporter, rejoiced:

> There is not a word of encouragement here for the big exploiters, not a word to hearten a murderous uprising, not a word to stir the greed of a dictator disguised as a deliverer, and not a word to expedite the sales of stocks and bonds in the United States by marauding corporations.[3]

A week later, on March 18, 1913, Wilson directed his righteous wrath at Dollar Diplomacy in China. As earlier noted, President Taft had forced the admission of Wall Street bankers into the six-power consortium for railroad construction in China. The tottering Chinese government was now seeking an additional $125 million loan from this group

[2] *Literary Digest,* XLVIII, 96 (Jan. 17, 1914). See also, M. E. Curti, "Bryan and World Peace," *Smith College Studies in History,* XVI, nos. 3–4 (1931).
[3] *New York World,* March 13, 1913, 10:3.

to bolster its administration. The American financiers, already suffering from misgivings and seeing greener pastures elsewhere, declared that they would need more than mere approval from the State Department. They would have to be actively encouraged by Washington to go ahead.

To the request of the bankers Wilson provided an answer—also in the newspapers. He declared that because the terms of the loan impinged upon China's sovereignty and might invite foreign intervention, American investors could expect no support from Washington. The next day the bankers announced their withdrawal from the enterprise. Wall Street, in the language of its enemies, had received a "knockout." Actually, the bankers were probably pleased to have this excuse to drop the Chinese hot chestnut.

Wilson's rebuff to Wall Street was not, from one point of view, a reversal. Taft had reversed traditional American policy; Wilson was merely returning to the well-worn course. As an idealist and reformer who had long distrusted the powerful "interests," Wilson no doubt derived satisfaction from rebuking them, but in doing so he plunged ahead in a manner that suggested both precipitancy and amateurishness. The conservative *Wall Street Journal* sneered, "Dollar Diplomacy was at least better than none at all."

Wilson's slap at Wall Street clearly appealed to the popular prejudice against Dollar Diplomacy, bankers, and trusts. But supporters of Taft complained about "deadly drifting." They argued that the United States, a trusted friend of China, might better have used its power positively to uphold the Open Door against the threatened encroachments of Japan. Wilson tacitly admitted his blunder when, in 1918, he prodded the bewildered bankers back into a new four-power China consortium, finally concluded in 1920. But by that time China was much weaker, and Japan had dug in more deeply.

THE ALIEN LAND CRISIS IN CALIFORNIA

The Japanese problem on the Pacific Coast again came to a boil at the outset of Wilson's administration. The Californians, ever sensitive to the "yellow peril," were disturbed by the high birthrate and unusual acquisitiveness of the Japanese. The statistics as to population and land-holding now cause such fears to appear ridiculous, but alarmists with slide rules could prove that the Japanese would elbow all the whites into the ocean within a century or so.

The issue was all the more explosive for having been postponed. The California legislature had seriously discussed legislation to debar the Japanese from owning land during the Roosevelt and Taft administrations, but vigorous protests from Washington had deferred the evil day. Wilson was handicapped at the outset, for the California legislature was

Republican, and quite willing to embarrass the Democratic administration on the Potomac.[4]

Alarmed by reports of giant protest meetings in Japan against land legislation, Wilson sent earnest telegraphic appeals to the California legislators. This episode is but another instance of the embarrassing blind spot in federalism. California seemed bent on provoking a war which the other forty-seven states would have to fight, while Washington remained powerless to intervene. The *Hartford Times* expressed an Eastern view when it remarked, "Of the two it might be cheaper to go to war with California than with Japan."

Unable to act effectively, Wilson nevertheless acted. He sent Secretary Bryan to California in April, 1913, to plead with the governor and legislature. The eloquence of the famed orator was not sufficient to prevent the passage of the alien land law, but his mission soothed Japanese sensibilities by demonstrating that Washington was sympathetic. The bill, as finally passed, forbade aliens ineligible to citizenship, like the Japanese, to own agricultural land. By not mentioning the Japanese outright, the law conveyed no direct affront to Japan and, by ingenious wording, observed the strict letter of existing treaty obligations.

But Tokyo, deeply resenting this thinly veiled discrimination, lodged several ringing protests in Washington. One of them was couched in such strong terms that it was returned to the Japanese ambassador to be toned down. Jingoes whooped it up on both sides of the Pacific, war preparations were hastened, and the Cabinet seriously discussed the imminence of an armed clash. But Bryan confided to the Secretary of Agriculture, "There will be no war. I have seen the Japanese Ambassador, and I am letting the old man down easy."[5] Partly as a result of Washington's conciliatory attitude, the crisis was surmounted.

THE PANAMA TOLLS TIFF

Another troublesome heritage from the Taft administration lay on Wilson's doorstep. In 1912 Congress had passed an act setting up regulations for the Panama Canal, which was then nearing completion. The most controversial clause specifically exempted American coastwise shipping, such as that plying between New York and San Francisco, from paying

[4] T. A. Bailey, "California, Japan, and the Alien Land Legislation of 1913," *Pacific Hist. Rev.*, I (1932), 42.

[5] D. F. Houston, *Eight Years with Wilson's Cabinet* (Garden City, N.Y., 1926), I, 67. On another occasion the ambassador asked Bryan if the reply of the United States to his protest would be final, and the Secretary answered, "There is nothing final between friends." Bryan later obtained some old swords from the War Department, had them beaten into miniature ploughshare paperweights, with the inscription, "Nothing is final between friends," and distributed them among a selected few. Stephen Gwynn, ed., *The Letters and Friendships of Sir Cecil Spring-Rice* (Boston, 1929), II, 274 n.

any tolls. This favoritism was frankly designed as a subsidy to force competing transcontinental railroads to lower their high rates, and as such appealed to the current antitrust prejudices of the voters.

But the Panama Canal Tolls Act of 1912 seemed to fly in the face of the Hay-Pauncefote Treaty of 1901, which plainly stated that "all nations" observing the rules would be required to pay the same rates. American legalists, including eminent lawyers like Taft and Knox, argued that "all nations" meant "all other nations," and that the act was not discriminatory because Congress had long since forbidden foreign vessels to engage in American coastwise trade. Besides, the United States, which had built the canal with its own money, was entitled to some concessions.

The British, who quickly perceived that the exemption of American traffic would raise the tolls for all other users, were angered by what they regarded as an act of bad faith. The Foreign Office lodged an emphatic protest in Washington, and suggested arbitration as a solution. But the Senate, under the Arbitration Treaty of 1908, was unwilling to give its two-thirds consent to such an alternative. The United States was almost certain to lose its case before a court consisting of foreigners representing other maritime nations.

Champions of honorable conduct on both sides of the Atlantic were distressed. The *New York Nation* insisted that the canal act was "a greater disgrace to this country than would have been a naval defeat in the waters off Colón." The British, who keenly remembered Cleveland's bellicose demand for arbitration in the Venezuela dispute, believed that what was sauce for the English goose was also sauce for the American gander. Walter Hines Page, the pro-British editor whom Wilson had recently appointed as Ambassador to London, reported:

> And everywhere—in circles the most friendly to us, and the best informed —I receive commiseration because of the dishonorable attitude of our Government about the Panama Canal tolls. This, I confess, is hard to meet. We made a bargain—a solemn compact—and we have broken it. Whether it were a good bargain or a bad one, a silly one or a wise one; that's far from the point.[6]

WILSON UPHOLDS HONOR AT PANAMA

The dispute with London was highly embarrassing to Wilson. He had been elected on a platform that had declared in favor of tolls exemption— a twist to the Lion's tail which had been highly popular with the large Irish element in the Democratic Party. But after wrestling with his conscience he concluded that the question was basically one of national honor, and that if reasonable doubts existed they should be resolved in favor of an honorable course.

[6] B. J. Hendrick, *The Life and Letters of Walter H. Page* (Garden City, N.Y., 1922), I, 249 (Page to Wilson, Sept. 10, 1913).

ISTHMIAN GAMES

EVENT No. 1—Extending the Cold Elbow.

British resent American position on Canal tolls controversy.
London Punch, 1912

After waiting to clear away some pressing domestic legislation, Wilson made a dramatic appearance before Congress, on March 5, 1914, to urge repeal of the discriminatory clause:

> Whatever may be our own differences of opinion concerning this much debated measure, its meaning is not debated outside the United States. . . . We . . . are too big, too powerful, too self-respecting a Nation to interpret with too strained or refined a reading the words of our own promises just because we have power enough to give us leave to read them as we please.[7]

Wilson closed by delicately hinting that his foreign policy elsewhere would be weakened if Congress did not give him "ungrudging" support in

[7] *Cong. Record,* 63 Cong., 2 sess., p. 4313.

dealing with the canal imbroglio. He evidently was hoping to make the United States a moral leader, and felt that he could not achieve his goal without repeal of the tolls exemption. Specifically, his anti-Huerta policy in Mexico was floundering badly, partly because the British, with their vital stake in Mexican oil, were recognizing President Huerta. Wilson may have felt, although there is no official record of a "deal," that the British would continue to give his Mexican policy lukewarm support if he pursued the honorable course regarding the Panama tolls exemption issue.

The British press warmly praised Wilson's forthright message to Congress. But in America the Anglophobes, with the vocal support of the Hearst press, emitted a pained outcry. Cartoons showed "the angular professor-President" cringing before the British throne. After a heated debate, the House passed repeal by a comfortable margin, but the real battle took place in the Senate. Behind the scenes, railroad lobbyists locked horns with shipping lobbyists. To the keen embarrassment of Wilson, a number of his own Democratic Senators, notably the Irish-supported O'Gorman of New York, opposed his cause, while a number of prominent Republicans endorsed it. Finally, on June 11, 1914, amid oratorical fireworks and near fist fights, repeal passed the Senate, 50 to 35. As a face-saving gesture of defiance, Congress specifically affirmed its right to re-enact tolls exemption at some future date.

Wilson's insistence on honorable conduct enhanced the prestige of the United States, and swept away the last major controversy in Anglo-American relations. With World War I and its bitter disputes fated to erupt the next month, the settlement of the tolls dispute proved to be an achievement of primary importance.

THE DOLLAR IS REVIVED IN NICARAGUA

The imminent completion of the Panama Canal—it was formally opened in August, 1914—intensified American interest in the Caribbean. In the banana lands of this region, as in China, Wilson was annoyed to find that his idealistic opposition to dollar diplomacy did not square with the realistic facts of international life.

The expiring Taft administration had drawn up a highly advantageous treaty with Nicaragua early in 1913. As finally drafted, it gave the United States a renewable ninety-nine year lease on the Great and Little Corn Islands of the Caribbean, and the privilege for a like period of establishing a naval base on the Pacific side on the Gulf of Fonseca. Most important of all, the pact granted the United States an exclusive option in perpetuity on the prospective canal route. For all these privileges the United States was to pay a rather meager $3 million, and this sum was to be used by the Nicaraguan government to meet its obligations to American bankers.

The evidence is clear that the Wall Street financiers were highly favorable to a United States protectorate over Nicaragua.

The Nicaragua canal-option treaty was another embarrassing legacy for Wilson and Bryan. While detesting Dollar Diplomacy, they could not ignore the priceless advantages of the pact, notably the removal of a rival canal route from possible foreign control. Bryan was finally persuaded not only to support the draft treaty but to strengthen it by adding an article authorizing American intervention, somewhat in the manner

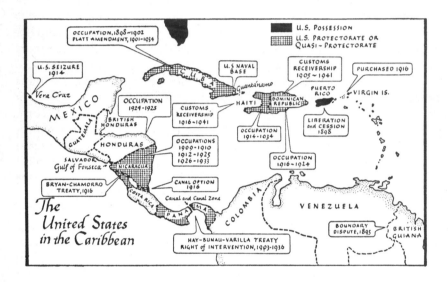

The United States in the Caribbean

of the Platt Amendment for Cuba. This unexpected development inspired the *New York Times* to remark that the new administration was making the "dollar diplomacy" of Taft and Knox "more nearly resemble ten-cent diplomacy." But the Senate balked at the Platt Amendment feature, and with this proviso eliminated, the pact was redrawn and approved in 1916. A number of Republican Senators voted for the new Bryan-Chamorro Treaty on the grounds that it was but a logical continuation by the Wilson Democrats of Taft's Dollar Diplomacy.[8]

The Nicaraguan treaty, so highly favorable to the United States, unfortunately stirred up a veritable hornet's nest. Three neighbors of Nicaragua—Costa Rica, El Salvador, and Honduras—claimed that some of the concessions granted to the Yankees were theirs. They appealed their case to the Central American Court of Justice, which had been created

[8] T. A. Bailey, "Interest in a Nicaragua Canal, 1903–1931," *Hispanic Amer. Hist. Rev.*, XVI (1936), 6.

In 1907 under the auspices of Washington. They won their case but lost their claim, for neither Nicaragua nor the United States accepted the decision. Thus undermined, the Court of Justice eventually collapsed amid the ruins of high hopes for international accord. Such were the unhappy fruits of dollar-lifeline diplomacy.

CREEPING DOWN THE CARIBBEAN

Wilson had earlier been an outspoken foe of imperialism, yet as President he carried out more armed interventions in Latin America than any of his predecessors. Upholding the Monroe Doctrine was important, but no less so to his idealistic way of thinking was lending a helping hand to revolution-cursed republics—what a later critic has called "missionary diplomacy."

The first of the Caribbean republics to require attention was the French speaking Negro republic of Haiti, which had fallen prey to financial chaos. A long procession of presidents had held office, most of them being elected for the short term ending with the next revolution—provided that they were not shot, poisoned, or blown to bits in the meantime.

The Haitian volcano finally erupted in 1915, when President Guillaume Sam engineered a cold-blooded butchering of some 160 imprisoned political foes. A vengeful mob dragged him from behind a dresser in the French legation, where he had taken refuge, and literally tore him limb from limb. Wilson found such disorders intolerable. Both Germany and France had earlier landed troops on a temporary basis, and the fear prevailed in Washington that they might defy the Monroe Doctrine by seizing a strategic spot from which they could menace the Panama lifeline.

United States Marines disembarked in July, 1915, and soon had the situation in hand. The Haitian regime was forced to sign a treaty which, in its stipulations for supervision and financial control, went much beyond the Platt Amendment protectorate for Cuba. The nature of the intervention is clearly betrayed in a telegram sent by Admiral Caperton to the Secretary of the Navy: "Next Thursday . . . unless otherwise directed, I will permit Congress to elect a president." [9]

The independence-loving Haitian Negroes resented wearing a foreign yoke, especially one imposed by white men, and American marines shot scores of them while "pacifying" the country. Liberals, both in America and abroad, held up their hands in horror at such brutality, while defenders of Wilsonian intervention pointed pridefully to the unprecedented new era of order and prosperity. But many Haitians, especially the "professional" revolutionists, protested that they were more interested in

[9] *Foreign Relations, 1915,* p. 431 (Aug. 7, 1915).

sovereignty than in solvency. Their once-free republic, they claimed, was but a "territory of the National City Bank" of New York.

Haiti's eastern neighbor, the Dominican Republic, presented a parallel if somewhat less spectacular threat to the Monroe Doctrine. For a half dozen years after Roosevelt had introduced customhouse control in 1905, this vexed land had enjoyed relative prosperity and tranquility. But the "insurrectionary habit" finally brought the United States marines in 1916. When the lawful regime refused to accept a Yankee-dictated treaty, a six-year military government was bodily established under the direction of the Navy Department in Washington. Some Dominican nonconformists were shot, and the Wilson administration carried to a logical conclusion the protective interventionism proclaimed by the Roosevelt Corollary of the Monroe Doctrine. Even though the bayonet-imposed dictatorship brought roads, prosperity, schools, and improved sanitation, disappointed politicians and genuine patriots alike were sleeplessly critical. They much preferred their own disorder to order imposed by Yankee soldiers.

The Danish West Indies (Virgin Islands) likewise bore an intimate relationship to the Monroe Doctrine. After the outbreak of World War I in 1914, many Americans feared that Germany might overrun Denmark and then take over her orphaned West Indies, which could then be turned into a submarine base against the United States and its Panama Canal.[10] In the summer of 1916, Washington concluded a treaty for the purchase of the impoverished islets, but only after informing Denmark that if German control seemed imminent, the United States would have to seize them. The war-inflated price was set at $25 million, as compared with the $7.5 million that Denmark had been willing to accept in 1867. This defensive purchase, which could be justified only on strategic grounds, further turned the Caribbean into a United States lake.

IDEALISM *VERSUS* MATERIALISM IN MEXICO

The Mexican tangle, another holdover from Taft, was the most persistently vexatious non-European problem to bedevil Wilson. Ever since 1877, when Porfirio Díaz began his three-decade dictatorship, the normally troubled relations of the United States with Mexico had been comparatively good. Strong-arm rule ("Díazpotism") had brought order—and order made the "Mexican cornucopia" safe for foreign investors. In the scramble for natural resources, notably the rich oil fields, the Yankees were able to outdistance their closest competitors, the British. By 1913 there were over 50,000 Americans in Mexico, and their investments totaled about $1 billion, or more than those of all the other foreign nations combined.

[10] C. C. Tansill, *The Purchase of the Danish West Indies* (Baltimore, 1932), pp. 467 ff.

A blow-up was inevitable, for if Mexico was rich, the Mexicans were poor. Despite order and outward evidences of prosperity, the 15,000,000 people were largely landless and poverty-stricken, reduced to a state of peonage. The forces of discontent found a leader in Francisco Madero, an impractical visionary, who, in May, 1911, succeeded in driving the eighty-year-old Díaz into exile. But the revolutionary wheel took an ugly and unexpected turn in February, 1913, when Victoriano Huerta, a full-blooded Indian and a spokesman for the propertied groups, deposed Madero. Several days later the imprisoned Madero was cold-bloodedly murdered in circumstances that pointed the finger of suspicion unwaveringly at Huerta.

During all these disturbances, which resulted in dismaying losses to American life and property, President Taft pursued a consistent policy of hands off. He was evidently hoping that the remaining weeks of his term would run out before a real explosion occurred. His do-nothingism elicited loud condemnation from many American newspapers, including those of Hearst, who had inherited a ranch in northern Mexico larger than Rhode Island. And when the brutal Huerta seized power in 1913, Taft, although not averse to demanding concessions for recognition, had failed to agree on terms by the time he left the White House.

The idealistic Wilson, unwilling to saddle the bloody-handed Huerta on the Mexican masses, flatly refused to recognize what he regarded as another Díaz. "My ideal," he declared, "is an orderly and righteous government in Mexico; but my passion is for the submerged eighty-five per cent of the people of that Republic who are now struggling toward liberty." [11] Wilson officially based his nonrecognition policy on the grounds that Huerta had come into office as the result of murder and that he did not truly represent the people, who craved reform. He summed up his views to a visiting Briton, "I am going to teach the South American republics to elect good men!" [12]

A MORALISTIC MEXICAN POLICY

Wilson's righteous attitude represented a sharp clash between idealism and legalism. From the days of Thomas Jefferson the United States had generally, though not invariably, pursued the policy of recognizing established governments, regardless of how they had come into office. A long list of powers had applied this simple test to Mexico and had accorded recognition. Among them was Britain, which saw in Huerta another "strong man" who would keep order, repress the masses, and permit British capitalists to exploit Mexican oil. The Royal Navy, which had

[11] Interview with Samuel G. Blythe, *Saturday Evening Post*, May 23, 1914, p. 3.
[12] R. S. Baker, *Woodrow Wilson: Life and Letters* (Garden City, N.Y., 1931), IV, 289. (Wilson to Sir William Tyrrell, Nov. 13, 1913.)

recently converted from coal burners to oil burners, was heavily dependent on the Mexican supply.

If Wilson had followed the path of least resistance, he would have closed his eyes to tyranny in Mexico and recognized "a government of butchers." Such acquiescence would have headed off a vast amount of criticism, including that of a prominent journalist, George Harvey, who demanded: "What legal or moral right has a President of the United States to say who shall or shall not be President of Mexico?" [13] But Wilson, who was troubled by a Presbyterian conscience, could not get the struggling Mexican masses out of his mind. He also suspected that the British oil interests were backing the "unspeakable Huerta." As a deep-dyed foe of trusts and bankers at home, he likewise hated the abuses of wealth abroad. He therefore adopted toward Huerta a policy of nonrecognition and noninterference which, in the circumstances, was really a policy of interference designed to reshape the government of Mexico.

The President further clarified his Latin-American policy in general and his Mexican policy in particular in a memorable address at Mobile, Alabama, on October 27, 1913. In ringing tones he asserted:

> We dare not turn from the principle that morality and not expediency is the thing that must guide us and that we will never condone iniquity because it is most convenient to do so. . . . It is a very perilous thing to determine the foreign policy of a nation in the terms of material interest. It not only is unfair to those with whom you are dealing, but it is degrading as regards your own actions.

Then, for good measure, Wilson threw in an arresting pledge:

> I want to take this occasion to say that the United States will never again seek one additional foot of territory by conquest. She will devote herself to showing that she knows how to make honorable and fruitful use of the territory she has. . . .[14]

This last statement was reassuring to the Latin Americans, who welcomed a retreat from the interventionist twist given to the Monroe Doctrine by Theodore Roosevelt. Yet such high-sounding words hardly squared with subsequent armed interventions in Mexico, Haiti, Santo Domingo, and Nicaragua, even though no territory was annexed.

COLD-SHOULDERING HUERTA

Wilson's Mexican policy of nonrecognition and "watchful waiting" assumed a more aggressive character when, in November, 1913, he formally insisted upon the resignation of that "desperate brute," Huerta. In his anti-Huerta policy he had the backing of the British, who were grateful to him for his fair stand on the tolls question. Then, in

---

[13] *North American Review*, CXCVIII, 740 (Dec., 1913).
[14] *Cong. Record*, 63 Cong., 1 sess., pp. 5846, 5645 in that order.

February, 1914, Washington lifted the existing arms embargo so as to permit war materials to reach Huerta's two leading opponents, white-bearded Venustiano Carranza and swarthy Francisco Villa. These two leaders were presumably carrying on the original Madero revolution of 1911.

Wilson was savagely criticized at home and abroad for thus prolonging anarchy in Mexico. A recognition of Huerta would supposedly bring peace and order; and order, not the welfare of the Mexican masses, was paramount in the eyes of foreign investors. In Europe, Wilson's policy was regarded as "impractical" and "idealistic." One Berlin newspaper branded it as "colossal arrogance." The German Kaiser reflected the spirit of the times when he queried, "morality [is] all right, but what about dividends?"

At home, Republicans condemned "deadly drifting" and demanded "robust representations." A dance step then popular was dubbed the "Wilson tango": one step forward, two backwards, a side step, and then a moment of hesitation. Advocates of a "strong policy" insisted that the President's blood was lacking in red corpuscles. One critic wrote, "He's a damned vegetarian, I believe." The virile Theodore Roosevelt cried, "He kissed the blood-stained hand that slapped his face."

American investors added their voices to the chorus of criticism. Every day of not recognizing Huerta was costing tens of thousands of dollars, to say nothing of lives. Altogether, from 1913 to 1915 more than seventy Americans were slain in Mexico. Even Ambassador Page wrote from London of intervening and shooting Mexicans until order could be restored—"shooting men into self-government," as he brutally phrased the process.

More ominous was the increasingly strident demand in Congress for intervention. In the Senate a leading advocate of armed action was Senator Fall of New Mexico, a mouthpiece of the oil interests. In the House men like Wingo of Arkansas were shouting, "I think those hearing me will live to see the Mexican border pushed to the Panama Canal." One of the Hearst papers sneered:

> Oh, say, can you see by the dawn's early light
> Any possible way for avoiding a fight?
> The Star-Spangled Banner, oh, long may it flap,
> While we're kicked by the Greaser and slapped by the Jap! [15]

But Wilson, steeling himself against pressure from the "favored few," remarked to his secretary: "I have to pause and remind myself that I am President of the United States and not of a small group of Americans with vested interests in Mexico." [16]

[15] *San Francisco Examiner*, March 13, 1914, p. 22.
[16] J. P. Tumulty, *Woodrow Wilson as I Know Him* (Garden City, N.Y., 1921), p. 146.

NATIONAL HONOR AT TAMPICO

Pressures continued to build up to a showdown with Mexico. The stubborn Huerta stood by his guns, and in fact gained additional support from Mexican patriots who resented the highhandedness of the Colossus of the North. The long-deferred flareup came on April 9, 1914, at Tampico, where a whaleboat of the United States Navy, with its flag plainly displayed, was loading supplies. The crew was arrested by the Mexicans and then marched through the streets for having violated martial law. Shortly thereafter the Americans were released, with oral expressions of regret that the ignorance of a subordinate should have caused the misunderstanding. But Admiral Mayo, commanding the American fleet, felt that there should be a more formal apology. Precipitately he delivered an ultimatum to the Mexican general in Tampico, to be complied with in twenty-four hours:

> . . . I must require that you send me, by suitable members of your staff, formal disavowal of and apology for the act, together with your assurance that the officer responsible for it will receive severe punishment. Also that you publicly hoist the American flag in a prominent position on shore and salute it with twenty-one guns, which salute will be duly returned by this ship.[17]

There was a curious inconsistency in Admiral Mayo's demanding a salute from a government that Washington would not recognize. The commanding Mexican general expressed regret in writing, and Huerta announced that he deplored the unfortunate incident. But he balked at saluting the American flag without the guarantee of a gun-for-gun return salute. Washington was unwilling to go this far, lest its action be interpreted as recognition. Many Americans, then and later, felt that sufficient apology had been forthcoming without further insisting on a salute.

Once Admiral Mayo's ultimatum had been issued, even the pacifist Secretary Bryan believed that the dignity and honor of the nation demanded that he be backed. Wilson, for his part, was determined to use this trifling incident as an excuse to seize the port of Vera Cruz, cut off revenues and arms, and thus force Huerta out. Extremists like Senator Chilton of West Virginia were crying, "I'd make them salute the flag if we had to blow up the whole place."

Wilson went before Congress on April 20, 1914, and in a solemn address asked for authority to interfere by force of arms in Mexico. He made it clear that the Tampico incident was but the culmination of a series of grievances, and that America's quarrel was with Huerta and

---

[17] *Foreign Relations, 1914,* p. 448.

his reactionary supporters, not with the Mexican people. After a two-day debate Congress gave its consent.

THE VERA CRUZ CRISIS

The shooting came on April 21, 1914, the day after the House had voted for intervention. A German merchantman was approaching Vera Cruz with a large cargo of arms, which might be used by Huerta against the United States. Aroused from a deep sleep early in the morning, Wilson telephoned orders to seize the port. American forces attained their objective later that day, but the defending Mexicans, while suffering much heavier losses, exacted a toll of nineteen dead and seventy-one wounded.[18]

Wilson embarked upon armed intervention, despite all the cover-up talk about national honor, primarily to overthrow Huerta. Yet the dogged "butcher" stood his ground, and even Carranza, his chief opponent, protested vehemently against this invasion of Mexico. American jingoes were demanding a full-dress war, but most Americans, including investors, evidently deplored the prospect of hostilities. Latin Americans were shocked, while elsewhere in the civilized world Wilson was being condemned for picking a fight over a small matter of punctilio.

Wilson was now out on the end of a limb. He could not risk the humiliation of withdrawal without atonement from Huerta. Yet a full-fledged Mexican war, which seemed to be the only other alternative, was unthinkable. It would be costly, bloody, and at variance with the hand's-off policy that he had proclaimed so proudly at Mobile.

At this critical juncture, the ABC Powers (Argentina, Brazil, and Chile) most opportunely stepped in with an offer of mediation. Wilson promptly and gratefully accepted this unexpected escape hatch. His evident determination to redeem the Mobile pledge of nonaggression caused sentiment in Latin America to rebound strongly, even hysterically, in favor of the United States.

Representatives of the ABC Powers, late in May, 1914, met with those of the United States and Mexico at Niagara Falls, Canada. After prolonged discussion, the delegates agreed upon a plan. It proved completely ineffectual because Carranza refused to accept it. Yet the Niagara Conference enabled the United States to avoid war, and it relieved the suspicions of the rest of the world as to Yankee designs on a weak neighbor.

President Huerta's days were now numbered. Beset by revolutionary armies, weakened financially, and crumbling under Wilson's pressures,

---

[18] See A. S. Link, *Wilson and the New Freedom* (Princeton, 1956), Ch. XI, for the incident. Ironically, the German merchantman landed its arms at another Mexican port.

he fled to Spain in July, 1914, the month after the Niagara Conference adjourned. He was succeeded by General Carranza. More than a year later, in October, 1915, Wilson finally recognized the Carranza regime as the *de facto* government of Mexico, despite the outcry from American Catholics, who deplored Carranza's attacks on the Church.

THE PERSHING PUNITIVE EXPEDITION

Peace did not descend like a dove on Mexico with the accession of President Carranza, who now showed only lukewarm enthusiasm for the reforms to which he had previously paid lip service. His chief lieu-tenant, illiterate Francisco Villa, a picturesque combination of blood-thirsty bandit and Robin Hood, soon raised the standard of revolt. In January, 1916, the followers of Villa showed their contempt for the

The United States and Mexico, 1914-1917

northern "gringo" by massacring eighteen American mining engineers at Santa Ysabel in cold blood. The temper of the American people rose to the boiling point, and a number of the more sober newspapers swung over to intervention. Hearst's rabidly interventionist *San Francisco Ex-aminer* cried: "On Mexico's blood-soaked soil the vultures tear the flesh and the coyotes gnaw the bones of our butchered and unburied dead." [19] On the floor of Congress the clamor for "cleaning up" Mexico rose to a crescendo. Representative Humphrey served notice that the day was "not far off when the people of this country, regardless of the attitude of the administration, will see that peace is brought to unhappy Mexico.[20]

Francisco Villa, scheming to involve his rival Carranza in war with

[19] *San Francisco Examiner,* Jan. 14, 1916, 18:2.
[20] *Cong. Record,* 64 Cong., 1 sess., p. 1638 (Jan. 27, 1916).

the United States, next raided across the border and sacked the town of Columbus, New Mexico, on March 9, 1916. Seventeen Americans lost their lives. Senator Ashurst of Arizona cried for more "grape shot" and less "grape juice." Senator Fall of New Mexico demanded the complete occupation of Mexico by an army of half a million men. To chastise Villa and end the border outrages, Wilson ordered General Pershing, with a force that ultimately numbered about 12,000 men, to pursue the bandit leader into Mexico and destroy his forces. Carranza grudgingly permitted the invasion to proceed, but not until a face-saving agreement had been entered into which permitted the pursuit of outlaws by either nation *in the future.*

Pershing's cavalry dashed deep into Mexico—more than three hundred miles—with commendable speed, and in spite of grave difficulties narrowly missed capturing Villa. But as the size and penetration of the American force increased, the Carranza regime redoubled its demands for withdrawal. Ugly incidents occurred, including a clash with Mexican troops at Carrizal which resulted in the killing of twelve Americans and the capturing of twenty-three. With the fruitlessness of the chase painfully apparent, and with a dangerous crisis developing with Berlin over the submarine, Wilson withdrew the Pershing expedition—"perishing expedition," it was dubbed—in February, 1917. The impending war with Germany would be enough of a handful without taking on Mexico as well.

Wilson left behind a snarling Carranza, a defiant Villa, and a revolution for the masses that had yet to run its bloody course. The confusion that attended the mobilization of the tiny Pershing expedition did nothing to deter the German war lords when they pushed America into the abyss with their ruthless submarine attacks. Carranza vented his hostility toward the Yankees by pro-German sympathies in World War I, and Mexico became a happy hunting ground for the Kaiser's secret agents.

IDEALISM IN MEXICAN DEALINGS

Wilson's Latin-American policy involved curious contradictions and shifts. Attempting to reverse Taft, he managed to reverse himself and carry out dollar diplomacy in the Caribbean on a much larger scale than his maligned predecessor. A foe of armed imperialism, he practiced a kind of moral imperialism. An avowed lover of peace, he landed marines in Haiti and Santo Domingo, and twice invaded Mexico. Determined to help the Mexican people, he helped keep Mexico in turmoil by departing from America's traditional recognition policy. He took strong positions, and then was forced to back down—shaking "first his fist and then his finger."

On the credit side of the ledger, Wilson kept steadfastly in view the liberation of the Mexican masses. He resisted a clamor for the conquest of all Mexico, and avoided a full-dress war during a period when hostilities might have helped his 1916 campaign for re-election. At the same time, he freed his hands for dealing effectively with Germany in World War I. Finally, he helped the cause of mediation and Pan-Americanism by deferring to the Latin-American powers in working out a settlement with Mexico.

Wilson even went so far in 1914 as to draft a general Pan-American treaty. It would mutually guarantee the territorial integrity and political independence of all the signatories—a kind of Pan-Americanizing of the Monroe Doctrine. He finally dropped this scheme in favor of the more sweeping guarantees of his proposed League of Nations. But to the very end he presented a puzzling mixture of hard-headed realism and star-reaching idealism.

SELECTED BIBLIOGRAPHY

The most recent scholarship is succinctly presented in A. S. Link, *Woodrow Wilson and the Progressive Era, 1910–1917* (New York, 1954); more fully in his *Wilson: The New Freedom* (Princeton, 1956). Richer detail appears in R. S. Baker, *Woodrow Wilson: Life and Letters* (8 vols., Garden City, N.Y., and New York, 1927–1939). See also Harley Notter, *The Origins of the Foreign Policy of Woodrow Wilson* (Baltimore, 1937). An impressive bibliographical study is R. L. Watson, Jr., "Woodrow Wilson and His Interpreters, 1947–1957," *Miss. Valley Hist. Rev.*, XLIV (1957), 207–236. Penetrating lectures appear in A. S. Link, *Wilson the Diplomatist* (Baltimore, 1957).

On the Far East, consult A. W. Griswold, *The Far Eastern Policy of the United States* (New York, 1938); Charles Vevier, *The United States and China, 1906–1913* (New Brunswick, N.J., 1955); Tien-yi Li, *Woodrow Wilson's China Policy, 1913–1917* (New York, 1952); R. W. Curry, *Woodrow Wilson and Far Eastern Policy, 1913–1921* (New York, 1957).

On Latin America, see S. F. Bemis, *The Latin American Policy of the United States* (New York, 1943); Carl Kelsey, *The American Intervention in Haiti and the Dominican Republic* (Philadelphia, 1922); D. G. Munro, *The United States and the Caribbean Area* (Boston, 1934); H. F. Cline, *The United States and Mexico* (Cambridge, 1953); J. F. Rippy, *The United States and Mexico* (rev. ed., New York, 1931); J. M. Callahan, *American Foreign Policy in Mexican Relations* (New York, 1932); G. M. Stephenson, *John Lind of Minnesota* (Minneapolis, 1935).

Useful articles are Selig Adler, "Bryan and Wilsonian Caribbean Penetration," *Hispanic Amer. Hist. Rev.*, XX (1940), 198–226; R. R. Hill, "The Nicaraguan Canal Idea to 1913," *ibid.*, XXVIII (1948), 197–211; C. C. Cumberland, "The Jenkins Case and Mexican-American Relations," *ibid.*, XXXI (1951), 586–607.

See footnotes of this chapter; Bemis and Griffin, *Guide*, pp. 500 ff.; *Harvard Guide*, Ch. 26.

7TH, 8TH, AND 9TH ED. REFS. See BIBLIOGRAPHICAL ADDENDUM, p. 1,017.

38

Waging Neutrality
1914-1915

> *It is difficult for people to think logically when their sympathies are aroused.*
>
> WOODROW WILSON, 1915

THUNDER ACROSS THE SEA

THE LONG-SMOULDERING European powder magazine finally exploded in the summer of 1914, when the flaming pistol of a Serb patriot murdered the heir to the throne of Austria-Hungary. Austro-Hungarian efforts to punish tiny Serbia touched off a chain reaction of war declarations, and in an incredibly short time most of Europe was ablaze. The Central Powers included Germany, Austria-Hungary, and later Turkey and Bulgaria. Their foes were the Allied Powers (the Allies), consisting principally of Britain, France, Russia, Japan, and later Italy.

The assassination of the Austrian heir caused only a brief flurry of excitement in the United States. Americans had heard the cry of "wolf" too often to believe that the pack was loose at last.[1] But when a bewildered nation finally realized that Europe was being sucked into a global war, the first reaction was to keep out of the senseless conflict. "Peace-loving citizens of this country," declared the *Chicago Herald*, "will now rise up and tender a hearty vote of thanks to Columbus for having discovered America." The *Wabash Plain Dealer* chimed in, "We never appreciated so keenly as now the foresight exercised by our forefathers in emigrating from Europe." The *Literary Digest* summed up newspaper reaction: "Our isolated position and freedom from entangling alliances inspire our press with the cheering assurance that we are in no

---

[1] Thirteen years earlier the *Baltimore American* had declared, "That great European war that is to start in the Balkans is again to the front, threatening as ever, but with its edges slightly frayed." *Literary Digest*, XXIII, 692 (June 8, 1901).

peril of being drawn into the European quarrel." [2] America felt strong, snug, secure; Europe could "stew in her own juice."

As one nation after another slipped into the abyss, President Wilson issued the routine proclamations of neutrality. But the American people could hardly avoid taking sides. This was a *world* war; and the United States, the historic asylum of the oppressed, contained a "menagerie of nationalities." Despite the magic of the melting pot, millions of "hyphenated" Americans could not completely forget the land of their birth and cultural heritage—German-Americans, Irish-Americans, Polish-Americans, and other "hyphenates." "America," wrote the British ambassador; "is no nation, just a collection of people who neutralize one another."

PRINCIPAL FOREIGN ELEMENTS IN U.S.

Census of 1910

[TOTAL U. S. POPULATION: 91,972,266]

Country of Origin		Foreign-born	Natives with Two Foreign-born Parents	Natives with One Foreign-born Parent	Total
Central Powers	Germany	2,501,181	3,911,847	1,869,590	8,282,618
	Austria-Hungary	1,670,524	900,129	131,133	2,701,786
Allied Powers	United Kingdom	1,219,968	852,610	1,158,474	3,231,052
	Ireland	1,352,155	2,141,577	1,010,628	4,504,360
	Russia	1,732,421	949,316	70,938	2,752,675
	Italy	1,343,070	695,187	60,103	2,098,360
Total for all foreign countries (including those not listed)		13,345,545	12,916,311	5,981,526	32,243,282

Intense bitterness developed between pro-Ally and pro-German sympathizers. The sharp-tongued British playwright, George Bernard Shaw, observed, "America, to judge by some of its papers, is mad with British patriotism, Polish nationality, and Belgian freedom." The *Toledo Blade* pointedly remarked, "United we stand, hyphenated we fall."

PRO-ALLY NEUTRALITY

President Wilson, from the beginning, favored a strict neutrality. When he foresaw that outbursts of sympathy for the belligerents would create grave difficulties, he issued an appeal to the American people, on August 18, 1914, urging them to be "impartial in thought as well as in action." But this was asking the impossible. As one editor insisted, "Only persons

[2] *Literary Digest*, XLIX, 215 (Aug. 8, 1914).

mentally unsexed or paralyzed" could be neutral in thought—"moral eunuchs," as another writer described them.

A vast majority of Americans wanted no part of the European blood bath. But on the whole their sympathies went out to Britain, France, and the other Allies, and against Germany, Austria, and their cohorts. Despite a century of Anglophobia and tail twisting, the American people could not forget their Anglo-Saxon blood and cultural heritage. This was notably true of the wealthier and better educated groups, including the Oxford-indoctrinated Rhodes Scholars. Moreover, relations with Britain had on the whole been friendly since the Venezuela blowup of 1895–1896; unusually friendly since the recent repeal of the Panama canal tolls exemption.

Yet America probably could not have developed any real enthusiasm for the Allies if France had not been among them. The United States, remembering 1778, seemingly owed an unrepayable debt of gratitude. From the pen of Robert Underwood Johnson came:

> Forget us, God, if we forget
> The sacred sword of Lafayette!

German-American relations, on the other hand, had not been genuinely friendly since the 1880's. By 1914 the American people had come to regard German militarism, navalism, imperialism, and commercialism as an international menace. Germany's ruthless invasion of Belgium, despite a solemn treaty obligation to respect her neutrality, merely confirmed the worst American suspicions. The offense took on a darker hue when the German chancellor blunderingly explained that the Belgian neutrality treaty was but a "scrap of paper." Americans deeply sympathized with "poor little Belgium" in her heroic but vain resistance; they were outraged by the destruction of the priceless library at Louvain and by the savage suppression of civilian resistance. The editor of *Life* declared with much emotion:

> For us the great, clear issue of this war is Belgium. If we see anything right at all in all this matter, Belgium is a martyr to civilization, sister to all who love liberty or law; assailed, polluted, trampled in the mire, heelmarked in her breast, tattered, homeless. . . . The great unconquerable fact of the great war is Belgium.[3]

But all this did not mean that the American people longed to get into the fight. Nor did it mean that they now loved Great Britain. Although the vast majority of those who took sides favored the Allies, this feeling was probably more anti-German than pro-British.[4] The people of the United States had long memories.

---

[3] *Life*, LXV, 20 (Jan. 7, 1915).
[4] Of the 367 editors who replied to a *Literary Digest* poll, 20 favored the Germans, 105 the Allies, and 242 neutrality. XLIX, 939 (Nov. 14, 1914).

FACT PLUS PROPAGANDA

British propagandists were later accused of having seduced America into the war. No one can deny that there was much Allied propaganda, but no one can determine its precise effect. For one thing, American opinion was clearly anti-German before the war began. For another, the American people were outraged by specific acts of Germany. The invasion of Belgium was a fact; the shooting of the British nurse Edith Cavell, an acknowledged spy, was a fact; the torpedoing of the passenger ship *Lusitania* was a fact. British propagandists undeniably embellished these facts, but their seed would have fallen on sterile soil without them.

British attempts to color the American mind involved two major instruments. The first was censorship of all cablegrams to the United States. American newsmen quickly learned that if they wanted their stories to get by the censors' scissors, they had better write as an Englishman would write. The result was that Americans came to view the war largely through Allied spectacles.

The second British weapon was an efficient propaganda organization in the United States. Understanding Anglo-Saxon psychology better than the Germans, the British were quiet, discreet, and effective. Their great success was in enlisting a number of influential Americans—preachers, teachers, politicians, and journalists—on the side of the Allies. These home-grown propagandists, many of them Rhodes scholars, did much to persuade their countrymen that England was fighting their fight. The Germans, thrown on the defensive by the invasion of Belgium, countered with a desperate and rather clumsy courtship of American opinion. A self-appointed guardian of Germany's honor, one Julius Meyer, poured out his soul to a New York editor:

> Down with England! Down with the boot-licking, kowtowing British hirelings in our press and in our Administration. . . . Up and at them! Enough of truckling to their good graces, enough of asking for fair play. . . . Up and at them! Up you Americans, who have not forgotten 1776! Up you Poles, Hungarians, Austrians, Czechs, Germans, Irish, Swiss, Scandinavians, up everybody, who stands for Old Glory first and all the time, for his fatherland next and the rest of the time. . . .[5]

The American people, while dismissing German denials as lies, believed many tales of Hunnish savagery that came out of Belgium. Among them were such barefaced inventions as the crucified Canadian, the German soap factory that used human corpses, and the Belgian babies with their hands cut off. There are always some atrocities on both sides in any great war, but in this case Allied offenses were hushed up.

The facts of German brutality, as exaggerated by Allied propa-

[5] *New York Evening Post*, Jan. 15, 1915, 8:6.

gandists, had a profound effect on American thinking. Before long many a citizen was convinced that the Kaiser, known as "the Beast of Berlin," had wantonly provoked the war; that when he had won it he would come over with millions of goose-steppers and make short work of the United States and its Monroe Doctrine; and that the lily-white Allies, including autocratic Russia, were fighting a purely defensive war for democracy. Countless Americans finally reached the point where they suspected that a man was not "100 per cent American" if he did not embrace all these conclusions.

The Wilson administration itself was not immune from Allied influence. Every member of the Cabinet, except one, had definite pro-Ally leanings. Secretary Bryan, who evidently was more genuinely neutral than the others, appeared to his colleagues as pro-German. Wilson himself was not only of British ancestry but a strong admirer of English culture and political institutions. He made a determined effort to pursue a strictly neutral course, but as the war ground on he generally found his sympathies becoming more and more pro-Ally. Occasionally in private he would betray himself. Once he burst out, "England is fighting our fight."

INTERNATIONAL ANARCHY IMPENDS

Wilson was faced with no easy task in keeping the nation out of war and at the same time maintaining its rights. The United States was not only the richest neutral state, but also the most important neutral carrier. Its shipping would inevitably run afoul of belligerent restrictions, just as it had during the Napoleonic upheaval.

Anticipating such controversies, an international conference in 1909 had drawn up the so-called "Declaration of London." This document, in general, was a codification of existing international law. But the restrictions thus imposed proved distasteful to "big navy" Britain, and as a result the Declaration was never put into effect.

When war finally erupted in 1914, Washington sought protection against arbitrary interpretations of international law by inviting the powers to accept the Declaration of London. Germany and Austria, faced with a strangling naval blockade, promptly expressed interest. But the British, who were unwilling to place hobbles on their dominant seapower, stood firm. Colonel House, Wilson's pro-Ally personal adviser, collaborating with the British ambassador in Washington, skillfully undermined the efforts of the State Department.[6] In the end the United States withdrew its proposal, and found itself once more on the shifting sands of the pre-1914 era.

Two nations locked in armed combat usually avoid flagrant violations

[6] C. C. Tansill, *America Goes to War* (Boston, 1938), pp. 144–146.

of international law. They are restrained in part by a desire to enlist the support of the rest of the world, or at least not to alienate it. But during the years from 1914 to 1917 every major power was involved in the conflict, except the United States. And the United States, though boasting the third strongest navy in the world, had only a tiny army, ranking in numbers with that of Persia. So, in general, no nation scrupulously observed any rule of international law if it felt that there was more to be gained than lost by modifying or flouting it.

In this war, as in other world wars, the maritime rules were interpreted, modified, or rewritten by the dominant sea power. There was no higher law; there was no other arbiter. If Britain had punctiliously observed the strict letter of international law, she would have partially shackled her navy, and probably would have lost the war. She therefore proceeded to take liberties with the traditional rules, justifying her "exceptional measures" by the age-old argument that this conflict had created "new," "peculiar," or "unusual" conditions. She also invoked "reprisals," "retaliation," and "military necessity." All this was highly objectionable to the neutrals, as well as to the enemy. But it was probably what any other power would have done in like circumstances. 'Necessity," as the German chancellor had himself remarked, "knows no law."

REWRITING INTERNATIONAL LAW

One of Washington's earliest disputes with Britain arose over contraband, which previously had embraced weapons and other articles used to fight a war. But London ultimately took the stand that in this highly mechanized conflict practically every important article, including foodstuffs, could be of direct or indirect aid to the fighting forces. Beginning with the Order in Council of August 20, 1914, the British arbitrarily redefined contraband, and intercepted American ships carrying forbidden items to the enemy. But London was careful not to add cotton to the list at first, because the South, which was suffering from the depression of 1913–1914, might have forced Washington to take strong measures. Even so, the governor of Texas demanded, in November, 1914, that "American ironclads" be sent "to England's door" to enforce the nation's rights. The eventual stoppage of virtually all American trade with Germany evoked strong protests from Washington, but Britain stood her ground.

The British navy also took unprecedented liberties with the right of visit and search. A belligerent warship, in exercising this right, had traditionally been permitted to halt a neutral merchantman on the high seas and inspect it for contraband. If none was found, the ship was allowed to go on its way; otherwise it was taken to a prize court for adjudication. But the British, again alleging "exceptional" conditions, altered this time-honored practice. Modern ships, they insisted, were so large that a thorough examination was impossible without bringing the vessel to port, where probers could even X-ray bales of cotton for hidden contraband. Besides, a British warship engaged in searching a merchantman on the high seas was a perfect target for a lurking submarine.

British cruisers, often on the basis of mere suspicion, forced neutral vessels to tie up for weeks in port, while evidence was being sought. This annoying practice not only caused loss to American owners but sometimes operated to the gain of British competitors. The British-born Secretary of the Interior, Franklin K. Lane, exploded:

> There isn't a man in the Cabinet who has a drop of German blood in his veins, I guess. Two of us were born under the British flag. I have two cousins in the British army, and Mrs. Lane has three. . . . Yet each day that we meet we boil over somewhat, at the foolish manner in which England acts. Can it be that she is trying to take advantage of the war to hamper our trade . . . ? [7]

THE ATROCITIES STILL GO ON

U.S. resentment against British practices.
McCutcheon in the *Chicago Tribune*, 1916

There were, of course, mitigating circumstances. The British paid for many of the cargoes they confiscated, and as a rule the American shipper realized a good profit, although perhaps not so much as he would have

---

[7] Charles Seymour, *Intimate Papers of Colonel House* (Boston, 1926), I, 459.

made if left alone. Many of the claims for damages that Washington brought against Britain were found to be legally unsupportable, and after the war they were dropped by mutual consent.[8] But law or no law, the British would not relax their grip on neutral commerce. They were fighting for their very existence, and to them American profits were a minor consideration.

PAPER BLOCKADES—1914 VERSION

Another grievance of the United States was the so-called British blockade, which was never officially proclaimed. The generally accepted practice had been to station warships near the ports of the blockaded country, just outside the three-mile limit. But Britain, again invoking the "exceptional" conditions of a war that involved long-range guns and submarines, early decided that the ancient course would be hazardous. Instead, His Majesty's warships took their station on the high seas, but not off German ports, in such a way as to intercept neutral commerce going to Germany. The British not only invoked against the United States its own Civil War doctrine of continuous voyage, (p. 324), but they improved upon it. They even went so far as to stop American merchantmen sailing to neutral countries adjacent to Germany, like Holland, or near enough to Germany, like Sweden, to act as "conduit pipes."

U.S. FOREIGN TRADE DURING WORLD WAR I [*]

	Dollars	*Index* (1914 = 100)
A. To Allied countries: England, France, Italy, Russia		
1914	$ 824,860,237	100.0
1915	1,991,747,493	241.0
1916	3,214,480,547	389.7
B. To Central Powers: Austria-Hungary, Germany		
1914	169,289,775	100.0
1915	11,878,153	7.0
1916	1,159,653	0.68
C. To Northern Neutrals: Denmark, Holland, Norway, Sweden		
1914	187,667,040	100.0
1915	330,100,646	175.8
1916	279,786,219	149.0

[*] Note the tremendous growth of Allied war trade; the almost complete cessation of commerce with the Central Powers; the shifting of some of that trade to the neutral "feeders"; and the curtailment of neutral commerce under British rationing.

The British could easily justify their restrictive action. To take one example, American lard exports to Denmark increased from practically

[8] See T. A. Bailey, *The Policy of the United States toward the Neutrals, 1917–1918* (Baltimore, 1942), p. 481.

nothing to 22,000,000 pounds during the first few months of the war. Obviously, the great bulk of this commodity was being transshipped to a Germany hungry for fats. Britain finally adopted quotas for neutral countries accessible to Germany, and forbade them to import substantially more than the prewar amounts. But British traders were often permitted access to markets that were thus denied Americans.

The British took a momentous step toward tightening their so-called blockade on November 3, 1914. Alleging that Germany had illegally sowed mines in open waters, they declared the North Sea a military area. They then proceeded to mine it so thoroughly that no neutral dared sail through without first stopping at a British port for sailing directions. Such instructions were withheld if the cargo was objectionable, and as a result all commerce sailing these waters was squeezed through the neck of the British bottle. This practice was so serious a departure from international usage as to work a grievous hardship on neutrals.

BOWING TO BRITAIN'S BLOCKADE

The United States did not tamely submit to the wiping out of its trade with Germany, for British restrictions hurt both American pockets and pride. Washington sent a number of strongly worded protests to London, some of them admirable expositions of pre-1914 international law.[9] The British countered—and most effectively—with delay. Their strategy was to take ample time in replying; to submerge the real issues in words; to concede little or nothing; and to hope that the next passing sensation in America, or the next outrage by Germany, would blunt American resentment. One German-American newspaper published a satirical British version of the "Star-Spangled Banner:"

> Then conquer we must, for the Yankee we trust
> To kindly forget that we are ever unjust;
> And the star-spangled banner we earnestly crave
> May enable Britannia to still rule the wave.[10]

London's strategy of delay was masterful, and what is more the State Department played the British game. The longer Washington deferred a showdown, the more perfect Britain's strangulation of Germany became, the more closely America was bound by economic ties to the Allied chariot, and the more likely a maddened Germany was to drive

[9] One day, when Ambassador Page was presenting a protest, his eye fell on the *Alabama* claims voucher in the sum of $15,500,000, which hung on the wall of the Foreign Office. Turning to Foreign Secretary Grey he jokingly said, "If you don't stop these seizures, Sir Edward, some day you'll have your entire room papered with things like that!" B. J. Hendrick, *The Life and Letters of Walter H. Page* (Garden City, N.Y., 1922), I, 391.

[10] Carl Wittke, *German-Americans and the World War* (Columbus, Ohio, 1936), p. 69 n.

the United States into war with her submarines. The British technique was later explained by Sir Edward Grey, then Foreign Secretary: "The Navy acted and the Foreign Office had to find the argument to support the action; it was anxious work. . . . British action preceded British argument; the risk was that action might follow American argument." [11]

Why did America fail to enforce what she so emphatically asserted were her rights? She had a powerful navy, and if she had seen fit to convoy her merchant ships, the British would have had to yield to her demands. England simply could not afford to quarrel with her chief munitions depot—as Sir Edward Grey himself confessed in later years.

DIPLOMATIC ALLIES OF THE ALLIES

One obvious explanation of America's surprising docility is that the Wilson administration was sympathetic with the Allies from the beginning. In addition, Wilson's most-trusted adviser, Colonel Edward M. House, was strongly pro-Ally. This well-intentioned but inexperienced Texan, who enjoyed being a power behind the throne, greatly influenced a number of Wilson's most critical decisions, generally to the advantage of the Allies.

The key diplomat abroad was the American ambassador in London, the author-editor Walter Hines Page, likewise without previous diplomatic experience. With his literary background, he soon became captivated by British society and culture. Before long he was thanking "Heaven I'm of their race and blood," and praising the English race as the one that had "guts." The British statesmen, notably the charming Sir Edward Grey, easily persuaded Page that the Allies were fighting America's battle for democracy, and that America herself should join them. In this frame of mind Ambassador Page had only contempt for the protests framed by the "library lawyers" in the State Department, and he either watered down his instructions or presented them in such a way that the British were not convinced of their seriousness. Sir Edward Grey reminisced:

> Page came to see me at the Foreign Office one day and produced a long despatch from Washington contesting our claim to act as we were doing in stopping contraband going to neutral ports. "I am instructed," he said, "to read this despatch to you." He read, and I listened. He then said: "I have now read the despatch, but I do not agree with it; let us consider how it should be answered!" [12]

Instead of faithfully representing the United States in England, as was his duty, Page represented the British cause to the government in Wash-

[11] Edward G. Grey, *Twenty-five Years, 1892–1916* (New York, 1925), II, 110.
[12] *Ibid.*, II, 110.

ington. IIis bias finally became so blatant that President Wilson wrote him off as "really an Englishman."

Perhaps more useful to the Allies was handsome Robert Lansing, an able international lawyer who served first as Counselor of the State Department, and then as Secretary of State after Bryan resigned in 1915. Warmly pro-Ally, he not only drafted many of the protests to London but exercised a strong influence on Wilson's judgment in a number of critical decisions. He also co-operated whole-heartedly with the British in their strategy of stalling. As he records in his *Memoirs:*

> . . . I saw with apprehension the tide of resentment against Great Britain rising higher and higher in this country. . . . I did all that I could to prolong the disputes by preparing . . . long and detailed replies, and introducing technical and controversial matters in the hope that before the extended interchange of arguments came to an end something would happen to change the current of American public opinion or to make the American people perceive that German absolutism was a menace to their liberties and to democratic institutions everywhere.[13]

It is not surprising that, between Page and Lansing, the British did not become unduly disturbed by American protests.

NURSING THE ECONOMIC "WAR BABIES"

Early in the war the Wall Street House of Morgan asked the State Department if there would be any objection to making a private loan to the French government. In a memorable letter to the President, dated August 10, 1914, Secretary Bryan sagely observed that "money is the worst of all contrabands because it commands everything else." He further pointed out that the bankers would probably use their influence with the press to support the cause to which they had lent money, thus making neutrality more difficult. Accordingly, in August, 1914, Bryan telegraphed J. P. Morgan that loans to belligerents, though legal, were not consistent with the true spirit of neutrality. The New York bankers, dubious from the start about the proposed French loan, decided not to go ahead without the blessing of the State Department.

But the iron hand of circumstance wrought a change of heart in Washington. At the outbreak of the war America had been wallowing in a cyclical depression, but the sudden mushrooming of war trade with Europe ushered in an era of feverish prosperity. The Allies at first did not need to borrow money for munitions in the United States; they could use the huge American debits in Europe. But as the months slipped by these

---

[13] *War Memoirs of Robert Lansing* (Indianapolis, 1935), p. 112. See also D. M. Smith, "Robert Lansing and the Formulation of American Neutrality Policies, 1914–1915," *Miss. Valley Hist. Rev.,* XLIII (1956), 59–81.

were rapidly exhausted. If credits or loans could not be obtained in the United States, the profitable boom in war supplies would collapse, and the nation would plunge back into the depression. In short, the munitions trade was about as essential to the economic life of America as it was to the military life of the Allies.

Faced with this crisis, Wilson made a momentous decision. He reversed the State Department's original ruling, and in October, 1914, privately and orally informed certain interested bankers that Washington would sanction the advancing of credits—but not loans. In the same behind-the-scenes manner Washington extended permission, in the late summer of 1915, to lend money outright. Several of the most important loans handled by the New York bankers were floated by popular subscription, notably the $500 million Anglo-French issue of 1915. The anti-British Hearst press and the pro-German element voiced violent opposition, while men carrying placards paraded up and down Wall Street proclaiming, "Billions for King George." When America finally entered the war, private bankers had advanced approximately $2.3 billion to the Allies in cash and credit, and only $27 million to Germany. Speaking for the House of Morgan, Thomas W. Lamont later declared:

> Those were the days when American citizens were being urged to remain neutral in action, in word, and even in thought. But our firm had never for one moment been neutral: we didn't know how to be. From the very start we did everything that we could to contribute to the cause of the Allies.[14]

The United States could have forced the Allies to respect its rights, some critics have charged, by clamping an embargo on these vast exports of war materials. Such a course was repeatedly proposed, especially in the early stages of the war by pro-Germans, but it ran head on into apathy. As the weeks slipped by, America's economic structure and prosperity became fatally intertwined with the Allied cause, so much so that the public would have raised a storm of protest against an embargo. The nation marched down the profitable but fateful path of least resistance.

MUNITIONS MONGERS

During the first six months of the war America was embroiled in virtually no serious disputes with Germany. Curiously enough, these two future foes were then contending with Britain for the freedom of the seas. But the mounting trade in war materials changed the picture drastically. The Americans were not only shipping enormous quantities of munitions to the Allies with which to kill Germans, but were soon advancing the necessary money from their own pockets in the form of credits and

[14] *Manchester Guardian*, Jan. 27, 1920, p. 68.

loans. The chief German-American propaganda newspaper in the United States cried: "We [Americans] prattle about humanity, while we manufacture poisoned shrapnel and picric acid for profit. Ten thousand German widows, ten thousand orphans, ten thousand graves bear the legend 'Made in America.' " [15]

The German and Austro-Hungarian governments naturally lodged vigorous protests against the ugly traffic in war materials. Washington correctly replied that private citizens in a neutral country could lawfully sell military supplies to a belligerent; in fact, the Germans themselves had done so in previous wars. Furthermore, the Secretary of State added, an embargo on munitions would operate so heavily to the advantage of the Germans, who were much better supplied with munitions factories than their enemies, as to constitute an unneutral act. Washington had no objection whatever to selling arms and ammunition to Germany. But if German ships could not get them because of the British navy, such were the misfortunes of war. In short, an embargo on munitions would favor Germany; the absence of one would favor the Allies. So again America followed the profitable and pro-Ally path of least resistance.

The United States undeniably had a legal right to forbid the export of military supplies, just as a number of the weak European neutrals did in order to conserve their scanty supplies. But such an embargo could be established only by act of Congress. By the time the American people came seriously to grips with the problem, the traffic had assumed such profitable proportions as to be able to defy its enemies. Washington therefore continued a policy of drifting that violated the true spirit of neutrality, although not its strict letter. At the same time, do-nothingism bound the nation's economy ever closer to the Allied cause, while so inflaming the German mind as ultimately to provide a partial justification—to the Germans at least—for unrestricted submarine warfare.

THE MENACE OF THE SUBMARINE

Relations with Germany entered upon an alarming new phase, on February 4, 1915, when Berlin announced that it would establish a war area around the British Isles and attempt to destroy all enemy merchant ships found within that zone. The official announcement further declared that this drastic step had become necessary because of Allied attempts to starve Germany by illegal practices, and that these practices had been acquiesced in by the neutral powers, including the United States.

This ominous German declaration brought inescapably to the fore the problem of using the submarine as a commerce destroyer. Interna-

[15] *The Fatherland*, June 9, 1915, 5:1. See also C. J. Child, "German-American Attempts to Prevent the Exportation of Munitions of War, 1914–1915," *Miss. Valley Hist. Rev.*, XXV (1938), 351–368.

tional law had long decreed that no belligerent warship could destroy an
unresisting enemy merchantman without first stopping it, ascertaining its
identity, and then making adequate provision for the safety of its passengers and crew. This practice had grown up during the days of the
sailing ship, when no merchant vessel dared tangle with a well-armed
warship. But the submarine was fragile, and a single shot or a well-
directed prow could easily send it to the bottom. In view of the fact that
many British merchantmen were armed with six-inch guns, the Germans
insisted that they would be foolhardy to emerge and give the conventional warning. Some earlier attacks by Allied merchant craft had
deepened this conviction.

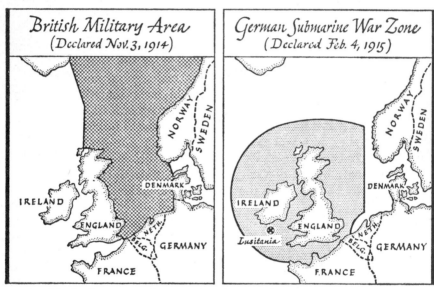

The blockading British, as already noted, repeatedly took liberties
with international law because of the "peculiar" nature of the conflict.
But when the Germans replied that because of "unusual" conditions they
too were justified in departing from the rules, they were met with the
Allied argument that torpedoing vessels without warning was so inhumane as to be unjustifiable. The Germans retorted that the slow
starvation of a large civilian population by means of an illegal blockade
was far more inhumane than sinking a few passenger ships without
warning.

The published German announcement of the war area pointed out that
the British had attempted to disguise their craft by flying neutral flags,
and that neutral ships, which might be unintentionally torpedoed, had
better avoid these waters. Nor could the submarine commanders always
be able "to save crew and passengers" (including Americans) traveling
on enemy merchantmen.

The Department of State, on February 10, 1915, vigorously protested against these "unprecedented" tactics, and solemnly declared that if American lives or vessels were lost, the Berlin government would be held to "strict accountability." Diplomatic language could hardly be stronger. Yet when, in November, 1914, the British had proclaimed the North Sea a military area—a liberty with the freedom of the seas comparable with the German war zone—not a word of official protest came from the United States. More than two years later Washington belatedly reserved its rights. As Bryan's *Memoirs* later observed: ". . . I submit the thought that the administration was lacking in neutrality—not in commission, but in omission; not the notes which were written, but the notes which were not written, threw the delicate machinery out of balance. . . ." [16]

THE *LUSITANIA'S* LAST TRIP

As soon as the submarine danger zone became effective, in mid-February, 1915, German torpedoes sent one Allied ship after another plunging to the bottom. The American public was aroused when, on March 28, 1915, the British passenger liner *Falaba* was sunk with the loss of one American citizen. Resentment flared again, on May 1, when the American tanker *Gulflight* was torpedoed (but not sunk) with a loss of three lives.

Yet American passengers continued to venture into the submarine zone on munitions-laden British liners. Secretary Bryan repeatedly urged the President to take steps to stop this practice, lest some terrible mishap occur. But Wilson steadfastly upheld the right of Americans to travel on belligerent merchantmen. The German representatives in the United States shared Bryan's fear; one of them lamented that "there will be hell to pay." The German Embassy even resorted to the highly irregular step of publishing an advertisement in the New York newspapers, on May 1, 1915, warning American passengers that they sailed on Allied vessels at their own risk.

Undaunted, an unarmed British passenger liner, the *Lusitania*, sailed from New York later that day. Her large passenger list contained the names of 197 Americans, who were undeterred by the German advertisement and by the daily loss of life in the submarine zone.[17] On May 7, 1915, when off the Irish coast, the *Lusitania* chanced to meet a German submarine, which, without any warning, launched a fatal torpedo. The ill-starred ship sank in eighteen minutes with a loss of 1198 persons, 128 of them American citizens.

[16] W. J. Bryan and M. B. Bryan, *The Memoirs of William Jennings Bryan* (Chicago, 1925), p. 404.

[17] T. A. Bailey, "German Documents relating to the 'Lusitania,'" *Jour. of Mod. Hist.*, VIII (1936), 320–337; T. A. Bailey, "The Sinking of the Lusitania," *Amer. Hist. Rev.*, XLI (1935), 54–73.

German apologists claimed that the sinking was justified because the *Lusitania* was carrying 4200 cases of small-arms cartridges, as well as other contraband of war. But the nature of the cargo had no legal bearing on the ancient rule that an unresisting and unarmed enemy merchantman must be adequately warned, with proper provision for the safety of passengers and crew, before being destroyed. The *Lusitania* was actually carrying secret orders to ram all enemy submarines on sight, and to this degree she was an offensively armed enemy warship, herself subject to being torpedoed on sight. But whatever the technicalities of the case, the indiscriminate killing of women, children, and babes in arms further turned world opinion against Germany.

For perhaps the first time the war was really brought home to the American people. The press rang with denunciations of what it regarded as "mass murder." The *New York Times* insisted upon a demand that "the Germans shall no longer make war like savages drunk with blood." The *New York Nation* lamented:

> It is a deed for which a Hun would blush, a Turk be ashamed, and a Barbary pirate apologize. To speak of technicalities and the rules of war, in the face of such wholesale murder on the high seas, is a waste of time. The law of nations and the law of God have been alike trampled upon. . . . The torpedo that sank the *Lusitania* also sank Germany in the opinion of mankind. . . . It is at once a crime and a monumental folly. . . . She has affronted the moral sense of the world and sacrificed her standing among the nations.[18]

A prominent clergyman declared, "It is a colossal sin against God and it is premeditated murder," while the well-known evangelist, Billy Sunday, cried, "Damnable! Damnable! Absolutely hellish!"

On May 12, 1915, just five days after the *Lusitania* tragedy, the British made public their Bryce Report on alleged German atrocities in Belgium. The document was designed for propaganda purposes, and the horrible evidence that it presented seems flimsy today. But the American people, stunned by the *Lusitania* "massacre" and reposing confidence in the beloved Lord Bryce (author of *The American Commonwealth*), were prepared to believe the worst about Germany. The *New York World* expressed a current thought when it declared that a government which would murder 1198 innocent noncombatants "would shrink at nothing done in Belgium."

WILSON WARS WITH WORDS

Angered though they were, the American people showed a remarkable willingness to suspend judgment. Only a handful of newspapers urged hostilities with Germany. There was considerable talk of war in the

[18] *New York Nation*, C, 527, 528 (May 13, 1915).

industrial East, which had become bound to the Allied cause by the golden chains of trade. But the Middle West, as the stronghold of German-American immigrants, and the far-away West seemed bent on maintaining peace. One Cabinet member found the Californians more interested in citrus fruits and good roads than in fighting. In brief, American opinion demanded strong words but shrank from resolute deeds. General Leonard Wood noted in his diary, "Rotten spirit in the *Lusitania* matter. Yellow spirit everywhere in spots."

Wilson was profoundly shocked by the catastrophe, but he steeled himself against letting the drowning cries of women and children divert his attention from the legal aspects of the problem. He was, moreover, too careful a student of American history to repeat President Madison's mistake of leading a disunited country into war. Three days after the *Lusitania* disaster, he addressed a large gathering in Philadelphia. Envisioning America's great moral mission, and emphasizing the ideal that was then guiding him in his troubles with Mexico, he asserted: "There is such a thing as a man being too proud to fight. There is such a thing as a nation being so right that it does not need to convince others by force that it is right." [19]

The phrase "too proud to fight" was quickly wrenched from its context and used maliciously against Wilson by his political foes. Theodore Roosevelt flayed "Professor Wilson," "that Byzantine logothete," who was supported by all the "flubdubs," "mollycoddles," and "flapdoodle pacifists." The Allies were bitterly disappointed. They had hoped that the United States would join them in their fight against the Central Powers.

The first American note to Berlin regarding the *Lusitania*, dated May 13, 1915, emphatically upheld the "indisputable" right of American citizens to sail the high seas, and demanded disavowal of the act and reparation for damages. In reply, the German Foreign Office adopted a strong tone. It argued at length that the *Lusitania*, because of its cargo of munitions and because of other circumstances, was not just "an ordinary unarmed merchant vessel." Though regretting the loss of American lives, the German Foreign Office asserted that the destruction of the liner was an act of "just self-defense." The United States ambassador in Berlin reported pessimistically: "I am afraid that we are in for grave consequences. It is the German hope to keep the *Lusitania* matter 'jollied along' until the American people get excited about baseball or a new scandal and forget. Meantime the hate of America grows daily." [20]

Wilson's second *Lusitania* note, that of June 9, 1915, was so strong as to alarm Secretary Bryan, who feared that it would trigger war. Unable to make his views prevail, he resigned spectacularly from the Cabinet.

[19] *New York Times*, May 11, 1915, 1:8.
[20] Seymour. *House Papers*, I, 454-455 (Gerard to House, June 1, 1915).

His departure at this critical time created the impression that the government was badly divided on the *Lusitania* issue, and consequently weakened Wilson's hand. An avalanche of abuse descended upon Bryan. The *New York World* insisted that his action was "unspeakable treachery," while the *Louisville Courier-Journal* cried that "men have been shot and beheaded, even hanged, drawn and quartered for treason less heinous."

Further diplomatic interchanges with Berlin failed to bring a prompt settlement of the *Lusitania* controversy, and American interest began to flag. The *Columbia* (South Carolina) *State* paraphrased John Paul Jones, "We have not yet begun to write." The bellicose Roosevelt muttered something about Wilson's last note having been "No. 11,765, Series B" on the subject.[21] Not until February, 1916, some ten months after the fatal torpedoing, did Berlin agree to assume liability for the loss of American lives and to pay a suitable indemnity. But Washington did not regard this concession as satisfactory, and the controversy was still dragging along when the United States went to war with Germany.

THE *ARABIC* BLUNDER

The Berlin government meanwhile recognized the danger of provoking America further, and on June 6, 1915, issued a secret order requiring submarine commanders to spare enemy passenger liners. A public order would have been a betrayal of weakness. This safeguard worked reasonably well until August 19, 1915, when a German submarine, in violation of instructions, sank the British passenger ship, *Arabic*, with a loss of two American citizens. Secretary Lansing, who had succeeded Bryan, seriously considered the severance of diplomatic relations, but feared that the country would not sustain the government.

The German ambassador in Washington, Count Bernstorff, was alarmed by the public outburst over the *Arabic*. On September 1, 1915, he gave the following reassuring statement to the State Department: "Liners will not be sunk by our submarines without warning and without safety of the lives of noncombatants, provided that the liners do not try to escape or offer resistance." [22] Bernstorff was not authorized to reveal these instructions, and their publication, though soothing to American public opinion, drew a sharp reprimand from Berlin.

The German government finally yielded to the insistent representations of the United States. On October 5, 1915, it announced that orders issued to the submarine commanders "have been made so stringent that a recurrence of incidents similar to the *Arabic* case is considered out of the

---

[21] See Russell Buchanan, "Theodore Roosevelt and American Neutrality, 1914–1917," *Amer. Hist. Rev.*, XLIII (1938), 775–790.
[22] *War Memoirs of Lansing*, p. 48.

question." Berlin also expressed regret that American lives should have been lost on the *Arabic,* and gave assurances that an indemnity would be paid.

The outcome of the *Arabic* case was a triumph—at least temporarily—for Wilsonian methods. Chief Justice White acclaimed it as "the greatest victory for American diplomacy in a generation." A feeling of relief swept over the country, and even ex-President Roosevelt was forced to concede that the result was "most gratifying." A clash with Germany might still be avoided if the submarine could be kept leashed.

SELECTED BIBLIOGRAPHY

The best summary of recent scholarship is A. S. Link, *Woodrow Wilson and the Progressive Era, 1910–1917* (New York, 1954). An older but sound account is Charles Seymour, *American Diplomacy during the World War* (Baltimore, 1934). The fullest one-volume treatment, strongly anti-Wilson, is C. C. Tansill, *America Goes to War* (Boston, 1938). See also Harley Notter, *The Origins of the Foreign Policy of Woodrow Wilson* (Baltimore, 1937); E. H. Buehrig, *Woodrow Wilson and the Balance of Power* (Bloomington, Ind., 1955); F. L. Paxson, *American Democracy and the World War: Pre-War Years, 1913–1917* (Boston, 1936); J. M. Blum, *Joe Tumulty and the Wilson Era* (Boston, 1951); Armin Rappaport, *The British Press and Wilsonian Neutrality* (Stanford University, Calif., 1951). Full details are given in R. S. Baker, *Woodrow Wilson: Life and Letters,* vols. V and VI (Garden City, N.Y., 1935, 1936). A misleading popularization is Walter Millis, *Road to War: America, 1914–1917* (Boston, 1935).

On propaganda and public opinion, consult H. C. Peterson, *Propaganda for War* (Norman, Okla., 1939); J. D. Squires, *British Propaganda at Home and in the United States from 1914–1917* (Cambridge, Mass., 1935); Carl Wittke, *German-Americans and the World War* (Columbus, Ohio, 1936); C. J. Child, *The German-Americans in Politics, 1914–1917* (Madison, Wis., 1939); J. M. Read, *Atrocity Propaganda, 1914–1919* (New Haven, 1941); Cedric Cummins, *Indiana Public Opinion and the World War, 1914–1917* (Indianapolis, 1945); Edwin Costrell, *How Maine Viewed the War, 1914–1917* (Orono, Me., 1940); J. C. Crighton, *Missouri and the World War, 1914–1917* (Columbia, Mo., 1947).

On international law and the blockade see Alice M. Morrissey, *The American Defense of Neutral Rights, 1914–1917* (Cambridge, Mass., 1939); the more critical Edwin Borchard and W. P. Lage, *Neutrality for the United States* (New Haven, 1937); and Marion C. Siney, *The Allied Blockade of Germany, 1914–1916* (Ann Arbor, Mich., 1957).

See footnotes of this chapter and the references at the end of the next; Bemis and Griffin, *Guide,* 655–672; *Harvard Guide,* Ch. 27.

7TH, 8TH, AND 9TH ED. REFS. See BIBLIOGRAPHICAL ADDENDUM, p. 1,020.

39

The Road to World War I
1915-1917

*If there is an alternative [to war], for God's sake,
let's take it!*

PRESIDENT WILSON, April, 1917

GERMAN SPIES AND SABOTEURS

RELATIVE QUIET reigned on the diplomatic front during the seven months
after the *Arabic* crisis, in August, 1915, primarily because German submarines refrained from killing American citizens. But a vast amount of
suspicion and ill will was stirred up by the plots of German secret agents,
particularly by their schemes to sabotage the American munitions trade.
The Allies, of course, did not become involved in such obstruction
because they had every reason to encourage the traffic. The most startling
revelations came when an American secret-service operative stole a brief
case from a key German espionage agent, Dr. Heinrich Albert, who
absent-mindedly let it out of his sight for a few moments in a New York
streetcar. The publication of some of his documents by the Washington
authorities, in August, 1915, sensationally confirmed suspicions of German sabotage.

Hardly less dramatic was the downfall of the Austro-Hungarian ambassador in Washington, Dr. Constantin Dumba. Some of his secret
papers relating to the fomenting of strikes in munitions factories fell
into the hands of the British, who in turn revealed them to the American officials. Dumba had violated the Eleventh Commandment for diplomats: "Thou shalt not get caught." In September, 1915, Secretary Lansing
requested his recall, and the luckless envoy, whose name suggested the
current slang for stupidity, was jeered out of the country. The *Boston Post*
gibed:

O Constantin Theodor Dumba,
You've roused Uncle Sam from his slumba:
    That letter you wrote,
    Got the old fellow's goat—
Now his path you'll no longer encumba.[1]

Evidence also fell into the hands of the State Department proving that Captain von Papen and Captain Boy-Ed, German attachés stationed in the United States, were implicated in plots. Adding insult to injury, von Papen had written to his wife, "I always say to these idiotic Yankees that they should shut their mouths. . . ." In December, 1915, Secretary Lansing requested the withdrawal of the two obnoxious officials.

These were but the most conspicuous figures among those implicated in undercover activity for Germany and her allies. Others, less notorious, were accused of planting bombs in American ships and factories. Their sinister hand was believed to be seen in the wrecking of the New Jersey Black Tom munitions plant, which blew up in 1916 with a loss of $22 million. Many of the alleged German plots were fabrications of fevered imaginations, but the witch-hunting hysteria that swept the country further turned the American mind against Germany and her allies. The *Chicago Herald* not unreasonably concluded that "where there are so many explosions there must be some Germans."

THE *SUSSEX* PLEDGE—WITH STRINGS

Early in 1916 Congress threatened to get out of hand and hamstring the President's leadership. A strong fear prevailed on Capitol Hill that Wilson was determined to plunge the country into war if more citizens were killed on belligerent merchantmen. Many Congressmen, responding to home pressures, threw their support behind two resolutions designed to warn Americans against traveling on armed belligerent passenger ships. The House of Representatives, according to the Speaker, was prepared to approve the McLemore resolution by a two to one vote. But Wilson, resenting this challenge to his policy, sent an emphatic letter to the chairman of the Senate Committee on Foreign Relations:

> For my own part, I cannot consent to any abridgement of the rights of American citizens in any respect. . . . Once accept a single abatement of right, and many other humiliations would certainly follow, and the whole fine fabric of international law might crumble under our hands piece by piece. What we are contending for in this matter is of the very essence of the things that have made America a sovereign nation. She cannot yield them without conceding her own impotency as a nation, and making virtual surrender of her independent position among the nations of the world.[2]

[1] *Boston Post*, Sept. 23, 1915, 12:3.
[2] *Foreign Relations, 1916 Supp.*, pp. 177–178 (Wilson to Stone, Feb. 24, 1916).

Largely as a result of strong political pressure from the White House, the two "scuttle resolutions" were disposed of, in March, 1916. The *New York Herald* rejoiced: "Pro-Germans are Swept to Defeat as the House Votes to Sustain American Rights." Yet American men, women, and children continued to embark on contraband-laden British liners, some of them armed, for submarine-infested waters. Whatever their rights, these people were just as dead, when killed, as if they had been wrong. And the consequences for the country were momentous.

The German submarine issue again burst into the headlines, on March 24, 1916. An unarmed French passenger ship, the *Sussex*, was torpedoed by an underseas marauder while crossing the English channel. Although severely damaged, the vessel limped into port with some eighty casualties, including injury to several Americans. The attack was a flagrant violation of the German *Arabic* pledge not to sink unresisting passenger ships without warning, and America was instantly aroused.

The ensuing crisis was the most dangerous yet to confront the United States. Diplomatically, the *Sussex* was by far the most important ship of the war. The submarine commander who torpedoed the vessel thought that he had attacked a warship, and his mistaken report to his superiors caused the Foreign Office at first to deny responsibility. This apparent duplicity further angered the American public and official Washington. Secretary Lansing favored an immediate rupture, but Wilson, faced with the Mexican crisis and a divided public opinion, recoiled from extreme measures. The stern note that Secretary Lansing finally sent to Berlin, on April 18, 1916, bluntly asserted:

> Unless the Imperial Government should now immediately declare and effect an abandonment of its present methods of submarine warfare against passenger and freight-carrying vessels, the Government of the United States can have no choice but to sever diplomatic relations. . . .[3]

The German reply, dated May 4, 1916, yielded to the major American demand. It declared that no more unresisting merchantmen—not just passenger liners—were to be sunk without warning and without proper humanitarian precautions. But a long "string" was tied to this pledge. Berlin assumed that Washington would now demand that the other belligerents respect "the laws of humanity"—that is, force Britain to relax her starvation blockade. Should such a relaxation not occur, Germany "would then be facing a new situation in which it must reserve [to] itself complete liberty of decision."[4] Wilson gratefully accepted the no-torpedoing assurances—but refused to accept the "string."

The so-called "*Sussex* Pledge" was consequently not a pledge at all. Berlin qualified it by insisting on conditions regarding the British blockade that were impossible of fulfillment. Yet Wilson won a deceptive dip-

---

[3] *Foreign Relations, 1916 Supp.*, p. 234.
[4] *Ibid.*, pp. 259–260.

lomatic victory—at least temporarily. He averted hostilities, maintained American prestige, and forced the Germans to muzzle, also temporarily, their most lethal sea weapon. But, ominously, he handed them a blank check which he could not honorably recall. He declared that if they reopened submarine warfare, he would have to sever relations—and that probably meant war. If and when they filled in the blank check, his hand would be forced. Wilson thus robbed himself of freedom of action.

THE HOUSE-GREY MORAL ENTANGLEMENT

With the conflict in western Europe bogged down in the mud and barbed wire of trench warfare, Wilson became convinced that the only sure way to keep America out of the struggle was to bring it to an end.

He had already taken a significant step toward a negotiated peace, in January, 1915, by sending his intimate personal adviser, the pro-Ally Colonel Edward M. House, on a mission to Europe. For a number of weeks the earnest Colonel was "jollied along" by the British, the French, and the Germans. The brutal truth is that both sides had already poured so much blood and treasure into the bottomless pit that they did not dare face their people without some fruits of victory. After an interview in England with King George V, House reported: "His idea seemed to be that the best way to obtain permanent peace was to knock all the fight out of the Germans, and stamp on them for a while until they wanted peace and more of it than any other nation." [5]

Early in 1916 the foot-loose Colonel House again reached Europe on another peace mission. Acting as Wilson's personal representative, he came to an agreement with Sir Edward Grey. The latter recorded the gist of their conversation in an extraordinary memorandum dated February 22, 1916:

> Colonel House told me that President Wilson was ready, on hearing from France and England that the moment was opportune, to propose that a Conference should be summoned to put an end to the war. Should the Allies accept this proposal, and should Germany refuse it, the United States would *probably* enter the war against Germany. [6]

Grey's memorandum of his understanding with House went on to say that even if such a gathering failed to secure peace, "the United States would [probably] leave the Conference as a belligerent on the side of the Allies. . . ." In short, House virtually committed the United States to becoming a member of the Allied coalition.

But the zealous Colonel exceeded his instructions. Wilson had authorized him to urge peace negotiations, and to promise that America

---

[5] Charles Seymour, *The Intimate Papers of Colonel House* (Boston, 1926), I, 385 (House to Wilson, March 1, 1915).
[6] *Ibid.*, II, 201–202. Italics inserted.

would throw her *"moral* force" against Germany and her allies if they should refuse to co-operate. There were already two safeguarding "probablies" in the House-Grey memorandum, a copy of which was forwarded to the President. Wilson, who could not completely ignore Congress, promptly watered down the document further by inserting a third "probably." He thus changed the original statement to read, "the United States would *probably* leave the Conference as a belligerent on the side of the Allies. . . ."

This statement, of course, was not a firm pledge by Washington, and the upshot was that the scheme for a negotiated settlement fell flat. Neither side desired a peace conference. Germany had the military advantage, and the Allies, confident of ultimately landing a knockout blow, did not want to be handicapped at the peace table by Wilson's embarrassing idealism. With the House-Grey memorandum tucked away in their files, the British could continue fighting with the comforting assurance that the United States, though outwardly professing neutrality, was morally committed to their side. The document also meant that London did not have to take too seriously American protests against Britain's blockading practices—practices that were slowly driving the Germans to desperation.

MAIL POUCHES AND BLACKLISTS

During the nine months following the *Sussex* pledge, in May, 1916, the German submarines were on their good behavior as far as the United States was concerned. American public opinion was left free to concentrate on the accumulation of grievances, old and new, at the hands of Britain. The ruthless suppression of an Irish revolt in the spring of 1916 added fuel to the flames.

Vastly annoying to red-blooded Americans was the British practice of opening United States mails, ostensibly in search of contraband en route to Germany. Resentment was increased by rumors that trade secrets were being filched from these letters and turned over to British commercial rivals. The *Brooklyn Eagle* was soon to lament, "Our mails are being held up by the British and sent down by the Germans."

After wordily refusing to make concessions on the mails, the blockade, and other complaints, the British suddenly turned the knife in the wound by proclaiming a blacklist, on July 18, 1916. This was a list of some eighty persons or firms in the United States, most of them German-connected, that were suspected of giving undercover aid to Germany. British subjects were now forbidden to trade with them.[7]

This latest slap from London caused the anti-British Hearst press and

[7] T. A. Bailey, "The United States and the Blacklist during the Great War," *Jour. of Mod. Hist.*, VI (1934), 14–35.

the pro-German partisans in the United States to rend the heavens. The strongly pro-Ally *New York Times* described the blacklist as "the most tactless, foolish, and unnecessary act of the British Government during the war." Even Ambassador Page in London was disgusted. Wilson, forsaking his normally pro-Ally bias for the one conspicuous period of the war, declared that the "poor boobs" in Britain had "got on his nerves." To Colonel House he confessed:

> I am, I must admit, about at the end of my patience with Great Britain and the Allies. This blacklist business is the last straw. I have told Spring-Rice [British ambassador] so, and he sees the reasons very clearly. Both he and Jusserand [French ambassador] think it is a stupid blunder. . . . Can we any longer endure their intolerable course? [8]

Washington protested vigorously against the blacklist, but was forced to base its case on international morals rather than international law. The plain truth was that Britain had a perfect legal right to forbid her own subjects to trade with certain firms in the United States. The strong tone of the American protest suggests that the Wilson administration, then in the midst of the 1916 campaign for re-election, was not overlooking the Irish and German vote. The British, recognizing their tactical error, gradually whittled down their blacklist as far as the United States was concerned.

An angered Congress faced squarely up to the possibility of a rupture with Britain. It clothed the President with retaliatory powers—never used—against nations that blacklisted Americans. At almost the same time it passed the Naval Act of 1916, the largest peacetime appropriation of its kind then on record. "Let us," insisted Wilson, "build a navy bigger than hers [Britain's] and do what we please." A showdown with England might well have come if the renewed submarine warfare of Germany had not diverted American attention.

Agitation for military preparedness had meantime been coming to a head, for far-visioned citizens like Theodore Roosevelt had early foreseen the danger of America's involvement in the war. Wilson, a pacifist at heart, had been cool to their clamor. But the tidal wave of public opinion, combined with Germany's submarine warfare, caused him belatedly to mount the bandwagon. In December, 1915, he urged a formidable military and naval program on Congress. The subsequent legislation of 1916, passed *two years after* the war had erupted, proved to be too little, too late, and largely of the wrong kind—big battleships rather than swift antisubmarine craft. The deterrent of a Big Stick was painfully absent when the German war lords decided to push America into the bloody abyss early in 1917.

[8] Charles Seymour, *American Diplomacy during the World War* (Baltimore, 1934), pp. 76–77 (July 23, 1916).

THE NATION VOTES FOR WILSON—AND PEACE

Interest in foreign affairs had meanwhile become partially eclipsed by the heated Presidential campaign of 1916. The Republicans passed by the vehemently pro-Ally ex-President Roosevelt, who was clamoring for armed intervention. Instead they picked their candidate, the heavily be-whiskered Charles Evans Hughes, from the cloistered Supreme Court. The Democrats renominated Wilson by acclamation in a wildly shouting convention that helped to provide impetus to the slogan: "He Kept Us Out of War."

Early in the campaign political wiseacres concluded that the hyphen-ated vote might well prove decisive. The Republicans took on the em-barrassing task of trying to woo the German-American element, while at the same time condemning Wilson for not having dealt more harshly with Germany in upholding American rights. In reply, the Democrats at-tempted to pin the mantle of pro-Germanism on the Republicans. The Democratic *New York World* challenged, "Can the Kaiser Defeat the President?" and defended Wilson for "the crime of being an American President instead of a German President."

Hughes, who condemned Wilson's "leisurely discussions" of the na-tion's rights, tried to "straddle" on the pro-German issue. He announced firmly that he was for "America first and America efficient." Such vague phrases led to his being renamed Charles "Evasive" Hughes, and to the quip that he had left the bench for the fence. Wilson, on the other hand, was accused by pro-German Irish-Americans of being "the best President England ever had." The violent Theodore Roosevelt, who was on fire to fight Germany, undoubtedly lost many votes for Hughes among German-Americans and peace-loving citizens by his ranting speeches against Wilson.

The campaign involved many issues—Mexico, the railroads, the tariff—but the leading one seems to have been the tacit promise of the Democrats to preserve neutrality. The country was plastered with placards bearing the slogan, "He Kept Us out of War." A Democratic appeal to working-men read:

> You Are Working;
> *—Not Fighting!*
> Alive and Happy;
> *—Not Cannon Fodder!*
> Wilson and Peace with Honor?
>   or
> *Hughes with Roosevelt and War?* [9]

[9] *New York Times,* Nov. 4, 1916, 6:4–8 (Paid advertisement).

A MATTER OF ROUTINE

PRESIDENT WILSON: "This calls for a note.—Mr. Secretary, just bring me in a copy of our No. 1 Note to Germany—'Humanity' Series."

A British view of Wilson's note-writing.
London Punch, 1915

On election night, when the first returns poured in, Hughes had evidently won by a landslide. But the voters of the Middle West and Far West, who were farther removed from the war and strongly set against participation, narrowly turned the tide for Wilson. The President did not receive a clear mandate to keep the country out of war, but his election was clearly made possible by citizens who hoped that he would do so. Wilson had promised nothing regarding the future, but many voters regarded the key slogan—"He kept us out of war"—as a virtual pledge.

WILSON THE GLOBAL PEACEMAKER

Shortly after the election, Wilson embarked upon a final desperate gamble to win a negotiated peace. He drafted an identical note appealing to both sets of belligerents to state specifically their war aims. But before he could present it the Germans stole his thunder by publishing, on December 12, 1916, a statement in which they indicated their willingness to discuss terms. This stroke left Wilson in an awkward dilemma. If he went ahead, the Allies would infer that Washington and Berlin were acting together. If he delayed, an opportunity to end hostilities would pass, and America might be dragged into the conflict by a resumption of submarine warfare. Wilson sent the note on December 18, 1916.

The Allies were sorely displeased with this presumed evidence of German-American collusion, and were mortally offended by Wilson's bold statement that "the objects which the statesmen of the belligerents on both sides have in mind in this war are virtually the same. . . ." The British and French particularly resented Wilson's attempt "to smoke them out" and force them to confess their secret war aims. If the Allies did so, their people might stop fighting. The outspoken British militarist, Sir Henry Wilson, fumed, "That ass President Wilson has barged in. . . ." Lord Northcliffe told Ambassador Page, "Everybody is mad as hell." The King broke down and wept. The Allied reply to Wilson's request for war aims, though more promising than Germany's, offered little hope. The Allies were determined not to yield to this "peace threat."

After prayerful thought, Wilson gave his reactions to the belligerent replies in a memorable address to the Senate—or rather to the world—on January 22, 1917. He suggested a league of nations for establishing world accord, and bluntly warned the embattled powers that only "peace without victory" could bring a permanent settlement. The American people generally greeted this far-visioned speech with enthusiasm. Senator Tillman of South Carolina, a Democrat, remarked that it was the "noblest utterance since the Declaration of Independence." But the frank phrase, "peace without victory," was a bucket of cold water to the Allies, who could not afford to accept a stalemate. As far as immediate objectives were concerned, the speech netted nothing. But it further magnified Wilson's stature as the emerging moral leader of the world.

THE BREAK WITH BERLIN

Germany provided her brutal answer to "peace without victory" by proclaiming, on January 31, 1917, an unrestricted submarine campaign. Henceforth her undersea craft would attempt to sink *all* ships—neutral or belligerent, passenger or merchant—in the war zone. As a slight but insulting concession, the United States might sail one ship a week to and from Falmouth, England, under severely restricted conditions. "The freedom of the seas," lamented the *Brooklyn Eagle*, "will now be enjoyed by icebergs and fish."

The all-out submarine campaign was a carefully calculated risk that the German military men had finally forced upon the civilian authorities. The war had reached a seeming deadlock. The unorthodox British block-ade, in which the United States acquiesced, was bringing shortages and hunger. With the lethal submarine, the Germans had a fairly good chance of winning; without it, they seemed doomed to lose. Their aim was to force England to her knees by ruthlessly cutting off supplies from all over the world, not merely munitions from America.

The Germans knew perfectly well that the unrestricted submarine campaign would shove the United States into the conflict. But they con-cluded, with considerable logic, that Britain would be starved out within a few months, long before the Americans could raise and train a formid-able army, much less supply it and transport it across the submarine-infested Atlantic. The United States, to be sure, had a powerful navy, but Britain already dominated the surface of the sea. With an eye to the tremendous traffic in munitions financed by American loans, the Germans reasoned that the Americans could scarcely help the Allies more as co-belligerents than they were then doing as neutrals. The German Minister of Marine privately insisted, "from a military point of view America is as nothing." [10]

To Wilson the German submarine announcement, though not com-pletely unexpected, came as a staggering blow. Until then, as had been true since the *Sussex* settlement eight months earlier, relations with Ger-many had been generally friendly, while those with Britain had de-teriorated badly. But Wilson had irrevocably committed himself to a break with Berlin in his *Sussex* ultimatum, and now the nation's plighted word required a diplomatic rupture. After much agony of spirit, he dramatically appeared before Congress, on February 3, 1917, to an-nounce the termination of diplomatic intercourse with Germany.

After the severance of relations, war was virtually inevitable. But Wilson still nourished the wishful thought that the Germans were bluffing, and that they would not commit "overt acts" against American ships and lives. His caution was understandable, for during these anxious weeks a vast number of citizens, perhaps a majority, were hoping for peace. "I could not move faster," Wilson remarked to his secretary, "than the mass of our people would permit."

The grim seriousness of Berlin was suddenly brought home to the American people by the Zimmermann note. On January 16, 1917, the Ger-

[10] Hans P. Hanssen, *Diary of a Dying Empire*, trans. by O. O. Winther (Blooming-ton, Ind., 1955), p. 170.

man Foreign Secretary, Zimmermann, had cabled the German minister in Mexico fantastic instructions. The latter, in the event of war with the United States, should strive for a German-Mexican alliance, while holding out to Mexico the bait of recovering Texas, New Mexico, and Arizona. He was also to arrange for Japan (one of the Allies!) to join the scheme.[11]

The incredible Zimmermann note was intercepted and deciphered by British authorities, who turned it over to the Washington officials. On March 1, 1917, the note was headlined in the press and created, Lansing thought, a profounder sensation than the submarine announcement itself. The American people were shocked to learn that Germany, if struck by the United States, would strike back with legitimate, if ill-chosen, diplomatic weapons. A tremendous wave of anti-German sentiment swept over the country, particularly into the hitherto apathetic Southwest and West. At this late date, Texans were not going to be reconquered by Mexicans. The Pacific Coast, with its "yellow peril" prejudice, was similarly aroused by the proposed overture to Japan. A more nearly united America had moved one step nearer the brink.

GERMANY "THRUSTS" WAR ON AMERICA

American shipping, fearful of submarine attacks, was meanwhile clinging to port. Great quantities of wheat and cotton were piling up on the wharves, and threatening to dislocate American economic life. On February 26, 1917, therefore, Wilson went before Congress and asked for authority to provide mounted guns for American merchantmen. The House approved this request by a strong majority, but a handful of "peace-at-any-price" Senators helped filibuster the bill to death. Red-blooded citizens branded the obstructers as "Iscariots" and "traitors," while more violent critics demanded that the dissenters be hanged. Wilson let himself go when he declared publicly that a "little group of willful men had rendered the great government of the United States helpless and contemptible."

But Wilson finally prevailed. After being assured by his legal advisers that authority could be wrested from existing statutes, he proceeded to arm American vessels anyhow. In March, 1917, the first American armed merchantmen put to sea with orders to fire on hostile submarines.

The country waited breathlessly for the "overt acts." In mid-March, 1917, some six weeks after the original submarine announcement, German undersea raiders ruthlessly sank four unarmed American merchant ships, with heavy loss of life. The Germans were now doing what they had threatened to do: waging war on United States shipping.

Wilson still did not want hostilities, but the initiative was out of his hands. One Philadelphia newspaper hit the nail on the head when it

[11] *Foreign Relations, 1917*, Supp. I, p. 147.

remarked that the "difference between war and what we have now is that now we aren't fighting back." The only recourse was to call Congress into special session and ask it to recognize the state of hostilities that Germany had brought about. Wilson's memorable war message, delivered to the joint houses of Congress on April 2, 1917, asked that body "formally" to accept the status of belligerency that had been "thrust" upon the United States. When he had finished, there was a moment of eloquent silence, and then deafening applause.

The fateful war resolution, formalizing the hostilities "thrust upon the United States," passed the Senate, on April 4, 1917, by a vote of 82 to 6. Among the dissenters were members of the "willful" group. On April 6 the House gave its approval by a count of 373 to 50. The rather surprising amount of opposition was concentrated in the isolationist and German-inhabited states of the Middle West. Only one of the negative votes in Congress represented the industrial East, which had a huge investment stake in an Allied victory and which was nearer geographically to the German menace. But the great mass of the American people by this time were resigned to fighting, even though there was little thought of sending a huge army overseas.[12]

THE WAGES OF UNNEUTRALITY

Why was the United States dragged into the European conflagration, despite two-and-one-half years of determination to stay out?

The German submarine was undoubtedly the immediate or precipitating cause. In a very real sense, America's war declaration bore the well-known trademark "Made in Germany." If the Germans had not launched their all-out submarine campaign, the United States would not have been drawn into the conflict when it was—possibly never.

But the American people, in pointing an accusing finger at the submarine, were prone to overlook their own responsibility for what befell them. Their large-scale assistance to the Allies in munitions and other contraband, coupled with Washington's acquiescence in the British blockade, drove the Germans to desperate expedients that ultimately involved the United States. A more even-handed neutrality might have averted a clash.

Both sets of belligerents flagrantly violated American rights—or what Washington insisted were American rights. Throughout the years of neutrality, the Allies did so more consistently and persistently than Germany. Why, then, did America not fight them?

The basic explanation is that Allied infractions hurt American property rights only. The United States could lodge protests against the seizure of ships, and collect damages later. But the German submarine took

[12] T. A. Bailey, *Woodrow Wilson and the Lost Peace* (New York, 1944), p. 14.

American lives, and there was no proper recompense for lives. As the *Boston Globe* remarked, "One was a 'gang of thieves'; the other was a 'gang of murderers.' On the whole, we prefer the thieves, but only as the lesser of two evils." Many Americans were so deeply disturbed by the submarine, and by its threat to historic freedom of the seas, that they proposed to fight a limited-liability war. They would pull out just as soon as Germany agreed to respect the nation's maritime rights.

Additional factors made easier the decision to fight when Germany attacked American shipping. Among them were anger over German sabotage and intrigue (Zimmermann note); German ruthlessness and militarism, as highlighted by Allied propaganda; fear that the Kaiser, if he crushed Europe, would ultimately attack the United States with overpowering force; the pro-Ally bias of a basically Anglo-Saxon nation; and the economic stake of American manufacturers and investors in the Allied cause. Finally, in March, 1917, some six weeks after the fateful submarine announcement, a Russian revolution overthrew the Czarist regime, and the American people could look forward to fighting beside the Allies without the black sheep of despotism in their camp.[13]

With the wisdom of hindsight, one can see that there were several ways by which America could have avoided the all-out submarine challenge. First, she could have kept her citizens and ships out of the combat zones, as was later done under the neutrality legislation of the 1930's—legislation that came one war too late. But to Wilson and many fellow Americans such a course was dishonorable and a base surrender of historic rights. Second, the nation could have lowered its standards of national honor, and simply have turned the other cheek. Norway, Sweden, and Denmark all stayed out of the war, although losing more of their nationals from submarine attacks than the United States did while neutral. But a proud and patriotic nation like the giant trans-Atlantic republic would not consent to being an international doormat.

In later years came the "revisionist" accusation that various pressure groups had stampeded America into declaring war. Among them were the propagandists, the bankers, and the munitions manufacturers. Such groups no doubt had some influence in shaping the policies in Washington that eventually goaded the Germans into their unrestricted sub-

---

[13] In later years writers alleged that the United States rushed into war to save the Allies, preserve the balance of power, and keep open the sea lanes to England. There was no rushing; eight weeks elapsed between the submarine announcement and the declaration of war. The Allies were not thought to be in need of saving; not until the United States got into the war was it revealed how badly off they were. As for keeping open the North Atlantic sea lanes, Germany's submarine warfare had been going on for more than two years, and not until after the United States entered the war did the tonnage losses become truly frightening. Nor did the United States "rush" into this conflict to "make the world safe for democracy" and to fight a war "to end war." These ideals were sloganized war aims that became prominent *after* the United States was forced in. See *ibid.*, Ch. I.

marine warfare. But in the final analysis America fought because she was attacked—the war was "thrust" upon her.

SELECTED BIBLIOGRAPHY

Most of the references cited at the end of the previous chapter are relevant, but note particularly the summary view of recent scholarship in A. S. Link, *Woodrow Wilson and the Progressive Era, 1910–1917* (New York, 1954). See also S. F. Bemis, ed., *The American Secretaries of State and their Diplomacy* (New York, 1929), X; Charles Seymour, *American Neutrality, 1914–1917* (New Haven, 1935); A. M. Arnett, *Claude Kitchin and the Wilson War Policies* (Boston, 1937); *War Memoirs of Robert Lansing* (Indianapolis, 1935); N. D. Baker, *Why We Went to War* (New York, 1936); A. L. and J. L. George, *Woodrow Wilson and Colonel House* (New York, 1956); Kent Forster, *The Failures of Peace* (Washington, 1941); S. R. Spencer, Jr., *Decision for War, 1917* (Rindge, N.H., 1953); M. J. Pusey, *Charles Evans Hughes* (2 vols., New York, 1951); Belle Case La Follette and Fola La Follette, *Robert M. La Follette* (2 vols., New York, 1953). Brief but perceptive is A. S. Link, *Wilson the Diplomatist* (Baltimore, 1957).

Revealing articles are A. R. Buchanan, "American Editors Examine American War Aims and Plans in April, 1917," *Pacific Hist. Rev.,* IX (1940), 253–265; H. C. Syrett, "The Business Press and American Neutrality, 1914–1917," *Miss. Valley Hist. Rev.,* XXXII (1945), 215–230; R. A. Billington, "The Origins of Middle Western Isolationism," *Pol. Sci. Quar.,* LX (1945), 44–64; A. S. Link, "The Middle West and the Coming of World War I," *Ohio State Archaeol. and Hist. Quar.,* LXII (1953), 109–121.

See footnotes of this chapter; Bemis and Griffin, *Guide,* pp. 655–672; *Harvard Guide,* Ch. 27.

7TH ED. REFS. See the relevant new titles at the ends of the previous two chapters. E. R. May, *The World War and American Isolation, 1914–1917* (Cambridge, Mass., 1959) is especially strong on the backgrounds of the German decision for unrestricted submarine warfare. The Chancellor (Bethmann-Hollweg), who here rises in stature, is shown to have been overborne by the military and by a public opinion embittered against the United States. The author rather surprisingly downgrades the Allied need for American munitions, and, not conceding that Germany was making war on the United States by mid-March, 1917, concludes that Wilson had an acceptable alternative in "armed neutrality." He overlooks the facts that this device was tried, and that when Germany began sinking American ships the only choices were limited war or large-scale war. K. E. Birnbaum, *Peace Moves and U-Boat Warfare: A Study of Imperial Germany's Policy towards the United States, April 18, 1916—January 9, 1917* (Stockholm, 1958) is even fuller than May on the German inner councils. The author concludes that Bethmann-Hollweg might have held out longer and that the Germans rejected Wilsonian alternatives because they were suspicious of Wilson's pro-Ally neutrality. The Kaiser played a minimal role in the final decision; Generals Hindenburg and Ludendorff had strong popular support. The German Ambassador in Washington sometimes softened his instructions and hence misled Wilson. For additional references see BIBLIOGRAPHICAL ADDENDUM, p. 1,021.

8TH AND 9TH ED. REFS. See BIBLIOGRAPHICAL ADDENDUM, p. 1,022.

Negotiating the Treaty of Versailles

Six million young men lie in premature graves, and four old men sit in Paris partitioning the earth.
NEW YORK NATION, 1919

ASSOCIATES OF THE ALLIES

THE TRANSITION from prolonged neutrality to active belligerency was not easy. Faithful to the hoary no-alliance tradition, the United States, at Wilson's insistence, did not become allied with the Allies, merely "associated"—hence the cumbersome term "the Allied and Associated Powers." But regardless of terminology, America poured out unstinted aid for the common cause.

Belligerency also brought a new viewpoint toward neutrality. The United States now became an active or silent partner of the Allies in "modifying" international law. But in the interests of consistency, Washington refused to support some of the Allied practices to which it had vigorously objected during the years of neutrality. Other practices that it had protested against only mildly were accepted and even refined. Conspicuous in this category were the blacklist and the economic control of neutrals near Germany or adjacent to her. But Washington was able to make out some kind of legal case for every device that it used—just as the Allies had been able to do before America entered the war.[1]

But co-belligerency was not achieved without friction. The recent disputes with Britain, notably those over the blacklist and mails, had left a bitter aftertaste. The German-Americans and particularly the Irish-Americans were acutely unhappy. Anti-British textbooks, keeping alive the traditional hatred, had been poisonously pervasive. When Admiral Sims went to England early in the war, Admiral Benson had warned

---

[1] See T. A. Bailey, *The Policy of the United States toward the Neutrals, 1917–1918* (Baltimore, 1942).

him: "Don't let the British pull the wool over your eyes. It is none of our business pulling their chestnuts out of the fire. We would as soon fight the British as the Germans." [2]

Britain made haste to cultivate her new "Associate." The *London Punch* rejoiced that "too proud to fight" had now become "proud to fight too." The King practiced baseball throwing and ate an American buckwheat cake, which he pronounced "good." On July 4, 1917—of all days—the Union Jack and the Stars and Stripes floated side by side over Westminster Abbey and the Houses of Parliament. The Americans, for their part, suddenly discovered that the anti-British textbooks were hurtful to Allied morale. One result was a rewriting campaign, in which the truth was grossly distorted.

Commissions of distinguished statesmen from the principal Allied powers, seeking to achieve closer accord, hastened to America to devise plans for a speedy victory. Their efforts were directed largely—and successfully—toward a much-needed co-ordination of effort. But American money and supplies, though lavishly provided, were not enough. The Allies were already scraping the bottom of their man-power barrel. The United States at length agreed to send an immense body of troops, ultimately over two million men. The American people would have accepted the German submarine challenge in 1917 with even greater reluctance if they had foreseen such large-scale participation.

THE IMPACT OF THE FOURTEEN POINTS

Wilson's moral leadership was enormously enhanced by America's active role in the conflict. For him the bitter pill of belligerency had been partially sweetened by the knowledge that the United States, as a cobelligerent rather than an onlooker, would be able to exercise greater influence in attaining Wilsonian ideals for a lasting peace. The republic had been forced into the conflict by German ruthlessness, but the American people could hardly be rallied to a great crusade by the slogan, "The World Must be Made Safe against the Submarine." Wilson attained a lofty emotional level by insisting that this was a "war to end war"—a war to make the world "safe for democracy."

In Wilson the man and the times providentially met. Using to the full his "Presidential pulpit," he held aloft with passionate conviction the principles for which the nation was fighting—or thought it was fighting. But these speeches were too long to lend themselves effectively to pamphleteering propaganda. Wilson remedied this deficiency admirably when, on January 8, 1918, he appeared before Congress and delivered his famous Fourteen Points address.

[2] E. E. Morison, *Admiral Sims and the Modern American Navy* (Boston, 1942), p. 338.

The Fourteen Points were designed as a capsuled statement of Allied war aims and hence as an engine of propaganda, both at home and abroad. Specifically, they were an attempt to offset the recent publication by the Russian Bolsheviks of the Czar's damaging secret treaties of imperialism with the Allies, and to encourage the Russians to stay in the conflict. Wilson further hoped that his statement of war aims would nerve the Allied peoples to fight harder, and weaken the resistance of the enemy nations by holding out to them the seductive hope of a just peace —not one of vengeance. In summary form Wilson's Fourteen Points program follows: [3]

1. Abolition of secret diplomacy.
   [The liberals in all countries would approve.]
2. Freedom to navigate the high seas in peace and war.
   [Pleasing to the Germans, who distrusted British sea power.]
3. Removal of economic barriers among the nations.
   [Reassuring to the Germans, who feared economic reprisals at the end of the war.]
4. Reduction of armaments.
   [Gratifying to taxpayers in all countries.]
5. Adjustment of colonial claims in the interest of both the inhabitants and the powers concerned.
6. Restoration of Russia and a welcome for her in the society of nations
7. The return of Belgium to her people.
8. Evacuation and restoration of French territory, including Alsace-Lorraine, taken by the Germans in 1871.
9. Readjustment of Italian frontiers "along clearly recognizable lines of nationality."
10. Free opportunity for "autonomous development" for people of Austria-Hungary.
    [An appeal to the submerged minorities of the ramshackle empire.]
11. Restoration of the Balkan nations and free access to the sea for Serbia.
12. Protection for minorities in Turkey.
13. An independent Poland.
    [Seductive to the Poles of Austria-Hungary and Germany.]
14. "A general association [League] of nations" to secure "mutual guarantees of political independence and territorial integrity to great and small states alike."

Wilson regarded his Fourteenth Point—the League of Nations—as the capstone point. The idea was not original with him. It had long been advocated by thinkers on both sides of the Atlantic, and since 1914 had received the backing of influential groups in the United States.[4]

In subsequent addresses Wilson elaborated, clarified, and supplemented the original Fourteen Points. He declared for a just, permanent, open peace, and stressed the desirability of consulting the wishes of the minority groups involved in the prospective settlements. This last ideal— Secretary Lansing called it self-determination "dynamite"—raised up

[3] *Cong. Record*, 65 Cong., 2 sess., pp. 680–681.
[4] See R. J. Bartlett, *The League to Enforce Peace* (Chapel Hill, N.C., 1944).

unrealizable hopes among subject peoples the world over. All the points and principles, totaling about twenty-three, are popularly referred to as the Fourteen Points.

Wilson's fascinating phrases proved to be a mighty instrument of propaganda. George Creel, head of the American Committee on Public Information, scattered over the world some sixty million pamphlets, booklets, and leaflets containing "Wilsonisms." In China, a translated volume of the President's speeches became a "best seller." In Poland, university men clasped hands when they met and soulfully uttered one word, "Wilson." In Italy, candles burned in lonely cottages before poster-portraits of the new Messiah risen in the West. The Allied military leaders, perceiving the propaganda value of the Fourteen Points, rained countless leaflets upon Germany and Austria-Hungary from balloons and airplanes. This aerial barrage was effective in spreading unrest among submerged minorities, and in weakening the morale of troops at the front.[5]

THE FOURTEEN POINTS DISARM GERMANY

Fresh man power from the aroused Western giant tipped the scales in favor of the Allies, and Germany's "military masters" foresaw their impending doom. By October, 1918, they had induced Berlin to propose to Wilson the calling of a conference that would make a peace based on the Fourteen Points. They chose Wilson, rather than the Allied leaders, because they assumed that the visionary ex-schoolmaster could be more easily handled. They especially feared that the embittered Allies would return a point-blank refusal, and thus make inevitable a bloody invasion of the Fatherland. They specifically hoped to trap Wilson into a cessation of hostilities that would enable them to re-form their lines and strengthen their position.

But in Wilson Germany picked the wrong man. Few chapters in American diplomatic history reveal greater skill than his series of interchanges with the German officials during October, 1918. He had consistently preached that America had no quarrel with the German people, only with their "military masters." He now indicated that the Kaiser and his following would have to be overthrown before an armistice could be agreed upon. The war-weary German people were not slow to take the hint. The pressure quickly became so intense that the Kaiser was forced to abdicate, on November 9, 1918, and flee the country to Holland, where he lived for his remaining twenty-three years "unwept, unhonored, and unhung."

[5] George Creel, *How We Advertised America* (New York, 1920), pp. 283 ff.; see also G. G. Bruntz, *Allied Propaganda and the Collapse of the German Empire in 1918* (Stanford University, Calif., 1938), pp. 212 ff.

President Wilson expressed his willingness to come to terms with Germany on the basis of his Fourteen Points and subsequent clarifying addresses. But the Allies, who had enthusiastically preached the gospel according to Wilson for war purposes, were far less enthusiastic about these principles for peace purposes. Long before America entered the war, these powers had made a number of secret treaties among themselves for the purpose of carving up the choicest possessions of the enemy. A strict application of the Fourteen Points would deprive them of their spoils. Britain likewise balked at accepting Point II, on freedom of the seas. She would not throw overboard the blockade, her chief offensive weapon, at the behest of the idealistic Wilson. The thrifty French peasants, for their part, were determined to have monetary payments for the heavy damages caused by the German invader. The Fourteen Points were not sufficiently clear on this issue.

The Allied objections to the Fourteen Points were serious, but Colonel House, who represented Wilson in Europe, held high cards. Economically, the Allies were hardly less dependent upon America for reconstruction than they had been for war. If Wilson should leave them in the lurch, the consequences might be calamitous. The Germans probably would be encouraged to fight to the last ditch, and without American assistance the Allies might not be able to extort satisfactory terms.

After Colonel House had delicately threatened to make a separate peace, the Allies grudgingly agreed to accept the Fourteen Points as the basis for negotiation. But they secured one important modification and one important elucidation. The reservation was that the Allies should retain complete liberty as regards freedom of the seas. The elucidation was that the restoration of evacuated territory by Germany should include compensation for damages to the civilian population—that is, reparations. Wilson much preferred an unreserved acceptance of the Fourteen Points, but he won a diplomatic victory, considering the secret aims of the Allies, in winning as much as he did.

The Armistice was formally signed on November 11, 1918. Wilson was not responsible for its terms. The instrument was drawn up and approved by the Allied military leaders, who thus plucked the fruits of victory without having to launch a costly invasion of Germany.

Yet the American people were badly frustrated by the outcome, for they had been keyed up to march on to Berlin and "hang the Kaiser." To leave the enemy's soil unseared seemed to many red-blooded citizens a betrayal of the honored dead. "Our answer to the Hun's twaddle," exclaimed the *Cleveland Plain Dealer,* "shall be more war." The *Charleston News and Courier* would have no bargaining "with the blood-stained gang of thugs and pirates . . . who deliberately . . . plunged the world into war." Prominent Republicans, like Senator Lodge of Massachusetts, feared a "soft peace." "Let us," cried ex-President Roosevelt, "dictate peace by the hammering guns and not chat about peace to the accompaniment of the clicking of typewriters." [6]

THE PARTISAN OCTOBER APPEAL

Wilson was much concerned about the forthcoming Congressional elections. Realizing that he faced a desperate fight with the Allies in securing a peace based on the Fourteen Points, he knew that his hand would be weakened by a setback at the polls. Accordingly, on October 25, 1918, he issued his famous appeal to the voters, beginning:

> If you have approved of my leadership and wish me to continue to be your unembarrassed spokesman in affairs at home and abroad, I earnestly beg that you will express yourselves unmistakably to that effect by returning a Democratic majority to both the Senate and the House of Representatives.[7]

During the war the popular slogan, sponsored by Wilson, had been: "Politics is adjourned." The Republicans in Congress had in fact supported parts of Wilson's war program more wholeheartedly than the Democrats. Now the Republican leaders cried out in anguish that Wilson had broken the truce. Actually, politics had not been "adjourned" during the war. Ex-president Roosevelt had for some time been waging a vigorous partisan campaign against Wilson, perhaps with the purpose of goading him into an indiscreet public declaration.[8] After a heated campaign, the voters tramped to the polls in November, 1918, and returned Republican majorities to both houses of Congress. But the victory was by no means of landslide proportions: the Republican control of the Senate rested on the paper-thin margin of two votes.

Post-mortems on the apparent repudiation of Wilson are all highly speculative. He might conceivably have lost even more support if he had not made the appeal. A reaction against the administration in the mid-term Congressional elections is normal, and it was to be expected in 1918, with the end of wartime sacrifices in sight. A number of Democratic leaders had urged Wilson to issue the appeal, and many Congressmen expressed delight at the assistance that it would presumably give them. Perhaps Wilson might better have asked for the election of Congressmen, both Democrats and Republicans, who would support him. If he had kept quiet and had won, he could have claimed a vote of con-

[6] D. F. Fleming, *The United States and the League of Nations, 1918–1920* (New York, 1932), pp. 30–31. See also H. R. Rudin, *Armistice, 1918* (New Haven, 1944).

[7] *New York Times*, Oct. 26, 1918, 1:6–7.

[8] President McKinley, a Republican, had made a less blunt appeal for Congressional support in 1898. It had not backfired, and Roosevelt had then publicly supported the President. On the election see Selig Adler, "The Congressional Election of 1918," *South Atlantic Quar.*, XXXVI (1937), 457–458; S. W. Livermore, "The Sectional Issue in the 1918 Congressional Elections," *Miss. Valley Hist. Rev.*, XXXV (1948), 29–60.

fidence. If he had kept quiet and had lost, he could have claimed that the result was of no particular significance. In any event, he had staked his prestige on the outcome, and on the basis of a legislative majority he was the only one of the leading statesmen at Paris not entitled to be there.

A HAND-PICKED PEACE COMMISSION

Wilson again startled the nation, on November 18, 1918, by announcing that he was going to Paris as a member of the American peace delegation. He evidently reasoned that only by appearing in person, and using his enormous prestige, could he secure the lasting peace on which he had set his heart.

A cry of protest arose from Wilson's critics, chiefly partisan Republicans. They insisted that no President had ever gone to Europe before, and that Wilson was needed at home to grapple with the pressing problems of domestic reconstruction. His going, moreover, was regarded as a manifestation of his "Messiah complex." Furthermore, he would be the only head of a delegation who had recently been "repudiated" by the electorate. Ex-President Roosevelt vehemently proclaimed that "Mr. Wilson has no authority whatever to speak for the American people at this time." [9] The argument also ran that the President could use his immense influence more effectively by acting through instructed representatives, as McKinley had done in 1898. In America, at one end of the cable, Wilson would be able to make his decisions unhurriedly, far removed from the personal pressure of Allied leaders, and closely in touch with American opinion and the headstrong Senate.

The Republicans received another rude shock on November 29, 1918, when the membership of the American Peace Commission was announced. In addition to Wilson, the group consisted of Secretary Lansing, Colonel House, General Tasker H. Bliss, and Henry White, an able career diplomat.

Republican foes of the administration were acutely unhappy. They complained bitterly that there was only one member of their party, Henry White, on the commission. And he was not an outstanding figure like Elihu Root or ex-President Taft, who branded the whole group "a cheap lot of skates." The Senators were offended on two counts. First, Wilson had not consulted them in advance; and second, he had not selected a single member from their ranks. The logical Republican was Lodge of Massachusetts, but he and Wilson hated each other. The Republicans, clearly the majority party, had helped fight the war; they now believed that they were entitled to better than 20-per-cent representation on the Peace Commission. The misfortune was that from Wilson's point of view

[9] *Kansas City Star*, Nov. 25, 1918, 1:2.

there were serious objections to taking along a prominent Republican, from either the Senate or private life. (McKinley had sent three Senators to Paris in 1898—one Democrat and two Republicans.)

Yet Wilson was bound to be the object of partisan attack, whatever he did. He was the only Democrat since Andrew Jackson to serve two consecutive terms, and he had pushed through Congress a sweeping program of domestic reform. These measures had trod on the toes of many big-business tycoons, who were preponderantly Republican and who were determined to turn back the clock to the good old days of conservatism. If the President were to dictate a liberal peace, his prestige would soar so high that he might run for a third term, or possibly hand-pick his successor. Wilson and his work had to be undone at all costs.

WILSON—THE NEW WORLD MESSIAH

Whatever the shortcomings of the American Peace Commission, it did not lack expert advice. Late in 1917, at the instance of Wilson, a group of specialists known as "The Inquiry" had assembled in New York City. Mostly college professors, they gathered and sifted a mountain of data—historical, economic, geographical, ethnographic—that might prove useful at the peace table.

Wilson sailed from New York on the *George Washington* in December, 1918, with a small army of experts from The Inquiry accompanying him. The great prophet arisen in the West—and apparently repudiated by his own people—was accorded a tumultuous, garlanded reception in France. *L'Europe Nouvelle* exclaimed, "Never has a king, never has an emperor received such a welcome." One woman wrote:

> Wilson, you have given back the father to his home, the ploughman to his field. . . . You have saved our fiancés; love blooms again. Wilson, you have saved our children. Through you evil is punished. Wilson! Wilson! Glory to you, who, like Jesus, have said: Peace on Earth and Good Will to Men! [10]

Delirious throngs turned out to cheer this American savior, who had helped hurl back the Germans and who seemed to promise an immediate millennium. Assuredly he would draw up a just peace—which, of course, meant grinding Germany down to the very dust.

While waiting for the Paris Conference to convene, Wilson journeyed to England, where he was warmly greeted. He next visited Italy, where the demonstration of blind devotion to "Voovro Veelson" was indescribable. One workingman declared:

> They say he thinks of us—the poor people; that he wants us all to have a fair chance; that he is going to do something when he gets here that will

[10] Quoted in G. B. Noble, *Policies and Opinions at Paris, 1919* (New York, 1935), p. 73.

make it impossible for our government to send us to war again. If he had only come sooner! I have already lost my two sons. Do you believe he is strong enough to stop all wars? [11]

The French and Italian leaders both made determined efforts to keep Wilson from the masses, lest his idealism weaken their imperialistic objectives. One Italian workingman is supposed to have remarked irreverently that if the Pope died Wilson might appoint a Protestant successor.

The Conference, which finally opened on January 12, 1919, got off on the wrong foot. The first of the Fourteen Points declared for "Open Covenants of peace, openly arrived at." Wilson did not mean that there was to be house-top diplomacy—that all the "birth pangs of the peace" were to be exposed to the public gaze. But he believed that the texts of treaties should be published so that the people would know in what way they had been bound. In short, secret diplomacy but open results.

American newspapers alone had sent more than a hundred of their ablest correspondents to report a blow-by-blow description of the Conference. But on the very first day the doors were locked in their faces, and a secretary finally came out and read a juiceless, five-line summary. The outcry of the newsmen was fearsome. Wilson fought valiantly for more publicity, for the United States was the one great nation whose aims could bear the full light of day. But the other powers did not want any more cats let out of the bag.

In the end, the scanty official statements were supplemented by "careful leakages," "grapevine" rumors, and other "drippings" from the Conference. One result was a most unfortunate atmosphere of suspicion and distrust. To add to the confusion, the French officials fed information to their press designed to poison the public against Wilson. The abuse became so savage that Wilson finally threatened to move the Conference to Geneva, whereupon the tone of the French newspapers miraculously changed.

THE "BIG FOUR" IN LABOR

The Conference had hardly got under way when the discovery was made that the hundreds of delegates from the twenty-seven Allied and Associated powers comprised too unwieldly a body for effective work. One British observer referred to the confusion as "that sense of riot in a parrot house." The Supreme Council or the Council of Ten was therefore assigned the task of grappling with the most important problems. It was composed of the two ranking delegates from each of the five big powers: Britain, France, Italy, Japan, and the United States. Its decisions, arrived at with the help of numerous experts, were reported from time to time to the plenary conference for final action.

[11] Norval Richardson, *My Diplomatic Education* (New York, 1929), pp. 182–183.

The Council of Ten, which in turn proved too cumbersome, was partially supplanted, in March, 1919, by the Council of Four or the "Big Four." Wilson, representing the richest and freshest of the powers, really occupied the driver's seat. The other members were Premier Vittorio Orlando of Italy, a genial and cultured gentleman; Prime Minister David Lloyd George of Great Britain, a magnetic, shifty, master politician; and Premier Georges Clemenceau of France, the seventy-eight-year-old "organizer of victory" known as "the Tiger." Grizzled, grey-gloved (to cover his eczema), fiery, cynical, he was a hard-bitten realist ever alert to the interests of France. Some of the time the group was the Council of Three, for Orlando was not infrequently absent. Three lone men in a room settling the fate of the world!

Speed was urgent, for Europe was exhausted and hungry. "The wolf," said Herbert Hoover, "is at the door of the world." The red cloud of Russian Bolshevism was spreading toward western Europe. Perhaps there would not even be a responsible government in Berlin when the time came to offer specific terms. A current saying in Paris was "Better a bad treaty to-day than a good treaty four months hence."

Despite the crying need of salvaging Europe first, the victors early turned to dividing the booty—the enemy's colonies. After a knock-down fight, and in conformity with Point V, Wilson successfuly resisted an outright partition. Instead, the powers were to become trustees of the conquered colonies under a mandate from the League of Nations. This half-loaf solution, which was a compromise between idealism and colonialism, generally turned out to be thinly disguised imperialism.

Wilson's overriding concern was the proposed League of Nations, which would insure a just and durable peace. But the Allied spokesmen, as well as many Republicans at home, insisted that the more pressing problem of a peace treaty be disposed of first, and that the League of Nations be fashioned later. Wilson vigorously objected, for he feared that if he did not get the League adopted at the outset, it would be shelved in the scramble for spoils. He was finally able to carry the day by the sheer weight of his prestige, by diplomatic skill, and by some old-fashioned log-rolling. In ignorance of the basic facts, he won the support of the Italians by promising them the Brenner frontier in the Tyrol with some 200,000 Germans—a disquieting violation of self-determination. At all events, the Conference voted, on January 25, 1919, to honor Wilson's wishes and make the League of Nations an integral part of the treaty.

Wilson himself was appointed chairman of the Commission to draft the Covenant of the League of Nations. Although European thinkers had long been at work on such an organization, he made the whole idea peculiarly his own. By laboring under intense pressure after hours, the Commission was able to patch together a draft in ten days. On February 14, 1919, Wilson triumphantly appeared before the entire Conference and read the completed League Covenant. "A living thing is born," he solemnly declared.[12]

By this time Wilson had been absent from home more than two months. He now found it necessary to return for the purpose of signing bills and explaining the League Covenant to the American people. Thus far he had done well. He had successfully resisted a snarling division of the booty, and he had committed the Conference to his capstone point, the League of Nations. His prestige, though waning, was still high. Perhaps the sequel would have been less tragic if he had remained in Washington, directing the subsequent negotiations by wire.

THE REPUBLICAN REVOLT IN THE SENATE

Before leaving Paris, Wilson sent a cablegram to the House and Senate committees concerned with foreign affairs, inviting them to dine with him at the White House and discuss the League of Nations. He also requested that Congress refrain from debating the subject until his arrival. But while he was on the high seas, the Senate opened fire. Senator Borah of Idaho assailed the League Covenant as "the greatest triumph for English diplomacy in three centuries of English diplomatic life," while Senator Reed of Missouri branded the League of Nations "a sort of international smelling committee."

The memorable gathering of the Senate and House committees took place on the evening of February 26, 1919. The President, who had agreed to answer questions regarding the League, was rigorously cross-examined. His friends thought that he appeared to good advantage; his critics thought otherwise. Republican Senator Brandegee of Connecticut remarked, "I feel as if I had been wandering with Alice in Wonderland and had tea with the Mad Hatter.[13]

On the last day of the Congress, March 4, 1919, the Senatorial foes of the League showed their teeth when Senator Lodge introduced the Republican Round Robin. It was signed by thirty-nine Senators or Senators-elect, more than the one-third plus one necessary to defeat the treaty. The most striking part of the ultimatum read:

> Resolved . . . That it is the sense of the Senate that while it is their sincere desire that the nations of the world should unite to promote peace and general disarmament, the constitution of the league of nations *in the form now proposed* to the peace conference should not be accepted by the United States. . . .[14]

The Round Robin then declared that the proposed league of nations should be considered only after peace had been made. Thus the Senate

[12] D. H. Miller, *The Drafting of the Covenant* (New York, 1928), II, 563.
[13] Fleming, *The United States and the League*, p. 134.
[14] *Cong. Record*, 65 Cong., 3 sess., p. 4974. Italics inserted.

served notice on the world, and particularly on the delegates at Paris, that it would approve no treaty embodying the League Covenant.

The Round Robin was greeted with warm praise by Republican foes of the President. "Woodrow Wilson's League of Nations died in the Senate tonight," rejoiced the *New York Sun.* George Harvey's *Harvey's*

THE CHILD WHO WANTED TO PLAY BY HIMSELF

PRESIDENT WILSON: "Now come along and enjoy yourself
with the other nice children. I promised that you'd be the
life and soul of the party."
London Punch, 1919

Weekly, which had been jeering at "the President's League of Nations Claptrap" and the "League of Denationalized Nations," cried "Honor and Praise" to Lodge, who had "fathered" the Round Robin, and to those who had co-operated in proclaiming it.

Smarting from these attacks, Wilson struck back before an enthusiastic audience in New York, on the evening of March 4, 1919. He defiantly revealed his strategy in an unfortunate combination of boast and threat:

> . . . When that treaty comes back, gentlemen on this side will find the covenant not only in it, but so many threads of the treaty tied to the covenant that you cannot dissect the covenant from the treaty without destroying the whole vital structure. The structure of peace will not be vital without the League of Nations, and no man is going to bring back a cadaver with him.[15]

Wilson did not think that the Senate would dare incur the odium of rejecting the entire treaty and breaking "the heart of the world."

THE FOURTEEN POINTS IN PERIL

The Round Robin stab in the back and the other attacks on Wilson were widely headlined in Europe. The foes of the President, thinking that he had been repudiated and that the League was now dead, took heart. When Wilson returned in mid-March, 1919, he was alarmed to discover that Secretary Lansing and Colonel House had, in his opinion, been too willing to make concessions during his absence. He halted the so-called movement to "sidetrack" the League, and dramatically declared that he would stand squarely on the decision to incorporate the League Covenant in the treaty. This whole disagreeable episode provides further ammunition for those who argue that only by being there in person could Wilson secure the kind of treaty that he envisioned.

The original draft of the League Covenant had been so hastily thrown together that it bristled with defects. Critics in America, many of them sincere and constructive, pointed to the desirability of amendment. They stressed the need of safeguarding the Monroe Doctrine, of exempting purely "domestic" issues like immigration and tariffs, and of providing a method for withdrawing from the League. Wilson finally succeeded in forcing the more reasonable of these demands into the Covenant; but in doing so he weakened his hand with his diplomatic adversaries, who insisted on equivalent concessions.

The chief battle was with France. The tough-minded Clemenceau remembered that the invader had been repelled by bayonets and bullets, not by flaming ideals. He was particularly skeptical of the Fourteen Points, which he apparently had never read. "God gave us his Ten Commandments," he said, "and we broke them. Wilson gave us his Fourteen Points—we shall see." [16]

Clemenceau's first demand was reparations for damages caused by the

[15] *New York Times,* March 5, 1919, 1:4.

[16] W. A. White, *Woodrow Wilson* (Boston, 1929), p. 384. "I can get on with you," said Clemenceau to House. "You are practical. I understand you, but talking to Wilson is something like talking to Jesus Christ!" *Lord Riddell's Intimate Diary of the Peace Conference and After, 1918–1923* (New York, 1934), p. 78.

Germanic invader. But to determine how much the fallen foe should and could pay would take too much time; hence the exact sum was left to the later decision of a Reparations Commission. This arrangement, in effect, was a blank check against Germany's economic resources.

When the Germans had laid down their arms in 1918, the understanding was clear that they would not be assessed war costs, only damages. But certain Allied leaders had promised their tax-burdened peoples to pluck huge sums from the German goose, and Wilson was finally persuaded to repudiate his public position and include Allied pensions. These virtually doubled the reparation bill, evoked anguished cries of betrayal from the Germans, and undermined the whole reparations program. When advised by one of his experts that the pension decision was illogical, Wilson shot back: "Logic? Logic? I don't give a damn for logic! I am going to include pensions."

PSEUDOSECURITY FOR FRANCE

Clemenceau's second demand was security against the horrors of 1914, when the German armies had thundered toward Paris. The French desired to occupy Germany to the Rhine River, or to create a buffer state there. But the placing of millions of Germans under the French flag would be a gross violation of self-determination. Wilson fought Clemenceau with all his soul, while the French press showered abuse upon the American idealist. Ray Stannard Baker found the President in the evenings "utterly beaten, worn out, his face quite haggard and one side of it and the eye twitching painfully; but the next morning he would appear refreshed and eager to go on with the fight." [17]

On April 3, 1919, at the peak of the crisis, Wilson was stricken with influenza. His temperature mounted to 103°, and he was seized with "violent paroxysms of coughing." Outside his bedroom, in the study, sat the other members of the Big Four. To their every demand the sick man replied, "No!" On April 7, his patience exhausted, he inquired when the liner *George Washington* could be made ready to take him back to the United States. Although one French spokesman sneered that the Americans "were going home to mother," this dramatic gesture may have played some part in breaking the deadlock.

The resulting compromise represented a balancing of interests. France was to occupy the Rhineland for fifteen years. The League of Nations would administer Germany's coal-rich Saar Valley for a like period, at the end of which the Saarlanders might by a plebicite determine their own fate. In return for these concessions by Clemenceau, Wilson and Lloyd George signed the Security Treaty of 1919, which promised France

[17] R. S. Baker, *Woodrow Wilson and World Settlement* (Garden City, N.Y., 1922), II, 43.

armed assistance in the event of another unprovoked attack by Germany. In one of the most fateful decisions of the post-war years, the United States Senate, true to its no-entangling tradition, never acted on the pact, and Britain was released from her obligation. France felt betrayed, for she now had neither the Rhineland nor security. If the three principal victors had kept this alliance intact, Adolf Hitler quite probably would not have unleashed the dogs of war twenty years later.

ITALY AND JAPAN SHOW THEIR HANDS

The next major crisis was precipitated by Italy. She had entered the war in 1915 on the side of the Allies, but only after being promised choice parts of the enemy's territory by the secret Treaty of London. She now put forth an additional demand for Fiume, the most valuable sea outlet of the newly created state of Yugoslavia. The city itself was inhabited predominately by Italians, but the Yugoslavs were far more numerous in the outskirts. On the basis of self-determination, Wilson sternly opposed the claim of Italy. When he found the Italian delegates unmoveable, he unwisely appealed over their heads to their own people, in April, 1919. The Italian leaders at the Conference left in a huff, their countrymen rallied enthusiastically behind them, and Wilson was denounced by the very masses that had shortly before idolized him. After the Paris Conference, Italy and Yugoslavia worked out a compromise on Fiume, with the result that Wilson won a belated but somewhat hollow victory for self-determination.

The politely bowing Japanese, who had been biding their time, now stepped forward to take full advantage of the Italian crisis. Having failed to secure a racial-equality declaration in the League Covenant, they were all the more determined to acquire Germany's economic rights in the Chinese province of Shantung, the birthplace of Confucius.[18] On the basis of treaties and actual armed conquest, they had a far better claim than Italy had to Fiume. Moreover, by a secret pact in 1917 Britain had agreed to support Japanese claims in Shantung and to Germany's Pacific islands north of the equator, in return for Japanese support of British claims to Germany's islands south of the equator.

Shantung contained some 30,000,000 Chinese, and Wilson feared a violation of self-determination if Japan were given so strong an economic foothold there. Yet if both the Japanese and the Italians bolted the Conference, it might collapse, and the precious League of Nations might die at birth. So Wilson wry-facedly swallowed a compromise by which the Japanese were to retain the economic holdings of Germany, and ultimately return the Shantung peninsula to China. (It was returned in 1923.) Japan also

[18] See R. H. Fifield, *Woodrow Wilson and the Far East: The Diplomacy of the Shantung Question* (New York, 1952).

received, under a League mandate, Germany's Pacific islands north of the equator—the Marshalls, Carolines, and Marianas—which later proved to be a thorn in America's flesh during World War II.

The concessions made to Japan at Paris smacked of expediency rather than justice, and proved highly damaging to Wilson's position as a champion of self-determination. The surrender of Shantung lent point to Clemenceau's alleged sneer that Wilson "talked like Jesus Christ but acted like Lloyd George." Back home the press teemed with such phrases as "Japan the possessor of stolen goods," "the crime of Shantung," "conspiracy to rob," "a damnable enterprise," and "the rape of Shantung."

THE VERDICT ON VERSAILLES

On May 7, 1919, the fourth anniversary of the *Lusitania* tragedy, the German delegates came to Versailles to receive the completed treaty. In one of the most dramatic moments in history, impressively staged by the French in the Trianon Palace, Clemenceau bitingly addressed the fallen foe:

> It is neither the time nor the place for superfluous words. . . . You have before you the accredited plenipotentiaries of all the small and great Powers united to fight together in the war that has been so cruelly imposed upon them. The time has come when we must settle our accounts. You have asked for peace. We are ready to give you peace.[19]

The Germans were then given an opportunity to study the bulky two-hundred-page treaty thus presented to them virtually on the point of a bayonet. They lodged furious but generally futile protests. In particular, they cried out against having been disarmed by a promise of the Fourteen Points, with two reservations, and then having this peace of vengeance rammed down their throats. But to no avail. Marshal Foch, at the head of the Allied armies, was ready to march. At the Hall of Mirrors, Versailles, the German delegates sullenly signed the treaty, on June 28, 1919.

The Treaty of Versailles proved to be one of the most abused and least perused treaties in history. Why was it not a better one? Why were so many of the Fourteen Points ignored, violated, or compromised away? Why did Wilson depart from Europe a fallen Messiah?

The basic answer is that Wilson shouldered an impossible task. Each nation had its own selfish aims, many of them guaranteed by the vexatious secret treaties, some of them mutually conflicting, and others sharply at variance with self-determination.

The first fruits of victory were the apples of discord. Wars usually unify allies in the face of the common enemy; the spoils of war tend to tear them apart. Clemenceau, who fought savagely for the aims of France, has been criticized for having been stubborn and selfish. But he was im-

[19] See Baker, *Wilson and World Settlement*, II, 501.

mediately responsible to the over-wrought French voters, and if he had not staunchly supported their interests, he would have been replaced by a man of sterner stuff. The same was true of all the other members of the Big Four, except Wilson, who enjoyed the security of a four-year term.

The United States, for its part, was unwilling to sacrifice any of its traditional policies or vital interests to insure a more satisfactory peace. It later refused, for example, to ratify the French Security Treaty, and it declined a bothersome mandate for Armenia. By failing to ratify the Treaty of Versailles, it accelerated a baleful chain of events involving disarmament, debts, and reparations.

Wilson's presence at Paris no doubt resulted in a "softer" settlement than otherwise would have been drafted. The victor may have peace or he may have vengeance but he cannot extract both from the same treaty. In general, there are two types of settlement: the victor's peace, which makes inevitable another war to undo it; and the peace of accommodation, which enables the vanquished to forgive and forget. The Treaty of Versailles fell between two stools. It was vengeful enough to arouse the Germans to burning anger, but it was not harsh enough to keep them safely enchained for more than one generation. Victory is not self-sustaining, and a dictated peace is no peace at all.

SECOND GUESSES

Too much haste went into the treaty. Wilson had favored a preliminary settlement to enable passions to cool, but his views did not prevail. There had to be a peace, and a speedy peace, or Europe might fall into complete chaos. With so many conflicting aims at Paris, there would have to be compromise or no agreement. So there was compromise—and some injustice.

Even so, there was much to be said for the treaty. Noteworthy was the liberation of millions of oppressed minorities, notably the Poles, in response to self-determination. Much more could be said for the treaty if the Allies had proceeded to carry out its terms in fairness and good faith, especially the pledge to reduce armaments. Lloyd George later argued that many of the ills blamed on the treaty were actually the fault of the men who executed it—or failed to execute it. The defection of the United States, whose influence would have been thrown on the side of moderation, caused the pact to become a different one—a harsher one— than the Germans signed. But given a Europe seething with war hatreds, perhaps the most remarkable feature of the Treaty of Versailles is that it was not more imperfect.

Wilson was deeply distressed by the outcome. A microscopic examination of the treaty reveals only about four of the Fourteen Points and subsequent principles—totaling twenty-three—completely intact. Wilson was compelled to compromise at every hand in order to save his precious League of Nations, which he was counting on to iron out the more serious injustices of the treaty. He was much like the mother who is forced to throw her younger children to the pursuing wolves in order to save her first-born son. Wilson was also hoping that America's participation with the ex-Allies would soften the terms of the pact. But only the future could tell whether the American people and the United States Senate would measure up to their new and unwanted responsibilities of world leadership.

SELECTED BIBLIOGRAPHY

The subject is treated from the American side in T. A. Bailey, *Woodrow Wilson and the Lost Peace* (New York, 1944). An able presentation of the whole picture is Paul Birdsall, *Versailles Twenty Years After* (New York, 1941). The most detailed work is R. S. Baker, *Woodrow Wilson and World Settlement* (3 vols., Garden City, N.Y., 1922).

Useful accounts by contemporaries are David Lloyd George, *Memoirs of the Peace Conference* (2 vols., New Haven, 1939); Robert Lansing, *The Peace Negotiations* (Boston, 1921); Edith B. Wilson, *My Memoir* (Indianapolis, 1939); E. M. House and Charles Seymour, *What Really Happened at Paris* (New York, 1921); C. H. Haskins and R. H. Lord, *Some Problems of the Peace Conference* (Cambridge, Mass., 1920); J. T. Shotwell, *At the Paris Peace Conference* (New York, 1937); Herbert Hoover, *America's First Crusade* (New York, 1942); Stephen Bonsal, *Unfinished Business* (Garden City, N.Y., 1944); Josephus Daniels, *The Wilson Era: Years of War and After, 1917–1921* (Chapel Hill, N.C., 1946).

Valuable secondary works are Allan Nevins, *Henry White* (New York, 1930); Frederick Palmer, *Bliss, Peacemaker* (New York, 1934); P. M. Burnett, *Reparation at the Paris Peace Conference from the Standpoint of the American Delegation* (2 vols., New York, 1940); René Albrecht-Carrié, *Italy at the Paris Peace Conference* (New York, 1938); L. L. Gerson, *Woodrow Wilson and the Re-Birth of Poland, 1914–1920* (New Haven, 1953); R. W. Curry, *Woodrow Wilson and Far Eastern Policy, 1913–1921* (New York, 1957); A. L. George and J. L. George, *Woodrow Wilson and Colonel House* (New York, 1956); A. S. Link, *Wilson the Diplomatist* (Baltimore, 1957).

Relevant articles are René Albrecht-Carrié, "Versailles Twenty Years After," *Pol. Sci. Quar.*, LV (1940), 1–24; R. H. Fifield, "Disposal of the Carolines, Marshalls, and Marianas at the Paris Peace Conference," *Amer. Hist. Rev.*, LI (1946), 472–479; Werner Levi, "American Attitudes toward Pacific Islands, 1914–1919," *Pacific Hist. Rev.*, XVII (1948), 55–64; J. L. Snell, "Wilson's Peace Program and German Socialism, January–March, 1918," *Miss. Valley Hist. Rev.*, XXXVIII (1951), 187–214.

See footnotes of this chapter; references at the end of the preceding and succeeding chapters; Bemis and Griffin, *Guide*, pp. 673–684; *Harvard Guide*, Ch. 27.

7TH, 8TH AND 9TH ED. REFS. See BIBLIOGRAPHICAL ADDENDUM, p. 1,024.

The Retreat to Isolationism
1919-1935

The League was defeated in the United States, not because it was a League of Nations, but because it was a Woodrow Wilson league, and because the great leader had fallen and there was no one who could wield his mighty sword.

T. W. GREGORY (WILSON'S ATTORNEY GENERAL), 1925

THE PARADE OF PREJUDICE

THE TREATY OF VERSAILLES, with the League firmly "riveted in" as Part I, faced a formidable array of critics in America. Partisan Republicans, smarting from six years of Democratic rule, had their knives sharpened for Wilson—that "drum-major of civilization." Most red-blooded Americans regarded the treaty as not harsh enough, while many liberals, like the editors of the *New York Nation* and the *New Republic*, regarded it as too harsh. They were especially aroused by the bartering away of the Fourteen Points and by the imposition of a victor's peace on Germany. "The treaty," said the *Springfield Republican,* "was dictated in a paroxysm of hate."

The "hyphenates" were also up in arms. A host of German-Americans condemned the treaty as a base betrayal of the Fatherland. The numerous Italian-Americans, tens of thousands of whom lived in Senator Lodge's Massachusetts, were embittered by Wilson's stand on Fiume. The Irish-Americans were indignant because the President had not antagonized Britain by pressing the cause of Irish independence at Paris. They were aroused by a League in which the component parts of the British Empire would have six votes to one for the United States. They were alarmed by Article X of the League Covenant, which seemed to guarantee the use of force to maintain the status quo and which, they felt, would hinder the attainment of Irish independence. Senator Hiram Johnson of California insisted that under Article X "The British Empire can demand American blood to subdue Ireland." The name of Wilson was repeatedly hissed by huge Irish-American crowds, who wildly cheered their own leaders. Two prominent Republicans approached the British ambassador in Washington and explained to him that, in using the Irish question to defeat Wilson and the League, they would assail England without mercy. But they wanted their British friends to know that all this was just politics.

ISOLATIONISM RESURGENT

Perhaps the most formidable opponents of the League were dead men: Washington, Jefferson, and Monroe. America was strong and self-sufficient, and her traditional policy of nonentanglement had served her well. Why should she become involved in a "League of Denationalized Nations," which might conceivably order American soldiers to Hejaz to protect King Hussein against the Bedouins? Why should the Stars and Stripes fly below the flag of some super-state? "One-hundred-per-cent Americanism," with editor William Randolph Hearst a leading trumpeter, became the slogan of the hour. The advertisement of an anti-League meeting in Boston read:

AMERICANS, AWAKE!

Shall We Bind Ourselves to the War Breeding Covenant?
It Impairs American Sovereignty!
Surrenders the Monroe Doctrine!
Flouts Washington's Warning!
Entangles us in European and Asiatic Intrigues!
Sends Our Boys to Fight Throughout the World by Order of a League!
"The evil thing with a holy name!" [1]

Everywhere one found a strong impulse to return to old isolationist ways. Wilson's inspiring leadership had keyed the American people up to a spirit of self-sacrifice that had even resulted in the prohibition of alcoholic beverages. But all this was changing. Victory had brought an emotional letdown—"the slump in idealism." It had also brought profound disillusionment with the imperialistic and bickering Allies. The war to make the world safe for democracy had not made the world safe for democracy, nor had it ended wars. Some twenty conflicts of varying dimensions were being waged in various parts of the world. About all that America had seemingly derived from the war was debt, inflation, prohibition, influenza, and ingratitude from Allies whom she had strained herself to help—while, of course, helping defeat the common enemy.

Disgust was deepening. Hundreds of thousands of American boys were returning from Europe, irritated by the gouging French shopkeepers and

[1] *Boston Herald,* July 8, 1919, 1:1–2.

most favorably impressed by the blonde German girls. Americans every-where were saying that Europe could jolly well "stew in its own juice." In the face of such widespread disillusionment, Wilson would have his troubles in arousing the people again—this time to a self-sacrificing ad-herence to the League. But the task was not an impossible one. Despite the noisy outcry of assorted critics, a strong majority of the people at first seem to have favored the Treaty of Versailles.

THE OPPOSITION FORMS IN THE SENATE

The momentous debate over the Treaty of Versailles centered in the Senate. The Senators, a majority of whom were Republicans, were in no mood to assist a Democratic President to a great personal triumph. Nor had Wilson shown much respect for what he called the "pigmy-minded" gentlemen on Capitol Hill. He had also assumed much legislative au-thority during the war, and Congress was now determined to reassert itself.

The leader of the Republican opposition in the Senate was the tall and aristocratically bewhiskered Henry Cabot Lodge, "ambassador from Massachusetts to the United States." A master parliamentarian and a skillful political leader, he was a man of considerable intellectual force, despite the quip that his mind was like the landscape of his native New England—"naturally barren, but highly cultivated." As the author of numerous books, he had been known as "the scholar in politics" prior to the advent of the scholarly Woodrow Wilson, and the two men came to hate each other intensely. Lodge had at first openly advocated *a* league of nations, but when Wilson began to champion such an organization, the Senator turned against it. His fight for a watered-down League of Na-tions strongly suggests that he was motivated largely by partisanship and hatred of the President.

When the Treaty of Versailles finally reached America, Lodge found the tide of opinion running so strongly for the League in Massachusetts that he despaired. "It's hopeless," he complained to Senator Borah of Idaho. "All the newspapers of my state are for it." [2] The best that he could hope for was "to Americanize" the treaty by adding a number of amend-ments or reservations, for which his party could take credit. The Re-publicans had enjoyed little opportunity to write the pact in Paris; now they could do some rewriting in Washington. Perhaps the stubborn Wilson would refuse to accept such a revised treaty, and in this even-tuality both he and his party could be saddled with the blame.

When the new Congress met in extraordinary session, in May, 1919, the Senate consisted of 49 Republicans and 47 Democrats. The Re-publicans were able to place a majority on the Senate Committee on

[2] See also C. O. Johnson, *Borah of Idaho* (New York, 1936), pp. 232, 233.

Foreign Relations, of which Lodge was chairman, and pack it with members unfriendly to the League. Control of this key committee was of great advantage to the foes of the treaty, for they could tie it up indefinitely until public opinion became confused and divided. Several years later Senator Moses of New Hampshire testified that if the rules of the Senate had permitted prompt action, "the Versailles treaty would have been ratified without reservations."

THE SENATE STALLS FOR TIME

The tide was still running strongly for the treaty when an unofficial version reached the Senate early in June, 1919. A clear majority of the American people seemingly favored ratification, with perhaps minor reservations. Thirty-two state legislatures had endorsed the League in concurrent resolutions, and two others conditionally. Thirty-three governors had gone on record as favoring a league of nations, while a *Literary Digest* poll of newspaper editors indicated the same trend. By May 1, 1919, Lodge himself admitted:

> . . . What I may call the vocal classes of the community, most of the clergymen, the preachers of sermons, a large element in the teaching force of the universities, a large proportion of the newspaper editors, and finally the men and women who were in the habit of writing and speaking for publication, although by no means thoroughly informed, were friendly to the League as it stood and were advocating it.[3]

But Lodge was by no means daunted. With time and money he might yet revamp the League. Time he had, because he could tie the treaty up in the committee. Money he secured by tapping the reserves of Henry Clay Frick and Andrew W. Mellon, two Republican millionaires who had been heavy beneficiaries of the pre-Wilson Republican tariff. The campaign of anti-League propaganda could now be launched with a full head of steam.

The printed treaty was laid before the Senate Committee on Foreign Relations in due season. There Senator Lodge read aloud the entire document of 264 quarto pages—a process that consumed two precious weeks. This totally unnecessary exhibition can be explained only on the ground that the Republicans wanted time to organize their opposition and wait for public opinion to weary of the League debate.

Even more time-consuming were the hearings before the Senate Committee on Foreign Relations. These ate up an additional six weeks. Though ostensibly held for the information of the Senate, the hearings were obviously designed in part to embarrass Wilson. The Committee summoned some sixty witnesses, whose remarks filled over 1200 pages of printed material. Some of those who testified, including Secretary Lan-

[3] H. C. Lodge, *The Senate and the League of Nations* (New York, 1925), p. 147.

sing, were able to throw real light on the treaty. Less defensible was the respectful hearing given to representatives of racial minorities. Self-appointed spokesmen appeared on behalf of the disappointed aspirations of a score of different groups, ranging from Ireland to Korea. The Senators solemnly listened to arguments for the breaking up of the British Empire, as if such a subject related to the Treaty of Versailles. The height of absurdity was reached when a woman with an Irish name argued the claim of Italy to Yugoslavia's Fiume.

Not content with these dilatory proceedings, Lodge arranged for a public conference between his committee and Wilson at the White House, on August 19, 1919. The President answered questions for some three hours, but he apparently did not succeed in changing the views of the Senators. In commenting on the affair afterward, he remarked "that Senator [later President] Harding had a disturbingly dull mind, and that it seemed impossible to get any explanation to lodge in it." [4]

WILSON TAKES THE LEAGUE TO THE COUNTRY

By early September, 1919, the treaty had plainly lost ground. It was bogged down in committee nearly two months after it had been presented, while the Senate hearings were stirring up an incalculable amount of rancor. Lodge and his colleagues were attacking the League with vigor on the floor of the Senate. The danger was great that the pact would be mutilated or even defeated unless heroic measures were taken.

In a desperate gamble, Wilson decided upon a barnstorming tour of the country. During the war, and even earlier, he had enjoyed considerable success in appealing over the heads of stubborn Congressmen to the sovereign people. He was convinced that if he could take his case to the masses, an aroused public opinion would force the Senate to act speedily and favorably.

The fighting President, now sixty-three years of age, undertook this strenuous journey against the advice of physicians and friends. Never robust, he was now weak, trembling, exhausted. Six years as Chief Executive, with the inferno of a World War and the madhouse of a Peace Conference thrown in, had taken a heavy toll. The Republican opposition at home, to say nothing of oppressive domestic problems and the heat of Washington, had further sapped his strength. Now he was insisting on a whirlwind campaign that would have taxed the endurance of Theodore Roosevelt in his prime. Wilson knew that he was taking a grave risk, but he was willing to sacrifice his life—as he had asked American soldiers to sacrifice theirs—in the cause of world peace.

Wilson left Washington on September 3, 1919. After speaking in Ohio

[4] D. F. Houston, *Eight Years with Wilson's Cabinet* (Garden City, N.Y., 1926), II, 17.

and Indiana, he passed on to the trans-Mississippi Middle West, where there was a strong German-American element. His receptions here, though enthusiastic, were not all that his friends might have desired. Wilson, of course, was not at his best. Already weary, he did not have time to prepare his speeches with customary care. He made some obvious errors of fact, and so far lost his customary dignity as to brand his adversaries as "contemptible quitters if they do not see the game through," and to challenge them to "put up or shut up." He was also under the handicap of placing the best possible interpretation on what he knew was an imperfect treaty. But when he reached Montana and Idaho, the demonstrations of enthusiasm were well-nigh unbelievable. The states of Washington, Oregon, and California warmed the President's heart. The West had re-elected him in 1916, and it was still with him.

The foes of Wilson were now thoroughly alarmed by his tumultuous receptions. Several of the Senators, notably the "irreconcilables" Borah of Idaho and Johnson of California, kept up the battle by "trailing" the President. They undertook to speak in some of the same cities a day or so later in opposition to the treaty. These orators, whose rabble-rousing talents were noteworthy, attracted enthusiastic, hat-throwing crowds. When Wilson's name was mentioned on one occasion, cries came back, "Impeach him, impeach him!"

THE CRIPPLED LEADER

Wilson's ovations reached a climax in Pueblo, Colorado, on September 25, 1919. The *Rocky Mountain News* reported that when he appeared "the entire audience arose and cheered for fully ten minutes." With tears in his eyes, the President pleaded for his League of Nations to end war, while the crowd roared its approval "time and time again." But this was the end of the trail for Wilson. Although he had planned to carry the fight into Lodge's New England—"the enemy's country"—his frail body, exhausted nervously and physically, refused to go on. The remaining speeches were cancelled, and he was whisked back to Washington, where several days later a stroke paralyzed one side of his body.

For weeks the President lay helpless, a shell of his former self, and as much a victim of the war, said his Attorney General, as the unknown soldier buried at Arlington. For seven-and-one-half months he did not meet his Cabinet. No outsiders were permitted to see him while he was most seriously ill. His coolness toward Colonel House and Secretary Lansing, both of whom had not seen eye to eye with him at Paris, developed into an open break. He failed to answer House's letters; he later dismissed Lansing from the Cabinet.

Who ran the government during this period is still something of a mystery, although Mrs. Wilson sorted out the official papers and allowed a few of the most important ones to be brought to her husband's attention. Passers-by noted the bars on the White House windows, put there years earlier for protection against the ball-playing Roosevelt children, and whispered about the "insane man" inside. But the President's mind apparently remained clear, and gradually some of his strength returned. The Republicans in the Senate arranged to have a "smelling" committee visit him to determine whether or not he was mentally sound. Senator Fall entered the sick chamber and remarked piously, "Well, Mr. President, we have all been praying for you." "Which way, Senator?" shot back the invalid.[5]

At the time Wilson was stricken, the League seems to have been gaining momentum. But the President's illness left public opinion confused and drifting, while depriving the Democrats in the Senate of their only effective leader. As the event proved, Wilson would have been well-advised to remain in the White House, conserving his strength and conciliating, so far as possible, the Senate opposition. A great deal of compromise had already gone into the treaty, and a little more might have saved it.

WILSON SPURNS THE LODGE RESERVATIONS

Two weeks before the President's collapse at Pueblo, the Senate Committee on Foreign Relations acted. The report of the Republican majority —a bitterly partisan document—proposed forty-five amendments and four reservations. After prolonged debate, the amendments were all rejected, primarily for the reason that the Paris Conference would have to be reconvened to make them valid.

The Senate next appended, by an almost solid Republican vote, fourteen so-called "Lodge reservations." These were all added by a simple majority vote, even though the entire pact would have to be approved by a two-thirds majority. Most of the reservations were irrelevant, inconsequential, or unnecessary. Some of them merely reaffirmed principles and policies, including the Monroe Doctrine and control of immigration and tariffs, already guaranteed by the Treaty of Versailles or by the Constitution of the United States.

The peculiar composition of the Senate, with its 49 Republicans and 47 Democrats, facilitated the passage of the Lodge reservations. The Republican group consisted of about twenty "strong reservationists," like Lodge; about a dozen "mild reservationists," like future Secretary of State Kellogg; and some sixteen "irreconcilables," like Borah of Idaho and Johnson of California. The "irreconcilables," fearing that the treaty would be approved anyhow, voted to add the reservations, and then voted against the reserved treaty. The "mild reservationists" might have been

[5] Edith B. Wilson, *My Memoir* (Indianapolis, 1939), p. 289.

persuaded to oppose the "strong" Lodge reservations and to support "mild" Democratic reservations. But Wilson did not defer sufficiently to them, and they were driven into the arms of Lodge.

Wilson repeatedly expressed a willingness to accept mild reservations, and had in fact worked out a list with the Democratic leaders that differed only slightly from that of Lodge. But he balked at any weakening of Article X, the "heart of the Covenant," which bound the United States to "preserve as against external aggression the territorial integrity and existing political independence" of the League members. Wilson feared, although the fear now seems exaggerated, that if he should consent to the Senate reservations, the Republicans would tack on others that he could not possibly accept. He declared emphatically that the Lodge reservations "emasculated" the entire treaty, even though ten of them applied to the League, and four rather harmlessly to the rest of the pact. He further believed that the Senate would eventually be forced into line, because "the alternative of going back to Germany to negotiate a new treaty is too absurd."

Though too feeble to lead, Wilson was still strong enough to obstruct. At the critical moment he wrote a letter to his Democratic following in the Senate:

> . . . In my opinion . . . [the Lodge resolution] does not provide for ratification but, rather, for the nullification of the treaty. I sincerely hope that the friends and supporters of the treaty will vote against the Lodge resolution of ratification.
>
> I understand that the door will probably then be open for a genuine resolution of ratification.
>
> I trust that all true friends of the treaty will refuse to support the Lodge resolution.[6]

The crucial vote came the next day, November 19, 1919. The treaty, with the fourteen Lodge reservations attached, was defeated by a vote of 39 yeas to 55 nays. The yeas consisted of thirty-five "reservationist" Republicans, plus four Democrats. The nays consisted of thirteen "irreconcilable" Republicans, together with the overwhelming majority of the Democrats, forty-two altogether, who loyally honored their fallen leader's request. A second-chance vote later the same day showed only a slight shift, 41 yeas to 51 nays, while an attempt of the Democrats to secure approval without any reservations lost, 38 yeas to 53 nays.

Thus the Democratic Senators voted down the treaty with reservations —the only form in which it could have been approved. As a consequence, the Republicans charged, with considerable force, that Wilson himself kept the United States out of the League of Nations. Isolationists jeeringly rewrote the 1916 slogan to read, "He Kept Us Out of Peace."

Jubilation reigned in many Republican quarters. Senator Borah ac-

[6] *Cong. Record,* 66 Cong., 1 sess., p. 8768. Letter dated Nov. 18, 1919.

claimed the result as "the greatest victory since Appomattox." The defeat of the treaty was, said the Republican *Cleveland News,* a "twin-victory of independence and democracy." On the other hand, critics of the Republican opposition regretted the "low political intrigue" and partisan obstruction of the Senate. One friend of the League bemoaned "the greatest tragedy since the crucifixion of the Saviour of Mankind."

FUMBLING THE SECOND CHANCE

But the treaty was not yet dead. About four-fifths of the Senate professed to favor it in some form, and a shocked public would not permit its quiet burial simply because the Senators could not agree on a few reservations. Senator Lodge was approached by representatives of twenty-six great national organizations, whose combined membership totaled 20,000,000 voters, and they urged immediate approval of the treaty. There can be little doubt that public sentiment in the country strongly favored approval of the treaty, though probably with some safeguarding reservations.

Under the lash of popular pressure, the Senate undertook to reconsider its rejection. Behind the scenes, Lodge entered into negotiations with the Democrats in an effort to work out a compromise on his reservations. But Senator Borah and other Republicans got wind of Lodge's "treachery," haled him dramatically before them, and threatened to depose him as majority leader and disrupt the party if he did not stand firm. Lodge hoisted the white flag, and the treaty came to a final vote on March 19, 1920. There were fifteen reservations this time, for a completely irrelevant declaration had been added in favor of Irish independence. As before, Wilson wrote a stern letter to the rudderless Democrats in the Senate, urging that the treaty with the hated Lodge reservations be rejected. He insisted:

> Either we should enter the league fearlessly, accepting the responsibility and not fearing the rôle of leadership which we now enjoy, contributing our efforts towards establishing a just and permanent peace, or we should retire as gracefully as possible from the great concert of powers by which the world was saved.[7]

The treaty failed to receive the necessary two-thirds majority by a vote of 49 yeas to 35 nays. The nays consisted of twelve "irreconcilable" Republicans (the "Battalion of Death"), plus twenty-three Democrats who remained stubbornly loyal. In view of the obvious fact that the plain alternatives were a treaty with reservations or no treaty at all, twenty-one realistic Democrats forsook their leader and voted for approval. If only seven of the faithful twenty-three had shifted their votes, the decision

[7] *Cong. Record,* 66 Cong., 2 sess., p. 4052 (March 8, 1920, Wilson's letter).

would have been reversed. The outcome cannot be blamed entirely on the two-thirds rule, for Wilson almost certainly would have pigeonholed a treaty with the Lodge reservations attached, as he had threatened. He asked for his way or nothing—and got nothing.

WHO KILLED THE TREATY?

Apologists for Wilson have frequently stated that even if he had accepted the Lodge reservations, the Allies would not have. But a financially prostrate Europe needed the co-operation of the United States so urgently that some kind of accommodation almost certainly could have been worked out.[8] Wilson simply did not give the Allies a chance to refuse or accept; he shouldered that grave responsibility himself.

Various elements combined to bring about the frustrating defeat of the treaty in America. Among them were public ignorance of the pact, confusion of thought, postwar disillusionment, jealousy of Senatorial prerogative, the Lodge-Wilson feud, and devotion to the isolationist tradition. Strangely enough, Washington, Jefferson, and Monroe could not keep America out of a war to end war, but they could keep her out of a League designed to end war. Wilson had mistakenly assumed that the American people would cast aside generations of tradition, and cheerfully shoulder the burdensome new responsibilities of world leadership.

In the final analysis, sectionalism and partisan politics caused the deadlock. Reservations broke the back of the treaty. The Lodge reservations were added by an almost solid Republican vote, and opposed by an almost solid Democratic vote. Wilson's most loyal followers came from the South, where men were still voting the way their fathers had shot in the Civil War.

The President's physical collapse, moreover, accentuated an ingrained stubbornness. Wilson might have perceived the wisdom of compromise if he had not been ill, and had not been secluded from the shifting currents of public opinion in a darkened sick room. But he was permitted to see only a few people, and these were loath to shock him into a relapse by presenting disagreeable truths. So Wilson, imperfectly informed, demanded a rejection of the Lodge-reserved treaty, and called for a "great and solemn referendum" in behalf of an unreserved treaty in the forthcoming Presidential election. Senator Ashurst of Arizona, a fellow Democrat, bitterly declared:

[8] The first set of Lodge reservations, rejected at Wilson's insistence on November 19, 1919, provided for approval by three of the four principal Allies: Britain, France, Italy, and Japan. France almost certainly would have adhered, and Britain and Italy probably. The revised Lodge reservations imposed much more difficult conditions, including acquiescence by *all* of the Allied and Associated Powers. See T. A. Bailey, *Woodrow Wilson and the Great Betrayal* (New York, 1945), pp. 240 ff.

As a friend of the President, as one who has loyally followed him, I solemnly declare to him this morning: If you want to kill your own child because the Senate straightens out its crooked limbs, you must take the responsibility and accept the verdict of history.[9]

HARDING: HIGH PRIEST OF NORMALCY

Following the second rejection of the treaty, in March, 1920, America was still technically at war with Germany and Austria-Hungary, nearly a year-and-a-half after the Armistice. The resulting uncertainty was disturbing to trade and other relationships. Congress therefore passed a joint resolution, in May, 1920, formally declaring hostilities at an end. But Wilson sternly vetoed what he regarded as a cowardly evasion of responsibilities, and confidently looked forward to an endorsement of the treaty in the approaching Presidential election.[10]

The Republican national convention, meeting in Chicago, had difficulty in framing an acceptable platform. Within the same party were "irreconcilables," "reservationists" of all stripes, and ardent advocates of the League. The platform that finally emerged was a masterpiece of double talk. It was so cleverly worded as to enable all shades of Republicans to support the party in the expectation that their views would prevail.

Deadlocked over a nominee, the convention finally compromised on the handsome but weak-willed Senator Harding of Ohio. A "regular" Republican, he could be easily managed by the Senate bosses. He had also been a supporter of the "strong" Lodge reservations, and had commended himself to the party leaders by a ringing declaration that the country needed "not heroics but healing; not nostrums but normalcy; not revolution but restoration. . . ."

Normalcy was what the voters wanted. Suffering from prolonged "moral overstrain," they were weary of being asked to exert themselves in behalf of noble ideals. Unlike the coldly reserved Wilson, Harding was warm-handed and effusive—"folksy." He was admittedly an intellectual lightweight—Wilson had sneered at his "bungalow mind"—but as one Republican Senator shortsightedly remarked, the times did not demand "first raters."

Meeting in breeze-swept San Francisco, the Democrats endorsed the League, although not opposing "mild" reservations. Their nominee for the Presidency, Governor Cox of Ohio, declared himself four-square for the League Covenant, as did his Vice-Presidential running mate, the vibrant, thirty-eight-year-old Franklin Delano Roosevelt.

[9] *Cong. Record,* 66 Cong., 2 sess., p. 4164.
[10] See W. M. Bagby, "Woodrow Wilson, a Third Term, and the Solemn Referendum," *Amer. Hist. Rev.,* LX (1955), 567–575, for the most recent scholarship on Wilson's angling for a third nomination.

THE SOLEMN MUDDLEMENT OF 1920

The ensuing campaign was a listless affair. By this time the voters were weary of the threadbare issue of the treaty, now nearly two years old. The Socialist *New York Call* declared that politically the League was "as vital as a dead cat in a gutter." The confused Harding wobbled all over his spacious platform, but his most consistent theme was that after the election he would consult with the "best minds" to work out "an association of nations for the promotion of international peace." In short, a Republican "Association" but not a Democratic "League."

The confusion thickened when 31 leaders—mostly Republicans and including Root, Hughes, and Hoover—signed a manifesto.[11] They announced that they were supporting Harding as the surest way of getting the country into the League. The Republican "irreconcilables," on the other hand, supported him as the surest way of keeping the country out. But such inconsistencies did not bother the voters unduly: "Back to Normalcy" was the winning slogan.

The result was a foregone conclusion. On the eve of the balloting the Wall Street odds were ten-to-one against Cox. Millions of eligible but apathetic voters stayed away from the polls. The rest rose up and swept Harding into office by an awesome vote of 16,152,200 to 9,147,353—a plurality of more than 7,000,000. "It was not a landslide," lamented Wilson's private secretary, "it was an earthquake."

Was Harding's triumph a popular repudiation of the League, as the "irreconcilables" gloatingly proclaimed? There were in fact dozens of issues in the campaign, and the result could hardly have been a mandate on any one of them. If the American people had been permitted to vote directly on the leading issue, they probably would have returned a majority in favor of the League of Nations with reservations. If the results were a mandate for anything, they were a mandate to relax—to get away from Wilsonian self-sacrifice and return to "normalcy." The crippled Wilson, not the dynamic Cox, had been running in the election.

As the sequel proved, Wilson actually condemned the League to death in America by injecting it into the campaign. He had asked for a mandate, and seemingly had secured an unfavorable one—by the prodigious plurality of 7,000,000 votes. Henceforth the professional politicians—a weak-kneed breed—shunned the League as they would have shunned a leper. Many of the defeated Democrats protested that there had been no true mandate, and that there ought to be one in the next election. But no politician will consent to rerun a race that he has already won, and the Republican leaders were content to stand pat.

[11] P. C. Jessup, *Elihu Root* (New York, 1938), II, 414.

ADVANTAGES WITHOUT OBLIGATIONS

Making peace with the enemy was the most pressing unfinished business piled on the doorstep of Harding's administration. Congress had gone to war in 1917 by passing a joint resolution; it got out by passing another. On July 2, 1921, it formally declared that hostilities had ceased, and reserved to the United States all the rights and privileges accruing to the victorious powers under the treaty settlements. In this inglorious manner, the nation claimed benefits without shouldering responsibilities.

In August, 1921, nearly three years after the Armistice, Washington signed separate treaties with Germany, Austria, and Hungary. Inasmuch as these pacts likewise reserved all benefits, the Senate gave its prompt approval. Thus the United States made peace with Europe—a one-sided peace of advantages without obligations.

What of co-operation with the League of Nations? The question was especially embarrassing because the thirty-one prominent Republicans had promised in 1920 that the election of Harding would be the surest guarantee of America's entry. Two of the "illustrious thirty-one"—Secretary of State Hughes and Secretary of Commerce Hoover—now sat in the new Cabinet. Secretary Hughes made an earnest effort to redeem these promises, but the violent outcry of the "irreconcilables" in the Senate forced him to retreat.[12] Their attitude was summarized by a statement attributed to Ambassador Harvey in London that the United States was "damned well out of the European mess."

The newly born League of Nations, orphaned by the United States, was cold-shouldered by its foster parent. Washington at first even refused to support the League's world health program. Letter after letter from the League Secretariat at Geneva to the State Department lay unanswered, partly through inadvertence, and evidently without the knowledge of Secretary Hughes. Not until September, 1921, did the Department, responding to a popular outcry, reply noncommittally to the fourteen unanswered communications.

President Harding, awed by his plurality of 7,000,000 votes, turned increasingly against the League. In his first message to Congress he announced that America would have nothing to do with it; in one of his last speeches he insisted that the issue was "as dead as slavery." Yet the League was too important to be ignored completely. American "unofficial observers" hung around its seat at Geneva, much like detectives shadowing a criminal. Thus was the proud American republic reduced to the practice of "keyhole diplomacy."

What of Harding's "Association of Nations," which had figured so prominently in the recent campaign? It was conveniently shelved, while

[12] See M. J. Pusey, *Charles Evans Hughes* (New York, 1951), II, 432.

the American people turned to the abnormal postwar problems of "normalcy." Like Mexico, Ecuador, Hejaz, and a few other nations that did not embrace the League, the United States was content to mind its own business. But the trouble was, remarked the *Hackensack* (New Jersey) *Evening Record* "that Uncle Sam must go to Europe to mind his own business." [13]

DEADLY DRIFTING IN THE TWENTIES

America's spurning of the League proved to be tragically shortsighted. After winning a costly war, the nation blindly kicked the fruits of victory under the peace table. Whether or not a potent international organization, with the United States carrying its end of the log, would have averted World War II will always be a subject for dispute. But there can

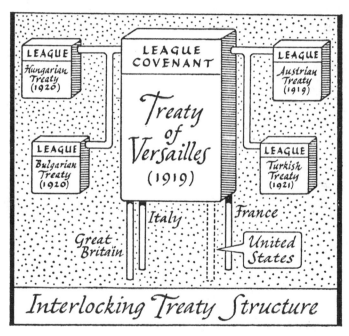

Interlocking Treaty Structure

be no doubt that the League was crippled at the start by the refusal of the mightiest power in the world to join it. The ex-Allies themselves were largely responsible for the coming of the Hitlerian conflagration in 1939, but they found convenient justification for their own spinelessness by blaming America for her lone-wolf course.

Responsibility for the ultimate collapse of the Treaty of Versailles can thus be laid, in some measure at least, at the doorstep of the United States. This complicated pact, tied in with the other peace settlements through

[13] *Literary Digest,* Jan. 13, 1923, p. 15.

the League Covenant, was a top-heavy structure that rested on a four-legged table. The fourth leg—the United States—was never put into place, and consequently the whole rickety edifice teetered for more than a decade before collapsing in ruins. The Europeans did not like this treaty structure, and would have devised a different one, possibly a more lasting one, if left to themselves. But, impoverished as they were, they accepted an unsatisfactory solution in order to humor their rich American uncle, as personified by President Wilson. And when the rich uncle rejected the lopsided monstrosity that he had helped design, they felt doubly betrayed.

THE GAP IN THE BRIDGE

A British view.
London Punch, 1919

Some critics have charged that America's most costly long-run mistake was not getting into the war but getting out of the peace. "Every time Europe looks across the Atlantic to see the American eagle," wrote the English novelist H. G. Wells, "it observes only the rear end of an ostrich." The United States, though the last great power to get into the war, was the first great power to pull out of the peace settlement. If the Big Three —America, Britain, and France—had remained united against Germany, the probabilities are that an Adolf Hitler would never have kicked over the apple cart in 1939. The defection of the United States promoted disunity between Britain and France, while facilitating the spectacular rise of the German dictator. The French, rendered insecure by the desertion of the United States, embarked upon a unilateral quest for security which in turn helped provoke Germany into rearmament and war.

The Reparations Commission provides a striking example. The understanding at Paris had been that America would be represented on this body and exercise an important moderating influence on it. But when the Senate rejected the treaty, France secured the upper hand and arranged for a crushing reparations bill to be presented to Germany. The resulting economic dislocations were fuel for the propaganda machine of Adolf Hitler in his meteoric ascent to power.

The United States, as the tragic sequel proved, hurt its own cause by a policy of negation. It wanted world peace, but was unwilling to pay for world peace. Even though the conduct of the Allies had been disillusioning, the republic had its own ends to serve by assuming its new war-born responsibilities. Instead of drifting aimlessly at the mercy of events, it might better have tried to control events in such a way as to avert another world catastrophe.

BACKDOOR CO-OPERATION AND THE WORLD COURT

A child must creep before it can walk, and the infant League of Nations got off to a wobbly start in 1920. The isolationist Republicans sneered at its successes and jeered at its failures. "About all the League of Nations has done so far," remarked the *Toledo Blade* with exaggeration late in 1922, "is to wish that the United States belonged." America of the prosperous 1920's revealed an almost incredible indifference to the fate of Europe. "A change of Ministers in France," asserted the *Los Angeles Times* in 1927, "is of less importance to the residents of Los Angeles than a change of grade on an important thoroughfare." [14]

President Harding, who was keenly aware of the anti-League temper of the country, continued to shun all official connection with the League of Nations. But, surprisingly enough, he did go so far as to urge, with appropriate reservations, American adherence to the World Court—the autonomous judicial arm of the League. Unlike The Hague Court of 1901, which provided panels of judges for special tribunals, the World Court was a permanent body for the settlement of international disputes. Its creation owed something to the example of the United States Supreme Court, and much to the inspiration and leadership of American legalists. Even without the official sanction of Washington, distinguished jurists like Elihu Root served on the tribunal.

Public agitation for membership on the World Court continued to mount in the days of Harding's successor, cautious Calvin Coolidge. The latter, like his predecessor, was anti-League but pro-Court. By the sum-

[14] Quoted in *Time*, IX, 28 (Feb. 14, 1927).

mer of 1924 popular pressures had so far built up that the platforms of both major political parties included declarations in favor of joining the League tribunal. In March, 1925, the House of Representatives, by an overwhelming vote of 303 to 28, passed a similar resolution.

But the Senate was not to be stampeded by public clamor. The thinning group of "irreconcilables"—Borah of Idaho and Johnson of California were still present—rallied to prevent what they regarded as a backdoor entrance into the League. The foes of adherence, arousing anew the emotions of the League fight, branded the World Court a "League Court," packed with "foreigners" hostile to the United States. Hearst's isolationist *New York American* cried: "Let America once get into this League Court House with its trap-doors and its panel walls and its false ceilings and its collapsible stairways and its packed bench, and she will find that she is involved, and she can not get out!" [15]

After a bitter debate, the Senate approved adherence to the World Court, in January, 1926, by a vote of 76 to 17. But acceptance was loaded down with five reservations, which were designed to safeguard what isolationists assumed to be America's interests. The fifth reservation, which proved to be the most troublesome, provided that the Court should never entertain a request for an advisory opinion on a dispute affecting the United States, without the consent of the United States. The members of the World Court were able to swallow all reservations, except the fifth, and during the ensuing nine years from 1926 to 1935 they made various attempts to work out an acceptable compromise with Washington.

The United States meanwhile had begun to take increasing notice of the League of Nations. At first unofficial American "observers" sat with the League committees in a "consultative" or "advisory" capacity to discuss purely nonpolitical problems, such as health regulations and white-slavery control. In 1924 American delegates were officially named to represent the United States at the Second Opium Conference of the League. Although they walked out of the sessions after a stormy debate, the ice was broken. By 1930 the United States had taken part in more than forty League conferences, all presumably nonpolitical and dealing with subjects like the suppression of obscene publications. By 1931 Washington had five permanent officials stationed at Geneva, all authorized to represent American interests before the League. Consultation, yes; commitment, no. And in 1934 the United States officially joined the International Labor Organization, which had been set up under the Versailles Treaty.

The anti-League Republican regimes from Harding to Hoover revealed a curious inconsistency. Although paying lip service to an isolationist course, they moved steadily toward a position of active if furtive co-

---

[15] Quoted in *Literary Digest*, Sept. 5, 1925, p. 11. For the full story see D. F. Fleming, *The United States and the World Court* (Garden City, N.Y., 1945).

operation with the League. The "irreconcilables" charged, with no little truth, that the United States was becoming a member of the League in all but name. Or, as the *Ohio State Journal* put it: "Our foreign policy seems to be that we won't belong to anything but are perfectly willing to butt in."

ESCAPING THE WORLD COURT "TRAP"

President Herbert Hoover, who took office in 1929, carried on the isolationist tradition of the Harding-Coolidge Republican dynasty. As a fabulously successful mining engineer in many foreign lands,[16] and as the head of gigantic relief projects in Europe both during and after World War I, he might have been expected to be an ardent international-ist in the Hay-McKinley-Roosevelt Republican tradition. But his experi-ences abroad had been such as to deepen a desire to shun foreign in-volvements. In keeping with Republican dogma, he announced in his inaugural address, March, 1929, that the United States would not join the League of Nations. He nevertheless continued the policies of Hard-ing and Coolidge, and co-operated increasingly with the League in dis-armament and numerous other nonpolitical activities.

President Hoover, like his three predecessors, strongly urged American adherence to the World Court. The issue had been in abeyance during the four years since 1926, when the members of the Court had balked at the Senate reservation regarding advisory opinions. Ex-Secretary of State Elihu Root, an eminent legalist, had finally devised a formula for reconciling existing differences. When President Hoover re-submitted the issue to the Senate in December, 1930, all signs indicated that American public opinion was favorable to the World Court. But the Hearst press, aided by other newspapers, cried that the tribunal was a "tool of the League of Nations"—a "den of international robbers." The rise of the dictators Mussolini and Hitler, to say nothing of Japan's current aggres-sions in China, seemed to underscore the wisdom of having fewer deal-ings with foreigners, rather than more. The die-hard "irreconcilable" Senators mustered impressive strength, and the showdown was postponed for five more years, when the Democratic Franklin D. Roosevelt was President.

Early in 1935 the clamor of public opinion, especially that of the better-educated groups ("best people"), became so irresistible that the stub-born Senate was forced to move. Preliminary estimates indicated that there were enough votes to secure adherence to the World Court, al-

[16] Hoover and his family were besieged in Tientsin, China, during the Boxer dis-orders of 1900. He later told how the beleaguered Americans rejoiced when they heard the band of the rescuing force playing "the precious strains of 'There'll Be a Hot Time in the Old Town To-night.'" W. S. Myers, ed., *The State Papers and other Public Writings of Herbert Hoover* (New York, 1934), I, 269.

though by a narrow margin. But at the eleventh hour the anti-Court forces rallied all their reserves. Father Coughlin, an influential "radio priest," burned the air waves with his denunciations, while editor Hearst urged his readers to telegraph their Senators in protest against the "League of Nations trap." A yellow snowstorm of telegrams, estimated at 200,000 and representing more than a million citizens, descended upon the Senate. Senator ("Kingfish") Huey Long, the Louisiana demagogue, shouted that adherence would mean cancellation of the Allied war debt to America, while the blind (physically) Senator Schall of Minnesota cried, "To hell with Europe and the rest of those nations!"

The final vote in the Senate, taken on January 29, 1935, was 52 yeas to 36 nays, seven short of the necessary two-thirds. The Court's friends were too timid; its foes too belligerent. "Thank God!" exclaimed the aging Senator Borah, while his "irreconcilable" colleague Senator Johnson declared, "This is one of the happiest days of my life. The Senate has averted a serious danger to our beloved republic." Henceforth the World Court issue was dead—as far as the United States was concerned.

SELECTED BIBLIOGRAPHY

A detailed analysis appears in T. A. Bailey, *Woodrow Wilson and the Great Betrayal* (New York, 1945), now incorporated in T. A. Bailey, *Wilson and the Peacemakers* (New York, 1947). An older and less critical account is D. F. Fleming, *The United States and the League of Nations, 1918–1920* (New York, 1932). The most recent scholarship on Lodge is J. A. Garraty, *Henry Cabot Lodge* (New York, 1953), in which the Senator appears to better advantage than in his own embittered *The Senate and the League of Nations* (New York, 1925). See also W. S. Holt, *Treaties Defeated by the Senate* (Baltimore, 1933) and R. J. Bartlett, *The League to Enforce Peace* (Chapel Hill, N.C., 1944). On the later history of the League and World Court consult D. F. Fleming, *The United States and World Organization 1920–1933* (New York, 1938). See also R. W. Logan, *The Senate and the Versailles Mandate System* (Washington, 1945); J. M. Cox, *Journey Through My Years* (New York, 1946); L. A. R. Yates, *The United States and French Security, 1917–1921* (New York, 1957); Selig Adler, "The War-Guilt Question and American Disillusionment, 1918–1928," *Jour. of Mod. Hist.*, XXIII (1951), 1–28. On the role of the Irish see C. C. Tansill, *America and the Fight for Irish Freedom* (New York, 1957). Brief but suggestive is A. S. Link, *Wilson the Diplomatist* (Baltimore, 1957).

See footnotes of this chapter; the references for the previous chapter; Bemis and Griffin, *Guide*, pp. 673–684; *Harvard Guide*, Ch. 27.

7TH, 8TH, AND 9TH ED. REFS. See BIBLIOGRAPHICAL ADDENDUM, p. 1,027.

CHAPTER

~~~~~~~~~~~~~~~~ *42* ~~~~~~~~~~~~~~~~

The Far East and Disarmament, 1917-1938

The problems of the Pacific are to my mind the world problems of the next fifty years or more.
GENERAL JAN SMUTS, 1921

RED BOLSHEVIKS AND BLACK GOLD

THE HARDING ADMINISTRATION, which took office in 1921, surprised many observers by not tossing all of Wilson's foreign policies into the ash can. The League, to be sure, was cold-shouldered. But in other important theaters the Republican regime carried forward Democratic policies under the vigorous leadership of Secretary Hughes. As will be noted later, the attempt of the Mexican government to confiscate American oil properties, under a retroactive interpretation of the Constitution of 1917, had brought a pained outcry from investors. The expiring Wilson administration took a firm stand against such practices, and the incoming Harding administration followed its lead with Secretary Hughes actively in command. The latter, who had narrowly failed to defeat Wilson for the Presidency in 1916, was generally and properly regarded as one of the "best minds" in Republican ranks.

The American people had developed a deepening distaste for the anti-capitalistic excesses of the Bolshevist regime in Moscow.[1] An hysterical "red scare" swept the country in 1919, with editors denouncing the bloody-handed Russian revolutionists as "assassins and madmen" and "beasts drunk from a saturnalia of crime." In the summer of 1920 Wilson's last Secretary of State, Bainbridge Colby, sternly refused to recognize a Russian regime that had subverted popular government. The masterful Secretary Hughes, in 1921 and again in 1923, likewise declined to extend recognition to a ruthless clique that had confiscated American property without recompense, repudiated lawful debts, and abused the

---

[1] See G. F. Kennan, *Russia Leaves the War* (Princeton, 1956).

hospitality of friendly nations by sending agents abroad to foment Communist revolution. This rigid and frigid policy of nonrecognition was not reversed until 1933, when the Democrats under Franklin D. Roosevelt returned to power.

Elsewhere oil, ordinarily a lubricant, was causing serious friction in Anglo-American relations. During World War I, the United States had dipped heavily into its own reserves of petroleum to float the Allies to victory. Modern navies had recently been converted from coal-burners to oil-burners, and the sea-dominant British agreed with Clemenceau that oil was "as necessary as blood in the battles of to-morrow." With a calculating eye to the future, British promoters had staked out their claims to the gigantic oil pool of the Middle East by securing a mandate from the League of Nations to Palestine and Mesopotamia. By 1919 British oil companies, which accounted for less than 5 per cent of the world's production, had cornered more than half of the world's known reserves. "Evidently John Bull aspires to be monarch of oil he surveys," wryly remarked one Virginia newspaper.

The United States, having contributed magnificently to the common Allied victory, could not take British monopolistic tactics lying down. The outgoing Wilson administration had insisted that America should not be without a voice in the parceling out of the spoils and the oils. Secretary Hughes vigorously upheld this view. At long last success crowned Washington's efforts when, in 1928, five American companies were admitted to an important Middle East petroleum combine.[2]

JAPAN'S PECULIAR INTERESTS IN CHINA

Relations with the Japanese, no less than with the British, suffered from the war. Early in the conflict Japan had joined the Allies on a limited basis, in response to her own imperialistic ambitions and the tug of the Anglo-Japanese alliance. Nipponese forces speedily seized the German islands of the North Pacific—the Marshalls, the Carolines, and the Marianas—and overran Germany's holdings in the Shantung province of China. Then, taking advantage of the death grapple of the European powers, Tokyo presented to Peking, in January, 1915, her notorious Twenty-one Demands. These encroached so sharply on Chinese sovereignty—particularly in Shantung, South Manchuria, and Eastern Inner Mongolia—as to arouse fears that Japan was determined to bang shut the Open Door. The Japanese attempted to keep their terms secret, but the Chinese cleverly contrived to let them leak out.

A storm of protest swept America, and the Japanese, their greed exposed, shamefacedly withdrew some of the more objectionable Demands.

[2] J. A. DeNovo, "The Movement for an Aggressive American Oil Policy Abroad, 1918–1920," *Amer. Hist. Rev.*, LXI (1956), 854–876.

Secretary Bryan, though conceding that "territorial contiguity creates special relations between Japan and these districts," insisted that the United States would not recognize any impairment of American rights in China, or of the political and territorial integrity of China, or of the Open Door.[3] Thus Bryan foreshadowed the doctrine of nonrecognition later promulgated by Hoover and Stimson, and used in a vain attempt to keep the Japanese out of China's Manchuria.

In the summer of 1917, some five months after America had entered the European war, Viscount Ishii, a distinguished Japanese diplomat, arrived in the United States to hammer out an understanding. His tactful speeches helped prepare the public mind for the ensuing negotiations with Secretary Lansing. Ishii tried to persuade the United States to recognize the "paramount interests" of Japan in China; Lansing sought to have Japan reaffirm the Open Door and the integrity of China. With neither side willing to yield ground, the negotiators found refuge in ambiguous language. The final exchange of notes, in November, 1917, recognized that "territorial propinquity creates special relations between countries," and that consequently Japan had "special [not paramount] interests in China. . . ." After the two diplomats had thus undermined the Open Door, they added a ringing reaffirmation of it.[4]

Secretary Lansing was severely criticized in America for his seeming surrender. In reply he asserted that by "special interests" in China he meant Japanese *economic* interests. But Tokyo, which regarded the agreement as something of a diplomatic victory, did not interpret "special interests" so narrowly. Actually, the Japanese gave up more than appeared on the surface. By a secret protocol attached to the Lansing-Ishii agreement the two governments agreed not to take "advantage of the present [wartime] conditions to seek special rights or privileges in China which would abridge the rights of the subjects or citizens of other friendly states."[5] Tokyo presumably objected to putting this secret understanding in the published notes for fear that such a concession would provoke an embarrassing uproar at home. At all events, the Lansing-Ishii published agreement, which indicated that Japan had gained more than she really had, deepened anti-Japanese prejudice in the United States.

America's recognition of Japan's "special interests" in China may have been the price paid for keeping Japan in the war. In his first conversation with Lansing, Ishii delicately remarked that Germany thrice had sought to persuade Japan to forsake the Allies. The hint was probably not lost on the American Secretary of State, who realized that America was in the midst of a desperate war with Germany, and in no position to alienate a nation possessing the strength of Japan.

[3] *Foreign Relations, 1915*, pp. 105–11.
[4] *Ibid., 1917*, p. 264.
[5] *Ibid., 1922*, II, 595.

AMERICA—THWARTER OF JAPAN'S ASPIRATIONS

Ugly developments at the Paris peace table in 1919 further increased tension between Japan and the United States.

The Japanese, who resented American discriminations against their emigrants, fought tenaciously for the inclusion of a statement favoring racial equality in the Covenant of the League of Nations. Wilson favored this proposal, but London frowned upon it. Fearing its effect on their millions of restless subjects in India and elsewhere, British spokesmen threatened to stir up the yellow press in America against such a concession. Wilson thereupon used his influence to defeat racial equality when the final vote was taken. The more violent Japanese journals attacked him viciously as a "hypocrite" and a "transformed Kaiser."

Then came the Shantung controversy. The purposeful Japanese, having lost out on race equality, forced Wilson to compromise on Chinese self-determination. The Hearst newspapers berated "wily, tricky, fight-thirsty Japan," while the conservative *Boston Transcript* decried this "insolent and Hun-like spoliation." Tempers were further inflamed when, during these same months, the Japanese showed their distaste for self-determination by ruthlessly crushing a revolt in Korea.

The ill-starred Allied intervention in Siberia further embroiled Japanese-American relations. Following the Bolshevik coup late in 1917, the Allies had been anxious to rally the Russians against Germany and her allies, and to prevent the Bolsheviks from permitting huge quantities of munitions to fall into German hands. Two Allied expeditions landed in North Russia in 1918, with the United States at Archangel contributing some 5000 men and suffering about 500 casualties.[6] But by far the most important intervention was in eastern Siberia, where an additional reason for interference was the rescue of an anti-Bolshevik force of Czechoslovaks, numbering some 50,000 men, then fighting its way eastward across Siberia in 1918.

The Japanese sent some 72,000 soldiers to Siberia; the Americans, 9000; the British and French, minor contingents. No binding agreement had been made in advance as to the relative size of forces, but the disproportionate strength of the Japanese aroused deep misgivings in the United States. President Wilson, who acted in the Russian interventions without Congressional sanction, consented to participation with the utmost reluctance. His primary purposes were to rescue the Czechs, to promote self-government by stable anti-Bolshevik groups, and to

[6] See L. I. Strakhovsky's two books: *The Origins of American Intervention in North Russia, 1918* (Princeton, 1937), and *Intervention at Archangel* (Princeton, 1944).

restrain Japanese imperialists from seizing territory in Siberia and North Manchuria, to the detriment of the Open Door.[7]

The muddled Siberian venture turned out badly. The Bolsheviks, reacting angrily against foreign interventions, took a considerable toll of American lives. The Japanese commander, who resented American chaperonage, was in constant hot water with General Graves, the head of the United States forces. When the last American contingent finally sailed from Siberia in 1920, leaving the field to Nippon, a Japanese band broke out with Stephen Foster's "Hard Times, Come Again No More." This evacuation was the signal for a renewed outburst in the Hearst press against alleged Nipponese treachery.

Wilson's increasing distrust of Japanese ambitions in eastern Asia was revealed in yet another way. Seeking to loosen Japan's growing economic foothold in China, he undertook, in November, 1917, to create a new four-power bankers' consortium. Critics were quick to remember that he had abruptly pulled the rug from under the old six-power consortium in 1913. The reluctant Wall Street financiers, after first receiving assurances of support from Washington, finally agreed to co-operate with Britain, France, and Japan. The Japanese, who were sorely displeased by the ill-disguised attempt of Wilson to thwart them, consented to join only after obtaining recognition of their "special position" in China's South Manchuria. The new consortium was formally signed on October 15, 1920.

THE SPECTER OF WAR WITH JAPAN

To add fuel to the flames, a disagreeable controversy flared up with Japan over the former German Pacific islet of Yap. As a key cable center, this tiny outpost was of importance to the United States in maintaining communications with China and other points in the Far East. At the Paris Peace Conference, Wilson had insisted that Yap be internationalized, and evidently believed that his views had prevailed. But Yap, together with Germany's other Pacific islands north of the equator, was awarded to Japan as a League of Nations mandate. Washington subsequently made vigorous representations to Tokyo in support of its claims. Many Americans, amused by the name of the island and its microscopic dimen-

[7] See Betty M. Unterberger, *America's Siberian Expedition, 1918–1920* (Durham, N.C., 1956), for well-balanced scholarship. See also J. A. White, *The Siberian Intervention* (Princeton, 1950); Pauline Tompkins, *American-Russian Relations in the Far East* (New York, 1949); C. A. Manning, *The Siberian Fiasco* (New York, 1952). In 1933 the Soviets abandoned their Siberian damage claims against the United States when Secretary Hull showed them documents proving that Washington was trying to preserve Russia's territorial integrity against Japan. *The Memoirs of Cordell Hull* (New York, 1948), I, 299.

sions, refused to take the dispute seriously. Under the title "Yap for Yappers," one humorist wrote a parody on a popular war song:

> Give us Yap! Give us Yap!
> The Yanks have put it,
> The Yanks have put it,
> The Yanks have put it,
> On the Map! [8]

But neither Washington nor Tokyo joked about Yap.

Far more alarming was the gigantic naval race in which Japan and America, as well as Britain, found themselves involved at the close of the war. Each had embarked upon ambitious programs and each was loath to stop while the others continued to build. Against whom was America constructing her enormous navy? Europe was prostrate; Britain was exhausted. Although die-hard Anglophobes were distrustful of England, the American public had generally settled on Japan as the rival to watch— and the Japanese knew it. War talk seethed on both sides of the Pacific. In Japan, student mass meetings were arguing methods of fighting the United States; in America, the "inevitable" war in the Pacific was being widely discussed. Alarmist books were pouring off the press, including Frederick McCormick's *The Menace of Japan* and Walter Pitkin's *Must We Fight Japan?*

Looming ominously in the background was the bugbear of the Anglo-Japanese Alliance. It had originally been aimed at Germany and Russia, both of whom had emerged prostrate from World War I. Big-navy zealots in America were insisting that the Alliance was now directed solely at the United States, and that in certain contingencies America would have to fight both Britain and Japan in the Far East. In December, 1920, London revealed that it would not consider the Alliance binding in the event of a war between America and Japan, but the Hearst press and other anti-Japanese spokesmen refused to trust this announcement. The Canadians also brought strong pressure to bear on Downing Street to modify or terminate the Anglo-Japanese Alliance; they did not want to get caught in the middle of a possible Anglo-American war. [9]

CALLING THE WASHINGTON CONFERENCE

The Republicans, who had blocked adherence to the League of Nations on Wilson's terms, suffered from guilty consciences when they viewed the ominous naval race. The League was designed to reduce armaments, yet its efforts were being crippled by the nonmembership of the most

[8] *New York Nation*, CIX, 328 (Sept. 6, 1919).
[9] J. B. Brebner, "Canada, the Anglo-Japanese Alliance and the Washington Conference," *Pol. Sci. Quar.*, L (1935), 45. See also C. N. Spinks, "The Termination of the Anglo-Japanese Alliance," *Pacific Hist. Rev.*, VI (1937), 321–340.

powerful nation in the world. A clear moral obligation rested on the new Harding administration to do something effective.

In December, 1920, the month after Harding's election, Senator Borah introduced a resolution in the Senate designed to bring about a tripower disarmament conference. Harding, who resented Borah's initiative, secretly tried to squelch the move. But both press and public enthusiastically sprang to its support. Chambers of commerce and mass meetings passed resolutions of endorsement. A monster petition was drawn up in St. Louis, and a great dial was erected in a public square. The hand moved forward with every thousand signatures; with every ten thousand a special courier left for Washington. Before such a tidal wave of sentiment the Borah proposal was approved by mid-1921, unanimously in the Senate and with only four dissenting votes in the House.

Secretary Hughes next sent informal inquiries as to the desirability of a Washington conference on arms limitation to London, Paris, Rome, and Tokyo. In line with British suggestions, he later broadened this invitation of July 8, 1921, to embrace not only arms but problems of the Pacific and the Far East. Four smaller powers were thus included: Belgium, China, Portugal, and the Netherlands. Hughes did not want to be put in the unfortunate position of being a "front" for Downing Street, and Britain was content to let the United States lead. She was reluctant to stir up the Irish and other Anglophobe elements in America, and unwilling to offend Japan by appearing too eager to junk the Alliance.

Japan was the only one of the powers to delay its response to Hughes' initial inquiry. Although supporting arms limitation, many Japanese strongly favored a continuance of the Alliance with Britain, and they feared that a multipower review of their recent grabs in the Far East might result in reverses. Japanese newspapers naturally surmised that a plot was on foot to trick Japan out of something.

DISARMAMENT ON THE POTOMAC

After Tokyo had carefully qualified its delayed acceptance, Secretary Hughes issued formal invitations to the eight select powers, on August 11, 1921. Each of the invitees sent distinguished statesmen to Washington. President Harding, unlike Wilson in 1918, gave the Senate ample representation on the American delegation. Indicative of the shifting balance of power was the fact that this conference—the most important of its kind yet to assemble—should be meeting in a capital of the New World.

When the delegates first assembled in beautiful Memorial Continental Hall, on November 12, 1921, the dynamic Secretary Hughes bowled them over. In an astonishingly candid speech he declared that the way to disarm was to disarm, and that the time to begin was at once—not in the distant future. He thereupon proposed a ten-year holiday in the construction of capital ships—that is, battleships and battle cruisers.[10] In addition, he would scrap other warships built and building, so that the navies of the three great naval powers—America, Britain, and Japan—would ultimately be left in the ratio of 5-5-3 in all categories. "Thus," he declared, "the number of capital ships to be scrapped by the United States, if this plan is accepted, is 30, with an aggregate tonnage (including that of ships in construction, if completed) of 845,740 tons." [11]

Hardly pausing for breath, Hughes proceeded to tell the British and Japanese delegates in a tomblike silence just what they should scrap— 19 and 17 capital ships respectively. In less than fifteen minutes, he destroyed 66 ships with a total tonnage of 1,878,043—more, as one British reporter put it, "than all the admirals of the world have sunk in a cycle of centuries."

The impact was tremendous. Congressmen, Senators, Supreme Court justices, and others broke into frenzied applause like that of a political convention. Tears streamed down the cheeks of ex-Secretary Bryan. The millennium was seemingly being ushered in. Newspapers ran banner headlines, as enthusiasm throughout the nation mounted to a fever pitch. Sermons and prayers in countless churches hailed Hughes as the savior of civilization. The president of the American Civic Association caught the spirit when he proposed that the antiquated cannon encumbering the public parks be taken to the dump yards.

Was Hughes' supercandid diplomacy a mistake? No major power could object if the United States sank its own navy. But to destroy the proud ships of other people was going dangerously far. Colonel Repington, a British reporter, recorded:

> It is an audacious and astonishing scheme, and took us off our feet. The few men to whom I spoke babbled incoherently. What will they say in London? To see a British First Lord of the Admiralty, and another late First Lord, sitting at a table with the American Secretary of State telling them how many ships they might keep and how many they should scrap, struck me as a delightfully fantastic idea.[12]

Secretary Hughes' audacious stroke, on the other hand, may have gained more than it lost. It started the conference in high gear and with tremendous momentum. It saved weeks of preliminary palaver and jockeying. It combined idealism with what was perhaps the only practicable formula for success. It captured the imagination not only of the United States but also of the other nations. One European dispatch declared that Hughes had become "a hero to all Europe's rank and file." Finally, his

[10] As defined at Washington, a capital ship was a warship, not an aircraft carrier, exceeding 10,000 tons or carrying guns in excess of 8 inches in caliber.

[11] *Conference on Limitation of Armament, Washington, November 12, 1921– February 6, 1922* (Washington, 1922), p. 62.

[12] Mark Sullivan, *The Great Adventure at Washington* (Garden City, N.Y., 1922), p. 27.

sensational proposal, which contrasted glaringly with the customary secrecy, helped mobilize world opinion behind the Conference and contribute to its success.

THE 5-5-3 RATIO IN CAPITAL SHIPS

The three great powers called upon to junk ships were faced with
different problems. The United States had *potentially* the most powerful
navy. Having also the longest purse, it could continue the armament race
to a point that would bankrupt war-burdened Britain and overpopulated
Japan. But the trump card of *potential* dominance was not so strong as it
appeared. In the first place, the British and the Japanese might be forced
to pool their navies in the face of a too-powerful United States. In the
second place, Senators Lodge and Underwood bluntly informed Hughes
that Congress, ever-conscious of the taxpayer, would not vote additional
burdens in order to attain the costly and unnecessary honor of ruling
the waves. "The thought of a national debt second to none," remarked
one Connecticut newspaper, "isn't quite so thrilling as the thought of a
navy second to none."

Britain, once undisputed mistress of the seas, was situated differently.
She still boasted the largest navy, but with the powerful German fleet
sunk, supremacy was less important than it had been. Her finances had
been so badly strained by the war that her taxpayers would welcome a
holiday in building. Secretary Hughes had reason to believe that the
British would agree to his 5-5-3 ratio, for in March, 1920, London had
revealed that it would be content to accept parity with the next greatest
naval power.[13]

The Japanese were far less tractable, for Secretary Hughes was asking
them to accept the small end of a 5-5-3 ratio. Ever sensitive to slights,
they insisted that the proportions proposed fell short of their defense requirements. Giant mass meetings in Japan, as well as impassioned newspaper editorials, supported demands for greater tonnage. The ratio of
10-10-7 would have been far more acceptable.

After protracted discussions, Tokyo consented to the Hughes ratio,
with a minor modification, on December 15, 1921. The alternative to concession was a ruinous naval race. But Japan insisted upon important safeguards. America agreed not to fortify further her Pacific islands (except
Hawaii), particularly the Philippines, Guam, Wake, and the Aleutians.
Without adequate bases on these outposts, the United States, even with
the 5-3 ratio, could not expect to attack Japan successfully in her home
waters. The British also agreed not to erect further fortifications on important island outposts, including Hong Kong.

[13] R. L. Buell, *The Washington Conference* (New York, 1922), p. 142. See also Y.
Ichihashi, *The Washington Conference and After* (Stanford University, Calif., 1928).

As far as naval limitation was concerned, the nonfortification agreement was the crucial compromise. Japan accepted a smaller naval ratio, but obtained greater security. Britain and America consented to leave certain of their insular possessions inadequately protected, but retained greater tonnage in capital ships.

THE FRENCH SECURITY PSYCHOSIS

France and Italy, the only other major naval powers, were not expected to throw a monkey wrench into the proceedings at Washington. The assumption was that they would both keep roughly what they had, thus leaving the over-all ratio at 5-5-3-1.7-1.7.

But at this point shell-shocked France threatened to wreck the conference. Fearing that a new German generation would follow in its fathers' goosesteps, the French quite logically insisted that security must precede disarmament. Resenting the failure of the United States Senate to honor Wilson's promises of assistance against future German aggression, they had embarked upon a lone-wolf course. They would seek security through Central European military alliances and their own army, which, despite accusations of imperialism, they made perhaps the most powerful in the world. They realized that the Washington Conference hoped to bring about arms limitation on land as well as on sea, and they perceived that their insistence on keeping their army would block progress in this direction. They were therefore carrying something of a chip on their shoulders. One Dallas newspaper later remarked, "France is for submarine limitation on land and cavalry limitation on sea."

French touchiness caused a good deal of unpleasantness at Washington. Before the war France had been a first-rank naval power. But in holding back the German hordes she had been forced to concentrate on her army, while her navy fell behind. She saw no reason why she should be penalized for defeating the German invader by having to accept a position of permanent naval inferiority, particularly since America and Britain had "welshed" on the Security Treaty of 1919. Finally, France deeply resented the implication that she was "decadent" and no longer counted.[14]

The French inferiority complex—and probably a horse-trading instinct as well—resulted in an astonishing demand for 350,000 tons of capital ships, or about twice as much as France was entitled to on the basis of existing strength. The essence of the Hughes plan was ratios based on craft built and building. If defense needs had been made the yardstick,

---

[14] When the French refused to sign the treaties unless the word "French" was placed before "English" in the clause stating that both texts were authentic, the ordinarily unruffled Root lost his temper and cried, "To hell with them! Let the whole business go to pot—I wouldn't care." Hughes conceded the point in the interests of harmony. P. C. Jessup, *Elihu Root* (New York, 1930), II, 465.

as the French proposed, the conference almost certainly would have broken up in fruitless wrangling.

The unexpected demands of the French alarmed the delegates, and in particular angered the British and the Americans. Through a "calculated indiscretion," the British permitted these extravagant claims to leak out and arouse a storm of criticism all over the world. A cartoon in the *New York World* showed France trying on a German spiked helmet. The Conference teetered on the brink of failure.

The crisis was not surmounted until Secretary Hughes had cabled a personal appeal to Premier Briand in Paris, and until the pressure of world opinion had converged on France. The French reluctantly consented to accept the inferior 1.7 ratio. But ominously they would permit no limitation on the numbers of cruisers, destroyers, or submarines. France regarded these smaller craft—the poor nation's navy—as necessary for protecting vital communications with her colonies and also for safeguarding her shores.

The Five-Power Naval Treaty of Washington, signed February 6, 1922, was to remain effective until 1936, when any one of the signatories might give a two-year notice of termination. There was to be a ten-year holiday in the building of new capital ships. After the scheduled scrapping of battleships and battle cruisers built or building, the capital ship strength of the five leading naval powers would be scaled down to 5-5-3-1.7-1.7. The aircraft carriers, with two exceptions, were not to exceed 27,000 tons or carry guns in excess of 8 inches. An upper limit of 35,000 tons and 16-inch guns was applied to battleships. There was no limitation whatever—and this was the fatal loophole—on submarines, destroyers, and cruisers, except that cruisers were not to exceed 10,000 tons or carry guns with a caliber larger than 8 inches.

THE FOUR-POWER PACIFIC PACT

The skeleton at the feast of the Conference was the Anglo-Japanese Alliance. As long as it existed, no satisfying naval ratio could be worked out. Many nervous Americans believed that in certain contingencies the naval strength of both Britain and Japan might be massed against the United States in the ratio of 8-5. But if the Alliance should be abrogated, the navies of Britain and America could theoretically "gang up" on Japan in the ratio of 10-3.

After prolonged discussion, the problem of finding a substitute for the Alliance was solved by the Four-Power Treaty, signed on December 13, 1921. Presented with poetical embroidery to the assembled Conference by Senator Lodge, it provided that Britain, America, Japan, and France agreed to respect one another's rights in the Pacific, and to refer future disputes in that area to a joint conference. The new pact further stipulated that if the rights of the four signatories were threatened by another power, they "shall communicate with one another fully and frankly in order to arrive at an understanding as to the most efficient measures to be taken, jointly or separately, to meet the exigencies of the particular situation." [15] This article was purposely left vague, but the clear implication was co-operative armed effort. The Four-Power Treaty was indeed a strange document for Senator Lodge, foe of foreign entanglements, to be sponsor-ing. One Senator sarcastically hailed him as "the father of a baby League of Nations."

Most significant of all, the Four-Power pact specifically terminated the Anglo-Japanese Alliance. It was the device by which the British could gracefully, though rather obviously, withdraw from their embarrassing commitments. The Japanese, quite naturally, were distressed by the somewhat abrupt severance of their tie with Britain. "We have discarded whiskey and accepted water," lamented one Japanese diplomat.

But the substitute had much to commend it. The four great powers bound themselves to respect one another's insular possessions and dominions in the Pacific. Although substituting a four-power agreement to talk for a two-power agreement to fight, the pact was in effect an en-largement of the old Anglo-Japanese Alliance. France, with a consequent boost to her wounded ego, was now included, as was the United States. In thus consenting to the treaty, America paid a cheap price for a termina-tion of the Anglo-Japanese Alliance and a guarantee, however illusory, of the Philippine Islands.

REHINGING THE OPEN DOOR IN CHINA

Despite all the fanfare about disarmament, any agreement at Washing-ton that ignored the explosive tensions in the Far East would be com-pletely unrealistic. Some of the Senators were threatening to attack the treaties unless the Conference lent a helping hand to China, especially in regard to Shantung. The issue confronting the revolution-torn Chinese was not so much disarmament as dismemberment, for their role thus far in relation to the Open Door had been largely that of the mat.

Under the driving leadership of Secretary Hughes, the weary delegates concentrated their attention on China—"the Sick Man of the Far East." The most important fruit of these labors was the Nine-Power Treaty of February 6, 1922. The signatories solemnly bound themselves to respect the "sovereignty, the independence, and the territorial and administrative integrity of China." They further pledged themselves to uphold "the principles of the Open Door" and to assist China in forming a stable government.

The United States seized the initiative in engineering the Nine-Power

[15] *Foreign Relations, 1922*, I, 35.

pact, although the British had proposed its outlines. Having surrendered her naval superiority, Britain was seeking an additional safeguard for her Far Eastern holdings. But the self-denying pledge embodied in the proposed Nine-Power Treaty was offensive to the Japanese, who, as one Pittsburgh newspaper remarked, found that the Open Door gave them "cold feet." Tokyo finally consented to sign only after both Britain and the United States had applied strong pressure.

LOOKS LIKE A DIFFICULT CASE

A divided China needs help at Washington Conference.
Brown in the *Chicago Daily News*, 1921

The Nine-Power Treaty proved to be the only formal and specific affirmation of the Open Door ever agreed to by the major powers, except Russia and Germany. John Hay's original notes had received only partial, evasive, or tacit acceptance. America's traditional policy in the Far East was now given, to all outward appearances, a broad, nine-power base—as strong a foundation as paper and ink could provide. The American delegation expressed the belief (or hope?) that the "Open Door in China has at last been made a fact."

But the Nine-Power pact was toothless. It was purely a self-denying pledge. The signatories did not bind themselves to defend the Open Door by force; in fact, the American public would not have sanctioned force. The effectiveness of the pact rested on the good faith of the contracting powers, and this turned out to be a frail prop. In no effective way, as events were to prove, did the treaty loosen Japan's favorable foothold in China's Manchuria.

THE AFTERGLOW OF THE CONFERENCE

The United States Senate eventually approved the treaties emerging from the Washington Conference. In general, they received warm support from the American press. A notable exception was the Hearst chain, which grieved over "the painted rattle called limitation of armaments," and assailed the Four Power Pacific pact as "a war breeder, not a peacemaker." Despite these pained outcries, the determined support of public opinion probably saved the pacts from becoming political footballs.

The most vigorous opposition in the Senate was concentrated on the Four-Power Pacific Treaty, which irreconcilable Senator Reed of Missouri denounced as "treacherous, treasonable, and damnable." Surprisingly enough, Senator Lodge reversed his obstructionist position on the League and fought for the new pact. When isolationist Senator Borah accused him of inconsistency, Lodge replied, "What are you going to do? It is an administration measure." [16] The treaty was finally approved, in March, 1922, with Democratic support and with only four votes to spare. But the Senate, ever cautious, tacked on a reservation declaring that "there is no commitment to armed force, no alliance, no obligation to join in any defense."

Other Far Eastern adjustments, although of no direct concern to the Conference, were by-products of the healthier atmosphere created at Washington or by the decisions reached there. In December, 1921, Japan agreed to a treaty conceding to the United States special cable rights on the disputed island of Yap. In January, 1922, the Japanese, under nudgings from Secretary Hughes, consented to pull their troops out of Russia's Siberia. In February, 1922, thanks to the good offices of the British and Americans at Washington, the Japanese agreed to evacuate Shantung on economic terms rather favorable to themselves.[17] And in April, 1923, more than a year after the Washington Conference had closed its doors, Japan consented to an annulment of the Lansing-Ishii agreement. It had once guaranteed her a favored position in China's Manchuria, but it now ostensibly conflicted with the Nine-Power Treaty. In short, Japan was induced or forced to retreat all along the line—to the acute dissatisfaction of her more vocal newspapers and politicians.

PROFIT AND LOSS AT WASHINGTON

The achievements at Washington in arms limitation, though widely acclaimed at the time, proved to be temporary and somewhat illusory. The door was left wide open for unrestricted building in smaller craft, while a tax-conscious American public fell victim to wishful thinking.

One unfortunate result was the impression that Uncle Sam had been the honest greenhorn at the poker table, bamboozled by be-spatted and

---

[16] Author's interview with Senator Borah, April 21, 1937. See also C. O. Johnson, *Borah of Idaho* (New York, 1936).

[17] R. H. Fifield, "Secretary Hughes and the Shantung Question," *Pacific Hist. Rev.,* XXIII (1954), 373–385.

monocled foreigners. Will Rogers, the rope twirling "poet lariat" of the 1920's, jeered that the United States never lost a war or won a conference. Critics repeatedly pointed out that Uncle Sam junked some thirty battleships and battle cruisers, completed or nearly completed, so that Britain might junk some of her obsolete craft, while still maintaining superiority in cruiser construction. The feeling that "Uncle Sap" had scrapped battleships while the others were scrapping blueprints prompted the *Irish World* of New York to brand the Conference as "an ominous triumph for British diplomacy." Actually, the three leading powers junked a total of seventy craft, with the United States junking the most.

Nor did the Far Eastern agreements escape criticism. If Japan chose to flout her paper promises and slam shut the Open Door (as she finally did in 1931), the United States could not stop her. The Japanese fleet was left without a rival in Asiatic waters. Admiral Sims of the United States Navy groaned ungrammatically, "Anybody can spit on the Philippines and you can't stop them."

The Washington Conference was in fact not a triumph for any nation. In general, it recognized existing realities and tried to freeze the status quo. Like all compromises, it was not completely satisfactory to any of the parties. The United States, to be sure, surrendered *potential* naval supremacy and *potential* fortifications on her Pacific islands. But the American delegation, sensing the mood of the taxpayers, regarded these potentialities as liabilities rather than assets. Fourteen years later, in 1936, when all restrictions on fortification had ended, the depression-ridden taxpayer was still unwilling to fortify Guam and the Philippines adequately.

Yet the Washington Conference, whatever its shortcomings, was clearly a landmark in history. It resulted in the first general international agreement for naval limitation, albeit in special categories and on the high seas. It did bring about a *temporary* halt to frantic naval building, with a consequent saving to the taxpayers and an easing of international tensions. The navies of the major powers in the Pacific were so scaled down that none could hope to attack another, in the adversary's home waters, with reasonable prospect of success. In the Far East, where the accomplishments of the Conference were less dramatic but perhaps more significant, the Open Door was given a new lease on life. The series of concessions and understandings made by Japan went far to scrap current suspicions. The general air-clearing dispelled the fetid atmosphere hanging over the Pacific and Far East, and made possible a more satisfactory recuperation from World War I than otherwise would have been possible.

Yet the Washington Conference interfered with the efforts of the League of Nations at Geneva to achieve genuine arms reduction. The Conference temporarily overshadowed and stole the thunder of the League, just as the anti-League Republicans, who hailed the assemblage as a true "peace conference," intended that it should. The lone-hand course of the United States, combined with the hollow results in disarmament, further crippled the arms-reduction program at Geneva.

The Washington Conference also befogged disarmament by strengthening the assumption that armaments are the basic cause of international distrust. A current belief was that big warships bring big wars; small warships, small wars; no warships, no wars. But armaments are not ordinarily so much a disease as a symptom of a disease: insecurity. Temperature is a symptom of a disease, and no regulation of the size, shape, and number of thermometers is likely to reduce fever or cure the disease. The "ever-logical" French were right when they insisted that security would have to precede disarmament. And in the end French insecurity proved to be not so much a French problem as a world problem.

THE DISARMAMENT DUD AT GENEVA

The Americans had rather naïvely assumed that the 5-5-3 ratio adopted at Washington for capital ships would by common consent be applied to auxiliary craft. But such fond hopes were shattered by continuing international friction. Britain and France were working at cross purposes; France and Italy were highly suspicious of each other; Japan had been grievously offended by the face-slapping American immigration law of 1924.

The naval race was now shifting ominously to nontreaty craft, that is, cruisers, destroyers, and submarines. The American public of the 1920's—obsessed with economy, prosperity, and peace—was unwilling to tax itself to build even the ships permitted by treaty. Parity with Britain was slipping away; superiority over Japan was melting away. From 1922 to 1930 the warships laid down or appropriated for by the leading powers numbered:

Japan	125
France	119
Italy	82
Britain	74
U.S.	11 [18]

President Coolidge, a penny-pinching New Englander who had succeeded Harding upon the latter's unexpected death in 1923, hoped for another spectacular stroke in disarmament. Proceeding on the theory that one good conference deserves another, he hastily and without proper diplomatic homework issued the call for a disarmament parley to meet at Geneva in 1927. Britain and Japan accepted the invitation, but France and Italy, for various reasons, declined.

[18] *Sen. Doc.*, No. 202, 78 Cong., 2 sess.

The Geneva Conference, as the *Wall Street Journal* feared, did not produce the scrapping of ships—just "scrapping." The American experts sought to extend the 5-5-3 ratio to smaller vessels, and to bring about a reduction in cruiser tonnage. The British, who insisted on seventy cruisers, were unwilling to concede parity. With their naval bases close together, they favored 7500-ton cruisers with 6-inch guns; the Americans, with bases far apart, favored 10,000-ton cruisers with 8-inch guns.

The politely bowing Japanese tried to serve as mediators, but the disputants proved unwilling to sink either their differences or their ships. In contrast with the Washington Conference, naval officers were "on top" rather than "on tap," and with understandable professional jealousy they were inclined to view global disarmament problems through a port-hole. To add to the confusion, three American shipbuilding concerns had on hand in Geneva a high-pressure and high-salaried lobbyist, W. B. Shearer, who did his suave best to promote discord. (The full revelation in 1929 of his scandalous activities led to a Senatorial investigation, and further turned the public mind against "merchants of death.")

After six weeks of fur-flying sessions, the Geneva conference broke up in complete failure, on August 4, 1927. The results were an embittering of British-American relations, a setback for the further limitation of armaments, and a keen disappointment to the American taxpayers. Within a year and a half Congress had authorized fifteen new 10,000-ton cruisers.

THE OUTCRY FOR OUTLAWING WAR

One important fruit of the futile Geneva Conference was an increasing belief that the way to promote peace was not to abolish arms but to abolish war. War-making nations should be regarded as outlaws or criminals. During the previous decade a small but vocal element in the United States had been urging that instead of laws *of* war there should be laws *against* war. Professor J. T. Shotwell of Columbia University, one of the leaders of this group, broached the idea to the French Foreign Minister, Aristide Briand. The latter, in April, 1927, announced that France was prepared to enter into a pact with the United States for the mutual outlawry of war.

American editors seized upon the idea, and the phrase "outlawry of war" caught the popular fancy.[19] Secretary of State Kellogg showed scant enthusiasm for the two-power French proposal: it might ensnarl the United States indirectly in France's defensive alliances. Yet the advocates of outlawry kept up their clamor. Senator Borah, a strange convert in-

[19] See J. E. Stoner, *S. O. Levinson and the Pact of Paris* (New York, 1943), and particularly R. H. Ferrell, *Peace in Their Time: The Origins of the Kellogg-Briand Pact* (New Haven, 1952); J. C. Vinson, *William E. Borah and the Outlawry of War* (Athens, Ga., 1957).

deed, persuaded the National Grange, with a membership of 800,000, to endorse a favorable resolution that he had prepared. Petitions bearing two million signatures poured in on Washington. Finally, in December, 1927, Kellogg proposed to Briand, as Borah and others had been suggesting, that the projected Franco-American pact be expanded to include the other powers.

Briand, with some reluctance, consented to the enlargement, for France's obligation to the League and to her allies envisaged defensive war. The proposed treaty was finally worded so as to permit defensive war but to outlaw war as "an instrument of national policy." On August 27, 1928, the Pact of Paris was formally signed by fifteen powers, and in succeeding months was approved by practically all remaining nations.

American opinion overwhelmingly favored the so-called Kellogg-Briand Pact, although hard-headed cynics were inclined to grumble. Some insisted that the treaty was a dangerous step toward membership in the League. Others noted that the pact permitted defensive war; and who ever heard of a nation that did not fight defensively? Others sneered that the treaty had no teeth, except the feeble pressure of world opinion; it was just "a New Year's resolution" or "a letter to Santa Claus."

AFTERMATH OF THE KELLOGG-BRIAND PACT

The Senate had few illusions about the agreement for abolishing war. Senator Reed of Missouri branded it an "international kiss," while Senator Glass of Virginia did not want people to think him "simple enough to suppose that it is worth a postage stamp. . . ." No formal reservations were attached to the treaty, but the Senate Foreign Relations committee did present an "interpretation" reserving the right of self-defense, the right to fight for the Monroe Doctrine, and the right not to enforce the treaty against violators.

Such was the tidal wave of public opinion that the Senate approved the Kellogg-Briand Pact, in January, 1929, by a vote of 85 to 1. The next order of business was the bill for constructing fifteen new cruisers, which shortly thereafter were approved. The *New York Evening Post* jibed, "If, after just having signed a peace treaty with twenty-six nations, we need fifteen new cruisers, how many would we have needed if we hadn't just signed a peace treaty with twenty-six nations?" [20]

The Kellogg-Briand Pact proved to be a monument to illusion. It was not only delusive but dangerous, for it further lulled the public, already prepared to lag behind in the naval race, into a false sense of security. Instead of outlawing wars, the treaty merely outlawed declarations of wars. Nations thereafter, always fighting defensively of course, tended to become involved in "incidents," not wars. Secretary Kellogg, who had

[20] *Literary Digest*, Feb. 23, 1929, p. 16.

taken many months to warm to the idea, was almost literally kicked into immortality by an aroused American public. He was awarded the Nobel Peace Prize for 1929, with a stipend of more than $46,000.[21]

Kellogg supplemented his new peace machinery by negotiating a series of bilateral arbitration treaties with about a score of nations. These pacts provided for the submission of justiciable disputes to the Permanent Court of Arbitration at The Hague, or to some other competent tribunal. The Senate, as usual, reserved the right to pass upon the nature and scope of each proposed arbitration, but more questions were now arbitrable under the new pacts than under the old Root treaties.

PAPER PARITY AT LONDON

President Hoover, an economy-minded Quaker who came to the White House in 1929, viewed the costly rivalry in cruisers and other lighter craft with dismay. A short time after his accession, a new Labor government came to power in London, headed by the Scotsman Ramsay MacDonald. In the mellower atmosphere produced by the Kellogg-Briand Pact and the change of regimes, preliminary negotiations for a disarmament conference began with the assumption that both nations were to enjoy parity in all categories of warships.

Events now moved rapidly toward a new five-power conference. President Hoover invited Prime Minister MacDonald to come to the United States, where he spoke effectively before the Senate. Friendly discussions continued at the President's summer fishing camp at Rapidan, Virginia, where the press pictured the two statesmen sitting on a log and informally settling the affairs of the world. The climax came on October 7, 1929, when Britain issued formal invitations to a disarmament conference at London, including France, Italy, Japan, America, and Britain.

The five-power sessions began in January, 1930, and this time the statesmen, rather than the admirals, were in command. France, still obsessed with security, demanded assurances of military support as the price of co-operation in arms limitation. Several members of the American delegation were rather favorable to the idea, but Hoover interposed a stern veto. Himself isolationist-minded, he was not unaware of opposition in the Senate to European entanglements. After prolonged arguments, the conferees in London completed a treaty on April 22, 1930, with France and Italy subscribing to only relatively unimportant clauses.

The London Conference proved to be only a limited victory for arms limitation. The glaring loophole of the Washington Treaty was plugged by placing an upper limit on all categories of warships. The Americans at long last were granted parity with the British in all types of vessels, not just capital ships and carriers. Replacement of capital ships under the

[21] See David Bryn-Jones, *Frank B. Kellogg* (New York, 1937).

Washington Treaty was postponed for five years, and nine capital ships then in commission were to be junked by Britain, America, and Japan. The taxpayers, in this one category at least, were thus saved millions of dollars.

The Japanese, though retaining the old 10-10-6 ratio in capital ships, improved their position and partially salved their injured pride. They gained complete parity in submarines. They also attained a 10-10-7 ratio in destroyers, as well as a slightly better than 10-10-6 ratio in cruiser tonnage. Yet such was the dissatisfaction of the superpatriots in Japan that the prime minister was assassinated, and the saber-rattling elements gained greater power.

The naval limitations at London would presumably stop competitive building. But the absence of complete adherence by France and Italy was most disquieting. The so-called "escalator clause" provided that if one or more nations not bound by the treaty, say Italy, should begin building in such a way as to jeopardize a signatory power, the ratios thus established would no longer be binding.

The American taxpayer, who had expected genuine arms reduction at London, read the results with sinking heart. The United States, to be sure, had won paper parity in cruisers and other craft but would have to spend about a billion dollars in order to build up to it. The *Chicago Tribune* scoffed, "We ought to be able to have a good first-class little war cheaper than that." But Hoover put the best face he could on the treaty by declaring that as compared with the standards discussed at the Geneva Conference in 1927, the United States would save about a billion dollars in six years.[22]

The Five-Power Naval Pact encountered rough sailing in the Senate. The Hearst press cried that the British and Japanese had "put something over" on the United States, and the Senators tried, without success, to force Hoover to submit his confidential papers. The treaty was finally approved on July 21, 1930, by a vote of 58 to 9, but the Senate showed its distrust by passing a resolution which declared that the United States was not bound by any secret understandings.

THE MIRAGE OF LAND DISARMAMENT AT GENEVA

The peace-loving Hoover co-operated wholeheartedly with the 51-nation World Disarmament Conference, which convened under League auspices in the quiet Swiss city of Geneva in February, 1932. After it had quibbled and dawdled for five months, he galvanized it into life by a sensational proposal. Among other things, he urged the abolition of

---

[22] On the London Conference see *The Memoirs of Herbert Hoover: The Cabinet and the Presidency 1920–1933* (New York, 1952) and H. L. Stimson and M. Bundy, *On Active Service in Peace and War* (New York, 1948).

offensive weapons, even though the distinction between "offensive" and "defensive" arms was impossible to establish in all categories. He also proposed that existing land armaments be reduced by approximately one-third. Although this scheme was enthusiastically received both in Geneva and America—"THANK HEAVEN FOR HOOVER!" exulted the head-lines—it was finally buried beneath oratorical flowers.

The new failure on the shores of Lake Geneva was not difficult to explain. The dictators were on the loose; Hitler was fast emerging in Germany. The French, quite understandably, were unwilling to disarm in advance of security guarantees—guarantees that the United States had "welshed on" and was unwilling to revive. Finally, the war-bent Japanese militarists, having seized China's Manchuria the year before, in 1931, launched a brutal attack on Shanghai while the conference was still in session. Security-conscious nations felt that they would be wiser to sharpen their swords than to beat them into ploughshares.

THE END OF THE DISARMAMENT DREAM

The depression-bedeviled Roosevelt administration, which took office early in 1933, cherished the hope of arms reduction, despite the feverish atmosphere created by the dictators. But the other powers continued to build up to their authorized quotas of ships, while the United States wishfully lagged behind. Finally, in the Vinson-Trammel Act of 1934, Congress bravely authorized the building of the navy to treaty strength, but less bravely failed to vote the money for construction.

The London Naval Treaty of 1930 had made provision for another conference in 1935. During the preliminary conversations the Japanese, on the grounds of prestige and security, made no bones about their determination to reject the short end of any ratio. As Ambassador Saito pithily explained, 5-5-3 sounded "to Japanese ears like Rolls-Royce—Rolls-Royce—Ford." In a fateful move Japan formally denounced the Washington Naval Treaty of 1922, on December 29, 1934, effective two years later.

The prospects were discouraging when the second London Naval Conference met late in 1935. The United States, with two long coastlines and far-flung possessions, was unwilling to concede parity to the Japanese delegates, who thereupon walked out. The treaty that emerged in March, 1936, contained some mild limitations on the size of naval craft, together with a number of "escape-hatch clauses." But the pact was virtually useless without Italy and Japan, and by 1938 the signatories had thrown overboard all trammels on naval construction.

President Roosevelt concluded that America could not risk falling farther behind in a madly rearming world, and in January, 1938, he asked Congress for a billion-dollar naval appropriation. The basic argument was that the United States needed a two-ocean navy, capable of meeting the combined fleets of the so-called aggressor nations—Japan, Italy, and Germany. With Japan invading China and Germany seizing Austria, the voices of the pacifists were drowned out, and in May, 1938, Congress passed the billion-dollar bill. America, with dangerous belatedness, now had both feet in the greatest naval race in history.

In retrospect, one may conclude that the United States, by spurning the League and Wilson's security commitment to France, helped create an atmosphere of insecurity in which effective disarmament proved impossible. Armaments are instruments of national policy, and any attempt to regulate them without regard for the factors that bring them into existence is doomed to failure. The United States, with wide ocean moats on each side and weak neighbors north and south, was in a much more favorable position than the other major powers, but it was unwilling to yield too much.

Disarmament is no simple problem in arithmetic. Land, sea, and air armaments are closely interrelated. Even parity in naval tonnage leaves disparity in types of craft, as well as an advantage with the nation enjoying better shipyards, bases, and other facilities. As one American newspaper remarked in 1929, "If you think it is a simple matter to establish naval parity, try to determine how many cows equal six sheep." Genuine disarmament was never attempted after World War I, merely arms reduction and limits on certain types of naval weapons. The only real disarmament was that forced upon the vanquished nations—and they rose again.

SELECTED BIBLIOGRAPHY

General works on disarmament are Merze Tate, *The United States and Armaments* (Cambridge, Mass., 1948), B. H. Williams, *The United States and Disarmament* (New York, 1931), and D. F. Fleming, *The United States and World Organization, 1920–1933* (New York, 1938). The most recent full-length treatment of the Washington Conference is J. C. Vinson, *The Parchment Peace* (Athens, Ga., 1956). Public opinion in relation to it is developed in C. L. Hoag, *Preface to Preparedness* (Washington, 1941). For Hughes' role see M. J. Pusey, *Charles Evans Hughes* (2 vols., New York, 1951). The Far Eastern backgrounds of the Washington Conference are well set forth in A. W. Griswold, *The Far Eastern Policy of the United States* (New York, 1938), while the purely naval aspects are clearly analyzed in Harold and Margaret Sprout, *Toward a New Order of Sea Power* (Princeton, 1940). Additional references on the Kellogg-Briand Pact are D. H. Miller, *The Peace Pact of Paris* (New York, 1928) and J. T. Shotwell, *War as an Instrument of National Policy* (New York, 1929). Hoover's policies are treated with verve in R. H. Ferrell, *American Diplomacy in the Great Depression* (New Haven, 1957).

See footnotes of this chapter and *Harvard Guide*, Ch. 28.

7TH, 8TH, AND 9TH ED. REFS. See BIBLIOGRAPHICAL ADDENDUM, p. 1,031.

43

Economic Foreign Policy between Wars, 1919-1939

We can not take our interest out of Europe without taking some interest in Europe.
ASHEVILLE TIMES, 1921

UNCLE SAM: THE WORLD'S PAWNBROKER

THE ROCK-RIBBED Republican regimes of Harding, Coolidge, and Hoover, with their big-business coloration, were in the saddle from 1921 to 1933. They carried over their political isolationism, born largely of tradition and disillusionment, into the realm of economic isolationism. The feverish boom-and-bust prosperity of the 1920's indeed seemed to justify their America-centered economic and political ingrowth.

This narrow postwar economic isolationism found vent in various ways. Fearing a horde of destitute Europeans, Congress in 1921, and more conspicuously in 1924, jerked away the historic welcome mat. By establishing quotas for certain nations, the new laws reduced to a trickle the net inflow of immigrants. Fearing not only Europeans but cheaply made European goods, the high-protection Republican Congresses also boosted the tariff to new heights in 1921, and more permanently in 1922.

The fateful postwar pattern of towering trade barriers was thus established. The *New York Herald* protested against the law of 1922 as "the damn-fool tariff," while the Democratic *Baltimore Evening Sun* prophetically declared: "A tariff wall that keeps foreign goods out may also keep American goods in; that unless we buy from the outside we can not sell to the outside." [1] But the voices of such prophets of doom were drowned out by grinding machinery and roaring blast furnaces.

Until the World War erupted in 1914, the United States had been a debtor nation, hating "the bloated British bondholder." American citizens,

---

[1] *Literary Digest,* February 26, 1921, p. 12.

to be sure, had invested many millions of dollars in foreign lands, but on balance Americans owed foreigners some three billion dollars more than foreigners owed them. The frightful destructiveness of the European conflict almost overnight changed the United States from a debtor to a creditor nation. By 1919 America was not only the wealthiest and freshest of the Great Powers, but the leading exporter and the chief moneylender to boot. Both the political and economic center of the world's gravity had shifted to the United States.

The credit side of Uncle Sam's ledger, at least on paper, grew increasingly favorable as the decade of the 1920's lengthened. The largest single item consisted of the so-called Allied debt of $10.350 billion, owed to the Washington Treasury. In addition, private investment capital had slopped over from a prosperous America into Europe and other continents by 1928 to the tune of $12 billion. In short, by 1928 the outside world was indebted to the American government or investors in the sum of about $20 billion.

The American people, befuddled by the complexities of international finance, did not adjust readily to their new role. They did not seem to realize that a creditor nation like the United States could not expect repayment of debts unless it was willing to let other nations earn the necessary dollars by exporting to it. Many Americans continued to believe that imports were basically bad.

THE CLAMOR FOR DEBT CANCELLATION

The guns had hardly grown cold when America's late allies began to agitate for a wiping out of the debt that they owed Washington. The principal debtors had come out of war with staggering casualty lists, mountainous tax burdens, strained currencies, and, in the case of Belgium and France, with gutted towns and factories, flooded mines, and torn-up topsoil. Approximately one-sixteenth of France lay devastated.

The Allies argued that the loans from Washington were not really loans at all but wartime subsidies to comrades-in-arms. America the Unready had entered the conflict thirty-two months after Germany invaded Belgium, and she had not been able to place an effective fighting force in France until at least another thirteen months had elapsed.[2] The Allied armies saved America by holding back the "Hun." During these anxious months, the United States could not provide men—only dollars for munitions, foodstuffs, and other Allied needs. The Allies provided not only money but the men who fired off the munitions. They were not ask-

---

[2] A favorite argument was that if America had entered the war from the beginning, as many Americans later insisted she should have, the conflict would have been shortened, and America would have had a far larger share of the casualties and the debt.

ing for their dead soldiers back; the United States should not ask for its dead dollars back. Was gold more precious than blood?

As for getting the money *back,* the Allies had received relatively little gold from the United States. The Washington government had raised the funds in the first place by selling Liberty Bonds to its own citizens, mostly at 4¼ per cent interest. The money thus poured into the Treasury had then been used for advancing credits to Allied agents, who purchased in America enormous quantities of military supplies, often at profiteering prices.

WAR AND POSTWAR FOREIGN LOANS OF U.S. GOVERNMENT

	Pre-Armistice [cash]	Post-Armistice [Cash & Supplies]	Total Indebtedness
To Allies:			
Great Britain	$3,696,000,000	$ 581,000,000.00	$4,277,000,000.00
France	1,970,000,000	1,434,818,945.01	3,404,818,945.01
Italy	1,031,000,000	617,034,050.90	1,648,034,050.90
Belgium	171,780,000	207,307,200.43	379,087,200.43
Russia	187,729,750	4,871,547.37	192,601,297.37
Romania		37,911,152.92	37,911,152.92
Greece		27,167,000.00	27,167,000.00
Cuba	10,000,000		10,000,000.00
Nicaragua		431,849.14	431,849.14
Liberia		26,000.00	26,000.00
To Countries Formed out of Allied Territory:			
Esthonia		13,999,145.60	13,999,145.60
Finland		8,281,926.17	8,281,926.17
Latvia		5,132,287.14	5,132,287.14
Lithuania		4,981,628.03	4,981,628.03
To Areas or Countries Formed Partially or Wholly Out of Enemy Territory:			
Poland		159,666,972.39	159,666,972.39
Czechoslovakia		91,879,671.03	91,879,671.03
Yugoslavia	10,605,000	41,153,486.55	51,758,486.55
Austria		24,055,708.92	24,055,708.92
Armenia		11,959,917.49	11,959,917.49
Hungary		1,685,835.61	1,685,835.61
	$7,077,114,750	$3,273,364,324.70	$10,350,479,074.70

The Allies, in effect, had borrowed not gold dollars but war materials that had gone up in smoke. The money, having been spent in the United States, had contributed to an unprecedented wartime prosperity. The Treasury had also enriched itself on the high income taxes and excess profits taxes resulting from these sales. In short, argued the Allies, the United States had already been repaid in prosperity. Some embittered

Europeans even went so far as to accuse the Americans of having deliberately stayed out of the war until they had made enough money to defray the costs of subsequent participation.

There were only three possible ways by which the ten-billion-dollar debt of the Allies could be paid. One was in gold. But the war-racked debtors did not possess enough gold to liquidate their entire obligation, and most of what they had was needed to support their own currencies. Another method of repayment was by services, such as shipping and the tourist trade. The flow of American tourists reached a new high in the 1920's, but still the Europeans, despite valiant gouging, could not raise anywhere near enough money. The third method was to pay with manufactured goods, which the debtors would have been delighted to sell. But the prompt erection of tariff barriers in postwar America proved to be an insuperable hurdle.

The European debtors speedily came to the conclusion that in the long run outright cancellation would best serve both them and the Americans. At the end of the Napoleonic upheaval, Britain had far-sightedly wiped the slate clean for her debtors, and had been repaid many fold by a prosperous Europe able to buy her goods. If Washington would do likewise, the British could afford to cancel France's heavy indebtedness to them, and the French could reduce their reparations bill to Germany to a more reasonable level. Thus Europe would revive, avoid a world-wide depression, and repay the Americans many times over as flourishing customers.

But Washington flatly refused to be taken in by any pretty little game of around-the-boards cancellation. It insisted that the loans had been made in good faith as loans, and that they were not tied up with any future German reparations. This position was technically sound but actually absurd: debts and reparations were inseparable Siamese twins.

THE CASE AGAINST CANCELLATION

The American arguments against cancellation were strong, though tragically short-sighted.

The money advanced was clearly a loan,[3] not a subsidy, despite the fact that at the time a few emotional Congressmen had referred to it as a gift. If these vast sums were not repaid, faith in international borrowing would receive a damaging blow. In the event of another war, the non-paying Allies could expect nothing but the glassy eye from rich Uncle Sam.

Even if the debts were cancelled—and here was the fatal stumbling block—they still would not be cancelled for the American taxpayer.

---

[3] French spokesmen pointed out that an ordinary commercial loan to a manufacturer is designed to produce wealth, from which both the principal and interest can be paid. The American loan to the Allies had largely gone for expended munitions.

Unless the Treasury repudiated outright its outstanding bonds, the tax-payers would have to dig down into their own pockets and make up the lost sum. "All those who would like to see America cancel the European debt," remarked one journal, "are requested to mail in their Liberty bonds." [4]

About a third of the so-called war debt was not a war debt at all but a series of post-Armistice commercial loans, designed to boost certain

"DOES ONE PANTS POCKET KNOW WHAT
THE OTHER IS DOING?"

Spencer in the *Omaha World-Herald*, 1932

countries back on their feet. The argument about fighting in a common cause was thus weakened. Considerable sums even went to nonbelliger-ents, like Finland, and to countries carved out of former enemy terri-tory, like Austria.

The late Allies, though pleading poverty, seemed to have plenty of money for everything except paying their just debts. American prohi-bitionists decried the heavy consumption of alcoholic liquor. Advocates of disarmament were quick to complain that the Europeans were arming to the teeth. Few Americans perceived that France, notably, was rearm-

[4] *Literary Digest*, Sept. 18, 1926, p. 17.

ing because she felt insecure, and that she felt insecure largely because
the United States had cancelled its commitments to help defend her. The
French, for their part, were disposed to retaliate by cancelling their
financial commitments to the United States. No city is going to disband
its fire department and its police force in order to pay the interest on its
bonded indebtedness.

Uncle Sam was also unhappy to note that some of the debtors had
fared far better than he at the peace table. They had made off with
German ships, valuable German colonies, oil-rich mandates in the Middle
East, and were about to make off with large German reparations. The
United States had not even been able to get an undisputed foothold on
the tiny island of Yap. The Americans could also point to a huge national
debt, heavy taxes, the high cost of living, widows, and pensions. "About
all America got out of Europe was its army," lamented the *Asheville*
(N.C.) *Times*. The United States had asked for nothing in the war, complained the anticancellationists, and had received less than nothing. "We
went across, but they won't come across," cried a prominent Ohio politician in the 1930's.

Actually, the United States had asked for a great deal and had obtained it: security against German aggression and militarism. This security
proved to be only temporary, owing largely to America's hasty withdrawal from Europe. But if Germany had defeated the Allies, the United
States presumably would have had to lay out many times the Allied war
debts in order to bolster its defenses.

JOHN BULL'S DEBT SETTLEMENT

The Treasury had originally made the Allied loans with the understanding that they would bear interest at 5 per cent, pending later arrangements for repayment. But more than three years after the Armistice
the war-improverished debtors were still unwilling to step up and pay.
Congress gave them a sharp prod when, in February, 1922, it empowered
a World War Foreign Debt Commission to conclude terms with the
backward borrowers, subject to Congressional approval of each settlement.

The proud British, though oppressively taxed, were the first to take
the hint. In better financial shape than some of their allies, to whom they
had re-loaned much of their American borrowings, they sent a special
mission to Washington early in 1923. It finally agreed to pay the obliga·
tion in full over sixty-two years, with the interest rate reduced from
5 per cent to an average of 3.3. The Americans preened themselves on
their generosity, for the lowering of the interest rate reduced the total
payment by 30.1 per cent. But the British, though trying bravely to uphold their tradition of good sportsmanship, grumbled over the two genera·

tions of "USury" to "Uncle $am." "For the next sixty years," lamented *London Opinion*, "the American flag is going to look to us like the $tars and $tripes." [5]

President Coolidge, the tight-lipped and tight-fisted Vermonter, continued Harding's policy of dunning the debtors.[6] "Well, they hired the money, didn't they?" was his classic remark. But the chief remaining debtors—France, Italy, and Belgium—were reluctant to follow Britain's noble example. Their principal worry was the difficulty of extracting reparations from Germany with which to meet their debts to Britain and America.

THE REPARATIONS TANGLE

Squeezing reparations blood from the German turnip proved to be no simple task. The Allied Reparations Commission, without the moderating influence of the United States, tentatively fixed the total bill in 1921 at about $32 billion, not counting many more billions in interest. The war-exhausted Germans might have made an earnest attempt to pay a reasonable sum, say $10 billion, but they threw up their hands in despair when faced with this astronomical figure. The sum was benumbing, largely because the United States, by spurning the Treaty of Versailles, had left the vengeful French in the driver's seat, and because America's debtors added to the reparations bill the sums they owed Washington.

When a complaining Germany failed to meet her payments, the French and Belgian armies in 1923 seized the Ruhr Valley—the industrial nerve center of Germany. They soon learned the bitter lesson that one cannot dig coal with bayonets or extract both beef and milk from the same cow. The outraged Germans embarked upon a program of passive resistance, with a consequent runaway inflation of their currency. The solid German middle class, which might have halted the later rise of Hitler, was wiped out. Reparations payments dried up.

Washington, although still denying the connection between debts and reparations, played an important but unofficial role in reviving Germany. Following a suggestion by Secretary Hughes, the Reparations Commission appointed two committees to study the German financial muddle. The better known of the two was headed by a well-known Chicago banker, General Charles G. Dawes, whose underslung pipe and picturesque profanity brought him headlines. The so-called Dawes Plan of 1924, in an effort to get Germany back on her financial feet, made provision for a loan of $200 million, half of which was to come from

[5] *Literary Digest*, March 24, 1923, p. 17.
[6] Coolidge's father reminisced, "It always seemed to me that Calvin could get more sap out of a maple tree than any of the other boys around here." E. E. Whiting, *President Coolidge* (Boston, 1923), p. 11.

American private bankers.[7] Reparations payments were to begin with a relatively modest 1 billion gold marks (about $250 million) and in five years stagger up to 2.5 billion gold marks a year (about $600 million). The total sum was left indefinite.

The Dawes plan, admittedly a stop-gap measure, gave way in 1929 to the Young plan. The new scheme was hammered out by the creditor powers in Paris, and bore the name of an unofficial American expert, Owen D. Young, Chairman of the Board of the General Electric Company. Germany was to make annual reparations payments for fifty-nine years, by which time she would have paid about $9 billion in principal and $17 billion in interest. The $9 billion represented a drastic reduction from the $32 billion originally assessed.

DUNNING THE DEBTORS

Once assured of regular reparations payments under the Dawes Plan of 1924, the chief debtors of the United States, except Russia, slowly came to terms. They were also prodded into line by the State Department's policy of frowning on private loans from America to those countries in default. So dire was the need for life-giving dollars that this financial bludgeon proved to be potent. In the case of no debtor nation was the principal reduced. In all cases except Austria the payments, principal and interest, were spread over sixty-two years—that is, two generations, one of them yet unborn. In every case the interest was reduced below the $4\frac{1}{4}$ per cent that the Treasury was still paying American citizens on Liberty Bonds.

Italy signed on the dotted line in November, 1925. On the basis of presumed "capacity to pay," the resources-poor Italians had their interest rate reduced to an average of 0.4 per cent from the originally contemplated 5 per cent. By a specious way of reckoning, these terms amounted to a cancellation of 80.2 per cent of the entire amount owed over the sixty-two year period, counting both interest and principal. The jut-jawed Italian dictator Benito Mussolini, with his saber-rattling tactics and his Black-Shirted following, had already aroused grave misgivings in America, and partly for this reason the softened terms were savagely condemned by a minority in Congress. Some critics felt that if Mussolini were forced to pay more, his war-making power would be less.

France, though possessing a large gold reserve, was still reluctant to pay "blood money," especially to a nation that owed her a debt of gratitude since the days of Lafayette. Still chasing the phantom of se-

---

[7] In 1925 the United States became a direct sharer in reparations when it agreed to accept $25 million a year under the Dawes Plan (for a potential total of about $600 million) to defray the costs of occupying Germany and to meet other claims.

curity, she continued to pile up arms and actually lent substantial sums
to her military allies in Central Europe. But the unfriendly policy of the
State Department regarding private loans acted as a powerful persuader,
and in April, 1926, French representatives reluctantly inked an agreement. The interest rate was scaled down to an average of 1.6 per cent,
which, by one way of calculating, amounted to a wiping out of 60.3 per
cent of the entire indebtedness over the 62-year repayment period. The
sum thus forgiven was equivalent to a cancellation of the sums borrowed
during the war, as contrasted with those borrowed after the Armistice.
This was generally true of all the debt settlements, except that with Britain.

THE DEBT AGREEMENTS *

Debtor	Funding Agreement Signed	Average Interest Rate Over 62-Year Repayment Period	Reduction of Entire Debt on 5 % Basis
Finland	May 1, 1923	3.3	29.8
Great Britain	June 19, 1923	3.3	30.1
Hungary	April 25. 1924	3.3	30.0
Lithuania	Sept. 22, 1924	3.3	30.5
Poland	Nov. 14, 1924	3.3	30.0
Belgium	Aug. 18, 1925	1.8	60.3
Latvia	Sept. 24, 1925	3.3	29.8
Czechoslovakia	Oct. 13, 1925	3.3	37.0
Esthonia	Oct. 28, 1925	3.3	29.9
Italy	Nov. 14, 1925	0.4	80.2
Romania	Dec. 4, 1925	3.3	37.1
France	April 29, 1926	1.6	60.3
Yugoslavia	May 3, 1926	1.0	75.9
Greece	May 10, 1929	0.3	72.1

* Russia repudiated outright her debt of $192,601,297; Armenia lost all vestiges of independence.
Special arrangements were made with Austria, Liberia, Cuba, and Nicaragua. The total interest
payments—$10,679,604,171.27—more than doubled the original debt. The reduced interest rates
about halved the original obligation.

Yet the French showed scant appreciation. They vented their wrath in
scathing editorials, hostile demonstrations against American tourists, and
a heart-rending parade of some 20,000 maimed French veterans in Paris.
The *New York Times* correspondent wrote of

> A battalion of pathetic little wheel-chairs, carrying legless men, some pro-
> pelled themselves, some pushed by nurses.
> Behind the legless men came the sightless men, a company of war blinded,
> each led by his wife or sister or some friend. Bravely they stept along,
> not to delay the faceless men who filed after. Frightful to see, yet in great
> dignity, these human remains, some with their faces hidden by bandages,
> others in all the horrors of misformed features.[8]

Final approval of the French agreement was delayed for three years, until
1929, when France was assured that the Young Plan would provide rep-

[8] *Literary Digest*, July 24, 1926, p. 7.

arations. The thrifty French made it clear that they would pay only as they were paid.

The payment of Allied debts to Washington was thus chained to Germany's reparations payments to the Allies. A curious financial merry-go-round began to revolve. An economic revival in Germany, combined with high interest rates, caused American private investors to lend her from 1924 to 1931 a total of about $2.250 billion. (Ironically, much of this

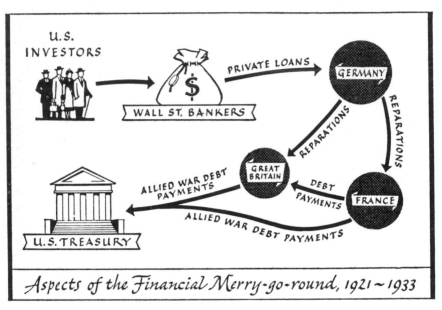

Aspects of the Financial Merry-go-round, 1921~1933

money went into rebuilding German industry, which formed the vitals of Hitler's devastating war machine.) During the same years, from 1924 to 1931, the United States received some $2 billion in payment on the war debts. The net effect was that American private investors lent the money with which Germany, through reparations, paid the Allies. They in turn paid the American Treasury.

THE HAWLEY-SMOOT TARIFF WALL

The catastrophic crash of the Wall Street stock market in October, 1929, heralded the Great Depression. American surplus capital for investment in Germany quickly dried up, German reparations payments to the Allies with these borrowings gradually dried up, and Allied debt payments to America ultimately dried up. Thus the depression, which started in America, spread to Europe, where worsening conditions, in an ever-widening vicious circle, deepened the depression in America.

A Republican Congress contributed powerfully to this dismaying cycle in 1930, when it passed the towering Hawley-Smoot Tariff bill. The existing rates of 1922 were already so high as to discourage many European imports, with which Allied debt payments could be made, and the new law added bricks to the wall. The wires to Washington hummed with protests from thirty-eight nations. A total of 1028 American economists, mostly academicians, addressed an appeal to President Hoover urging him to veto the bill. With prophetic vision, critics pointed out that the measure would reap a harvest of ill will, end a promising worldwide trend toward reasonable tariffs, stimulate retaliation, impede intergovernmental debt collections, and worsen the depression. But Hoover, no doubt realizing that a veto would damage his party in the forthcoming Congressional elections, not only signed the Hawley-Smoot bill but defended it vigorously, both then and later.[9]

The Hawley-Smoot Tariff no doubt greatly darkened the already gloomy international picture. Foreign exporters, unable to sell their products in America, could not build up dollar credits with which to buy American automobiles and other items. International trade is a two-way street, and as a rule nations cannot buy from their neighbors if their neighbors will not buy from them. Boosting tariffs is a game that two can play, and many nations, either for self-protection or as a reprisal, jacked up their rates or erected spite fences. Britain abandoned her historic free-trade policy, and bound the parts of her empire, including Canada, more closely to herself in imperial preference arrangements. Other nations engaged in boycotts of American goods, and in various other ways sought to quarantine the United States economically. The result was an intensification of narrow economic isolation and a worsening of that financial and political chaos which finally spawned Adolf Hitler.[10]

THE ONE-YEAR HOOVER HOLIDAY

In the spring of 1931 the depression in Europe reached panic proportions when a banking crisis struck Austria and spread rapidly into Germany. A complete collapse would certainly end the payments of the socalled war debts to Washington, and in addition wipe out the hundreds of millions of dollars invested privately by American citizens in Europe since 1918.

President Hoover, impressed with the need for drastic medicine, proposed a general moratorium in June, 1931. All payments on reparations and war debts were to stop for a breathing-spell period of one year. Congress was not then in session, and to create confidence in its final approval, Hoover gave out the names of certain Congressional leaders

---

[9] See *The Memoirs of Herbert Hoover: The Cabinet and the Presidency, 1920–1933* (New York, 1952), Ch. 41.

[10] J. M. Jones, Jr., *Tariff Retaliation: Repercussions of the Hawley-Smoot Bill* (Philadelphia, 1934).

favorable to the scheme. But he revealed that he was still inflexibly opposed to cancellation of the war debts, or to any official linking of German reparations with payments to the Washington Treasury.

The next step was to win the approval of those nations entitled to reparations from Germany. France proved to be the major roadblock. Hoover had not consulted her in advance, and her traditionally thin-skinned pride was hurt. As the nation that had suffered the greatest damage from the German invader, she demanded ironclad assurances that the existing reparations payments would be renewed at the end of the proposed holiday. Not until such assurances were received, some of them from Hoover by the new trans-Atlantic telephone, did Paris grudgingly accede. But the two-week delay worsened the financial disaster in Austria and Germany, and further played into the hands of the fast-emerging Adolf Hitler.

The economic blood-transfusion provided by the "Hoover holiday" brought new hope. A wave of optimism carried prices up with a rush on the stock markets of the world; many Europeans hailed the moratorium as America's re-entry into international affairs. Public sentiment responded enthusiastically in the United States, especially among bankers who saw that immediate relief might salvage their private loans abroad. Editorial opinion favored the moratorium in the ratio of about ten to one, although editor Hearst declared himself as "uncompromisingly opposed to any further reduction of the war debt." Newspapers like the *Wichita Eagle* feared, with good reason, that when the year had ended "Europe may want to place the accent on that *more* in *mor*atorium."

Congress approved the moratorium by sweeping majorities, in December, 1931. At the same time it rejected a recommendation by Hoover that steps be taken to re-examine the war debts in the light of the financial emergency. Belatedly, an increasing number of businessmen were now saying that cancellation would improve economic ills. But the Treasury was running a heavy deficit; and if Congress would not cancel when the books were in the black, it certainly would not do so when they were in the red.

THE REPARATIONS-DEBT DEADLOCK

In the autumn of 1931, with the depression still acute, Premier Laval of France was invited to come to America for a discussion of recovery policies. The swarthy, black-mustached "peasant premier" (shot in 1945 by his own people for collaboration with Hitler), engaged in a three-day discussion with Hoover. At the end of the conferences, the two men issued a guarded statement favoring "monetary stability."

The European debtors were inclined to regard the Hoover-Laval understanding with unwarranted optimism. They concluded that if they scaled down their reparations bill to Germany, the United States might be persuaded to reduce the debt payments proportionately. Meeting at Lausanne, Switzerland, in June, 1932, the debtor nations lowered the German reparations to a modest $714 million. This figure, when compared with the original $32 billion, amounted almost to cancellation. But the joker was that the United States would have to consent to a downward revision of the war debts.

The alleged trick by the debt-dodgers at Lausanne aroused a furor in the United States. If Washington were to waive debt payments in order to reduce reparations, then the American taxpayers indirectly would be paying Germany's reparations. The Hearst press, other journals, and members of Congress struck back angrily at the "league of debtors." An aroused Senator Borah extracted a statement from President Hoover that reparations were a "strictly European problem," and that the United States was "not a party to, nor in any way committed to any such agreements." [11] The American press loudly applauded this emphatic declaration. But the debtors were highly displeased. One Parisian daily, *La Liberté,* declared that "Americans are the only race which passed directly from barbarism to decadence without knowing civilization."

The discouraged debtors wisely forbore to push their pleas during the Presidential election campaign of 1932. But in November, after the Democratic Franklin Roosevelt had overwhelmed Herbert Hoover, they renewed their requests for relief. Hoover, now a lame-duck President unwilling to make long-range commitments, arranged for two White House conferences with Roosevelt. But the two men were unable to come to an agreement. Roosevelt apparently did not care to tie his hands in advance with a joint commitment, and he felt that the problem of economic recovery should be attacked on a wide front at home rather than from abroad. Unofficially he remarked somewhat airily to reporters that the war-debt tangle was "not my baby."

Late in 1932 the State Department displayed a willingness to discuss debt revision, but not until after receiving the payments due in December —the first since the moratorium. But such generosity came too late. On December 15, 1932, six of the debtors defaulted outright, the most conspicuous among them being France and Belgium. The baby that Roosevelt had been loath to recognize lay bawling on the White House doorstep when he took office, in March, 1933.

DISRUPTING THE LONDON ECONOMIC CONFERENCE

Franklin D. Roosevelt was not new to Washington or to the national stage. He had served capably under Woodrow Wilson as Assistant Secretary of the Navy for seven years, and had fallen under the spell of his

[11] W. S. Myers, ed., *The State Papers and Other Public Writings of Herbert Hoover* (Garden City, N.Y., 1934), II, 235.

wartime idealism. Born to a well-to-do New York family, and afforded the opportunity to travel and study abroad, he came to the White House with an unusual cultural background and a broad cosmopolitan outlook. Although the Democrats had been out of power for twelve years, the new administration did not make a sharp break with the past in foreign affairs.

In June, 1933, with the depression still in an acute stage, a multipower Economic Conference convened in London. The most pressing international economic problems were Allied war debts, tariff barriers, and monetary stabilization. Roosevelt opposed any sweeping concessions on the tariff, and flatly ruled out any discussion of the war debts. "That stays with Poppa—right here," he said.[12] With the world suffering from many interconnected economic ills, a concentration on monetary stabilization was, observed the *Dallas News*, like holding a "surgical clinic limited to academic discussion of the stomach ache."

The Conference seemed to be making some laborious headway when the gold-bloc nations undertook to commit the United States to a currency-stabilization program. Roosevelt had recently taken the nation off the gold standard, and his devaluation of the currency was evidently bringing some feeble blushes of economic recovery. Many nervous Americans feared that stabilization would erase these slight gains. Roosevelt himself concluded that recovery, like charity, begins at home. On July 2, 1933, while vacationing on a United States cruiser in the North Atlantic, he hastily dashed off a radio message to the London Conference, in which he sharply rebuked the delegates for concentrating on currency stabilization to the exclusion of "fundamental economic ills."

This ringing assertion of economic independence, published in America on Independence Day, evoked stirring applause. Rumors of currency stabilization at London had already produced a disquieting fall in prices. Some American newspapers even went so far as to hail the President's bombshell message as a "new Declaration of Independence."

But in London the reaction was violent. The delegates were angered by the scolding tone of Roosevelt's pronouncement, and by his blunt refusal to consider currency stabilization after having agreed to do so. Secretary of State Hull, who headed the American delegation, labored manfully to prevent an immediate breakup of the Conference. It lingered on impotently for several more weeks, and then adjourned virtually empty-handed.[13]

The aftermath was ominous. The United States, already the unpopular international banker, was bitterly blamed for the fiasco. But so chaotic were world conditions that substantial agreement probably could not have been secured, even if Roosevelt had not pulled the rug from under the delegates. At all events, the disheartening exhibition of futility at London

[12] J. M. Burns, *Roosevelt: The Lion and the Fox* (New York, 1956), p. 179.
[13] See Raymond Moley, *After Seven Years* (New York, 1939), Ch. VII.

did nothing to cushion the depression, dealt a heavy blow at international co-operation, and accelerated the worldwide drift toward isolationism, big-navyism, and extreme nationalism. A few months later Adolf Hitler withdrew Germany from both the current Disarmament Conference at Geneva and the League of Nations, and within two more years had embarked upon a fateful program of rearmament. Money that had formerly gone into German reparations was now going into German guns.

THE DEATH OF THE DEBTS

The United States, by its refusal to reconsider the war debts in the light of the world-wide depression, finally drove its debtors to the wall. As the *Ohio State Journal* queried, "Shall we cancel the debts or just not

HARMONY IN EUROPE

Thomas in the *Detroit News*, 1932

get the money?" The American public, except notably some internationalists and academicians, clearly preferred forced repudiation to voluntary cancellation. When the next installments fell due, in June, 1933, Italy and Britain, rather than default outright, as France and several other nations had done in 1932, made a "token payment." This was a relatively small sum acknowledging the existence of the debt "pending a final settlement."

American public opinion was highly dissatisfied with the token-payment dodge. Congress took a hand when, in April, 1934, it passed the Johnson Act, sponsored by the "irreconcilable" Senator Hiram Johnson of California. It provided that no person or private corporation under American jurisdiction could lend money to a government that was in default to the United States. This spiteful measure was correctly interpreted as an attempt to club the debtors into line, for they would presumably need to borrow again from the United States in the event of World War II.

The burning question now was: Did a token payment constitute a default? The Attorney General ruled that in the future the European nations would have to honor their obligations fully, if they were not to be regarded as defaulters under the Johnson Act. The debtors had now come to a dead end. They either could not or would not pay in full, and they would get no credit for part payments. So all of them, except Finland, defaulted outright on June 15, 1934.

The Finnish debt was in a class by itself. "Brave little Finland" had not been an ally; she had been formed out of Russian territory. She had secured a relatively small post-Armistice loan from the United States, some $8.281 million, for foodstuffs and other supplies. Being thrifty and having established a favorable dollar balance in America, she could make her relatively small payments without serious difficulty. During the 1920's and 1930's her distance runners and javelin throwers performed prodigiously at the Olympic games. A sports-mad America loudly applauded the Finns' fleet feet and financial fidelity, while illogically condemning the late Allies, who had incurred serious internal damage and vastly heavier debts in fighting a common enemy.

THE FRUITS OF FISCAL FOLLY

All the unpaid debts, except Finland's, were defunct by 1934. As the years lengthened, the original obligation of some $10 billion swelled with back interest to well over $16 billion. From time to time there was some little agitation in the United States to invite Britain and France to hand over some or all of their West Indian islands as payment of their debts. But with America's involvement in World War II, and with the vastly larger lend-lease credits to the new Allies, the old accounts were largely forgotten. The scornful nickname of "Uncle Shylock" that Europeans applied to Uncle Sam seemed apt; Shylock did not get his money either.

With the wisdom of 20/20 hindsight, one can now see that the United States should have wiped out the debts at the outset, and taken payment in world recovery. Since the loans were largely destined to be gifts anyhow, the gifts might well have been given graciously. Uncle Sam may not have sent hogsheads of gold dollars to Europe, but he certainly collected hogsheads of ill will and barrels of epithets, including "vampire" and "bloodsucker." Many Americans came to think more kindly of their whimpering German foe than of their ungrateful allies, and the ominous trend toward narrow isolationism and storm-cellar neutrality was accelerated.

Nations do not live in watertight compartments, and a fateful interrelationship existed among tariffs, debts, reparations, armaments, and security. Washington's hard-fisted policy undoubtedly deepened the depression and sped the emergence of Adolf Hitler. Straining to collect $10 billion, the United States shortsightedly contributed to the coming of a world war that cost it over a third of a trillion dollars.

The basic blame belongs to the American people, not to Congress or the White House. The taxpayers simply would not permit cancellation, and the more isolationist they were the more anticancellationist they became. International finance is infinitely complicated, and the American public unfortunately was called upon to make decisions regarding debts that had to be based on ignorance. The people—and this included many bankers and "hard-headed businessmen"—naturally thought of the debt as a loan from a local banker or a bill owed to a downtown merchant. "Tell your grocer," suggested the *Washington Post*, "about the British discovery that whoever tries to collect a debt will be ruined." [14] But even a banker will change the terms of the mortgage in the light of changed conditions, rather than force both the debtor and himself into bankruptcy.

RECOGNITION FOR RED RUSSIA

The Great Depression, which killed the war debts and reparations, curiously gave life to a movement to recognize Soviet Russia.

The American people had never been hostile to the Russian masses—witness the gigantic famine relief program of 1921–1923—but abhored the Bolshevist government of Russia. Successive administrations since 1917 had steadfastly refused to recognize the Moscow regime, even though it abandoned outright Communism in 1921 for a form of state capitalism. The Communists had flatly repudiated the Czarist debts to Washington, had declined to recognize the claims of American citizens resulting from revolutionary disturbances, and were sleeplessly seeking to overthrow "the damned rotten" capitalistic governments through subversive propaganda. For more than a decade after 1918 Washington's policy of nonrecognition was applauded by American conservatives and denounced by liberals, who constituted a relatively small minority. Yet other nations recognized the Soviet Union, and America's cold-shoulder treatment was evidently not weakening the Red regime.

By 1933 the withering depression had brought a change of heart in America. Repudiation of debts was now fashionable; even France had

[14] *Literary Digest*, Feb. 18, 1933, p. 11.

"welshed." The slight American trade with Russia was falling off, and many straw-clutching souls believed that recognition might open up a vast new market and relieve unemployment. Japan was on the rampage in China, and Hitler was on the rise in Germany. If recognition would strengthen the prestige of the Russians, they might be in a better position to halt these twin menaces. Roosevelt, moreover, was a militant liberal, not bound by the conservative dogmas of his Republican predecessors.

After lengthy negotiations with the Soviets, an agreement was concluded in Washington, in November, 1933. In return for formal recognition, Moscow agreed to grant freedom of worship to Americans in Russia, and to discontinue Communist propaganda against the United States. A further consideration of claims, debts, and loans was postponed.[15]

With the passage of time, recognition came to be deplored in America as a cruel hoax. The prospect of trade had baited the trap—the Russians had talked glibly of placing a billion dollars worth of orders—yet trade with Russia rapidly sank. The Soviets had evidently counted on a huge loan from the United States, and when it was denied them, partly because of the antidebtor Johnson Act of 1934, they dropped their discussion of debts, amid cries of bad faith on both sides. "Lending money to Russia," declared the *Wall Street Journal*, "would be borrowing trouble." The Communists, moreover, continued their brazen propaganda in the United States, despite their solemn pledge to desist.

When the formal hand of recognition was extended in 1933, American public opinion quite obviously favored the move, although die-hard conservatives wailed dolorously. The establishment of official relations, which would clearly facilitate diplomatic intercourse, was merely recognition of the disagreeable fact that the Moscow regime had securely fastened itself on the backs of the Russian masses. Recognition did not necessarily mean approval. There was indeed something inevitable in America's officially recognizing, after sixteen long years, a country containing 160,000,000 inhabitants and occupying one-sixth of the earth's surface. The two nations were now on official speaking terms—or rather name-calling terms.

TARIFF WHITTLING BY RECIPROCAL AGREEMENT

The advent of the Roosevelt administration in 1933 foreshadowed a sharp reduction of the Hooverian Hawley-Smoot Tariff of 1930. The Democratic Party was traditionally wedded to low tariffs, and Secretary of State Hull, a former long-term member of Congress, was a life-long advocate of lowered barriers. He believed that trade was the handmaiden

[15] An able book on the subject is R. P. Browder, *The Origins of Soviet-American Diplomacy* (Princeton, 1953). See also G. S. Moyer, *The Attitude of the United States towards the Recognition of Soviet Russia* (Philadelphia, 1926).

of peace and that economic warfare paved the way for shooting warfare. The Great Depression was still in its acute stage, and many experts believed that unclogging the channels of trade would promote world recovery.

A Congress subservient to Roosevelt passed the Reciprocal Trade Agreements Act in June, 1934. It left the maligned Hawley-Smoot Tariff on the books, but clothed the President with power to lower the existing rates by as much as 50 per cent for those nations willing to make reciprocal concessions. One refreshing feature of these trade pacts was that they would not have to run the Congressional gauntlet, with the usual danger of rejection, mutilation, or log-rolling amendment. The Reciprocal Trade Act also incorporated the most-favored-nation-principle in its unconditional form. For example, if an American bilateral agreement lowered the duties on coffee from Brazil, the same reduction automatically applied to all other coffee-exporting countries, provided that they did not discriminate against American goods.

Secretary Hull, who was accused of being a fanatic on the subject, pushed the reciprocal trade pacts with unflagging zeal. By 1947 he and his successors had negotiated agreements with twenty-nine nations, thereby achieving a substantial reduction on duties affecting 70 per cent of America's imports. The original act, with some modifications, was renewed by subsequent Congresses for periods ranging from one year to three years, and always in the face of considerable high-tariff Republican opposition.[16] Ironically enough, Secretary Blaine had fathered the reciprocal trade policy, but dyed-in-the-wool Republicans were loath to recognize the Blaine baby in Democratic clothing.

The reciprocal trade agreements program naturally became a subject of heated controversy. Wool growers, for example, could not appreciate why their interests should be sacrificed to the welfare of the nation as a whole. Nor could reciprocal traders prove that the program contributed substantially to pulling the nation out of the depression. But there can be no doubt that the Hawley-Smoot Tariff was substantially whittled down; political log-rolling was largely eliminated from tariff-making; and international good will, particularly in Latin America, was greatly improved as trade with the United States increased.

FREEDOM FOR (FROM?) THE FILIPINOS

The Great Depression, which blighted almost everything else, actually brightened hopes of Philippine independence. Every President since McKinley had held out the prospect of freedom, but for various reasons

---

[16] Beginning with 1947, when the United States became a party to GATT (General Agreement on Tariffs and Trade) numerous bilateral tariff pacts were combined into a multilateral program, thus further lowering trade barriers.

the glorious day was repeatedly deferred. As long as there was a good chance of extracting riches from the tropical archipelago, American promoters were reluctant to pull out.

The depression finally convinced the American people that the islands were a hopeless economic liability. Tens of thousands of unemployed white laborers on the Pacific Coast resented the influx of thousands of low-wage Filipinos. Hard-pressed American sugar growers complained bitterly about the importation of duty-free Philippine sugar. The home-front producers of cordage, cotton-seed oil, dairy products, and other commodities were similarly vocal. In addition, the Japanese war lords were running amuck in Manchuria, and the American public was begin-ning to perceive that the Philippine Islands, on which millions had al-ready been spent in fortifications, were virtually indefensible against Japan. Military necessity, economic stresses, and past promises all called for a speedy divorce.

Agitation for Philippine independence snowballed late in the de-pression-cursed Hoover administration. But determined opposition came from American investors, imperialists, and big-navyites. In the end, the agriculture-labor lobby in Congress proved too strong. One independence bill, repassed over President Hoover's emphatic veto in 1933, was spurned by the Philippines as too unfavorable. But the Tydings-McDuffie Act, approved by President Roosevelt in March, 1934, was unanimously ac-cepted by the Philippine legislature on May 1, 1934—thirty-six years to a day after Dewey's smashing victory at Manila.

The Tydings-McDuffie Act provided for complete independence after a ten-year transitional period, at the end of which the United States would withdraw all military bases. Naval establishments were left for future dis-cussion. The Filipinos, though relieved, were not altogether happy. Their economic life had become so heavily dependent on a tariff-free America for markets that prostration appeared to be the price of independence.

The decision to abandon the Philippines, finally implemented in 1946, was fraught with fateful significance. Rather than freeing the islands, the United States freed itself from the islands. The basic motives were not altogether high-minded. The United States gained some credit with the anticolonial peoples of eastern Asia, but suffered much criticism from the shaky European colonialists who deplored this incendiary example. On the other hand, America's scuttle-and-run policy in the face of Japan's aggressions cost the nation "face," and did nothing to dampen the mad ambitions of the Nipponese war lords. They were to be heard from again.

SELECTED BIBLIOGRAPHY

A general introduction is B. H. Williams, *Economic Foreign Policy of the United States* (New York, 1929). See also Herbert Feis, *The Diplomacy of the*

Dollar: First Era, 1919–1932 (Baltimore, 1950). The most useful single volume on debts and reparations is H. G. Moulton and Leo Pasvolsky, *War Debts and World Prosperity* (New York, 1932). Indispensable for most aspects of the Roosevelt years are *The Memoirs of Cordell Hull* (2 vols., New York, 1948). See E. E. Robinson, *The Roosevelt Leadership, 1933–1945* (Philadelphia, 1955) for a critical appraisal. Additional material on Russian recognition appears in Meno Lovenstein, *American Opinion of Soviet Russia* (Washington, 1941); F. L. Schuman, *American Policy toward Russia since 1917* (New York, 1928); T. A. Bailey, *America Faces Russia* (Ithaca, N.Y., 1950); W. A. Williams, *American-Russian Relations, 1781–1947* (New York, 1952). Hoover's policies are analyzed in R. H. Ferrell, *American Diplomacy in the Great Depression* (New Haven, 1957).

See footnotes of this chapter and *Harvard Guide,* Chs. 28, 29.

7TH ED. REFS. Joseph Brandes, *Herbert Hoover and Economic Diplomacy: Department of Commerce Policy, 1921–28* (Pittsburgh, 1962) concludes that Hoover pursued narrow economic nationalism so vigorously as to usurp the functions of the State Department. His foreign economic involvements were inconsistent with his political isolationism; he tried to promote American economic opportunity abroad while restricting that of foreigners in dealing with America. H. G. Warren, *Herbert Hoover and the Great Depression* (New York, 1959) deals with the foreign repercussions of the Hawley-Smoot Tariff, as well as Hoover's stubbornness and misuse of statistics in representing it as moderate. L. P. Lochner, *Herbert Hoover and Germany* (New York, 1960) is a eulogistic account of Hoover as the benefactor of Germany; some new material on the moratorium is reproduced from Hoover's diary. E. E. Morison, *Turmoil and Tradition: A Study of the Life and Times of Henry L. Stimson* (Boston, 1960) criticizes the moratorium as too little and too late (Hoover's advisers urged two years instead of one), and contends that Hoover was not considerate of France. A. M. Schlesinger, Jr., *The Age of Roosevelt: The Coming of the New Deal* (Boston, 1959) shows that foreign trade increased after the reciprocity agreements but the causal relationship cannot be proved. The author attributes the failure of the London Economic Conference largely to poor planning by Washington and to the inharmonious and inept American delegation. (Hard-drinking Senator Pittman of Nevada chased a man through a hotel corridor with a bowie knife, but engineered an international agreement on silver.) Schlesinger concludes that acquiescence in the general purposes of the conference would not have ruined the New Deal, and that approval of empty resolutions would have been better than exploding a bombshell. Jean-Baptiste Duroselle, *De Wilson à Roosevelt: Politique extérieure des États-Unis, 1913–1945* (Paris, 1960) is a creditable survey by a French scholar, especially full on economics. G. E. Wheeler, "Republican Philippine Policy, 1921–1933," *Pacific Hist. Rev.,* XXVIII (1959), 377–390 discusses the factors, including strategic and economic, that paved the way for a dump-the-Philippines decision.

8TH AND 9TH ED. REFS. See BIBLIOGRAPHICAL ADDENDUM, p. 1,034.

44

Good Neighbors South and North, 1917-1941

> *In the field of world policy I would dedicate this nation to the policy of the good neighbor—the neighbor who resolutely respects himself and because he does so, respects the rights of others.*
>
> FRANKLIN D. ROOSEVELT, INAUGURAL ADDRESS, March 4, 1933.

UNCLE SAM: THE BAD NEIGHBOR

THE CARIBBEAN SEA had become virtually a Yankee lake before World War I. Puerto Rico, Spain's last remnant, fell to American invaders in 1898. Cuba became a protectorate under the Platt Amendment of 1901, after which there were repeated troop landings. Panama, with its Canal Zone leased to Uncle Sam in perpetuity, was born a puppet in 1903—and remained one. Bankrupt Santo Domingo submitted to a financial receivership in 1905, under the hated Roosevelt Corollary of the Monroe Doctrine. A major intervention by the marines followed in 1916. The plight of Nicaragua was essentially the same: a financial protectorate in 1911, and American troops later. The grip of the *yanqui* tightened in 1916 with the Bryan-Chamorro treaty for the Nicaraguan waterway route, with important leaseholds near each end. Haiti likewise felt the paternal hand of Washington when disorders brought troops in 1915, and financial supervision the next year.[1]

World War I introduced new complications. The United States purchased the Virgin Islands in 1917, rather than run the risk of their falling into German hands. General Pershing's frustrating pursuit of Villa ended

---

[1] Franklin D. Roosevelt, candidate for Vice-President in 1920, indiscreetly and somewhat inaccurately boasted that while Assistant Secretary of the Navy he had written the constitution of Haiti himself. Frank Freidel, *Franklin D. Roosevelt: The Ordeal* (Boston, 1954), pp. 81–82.

early in 1917, on the eve of war with Germany. The invaders left the Mexican people resentful over this pollution of their soil, while harboring bitter memories of the brutal bombardment and occupation of Vera Cruz in 1914. Mexican hatred manifested itself during World War I in the harboring or promoting of much pro-German activity, to the great annoyance of the neighboring Yankees.

Yet "democratic" Latin America generally supported the war to make the world "safe for democracy" from 1917 to 1918. Seven republics remained nominally neutral, including Mexico, Argentina, and Chile. Five severed relations, including marine-occupied Santo Domingo. Eight declared war on Germany, including coffee-producing Brazil, the traditional friend of the United States in Latin America, and four Yankee-dominated republics of the Caribbean: Panama, Nicaragua, Haiti, and Cuba.[2]

The Latin Americans on the whole responded favorably to Wilson's wartime leadership. With their strong idealistic bent they became ardent advocates of the League of Nations, although ironically some of their enthusiasm sprang from the prospect of using it to thwart the aggressions of the Colossus of the North. But when the United States repudiated the League, and Wilson's orphaned brain child got off to a feeble start, American prestige dropped to new depths. A common attitude was reflected in the Latin-American sneer, "There is no God but the dollar and the Yankee is his prophet."

The World War ended in 1918, but friction with Mexico did not. The Mexican Constitution of 1917, promulgated under President Carranza's auspices by a rigged convention, was a flaming revolutionary document dedicated to the principle "Mexico for the Mexicans." Pro-labor and pro-landless, it was also violently anti-Catholic and antiforeign. Most alarming to outside exploiters was Article 27, which vested in the nation ownership of all subsoil properties, including minerals and oil. President Carranza declared in 1918 that this clause was retroactive, whereupon American oil and mining promoters redoubled their cries of "confiscation" by a "godless and socialistic" regime.

A temporary adjustment of the oil squabble was finally threshed out. Secretary of the Interior Fall, who was later jailed for his part in the Teapot Dome oil scandal, kept up the pressure. Washington even used the old Wilsonian club of withholding recognition from General Obregón, the new strong-man president of Mexico. In 1923, after patient negotiations, the Mexican government gave a tacit pledge that Article 27 would not be applied retroactively, and Washington in turn expressed its satisfaction by recognizing Obregón as president. Thus ended a trouble-fraught era.

[2] See T. A. Bailey, *The Policy of the United States toward the Neutrals, 1917–1918* (Baltimore, 1942), Ch. X.

BAYONETS IN SANTO DOMINGO AND NICARAGUA

The Harding-Coolidge era ushered in a happier day in relations with Latin America. The Wilsonian role of "Policeman of the Caribbean" had come under fire in the Presidential campaign of 1920, and Secretary of State Hughes embarked upon a more conciliatory course.

Santo Domingo, perhaps the ugliest example of Yankee dictatorship, benefited from this more enlightened policy. The United States in 1924 concluded a hope-giving treaty, under which the marines sounded taps and departed. But a financial adviser remained to keep customs receipts out of the hands of grafting politicians, and to reimburse Santo Domingo's foreign creditors. Supervision from Washington did not end until 1941.

Less auspicious was the fate of Nicaragua, with its optional canal route and its latent threat to the Panama lifeline. In 1925 the marines ended their thirteen-year guardianship, for by then the nervous New York bankers had been paid off. But the Liberals, long out of power and plunder, raised the standard of revolt against the entrenched Conservatives. The bayonets of the marines returned in 1926.

The crisis in Nicaragua rapidly deepened. The Washington authorities, hoping to speed stability, rather hastily recognized the Conservative government of Díaz. Mexico, already involved in serious new difficulties with the United States over oil expropriation, recognized and sent munitions to the rival Liberal regime of Sacasa. The Coolidge administration in turn clamped an embargo on arms to Sacasa, while allowing American-financed munitions to flow freely to Díaz. In 1927, when Sacasa seemed to be winning out, President Coolidge landed several thousand marines to fight what critics called his "private war" but actually, at the request of Díaz, to protect American lives and property.

The conflict in Nicaragua, waged without a declaration of war by Congress, aroused a storm of opposition in the United States. Most of the uproar came from liberals, anti-imperialists, and Democrats—the party of the "outs." In Congress, one Democrat cried quite irrelevantly, "Oh, Monroe Doctrine, how many crimes have been committed in thy name?" —to the accompaniment of cheers from the Democratic side. Smarting under these attacks, President Coolidge sent a message to Congress early in 1927, in which he stressed the safeguarding of American lives and property, and the prevention of foreign infiltration into the Isthmus. Several months later he asserted, "We are not making war on Nicaragua any more than a policeman on the street is making war on passersby."

The log jam was broken by Colonel Henry L. Stimson, Hoover's future Secretary of State, whom Coolidge sent as a personal representative to Nicaragua in April, 1927. Stimson induced most of the factions to surrender their rifles and submit to an American-supervised election.[3] The results of the balloting were so satisfactory that both political parties, Conservatives and Liberals, united in requesting similar supervision of the ballot boxes four years later. In one of these American-chaperoned elections, the ingenious Yankees eliminated "repeating" by staining the fingers of the voters with mercurochrome. On the whole, Colonel Stimson's patient diplomacy contributed to a betterment of relations with Nicaragua.

The final withdrawal of the American marines was delayed several years, until 1933, by the opposition of one rebel leader, General Sandino. Regarded as a "bandit" by Washington and as a *"patriota"* by many Nicaraguans, he and his ragged following made life miserable for the occupying force. He was treacherously shot by Nicaraguan officers in 1934, after he had surrendered his arms.

MEXICAN MISUNDERSTANDINGS

A major crisis with Mexico paralleled and was inflamed by that with Nicaragua.

The ultraliberal Constitution of 1917 was the bone of contention. President Calles, an iron-jawed son of poverty, alarmed the foreign oil companies in 1925 by reversing President Obregón's assurances and making retroactive the expropriation of subsoil properties.[4] Seeking to implement the constitution further, he launched violent attacks on the big landholders, on employers of labor, and on the Roman Catholic Church. The clergy, in resisting the deportation of foreign priests and the closing of church schools and convents, went on a "strike," and for three years there was no public Mass in all Mexico.

A new clamor for war with Mexico arose in the United States. The oil companies released tons of propaganda, in which they demanded armed intervention for the protection of their alleged rights. The Knights of Columbus and other Roman Catholic groups organized protest meetings and published their appeals in the newspapers. Secretary Kellogg was so indiscreet as to add fuel to the flames by publicly declaring in 1925, "The Government of Mexico is now on trial before the world." In 1926, and particularly in 1927 at the height of the Nicaragua crisis, he ineptly gave new life to the war scare by resurrecting the Bolshevik bogey. He declared that Soviet agents, harbored in Mexico, were encouraging the Nicaraguans to resist Yankee aggression. Relations between the United States and its southern neighbor could hardly have been worse, short of a complete rupture in diplomatic relations.

[3] H. L. Stimson, *American Policy in Nicaragua* (New York, 1927); H. L. Stimson and M. Bundy, *On Active Service in Peace and War* (New York, 1947).
[4] See W. C. Gordon, *The Expropriation of Foreign-Owned Property in Mexico* (Washington, 1941).

At this critical juncture, in September, 1927, President Coolidge happily appointed his former Amherst College classmate, Dwight W. Morrow, as ambassador to Mexico. Although a rank amateur in diplomacy and a partner in the banking House of Morgan, he had none of the stuffiness of the striped-pants professional. Before leaving for his new post he remarked, "I know what I can do for the Mexicans. I can *like* them." His sympathetic and friendly approach, combined with insight and tact, wrought an amazing change of opinion among the Mexican people. He was even greeted on his travels with enthusiastic cries of approval. To give dramatic point to the new cordiality, Morrow arranged to have the aviator Charles A. Lindbergh, recent solo conqueror of the Atlantic, to fly to Mexico City late in 1927. The reception accorded "the Ambassador of the Air" was so overwhelming as to prompt the *Philadelphia Evening Ledger* to suggest that the conduct of all foreign affairs be turned over to the airmen. The *New York Sun* suggested as a new version of the old floral slogan: "Say it with flyers."

In this mellowing atmosphere, Morrow achieved a spectacular diplomatic triumph—in a sense the first real beginnings of the embryonic Good Neighbor policy. First of all, he established a solid friendship with President Calles, whom he met repeatedly on a face-to-face basis. Late in 1927 the Mexican Supreme Court, under pressure from Calles, decreed that foreign companies which had begun to work their subsoil properties before 1917 might retain ownership. Morrow also helped persuade Calles to slow down his land-seizure program and end his violent anti-Catholic crusade. The bells in the cathedrals rang again.

With the Mexican storm clouds clearing, the Sixth International Conference of American States met at Havana, Cuba, in January, 1928. President Coolidge, arriving inappropriately on a battleship, opened the sessions in person. The atmosphere was electric, for the presence of the American marines in Nicaragua was bitterly resented, and the skeleton of intervention threatened to burst from the closet at any moment. On the last session of the Conference the eruption finally occurred during a debate over a resolution that "no state has the right to intervene in the internal affairs of another." Ex-Secretary Hughes turned the tide and headed off a final vote when, in a supreme effort, he defended the right of "interposition of a temporary character" to prevent Americans from being "butchered in the jungle." This was the last major stand of intervention; within five years Washington officially renounced it.

HOOVER PIONEERS FOR THE GOOD NEIGHBOR

President-elect Hoover, shortly after his triumph at the polls in November, 1928, embarked upon a seven-week good-will tour which took him to more than half of the Latin-American republics. The enthusiasm was spotty. The distinguished visitor rather ominously came on a battleship (penny-pinching Coolidge had preferred a cruiser for him as less expensive), and as Secretary of Commerce for nearly eight years he had been indirectly tarred with the interventionist policies of Harding and Coolidge. One Cuban journal sourly declared that the trip would not help the republics "practically strangled by United States imperialism":

> If Mr. Hoover wants to conquer the immediate sympathy of Latin America, he should at once announce a change in the policy of his country, declaring that the Monroe Doctrine does not mean that the American continent is only for the United States, that Haiti will be evacuated, that Nicaragua shall be freed from foreign yoke, that Cuba will see the quick abrogation of the Platt Amendment, that our commercial treaties will cease being one-sided affairs, that our countries will be free to manage their own affairs as they deem fit, and that the United States is a real friend in fact, and not a conqueror.[5]

Yet the good-will tour seems to have generated some good will. The hitherto snubbed Latin Americans could hardly fail to be flattered by this unprecedented evidence of interest in them. The ovations were particularly heart-warming in Brazil, the traditional friend and coffee bag of the United States. While on the tour, Hoover suggested the formula by which the Tacna-Arica territorial dispute, a half-century running sore between Chile and Peru, was amicably settled in 1929 by a division of the area. Finally, by repeated emphasis on both the theme and slogan "Good Neighbor," Hoover gave promise of happier days to come.[6]

When the curtain officially rose on his administration in 1929, Hoover revealed his determination to accelerate "the retreat from imperialism" in Latin America. In his inaugural address, he confidently announced that "we have no desire for territorial expansion, for economic or other domination of other peoples." Alluding in his first annual message to the United States Marines in Nicaragua and Haiti, he declared that "we do not wish to be represented abroad in such a manner."

Perhaps more heartening was the semi-official Clark *Memorandum on the Monroe Doctrine*. Prepared in 1928 by J. Reuben Clark, then Undersecretary of State, this 236-page document flatly repudiated the interventionist twist given the famed Doctrine by Theodore Roosevelt in 1904. Arguing that the numerous Caribbean interventions had not been justified by the original Monroe Doctrine, the memorandum went on to say that the dictum of 1823 "states a case of United States *vs.* Europe, and not of the United States *vs.* Latin-America." The right of intervention was not surrendered, only the right to intervene under the aegis of the Monroe Doctrine—a policy designed for defense, not domination. Hoover's new Secretary of State, Colonel Stimson of Nicaraguan

---

[5] *Literary Digest*, Dec. 8, 1928, p. 15.
[6] Alexander DeConde, in *Herbert Hoover's Latin-American Policy* (Stanford, 1951), finds the beginnings of the Good Neighbor. See also *The Memoirs of Herbert Hoover: The Cabinet and the Presidency, 1920–1933* (New York, 1952).

mediation fame, approved the hand-tying Clark *Memorandum*, although it was not published until 1930, a year after he took office. Subordinate officials in the State Department, as well as Hoover, treated the statement as unofficial and unimportant. Yet the avowed intent to keep hands off Latin America helped to foster Good Neighborism.

THE DEPRESSION AND GOOD NEIGHBORISM

The Great Depression subjected the new policy of nonintervention to a severe test. A rash of revolutions, partly the result of economic maladies, broke out in Latin America. Disorders in Mexico and Brazil threatened serious complications, but in both cases Washington embargoed arms to the rebels and remained on the sidelines. When the revolutionists triumphed in Brazil, the State Department accorded prompt recognition. This was a conspicuous example of a further retreat from the old Wilsonian policy of interference by using the nonrecognition bludgeon. Henceforth the warm hand of brotherhood would generally be extended to *de facto* regimes, whether of saints or sinners, legitimate rulers or blood-stained usurpers.

The good will laboriously built up by Hoover south of the border unhappily received a severe jolt from the Hawley-Smoot Tariff of 1930. The Latin Americans, already knee deep in the depression and long sensitive to Yankee economic barriers, reacted bitterly. They regarded the new tariff law as a deliberate blow below the trade belt, and their anger mounted accordingly.

Yet the impact of the depression on Latin American relations was not wholly bad. It contributed to a less aggressive and less predatory attitude by the *norteamericanos*. Potential investors in the United States had much less money to invest. Huge sums that they had sunk into Latin America were now represented by worthless securities that might well have been used for wall paper. The so-called Yankee exploiters were themselves exploited to the tune of billions of dollars—Dollar Diplomacy in reverse gear. With investments thus gone sour, American citizens who had surplus capital betrayed little eagerness to invest it below the border, and consequently they were less inclined to bring pressure on Washington to send down the marines.

The stage was set for troop withdrawals. In 1932, perhaps the worst year of the depression, the United States concluded a treaty with Haiti providing for the departure of the marines. Although the Haitian legislature turned it down because of a remnant of financial supervision, the handwriting was clearly on the wall. In Nicaragua, early in 1933, the marine buglers sounded their last shrill notes. Herbert Hoover, the Engineer in Politics, thus happily engineered the foundation stones of the Good Neighbor Policy.

ROOSEVELT CHAMPIONS GOOD NEIGHBORLINESS

Franklin D. Roosevelt baptized, publicized, and glamorized the Good Neighbor Policy, even if he did not invent it. As the liberal leader of a Democratic Party that was anti-Big Banker and anti-Big Business, he seemed to be divinely appointed to carry the new policy to fruition. In his inaugural address he dramatically dedicated the United States to the role of "the Good Neighbor," in both hemispheres. He worked hand in glove with Secretary of State Cordell Hull, "the last of the log-cabin statesmen," who became a zealot for the reciprocal trade agreements program. The consequent reduction of tariff duties for co-operating Latin American states took much of the sting out of Hoover's Hawley-Smoot Tariff, and contributed to a more wholesome atmosphere south of the Rio Grande.

The Latin Americans were still highly skeptical as preparations went forward for the Seventh International Conference of American States, in Montevideo, Uruguay, late in 1933. They remembered all too keenly the Sixth Conference at Havana in 1928, where ex-Secretary Hughes had fought valiantly for the right to intervene. When Secretary Hull, the head of the American delegation approached Montevideo, he was greeted with billboard signs, "Down with Hull." But when the ghost of intervention rose again, he delighted the delegates by supporting a pact which declared that "No state has the right to intervene in the internal or external affairs of another." The Montevideo Conference adjourned amid every indication of a new cordiality toward the old Colossus of the North. The United States Senate approved the pact without a dissenting vote, and with only one mild reservation.

Franklin Roosevelt vigorously supported the new policy of nonintervention, even though it meant reversing completely the preventive interventionism of his distant cousin, Theodore Roosevelt.[7] Grave disorders in Cuba, springing from the world-wide depression and the bloody rule of Machado "the butcher," sorely tried Washington's patience. But troops were not landed, though warships arrived in Cuban waters and the old nonrecognition bludgeon was used temporarily with good effect. But by this time the Platt Amendment had clearly outlived whatever usefulness it had ever enjoyed. To the intense delight of Cubans, and the joy of Latin Americans everywhere, Washington signed an epochal treaty in May, 1934, releasing Cuba outright from the thirty-three-year old hobbles of the Platt Amendment.

[7] One irreverent commentator, paraphrasing Job I, 21, quipped: "A Roosevelt gave and a Roosevelt hath taken away, blessed be the name of the Roosevelts." A comprehensive general account is E. O. Guerrant, *Roosevelt's Good Neighbor Policy* (Albuquerque, N.M., 1950).

The new deal for Latin America was in evidence elsewhere. Roosevelt revived the Hooverian proposal to evacuate Haiti, and under the Executive agreement of 1933 the marines folded their tents in 1934. Although financial control extended until 1941, the departure of the American troops ended a twenty-year occupation. For the first time since 1915 no U.S. troops trod Latin-American soil. None returned until 1965, when President Johnson ordered the Dominican intervention (p. 901).

NONINTERVENTION TRIUMPHANT

The darkening menace of the dictators on the European horizon prompted Roosevelt, in 1936, to propose a special Inter-American Conference for peace. Buenos Aires, in Argentina, was selected as the site, and the polio-crippled President journeyed by sea the seven thousand miles as "a traveling salesman for peace." Following an enthusiastic reception, he opened the Conference with a dramatic speech, in which he declared that non-American states seeking "to commit acts of aggression against us will find a Hemisphere wholly prepared to consult together for our mutual safety and our mutual good."

This clear invitation to make the Monroe Doctrine multilateral against the dictators was not then accepted; conflicting jealousies and prior obligations to the dying League of Nations imposed a barrier. The Conference instead adopted a consultative pact for further co-ordinating the existing peace machinery. It likewise adopted a protocol again endorsing nonintervention. Prompt acceptance by the United States, without any strings whatever, provided gratifying evidence that the new policy of no-interference was more than temporary.

Nonintervention received its acid test in a renewal of the oil controversy with Mexico, with which relations had been reasonably good since the Morrow settlement in 1927. Following the refusal of the foreign companies to meet the demands of Mexican strikers, the government in 1938 expropriated the oil properties. The American concerns involved valued their holdings, perhaps extravagantly, at some $260 million. The right of the Mexican government to expropriate could not be successfully challenged, provided that proper compensation was paid. But on this point there was grave doubt. Again a clamor rose in the United States from the oil companies for strong-armed intervention.[8] But President Roosevelt, ably supported in Mexico by genial Ambassador Daniels, kept a tight rein. He was pledged to nonintervention, he valued the labor vote in America, he distrusted big business, and he coveted Mexican co-operation in the impending showdown with the dictators.

A sweeping compromise settlement, involving also agrarian lands, was finally reached with Mexico in November, 1941, the month before the

[8] See B. M. McConnell, *Mexico at the Bar of Public Opinion* (New York, 1939).

sneak Japanese attack on Pearl Harbor. The American oil companies ultimately received about $42 million, or less than one-sixth of what they demanded. Even making allowance for exaggerated claims, their interests were substantially sacrificed to the larger national interest—the success of the Good Neighbor Policy and the defense of the democracies against the dictators. One gratifying result was that Mexico entered World War II as a co-operative ally of the United States, rather than the snarling neighbor she had been in World War I.

CLOSER CONTACTS WITH CANADA

The Good Neighbor Policy embraced Canada, no less than Latin America, and there it likewise bore wholesome fruit.

But the northern orchard required much cultivation. The noxious weeds of the rigged Alaska boundary settlement of 1903 and of the abortive reciprocity agreement of 1911 remained. They choked out any lingering hopes of annexation, and helped to turn Canada toward a high-protectionist course. In 1914 the Canadians plunged into World War I promptly on the side of Mother England. America stayed on the sidelines, counting her profits while Canada counted her dead. The United States finally entered the conflict, belatedly in Canadian eyes, and then claimed extravagant credit for the final victory—"The Yanks did it!" Canadian resentment was not salved when America, after forcing the League on the world, ran off and left the waif on the doorstep of Geneva.[9]

The American prohibition of alcoholic liquors in the 1920's struck the Canadians as silly and troublesome, though profitable. Countless cases of Scotch whisky, "just off the boat," leaked down across the American border, where constant friction developed with prohibition agents. As further evidence of her complete independence, Canada by 1927 was represented in Washington by a full-fledged minister, much of whose time was taken up with these irritating incidents. The most spectacular outrage of all involved the pursuit and sinking in 1929 of a Canadian-registered rum-runner, *I'm Alone,* off the Louisiana coast, with the loss of one life. The dispute was finally referred to two arbiters, who in 1935 required appropriate apologies and indemnities of the United States, even though the real owners were American bootleggers.

The coming of the Franklin Roosevelt administration and the repeal of prohibition in 1933 heralded a new day. The Hooverian Hawley-Smoot Tariff had goaded the Canadians into retaliating with higher tariffs and extending preferential rates to associate members of the Empire. One of Secretary Hull's major reciprocal trade agreements, concluded in 1935,

---

[9] See H. L. Keenleyside and G. S. Brown, *Canada and the United States* (New York, 1952), Ch. X. A less comprehensive survey is J. M. Callahan, *American Foreign Policy in Canadian Relations* (New York, 1937).

brought about a substantial lowering of tariff barriers and a reduction of ill feeling on each side of the border.

A troublesome legacy from the later Hoover years was the St. Lawrence Waterway Treaty, signed in 1932. It provided for the deepening of the St. Lawrence-Great Lakes Waterway so as to transform the lake ports into seaports, and for the development of electric power. Strong opposition arose in the Senate, especially from members who did not want the government to enter the power business or who feared that traffic would be diverted from the railroads. In March, 1934, the proposal failed of the two-thirds vote by 46 yeas to 42 nays. But President Roosevelt was not greatly disturbed: he blandly announced that the scheme would one day be adopted, "just as sure as God made little apples." This prediction came true twenty years later. (See p. 828.)

The menacing rise of the dictators in Europe served to draw Canada and the United States closer together than ever before. Roosevelt sensationally declared in a speech at Kingston, Canada, in 1938: "I give you my assurance that the people of the United States will not stand idly by if domination of Canadian soil is threatened by any other empire." [10] The Canadians enthusiastically applauded what was widely regarded as an extension of the Monroe Doctrine to their soil. Although Roosevelt's declaration seems to have been the first official coupling of the Doctrine with Canada, the no-transfer principle of the original dictum had always applied to all North America and South America.

PAN-AMERICANISM AT LIMA AND PANAMA

The startling gains of the European dictators, highlighted by the surrender of the Western democracies to Hitler at Munich in 1938, caused the United States to look with increasing apprehension to the leaks in the Latin-American dike. German and Italian propagandists were sleeplessly active, especially in Argentina, where hundreds of thousands of German and Italian immigrants lived.

Argentina was the chief obstacle in the path of effective Pan-American action against the dictators. Aside from blood relationships and commercial ties with dictator-cursed Germany and Italy, she was jealous of Uncle Sam's leadership, and resentful of his tariff barriers against Argentine beef and grain. She was also suspicious of Washington's traditional friendship with her great rival Brazil. Unlike Argentina, Brazil produced coffee and other products which were not grown in the United States and against which tariff protection was not deemed necessary.

The Eighth International Conference of American States, which convened at Lima, Peru, late in 1938, was concerned mainly with concerted action against aggression by the European dictators, Hitler and Mus-

[10] *New York Times*, Aug. 19, 1938, 1:1.

solini. The special Pan-American conference at Buenos Aires two years earlier had provided for consultation in the face of danger, but had left unanswered the question of how. Secretary Hull grappled manfully with this problem, even though the Argentine Foreign Minister unaccountably left the Conference and remained incommunicado among the Chilean lakes. The famed Declaration of Lima, approved unanimously on Christ-

The Hemispheric Safety Belt 1939

mas Eve, 1938, not only supported common action by the American republics to meet a common danger, but provided that the foreign ministers of all of them should meet upon the call of any one of them.

The first conference of foreign ministers met at Panama in September, 1939, a few days after Hitler's Germany had shattered the peace of Europe by his invasion of Poland. Acting with surprising unanimity and dispatch, the assemblage adopted the Declaration of Panama. This document proclaimed a "safety belt" around the Americas south of belligerent Canada, ranging from some 300 to 1000 miles in width, and warned the combatants to refrain from warlike action within that area. But the so-called "chastity belt" proved ineffective. The American republics were unwilling to use force to uphold it, and neither set of belligerents was willing to accept this upstart restriction upon traditional freedom of action.[11] Yet the Declaration of Panama was concrete evidence of a willingness to take common action not only to provide hemispheric defense, but to avert involvement in the European war.

MULTILATERALIZING MONROE'S DOCTRINE

The spectacular collapse of the Low Countries and France, under Hitler's sledgehammer blows in May and June, 1940, posed an immediate threat to the security of the Americas. Britain might momentarily go under, and with her the powerful fleet that stood between the Western Hemisphere and the power-mad dictators. The American people for perhaps the first time became keenly aware of the relationship between the Monroe Doctrine and a friendly British navy.

One burning question was what to do with the orphaned colonies of Denmark, Holland, and France, especially the Dutch and French West Indies and Dutch and French Guiana. Their seizure by Hitler would constitute an intolerable threat to the Panama Canal, the Caribbean commercial lifeline, and perhaps the mainland of the United States. Even before France formally surrendered, Congress overwhelmingly passed a resolution, in June, 1940, firmly opposing the transfer of territory in the Western hemisphere "from one non-American power to another non-American power." The Berlin Foreign Office responded in such defiant terms as to deepen American fears of Hitler's designs.

The downfall of France spurred the meeting at Havana, in July, 1940, of the second Conference of the Foreign Ministers of the American republics. The most notable fruit, despite Germany's threats of postwar economic reprisals, was the Act of Havana. This declaration provided that the colonies of European powers, if in danger of falling into hostile hands, might be taken over and administered jointly by the American republics, pending the independence or restoration of the jeopardized territory. If the need for haste was imperative, individual nations like the United States might move in temporarily, subject to later review. (Such a drastic step did not prove necessary.) A treaty implementing the Act of Havana was approved by the necessary two-thirds of the American republics early in 1942.

[11] For example, three British cruisers fought the German pocket-battleship *Graf Spee* in a spectacular action off the Uruguyan coast, in December, 1939. Winston Churchill, *The Gathering Storm* (Boston, 1948), pp. 518–526.

The Act of Havana was a milestone in both the history of Pan-Americanism and of the Monroe Doctrine. It was not only an epochal act of joint defense but the most striking step yet taken toward the multi-lateralization of the Monroe Doctrine. The original dictum of 1823 had been a stick which the United States had held unilaterally over the heads of potential intruders. Now twenty other pairs of smaller hands would help hold the club. In dire emergencies, the Latin-American republics would even permit Uncle Sam to swing the club all by himself. Their official willingness to do so was proof not only of the gravity of the crisis but also of their new faith in the Good Neighborliness of the onetime Colossus of the North.

Canada, no less than Latin America, demanded attention, particularly in view of the possible destruction of the British navy and a Hitlerian invasion. In August, 1940, President Roosevelt invited Prime Minister King to Ogdensburg, New York, during army maneuvers. There they agreed upon procedures for setting up the Permanent Joint Board of Defense, which would study common defensive problems. Why should a technical neutral like the United States be making a military pact with a belligerent like Canada? The answer is that the American people clearly realized that the defense of Canada was also the defense of the United States, and they were prepared to back up their conviction with force.[12]

The historic Rush-Bagot disarmament agreement of 1817 was modified in 1940, and again later, to permit ship construction and other naval activity on the Great Lakes. The calm waters of the lakes were ideal for training with aircraft carriers, and the shipyards were needed to build smaller craft for the desperate struggle against Hitler. With the two northern neighbors now virtual allies, not enemies, the old restrictions born of suspicion no longer had reality.

GOOD NEIGHBORISM PAYS OFF

The United States in 1940–1941 was not content with such pronouncements as the Panama "safety belt" and the Havana multilateralization of the Monroe Doctrine. The Division of Cultural Relations of the Department of State engaged in an extensive program to combat German Nazi propaganda in Latin America. A steady stream of good-will missions flowed south from the United States, consisting of academicians, journalists, and actors like Douglas Fairbanks, Jr. There was some little resentment among the Latin republics against this obvious, eleventh-hour courtship—"good-will slumming," it was cynically called. But the results on the whole seemed reassuring.

Further steps were taken to bolster hemispheric defense. A half dozen

[12] Gallup found, in June, 1940, that Americans with opinions favored defending Canada in the ratio of 87% to 13%. *Pub. Opin. Quar.,* IV, 553.

or so military, naval, and economic missions were sent to Latin America, or received from Latin America in the United States. Washington increasingly opened its capacious coffers and advanced loans in strategic spots. A half dozen or so of the republics, either formally or informally, made available their defense facilities in the common cause.

A partial hatchet-burying was even achieved with jealous Argentina. Yankee tariff barriers against Argentine grain, combined with quarantines on meat, had resulted in such bitterness that late in 1940 Buenos Aires

THE ONLY "PAN-AMERICAN RAT HOLE"

Bishop in the *St. Louis Star-Times*, 1943

proclaimed a temporary embargo on all United States imports. But in the face of the Hitlerian menace, an important trade agreement was signed in October, 1941, on the eve of Pearl Harbor.

The violent attack of the Japanese on the United States in 1941 brought heart-warming manifestations of solidarity from the sister republics. This response contrasted most favorably with 1917–1918, when Mexico was downright unfriendly and other states flirted openly with Germany. The danger to the Western Hemisphere, to be sure, seemed much more acute in 1941 than in 1917. But more than that, the Good Neighbor Policy had achieved a common understanding. At long last Pan-Americanism had been transformed from a flowery phrase to a functional fact.

SELECTED BIBLIOGRAPHY

The best general surveys are S. F. Bemis, *The Latin-American Policy of the United States* (New York, 1943) and H. L. Keenleyside and G. S. Brown, *Canada and the United States* (rev. ed., New York, 1952). See also G. H. Stuart, *Latin America and the United States* (5th ed., New York, 1954). On the Caribbean, consult Dexter Perkins, *The United States and the Caribbean* (Cambridge, Mass., 1947) and J. F. Rippy, *The Caribbean Danger Zone* (New York, 1940). The most recent survey is H. F. Cline, *The United States and Mexico* (Cambridge, Mass., 1953). See also J. F. Rippy, *The United States and Mexico* (rev. ed., New York, 1931) and J. M. Callahan, *American Foreign Policy in Mexican Relations* (New York, 1932). On the Roosevelt Good Neighbor era, consult books by two participants: Sumner Welles, *The Time for Decision* (New York, 1944) and *The Memoirs of Cordell Hull* (2 vols., New York, 1948); also Dexter Perkins, *A History of the Monroe Doctrine* (rev. ed., Boston, 1955). On special areas see A. P. Whitaker, *The United States and South America: the Northern Republics* (Cambridge, Mass., 1948) and *The United States and Argentina* (Cambridge, Mass., 1954). Hoover is briefly considered in R. H. Ferrell, *American Diplomacy in the Great Depression* (New Haven, 1957).

See footnotes of this chapter and *Harvard Guide*, Chs. 28, 29.

7TH ED. REFS. Bryce Wood, *The Making of the Good Neighbor Policy* (New York, 1961) downgrades Hoover's pioneering effort and credits F.D.R. with shaping a new concept: the interest of the nation is superior to that of private investors. The liberal New Deal domestic policies helped induce the Latin Americans to have faith in Washington's promises. D. M. Dozer, *Are We Good Neighbors?: Three Decades of Inter-American Relations, 1930–1960* (Gainesville, Fla., 1961) is a useful survey which stresses Hoover's alleged hypocrisy in proclaiming nonintervention while continuing it in the Caribbean; F.D.R.'s great popularity; and trade improvement under the Good Neighbor Policy. J. L. Mecham, *The United States and Inter-American Security, 1889–1960* (Austin, Tex., 1961) deals in broad terms with the Good Neighbor, while emphasizing the inter-American conferences. E. D. Cronon, *Josephus Daniels in Mexico* (Madison, Wis., 1960) shows how this unlikely ambassador became immensely popular by championing the interests of the Mexicans (sometimes in disregard of instructions) and the long-range interests of the United States as against the short-range interests of American investors. Morrow had represented American capital; Daniels represented the Mexican people. Sister M. Elizabeth Rice, *The Diplomatic Relations between the United States and Mexico as Affected by the Struggle for Religious Liberty in Mexico, 1925–1929* (Washington, 1959) describes Morrow's mediation in temporarily settling the church-state controversy. The church lost more. Morrow deserves much credit, but when he had to choose between American policy and the Vatican, he chose the former. For further 7TH, 8TH, AND 9TH ED. REFS. see BIBLIOGRAPHICAL ADDENDUM, p. 1,036.

CHAPTER

45

Japan, Neutrality, and the Dictators, 1923-1939

There must be positive endeavors to preserve peace.
FRANKLIN D. ROOSEVELT, October 5, 1937
(QUARANTINE SPEECH)

A SLAMMED DOOR FOR JAPANESE

FOR TWO YEARS after the cloud-dispelling Washington Disarmament Conference of 1921–1922, relations between Japan and America were relatively friendly. The frightful Tokyo-Yokohama earthquake of 1923, with its toll of more than 90,000 lives, elicited an outpouring of sympathy and assistance from the United States to which the Japanese responded with gratitude. But overnight the American Immigration Act of 1924 changed cordiality to a burning sense of injustice.

With the existing Emergency Quota Act of 1921 about to expire, Congress was determined to erect new bars against the destitute masses of Europe. The proposed law of 1924 would permit foreign nations to send yearly a maximum of 2 per cent of the number of their nationals residing in the United States in 1890. Secretary Hughes estimated that on this basis the Japanese would be allowed not more than 250 a year—certainly not "a yellow horde."

But anti-Japanese agitators on the Pacific Coast cried out against a quota for Japan. The Gentlemen's Agreement of 1908, under which Tokyo voluntarily withheld passports from coolies coming to the United States, had proved somewhat leaky. Resorting to the "picture bride" scheme, Japanese males in America could lawfully import wives from Japan, with a consequent bumper crop of babies.

Pressures from the Pacific Coast for complete exclusion became so insistent that the Immigration Bill of 1924, as finally drafted, completely barred "aliens ineligible to citizenship." The phrase "aliens ineligible to citizenship," although embracing all Orientals, hit the Japanese a stag-

692

gering blow. It was not only an abrupt abrogation of the long-standing Gentlemen's Agreement, but it was a discriminatory slap at the sensitive Japanese, by far the largest Oriental group affected.

Secretary Hughes, alarmed by the possible consequences of this bill, urged Ambassador Hanihara, the Japanese envoy in Washington, to draw up a detailed explanation of Japan's position. Hughes hoped that Congress might thus be persuaded to put Japan on a quota basis. But the concluding paragraph of Hanihara's statement most ill-advisedly, though truthfully, referred to the "grave consequences" that complete exclusion would have on Japanese-American relations.[1]

The Ambassador's blundering note hastened rather than halted the impending legislation. The anti-Japanese press in America was bitterly aroused by this "veiled threat" of war. The *Seattle Times* branded it "the most insolent message this Government has ever received," while the *Cincinnati Enquirer* believed that the "entrance of foreigners into this country is a privilege to be granted, not a right to be demanded." President Coolidge urged a postponement of discriminatory action against Japan, in the hope that the same end could be achieved by the quiet and face-saving processes of treaty negotiation. But Congress, ever jealous of its right to control immigration, quickly approved Oriental exclusion by overwhelming majorities. Coolidge finally signed the general Immigration Law of 1924 with great reluctance, and only because he felt that the country urgently needed it. If the Japanese-exclusion clause had stood alone, he would have vetoed it.

JAPAN LOSES FACE

The race-conscious people of Japan, ever sensitive to slights, reacted violently against the new legislation. The Japanese press teemed with denunciations of this "outrageous enactment." The Stars and Stripes were desecrated; monster "hate everything American" mass meetings were held; a movement to boycott American goods was begun. One embittered merchant hung over his shop this sign: "DON'T ASK AMERICAN GOODS & AMERICAN DO NOT ASK ME. I DON'T LIKE YANKEE MONKEY." An obscure Japanese superpatriot disemboweled himself in protest near the United States embassy in Tokyo. The date on which the law became effective was declared National Humiliation Day in Japan. The liberal friends of America in Japan were discredited; the illiberal military elements were emboldened to launch out upon an anti-American, imperialistic course. They finally got into the saddle, and drank deep of revenge at Pearl Harbor.

The United States, as Tokyo was the first to admit, had a perfect legal

[1] See M. J. Pusey, *Charles Evans Hughes* (2 vols., New York, 1951); R. W. Paul, *The Abrogation of the Gentlemen's Agreement* (Cambridge, Mass., 1936).

right to adopt any type of immigration act it chose. But Congress, with blind impetuosity, forgot that purely "domestic" laws can often produce the most serious foreign complications. The goal of Japanese exclusion could have been achieved, and the good will of a powerful nation could have been retained, by more diplomatic methods. Congress paid much too high a price in hate for the spiteful satisfaction of excluding about 200 Japanese immigrants a year.

From 1924 to 1931 American advocates of a quota for Japan made encouraging progress. They were spearheaded by educators, clergymen, church organizations, and particularly by commercial groups, which were pinched by the Japanese boycotts. But in 1931 the Nipponese militarists unsheathed the sword in Manchuria, and two turbulent decades had to pass before Japan was put on a quota basis.[2]

JAPAN'S MANCHURIAN MACHINATIONS

A curtain-raiser for Japan's seizure of China's Manchuria came in the Russo-Chinese clash of 1929. A resurgent Nationalist China, seeking to weaken the Soviet sphere of influence in North Manchuria, arrested certain Russian Communist agents and seized tell-tale propaganda documents. The Soviets responded with a full-fledged invasion of Manchuria, and speedily forced the Chinese to accept terms of peace.

Both Russia and China were recent signatories of the Kellogg-Briand Pact of 1928, which completely renounced aggressive war. Secretary of State Stimson, a strong advocate of collective security, energetically sought to marshal support from the other powers to bring about a cease fire. But his vigorous intervention had no demonstrable bearing on the outcome, and Moscow stingingly rebuked him for brashly giving advice to a government which Washington did not then even recognize. The whole episode further advertised the weakness of China, the hollowness of the Kellogg-Briand Pact, and the futility of trying to halt determined aggression with the wrist-slap of world opinion. These lessons were not lost on Japan's ambitious militarists.

If Russia had a traditional sphere of interest in North Manchuria, Japan had one in South Manchuria—one that was even more vital to her livelihood. A reawakening China was likewise attempting to re-establish her authority in this coveted outer province, where ugly anti-Japanese incidents were recurring. The military elements in Japan, seeking to assert their independence of civilian control, brazenly forced a showdown. "Japan's chief trouble," noted the *Erie Times*, "seems to be a truck complex on an Austin chassis."

[2] See E. Tupper and G. E. McReynolds, *Japan in American Public Opinion* (New York, 1937). The Chinese were put on the quota in 1943; the Japanese (and other Orientals), after the war, by the McCarran-Walter Act of 1952.

On the night of September 18, 1931, an explosion, evidently staged by the Japanese militarists, slightly damaged the Japanese-controlled South Manchurian railroad.[3] The Mikado's armed forces, in retaliation, rapidly overran most of the key Chinese positions in South Manchuria. The speed and precision of these thrusts seemed to be positive proof of an elaborately preconceived plan.

Japan's naked aggression was a violation of the League Covenant, the Nine-Power Pact of 1922, and the Kellogg-Briand Pact of 1928. Washington, as a party to the last two instruments, was prompted to lodge solemn protests with Tokyo. But the American people, depression-mired and isolationist-bent, opposed strong action, either alone or jointly with the League. Accordingly, Secretary of State Stimson, though an avowed internationalist, at first favored encouraging Japan and China to settle their quarrel by direct negotiations.

UNCLE SAM SIDLES UP TO THE LEAGUE

There is no real basis for the myth that in 1931 Washington proposed boycotts against Japan which the British and French rejected. On the contrary, Secretary Stimson rebuffed such overtures from the League, although indicating that the United States Navy "probably" would not interfere with an embargo. The peace-loving President Hoover, who was much less of an internationalist than Stimson, set his face like flint against involvement in the Far Eastern quarrel.

Energetic steps by the League powers, even without the United States, might have brought Japan sharply to book in 1931, and averted the calamitous chain of events that followed. But depression-ridden Britain and France, fearing war and hoping to preserve trade and investments in the Far East, had no stomach for taking resolute action, even with the acquiescence of the United States.

While the well-oiled Japanese military machine continued to roll relentlessly into Manchuria, the United States, in October, 1931, took a precedent-shattering step. Responding to an invitation from Geneva, it officially designated a representative to sit with the League Council. But he was carefully instructed to take part in the discussions only insofar as they related to America's obligations under the Kellogg-Briand Pact. Otherwise he was to act solely in the capacity of "observer and auditor." Washington had hitherto shunned the League, and Tokyo naturally regarded the presence of the American agent as deliberately unfriendly.[4]

[3] See R. H. Ferrell, "The Mukden Incident: September 18–19, 1931," *Jour. of Mod. Hist.*, XXVII, 00–72 (March, 1055).
[4] Useful monographs are S. R. Smith, *The Manchurian Crisis, 1931–1932* (New York, 1948); Robert Langer, *Seizure of Territory: The Stimson Doctrine and Related*

After fruitless attempts to compel the Japanese to disgorge Manchuria, the League was forced to temporize. It appointed, at the suggestion of Tokyo and with the approval of Washington, a neutral commission of five, headed by Lord Lytton, to study the crisis at first hand. One member of the group was Major General Frank R. McCoy, an able United States army officer released from active duty for this assignment.

Even these indirect and gingerly efforts at co-operation with the League evoked an angry outcry from the isolationist press of the United States. The *New York Daily News* warned, "Let's shinny on our side of of the street," while an editorial in Hearst's *New York American* bore the caption, "Stimson's Folly." The probabilities are that majority opinion in America did not support the administration's course. President Hoover felt called upon, in his annual message of December, 1931, to assure the nation that he had retained complete freedom of action.

THE NONRECOGNITION BLUDGEON

In January, 1932, after Japan had crushed the last effective resistance in Manchuria, Stimson made a dramatic gesture. Restrained both by President Hoover and by American isolationist opinion from acting vigorously with the League, he addressed an identical note to both Japan and China. Serving notice on them that Washington would not accept any arrangement in Manchuria hurtful to American rights, he declared that the United States "does not intend to recognize any situation, treaty, or agreement which may be brought about by means contrary to the covenants and obligations" of the Kellogg-Briand Pact.

This policy of refusing to recognize gains achieved by force, soon to be known as the Stimson or Hoover-Stimson Doctrine, was not basically new. President Hoover later stated that he found inspiration for it in Secretary Bryan's note to Japan of May 11, 1915, protesting the Twenty-one Demands on China. But the Hoover-Stimson version broadened the base of the nonrecognition doctrine by invoking the Kellogg-Briand Pact, which virtually all nations had endorsed. Thus Washington, while avoiding economic sanctions or other strong-armed measures, would establish a moral sanction against aggression. The diplomacy of condemnation would be a cheap and conscience-satisfying substitute for armed intervention.[5]

Secretary Stimson hoped that both Britain and France, whose finan-

---

Principles in Legal Theory and Diplomatic Practice (Princeton, 1947); P. H. Clyde, "The Diplomacy of 'Playing No Favorites': Secretary Stimson and Manchuria, 1931," *Miss. Valley Hist. Rev.*, XXV (1948), 187–202.

[5] On the Far East crisis see *The Memoirs of Herbert Hoover: The Cabinet and the Presidency, 1920–1933* (New York, 1952). The Stimson viewpoint appears in H. L. Stimson, *The Far Eastern Crisis* (New York, 1936) and H. L. Stimson and M. Bundy, *On Active Service in Peace and War* (New York, 1947).

cial investment in the Far East was vastly larger than America's, would staunchly uphold the nonrecognition doctrine. But the British stake in China was far south of Manchuria, and London responded to Stimson's invitation by professing faith in Tokyo's assurances regarding the Open Door. The rampaging Japanese militarists were not stopped for one moment by Stimson's disapproving note. They recognized that the isolationist and pacifistic United States, acting alone and bogged down in the depression, was in no position to stop them by force. Sticks and stones might break bones, but not paper barricades and moral sanctions.

Public opinion in America, eager to avoid a clash at all costs, warmly supported the cut-rate substitute for force known as the Hoover-Stimson Doctrine. Yet there was a bitter undercurrent of criticism from observers who argued that the note was as useless as it was dangerous. The *Philadelphia Record* entitled an editorial, "Don Quixote Stimson and the Japanese Windmill," while the *Chicago Tribune* hoped that Washington would stop "sticking pins into Japan." Certain cynics were inclined to excuse the Japanese on the ground that they had merely done what the other powers, including America, had long been doing. "Be patient," counseled the *Los Angeles Times*. "When Japan gets her India or her Panama she will oppose land-grabbing too."

THE SHANGHAI ASSAULT

American opinion overwhelmingly sympathized with the Chinese underdog in Manchuria. But it sympathized lukewarmly. The Far East was far away; the dreary depression was close at home. "The American people," asserted the *Philadelphia Record,* "don't give a hoot in a rain barrel who controls North China."

But the lid blew off at Shanghai in January, 1932. Smarting from a boycott inspired by the Manchurian invasion, Japanese troops landed and clashed with the Chinese forces stationed there. During the ensuing fighting, thousands of men, women, and children were bombed or burned to death—at a time when the aerial bombardment of civilians was regarded as utterly uncivilized. A wave of revulsion swept the United States. Editorial pages bristled with such expressions as "insane imperialism," "running amuck," and "beyond the pale of civilized warfare." A few American hotheads urged a declaration of war against Japan. Many more, including prominent figures like President Lowell of Harvard University, advocated a boycott of Japanese goods. By late February, 1932, the *New York Times* could announce that some five thousand civic leaders had signed petitions urging such a course, and many dime-store knick-knacks lay unsold. But a strong body of American opinion—probably a majority—opposed economic sanctions as too dangerous.

Other alternatives were weighed. Secretary Stimson, growing increasingly bold, urged co-operation with the League in imposing a boycott. But President Hoover, true to his Quaker background, again put his foot down. To him, boycotts meant bayonets; embargoes meant bombs. The American Pacific fleet was nevertheless stationed conspicuously in Hawaiian waters, and Secretary Stimson believed that its presence had a sobering effect on the Japanese.[6]

In February, 1932, Stimson urged London to join with Washington in an invocation of the Nine-Power Treaty of 1922 against Japan. He hoped that such co-operative action would pave the way for economic sanctions by the League, which Congress in turn would support. Despite repeated trans-Atlantic telephone appeals from Stimson, Sir John Simon, the British Foreign Secretary, refused to go along. The latter has been savagely criticized for failing to grasp America's outstretched hand during one of the few periods since World War I when she was prepared to extend it. But Sir John no doubt remembered that the League's suggestion of economic sanctions in 1931, at the time of Japan's Manchurian coup, had been spurned in Washington. He preferred to work within the League of Nations, rather than with a power outside it. He probably also perceived that in no case would American opinion permit Congress to impose an economic boycott.

Conventional diplomacy ran its course, as Washington contented itself with paper protests to Tokyo whenever American interests were injured at Shanghai. After the Japanese had recovered face by finally driving out the defending Chinese army, they yielded to joint pressure from America and the other powers. Their withdrawal, in May, 1932, was a belated victory for multipower co-operation, in which the British, their vital interests in China now jeopardized, played a leading role.

NONRECOGNITION OF PUPPET MANCHUKUO

The Japanese imperialists had meanwhile contrived, on February 18, 1932, to proclaim in Manchuria the new state of Manchukuo. Nominally independent, it was obviously a puppet of Tokyo.

This brutal challenge to the Hoover-Stimson Doctrine of nonrecognition did not go unanswered. Secretary Stimson, reluctant to suffer another rebuff by approaching Tokyo directly, prepared a letter to Senator Borah, Chairman of the Senate Committee on Foreign Relations, and gave it to the press on February 23, 1932. It referred to the Nine-Power Pact of 1922 for the protection of China, and further proclaimed that the United States would insist on its treaty rights in the Far East. Stimson then directed

[6] For a highly critical account see R. N. Current, *Secretary Stimson: A Study in Statecraft* (New Brunswick, N.J., 1954); also his "The Stimson Doctrine and the Hoover Doctrine," *Amer. Hist. Rev.*, LIX (1954), 513–542.

attention to his nonrecognition doctrine, and invited the other nations of the world to embrace it.

The letter to Borah had an immediate impact. Scores of American journals ranked it with the great documents of American history, although some cynics, like the *Honolulu Star-Bulletin,* thought that "after Stimson has got through invoking the Nine-Power Treaty, he might try the Ten Commandments." Nevertheless, Stimson could boast of a feather in his cap when, in March, 1932, the Assembly of the League of Nations unanimously adopted an anti-Japanese resolution which incorporated almost verbatim the Hoover-Stimson Doctrine of nonrecognition.

Yet with each passing month Manchukuo seemed more firmly established. The exhaustive report of the League's Lytton Commission, published in September, 1932, condemned Japan's invasion, although noting that the Chinese had given serious provocation. The Assembly of the League endorsed the findings of the investigators, and the State Department declared itself to be in "substantial accord" with the report. The result was that instead of driving Japan out of Manchuria, the League drove Japan out of the League. In March, 1933, Tokyo gave the prescribed notice of withdrawal, effective two years later. Thus the birth cries of Manchukuo heralded the death rattle of the League.

In grappling with the Sino-Japanese crisis of 1931–1932, Washington showed a remarkable willingness to depart from its traditional policy of co-operation in the Far East and "go it alone." Neither President Hoover nor American opinion would support joint-power economic sanctions or military intervention. The paper bullets of moral sanctions were all they would fire. The British and French, fully aware of America's isolationist mood and her nonmembership in the League, found further support in Washington's aloofness for their own timorous course. The inability of the powers to act in unison proved that the Kellogg-Briand Pact was a parchment pretense, and that the League could be bluffed with impunity.[7] In a very real sense the Open Door collapsed, the League fell apart, collective security perished, and World War II began in 1931 on the windswept plains of Manchuria.

THE RAPE OF ETHIOPIA

Japan's successful flouting of the League in 1931–1932 was not lost on the fast-rising dictators in Europe. In October, 1933, Chancellor Hitler abruptly withdrew Germany from the General Disarmament Conference at Geneva and from the League of Nations as well. In March, 1935, he announced that he would openly rearm, in defiance of the Treaty of Versailles. He argued that Germany was released from this obligation by

[7] See Sumner Welles, *The Time for Decision* (New York, 1944), p. 279.

the failure of the Allies to honor their own pledges to reduce armaments.

Late in 1935, the Italian dictator Mussolini undertook to recreate the glories of the Roman Empire in Africa by brazenly seizing semidefenseless Ethiopia. The League of Nations this time had the fortitude to brand Italy an aggressor and to impose economic sanctions. But it failed to include on the prohibited list a few crucial items, such as oil, which would have forced Mussolini's war machine to a grinding halt.

Britain and France were reluctant, with Hitler on the rise, to push Italy into a shooting showdown. They found further excuse for their caution in the realization that certain non-League nations, notably the United States, might continue to ship oil.[8] Washington appealed to American exporters to impose a voluntary "moral embargo" on shipments to Italy, and although this "honor system" met with limited success, the League again was weakened by the nonmembership of the United States. The Roosevelt administration, fearful of an isolationist uproar, made no bones about its reluctance to co-operate officially with the League in imposing sanctions. Yet it indicated that it would not sabotage them.

Hitler took advantage of the Ethiopian crisis, in March, 1936, by boldly reoccupying the Rhineland, in flagrant defiance of what was left of the Treaty of Versailles. The French had the military power to stop him in his tracks, but they and the British, who coveted German trade, fell prey to divided counsels. From then on Hitler was unstoppable. "Appeasing" the dictators by permitting them small gains in the hope of averting bigger losses merely whetted their appetites for more.

THE NATIONAL NEUTRALITY NEUROSIS

As ominous warclouds continued to gather in Europe, the American people stood at the crossroads. They could attempt to halt the dictators and avert war by throwing their weight on the side of the League of Nations and collective security. Or responding to their fears and their traditions, they could try to stay out of war by retreating to the storm cellar of neutrality. They chose the timorous, short-range course.

The decision for neutrality—spurred by postwar disillusionment, war debts, and depression—was largely inspired by the current phobia against the munitions manufacturers. In 1934–1935 an avalanche of lurid books and articles poured from the press, describing the fantastic profits of these "merchants of death," their interlocking international ties, and their skulduggery in fomenting wars so as to sell military hardware.[9]

In response to an overwhelming public sentiment, a Senate Committee,

[8] See Herbert Feis, *Seen from E.A.* (New York, 1947).
[9] For example, see H. C. Engelbrecht and F. C. Hanighen, *Merchants of Death* (New York, 1934).

headed by Gerald P. Nye of North Dakota, began to hold luridly publicized hearings on the munitions traffic. The sinister fact was brought
out—though hardly news—that the American bankers and munitioneers
had reaped fabulous profits during the neutrality period of 1914–1917.
The popular conclusion seemed justified, though quite contrary to historical evidence, that these "blood-suckers" had dragged the United States
into World War I to make more profits and to protect their loans. A
swelling demand rose from the public that Congress prevent the nation's
entry into another conflict by prohibiting this nefarious traffic. The
German submarine of 1917 now seemed to be a minor culprit, and involvement in World War I a colossal blunder.

With the Italo-Ethiopian crisis threatening to plunge the world again
into chaos, Congress hastily passed the Neutrality Act of 1935. Whenever the President should proclaim the existence of a war, he could forbid
the sale or transportation of munitions to the belligerents. He was further
empowered to warn American citizens that they traveled on belligerent
ships *at their own risk*. (The sunken *Lusitania* was still fresh in mind.)
The President and the State Department both favored a more flexible
measure that would permit them to deny munitions to the aggressor,
while making them available to his victim. But a neutrality-minded Congress, with the strong backing of public opinion, overwhelmingly voted
for strait-jacket neutrality. Roosevelt reluctantly signed the bill.

With the European crisis still menacing, Congress the next year passed
the Neutrality Act of 1936. While including the basic provisions of the
first law, it broadened them and made them even more rigid. Loans were
forbidden the belligerents, except for ordinary commercial transactions.
As a means of upholding the Monroe Doctrine, arms could be exported
to a Latin-American state at war with a non-American state. Finally, the
President was required to extend the law to such additional nations as
joined the ranks of the belligerents. If France and Britain, for example,
should go to war to defend Ethiopia against the aggressor Mussolini, the
President would have to embargo munitions and loans to them.

HEAD-IN-THE-SANDS NEUTRALITY LAWS

The outbreak in 1936 of a three-year civil war in Spain revealed glaringly that the neutrality law did not apply to internal conflict. The pro-
Catholic General Franco, who led the rebels, was undertaking to overthrow the existing Loyalist regime, which had proved anticlerical. Franco
was openly supported with arms and men by both Hitler and Mussolini;
the Loyalists to a lesser degree by the Russians. The confused American public was generally indifferent to the outcome, although a small
plurality favored the Loyalists and a smaller group, chiefly in Roman

Catholic centers, favored Franco.[10] Several thousand American volunteers fought for the Loyalists, who were believed to be upholding the cause of democracy.

The traditional policy of the United States, notably in dealing with Latin America, had been to export arms to the legitimate regime, in this case the Loyalists. But so strong was the antiwar feeling in America that Congress, responding to the leadership of President Roosevelt, extended the existing neutrality legislation to civil conflict with only one dissenting vote in both houses, January 6, 1937.

Franco fought on to victory, and then clasped hands in gratitude with his fellow dictators. The Loyalists, if triumphant, might have joined hands with the Soviets, whose support chilled anti-Communist America. Thus the democracies, desperately determined as they were to stay out of the Spanish war, condemned a fellow democracy to death. While standing on the sidelines, they passively encouraged a conflict that proved to be both a testing ground and a small-scale dress rehearsal for World War II.

In 1937, after more mature reflection and in the face of the deepening crisis in Europe, Congress enacted "permanent neutrality." The revamped law, which also applied to civil conflict, reaffirmed the main provisions of the act of 1936 regarding the nonsale and nonexport of munitions, the extension of loans, and the exemption for Latin America. Travel on belligerent ships was now made unlawful, not just at the passenger's risk.

The question arose as to what should be done about raw materials like copper and oil, which were as vital to war-making as munitions themselves. Profit-conscious America, though wedded to neutrality, was unwilling to deny herself all such trade. As a compromise, the law provided that the President could list certain commodities, and these would have to be paid for upon delivery and taken away in the ships of the buyer. This so-called "cash-and-carry" provision was limited to two years.

The Neutrality Act of 1937, although eliminating some of the dangers that had drawn America into World War I, was highly vulnerable to criticism. It was hardly true neutrality, for it extended favored treatment to Latin America and to those sea-controlling nations, like Britain, that could take full advantage of the "cash-and-carry" provision. While not abandoning freedom of the seas, the United States served notice that it would not fight in all cases to uphold its historic policy. It would safeguard its rights by refusing to exercise them. Instead of employing its vast power to support the democracies against aggression, and thus control events in its own interests, it would permit itself to be tossed about at the mercy of events.

[10] A Gallup poll (Jan. 11, 1937) found 12% pro-rebel, 22% pro-Loyalist, and 66% for neither. Hadley Cantril, ed., *Public Opinion* (Princeton, 1951), p. 807. See also F. J. Taylor, *The United States and the Spanish Civil War* (New York, 1956), and the pro-Loyalist C. G. Bowers, *My Mission to Spain* (New York, 1954).

The storm-cellar legislation of the 1930's presumably encouraged the dictators by serving notice that their victims could expect no aid from the rich Uncle Sam. But the extent of such encouragement has probably been exaggerated. One did not have to know much about American government to realize that what Congress passes, Congress can also repeal.[11]

In retrospect, the United States was one war too late in its attempt to legislate itself into neutrality. Such legislation might have prevented embroilment in World War I. But timed as it was, it tended to accelerate World War II, into which the United States was ultimately sucked.

INTERNATIONAL GANGSTERISM

The troubled events of the mid-1930's deepened the urge of the American people to cower in the storm cellar of neutrality. Naval limitations had collapsed completely. The dictator nations were uniting in a new unholy alliance against the democracies. Drawn together by joint participation in the Spanish Civil War, Hitler and Mussolini in 1936 clasped hands in an anti-Communist alliance, popularly known as the Rome-Berlin Axis. Later that same year Germany and Japan formed an anti-Comintern pact, nominally aimed at the Moscow-directed Communist International, but actually at the Soviet Union itself. In 1937 Mussolini joined their ranks. The world now witnessed an antidemocratic, anticommunistic Rome-Berlin-Tokyo Axis. The disappointed "have not" nations of the world, with their crowded populations and limited resources, were evidently determined to improve their lot at the expense of the "have" nations.

Tensions were meanwhile mounting in the Far East. Following the Japanese withdrawal from Shanghai in 1932, Washington persisted in its nonrecognition of Japan's puppet Manchukuo. Despite Tokyo's bland assurances about American rights there, the Open Door was evidently being closed on the fingers of American merchants. The subsequent protests of the State Department were wasted paper.

From time to time, Japanese official spokesmen, notably in 1934, attempted to proclaim what they called a Japanese Monroe Doctrine. The basic concept was "Asia for the Asiatics," or rather China for the Japanese, to the exclusion of America's Open-Door rights. Washington flatly refused to see any connection whatever between the defensive doctrine of Monroe and the aggressive doctrine of Tokyo.

Not content with Manchukuo, the Japanese expansionists cast covetous eyes on neighboring Chinese provinces. After annexing adjoining Jehol to their puppet Manchukuo, they sought to acquire China's northern

[11] The extended debate in Congress during mid-1939 over lifting the arms embargo gave the world a warning several months before Hitler attacked Poland.

provinces by fomenting separatist movements there. Such bare-faced attempts at grab met with firm remonstrances from Washington.

THE UNDECLARED "CHINA INCIDENT"

An ugly turn for the worse came on July 7, 1937, when fighting broke out at the Marco Polo bridge between Chinese troops and a Japanese detachment stationed near Peiping. Reinforcements poured into North China from Japan. Formal declarations of war had gone out of style with the Kellogg-Briand Peace Pact, and this conflict, known as the "China Incident" or the "China Affair," was not officially declared for four-and-one-half years.

The next month, August, 1937, heavy fighting erupted at Shanghai, again with frightful loss of life among the teeming population. As in 1932, the American public was appalled by the slaughter of civilians, and its heart went out to the Chinese underdog.[12] After the incidental killing or injuring of several American citizens on American ships, a strong demand arose in the United States for complete withdrawal from the danger zones.

President Roosevelt, though morally bound to do so, declined to invoke the Neutrality Act of 1937 in the "China Incident." Technically he was justified, for there had been no formal declaration of war. But his real reason was that both he and the American people were warmly pro-Chinese. The application of the neutrality law to both the aggressor and his victim would work a greater hardship on China, even though Japanese imports from the United States were much larger than the trickle flowing to China.

But Roosevelt finally took a strong verbal stand in his sensational "Quarantine Speech," delivered on October 5, 1937 at Chicago, the so-called isolationist capital of America. Deploring the recent outburst of "international lawlessness" in China as threatening to involve the United States in a world war, he proposed that those nations stirring up "international anarchy" be quarantined. As he declared in denouncing the dictators:

> The peace, the freedom, and the security of 90 percent of the population of the world is being jeopardized by the remaining 10 percent, who are threatening a breakdown of all international order and law. Surely the 90 percent who want to live in peace under law and in accordance with moral standards that have received almost universal acceptance through the centuries, can and must find some way to make their will prevail. . . . There must be positive endeavors to preserve peace.[13]

[12] In October, 1937, Gallup found sentiment 59% to 1% against Japan. In February, 1940, it was 77% to 2%. Cantril. *Public Opinion,* pp. 1081–1082.
[13] Department of State, *Press Releases,* Oct. 9, 1937, pp. 278–279.

The phrase "positive endeavors" indicated that Roosevelt was ready to impose economic sanctions on Japan. Advocates of collective security, both at home and abroad, applauded. But a wild outcry arose from the isolationists against involving the nation in broils with which it had no direct concern. This outburst, though a minority view, evidently caused Roosevelt to soft-pedal his idea of "quarantining." Any attempt at drastic measures without popular support would rip the nation wide apart. Yet a large number of American citizens privately instituted anti-Japanese boycotts, which put a partial pinch on Japan.

In November, 1937, the month after the backfiring "Quarantine Speech," an eighteen-power conference met at Brussels, Belgium, to grapple with the Far Eastern hornet's nest. The United States accepted full membership, but Germany refused to attend and Japan declined to be haled into court. The conclave was thus foredoomed to failure. Japan apparently could be stopped only by force, and neither Britain nor America, the two greatest naval powers, was willing to use force.

CONTINUING CRISIS IN CHINA

The Japanese invasion of China was meanwhile degenerating into an orgy of lust and loot. At various times American citizens, male and female, were subjected to slapping and stripping by arrogant Nipponese soldiers. Some American schools and hospitals were damaged by aerial bombers, despite the huge American flags painted on their roofs.

The most sensational incident of all came on December 12, 1937, when Japanese aviators bombed and sank a United States gunboat, the *Panay*, on the Yangtze River in broad daylight. Two men were killed and some thirty wounded; escaping survivors were repeatedly machine-gunned. The vessel was so plainly marked and the visibility was so clear that the incident could hardly have resulted from mistaken identity. One plausible explanation was that hot-headed Japanese officers, defying the Tokyo government, had thus vented their contempt for Yankees.

The American people were shocked by this wanton attack, which also involved the destruction of three Standard Oil tankers. Cartoonists represented the Japanese ambassador as saying, "So sorry—excuse please," while the bodies of mangled American sailors lay about. Washington promptly demanded apologies, reparation, and adequate precautions against the repetition of such an outrage.

The Tokyo Foreign Office, put in a bad light by irresponsible military men, made haste to tender the most profound apologies and pay full monetary reparation—$2,214,007.36. Thousands of Japanese subjects attempted to make amends through private gifts. In these circumstances, the crisis quickly blew over.

The American public viewed the entire *Panay* incident with surprising calm, quite in contrast with their reaction to the destruction of the *Maine* in 1898. The Far East was on the other side of the world; Americans had already been killed there incidentally; America was being plunged deeper into the depression; and many citizens felt keenly that they should not be inveigled into fighting China's battles.

The strength of the peace-at-any-price feeling was reflected in Congressional action on the proposed Ludlow Amendment, which would require a nation-wide referendum on a declaration of war, except for

JAPANESE MASS PRODUCTION OF NOTES

Berryman in the *Washington Evening Star*, c. 1937

actual invasion. Shortly after the *Panay* bombing, and under great pressure from President Roosevelt, the proposal was shelved in the House of Representatives by the shockingly narrow vote of 209 to 188.[14]

As the "China Incident" dragged on, the Open Door became more and more bullet pocked. Little was achieved in 1938 when Washington, with some slight success, imposed a "moral embargo" on the sale of aircraft to Japan. In response to vigorous protests from the State Department against repeated violations of American rights, Tokyo took the position, late in 1938, that new circumstances had rendered old principles void. In short, the Open Door and the treaties that buttressed it were dead. But

[14] A poll by *Fortune* magazine revealed that a majority of the people favored complete withdrawal from China. XVII, 109 (April, 1938).

if the United States would recognize this changed era, and co-operate with Japan's New Order for East Asia, Americans might hope for a larger volume of trade than they had enjoyed under the chaotic and unprosperous old order. Unwilling either to co-operate or to fight—"to shut up or put up"—Washington could do little more than reserve American rights and arrange for a loan of $25 million to the Chinese government through the Export-Import Bank.

Continued flouting of Western rights in China by the Japanese invader finally brought more resolute action by Washington. In July, 1939, out of a clear sky, the State Department gave Tokyo the necessary six-months' notice for the termination of the existing commercial treaty of 1911. This stroke was obviously designed to bring pressure on Japan by clearing the way for an embargo on war supplies. The effect on Tokyo was sobering. The next month, August, 1939, Russia and Germany stunned the democratic world by signing their fateful nonaggression pact. Russia was thus left with a freer hand to deal with the Far East, and her strengthened position evidently caused the Japanese to adopt a more conciliatory tone in their dealings with Washington.

THE MUNICH SELL-OUT

A world already ablaze in the Far East was further inflamed by the fanaticism of Adolf Hitler in Germany. Elbowing his way into power as Chancellor in 1933, he inaugurated an era of sadistic anti-Jewish persecutions, which attained a new ferocity in 1938. The American public, including Jewish citizens in the metropolitan centers, reacted indignantly and urged Washington to protest. Technically speaking, the abuse of Jews in Germany, like that of Negroes in America, was a purely domestic problem, and the State Department was hardly in a position to remonstrate effectively. President Roosevelt and prominent members of his administration nevertheless expressed emphatic disapproval. Among them were the acid-tongued Secretary of the Interior Ickes, who openly condemned Hitler as a "brutal dictator."

Suddenly, in March, 1938, Hitler bloodlessly seized and annexed German-speaking Austria. The democratic powers, wringing their hands in an agony of indecision, prayed that this grab would be his last.

But in the autumn of that same year, 1938, Hitler provoked the most dangerous postwar crisis to date. His bullying demand was for the Sudetenland—the German-inhabited portion of his eastern neighbor, Czechoslovakia. The Czechs, who stood firm during this "war of nerves," mobilized their respectable army and counted on their defensive alliance with France and Russia. Hitler was determined to attack, even though his troops were not yet ready for a full-scale invasion. The nations of Europe seemed to be trembling on the brink of World War II, with

Hitler's Germany and Mussolini's Italy arrayed against Czechoslovakia, France, Russia, and Britain.

President Roosevelt, fearing that a general flare-up would jeopardize the United States, kept the wires to Europe hot. Late in September, 1938, he cabled two desperate, last-minute appeals to Hitler and one to Mussolini. The Italian dictator called Hitler on the telephone, and the latter agreed, whether as a result of Roosevelt's intervention or not, to discuss the dispute at Munich. Probably an appeal from London contributed more to this momentous decision.

The conclave at Munich did its melancholy work in two days, September 29-30, 1938. Present were the two strutting dictators, Hitler and Mussolini, and the nerve-shattered premiers of Britain and France. The Soviet Union, although vitally interested in the fate of Czechoslovakia, was not invited—and this snub by the democracies tended to drive Moscow closer toward the embrace of Hitler. The British and French, fearful that their undefended cities would be gutted by Germany's powerful bombing fleets, induced Czechoslovakia to yield the Sudetenland to Hitler, and thus avert a global holocaust. The Czechs were thus sold down the Danube River to purchase an uneasy peace.

The word "Munich" forthwith became the synonym for "appeasement"—the practice of trying to "appease" the insatiable power-lust of the dictators by giving them by degrees what they demanded. Prime Minister Chamberlain, caricatured with an umbrella, returned to London wishfully declaring that he had brought back "peace in our time." Hitler, to be sure, had stated at Munich that the Sudetenland "is the last territorial claim which I have to make in Europe." [15] But the sequel was to prove that both statements were tragically incorrect: Munich was merely surrender on the installment plan.

HITLER RUNS AMUCK

The Roosevelt administration was evidently moving toward more active support of the democracies against the dictators in the months after Munich. In his message to Congress of January 4, 1939, the President strongly hinted at the desirability of boycotting the "aggressor governments." Rumors that Washington was selling the most modern types of American aircraft to the French spurred rumors of a secret military alliance. The isolationists and other foes of the administration emitted a roar of protest, which increased in intensity when the President was alleged to have said in private, "The frontier of the United States is in France." Isolationist fears were not completely quieted when Roosevelt insisted that some "boob" had invented that "deliberate lie."

Hitler waved another lighted torch over the European powder maga-

[15] W. S. Churchill, *The Gathering Storm* (Boston, 1948), p. 345.

zine, in March, 1939, when he forcibly absorbed what was left of mutilated Czechoslovakia. The hollow mockery of appeasement at Munich became transparently clear. The State Department vigorously but vainly condemned in public this act "of wanton lawlessness and arbitrary force."

With Europe teetering on the brink of catastrophe, Roosevelt urged Congress to revise the Neutrality Act of 1937. His aim was to discourage the saber-rattling dictators by serving notice on them that in the event of war the munitions factories of America would be available to the democracies—France and Britain. But a determined isolationist bloc in Congress, strongly supported by proneutrality sentiment throughout the country, stymied all efforts at revision.

Hitler, his appetite increased by appeasement, had meanwhile stepped up his demands upon Poland for the Polish Corridor and Danzig. Both of these German-inhabited areas had been torn from the side of Germany by the Treaty of Versailles. The Poles, stiffened by their western allies, France and Britain, resolutely resisted these demands, and insisted upon peaceful negotiation.

The key to the diplomatic puzzle was dictator Joseph Stalin, the Sphinx of the Kremlin. Fearful of Hitler's aggressions, he was attempting in the summer of 1939 to negotiate a defensive alliance with Britain and France. When the two western democracies tried to drive too hard a bargain, Stalin went behind their backs. To the amazement and consternation of the outside world, he concluded with Hitler, on August 23, 1939, a nonaggression pact. A secret agreement at the same time assured Stalin of his share of Poland when the imminent partitioning took place.

The Russo-German pact in effect gave Hitler a green light for the invasion of Poland and the starting of World War II. There had been much loose talk in the Western democracies of egging Hitler on Stalin so that the twin menaces would bleed each other white in the vastnesses of Russia, while the democracies remained secure. Stalin now cleverly contrived to turn Hitler against the democracies in the expectation that they would bleed one another white, while he emerged supreme.

Hitler was now unrestrainable. With Poland deprived of any possible Russian assistance, and with her French and British allies far distant, he pressed his advantage to the hilt. The Poles, unwilling to be the victims of another bloodless bargain, refused to budge. While Hitler insisted on either his terms or war, the urgent appeals of President Roosevelt fell on deaf ears. On that memorable September 1, 1939, Hitler, unable to bluff the Poles and impatient of further parley, gave the fateful orders, and the mechanized German hosts burst into Poland.

Britain and France both honored their alliance with the Poles. After Hitler had spurned their demands to withdraw, they declared war on Germany, September 3, 1939. Two days later President Roosevelt issued the routine proclamations of neutrality and invoked the strait-jacket Neutrality Act of 1937. The long-dreaded and long-prophesied World War II had at last erupted.

SELECTED BIBLIOGRAPHY

Useful surveys on the Far East are A. W. Griswold, *The Far Eastern Policy of the United States* (New York, 1938); T. A. Bisson, *America's Far Eastern Policy* (New York, 1945); and F. C. Jones, *Japan's New Order in East Asia: Its Rise and Fall, 1937–45* (New York, 1954). Intimate details from Tokyo are presented in J. C. Grew, *Turbulent Era: A Diplomatic Record of Forty Years, 1904–1945* (2 vols., Boston, 1952) and in his *Ten Years in Japan* (New York, 1944). The Hoover-Stimson policies are described in R. H. Ferrell, *American Diplomacy in the Great Depression* (New Haven, 1957).

The most valuable brief introduction to the European crisis is W. L. Langer and S. E. Gleason, *The Challenge to Isolation, 1937–1940* (New York, 1952). Indispensable is *The Memoirs of Cordell Hull* (2 vols., New York, 1948). A critical study is E. Borchard and W. P. Lage, *Neutrality for the United States* (New Haven, 1937); see also C. G. Fenwick, *American Neutrality: Trial and Failure* (New York, 1940). C. A. Beard stacks the cards against Roosevelt in his *American Foreign Policy in the Making, 1932–1940* (New Haven, 1946), while Basil Rauch becomes something of an apologist in *Roosevelt: From Munich to Pearl Harbor* (New York, 1950). A revealing article is Dorothy Borg, "Notes on Roosevelt's Quarantine Speech," *Pol. Sci. Quar.,* LXXII (1957), 405–433.

See footnotes of this chapter and *Harvard Guide,* Ch. 29.

7TH ED. REFS. W. S. Cole, *Senator Gerald P. Nye and American Foreign Relations* (Minneapolis, 1962) finds the Senator's isolationism rooted in the anti-Eastern, anti-Wall Street agrarianism of the Middle West. The isolationists of this era tended to be liberals in domestic affairs; by the time of Pearl Harbor, and especially later, they shifted to conservatism. R. A. Divine's *The Illusion of Neutrality* (Chicago, 1962) is highly critical of the patchwork, self-defeating neutrality legislation, particularly since it withheld American influence from the shaping of events. F.D.R. reluctantly accepted nonflexible legislation, partly because he did not want to jeopardize his New Deal program. D. A. Puzzo, *Spain and the Great Powers, 1936–1941* (New York, 1962) has one chapter on the United States which relates isolationism and Catholicism to nonintervention; a number of the leading actors (except Hull) came to regard nonintervention as a mistake. *The Memoirs of Anthony Eden: Facing the Dictators* (Boston, 1962) reveal that uncertainty as to American exports influenced Britain in not supporting oil sanctions at the time of the Italo-Ethiopian crisis. Foreign Secretary Eden favored closer co-operation with Washington against Japan and against the European dictators than did Prime Minister Chamberlain; over a proposal by F.D.R. for a joint *démarche* to halt the dictators the two Britons parted company.

For further 7TH, 8TH, AND 9TH ED. REFS. see BIBLIOGRAPHICAL ADDENDUM, p. 1,038.

46

World War II: Through Lend Lease, 1939-1941

We must be the great arsenal of democracy.
FRANKLIN D. ROOSEVELT, December 29, 1940.

DICTATORS ON THE LOOSE

WHEN HITLER unleashed the dogs of war in 1939, the American people had already taken their stand. An overwhelming majority wanted to stay out of the conflict, but a large body, which grew into a strong majority, feared that America would be unable to do so. Approximately 90 per cent of the American people distrusted Hitler and hoped that the allied democracies—France, Britain, and Poland—would win. Unlike 1914, there was no pro-German element worthy of the name.[1]

Foreign propaganda, unlike 1914–1917, was of little significance. The Germans made some effort to cultivate American sympathy, but their seeds fell on barren ground. The Allies, generally speaking, refrained from large-scale propaganda activity. One does not waste money and energy in assaulting a fortress already won.

The most effective propaganda work, as in 1914–1917, was done by volunteer groups in America. As the lines were drawn by 1940, the most vocal noninterventionist organization was the America First Committee, with its center in isolationist Chicago and its leading orator the famed aviator, Colonel Charles A. Lindbergh. The leading interventionist organization was the Committee to Defend America by Aiding the Allies, with the noted journalist William Allen White as its first head. Its avowed objective was to keep America out of the war by giving the Allies enough material aid so that they could defeat the Axis menace. "The Yanks are not coming" ought to be, avowed White, the unofficial slogan of his com-

[1] Gallup (October, 1939) found that 84% were pro-Ally, 2% pro-German, and 14% without opinion. *Pub. Opin. Quar.*, IV, 102. See H. Lavine and J. Wechsler, *War Propaganda and the United States* (New Haven, 1940).

mittee. But as the war ground on, the organization became more openly interventionist, and White dropped out.[2]

Momentous changes had occurred in the standards of international conduct since 1914. The naked aggressions of the dictators in the 1930's had caused the aerial bombing of civilian centers to become recognized as a new refinement of "civilized warfare." Treaties had become whole wastebaskets full of paper; nonaggression pacts were made to lull the prospective victim into a false sense of security. Unoffending neighbors were assaulted with devastating suddenness. International law—one-way international law—was cynically used by the dictators to justify prior violations of international law, and to prevent weak nations from joining effectively in their own defense. Hitler, who commanded the most terrifying striking power yet amassed, had little respect for the force of world opinion. The only language he really understood was the language of superior force.

The unvarnished truth is that by the late spring of 1940, if not earlier, Hitler had virtually abolished neutral rights and unofficially declared war on all the democracies—including the United States. The rape of Czechoslovakia, Poland, Norway, Denmark, Holland, Belgium, and Luxemburg should have provided adequate warning. But the American people were reluctant to recognize Hitler's challenge. Many disillusioned souls lamented the blunder of having entered World War I. Others, remembering the munitions scandals uncovered by the Nye Senate Committee, steeled themselves against being gulled again by the munitioneer, the profiteer, the financier, and the sloganeer. Immense numbers of America Firsters regarded this conflict as just another European war of imperialism. Five years of neutrality debate and legislation had not only strengthened the isolationists, but had developed a neutrality-at-any-price complex.

THE FINNISH INTERLUDE

When war erupted in 1939, many Americans assumed that the conflict would follow the familiar pattern of 1914–1918. The supposedly impregnable concrete Maginot Line on France's eastern border would hold Hitler at bay. The strangling noose of Britain's blockade would slowly choke Germany into starvation, and Berlin would be forced to sue for peace, as in 1918.

But surprises were speedily forthcoming. German mechanized divisions speedily overran Poland, while Stalin came in for his prearranged share of the loot. Yet the lesson of the Polish preview meant little to the Allied

---

[2] Careful studies of the two committees are W. S. Cole, *America First: The Battle Against Intervention* (Madison, Wis., 1953), and Walter Johnson, *The Battle Against Isolation* (Chicago, 1944). See also W. S. Cole, "America First and the South, 1940–1941," *Jour. of Southern Hist.*, XXII, 36–47 (Feb. 1956).

countries. They went ahead with their business-as-usual plans for waging the conflict, while the bored journalists wrote disgustedly of the "phony war."

Unexpected excitement developed late in 1939 over the Finnish crisis. Joseph Stalin, not trusting his dictator-accomplice Adolf Hitler, sought to secure from Finland certain strategic areas that would enable him to bolster his defenses against Germany. "Brave little Finland" resolutely refused the proffered exchange of territory. Late in November, 1939, the Soviet Union spurned Washington's offer of good offices and assaulted its tiny neighbor. Russian aircraft, in defiance of an appeal from Roosevelt, heavily bombed civilian centers.

The sympathies of America went out overwhelmingly to the democratic Finns. They not only paid their debts but were fighting in self-defense against a bullying Communist aggressor.[3] President Roosevelt promptly denounced the Soviet invasion as "wanton disregard for law," and called for a moral embargo on the shipment of airplanes and other war materials to Russia.

After white-clad Finns on skis had administered initial defeats to the overconfident Russians, enthusiasm for Finnish relief rose to new heights. Finland was granted a moratorium on her debt payments, while Congress made available a total loan of $30 million for agricultural and civilian supplies and other nonmilitary purposes. The Finns desperately needed airplanes and tanks, not plows and harvesters. But so determined was American public opinion not to become involved in this conflict that nothing more was possible.

Finland was finally flattened by the Russian steam roller in March, 1940. The American people consoled themselves with the thought that even if they had sent over arms, these weapons probably would not have arrived in time or in sufficient quantity to have any real effect. The whole dismal affair further embittered Russian-American relations, and again revealed the feeble-willed democracies in the role of coming forward with "too little" and that "too late."

UNNEUTRALITY SHORT OF WAR

The existing Neutrality Act of 1937 flew in the face of two basic American desires: to stay out of the war and to help the democracies win it. The Allies, although assaulted by a Germany armed to the teeth, could not legally buy a single cartridge in the United States. The cash-and-carry clause of the Neutrality Act of 1937, valid for only two years, had expired in May, 1939. American merchantmen, laden with the vital raw

[3] A Gallup poll (Dec. 31, 1939) showed that 88% were pro-Finnish, 1% pro-Russian, and 11% without opinion. *Pub. Opin. Quar.*, IV, 102. See A. G. Mazour, *Finland between East and West* (Princeton, 1956).

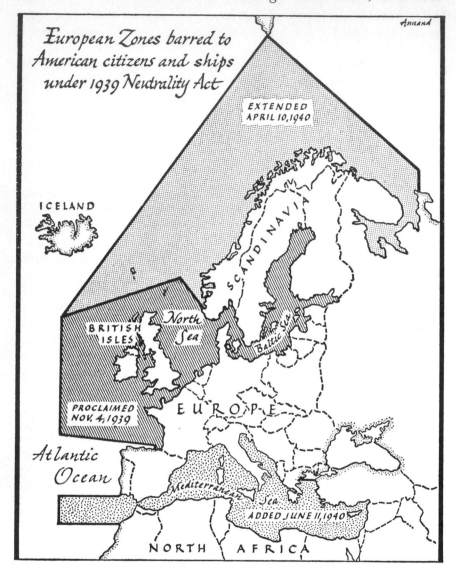

European Zones barred to American citizens and ships under 1939 Neutrality Act

EXTENDED APRIL 10, 1940

ICELAND

SCANDINAVIA

BRITISH ISLES

North Sea

Baltic Sea

EUROPE

PROCLAIMED NOV. 4, 1939

Atlantic Ocean

Mediterranean Sea

ADDED JUNE 11, 1940

NORTH AFRICA

materials of war like copper and oil, were now free to steam into the submarine-infested combat zones. Dangerous incidents, like those of 1917, seemed bound to drag America into the conflict.

Keenly aware of the need to revamp the Neutrality Act, Roosevelt called Congress into special session less than two weeks after Hitler's invasion of Poland. To help the democracies resist aggression—although he did not put it that baldly—he recommended a repeal of the arms embargo. To insulate the United States against the conflict, he urged a re-enactment of the expired cash-and-carry safeguard and a restriction against American ships and citizens sailing into the danger zones.

The ensuing debate, in Congress and out, was one of the most stormy and momentous in American history. Noninterventionists insisted that a repeal of the arms embargo was unneutral, because it would change the rules after the game had begun so as to help one side against the other. They further argued that the United States, after again developing a huge vested interest in the munitions business, would slither into the conflict.

The repealists, for their part, declared that the existing straight-jacket legislation was basically unneutral.[4] It merely served to throw American influence on the side of the "aggressors." Hitler, they argued, would never have attacked Poland if he had been assured that his victims could secure weapons from the United States. But some of the repealists were candid enough to point squarely to self-interest: America's defenses would be bolstered by a victory for the democracies.

The question of setting up danger zones into which American ships could not sail aroused violent controversy. The noninterventionists believed that any other course would lead directly to shooting. The interventionists feared that such a prohibition would leave small neutrals like Norway completely at the mercy of Hitler, and would be an abdication of America's sacred principle—freedom of the seas.

Both the friends and foes of repeal had one thing in common: they professed a desire to keep America out of the war. Those citizens opposing repeal would insure neutrality by ignoring the conflict; those favoring repeal would ensure neutrality by helping the Allies keep the fight on the other side of the Atlantic.

The Fourth Neutrality Act—that of 1939—was finally approved by comfortable majorities in both houses during November, 1939. Despite loud outcries from Berlin, the arms embargo was lifted and American ships were forbidden to enter the danger zones. But the Allied purchasers of war materials would have to operate on a "come-and-get-it" and "cash-on-the-barrelhead" basis.

The revised law was basically a compromise. The noninterventionists gave up the arms embargo in order to get the danger zone; the repealists accepted the danger zone in order to get a repeal of the arms embargo. The new Act of 1939, though losing most of the old teeth, retained certain restrictions of the former law, notably those regarding loans to warring nations and travel on belligerent ships. The preamble specifically stated that the United States, while declining to exercise certain of its "rights or privileges," was not abandoning them. Thus Congress made one final but futile attempt at "storm-cellar" neutrality.

[4] Gallup (Sept., 1939) found the arms embargo repeal favored by about 50% and the danger zone by about 84%. *Pub. Opin. Quar.*, IV, 105–106.

ANNULLING NEUTRAL RIGHTS

Ominously, World War II took up where World War I had ended. The *Lusitania*—the first passenger liner to be sunk without warning—went to the bottom in 1915, when the conflict was nine months old. The *Athenia,* a British passenger ship, was destroyed on the first day of the new war by a German submarine, without warning and with heavy loss of life. Other weapons and devices of World War I were adopted at the outset of hostilities, or soon thereafter, and a new era of international anarchy was foreshadowed.

The United States attempted, without success, to halt the melting away of neutral rights. The futile "safety belt" around the Americas, adopted at Panama in 1939, has already been described. Five days after the declaration of war, the Allies announced what amounted to a long-range blockade of Germany in retaliation for Hitler's ruthless submarine attacks. Berlin promptly responded with a counterblockade of Allied coasts. In November, 1939, the Germans launched a lethal attack on Allied shipping with floating magnetic mines. The Allies retaliated by extending their so-called blockade to enemy exports as well as to imports. They even included noncontraband goods that were exported through adjoining neutrals in neutral vessels, contrary to the ancient dictum "free ships, free goods."

The United States, as in World War I, did not submit to these encroachments on freedom of the seas lying down. Washington again protested against forcing American ships into British control stations, where they suffered prolonged detention while undergoing search.[5] The American public, as in 1916, became aroused over the searching of mails, and particularly over the dramatic story that British authorities in Bermuda had removed pouches from an airplane at the point of bayonet. Washington's protests were weakened by the fact that in 1917–1918 the United States, as a belligerent, had acquiesced in or employed such devices as blacklists, expanded contraband lists, and control of imports to neutral nations.

The British must have perceived that Washington, in lodging its protests, was merely going through motions for the sake of the record. The American people quite obviously wanted the democracies to win, and consequently Downing Street held firm. Curiously enough, until the collapse of France in 1940 practically all of America's diplomatic disputes were with the Allies. This situation presents a striking similarity to the period of World War I before Germany began her all-out submarine attacks.

[5] See S. S. Jones and D. P. Myers, ed., *Documents on American Foreign Relations* (Boston, 1940), II, 705 ff.

THE FALL OF FRANCE

The so-called "phony war" came to an abrupt end in the spring of 1940, when the German armies suddenly engulfed both Denmark and Norway, without warning and without a declaration of war. In May, 1940, also without warning and in violation of solemn nonaggression pledges, Hitler assaulted neutral Belgium, Holland, and Luxemburg. Within twenty days the British armies were driven out of France, and but for the so-called "miracle of Dunkirk" would have been annihilated. Early in June, 1940, Mussolini, coveting a jackal's share of France's carcass, pounced upon his neighbor from the rear.

In desperation, France appealed to Roosevelt for "clouds of planes." But the President, who was fully aware of isolationist sentiment and the sole power of Congress to declare war, found his hands tied. He could do no more than extend his "utmost sympathy" and promise all the arms that America could spare—without military commitments.

Prostrate France, her "impregnable" Maginot Line flanked, signed an armistice with her conqueror, on June 22, 1940. Hitler staged the ceremony, with a gleeful eye on the ironies of history, in the same railway car on the same spot in the same forest where the Armistice of 1918 had been concluded.

These six weeks that shook the world shook the American "Maginot minds" out of their complacency. Britain, the last bastion of democracy in all Europe, might go under at any moment. A woefully unprepared United States would, in this event, be forced to defend the Americas against a ruthless dictator who would have the economic and military power of Europe behind him—and perhaps the British navy as well.

The panicky feeling that swept the United States was best reflected in a sudden upsurge of preparedness activity. Under the driving leadership of Roosevelt, Congress voted nearly $18 billion in a relatively few weeks. But drafting manpower proved to be more difficult than appropriating money. Not until September, 1940, and only after vehement opposition from the isolationists, did Congress pass a conscription law. This measure authorized the first peacetime draft in American history.

The fall of France also forced the United States to abandon its technical neutrality toward Britain in favor of an unneutrality that would bail out Britain. In April, 1940, following Hitler's assaults on Denmark and Norway, Washington "froze" the assets of those two countries in America so that such funds would not be available to the aggressor. These were the first in a long series of "freezings." Every major aggressive move by the dictators elicited condemnation from Washington, and in several cases promises of help for the victims. The State Department consistently refused to recognize the fruits of aggression, and maintained formal diplomatic relations with a number of governments-in-exile. In a memorable speech on the day Italy entered the war against France, Roosevelt proclaimed with startling directness that "the hand that held the dagger has struck it into the back of its neighbor." [6]

Unneutral deeds followed unneutral words. In June, 1940, Washington worked out a clever trade-in scheme, under an almost forgotten law of 1917. The government would turn over to the American airplane manufacturer a number of planes already constructed, to be replaced by more recent models being built. The private manufacturer would then transfer the older craft to the British. Washington also sold to private concerns a vast amount of old military equipment, with the understanding that it would be resold to the British. This process involved about 600,000 rifles and 800 cannon, as well as huge stocks of machine guns, mortars, and ammunition, all of which proved a godsend to Britain. These transactions in their final stages did not involve the United States government, and technically Washington kept its skirts clean as far as international law was concerned.

As time passed, these transparent subterfuges were largely dropped. Washington ruled that American airplanes could be flown directly to Canada, without having to stop at the border to be pulled or pushed across. It allowed thousands of British pilots to train in Florida, where flying conditions were better than in Canada. It permitted damaged British warships to undergo extensive repairs in American shipyards. All such activity, of course, was not neutrality. But this was a war in which Hitler, by brazenly assaulting neutrals, had rendered neutrality meaningless and dangerous. America preferred to bolster Britain, at the cost of neutrality, rather than let Britain collapse and then have to face the fury of Hitler alone.

THE DESTROYER-BASE DEAL

In the summer of 1940, while Hitler was vainly trying to bomb Britain into submission, American interventionists increased their clamor for large-scale assistance. Many of them harped on the theme that the United States Navy had left over from World War I some fifty overage, four-funnelled destroyers. These craft were of no immediate use to the United States, but they might prove the salvation of Britain in combating Germany's submarine blockade and in repelling invasion by Hitler's mechanized armies.

Responding to such pressures, Washington announced the momentous destroyer-base deal, on September 3, 1940. Roosevelt, in an Executive agreement, promised to turn over the fifty vessels directly to Britain. The British, for their part, made outright gifts of sites for bases on

[6] *New York Times,* June 11, 1940, 1:4.

Newfoundland and Bermuda for ninety-nine years. At the same time, they granted rent-free leases, for ninety-nine years, on six additional sites ranging from the Bahamas to British Guiana. Almost simultaneously, but not as a formal part of the deal, Downing Street quieted fears that Hitler might use the fifty destroyers against America when it gave a formal pledge never to sink or surrender the British fleet.

The destroyer-base deal soon touched off a furious debate in the United States. Few discerning citizens questioned the value of these potential bases, for with air power growing in destructiveness the sites could be used to fend off or forestall possible German attacks on the United States. Few thoughtful Americans could deny the usefulness of the destroyers to Britain.[7] But many Americans sharply challenged the way in which the transaction was carried through —by a simple Executive agreement, without the advice and consent of the Senate. The non-interventionists in particular were up in arms. "The United States," declared the *New York Daily News*, "has one foot in the war and the other on a banana peel."

President Roosevelt's coup was clearly vulnerable to criticism. The transfer of fifty warships from the navy of the United States to that of a belligerent was not only a gross violation of neutrality, but also of pre-Hitler international law. Berlin could have found complete justification in this act for a declaration of war. The disposal of public property in such a fashion presumably violated a domestic law as well. But Roosevelt's attorney general prepared a labored defense, much of which hinged on the place-

---

[7] Gallup found (Aug. 17, 1940), two weeks before the deal was consummated, that of those with opinions on selling the destroyers, 62% were favorable, and 38% opposed. *Pub. Opin. Quar.*, IV, 710. For the British side see W. S. Churchill, *Their Finest Hour* (Boston, 1949). The "theme" reads, "How the British people held the fort ALONE till those who hitherto had been half blind were half ready."

ment of a comma—"the Battle of the Comma." As for the President's not seeking the prior approval of Congress, the stock answer was that Congress was slow and windy, and that by the time the isolationists had all had their say, Britain might have been knocked out. Public opinion on the whole acquiesced in the deal, despite the bitterness of the noninterventionists and many partisan Republicans. Congress finally and indirectly put the seal of its approval on the transaction when it voted money for the development of the ninety-nine year bases.

With the destroyer deal consummated, the United States virtually abandoned any remaining pretense of neutrality. The American people refused to sit on the side lines, shackled by neutrality and international law, while Hitler rode roughshod over neutrality and international law. They were determined, by an overwhelming majority, to stay out of the war. But they were no less determined to lend unneutral assistance to a fellow democracy—again "the world's last hope"—in its desperate struggle for survival. The old concepts of neutrality thus went out the window in favor of self-interest.

SHATTERING THE TWO-TERM TRADITION

In 1940, as in the Wilson-Hughes campaign of 1916, American diplomacy felt the paralysis of a Presidential campaign. President Roosevelt had to move cautiously in his program of aid to the Allies, because the isolationists opposed that policy, and because the Republicans opposed the administration.

Roosevelt finally consented to accept the nomination for an unprecedented third term. He explained that he could not withhold his experienced hand in this grave crisis, despite his personal desire to return to private life. His critics hotly charged that, drunk with power, he really wanted to hang on, and that he had arranged to have himself "drafted." The Democratic platform pledged abstention from "foreign wars" and promised aid to nations resisting aggression. The Republicans nominated the dynamic and tousle-haired Wendell Willkie, an interventionist who had rocketed from political nothingness within a few short weeks. Their platform likewise pledged aid to peoples resisting aggression and proclaimed opposition to "a foreign war."

In foreign affairs there was little to choose between the platforms and speeches of the two candidates. Both Roosevelt and Willkie promised aid to the Allies; both promised to bolster the nation's defenses; both promised to keep the nation out of war. Roosevelt was later embarrassed by some of his ringing declarations, particularly the one at Boston, where he proclaimed, "I have said this before, but I shall say it again, and again and again. Your boys are not going to be sent into any foreign wars." [8]

[8] *New York Times,* Oct. 31, 1940, 14:3.

Willkie deserves immense credit for his role as one of the founding fathers of a bipartisan foreign policy. He might have convulsed the country, and weakened the hand of the President abroad, by loudly condemning the drift toward interventionism. But favoring the cause of the Allies, and putting patriotism above partisanship, he helped save both military conscription and the destroyer deal, although objecting to the "dictatorial action" involved in the latter transaction.

In ordinary times the Republicans might have been able to defeat Roosevelt by their charge that junking the two-term tradition was the entering wedge for a dictatorship. But these were no ordinary times. One of the most effective arguments used by the Democrats was that Hitler and his fellow dictators hoped for the defeat of Roosevelt. Many voters believed that Roosevelt's experience was needed in this crisis; that he would prove more effective than Willkie in achieving preparedness; that one should not "swap horses in mid stream"; and that Roosevelt would be a more inspiring war leader should the United States be sucked into the abyss.[9] "Better a third term than a third rater" was a Democratic rallying cry.

The nation tramped to the polls in November, 1940. Roosevelt won by a landslide in the electoral college, although his opponent polled an impressive popular vote. There was no rejoicing in Berlin or Rome or Tokyo.

LEND-LEASE LARGESSE

His hands freed by the election, Roosevelt could now turn to the task of rendering large-scale assistance to beleaguered Britain. The British were rapidly reaching the end of their financial tether. But to lend them billions of dollars would produce economic dislocations at home and abroad, and inevitable postwar friction over repayment. With a keen memory of the defunct Allied war debts, Roosevelt declared that he was going to get rid of the "silly, foolish old dollar sign." He used the analogy of lending garden hose to a neighbor, whose burning house endangers one's own, and then expecting it back when the fire is out. Similarly, Roosevelt would lend arms and other assistance directly to those nations resisting aggression, and expect a return of this equipment or replacements for it when the fire was out. Such was his historic lend-lease scheme.

The lend-lease bill, symbolically numbered 1776, was introduced into Congress in January, 1941, and rather misleadingly named, "An Act Further to Promote the Defense of the United States." The ensuing debate compared in bitterness and volume with that over the repeal of the arms embargo in 1939. The Aid-the-Allies group warmly backed lend-lease as a "defense" measure that would help Britain defeat the European aggressors and at the same time keep America out of the conflict. The

[9] For opinion polls on these points see *Pub. Opin. Quar.*, V, 135, 137.

America First zealots denounced this "blank-check bill"—this "Dictator, War, Bankruptcy Bill"—as a sure guarantee of war. Mothers kneeling on the steps of the capitol exhibited the sign:

Kill Bill 1776
Not our Boys

Republican Senator Taft of Ohio, a leading isolationist, scoffed that "Lending war equipment is a good deal like lending chewing gum. You don't want it back." Isolationist Senator Wheeler of Montana, referring to the earlier plowing under of surplus crops, branded the scheme as one designed "to plow under every fourth American boy."

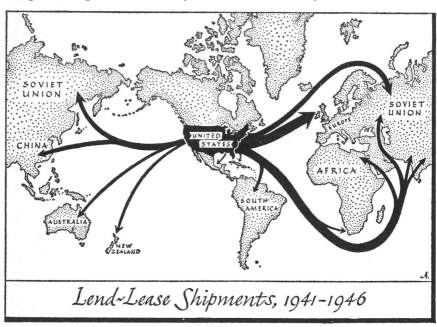

Lend-Lease Shipments, 1941-1946

Despite vehement opposition, the lend-lease bill carried. American public opinion rather strongly favored it as a means of fending off the war. But if the people could have foreseen that it would lead to involvement by gradual steps, they no doubt would have been less enthusiastic.[10] The final vote was 60 yeas and 31 nays in the Senate; 317 yeas and 71 nays in the House. Thus the United States formally pledged itself, to the limit of its enormous industrial and financial resources, to lend "defense articles" to those governments "whose defense the President deems vital to the defense of the United States."

The lend-lease act, which sanctioned the expenditure of an ultimate $50 billion, must take high rank among the most momentous laws ever

[10] By March, 1941, Gallup found 56% favorable, 27% opposed, 8% qualified, and 9% without opinion. *Ibid.,* V, 325.

passed by Congress. It was more than an abandonment of neutrality, because neutrality had already been abandoned. It was an unofficial declaration of war on the war-mad dictators—or rather a belated acceptance of the fact that the dictators had already unofficially declared war on all the democracies, including the United States. The lend-lease law proclaimed a tacit, nonshooting alliance with Britain and other nations whose resistance to aggression merited American support. Militarily and diplomatically this "aid-to-democracies-bill," which greatly boosted British morale, was one of the grand climaxes of the war.

Unlike the destroyer deal, lend-lease was no simple Executive agreement cooked up behind drawn curtains. It was debated "over every cracker barrel in the land," supported by a respectable majority of the voters, and passed by wide margins in Congress. The American people, through their regularly elected representatives, had spoken. They still hoped to stay out of a "shooting war," but they were willing to stake the democracies to victory even at the risk of involving themselves.[11]

INCREASING TENSIONS WITH HITLER

The American occupation of Denmark's Greenland, in April, 1941, proved to be another long stride toward an undeclared war with Germany. A German lodgment in this area would constitute an intolerable threat to the mainland of the United States and to the lend-lease lifeline to Britain. The State Department entered into negotiations with the Danish minister in Washington, Henrik Kauffmann, for Denmark's motherless colony. Acting solely on his own responsibility, he signed an agreement permitting the United States to occupy Greenland during the emergency for defensive purposes and without detriment to Danish sovereignty.

Diplomatic complications speedily ensued. The Hitler-dominated government in Copenhagen promptly disavowed the Greenland deal, and forthwith recalled Kauffmann. Secretary Hull refused to recognize the recall, while continuing to regard Kauffmann as the regularly accredited minister. The United States, in dealing with an unprincipled adversary, was thus forced to fight the devil with fire. As a step toward hemispheric defense, and as a means of bolstering the Monroe Doctrine, the occupation of Greenland was completely in line with the recommendations approved by the American foreign ministers at Havana in the summer of 1940.

Relations with Berlin meanwhile continued to deteriorate. Following a brutal German attack on the neutral Egyptian steamer *Zam Zam*, in May 1941, with injury to several Americans, Congress authorized the

[11] In January and April, 1941, Gallup found 68% to 67% favoring aid at the risk of war. *Ibid.*, V, 481.

seizure of the scores of foreign ships, many Axis owned or controlled, immobilized in United States ports. Many of them were transferred to the British flag. Later that same month President Roosevelt startled the nation with a proclamation of unlimited national emergency.

Then, on May 21, 1941, the American merchantman *Robin Moor* was torpedoed and shelled in the South Atlantic by a German submarine.

BLACKOUT

The dark menace of Nazi Germany.

Holland in the *Nashville Banner, c.* 1940

This was the first United States vessel of any kind to be deliberately sunk by German hands, either in or out of the war zones. American public opinion was shocked and angered, even though no lives were lost. Senator Carter Glass of Virginia expressed the views of countless interventionists when he cried, "I think we ought to go over there and shoot hell out of every U-boat."

Hitler's spokesmen defended the sinking by alleging that the *Robin*

Moor was carrying contraband of war to Britain's South Africa. Yet the Germans, in forcing the passengers and crew into small boats hundreds of miles from land, had not made provision for their safety in accordance with international law and the London protocol of 1936, which Berlin had freely signed. Roosevelt angrily denounced this act of "piracy," but Germany rejected his claims for damages. Washington in retaliation "froze" all German and Italian assets in the United States, and ordered all German and Italian consulates, as hotbeds of subversive activity, to be closed. Berlin and Rome retaliated in kind.

The *Robin Moor* opened a new chapter in German-American relations. Until then, Washington had little justification for complaint against the Germans, as far as America's specific rights were concerned. But it had much reason to complain of Hitler's ruthless attacks on the community of nations, of which the United States was a leading member. On purely legalistic grounds, Berlin had much better grounds for protest against America's unneutral aid to the Allies than America had for complaint against Germany's infractions of America's rights. The lend-lease act widened the breach irreparably. The United States was now a virtual co-belligerent of the Allies. Hitler, with bitter memories of America's role in terminating World War I, did not wish to provoke a showdown yet. But henceforth the German submarine commanders, pursuant to orders, could hardly be expected to refrain from defending themselves against American destroyers escorting lend-lease supplies to Britain.

SELECTED BIBLIOGRAPHY

A capital bibliographical article is W. S. Cole, "American Entry into World War II: A Historiographical Appraisal," *Miss. Valley Hist. Rev.*, XLIII (1957), [1] 595–617. Outstanding are W. L. Langer and S. E. Gleason, *The Challenge to Isolation, 1937–1940* (New York, 1952) and *The Undeclared War, 1940–1941* [2] (New York, 1953). Much the same ground is covered in briefer compass in D. F. Drummond, *The Passing of American Neutrality, 1937–1941* (Ann Arbor, [3] Mich., 1955). Important contributions by participants are *The Memoirs of Cordell Hull* (2 vols., New York, 1948); H. L. Stimson and M. Bundy, *On Active Service in Peace and War* (New York, 1948); R. E. Sherwood, *Roosevelt and Hopkins* (New York, 1948); and Sumner Welles, *The Time for Decision* (New York, 1944). C. A. Beard's biased indictment of Roosevelt in *American* [4] *Foreign Policy in the Making, 1932–1940* (New Haven, 1946) is offset in part by Basil Rauch's conspicuously friendly *Roosevelt: from Munich to Pearl Harbor* [5] (New York, 1950). A critical appraisal is E. E. Robinson, *The Roosevelt Leadership, 1933–1945* (Philadelphia, 1955). [6]

See footnotes of this chapter; references at the end of the next chapter; and *Harvard Guide*, Chs. 29–30.

7TH, 8TH, AND 9TH ED. REFS. See BIBLIOGRAPHICAL ADDENDUM, p. 1,041.

47

The Road to
Pearl Harbor

*I ask that the Congress declare that since the un-
provoked and dastardly attack by Japan on Sunday,
December seventh, a state of war has existed between
the United States and the Japanese Empire.*
PRESIDENT ROOSEVELT, WAR MESSAGE,
December 8, 1941.

JOSEPH STALIN: STRANGE BEDFELLOW

THE DEMOCRATIC WORLD received a totally unexpected boon when, in 1941, Hitler and Stalin came to blows. Having brutally divided Poland and the Baltic spheres of influence in 1939, they attempted to partition additional spoils. When Stalin stubbornly insisted on Russian ascendancy in the Balkans, Hitler astounded the world, on June 22, 1941, by launching a devastating surprise attack on his partner in the nonaggression pact of 1939. Overnight the entire complexion of the war was drastically changed.

The American people, up to this time, had been profoundly distrustful of Stalin. He had given Hitler the green light for the assault on Poland, and then had come in for the kill. He had next ruthlessly wrested territory from his neighbor, Finland. Needing additional defense in depth against Germany following the premature collapse of France, he had absorbed the independent Baltic states of Lithuania, Latvia, and Esthonia, and had seized two areas in Romania. He had, moreover, distressed the American people by his notorious purge trials of 1937–1938, and by his continued Communist propaganda in the United States, despite solemn pledges in 1933 to desist.

Hitler's fateful attack on the "Mongol halfwits" of Russia wrought a revolution in American opinion. Stalin—the cynical, self-seeking, iron-fisted aggressor—suddenly became a most welcome ally of those nations who were seeking to halt Hitlerism. President Roosevelt promptly issued promises of aid to Moscow, and soon made some military supplies available. In about four months, after investigating Stalin's capacity to resist, he provided the first installments of lend-lease assistance to Russia that ultimately totalled a staggering $11 billion.

No less astonishing was the reversal of American opinion regarding Finland. Alleging prior attacks, Russia reopened war with her, and the Finns, forced into bad company, fought back with Hitler's help. Many of the same Americans who had applauded Finnish victories the year before were now hoping for Russian victories, while Washington vainly tried to persuade Finland to drop out of the war. The Berlin press screamed "criminal intervention" and "Jewish impudence."

The American people, especially diehard conservatives, were not altogether happy over "Bloody Joe" Stalin, their new ally. If Russia won, they asked, would not communism, which was as bad as Naziism, engulf all Europe? Would Stalin prove to be a co-operative associate at the peace table? Roman Catholic and other religious denominations were deeply disturbed by the long-continuing persecutions directed against the Greek Orthodox Church in Russia. "I have no more confidence in Stalin," presciently declared Archbishop Curley of Baltimore, "than I have in Hitler." American isolationists saw in the unexpected boon of a Russo-German war additional evidence that the two dictators should be allowed to slit each other's throats on the frozen wastes of Russia. The democratic world would then emerge strong and triumphant.

If the two menaces would only bleed each other white, all would be well. But the great majority of the military experts confidently predicted that Russia would collapse in a few short weeks, and then Hitler, after overrunning Britain, would bestride the Western World like a colossus. With Nazi Germany the immediate menace, Washington decided to send all possible aid to Stalin, short of war, and pray that he would stay afloat. The American people—and the administration—believed in combating the worse menace first, and then coping with the Communist menace, if any, later. As the passing weeks revealed unexpected powers of resistance in Russia, critics of Roosevelt, notably ex-President Hoover, declared that Stalin could have held out without American help. But the public, backed by the experts, was unwilling to take a chance, and the facts *as then known* tended to support the wisdom of such a course.

INCREASING COBELLIGERENCY WITH BRITAIN

Significant moves toward joint Anglo-American military action meanwhile were on foot. Early in 1941, parallel with the lend-lease debates in Congress, prolonged discussions were secretly held in Washington between American and British military officials. The conferees worked out arrangements for perfecting lend-lease aid, and for co-ordinating military and naval activity should the United States be drawn into the war. The crucial decision was reached that in the event of American belligerency, the overthrow of Germany would be given top priority over that of Japan. The reasoning was that if Japan fell, Hitler would still be strong; if Hitler fell, Japan's days would be numbered. By this time Roosevelt was veering strongly toward the belief that, in the interests of national security, an Axis victory had to be prevented at all costs, even American participation. But because of vehement isolationist sentiment, he did not feel that he could proclaim this belief from the house tops. He still talked publicly in terms of sending lend-lease aid so that the war could be kept on the other side of the Atlantic.

As German submarines intensified their attacks on British freighters carrying lend-lease arms from America, Iceland took on increasing importance as a bastion protecting the North Atlantic sea lanes. This strategic island had declared its independence of Denmark following Hitler's occupation of the mother country. The British had then taken the orphaned area under their protective wing. In July, 1941, Roosevelt announced arrangements with the Icelandic government under which American troops, for the duration of the emergency, would gradually take over from Britain the burden of defending the island. This new Executive agreement, which received strong public support,[1] was but one more fateful step by technically nonbelligerent America in the direction of cobelligerency with Britain.

THE ATLANTIC CHARTER

In line with his policy of limited cobelligerency, Roosevelt arranged, in August, 1941, for a secret meeting on warships with Prime Minister Winston Churchill, off the Newfoundland coast. Extreme precautions were taken against attacks by lurking German submarines. The major purposes were to discuss lend-lease, common defense, and a stiff joint policy against further Japanese aggression in the Far East. As a kind of afterthought, the two statesmen issued a press release—not a formally signed document—setting forth their common aims for a peace program.

This so-called Atlantic Charter embraced eight points, which are here given in abbreviated form:

1. No territorial or other aggrandizement for either Power.
2. No territorial changes contrary to the wishes of the people concerned (*i.e.*, self-determination, one of the later Fourteen Points of Wilson; in part also Points V and XII of the Fourteen).
3. The right of people to choose their own forms of government; restorations of governments to those deprived of them (*cf.*, territorial restoration, Points VI, VII, VIII, XI of the Fourteen).

[1] Gallup (July 24, 1941) found 61% approving, 17% disapproving, and 22% without opinion. *Pub. Opin. Quar.*, V, 686.

4. Access by all nations, victor and vanquished, to the trade and raw materials of the world (*i.e.*, Point III of the Fourteen).
5. International collaboration for improved labor standards, economic advancement, and social security. (A combination of later objectives of the League of Nations and of Roosevelt's New Deal.)
6. A peace of security with freedom from fear and want (*i.e.*, two of Roosevelt's famous Four Freedoms, the other two being freedom of speech and worship).
7. A peace that "should enable all men to traverse the high seas and oceans without hindrance" (*i.e.*, freedom of the seas, Point II of the Fourteen.)
8. Abandonment of force; disarmament of the aggressor nations pending establishment of a "permanent system of general security" (League of Nations [?], Point XIV of the Fourteen); lightening of armament burdens (*i.e.*, Point IV of the Fourteen).[2]

The rumored secret meeting of Roosevelt with Churchill had led American opinion to expect some kind of world-shattering pronouncement. The immediate reaction was one of disappointment, for the Atlantic Charter was largely a mixture of the Rooseveltian New Deal and the Wilsonian Fourteen Points. The Roosevelt-Churchill declaration was clearly designed to establish an Anglo-Saxon peace, and it could hardly be used to disarm Germany in the manner of the Fourteen Points. In fact, "Nazi tyranny" was to be overthrown by force. The eight-point charter, like the fourteen-point Wilson program, was enheartening to those liberals who hoped for a better postwar world, and encouraging to conquered peoples, like the Poles, who had fallen under the heel of Hitler and Stalin. When these promises were not fulfilled, bitter cries of betrayal again burst forth.

The Atlantic Charter, from the standpoint of the United States, was in effect a formal acceptance of full responsibility for the defeat of Hitler and the establishment of a democratic peace. The isolationists denounced the agreement as one more move toward open collaboration with Britain, as indeed it was, only the public was not informed of the most secret understandings. The *Chicago Tribune*, a powerful mouthpiece of isolationism, demanded to know what business Roosevelt had to discuss these matters with the head of a state already at war. The *Tribune* was unprepared to concede that in a very real sense the United States was already at war, and that the Atlantic Charter was a tacit alliance with Britain.

LEND-LEASE LEADS TO CONVOY

The issue of delivering lend-lease shipments to Britain come dramatically to the fore in the spring and summer of 1941. By the terms of the Neutrality Act of 1939, such military supplies could not be sent from American ports in American ships. With "wolfpacks" of German subma-

[2] Text in *Department of State Bulletin,* V, 125 (Aug. 16, 1941).

rines sinking British freighters, the American people were now perceiving the illogic of providing arms without guaranteeing delivery. During the stormy debate in Congress over lend-lease, the foes of the measure had prophesied that lend-lease would lead to convoying, convoying would lead to shooting, and shooting would lead to war. But administration spokesmen repeatedly shunted aside the disagreeable issue of convoying. From their point of view the proper strategy was to commit the nation to irrevocable courses one step at a time, and not to arouse unnecessary opposition by peering too far into the future.

The United States finally waded into the chill water of convoying by degrees. In April of 1941 Roosevelt established naval patrols which, partly under sanction of the Panama "chastity belt" of 1939, radioed the position of German submarines to nearby British warships and airplanes. The occupation of Iceland by American troops in July, 1941, opened a major breach in the dike. President Roosevelt, as commander-in-chief, issued orders that resulted first in the convoying of American ships to Iceland, then neutral ships, then British ships. Lend-lease goods were thus shepherded to Iceland by American destroyers, and then British patrols escorted them the rest of the way to the United Kingdom. These grave decisions, made solely in the White House, seem to have been favored by a majority of the American people.[3]

Ugly incidents were inevitable. As early as April 10, 1941, the U. S. destroyer *Niblack* dropped depth bombs in the vicinity of what was assumed to be a German submarine. Early in September, 1941, Washington reported that a U-boat had fired two torpedoes at the destroyer *Greer,* en route to Iceland, and that the latter had retaliated with numerous depth charges. (More than a month later, the Navy Department revealed that the *Greer* had been trailing the U-boat for three-and-one-half hours and broadcasting the latter's position to nearby British air patrols before the submarine turned and attacked.)

President Roosevelt, smarting from the *Greer* attack and the sinking of two American-owned merchantmen, broadcast a sensational radio message to the American people, on September 11, 1941. He declared that henceforth the United States, not content with merely repelling attacks, would defend freedom of the seas by striking first at all Axis raiders operating within the American defensive areas. The isolationists loudly protested that the President, by issuing shoot-at-sight orders, was usurping the war-declaring powers of Congress. His repeated references to freedom of the seas showed that he was attempting to make drastic courses more acceptable to the public by clothing them in the mantle of an ancient American doctrine. That historic doctrine actually had no relation to the armed

[3] Gallup (June, 1941) found 55% favorable to convoy. See *Pub. Opin. Quar.,* V, 485, 680.

convoying of gift lend-lease munitions through German-proclaimed war zones to the enemies of Germany.

CONVOY LEADS TO SHOOTING

Roosevelt next sent a vigorous message to Congress, on October 9, 1941, urging a repeal of the "crippling provisions" of the Neutrality Act. He specifically requested authority to arm American merchantmen for defensive purposes against "modern pirates," and he urged a termination of the combat areas so that American ships could carry lend-lease aid directly to those countries fighting aggression. Senator Glass eloquently expressed interventionist approval when he declared that "we should repeal the whole damn thing." Although a powerful isolationist minority insisted that repeal was one more step toward war, the country as a whole seemingly favored the change.

In mid-October, 1941, came news that the U.S. destroyer *Kearny*, operating southwest of Iceland, had been damaged by a torpedo with a loss of eleven lives. Later information revealed that she had been engaged in a full-fledged battle with German submarines. Roosevelt responded in a sensational Navy Day speech with the declaration that "America has been attacked" by German "rattlesnakes of the sea," and notwithstanding a desire to avoid war, "the shooting has started."

Late in October, 1941, the American destroyer *Reuben James* was torpedoed and sunk off Iceland while engaged in convoy duty. This was the first armed national ship of the United States to be destroyed by Germany, and the loss of life was heavy, totaling about one hundred officers and men. Such incidents were not welcome to Hitler, who was desperately anxious to knock Russia out of the war before trying conclusions with the same Western giant that had humbled Germany in 1918. His submarine commanders were under strict orders to avoid fighting, except in those situations where American forces endangered German craft.[4]

The German torpedoings undoubtedly accelerated action in Congress for a partial repeal of the Neutrality Act of 1939. In November, 1941, both houses of Congress, although retaining the ban on loans to belligerents and travel on belligerent ships, removed the most serious restrictions. Henceforth American merchant ships, armed or unarmed, could legally go anywhere, including the danger zones, carrying any kind of cargo, including munitions. American opinion, despite the impassioned outcries of the noninterventionists, seems to have favored by a comfortable margin this momentous stride toward deeper involvement.

Storm-cellar neutrality was thus officially junked in 1941. The Act of

[4] H. L. Trefousse, *Germany and American Neutrality, 1939–1941* (New York, 1951), p. 122.

1939, far from being a failure, as the interventionists charged, was too successful. Prior to partial repeal, no American merchant ship was ever sunk in the combat areas proclaimed by the President because none could legally go there. Such a prohibition in 1917 might have kept the United States out of war. But this was 1941, and the American people, determined to send succor to Britain, did not wish to be kept out of the danger zones. While remaining technically neutral, they wanted to engage in belligerent deeds; and when they found that the Neutrality Act tied their hands, they got rid of its main shackles. But by this time the nation was engaged in a limited and unofficial shooting war in the Atlantic. The official blowup came in the Far East, where the American public was hardly expecting it.

THE RISING SUN MOVES SOUTHWARD

Tension between Tokyo and Washington had grown increasingly ominous, particularly since the fall of France in June of 1940. The preoccupation of the democracies with the menace of Hitler left the Japanese free to make giant-boot strides toward what they called the "New Order in East Asia" and "the Co-Prosperity Sphere in Greater East Asia." Europe's distresses cleared the road for Japan's imperialistic successes in China and elsewhere.

The diplomatic tug-of-war in the Far East took various forms. Washington steadfastly refused to recognize territorial changes achieved by force; insisted upon the sanctity of the sagging Open Door; and protested against damage to American property and indignities to American citizens. The Japanese, for their part, argued that as soon as "third powers" stopped their interference, the "China Incident" would be liquidated and peace would descend like a dove on the Far East. Tokyo also held out the bait that "third powers" which co-operated with the New Order might expect a fair share of trade and investment. This share, the Japanese insisted, would be greater under the new era of peace and order established by Nippon than ever before.

The bolstering of China as a dike against Japanese imperialism was a major objective of Washington. The Roosevelt administration provided large loans to the Chinese, and refused to invoke the Neutrality Act, lest it cut off the trickle of supplies going to China over the famed road from Burma. Yet, rather inconsistently, Washington permitted vast quantities of scrap iron, gasoline, and other war materials to flow across the Pacific to Japan for use in her war against China.

The American public, which was overwhelmingly pro-Chinese, almost as overwhelmingly favored cutting off these supplies from the Japanese war machine.[5] Washington was free to impose such embargoes by January, 1940, when the commercial treaty of 1911 with Japan, denounced by

[5] See *Pub. Opin. Quar.*, V, 148.

the United States six months earlier, ceased to be effective. But Roosevelt resolutely refused to proclaim an embargo for fear that the Japanese would be driven south to the oil reserves of the semidefenseless Dutch East Indies. The policy of Washington was to conciliate the nonmilitaristic elements in Japan, and to postpone the evil day of a showdown until the ABCD powers (Americans, British, Chinese, Dutch) were better prepared to halt the aggressive men of Nippon. Roosevelt was able to continue "appeasing" Japan because American opinion, although numerically strong in favoring an embargo, was lacking in intensity.

The policy of appeasing Japan underwent sharp modification in the spring of 1940. The Netherlands and France collapsed, thus presenting the Japanese with a heaven-sent opportunity to seize such orphaned colonies as French Indo-China and the Dutch East Indies. When Tokyo revealed a covetous interest in these rich prizes, Roosevelt jarred the Japanese, on July 25, 1940, by banning the export without license of petroleum, petroleum products, and scrap metal. Six days later he decreed that the sale of aviation gasoline was to be restricted to the nations of the Western Hemisphere.

This was the beginning of an economic noose around Japan that finally caused her to burst out at Pearl Harbor. The new regulations, of course, were technically nondiscriminatory. But the Japanese, whose war machine was in danger of grinding to a halt without American aviation gasoline and scrap metal, lodged vigorous protests in Washington.

THE ECONOMIC CRACKDOWN ON JAPAN

The restraining hand of Uncle Sam may have held Japan back from the riches of the Dutch East Indies in the summer of 1940, but not from those of French Indo-China. In September, 1940, Tokyo put the screws on the Hitler-dominated French government and extorted strategic bases in northern Indo-China. Secretary Hull roundly condemned this fresh act of aggression, and Washington retaliated by agreeing to lend China an additional $25 million.

A world already steeled against surprises was jolted, in September, 1940, by the news that Japan had signed a treaty with the Axis partners, Germany and Italy. The signatories solemnly agreed to attack jointly any power, say the United States, that should make war on any one of them. Russia, then the only other important nonbelligerent, was specifically exempted. No one could doubt that the pact was tailored to discourage the United States from going to war against either the Axis dictators or the Japanese, lest the Americans have a two-ocean war on their hands.

The Roosevelt administration, apparently in an effort to head off the tripartite pact, took a bold step. On September 26, 1940, it proclaimed an embargo on all iron and steel scrap, except to the Western Hemisphere and Great Britain. The earlier proclamation of July, 1940, had required the *licensing* of scrap metal. The new proclamation of September, 1940, provided for embargoing it—and on a discriminatory basis.

Relations between America and Japan continued their ominous decline. Washington dismissed the new triple alliance—Germany, Italy, and Japan—as something that did not alter the existing realities, and many Americans shrugged it off as a colossal bluff. The State Department nevertheless warned Americans to leave the Far East, and stepped up its loans and other assistance to embattled China.

The Japanese scored a significant point in the diplomatic chess game when, on April 13, 1941, they concluded their five-year treaty of neutrality with Moscow. Each party pledged itself to remain neutral, if the other should become involved in war. Hitler's assault on Russia was some two months in the future, and Japan was clearly trying to protect her rear from an attack should she become involved in hostilities with the United States. The threatening implications of the Tokyo-Moscow pact were not lost on Washington.

New golden opportunities were presented to Japan in June, 1941, when Hitler launched his tremendous assault on Stalin. Taking advantage of Europe's distresses, Tokyo promptly made new demands on the Hitler-controlled French government for bases in southern Indo-China, in addition to those already extorted in the north. When France was forced to knuckle under, Washington stoutly condemned this new act of aggression.

Washington backed up its wordy protest against the Indo-China coup with drastic deeds. Roosevelt jolted Tokyo, on July 25, 1941, by an order freezing all Japanese assets in the United States. Britain and the Netherlands followed suit, with the result that the embargo on war materials to Japan was now virtually complete. The Japanese were stunned. They were not only cut off from outside oil supplies, but they had on hand petroleum stocks for only twelve to eighteen months of wartime consumption. As the oil gauge dropped, the Japanese war lords concluded that they must either seize essential oil reserves or abandon their schemes for a "New Order" in the Pacific. In these circumstances, the Big Freeze was a blow hardly less jarring to the Japanese than their later assault on Pearl Harbor was to the Americans. As Nippon's war supplies continued to melt away and as the diplomatic deadlock tightened late in 1941, the Japanese leaders felt that they had only two alternatives: to knuckle under or to burst out.

LAST-DITCH NEGOTIATIONS WITH TOKYO

The efforts of the diplomats to halt war-mad Nippon with words continued to be futile. At the Atlantic Conference in August, 1941, Roosevelt and Churchill had worked out a threatening protest against Japanese aggression, but Washington later presented it to Tokyo in a watered-down form. The next month, September, 1941, hope sprang anew when the conciliatory Prince Konoye, the Japanese Premier, indicated a willingness to meet with Roosevelt in a Pacific conference, perhaps at Honolulu. But the President, fearing that the Japanese were plotting a propaganda victory by placing the onus for a diplomatic breakdown on America, insisted on specific concessions in advance. Konoye, suspecting that the news of such commitments would leak out and destroy him, was unwilling or unable to yield.[6] The proposal for a conference was dropped, the Konoye ministry fell the next month, and a militaristic group, ominously headed by the unsmiling and truculent General Tojo ("The Razor"), took over. The drift toward war continued with seeming inevitability.

The new regime nevertheless decided on one final attempt to break the deadlock with America. Early in November, 1941, Tokyo announced that a special envoy, Saburo Kurusu, was flying to Washington, there to assist the regular ambassador with Japan's "last proposals." On reaching San Francisco the smiling Kurusu, who had married an American wife, indicated that the prospects were not good but that he hoped to "go through the line for a touchdown." Given the existing crisis, there was indeed little hope for peace. The United States was already engaged in a limited shooting war with Hitler's submarines in the Atlantic, and the Japanese, if they were not to back down, would ultimately be forced to fight their way through America's economic barricades.

The Japanese presented their final terms on November 20, 1941, when they offered to withdraw their troops from southern Indo-China to northern Indo-China. In return for this rather hollow concession, the United States, among other benefits, would have to restore commercial relations to the prefreezing basis, supply Japan with a required quantity of oil, and refrain from measures that would prevent a Japanese victory over China in their undeclared war. Upon the restoration of peace in East Asia, Tokyo was willing to remove all Japanese troops from Indo-China, and agree not to make any armed advances into southeastern Asia and the South Pacific. These proposals were of course spurned by Washington, which had consistently pursued a policy of bolstering China against Japanese aggression.

At this point Secretary Hull seriously considered a three-month's truce or *modus vivendi* with Japan. Roosevelt's basic policy of helping Britain and Russia against Hitler would be greatly weakened if the United States should become involved in a two-ocean war with Japan in the Pacific. The American army and navy, woefully unprepared to grapple with

---

[6] Ambassador Grew and others have argued that a great opportunity for peace was missed when the Konoye conference was spurned. J. C. Grew, *Turbulent Era* (Boston, 1952), II, 1301 ff. Subsequent revelations cast serious doubt on this theory.

Japan's military might in the Far East, were begging for time. President Roosevelt, who confessed that "I simply haven't enough navy to go around," was quite anxious to "baby Japan along" for a while longer. The scheme that Secretary Hull had in mind involved a partial resumption of trade with Japan, and a limitation on Japanese troops in Indo-China.

The Hull proposal for a three-month truce was finally pigeon-holed. It offered so little to the Japanese that they almost certainly would have rejected it. But the furious opposition of the Chinese Nationalist leaders perhaps more than anything else killed the scheme. China, understandably enough, had no desire to be sold down the Yangtze River to buy time for the United States. Generalissimo Chiang Kai-shek naturally wanted war to erupt between America and Japan, for in it lay his best hope for success in the long drawn-out conflict. The fear spread in Washington that the proposed three-month *modus vivendi* might so dishearten the Chinese as to cause them to drop out of the war. Such an eventuality was regarded as catastrophic. China was not only bogging down large Japanese armies, but was regarded as a potential springboard for the invasion of the Japanese homeland if war should erupt between Japan and the United States, as seemed almost inevitable.

The Roosevelt administration, when faced with the risk of losing a valuable ally, preferred to force the issue to a showdown with Japan, even though the Army and Navy were badly unprepared. There was also strong opposition in America to "appeasing" Japan further. Secretary of the Interior Ickes wrote in his diary that he was prepared to resign and devote himself to "raising hell generally." [7]

PRELUDE TO PEARL HARBOR

Secretary Hull, instead of presenting his three-month *modus vivendi* to Tokyo, responded to the Japanese proposals of November 20 with his uncompromising note of November 26, 1941. It was one of the most fateful documents in American history.

Hull nailed his colors to the mast. Japan was to withdraw all her armed forces from *both* China and Indo-China, and lend her support to the Chinese Nationalist government of Chiang Kai-shek. As a pledge of good behavior, Tokyo was to enter into a multilateral nonaggression pact with America designed to guarantee the stability and territorial inviolability of East Asia. Partially to sweeten this bitter pill, Washington would grant Japan a favorable trade agreement, unfreeze Japanese assets, cooperate in the stabilization of the dollar-yen rate, and work for the abolition of extraterritoriality in China.

[7] *The Secret Diary of Harold Ickes* (New York, 1954), III, 655. See also I. C. Y. Hsu, "Kurusu's Mission to the United States and the Abortive *Modus Vivendi*," *Jour. of Mod. Hist.*, XXIV (1952), 301–307.

Hull was painfully aware that the presentation of his terms probably meant the end of negotiations. The next day he privately remarked to the Secretary of War that he had washed his hands of the problem, and that it now lay in the laps of the army and navy. On December 1, 1941, the Tokyo government secretly made the final and fateful decision for war. On the same day it firmly rejected the American terms, but requested that the negotiations be continued. The ensuing conversations were deliberately designed to lull the Americans, while a carefully trained Japanese carrier force, which had left its rendezvous for Hawaii on November 25 (Washington time), prepared to strike from the skies after receiving by radio Tokyo's war decision of December 1. The fleet could have been recalled within twenty-four hours of its assault on December 7, if Washington had unexpectedly made last-minute concessions in the deadlocked negotiations.

But the time for concession had clearly passed. The United States had flatly insisted that Japan pull out of China, bag and baggage. The Japanese, after four-and-one-half years of bloody losses, would suffer an intolerable loss of face and position if they did so. In the last analysis, Washington forced a showdown over China. This policy could hardly be justified by America's relatively small stake in China, whether missionary, investment, or trade. The only reasonable justification was that the continued militaristic expansion of Japan in the Far East—with its challenge to law, order, peaceful processes, and territorial integrity—posed an intolerable threat to the future security of the United States. From the standpoint of Japan, America was the aggressor. But so is the citizen trying to halt a bank robber, who asks only to be allowed to go about his business.

The explosion of the Far Eastern powder keg was now perilously near. While the Japanese were deliberately stalling the conversations in Washington, reports came through that Japan was massing troops in Indo-China for an invasion of Thailand. On December 2, 1941, Roosevelt anxiously asked Tokyo for explanations. When no satisfactory reply was forthcoming, he resorted to the extraordinary step of appealing personally to Emperor Hirohito, on December 6, for a withdrawal of Japanese armed forces from Indo-China.[8]

Japan's reply came the next day in the form of a paralyzing surprise assault at Pearl Harbor. It crippled the air force there, inflicted some 3000 casualties, and destroyed or immobilized a large number of warcraft, including seven battleships—the backbone of the Pacific fleet. The plan of the Japanese was not to invade Hawaii or the American mainland but to prevent the American navy from interfering with their simultaneous attacks on British, Dutch, and American possessions in the Far East. This short-range strategy was eminently successful.

[8] *The Memoirs of Cordell Hull* (New York, 1948), II, 1091–1092.

THE SEARCH FOR SCAPEGOATS

The background of the Pearl Harbor assault reads like a cloak-and-dagger mystery. Late in 1940, a year or so before the fatal attack, ingenious American experts had succeeded in "cracking" the main Japanese diplomatic code. During the succeeding months, the State Department was privy to the secret messages exchanged between Tokyo and its representatives in the United States. Official Washington knew, shortly before Pearl Harbor, that the Japanese were going to strike somewhere, for one decoded dispatch read that after the deadline date in late November "things are automatically going to happen." Then why the gigantic surprise party at Pearl Harbor?

The circumstantial evidence, according to a group of Roosevelt's critics, damns the President. Some of the extreme "revisionists" have gone so far as to charge that he wanted to get the nation into war with Japan, and that he criminally exposed the fleet at Pearl Harbor so as to lure the Japanese into an attack and arouse the nation behind him. Under the Constitution he dared not strike the first blow himself, and he might have had difficulty in getting a war declaration from Congress in advance. So he allegedly resorted to this fiendish expedient of deliberate exposure.

The trap-baiting theory assumes that Roosevelt was either a wholesale murderer or a madman or both. If he was determined to go to war with Japan, he certainly wanted to be known to history as the President who won it. One does not go about winning a war by arranging for the destruction of one's battleship fleet on the very first day of hostilities. In view of the unpreparedness of the armed forces, he would have preferred to "baby Japan along" for a while longer. But having stood firm on the China issue, he knew that Japan was preparing to break out somewhere. When the blow finally fell, he and many of his associates evidenced relief.[9] The period of uncertainty had ended, and the United States could cast aside all pretense and fight openly to halt Japanese aggression. But this does not mean that the President planned Pearl Harbor.

The basic reason for the surprise is that the American officials, military and civilian, were either confused, obtuse, asleep, or looking the wrong way. The question of who was most soundly asleep is one of internal administration rather than diplomatic history, and it will be debated endlessly. Certainly there were enough warning signs, such as the burning of secret papers by the Japanese Embassy in America, to enable alert observers to put the pieces of the puzzle together. Most Americans simply assumed that the Japanese would not be foolhardy enough to attack Hawaii, or that they did not have the strength to do so effectively.

[9] H. L. Stimson and M. Bundy, *On Active Service* (New York, 1947), p. 394.

The day before Pearl Harbor, word reached Washington that two large Japanese task forces were steaming southward along the East Asia coast. The blow was expected to fall on Thailand, British Malaya, the Dutch East Indies, or the Philippines. American eyes were focused on these areas, and properly so, for the *major* blow did fall on all of them. The attack on Pearl Harbor was merely a hit-and-run raid.

The element of treachery in the Japanese attack should have surprised no keen onlooker. Declarations of war, although still required by international law, had gone out of fashion in the law-flouting Age of the Dictators. And the Japanese since 1894 had shown a conspicuous tendency to shoot first and declare war afterward.

Contrary to a persistent legend, the Japanese were not prodded into the attack on Pearl Harbor by their German ally. Hitler, in a curious lapse from his policy of not provoking the United States until he had smashed Russia, had blindly given Tokyo a blank-check promise of support about two days before the assault. He was probably more surprised than Roosevelt when the Japanese unexpectedly attacked Pearl Harbor, but he backed them up in the vain hope that they would reward him by being co-operative allies.[10]

POSTSCRIPT TO PEARL HARBOR

The hara-kiri gamble of the Japanese at Pearl Harbor proved to be a blunder of colossal proportions. The damage inflicted was heavy, but not irreparable. If the Japanese had continued their Hitlerian tactics of piecemeal penetration, if they had moved step by step into Thailand, British Malaya, the Dutch East Indies, and even the Philippines, they would have presented the American people with agonizing decisions. The isolationists elements, spearheaded by the America First group, were still large, noisy, and obstructive.

Fortunately for American unity, the decision for war was snatched from the hands of the United States. Shortly before Pearl Harbor, Roosevelt had discussed with his Cabinet the wisdom of sending a message to Congress recommending war, and his advisers agreed that such a resolution would be approved. This, of course, was problematical. Even granting final approval, there would have been last-ditch opposition from a powerful minority, who no doubt would have cried, "Why fight for British, Dutch, and French imperialism in the Far East?" The debate would undoubtedly have been bitter, disruptive, and prolonged, with consequent harm to American morale and the preparedness effort. As late

[10] Trefousse, *Germany and American Neutrality*, pp. 147–153. The Japanese presumably attacked partly because Russia seemed to be collapsing under Hitler's blows.

as 1945, more than three years later, eight out of ten Americans believed that Roosevelt should have been trying to keep the nation out of war at the time of Pearl Harbor.[11]

The foul blow struck by Japan forthwith banished partisanship and confusion, and galvanized the American people into action as one nation. The torpedoes and bombs that sank the American battleships at Pearl

RISING AS ONE MAN

The day of Pearl Harbor.

Orr in the *Chicago Tribune*, 1941

Harbor also sank "America Firstism." "The only thing now to do," declared isolationist Senator Wheeler, "is to lick hell out of them."

Congress, responding to an overwhelming national cry for revenge, moved speedily and decisively. The war resolution placed before it asked not for a declaration of war but for a recognition of the "state of war" which "has thus been thrust upon the United States." On December 8, 1941, the day after Pearl Harbor, the Senate approved the war resolution 82 to 0. The House vote on the same day was 388 to 1, with the

[11] National Opinion Research Center, *Opinion News*, April 3, 1945, p. 1.

sole negative voice coming from Miss Jeannette Rankin of Montana, who had opposed war with Germany in 1917.

Germany and Italy, the Axis partners of Japan, likewise spared the United States the agony of a decision. Many Americans were determined to fight a private war of vengeance in the Pacific against the treacherous Japanese, who had struck below the belt while still negotiating. An angry debate in Congress over a war resolution against Hitler and Mussolini would have added to the national disunity. But on December 11, four days after Pearl Harbor, Germany and Italy declared war on the United States. That same day Congress responded with formal war resolutions. Against Germany the count was 88 to 0 in the Senate and 393 to 0 in the House; against Italy the count was 90 to 0 in the Senate and 399 to 0 in the House. This unprecedented unanimity was largely a recognition of the fact that war had already been declared on the United States, and that the only possible response was retaliation in kind.

CALLING A HALT TO AGGRESSION

To the bitter end, the American people were torn by contradictory desires. They overwhelmingly wanted the victims of aggression to win, yet they overwhelmingly wanted to stay out of the conflict. With the British, Russians, and Chinese all in grave danger of collapsing, America was willing to help them at the risk of war—all the while hoping to stay out of war. In the event of a shooting showdown, the American people did not want to face the dictators alone, without Britain, Russia, and China as allies. They had little faith in the intentions of the Japanese militarists, and none whatever in the promises of Hitler. His hollow assurances to his victims had preceded the overrunning of a half dozen or so sovereign peoples, beginning with the Czechs.

The American First propagandists belittled the menace of Hitler. They declared that he had no designs on the Americas, and that even if he had the United States fleet would prevent his coming. But the American people—the polls indicated more than seven out of ten—believed that Hitler would not be satisfied until he had conquered everything. To be sure, he declared in November, 1941 that "As far as I am concerned, South America is as far away as the moon." Yet he had also insisted in 1938 that he did not "want any Czechs." The American people, when faced with Hitler's sorry record of broken promises, pledges, and pacts, were simply unwilling to take a chance. If they guessed wrong, they would lose everything—including their most priceless possession, liberty.

The American people were determined to resist the aggressors, even at the risk of a war that they hoped would never come. In these circumstances, any mutually satisfactory compromise was impossible, whether in Berlin, Rome, or Tokyo. In the Pacific, time was on the side of the United States, as Japan's oil reserves continued to drop. The tick of the clock drove the Japanese to the madness of Pearl Harbor. If they had deliberately tried to work out a scheme for uniting America behind President Roosevelt, they could hardly have been more successful.

SELECTED BIBLIOGRAPHY

All the references cited at the end of the previous chapter are relevant, but W. L. Langer and S. E. Gleason, *The Undeclared War, 1940–1941* (New York, 1953) is an outstanding survey. Briefer is D. F. Drummond, *The Passing of American Neutrality, 1937–1941* (Ann Arbor, Mich., 1955). See also Sumner Welles, *Seven Decisions that Shaped History* (New York, 1951); T. Kase, *Journey to the "Missouri"* (New Haven, 1950); F. C. Jones, *Japan's New Order in East Asia* (New York, 1954).

The best-balanced detailed account of the events leading to Pearl Harbor is probably Herbert Feis, *The Road to Pearl Harbor* (Princeton, 1950). See also Walter Millis, *This is Pearl!* (New York, 1947) and S. E. Morison, *The Rising Sun in the Pacific, 1931–April, 1942* (Boston, 1948). Bitterly anti-Roosevelt and in varying degrees unreliable are C. A. Beard, *President Roosevelt and the Coming of the War* (New Haven, 1948); H. E. Barnes, ed., *Perpetual War for Perpetual Peace* (Caldwell, Idaho, 1953); George Morgenstern, *Pearl Harbor: The Story of the Secret War* (New York, 1947); W. H. Chamberlin, *America's Second Crusade* (Chicago, 1950); F. R. Sanborn, *Design for War: A Study of Secret Power Politics, 1937–1941* (New York, 1951); C. C. Tansill, *Backdoor to War* (Chicago, 1952); Admiral R. A. Theobald, *The Final Secret of Pearl Harbor* (New York, 1954); and H. E. Kimmel, *Admiral Kimmel's Story* (Chicago, 1955). See also R. N. Current, *Secretary Stimson* (New Brunswick, N.J., 1954), which is likewise highly critical. More favorable is his "How Stimson Meant to 'Maneuver' the Japanese," *Miss. Valley Hist. Rev.,* XL (1953), 67–74. The story of the attack on Pearl Harbor is told in Walter Lord, *Day of Infamy* (New York, 1957).

An excellent essay on the literature of Pearl Harbor is Louis Morton, "Pearl Harbor in Perspective: A Bibliographical Survey," *U.S. Naval Institute Procs.,* LXXXI (1955), 461–468. See also Herbert Feis, "War Came at Pearl Harbor: Suspicions Considered," *Yale Review,* XLV (1956), 378–390, and R. H. Ferrell, "Pearl Harbor and the Revisionists," *The Historian,* XVII (1955), 215–233.

See footnotes of this chapter and *Harvard Guide,* Chs. 29–30.

7TH ED. REFS. E. E. Morison, *Turmoil and Tradition: A Study of the Life and Times of Henry L. Stimson* (Cambridge, 1960) emphasizes the inflexibly moralistic position of Secretary of War Stimson regarding Japan. R. H. Dawson, *The Decision to Aid Russia, 1941* (Chapel Hill, N.C., 1959) contends that despite opposition (especially Catholic) lend-lease to Russia ("Lenin-lease," said Representative Fish) seemed the least dangerous of several possible alternatives designed to bolster the Allies; F.D.R. was not in a good position to attach strings to lend-lease in November, 1941.

For further 7TH, 8TH, AND 9TH ED. REFS. see BIBLIOGRAPHICAL ADDENDUM, p. 1,043.

48

Diplomacy for Victory
1941-1945

It is fun to be in the same decade with you.
ROOSEVELT TO CHURCHILL, CABLEGRAM, 1942

THE NATIONS UNITED

THE FIRST YEAR of the war went badly for the United States and its Allies. Russia was reeling under Hitler's blows; bomb-shattered Britain had lost her Mediterranean lifeline to Italy; German tanks were smashing across North Africa toward the Suez Canal; Hitler's submarines in the Atlantic were taking a ghastly toll of Allied shipping; the Japanese were hammering at the gates of India, Australia, and Alaska; and China was cut off from land communications with the free world.

Time was the most precious commodity. The well-justified fear prevailed that the Japanese, after digging in so deeply that they could not be dislodged, would remain in control of half of the world's population. The longer the war lasted the more likely a German secret weapon that would forestall an invasion of Hitler's Europe from the British Isles. The United States—the famed industrial colossus—would have to retool itself for war production while there was yet time.

Unity was another crying need of the hodgepodge of nations forced into the war against the Axis. They enjoyed an overwhelming share of the population and resources of the globe, and if they could only co-ordinate their vast strength in time, they were almost certain to win.

The most significant single stride toward unity came two weeks after Pearl Harbor, when Prime Minister Churchill and his advisers arrived in Washington for extended discussions with Roosevelt and other co-belligerents. The upshot was the epochal Declaration of the United Nations, dated January 1, 1942, and signed by the representatives of twenty-six countries at war with the Axis. This solemn covenant bound

743

the signatory nations to the principles of the Atlantic Charter, assured the full employment of their resources against the common enemy, and pledged no separate armistice or peace. Nations not yet at war with the Axis could sign later, as fifty-one ultimately did.

The Declaration of the United Nations is of supreme importance in American diplomatic history. It not only insured unity for war but provided the embryo of a new world organization for peace—the United Nations. It was in effect a binding military alliance, and as such a spectacular departure from America's hoary tradition of nonentanglement. It was not a treaty formally approved by the Senate, but an Executive agreement signed by the President. It was immediately, enthusiastically, and widely acclaimed in the United States. This spontaneous reaction revealed not only the desperate need of the Allies for unity, but also the growing maturity of the American people in dealing with international affairs.

Yet unity was seriously weakened by confusion in the United States regarding war aims. Most Americans knew what they were fighting *against* rather than what they were fighting *for:* the republic had been foully attacked and the aggressors would have to be punished. There was heated dispute as to whether Chancellor Hitler or Emperor Hirohito was Public Enemy Number One. Millions of Americans believed that they had a private score to settle with treacherous Nippon, and that "the war of imperialism" in Europe was not their war. Fortunately, the strategy of "getting Hitler first" had been adopted in Washington early in 1941, and Roosevelt carried it through despite the outcries of a dangerous minority.[1] This unpleasant episode was but another illustration of the power of an ignorant and misdirected public opinion.

The American and British peoples, welded by a common foe, enjoyed unusually intimate relations. Canadian industry was further meshed with that of the United States, and joint enterprises were pursued with harmony, notably the gigantic "Alcan" highway to Alaska. The presence of American troops in British outposts, notably Australia, established new relationships and increased the number of war brides. The United Kingdom, which became a gigantic base for mounting the D-day invasion of Europe, took on a new importance. Although London and Washington often differed sharply on the handling of common problems, these disputes were but relatively minor ripples on the surface of a new cordiality. By early 1945 the old traditions and hatreds had so far melted away that six out of ten Americans could favor a permanent military alliance with Britain.[2]

[1] A *Fortune* magazine poll showed (February, 1942) that a plurality of voters, 46.8%, favored "getting Hirohito first."

[2] *Pub. Opin. Quar.,* IX, 47.

MORAL TONIC FOR CHINA

The unity of the United Nations was badly strained by China. The Chinese people, ravaged by four years of war with Japan, expected deliverance after Pearl Harbor. Instead, the myth of white supremacy received a shattering blow when the British, Dutch, French, and Americans were hurled out of the Far East by the Mikado's minions. The strategy of "getting Hitler first" left pitifully short rations for the Chinese. The danger impended that China, potential springboard for the Allied invasion of Japan, would be forced to hoist the white flag of surrender.

Emergency measures were taken by Washington to boost Chinese morale. After Japan had cut off the Burma Road, the United States established a kind of aerial Burma Road. American aviators, flying from India, scraped "over the hump" of the world's loftiest mountains with a mounting driblet of military supplies.

The State Department, reacting to Japanese accusations that the West would continue its exploitation and discrimination in the Orient, made a dramatic move in the autumn of 1942. It announced that the United States was prepared to sign a treaty renouncing its extraterritorial and other special privileges in China, some of them nearly one hundred years old. The ensuing negotiations proceeded rapidly, paralleling similar concessions by the British, and the new pact was formally signed in January, 1943. As a juridical declaration of independence for China, it went far toward removing from her the stigma of semicolonial status, and toward putting her on an equal footing with the other United Nations.

Immigration and naturalization barriers against the Chinese were the next to fall. As a sop to China and a slap at Japan, Congress passed a morale-boosting law in December, 1943. It made thousands of Chinese aliens in America eligible for citizenship, and permitted 105 immigrants to enter annually on a quota basis. But the discrimination in the Act of 1924 against other Orientals, including Japanese, still remained.[3]

The fixed policy of Roosevelt during the war years was to groom China, despite her glaring weaknesses, as one of the Big Five powers. But the American people were disturbed by evidences of antidemocratic practices, by friction between Chiang Kai-shek and United States General Joseph W. ("Vinegar Joe") Stilwell, and by reports that Chiang was much more interested in using American lend-lease supplies to fight the Chinese Communists than the Japanese invaders.[4] But there seemed to be wisdom in bolstering China as an Asiatic counterpoise against a po-

---

[3] Orientals were finally placed on the quota basis by the Walter-McCarran Immigration Act of 1952.

[4] See J. W. Stilwell, *The Stilwell Papers* (New York, 1948).

tentially resurgent Japan. China was to be mistress in her own house, and under no compulsion to grant special privileges to outsiders.

The multipower Open Door was presumably dead, for it had enjoyed vitality only when the Chinese were too weak to protect themselves against outside extortion or aggression. The assumption in Washington was that henceforth a strong and fully sovereign China would be a faithful guardian of the Open Door—her own Open Door. Unhappily, the eventual triumph of the Communists in 1948–1949 completely dashed all such hopes.

SUSPICIOUS SOVIETS

The weakest link in the unity of the United Nations was Russia. She was the key to victory, for her stout warriors "clawed the guts" out of the German army and saved the Western Allies. She was the key to peace, for she was potentially the greatest power, and could become, if she refused to co-operate, the world's greatest menace.

The truth is that Communist Russia was deeply suspicious of her "capitalistic" bedfellows. They had in 1918–1920 opposed Bolshevism with both money and armed intervention, and they had been slow to extend the right hand of official recognition. The United States had been the slowest of the major powers. The Western nations had rebuffed Soviet proposals for disarmament in the 1920's—probably made insincerely—and had left Russia out in the cold at the time of the Munich sell-out of 1938. On the eve of the German invasion of Poland in 1939, certain outspoken groups in France and England wanted to egg Hitler onto Stalin so that the two menaces would kill each other off. Instead, Stalin turned the tables in his fateful nonaggression pact of 1939 with Hitler.

Territorial changes had generated additional friction with Moscow. When Stalin seized his prearranged share of Poland after the Hitlerian invasion of 1939, both America and Britain registered opposition. They not only refused to recognize this brutal partition but granted formal recognition to the anti-Soviet Polish government-in-exile in London. When Russia in 1939–1940 undertook to wrest territory from Finland in order to protect Leningrad, the Western powers—Britain, France, and America—took steps that verged on war. When France collapsed in 1940 and Stalin sought to put more territory between himself and Hitler by absorbing the formerly Czarist Baltic states of Lithuania, Latvia, and Esthonia, the State Department flatly refused to recognize these changes. More than that, it persisted in maintaining official relations with the Washington embassies of all three defunct nations.

After Pearl Harbor, Stalin voiced new grievances. He was irritated by America's willingness, even in the name of military expediency, to deal with Fascist elements in France and Italy. He was irked by Washington's refusal to break relations with Finland, long after the Finns, hoping to regain their lost territory, had gone to war with him and were attacking Leningrad. He was dissatisfied with the quantity of lend-lease supplies which America, colossus of production, was able during 1942 to send him over circuitous and hazardous routes.

THE PIED PIPER OF MOSCOW

Russian bayonets shepherd the Baltic states into the
U.S.S.R.

Elderman in the *Washington Post*, 1940

Most galling of all to Moscow was the reluctance of Britain and America to open a real second front in France until their preparations were perfected. The suspicion grew in the Kremlin that the Allies, fearful of a dominating postwar Russia, wanted her "bled white" before they shed their own precious blood. When Drew Pearson, the indiscreet key-hole columnist, charged the State Department with officially pursuing this "bleed-white" policy, Secretary Hull indignantly replied that such accusations were "monstrous and diabolical falsehoods." Even after the Allies opened their spectacular campaigns in North Africa and Italy, in 1942–1943, Stalin declined to recognize these operations as real second fronts because they engaged so few of the common enemy.

Irresponsible agitators in America, unconsciously parroting Hitler's propaganda, were predicting that the next world war would be fought against the Communist menace. These fears multiplied as the Soviet armies surged toward Berlin. The Russian army newspaper, *Red Star,* complained bitterly of such a headline in Hearst's *New York Journal-American* as "RED WAVE THREATENS TO DROWN CHRISTIAN CIVILIZATION," and of a headline in the *Chicago Tribune,* "SOVIET UNION IS ONLY AGGRESSOR IN THE WORLD."

THE SHADOW OF THE HAMMER AND SICKLE

American suspicions of Russia, on the other hand, were well founded. During the 1920's and 1930's the Soviet leaders had sleeplessly sponsored propaganda for world revolution through the Communist International— the Comintern for short. A year-and-a-half after Pearl Harbor the Russians endeavored to allay Western anxieties by announcing, in May, 1943, that the Comintern had been dissolved. A year later the Communist party in the United States formally disbanded, although reconstituted as a supposedly nonpartisan group. Both of these apparent concessions were temporary, illusory, and deliberately designed to deceive the capitalistic world.[5]

Other events of the 1930's had aroused deep distrust in the United States. Prominent among them were the bloody Soviet purges of high officials, restrictions on personal liberty, rigorous control of the press, and atheistical attacks on religion—Karl Marx's "opiate of the masses." Roman Catholics continued to be distressed by repeated attacks on the Greek Orthodox Catholic Church. Stalin's assault on Finland in 1939, plus the seizure of the three Baltic states in 1940, may have been justified in the Kremlin by strategic necessities, but to the outside world they all spelled naked aggression.

Soviet mistrust of the capitalistic world lingered long after the Japanese assault on Pearl Harbor had caused the Americans to become comrades-in-arms. The Russians refused to share their military secrets, spied on their Allies, were reluctant to make known their most pressing needs so that lend-lease supplies could be provided, and obstructed the movements of American military personnel sent there to assist them. Seemingly the Soviets regarded World War II as merely one more campaign in

---

[5] The Comintern, after several years underground, emerged in 1947 as the Cominform. In 1945, the Communist Party of the United States was formally reconstituted.

the conflict with capitalism. They wanted no capitalistic agents snooping around their country and collecting information that would be useful in the coming showdown.[6]

President Roosevelt, who had not read much Communist literature, believed that the best way to wean the Soviets away from their nasty ideas of world revolution and make them co-operative Allies was to treat them generously. The hardened conspirators of the Kremlin were not melted. The truth is that America showered lend-lease supplies upon Russia with such generosity as to arouse suspicions as to Roosevelt's motives. The original decision to send lend-lease to Russia prior to Pearl Harbor is perhaps not so questionable as the decision to continue it after 1943. By then the tide had turned, a Russian victory was only a matter of time, the Kremlin was still highly unco-operative, and concessions might have been extorted by a judicious throttling down of the lend-lease spigot.

Stalin's policy toward Japan during the war evoked much bitter criticism in America. In particular, the Soviets were condemned for failing to attack the Japanese in the rear, and also for refusing to offer Siberian bases to American bombers so as to shorten the war in the Pacific. Such critics seem not to have realized that Russia had to marshal all her strength to beat back Germany. If she had attacked Japan, she would have been nutcrackered between two foes, and her Siberian bases would probably have been useless to both herself and her allies.

THE FIGHTING FRENCH

Relations with France, no less than with Russia, created delicate problems. The German invaders had occupied the northern and western part of the fallen republic since 1940. The technically neutral remainder, including a vast overseas empire, was left under a Hitler-dominated puppet government at Vichy, headed by Marshal Pétain, the eighty-four-year-old hero of World War I. Outside France a determined band of French patriots, led by the austere General de Gaulle, maintained headquarters in London and defied the aged Pétain.

Washington continued diplomatic relations with the Vichy regime, which was the only legal government of France. At the same time, the United States extended lend-lease aid to the fugitive de Gaullists and encouraged them in various other ways. The policy of "appeasing" the Vichy government, the so-called "stooge" of Hitler, evoked violent protests from many American "liberals." But a severance of relations would have involved a withdrawal of all consular and diplomatic officials from

[6] J. R. Deane, *The Strange Alliance* (New York, 1947). General Deane was an American liaison officer in Russia. See also E. D. Stettinius, Jr., *Lend-Lease* (New York, 1944); W. H. Standley and A. A. Ageton, *Admiral Ambassador to Russia* (Chicago, 1955).

Vichy France and French North Africa. These agents did invaluable work in smoothing the path for the Allied invasion of North Africa, and in keeping the powerful French fleet, still under the orders of Vichy, from falling into Hitler's hands. The Allied surprise assault on French North Africa, led by General Eisenhower in November, 1942, enabled Washington to tear off the mask and reveal that all along it had been trafficking with Vichy primarily for military purposes.[7]

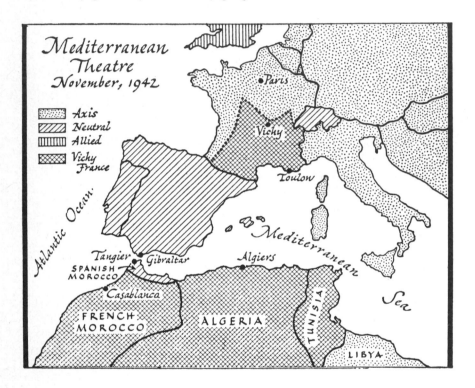

The daring attack on North Africa, while removing some old complications, created new ones. The Allies, who deeply distrusted General de Gaulle, chose as their tool General Giraud, a gallant French officer famous for spectacular escapes from German prisons during two world wars. Smuggled into North Africa by airplane, he ordered the French troops to end their resistance to the Allies, but he was not obeyed. At this perilous juncture Admiral Darlan, Vice-Premier of Vichy France, was on

[7] The backgrounds appear in Paul Farmer, *Vichy: Political Dilemma* (New York, 1955). Favorable to the State Department is W. L. Langer, *Our Vichy Gamble* (New York, 1947), the best single study. Highly critical of Langer is Louis Gottschalk, "Our Vichy Fumble," *Jour. of Mod. Hist.*, XX (1948), 47–56; also Ellen Hammer, "Hindsight on Vichy," *Pol. Sci. Quar.*, LXI (1946), 175–188. The American ambassador at Vichy, Admiral W. D. Leahy, tells his story in *I Was There* (New York, 1950).

the ground for the ostensible purpose of visiting his polio-stricken son. Although distrusted by the Allies as a leading collaborationist, he evidently perceived that Hitler might now be beaten, and he revealed a willingness to order a cease-fire. General Eisenhower agreed to accept his cooperation, and the Allied landings were made with surprisingly few casualties.

The assistance of turncoat Darlan, though savagely criticized in America, was of undeniable military value. More important perhaps than the saving of lives was the saving of time. Prolonged French resistance might have tempted Hitler to imperil the entire invasion by a lightning thrust through Spain. But the undercover dealings with Darlan were understandably distasteful to de Gaullists, to many British, to Communists, and to American liberals, especially "professional liberals." The United States was accused of grooming this hated Vichyite as a Fascist dictator of postwar France, to the discouragement of democratic elements in France and elsewhere. Many critics were evidently more determined to win a victory for liberalism than to win the war against Hitlerism. Darlan finally relieved Washington of further embarrassment when he died from an assassin's bullet, on Christmas Eve, 1942.

General de Gaulle, defying efforts to squelch him, continued to pop up like a jack-in-the-box. Despite his brusque manner and presumed Napoleonic ambitions, he had won a wide following for himself in France. Following the invasion of his homeland by Allied armies, his Committee of National Liberation was finally recognized by the Allies, in October, 1944, as the provisional government of France.

Roosevelt's French policy was clearly one of opportunism in the interests of winning the war. With fearsome secret weapons in the making, the delays that would result from trying to shape the postwar world along democratic lines seemed dangerous. "Temporary expediency" was the price that the Allies were prepared to pay for precious time—and victory. Roosevelt, in another connection, recalled a pertinent Balkan proverb: "In times of great peril, my son, you may walk with the Devil until you have crossed the bridge."

THE "APPEASEMENT" OF SPAIN

Closely connected with the surprise North African invasion and the "diplomacy of expediency" was Franco's Spain. The Spanish dictator, after riding into power with the openly "secret" help of Hitler and Mussolini, repaid his debt with noisy sympathy for the Axis. He even permitted the volunteer Spanish Blue Division to serve with the German army against Communist Russia. If Franco had been driven into the arms of his fellow dictators, the results would have been calamitous. The western Mediterranean would have been cut off, the African coast and outlying islands would have become Axis bases, the North African invasion would have been thwarted, and the war might have been lost by the Allies or pro-longed interminably.

The projected Allied invasion of North Africa underscored the de-sirability of keeping Franco in line. A distinguished Catholic layman, the historian Dr. Carlton J. H. Hayes of Columbia University, was drafted as ambassador to Spain to carry out this harrowing assignment. His efforts met with considerable success, despite anguished cries of "appeasement" from liberal and leftist elements in America who at times seemed more eager to fight Franco than to destroy Hitler.[8]

Anxious moments followed the invasion of North Africa. Roosevelt immediately assured Franco that the United States had no designs on Spanish territory. As an added precaution, the Allies detached a large force to guard against a possible flank attack from Spanish Morocco, where Franco had an army of some 150,000 men. At the same time, Washington sought to convince the Spaniards of the blessings of neu-trality by permitting them to receive—"appeasement" again—cargoes of urgently needed supplies, especially petroleum.

With the North African campaign a smashing success, the United States and Britain were free to clamp down on Franco. In previous months the Allies had been able to secure needed shipments of Spanish ore, while limiting them to Hitler, by "preclusive buying"—the "battle of the checkbooks." Now Spain could be forced into line by suspending oil shipments. As the fortunes of the Allies improved, the wily Franco gradually veered from pro-Axis nonbelligerency, to neutrality, and finally to neutrality favorable to the Allies—in short, from malevolent to benev-olent neutrality. "Appeasement" thus had the virtue of contributing to military success. Perhaps Franco was overappeased, but in the dark days of 1942–1943 Washington believed that it was better to be safe than sorry.

THE REDISCOVERY OF LATIN AMERICA

The devastating attack on Pearl Harbor aroused not only the United States but Latin America as well. In the words of the Havana declaration of 1940, an attack upon one was an attack upon all. Most of the twenty republics promptly severed relations with the Axis or declared war, and even such laggards as Chile and Argentina extended unneutral privileges to their belligerent sisters. The nations that acted with the most vigor were located in or near the Caribbean danger zone, where the influence

---

[8] See C. J. H. Hayes, *Wartime Mission in Spain, 1942–1945* (New York, 1945), which abounds in examples of how ignorant public opinion at home hampered the larger strategical purposes of the Washington government. See also Herbert Feis, *The Spanish Story* (New York, 1948).

of Uncle Sam was strong and where his navy could most easily provide defense.

The Pan-American machinery that had been so laboriously constructed in the 1930's was quickly thrown into high gear. In January, 1942, the darkest days of the war, the Third Meeting of Ministers of Foreign Affairs assembled at Rio de Janeiro, the hospitable capital of Brazil. The primary goal of the United States and its co-belligerents was to secure unanimous agreement on a resolution binding all the American republics to sever relations with the Axis. But Argentina and Chile, which were farthest removed from the protecting naval arm of Uncle Sam, led a successful fight to make the declaration recommendatory rather than mandatory. Even in its watered-down form the resolution, which was unanimously adopted, preserved the Pan-American front, while striking a blow at the Axis propagandists who had reckoned on disunity. Within a day after adjournment, all the Latin-American republics that had not done so severed relations with the Axis, except Argentina and Chile.

Brazil, traditionally the most friendly of the major Latin-American countries toward Washington, was the first South-American nation to declare war. The Portuguese-speaking republic and the great Republic of the North were by far the two largest republics in the Americas. They were also the most important non-Spanish nations in the Pan-American concert. They exchanged products, such as coffee for manufactured goods, that were largely complementary rather than competitive. During the war years the United States also shipped large quantities of lend-lease supplies to Brazil, and extended substantial loans for industrial purposes. Brazil, for her part, was the only Latin-American nation to send an expeditionary force to Europe, and she provided air bases that were of immense value in ferrying reinforcements across the "Atlantic narrows" to North Africa.

The war years were something of a honeymoon period for the republics to the south. One wit observed that in 1492 Columbus discovered America; in 1942 the United States discovered Latin America. The Good Neighbor of the North not only extended lavish loans but, among other activities, purchased immense quantities of raw materials at generous prices. Bolivian tin was especially prized, for the Japanese had cut off the invaluable Malayan source. The Latin Americans were quite content to make hay, at the expense of rich Uncle Sam, while the sun of Hitlerism shone.

The costliness of this war program stirred up a storm of criticism in the United States. Senator Butler of Nebraska charged that "Good Neighborism" had become "Rich Uncleism," and extravagantly estimated that in three years Uncle Sam had squandered some $6 billion in hemispheric "boondoggling." The Latin Americans reacted angrily to these loose accusations. They did not like to be told that the Good Neighbor policy was but a marriage of convenience, and that a divorce suit might be expected just as soon as the shadow of Hitler had passed.[9]

THE ARGENTINE PROBLEM CHILD

Argentina continued to be the least co-operative nation in the All-America lineup. As the wealthiest and most progressive of the Latin-American states for about half a century, she regarded herself as the natural leader of her sister republics, and resented the overshadowing dominance of Uncle Sam. If she could not lead, she would not follow. The jealousy of the would-be Colossus of the South for the so-called Colossus of the North explains why Argentine statesmen for several decades had consistently sought to checkmate the United States at international conferences.

Back of this superiority complex lay economic rivalry. Argentina's twin kings—meat and wheat—were unwelcome competitors in the United States. Uncle Sam's tariff barriers and meat-quarantine restrictions, chiefly against hoof-and-mouth disease, were regarded as foul blows. The witticism is that one can insult an Argentinian's mother but not his meat.

Argentina's great export market was Europe, and she did not want to antagonize potential postwar customers, Hitlerian or otherwise. She was not prepared to gamble on an Allied victory, particularly in the dark days of 1942. Her policy, as well as that of neighboring Chile, seems to have been not so much pro-Axis as pro-"playing it safe."

The pro-Fascist and promilitarist bent of Argentina had still other roots. She had a deep-seated dictator tradition; she boasted a large German and Italian immigrant population; and she harbored native Fascist elements who admired Dictator Franco of Spain. She also eyed with mounting distrust the loans and lend-lease supplies with which Uncle Sam was strengthening the military muscles of her arch-rival, neighboring Brazil.

A military coup by the "colonel's clique" in 1943 ushered in new complications for Argentina. Presumably fearing reprisals from the Allies, she belatedly broke relations with Japan and Germany in January, 1944. Yet subsequent developments inspired the State Department publicly to denounce Argentina for "deserting the Allied cause." A protesting crowd in Buenos Aires, demonstrating before the United States Embassy, carried a banner proclaiming, "Argentina Wears Long Pants." The Washington government, rejecting demands for a rigid boycott, cracked down when it froze Argentine gold stocks and tightened shipping regulations. The Roosevelt administration, in addition to economic pressures, was evidently falling back on the old Wilsonian policy of nonrecognition, moral castigation, and diplomatic quarantine.

[9] See S. F. Bemis, *The Latin American Policy of the United States* (New York, 1943).

With the diplomats thus deadlocked and the war in Germany roaring to an end, an Inter-American Conference on Problems of War and Peace met in Mexico City early in 1945. The site was Chapultepec Castle, which, ironically, the Yankee invader had stormed in 1847. The major purposes of the delegates were to strengthen Pan-American solidarity, to intensify the war effort, and to lay the foundations for postwar stability. The most significant resolution was the Act of Chapultepec, which in effect made all the American republics co-guardians of the Monroe Doctrine, *even against an American* aggressor. Thus the Monroe Doctrine, multilateralized at Havana in 1940, was expanded at Chapultepec into a kind of Pan-American defense doctrine. The "absent sister" Argentina caused much embarrassment, but the conference resolved that if she would subscribe to the principles of Chapultepec and enter the war, she would be eligible for admission to the United Nations.

Hitler's dream of a thousand-year Reich was rapidly crumbling when Argentina finally fell into line. As an act of deathbed conversion, she unenthusiastically declared war on Japan and Germany on March 27, 1945, and adhered to the Act of Chapultepec. The United States and the other American republics responded by lifting economic restrictions and resuming full diplomatic relations. Yet grave doubts existed as to the sincerity of Argentina's repentance. Paradoxically, the United Nations had fought to make the world safe against Fascism, but the war came to an end with the most important center of Fascism, except possibly Franco's Spain, defiantly entrenched in the Western Hemisphere.[10]

TURNCOAT ENEMIES AND NERVOUS NEUTRALS

Diplomatically, the enemy nations presented a confusing picture. All of Hitler's satellites—Italy, Hungary, Bulgaria, Romania, and Finland—not only dropped out of the conflict but turned against the German dictator.

The Italian people, who had been led into war by the bullying Benito Mussolini, did not have their hearts in the fight. After the Allied invasion of Sicily, in July, 1943, Italian resistance wilted rapidly. Mussolini was deposed and a new government under Marshal Badoglio, the Fascist-tainted conqueror of Ethiopia, came to terms with the Allies. Liberal elements in America, especially those who had decried the trafficking with Vichy, Darlan, and Franco, were noisily critical of the dealings with Badoglio. But the Germans had to be driven out of Italy, and, as in North Africa, the Allied military leaders preferred to get on with the fighting and worry about local politics later. After turncoat Italy had declared war on Hitler, in October, 1943, she was accepted by the Allies as a co-belligerent.

Finland was even more of a diplomatic curiosity. On the day of Pearl

[10] See A. P. Whitaker, *The United States and Argentina* (Cambridge, Mass., 1954).

Harbor the Finns, having won back their lost territory, were attacking Russian lines before Leningrad in uneasy partnership with Hitler. America's admiration for debt-paying Finland was such that Congress could not bring itself, despite bitter protests from Moscow, to declare war on her. Washington finally severed relations in June, 1944, and the next year, after the Russians had again crushed the Finns, resumed diplomatic intercourse. "Brave little" Finland was then permitted to pay further installments on her debt.

The neutral nations of Europe—Eire, Switzerland, Sweden, Turkey, Spain, Portugal—played varying roles. Portugal made available to the British (and Americans) antisubmarine bases in the Azores, and responded to joint Anglo-American pressures by cutting off from Germany all shipments of steel-hardening wolfram. Sweden in 1944 likewise yielded to joint Anglo-American pressure and severely curtailed her exports of iron ore and steel ball bearings to Germany. The Turks, who were seriously threatened by Hitler's invasion of Russia and North Africa, received invaluable lend-lease aid from the United States. When the Nazi tide receded, Washington joined with London in forcing Turkey to break both economic and diplomatic ties with Hitler. The Turks finally declared war on disintegrating Germany in 1945, and joined the United Nations in the eleventh hour of the conflict.

American public opinion was highly critical of the economic assistance rendered by Turkey, and especially by Sweden, to the Nazi war lords. The truth is that during most of the conflict neither nation was in a position to resist Hitler's demands, and that both helped the Allied cause by not provoking Nazi conquest.

SELECTED BIBLIOGRAPHY

Indispensable is Herbert Feis, *Churchill, Roosevelt, Stalin* (Princeton, 1957). Important accounts by participants are R. E. Sherwood, *Roosevelt and Hopkins* (New York, 1948); *The Memoirs of Cordell Hull* (2 vols., New York, 1948); H. L. Stimson and M. Bundy, *On Active Service in Peace and War* (New York, 1947); and W. S. Churchill, *The Grand Alliance* (Boston, 1951); *The Hinge of Fate* (Boston, 1950); *Closing the Ring* (Boston, 1951); *Triumph and Tragedy* (Boston, 1953). The difficulties with Russia are dealt with briefly in T. A. Bailey, *America Faces Russia* (Ithaca, N.Y., 1950) and W. A. Williams, *American-Russian Relations, 1781–1947* (New York, 1952).

Domestic backgrounds appear in Roland Young, *Congressional Politics in the Second World War* (New York, 1956). See also H. B. Westerfield, *Foreign Policy and Party Politics: Pearl Harbor to Korea* (New Haven, 1955).

See footnotes of this chapter; the references at the end of the next chapter; and *Harvard Guide*, Ch. 30.

7TH, 8TH, AND 9TH ED. REFS. See BIBLIOGRAPHICAL ADDENDUM, p. 1,047.

49

Founding the United Nations 1941-1945

We have learned that we must live as men, and not as ostriches, nor as dogs in the manger. We have learned to be citizens of the world, members of the human community.
FRANKLIN D. ROOSEVELT, 1945

UNCONDITIONAL SURRENDER

THE INTIMATE personal relationship between President Roosevelt and Prime Minister Churchill facilitated Anglo-American co-ordination to a remarkable degree. The first meeting of the two statesmen—off Newfoundland, at the time of the Atlantic Charter, and in Washington, at the time of the Declaration of the United Nations—had gone off smoothly. The third meeting occurred in June, 1942, when Churchill, cigar embedded in his cherubic face, flew into Washington for discussions of high strategy. The conferees issued optimistic statements to offset recent reversals to Allied arms, and promised an attack that would relieve Hitler's pressure on Russia.

The spectacular North African thrust, which partially redeemed the Allied promise of action, necessitated another high-level conference. This time Roosevelt, amid strictest secrecy, flew the Atlantic for the first time and met with Churchill at Casablanca, French Morocco, in January, 1943. Stalin, though cordially invited, presumably had his hands full directing the giant Soviet offensive. The conferees agreed to launch an invasion of Sicily and Italy, to open a full-fledged second front somewhere, and to wage war relentlessly until the enemy surrendered unconditionally. In fact, Roosevelt requested that this meeting be called the "Unconditional Surrender Conference."

"Unconditional surrender" proved to be one of the most hotly debated decisions of the entire war. Many critics agreed with isolationist Senator

Wheeler of Montana that the policy was "brutal" and "asinine." The strongest criticism was that "unconditional surrender" disheartened those liberal elements in Germany who might have overthrown Hitler and shortened the war. This allegation is difficult to prove, because the German liberals were notoriously few and timid, and because Hitler's henchmen wielded ruthless power. But there can be no doubt that the Allied refusal to negotiate terms with Germany left that nation at the end of the war without a government, and facilitated the four-power regime that opened a Pandora's box of trouble. The complete collapse of both Germany and Japan, though perhaps unavoidable, upset delicate balances of power in two hemispheres, while paving the path for Soviet ascendancy.

The reasons *at the time* for unconditional surrender were persuasive. The Russians were highly suspicious of the Allied failure to establish a genuine second front, and they feared that the Allies might make a separate peace with Hitler. "Unconditional surrender" "appeased" them to some degree, and possibly counteracted any impulse on their part to come to terms with Germany.

The ghost of Woodrow Wilson, moreover, was near the shoulder of Franklin Roosevelt at Casablanca. The latter's memory went back to the mistakes of 1918. The Germans had then been granted terms based on the Fourteen Points, and had subsequently cried "betrayal." Their armies had marched home, thereby giving rise to the legend that they had not been beaten but merely stabbed in the back by Jews and other disloyal elements. The conquering American forces had halted short of German soil in 1918, and the subsequent feeling of frustration had produced a bitter harvest of disillusionment in the United States.

Unconditional surrender would avert all these difficulties, though creating others. The goal of smashing Hitler would key the United States up for greater sacrifices, while postponing disruptive discussions with the Allies over what to do with the fallen foe. The American people, now bitterly aroused against the brutality of the dictators, generally applauded "unconditional surrender." [1]

SOVIET-AMERICAN SOLIDARITY

The meshing of plans for an effective second front required two more high-level conferences between Churchill and Roosevelt. The first occurred in Washington during May, 1943. The second took place during August, 1943, in high-cliffed Quebec, where the decision was reaffirmed to launch a full-scale invasion of French Normandy in May, 1944. A repre-

[1] One survey found opinion 81% favorable. *Opinion News*, March 20, 1945, p. 2. See J. L. Chase, "Unconditional Surrender Reconsidered," *Pol. Sci. Quar.*, LXX (June, 1955), pp. 258–279.

sentative of China was present to participate in discussions regarding the Burma-China front.

Co-ordination among America, Britain, and China was proceeding smoothly, but that with Russia was not. Stalin was deeply distressed by the repeated postponements of a real second front. Even while the Quebec conference was meeting, the Soviet army journal *Red Star* complained that the operations of the Allies in the Mediterranean had "failed to divert a single German division" from Russia. Soviet-American relations were dangerously strained by the late summer of 1943.

At this critical point Secretary of State Hull stepped into the breach. Although seventy-two years old and suffering from poor health, he boarded an airplane for the first time and undertook the wearisome trip to Moscow. There, in October, 1943, he conferred at length with British Foreign Secretary Eden and Soviet Foreign Commissar Molotov. The discussions, which involved the first high-level meeting of the Big Three, proceeded with gratifying cordiality, and on the last night Stalin played host to the delegates at a vodka-lubricated dinner in the Kremlin.

The Moscow Conference was perhaps more memorable for clearing away fetid air than for any concrete achievements. Stalin was assured that preparations were well advanced for the second front in France, and he was so pleased as to promise that when the European war ended he would enter the conflict against Japan. In the long view the most important declaration of the conference pledged the powers—and here the Chinese ambassador signed—to establish a new organization for peace [the United Nations].

The Moscow Conference, which broke the log-jam of nonco-ordination, was one of the major Allied victories of the war. Henceforth the Soviet Union was actively represented in high-level Allied discussions dealing with subjects not directly involving Japan. Secretary Hull returned to Washington a conquering hero, and responded to an unprecedented invitation from Congress to make a personal report on his trip.

GRAND STRATEGY AT THE SUMMIT

A high-level conference on the Far East now seemed imperative, for the tide of battle was turning heavily against Japan in the Pacific. Roosevelt journeyed secretly to Cairo, Egypt, where he took part in important deliberations late in November, 1943. Winston Churchill and Chiang Kai-shek were present, with the chic Madame Chiang, who had studied at an American college, serving as interpreter. The Soviets, who did not want to provoke war with Japan prematurely, were represented by a delegate when non-Japanese subjects claimed attention. At long last Chiang had his feet under the same table with Roosevelt and Churchill in an effort to co-ordinate Allied blows.

The ensuing Declaration of Cairo was one of the diplomatic highlights of the war. The three powers, while disclaiming territorial designs, pledged themselves to fight Japan until "unconditional surrender." The Japanese would be deprived of all Pacific islands acquired since 1914, whether by capture or mandate from the League of Nations. Japan would also be forced to return former Chinese territory, notably Manchuria, Formosa, and the Pescadores. Japanese-dominated Korea was promised her independence "in due course"—a vague phrase that alarmed Korean patriots, and properly so. The Cairo Declaration was thus a public pledge to squeeze the Japanese genie back into the pre-Perry bottle. It may have steeled the sons of Nippon to a more fanatical resistance, but on the other hand it bolstered the morale of the Chinese, Koreans, and other exploited peoples of the Far East.

Roosevelt and Churchill next secretly enplaned for the Iranian capital, Teheran, for a memorable and long-deferred meeting with Marshal Stalin, November 28–December 1, 1943. Roosevelt, who jocularly referred to the Soviet dictator as "Uncle Joe," had long been eager to meet the hardened conspirator of the Kremlin and melt him with an application of the famous Roosevelt charm. "Stalin—I can handle that old buzzard," he once remarked jauntily to an intimate. The Soviet leader, burdened with heavy military responsibilities, would go no farther than Iran from his home base, so the crippled Roosevelt had to come to him.

The Teheran Conference went off harmoniously, although there is no evidence that Stalin was ever swayed from the Communist goal of world revolution by Roosevelt's "charm." Final commitments were made for a full-fledged invasion of France in the late spring of 1944, and for a simultaneous offensive by the Soviets from the east. This decision cleared the air and pleased the Russians, who could no longer complain of being step-brothers in arms. Diplomatically, the Teheran Conference was perhaps most important in reducing tensions by establishing for the first time a personal relationship among the leaders of the Big Three.

The smashing success of the second front, launched in France in June, 1944, necessitated another Roosevelt-Churchill conference to deal with Germany as well as with Japan. The conferees again met in Quebec, in September, 1944. They decided, among other things, on the location of the British and American zones of postwar Germany, thereby clearing the way for the later Soviet and French zones. An unfortunate blunder was the temporary adoption by Roosevelt and Churchill of the Morgenthau plan. Henry Morgenthau, Jr., the Secretary of the Treasury, and an influential associate of the President, was so disturbed by Nazi brutalities as to propose a scheme for punishing industrial Germany by reducing her to an agrarian economy—"a potato patch," the phrase went. Roosevelt, repenting of his hasty decision at Quebec, dropped the scheme a month later. But the punitive plan played into the hands of German propagandists, along with "Unconditional Surrender." The "Morgenthau mentality" unfortunately lingered on in the postwar treatment of Germany.[2]

ROOSEVELT THE FOURTH TERMER

As the Presidential election of 1944 approached, Roosevelt was the inevitable choice of the Democrats for a fourth nomination. He was, to be sure, showing the strain of three terms, but he had no other rival. With a war and a peace yet to be won, he seemed more than ever the "indispensable man."

The Republicans turned to Thomas E. Dewey, the dapper and dynamic young prosecutor-governor of New York. Old-line party members were annoyed by his recent advocacy of international co-operation, and as an antidote they chose as his running mate Governor Bricker of Ohio. The handsome Ohioan was an isolationist who vaguely preached "co-operation without commitments," and who was damned in some quarters as an "honest Harding." The greater enthusiasm of the convention for the Vice-Presidential nominee led to the quip, "The delegates loved Bricker but married Dewey."

To an unusual degree foreign affairs were kept out of the dusty arena of 1944. The Republican nominee could no doubt have disrupted the nation by stirring up a bitter controversy over Roosevelt's conduct of the war, and over Washington's tentative plans for world co-operation. But Dewey commendably put patriotism above party. With foreign policy thus soft-pedaled, the Republicans concentrated their ire and fire on the domestic shortcomings of the Democrats. The rich baritone voice of Dewey tirelessly hammered home the slogan, "That's why it's time for a change!" In foreign affairs the burning question was: Which party could be trusted to win the war and negotiate a lasting peace?

The arguments for Roosevelt, the constitutional commander-in-chief, were strong. He was winning the war, and one should not change commanders any more than quarterbacks when one's side is gaining the upper hand. The President, who was on intimate terms with Churchill and Stalin, had laid the ground work for peace. He should be permitted, so his boosters claimed, to finish the job.

If the young and inexperienced Dewey favored international co-operation, a powerful and noisy bloc of his supporters definitely did not. The Republicans in 1920 had similarly promised to work for world collaboration, but the isolationist wing had secured control of Warren G. Harding and had refused to carry out these pledges. The Democrats did not fail to stress this betrayal in such doggerel as:

[2] See Henry Morgenthau, Jr., *Germany is Our Problem* (New York, 1945).

Dewey, Tom,
    On matters foreign,
Sounds a lot like
    Harding, Warren.

The Allies were quietly praying for Roosevelt, the known quantity, while the German Nazis were pulling for Dewey.

The results of the election of 1944 were widely heralded as a victory for international co-operation. Roosevelt was swept to victory by the votes of many who opposed his domestic policies but who favored his foreign policies.[3] Like overripe apples, many isolationist members of Congress fell at the polls, including Senator Nye of munitions-investigation fame and godfather of the neutrality legislation. Sixteen newly elected Senators of both parties, in an unprecedented declaration, pledged their support to the President. Politicians could not safely ignore the mounting pressure of internationalist sentiment.

SECRET DEALS AT YALTA

Following the Presidential election, a final conference of the Big Three seemed imperative to grapple with the problems of a collapsing Germany and a doomed Japan. President Roosevelt, his health obviously failing under the strain of three full terms, sailed to Yalta, a beautiful ex-Czarist resort on the relatively warm southern shore of the Crimean Peninsula. There, early in February, 1945, he met for a week with Churchill and Stalin. He then returned to Washington and made his last personal report to a joint session of Congress—for the first time sitting down. Perceptibly ageing, he complained that the ten-pound steel braces bothered his legs.

The men of Yalta announced that they had worked out plans for the unconditional surrender of Germany. The fallen Reich was to be divided into three zones of occupation, with France being invited to take over a fourth. (Details appeared in the secret agreement published March 25, 1947.) Germany was to be disarmed, her war criminals were to be punished, and she was to pay reparations for the damages she had caused. (Details on reparations appeared in the secret agreement published March 19, 1947.) [4]

The Yalta Conference released the announcement that a meeting of the United Nations would be held in San Francisco, beginning April 25,

---

[3] One poll showed that 63% preferred Roosevelt at the peace table to 26% for Dewey. *Pub. Opin. Quar.*, VIII, 335.

[4] Publication at the time would have played into the hands of Nazi propagandists. See J. L. Snell, ed., *The Meaning of Yalta* (Baton Rouge, La., 1956), a good general work on the subject. See also Herbert Feis, *The China Tangle* (Princeton, 1953); E. R. Stettinius, Jr., *Roosevelt and the Russians: the Yalta Conference* (Garden City, N.Y., 1949); J. F. Byrnes, *Speaking Frankly* (New York, 1947); W. S. Churchill, *Triumph and Tragedy* (Boston, 1953).

1945, to frame a world organization for peace. The conferees promised that they would later make public the formula they had threshed out for voting procedures in the Security Council of the United Nations. (These secret arrangements were revealed nearly three months later, at the time of the San Francisco Conference.)

UNCORKED AT LAST!

The secret papers of Yalta, published ten
years later, created a sensation.

Costello in the *Knickerbocker News*
(Albany), 1955

Roosevelt also secretly agreed at Yalta that Russia might have three votes in the Assembly of the embryonic United Nations, including one each for the Ukraine and White Russia. The objective was partially to offset the six votes of the British Commonwealth. Roosevelt reserved the right to ask for three votes for the United States, should the Senate need this sop, but he later renounced the privilege. The news of this secret deal leaked out late the next month, and further black-eyed the Yalta Conference. Apologists for Roosevelt could hardly defend the inept publicity, but they could argue that the concessions to Moscow were unimportant. The Russians were fully protected by a veto in the Security Council, and two more votes in the Assembly then seemed immaterial.

THE PLIGHT OF POLAND

The published announcement at Yalta seemed to herald a new day for Poland and the other liberated nations of Central Europe, then partially or wholly occupied by Soviet troops. The Big Three solemnly agreed to facilitate "free elections" in all of these countries, in harmony with the Atlantic Charter. Specifically, the government of Poland was to be reorganized on "a broader democratic basis," with both non-Communists and Communists represented, and it was to be committed to "free elections."

Stalin's subsequent breaking of his "free-election" pledge proved to be one of the great eye-openers of the postwar era. Roosevelt was accused of having naïvely reposed faith in the word of a dictator who was notoriously untrustworthy, and of thus having sacrificed Poland to Soviet imperialism. The apologists for the President replied that Stalin, with a powerful Red army at his back, was in a position to work his will anyhow. His co-operation in building a better tomorrow was urgently needed, and Roosevelt, with much public support, believed that more was to be gained by trust than distrust. At all events, a pledge was written into the Crimean Charter which, when flagrantly violated by Stalin, strengthened the moral cause of the Western democracies by clearly highlighting Soviet duplicity.

The new boundaries of Poland, as outlined in the Crimean Charter, aroused heated controversy at the time. Poland was to have her Russian-inhabited areas cut off in the east by roughly the Curzon Line, but was to be compensated by German territory to the west and north. This decision, which handed over to the Soviets about one-third of pre-1939 Poland, aroused bitter denunciation among powerful Polish and Roman Catholic groups, both in America and abroad. Polish-descended Congressman O'Konski of Wisconsin, supported by Congressman Lesinski of Michigan, assailed the "crime of Crimea" as a "stab in the back" for Poland and as a "second Munich." Yet the American public, recognizing that these controversial arrangements involved compromise, generally approved the published results.[5] The secret deals that were later revealed came as a bucket of cold water.

THE PRICE TAG FOR STALIN'S ARMY

Choice bait was dangled before Stalin at Yalta to induce him to enter the Far Eastern conflict after Hitler was crushed. Roosevelt's military advisers, not yet realizing how near Japan was to collapse, calculated that a successful assault on the main Japanese islands would take about

---

[5] Gallup (March 10, 1945) found 61% favorable, 9% unfavorable, and 30% undecided. *Pub. Opin. Quar.*, IX, 95.

eighteen months and cost up to a million casualties. If Stalin could be persuaded to attack the Japanese armies in Manchuria and Korea, he would pin down large numbers of troops and save the lives of countless American boys. But why should he fight to save American boys? He had already suffered immense losses in "meat-grinder" fighting with the Germans, while the Allies had allegedly dragged their feet in opening a second front.

Stalin was in a position to drive a stiff bargain. The terms, temporarily kept secret from China for fear of leaks, were not published for exactly one year. The Soviets did not want to goad Japan into an attack until they were ready. Stalin agreed to enter the Far Eastern war "two or three months" after the conflict in Europe had "terminated." In return, he would receive the following rewards:

1. Outer-Mongolia, once China's, would continue as a Communist satellite of the Soviet Union.
2. The "lost fruits" of the Russo-Japanese war were to be returned, including the southern half of Sakhalin Island. In Manchuria, the port of Dairen was to be internationalized and Port Arthur was to be leased to Russia as a naval base. The railroads of Manchuria were to be operated jointly by the Chinese and Soviets, with "the pre-eminent interests" of Russia safeguarded and China retaining "full sovereignty."
3. The Kurile islands, once partially Russian, were to be handed over to the Russians.

Where did Chiang Kai-shek, who was not an ally of Russia, fit into all this? His acquiescence would be necessary regarding Manchuria and

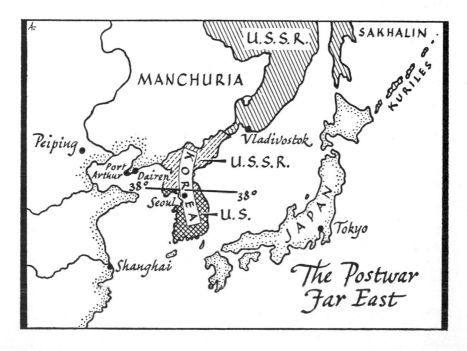

The Postwar Far East

Outer Mongolia, and Roosevelt in the same secret agreement specifically undertook to secure it. Critics of these arrangements later condemned the President for having gone behind Chiang's back, and for having unethically promised Stalin partial control of the same Manchuria which Roosevelt had promised at Cairo to return to Chiang. On the other hand, Stalin agreed to negotiate with China a pact of friendship and alliance for the purpose of helping the Chinese rid Manchuria and their other territories of the Japanese invader. The war-weary Chinese Nationalists, although later haggling over the terms regarding Outer Mongolia and Manchuria, were pleased with the prospect of recognition and assistance from the Soviet Union. In fact, since mid-1943 Chiang had been urging Washington to promote a friendly understanding between the Nationalists and the Russians. (For the treaty of 1945, see p. 774.)

Critics of Roosevelt—and Churchill—had a Roman holiday when the secret Far Eastern terms were later published. They accused the President, allegedly sick and feeble-minded, of having betrayed China in return for help that was not needed to crush Japan. The best that can be said in his defense is that he had to rely on the advice of his experts regarding the need for Soviet military aid; that the Yalta agreement, if honored by Stalin, actually set limits to Russian domination in China; and that the Soviets could deploy such powerful military forces that they were in a position to seize what they wanted anyhow. The subsequent charge that China went down the Communist drain primarily because of the Yalta "betrayal" is impossible to substantiate and inherently improbable.[6] As a matter of fact, no territory was actually taken away from China; Manchuria was taken away from Japan and restored to China. Outer Mongolia was already alienated from the Chinese.

Even so, Yalta became a kind of dirty word in American thinking. The stain of secret diplomacy and under-the-table deals would not wash off. The Soviets certainly would have come into the war with or without a prior agreement, and they might have seized more than they were awarded at Yalta if left alone. But there was a glaring inconsistency in turning back the hands of the clock and restoring their influence in Manchuria. John Hay's Open Door policy had been largely designed to jockey them out. And the balance of power in the Far East was further unbalanced in favor of the Soviets, who, despite ample wartime evidence to the contrary, were wishfully expected to be co-operative. As was so often the case in World War II, overconcentration on short-run military victory resulted in a long-run moral defeat. The whole unsavory episode also lent color to the charge that Roosevelt had treacherously permitted Communists to infiltrate the State Department and betray the best interests of the United States. The path was further paved for Senator McCarthy and the anti-Communist hysteria of the 1950's.

[*] Snell, *The Meaning of Yalta*, p. 197.

IN TIME OF WAR PREPARE FOR PEACE

The tragedy of the Wilson-Lodge deadlock of 1919–1920 continued to cast a long shadow over current schemes for a new world organization. Partisan politics would have to be leashed and the Senate would have to show a co-operative spirit before definite plans for a new international order could be jelled. Secretary Hull took a giant stride toward bi-partisanship when, early in 1942, he launched his Advisory Committee on Postwar Foreign Policy. It was gradually expanded to include leading members of both parties in the Senate. Republican governors and other leaders grasped the extended hand of bi-partisanship when, in September, 1943, they met at historic Mackinac Island, Michigan, and pledged their support to an international organization for peace.

Congress gradually fell into line. The House of Representatives, in June, 1943, passed the Fulbright resolution by a resounding vote of 360 to 29. In broad terms it committed the United States to support a future organization for peace. Representative Fish of New York, a rabid isolationist, was but a voice crying in the wilderness when he branded this "pious declaration" a "mirage." "Let's win the war," he sneered, "and then fight it out with our allies."

Later in the year, November, 1943, the Senate, over the quavering opposition of the still "irreconcilable" Senator Hiram Johnson of California, approved a resolution similar to that of the House by the lopsided vote of 85 to 5. The Senate thus promoted the cause of peace by signing in advance a blank check to support any reasonable plan for a postwar organization. All these pronouncements helped remove the disruptive debate over isolationism from the Roosevelt-Dewey Presidential campaign of 1944.

The economic foundation stones of peace had meanwhile been receiving expert attention. In July, 1944, the United Nations Monetary and Financial Conference, involving some 1300 specialists, met at the fashionable Bretton Woods resort, in the mountains of New Hampshire. The representatives of forty-four nations engaged in protracted discussions, and finally came to an agreement on a two-pronged plan. First, an international loan fund of $8.8 billion would help stabilize national currencies and facilitate payments across international boundaries. Second, a World Bank capitalized at $9.1 billion would provide loans to needy nations, primarily for reconstruction and economic development. American bankers protested loudly against government competition with their business, and prospects were that the Bretton Woods agreement would encounter stormy weather in Congress.

The political counterpart of the Bretton Woods Conference was the six-week Dumbarton Oaks Conference. It was held from August 21 to October 7, 1944, at Dumbarton Oaks, a beautiful Harvard-owned colonial residence on the outskirts of Washington. Pursuant to the understanding reached by Secretary Hull in Moscow with Stalin, the representatives of the Big Four—America, Britain, Russia, and China—hammered out a tentative draft of the charter for the yet unborn United Nations organization. The Soviets, fearing the anti-Communist prejudices of other nations, were determined to have a veto voice in the forthcoming Security Council. This roadblock was not removed at Dumbarton Oaks but at Yalta, where Roosevelt, Stalin, and Churchill worked out a compromise on voting procedures. The call then went forth from the Big Three for a conference at San Francisco to whip the Dumbarton Oaks draft into the charter of the United Nations.

SECOND CHANCE AT SAN FRANCISCO

In preparing for the San Francisco Conference, Roosevelt was at pains to avoid the more costly mistakes of Wilson at Paris in 1919. The American delegation of eight members was clearly bi-partisan: four Democrats, three Republicans, and one independent Democrat. The Senate was adequately represented by two leading members,[7] and the House also with two. Secretary Cordell Hull, who had been forced to resign because of ill health, was made a member and senior adviser, although unable to go to San Francisco. The titular head of the delegation was the new Secretary of State Edward R. Stettinius, Jr., a prominent businessman new to foreign affairs. The assumption was that Roosevelt planned to be his own Secretary of State.

Roosevelt at San Francisco was faced with a simpler task than Wilson at Paris. The conclave in California was not to concern itself with the terms of peace but to mold the draft prepared at Dumbarton Oaks into a new charter for world organization. Unlike the League Covenant, the Dumbarton Oaks plan had been published well in advance, and critics had ample time for microscopic examination. In contrast with the secrecy at Paris, forty-two national organizations, including the National League of Women Voters, were invited to send consultants to San Francisco.

Most important of all, the new United Nations Charter was to stand on its own feet. Unlike the League Covenant, it was not to be shackled to the ball and chain of a punitive peace treaty.

Preparations for the San Francisco conference were proceeding favorably when Roosevelt suddenly died on April 12, 1945, less than two weeks before opening day. Germany was collapsing, and a peace had to be made. At a time when leadership of the highest order was needed, the leader's hand fell limp. The nation was stunned.

[7] Highly important was Republican Senator Vandenberg, who had recently switched from isolationist to internationalist. See A. H. Vandenberg, Jr., ed., *The Private Papers of Senator Vandenberg* (Boston, 1952).

But the shock of Roosevelt's death passed quickly. Harry S. Truman, the inexperienced and unbriefed Vice-President, partially revived confidence by announcing that the conference in San Francisco would be held on schedule. The unexpected death of the President seems to have aroused in politicians a deeper sense of their responsibilities. Forty Republican Senators promptly volunteered an unprecedented pledge of support, quite in contrast with the Lodge-sponsored Round Robin of 1919. Marshal Stalin, who had hitherto betrayed indifference by naming only minor delegates to the conference, responded to an earlier American appeal by sending Foreign Commissar Molotov.

CONTROVERSY AT THE UN CONFERENCE

With flags flapping at half-mast in honor of Roosevelt, the United Nations Conference opened on April 25, 1945. The representatives of forty-six countries—ultimately fifty—were keenly conscious that civilization must not fumble its second chance.

The aggressive attitude of the Russians got the Conference off to a shaky start. Invoking the secret agreement with Roosevelt at Yalta, they expanded their representation to three, including the quasi-independent Ukraine and White Russia. They also insisted that the Communist regime in Poland, which they were propping up, be allowed a seat. But the British and Americans, claiming that Moscow's hand-picked Communist government did not measure up to the democratic standards agreed upon at Yalta, denied Poland representation. Fascist-tainted Argentina, on the other hand, was seated in the face of the violent objections of the Russians, and largely because she had come through with an eleventh-hour declaration of war against the Axis.

The Big Four had meanwhile been meeting privately in Secretary Stettinius' penthouse apartment atop the Fairmont Hotel. This group, in addition to Stettinius, consisted of Foreign Secretary Eden of Britain, Foreign Commissar Molotov of Russia, and Foreign Minister Soong of China. So smoothly did their discussions proceed that, by May 5, 1945, they had agreed upon twenty-two of the scores of amendments proposed to the Dumbarton Oaks draft. With this ground gained, and with the problems of peace pressing in Europe, Molotov, Eden, and other leading figures enplaned for home. The drudgery of committee work was left to competent if less distinguished hands.

The first major crisis of the conference concerned the fate of backward or dependent peoples. The Soviets, whose propaganda hypocritically pilloried imperialism and colonialism, demanded a liberal policy. The British, French, and Americans, all tarred in varying degrees with the brush of imperialism, were hesitant. In particular, the Americans were determined to retain the strategic islands in the Pacific so dearly purchased from the Japanese with American blood. A compromise finally emerged in the form of a Trusteeship Council, together with a rather vague promise of ultimate independence for subject peoples. The United States was thus left free to secure the coveted islands under a trusteeship, and did in 1947.[8]

A second and more serious crisis arose over regionalism. The Soviets professed to fear that regional security pacts, like the Pan-American concert recently perfected at Chapultepec, would cripple the United Nations organization. But the American republics stubbornly refused to junk their recently perfected front in order to appease Stalin. After discouraging days of deadlock, a formula was devised (Article 51) by which regional groupings could still work usefully for defense and peace within the United Nations organization. This concession took on immense importance in later years, and permitted "regional" defense alliances like the original North Atlantic Treaty Organization (NATO).

The third and most ominous crisis developed over the proposed veto by the big powers in the Security Council. The Soviets, relying upon assurances at Yalta, insisted that any one of the Big Five be privileged to veto any decision whatsoever in the Council—even a motion to permit debate. The small powers, ever sensitive to big-power domination, bitterly resented this attempt at "gag rule" by the anti-democratic Soviets.

The dangerous deadlock was finally broken by a personal appeal to the Kremlin by Harry L. Hopkins, adviser to President Truman. Stalin gave way. The welcome news, when announced to the delegates in San Francisco, elicited a spontaneous cheer. The great powers would still retain their veto in the Security Council on all nonroutine questions of substance, but they would permit the small nations to bring controversial issues before them for debate. An appeal could thus be made to the forum of world opinion. The United States, one should note, would probably have taken the lead in insisting on the big-power veto if the Soviet Union had not. Without it, the Senate could not have been counted on to act favorably.

A NEW CHARTER IS BORN

The United Nations Charter was noteworthy for the unprecedentedly large voice that it gave to the small powers. Throughout the conference they had demanded more influence, had fought big-power domination, and had proposed numerous amendments. Perhaps most important of all, in the light of subsequent crises, they were permitted to turn the General Assembly into a kind of town meeting of the world. Through freedom of

[8] See below, p. 788. Polls taken from 1942 to 1945 showed that the American people favored retaining naval bases, while emphatically rejecting territorial imperialism. *Opinion News*, Sept. 4, 1945, p. 1.

debate and recommendation, they were privileged to mobilize the potent force of world opinion against wrongdoing. The Soviets naturally opposed such latitude, although without success.

With the last log-jams broken, the Conference wound up its labors. President Truman flew out to San Francisco to close the deliberations, and the delegates unanimously approved their handiwork, on June 25, 1945, exactly two months after the opening session. The formal signing of the leather-bound charter took place the next day. The Chinese delegation, whose country had suffered the longest in the war, first brushed its signatures.

The United Nations charter was probably as satisfactory a document as could have been framed at that time. There was much about it to suggest the old League of Nations, notably the Security Council, dominated by the Big Five; the Assembly, dominated by the small powers; and the new International Court of Justice, popularly known as the World Court. But there were many changes for the better. The new Economic and Social Council, with large investigatory authority, highlighted the emphasis on "the dignity and worth of the human person." The same could be said of the provisions for trusteeship, which resembled the old mandate system of the League of Nations. Perhaps most important of all, the machinery was set up for continuous consultation.

Much was expected of an international police force, to be made up of contingents from the various nations and to be under the direction of the Security Council. But its effective creation was delayed in subsequent years by the obstruction of the Soviet Union.

Whatever the weaknesses of the United Nations Charter, the delegates had blueprinted the machinery for the boldest experiment in international organization yet adopted by man. If supported by leaders of good will and amended to meet changing conditions, it held promise of mitigating the age-old curse of war. The statesmen of 1945 were not out to make the world safe for democracy; they were out to make the world safe.

THE SENATE MAKES AMENDS—ONE WAR LATE

Overwhelming popular support speeded deliberations in the United States Senate on the new United Nations Charter. The Senate Foreign Relations Committee, as in 1919, arranged for public hearings, but Chairman Connally of Texas, unlike Lodge in 1919, sternly held his watch over the witnesses. A few "cranks" branded the Charter a "Communist plot" and a "godless and unconstitutional" document framed by a lot of wicked foreigners, but these silly objections merely underscored the weakness of the opposition.

Serious criticisms were nevertheless raised before the Senate Committee. These mainly concerned the absolute veto of the Big Five, as well as the commitment to send American troops overseas as part of a United Nations police force. But after only five days of hearings the committee voted, 20 to 1, to report the Charter without a single reservation or amendment. The aged "irreconcilable" of 1919, Johnson of California, sent in the sole dissent from his sickroom.

Various straws in the wind indicated that Senate approval of the United Nations Charter was a foregone conclusion. The House of Representatives had already passed, 345 to 18, the Bretton Woods Bill, which implemented the recommendations of the Bretton Woods Conference. On July 19, 1945, the Senate added its approval by the lop-sided vote of 61 to 16. Conspicuous among the dissenters was isolationist Senator Taft of Ohio, who denied that modern wars have economic roots and who feared that Uncle Sam would become a kind of international Santa Claus.

The formal debate on the United Nations charter, beginning in July, 1945, produced few fireworks. Senator Connally of Texas, one of the two Senatorial delegates at San Francisco, referred dramatically to the killing of the League Covenant when he cried, "Can you not still see the blood on the floor?" Isolationist-minded Senators, thinking more of the next election than of posterity, succumbed to tremendous public pressure for action.[9] Senator Wheeler, who in a three-hour speech branded the charter "a declaration of pious intentions," concluded that he would vote for it anyhow. After only six days of debate, in contrast with the futile eight months on the League Covenant, the United Nations Charter was approved, on July 28, 1945, by a vote of 89 to 2. Senator Johnson of California sent word from his deathbed that if present he would have voted nay.

To paraphrase a proverb, an isolationist convinced against his will is of the same opinion still. To an increasing degree the battle of the next decade was not to be between isolationism and internationalism, but between weak internationalism and strong internationalism.

SOFTENING UP JAPAN

Now that Germany had surrendered and Japan was teetering, a final Big Three conference was imperative. President Truman, *even six months after Yalta,* was most anxious to get a reaffirmation of the Soviet pledge to enter the Far Eastern war.[10] He sailed to Europe on a United States cruiser, and in a Potsdam palace near Berlin met with Stalin and Churchill, later replaced by Clement Attlee after an electoral overturn in Britain. The seventeen-day conference, from July 17 to August 2, 1945, proceeded

---

[9] Gallup (July 25, 1945) found opinion 66% favorable, 3% unfavorable, and 31% undecided. *Opinion News,* August 7, 1945, p. 6.
[10] *Memoirs by Harry S. Truman* (Garden City, N.Y., 1955), I, 411.

in an atmosphere of restrained cordiality. Truman on one occasion entertained Stalin with a piano rendition of Paderewski's Minuet in G.

On the fateful day before the Potsdam Conference formally met, American scientists exploded, on an experimental basis, the first atomic bomb in history—near Los Alamos, New Mexico. Stalin, when informed of the epochal event by Truman, did not seem unduly impressed.[11] Unknown to the Americans, Soviet spies had presumably secured full knowledge of the atomic bomb and the forthcoming test. Probably Stalin was more impressed with the need of getting into the war against Japan before it had ended, and while he was able to collect the wages exacted at Yalta. This urgency was further underscored by the peace feelers that the Japanese were putting out through neutral Russia. Even though such overtures did not include "unconditional surrender," they revealed that Japan was in desperate straits.[12]

The first momentous document to emerge from Potsdam was a surrender ultimatum addressed to Japan on July 26, 1945. It was partly designed to weaken Japanese resistance by assurances of nonenslavement. Japan was to be disarmed, occupied, shorn of her fifty-year conquests, and deprived of her economic war potential. Yet she would be permitted access to raw materials after the war, and allowed an opportunity for democratic self-development. If she did not surrender, she would be destroyed (by yet unannounced atomic bombs). The Soviets, who were still two weeks away from a declaration of war on Japan, were not parties to this ultimatum.

Of more immediate concern to the Russians at Potsdam was another document, issued August 2, 1945. It was a blueprint for the control of Germany and for the settlement of numerous European problems, including provisional territorial adjustments in Germany and Poland. Germany was not only to be de-Nazified and disarmed, but her leaders were to be punished as war criminals and her resources were to be used to repair damages inflicted on her neighbors.

Then came the eight days that shook the world. Japan did not respond satisfactorily to the surrender ultimatum, even though tens of thousands of leaflets threatening destruction were showered from the skies. On August 6, 1945, a lone American airplane dropped a single atomic bomb on Hiroshima, a war-production center of secondary importance, and virtually wiped the city off the map. The scientists of Germany and Japan had already done some work with nuclear fission, but in the Battle of the Laboratories the United States achieved a stunning success, outdistancing Germany by a wide margin. The flash that flattened Hiroshima was the dawning light of a new age—military, diplomatic, industrial.

Stalin now redeemed one of his promises at Yalta by declaring war

[11] *Ibid.*, p. 416.
[12] See R. J. C. Butow, *Japan's Decision to Surrender* (Stanford, Calif., 1954).

on Japan, August 8, 1945. This was exactly the deadline date, set at Yalta, of "two or three months" after the surrender of Germany. So eager was Stalin to be in for the kill that he took the plunge six days *before* he had secured a treaty with China confirming the fruits of Yalta. After he had overrun Japanese resistance in Manchuria in a six-day "victory parade," he finally concluded his promised pact with Chiang's Nationalist China, announced August 14, 1945, the day Japan surrendered. The Soviets, in return for their foothold in Outer Mongolia and Manchuria, agreed to aid the Nationalists rather than the Communists, to refrain from meddling in China's internal affairs, and to recognize Chinese sovereignty in Manchuria. Subsequent events revealed the hollowness of these assurances, though for the most part they were initially kept.

ATOMIC ARMAGEDDON

The days of Japan's bamboo empire were now numbered. After Tokyo had failed to capitulate, despite further warnings of doom, the Americans dropped a second atomic bomb, this time on another secondary war-production center, Nagasaki, on August 9, 1945. The next day Japan sued for peace, though attempting to salvage the 2000 year-old throne of the god-emperor Hirohito. The surrender did not turn out to be completely "unconditional." The Japanese saved some face when their enemies agreed, on August 14, that the Emperor might be retained, subject to the orders of an Allied supreme commander. One of the saddest might-have-beens of history is that these terms could have been accepted two weeks or so earlier, thereby forestalling the dropping of the atomic bombs and the entrance of Russia into the war.

Nineteen days later, on September 2, 1945, the final terms of surrender were signed in Tokyo Bay, on the United States battleship *Missouri*. The flag of Commodore Perry had been flown across the Pacific from Washington for the ceremony. How painfully different this signing was from the one that had taken place ninety-one years earlier, only a short distance away, on the sacred soil of Nippon!

Unhappily, the mushroom-shaped cloud of the atomic bomb cast a pall over the victory celebrations in America. Neither British nor American leaders had hesitated to use the horrible new weapon to shorten the war and save lives.[13] But when postwar observers discovered that Japan would have collapsed within a short time without this horrible slaughter, consciences became increasingly troubled. More than that, bomb-dropping was a game that two could play. Before World War II, the United States had been relatively invulnerable to foreign attack.

[13] See *Truman Memoirs*, I, Ch. 26; W. S. Churchill, *Triumph and Tragedy*, Bk II, Ch. 19; H. L. Stimson and M. Bundy, *On Active Service in Peace and War* (New York, 1947). Critical of Stimson is R. N. Current, *Secretary Stimson* (New Brunswick, N.J., 1954).

Now, thanks to the ingenuity of those Americans who had developed the airplane and the atomic bomb, the day would come when the United States could be virtually wiped out overnight by a sneak attack.

The Age of Extermination had dawned. The nations of the world would have to iron out their differences or atomize their civilization off the face of the planet. The implications of these alternatives for both American strategy and diplomacy were staggering.

SELECTED BIBLIOGRAPHY

Indispensable is Herbert Feis, *Churchill, Roosevelt, Stalin* (Princeton, 1957). The best accounts by participants are R. E. Sherwood, *Roosevelt and Hopkins* (New York, 1948); *The Memoirs of Cordell Hull* (2 vols., New York, 1948); J. F. Byrnes, *Speaking Frankly* (New York, 1947); and *Memoirs by Harry S. Truman: Year of Decisions* (New York, 1955), vol. I. Relevant books by Sumner Welles, former Under Secretary of State, are *The Time for Decision* (New York, 1944); *Seven Decisions that Shaped History* (New York, 1951); *Where are we Heading?* (New York, 1946). The Japanese point of view appears in T. Kase, *Journey to the "Missouri"* (New Haven, 1950). Important military memoirs are D. D. Eisenhower, *Crusade in Europe* (Garden City, N.Y., 1948) and E. J. King and W. M. Whitehill, *Fleet Admiral King* (New York, 1952). A general account is W. L. Neumann, *Making the Peace, 1941–1945* (Washington, 1950).

See also footnotes of this chapter; the bibliography of the previous chapter; and *Harvard Guide*, Ch. 30.

7TH ED. REFS. On the speculative subject of unconditional surrender, Paul Kecskemeti, *Strategic Surrender: The Politics of Victory and Defeat* (Stanford, Calif., 1958) holds that it did not prolong the war with Germany: the last-ditch fighting was with Russia, which soft-pedaled unconditional surrender. But the Nazis did use this issue in their war propaganda, and it did cause delays in regard to Italy and Japan. Anne Armstrong, *Unconditional Surrender* (New Brunswick, N.J., 1961) contends that this policy prolonged the war and cost countless thousands of lives by weakening anti-Hitler elements and steeling the Germans to a fanatical resistance. Trumbull Higgins, *Winston Churchill and the Second Front, 1940–43* (New York, 1957) argues that Churchill, determined to avoid the heavy casualties of a cross-channel operation, led the United States into "periphery pecking," notably the North African invasion. Willard Range, *Franklin D. Roosevelt's World Order* (Athens, Ga., 1959) concludes that F.D.R., despite charges of a jumping-jack mentality, had definite goals of global good-neighborhood and clung to them with remarkable consistency. D. B. Johnson, *The Republican Party and Wendell Willkie* (Urbana, Ill., 1960) emphasizes Willkie's vital role in prodding the Republicans toward internationalism and in contributing to the founding of the UN; his bestseller *One World* was most effective. For extensive references to Yalta and the decision to drop the atomic bomb, see BIBLIOGRAPHICAL ADDENDUM, p. 1,049.

8TH AND 9TH ED. REFS. See BIBLIOGRAPHICAL ADDENDUM, p. 1,050.

50

The Rift with the Soviets
1945-1947

> We may well ask, "Why have they [the Soviets]
> deliberately acted for three long years so as to unite
> the free world against them?"
>
> WINSTON CHURCHILL, 1949

UNFINISHED BUSINESS

URGENT PROBLEMS of an economic and humanitarian nature lay piled on the tables of the diplomats when the war finally jarred to a close. "It is now 11:59 on the clock of starvation," warned Herbert Hoover.

A temporary organization, the United Nations Relief and Rehabilitation Administration (UNRRA), was launched late in 1943, when representatives of forty-odd nations signed an agreement at the White House. Its primary purpose was to help the liberated peoples of Europe and the Far East to get back onto their feet. The uninvaded member nations were invited to contribute to the budget of UNRRA a small percentage of their incomes in 1943. The United States, as the wealthiest participant, became the chief financial backer and leader of this vast humanitarian enterprise. When the books were closed in 1947, huge quantities of urgently needed food and other supplies had been shipped to China and the nations of Europe, notably Poland, Italy, Yugoslavia, Czechoslovakia, Greece, and Austria.

Hardly less clamorous was the problem of the several million Displaced Persons (DP's), all of whom had been uprooted by the war and many of whom dared not return to their Communist-enslaved homelands. The American people were more generous in sending money to Europe than they were in inviting the impoverished peoples of Europe to their shores. Painful memories of unemployment during the Great Depression were still fresh. Finally, in June, 1948, Congress made a belated beginning when it voted to set aside quota restrictions and admit 205,000. The treatment of these DP's—Delayed Pilgrims, someone has called them—was harshly criticized as overcautious, and the sifting process was widely condemned as discriminating against Catholics and Jews.

The settlement of lend-lease obligations, on the other hand, presented a far prettier picture than the prolonged wrangling over Allied debts after World War I. The total account at the end of World War II was approximately $50 billion, of which about $31 billion had gone to the British Empire and $11 billion to the Soviet Union. This staggering total was reduced some $10 billion by reverse-lend lease—that is, the supplying of goods or services for the United States at the other end. By late 1953, adjustments had been threshed out with all the major debtors, except the Soviet Union. As of that date, the settlement agreements had reduced the total to be paid to about $1 billion, which amounted to approximately three cents on the dollar.

The liquidation of the lend-lease account was both more generous and more realistic than that of the war-debt account following World War I. The original lend-lease agreements had stipulated that the ultimate terms should "promote mutually advantageous economic relations." Happily, this far-visioned formula was generally followed in making the necessary reductions.

THE COMMUNIST CHALLENGE

When the war ended with an atomic bang in 1945, the American people still retained a vast reservoir of good will toward their valiant Russian ally.[1] He had saved their hides while saving his own. Not only were Americans counting on Soviet co-operation to create a warless world, but many of them favored lending Russia money and technical assistance to repair the ravages inflicted by the Nazi invader.

But the Kremlin rudely slapped aside the outstretched American hand, presumably because co-operation with the capitalistic West would retard the Communist revolution. The ideal of One World thus collided head on with the actuality of the Communist world. The resulting deadlock was the most momentous and terrifying single development of the postwar years.

By the summer of 1946, if not earlier, the various public opinion polls in the United States revealed disquieting conclusions. The American people did not regard Russia as a peace-loving nation, and they did not trust her to co-operate with the United Nations. Her dominance over her satellite neighbors, they felt, was prompted by aggressive rather than defensive designs, and they were convinced that the Kremlin was bent on enchaining the entire globe. Not only was another war probable within twenty-five years, most Americans believed, but the Russians were the most likely to start it.

[1] Wendell Willkie's best-selling *One World* (New York, 1943) captured this spirit.

The Soviets thus unwittingly engineered a psychological Pearl Harbor. Crying "capitalist encirclement," they were bolstering their armed forces while the democracies were demobilizing theirs. Within a few short months the aggressive tactics of Moscow had awakened the American people to the true nature of the Communist conspiracy. Thus forewarned and alerted, the United States undertook to revamp its foreign policies and bolster its defenses in a determined effort not to be caught napping again.

THE BLAME FOR THE BREAK

Who was responsible for the shattered dream of One World? Apologists for Russia have insisted that the Soviets turned against America because America first turned against them. They further allege—the Myth of the Empty Chair—that if Roosevelt had not come to an untimely end, he would have been able to co-operate with the Kremlin.

The naked truth is that by mid-March, 1945—one month before the President's death—the Soviets were clearly taking over Poland and Romania as satellites in violation of their solemn pledges at Yalta. Roosevelt died knowing, or strongly suspecting, that he had failed in his gigantic gamble to wean Stalin away from his dangerous ideals by kind words and lend-lease largesse. The Russian leaders, although soft-pedaling Communist world revolution during the desperate days of World War II, had never really abandoned it. They had cleverly deceived the Americans, who in turn were in a mood to deceive themselves.

American military strategy, moreover, played directly into the hands of the Soviets. The forward-dashing American columns might have captured Berlin and Prague after costly fighting. But pursuant in part to arrangements made earlier with the Soviets, the Red Armies were allowed to enter these capitals as liberator-conquerors. The Americans kept their agreements, while hoping that the Russians, despite mounting evidence to the contrary, would keep theirs. The "liberating" Reds thus further entrenched themselves on the soil of the neighboring satellites.

Less defensible was the overhasty withdrawal of the American armies from Europe, and the consequent creation of a power vacuum into which the Soviets speedily moved. Short-sightedly assuming that victory is self-perpetuating, and that wars end with the shooting, the American public demanded a speedy dismantling of one of the most potent striking forces ever assembled. Roosevelt himself was privately committed to bringing the troops home at the earliest possible date. The men in uniform staged incredible "I Wanna Go Home" demonstrations, and they were backed to the hilt by lonesome wives, mothers, sweethearts, and children ("Bring-Daddy-Back-Home" clubs). As in 1918, the American fire department withdrew before the fire was completely out. Winston Churchill expressed the opinion in 1949 that only the existence of the atomic bomb, a temporary monopoly of the Americans, kept the Soviets from sweeping to the English channel.

The atomic bomb—a veritable apple of discord—aroused genuine fear in the Soviet Union. A tiny but vocal group of Americans, including ex-Governor Earle of Pennsylvania, was demanding a "preventive war" while the United States had this frightful new weapon and the Soviet Union did not. The "rattling of the atomic bomb" became louder when American forces retained bomber bases within striking distance of Russia's industrial vitals, and undertook impressive naval demonstrations in the Mediterranean. Soviet suspicions deepened as Washington delayed or halted lend-lease shipments, and as the American public grew increasingly cold toward a proposed postwar loan of $6 billion.[2]

THE FIRST BATCH OF PEACE TREATIES

The machinery for producing peace treaties with the satellites was repeatedly thrown out of gear by Soviet monkey wrenches. Nothing better illustrated the mounting friction between East and West.

The foreign ministers of the victorious powers met in London, in September, 1945, primarily to begin work on the Italian treaty. Unable to agree even on procedural matters, they adjourned after three weeks of fruitless wrangling, chiefly between Secretary of State James F. Byrnes and the Soviet representative, V. M. Molotov, a hardened old Bolshevik. The current quip was, "Molotov fiddles while Jimmy Byrnes."

The peace machinery continued to grind slowly and intermittently. First there were conferences of the foreign ministers of the Big-Four powers in Moscow and Paris, late in 1945 and early in 1946. The chief stumbling block at Paris was the noisy demand of Communist Yugoslavia, backed no less noisily by Communist Russia, for Italy's Adriatic port of Trieste. This particular obstacle was not cleared away until the delegates finally agreed to internationalize the city under the United Nations auspices.[3]

Progress was being made—painfully. A twenty-one nation conference assembled in Paris, in mid-1946, and brought forth a litter of five treaties. The Big-Four ministers, next meeting in New York, haggled bitterly over these drafts. The final versions were formally signed in Paris, in February, 1947, nearly two years after the collapse of Hitler.

This batch of treaties involved Finland, Hungary, Bulgaria, Romania, and Italy. The United States, which had not declared war on Finland, was not a party to the Finnish pact, but was a signatory of the others. The treaties were not popular with the American people, who loudly objected to the

---

[2] In October, 1945, Gallup found 27% favorable to the loan, with 60% unfavorable, and 13% without opinion. *Pub. Opin. Quar.,* IX, 533.

[3] The explosive Trieste issue was finally settled by a division of the disputed area between Italy and Yugoslavia, on October 5, 1954. The Soviets, surprisingly, acquiesced.

reparations that gave the Soviets an undue amount of continuing influence. But the Senate, realizing that these arrangements were the best obtainable, approved them without enthusiasm.

The treaty with Italy was showered with brickbats by powerful Italian-American groups in the United States, largely because it provided for the payment of reparations to the Soviet Union. Many Americans feared that when the Allied troops left Italy, the militant Communist party would take over. The Senate finally approved the pact, 79 to 10, after hearing arguments that the United Nations would help defend Italian democracy when the foreign bayonets had departed. The treaty was also denounced in Italy, where a former prime minister publicly regretted that Columbus had ever discovered America.

FOUR-POWER FRICTION IN GERMANY

The German Reich, in accordance with the unrealistic arrangements made at Yalta and Potsdam in 1945, was chopped into four administrative zones: the American, the British, the French, and the Soviet. The rubble heap known as Berlin, deep in the Russian zone, was likewise cut into four sectors.

The vengeful Morgenthau plan, designed to turn Germany into a

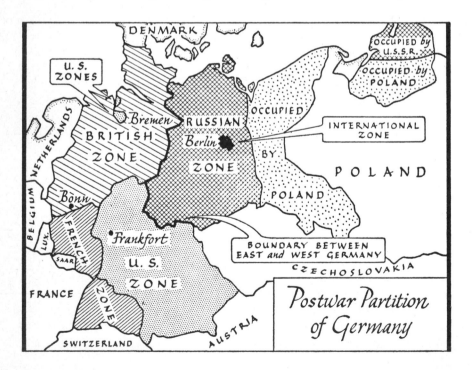

Postwar Partition of Germany

"potato patch," had been quickly discarded after its adoption at Quebec in 1944. The simple truth was that an agrarian economy could not begin to support the teeming millions of Germany. Even before the war ended, Washington had become keenly aware that a re-industrialized German Reich was vital to the economic recovery of Europe. More than that, Germany had become a crucially important dike against the westward surge of Soviet communism. Washington therefore threw its postwar support behind a rehabilitated but shackled Germany—de-Nazified, demilitarized, and democratized.

The French security obsession, so troublesome after World War I, again raised its head after World War II. The people of France, their soil thrice polluted since 1870 by the German hobnailed boot, were vehemently opposed to a revitalized Germany. In an effort to quiet French fears, Secretary of State Byrnes in 1946 offered the other members of the Big Four a twenty-five year treaty designed to keep Germany demilitarized. Despite this startling departure from America's no-alliance tradition, Byrnes and his successor raised the time limit to forty years. But the Soviets, who also feared a resurgent Germany, complained that such guarantees did not go far enough.

Reparations from Germany also proved to be a meaty bone of contention. The Russians, insisting that they had been promised $10 billion at Yalta, began to seize manufactured goods from current German production. The Americans replied that the $10 billion had been accepted merely as a *basis for discussion*. They further argued that while the Russians might properly remove factories, they were violating the Potsdam Agreement and discouraging German incentive when they carted away the output of those factories. One obvious goal of Moscow was to leave the Germans so impoverished that they would be willing to follow the Pied Piper of Communism and so weak as not to constitute a future menace.

The Soviets were also eager to turn Germany into a satellite state. They set up a puppet Communist party in their own zone, and through it drenched the other three zones with propaganda—all in violation of the Potsdam agreement. They also retained hundreds of thousands of German prisoners of war, likewise contrary to agreement, and presumably for purposes of Communist indoctrination.[4]

WAR CRIMES AND THE TWO GERMANYS

The Soviets managed to co-operate more satisfactorily with their three Western allies in bringing the leading Nazi war "criminals" before the bar of justice, at Nuremberg, Germany. These trials were designed to establish an international law governing war crimes, and thus deter future

[4] See General L. D. Clay, *Decision in Germany* (Garden City, N.Y., 1950).

aggressors by promising a noose instead of a halo. The proceedings were criticized to some extent in the United States as "judicial lynchings." They seemed to fly in the face of the *ex-post-facto* principle, deeply imbedded in the American Constitution, that no man should be punished for an offense that was not a crime when the deed was committed.

The trials nevertheless ground on. Finally, on October 1, 1946, nineteen leading Nazis were found guilty. Twelve were sentenced to death, but the blubbery Herman Goering cheated the gallows by swallowing poison in his cell. Trials of smaller-fry Nazis for varying crimes went forward for many months.

The Postwar Zones of Austria

The deadlock in Austria, which likewise was carved into four zones, proved hardly less vexatious than that in Germany. Washington regarded the Austrians as a liberated people, on the theory that they had been raped by Hitler in 1938. Moscow regarded them as a subject people, on the theory that they had been willingly seduced. Serious friction developed between Moscow and the Western Powers over such controversies as reparations and the Soviet seizure of Austro-German assets.

The four-way tangle in Germany could not go on indefinitely. The Potsdam agreement of 1945 had stipulated that Germany should be treated as an economic unit. Yet the Soviets flatly refused to send food from their predominantly agricultural zone to the industrialized western zones. There was considerable truth in General Clay's witticism that in the division of Germany the Russians got the agriculture, the British the industry (the Ruhr), and the Americans the scenery. The British and Americans, burdened with heavy occupation costs and seeking to make their own zones self-sufficient, finally arranged for a bizonal economic merger late in 1946. The Soviets thereupon gave vent to outraged outcries that the Potsdam pact had been broken by the establishment of "Bizonia."

A giant-boot stride toward an independent West Germany was taken when the French were persuaded to merge their zone with the British and American zones. "Trizonia" thus became the basis for the new German Federal Republic, under a constitution framed by the Germans at Bonn in 1949. But grave trouble still loomed ahead. There were two Germanys and two Berlins, each caught in the middle of an East-West tug of war, and each striving to be the magnet that would draw the other to itself.

THE CHINESE PUZZLE

On the other side of the globe, the prospects for Chiang Kai-shek's Nationalist government seemed far from hopeless when World War II ended. The Soviets, to be sure, had secured a strong foothold in China, thanks to the "sell out" at Yalta as accepted by Chiang in the Sino-Soviet "friendship" treaty of August 14, 1945. But at the same time Stalin had solemnly bound himself to support the Nationalist government as against the Communists. The Americans had rendered Chiang invaluable help in air-lifting three Chinese armies to the northern and eastern regions, and United States marines had seized and held vital seaports along the China coast for the Nationalists.

But the picture in Manchuria, the industrial heart of China, rapidly darkened. When the Soviet armies withdrew in 1946, they systematically wrecked or removed most of the factory machinery. They also delayed their departure so as to assist the Chinese Communists, who speedily enlarged their foothold with captured Japanese arms conveniently "abandoned" by the Russians. Before long the Communists were secretly receiving co-operation and assistance from the Soviets, who thus betrayed their pledges to Chiang in the treaty of 1945.

The rapid deterioration of the Nationalist position aroused grave fears in the Occidental world. The United States was beginning to perceive with increasing clarity that the Chinese Communists, as disciples of Karl Marx, were not mere "agricultural reformers." They were ideological cousins, if not outright bedfellows, of the Soviets.

General George C. Marshall, fresh from his wartime laurels as United States Chief of Staff, was sent to China on a last-chance mission late in 1945. His was the thankless task of making one supreme effort to end the protracted internal strife between Communists and Nationalists. After about a year of wearisome negotiations, he was finally forced to confess failure. He had learned to his sorrow that communism can no more compromise with free enterprise than fire can with water.[5] Returning home in 1947, Marshall was sworn in as Secretary of State to succeed James F. Byrnes. The drafting of high-ranking generals for the diplomatic service, though criticized as a drift toward dictatorship, merely accentuated the fact that the war was now being continued by other means. The most pressing problems were those of power politics.

THE COMMUNIZATION OF CHINA

The grip of Chiang's Nationalist regime gradually weakened, largely because its inefficiency and corruption were undermining the confidence

THE BEAR THAT WALKS LIKE A DRAGON

Soviets use Asian nationalism for Communist infiltration.
Fitzpatrick in the *St. Louis Post-Dispatch*, 1954

[5] See Herbert Feis, *The China Tangle* (Princeton, 1953).

of the Chinese people. When conditions become hopeless enough, the masses will turn in desperation to almost anything—even the chains of communism.

Washington nevertheless continued to send haphazard financial and military aid to Chiang, though cutting off arms in 1946–1947. Altogether this assistance, since mid-1945, amounted to about $2 billion in money alone, to say nothing of military supplies and other succor. The Chinese Communists, who regarded the United States as their chief foreign enemy, condemned this support. The truth seems to be that during these crucial postwar years Washington openly aided Chiang on a far larger scale than the Soviet Union secretly helped the Communists.

The dam began to break late in 1948, when the Communists overran Manchuria and pushed southward into the heart of China. In desperation, the glamorous Madame Chiang Kai-shek flew the Pacific to Washington, vainly seeking large-scale support for her faltering husband. In 1949 Chiang was finally forced to flee the mainland of China with the shattered remnants of his army, and set up his refugee Nationalist government on the offshore island of Formosa.

The collapse of China was undeniably the most staggering blow yet suffered by the free world in its life-and-death struggle against Communism. With a half billion or so Chinese now in the Communist camp, a frightening shift had occurred in the world balance of power. The Moscow Communists had started from scratch in 1917. Now, thirty-two years later, they controlled about one-fourth of the world's land and over one-third of its population. Their shackled people numbered about 900,000,000. If one concedes that Washington forced a showdown with Japan over China on the eve of Pearl Harbor, then the United States had been robbed of the major fruit of World War II in the Far East.

WHO "LOST" CHINA?

Second-guessers in America now had their inning. Critics of the Truman administration, chiefly Republicans, angrily charged that the catastrophe had been plotted by Communists in the American diplomatic service who had thwarted the prompt dispatching of effective aid. The evidence is strong that only a powerful United States force could have turned the tide shortly after the war, at least temporarily. But with American opinion vehemently supporting the "I-wanna-go-home" movement, the sending of such an expeditionary force to China was simply out of the question. Nor can one prove that Chiang fell primarily because of the absence of arms. Enormous quantities of American munitions actually fell into the hands of the Communists, either through capture or sell-out by corrupt Nationalist leaders. When a regime has forfeited the confidence of its own people, dollars and bayonets are not likely to prop it up for long. The charge that the United States "lost" China is weakened by the simple fact that the United States never had China to lose.

Washington's semipassive attitude toward China severely strained the bipartisan foreign policy established during the war and the postwar years. The Republicans, who had generally gone along with the Democratic administrations in their policies toward Europe, refused to take any responsibility for the disaster in China. They insisted, often angrily, that they had not been properly consulted in advance. Many of them continued to demand further financial aid for the Nationalists, even at the expense of the recovery in Europe, and even after Chiang had fled to Formosa.

The State Department, hoping to head off what it regarded as expensive injections into the dead dragon of Nationalist China, issued a sensational White Paper, on August 5, 1949. This handpicked collection of documents not only absolved the United States of responsibility for Chiang's collapse, but put the blame squarely on the Nationalist regime—a regime that was represented as inept, selfish, purblind, and faithless. This astounding denunciation of a friendly government, though condemned by many Republicans, received wide public support.[6]

Most Americans were evidently resigned to Washington's policy of waiting for "the dust to settle." There seemed little point in further antagonizing the victorious Communists, with whom devotees of the Open Door still hoped to do business. Optimists could always hope that some 500,-000,000 war-ravaged Chinese would prove to be a millstone around the necks of the Soviets, or perhaps become so powerful as to throw overboard their Soviet tutors. (This hope became a reality in the 1960's.)

A DOSE OF DEMOCRACY FOR JAPAN

The rehabilitation of Japan, in glaring contrast with China, presented one of the brighter spots in the troubled Far East. The United States, as the principal conqueror, was chiefly responsible for the Allied military occupation. Soviet Russia had only an advisory voice on the Four-Power Allied Council for Japan, and hence was unable to snarl up the administration, as she did in Germany. Five-starred General Douglas MacArthur sat firmly in the driver's seat, while an eleven-power Far Eastern Commission in Washington ventured to send out directives to him.

The able but highhanded MacArthur evoked emphatic but futile protests from the Soviets, who did not relish being dosed with their own dictatorial medicine. Unable to make satisfactory headway in communizing Japan, the Russians blocked all progress toward a peace treaty with

[6] As early as May 27, 1949, Gallup discovered that only 22% favored help for China, as compared with 55% a year before. *Pub. Opin. Quar.*, XII, 548. Gallup found (Sept. 18, 1949) that a selected group of informed persons blamed the United States, in the ratio of 53 to 26, for not sending more help. By August 13, 1954, only 1 adult in 14 blamed Washington. Gallup Release.

Tokyo, except on their terms. They also continued to retain hundreds of thousands of Japanese prisoners of war, contrary to agreement but clearly for purposes of Communist indoctrination.

General MacArthur, the Yankee Mikado with a Greek-god bearing, molded the new Japan with an imperious hand. The leading Japanese war lords, including ex-Premier Tojo, were given a protracted war crimes trial and executed in December, 1948. The attempt to bring American "de-mok-las-sie" to Japan went forward with unexpected smoothness. The new MacArthur-dictated constitution of 1947 not only renounced war but also armed forces. These reforms were urged by the United States largely because of the lingering belief that the Soviets would prove co-operative and peace-loving. But when China fell to the Communists, and the free world found itself in desperate need of building up Japan as a bastion against Soviet penetration, Americans regretted that they had caused the Japanese to swear off war. Subsequent efforts by Washington to rearm Japan brought charges of inconsistency. At all events, the Japanese acquiesced in the American occupation with surprising docility, and presumably in the knowledge that they would get time off for good behavior—as in fact they did in the subsequent "soft" peace treaty of 1951.[7]

CURTAINS FOR PHILIPPINE COLONIALISM

Farther south, the Philippine Islands were formally granted their long-promised independence in colorful ceremonies at Manila on America's Independence Day, July 4, 1946. The United States agreed, among other concessions, to pay the infant republic $620 million for damages sustained in fighting the Japanese, and to grant a preferential tariff. In return, American citizens were to enjoy equality with Philippine citizens in exploiting the rich resources of the archipelago. The United States also retained twenty-three military and naval bases as leaseholds on a ninety-nine year basis. These outposts seemed all the more desirable as the tides of Communist aggression swirled deeper into southeastern Asia.

The United States thus emerged as a leading champion of anticolonialism in Asia. Returning to its ancient ideals, the republic spectacularly renounced the most embarrassing remnant of its imperialistic deviation of 1898. Like many another sinner who has "got religion," Uncle Sam put strong pressure on the other colonial powers in Asia to go and do likewise. The complete liquidation of Dutch imperialism, and the substantial liquidation of French and British colonialism in the Far East, were attributable in some degree to the potent influence of Washington. The European powers, notably the Dutch, were not too happy about being

[7] See E. M. Martin, *The Allied Occupation of Japan* (Stanford University, Calif., 1948), and R. A. Fearey, *The Occupation of Japan: Second phase, 1948-50* (New York, 1950).

evicted from their profitable colonial real estate, and they muttered unpleasantly about the self-righteous United States.

Yet, strangely enough, the Russians stole the show in the Far East as advocates of anticolonialism. While hypocritically practicing world-wide Communist imperialism, and while subjugating about 100,000,000 satellite neighbors in a flagrant application of colonialism, they posed in the Far East as the champions of anticolonialism against the British, Dutch, and French. Their propaganda was surprisingly successful, largely because the Asiatics had long and bitter memories of European exploitation. Uncle Sam was shoring up these nations in Europe as a bulwark against communism, and his association with them inevitably caused some of the tar of colonialism to rub off onto his clothes.

LAUNCHING THE UN

The new world forum known as the United Nations was officially unveiled in 1946, when the Assembly and Security Council convened for the first time in London. After voting to establish a permanent home in the United States, the organization found temporary quarters in the New York suburban area. In 1951–1952 it moved into its present headquarters in a magnificent, thirty-nine story, glass skyscraper located on a Manhattan site donated by John D. Rockefeller, Jr.

The judicial arm of the United Nations, unlike the ill-fated World Court of the League, received a friendly reception in America. In August, 1946, the Senate voted, 60 to 2, to adhere to the new International Court of Justice. But this acceptance was watered down when the Senators, yielding to their time-honored fears, voted to exempt from "compulsory jurisdiction" all disputes involving domestic affairs, such as tariffs and immigration. The United States thus reserved the right, under the famous Connally Reservation, to be the sole judge of what was "domestic."

Washington was eager to retain, under a trusteeship of the United Nations, the small but strategically important Japanese mandated islands in the Pacific—the Marianas, Marshalls, and Carolines. These hard-won outposts were the only territorial gains that the American people desired from the war. The Security Council finally awarded them to the United States, in April, 1947, but not until President Truman had bluntly announced that the islands would be kept anyhow.

The Soviets, who at first had shown scant enthusiasm for the UN, quickly seized upon it as a tool for spreading communist propaganda and combating anti-Communist forces. Bitterly anti-Fascist, the Russians had a large hand in pushing through the UN Assembly a resolution recommending the withdrawal of ambassadors from Franco's Spain. They used their veto in the Security Council to block an investigation of Communist activity in Greece. They likewise temporarily blackballed the admission of new states with alleged "Fascist" coloration, such as Ireland and Portugal, presumably because such nations would vote with the "capitalistic" camp.

Most alarming of all was Moscow's hostility to America's plans for the international control of atomic energy. Washington, with unique generosity, offered to share its terrible "secret," provided that adequate safeguards were erected. The chief barrier to such safeguards was the unwillingness of the secretive Soviets to permit international inspectors from the "capitalistic" countries to prowl around their homeland. The Russians further demanded that the atomic bomb first be outlawed, and that the United States destroy its stockpiles of atomic bombs, preparatory to a world-wide arms reduction. The American people, already dismayed by Soviet behavior, were naturally unready to throw away their potent new weapon.[8]

The atomic deadlock was further intensified on September 23, 1949, when President Truman announced that the Russians had recently exploded a nuclear bomb. The United States had enjoyed its monopoly for only four short years after the war. New and terrifying power relationships were taking shape. Short of a preventive war, from which civilized opinion shrank, the day was inevitably coming when the Soviet Union would be able to destroy the United States as completely as the United States would be able to destroy the Soviet Union.

THE VETO VIRUS

The abuse of the veto in the Security Council by the Soviets brought partial paralysis to the United Nations. The original intent of the Western democracies had been that this weapon would rarely be used, and never to obstruct procedure or choke off debate. But the Russians, perceiving that they were heavily outnumbered by the "capitalistic" powers, wielded the veto from the outset in a routine and ruthless fashion.

The case of Iran (Persia) early spotlighted the widening chasm between Russia and the democracies. When the deadline came in 1946 for the Russians to evacuate this oil-rich land, the Red army remained. The Iranians, over the wrathful objections of the Soviets, brought their case before the Security Council. The Russian delegate stalked out and continued to absent himself whenever the issue was discussed. Pressure from world opinion, the United Nations, and the United States finally induced the Soviets to withdraw from Iran, but the basic issue was only postponed.

The United Nations thus proved to be a cruel disappointment to the ordinary American, who had earnestly prayed for an iron-clad guarantee against future war. Cynics belittled its solid achievements in helping to

[8] Gallup found in December, 1946, that 72% were opposed to destroying the bombs made and discontinuing the manufacture of others. *Pub. Opin. Quar.*, XI, 139.

bring peace to places like Iran, Indonesia, and India, and overlooked entirely its real but unspectacular progress in social and economic welfare. The suspicion grew in America that the Soviets had joined the United Nations merely to snarl it up, while using it as a global sounding board for their Communist propaganda. Violent charges of "warmongering," first flung by the Soviet delegate in 1947, strengthened this belief.

The United Nations Charter made provision for an international police force to keep the peace, but largely because of Soviet obstruction such a contingent was not organized. A popular drive began to develop in America to strengthen the UN by equipping its toothless gums with adequate dentures. The United World Federalists, who envisioned eventual world government, were conspicuous in their demands for a more powerful organization. In 1948 sixteen United States Senators of both parties demanded a drastic revision of the United Nations, with or without Russia.

But the alternatives to worrying along with the existing UN charter were uninviting. The Russians could veto any amendment, as well as any move to expel them from the United Nations. To secede from the UN and leave Russia alone with the corpse she had strangled in the cradle, would merely widen the growing gulf between East and West. There was at least some comfort in the fact that as long as the Soviets were throwing hot words in the forum of the UN, they were not throwing hot lead on the field of battle.

THE IRON CURTAIN CLANGS DOWN

The oft-invaded Russians were determined to strengthen themselves against future foes by marshaling subservient satellite nations on their flanks. The descent of Moscow's "iron curtain" around the neighbors of the Soviet Union aroused the American people, more than anything else, to the nature of the Communist peril.

Soviet darkness gradually enshrouded Romania, Bulgaria, Albania, and Hungary, as Moscow-manipulated stooges took command. Washington, appealing to Stalin's unredeemed pledges at Yalta, lodged repeated protests with Moscow against coercion and intimidation. But in Soviet thinking security ranked higher than capitalistic conceptions of honor. Washington also made repeated representations to the satellites themselves—and with no greater success—against such offenses as the execution of political prisoners and the persecution of religious leaders.

Night likewise descended over Poland when a Soviet-dominated regime took control in 1945, also in defiance of Stalin's pledges at Yalta. After exasperating delays, the farcical "free and unfettered" election, also promised at Yalta, was held in 1947. The Communists polled about 90 per cent of the vote, although the American ambassador reported that in an honest election the opposition party would have won about 60 per cent of the votes.[9] Washington's protests against the flouting of the Yalta pledges were wasted paper and ink.

Yugoslavia, a Communist satellite under the iron hand of Marshal Tito, presented special problems. The Yugoslavs reacted violently against America's opposition to their proposed grab of the Italian-Yugloslav city of Trieste, at the head of the Adriatic Sea. The internationalization of the city created a witches' cauldron, and numerous clashes ensued between the Yugoslav soldiers, on the one hand, and the American and British occupying troops, on the other.

The Tide of Communism

The Western world breathed easier in 1948, when Tito parted company with Moscow, amid angry words. While still a Communist, he preferred his own local brand to that dictated by Moscow. Just as Roosevelt grasped the bloody hand of Stalin when he split with Hitler in 1941, so Truman grasped the bloody hand of Tito when he split with the Kremlin in 1948. In the hope of encouraging "Titoism" or independence among the other satellites of Moscow, the United States dispatched arms and supplies to Tito. In less than ten years these subventions amounted to about $2 billion, despite considerable opposition in America to underwriting any form of communism. As in the days of the Franco-American Alliance of 1778, a common danger was still making strange bedfellows.

[9] See A. B. Lane, *I Saw Poland Betrayed* (Indianapolis, 1948).

BAILING OUT BRITAIN

The westward sweep of Communism served as a constant reminder that Britain, in 1945 as in 1940, was the only dependable major bulwark of democracy left in Europe. Yet the British, to whom foreign trade was life blood, emerged from six years of war with ships sunk, markets closed, and overseas capital bleeding away. Like most other nations, Britain was forced to buy more goods from Americans than Americans bought from her, and consequently her dollar balances in the United States were fast disappearing. This "dollar hemorrhage" afflicted most other countries. It further underscored the fact that the American giant was not only the last great stronghold of capitalism but the world's creditor to boot.

The British, jarred by the sudden termination of lend-lease in 1945, sought a gift or at least an interest-free loan from their rich American cousins. Late in 1945 a fifty-year agreement was concluded which provided for $3.75 billion at the low interest rate of 2 per cent. In return, Britain bound herself to abandon certain preferential trade practices that restricted the free flow of goods. Certain outspoken Britons, not overjoyed by these terms, sneered at tight-fisted Uncle Sam—"old Uncle Shylock"— and expressed fears that England would soon become the forty-ninth state.

The debate in Congress over the British loan, despite the obvious need for haste, dragged along for seven long months. There Uncle Sam was condemned as a Santa Claus rather than a Shylock. Critics pilloried Britain as a poor credit risk (she had "welshed" after World War I), recalled America's generosity during World War II, and pleaded for the overburdened taxpayer. One jingle ran:

> There will always be a U.S.A.
> If we don't give it away.

The recent triumph of the Labor government in Britain, with the consequent sharp turn toward socialism, also inspired much criticism. Congressman Celler of New York was quoted as saying that the loan would "promote too damned much socialism at home and too damned much imperialism abroad."

The Truman administration realistically urged that the loan be approved on the basis of America's self-interest. Britain's recovery was essential for world recovery, without which the prosperity of the United States would presumably wither away. Other supporters of the loan, foreshadowing the arguments for the Marshall Plan the next year, urged that Britain be bolstered as a dike against Communism. Some grateful citizens even argued that wealthy and unscathed America owed the British an enormous debt for having held out alone against Hitler in 1940.

The British loan was never popular in the United States, and the public opinion polls indicated that it never commanded majority support.[10] The final vote in Congress, in July, 1946, was favorable but relatively close: 46 to 34 in the Senate and 219 to 155 in the House. Ironically, the long delay in Congress during an era of rising prices caused the purchasing power of the loan to shrink far below what the British had committed themselves to repay.

A HAVEN FOR JEWS

The Palestine problem came to a boil at the time of the debates over the British loan, and got in its way. The Jews had long dreamed of securing a national haven in their ancestral lands. With tens of thousands of their co-religionists uprooted by the war, and some six million butchered by the Nazis, they were determined to get it. But the Arabs, who outnumbered the Jews about two to one in Palestine, had established prior rights through centuries of residence, and they could not be elbowed aside without grave injustices.

The British also were heavily involved. As holders of an old League of Nations mandate over Palestine, they had obligations to the Arabs. In a series of heart-rending scenes, British naval patrols turned back a number of steamers laden with destitute Jewish refugees within sight of the Promised Land.

The United States, needing oil and bases in the Middle East to curb Soviet Russia, was also reluctant to alienate the Arabs and drive them into the arms of the Kremlin. But if the Arabs had the oil, which was far away, the American Jews had the vote, which was near at hand. Jewish-Americans, especially those in New York, might turn the forthcoming Presidential election of 1948 against President Truman.

Truman indicates in his memoirs that he was motivated largely by humanitarianism, but the circumstances suggest that he was not immune to politics. In October, 1946, he publicly repeated his desire that 100,000 Jews be admitted to Palestine. Several days later his prospective opponent in the Presidential sweepstakes, Governor Thomas E. Dewey of New York, trumped this ace with a demand for several hundred thousand.

The financially exhausted British finally dumped their Palestine burden on the doorstep of the United Nations, early in 1947. A scheme for partitioning the troubled Holy Land between Arabs and Jews was adopted by the UN Assembly later that year, with the Arab delegates violently dissenting. The experts in the State Department, thinking of America's enormous strategic interest in retaining the good will of the Arabs, vigorously opposed partition. But President Truman, whether influenced by humanitarianism or politics, applied pressure to help force partition through the United Nations. The Soviets during these postwar years seldom voted

[10] See *Pub. Opin. Quar.*, IX, 533.

with the United States on a major issue, but this time they did. Evidently they were hoping to stir up troubled waters in which they could profitably fish. These hopes were abundantly fulfilled.

The Jewish Zionists, their long-deferred goal in sight, moved rapidly. With Palestine already involved in civil strife with the Arabs, they announced the formation of the new state of Israel, on May 14, 1948. About eleven minutes after this proclamation, President Truman, presumably with an eye to the impending election, stole a march on other nations by hastily extending *de facto* recognition.[11]

The infant state of Israel—a child of battle—was soon attacked on several sides by Arab armies. The invaders were hurled back by numerically inferior but better trained Jewish forces, who received aid in money and man power from their co-religionists in the United States. Mediation by the United Nations brought a halt to the fighting in 1949, with the distinguished American Negro, Dr. Ralph J. Bunche, winning plaudits for his role in the negotiation. A new state thus saw the light of day, in circumstances as fantastic as those related in the Arabian nights.

As far as America was concerned, the partition of Palestine presented a curious clash of motives. Short-range humanitarian and political interests eclipsed long-range economic and strategic interests. The Arab nations, sitting on the richest oil pool in the world, had been friendly to the United States when the war ended. Franklin Roosevelt had promised them sympathetic treatment. But after they had been humiliated by Jews bearing American arms, they spat when they spoke the hated word "American."

The picture was further clouded by the presence of approximately one million bedraggled and uprooted Arabs. Expelled from Israel by the war, they were festering nearby in idleness, poverty, and semistarvation in hate-ridden camps for displaced persons. The Israeli were not willing to let them return, while the Arabs themselves were unwilling to resettle elsewhere. Meanwhile, supported largely by American dollars, these luckless refugees continued to eke out a miserable existence as pawns in the game of power politics. Grave trouble loomed ahead.

SELECTED BIBLIOGRAPHY

Helpful surveys are J. C. Campbell, *et al, The United States in World Affairs, 1945–1947* (New York, 1947) and *The United States in World Affairs, 1947–1948* (New York, 1948). Extremely valuable are the *Memoirs by Harry S. Truman* (2 vols., Garden City, N.Y., 1955), Vol. I. Two other books by participants must not be overlooked: J. F. Byrnes, *Speaking Frankly* (New York, 1947) and W. B. Smith, *My Three Years in Moscow* (Philadelphia, 1950). More generalized accounts are T. A. Bailey, *America Faces Russia* (Ithaca, N.Y., 1950); V. M. Dean, *The United States and Russia* (Cambridge, Mass., 1948); K. S. Latourette, *The American Record in the Far East, 1945–1951* (New York,

[11] *Memoirs by Harry S. Truman* (Garden City, N.Y., 1956), II, 164.

1952); H. M. Vinacke, *The United States and the Far East, 1945–1951* (Stanford University, Calif., 1952); and F. E. Manuel, *The Realities of American-Palestine Relations* (Washington, 1949). See also J. A. White, "As the Russians Saw Our China Policy," *Pac. Hist. Rev.*, XXVI (1957), 147–160.

See footnotes of this chapter and *Harvard Guide*, Ch. 30.

7TH ED. REFS. See new references at end of previous chapter. John Spanier, *American Foreign Policy Since World War II* (rev. ed., New York, 1962) is comprehensive in scope. J. F. Byrnes, *All in One Lifetime* (New York, 1958) adds some interesting details on Yalta and Russian relations to his earlier *Speaking Frankly;* he flatly denies that Truman ever scolded him for "babying the Soviets." Alfred Steinberg, *The Man From Missouri: The Life and Times of Harry S. Truman* (New York, 1962) is anecdotal and journalistic. F. L. Schuman, *The Cold War* (Baton Rouge, 1962) is a brief book presenting several stimulating lectures. D. F. Fleming, *The Cold War and Its Origins, 1917–1960* (2 vols., New York, 1961), though detailed and documented, rather consistently blames the United States and exculpates the Soviet Union. J. L. Snell, *Wartime Origins of the East-West Dilemma over Germany* (New Orleans, 1959) describes the retreat from revenge and dismemberment, in view of the rising Soviet threat; the U.S. policy was one of haphazardness, evasion, and postponement. Eugene Davidson, *The Death and Life of Germany* (New York, 1959) concludes that Soviet rudeness, perhaps as much as American humaneness, prompted the United States to help. Eugene Davidson, "The Nuremberg Trials and One World," in G. L. Anderson, ed., *Issues and Conflicts* (Lawrence, Kans., 1959) casts doubt on the fairness of the trials; the guilt-stained Russians were improper judges. W. L. Dorn, "The Debate over American Occupation Policy in Germany in 1944–1945," *Pol. Sci. Quar.*, LXXII (1957), 481–501 emphasizes the influence of Secretary of the Treasury Morgenthau in formulating the punitive occupation policy of the postwar years. General A. C. Wedemeyer, *Wedemeyer Reports* (New York, 1958) is an embittered book by a top American war planner: he is anti-British, anti-Roosevelt, and anti-Communist, while pro-German, pro-isolationism, and pro-Chiang Kai-shek. He thinks that withholding American aid from Nationalist China at a critical time led to the Communist triumph; he claims that his famous confidential report on China was suppressed by Washington. Kazuo Kawai, *Japan's American Interlude* (Chicago, 1960) is a revealing analysis by an American-educated Japanese who was editor of the Nippon *Times*. He believes that on the whole the occupation was "a magnificent success," largely because of MacArthur and despite the crudeness of some of America's carpetbaggers. But the United States tried to go too far too fast in "conferring democracy from above," and a sourness was beginning to set in when the occupation ended. Tang Tsou, "The American Political Tradition and the American Image of Chinese Communism," *Pol. Sci. Quar.*, LXXVII (1962), 570–600 describes how Americans deceived themselves into thinking the Communists simple "agrarian reformers." Tang Tsou, *America's Failure in China, 1941–1950* (Chicago, 1963) is a perceptive critique, impressively detailed and documented, which explains America's failure in terms of an unwillingness "to go to war in the defense of American principles and interests in China." But American public opinion was never willing to back such a policy, and the men in Washington were aware of this feeling. Nadav Safran, *The United States and Israel* (Cambridge, Mass., 1963), argues that the Truman-backed partition of 1948 was the best alternative for the U.S.

8TH AND 9TH ED. REFS. See BIBLIOGRAPHICAL ADDENDUM, p. 1,052.

51

The Cold War
1947-1950

> *Let us not be deceived—we are today in the midst of a cold war.*
>
> BERNARD BARUCH, April, 1947

THE TRUMAN DOCTRINE

THE NAKED AGGRESSIONS of Moscow had, by early 1947, swung American opinion around in favor of a "get-tough-with-Russia" policy. President Truman, aware of imminent Communist inroads and confident of strong public backing, prepared to take resolute action. As he privately remarked, "I'm tired of babying the Soviets."

The time for decision came in February, 1947. The overburdened British shocked Washington by announcing that they could no longer provide full-scale economic support for the "rightist" government of Greece. When they withdrew their assistance, the Communist guerrillas, who were receiving help from their Communist neighbors to the north, would no doubt seize control. Greece would then gravitate into the Soviet orbit. The position of Turkey, on which Moscow was exerting heavy pressure, would become untenable. The strategically vital eastern Mediterranean would presumably fall like a ripe pear into Communist hands, and the impact on the free world would be catastrophic.

President Truman, after hurried conferences with military and Congressional leaders, made a surprise appearance before Congress, on March 12, 1947, to present an epochal pronouncement. In solemn tones he described the plight of war-racked Greece, and then declared:

One of the primary objectives of the foreign policy of the United States is the creation of conditions in which we and other nations will be able to work out a way of life free from coercion . . . . We shall not realize our objectives, however, unless we are willing to help free peoples to maintain their free institutions and their national integrity against aggressive movements that seek to impose upon them totalitarian regimes. [Applause.] This is no more than a frank recognition that totalitarian regimes imposed on free peoples, by direct or indirect aggression, undermine the foundations of international peace and hence the security of the United States.[1]

Truman thereupon concluded that "it must be the policy of the United States to support free peoples who are resisting attempted subjugation by armed minorities or by outside pressures." With this goal in view, he requested an appropriation of $400 million for economic and military succor to Greece and Turkey. This, he conceded, was a "serious course," but the alternative to drifting was "much more serious. [Applause.]" The implication was clear that Congress had better expend a modest amount of the taxpayers' money than later expend the taxpayer himself. When Truman concluded, Congress arose as one man to applaud—except for one left-wing member.

CASH FOR "CONTAINMENT"

The Truman Doctrine was the major opening gun in what journalists called the "cold war"—a war waged by means other than shooting. It also inaugurated in a spectacular way the new policy of "containment" or the attempt to stem Soviet advances in vital spots.[2] The public, though now willing to halt Russian aggression by risky measures, was momentarily stunned by the President's blast. But the feeling was general that while the "Truman Doctrine" was fraught with peril, a policy of dangerous do-nothingism was even more perilous. The only two major groups to express strong hostility were the left-wing "liberals," for whom Henry A. Wallace was a spokesman, and the old-line isolationists, for whom the *Chicago Tribune* was a leading mouthpiece.[3]

Critics of the Truman Doctrine advanced numerous and weighty arguments. It would cost too much, for the initial appropriation would be but a drop in the bucket. It would create the bad precedent of sticking the national nose into the internal affairs of other nations. It would goad into war the Soviet Communists, who could not be fought with mere dollars. It would bypass the United Nations and weaken that organization at the very time when it was getting off to a wobbly start.

As far as the UN was concerned, Truman had clearly taken lone-hand action because of the inevitable delaying tactics of the Soviets. But he had gone so far out on the end of a limb that he could not be repudiated without

---

[1] *Cong. Record,* 80 Cong., 1 sess., p. 1981 (March 12, 1947).

[2] The reputed author of "containment" was George F. Kennan of the State Department, whose views, published anonymously at the time, later appeared in his *American Foreign Policy* (Chicago, 1951), pp. 107–128.

[3] The Truman Doctrine grew in popularity. In March, 1947, the loan to Greece was supported by 56%; that to Turkey by only 49%. The sending of military advisers was less popular. *Opinion News,* April 15, 1947.

weakening the United States in the eyes of the world at a critical hour. Senator Vandenberg of Michigan, who with a majority of his Republican colleagues continued to support a bipartisan foreign policy, helped to push through Congress a face-saving amendment. It stipulated that whenever the United Nations was prepared to take over the burden, the United States would lay it down.

FOUR-HEADED BEAR

Goldberg in the *New York Sun*, 1946, courtesy of the
New York Sun, Inc.

After a windy debate of about two months, Congress approved the initial Truman Doctrine appropriation of $400 million on May 15, 1947. The vote, which reflected wide public support, was 67 to 23 in the Senate and 287 to 107 in the House.

The Truman Doctrine was of incalculable significance. It enabled America to seize the offensive in the Cold War to "contain" communism. Although applied to Greece and Turkey, it was general in scope and led by direct steps to the vastly more important Marshall Plan and the North Atlantic Treaty Organization (NATO). It was a kind of lend-lease—this time against communism rather than fascism. It reversed the nonintervention principle of the original Monroe Doctrine, but like the Monroe Doctrine it aimed at long-range defense.[4]

THE MARSHALL PLAN

Once the American people had accepted the principle of helping independent governments resist communism, they gradually perceived that stopgap aid for only Greece and Turkey was merely sending a boy on a man's errand. War-blasted Western Europe, further scourged by the icy winter of 1946–1947, was not making the necessary economic recovery. Local Communist groups were deliberately sabotaging progress by strikes and other incendiary tactics. If the chaos that was so favorable to communism should develop, the Communists would probably seize control of Italy and France. All Western Europe would then fall into their grip, and Moscow's influence would sweep to the English Channel.

Into the breach boldly stepped the Secretary of State, General Marshall. Speaking at the Harvard University commencement exercises, on June 5, 1947, he announced a policy that forthwith dwarfed the Truman Doctrine. He suggested that the nations of Europe get together, devise long-range plans for economic recovery, concentrate on self-help and mutual assistance, and present to Washington a specific statement of their needs. The United States would then support them with financial help "so far as it may be practical. . . ."

The Marshall speech did not at once make a great splash in the United States.[5] It was not a clear-cut promise, and it put the burden of initiative squarely on Europe's shoulders. But gradually the American people perceived that the Marshall scheme was no unilateral Truman Doctrine aimed at military aid or temporary relief. It was an inclusive plan, and so designed by Truman, looking toward long-range rehabilitation.

The foreign ministers of France and Britain, recognizing the breathtaking implications of Marshall's overture, seized the initiative. They arranged for a meeting at Paris, to which the Soviet foreign minister, V. M. Molotov, was also invited. After a short but stormy stay, he finally walked out, thus spurning an enviable opportunity to tie up the Marshall Plan with obstructionism.

The British and French thereupon issued invitations for a general conference at Paris, to which twenty-two nations were invited—all Europe west of Russia except Fascist Spain. The eight nations under the shadow of the Kremlin declined, or were forced to spurn the "imperialist" plot, cooked up for "the enslavement of Europe." They were Albania, Bulgaria,

[4] Monroe promised to stay out of Greece; Truman urged America to go into Greece.

[5] Gallup found (July 23, 1947) that of the 49% who had heard of the Marshall proposal, 57% were favorable, and 21% opposed. *Pub. Opin. Quar.*, XI, 495.

Czechoslovakia, Finland, Hungary, Poland, Romania, and Yugoslavia. The sixteen that accepted were Austria, Belgium, Britain, Denmark, Eire, France, Greece, Iceland, Italy, Luxembourg, the Netherlands, Norway, Portugal, Sweden, Switzerland and Turkey. Representatives of these sixteen Marshall Plan countries, meeting in Paris from July to September, 1947, finally wove their "shopping lists" of help desired from America into an integrated program.

One defiant answer of Moscow to the Marshall Plan was the nine-nation Communist Information Bureau (Cominform), announced on October 5, 1947. It was in effect a revival of the Old Comintern, which ostensibly had been disbanded in 1943. The new agency was openly designed to promote communism by sabotaging the economic recovery of Europe under the Marshall Plan. At the same time the Kremlin, through the counter Molotov Plan, would attempt to shackle its satellites together as an economic whole. They would fight all schemes to spread capitalism eastward.

MARSHALING MARSHALL DOLLARS

The scene now shifted to Washington, where President Truman submitted his Marshall Plan estimates to Congress, in December, 1947. They embraced $17 billion for four-and-one-quarter years, with an initial outlay of $6.8 billion for the first fifteen months. The debate in Congress then began in earnest, and despite the urgent need for haste, consumed more than three precious months.

Advocates of the Marshall Plan, though appealing to simple humanitarianism, stressed the bread-and-butter argument that a prosperous Europe was essential for America's own prosperity. Industrial and agricultural groups, worried about their overseas markets, warmly seconded this view. But the necessity of halting Soviet communism was no doubt the compelling argument. The Marshall Plan was admittedly a calculated risk, but it was cheaper than war. If successful in redressing the European balance, it might head off a conflict that would be infinitely costly and destructive.

Critics of the Marshall scheme charged that it was just another "Operation Rathole." "Uncle Santa Claus" had already poured too much money into the pockets of ungrateful Europeans—about $12 billion in various loans and handouts since mid-1945. America had better make herself strong at home, conserve her resources, and help her own needy people. Otherwise she would offend the Soviets (who were already offended), divide Europe (which was already divided), and lay herself open to the Russian charge (which had already been made) of "dollar imperialism." The whole device, cried Henry A. Wallace, was a "Martial Plan."

The Kremlin unwittingly helped spur the languishing Marshall Plan appropriation through Congress. The Communist coup of February, 1948,

in Czechoslovakia had a profound effect, especially the suicide of the beloved Foreign Minister Masaryk under circumstances that suggested foul
play. Hardly less disturbing was Moscow's strong-arming of "Brave little"
Finland into a distasteful alliance. These alarming developments not only
increased enthusiasm for the Marshall Plan, but sped through Congress
an unprecedented peacetime conscription law and an appropriation for
a potent airforce.

The debate on Marshall aid at length ended. The legislators, who were
unwilling to bind future Congresses by a long-term appropriation, finally
voted $6.098 billion for various purposes during the first twelve months.
The tacit understanding was that similar sums would be forthcoming

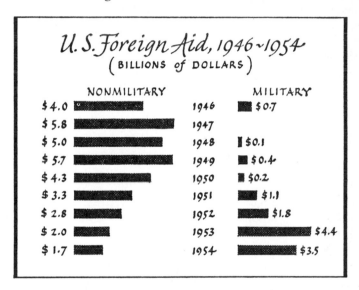

U. S. Foreign Aid, 1946~1954
(BILLIONS of DOLLARS)

NONMILITARY		MILITARY
$4.0	1946	$0.7
$5.8	1947	
$5.0	1948	$0.1
$5.7	1949	$0.4
$4.3	1950	$0.2
$3.3	1951	$1.1
$2.8	1952	$1.8
$2.0	1953	$4.4
$1.7	1954	$3.5

through the next three years. This measure, after passing the House 329
to 74 and the Senate 69 to 19, was signed by Truman on April 3, 1948.

The Marshall Plan—officially called the European Recovery Program
(ERP)—was approved just in time to influence the Italian election. The
militant Communist Party, crying "Death to Truman," was threatening to
seize control and undermine the position of the democracies in Europe.
The Italian people, thus confronted with the choice between the concrete
aid of the Marshall Plan and the pie-in-the-sky promises of communism,
returned a smashing verdict against the Communists.

The Marshall Plan, which turned out to be a spectacular success, was
an epochal step in both foreign policy and postwar recovery. This economic blood transfusion—altogether $10.25 billion in three years—took
the Europeans off their backs and put them on their feet. It halted the
westward surge of communism. It was one of the major steps in the evolution of the North Atlantic Treaty Organization (NATO). It was interven-

tion of a sort—or counterintervention against the Communists—but intervention designed to create the economic and political conditions in which free men could make a free choice of government. The Marshall Plan deservedly takes high rank among "the most unsordid acts in history." The money, to be sure, was given but it was given largely for what were deemed to be the best interests of the United States.

AIRLIFTS AND AIRWAVES

Berlin was perhaps the first critical area to suffer from Soviet resentment against the Marshall Plan. Moscow had long been disturbed by the success of the British, Americans, and French in unifying their German zones and in establishing currency reform. On June 24, 1948, therefore, the Soviets shut off all non-Russian traffic to Berlin, except by air. They evidently reasoned that America, Britain, and France, unable to supply the garrisons and populations in their sectors, would abandon the city. It would then become a rallying point for the Soviets in the unification of an all-Communist Germany.

President Truman, supported by the British, promptly and courageously refused to be run out of Berlin. In arriving at this decision, he correctly interpreted the mood of the American people.[6] American and British airmen speedily inaugurated the Berlin airlift, through which they undertook the gigantic task of supplying not only their garrisons but the needs of some 2,500,000 people as well. "Operation Vittles," as it was called, at one time was flying in some 4500 tons of supplies a day, including coal—expensive coal.

The Berlin blockade backfired badly on Moscow. There were some ticklish scrapes with Russian fighter planes, and the peace of the world lay with the trigger fingers of Soviet airmen. But President Truman and his associates properly concluded that the Russians did not want to fight—otherwise they would have let war come then and there. The West gained in popularity with its fallen German foes, while the Soviets sank even lower. The Berlin airlift thus proved to be a stimulant to the formation of the West German Republic, and also an important step toward the North Atlantic Alliance. The Russians, pinched by a counterblockade of their zone by the West, finally agreed to end their blockade of Berlin in 1949, after about a year's trial.

Spectacular episodes meanwhile had further highlighted the pervasiveness of Soviet communism. The House Committee on Un-American Activities, which had been flushing out small-fry Communist conspirators, finally emerged with big game. It found evidence that in 1937–1938 Alger Hiss, then an official in the State Department, had betrayed important

---

[6] One national poll (Sept. 15, 1948) showed that 85% were for staying in Berlin, 7% were for leaving, and 8% were undecided. *Pub. Opin. Quar.*, XII, 764. For the whole story see L. D. Clay, *Decision in Germany* (Garden City, N.Y., 1950).

secrets to Soviet agents. After two sensational trials, Hiss was found guilty of perjury in 1950, and sentenced to a prison term of five years.

Such incidents induced the American people, despite a natural aversion to such methods, to try to match weapons with the Soviets on the propaganda front. When World War II had ended, an economy-minded Congress was giving niggardly support to an informational and cultural program, popularly known as the "Voice of America." It was designed to instruct other people in the American way of life, through radio and other agencies, and thus combat communism. As the wholesale propaganda activities of the Soviets became more blatant, and as the conviction deepened that the only way to bring the truth to the Russians and their satellites was by a short-wave radio, Congress pricked up its ears. Early in 1948 it put the "Voice of America" on a permanent basis with more adequate funds, although they were far short of what the Soviets were spending.[7] The American short-wave radio program had serious defects, but its partial success was attested by persistent Soviet efforts to "jam" its broadcasts.

THE TRUMAN "MIRACLE" OF 1948

The Republicans, who had been the "outs" for sixteen long years, were confident of victory as the Presidential campaign of 1948 approached. They enthusiastically renominated their previous candidate, the dapper Governor Dewey of New York. The prospects of President Truman, who received the Democratic nomination, seemed hopelessly weakened when the Southern wing of his party—the "Dixiecrats"—bolted in protest against his program of civil rights for Negroes.

Truman and Dewey, concentrating their fire on domestic problems, succeeded fairly well in keeping foreign policy on the new bipartisan level. Dewey condemned the administration for its "wobbling and fumbling" tactics, rather than for its over-all policy and objectives. While demanding a "firm" stand toward Moscow, he urged more aid for the faltering regime of Chiang Kai-shek. "Harassed Harry" Truman, undaunted by the seeming odds against him, toured the country in a whistle-stop campaign which struck hard at the short-sighted Republican isolationism since 1920.

The already confused campaign was complicated by the antics of Henry A. Wallace. An idealist and visionary who hated war, he had been forced out of Truman's Cabinet as Secretary of Commerce for publicly advocating a go-easy-on-Russia policy while the Secretary of State was publicly advocating a get-tough-with-Russia policy. Wallace thereafter pulled no punches, both at home and abroad, in hammering at the bipartisan anti-

---

[7] Gallup found that in June, 1947, a plurality of 46% was opposed to short-wave broadcasts to Russia, but by December, 1948, 58% were favorable to spending as much in Europe for propaganda as Russia was. *Pub. Opin. Quar.*, XI, 493; XIII, 171. A separate organization, divorced from the State Department and known as the United States Information Agency, was set up in 1953 to handle propaganda.

Soviet policy of Washington. In May, 1948, he touched off what his followers called a "peace scare" by addressing an open letter to Marshal Stalin, to which the latter replied cordially. This bypassing of the State Department was probably a violation of the Logan Act of 1799, which as revised forbade unauthorized negotiations with foreign governments regarding issues in dispute with the United States.

Wallace finally made good his threat to head a third party when he further split the Democrats by accepting the Progressive nomination in July, 1948. His platform denounced the Truman doctrines as allegedly inspired by Wall Street and professional militarists. It also condemned the recent peacetime draft, and demanded an end to the stalemate in Soviet-American relations. The views of the Wallaceites attracted many "liberals" and disaffected elements, who naturally received noisy backing from the American Communists. Wallace undoubtedly weakened the position of the United States, and may have encouraged the Kremlin to continue its stiff-necked course.

Truman scored an incredible upset, partly because of his own vigor but largely because of Dewey's vagueness. Nobody seemed to be for him except the voters. Wallace polled only 1,156,103 votes out of more than 48 million cast, although he was unable to get his name on the ballot in some states. This evidence that the nation was behind Washington's "firm" Soviet policy may have had a sobering effect on the Kremlin, which began to adopt a somewhat more conciliatory tone.

THE "BOLD NEW" POINT FOUR PROGRAM

Enheartened by his triumph, Truman highlighted his inaugural address by urging, under Point Four, a "Bold New Program." It ranks in significance with the Truman Doctrine and the Marshall Plan.

The Point Four program was breathtaking in its global coverage, for it embraced most of the underdeveloped and backward countries of the earth. It was not a "giveaway" program, like the Marshall Plan, but a Technical Assistance Program. The underprivileged nations would be taught by American technicians how to help themselves. The United States would export skills and "know-how" rather than money.

The Bold New Program combined idealism with hard-headed realism. If impoverished nations could become prosperous, they would prosper the United States by providing rich markets. At the same time, the reduction of poverty would reduce the appeal of communism, and thus help in the crusade to "contain" the communistic imperialism of Moscow.

The new program would cost money, although the outlays would be small as compared with the Marshall Plan. But Truman preferred to spend millions to prevent people from becoming Communists rather than spend billions to shoot them after they became Communists. The Marshall Plan had been a short-range "crash" program, designed to revive the war-ravaged countries of Western Europe as buffers against communism. Point Four was a long-term program, designed to help backward countries anywhere that were willing to accept technical guidance.

The Point Four program got under way slowly in 1950 with a modest appropriation of $34.5 million. By the end of the next year trainees had come to America from more than a score of nations, and aid had been extended to thirty-four countries, ranging from India to Iran, from Paraguay to Liberia. By 1953 the public and Congress were so favorably impressed with the results that they raised the annual appropriation to $155.6 million, which was negligible when compared with the annual defense budget.

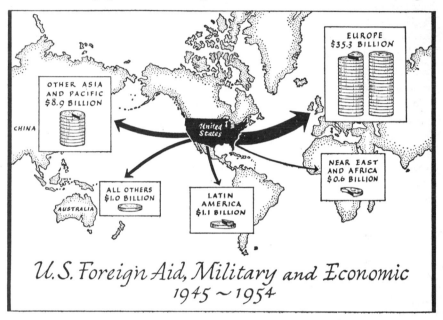

U. S. Foreign Aid, Military and Economic 1945 ~ 1954

The practical results of the long-range Truman program were soon evident in many theaters. Increasing the food supply was a primary objective, and this was achieved through such contributions as improved seeds and fertilizers. The eradication of disease was no less important, whether of typhus in Iran or malaria in Peru and Burma. The benefits were also seen in transportation, monetary reform, irrigation programs, and hydroelectric installations. Above all, in vocational schools American experts taught the natives how to teach natives to employ the necessary skills. On a dollar-for-dollar basis, none of the enormous expenditures of the years after World War II returned such rich dividends in good will and support for America's foreign policies as the Point Four scheme.[8]

The underprivileged nations of Latin America were a major concern of the "Bold New Program." Poverty and disease provided a lush culture

[8] See J. B. Bingham, *Shirt-Sleeve Diplomacy: Point 4 in Action* (New York, 1954); Eugene Staley, *The Future of Underdeveloped Countries* (New York, 1954).

bed for the Communists, whose slogan was "Down with Yankee Imperialism." The Latin Americans, moreover, were aggrieved to see so many billions being poured into Europe under the Marshall Plan, especially after the deluge of American dollars during the critical war period. The Point Four program did something to assuage their bitterness, to create a firmer front in Latin America against communism, and to strengthen the Pan-American ideal.

THE TRUCE WITH ARGENTINA

Argentina continued to be the most formidable obstacle to an all-American front. The dynamic and power-hungry Colonel Perón succeeded in consolidating his dictatorship late in 1945, despite the vigorous protests of United States Ambassador Braden. In the midst of the controversy Braden was brought home to become Assistant Secretary of State, in which capacity he pursued a strong anti-Perón policy.

The Department of State, in a thinly veiled attempt to defeat Perón in the forthcoming Presidential election, published a dynamite-laden Blue Book in February, 1946. It consisted of captured German documents, which exposed Nazi influence in Argentina and implicated Perón himself in a conspiracy with the Nazis to undermine the governments of neighboring republics. The followers of Perón, denouncing the act of Washington as gross intervention, raised the cry, "Perón or Braden!" "Yankee interference" no doubt swung many votes to Perón, who won by a comfortable margin.[9]

The United States, unwilling to sacrifice the Good Neighbor Policy or resort to old brass-knuckle methods, was now forced to back down. Secretary Byrnes announced in April, 1946, that Washington would welcome black-sheep Argentina into the fold if she would fulfill her pledges, made at Chapultepec in 1945, and stamp out Nazi infection. The Argentine regime subsequently cracked down on the Nazis more gently than the United States liked, but in June, 1947, President Truman proclaimed that Buenos Aires had carried out its commitments. Henceforth Washington managed to hold its nose and get along after a fashion with Perón, who, after all, was anti-Communist. Patience paid off in 1955, when the dictator was forced into exile by his own people.

PAN-AMERICANISM COMBATS COMMUNISM

With Argentina now in a more agreeable frame of mind, a special conference of the American states, long deferred, was scheduled to meet at Rio de Janeiro (Brazil), in August, 1947. It was designed to put into more permanent form the defensive arrangements that had been adopted

[9] See A. P. Whitaker, *The United States and Argentina* (Cambridge, Mass., 1954).

at the Chapultepec Conference in 1945. The lengthening shadow of Soviet aggression provided a sharp spur to prompt and effective action. Attesting to the importance of the parley, the President of the United States journeyed south to close the meetings, amid shouts of "Viva Truman!"

The most memorable fruit of the conference was the Treaty of Rio de Janeiro—an epochal achievement in regional security and interlocking defense pacts. It provided for action by all of the contracting nations against an armed attack on any American republic, even from an American state like Argentina, pending measures by the Security Council of the United Nations. This historic pact, which the United States Senate approved 72 to 1, further strengthened the multilateralization of the Monroe Doctrine. It was by all odds the most significant inter-American agreement to date. It was also the first regional defense pact, as envisioned by Article 51 of the United Nation Charter. As such, it served as both a model and a precedent for the multipower North Atlantic Treaty of 1949.

The next regular International Conference of American republics—the ninth since 1889—met at Bogotá, Colombia, early in 1948. The Latin Americans, pinched by a postwar economic slump and eyeing the Marshall Plan plums with envy, hoped for generous aid through a "little Marshall Plan." The suggestion of President Truman that a mere half-billion dollars be made available through the Export-Import Bank in Washington left them cold. But Secretary Marshall himself, who headed the American delegation, regarded as the most urgent business the fashioning of an anti-Communist pact. As if to give point to his pleas, a frightful local revolt, in which Communists presumably had a large hand, wrecked the city and took hundreds of lives. The conference was forced to suspend its labors for several days, at the end of which time it was ready to take strong steps to unite the Americas against the Red peril. These included the adoption of an anti-Communist resolution, the establishment of a defense council, and the formation of the Charter of the Organization of American States.

The Soviet threat thus caused the American republics by 1948 to draw together more closely than ever before. But below the seeming solidarity there were rankling grievances. The Latin-American states, although not war ravaged and not on the firing line of communism, could not readily understand why Uncle Sam was unable to shower his inexhaustible dollars southward as well as Europe-ward.

THE 12-POWER NORTH ATLANTIC PACT

The menace of Moscow elsewhere brought further noteworthy developments. In March, 1948, five nations of Western Europe—Britain, France, Belgium, the Netherlands, and Luxembourg—signed at Brussels a fifty-year defensive pact. By its terms they solemnly bound themselves to aid one another against an attack by an aggressor. The United States, as their chief economic underwriter and as a leader of the anti-Communist nations, was irresistibly drawn toward the new alliance.

Washington was in a receptive mood. In June, 1948, nearly three months after the birth of the Brussels pact, the United States Senate passed the Vandenberg resolution by the lopsided vote of 64 to 4. It affirmed American support for regional security pacts like the one recently adopted by the five European nations. With this green light plainly flashing, the State Department pressed negotiations to include the United States in the union. Moscow loudly proclaimed that Washington was weakening the United Nations (which the Soviets had already weakened), and was forming an aggressive bloc (which the Soviets had already formed by a network of treaties with their satellites). Regional security pacts conformed to both the letter and spirit of Articles 51 and 52 of the UN Charter, and the proposed Atlantic alliance was clearly defensive rather than aggressive.

Representatives of twelve nations, with appropriate white-tie pageantry, finally met in Washington to sign the North Atlantic Treaty, on April 4, 1949. The charter members were the United States, Canada, Britain, France, Italy, Belgium, the Netherlands, Luxembourg, Norway, Denmark, Iceland, and Portugal. After paying their respects to the UN, they stipulated that an attack by an aggressor on one of them would be an attack on all of them. They further proclaimed that each of the other signatory nations, in the event of an assault on one member, would take "such action as it deems necessary," including "armed force." This pledge did not flatly commit the United States to war, or remove from Congress the war-declaring power. But it was a moral commitment to aid the victims of aggression for at least twenty years.

NONENTANGLEMENT BECOMES ENTANGLEMENT

The North Atlantic Pact was precedent-shattering. It was unquestionably a formal treaty of alliance, the first the United States had ever concluded in peacetime with a European power or powers. Yet such was the growing fear of the Soviet menace that this drastic departure from tradition met with widespread favor in America.[10] The conviction was general that if World War III broke out, the republic would be sucked into it at the outset. The only sensible alternative seemed to be to attempt to avert it, as the United States had been unable or unwilling to do in 1914 and 1939, by serving notice on potential aggressors that they would have to reckon with America's might from the very outset. The loudest opposition to the alliance came from the last-ditch isolationists, from the Henry Wallaceites,

---

[10] Gallup found that 67% favored ratification and 12% opposed. Gallup Release, May 18, 1949. The Rio Pact of 1947 was a defensive pact but hardly a military alliance. No member could be required to use force against its will.

and from the Communists. The leading Communist organ, the *New York Daily Worker,* branded the pact "International Murder, Inc."

The epochal North Atlantic Pact was approved by the Senate, in July, 1949, by a vote of 82 to 13. There was surprisingly little opposition. A few die-hard isolationists feared foreign entanglements, a loss of the war-declaring power of Congress, and commitments to heavy and dangerous defense expenditures. Opponents of the pact made a determined effort to relieve the United States of any obligation to rearm Western Europe, but such proposed amendments were beaten down by heavy majorities.

One presumed by-product of the North Atlantic Pact was the lifting of the Berlin blockade. Three weeks after the signing of the alliance the Soviets, in what may have been an attempt to head off American ratification, agreed tentatively to end the stoppage. The formal lifting came on May 12, 1949. The Soviets seemed less aggressive and self-assured, perhaps because of the success of the Marshall Plan, the Berlin airlift, and the Atlantic Treaty.

The threat of Russian communism had thus brought about a major revolution in American foreign policy within a few short years. The United States had reversed its Monroe Doctrine in relation to Greece by accepting the Truman Doctrine. It had forsaken nonintervention by promoting the Marshall Plan. It had tossed overboard the no-alliance tradition by signing the Atlantic Pact. It had adopted peacetime conscription and a wartime military budget. It had embarked upon all such departures with extreme reluctance but basically in response to the instinct of self-preservation. The new American policies—all defensive in their outlook—were actually authored more by the men in the Kremlin than by the men in Washington. The American people had hoped for a peaceful world after World War II, but the aggressions of the Soviets simply would not permit them to drop their guard.

MILITARY AND ECONOMIC DIKES

The twelve-power Atlantic Pact of 1949 got off the ground slowly but hopefully. Early in 1950 eight Western European nations signed agreements with Washington under which they would receive, as a starter, one billion dollars worth of American arms. Ex-General Dwight D. Eisenhower, laying aside his cap and gown as president of Columbia University, took on the formidable task of creating an army for NATO (North Atlantic Treaty Organization). Each member country was expected to contribute appropriate contingents.

The hodge-podge NATO army grew with dismaying slowness, especially in view of the Soviet Union's preponderant military strength. The American people, on the whole, were willing to send a few divisions of troops to Europe, rather than keep them at home for a last-ditch defense.

But prominent Republicans of an isolationist tinge, notably ex-President Hoover and Senator Taft, tried to halt or limit the commitment of American soldiers abroad.

The NATO nations of Western Europe meanwhile continued to make encouraging military and economic headway. Anti-Communist Greece and Turkey, both with respectable armies, were admitted to NATO in September, 1951, thereby bringing the number of allies to fourteen. The economic integration of Western Europe went forward promisingly, notably with the negotiation and ratification, in 1951–1952, of the six-nation Schuman coal-steel pool.

Marshall Plan dollars continued to have a tonic effect. The Economic Co-operation Administration (ECA), created in 1948 to administer the Marshall Plan, gave way in 1951 to the Mutual Security Agency (MSA) under W. Averell Harriman, later governor of New York. The initial Mutual Security Appropriation Bill made available $7.428 billion for various kinds of foreign aid—economic, military, and technical.

The fruits of this overseas assistance, though costly to the American taxpayer, on the whole proved gratifying. In 1950 a number of the fourteen NATO nations could proudly report that their industrial output topped that of 1938—the year before Hitler smashed into Poland. Several of the recipient countries candidly announced that they needed no further help, and various European spokesmen, hitting at America's moderate tariff barriers, demanded "Trade not Aid." Communist agitators in various Western European countries added the cry, with mounting vehemence, "Yankee, go home!"

Unhappily the economic recovery of Europe brought little relief to the groaning American taxpayer. As financial handouts from Washington fell off, increased military appropriations took up the slack. All foreign aid programs were reorganized in August, 1953, under the Foreign Operations Administration (FOA). Serving as the world's bank and arsenal had brought heavy expense, to say nothing of a mixture of gratitude and ingratitude from the beneficiaries. But the foreign-aid program received solid support from the American people, who were grimly determined to halt the Soviet surge.[11]

THE REBIRTH OF THE GERMAN REICH

A Germany rising from her rubble was the key problem of Central Europe. Her continued division into democratic West Germany and Communist East Germany stimulated German nationalism and a passion for unity. Yet the Russians, working through Communist puppets, stolidly refused to discontinue rearming and reoccupying East Germany. They had valid

[11] Gallup (Aug. 24, 1951) found 2 to 1 support among informed respondents. *Ibid.*

reason to fear that East Germany would rotate out of the Soviet orbit, once the Red Army was withdrawn.

The amazing economic and political resurgence of West Germany, with its 50,000,000 bustling people, made the problem of Germany more pressing. The creation of the German Federal Republic in 1949, with its capital at historic Bonn on the Rhine, evoked menacing noises from Moscow. In the same year, Washington agreed to make Germany a full-fledged participant in the European aid program, and the Allies discontinued their dismantling of German war-making industry. The determination of the victors to keep Germany disarmed forever was plainly weakening.

The possible rearmament of West Germany took on a different complexion as the menace of Soviet communism mounted and when the Korean War broke out in 1950. German manpower seemed critically necessary if the NATO armies were to meet the threat of Moscow on anywhere near equal terms. Yet German guns that could shoot eastward against Communists could also shoot westward against the democracies.

A promising scheme for a denatured German army, originally proposed by the French, was the European Defense Community (EDC). The Germans would merge their quota of troops with a six-nation EDC force within NATO, and thus eliminate the threat of a German national army. The other nations concerned, including the United States, gave their approval in 1952, but the French dragged their feet. Still bearing the teeth marks of Nazi aggression, and fearing that a new generation of Germans would follow in its fathers' footsteps, they seemed more willing to face the dangers of Soviet aggression than have German soldiers stationed on their soil, even in EDC uniforms. Despite threats from Washington that German sovereignty might have to be recognized anyhow, the French National Assembly spurned the EDC scheme in August, 1954, with a solid bloc of Communist delegates gleefully voting to sidetrack it.

Speedy work by the Western diplomats, notably Britain's Foreign Secretary Eden, resulted in a miraculous comeback from the EDC debacle. French misgivings were partially quieted by an unprecedented British commitment to maintain four divisions of troops in Western Europe. A series of agreements was concluded in October, 1954, when a fifteen-power parley met in Paris, consisting of fourteen NATO nations plus West Germany. The resulting pacts were designed to bring a near-sovereign and rearmed West Germany into NATO under the supervision of the countries of the Western European Union. The hope was that the Germans would contribute twelve urgently needed divisions to the common cause.

West Germany was admitted to NATO, as a full-fledged member, in 1955. The sovereign Germans were now committed to rearmament and co-operation with the West, even though in subsequent months their arms program lagged alarmingly.

TITO AND FRANCO—IDEOLOGICAL ANTIPODES

The menace of Moscow continued to force the United States to keep company with mismated ideological bedfellows.

Tito, the Communist dictator of Yugoslavia, had been a welcome if distrusted quasially of the Western World since his break with Stalin in 1948. Although still an outspoken Communist, he was not of the Moscow breed. The condemnations heaped upon him by the Kremlin were but another case of the pot calling the despot black. Yet Tito, though not completely respectable in American eyes, was anti-Soviet. And in the life-and-death struggle between East and West, the West could not afford to probe too deeply into the past of its allies.

American aid, with some misgivings, continued to go to Tito. Tanks, artillery, and other military supplies bolstered his underequipped but highly esteemed army. In addition, Washington provided substantial loans, supplies of food, and other assistance. Even though Tito was unwilling to renounce communism or enter into a direct military alliance with the West, these costly subventions received some support from the American public. In August, 1954 Tito became indirectly bound to NATO when he entered into a formal alliance with two of its members, Greece and Turkey.

Aid to Tito was a calculated risk. The fear was ever present that he would bury the hatchet with the Kremlin, as he did ultimately in 1956, and that his American tanks would be used to crush American boys. But the need to encourage "Titoism" among the other satellites of Moscow seemed to justify the risk, and the subsequent uprisings in Poland and Hungary in 1956 provided some justification for this policy.

Fascist Franco of Spain, like Communist Tito of Yugoslavia, took on a better odor as the cold war grew hotter. Anchored below the rugged Pyrenees mountains, Catholic Spain was regarded in America as a valuable fall-back zone, should the Soviet divisions engulf Western Europe. Franco had a large though ill-equipped army, and his people had already shown a last-ditch determination to fight Moscow's communism. Mounting sentiment developed in the United States for admitting Franco to both the UN and NATO, and for providing Franco with urgently needed economic and military aid.[12]

As the menace of the Kremlin increased, Washington veered slowly around toward lending Franco a helping hand. In 1950 the Export-Import Bank in Washington granted Madrid a loan of $62.5 million, and President Truman announced the appointment of the first full-fledged Ambassador to Spain since 1945. Late in 1953 an extraordinary Executive agreement was signed in Madrid. Spain, in return for at least $226

[12] Gallup had found as early as June, 1951, that 65% of informed voters favored aid to Franco, with 26% disapproving, and 9% without opinion. *Ibid.*

million in economic and military aid, granted the United States the use of key air and naval bases.

The deal with Franco, though unpopular with many American and European liberals, was stoutly defended by Washington as realistic. Spanish bases, especially for American planes carrying nuclear bombs, seemed necessary for insuring the good behavior of the Soviet Union. Americans could like Franco's defenses without liking his dictatorship.

THE DAWN OF THE HYDROGEN AGE

A fateful epoch ended when Stalin—once the Man of Steel—died in March, 1953. The Western World hoped that a violent quarrel over his successor might bring an easing of tensions. But so ruthless was the Communist machine that the succession, with scarcely a grinding gear, passed

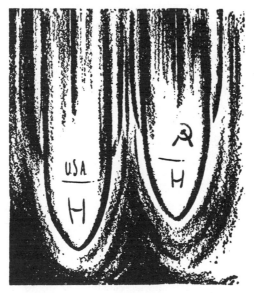

"LOOK! WE'RE OUT IN FRONT!"

Little in the *Nashville Tennessean,* 1953

on to beefy Georgi M. Malenkov. At first the new regime sang a sweeter tune, no doubt in the hope of lulling the West into dropping its guard, but relations were soon back on the old unhappy track.

The horrifying tick of the atomic time-bomb continued to jar on already taut nerves. All efforts at nuclear disarmament in the United Nations sank on the rock of Soviet obduracy. Moscow simply would not consent to adequate international inspection, without which any agreement was folly.

The geographical defenses of the United States, within a few short years, had been vastly weakened by two inventions, ironically perfected by Americans themselves—the airplane and the atomic bomb. Hitherto America had been the only major power whose soil was not immediately vulnerable to an almost overnight attack by a powerful neighbor. Now, in a science-shrunken world, the United States and all other nations were exposed to an atomic Pearl Harbor.

The race in "nation-busting" weapons accelerated. In January, 1950, President Truman gave orders for making a hydrogen bomb, vastly more destructive than the atomic bomb. The Washington strategists assumed—and correctly so—that the Russians were breathing on America's neck in the atomic race. Late in 1952 reports leaked out that American scientists had detonated a hydrogen bomb in the Pacific. The Soviet Union, not to be outdone, proclaimed the explosion of a hydrogen device, in August, 1953.

The incredible new H-bomb, several hundred times more lethal than either of the atomic bombs dropped on Japan, was hailed in some quarters as making another global conflict less likely. Like two scorpions in a bottle, the Communist World and the Western World seemed capable of destroying each other in a double-suicide war. In this unhappy event, there would not be much of the world left for the Communists to communize. Peace through mutual terror, with occasional "brush-fire" outbreaks, might be the best that the world could hope for in its quest for peaceful co-existence.

SELECTED BIBLIOGRAPHY

The volumes published for the Council on Foreign Relations entitled, *The United States in World Affairs,* and prepared by various authors, are useful, as are the studies published by the Brookings Institution under the title, *Major Problems of United States Foreign Policy.* Invaluable first-hand material appears in the *Memoirs by Harry S. Truman* (2 vols., Garden City, N.Y., 1956). For an inside story by a State Department official on the backgrounds of the Truman Doctrine and the Marshall Plan consult J. M. Jones, *The Fifteen Weeks* (New York, 1955). See also G. F. Kennan, *Realities of American Foreign Policy* (Princeton, 1954) and Sumner Welles, *Where are we Heading?* (New York, 1946). Background material appears in Merle Curti and K. Birr, *Prelude to Point Four: American Technical Missions Overseas, 1838–1938* (Madison, Wis., 1954).

See also footnotes of this chapter and *Harvard Guide,* Ch. 30.

7TH ED. REFS. See the general new references at the end of the previous chapter. For additional new references see BIBLIOGRAPHICAL ADDENDUM, p. 1,054.

8TH AND 9TH ED. REFS. See BIBLIOGRAPHICAL ADDENDUM, p. 1,055.

52

Communism and
the Korean Conflict

*For all of us the future is shadowed by mushroom
clouds and menaced by godless men, addicted to force
and violence and the continuance of anarchy among
nations.*

PRESIDENT EISENHOWER, 1954

THE AGE OF SUSPICION

As THE 1950's lengthened, American foreign policy abroad came to be
jeopardized by anti-Communist hysteria at home. The Red hunt was
partly spurred by the fear and insecurity resulting from the frightening
gains of the Communists in the Cold War, especially in Asia. The American people fell victim to a natural desire to find scapegoats for all these
setbacks.

The Truman administration, naturally seeking to cover up its political
mistakes, was partly responsible for inviting the Red probe among suspected subversives in the government. The President himself scolded the
Republicans in Congress for being diverted by "Red herrings," while
neglecting much more pressing matters. Truman, and especially his suave
Secretary of State, Dean Acheson, were accused of being too velvet-
gloved in handling Communist-tainted officials. Early in 1950, Acheson
was so ill-advised as to announce that "I do not intend to turn my back"
on the convicted spy-perjurer, Alger Hiss.

Into this feverish atmosphere of "Hiss-teria", in 1950, stepped burly,
free-swinging Senator McCarthy of Wisconsin, hitherto unknown to
fame. In a speech in West Virginia he claimed that he held "here in my
hands" the names of 205 known Communists then employed in the State
Department. (Not one was ever proved to have been a Communist.) As
the head of a Senate investigating committee, McCarthy made other
accusations, many of them poorly supported, and some of them behind

the cloak of Senatorial immunity. A few custodians of American overseas libraries, fearful for their jobs, began to remove or burn "hot" books by left-wing authors. All this was disagreeably reminiscent of Hitler's book-burnings, and incalculably damaging to American attempts to promote democracy abroad, especially in Germany.

Undue concentration on the issue of Communists in government un-doubtedly hampered the United States in its prosecution of the cold war against communism. With the possible exception of President Eisenhower, Senator McCarthy by the mid-1950's became the best-known American abroad. Many prominent citizens, including Vice-President Nixon, feared that the republic might be burning down the barn of basic American freedoms in order to get rid of a few Communist rats. While Com-munists were on the rampage abroad, American investigators were directing attention to those under the bed.

The effects of McCarthyism on American foreign policy were dis-heartening. The inquisitors admittedly drove a few Communists and other left-wingers to cover, but the morale of the foreign service re-ceived a staggering blow. Honest mistakes of judgment, notably in connection with the collapse of China, were now regarded as Moscow-inspired sabotage. Senator McCarthy extravagantly branded the Demo-cratic administrations as "twenty years of treason." Foreign service officers abroad, whose candid observations were indispensable for the guidance of policy-makers in Washington, were now under pressure to gloss over unfavorable conditions, lest their careers be ruined in later months by "headline happy" Senatorial probers.[1]

Powerful but unsophisticated Uncle Sam had been thrust into the role of world leadership, but other nations doubted his ability to carry the banner. Americans were beginning to fear one another more than Soviet Communists, and Senator McCarthy's tactics were actually playing into the hands of the enemy in the cold war. America's prestige abroad rose somewhat when, late in 1954, the Senate formally condemned McCarthy, 67 to 22, for his contemptuous, abusive, and insulting conduct toward his colleagues. The Senator speedily went into an eclipse, and died of a liver ailment in 1957.

A REJUVENATED JAPAN

Conquered Japan, like conquered Germany, gradually gained in re-spectability. Time softens the bitterness of war. The United States, faced with both the rising tide of communism and the Korean conflict, sought to rearm Japan and make her a bulwark of democracy in East Asia. But

[1] See letter by five distinguished former diplomats to the *New York Times,* Jan. 17, 1954.

the once-militant Japanese, sobered by the war and the pacifistic teachings of General MacArthur, took to rearmament slowly and lukewarmly.

Pressures for making a peace treaty with Japan, despite bitter Soviet obstruction, finally became irresistible. In the teeth of Russian protests, arrangements were perfected for a fifty-odd nation conference at San Francisco, in September, 1951. After the adoption of rigid rules of procedure, the presiding officer, Secretary Acheson, gaveled down Russian filibustering protests. The treaty, with appropriate television ceremony, was formally signed on September 8, 1951, with the Communist-bloc nations abstaining. At the same time the United States and Japan concluded a bilateral security treaty which permitted the stationing of American troops on Japanese soil for an indefinite period. Subsequently, on February 28, 1952, the two nations signed a pact which would permit the United States to retain military bases in Japan for defensive purposes.[1a]

The Japanese treaty, though bitter medicine for the Soviets, was generally satisfactory to the Western World. As a result of the six-year cooling off period, the pact was not punitive but a "Peace of Reconciliation" —one that would let bygones be bygones. The United States Senate, by lopsided majorities, approved the treaty and the related security arrangements on March 20, 1952. Japan regained her sovereignty when the pact took effect, and forthwith began to show more independence toward her conqueror. Japanese Communists, in particular, were loud in their condemnation of the continued presence of American troops on Japanese soil.

The treaty with Japan also became an essential stone in the arch of a Pacific security edifice. About a week before the signing in San Francisco, the United States and the Philippines agreed upon a mutual defense treaty, on August 30, 1951. Two days later, Washington concluded a similar defensive pact with Australia and New Zealand. Designed in part to quiet fears inspired by a reviving Japan, it was known as ANZUS from the initials of the three powers—Australia, New Zealand, and the U.S. Less firm an alliance than NATO, it provided for periodic consultation for defensive purposes, and in subsequent years a number of meetings were held.

THE TWO CHINAS

A sharp controversy developed in the United States over what should be done with Chiang Kai-shek, following his escape to Formosa, in December, 1949, with several hundred thousand orphaned troops. The Truman administration, which had washed its hands of Chiang, barred

[1a] See B. C. Cohen, *The Political Process and Foreign Policy: The Making of the Japanese Peace Settlement* (Princeton, 1957).

military aid to Formosa but permitted limited assistance under the general foreign relief program. This policy was in line with American opinion, which likewise had written off Chiang's cause on the Chinese mainland as hopeless.

But many leading Republicans assailed the "ditch-Chiang" decision. Curiously enough, isolationist-inclined spokesmen, like Senator Taft and ex-President Hoover, were prepared to fight for Formosa, while vehemently opposing the halting of communism by force in Europe. These Asia-first Republicans ("Asialationists") further argued, with the bogey of Alger Hiss ever in the foreground, that China had collapsed because treacherous Communists in the State Department had sabotaged any effective aid to Chiang.

The next pressing problem was what attitude to take toward the Communist government in Peiping, which had fixed its tentacles securely on China's silent millions. Great Britain, with a huge trade stake in East Asia, made haste to recognize the Communist regime, but the latter made no haste to recognize Britain. Peiping, to be sure, spoke for about a half billion Chinese, and traditional American policy was to recognize *de facto* governments. But Washington, responding to public pressure and returning to the moralizing of Woodrow Wilson, declined to extend the friendly hand of recognition.[2] Americans not only disapproved of communism, but they had no assurance, in the light of previous experience, that United States foreign service officers would not be mishandled. Washington was prepared to wait until Peiping was able to give convincing assurances of good behavior.

The Soviet Union naturally became the thick-and-thin champion of its Peiping protégé. On February 14, 1950, Moscow signed with Red China a 30-year mutual aid pact, which bound each nation to come to the aid of the other if attacked by a resurgent Japan or the Western allies. At the UN meeting on Long Island, the Soviets loudly demanded the unseating of the Nationalist Chinese delegate, who did not represent the Chinese people, and the seating of a Communist delegate, who did. When rebuffed, the Russian delegate huffily staged a protracted walkout. The Washington officials, backed by an overwhelming public opinion, naturally opposed the seating of a Communist puppet from Peiping. This attitude hardened when the Communist Chinese intervened in the Korean war in 1950, and began killing the soldiers of the UN, including those of the United States. The ideals of the United Nations, as expressed in the Charter, were then so widely at variance with the actions of the Chinese Communists as to render admission unthinkable.[3]

[2] Gallup found the count (June 2, 1950) 16% favorable, 40% opposed, and 44% without opinion. Gallup Release.

[3] Gallup found (July 25, 1954) that 78% of the respondents opposed seating Communist China in the UN. *Ibid.*

THE KOREAN COCKPIT

At the end of World War II, Japan's mainland possession of Korea was temporarily occupied by both Russian and American troops, with the 38th parallel separating them. In their northern zone the Soviets set up a puppet Communist clique and trained a Communist army. Determined to prevent the formation of a free South Korean government, the Russians fought against its establishment; and when they failed in their efforts, they flatly vetoed its admission to the UN.

The Americans, in their southern zone of Korea, attempted to foster a democratic order—despite Communist agitation, internal dissension, and economic prostration. The Soviets in their zone had only to make a minority Communists. The Americans had to make a majority democratic and keep them that way—at great expense to the taxpayers back home.

A new era opened in June, 1949, when the American troops, after nearly four years of occupation, withdrew from South Korea, leaving behind only a few technical advisers. The fear was expressed at the time that Communist forces might come swarming down from the north. Secretary of State Acheson, in a memorable speech on January 12, 1950, indicated that Korea was not within the "defensive perimeter" for which the United States would fight, although he did note that the protection of such areas was still a responsibility of the UN. This address was later condemned as an invitation to Communist aggression.

The lid finally blew off on June 25, 1950. A North Korean army— Russian-trained, Russian-equipped, and presumably Russian-inspired— suddenly lunged southward across the borderline 38th parallel with the object of engulfing UN-sponsored South Korea. The assault was evidently made in the expectation that a weak-kneed UN would act either too late or not at all.[4]

But the Security Council of the UN, then meeting on Long Island, moved swiftly under proddings from Washington. The Russians were unable to cast the usual crippling veto, because their delegate was still absent in protest against the nonseating of Communist China. On June 25, 1950, the day of the invasion, the Security Council unanimously branded North Korea the aggressor, urged a cease-fire, and called upon the members of the UN "to render every assistance" in bringing about a restoration of peace.

The long-dreaded shooting had now begun in the hitherto cold war, even though the Soviet Union was doing the shooting by proxy through puppets. The life of the UN hung by a hair. The events of 1931, when the League of Nations had quailed before Japan's attack in Manchuria, seemed to be repeating themselves like a groove-stuck phonograph

[4] See *Memoirs by Harry S. Truman* (Garden City, N.Y., 1956), II, Ch. 22.

record. If the UN failed, all hope of collective security would presumably perish—and World War III would become virtually inevitable. Speed was desperately needed. Truman would have to move rapidly, if at all, for a full-dress Congressional debate on intervention in Korea would consume so much time as to guarantee the fall of South Korea. The cautious course in Washington would have led to the conclusion that Korea was not essential for the defense of Japan, and that the clash in Korea was merely a civil war which was of no real concern to either the UN or the United States.

HISTORY DOESN'T REPEAT ITSELF

Truman rushes UN to the rescue.
Low in the *London Daily Herald*, 1950. By special permission.

But Truman again took a resolute stand. As commander-in-chief he issued the order on June 27, 1950—two days after the invasion began— for American air and naval forces to resist Communist aggression in Korea. At the same time, he ordered the navy to neutralize Formosa by preventing attacks from Formosa on China or from Communist China on Formosa—a step which Peiping claimed was a direct blow at itself. Later, on that fateful June 27, the Security Council formally called upon the members of the UN for military assistance. Three days later, when the stopgap American forces proved woefully inadequate, Truman ordered a substantial part of the unseasoned United States troops in Japan to go to Korea

Truman's courageous and decisive action *at the time* won reassuring applause from both the public and Congress, quite in contrast with the noisy condemnation when the going got rougher.[5] Weary of appeasement and barefaced Communist aggression, the American people were determined to draw the line somewhere—and that line happened to be the 38th parallel.

MILITARY SEESAW IN KOREA

The Korean conflict, though officially a United Nations action, was overwhelmingly an American responsibility. Only sixteen of the sixty member nations sent armed contingents, and all but one were tiny, partly

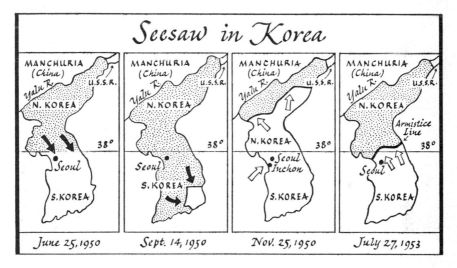

because of heavy commitments elsewhere. The United States furnished the great bulk of the air units, of the naval forces, of the supplies, and of the money—over $15 billion. Except for the Republic of [South] Korea, it provided most of the men. More than a million Americans served, of whom about 150,000 suffered casualties, including some 33,000 battle deaths. Under authority of the UN, President Truman appointed General Douglas MacArthur as commander of the international force.

The tide of battle at first went badly for the UN. The North Koreans, driving southward relentlessly, pinned the American and other UN troops to a small southeastern beachhead. Then suddenly, on September 15, 1950, General MacArthur turned and caught the Communists on the flank by an amphibious attack at Inchon. The trapped North Koreans

[5] Shortly after Truman's intervention Gallup found 81% favorable, 13% opposed, and 6% without opinion. Summary in Gallup Release, Jan. 21, 1951.

either surrendered or fled northward in panic toward the sanctuary of the 38th parallel, closely followed by their enemies.

Should the fleeing foe be pursued across the surveyor's line? There seemed little point in permitting the North Koreans to rally, regroup, and then attack again at their convenience. American opinion was strongly in favor of finishing the job, and the UN Assembly, in October, 1950, rather vaguely authorized the crossing by MacArthur, after the South Koreans had already crossed.[6] Ominously, the Chinese Premier, Chou En-lai, had earlier served a public warning that China would not "supinely" stand aside if North Korea was invaded. This threat was short-sightedly dismissed at the time as pure bluff.

But Peiping was not bluffing. Late in 1950, as the victorious Americans drove northward toward China's border, contingents of "Chinese volunteers" caught MacArthur's overextended lines on the flank and rear. The Americans and their associates were hurled southward across the 38th parallel, in a frostbitten, humiliating retreat. There, early in 1951, they finally regrouped forces and regained much lost ground.

The intervention of China, though unofficial, drastically altered the complexion of the conflict. Many Americans were convinced that World War III had already started. Certainly there could be no doubt as to the hostility of the Chinese, and General MacArthur was eager to improve his position by bombing their supply bases in Manchuria and by blockading their coasts. Washington resumed the sending of arms to the Nationalist Chinese in Formosa, while the House and Senate demanded a denunciation of Peiping as an aggressor. Early in February, 1951, and in the face of determined opposition by the Communist nations, the UN Assembly formally condemned Communist China, 44 to 7.

The stinging military defeat inflicted by the Chinese, far from arousing the American public, as might have been expected, had precisely the opposite effect. Republicans, in particular, branded the conflict "Mr. Truman's War." A majority of the American people believed that not only was intervention a mistake but that the United States ought to pull out of Korea.[7] A barrage of criticism was also directed at the feet-dragging UN allies, who allegedly were willing to fight to the "last American."

THE MacARTHUR REMOVAL

A disagreeable difference of opinion gradually developed between the deflated General MacArthur and the anxious Washington authorities,

---

[6] Gallup (Oct. 13, 1950) found 64% favorable, 27% opposed, and 9% without opinion. Gallup Release.

[7] Gallup found (Jan. 21, 1951) the vote for pulling out altogether 66% yes, 25% no, and 9% no opinion. *Ibid.*

military and civilian. Believing that "There is no substitute for victory," MacArthur was eager to strike effectively at his enemy by bombing what he called the Chinese "privileged sanctuary" in Manchuria, and by importing a part of Chiang's army from Formosa. But bombing Chinese soil was dangerous business. The Russians were bound by the terms of their 1950 alliance to come to the aid of China, and there was grave danger that a full-fledged conflict would erupt in the Far East.

The Truman administration tried to restrain the headstrong MacArthur, for it had no desire to pour American boys down the sinkhole of an all-out Asiatic war. But the outspoken general undertook, by various means, to shape over-all policy to his thinking, rather than act as the executor of over-all policy. His attitude was alarming to America's UN associates, especially the war-scarred British, as well as to Washington itself.

Truman's patience at length gave way. Determined to assert civilian control over the military and to uphold the principle that broad policy should be made in Washington, he summarily removed General Mac-Arthur from all his commands, on April 11, 1951. Even granting the correctness of Truman's views, his brutal treatment of a distinguished public servant was a blunder of the first water. The President might better have shown the General the door rather than kicking him out the fifth story window. Public opinion in America reacted hysterically in favor of the dethroned idol, who returned to receive a hero's welcome.[8]

The removal of MacArthur touched off a nation-wide "great debate" on foreign policy. The five-starred General made a dramatic speech before Congress, in which he urged that the Far East be viewed in global perspective. The truth is that he himself had twisted the picture somewhat out of focus. Members of the UN, notably Britain, were vehemently opposed to starting World War III, but many American "go-it-aloners," principally old-line Republican isolationists, favored defying the UN. The danger of fighting without allies impressed itself on the Truman administration, which had "the courage to be timid." General Bradley, of the Joint Chiefs of Staff, testified before a Senate committee that a full-dress conflict with China would be "the wrong war, at the wrong place, at the wrong time, and with the wrong enemy."[9] Public anger over the MacArthur removal gradually cooled, and the aging general was allowed, as he put it, to "fade away."

THE KOREAN TRUCE TALKATHON

A ray of hope shot through the war-cursed world on June 23, 1951, when the Russian delegate to the UN proposed discussion of a cease fire

[8] Gallup (May 16, 1951) found 66% favoring MacArthur, 25% Truman, and 9% without opinion. *Ibid.*

[9] On the issue of an all-out war in the Far East, Gallup found (Feb. 28, 1951) 77% opposed, 14% for, and 9% without opinion. *Ibid.*

and an armistice. He was obviously speaking for the Chinese and North Korean Communists, who had suffered bloody losses in matching man-power against firepower in "human wave" attacks. Peiping endorsed the "cease-fire" suggestion, but stipulated that all foreign troops must evacu-ate Korea—a proposal that would leave South Korea again at the mercy of the aggressor. American opinion not only favored a truce but an end to what Senator Taft branded an "utterly useless war."

Truce negotiations opened on July 10, 1951, at a neutralized site near the 38th parallel, and continued intermittently for over two years. Heavy fighting erupted sporadically, and the peace talks were repeatedly broken off by the UN spokesmen after incredible Communist delays. The sus-picion prevailed that the Communists were using a verbal smoke screen to strengthen their badly mauled divisions.

The sickening truce stalemate in Korea would have seemed farcical had it not been so tragic. Some progress was made in November, 1951, when the negotiators tentatively agreed that the cease-fire front between North and South Korea should be drawn where the shooting stopped. But the United States steadfastly refused to withdraw all UN troops from South Korea. The Communists meanwhile undertook to make anti-American propaganda by fomenting bloody riots in UN prison camps, and by trumped-up charges that the United States was using murderous germ warfare ("microbe killers").

Prisoners of war captured by the UN forces now proved to be the most serious stumbling block. The Communists, who insisted on a return of these captives, increased their demands when they learned that about 85,000 of 170,000 prisoners were refusing to go back to Red tyranny. Many Communist soldiers had surrendered on the strength of promised protection, and the UN could not honorably go back on these assur-ances by returning the prisoners. The Communists, not to lose face, were determined to have their vassals back. The deadlocked Korean issue was now tossed into the whirlpool of the Presidential campaign of 1952.

THE PRO-EISENHOWER UPHEAVAL

Long before convention time, a tremendous "We-Like-Ike" ground swell had developed for General Dwight D. ("Ike") Eisenhower as the Republican Presidential standard-bearer. The genial General, a rank amateur in politics, was nominated at Chicago after a close and bitter struggle with Senator Taft of Ohio. Eisenhower, with wide experience abroad, represented the internationalist wing of his party. Taft repre-sented the isolationist or "dinosaur wing," which, Democratic critics charged, was attempting "to repeal the 20th Century." The Republican platform assailed the Democrats for having lost China to the Com-munists, for having "plunged us into war in Korea without the consent of our citizens through their authorized representatives in the Congress," and for fighting "without will to victory."

The Republicans, sharply challenging the Democratic nominee Adlai Stevenson, undertook a crusade against Democratic "plunder at home and blunder abroad." Eisenhower, who was famed as a conciliator, first made his peace with isolationist Senator Taft in what the Democrats dubbed a "Munich" surrender. This obvious attempt to appease the isolationist wing of the party led to the quip that Taft had "lost the nomination but won the nominee." Eisenhower hit hard at corruption and "Communist coddling" in Washington, and won enthusiastic acclaim by promising to go to Korea in person in an effort to bring the fighting-talking deadlock to an end. Democrats retorted with the cry, "grandstand play," and declared that the place to end the war was in Moscow, not in Korea.

Foreign affairs figured to an unusual degree in the campaign and probably proved decisive. The American people, never noted for patience and long accustomed to quick successes, were in an ugly mood. Three "C's" relating to foreign affairs carried much weight—Corea (old spelling), loss of China, and Communist "coddling." In addition, there were the three "C's" involving domestic affairs—corruption, cost of living, and need for a change. Korea, with its bloody and frustrating futility, was a dead horse tied to the necks of the Democrats. The voters by a wide margin believed that the experienced, five-starred Eisenhower could solve this Far Eastern puzzle better than the less colorful, less famed Stevenson.[10]

The glamorous General won in a landslide. The outcome was largely a vote of confidence in him and his radiant personality, for he not only ran far ahead of his ticket but cracked the Solid South wide open. The Republicans won control of Congress by only a paper-thin margin. For the most conspicuous time in American history, the party in power was evicted in the midst of piping prosperity. The voters freely admitted that the Democratic party had done more for their economic welfare than the Republicans, but they voted against their pocketbooks. Such was the personality of "Ike," anger over "the mess in Washington," and resentment against the "mass-murder trap" in Korea.[11]

CEASE-FIRE IN KOREA

The Eisenhower administration started with an encouraging display of energy. A prominent Wall Street lawyer, John Foster Dulles, became Secretary of State. He was already an experienced diplomat, and had

---

[10] Gallup on this point (Nov. 6, 1952) recorded the respondents 67% for Eisenhower, 9% for Stevenson, and 24% noting no difference. *Ibid.*

[11] Postelection Gallup polls (Jan. 21, 1953) showed that the two most important issues helping Eisenhower were corruption and Korea. *Ibid.*

played a stellar role in negotiating the Japanese peace treaty. On February 2, 1953, Eisenhower announced, with considerable fanfare, that the United States Far Eastern fleet was to end the neutralization of Formosa, thereby unleashing Chiang for attacks on the Chinese mainland. Actually, such hit-and-run raids had been going on for some time.

The truth is that the new administration made no sharp break in foreign policy with the old. Despite bold talk about "liberation not containment" and "seizing the offensive" in the cold war, Washington was soon back on the well-worn path of "containment." Eisenhower, himself internationalist-minded, encountered noisy opposition from the Taft-Bricker isolationist group. His most pressing problem was to get the two wings of the party—internationalist and nationalist—to flap together. On foreign aid and other kindred problems the Democrats, steeped in the Roosevelt-Truman tradition, supported Eisenhower's foreign policy more faithfully than many of his own nominal followers. Economy-minded Republicans engineered heavy reductions in Eisenhower's recommended foreign-aid program. The President was so deeply disturbed that he actually gave serious thought to founding a new political party.[12]

Progress, though halting, was meanwhile snailing forward on the blood-soaked Korean peace front. Eisenhower made his promised visit to Korea in December, 1952—a three-day stay—but many months dragged by before the deadlock was broken. The Communists reluctantly agreed to permit a neutral commission to handle the UN-held prisoners who did not want to go home. But President Syngman Rhee, the gnarled and stubborn old leader of South Korea, violently opposed any terms that would leave his country divided, and in a one-man "Rhee-bellion" threatened to go-it-alone. With the evident intent of disrupting the peace negotiations, he suddenly freed 27,000 North Korean anti-Communist prisoners of war, in June, 1953, in flagrant defiance of the UN. The Communists were clearly eager to call off the fighting, for otherwise they would have broken off negotiations following Rhee's incendiary tactics.[13] At length the doughty Korean president grudgingly consented to terms, but only after receiving assurances of economic and military support from Washington. The United States was evidently going to have its hands full in restraining him from attempting to unite all Korea by force of arms.

The Korean armistice was finally concluded on July 27, 1953, after three years of fighting, including two of truce-talking. It provided for a cease-fire on existing battle lines, a processing of prisoners, and a political conference to arrange for an evacuation of troops and a peaceful settlement of the whole Korean question. Amid UN charges of tortures,

[12] R. J. Donovan, *Eisenhower: The Inside Story* (New York, 1956), pp. 151–153.
[13] For the undocumented story that Secretary Dulles and Eisenhower forced a truce settlement by their clear determination to fight through to victory, even with atomic bombs, see J. R. Beal, *John Foster Dulles* (New York, 1957), pp. 181–84.

atrocities, and illegally withheld prisoners, a neutral commission arranged to send back to communism those UN captives who wanted to return. The others were released after being harangued, on the whole unsuccessfully, by Communist interrogators under neutral supervision.

The fears of the South Koreans were to some extent quieted by a mutual security pact with the United States. Signed October 1, 1953, it passed the Senate on January 26, 1954, by a vote of 81 to 6. Each nation bound itself to consult with the other in the face of threatened attack, and "to meet a common danger in accordance with its constitutional processes." This commitment to intervene was carefully worded so as to be more moral than legal.

CASTING KOREAN ACCOUNTS

The truce was but an uneasy truce—not a peace treaty. Although the fighting had stopped, the riddle of a divided Korea's political future remained unsolved. The end of the shooting was accepted in the United States with a weary sigh of relief; there was no dancing in the streets.[14] Neither side, as in the War of 1812, was able to impose its will on the other, and the cease-fire was proof of a military stalemate rather than a satisfying victory.

Yet the U.S.-UN intervention in Korea was a move of incalculable significance. No one could charge that the new international organization had died in the rice paddies of Korea because the United States had failed to shoulder its responsibilities. For the first time in history a multipower international organization had intervened effectively with a large-scale force. For the first time in the cold war the Communists had been stopped dead in their tracks. They had not only suffered enormous casualties, but had wound up with 1500 square miles less territory than when they had started. Would-be aggressors could take notice.

The UN, located since 1951 in its magnificent glass-brick home in New York City, emerged from the Korean crisis with enhanced prestige. But its laurels would have been brighter if it had not forced Uncle Sam to carry the lion's share of the burden, and if it had been able to win a decisive military triumph.

Communist China, ominously, emerged from the fighting as a new and potent force in the world balance of power. With a formidable air armada and a huge army trained in modern tactics, she was in a position to throw her might elsewhere in eastern Asia. But her intervention in Korea bolstered American determination not to recognize her, or to allow her to "shoot her way" into the United Nations as a replacement for the exiled Formosa regime. To do so—at least until she had shown convincing

---

[14] Gallup noted responses in May to the truce as 84% favorable, 12% unfavorable, and 4% without opinion (July 31, 1953). Gallup Release.

signs of good faith—seemed like a betrayal of the UN and of the American boys who had shed their blood in Korea under its flag. Most Americans dismissed as wishful thinking the arguments by British and others that the UN welcome mat would insure Peiping's good behavior.

"NEW LOOK" DIPLOMACY

Once the Korean deadlock was broken, the Eisenhower administration could move with greater vigor on other fronts. Substantial cutbacks were achieved in conventional war appropriations by a "new look" at defense. The avowed intention was to concentrate on "instant" and "massive" retaliation, presumably with nuclear weapons, against aggression by Communist foes.

Eisenhower also endeavored, without conspicuous success, to revive the bipartisan ideal in foreign policy. For one thing, he was hampered by intraparty strife within his own Republican following. Senator Taft died of cancer in July, 1953, and a vacuum developed in the Senate leadership. Isolationist Senator Bricker openly challenged Eisenhower's treaty-making powers by sponsoring a proposed constitutional amendment. Among other restrictions, it required Congressional (including Senatorial) approval of Executive agreements. The swift-moving nature of the international crises called for more Presidential discretion rather than less, and the White House voiced determined opposition. The original Bricker amendment was at length rejected, and a watered-down substitute failed in the Senate, on February 26, 1954, by the margin of one vote.

A noteworthy achievement was the approval by Congress, in May, 1954, of the St. Lawrence seaway, "the Socialistic ditch" which had been in abeyance since first formally proposed in 1932.[15] The iron-ore reserves of the Lake Superior region had been deeply gouged during World War II, and the United States was recognizing the desirability of tapping the immense mineral resources of Labrador by a rail-and-water route to the Great Lakes. The Canadians, moreover, were threatening to build the seaway themselves if their neighbor continued to be unco-operative. Such considerations finally brought the public and Congress around to support the joint Canadian-American project.

Eisenhower's assertion of leadership showed itself spectacularly in connection with the nuclear arms race. In a dramatic speech before the UN General Assembly in New York, on December 8, 1953, the President proposed that the nations pool their fissionable materials for peaceful industrial purposes. The civilized world rejoiced at the atoms-for-peace

---

[15] Gallup (April 16, 1954) found informed voters favoring joint participation 11 to 1. Gallup Release. The vote in the House was 241 to 158 (May 6), and that in the Senate was a voice vote (May 7).

plan; and although the usual sour note was at first sounded by the Kremlin, the United States and its allies proceeded to put the scheme into effect on a limited scale. Four years later the Senate approved a treaty authorizing the plan on a global basis.[16]

Relations between the United States and India, now fast emerging as a power in Asia, were meanwhile being subjected to severe strains. This teeming nation of some 350,000,000 people, though vulnerable to communism, was seeking under Prime Minister Nehru to maintain a "neutralist" stand—"Nehrutrality"—between East and West. The position of India was complicated by a bitter territorial dispute with neighboring Pakistan, a nation of 75,000,000 souls basically anti-Communist.

In May, 1954, in the face of indignant protests from India, Washington agreed to supply Pakistan with arms under a mutual defense pact. The United States intended that these weapons should be used to stem communism; the Indians suspected that they would be turned by rival Pakistan against themselves. Despite clear-cut assurances from Washington, American prestige in India sank to a new low point. Millions of hungry and depressed Indians had long been disturbed by what they regarded as the indifference, lack of sympathy, and racial prejudice of the Americans. Washington's arming of Pakistan confirmed their worst fears.

COMMUNISM IN THE CARIBBEAN

The shadow of the Soviet hammer and sickle had meanwhile been falling on Uncle Sam's own back yard. Communist movements of considerable vigor existed in many of the Latin-American countries, which were not so much worried as Washington by the menace of Moscow. As between Soviet communism and Yankee interventionism, a host of Latin Americans found Soviet communism less alarming. Good Neighborism had also been deteriorating since the lavish hand-out days of World War II, and especially as a result of Washington's slighting of Latin America in postwar loans and subsidies. Some Latin Americans were in fact pleased by the prospect of having the Yankee Colossus of the North taken down a peg by the Soviet Colossus of the East.

By 1954 a Red danger spot had developed in the Central American Republic of Guatemala, within easy bombing range of the Panama Canal. A Communist-tinged government had won control of this backward banana land, and in 1953 had seized the holdings of the powerful United Fruit Company. Washington protested against the inadequate compensation to the giant corporation, but Guatemala registered defiance.

Against this Reddish background, the tenth Inter-American Conference gathered at Caracas, Venezuela, in March, 1954. An undercurrent of hostility against the United States was prevalent, and the delegates over-

[16] See p. 846.

looked few opportunities to twist Uncle Sam's coattails. Under strong pressure from Washington, the Conference approved a resolution, with a lone dissent from Communist-tainted Guatemala, branding as a "threat" Communist infiltration of the Americas.

The crisis in Guatemala rapidly came to a head. In May, 1954, a large cargo of arms for the Guatemalan army slipped in from behind the Iron Curtain by way of Poland. Secretary of State Dulles publicly branded the attempt of Moscow to infiltrate this hemisphere as a violation of the Monroe Doctrine, and the United States began to airlift munitions to Guatemala's neighbors. Anxieties in Washington eased, in June, 1954,

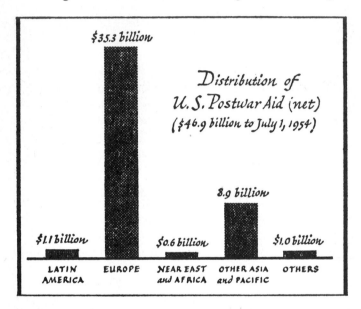

Distribution of
U. S. Postwar Aid (net)
($46.9 billion to July 1, 1954)

| LATIN AMERICA | EUROPE | NEAR EAST and AFRICA | OTHER ASIA and PACIFIC | OTHERS |
| $1.1 billion | $35.3 billion | $0.6 billion | $8.9 billion | $1.0 billion |

when an army of Guatemalan exiles invaded their native land and speedily overthrew the Red-infiltrated regime. But the United States did not escape unscathed. Communist agitators in Latin America blamed the Yankees for backing the rebels, and in Chile irate students burned effigies of President Eisenhower.[17]

The Guatemalan revolution was a clear-cut victory for the United States and for hemispheric solidarity. For the first time since the outbreak of the Cold War a Communist government had been overthrown by its own people, albeit with foreign aid. Yet the wretched conditions still continued that had caused Red doctrines to take root in Guatemala and elsewhere in Latin America. Uncle Sam would do well to look south of the Rio Grande, and help promote land redistribution and other desired

[17] For the episode, see P. B. Taylor, Jr., "The Guatemalan Affair: A Critique of United States Foreign Policy," *Amer. Pol. Sci. Rev.*, L (1956), 787–806; U.S. Dept. of State, *A Case History of Communist Penetration: Guatemala* (Washington, 1957).

reforms, especially those relating to a spread of national income. Otherwise the menace of communism in the Americas was bound to become more acute.

CRISIS IN INDO-CHINA

Following the uneasy Korean truce, Communist pressure shifted to Indo-China. There the Communist Viet Minh rebels, increasingly aided by Communist China, had been fighting the French-led Viet Nam loyalists since late 1946.

The Post-Geneva Far East

French Indo-China was of crucial importance to the Western World, both economically and strategically. Fertile and well-watered, it was often referred to as "Asia's rice bowl." If the Communists triumphed, the United States feared that all the states of Southeast Asia would collapse like a row of falling dominoes. Washington, at the risk of appearing to bolster colonialism, contributed about $3 billion in military aid to help the hard-pressed French. The American people were generally favorable to this support, but, with the Korean slaughter-pen still fresh in mind, they vigorously opposed sending in troops.[18]

A nineteen-nation conference finally assembled at Geneva, in April, 1954, to discuss the fate of both Korea and Indo-China. Sixteen countries that had fought for the UN in Korea sent delegations, as did the U.S.S.R., North Korea, and Communist China. The Communist negotiators held the high cards. The tide of battle in Indo-China was running their way at Dienbienphu, and the longer they delayed the stronger their position became. At one juncture certain top officials in Washington evidently favored sending in carrier-based planes loaded with lethal bombs to help the French, provided that the French and British would co-operate fully.[19] But the British, now in a mood for appeasement, were unwilling to take effective joint action until negotiations at Geneva had broken down or otherwise terminated.

The French, without the backing of allies, had little choice. They were desperately eager to end the blood-draining war, now seven-and-one-half-years old, on any terms that would preserve a semblance of honor. An agreement was finally secured among the nine powers most directly involved. On July 21, 1954, the Communists agreed to a "provisional military demarcation line" along the 17th parallel, retaining northern Viet Nam, with 13,000,000 people, and leaving the fate of South Viet Nam, with 10,000,000 people, to a general election in 1956 (never held).

Geneva was another signal victory for communism; another grievous setback for the West in the cold war. Although greeted with weary satisfaction in France and Britain, the settlement was condemned by many American "Asia-firsters" as a "Far Eastern Munich." Washington, loath to endorse any of these arrangements, acquiesced without approving. About the best that could be said was that the shooting had stopped—at least temporarily. But the Communists were left free to strike, either directly or through infiltration, at a time of their own choosing. The trap was thus set for America's fateful involvement.

SEATO—AN ASIATIC NATO

The crumbling of Western defenses in the Far East prompted the United States to form a South East Asia Treaty Organization (SEATO) to parallel the European North Atlantic Treaty Organization (NATO). Delegates from eight interested nations met at steaming Manila in September, 1954—the United States, Britain, France, Australia, New Zealand, the Philippines, Thailand, and Pakistan. Four "neutralist" states—India,

---

[18] Among informed respondents, Gallup discovered (June 5, 1953) that 56% favored sending arms, 28% opposed, and 16% were without opinion. There was ten to one opposition to ground troops (Sept. 18, 1953). Gallup Releases.

[19] See Donovan, *Eisenhower*, p. 266; Beal, *John Foster Dulles*, pp. 206–212.

Indonesia, Burma, and Ceylon—cast a wet blanket on the proceedings by refusing to become involved in the open struggle against communism.

The discussions at Manila were hastened by signs that the Chinese Communists were about to launch their long-threatened invasion of Formosa. After only three days of formal deliberation the delegates, on September 8, 1954, signed a noteworthy defense pact. The treaty bound the signatories, in the event of aggression or subversion (presumably Communist), to "consult immediately" for defense measures in accordance with each nation's "constitutional processes." The delegates also signed a Pacific Charter, which pledged their nations to promote self-government as an answer to Communist charges of colonialism.

The SEATO pact was obviously not a hard-and-fast military alliance, like NATO, but a rather vague consultative pact with some moral commitment. Yet it was the best that could be hoped for, and as a foundation stone it was better than nothing. It was supplemented some three months later by the conclusion of a mutual defense treaty between the United States and the Chinese Nationalist regime on Formosa. The West, although clearly on the defensive, was not going to allow the East to go by default.

SELECTED BIBLIOGRAPHY

Annual surveys are provided by the Council on Foreign Relations in volumes entitled *The United States in World Affairs*, and by the Brookings Institution, in *Major Problems of United States Foreign Policy*. Of great value are the *Memoirs by Harry S. Truman* (Garden City, N.Y., 1956), II (*Years of Trial and Hope*). Intimate glimpses are provided in R. J. Donovan, *Eisenhower: The Inside Story* (New York, 1956), and in J. R. Beal, *John Foster Dulles* (New York, 1957). A timely analysis is N. A. Graebner, *The New Isolationism* (New York, 1956). Much of the literature is ephemeral, but note Senator R. A. Taft's isolationist *A Foreign Policy for Americans* (Garden City, N.Y., 1951); Chester Bowles' *Ambassador's Report* [India] (New York, 1954), J. J. McCloy, *The Challenge to American Foreign Policy* (Cambridge, Mass., 1953); and G. F. Kennan, *Realities of American Foreign Policy* (Princeton, 1954). A critical treatment of MacArthur is R. H. Rovere and A. M. Schlesinger, Jr., *The General and the President* (New York, 1951); uncritical is C. A. Willoughby and J. Chamberlain, *MacArthur, 1941–1951* (New York, 1954). See also John Norman, "MacArthur's Blockade Proposals against Red China," *Pacific Hist. Rev.*, XXVI (1957), 161–174. Illuminating is L. M. Goodrich, *Korea; A Study of United States Policy in the United Nations* (New York, 1956). See footnotes of this chapter and the *Harvard Guide*, Ch. 30.

7TH, 8TH, AND 9TH ED. REFS. See BIBLIOGRAPHICAL ADDENDUM, p. 1,057.

World Tensions and the Middle East Crisis

We have shown . . . our dedication to the principle that force shall not be used internationally for any aggressive purpose and that the integrity and independence of the nations of the Middle East should be inviolate.

PRESIDENT EISENHOWER, 1957

THE FAR EASTERN TINDERBOX

THE NATIONALIST CHINESE island of Formosa, against which the Chinese Communists were evidently preparing for an all-out assault late in 1954, threatened to mousetrap the United States in another Korean War. Unless Washington announced in advance its determination to fight, President Eisenhower might be confronted with Truman's painful dilemma of either acting without the authorization of Congress or acting too late. Better yet, a stern warning might ward off the impending attack altogether.

The upshot was the unprecedented Formosa Resolution, which Eisenhower formally requested of Congress on January 24, 1955. After only four days of debate, the legislators handed him a signed blank check. Declaring that a friendly regime on Formosa was essential for the defense of the United States, the joint resolution went on to say:

> That the President of the United States be and he hereby is authorized to employ the Armed Forces of the United States as he deems necessary for the specific purpose of securing and protecting Formosa and the Pescadores against armed attack, this authority to include the securing and protection of such related positions and territories of that area now in friendly hands. . . .[1]

[1] *U.S. Statutes at Large*, LIX, 7 (resolution signed Jan. 29, 1955). The resolution purposely left vague the question of defending the nearby islands of Quemoy and Matsu, which were held by the Nationalists. See J. R. Beal, *John Foster Dulles: A Biography* (New York, 1957), pp. 220–221.

The Formosa Resolution received overwhelming support from both public opinion and Congress. The vote was 410 to 3 in the House and 85 to 3 in the Senate. The objection was feebly voiced that the President, as commander-in-chief, already had the authority to employ the armed forces, and Senator Morse of Oregon complained that "Eisenhower is passing the buck." Actually, the Formosa Resolution both weakened and strengthened the hand of the Executive in foreign affairs. It narrowed his freedom of action by establishing the precedent of seeking Congressional approval in advance; it strengthened his position by forestalling the possibility of Congressional criticism.

The warning signal known as the Formosa Resolution evidently had a sobering effect on the Chinese Communists. In succeeding months the atmosphere gradually improved, notably when the Peiping government agreed to release certain Americans long held prisoners. But American public opinion remained steadfast in its determination not to recognize the Communist regime or admit it to the UN.[2] Washington adamantly continued its embargo on commerce with Communist China, although the trade-hungry British and other ex-allies of the Korean War stirred up much criticism when they relaxed their restrictions in 1957.

The survival of South Viet Nam proved to be one of the few pleasant surprises in the Far East. Seemingly doomed to fall like a ripe pear to Communist infiltrators from North Viet Nam, this lush tropical land raised up a resolute leader in the person of Ngo Dinh Diem. Aided by a generous outpouring of American dollars, he grappled so effectively with the chaotic problems as to inspire new hope that he might yet fend off the bamboo curtain of communism that was feared at Geneva in 1954 (p. 832).

THE SOVIET SMILING OFFENSIVE

A change in Soviet leadership after the resignation of Premier Malenkov in February, 1955, brought a sharp shift in tactics. The new premier was the grandfatherly and white-goateed N. A. Bulganin, at whose elbow stood N. S. Khrushchev, the burly and indiscreetly outspoken First Secretary of the Communist Party. The chill blasts from the Kremlin had failed to induce the Western World to discard its defensive wraps; perhaps the bright sunshine of Soviet smiles would prove more persuasive. The coos of peaceful co-existence now replaced the raucous cries of world revolution. One happy result of the new policy was a lifting of the Iron Curtain to a limited number of American tourists, and a welcoming by the United States of visiting Soviet delegations of agriculturalists and journalists.

Bulganin and Khrushchev proved to be sensationally successful as

[2] In July, 1956 public opinion on Peiping's admittance to the UN was 74% against, 11% for, and 15% without views. Gallup Release, Feb. 22, 1957.

globe-trotting salesmen for peace. They ventured into such faraway lands as India and Burma, where they were enthusiastically acclaimed by immense crowds. They were lavish with their promises of economic aid, and this disconcerting new development in the Cold War was a recognition of the fact that American assistance to backward countries had proved effective. But the American taxpayers, who had supported the expenditure of millions of dollars in India, were shocked by the enthusiasm with which the masses there greeted vague Soviet assurances. Evidently an ounce of Soviet promise, when wrapped in brightly colored anticolonial propaganda, was worth more than a pound of American performance.

Pressures had meanwhile been mounting for a meeting "at the summit" of the heads of the Big Four: President Eisenhower, Premier Bulganin, Prime Minister Eden of Britain, and Premier Faure of France. American public opinion was strongly in favor of this oft-proposed conference.[3] But President Eisenhower, remembering the pitfalls laid for his predecessors at Yalta and Potsdam, was slow in warming to the idea. The prospects became more favorable in 1955, when the Soviets finally agreed to end their ten-year military occupation of Austria. The Big-Four powers thereupon signed a treaty restoring sovereignty to that tiny nation, and later in the year they pledged themselves to recognize its perpetual neutrality. With the Austrian log-jam thus broken, final arrangements were facilitated for the Big-Four conference, and on July 18, 1955, the conferees began their week of labor by the quiet Swiss waters of Lake Geneva.

The Geneva "Summit Conference" turned out to be a personal triumph for President Eisenhower. Radiating friendliness and warmth, he evidently made headway in convincing the Soviet leaders of America's sincere desire for peace. He electrified the conference, and disturbed the secretive Soviets, by his open-skies inspection proposal. He had in mind that the Russians and the Americans should exchange blueprints of military establishments and permit mutual aerial inspection so as to quiet fears that one side was secretly building against the other.[4] The eversuspicious Soviets, as might have been predicted, scowled upon the scheme: Khrushchev later said that it was like peeping into one's bedroom after the curtains were drawn. But the West did score an important point in the propaganda game, while planting seeds that might one day yield a harvest.

The Geneva Summit Conference, like many another windswept peak, on the whole presented a barren aspect. No progress was made in grappling with prickly problems like the unification of Germany. The only real agreement was on a conference of the Big-Four Foreign Ministers (the "Little Four"), which met in Geneva in October, 1955, and

---

[3] Gallup found 8 out of 10 respondents favoring the Geneva Summit Conference. *Ibid.*, July 17, 1955.

[4] See R. J. Donovan, *Eisenhower: The Inside Story* (New York, 1956), p. 344.

finally broke up in complete deadlock. But the delusively friendly "Spirit of Geneva" spread abroad, and the world breathed easier. The grinning Eisenhower was photographed with the smiling Bulganin, and the Russians cleverly made use of this picture among their enchained satellites to support their claim that the United States was finally embracing peaceful co-existence.

HUNGARIAN HORRORS

A confusing new twist of Soviet policy came in February, 1956, when Khrushchev assailed Stalin in a secret speech before a Communist Party Congress in Moscow. Even a donkey can kick a dead lion, and Khrushchev denounced his former chief as a ruthless and bloody bungler. The resulting desanctification of Stalin resulted in a sudden shift in the party line abroad, where the departed dictator had long been extolled as a demigod. Cruel disillusionment disrupted the ranks of Communists in other countries, including the United States. Many of the faithful angrily tore up their party-membership cards.

A more conciliatory Soviet foreign policy temporarily followed the de-haloing of Stalin. After earlier overtures the Russian leaders came crawling to Tito, whom they had long denounced as a "fascist hireling," and signed a pact in June, 1956, proclaiming that there were "differing roads to socialism." Much soul-searching followed in Washington, where the policy of sending arms to Tito again came under sharper scrutiny.

In the wake of de-Stalinization bloody riots broke out in Poznan, Poland, in June, 1956, among workers who were protesting against Communist-imposed conditions. The Poles finally gained some semblance of autonomy in October, 1956, when they managed to elect their own Communist Party chief in defiance of strong pressures from Moscow.

Anti-Stalinist demonstrations in Hungary, in October, 1956, quickly flared into a large-scale revolt among a people whose passion for liberty was traditional. Carried away by the heady champagne of freedom, the Hungarians boldly renounced the Warsaw military pact, which bound them to the Soviet Union. This was going too far for the Russian leaders. Treacherously massing a formidable array of tanks near Budapest, they slaughtered hundreds of the rebels and installed a puppet regime subservient to Moscow.

The American people were stirred to their depths by the Hungarian uprising, as they had been in 1849, when the Russian Cossacks had crushed Kossuth. Washington temporarily lifted immigration bars to permit many thousands of Hungarian refugees to reach America, although by no means all those who wanted to come. An outpouring of American medical supplies and other relief likewise flowed from generous hearts. But in response to frantic appeals for armed intervention, the

United States could do nothing effective, except perhaps to threaten Moscow with atomic warfare—and that might touch off World War III. Cruel though the conclusion was, the policy makers in Washington deemed it better that a rebellion should die rather than a world should perish.

Both the United States and the United Nations lost face. The repeated resolutions of the General Assembly, which called on the butchers of

"I'LL BE GLAD TO RESTORE PEACE TO THE MIDDLE EAST, TOO"

Herblock in the *Washington Post*, 1956

Budapest to withdraw and to permit UN investigators to enter Hungary, were ignored by Moscow. The conclusion was confirmed that when one of the great powers chose to defy the UN, it could do so with impunity. The United States was blamed by embittered Hungarians for having encouraged them to rise through its widely heralded policy of "liberation," and then leaving them in the lurch. Desperate people often read more into such appeals than is intended, and American radio programs beamed to Hungary were rather unfairly condemned, both by Hungarians and Russians, for having touched off the revolt.

The Russians lost even more face. The blood of Budapest did not wash off easily. More Communists abroad tore up their party cards, and even "neutralist" states like India were moved to protest against the brutality of the Soviets. Tito temporarily parted company again with Moscow after his honeymoon with Bulganin and Khrushchev. The Russians were disturbed by the unreliability of their own troops, by the defection of satellite troops, and by the failure of Communist indoctrination to "take" among the people of Hungary, especially the youth. The exhibition of Hungarian heroism and Russian brutality won a great propaganda victory for the West. But bleeding Hungary still lay in chains, while the contemporaneous British-French-Israeli attack on Egypt weakened the moral position of the Western world.

THE MIDDLE EAST MUDDLE

The fear had existed since the end of World War II that the Soviets, none too rich in oil, would move into the Middle East, whose hot sands covered the greatest known oil pool. This critical area threatened to erupt

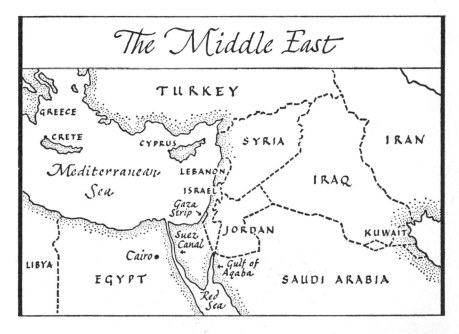

in 1951 when the Iranians, under their weeping Premier Mossadegh, nationalized the British oil refineries. If the British had resorted to strong-armed measures, as they were sorely tempted to do, the Russians probably would have invaded Iran in force, with calamitous consequences. Fortunately for peace, Mossadegh overplayed his hand, and following his internal overthrow, Washington used its good offices to achieve a peaceful settlement of the Anglo-Iranian controversy in 1954.

Yet the Middle Eastern dikes needed bolstering. The American policy of containment had given birth to NATO (North Atlantic Treaty Organization) and to SEATO (Southeast Asia Treaty Organization). A Middle Eastern Treaty Organization (METO) seemed desirable defensively, and in response to urgings from Washington the northern-tier states joined in the Baghdad Pact (1955): Turkey, Iraq, Iran, and Pakistan, with the added membership of Great Britain. The Soviet Union was now confronted with a solid block of territory, albeit poorly defended, all the way from the Mediterranean Sea to the gates of India. The United States, unwilling to get involved in the clashing ambitions of the Middle East nations, did not formally join the Baghdad Pact, although co-operating with several of its important committees.

The uneasy truce between Israel and her Arab neighbors, concluded in 1949, continued to worry Washington. The United States was reluctant to sell arms to either the Israeli or the Egyptians, because it hoped for a balance of power in which neither side would feel strong enough to attack the other. President Nasser of Egypt, after vainly seeking weapons from Washington, exploded a bombshell when he announced, on September 27, 1955, that he had arranged to exchange Egyptian cotton for munitions from Communist-dominated Czechoslovakia.

Cairo's cotton-for-arms deal definitely chilled American interest in the proposed high dam at Aswan, on the upper Nile. The construction of this giant project, whose cost was estimated at some $1.3 billion, would add about 25 per cent to the arable land of poverty-stricken Egypt. The United States, in harmony with its program of assistance for backward countries, had joined with the British in offering a grant of $70 million to initiate the enterprise. President Nasser, an energetic and strong-willed nationalist, delayed official acceptance and, to improve his bargaining position, hinted at better terms from the Soviet Union. He then compounded this offense by formally recognizing Communist China, to which the United States was still turning the cold shoulder.

CRISIS IN CAIRO

The rasping tactics of Nasser merely accelerated a mounting sentiment in the United States for pulling out of the dam project in Egypt. Tax-conscious citizens favored paring down foreign aid; surplus-cursed cotton growers in the South opposed taking tax dollars from their pockets to irrigate lands which would grow competing cotton; Jewish-Americans cried out against strengthening Egypt, the undying enemy of Israel. The mortgaging of Egyptian cotton for Communist arms, moreover, implanted grave doubts as to Egypt's ability to finance the high dam. Worst of all, the slippery Nasser seemed cast in the role of a blackmailer: if Washington did not lend him money, then he would turn to the Soviets, whose technicians would proceed to infiltrate Egypt and prepare for a Communist take-over. This kind of thing could become catching all over the world. America's friends would get little aid, while her enemies would blackmail her into bankruptcy.

Secretary Dulles, bending to all these pressures and acting in concert with London, flatly withdrew the dam offer, on July 19, 1956. This not unexpected jerking of the rug from under Nasser brought cheers from red-blooded Americans, even though the diplomatically prudent course would have been to protract negotiations until they died in the desert sands. As it was, Nasser was made a laughing stock before the entire world.

A week later Nasser, as probably preplanned, reacted by seizing the Suez Canal, which was then owned by foreign stockholders, chiefly French and British. He announced that he was going to use the surplus revenues to finance the high dam on the Nile. A case could be made out for his legal right to nationalize the canal, provided that the stockholders were properly recompensed, and provided that the waterway was kept open on equal terms to all shippers. But the British and French, seeing in Nasser a Middle Eastern Hitler who would hold a razor's edge against their economic jugular vein, were eager to seize the canal outright.

Secretary Dulles labored manfully to prevent a resort to force, which was expressly forbidden in such circumstances by the UN charter. Repeatedly dissuading the British and French from strong-arm measures, he proposed a Suez Canal Users' Association (SCUA) to negotiate terms with Nasser. But with the passage of time the unyielding Nasser seemed more firmly in control, and the British and French were increasingly angered by what seemed to them an attempt by Secretary Dulles to stab in the back the Suez Canal Users' Association which he had sponsored. Finally driven to desperation, the British and French surprised Washington and astounded the civilized world, on October 31, 1956, by launching an attack on the Suez area, following an Israeli thrust two days earlier.

THE PEOPLE STILL LIKE IKE

The flaming Suez crisis further complicated the Presidential campaign of 1956. The immensely popular but obviously ageing Eisenhower, now sixty-five years old, was again drafted by the Republicans, despite a recent heart attack followed by an emergency intestinal operation. "The world needs Eisenhower," proclaimed the Republicans, in referring to the confidence that his moral stature commanded abroad. They might have added that the party needed him, for it probably could not have won with any other candidate. The Democrats again nominated the polished ex-governor Adlai Stevenson, whom anti-intellectuals dubbed an "egghead."

Domestic difficulties eclipsed foreign issues in the early stages of the campaign. The Republicans pointed with pride to the balanced budget, the reduced taxes, the unprecedented prosperity, the Washington house-cleaning, and the era of blessed peace following Eisenhower's ending of the Korean War. The Democrats viewed with alarm the President's precarious health, the plight of the farmer, and favoritism toward Big Business. The general welfare, they charged, was being subordinated to General Motors.

Stevenson spectacularly shifted the spotlight to foreign affairs in the closing weeks of the campaign. With more candor than caution, he declared that serious study ought to be given to reducing the military draft. He also advocated a cessation of nuclear-bomb tests, lest they pollute the atmosphere permanently and jeopardize future generations. Republicans replied by jeering at Stevenson as a starry-eyed amateur. At a time when world tension was mounting, they insisted, the reduction of armed forces and the stopping of nuclear experiments would be supreme folly. General Eisenhower, the renowned military man and world leader, could be counted on to keep the nation's guard up.

The tragic Hungarian uprising, followed closely by the British-French-Israeli attack on Egypt, came most embarrassingly in the last ten days of the Presidential campaign. The Democrats made some political hay by condemning the administration for having permitted the crisis to develop, and then for having given assurances that it was being worked out peacefully. But on balance the Hungarian and Suez crises probably made votes for General Eisenhower. If World War III was just around the corner, a battle-seasoned commander was evidently needed in the White House.[5]

Eisenhower won in a landslide more overwhelming than that of 1952. It was a popularity contest, said one critic, not an election. But if the voters "liked Ike," they had much less affection for his party. Despite the exhilarating ride on his coattails, the Republicans fell short of winning a majority in either house of Congress—a failure without precedent in a Presidential triumph of these proportions.

FORSAKING ALLIES FOR THE UN

The election-eve explosion at Suez had been triggered by the Israeli, who, infuriated by repeated raids from Egyptian soil, launched an all-

[5] Dr. Gallup found, after the election, that the reason most often given for voting for Eisenhower was the belief that he could best handle the international crisis. Gallup Release, Nov. 28, 1956.

out attack on Egypt, beginning October 29, 1956. Two days later came the joint British and French assault on the Suez area. Whatever the avowed reasons for the attack, London and Paris were plainly determined to depose President Nasser and establish international control over the vital waterway.

The American people were profoundly shocked. The British and French, remembering Secretary Dulles' earlier opposition to armed intervention, had deliberately kept Washington in the dark so as to prevent last-minute interference. The timing of their attack was such as to suggest barefaced collusion with Israel, and the assault clearly weakened the moral stand of the free world against simultaneous Soviet aggression in Hungary. Many Americans assumed, whether correctly or not, that the NATO allies, Britain and France, had treacherously made their move so as to take advantage of the political paralysis produced by the Presidential campaign.

Washington stood at the crossroads. Seeking to patch up the ruptured NATO alliance, and ignoring the prohibition in the UN charter against force, it could back up its allies in this dangerous Egyptian venture. If it did so, it would reveal that it had one standard of conduct for its friends and another for its foes. The result would be an almost certain breakdown of the UN, and the costly sacrifices of American boys in Korea to salvage the UN would have been in vain.

President Eisenhower promptly chose morally high ground. He threw his full support behind the UN in an effort to bring about a cease-fire and the withdrawal of the Anglo-French-Israeli invaders from Egypt. The British and French naturally tied up the Security Council with their veto, but the Assembly took on a new importance as it provided a sounding board for outraged world opinion. The Soviet leaders openly talked of nuclear war against Britain and France, and threatened to pour Russian "volunteers" into Egypt. The British Commonwealth began to crack at the joints as certain members, notably Canada and India, gave signs of breaking away.

In the face of all these pressures, including resolutions by the UN Assembly, the Anglo-French-Israeli forces were pulled out. A special UN police force was sent to the Suez area to preserve order following the Allied withdrawals. The Israeli were most reluctant to yield the conquered territory, but they finally gave way in response to assurances from Washington that they would receive American diplomatic support for their claims against Egypt.

The United States salvaged more from the Suez crisis than had at first seemed possible. Its lofty stand for international morality won acclaim from the Arab nations and other victims of Western colonialism, while angering the frustrated British and French. The United States seemed to be keeping company with the Soviets and the Arabs, while opposing its

Western allies. The sabotaging of the canal by Nasser interrupted traffic for some five months, and the first impulse of the United States was to let the British and French lie in the oil-dry bed they had made for themselves. But the Americans, soon perceiving that the economic collapse of Western Europe would undo the work of the Marshall Plan, headed off catastrophe by supplying American oil. The UN, though unable to force the Russians out of Hungary, emerged with new laurels, and the successful precedent of a UN police force brought renewed hope for the future.

But the Middle East crisis was by no means solved. Nasser, though badly mauled, emerged with most of the high cards and in complete control of the canal. The French and British, forced to suspend their blow in mid-air, had betrayed their basic weakness to the entire world. A power vacuum had developed in the Middle East, and if the United States did not move in, the Soviet Union probably would.

THE EISENHOWER DOCTRINE

President Eisenhower's response to the Middle Eastern emergency took the form of a proposal, on January 5, 1957, that paralleled the Formosa Resolution. Again asking Congress for a signed blank check, he requested authority to provide American economic aid and armed support to any Communist-threatened nation in the Middle East that requested it.

American public opinion generally favored the so-called Eisenhower Doctrine, even though the *Chicago Tribune* branded it "a goofy design for foreign meddling." [6] But the response of Congress was less prompt and less enthusiastic than it had been at the time of the Formosa Resolution. There were complaints about cost, about goading the Soviets into war, and about trying "to pass the buck to Congress." But Communist aggression would probably result in American intervention, and with Korea ever fresh in mind, Congress perceived the wisdom of trying to head off such aggression by a ringing declaration of America's intention to act energetically.

After some two months of debate, the revised Eisenhower Doctrine received the stamp of Congressional approval in March, 1957. The vote in the Senate was 72 to 19; in the House, 350 to 60. The joint resolution authorized the President to use $200 million for economic-military aid to the Middle East, and the key clause read:

> Furthermore, the United States regards as vital to the national interest and world peace the preservation of the independence and integrity of the nations of the Middle East. To this end, if the President determines the

[6] Dr. Gallup (*ibid.*, Feb. 3, 1957) found the voters favoring economic aid in the ratio of 70% to 19%; sending war materials in the ratio of 53% to 34%; and dispatching troops in the ratio of 50% to 34%.

.necessity thereof, the United States is prepared to use armed forces to assist any such nation or group of such nations *requesting* assistance against armed aggression from any country controlled by international communism . . . [Italics inserted].[7]

The resolution as thus amended placed full responsibility on the President, and required the Middle Eastern nations specifically to request military assistance.

The Eisenhower Doctrine, though not directly invoked, was given an opportunity to show its teeth in the spring of 1957. An attempt by pro-Soviet schemers to overthrow the government of Jordan—a coup evidently plotted by Nasser of Egypt—narrowly missed success. At the height of the crisis Washington ostentatiously dispatched the powerful 6th fleet, including the mighty carrier *Forrestal,* to the eastern Mediterranean. Happily for the United States, King Hussein of Jordan showed unexpected firmness in riding out the storm, and accepted $10 million from Washington, without any commitment under the Eisenhower Doctrine.

The victory for the West in Jordan was soon offset by an alarming setback in Syria. A pro-Soviet military group vaulted into the saddle in August, 1957, and menaced the Middle East with the prospect of a strategic Communist beachhead. One alarming manifestation of the new shift was the heavy importation of Russian arms, to which the United States responded by airlifting weapons to Syria's neighbors. This spectacular countermove brought angry charges of warmongering from the Communist camp, bitter protests from Syria, and uneasiness among foreign observers who feared another explosion of the Middle Eastern powder keg.

The much-ballyhooed Eisenhower Doctrine was plainly a round plug in a square hole. Designed to check overt aggression, it was unable to cope with covert infiltration. Syria and Egypt denounced it, while other Middle Eastern nations were reluctant to beg for aid from a United States that was also aiding the hated Israeli.

AN UNCERTAIN FUTURE

The wounds inflicted on the North Atlantic Alliance by the Suez crisis gradually scarred over, and the United States joined the British and French in trying to induce Nasser to operate the canal on more liberal terms. Fears that the Alliance would break up were dispelled by the evident dependence of the British and French on American support. At the historic Bermuda conference between President Eisenhower and the British Prime Minister Macmillan, in March, 1957, the United States agreed to supply Great Britain with guided missiles. The dependence of the British on their American ally was thus increased in this quarter.

[7] Public Law 85-7; 85 Cong. H. J. Res. 117.

Such dependence lessened when, in the spring of 1957, the British unveiled their own hydrogen bombs in the Pacific testing grounds. America, Russia, and Britain now had the hydrogen bomb; the question was who would be fourth and fifth.

The peaceful uses of atomic energy temporarily regained the headlines in the late spring of 1957. The United States Senate, after warm debate and by a vote of 67 to 19, approved the Atoms-for-Peace Treaty on June 18, 1957. This scheme, which was an implementation of Eisenhower's atoms-for-peace proposal of 1953, provided for the sharing of fissionable materials by the great powers through the International Atomic Energy Agency. The 80-nation treaty had already been ratified by nine nations, including Soviet Russia.

Hopes for halting the feverish arms race brightened anew in the summer of 1957, as a subcommittee of the UN carried forward its deliberations in London. But the Soviets in the end applied the usual wet blanket. On August 26, 1957, eleven days before the wrangling ended in complete deadlock, Moscow announced the recent test-firing of the first successful intercontinental ballistic missile. Once the Soviets had an arsenal of such weapons, equipped with hydrogen-bomb warheads, they could bring into almost instant jeopardy every important urban and strategic center in the world.

The skeptics who pooh-poohed the ability of Russia to perfect a weapon on which American scientists were still laboring were soon rocked back on their heels. On October 4, 1957, without previous fanfare, the Soviets astounded the civilized world by launching into outer space the first man-made earth satellite. They thus scored a tremendous propaganda victory in the Cold War—a scientific Pearl Harbor. At one stroke they spectacularly demonstrated the advanced state of their science, the lagging efforts of the Americans, and the Soviet potential for wiping out all enemies and dominating the world. A month later, on November 3, Soviet scientists provided a new jolt when they put aloft a much heavier earth satellite which contained a live dog for experimental purposes.

While the Russians were thus impressing the "backward" nations, the United States was advertising from the housetops its prejudice against colored peoples when the school-integration crisis came to an angry boil at Little Rock, Arkansas. On September 24, 1957, President Eisenhower sent in federal bayonets to protect nine Negro children attending the Central High School. At a time of all times when national unity was imperative, the nation was being convulsed with internal disunity.

Some little ground was apparently retrieved at the first NATO "summit" conference, which assembled in Paris during December 1957. President Eisenhower, recovering from a mild stroke, turned on his famed charm in an heroic effort to achieve greater Allied unity. The result was a compromise. As a concession to the strong-hearted, the United States would supply intermediate-range missiles to NATO partners willing to accept them despite Soviet threats. As a concession to the faint-hearted, NATO would seek further negotiations with Russia on disarmament.

The future looked grim. The Soviets were scoring alarming gains in their economic warfare abroad and on the propaganda front. Their two earth satellites had shaken faith in the scientific superiority of the United States. The deterrent power of American arms had been gravely weakened, while the Russians were threatening to gain commanding supremacy. The United States would have to exert itself mightily, even at the cost of heavier taxes, red-ink financing, and higher defense outlays. The alternative would be the triumph of the Communist world revolution.

SELECTED BIBLIOGRAPHY

A useful analysis is presented in R. P. Stebbins, *The United States in World Affairs, 1956* (New York, 1957). See also N. A. Graebner, *The New Isolationism* (New York, 1956). Herbert Agar, *The Price of Power: America Since 1945* (Chicago, 1957) is a broad interpretation. Journalistic accounts are J. R. Beal, *John Foster Dulles: A Biography* (New York, 1957) and R. J. Donovan, *Eisenhower: The Inside Story* (New York, 1956). See also Chester Bowles, *Ambassador's Report* (New York, 1954) and A. E. Stevenson, *Call to Greatness* (New York, 1954). A capital account is H. A. Kissinger, *Nuclear Weapons and Foreign Policy* (New York, 1957).

7TH ED. REFS. D. F. Fleming, *The Cold War and Its Origins, 1917–1960* (2 vols., Garden City, N.Y., 1961) is detailed but marred by a pro-Soviet bias. D. J. Dallin, *Soviet Foreign Policy after Stalin* (Philadelphia, 1961) is better balanced. Richard Goold-Adams, *John Foster Dulles* (New York, 1962) is a sophisticated and surprisingly fair appraisal by a British journalist. Deane and David Heller, *John Foster Dulles: Soldier for Peace* (New York, 1960) is popularized, adulatory journalism. Roscoe Drummond and Gaston Coblentz, *Duel at the Brink* (Garden City, N.Y., 1960) is a balancing of pros and cons, on the whole favorable to Dulles but unfavorable to Eden, who had tried to block Dulles' appointment as Secretary of State. See also the highly critical sketch of Dulles by H. J. Morgenthau, in N. A. Graebner, ed., *An Uncertain Tradition* (New York, 1961). Sherman Adams, *First-Hand Report* (New York, 1961), by Eisenhower's loyal lieutenant, declares that the President was less willing to fight than Dulles during the recurrent crises and was fully consulted before any final decision, even though the Secretary had a remarkably free hand. Adams thinks that Eisenhower overestimated the seriousness of the Lebanon crisis in 1958. *The Memoirs of Anthony Eden: Full Circle* (Boston, 1960) present a labored, anti-Dulles apology for the Suez debacle; Eden claims (contrary to Sherman Adams) that he was not advised in advance of the withdrawal of the dam offer. He feels that the Suez intervention averted World War III, as did his refusal to go along with Dulles in Indo-China. Lionel Gelber, *America in Britain's Place* (New York, 1961) notes that Washington's opposition to force strengthened Nasser at the time of the Suez crisis, while the U.S. Sixth fleet in the Mediterranean openly interfered with the British and French joint operation. J. C. Campbell, *Defense of the Middle East* (New York, 1958) assesses the Suez Crisis and the Eisenhower Doctrine. For further 7TH ED. REFS., as well as 8TH AND 9TH ED. REFS., see BIBLIOGRAPHICAL ADDENDUM, p. 1,059.

54

The End of the Eisenhower Era

> *We face a hostile ideology—global in scope, atheistic in character, ruthless in purpose, and insidious in method.*
>
> PRESIDENT EISENHOWER
> Farewell Address
> January 17, 1961

NUCLEAR NIGHTMARES

THE SHOCK of the first Soviet earth satellite (Sputnik), launched late in 1957, spurred the United States into frantic efforts to regain lost prestige. After a series of humiliating fizzles, American scientists succeeded in orbiting a succession of space vehicles. These were generally smaller in size but larger in number and more significant in their scientific contribution than those of the USSR. But the Russians, who had concentrated on mightier booster power, scored another impressive "first," on April 12, 1961, when they spun a man around the earth and brought him back alive. Not until nearly a year later could the Americans duplicate this dazzling feat.

The fantastic race into space was intimately connected with both diplomacy and defense. Spectacular achievements in the heavens were bound to impress the uncommitted one-third of the world, and perhaps convince it that the overnight road from oxcarts to rocket ships lay through communism. As for defense, technological advances meant bigger and better intercontinental missiles, and the possible domination of the world through the domination of outer space.

As the 1950's lengthened, the Dulles-Eisenhower doctrine of deterring the Soviets by the threat of nuclear "massive retaliation" came under increasing fire. It had the merit of being relatively cheap; and the budget-balancing Eisenhower regime was bent on getting "more bang for the buck." But in the absence of strong "conventional forces," the alternatives in a diplomatic showdown were either a backdown or a blowup. Washington's global strategy was based on the assumption that the United States would never be the first to fire a nuclear salvo. After losing 100 million or so of its own people, it would have enough bombs and missiles left to retaliate against a Soviet "first strike" with a devastating "second strike" that would wipe out 100 million or so Russians.

In the face of these terrifying prospects, world-wide pressures for disarmament increased. But the subsequent negotiations with Russia, at Geneva and elsewhere, quickly slid into the well-worn rut. The Soviets, looking upon outsiders as spies, demanded disarmament without acceptable on-site inspection. The Western world, looking upon the Soviets as potential cheaters, did not trust Moscow's promises. In an atmosphere of mutual distrust, deadlock continued.

NIXON'S LATIN-AMERICAN ORDEAL

A sharp dip in the Eisenhower prosperity, with a consequent blight abroad, brought relations with Latin America to a focus in 1958. Communist agitators harped on long-festering grievances: the persistence of Yankee economic imperialism; the slighting of Latin America in foreign-aid handouts; the bolstering of ruling classes that were fighting land redistribution and other overdue reforms; and the tolerating and even decorating of sadistic dictators. The impoverished masses of Latin America, stirred by the world-wide "population explosion" and the "revolution in rising expectations," were not always going to be content to live in shanty-town huts and subsist off garbage dumps.

Seeking to salvage Good Neighborism and implement Eisenhower's "Good Partner" Policy, Vice-President Richard M. Nixon embarked upon a goodwill tour of Latin America in April, 1958. His red-carpet reception went off reasonably well at first, but in Lima (Peru) anti-Yankee crowds, yelling *"Fuera Nixon"* ("Nixon get out"), shouted down the visiting dignitary and subjected him to a barrage of stones.[1] In Caracas (Venezuela) a larger and uglier mob, bespewing Nixon and his party with tobacco-stained spittle, and shouting *"Muera Nixon"* ("Death to Nixon"), beat in the glass windows of his limousine with iron pipes. Miraculously, no one was killed. Back in Washington, President Eisenhower, fearing for the safety of his second-in-command, ordered a large body of paratroopers to be readied for a possible rescue mission. A shudder of apprehen-

[1] Nixon gave a "healthy" kick in the shins to one tormentor who spat full in his face. R. M. Nixon, *Six Crises* (Garden City, N.Y., 1962), p. 204. It should be noted that in 1953 and 1954 President Eisenhower had presented the Legion of Merit to Dictator Odría of Peru and Dictator Pérez Jiménez of Venezuela. Nixon visited both countries after these men had been ousted, and there anti Yankee resentment ran the highest.

sion ran through Latin America at the prospective revival of bayonet-supported intervention, abandoned by Franklin Roosevelt in 1933.

Not all the stones, spit, and spite came from Communists. Left-wingers were active, but they were by no means alone. An ex-President of Costa Rica, while deploring the vulgar behavior of the mob, testified that the United States had first spat on all Latin America by bolstering, decorating, and even sheltering torture-chamber dictators. Latin Americans could not retaliate by spitting on the entire United States: all they could do was to take it out on the Vice-President of the United States.[2]

The Nixon nightmare was a jarring reminder that Americans had too long taken their southern neighbors for granted. Heroic measures were necessary if the Communists were not to triumph, as they were doing in Cuba. Congress, which had been showering billions of dollars upon Europe and Asia, would have to look southward. The Eisenhower administration did manage to secure Congressional authorization for stepped-up foreign aid, but the gigantic Alliance for Progress plan, fully launched by the next administration, was to come later (see p. 870). Vice-President Nixon was its unwitting godfather.

THE LEBANON LANDING

The Eisenhower Doctrine of 1957, designed to thwart Communist aggression in the faction-torn Middle East (see p. 844), received its baptismal test in the summer of 1958. Tiny Lebanon, bordering the eastern Mediterranean (see map, p. 839), was beset with disorders from within (partly Communist fomented) and menace from without. The ambitious President Nasser of the new United Arab Republic (then combining Egypt and Syria) was casting covetous eyes on this troubled land. The blowup came on July 14, 1958, when the pro-Western king of Iraq was murdered, and a take-over of his country by Nasser seemed imminent. The president of Lebanon, fearful of a chain reaction, appealed to Washington for help.

With startling celerity, President Eisenhower honored the doctrine that bore his name.[3] Seeking to protect American lives and preserve world peace by forestalling aggression, he ordered American marines to land

[2] For this remarkable statement by José Figueres, see Lewis Hanke, *Mexico and the Caribbean* (Princeton, 1959), pp. 105–107. Nixon himself concluded that Washington should extend a coldly formal handshake to the dictators but a warmly approving *abrazo* to the democratic leaders. *Six Crises*, p. 228. The United States could not win: if it overthrew the dictators, it was guilty of intervention; if it recognized them, it was guilty of collaboration.

[3] For Eisenhower's statement, see *Department of State Bulletin*, XXXIX, 185 (August 4, 1958). Strictly speaking, the United Arab Republic was not a Communist-controlled state, within the obvious meaning of the Eisenhower Doctrine, but by this time President Nasser had formed intimate economic and political ties with the Kremlin. Dulles himself evidently did not invoke the Eisenhower doctrine.

in Lebanon the day after the assassination. (With additional units they ultimately totaled some 14,000 men.) Although the landings were completely unopposed, Soviet rocket-rattlers uttered dire warnings about the "brink of disaster" and the guns that were "already beginning to shoot." But the five-star general in the White House did not flinch, even though the bulk of "neutralist" and much of Western opinion seemed hostile to the "war-mongering" United States.

Tensions were greatly eased late the next month (August, 1958) by a dramatic switch in the UN Assembly. The Arab nations themselves successfully sponsored a resolution under which they agreed not to interfere in one another's internal affairs. With a peaceful solution thus insured, the United States pulled out its troops in October, 1958, and the crisis dropped from a high boil to a low simmer.

The after-shocks of the Lebanon landing were far-reaching. The UN had again demonstrated its worth as a safety valve and mediatory agency. The prestige of the United States shot up as it demonstrated a will and an ability to take resolute action in restoring stability to a war-threatened area. By withdrawing troops when order was insured, Washington gave the lie to Communist charges of "imperialistic aggression." But Eisenhower's rather precipitate action exposed the basic flaw in the Eisenhower Doctrine: it was aimed at external Communist aggression and was not equipped to parry the insidious hand of subversion.

Elsewhere the Middle East continued to smoulder ominously. Late in 1958 President Nasser, his aggressive nationalism undampened, accepted Soviet terms for constructing the High Dam on the Nile. With assassination-torn Iraq now tottering, the anti-Soviet Baghdad Pact—including Turkey, Iran, Iraq, Pakistan, and Britain—seemed more anemic than ever, even with Washington's continued co-operation. Iraq, turning neutralist, finally dropped out of the pact completely in March, 1959, taking with it Baghdad, the fabled capital city of the alliance.

A revamped pact was now fashioned to replace the old one. Christened the Central Treaty Organization (CENTO), with its seat at Ankara, the capital of Turkey, it was officially proclaimed on August 19, 1959. If the Baghdad Pact was a frail reed, this one was frailer—embracing only Turkey, Iran, Pakistan, and Britain. The United States, as in the case of the old pact, recoiled from formal membership. But on March 5, 1959, President Eisenhower concluded Executive Agreements with each of the three Middle East members, and these commitments in effect bound Washington to defend them with armed forces in certain critical contingencies.

CENTO, already weakened, received a new jolt late in 1962. The Pakistani, angered by the shipment of American arms to their arch-rival India during the China-invasion crisis (p. 882), gave disquieting signs of wanting to pull out and sidle up to Communist China.

GUNFIRE OFF FORMOSA

In the Far East, unofficial relations with Red China, technically on a war footing since the Korean intervention of 1950, remained envenomed. An intensive hate-America campaign was being whipped up by the fanatics in Peking, who assailed the "wolfish imperialism" of the "ferocious and cunning butchers" in Yankeeland. Washington, for its part, continued to deny recognition to the Communist government, and persisted in its costly program of propping up the orphaned Nationalist regime of Chiang Kai-shek on Taiwan (Formosa). The aging Generalissimo still insisted that he would return triumphantly to China with his American-equipped army.

Chiang continued to cling precariously to two tiny island groups a half dozen or so miles from the Chinese mainland: Quemoy and Matsu. They served as observation centers, warning posts, and espionage nests, as well as bases for harassing the commerce of two of Communist China's largest ports.

The Chinese Communists, taking advantage of the Lebanon crisis, reopened a furious artillery bombardment of the Quemoys on August 23, 1958.[4] Chiang had made the "rather foolish" move, according to Secretary Dulles, of committing some 90,000 troops, or about one-third of his effective force, to this highly vulnerable outpost. American critics of the Generalissimo charged that he was trying to suck the United States into an atomic Armageddon; and why die for Quemoy? They also insisted that these beleaguered rocks were not necessary for the defense of Formosa, some 120 miles distant, especially since the U.S. Seventh Fleet stood ready to repel an invasion. But Chiang, who could ill afford to sacrifice so many men, flatly refused to pull back. The Seventh Fleet was therefore ordered to escort Nationalist supply ships, though prudently keeping outside the three-mile limit.

Peking appears to have been restrained by the evident determination of the United States to fight if the push against the Quemoys seemed about to blossom into a full-fledged invasion. The Formosa Resolution, passed by Congress in 1955 (see p. 834), was so deviously worded as to authorize the President to defend Quemoy and Matsu, even though these islets were purposely left unmentioned. Secretary Dulles flew out to Formosa to put pressure on President Chiang. After three days of earnest talks, the two men issued a joint announcement, on October 23, 1958, stating that Nationalist China had renounced military force as a

---

[4] The first heavy bombardment had occurred on September 3, 1954. Gallup found that 91 per cent of informed Americans preferred turning the Quemoy-Matsu problem over to the UN rather than committing American forces to Chiang's defense. Gallup Release, September 26, 1958.

means of regaining the Chinese mainland. This public scuttling of a long-established American policy—that of helping the Nationalists to return—calmed the Formosan typhoon. The Communist bombardment of the Quemoys then tapered off after first having been reduced, oddly enough, to even-numbered days.

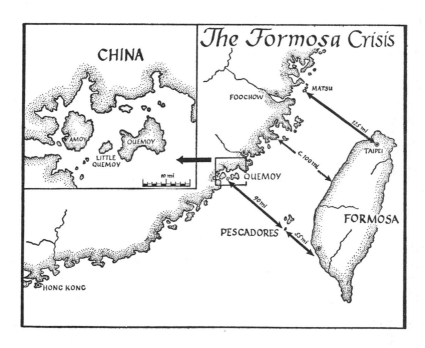

Secretary Dulles regarded his stand on Quemoy and Matsu as one of his most brilliant strokes of "brinkmanship"—that is, going to the very brink of war and forcing one's adversary to back down by risking war to preserve peace. But critics condemned his "Formosan folly." They insisted that Chiang's lost-hope regime represented only the Seventh Fleet, that he was not worth a nuclear war, and that Dulles was applying the teen-age game of "chicken" to the explosive problems of the atomic age.

THE BERLIN TIME BOMB

The dilemma of the two Germanies—the Communist East and the democratic West—continued to be the most critical of the Cold War. The men in the Kremlin, with bitter memories of German invasions in two world wars, could not permit this militaristic menace to rise again. They had opposed with dire threats the creation of a democratic West Germany and its joining the North Atlantic Treaty Organization (NATO). They could not risk a free election in Communist-controlled

East Germany, for this economically sagging satellite might vote to join thriving West Germany.

Most vexatious of all was four-sectored Berlin, deep in the heart of East Germany (see map, p. 780). The Russian sector of the city was now the capital of East Germany; the American, British, and French zones were occupied by some 11,000 troops, 5000 of them American. West Berlin, partner in the prosperity of West Germany, was mockingly wealthy; East Berlin, under a stooge Communist regime, was shockingly threadbare. Tens of thousands of East Germans, many of them university trained people, were pouring into West Berlin, and from there into job-plentiful West Germany. The very existence of the West Berlin show window was potent anti-Communist propaganda: Soviet Premier Khrushchev growled that it was a "bone in the throat."

The Western allies persisted in a strongly legalistic stand. They insisted that the four-power occupation of Berlin rested on a solemn wartime agreement, and that it would have to be continued until a peace treaty was signed with a united Germany.[5] Since Moscow would not permit Germany to unite, except on Communist terms, the dangerous deadlock continued. With each passing year, a permanent division of Germany seemed more likely, and this the West German government of Chancellor Adenauer vehemently opposed.

Premier Khrushchev, his patience wearing thin, stunned the Western world, in November 1958, by delivering a virtual ultimatum. Publicly terminating the relevant wartime agreements, he proposed that Berlin be made a "free city," and warned that Soviet occupation functions would be turned over to the Communist East Germans within six months. East Germany presumably would demand that the three Allies pull out. If they refused to budge, the East Germans could starve them out by cutting off the approaches to the city. The occupying powers would then have two choices: to turn tail or try to bull their way in with tanks and trucks. If the well-armed East Germans resisted this "invasion," then war would erupt. If the Soviets came to their aid, World War III would presumably be triggered.

To the United States and the other Western powers the only possible course was to hold the line and pray that Khrushchev was bluffing. His seductive talk about making Berlin a free city rang hollow: Communist take-overs in "free" Czechoslovakia strongly suggested that the "free city" would soon become a "slave city." After high-sounding pledges to the West Berliners, American prestige would suffer an irreparable blow if Washington betrayed 2,250,000 free Germans. One possible road to appeasement was to grant a limited recognition to East Germany. But this

---

[5] One distinguished authority argued that the 1945 agreements had been violated by all parties, especially by the West. Quincy Wright, "Some Legal Aspects of the Berlin Crisis," *Amer. Jour. of Internat. Law*, LV (1961), 959–965.

would drive another nail into the coffin of unification and alienate West Germany, whose contribution of manpower to the NATO armies was indispensable. Meanwhile the six-month time fuse continued to sputter.

THE "MARTYRDOM" OF DULLES

Secretary of State Dulles, suffering agonies from a recurring intestinal cancer, resigned in April, 1959, at age seventy-one. He died five weeks later. His successor was Christian A. Herter, sixty-four years of age, tall, kindly, and soft-spoken but partially crippled by arthritis. Formerly a member of Congress and a governor of Massachusetts, and recently Undersecretary of State, he was a man of wide diplomatic experience and unusual abilities, but he did not have Dulles' flair for bursting into the headlines.

The reputation of Dulles had undergone a miraculous rehabilitation since 1956. The British and French distrusted "that terrible man," whose evasiveness and self-righteousness had driven them to the madness of Suez and had almost demolished the North Atlantic Alliance.[6] But in succeeding months, as Dulles doggedly clung to his post, relations with the two allies had risen from disastrous to endurable. His dedication to his job, his beaverish industry, his capacity for "taking infinite planes" (he traveled about 500,000 miles in visiting nearly 50 countries), and his courage in carrying on while dying of cancer transformed him into something of a martyr.

But many critics, chiefly Democrats, continued to find fault with the jet-propelled Secretary. They charged that there was more noise than newness in his "new look" policies. Despite high-sounding catchwords like "massive retaliation," "unleashing Chiang," "agonizing reappraisal," "liberation" (e.g., Hungary in 1956), he had actually traveled the well-rutted road of containment laid out by Truman. "Massive verbal retaliation," the criticism ran, had been his long suit. His "airborne diplomacy" tended to paralyze decision-making in Washington while he was absent, and his usurping of ambassadorial functions while abroad threw the delicate machinery out of gear.

But Dulles had his defenders. They noted that he had extended military containment to the Middle East and the Far East by promoting a network of alliances (Baghdad Pact, SEATO). He had stood firm on Korea, on Indo-China, on the Formosa Straits, and on Berlin, even though his inflexibility had often led to deadlock. His successors were as guilty of "perpetual motion" as he was. He had, moreover, maintained excellent relations with Congress (unlike his predecessor Acheson), at the price of permitting the right-wing McCarthyites in the Senate to wreck the

---

[6] See Richard Goold-Adams, *John Foster Dulles: A Reappraisal* (New York, 1962), by a British journalist.

morale of the State Department by purging it of "disloyal" employees. And although the Soviet Union was stronger—perhaps inevitably after its nuclear breakthrough—Dulles had won Moscow's bitter respect by substantially holding the line all over the world.

The death of Dulles placed new burdens on the semi-invalid Eisenhower. Operating on a limited work schedule, he had allowed Dulles a freer hand than any other Secretary in modern times, and generally had approved his recommendations without much question.[7] Not reposing the same confidence in Secretary Herter, Eisenhower was forced to curtail his golfing and grasp the helm himself.

The outburst of energy displayed by the "new Eisenhower" was amazing. Among other trips, he embarked upon an eleven-nation goodwill safari, in December, 1959, which took him all the way to India and during which he grinned his way through showers of confetti. Early in 1960 he visited Latin America, and although he got a whiff of tear gas in Montevideo while student demonstrators were being dispersed, he was warmly received. His radiant sincerity and goodwill no doubt were impressive reflections of the nation's desire for peace, but Democrats grumbled that stagecraft was no substitute for statecraft.

KHRUSHCHEV COURTS AMERICA

The demise of Dulles smoothed the way for a more intimate relationship with Khrushchev. For many months the pudgy Premier had been clamoring for a conference "at the summit" to solve current problems, including the crisis he had deliberately stirred up over Berlin. He argued that not the hired hands but the heavyweights could arrive at solutions. Dulles and Eisenhower had both feared that "summiteering" would quickly degenerate into a propaganda circus, like that staged by the USSR at Geneva in 1955. They balked at any further top-level parleys as long as there were no real assurances of success and no convincing proofs of good faith on the part of Moscow. Patient discussions and careful homework at the ambassadorial levels seemed imperative if the preliminary obstacles were to be cleared away. Negotiations under glaring lights, with a nation's prestige on the line and the people back home clamoring for no-surrender, seemed like the acme of futility.

With Dulles gone, Eisenhower relented and invited Khrushchev to visit America, during September, 1959, in the hope of defrosting the Cold War. Many American conservatives protested, fearing that World War III would erupt if Khrushchev were assassinated by some refugee from communism. Jetting into the outskirts of Washington on a Soviet plane (the world's largest), he received a courteous but cool welcome:

[7] Goold-Adams concludes that Dulles exercised more power than any other modern American except Franklin Roosevelt. *Ibid.,* p. 300.

the crowds turning out to see the chief Red were curious but notably silent. Then he went on to appear before the UN Assembly in New York, where, on September 18, 1959, he delivered a sweeping total-disarmament speech, obviously for propaganda effect. It proved to be the same old no-inspection salad with Russian dressing.

Khrushchev's thirteen-day tour of the United States resembled that of an American politician campaigning for office. He evidently thought of himself as a kind of traveling supersalesman for communism. Alternately bland and boorish, grinning and growling, docile and domineering, he left the impression, perhaps calculated, of a temperamentally unstable figure ruthlessly wielding immense power. "He uses rather than loses his temper," Vice-President Nixon had noted.

The highlight of Khrushchev's visit was a two-day meeting with Eisenhower at the latter's rustic retreat at Camp David, Maryland, September 25–27, 1959. The two men emerged from their secrecy-enshrouded talks to announce that they were prepared to negotiate existing disputes, including embattled Berlin, without the ticking of a time bomb. The six-month ultimatum had expired four months earlier.

SPIES IN THE SKIES

The friendly "spirit of Camp David" helped clear the air for the long-discussed "summit conference," involving Khrushchev, Eisenhower, President de Gaulle of France, and Prime Minister Macmillan of Britain. But on the eve of the meeting, scheduled for May 16, 1960, American spokesmen and Khrushchev had both publicly taken frozen positions on the crucial Berlin issue, and neither side could retreat without intolerable loss of face.

A ready-made excuse for rupturing the summit meeting came with the sensational spy-plane affair. For about four years, the United States had been engaging in photographic espionage over the Soviet Union with high-flying U-2 airplanes, especially designed to soar above the range of anti-aircraft fire. On May 1, 1960, one of these one-man planes was shot down some 1,200 miles inside the Soviet Union, near a vital industrial center.

Then the bungling began. Two separate American agencies, evidently working at cross purposes, haltingly tried to lie their way out. On May 6, 1960, a State Department spokesman announced that "There was absolutely no—N-O—no—deliberate attempt to violate Soviet air space . . . [and] never had been." [8] Further clumsy and conflicting denials followed, and on May 9, Secretary of State Herter confessed that the White House had known all along about the U-2's. Surprisingly, he left the impression that the flights would continue if American security required them.

[8] David Wise and Thomas B. Ross, *The U-2 Affair* (New York, 1962), p. 93.

Khrushchev offered Eisenhower an "out" by saying that he did not believe the President to be responsible for ordering the incursions. The President might then have axed some underling, but with a candor unprecedented in diplomacy, he publicly assumed all responsibility for the spy-flights. More than that, he defended them as necessary: the Soviets had threatened to "bury us" with nuclear missiles, and he deemed it necessary to peek behind the Iron Curtain in an effort to avoid another Pearl Harbor surprise party. In short, Washington had spied, denied, lied, and defied. Soviet sovereignty was frontally challenged.

The espionage-expert Soviets, who could have hushed up the U-2 affair, were outraged or professed to be. Khrushchev, admitting that he had known about the overflights while at Camp David, condemned the duplicity of his "fishy" friend. The Soviets threatened to obliterate with their missiles those neutral "accomplices" who maintained the bases from which the flights originated. Washington promptly retorted by promising to defend its allies if they were assailed.

The summit parley now seemed pointless. At Paris, but too late to do much good, Eisenhower announced that he had suspended the U-2 flights, and that they would not be resumed. He thus seemed to yield to pressure, but not in time to get credit for his concession. Khrushchev stormed into Paris demanding that Eisenhower apologize for the insult and punish those responsible for it. The President obviously would not punish himself, so the Summit Conference collapsed before it could get off the ground. A still-smiling Eisenhower, who had endured Khrushchev's vulgar abuse in silence, returned home with his popularity greatly enhanced. Remembering that he had kept his dignity, but forgetting that this was one of the most badly bungled diplomatic episodes in American history, the banner-makers proclaimed, "THANK YOU, MR. PRESIDENT."[9]

THE U-2 BACKFIRE

The strict letter of international law was on the side of the Russians, who for centuries had been obsessed by secrecy. Flights over the territory of a sovereign nation in peacetime were clearly illegal, and Americans, as Moscow pointed out, would have resented Russian spy planes over Kansas City. The aggrieved Soviets sought to have the Security Council of the UN brand the United States an aggressor for having sent

[9] According to Gallup (Release of June 8, 1960), Eisenhower's personal popularity rose sharply after the U-2 affair, which the public believed he had handled well, considering the circumstances. But ex-candidate Adlai Stevenson charged that the administration "handed Khrushchev the crowbar and sledgehammer" with which to wreck the Paris conference. Senator John F. Kennedy remarked that Eisenhower might have "expressed regrets"—a statement for which he was attacked during the presidential campaign later that year. Wise and Ross, *The U-2 Affair*, pp. 172, 174.

unarmed planes with single aviators over their territory. But since the Russians notoriously maintained a large army of spies, they did not come into court with clean hands. (Conventional espionage, depending on the means used, is ordinarily a violation of domestic rather than international law.) Ambassador Henry Cabot Lodge, defending the United States at the UN, displayed a large wooden American eagle, taken from the American Embassy in Moscow, which Soviet agents had obviously "bugged" with a secret listening device. The Russian charge of "aggressive acts" proved to be so farfetched that it was voted down by the Security Council, 7 to 2.[10]

The U-2 affair was a besmirching blow to the national image, especially to the holier-than-thou assumption that Americans would not stoop to snooping. Communist propagandists had a hypocritical field day. American diplomacy, to the dismay of NATO allies and other well-wishers, was revealed as bungling, inept, and naive. All great nations spied; but none admitted it. Complete silence would have been better than lying denials, even though the American newshawks were clamoring for statements. "We are investigating" or "Regrettable, if true" might have served, especially in the light of the Communist record of fabricating evidence.

The unaligned nations were unnerved by Moscow's threats of nuclear retaliation if they served as bases for spy planes. The revelation that three U-2's were based in Japan helped arouse mob demonstrations against the government and the pending mutual security treaty with the United States. (The spy planes were removed but the treaty was ratified the next month, June, 1960.) The outbursts finally became so violent that Eisenhower was forced to cancel a visit to Japan during his goodwill tour of the Far East. Loss of face was better than possible loss of life, even though the Communists celebrated another propaganda victory.

All hope of relaxing cold-war tensions went down the drain. The peppery Premier Khrushchev abruptly cancelled the invitation he had issued to his "fishy" friend for a goodwill visit to Russia, and announced that he would deal only with Eisenhower's successor.

Determined to make propaganda at some kind of summit meeting, Khrushchev invited himself to the UN and arrived in New York, September, 1960, for a twenty-five day stay. His menacing presence forced the unprecedented attendance of eleven heads of state and thirteen of government, including President Eisenhower, who refused to meet his uncouth tormentor. Khrushchev flexed his nuclear muscles when he

[10] See *Department of State Bulletin*, XLII, 961 (June 13, 1960), for the text of the Soviet resolution. The Russians argued that since they had rejected Eisenhower's "open skies" proposal at Geneva in 1955, he had set about to open the skies slyly. Actually, the U-2 program, until it came a cropper, was a brilliant espionage coup.

boasted that the Soviets were grinding out missiles like sausages. He attempted to shout down Prime Minister Macmillan of Britain, he branded the UN a "spittoon," and he removed a shoe, waved it menacingly at a speaker, and pounded it on the desk. Such outrageous conduct shocked and disgusted many of the delegates, including the rapidly growing Afro-Asia bloc, which the Soviets were trying to woo.

CASTRO COMES DOWN FROM THE HILLS

Incredibly enough, Cuba emerged in 1959 as a major piece on the Cold War chessboard. After seizing power again in 1952, the dictator Fulgencio Batista had kept order, and had encouraged heavy American investments, partly no doubt to insure continuing support from the United States. Washington, in the interests of stability and security, not only recognized his dictatorship but sold him arms and continued to provide military training missions.

Cuba had long been ripe for revolution. The plush gambling casinos and tourist resorts in Havana, operated largely with United States capital (some of it gangster), contrasted glaringly with the shacks of the populace. Poverty stalked the land; prolonged unemployment followed the seasonal sugar-cane cutting; the most fertile soil was heavily concentrated in a few hands, including Yankee-owned corporations.

Tall, broad-shouldered, and black-bearded, Dr. Fidel Castro, a law graduate and the youngish son of a well-to-do family, emerged as the "maximum leader." After an earlier failure, he renewed his guerrilla warfare in 1956 with some eighty unshaven followers. He finally managed to secure a supply of modern weapons from private Cuban sources in the United States, while Washington, beginning in March, 1958, clamped down an embargo on further arms to Batista. Suddenly, on January 1, 1959, the graft-rotten dictatorship collapsed like a Hollywood set, and the deposed tyrant fled the country with a reputed $200 million in graft, all the while condemning the Yankees for nonsupport.

At first the heroic Castro had many sympathizers in the United States, so obvious was the need for reform. Washington accorded his government formal recognition in the surprisingly short time of one week. But the cigar-smoking premier, visiting the United States unofficially in April, 1959, appears neither to have received any offers of large-scale financial aid nor to have sought them. During these critical months he professed dedication to democracy; but whether he would have taken this high road if he had received adequate economic assistance is debatable. The circumstantial evidence is strong that he was determined to have a real revolution; that he did not wish to tie his hands by binding himself to Washington; and that he needed Uncle Sam as both a whipping boy and an ogre if he hoped to achieve his ends.

Misgivings about Castro had meanwhile mounted. Amid cries of "*Paredón*" ("To the wall") hundreds of ex-followers of Batista were lined up and shot down after "kangaroo court" trials. Some of these thugs richly deserved their fate, but American outcries against this un-American "blood bath" evoked retorts from the Castroites that Batista's butcheries had inspired no such protests. Then followed wholesale confiscations of United States land and other properties, without any real prospect of repayment. "We will take and take," boasted Castro, "until not even the nails of their shoes are left." [11] Notorious Communists soon began to emerge as leading officials; the press was muzzled; free thought was stifled; long-promised elections were forgotten; and tens of thousands of Cuban refugees fled to Florida and elsewhere.

Taking the offensive, the Castroites drenched the other nations of Latin America with Communist propaganda, both by powerful radio transmitters and the printed word. Castro even tried to "export" his revolution to several nearby Caribbean countries, including Panama, where some eighty armed men abortively landed in April, 1959. United States naval patrols helped to intercept such forays. In short, the island of Cuba, thrust up below the soft underbelly of the United States, was being turned into a Communist beachhead for the subversion of Latin America.

With his potent propaganda machine and multihour television harangues, Fidel Castro undoubtedly enjoyed fanatical support in Cuba, especially among the peasant beneficiaries of his so-called land redistribution. To them he was a bearded Robin Hood who robbed the rich and gave to the poor. His hand was further strengthened by Yankee protests against the wholesale execution of ex-followers of Batista, the granting of asylum to others, and the permitting of hit-and-run airplane and boat raids from American soil. The underdog Cuban revolutionists thought it great fun to kick mighty Uncle Sam in the shins, knowing full well that he would not dare alienate world opinion by flouting Franklin Roosevelt's nonintervention policy, or the Charter of the UN, or the Charter of the Organization of American States.

CRACKING DOWN ON CUBA

Castro's contempt was hard for Americans to take. They found patience all the more difficult because they were consuming about one-half of Cuba's billion-dollar sugar crop and paying a bonus of two cents a pound above the world price, or approximately $150 million annually. Finally, in reprisal for the confiscation of American properties (all told worth about $1.5 billion), Washington cut off Cuban sugar imports and

[11] K. E. Meyer and Tad Szulc, *The Cuban Invasion: The Chronicle of a Disaster* (New York, 1962), p. 62.

imposed an embargo on virtually all shipments from the United States, except medicine and food. The Castroites, having branded the favorable bonus arrangements "economic slavery," now branded their termination "economic aggression." Washington hoped that when Castro ran out of oil and the parts for his American machines, he would have to come to heel.

"DON'T MESS AROUND WITH US CUBANS"

Premier Khrushchev, with false beard, backs Castro.

Werner in the *Indianapolis Star*, 1960

Soviet agents, ever ready to fish in tropical waters, had already swarmed onto the scene. On February 13, 1960, they signed a sweeping trade pact with Cuba under which they agreed to buy 5,000,000 tons of sugar over a five-year period, without a bonus. They also arranged to supply numerous technicians, large shipments of oil, and enormous quantities of arms with which to equip Castro's militia, both male and female. Khrushchev boasted of his ideological kinship with the Robin Hood of the Caribbean, and threatened to rain rockets on the United States should it intervene. As for the Monroe Doctrine, he declared that it was dead and that the only thing left to do was "to bury it, just as you bury anything dead, so it will not poison the air." [12]

[12] *Ibid.*, p. 72. Khrushchev backed water when he later declared that his threat to use rockets was merely "symbolic."

Americans were alarmed by this violation of their revered Doctrine, and the State Department ringingly reaffirmed its vitality.[13] President Monroe had warned the European powers not to impose their systems on the Americas, and the principle seemed fully applicable to a Communist system imposed by Moscow, even though Fidel Castro was a willing stooge. On December 2, 1961, during a radio-TV broadcast, he proclaimed, "I am a Marxist-Leninist and will be one until the day I die." He further confessed that he had earlier concealed his Communist views for fear of alienating bourgeois support during his rise to power.

Washington was bound by its membership in the Organization of American States to refrain from single-handed intervention reminiscent of the pre-Good Neighbor days. Agreement among twenty nations on resolute steps was virtually impossible, largely because left-wing groups in many of the Latin-American countries sympathized with Fidel Castro's social reforms (*fidelismo*), and because they relished the humiliation of the hated Colossus of the North. At a meeting of foreign ministers of the American states, in Santiago, Chile (August 12–18, 1959), the best that the United States could muster was a vague, slap-on-the-wrist declaration which condemned totalitarianism and reaffirmed faith in democracy, without specific mention of Cuba. A subsequent meeting of foreign ministers, assembled at San José, Costa Rica, August 16–21, 1960, also condemned "extracontinental" intervention in the Americas, but again did not mention Cuba or authorize sanctions.[14]

Fidel Castro had meanwhile stepped up his campaign of vilification against the United States, while frenzied crowds chanted, "*Cuba sí, Yanki no.*" Among other concessions, he demanded the return of the American naval base site at Guantánamo, granted in 1903 and reaffirmed in what amounted to perpetuity by the treaty of 1934. He administered a stinging slap when, on forty-eight hours notice, he ordered the United States to reduce its embassy staff in Havana from an alleged three hundred persons to eleven. President Eisenhower, whom Castro had dubbed a "gangster" and the "senile White House golfer," promptly severed diplomatic relations on January 3, 1961, only seventeen days before his successor was to inherit the prickly problem.

THE NOMINEES OF 1960

As the time neared for picking a successor to President Eisenhower, problems involving foreign affairs overshadowed all others, even "gut

---

[13] July 14, 1960. *Department of State Bulletin*, XLIII (August 1, 1960), 170–171.

[14] The San José conference did vote economic sanctions and a diplomatic quarantine against the brutal Dominican regime of Dictator Trujillo, who had been recently implicated in an assassination attempt against the President of Venezuela. Trujillo was himself assassinated in 1961, and the next year the Dominicans participated in a free election for the first time since 1924.

issues" like unemployment. The overwhelming preoccupation was how to preserve the precarious peace in the cold war.[15]

A mature and experienced leader in Washington was urgently needed. President Eisenhower, declaring that the White House was no place for "on-the-job training," cast his mantle of the Presidency upon Vice-President Nixon. The ambitious and able Vice-President had in fact shouldered far more responsibilities than any of his predecessors, and Eisenhower had dispatched him to many lands on goodwill missions. Nixon's popularity had shot up spectacularly in 1958, following his exhibition of courage ("foolhardiness," said the Democrats) in South America under a spit-and-stone barrage. His stock had risen further the next year when, at the opening of an American exhibition in Moscow, he had stood up to the bullying Khrushchev and defended democracy in an impromptu television debate in a model kitchen ("Kitchen Summit Conference"). Nixonites played up a photograph showing their hero jabbing a defiant finger at the portly premier. The inference was that he would be able to handle the Russians.

The Republican convention in Chicago, on the one-hundredth anniversary of Lincoln's nomination in the same city, unanimously chose Nixon on the first ballot. His running mate was handsome Ambassador Henry Cabot Lodge, Jr. (grandson of Woodrow Wilson's archfoe), also experienced in foreign affairs as American representative at the UN. Republicans hammered home slogans such as "Experience Counts" and "They Understand What Peace Demands."

The victory-starved Democrats, meeting in Los Angeles, nominated on the first ballot a young, dynamic, and wealthy Senator from Massachusetts, John F. Kennedy. But the galleries were "Madly for Adlai"—the "experienced" but shop-worn Adlai Stevenson, already a two-time loser. Aside from a Boston-Harvard accent, Kennedy was presumably handicapped by his Catholicism (no Catholic had yet been elected President), by his youth (he was 43 to Nixon's "mature" 47), and by his "inexperience" in grappling with world affairs. But he had sat for fourteen years in Congress, a part of that time as a member of the Senate Committee on Foreign Relations, and had travelled extensively abroad, both as a private citizen and as a member of the armed forces during World War II.[16]

[15] Gallup found that of twelve world-wide centers sampled, only the United States and Norway (Oslo) voted "keeping the peace" the number one problem. The anxiety of far-removed America presumably reflected the weight of responsibility on the most powerful free nation, as well as an increased awareness of the international situation. World Gallup Poll News Service, November 16, 1958.

[16] In 1938, while twenty-one years old, Kennedy had served for a time as secretary to his isolationist father, Ambassador Joseph P. Kennedy, in the London Embassy. He subsequently published a book on these appeasement years entitled *Why England Slept* (New York, 1940).

TWO YOUNG MEN IN A HURRY

As regards foreign affairs, the two candidates generally saw eye to eye on basic issues. But Kennedy harped on the accusation that America had lost much of her prestige and power under Eisenhower—eight years of standpattism, do-nothingism, and obsession with a balanced budget in an unbalanced world. With the Soviets presumably forging ahead in missile development and rate of economic growth, he declared that the nation must regain its paramount position.

Nixon was forced into the position of defending the middle-of-the-roadism of a dying administration. He denied that America's prestige had sagged, although a confidential official survey indicated otherwise. He denied that the United States was falling behind the Soviets economically: they were coming up faster because they had farther to come. He denied that there was a "missile gap"—and subsequent revelations supported his position.

The highlight of the campaign was a series of four joint television appearances, popularly called "debates." Nixon, a clever speaker, welcomed these clashes, but at best he barely held his own, and no doubt contributed to his defeat by sharing an immense audience with a less prominent man.[17] On certain issues, Nixon managed to seize the offensive. He accused his opponent of appeasement when Kennedy indicated that he would yield the offshore islands of Quemoy and Matsu, difficult to defend, so as to concentrate on the defense of Formosa itself. With an impressive display of moral indignation, Nixon condemned Kennedy for being "dangerously irresponsible" in advocating the support of Cuban refugees who were seeking to overthrow Castro. (Ironically, Nixon was then backing top-secret plans for the abortive Bay of Pigs invasion that came the next year.)[18] Under Nixon's hammering, Kennedy modified his stand on both Cuba and the offshore islands.

On election day Kennedy triumphed by the wafer-thin margin of 49.7 per cent of the popular vote. The results could not properly be regarded as a mandate from the voters for or against anything. There was no real clash on the fundamentals of foreign policy. Both men were anxious to see the nation moving forward: one claimed that it was, the other that it was not. Kennedy's poor-mouth downgrading of American power and prestige, so alien to the American character, was certainly not so com-

---

[17] One could question the wisdom of having Presidential candidates, standing nervously before half the nation, make off-the-cuff responses to dynamite-laden questions.

[18] See Nixon, *Six Crises*, p. 354. Nixon here accuses Kennedy of having been briefed by the CIA on the Cuban invasion, and of having jeopardized the operation by bringing up the subject. Ex-CIA director Allen W. Dulles denied that Kennedy had been briefed. *New York Times*, March 21, 1962.

forting as the cheery diagnosis by the "experienced" Nixon. But many voters were so deeply jarred by successive cold-war setbacks that they were willing to listen to disagreeable realities and welcome a change of the guard.

AN OLD GENERAL FADES AWAY

President Eisenhower ended his eight-year stint in January, 1961, with his personal popularity still astonishingly high. He almost certainly could have been re-elected if the 22nd Amendment had not raised a forbidding hand. The pessimistic prediction by experts that the two-term restriction would turn him into a "lame duck" was not borne out by events: he exercised more energetic leadership, especially in foreign affairs, in his last two years than during any other comparable period.

The charge that Eisenhower was a mark-time general, wedded to the status quo, was not without some force.[19] Certainly the Soviets had grown stronger, relatively and absolutely, but probably this shift was inevitable. Few significant, forward-looking new policies in foreign relations were launched under Eisenhower's stewardship. He had continued the Democratic commitment to containment through economic and military aid. He had persuaded Congress to renew the reciprocal trade agreements of his predecessors, though with modifications.[20] He had "stood up to" the Russians without appeasement, he had refused to budge on Berlin, he had declined to recognize Red China, he had opposed Peking's entry into the United Nations, he had held fast on Formosa, and he had taken a firm stand on Laos. But he had "lost" Cuba in the same sense that Truman had "lost" China.

As for friends and neighbors, the fifteen-nation NATO alliance had weathered the Suez setback, though still creaking at the joints. Relations with Latin America had received a higher priority since the Nixon "illwill tour" of 1958. Commercial relations with Canada were tightened by the completion in 1959 of the St. Lawrence Waterway (see p. 828), which turned lake ports into seaports. The increasing economic enmeshment with Canada, and particularly the heavy inpouring of American dollars, aroused grave misgivings among the Canadians. They had no desire to become a kind of northern "banana republic," dancing to strings pulled by the Colossus of the South.

General Eisenhower's keenest disappointment was his inability to place the dove of peace on a secure perch. Yet he could proudly boast that he had involved the nation in no foreign war during his eight

---

[19] For a critical view of Eisenhower's foreign policy by his one-time speech writer, see E. J. Hughes, *The Ordeal of Power* (New York, 1963), especially pp. 340–341.

[20] Congress, in August, 1958, granted the President a four-year extension of the Reciprocal Trade Agreements Act. It was the eleventh extension.

America Faces the Future 867

years, which witnessed the windup of the Korean conflict. The nation was still immensely strong and, with the power to atomize any possible antagonist, was undisputed leader of the free world. But with overwhelming power went the responsibility of providing energetic and far-visioned leadership for an atomically fused and potentially explosive globe.

SELECTED BIBLIOGRAPHY

See the general works listed at the ends of the previous four chapters. The most useful annual surveys are those for the relevant years by R. P. Stebbins, under the title *The United States in World Affairs* and sponsored by the Council on Foreign Relations. A valuable global assessment is W. W. Rostow, *The United States in the World Arena* (New York, 1960). A brief scholarly interpretation is J. W. Spanier, *American Foreign Policy Since World War II* (rev. ed., 1962). Relevant also is Lionel Gelber, *America in Britain's Place* (New York, 1961). Personal observations by participants appear in R. M. Nixon, *Six Crises* (New York, 1962); Sherman Adams, *Firsthand Report* (New York, 1961); L. L. Strauss, *Men and Decisions* (New York, 1962); E. J. Hughes, *The Ordeal of Power* (New York, 1963). See also J. C. Campbell, *Defense of the Middle East* (New York, 1958); A. D. Barnett, *Communist China and Asia: Challenge to American Policy* (New York, 1960); Hans Speier, *Divided Berlin: The Anatomy of Soviet Blackmail* (New York, 1961). See also LATIN AMERICA in the GENERAL BIBLIOGRAPHY and William Benton, *The Voice of Latin America* (New York, 1961). On Castro useful accounts are R. F. Smith, *The United States and Cuba: Business and Diplomacy, 1917–1960* (New York, 1960); Theodore Draper, *Castro's Revolution* (New York, 1962); H. L. Matthews, *The Cuban Story* (New York, 1961); Daniel James, *Cuba: The First Soviet Satellite in the Americas* (New York, 1961); Ruby H. Phillips, *Cuba: Island of Paradox* (New York, 1959); W. A. Williams, *The United States, Cuba, and Castro* (New York, 1962). Enthusiastically pro-Castro are C. W. Mills, *Listen Yankee!* (New York, 1960) and Leo Huberman and P. M. Sweezy, *Cuba: Anatomy of a Revolution* (New York, 1960). The conservative ex-Ambassador E. E. T. Smith tells his pro-Batista side of the story in *The Fourth Floor* (New York, 1962). See also B. G. Bechhoefer, *Postwar Negotiations for Arms Control* (Washington, 1961); L. P. Bloomfield, *The United Nations and U.S. Foreign Policy* (Boston, 1960); Klaus Knorr, ed., *NATO and American Security* (Princeton, 1959). A perceptive brief analysis, with complementary documents, is N. A. Graebner, *Cold War Diplomacy: American Foreign Policy, 1945–1960* (Princeton, 1962).

8TH ED. REFS. George R. Packard III, *Protest in Tokyo: The Security Treaty Crisis of 1960* (Princeton, 1966), is a scholarly analysis of the Japanese riots that forced the cancellation of Eisenhower's visit. The author sees in the uproar a manifestation of the Japanese mood rather than an international Communist conspiracy. See also references for preceding chapter.

9TH ED. REFS. See BIBLIOGRAPHICAL ADDENDUM, p. 1,060.

55

New Frontier Diplomacy

Today, every inhabitant of this planet must con-
template the day when this planet may no longer
be habitable. . . . The weapons of war must be
abolished before they abolish us.
PRESIDENT KENNEDY, Sept. 25, 1961

NEW FRONTIERS ON THE POTOMAC

ON A WINTRY JANUARY 20, 1961, the youngest President-elect ever to
enter the White House (then 43) took over the reins from the oldest
President (then 70) ever to leave it. In keeping with his promise to
"get the country moving again," Kennedy unveiled his New Frontier—
a liberal program designed to provide wider horizons for the American
economy and spirit. But the New Frontiersmen were harassed by toma-
hawk-wielding Indians in the persons of conservative Democrats, who
united in Congress with conservative Republicans to block important
legislation. During the first two years, at least, Congress dealt more
gently with programs involving foreign policy than those involving
domestic reform.

The selection of a new Secretary of State provided a surprise. Adlai
Stevenson, the uncrowned king of the party, was in line with the Clay-
Seward-Blaine-Bryan tradition; but he had held off mounting the Ken-
nedy bandwagon and was instead appointed Ambassador to the UN.
The President's choice was a virtual unknown—Dean Rusk, a former
Rhodes Scholar, college professor (political science), and head of the
Rockefeller Foundation. Quietly professorial in manner and lacking the
showmanship of Dulles, he had already served for some five years in
the Department of State.

The Kennedy administration marked no sharp break with the past in
foreign affairs. But one important reversal involved the Dulles-Eisenhower concept of "massive retaliation," which could well mean nuclear
war or nothing, holocaust or humiliation. Embracing a "damn the defi-

cits" philosophy, Kennedy strove to build up conventional forces so that he could control "brush-fire" wars without reducing the globe to radioactive rubble.

Kennedy also stepped up the "space race" with the Russians. Before 1963 ended the Americans could boast of having four times put a man into orbit, though they were substantially behind the Soviets in this area. Kennedy likewise committed the nation to an astronomically costly program—with an estimated price tag of from $20 to $40 billion—of beating the Russians to the moon by 1970. There were sound reasons of strategy, prestige, and scientific exploration behind this gamble, but opponents of "lunar lunacy" complained that more mundane problems deserved priority.

A more earthy new concept—the Peace Corps—brought a warm heart to the cold war. During the campaign of 1960 Kennedy had endorsed the idea of having the government send abroad specially trained men and women who would share their skills with the underprivileged. They would concentrate on such projects as education, irrigation, sanitation, and agriculture—in short, a demonstration of democracy at work. This scheme, when first proposed, was condemned by critics as too starry-eyed, too expensive, and too much of a temptation to draft-dodgers. But the work done by these dedicated peace corpsmen—called "the poor gringoes" in Latin America—proved so helpful that the host countries soon requested more than could be trained. In certain areas the cry "Yankee, Go Home" was replaced by "Send Us More Peace Corps Volunteers." In September, 1961, a once-skeptical Congress passed by wide margins a bill to put the Corps on a permanent footing. Few, if any, investments of the Cold War returned such rich dividends in good will as this relatively inexpensive project. The Chinese Reds branded it "the Penetration Corps." [1]

ALLYING FOR PROGRESS

Vice-President Nixon's tour in 1958 had touched off considerable talk of a Marshall Plan for Latin America. After Castro's Cuba had sounded a new alarm, the Eisenhower administration was prepared to promise $500 million at the economic conference at Bogotá, Colombia, in September, 1960. Cynical Yankeephobes in Latin America labeled the then nameless scheme the "Fidel Castro Plan," and gave thanks (*"Gracias, Fidel"*) for the boat-rocking revolutionist who had forced the United States to abandon its *mañana* tactics.

Early in the New Frontier days, President Kennedy threw his full

[1] By the end of 1963 there were some 5000 Peace Corps volunteers in about 50 countries. Public opinion early endorsed the idea about 7 to 1. Gallup Release, February 1, 1961.

weight behind a new ten-year, ten-point $20 billion program. He not only attached to it a glamorous name, "Alliance for Progress" (*Alianza para Progreso*), but urged Congress to launch it by voting the initial $500 million. The appropriation was forthcoming in May, 1961. The next significant step came in August at a meeting of the Inter-American Economic and Social Council in Punta del Este, Uruguay, held in a converted Uruguayan gambling casino. The Kennedy administration itself gambled when it pledged the nation to provide the major part of $20 billion over a ten-year period. The assembled delegates of nineteen Latin American governments (Cuba excepted) formally subscribed to the historic charter of the Alliance for Progress, on August 17, 1961. President Kennedy demonstrated his personal interest in the fate of the new program when, accompanied by his bewitching young wife, he toured Venezuela and Colombia in December, 1961, and Mexico in June, 1962.[2]

Like the Marshall plan for Western Europe in 1947, the Alliance for Progress was tailored to encourage the Latin Americans to help themselves. It was not to be just another handout from Uncle Sam's bulging money bags. The theory was that if the alarming Communist penetration (*fidelismo*) was to be halted, then the appalling poverty which bred discontent would have to be eliminated, especially in those areas notoriously suffering from the "population explosion." Specifically, the Washington planners had as goals improved housing, medical care, sanitation, and education. Also high on their list was a more equitable distribution of land, which the large holders were adept at monopolizing, and a fairer apportionment of taxation, which the wealthy were ingenious in evading.

The Alliance for Progress was not an alliance and it did not progress satisfactorily. The rich naturally wanted to remain rich, blind to the fact that their blindness was hastening a Communist takeover. Dollars from Yankeeland, instead of profiting the poor, all too often found their way into the wallets of the wealthy, and from there into Swiss banks. Attempts by Uncle Sam to police the spending of his money invariably led to charges of undue influence or unfriendly interference, contrary to the noninterventionism of the Good Neighbor policy. Right-wingers in Latin America resented the Alliance as undermining capitalism; left-wingers denounced it as patching up capitalism. Little could be accomplished as long as the Alliance had to work through governments unwilling or afraid to support needed reforms.

[2] "Juan" and especially "Jackeline" Kennedy made a deep impression in Mexico. One greeting sign read: *"Gringo no, Jacki sí."* See also Lincoln Gordon, *A New Deal for Latin America: The Alliance for Progress* (Cambridge, Mass., 1963). In a useful analysis of reciprocal attitudes, Milton S. Eisenhower gives his presidential brother credit for having started the Alliance for Progress: *The Wine Is Bitter; The United States and Latin America* (New York, 1963).

THE BAY OF PIGS BLUNDER

Tens of thousands of Cuban refugees had fled to Florida, and in March, 1960, President Eisenhower had authorized the training of a small band for the possible invasion of the island. The management of the risky scheme was entrusted to the Central Intelligence Agency (CIA), later dubbed the "Cuban Invasion Authority." This cloak-and-dagger organization, with an immense secret budget reputed to be about

Mauldin in the *St. Louis Post Dispatch*, 1962

$1 billion annually, had helped engineer the overthrow of the Communist-tainted regime in Guatemala in 1954 (see p. 829), and it brashly expected to "Guatemalize" Cuba. The tiny army of some 1500 Cuban refugees was secretly trained in Guatemala by American officers and armed with American weapons and equipment, including obsolete aircraft.

The newly inaugurated Kennedy found the Cuban-invasion baby on the White House steps, and he had to adopt it or abandon it. The pressures to adopt were strong, especially since he had promised in the recent campaign to do something about Cuba, and since American opinion was reacting with mounting anger to Castro's calculated insults. But Kennedy insisted, and so announced on April 12, 1961, that in no circumstances would United States armed forces become *directly* involved.

The invasion was launched five days later, at the Bay of Pigs (Bahía de Cochinos), on the southern coast of Cuba. After a momentary success, the invaders were forced to surrender when Castro won control of the air. Kennedy was under great pressure to rush in American aircover, allegedly promised, but in an agonizing decision he stood firm on his pledge of no direct intervention. Complete collapse rapidly ensued, which was perhaps fortunate for the United States. Castro had a militia force of some 250,000 men and women, and quick failure was probably better than slow success, with the attendant dangers of deeper American involvement and possible Soviet intervention.

This madcap operation was a staggering blow to the nation's prestige, about which Kennedy had waxed so eloquent in the recent Presidential campaign.[3] Despite vehement American denials, the invasion had come after all. An aggrieved Castro, resorting anew to the UN sounding board, could redouble his charges of Yankee aggression. The Washington government had violated, at least in spirit, its own neutrality laws. It had violated the spirit, if not the letter, of the United Nations Charter, which forbids aggression, and also of the Organization of American States, which forbids unilateral aggression against a fellow member. The Kennedy administration had kept in the dark its own representative at the UN, Adlai Stevenson, who unwittingly lied before the whole world when he denied American complicity in an invasion which was even then starting. Altogether, the holier-than-thou image which Uncle Sam had fostered was hideously besmirched.

CASTRO CASTS ACCOUNTS

The Central Intelligence Agency had bungled the job scandalously. The expedition could succeed only if a large number of anti-Castro Cubans rose up to greet it. But the CIA failed to alert the Cuban underground, and a vigilant Castro rounded up tens of thousands of suspects. Especially repulsive to the Cuban people was the presence of former Batista reactionaries among the leaders of the invasion, some in the invasion force itself. Critics in the United States were also disturbed to find that the CIA, a virtual law unto itself, had not only undertaken to execute high policy but also to make it—to the consequent confusion

[3] Surprisingly, after this fiasco, Kennedy's popularity shot up to 83 per cent, obviously in a rally-behind-the-President spirit. Gallup Release, May 7, 1961.

of the Department of State and related agencies.[4] But Kennedy, who could easily have found scapegoats, manfully assumed "full responsibility" for the fiasco. Critical Republicans were quick to jeer that he had "got the country moving again"—downhill.

Abroad, the reactions to the blunder were almost uniformly unfavorable. The British and French remembered their abortive Suez invasion, when a self-righteous Eisenhower had forced them to back down. Others, recalling the Soviet butcheries in Hungary in 1956, noted that the United States, guilty of "a Hungary in reverse," was now in a poor position to accuse the Russians or the Chinese of aggression. At the height of the crisis, Khrushchev promised "all necessary assistance" to resist this "gangsterism," while crowds of Russians milled before the American Embassy in Moscow shouting, *"Kuba da, Yankee nyet"* ("Cuba yes, Yankees no"). A number of the more important Latin American nations, especially those Red-tinged, cried out against this reversal of Good Neighbor Roosevelt's nonintervention policy. A thousand or so demonstrators stoned the United States Embassy in Bogotá, Colombia, screaming *"Cuba sí, Yankee no!"*

Castro, far from being crushed, bounced back stronger than ever. The bearded David had indeed triumphed over the mighty Yankee Goliath. Washington appeared to be willing to wound secretly but afraid to strike openly. The episode evidently sobered and settled President Kennedy, but the Soviets seem to have concluded, mistakenly, that the inexperienced young man in the White House lacked the iron nerve for "brinkmanship."

The 1100 or so men rotting in Cuban jails continued to weigh heavily on the Kennedy conscience and on that of the American people. Fidel Castro, arguing that he had suffered much damage and heavy expense, demanded a stiff indemnity (ransom), which was finally set at about $53 million in food and badly needed medical supplies. The Washington authorities in effect waived the Logan Act, which forbade non-official negotiations. They encouraged unofficial intermediaries both to negotiate with Castro and to secure the necessary funds from private sources, which in turn were granted generous tax exemptions.

The ransom of some 1100 prisoners, while an act of humanity, revealed a sharp inconsistency of policy. The existing American embargo, designed to bring Castro to his knees, was definitely undermined by this wholesale human barter. Critics declared that the invaders (who had taken their chances) should have stayed in jail, and that the United States should not have salved the Kennedy conscience and strength-

---

[4] This alarming cross-purpose activity was going on elsewhere, notably in Laos, where CIA agents were notoriously undercutting the policy being implemented by foreign service officers.

ened communism by paying what Republican Senator Goldwater branded international "blackmail."

THE BERLIN WALL

Jolted by the Cuban debâcle, President Kennedy stiffened toward Moscow. Journeying to Europe for exploratory talks with the Western leaders, he met with Premier Khrushchev at Vienna, early in June, 1961, in a tense, two-day conference. The millionaire President and the ex-coal miner, although agreeing on a neutralized Laos, disagreed sharply on Germany, disarmament, and a ban on nuclear testing. Kennedy returned visibly shaken by the belligerent steeliness of his opponent.

Khrushchev next deliberately stirred up the Berlin embers. On June 15, 1961, he again threatened to turn the controversial city over to East Germany by the end of the year unless the Western powers recognized the sovereign status of his puppet. But Kennedy, far from quailing, dramatically asked of Congress authority to strengthen the nation's defenses and to call up 250,000 reservists. His request was promptly and overwhelmingly honored on July 31, 1961, and thousands of unhappy reservists were wrenched from their jobs to rejoin the armed forces. Kennedy's evident determination not to be bullied out of Berlin seems to have had a moderating influence on Moscow.[5]

The next Soviet move was the sudden erection of a wall or barricade between East and West Berlin, in August, 1961, subsequently extended along the entire border between East and West Germany. This startling closure of the escape hatch, through which thousands were fleeing to freedom, inexplicably caught the Western powers flatfooted. Critics demanded to know why American tanks had not pushed over the wall before it could be solidly built. But the danger was ever present that tough-fisted measures would beget shooting and shooting would beget World War the Last. The best response that the United States could make was to add 1500 men to its tiny Berlin garrison of 5000.

The Wall, though ending Communist irritation over the population drain, was actually a monument to failure. On one side lay freedom and prosperity; on the other slavery and poverty. Hundreds of East Berliners risked their lives—and often lost them—in tunneling, jumping, swimming, driving, or running to freedom, frequently amid a hail of bullets. The Wall in fact proclaimed that East Germany was a huge, barbed-wire concentration camp, with its 18 million citizens imprisoned therein. The free world could hardly have hoped for a better propaganda exhibit.

[5] Dr. Gallup found (September 15, 1961) that 64 per cent of his respondents favored the United States' fighting its way into Berlin should Communist East Germany close all approaches.

Moscow's most recent deadline on Berlin expired quietly on December 31, 1961, and the American reservists were demobilized. Kennedy clearly meant business, but the disturbing question was: Did Khrushchev know that he did?

POISON IN THE SKIES

Negotiations over disarmament likewise remained deadlocked. The stumbling block, as always, was the unwillingness of the West to consent to pledges that were not reinforced by adequate on-site inspection. But the Russians, highly suspicious since early Tsarist days of foreign snooping, would accept no iron-clad guarantees against cheating. A special Anglo-American-Russian conference on the discontinuance of nuclear testing had dragged along drearily at Geneva since October, 1958. Although no real progress was made, the world was being spared open-air nuclear tests by the great powers, for on March 31, 1958, the Soviets had voluntarily proclaimed a moratorium on further nuclear blasts. A sense of relief swept over a world that was fearful of the effects of fallout on health and heredity.

At Geneva, increasing Soviet disinterest in negotiating indicated that something was in the wind. The thunderclap came on August 31, 1961, when the Russians proclaimed that they would resume open-air nuclear testing. They evidently realized that the United States was ahead in the quantity and quality of its nuclear arsenal; they were determined to close the gap and, if possible, attain a lead.

Much of the civilized world was shocked by this abrupt termination of the Soviet moratorium.[6] But the response of the neutralist nations like India was surprisingly mild, quite in contrast with the shock waves of condemnation that beat around the world whenever the Americans undertook to spew radioactivity into the atmosphere.

The United States simply could not permit the Russians to gain the upper hand in the nuclear arms race. They might even perfect anti-missile missiles that would paralyze America's deterrent force. Neutralists, Communists, pacifists, and geneticists alike cried out against America's testing, but President Kennedy, custodian of the nation's security, reluctantly announced that nuclear tests would be resumed.[7] Before issuing

---

[6] The accusation that the Soviets had broken a binding promise ignores the fact that their voluntary moratorium was predicated on other nations not testing, and France had tested. Moreover, President Eisenhower had publicly reserved the right to resume nuclear tests after December 31, 1959. *Public Papers of the Presidents of the United States: Dwight D. Eisenhower: 1959* (Washington, 1960), p. 883.

[7] Gallup polls showed that in fifteen foreign centers, eleven of them America's allies, only Australia (Melbourne) favored a renewal of the tests. American opinion seems to have approved them by a 58 to 33 margin. Public Opinion News Service, Release, June 1, 1958.

the final orders he offered to hold the line if Moscow would sign a treaty banning such testing in the future. But the Soviets, angrily charging blackmail by the Yankee "atom-mongers," returned a blunt refusal. They believed that since the United States had been the first to test, they ought in all fairness to be the last. By this reasoning there would always be one power demanding the last blast.

The exclusive nuclear club was growing fearsomely. America, Russia, Britain, and France all had varying degrees of thermonuclear capability; Communist China was reported to be working furiously on nuclear bombs. The point of no return would soon be passed, if it had not been already. Some kind of agreement seemed imperative to end the arms race before it ended the human race.

THE CONGO IN CONVULSION

One of the most striking changes of the mid-century decades was the sudden emergence of some thirty new African nations from the guardianship of colonialism into the blinding sunlight of independence. In general these peoples, many still bound by tribal loyalties, were poorly prepared for self-government. Yet they were routinely admitted to the UN, where they joined the ex-colonial nations of Asia to swell the potent Afro-Asia bloc. By May of 1963 it had come to number fifty-eight members out of a total of one hundred and eleven. For the first time the United States was facing the frustration of being outvoted in the "Tower of Babble" known as the UN Assembly by tiny, immature states.

The once-Belgian Republic of the Congo became an incredibly confused storm center, and one that threatened to involve the major powers in World War III. The Belgians, suddenly confronted with anticolonial riots, were forced to give this huge area its independence on June 30, 1960, without yet having trained competent political leaders. The Europeans were forthwith subjected to an orgy of looting, raping, and murdering, as the drunken native troops mutinied against their white officers. The Belgians understandably reacted by halting the withdrawal of their troops and sending others back in.

The erratic Congolese Premier Patrice Lumumba, a former postal clerk, appealed to the UN for help against this renewed Belgian "aggression." He made it clear that he would turn to Moscow if assistance were not promptly forthcoming. The Soviets, whose agents had already infiltrated the Congo, voted with the United States and the other members of the Security Council in supporting a resolution (8 to 0) designed to eject the Belgian "imperialists" and restore order. A neutralist UN police force, ultimately numbering over 20,000 men, moved in under a Swedish commander.

The Congo problem was economic as well as political. Katanga province, rich in copper, cobalt, and other minerals, had proved a veritable bonanza to Belgian and other foreign investors. They naturally wished to continue exploiting it by encouraging a separatist movement under mercurial Moise Tshombe, who formally seceded in July, 1960. But the rest of the Congo was so resources-poor that it could not exist as a

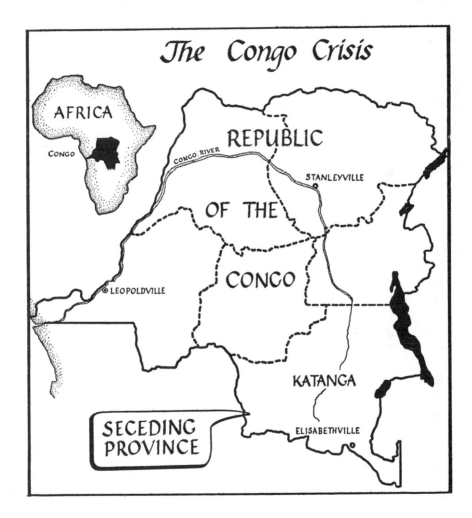

viable state without resources-rich Katanga sharing its wealth and taxes with its impoverished brethren.

A major objective of the UN was to induce Katanga to confederate with its sister provinces. Washington strongly supported this policy, partly because of pressure from many of the African nations, which feared that fragmentation would invite further colonialism. When persuasion in the Congo failed, UN forces engaged in pitched battles, not always successfully, with Katanganese troops commanded by Belgians and other white "mercenaries."

THE UN FIGHTS FOR PEACE

The Soviets, after having voted for the Congo intervention, by now had turned violently against it. Their agents had been run out; the allegedly pro-Communist Lumumba had been murdered. They flatly refused to contribute their share to the heavy costs of this "imperialistic" venture, and the similar refusal of France, Belgium, and numerous other nations brought the UN perilously close to bankruptcy and the withdrawal of its troops. Only an emergency bond authorization of $200 million in 1962, with the United States agreeing to buy as much as $100 million on a dollar-for-dollar matching basis, averted disaster.

The UN's Katanga venture aroused biting criticism in America, especially among right-wing groups. The multination organization was designed to police the peace, not break it; to avert war, not make it. Moise Tshombe, the Katanga leader of a minority group, was anti-Communist, in sharp contrast with certain other Congolese. He was also a secessionist (in the Southern tradition) and semed to be a self-determinist (in the Woodrow Wilson tradition). If there had been a UN in 1776, declared critics, George III would have invited in a UN army to crush secessionist George Washington. Foes of the UN viewed its possible collapse with ill-concealed glee. Conspicuous among them were dedicated ultra-conservatives like the Daughters of the American Revolution, who for years had been clamoring to take the U.S. out of the UN and the UN out of the U.S.[8]

The Kennedy administration vigorously backed the UN and the Congolese government in a final desperate effort to corral Katanga. Protracted conflict might easily bankrupt both the UN and the Congo regime, while turning Central Africa into the vortex of World War III. The speedy delivery of large quantities of American military supplies spurred the UN forces on, and in January, 1962, Tshombe was crushed. The central government could now anticipate stronger political and financial support. The prestige of the UN rose, despite charges of partiality and undue force, as it scored an impressive victory for world order. But deep scars remained, and the problem of unifying the Congolese tribes was far from solved. Especially alarming was the continued refusal of UN members like Russia and France to contribute financially to the preservation of peace in the Congo.

[8] But Gallup found Americans giving a 90 per cent vote of confidence to the UN; only 5 per cent favored withdrawal. February 9, 1962. The selection of New York City as the home of the UN was in some respects a blunder. Non-white delegates from the new African nations were humiliated by discrimination, and espionage agents from Communist countries were a constant irritant, as were various demonstrators.

THE FAR EAST IN FERMENT

Even in the days of Eisenhower, Japanese nationalism, neutralism, and communism had proved disquieting. Opposition was mounting against the continued presence of United States bases on the main islands of Japan, as well as on Okinawa, where the land-pinched Okinawans resented the huge American outlay. The war-ravaged Japanese still clung to neutralism with their hearts, while their heads pointed to the wisdom of collaborating with the West. General MacArthur had hammered home the nuclear-taught folly of militarism, and the people of Japan showed no enthusiasm for taking a stand with Uncle Sam against Communist ideology. Jammed onto small islands and needing overseas markets, they were eager to develop extensive outlets in Communist China, despite scowls from Washington.

Korea continued to be anything but the "Land of the Morning Calm." In April, 1960, the gnarled and dictatorial Syngman Rhee was forced to flee in the wake of bloody student riots against rigged elections. A military junta, flouting democracy, undertook to restore order and eliminate graft. Large-scale American aid nevertheless continued to flow in, and some 50,000 American troops stood ready to repel another invasion from the north. Technically, South Korea and the UN were still at war with North Korea and Communist China: the armistice line was being uneasily held, and each side repeatedly accused the other of violating the armistice agreement. A renewed eruption might occur any day.

President Kennedy inherited all these Far Eastern problems and others as well, including Laos and South Vietnam (see map, p. 831). Despite scandalous wastage of American financial aid, Laos was in grave danger of falling to Communist-supported jungle fighters. The fear prevailed that if strategic Laos fell to the Reds, its neighbors, especially South Vietnam, would be the next Communist target for a salami-slicing conquest of Southeast Asia.

At the outset, Kennedy took a firm stance. He declared emphatically, on March 23, 1961, that to prevent the loss of Laos he would pursue a policy aiming at independence, peace, and neutrality. Armed intervention might well trigger another Korea, under circumstances far less favorable to American fighting men. Within ninety days after his inauguration, Kennedy had evidently decided to pull back to South Vietnam as a more defensible bastion, and if necessary to write off Laos. Republican partisans sneered that first he shook his fist and then his finger. But he took energetic action in mid-May, 1962, when, following major Communist gains in Laos, he threw some five thousand troops into neighboring Thailand. Welcomed by eager Thais, some of them remained until the following December as a steadying influence, despite the routine Communist cries of "imperialistic aggression."

American delegates participated in a fourteen-power conference at Geneva which, on July 23, 1962, agreed on the neutralization and independence of Laos. The quarreling Laotian factions agreed to prop up a neutralist government, combining the three antagonistic elements: Communist, neutralist, and pro-Western. Conservatives in America cried "appeasement" and "a Far Eastern Munich," for previous experience with coalitions indicated that Communist participation usually led to Communist domination. Subsequent violations of the truce agreements by the Communists boded ill for the future peace of Southeast Asia.

Kennedy's decision to hold the line in pro-Western South Vietnam inescapably meant increasing entanglement and undeclared war. Autocratic-aristocratic President Ngo Dinh Diem, unpopular at home and distrusted abroad, was waging a losing battle with Communist guerrillas. Kennedy sent in military "advisers," then American helicopters ("sky cavalry"), and then military personnel. Inevitably United States service men were killed.[9] If the Americans were to succeed where a large French army had failed after seven years of frustrating fighting, then a vast amount of blood and treasure would have to be poured into the steaming jungles of South Vietnam.

RED DRAGON OVER ASIA

Communist China continued to be the overshadowing storm cloud in the Far East. With an exploding population of some 700,000,000 and a large, well-disciplined army, Peking was an ever-present threat to weak neighbors.

The West could take some comfort from the widening rift between the Soviets and their Oriental protégé over how best to "bury us." The Russian Communists, with their revolution more than four decades old, had lost much of their initial zeal and were allegedly falling victim to "creeping private enterprise." The Chinese, with the fanaticism of recent converts, had become more Communist than their teachers, whom they openly accused of the ideological treason of being "soft on capitalism." The Soviets, now a "have got" nation, interpreted Marxist-Leninism as endorsing world revolution by competitive peaceful coexistence (except wars of "liberation"). The Chinese, still a "have not" nation, interpreted Marxist-Leninism as endorsing aggressively warlike means. They argued that a nuclear war would extinguish imperialism, not mankind. If this catastrophe occurred, they could afford to lose half their population and

---

[*] On April 25, 1962, Kennedy issued an executive order to the effect that American servicemen wounded in the Vietnam action would be awarded Purple Hearts. Early in 1963 some 10,000 American servicemen were reported to be in South Vietnam, involved in another undeclared war. By the summer of 1963, over seventy had been killed. Further complications developed in August, 1963, when the pro-Catholic Diem regime cracked down on the dissenting Buddhist majority.

still emerge *the* dominant power. Perhaps the Soviets had created a Frankenstein's monster, and would one day have to ally themselves with the West to keep it caged. Peaceful coexistence between Russia and China loomed as a real problem.

Meanwhile Washington and Peking refused to speak to each other officially. Meaningful recognition is a two-way street, and both governments failed to see eye-to-eye on this thorny issue. In successive Presidential elections, the American people had presumably endorsed nonrecognition, and for a politician to advocate recognition would be to cut his political throat. Nonrecognition implied disapproval of communism; a hope that the Peking dictatorship would collapse if unacknowledged; a desire to encourage Chiang's glimmering prospects; a protest against a regime that not only confiscated American property and mistreated American citizens but waged an intensive hate-America campaign. In keeping with nonrecognition, Washington refused passports to American travelers and newsmen seeking to penetrate the Bamboo Curtain, and maintained an embargo on commerce, initiated in 1950 during the Korean conflict. But subsequently some of America's allies, notably Britain, developed a substantial trade with Communist China, much to the annoyance of conservative spokesmen in the United States.

TWO CHINAS AND THE UN

Official Washington also flintily opposed the admission of Red China into the UN. Foreign critics of this position, notably neutralist India,[10] contended that there could be no United Nations without the most populous of all nations; that China would be less of a menace if she could let off steam in UN debates; and that she would be subject to such sanctions as the organization might impose on a fellow member. Nothing could be more ridiculous, ran the argument, than to continue to recognize the "rump regime" of Chiang as the legal government of a vast land that he did not govern and never would.

Apologists for the American policy of nonadmission replied with weighty arguments. They insisted that although the UN was not exactly a Good Boy's Club, Communist China could hardly qualify under the Charter as a peace-loving nation: she had been technically at war with the UN since her stab-in-the-back attack on the UN forces in Korea in 1950. In 1959 she had crushed the autonomous government of Tibet with brutal force. The seating of Communist China in the UN would mean

[10] Gallup found that the people of New Delhi (India) favored the admission of Red China by a vote of twelve to one; in the United States two out of three voters were opposed. Of the people polled in fourteen nations, only the United States and the Netherlands had a majority against seating. World Gallup Poll News Service, November 19, 1958, release. Washington's pressures on certain "kept" nations contributed to the continued exclusion of Red China from the UN.

the unseating of Chiang's representatives; and the American people, after their multibillion dollar investment in the Generalissimo, would not willingly consent to such a betrayal.

Washington was gradually losing its decade-old battle to blackball Peking at the UN when, in October, 1962, the picture sharply changed. Communist China brought a boundary dispute with India to a climax by launching an overwhelming attack on its neighbor's mountainous outposts. The assault would have been deliciously ironical if it had not been so tragic. The neutralist Premier Nehru of India had been an outspoken apologist for both Red China and Red Russia, while habitually moralizing about the wickedness of the United States in standing up to the Communists. But the devastating assaults by the Chinese on the ill-prepared Indians forced Nehru to swallow his pride and beg for military aid from the "war-mongering" Yankees. Avoiding I-told-you-so's, Washington speedily flew in quantities of military hardware, in pursuance of its established policy of bolstering the largest democracy in Asia and the second most populous nation in the world. Such an energetic response may have contributed to Peking's unilateral proclamation of a cease-fire on November 21, 1962. At all events, Red China's furious clawing on the Roof of the World embarrassed her friends in the UN.

BALLISTIC BLACKMAIL IN CUBA

Fidel Castro had meanwhile been slyly setting the stage for the hottest hour of the Cold War. Following the Bay of Pigs repulse, the loquacious leader continued to bolster his forces in preparation for another invasion. Lavishly provided with shiploads of modern weapons by the Russians, he maintained the second largest army in the Western Hemisphere. Soviet spokesmen repeatedly assured the United States that these weapons were of short range, and for defensive purposes only.

Official Washington was stunned, in mid-October, 1962, by aerial photographs revealing that hundreds of Russian technicians were feverishly emplacing some forty nuclear missiles possessing an estimated range of 1000 to 2000 miles. With this supplement to his long-range missiles in Russia, Khrushchev could "get tough" on Berlin; and Washington, facing nuclear suicide, would presumably have to submit. Cuba's made-in-Moscow muscle was in a sense defensive, because the United States would never dare attack the island if the immediate result would be to wipe out America's major cities. At the same time, Castro would have a free hand to "export" his revolution to the rest of Latin America.

Turning Cuba into a missile-launching pad, and thereby upsetting the world balance of power, constituted the most lethal challenge ever to confront the Monroe Doctrine. Working through his tool Castro, Khrushchev could presumably cow the United States and take over the

Western Hemisphere. The presumed menace of the Holy Alliance in 1823 seemed child's play when compared with this horrifying prospect.

President Kennedy decided to move swiftly in the few days that remained before the Soviet missiles became operational. There was no time for long-winded discussions in the UN or with NATO allies, though he did confer with Congressional leaders.[11] In a nationwide television appearance, on October 22, 1962, he grimly announced that he would impose a "quarantine" on all ships carrying offensive weapons to Castro's Cuba. So grave was the crisis and so convincing the photographic evidence that the Organization of American States, in an unusual display of unity, voted unanimously to support Uncle Sam. Missiles that could shoot north could also shoot south.

Crackingly tense days followed. International law does not sanction a blockade in time of peace, though Kennedy called it a "quarantine," and though the Cold War was hardly peace. The blockage of merchant ships on the high seas in peacetime ran afoul of the hallowed American principle of freedom of the seas. (Oddly enough, two basic policies here clashed: freedom of the seas and the Monroe Doctrine.) The United Nations Charter forbade the use of force or threats of force in such instances, except in "self-defense if an armed attack occurs" (Article 51); and Cuba had not started shooting yet. (Some legalists argued that in this instance the potential danger was so great as to constitute "an armed attack.") If Soviet ships refused to stop and be searched for offensive weapons, American commanders were authorized to fire upon them. Russian submarines prowled Caribbean waters, and if they shot back, World War III would be unleashed.

Fortunately, the avenues of negotiation were kept open. Kennedy communicated directly with Khrushchev at the most critical stage, and the Secretary-General of the UN did yeoman mediatory work. Kennedy had not specifically invoked the musty Monroe Doctrine, but the principle was clearly present.[12] A deadly earnest United States was not bluffing: if the Soviets did not take their missiles out of Cuba, American armed forces would seize or destroy them, Russian technicians and all. And this would be war—probably a nuclear holocaust.

[11] In September, 1962, Congress had overwhelmingly passed a resolution expressing American determination to use whatever means were necessary to block the expansion of Cuban power. The vote was 384 to 7 in the House and 86 to 1 in the Senate, and followed an announcement on September 25 that the Soviets would build a $12 million base for "fishing boats" (submarines?) in Cuba.

[12] Kennedy, like Seward in dealing with Maximilian, did not have to invoke the Monroe Doctrine: self-defense was enough. To have invoked it would have stirred up argument as to whether it was dead or even applicable, since the United States had intervened repeatedly outside the Western Hemisphere. This whole episode is further proof that freedom of the seas is a shackle to the big-navy power. *The American Journal of International Law,* LVII, July, 1963 has a half dozen articles which hold that the Cuban quarantine, which involved self-preservation, was within the framework of international law.

KHRUSHCHEV KNUCKLES UNDER

Happily for peace—and sanity—Khrushchev veered away from the collision course: he did not desire a nuclear incineration over Cuba. He had gravely miscalculated the fiber of Kennedy and the vital concern of the American people, reaching far back into the nineteenth century, for their "soft underbelly." A number of Cuba-bound Soviet ships turned back, and the others never challenged the blockade. After anxious interchanges, a compromise settlement was announced on October 28, 1962. Khrushchev agreed to pull his offensive weapons out of Cuba, under verification by UN representatives; Kennedy agreed to lift the "quarantine" and not to invade the island.

The Kennedy-Khrushchev agreement was never fully honored. The Soviets, with remarkable speed, apparently crated all their missiles and shipped them home, together with some long-range bombers. But a jilted Castro, humiliated before the world, defiantly stood on his sovereignty by refusing to permit on-site inspection. As long as he did so, Kennedy was released from his provisional no-invasion pledge.

The Soviet Communists, who traditionally knew how to practice strategic retreat, suffered a spectacular setback. But their propaganda machine ground out the "line" that since they had gone to the defense of Castro, and since they had extorted a no-invasion pledge, they had saved Cuba. Hence the missiles were no longer needed. As custodians of the dove of peace, they had averted catastrophe and "saved civilization" at a time when the "adventuristic warmongers" of the Pentagon seemed insanely bent on a nuclear war. But the Chinese Communists were not deceived: they accused Moscow of "capitulationism" for having turned tail and betrayed the Cuban comrades. Khrushchev sternly reminded them that although Uncle Sam might be a "paper tiger," he had "nuclear teeth." In the ensuing months the Kremlin, presumably thrown off balance, soft-pedaled the explosive Berlin issue.

COEXISTENCE WITH CASTRO

Both the Soviets and Castro emerged with ruptured reputations. Posing as peace-loving supporters of Cuba, the Russians had blandly lied about their intentions while sneaking missiles and troops into the island. Castro had proclaimed, "Cuba is not alone." But when the crunch came, Khrushchev left him in the lurch, nakedly revealed not as the "maximum leader" but as an expendable tool of Soviet ambitions. The eyes of Latin-American nations, several of which volunteered military assistance, were opened as never before to the dangers of a romance with the Reds.

The prestige of the United States rose correspondingly; Kennedy's unflinching diplomacy largely erased the Bay of Pigs blot. For once, Washington had seized the offensive and had caught the Russians with their missiles down. Enheartened by America's decisive leadership, the principal NATO allies had given Kennedy their support, notably Britain and France, both of which nursed memories of American nonsupport at the time of the Suez attack.

Politically, the Cuban crisis was a godsend to Kennedy, whose popularity rocketed.[13] Republican orators during the concurrent Congressional campaign had been assailing the administration for permitting the obvious Soviet arms build-up in Cuba, and they had been clamoring for a full-scale blockade or outright bombing. Kennedy's bold stroke took the wind out of their oratory, and in next month's elections the Democrats scored a satisfying victory. "We were Cubanized," moaned the Republicans. Yet they denied that Kennedy had won more than a negative triumph: he still had a defiant Castro and entrenched communism on his hands, plus some 17,000 hard-to-move Russian troops.

In subsequent months Washington continued its policy of trying to isolate Castro politically while strangling him economically. Constant pressure was exerted on Moscow to remove the Soviet troops. Embargoes on American exports to Cuba were retained, while the policy was tightened of denying certain return-trip American cargoes to foreign ships supplying the troubled island. The hope was that Castro and his subverted revolution would slowly wither behind his Sugar Cane Curtain.

THE DEFENSE OF THE DOLLAR

President Kennedy continued the established postwar policy of pouring dollars into backward countries that were in danger of going Communist. But the long-suffering American taxpayer and budget-paring Congressmen were beginning to wonder if foreign aid was a boon or a boondoggle. In 1962 a rebellious Congress, wielding a meat-axe, chopped off more than a billion dollars from Kennedy's recommended figure, leaving a postwar low of $3.9 billion. In certain "expectant" nations, notably Laos, the wastage had been frightful and the results futile, if not harmful. The heavy emphasis on arms likewise raised doubts as to whether guns should be thrust into the hands of men who needed plows. Criticism was also rising against aid to Marshal Tito of Yugoslavia, who seemed to be embracing Khrushchev with one hand while blackmailing Uncle Sam with the other.

[13] Kennedy's popularity shot up to 74 per cent approval; his recent sending of federal troops to Mississippi during the school-integration crisis had brought a slump. Gallup Release, December 5, 1962.

Few clear-thinking American leaders were demanding that foreign aid be choked off completely.[14] If imitation is the sincerest form of flattery, the Soviets were complimenting the Americans by pouring rubles into backward countries, sometimes more lavishly and often to better advantage. Even the semistarved Chinese Reds were scraping together aid for their ideological bedfellows in Albania and Cuba. The conviction was growing in America that West Germany and other prosperous Western

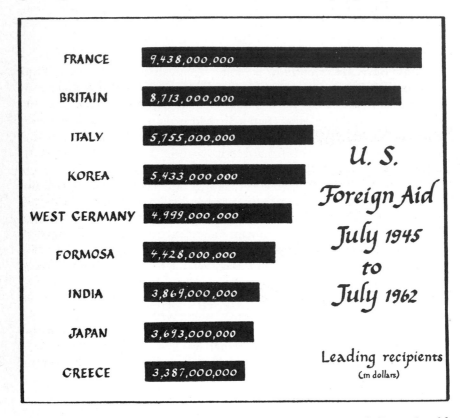

FRANCE	9,438,000,000
BRITAIN	8,713,000,000
ITALY	5,755,000,000
KOREA	5,433,000,000
WEST GERMANY	4,999,000,000
FORMOSA	4,428,000,000
INDIA	3,869,000,000
JAPAN	3,693,000,000
GREECE	3,387,000,000

U. S. Foreign Aid July 1945 to July 1962

Leading recipients
(in dollars)

nations, boosted back onto their feet with Marshall Plan dollars, should begin to shoulder their share of the burden, as indeed they were doing to a considerable extent.

The agitation for cutbacks in foreign aid was intensified by a hemorrhaging of gold from America, developing seriously in 1958 and largely the result of maintaining costly overseas forces and programs. Once-flush Uncle Sam was forced into the humiliating position of urging his

[14] A Gallup Release (Feb. 3, 1963) showed that the public supported foreign aid to the extent of 58 per cent for to 30 per cent against, as compared with 51 per cent for to 33 per cent against in March, 1958. Many respondents, annoyed by nonsupport from beneficiaries during international crises, called for more discrimination in getting "our money's worth."

ex-enemy, West Germany, to co-operate in preserving the dollar balance. Drastic economies during the early Kennedy years eased the Treasury over the acute stage, but the leakage continued to be serious and the whole world could see that the seemingly "bottomless" money bags of Uncle Sam actually had bottoms. By mid-1963 the United States had sent abroad about $100 billion in post-World War II loans and grants.

THE COMMON MARKET THREAT

An exciting development of the late 1950's and the early 1960's was the emergence, with American encouragement, of an embryonic United States of Europe. Six highly industrialized nations of Western Europe—France, West Germany, Italy, Belgium, the Netherlands, and Luxembourg—had gradually drawn together to form an economic union known as the Common Market (European Economic Community). A distinguishing feature was the mutual lowering of tariff walls, with a consequent inrush of prosperity.

But perhaps more significant for the future was the fact that economic integration foreshadowed political integration. The aging President de Gaulle of France and the aged Chancellor Adenauer of West Germany, though once hereditary foes, had so purposefully tied together their two economies—notably in coal, iron, and steel—that the two nations could hardly make war on each other in the future.[15] A United States of Europe would present to the world a potent "third force," in population and economy perhaps even more powerful than either the United States or the Soviet Union. This epochal integration was especially disturbing to the men of Moscow, who denounced it as "imperialistic" and "monopolistic." Capitalism, far from decaying from within, was experiencing a wondrous rebirth. The most conspicuous decay seemed to be occurring within the ranks of the Communist parties of Western Europe.

The Common Market countries, with their common tariff barrier and about 170,000,000 consumers, threatened to make heavy inroads into the export markets of the United States, especially in farm products. President Kennedy emphatically expressed his conviction that America must either "trade or fade." The Reciprocal Trade Agreements Act was about to expire, and he urged upon Congress a new Trade Expansion Act, which would give him sweeping powers to raise or lower or eliminate tariffs so as to meet the competition of the Common Market. By surprisingly wide margins, he won a smashing victory when Congress, in October, 1962, granted him substantially what he requested. America

[15] De Gaulle and Adenauer formally turned a bloody page of history when, on January 22, 1963, they signed in Paris the Franco-German Treaty of Cooperation.

was indeed showing surprising maturity in facing up to the challenge of a fast-changing economic world.

NATO: A FORCE OR A FARCE?

Intimately related to the Common Market was the fate of the fifteen-nation NATO pact, still the major dike against a Soviet lunge into Western Europe. This alliance had never attained its blueprinted strength, and by early 1963 could field only some 25 divisions, as compared with perhaps 175 for the Communist bloc. The French, as feet-dragging allies, had drained off much of their promised support during their seven-year struggle against the rebellious Algerians. The United States itself maintained several hundred thousand troops in Europe, while also relying on nuclear missiles emplaced on the soil of its allies.

Coalition diplomacy—getting all fifteen clocks to strike at once—is difficult at best. Here the complexities were compounded. First, the United States was militarily so powerful that the other members of the alliance seemed like pale shadows: the mighty republic had enough nuclear power to kill every human being on the globe twenty-five or so times over. Second, as Europe became stronger and more prosperous, it became less dependent on American support and hence more restive. Third, the once-great powers—Britain and notably President de Gaulle's France—did not take kindly to the role of poor relations. Their unproclaimed slogan was: "No annihilation without representation."

The British and French both desired a nuclear deterrent of their own, for they feared that America might leave them in the lurch during a purely European showdown. The British had detonated their first atomic bomb in 1952; and American and world opinion had exerted heavy pressure on France not to embark upon such a course. But De Gaulle plunged ahead with grim determination, and the French exploded their first atomic device in the Sahara in 1960.

To the Kennedy administration this duplication of nuclear programs was intolerable. The Alliance did not require more nuclear weapons: the United States possessed about 97 per cent of the West's atomic arsenal. The need was for adequate ground forces, which the European allies should and could provide but which they would not if they "wasted" their money on relatively puny nuclear weapons. President Kennedy's ideal was to establish under NATO a common nuclear deterrent, rather than a fragmented one with many nervous fingers near many different buttons.

DICTATION WITHOUT DOMINATION

Under the cocoanut palms of Nassau, in the British Bahamas, Kennedy finally threshed out an agreement with Prime Minister Macmillan of

Britain, late in December, 1962. The United States promised to sell Polaris nuclear missiles, to be fired from hard-to-locate submarines, while the British would provide additional submarines. A NATO nuclear force was to be established with American help, and Britain would turn over her nuclear strength to the NATO command, except when the British decided that their "supreme national interests are at stake."

Kennedy offered similar terms to President de Gaulle, who, annoyed by the secret Anglo-American conclave at Nassau, returned a blunt *"non."* Rigidly determined to regain France's lost prestige (*grandeur*), he would go it alone or not at all. At the same time, jealous of sharing the leadership of Western Europe with Britain, he brushed off Washington's pressures and dramatically slammed the door, in January, 1963, on London's belated bid to enter the not-so-common Common Market. He seemed determined to squeeze British and American influence from the continent of Europe.

Kennedy indicated late in 1962 that he who sits in the driver's seat should do the driving, but his more aggressive leadership made for friction. The British and French resented it, while Washington's public scolding of Canada for remissness in honoring defense commitments backfired in February, 1963. The Canadian government fell, and Prime Minister Diefenbaker, declaring that Canada was "an ally but not a satellite," went to the country with an unsuccessful anti-American campaign. One British writer suggested that Kennedy was not a football coach but the leader of a fifteen-member orchestra, many of whose members wanted to play first violin.

NATO was clearly in trouble. In the more relaxed atmosphere after the Cuban crisis, the cohesive plaster of a common danger seemed to be dissolving. Washington was unable to take full advantage of the Sino-Soviet split in the Communist camp because of the split in its own. With the United States emplacing increasing numbers of intercontinental ballistic missiles at home, it was becoming less dependent on bases and allies abroad. Yet, in the interests of its own security, it could not wash its hands of its European allies, as they well knew.

In a dramatic effort to prevent the polarization of power around Gaullist France, Kennedy undertook a ten-day tour of Western Europe, June 23 to July 2, 1963. His first and most impressive reception occurred in West Germany, where street-lining masses shouted "Ken-ne-DEE" and where his emphatic assurances of continued military support, in several widely televised speeches, drew enthusiastic acclaim. In West Berlin, where he grimly viewed The Wall, he was made an honorary citizen. He assured the cheering throng that in the sense that he too favored human freedom *"Ich bin ein Berliner"* ("I am a Berliner.") He then made a sentimental-political journey to his ancestral home (Ireland), after which he conferred briefly in England and Italy with leading statesmen.

Kennedy's barnstorming tour, though undertaken with misgivings, was a gratifying success. Khrushchev hastened to East Berlin on a fence-mending countervisit, but the crowds were markedly smaller and quieter. De Gaulle, who had frostily withheld an invitation, responded by journeying to West Germany, there to try to keep Adenaeur in line. French spokesmen declared that while they did not doubt Kennedy's sincerity in promising armed assistance, he could not bind his successors ten years later. Hence France would have to develop her own nuclear arsenal. At all events, the Kennedy trip clearly had a tonic effect on languishing NATO. "Yankee, Go Home" might be the watchword of the Gaullists, but not of the more cautious and less ambitious West Europeans.

THE TEST-BAN TREATY, LTD.

The Kremlin had meanwhile begun to show surprising signs of warm-ing up to the West. The thaw was generally attributed to the heat generated between the two Red giants, for if Kennedy had his de Gaulle, Khrushchev had his Mao Tse-tung. In July, 1963, the Sino-Soviet ideological conference in Moscow collapsed, in an atmosphere blue with charges and countercharges. Perhaps the Soviets wanted to prove to Peking that coexistence and economic competition with the West were possible. Perhaps they foresaw ultimate war with their Oriental comrade, whose contiguous frontier and proliferating population augured trouble. Perhaps they were seeking to pressure the Chinese into abandoning the nuclear bomb.

Whatever his motives, Khrushchev startled the Western world, on July 2, 1963, by proposing a nuclear test-ban agreement, coupled with a nonaggression pact between the West and the Communist bloc. The Americans and British, who had been urging such a ban for years, eagerly embraced the test-ban scheme, while rejecting the nonaggression pact. It would involve the consent of the 15-nation NATO alliance, and would certainly be vetoed by West Germany, which detected a booby trap for securing recognition of a permanently separated East Germany.

The nonaggression pact was put aside, but not abandoned by Khrushchev, while the American and British negotiators haggled with the Soviets in Moscow for ten days. The United States representative, W. Averell Harriman, former ambassador to the USSR, played a stellar role. With all three parties evidently agreed to agree, progress was rapid, and the completed treaty was formally signed on August 5, 1963, amid much pageantry. Leaving no stone unturned, Kennedy had arranged to fly in to Moscow six prominent United States Senators, four Democrats and two Republicans.

The 900-word treaty was short, simple, clear—and limited. It prohibited further nuclear tests in the atmosphere, in outer space, or under the water. Underground tests might continue without restriction; they could not be so easily detected, and the Soviets had long since spurned cheat-proof inspection. Other nations were invited to adhere, and most of them soon did. De Gaulle, as feared, returned a flat *"non."* He was joined by Communist China, which would not be lured into a self-denying trap by the "dirty fraud" of the Kremlin "freaks and monsters."

The partial test-ban treaty, like the Kellogg-Briand Pact before it, was given an extravagant billing. It did not limit the current arms race or arms stocks in the slightest degree. The signatories could shake off this shackle by giving three months' notice, if "extraordinary events" so required. If honored, the pact would reduce the radioactive fallout that was poisoning the atmosphere, and limit the proliferation of nuclear weapons. It would bring moral pressure to bear on France and Communist China to avoid dirtying the atmosphere further. By relaxing tensions between East and West, it might slow down the frantic arms race and even serve as the opening wedge for a genuine disarmament agreement. It was generally hailed as a symbol, more for what it portended than for what it promised. Feeble though it seemed to be, it was the first completed treaty on arms limitation after eighteen years of negotiations between East and West.

American public opinion—especially the fallout-conscious "mother vote"—overwhelmingly favored the hope-freighted pact. Despite the fear that the now-smiling Soviets must be up to something, the gamble did not seem unduly risky in view of the built-in "escape hatch." In extended Senatorial hearings, the pluses were carefully weighed against the minuses. Republicans were reluctant to stick a feather in the Kennedy cap on the eve of a presidential election, but to have rejected the treaty, now that it was signed, would have put America in the same camp with Communist China. Under the lash of public opinion the Senate finally gave its approval, September 24, 1963, by the lopsided vote of 80 to 19, or 14 more than the necessary two-thirds. The hope was that this "historical breakthrough" might be the beginning of a new era, but the fear was it would prove to be one more disappointment of the old.

Certainly the international scene was troubled and confused. World communism, despite Western fears, was clearly not monolithic: newly fragmented centers of power were forming. With Moscow now less able to crack the whip over fanatical world revolutionists, new problems were rising. Coexistence with the Communist world—and even with independent-minded NATO allies—presented increasing difficulties. More than ever patient diplomacy of the highest order was urgently needed.

SELECTED BIBLIOGRAPHY

Many of the titles listed in the bibliographies of the last five chapters are relevant. The most useful general coverage is R. P. Stebbins, *The United States in World Affairs, 1961* (New York, 1962). Speeches of Secretary of State Dean Rusk, edited by E. K. Lindley, have been published as *Winds of Freedom* (Boston, 1963). A journalistic account of the Bay of Pigs affair is

Tad Szulc and K. E. Meyer, *The Cuban Invasion: The Chronicle of a Disaster* (New York, 1962). The crisis of October, 1962 is dealt with in J. Daniel and J. G. Hubbard, *Strike in the West* (New York, 1963). On Latin America consult A. A. Berle, *Latin America: Diplomacy and Reality* (New York, 1962); J. C. Dreier, ed., *The Alliance for Progress* (Baltimore, 1962); P. A. Ray, *South Wind Red: Our Hemispheric Crisis* (Chicago, 1962). An anti-Yankee denunciation by a noted Spanish scholar is Salvador de Madariaga, *Latin America between the Eagle and the Bear* (New York, 1962). On Africa, see M. N. Hennessy, *The Congo: A Brief History and Appraisal* (London, 1961); Smith Hempstone, *Rebels, Mercenaries, and Dividends: The Katanga Story* (New York, 1962). On the Far East consult C. A. Buss, *The Arc of Crisis* (New York, 1961); James Cary, *Japan Today: Reluctant Ally* (New York, 1962); O. E. Clubb, *The United States and the Sino-Soviet Bloc in Southeast Asia* (Washington, 1962); Charles Wolf, *Foreign Aid: Theory and Practice in Southern Asia* (Princeton, 1960). See also Arnold Wolfers, *Discord and Collaboration: Essays on International Politics* (Baltimore, 1962); H. C. Allen, *The Anglo-American Predicament; The British Commonwealth: The United States and European Unity* (New York, 1960).

8TH ED. REFS. Arthur M. Schlesinger, Jr., *A Thousand Days: John F. Kennedy in the White House* (Boston, 1965), is a brilliant mixture of history and memoir by a member of the White House staff especially concerned with foreign policy. An admirer of J.F.K., he thinks the President was really finding himself when cut down and that President Johnson harvested much undeserved credit for the labors of his predecessor. Kennedy's contemplated dropping of Secretary Dean Rusk, as reported by Schlesinger, caused the Secretary (who continued in office) considerable embarrassment. Theodore C. Sorensen, *Kennedy* (New York, 1965), is another valuable memoir by a presidential assistant closer to the throne than Schlesinger. More discreet, Sorensen is primarily concerned with domestic affairs. He reveals that after the Vienna meeting, Khrushchev entered into an extensive secret correspondence with Kennedy which helped keep lines of communication open during the Cuban missile crisis. Roger Hilsman, *To Move a Nation: The Politics of Foreign Policy in the Administration of John F. Kennedy* (Garden City, N.Y., 1967), provides more of the inside story by a high-ranking State Department official who was a strong admirer of Kennedy. The author is especially revealing on the Congo, the Cuban missile crisis, and the involvement in Laos and Viet Nam. The role of the CIA looms large throughout. Pierre Salinger, *With Kennedy* (Garden City, N.Y., 1966), by Kennedy's ebullient press secretary, is not particularly revealing on foreign affairs, although there are gossipy glimpses of Khruschev and other Soviet dignitaries. Elie Abel, *The Missile Crisis* (Philadelphia, 1966), though journalistic, is reasonably reliable and recaptures the breathlessness of the "crunch." It reveals that the President's brother Robert first suggested that the government ignore Khrushchev's last message (a tough one) and respond to the previous message (a milder one) as a basis for compromise (pp. 198–99). David L. Larson, ed., *The "Cuban Crisis" of 1962: Selected Documents and Chronology* (Boston, 1963), is a revealing compilation of key documents. Detailed general coverage appears in Richard P. Stebbins, *The United States in World Affairs, 1962* (New York, 1963) and *The United States in World Affairs, 1963* (New York, 1964). Robert F. Kennedy's posthumous *Thirteen Days: A Memoir of the Cuban Missile Crisis* (New York, 1969) provides some intimate details without altering the generally known outlines of the Cuban crunch. Emphasis is placed on the alleged bellicosity of the military men.

9TH ED. REFS. See BIBLIOGRAPHICAL ADDENDUM, p. 1,061.

56

The Ordeal
of Lyndon Johnson

*But we are not about to send American boys nine or
ten thousand miles away from home to do what
Asian boys ought to be doing for themselves.*
PRESIDENT JOHNSON, October 21, 1964

THE TORCH IS PASSED

PRESIDENT KENNEDY, continuing his efforts to improve Soviet-American relations, achieved something of a coup when, on October 9, 1963, he announced approval of the sale to Russia of some $250 million worth of wheat and wheat flour. Massive crop failures in the Soviet Union had forced the Communists, hat in hand, to seek grain from the capitalist West. Right-wing Americans were vehement in their opposition. Why feed your adversary when you can starve him into submission?

But Kennedy, strongly backed by public opinion, concluded the deal.[1] America was glutted with a price-supported wheat surplus, much of which was being expensively stored (while deteriorating) in huge containers. Moreover, the sale to Russia would aid American business and provide enough money to help stem the hemorrhaging of gold resulting from the increasingly adverse balance of payments. Finally, there was no proof that a hungry and desperate Communist was more peaceful than a well-fed one.

President Kennedy had about come of age, diplomatically speaking, when he was tragically murdered by hidden rifle fire in Dallas, Texas, November 22, 1963. Vice-President Johnson, the tall Texan, promptly assumed the Presidency with whirling-dervish energy. A veteran of the House and Senate, he had long been more concerned with domestic

---

[1] A Gallup Release (Oct. 25, 1963) reported that of those with opinions the favorable response ran two to one.

problems than foreign affairs. Yet he was no greenhorn in diplomacy. As Vice-President, he had sat in Cabinet meetings and other high-level conclaves. As "America's traveling ambassador" under President Kennedy, he had journeyed over 100,000 miles and had exchanged views with important personages in some thirty countries, including Viet Nam.

Bothersome problems remained from the Kennedy administration. By far the most vexatious was the decades-old war in South Viet Nam, now largely a civil conflict in which America, supporting the anti-Communist regime, was still embroiled (technically) in an "advisory" capacity. President Kennedy had increased the 700 or so military advisers sent by President Eisenhower to about 16,000. This substantial intervention did not save the scandal-ridden regime of autocratic President Diem and his brother in Saigon. Both men were murdered in a military coup, November, 1963, earlier in the month in which Kennedy was assassinated. Official Washington was visibly relieved to be rid of the despotic Diem, but a succession of corrupt and collapsible governments ensued which, as will be noted later, made almost inevitable a larger American commitment.

CUBA, CASTRO, AND THE CANAL

Fidel Castro's Cuba, exporting both sugar and sedition, continued to be an official worry. Late in 1963 Washington imposed new boycott restrictions on Western ships trading with the Cubans. It followed up this turn of the screw by curtailing military aid to five offending nations, including the NATO allies Britain and France. The Organization of American States (OAS) had meanwhile substantiated charges that Cuban arms were being smuggled into Latin America, notably Venezuela, for Communist subversion. As a reprisal, the Organization of American States, in July, 1964, voted to impose economic sanctions on Cuba and to bar all OAS members from official relations with Havana.[2]

The Castroites, with heavy financial support from Moscow, continued their Communistic course. The Chinese Communists, now bitter ideological rivals of the Russians, embarked upon competitive aid. But when they failed to deliver promised shipments of rice, Castro turned angrily against Peking in 1966, accusing his Chinese "comrades" of attempted "blackmail" and classing them with "Yankee imperialists." As far as America was concerned, a partial lifting of the sugarcane curtain came in November, 1965, when Castro agreed to permit 3,000 to 4,000 unhappy Cubans to leave each month on "mercy flights" to the United States.

Farther south, a shocking anti-Yankee outburst, with some Communist

[2] The independent-minded Mexican government continued to recognize the Castro regime.

overtones, flared up in Panama, on January 9, 1964. The Panamanians, still chafing under the lopsided treaty of 1903, had secured a concession from Washington that the Panamanian flag should always fly beside the Stars and Stripes in the leased Canal Zone, on a separate-but-equal basis. Superpatriotic Americans in the Zone ("Zonians") resented this new regulation. When some high-spirited high school youths refused to honor it, shooting erupted which resulted in the deaths of some twenty-five persons, four of them American soldiers. Panama promptly broke diplomatic relations with Washington and took her complaints in vain to both the UN and the Organization of American States.

President Johnson, in response to public pressures, could have used the iron fist against tiny Panama.[3] Instead he used the velvet glove. Negotiations to appease the Panamanians rocked along until after the November Presidential election in the United States. Then President Johnson announced, in December, 1964, that he would propose a renegotiation of the hated treaty of 1903 and the building of a new sea-level canal. The old one was now too slow, too congested, too vulnerable to sabotage and bombing, and too small for larger ships, including American aircraft carriers.

In June, 1967, the presidents of the two countries announced agreement on three new pacts. The first would terminate the treaty of 1903 and give Panama greater control over the Zone and the canal. The second would provide for joint defense. The third would smooth the path for rebuilding the waterway at sea level, possibly by nuclear excavation. But patriotic Panamanians, unwilling to be second-class citizens in their own country, demanded greater control of the existing canal and the unbuilt one. The local political situation became so explosive that the triple package was shelved in Panama, at least temporarily.

PRESIDENT DE GAULLE—UNRELIABLE ALLY

Even before Kennedy's murder, the fifteen-nation NATO coalition was evidently on the verge of collapse. This was notably true of the eastern anchors, Greece and Turkey, which were periodically at daggers drawn over the alleged mistreatment of the Greeks and Turks among the citizens of Cyprus.

The need for NATO, originally designed to contain Russia, seemed less imperative than in 1949. The Communist satellite nations of the Warsaw

[3] Dr. Gallup found that among the 64 per cent of his respondents who had followed the dispute, the vote ran 6 to 1 against making concessions to Panama for greater control over the Canal. This response indicated that there would be considerable opposition to a revised treaty in the United States Senate. Gallup Release, February 12, 1964.

Pact—the Kremlin's answer to NATO—had already shown their restiveness. A formidable Red China, fast stockpiling nuclear weapons, loomed on Russia's lengthy Siberian border as a monster, itself to be "contained." Finally, the revived European nations were in better shape than in the 1940's to defend themselves, especially de Gaulle's France, which was expanding its second-class nuclear arsenal.

President de Gaulle continued his role as the chief disrupter of the Western alliance. Dispelling dreams of a United States of Europe, he was determined to pursue policies almost exclusively in the interests of France, as he conceived them. His repeated attacks on the American dollar, with an increase in the disturbing gold drain to Europe, deepened antagonism in the United States. Americans who remembered their outpouring of aid in two world wars complained bitterly of ingratitude, while recalling that France still owed about $7 billion on the debt of World War I.[4]

De Gaulle, who had already withdrawn some French forces from the NATO command, dealt the alliance a body blow with two announcements in March, 1966. As of July 1, 1966, all remaining French units would be detached, and as of April 1, 1967, all foreign troops and installations not under French authority were to be removed from French soil.[5] This eviction notice would cost the United States hundreds of millions of dollars and accelerate the distressing dollar drain. After Washington had vainly protested against what it regarded as a premature abrogation of the alliance, NATO reluctantly agreed to move its military headquarters from France to Belgium.

De Gaulle claimed that France still belonged to NATO and had no intention of leaving at a later date. But in view of his overtures to the Communists, whether in Moscow or Peking, his trustworthiness as an ally was further suspect in Washington. Additionally, he barred Britain from the Common Market, angered Canada by blatantly encouraging French-Canadian separatism, and self-righteously assailed America's participation in the French-started Viet Nam conflict.

The Viet Nam deathtrap created problems with still other NATO nations. The British and other allied shippers, to the exasperation of Americans, continued their profitable trade with North Viet Nam. The British Labour government was under heavy fire at home for its support, albeit lukewarm, of the United States. Finally, West Germany resented the withdrawal of thousands of American troops for service in Viet Nam, and with good reason feared even greater redeployment.

[4] This figure, which included accumulated interest to June, 1967, was about double the original debt. See above, pp. 657–667. The other defaulting debtors were in generally the same situation, with Britain owing even more than France.

[5] For the exchange of the French and American *aides-mémoire* on this subject, see the *Department of State Bulletin*, LIV (April 18, 1966), 617–618; *ibid*. LIV (May 2, 1966), 699–703.

FROM KHRUSHCHEV TO KOSYGIN

The months following the Cuban missile climbdown of 1962 had brought a perceptibly more relaxed atmosphere (*détente*) to Soviet-American relations. But abundant friction points remained. The East Germans, with the obvious backing of the Kremlin, made periodic attempts to throttle access to West Berlin. Occasionally Soviet fighter planes would force down American aircraft that wandered into Communist airspace.

A promising stride forward was taken on June 1, 1964, when the USSR and the U.S., on Washington's initiative, signed a consular convention in Moscow—the first bilateral treaty the two regimes had ever concluded.[6] Specific rules were elaborated, with new safeguards for American citizens, for the establishment of additional consulates. But because overstaffed Soviet embassies and consulates were suspected centers of espionage, the pact encountered violent criticism from American conservatives. Not until nearly three years later—March 16, 1967—did a suspicious Senate vote its approval, 66 to 28, or a margin of 3 votes over the necessary two-thirds.

Another gain for sanity came on October 14, 1964, when Premier Khrushchev—theatrical, unpredictable, and bullying—was unexpectedly sacked and demoted to the rank of an "unperson." His successor was the more temperate Premier Kosygin, who resorted to less bluster and bomb-rattling. The path was cleared for more cordial relations, especially in view of the violent split between Moscow and Peking. But the accession of Kosygin roughly coincided with President Johnson's widening of the war against Communist North Viet Nam, which was receiving heavy shipments of arms from China and Russia, including sophisticated weapons that were to destroy hundreds of American planes. A priceless opportunity to drive a deeper wedge between Moscow and Peking evaporated as American policy in Viet Nam tended to drive the quarreling yokefellows somewhat closer together.

The Soviet Premier Kosygin, attending the UN sessions in New York on the Arab-Israeli crisis (p. 907), arranged for a so-called summit conference with President Johnson on June 23 and 25, 1967. They chose a compromise site, halfway between New York and Washington, at the home ("Hollybush") of the President of Glassboro State College, Glassboro, New Jersey. At the end of the parley, President Johnson reported that he had discussed the Middle East crisis, limitation of nuclear arms, and the Viet Nam War. His sagging popularity shot up temporarily as a result of the "Spirit of Hollybush," but skeptical observers concluded that nothing significant had resulted. The Soviets had repeatedly proclaimed

[6] For text, see *Department of State Bulletin*, L (June 22, 1964), 979–985.

that tensions could not be relaxed until the American "imperialist aggressors" had pulled out of Viet Nam.

NUCLEAR NONPROLIFERATION

Snail-like progress was meanwhile being made toward limiting nuclear warfare. On January 27, 1967, a pact for the peaceful uses of outer space was signed by 60 nations of the UN. Surprisingly, the treaty was unanimously approved by the United States Senate on April 25, and by the Soviets on May 19. As only the U.S. and the USSR had developed a substantial program for outer space, their approval made general acceptance a virtual certainty.

One significant byproduct of the get-together at Glassboro may have been greater impetus to a multipower treaty to end the proliferation of nuclear weapons. After months of wearisome negotiation, the Soviet Union and the United States jointly submitted to the UN Disarmament Conference at Geneva, on August 24, 1967, a treaty to halt the spread of nuclear weapons. The General Assembly in New York approved the pact on June 12, 1968, by the lopsided vote of 95 to 4, with 21 abstaining.[7] The treaty was to enter into force when ratified by the United States, Soviet Russia, Great Britain, and forty other signatories. The two newer nuclear powers could be counted on not to approve: France, which had absented itself during the final vote, and unrepresented Communist China, which denounced "the plot" cooked up by America and Russia.

The nonproliferation pact, when properly concluded, bound the signatory states with nuclear stockpiles not to supply such weapons to nations not possessing them. The non-nuclear countries that ratified agreed, for their part, not to manufacture such devices. President Johnson hailed the treaty as an epochal gain for peace, because the more nations there were with nuclear arsenals, the more likely the world was to blow itself up, whether through accident or design.

A ceremonial signing in Washington, Moscow, and London by the three leading nuclear powers, on July 1, 1968, also brought hope that a breakthrough might be achieved in limiting competitive anti-missile missiles. Both the Soviets and the Americans were moving toward elaborate defensive screens, at an estimated cost to the United States of some $40 billion. The prospect of a mutual missile moratorium, designed to head off such a ruinous race, was heartily welcome to the tax-burdened peoples of both countries. (The pact became effective on March 5, 1970.)

---

[7] A number of nations had grave misgivings about entrusting their protection to the existing nuclear powers. Among the four that voted negatively were Albania and Cuba; among the abstainers were India, Argentina, Brazil, Portugal and Spain.

THE REPUDIATION OF GOLDWATERISM

As the Presidential sweepstakes of 1964 neared, Lyndon Johnson loomed as the overwhelming choice of the Democrats for nomination "in his own right." A master "wheeler-dealer," arm-twister, and energizer, he had driven an impressive amount of domestic legislation through Congress in his "nine miracle months." He was nominated by acclamation in a carefully ringmastered convention in Atlantic City, on August 26, 1964. The platform stressed peace and prudence abroad (ironical words), as well as help for the underprivileged and impoverished at home—or what came to be called the Great Society.

The Republicans meanwhile had embarked upon a suicide course. The right-wing extremists, though a clear minority of the party, secured control of the convention, held at San Francisco's famed Cow Palace in July, 1964. They ruthlessly rammed through the nomination of their gray-haired idol, handsome Senator Barry M. Goldwater of Arizona, amid scenes of near hysteria.

Goldwater, a major general in the Air Force Reserve, was the rugged, two-fisted type. Suspicious of Soviet wiles, he had alienated the "mother vote" by opposing the Nuclear Test Ban Treaty of 1963. He believed that the administration was "soft on Communism" and that the Communists ought to be halted, if necessary, by brute force. While seeking to contain Communism abroad, he rather inconsistently urged a meat-axing of foreign aid, which was largely designed to curb Communism. A foe of Big Government, he also inconsistently demanded a reduction of the federal budget while immensely increasing expenditures for the armed forces. At heart a go-it-aloner like de Gaulle, he condemned the NATO alliance. He lambasted the "no-win" war in Viet Nam, called for further defoliation of the jungles with chemicals, and indiscreetly proposed that American field commanders be authorized to use tactical nuclear explosives at their own discretion. Shooting impulsively "from the lip," he gave the impression of recklessness abroad and heartlessness at home.

President Johnson, in ringing words that came back to plague him, repeatedly assured the voters that the war in Viet Nam was an Asian war which would have to be fought by Asians. These statements seemed to be a pledge that substantial numbers of American boys would never be committed to the meatgrinder of Viet Nam.

An ugly turn came, August 2–4, 1964, when North Vietnamese torpedo boats reportedly attacked two American destroyers operating in the Gulf of Tonkin, off North Viet Nam, in international waters. Smarting under Goldwater's charges of "softness" on Communism, Johnson reacted, perhaps over-reacted. On August 4, the day of the second attack, he ordered

American aircraft to blast North Vietnamese boats and naval installations
along about 100 miles of the coast. The American public enthusiastically
applauded this resolute act of red-blooded Americanism.[8]

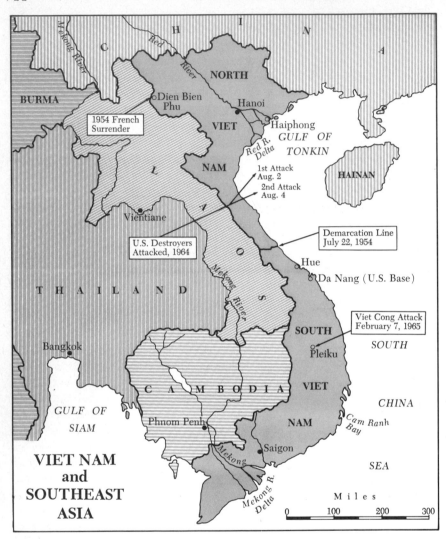

VIET NAM
and
SOUTHEAST
ASIA

Johnson capitalized on the overwhelming applause to ask Congress for
the blank-check Gulf of Tonkin Resolution. It specifically supported him

[8] Whatever its motivations, the bombing was good electioneering. Dr. Gallup found
that popular approval of Johnson's handling of the Viet Nam situation shot up from
38 per cent to 71 per cent, with 16 per cent unfavorable, and 13 per cent without
opinion. Gallup Release, August 26, 1964. In succeeding weeks, popular approval
weakened greatly.

in his determination "to take all necessary measures to repel any armed attack against the forces of the United States and to prevent further aggression." Stating further that the peace and security of Southeast Asia were "vital" to the "national interest," the resolution authorized the President to take all necessary steps to help those freedom-seeking states of the area that sought such assistance.[9] This fateful enactment passed the House on August 7, 1964, 416 to 0, and the Senate, 88 to 2. Many members of Congress, who did not foresee what they were blindly sanctioning, later regretted having voted approval.

The worrisome international situation operated to the advantage of the "prudent" Johnson and against the "trigger-happy" Arizona "cowboy." About two weeks before the election, Khrushchev was unhorsed, and the Chinese Communists detonated their first nuclear device, thus becoming unwanted member Number Five of the exclusive Nuclear Club. An experienced hand on the tiller seemed imperative. On November 3, 1964, President Johnson buried Barry Goldwater with an unprecedented 61.1 per cent of the popular vote, including hundreds of thousands of Republicans who feared the Senator's itchy nuclear finger. The results seemed to be an emphatic demand from the American people not to escalate the war in Viet Nam.

THE DOMINICAN DIVERSION

On April 24, 1965, a bloody revolt, which ultimately claimed about two thousand Dominican lives, erupted against the rightist-oriented and Washington-supported government in Santo Domingo. The fighting rapidly became so furious that the American Ambassador, unanimously supported by his eight subordinates, urged the President to intervene for the protection of hundreds of American lives. Four days after the outbreak, Johnson reluctantly helicoptered in several hundred American troops, who ultimately numbered about 25,000. Such iron-fisted interference violated solemn commitments to the Organization of American States and the United Nations. But President Johnson, concluding that the crisis did not permit windy debate, resolved to be illegally safe rather than legally sorry.[10]

Four days after the first marines landed, a grim-faced Johnson appeared

[9] Specifically, any member of the Southeast Asia Collective Defense Treaty, "or protocol state," which would include South Viet Nam. Text of resolution in *Department of State Bulletin*, LI (Aug. 24, 1964), 268.

[10] C. G. Fenwick, "The Dominican Republic: Intervention or Collective Self-Defense," *American Journal of International Law*, LX (1966), 64–67, finds partial justification in the self-defense doctrine; R. T. Bohan, "The Dominican Case: Unilateral Intervention," *ibid.*, 809–812, takes issue with Fenwick and deplores the precedent for unilateral intervention.

on television to justify his action. This time he not only stressed the saving of American lives but the averting of a Communist coup. Alluding to the Castro-style takeover of Cuba, he made it clear that he was not going to sit back and see the Dominican Republic become another Caribbean cancer.[11] This injection of the Communist "bogey" added fuel to the controversy, partly because the State Department could name only a few known Communists.[12]

The unexpected landing of the troops, some of whom killed or were killed while returning hostile fire, aroused Latin Americans in general and liberal Americans in particular. Not once since Franklin Roosevelt's disavowal of intervention in 1933 had unfriendly marine bayonets desecrated Latin American shores. Outraged Latinos decried the flouting of a sacred pledge, and many of them feared that henceforth they could not enjoy the right of revolution without undue interference from Big Brother in Washington. Signs urging "Go Home, Yankee" were widely displayed. The reservoir of good will that Uncle Sam had expensively built up since 1933—from the hope-giving Good Neighborism to the limping Alliance for Progress [13]—seemed to be disappearing in the Caribbean cauldron.

Fortunately for improved relations, Washington persuaded the Organization of American States, by a vote of 14 to 5, to authorize an Inter-American Peace Force. Ultimately five Latin American nations sent at least token manpower.[14] Command of the entire body of troops, though overwhelmingly from the United States, fell to a Brazilian general, who had the second largest contingent. In this way the Yankee-haters were partially appeased.

With the blessing of the Organization of American States, the Dominican Republic held new elections in June, 1966, and the moderate right-of-center candidate defeated his moderately leftist opponent by a surprising margin. Evidently the Dominicans preferred calm to continued chaos. The Yankee troops gradually left for home, and in September, 1966, the Inter-American Peace Force officially disbanded, although sporadic terrorism continued. Washington's determination not to revert to the old "gunboat policy" of the Big Stick years was somewhat reassuring to the Latin Americans, but they could not be certain that the Northern

[11] *Department of State Bulletin*, LII (May 17, 1965), 744–748, speech of May 2, 1965.

[12] Many of the 58 to whom Johnson referred could hardly qualify as card-carrying Communists. American public opinion supported the intervention. Of the 80 per cent who were aware of the crisis, Gallup found 76 per cent favorable, 17 per cent unfavorable, and 7 per cent without opinions. Gallup Release, June 2, 1965.

[13] The Alliance for Progress (p. 870) was not living up to expectations, but it probably was better than nothing.

[14] They were Brazil (with the second largest contingent of some 1,300 men), Costa Rica, Honduras, Nicaragua, and Paraguay. John B. Martin, *Overtaken By Events* (Garden City, N.Y., 1966), p. 699. Martin was a former U.S. Ambassador whom President Johnson sent to Santo Domingo on a special mission.

Colossus would not come again if he felt that conditions required his "helping" hand. The Dominican wound would be a long time healing.

JOHNSON WIDENS THE WAR IN VIET NAM

The successive regimes in Saigon that followed the murder of President Diem, in November, 1963, proved to be weak, inefficient, corruption-riddled, and beset by factions (Buddhists versus Catholics). The Viet Cong rebels, whose political arm was the National Liberation Front, were gaining strength. Generously supplied with additional arms from North Viet Nam, China, and Russia, they were clearly winning the upper hand and endangering the elaborate bases being constructed by the Americans.

Justification for more vigorous action came on February 7, 1965, when a Viet Cong force staged a night raid on the American barracks at Pleiku, South Viet Nam, killing eight men and wounding over 100, while destroying several aircraft. In retaliation, President Johnson ordered a number of increasingly destructive bombing raids on military targets in North Viet Nam.[15] Gradually stepped up, these forays caused heavy incidental damage to nonmilitary structures and considerable loss of civilian life, including residents of the capital, Hanoi.

Less than a month after the first large-scale bombings, Washington announced (March 6, 1965) that two battalions of marines were being dispatched to South Viet Nam. They began to disembark two days later. These, one should note, were the first combat troops (non-advisory) to be dispatched in substantial numbers. President Johnson thus chose to escalate the war, despite his electoral promises of 1964, in what he conceived to be the national interest. Determined to demonstrate that Communist aggression did not pay, he probably was unduly persuaded by his advisers that he could achieve a cheap and easy victory, where the French had failed, with overwhelming air superiority. Seldom has awesome power proved so impotent.

The jungle-and-rice-paddy conflict rapidly widened until it had become the third largest foreign war in American history. By mid-1968 it was costing some $30 billion a year, sucking in over a half million servicemen, and attracting increasing numbers of North Vietnamese regulars. The casualty toll had mounted to more than 25,000 American battle deaths, to say nothing of the more than 100,000 wounded. The dirty little war had become a dirty big one.

---

[15] Gallup found the retaliatory air strikes strongly favored, with 67 per cent responding "yes," 15 per cent "no," and 18 per cent "no opinion." Gallup Release, February 16, 1965. General Curtis E. LeMay, Chief of Staff of the Air Force, had earlier advocated bombing North Viet Nam, saying, "We are swatting flies when we should be going after the manure pile." Roger Hilsman, *To Move a Nation* (Garden City, N.Y., 1967), pp. 526–527.

DEEPENING VIET NAM QUICKSANDS

America had become deeply involved in this tragic trap in May, 1950, when President Truman agreed to support the French against the Communist guerrillas of Ho Chi Minh with money and military hardware, altogether costing some three billion dollars. The reasoning in Washington was that the Communists, having subverted China in 1949, were a huge monolith, with the directing brain in Moscow. When the Chinese Reds and the Russian Reds split openly in the 1960's, and noisily advertised that Communism was no monolith, justification for the American presence was more difficult. But so heavily involved were the Americans by this time that they had to find other reasons for justifying the prodigal expenditure of men and money, such as moral obligations, national security, and commitments to the Saigon regime.[16]

MARX SADLY VIEWS THE NON-MONOLITHIC COMMUNIST WORLD

Bastian in the San Francisco *Chronicle*.

The Washington administration, after spurning earlier peace feelers from North Viet Nam, repeatedly tried to extricate itself from the mon-

[16] Late in 1964, several months after the Bay of Tonkin incident, Gallup sought reasons for the American presence. A total of 49 per cent replied "stopping the spread of Communism," 6 per cent stressed the moral obligation to the free world, 3 per cent mentioned security, 2 per cent referred to the legal commitment, and 31 per cent were unable to give any reason. Gallup Release, December 2, 1964.

soon mud. In a nationally televised speech at The Johns Hopkins University in Baltimore, April 7, 1965, Johnson brandished the bludgeon and waved the carrot. He declared that while he was prepared to fight through to victory, he was also prepared to negotiate unconditionally and to back a billion-dollar program for the economic rehabilitation of Southeast Asia, including North Viet Nam. The next year (October 24–25, 1966), in a seven-nation summit conference at Manila made up of representatives of the countries fielding troops in South Viet Nam, Johnson pledged a withdrawal of American forces within six months after a satisfactory withdrawal by North Viet Nam.

The hard-bitten North Vietnamese regime in Hanoi rejected all such formulas as "swindles," possibly because American planes had inopportunely dropped bombs on civilian centers when Hanoi had earlier shown some responsiveness to peace feelers.[17] Realizing that Americans were notoriously short on patience, Hanoi was evidently convinced that eventually it could wear down the national will to win. It persistently refused to negotiate unless the Americans ended the bombing and withdrew their troops. It argued that North Viet Nam was not blasting Yankee cities and that it should not bribe its adversary into not doing what he should never have started. Several unilateral "bombing pauses" by the Americans resulted in nothing but an increased flow of troops and supplies from North Viet Nam (while American supplies were pouring into South Viet Nam).

BOMBS HEARD ROUND THE WORLD

The brutal and futile war in Southeast Asia cast an evil shadow on America's relations with many nations. Articulate world opinion, reflecting a David-versus-Goliath sympathy, turned heavily against the United States. U Thant, Secretary General of the UN, repeatedly vented his displeasure. Embattlement abroad also created embroilment at home. The costly conflict accelerated the alarming dollar drain, seriously unbalanced the national budget, sharply reduced foreign aid appropriations, escalated the current inflation, hamstrung the War on Poverty ("Make War on Poverty, not People"), and curtailed help for disadvantaged Negroes. The republic was trying to police the world but could not police its own streets. Viet Nam, critics charged, was causing Johnson's Great Society to become Johnson's Great Fiasco.

The United States did receive some direct outside aid in Viet Nam, but mostly of a token nature. Australia, New Zealand, the Philippines, and Thailand contributed a few thousand men, in various categories. South Korea sent about 50,000 troops. But, as in the Korean War, Uncle Sam, among outsiders, carried the lion's share of the burden.

[17] A journalistic account of several alleged diplomatic mixups, possibly because of forgetfulness in not countermanding orders already issued, is David Kraslow and Stuart H. Loory, *The Secret Search for Peace in Vietnam* (New York, 1968).

The Red Chinese stepped up their hate-America campaign, joined with the Russians in supplying the North Vietnamese with arms, and shot down American planes violating their air space. They also indicated their willingness to send in hordes of "volunteers," as they had done in Korea in 1950. The United States had violated a fundamental military precept in becoming again involved in a land war with a nation contiguous to the "inexhaustible" manpower of China.

American bombing near the Chinese border, with incidental damage to Russian and Chinese shipping, posed the grave danger that World War III would be triggered in Asia. Whenever the North Vietnamese seemed willing to talk terms with the "imperialist aggressors," Communist China, though torn with internal disorders, expressed ominous displeasure.[18] Neither Peking nor Moscow was any more willing to see the capitalists triumph in Viet Nam than Washington was to see the Communists triumph. Each side regarded the other as the aggressor, and each was keenly aware of the so-called lessons of Munich.

REPERCUSSIONS IN EAST ASIA

Cambodia, which bordered South Viet Nam, severed diplomatic relations with Washington in 1965, following alleged violations of its territory by American forces. Washington, with equal reason, charged Cambodia with providing sanctuary for the shadowy Viet Cong.

The North Vietnamese were funneling men and supplies into South Viet Nam over the Ho Chi Minh trail, which, for many miles, ran through the charade known as neutralized Laos. In counter-violation of its neutrality, American planes secretly engaged in heavy aerial bombing of Laotian jungles.

Thailand, which was threatened by Communist guerrillas in the east, welcomed American help. Huge military installations were built on Thai soil, from which bombing raids, at first on a hush-hush basis, were launched by the Americans against North Viet Nam. In Thailand, as in South Viet Nam, increasing friction developed with the populace over the Americanization of the country. Anti-imperialists, especially in North Viet Nam, naturally viewed the enormous bases as evidence that imperialist Uncle Sam was in the Far East to stay.

The Japanese, many of whom resented the attack by white men on Asians, were critical of America's involvement in Southeast Asia. The clamor increased when the Americans used Japan's island of Okinawa as the primary staging area for their combat operations in North Viet Nam.

The North Koreans, who had increasingly provoked minor clashes and

---

[18] During these years Red China was routinely denied membership in the United Nations, which it was unwilling to join, except on its own terms, which were so sweeping as to be unacceptable to most UN members.

casualties along the armistice line of 1953, showed their contempt for a United States that was bogged down in Viet Nam. On January 23, 1968, the North Koreans seized the American intelligence ship *Pueblo,* which allegedly had penetrated their territorial waters, and imprisoned the crew of some eighty men. Outraged by the "insolence" of this tiny nation, many Americans demanded devastating measures, if necessary, to rescue the ship and its crew. But the Johnson administration, with one costly conflict on its hands, did not want to spark another Korean war, which might well cost tens of thousands of lives, in return for the unlikely rescue of eighty men.

After exasperating negotiations, Washington's patience was rewarded eleven months later, when the men were released after the United States had admitted guilt and signed an apology for violating Korean waters. By bizarre prearrangement, the "confession," obviously extorted under duress, was openly repudiated before and after the signing. The humane but awkward solution raised doubts as to the worth of America's word, and definitely played into the hands of Communist propagandists.

THE SIX-DAY ISRAELI-ARAB WAR

The dangers of weakening one's diplomatic hand by military overcommitment elsewhere were further driven home in June, 1967, by a frightening explosion in the Middle East.

The truce that had ended the Israeli-Egyptian war in 1956 lasted nearly eleven years, with the Arabs repeatedly proclaiming their undying determination to destroy the state of Israel and to restore an Arab Palestine. Repeated forays from Syria brought a smashing aerial reprisal by the Israelis in April, 1967. As the tension mounted, President Nasser of Egypt, plentifully equipped with Soviet tanks and planes, demanded the withdrawal of the neutral United Nations peacekeeping force, which had long stood between him and Israel on the Egyptian side of the line.

With the UN police gone, Nasser, on May 22, 1967, closed to Israeli shipping the narrow mouth of the Gulf of Aqaba, which provided access to Israel's only backdoor port. President Johnson, speaking for a nation that had long advocated freedom of the seas, urged Nasser to lift the blockade, explaining that America had long considered the entrance to the Gulf of Aqaba an "international waterway." [19]

Tiny Israel was now threatened with both suffocation and strangulation. The United Nations, tied up in knots by the pro-Arab Soviet veto, was powerless. The great maritime nations, notably Britain and the United States, hemmed and hawed as they discussed ways of reopening the disputed straits. The desperate Israelis, concluding that they could rely on no one but themselves and the God of Abraham, launched a preemptive

[19] *Department of State Bulletin,* LVI (June 12, 1967), 870–871.

lightning war (June 5–10, 1967) which completely routed their neighboring Arab foes and blocked the Suez Canal.

On June 6, 1967, when the Arab forces were clearly flattened, the Security Council of the UN adopted a Soviet-backed proposal for a cease fire. The same day Nasser broke diplomatic relations with the United States, mistakenly accusing the Americans and the British of having used their warplanes to aid Israel. Many observers feared that the Soviets might intervene to save their expensively equipped protégés, but dangers of a misunderstanding were reduced by the use of the Hot Line. (This was the instantaneous teletype communication established between Moscow and Washington by President Kennedy after the Cuban missile crisis.)

Another teetering truce came after another quick-thrust war that settled little and unsettled much. Israel now held greatly enlarged territory and more defensible frontiers, to which she defiantly clung pending guarantees of recognition and security. President Johnson, who had pursued a neutral course, declared that Washington could not recognize the forcible and unilateral unification of Jerusalem by the Israelis. Yet he was prepared to continue the long-established policy of seeking a peaceful balance in the Middle East between the contending forces.

From the standpoint of Washington, there was one fortunate aspect of this devastating little war: it ended before the United States, already overextended in Viet Nam, could become involved in a crisis that might well have detonated World War III. But the Middle East remained a powder keg.

THE GREAT DEBATE ON VIET NAM

The Viet Nam conflict was beyond doubt the most unpopular foreign war in American history, not even excepting Korea. The mounting wrath of the people provides a classic example of how an aroused public opinion can force a sharp turnabout in official policy.

Concerted popular resistance began in 1965, after President Johnson had started the large-scale aerial bombing and had sent in ground troops. Criticism was initially headlined by marathon "teach-ins" in the colleges, organized by "Vietniks." Mounting defiance resulted in the public burnings of draft cards ("Hell No, We Won't Go"), and in various mass demonstrations, including one at the Pentagon in Washington. Cynical youths chanted, "Hey, Hey, LBJ, How Many Kids Did You Kill Today?" Counter demonstrations were also staged, some of them impressively large, in support of the administration. Those citizens who supported escalation were called "hawks," while those who favored extrication were dubbed "doves."

The opinion polls showed, as in the case of Korea in 1950, that initially the Viet Nam intervention enjoyed strong public support. But as the bill mounted, in gold and gore, and the war seemed interminable and unwinnable, the American people became restive, and the tide began to turn. Such opposition no doubt brought some hope to Hanoi, which had counted on war weariness to help achieve ultimate victory. Though some of the protest in America may have been engineered or supported by Communists or Communist sympathizers, they alone could not begin to account for the tidal wave of condemnation that gradually welled up. Repeated assurances from the administration that victory was just around the next rice paddy, and that a few more American soldiers would turn the trick, widened Johnson's so-called Credibility Gap.

Much of the antagonism to the war was channeled through the Senate Foreign Relations Committee, headed by Senator Fulbright of Arkansas. He arranged for a series of widely viewed televised hearings, beginning early in 1966, and featuring a parade of prominent witnesses. Secretary of State Rusk held doggedly to the administration line but other experts were highly critical, including George F. Kennan, the reputed architect of containment in 1947. He testified that he had never interpreted containment to mean the use of armed force, particularly in hot spots all over the world. He stated bluntly that if the nation were not already heavily committed in Viet Nam, he could think of "no reason why we should wish to become so involved. . . ."[20]

DISSENTING DOVES

The doves charged that the Viet Nam war was illegal because Congress, as required by the Constitution, had never formally declared it. It was immoral because it was a no-front, no-rear conflict which involved the indiscriminate killing of civilians, friendly or otherwise, with murderous new weapons, including "improved" napalm. It had caused America to betray her own revolutionary traditions because she had become the aggressor in a civil war between a people who spoke the same language and who resented the interference of a foreign nation.

The United States, moreover, was violating the Wilsonian principle of self-determination by conniving at the flouting of the general elections stipulated in the Geneva Agreements of 1954 (see p. 832). If the elections had been held, and the people had voted for Ho Chi Minh (as then seemed certain),[21] an unvivisected Viet Nam might well have refused to

[20] J. William Fulbright, ed., *The Vietnam Hearings* (New York, 1966), p. 108. This is a convenient compilation of the first hearings. See also his *Old Myths and New Realities* (New York, 1964); *The Arrogance of Power* (New York, 1966).

[21] President Eisenhower later wrote that if the elections had been held as "of the time of the fighting, possibly 80 per cent of the population would have voted for the Communist Ho Chi Minh. . . ." Dwight D. Eisenhower, *Mandate for Change, 1953–1956* (Garden City, N.Y., 1963), p. 372.

follow the dictates of Peking, as Tito had spurned those of Moscow in 1948. The Vietnamese, in fact, boasted a centuries-old enmity toward the Chinese.

Asians, declared the doves, should be allowed to fight their own wars, as President Johnson had assured the voters in the 1964 campaign. President Eisenhower's initial promise of support for President Diem in 1954 had been invalidated by Diem's failure to carry out contingent reforms, as was true of the succeeding "puppet" governments in Saigon. At all events, any such commitments were plainly superseded by President Johnson's election pledge not to pour in American boys.

The doves further argued that the war could not be won by any conventional means that the nation had the will to employ. Nuclear bombs would merely result in creating a desert and calling it peace. If the United States should win the war in these circumstances, it would in fact lose the peace. The Vietnamese people, many of whom resented the "Americanization" of South Viet Nam, were becoming bystanders in their own war. Many of them hated the Yankee and wanted him to go home, except conspicuously for the pimps and prostitutes at the bottom of the social scale and the corrupt, dollar-draining bureaucrats at the top. The regime would obviously collapse overnight if the Americans pulled up stakes.[22] The war could not be won unless the men-in-the-rice-paddy were won under the American pacification program, and this scheme faltered as the Viet Cong methodically slaughtered the village leaders. The United States had fallen so low in world opinion that it would seem to save face rather than lose face if it pulled out. France had lost face in 1954 but had gained prestige.

HIGH-FLYING HAWKS

The hawks stated their rebuttal with vigor. The President could constitutionally send troops wherever he chose, and the Gulf of Tonkin Resolution provided clinching legal authority. If the members of Congress did not like it, they could repeal it and withdraw financial support from the boys in the jungles (something that would have been political suicide). The war was no more immoral than any other: in this jumbled-up type of fighting, civilians were bound to be hurt. The onus of immorality was on the Viet Cong aggressors, who butchered and beheaded in barbaric fashion.

The United States, the hawks insisted, was not the aggressor. The Americans were there by request of the legal Saigon government, in re-

---

[22] The Thieu–Ky military clique that was elected in September, 1967, polled about 35 per cent of the vote cast, amid numerous charges of fraud, and subsequently clapped the runner-up peace candidate into jail.

sponse to prior intervention by North Viet Nam.[23] If the war had ever been purely a civil war, it no longer was, with thousands of North Vietnamese troops present, backed by numerous Russian and Chinese technicians. Free elections, as contemplated for 1956, were impossible under Communist auspices.

The hawks further contended that Johnson's campaign promises were made when conditions were radically different. At that time the South Vietnamese seemed capable of pulling through without American bombing or troops. The war, moreover, contributed to a containment of Communism that was in America's interest. Otherwise the remaining small nations of Southeast Asia would collapse like "falling dominoes" and force an American retreat to the beaches of Hawaii, perhaps California.[24] If the United States turned tail, the Communists would murder hundreds of thousands of Roman Catholics and others who had fled from North Viet Nam in 1954 and who had pinned their faith on American promises. If Washington should prove faithless to its word, world order would be irreparably undermined. America's allies, some forty in number, would lose all faith in her and make what terms they could with Communism. Finally, the United States had never failed to win a war (except, one should note, the War of 1812 and the Korean War), and the national honor would be besmirched if it should lose one now.

The more militant hawks cried out against any form of appeasement. They concluded from the Munich surrender of 1938 that compromise, concession, and de-escalation would only be quitting on the installment

[23] This is a disputed point, but there can be little doubt that there was some North Vietnamese involvement with the Viet Cong from the beginning, although not on a considerable scale until about 1958, when American advisers were appearing in numbers. Washington, though not signing the Geneva Agreements of 1954 (see p. 832) had pledged itself not to use "force" to upset them, but when "aggression" was renewed, with the obvious encouragement of North Viet Nam, the United States felt released from this pledge. For a lengthy justification by the State Department Legal Adviser, see Leonard C. Meeker, "The Legality of United States Participation in the Defense of Viet-Nam," *Department of State Bulletin*, LIV (March 28, 1966), 474–489, which argues that North Viet Nam violated the Geneva Accords from the beginning. For a strong rebuttal, see Quincy Wright, "Legal Aspects of the Viet-Nam Situation," *Amer. Jour. of Internat. Law*, LX (1966), 750–769, which holds that the U.S. position was illegal in the view of traditional international law. No appreciable number of North Vietnamese came before 1958, and by that time Saigon had voided the cease fire by non-compliance with the obligation to hold elections in 1956. The Gulf of Tonkin reprisal, argues the author, was not a legal reprisal because it did not involve a prior attempt to seek redress from the presumed attacker. Arguing learnedly from the same set of facts, John N. Moore, in "The Lawfulness of Military Assistance to the Republic of Viet-Nam," *ibid.*, LXI (1967), 1–34, fully supports the American intervention. Wolfgang Friedmann, "Law and Politics in the Vietnamese War: A Comment," *ibid.*, 776–785, scrutinizes both the Wright and Moore articles and concludes that the U.S. relied not on international law but on national power.

[24] The falling domino theory—that if one Asian state fell to Communism, its neighbors would also fall—had not been borne out in practice. Communist China, the biggest domino of all, had fallen in 1949, but none of its neighbors had toppled.

plan.[25] Yielding of ground would merely demonstrate that the super-powerful United States was really a "paper tiger," as the Chinese Reds tirelessly charged. The morale of all South Viet Nam would collapse, and America's bloody, billion-dollar sacrifices would have been in vain. The Communists were committed to "wars of national liberation," and if they succeeded in their guerrilla aggression, all confidence in halting them would evaporate, from Berlin to Burma.

America's hard-nosed position in South Viet Nam had already encouraged the smaller nations of Southeast Asia to rebuff the malign hand of Communism. The hawks could point with satisfaction to the bloody crushing by Indonesia, in 1967, of an alleged attempt by the Chinese Communists to take over a nation of some 100,000,000 souls. This falling domino had fallen into the Western camp.

As for provoking the Chinese into World War III, this was most unlikely. Chaotic China was but a "paper dragon": it had fallen out with Russia; the Red Guards had created chaos; and Peking knew that extremists in the Pentagon would like nothing better than to bomb in the bud Chinese nuclear capability. Such was the hawk case.

THE RISING ANTI-WAR TIDE

The doves and the hawks sported varicolored feathers. The more extreme hawks, like Governor Ronald Reagan of California, urged that bomb-pocked North Viet Nam be pulverized into submission and that the boys then be brought home in a hurry with victory emblazoned on their banners. The extreme doves, a growing minority, clamored for a speedy pullout, leaving the Vietnamese to settle their own differences in their own way. By late 1967 most Americans, while not proposing an immediate pullout, evidently favored bringing the war to an honorable end on terms that would save face and permit the South Vietnamese to stand on their own feet.

On January 30, 1968, the Viet Cong guerrillas, who had suffered some bad beatings, launched a well-coordinated and totally unexpected offensive against more than 30 key cities and towns, including Saigon itself and the American embassy there. Although this Tet holiday offensive was repulsed with heavy losses on both sides, the surprising bounceback of the Viet Cong proved that the war was far from won. The effect on American opinion strikingly resembled that of MacArthur's Korean reverse late in

[25] Arthur M. Schlesinger, Jr., has suggested that the misapplication of the lessons of Munich may already have done more harm than Munich itself. *The Bitter Heritage* (Boston, 1967), p. 89. Secretary Rusk, publicly defending his Viet Nam policy, repeated in classic form the Hitler-appeasement analogy. The New York *Times*, Dec. 9, 1967. The weakness of the Munich analogy in its application to Viet Nam is analyzed in Howard Zinn, *Vietnam: The Logic of Withdrawal* (Boston, 1967), pp. 85–88.

1950. Popular support for the war dropped dramatically, and criticism of Johnson's handling of it increased spectacularly.[26]

The doves now found an unexpected champion in the little-known, soft-spoken Senator Eugene McCarthy of Minnesota. Running in the Democratic Presidential primary in New Hampshire, on March 12, 1968, he polled an incredible 42 per cent of the vote to 49 per cent for President Johnson. Five days later, Senator Robert F. Kennedy of New York, belatedly recognizing the rising strength of the anti-war tide, threw his hat into the ring. His dovish position and the Kennedy name were expected to have a strong appeal. Up to this point President Johnson had repeatedly avowed his determination to blast his way to the peace table, presumably on the theory that if past medicine fails, double the dose. General Westmoreland, commanding in Viet Nam, was reportedly asking for some 200,000 more troops, to add to the 535,000 already there.

JOHNSON'S GREAT RENUNCIATION

Then came one of the most amazing reversals in American history. President Johnson was obviously weary, plainly discouraged, visibly ageing, and possibly unwell. His popularity was plummeting. He faced a struggle for renomination by his own party, and possible defeat by the Republicans in 1968, quite in contrast with his landslide victory of 1964. He could bow out with honor by sharply changing course in Viet Nam, closing the Credibility Gap, reuniting the country, promoting the chances of peace, and increasing his stature as a statesman who was not angling for re-election. He could run for his place in history rather than for another term in the White House.[27]

Whatever his motives, Johnson took to television, on March 31, 1968, with a bombshell message. He announced emphatically that he would not accept another nomination, and that he would de-escalate the war unilaterally. Future bombings of North Viet Nam would be limited to the narrow and scantily populated southern sector (below the 20th parallel), and the troop reinforcements requested would be not the talked-about

[26] The day before Johnson announced his non-candidacy for 1968, Gallup reported that 26 per cent approved his conduct of the war, 63 per cent disapproved, and 11 per cent were of no opinion. Gallup Release, March 31, 1968. Much of the dissent, of course, came from those who felt that he should go all-out. Gallup had also found (Release of Mar. 10, 1968) that 49 per cent regarded the Viet Nam involvement as a mistake, 41 per cent thought it was not, and 10 per cent were without opinion. Corresponding figures for August, 1965, had been 24 per cent, 61 per cent, and 15 per cent. In late February, 1968, the hawks outnumbered the doves more than 2 to 1; by May 1, 1968 (Gallup Release) they were even at 41 per cent each.

[27] Immediately after Johnson's renunciation of March 31, his popularity shot up spectacularly, from a 36 per cent approval of his overall performance to a 49 per cent approval. Approval of his conduct of the war rose from 26 per cent to 41 per cent. Gallup Release, April 17, 1968.

200,000 but a nominal 13,500. Johnson hoped that these substantial concessions would cause Hanoi to come to the conference table.

Copyright 1968 Los Angeles Times Syndicate

AGING PROCESS

President Johnson Ages Under the Strain.
Copyright 1968 Los Angeles Times Syndicate.

The North Vietnamese and the Americans, after weeks of haggling over the site, agreed, on May 3, 1968, to meet in Paris to talk about talks. They inflexibly repeated their demand that all bombing and other acts of war against North Viet Nam cease unconditionally before there could be meaningful discussions. Washington was unwilling to make this concession in view of the increasing infiltration of North Vietnamese troops and supplies into South Viet Nam, following the partial limitation on bombings. No measurable progress was made at Paris during the early meetings, and the pattern of the prolonged Korean negotiations seemed to be repeating itself in a dialogue of the deaf. Political experts speculated that Hanoi was holding back pending the outcome of the upcoming Presidential election, which might bring to the White House a candidate who had never identified himself with Johnson's hard line.

A THREE-WAY RACE TO THE WHITE HOUSE

Following President Johnson's dramatic "abdication," March 31, 1968, a three-cornered contest developed among the Democrats for his crown. Vice-President Humphrey, virtually a prisoner of White House policies, enjoyed the support of the Democratic establishment, including the machine politicians. He urged a continuation of the limited bombing of North Viet Nam until the enemy was forced to make reciprocal concessions that would lead to "an honorable peace." His two chief rivals were dovish Senator McCarthy and dovish Senator Robert F. Kennedy. McCarthy received near-fanatical support from anti-war young people of college age (the so-called Children's Crusade). Kennedy, after developing impressive momentum in the primaries, was fatally shot in Los Angeles on the night of his narrow victory over McCarthy in California. Humphrey then loomed larger as the man to beat for the nomination.

Early in August, 1968, the victory-starved Republicans gathered in Miami Beach, Florida, gloating over the deep divisions among the Democrats and the unpopularity of lame-duck President Johnson.[28] The "new" Richard M. Nixon, a middle-of-the-roader who leaned toward the right, had the nomination sewed up on the first ballot. Among his assets were an increased maturity; a strong advocacy of "law and justice"; an insistent demand for greater economy in government, including the already slashed foreign aid program;[29] and a hard-nosed position on Viet Nam.

The faction-rent Democrats met in Chicago late in August, 1968, despite threats from anti-Viet Nam militants that the proceedings would be disrupted. Vice-President Humphrey, as anticipated, triumphed on the first ballot: his chief rival, Senator McCarthy, simply did not have the necessary machine-garnered votes. The chief battle erupted over the plank in the platform relating to Viet Nam. The McCarthyites argued for an *unconditional* termination of the bombing, followed by negotiations for a phased withdrawal of all foreign troops. The Humphreyites (echoing President Johnson) demanded a cessation of the bombing only when such action would not endanger American lives and when there was evidence of an appropriate response from Hanoi. After a heated three-hour debate, the McCarthyite substitute lost by a vote of 1567¾ to 1041¼, amid "Stop the War" chants. Many of the dissenting doves remained bitterly unreconciled.

Fireworks were provided during the convention by the "Battle of Chicago." Thousands of young agitators gathered to demonstrate for

[28] Approval of Johnson's stewardship sank to a new low of 35 per cent in August, largely because of Viet Nam. Gallup Release, September 4, 1968.

[29] Congress had cut the outlay in 1968 to about $1.6 billion, the lowest foreign aid appropriation since the end of World War II. In 1967 several other nations had contributed a larger percentage of their gross national product than the United States.

McCarthy and peace, while condemning the military draft and the Viet Nam War. Flaunting Viet Cong flags and chanting "Ho, Ho, Ho Chi Minh," many taunted or defied the blue-helmeted police ("pigs"), who over-reacted with billy clubs in riotous scenes that were widely telecast, at home and abroad. Scores of citizens were injured, but no one died, except, cynics observed, the Democratic Party. Senator McCarthy's disenchanted followers did not fall in behind Humphrey *en masse*, and not until a week before the election did McCarthy, with obvious distaste, come out for Humphrey.

The campaign was complicated by a "spoiler" American Independent party, headed by ex-Governor George C. Wallace of Alabama. Appealing primarily to fear and white racism, he promised a "law and order" crackdown on criminals, rioters, looters, and other "anarchist" demonstrators. Abroad, he would smash the Vietnamese into submission. Lending punch to his promise, he chose as his running mate General Curtis E. LeMay— the same LeMay who had urged blasting North Viet Nam back "into the Stone Age."

THE THIRD RAPE OF CZECHOSLOVAKIA

Midway between the conventions at Miami and Chicago, a frightening crisis developed in Czechoslovakia. Created in 1918 as a promising democracy, this ill-starred nation had experienced a short and tragic history. Vivisected and then seized by Hitler in 1938–1939, it was liberated in 1945 and then taken over by the Soviet Communists in 1948. After twenty years under Moscow's heel, the Czechoslovaks were edging daringly toward the heady wine of democracy and freedom. If they succeeded in shedding Russian shackles, the contagion of liberty might spread to the other Soviet satellites in the Warsaw Pact.[30] These subservient peoples might then break away like falling dominoes, and the Red army's defensive-offensive position on Russia's western frontier would be gravely weakened. The Kremlin still feared the virus of freedom at home and especially the revival of a unified and nuclear-armed Germany abroad.

After some hesitation, the Soviets suddenly overran Czechoslovakia on the night of August 20–21, 1968, with a massive display of tanks, accompanied by several hundred thousand troops. They encountered little organized resistance; only a few dozen Czechoslovaks vainly sacrificed their lives. Evidently for the sake of appearances, the Russians also

---

[30] The Warsaw Treaty Organization was created by the Soviets in 1955 as an answer to the North Atlantic Treaty Organization and to the rearmament of West Germany. It originally included Russia, East Germany, Poland, Hungary, Bulgaria, Czechoslovakia, Romania, and Albania, which had moved into the Red Chinese orbit in the early 1960's and which withdrew from the Warsaw Pact following the Soviet invasion of Czechoslovakia in 1968. Romania, exhibiting democratic tendencies, was highly unreliable.

brought in Communist troops from four Warsaw Pact countries: East Germany, Poland, Hungary, and Bulgaria. Under the iron fist of Moscow, the Prague government was forced to reverse its democratization and sign a treaty legalizing the presence of Soviet troops.

President Johnson issued a vigorous protest over nationwide television and radio, calling upon the invaders to withdraw. He pointed to the obvious violation of the United Nations Charter, to the nonexistence of external aggression, and to the absence of a Czechoslovak invitation (despite Moscow's allegations to the contrary).[31] Yet America's hands were not entirely clean. Critics, both at home and abroad, pointed to the recent armed intervention in the Dominican Republic, and the continuing bloody intervention in Viet Nam.

THE CZECHOSLOVAK AFTERMATH

Few events of the post-1945 years produced such alarming global reverberations as the Czechoslovak coup.

The Cold War became hotter, and all immediate hopes of a real *détente* with the USSR were dampened. The Kremlin leopard had obviously not changed its spots; moreover, the Soviets had proved themselves dangerously unpredictable. The ruling clique was obviously putting security and domination above all else, just as ruthlessly as it had in Hungary in 1956. It promptly resumed jamming the Voice of America radio broadcasts, which had been permitted on the airwaves since 1963. In crushing Czechoslovakia, the Kremlin revealed fear and weakness rather than security and strength.

The necessity of beefing up faltering NATO was revealed by this upsetting of the balance of power. Those optimists who had argued that the alliance was no longer needed, in view of the growing cordiality with Moscow, were unmasked as false prophets. President de Gaulle of France, who had ejected NATO from French soil and who had been courting the Soviets, now looked less than omniscient. The Alliance representatives, meeting in Brussels, served stern notice that further aggression in Europe or the Mediterranean would result in "grave consequences." The first Soviet rape of Czechoslovakia in 1948 had caused NATO to be born; the second in 1968 created a strong demand that it be reborn.

The weakness of the United Nations was again highlighted. Even so feeble a wrist slap as a condemnatory resolution in the Security Council was killed by a Soviet veto. Simultaneously, the inability of the Americans to influence events in Eastern Europe was again headlined, as during the

---

[31] *Department of State Bulletin,* LIX (Sept. 9, 1968), p 261. Address of August 21, 1908. When the Russians crushed Hungary, in 1956, the West was likewise morally weakened by the simultaneous attack of Britain, France, and Israel on Egypt.

Hungarian uprising of 1956. Overcommitment in Viet Nam did nothing to strengthen America's military posture.

The Czechoslovak crisis gave the Viet Nam hawks in America further ammunition for their tough position. The Soviets, who were major suppliers of weapons to the North Vietnamese, had evidently demonstrated anew that Communists could not be trusted. The Kremlin thus provided additional support for the view that the bombing should be continued (or expanded) until the Hanoi Communists and their backers knuckled under.

Renewed distrust of the Russians increased pressure in Congress for building a $40 billion anti-missile missile system, and dampened the recently kindled prospects of mutual agreement with the Soviets in this area. The Czechoslovak crisis also accelerated the arms race in the Middle East and elsewhere.[32]

The nuclear nonproliferation pact, still before the Senate, was endangered. Why make a treaty that would involve trusting a nuclear nation which had shown itself unworthy of trust? Candidate Nixon, contrary to Humphrey, demanded that action on the treaty be deferred, and deferment threatened defeat.

Ironically, the men in the Kremlin, who had long distrusted Nixon, played into his hands by their brutal crushing of freedom-craving Czechoslovakia. Renowned as a lifelong anti-Communist and distruster of Moscow, he seemed more than ever to be the man of the hour.

THE TRIUMPH OF THE "NEW" NIXON

The Presidential primary elections had indicated that the burning issue would be Viet Nam, but after the derailing of dovish Senator McCarthy, the voters had no clear-cut choice. A much sharper clash developed over "law and order," basically a euphemism for "keeping the Negro in his place." A majority of Americans with opinions evidently regarded involvement in Viet Nam as a mistake but hoped to de-Americanize the conflict by turning it over to the South Vietnamese. Yet most of them opposed a bombing halt without some sign or assurance of reciprocal concessions.[33]

Nixon, who had taken a bellicose stance while campaigning for the nomination, declared that he knew how to "end the war" and "win the peace," if elected. But he refused to unveil his scheme, he explained, for fear of undercutting the stalemated peace negotiations in Paris.[34] Patriotism and expediency thus joined hands.

[32] Presidential candidates Nixon and Humphrey both spoke in favor of selling jet fighter aircraft to Israel. This position was probably influenced in part by the challenge to the U.S. Sixth Fleet in the Mediterranean resulting from the formidable Soviet naval buildup in that area following the Israeli-Arab war of June, 1967.

[33] Gallup Releases, August 11, October 6, 1968.

[34] A strong point for Nixon was that the new Eisenhower-Nixon administration in 1953 had brought the Truman-started Korean involvement to an end.

A dramatic breakthrough came on October 31, 1968, less than a week before the election. President Johnson announced that the next day all bombing of North Viet Nam would cease, pending fruitful discussions at Paris between the Americans and South Vietnamese on the one side, and the North Vietnamese and the National Liberation Front (Viet Cong) on the other. The implications were that this declaration was approved by all parties concerned, and that if the North Vietnamese stepped up the fighting, the bombing would be resumed.

All three Presidential candidates, with varying degrees of enthusiasm, expressed the hope that this declaration would lead to an honorable peace. Humphrey was especially pleased because the bombing pause undoubtedly boosted his stock with the dovish element, notably the McCarthyites. Some of his opponents declared that the whole scheme was an electioneering device; if so, it came too late in the game. President Thieu of South Viet Nam, after apparently acquiescing, dampened the last-minute peace hopes by declaring that his representative would not sit down at the same peace table in Paris with the Viet Cong. (After the election he changed his tune.)

On November 5, 1968, Nixon won the White House in a cliffhanging election which entitled him to 32 more than the necessary 270 electoral votes, but only 43.4 per cent of the popular vote.[35] Only two other Presidents, Lincoln in 1860 and Wilson in 1912, had attracted less popular support since 1824. Both houses of Congress remained Democratic, and this oddity was without precedent in modern times. Clearly the Republican Nixon had no popular mandate for anything.

What the result portended for foreign affairs no prophet could safely predict. Even in those contests for the House and Senate in which doves ran against hawks, the results were not conclusive on Viet Nam. Many hawks voted for Governor Wallace; many doves finally voted for Hubert Humphrey. The election was so close that any one of three men concerned with foreign affairs could have turned it: Premier Kosygin (who was associated with the Czechoslovak crisis), Senator McCarthy (who dragged his feet),[36] and President Thieu (who threw a wet blanket on hopes of peace).

Nixon, who had promised the voters "no more Viet Nams," was relatively free to bring about an "honorable peace" in his own way. His triumph seems to have hinged primarily on a desire for a change and a protest against existing grievances—high taxes; inflation; big spending by big government; organized crime; the so-called coddling of criminals by the courts; demonstrations, riots, and looting by minority groups; the inequitable military draft; and the "no-win" war. Many of those who favored

---

[35] The popular vote ran as follows: Nixon (43.4 per cent); Humphrey (42.7 per cent); and Wallace (13.5 per cent).

[36] McCarthy blamed Humphrey for not having come out in favor of a conditional halting of the bombing of North Viet Nam much sooner than he eventually did.

continued fighting in Viet Nam were isolationists who wanted to get the shooting over with in a hurry and bring the boys back. The nation evidently wanted less strife at home and less grief abroad.

A break in the Paris stalemate occurred on January 16, 1969, only four days before the end of President Johnson's stewardship. After eight months of sparring about the shape of the conference table and other procedural trivia, the three sets of delegates from Viet Nam agreed with the American representatives to begin discussion of substantive issues. President Johnson thus ended his tenure on something of an upbeat. But students of Communist techniques freely predicted that there would be a prolonged Korea-type negotiation against a background of fierce fighting.

SELECTED BIBLIOGRAPHY

Broad yet detailed coverage appears in Jules Davids, *The United States in World Affairs, 1964* (New York, 1965), and in Richard P. Stebbins, *The United States in World Affairs, 1965* (New York, 1966) and *The United States in World Affairs, 1966* (New York, 1967). Journalistic in nature are Philip L. Geyelin, *Lyndon B. Johnson and the World* (New York, 1966), and Rowland Evans and Robert Novak, *Lyndon B. Johnson: The Exercise of Power* (New York, 1966). Broader in scope is Seyom Brown, *The Faces of Power: Constancy and Change in United States Foreign Policy from Truman to Johnson* (New York, 1968). Useful for their respective subjects are John Plank, ed., *Cuba and the United States: Long Range Perspectives* (Washington, D.C., 1967), and Sheldon B. Liss, *The Canal: Aspects of United States-Panamanian Relations* (Notre Dame, Ind., 1967). On the Dominican intervention consult John B. Martin, *Overtaken by Events* (Garden City, N.Y., 1966) [by the ex-ambassador], and two journalistic treatments: Tad Szulc, *Dominican Diary* (New York, 1965), and Dan Kurzman, *Santo Domingo: Revolt of the Damned* (New York, 1965). There is a plethora of ephemera on Viet Nam, but for present purposes the most valuable single work is probably George McT. Kahin and John W. Lewis, *The United States in Vietnam* (New York, 1967). See also Richard N. Goodwin, *Triumph or Tragedy: Reflections on Vietnam* (New York, 1966); Jean Lacouture, *Vietnam: Between Two Truces* (New York, 1966); Robert Shaplen, *The Lost Revolution: The U.S. in Vietnam, 1946–1966* (rev. ed., New York, 1966); Bernard Fall, *The Two Viet Nams* (2nd rev. ed., New York, 1967); and Robert F. Kennedy, *To Seek a Newer World* (Garden City, N.Y., 1967). Important legal aspects are examined in Richard A. Falk, ed., *The Vietnam War and International Law* (Princeton, 1968). Two scholarly books on related topics are Cecil Van Meter Crabb, Jr., *The Elephants and the Grass: A Study of Nonalignment* (New York, 1965), and Henry A. Kissinger, *The Troubled Partnership: A Re-appraisal of the Atlantic Alliance* (New York, 1965). George W. Ball, a former Undersecretary of State, has some perceptive views on Viet Nam and other problems in *The Discipline of Power* (Boston, 1968).

9TH ED. REFS. See BIBLIOGRAPHICAL ADDENDUM, p. 1,061.

57

Nixonian Foreign Policy

> . . . *America cannot—and will not—conceive* all
> *the plans, design* all *the programs, execute* all *the*
> *decisions and undertake* all *the defense of the free*
> *nations of the world.*
>
> PRESIDENT RICHARD M. NIXON, Message to
> Congress, Feb. 18, 1970.

VIETNAMIZING THE VIET NAM WAR

PRESIDENT NIXON, a seasoned global traveler, had long shown a keen interest in foreign affairs and regarded himself as having a special aptitude for handling them. Famed as a headline-catching, hard-hitting anti-Communist, he seemed to relish the give-and-take of diplomatic combat. He chose as his Secretary of State a close friend and confidant, William P. Rogers, a wealthy lawyer in his mid-fifties who had accumulated some modest experience in diplomacy, notably as a former member of the U.S. delegation to the U.N. General Assembly. Obviously somewhat self-effacing, he was to be spectacularly upstaged by Nixon's brilliant special adviser on foreign affairs, Dr. Henry A. Kissinger, a bespectacled and German-accented Harvard professor of government in his mid-forties who had written extensively on nuclearized foreign policy and who had served as consultant to the Department of State. As a globe-girdling "mystery man," he assisted the President as theoretician, advance agent, and jaw-to-jaw negotiator, whether in Paris or Peking, Saigon or Hanoi. He was dubbed "Super-Kraut" and "The most powerful Number-two Man in history."

The no-end, no-win war in Viet Nam still convulsed the country, and Nixon was determined to have more calm at home and less confrontation abroad. No doubt remembering his 1968 campaign slogan, "Bring us together again," he urged the people in his inaugural address "to lower our voices" and to "stop shouting at one another." The Truman Doctrine of 1947 had aimed at containing Communism the world over, but the disillusioning experience in Viet Nam had revealed that America was dangerously overcommitted. Uncle Sam could no longer attempt to play the self-appointed role of "Policeman for the World."

Clearly the most pressing candidate for disengagement was Viet Nam. In his recent campaign for the Presidency, Nixon had spoken of his "secret plan" for ending the war. The scheme that he finally unveiled from the White House was "Vietnamization"—or gradually turning the conflict over to the South Vietnamese as they developed strength (with essential American money and military hardware) to have a "reasonable chance" of surviving. This "new" policy was hardly new, because the old policy of President Johnson had been to de-Americanize the fighting as soon as feasible. But Nixon put fresh emphasis on "winding down" the war in such a way as to permit America to retreat from the combat without appearing to suffer defeat and without betraying its South Vietnamese protégé.

American opinion, while regretting the continuing enmeshment, accepted "Vietnamization" as the most promising way out of the quagmire, and largely for this reason Nixon was able to pursue his policy to the end, despite slow-motion results.[1] The process was a compromise between complete turn-tail withdrawal, which a vocal minority favored, and re-escalation, which a smaller minority demanded. By the end of his first four years Nixon had gradually reduced the American troop levels of some 550,000 men to a "residual force" of some 23,700 noncombat soldiers.

Vietnamization obviously required South Vietnamese approval, and in June, 1969, President Nixon flew to America's Midway Island to meet approximately midway with President Thieu, the military President and quasi-dictator of South Viet Nam. On June 8, 1969, during the one-day session, Nixon announced the "immediate" pullout of the first 25,000 men.[2] Critics wondered aloud how the South Vietnamese could "hack it" alone when, with more than a half million American troops aiding them, they could not win.

THE NIXON DOCTRINE AND MASS MORATORIUMS

Man's age-old dream became reality on July 20, 1969, when two American astronauts astonished the world and enhanced their nation's prestige by becoming the first men to reach the moon. Such was the spectacular fruit of a $24 billion program launched in 1961 under President Kennedy. By fortunate planning, President Nixon enplaned two

[1] Between January and November, 1969, Dr. Gallup found that those with opinions favored the phased withdrawal by majorities ranging from 53% to 58%. Late in November, immediate withdrawal was opposed by 74% and favored by 21% of those with opinions. Gallup Release, Nov. 27, 1969.

[2] *Department of State Bulletin*, LX (June 30, 1969), p. 549.

days later for a nine-day, eight-nation tour of Asia and Europe, by way of Guam, the Philippines, and Viet Nam. He arranged to watch the splashdown of the returning astronauts in the Pacific, and he basked in their moonglow when he personally greeted the returning heroes.

While stopping at Guam, and with special reference to the Viet Nam morass, Nixon announced the so-called "Guam Doctrine," later officially baptized as the "Nixon Doctrine." Its most pressing purpose was to announce that the United States would never again become heavily involved with manpower in attempting to solve Asia's problems. In its refined form the new policy applied "to all our international relationships," whether in Asia or Europe, and in Asia its implementation involved continued withdrawals of troops from Viet Nam, Korea, and Japan. Specifically, the Nixon Doctrine embraced three basic precepts:

> The United States will keep all its treaty commitments.
> We shall provide a shield if a nuclear power threatens the freedom of a nation allied with us or of a nation whose survival we consider vital to our security and the security of the region as a whole.
> In cases involving other types of aggression, we shall furnish military and economic assistance when requested as appropriate. But we shall look to the nation directly threatened to assume the primary responsibility of providing the manpower for its defense.[3]

In essence, as regards the quicksands of Asia, the United States would count on its friends to provide the bulk of the cannon fodder when they were attacked. America would help only those who would help themselves, for there would have to be "shared burdens and shared responsibilities." As Defense Secretary Melvin R. Laird put it, "America will no longer try to play policeman to the world. Instead, we will expect other nations to provide more cops on the beat in their own neighborhood."

The Nixon Doctrine was acceptable enough as a policy for the future, but Viet Nam was ever present. "Vietnamization" continued to come under blistering fire from those Americans who favored a speedy evacuation, but at most they never represented more than a third or a fourth of the population. In October and November, 1969, "peaceniks" staged giant antiwar demonstrations ("The Viet Nam Moratorium"), with crowds ranging from 100,000 on the Boston Common to 250,000 in Washington, D.C. Again, late in March, 1971, about 200,000 protesters marched in the nation's capital. But Nixon, who knew from the public opinion polls that "the great silent majority" were behind his policy, or what they conceived it to be, refused to be swayed by "mobs" in the

---

[3] On Guam the President outlined his policy to newsmen, with direct quotation forbidden. The above refined and expanded official version appears in *United States Foreign Policy, 1969–1970: A Report of the Secretary of State* (Washington, D.C., 1971), pp. 35–37.

street. Indeed, such exhibitions proved counterproductive; a Gallup poll found only one in five persons supporting the demonstrators.[4]

THE CAMBODIAN AND LAOTIAN INCURSIONS

As fate would have it, South Viet Nam was bordered on the west by Cambodia and Laos. The neutrality of both of these nations had long been flouted by the North Vietnamese, particularly in transporting supplies or accumulating them for attacks on South Viet Nam. Repeated American bombing forays over both Laos and Cambodia had evidently proved more annoying than effective. From a purely military standpoint, the United States would be fully justified in attacking North Vietnamese staging areas in Cambodia, thus weakening the enemy, hastening Vietnamization, and making less hazardous the withdrawal of American troops from South Viet Nam.

In response to an appeal from the Cambodian government for aid, Nixon sent American troops plunging into Cambodia, April 30, 1970. His ostensible purpose was to wipe out the enemy's advance bases and accumulated supplies. But the effect was to widen the war rather than to narrow it—to "Indochinaize" rather than "Vietnamize" it. Outraged critics at home feared that the new thrust, rather than hastening the departure of American troops, would soak up more.

Angry demonstrations against the war had meanwhile been continuing, especially on college campuses, where many worried enrollees were eligible for the draft. On May 4, 1970, four days after the Cambodian thrust began, harassed Ohio National Guardsmen deliberately discharged their rifles into a crowd of students at Kent State University, killing four and wounding nine others. Shock waves of outrage swept the nation. The next day Nixon promised to withdraw the American troops from Cambodia gradually, within a two-month period, and not to permit them to penetrate deeper than twenty-one miles without the consent of Congress. He kept his pledge after the invading Americans had captured some rather disappointing caches of rice and arms.

Yet the administration hailed the Cambodian incursion as a huge success, even though the enemy, evidently forewarned, had moved his strategic headquarters elsewhere. The public evidently believed the President's assurances that the bold stroke would hasten the dawn of peace. Gallup polls showed a sharp rise in public approval of Nixon's handling of the Presidency to 57 per cent, while the same respondents expressed emphatic disapproval of student demonstrators.[5]

The marathon peace talks in Paris, involving the United States and South Viet Nam on one side and North Viet Nam and the Viet Cong

[4] Gallup Release, Nov. 27, 1969.
[5] Gallup Release, May 10, 1970.

on the other, ended their second fruitless year on January 18, 1971. All that the conferees had agreed on was the shape of the conference table! The next month the spotlight shifted to Laos. There the United States sponsored an invasion by South Vietnamese troops, with the evident intention of cutting off supplies funneling down the Ho Chi Minh trail from North Viet Nam. Despite massive assistance from about 1,000 American aircraft, the invaders were hurled back in panicky retreat. Public approval of Nixon's managing of the Vietnamese War temporarily dropped to disapproval, while the majority belief that involvement in Indochina was a mistake climbed to the highest point thus far. Confidence in the government suffered another heavy blow in June, 1971, when *The New York Times* published top-secret Pentagon papers which revealed how scandalously previous administrations had deceived the public in regard to Viet Nam.

PING PONG DIPLOMACY

Ugly though the war in Viet Nam was, it had the happy side effect of promoting an astonishing new relationship between the United States and Red China (The People's Republic of China). The Peking government, next to Russia the chief supplier of war matériel to the North Vietnamese, could conceivably be induced to pressure Hanoi to end the fighting. One prime advantage of a cease-fire would be to remove the ever-present danger that risky American operations near the Chinese border (as in Korea in 1950) might force Red China fully into the conflict.

A diplomatic breakthrough to Peking would not be easy. The United States, fearing a communized China, had faithfully supported Chiang Kai Shek's rump refugee government in Taiwan since 1950. Washington had declined to open diplomatic relations with Peking, and for two decades had successfully fought the admission of Red China to the U.N. Additionally, masses of Chinese "volunteers" had attacked the U.N. forces (including U.S.) in Korea in 1950, and the armistice of 1953 had not yet formalized peaceful relations. President Nixon, who had climbed to political fame as a relentless Red-baiter, could hardly be expected to extend the olive branch, especially since he headed the party that embraced the largest bloc of anti-Communist conservatives.

Yet more than twenty years had passed since the triumph of the Chinese Communists in 1949, and power alignments were shifting. China had not only become a nuclear power in 1964, but was developing a fearsome arsenal of intercontinental ballistic missiles. The fiction that Chiang's tiny offshore island of Taiwan represented Mainland China could not be maintained much longer. Indeed, with the admission of many new "developing" nations to the United Nations, Uncle Sam was yearly being cast in the role of the boy at the dike in his efforts to hold back Peking.

In the early 1960's, Russia and China had angrily split over their interpretation of Marxist-Leninism, thereby fully revealing that Communism was not a fearsome monolith under the iron direction of Moscow. The necessity of holding the anti-Communist ramparts in Viet Nam seemed to the United States less compelling. But more important, Russia and China were at each other's throats, massively preparing for a possible war with each other, and actually engaged in some minor fighting along their borders. Why should Washington not take advantage of this opportunity to play Moscow and Peking off against each other, while reaping solid diplomatic and commercial advantages from both? A President whose anti-Communist credentials were gilt-edged would be less susceptible to charges of a sellout than his Democratic predecessors.

Nixon, who openly expressed a desire to visit China, was rather subtle in his approach to Peking. In 1969, Washington eased somewhat its official trade and travel restrictions. Then, on April 6, 1971, Peking invited U.S. table tennis players to China, where, as expected, they were soundly beaten by the world champions. Nixon responded by further easing and then ending the two-decades embargo on trade (June 10, 1971). The next month, July 15, 1971, he surprised a huge television and radio audience by announcing his acceptance "with pleasure" of an invitation to visit China some time "before May" of 1972. He assured "old friends" (Chiang's Taiwan) that their interests would not be sacrificed. Taiwan was unhappy; Moscow was cool; the two Viet Nams were apprehensive.

The tide was clearly turning in favor of Red China's admission to the U.N., with the concurrent expulsion of Taiwan (Republic of China). Sports-minded America, after the ping-pong invitation, became markedly more friendly to Peking; for the first time in twenty-one years more citizens favored than opposed the seating of Red China.[6] Anticipating the inevitable, the State Department announced, August 2, 1971, that it would support the admission of Red China but would oppose the expulsion of its protégé, Taiwan. Such was the so-called Two-Chinas policy. But on October 25, 1971, the U.N. Assembly resoundingly approved, by a vote of 76 to 35, a resolution to admit Red China and expel Taiwan, a charter member. Many delegates from Communist nations and pro-Communist third-world countries burst into cheers and joyfully or tauntingly clapped their hands, while one Tanzanian danced an impromptu jig in the aisle. President Nixon, speaking through his press secretary, denounced "the shocking demonstration" of "undisguised glee" and "personal animosity" toward the United States.[7]

---

[6] One tally was 45% yes, 38% no, and 17% no opinion. Gallup Release, May 30, 1971.

[7] *Time,* Nov. 8, 1971, p. 17.

THE PRESIDENT IN PEKING

Nixon's unprecedented and globally televised China visit was eventually scheduled for the last eight days of February, 1972. When the President deplaned at Peking, only a corporal's guard of officials was there to meet and greet him, including Premier Chou En-lai, with whom Nixon cordially shook hands. Although a Chinese band played the "Star Spangled Banner" recognizably, there were no wildly cheering crowds—in fact, there were no crowds at all. Sandwiched between dinners of exotic food and innumerable glass-clinking toasts, Nixon engaged in lengthy private talks with Premier Chou and Chairman Mao, the aged but still powerful Communist leader. A high point of the visit was Nixon's walk on the undulating Great Wall of China, which was several centuries older than Christ. This historic Wall-walk seemed almost as eerie as the first moonwalk of the American astronauts, less than two years earlier.

The finale was a joint communique, released February 27, 1972. It proved to be more a reaffirmation of the views held by both sides on controversial issues than an affirmation of new shifts of policy. The United States repeated its evident determination to pull out of Viet Nam and declared its "*ultimate* objective" to be "the withdrawal of all U.S. forces and military installations from Taiwan." Both sides agreed that they would seek "normalization of relations" through increased contacts.[8]

Post-mortems about reopening the Open Door in China were grossly exaggerated. Like Perry in Japan (1853–1854), Nixon had little more than a foot in the door, but his old-fashioned balance-of-power gambit was an encouraging beginning toward more fruitful contacts. If the United States received little, it conceded little.

Diplomatically speaking, the visit was more important for its falling-domino effects elsewhere than for any concrete concessions. Taiwan was deeply disturbed, despite new assurances by the State Department of America's support. Japan, America's chief ally in Eastern Asia and already a potent economic rival, lost much face from the "Nixon shock (*shokku*)." Tokyo had not been consulted in advance about the trip, and fearing that its interests would be sacrificed, took steps to appease China, the ancient enemy.[9] The leaders of South Viet Nam and North Viet Nam suspected that they had been sold down the Yangtze River: South Viet Nam because China was an enemy, and North Viet Nam because China was a prime supplier of arms. If the United States had been fighting in South Viet Nam for a decade to hold back Chinese

---

[8] Text of communique, *Department of State Bulletin,* LXVI (March 20, 1972), 435–438.

[9] In September, 1972, Premier Tanaka of Japan visited Peking to express regret and repentance for Japan's past aggression. Both parties agreed to end the state of war (begun in 1937) and to establish diplomatic relations. Immediately thereafter, Tokyo severed diplomatic relations with Taiwan.

Communism, as alleged, what was Nixon doing kow-towing in Communist China? No doubt Peking weakened itself greatly in its competition with Moscow for the allegiance of the uncommitted Third World.

If Nixon's friendly overtures to China were intended to put pressure on the Kremlin, his ploy evidently worked. Peking could now concentrate more fully on the Russian border menace. Moscow could not be sure as before that Uncle Sam would remain on the sidelines if the Russians should launch a preventive nuclear strike before the Chinese were able to fill their nuclear arsenal. The Soviets evidently feared that America and China, both now nuclear powers, were scheming to "gang up" on them; the controlled Russian press denounced Nixon's summit negotiations in Peking as a "dangerous plot." Rather than quietly remain the victims of a triangular power play, the Russians invited Nixon to Russia in October, 1971. The conferences were later scheduled for May, 1972.

MINING AND BOMBING DIPLOMACY

Fighting in Viet Nam suddenly escalated anew to an alarming level on March 30, 1972, when massive units of the North Vietnamese army, spearheaded by foreign-built tanks, burst into and through the Demilitarized Zone (DMZ) separating North Viet Nam and South Viet Nam. The South Vietnamese defenders, hurled back, lost considerable areas, although supported by intense bombing from U.S. aircraft. Nixon's whole Vietnamization program trembled in the balance, and the thousands of remaining American troops were endangered.

President Nixon regarded the crisis as so serious as to warrant a daring gamble. On May 8, 1972, he announced his intention to bomb transportation lines and military installations in North Viet Nam, including Hanoi and Haiphong. More than that, he issued orders to drop mines in the principal harbors of North Viet Nam. One of his main purposes was obviously to cut off oil and other supplies pouring in from Russia and China.

A grave danger loomed that Chinese and Russian merchant ships would suffer such damage that both China and Russia would openly intervene, thereby triggering World War III. (Moscow claimed damage to at least four Soviet ships.) Both Moscow and Peking did protest, but their protestations were surprisingly mild. With Russian and Chinese troops glaring at one another over their elongated borders, both rivals had no desire to become involved with America. In their own interests they both welcomed a mutual understanding.

Nixon, who had earned a reputation as a poker player while a naval officer in World War II, had gambled and won. He showed that America —no "paper tiger"—had not only the power but the will to use it. Right-wing Americans enthusiastically applauded, for they felt that if North Viet Nam had been bombed "back into the stone age" much earlier, the war would have ended much sooner. The pollsters found a strong majority of the respondents favoring Nixon's two-fisted policy.[10]

Another fear was that an angered Kremlin would cancel the Moscow "summit" with Nixon, scheduled for late May, 1972. (President Eisenhower had been disinvited in 1960, following the spy-plane fiasco.) But the success of the recent Sino-American reconciliation in Peking, to say nothing of serious internal Soviet difficulties, evidently prompted the Russians to carry through the planned reception. Nixon presumably had reckoned on these odds when he opted for the heavy bombing and mining of North Viet Nam. Yet both Russia and China lost face when they failed to back their North Vietnamese "client," which as a result probably became more willing to consider a cease-fire.

NIXON IN THE KREMLIN

Many boulders lay in the path of a successful ascent to the Moscow summit. Cold War rivalry, with foreign-armed surrogate states such as North and South Korea and North and South Viet Nam engaging in hot war, had been grinding on for about a quarter of a century. The fantastic Soviet-American race into space, climaxed by the first man on the moon, had increased both rivalry and financial burdens on both sides. The Soviets were rapidly building a powerful modern navy which in some types challenged or rivaled that of the United States. For years, Russian vessels had dashed dangerously close to American ships in the hair-raising game of "sea chicken." The Soviets were expanding their naval presence into the Mediterranean (once regarded as an American-NATO lake), and even into Cuban waters and the Indian Ocean. In 1971–1972, Moscow was charging cost-of-education exit fees up to $25,000 of Jews (and others) seeking to leave for Israel. This imposition stirred up disagreeable incidents against Soviet officials and agencies in America, while street demonstrators displayed placards reading, "Ransom No! Let My People Go."

Yet various factors were making for a more conciliatory attitude in the Kremlin than might otherwise have been expected. The ever-present nightmare of a Germany that was reunited, resurgent, and nuclearized largely disappeared on August 12, 1970, when Chancellor Willy Brandt of West Germany signed in Moscow an epochal nonaggression treaty with the USSR. Among other provisions, it formally recognized the existing frontiers of a divided German nation. Three months later, on November 18, 1970, Brandt concluded a pact with neighboring Poland

[10] A Louis Harris poll, published early in September, 1972, found 55% approval and 32% disapproval.

which renounced force and acknowledged the permanent loss to Poland of former German territory held by her since 1945. A year later Chancellor Brandt received the Nobel Peace Prize for his efforts in lessening East-West tensions.

Meanwhile, in this more relaxed atmosphere, the long-burning Berlin issue cooled off. On September 3, 1971, ambassadors of the four powers administering four-sectored Berlin—the U.S., the USSR, Britain, and France—signed a quadripartite agreement permitting unhindered civilian access to Berlin and the end of various forms of transport discrimination by Russia and East Germany.[11] For the first time, Western access rights were to be guaranteed, as memories of the air-lift Berlin blockade of 1948–1949 further faded. With tensions thus eased in Central Europe, there was increasing talk on both sides of a "mutually balanced" reduction of arms between the West's NATO and the East's Moscow Pact allies.

Internal conditions in Russia also favored a friendlier Soviet-American relationship. The Soviet masses, long denied shoes, clothes, and other quality goods in abundance, were exhibiting restiveness. Bad harvests were so reducing grain supplies that enormous shipments were urgently required from abroad, especially the United States. The Soviet Union, with its relatively low production per man-hour, also needed modern technological equipment. America was by far the most important potential supplier, and the republic, facing an "energy crisis" and shortages of raw materials, appeared willing to embark upon a mutually advantageous interchange. So it was that when Nixon went to Moscow he was playing from a hand of considerable strength in a rather favorable atmosphere.[12]

NUCLEAR ARMS LIMITATION—NOT DISARMAMENT

President Nixon had previously visited Russia four times, but in May, 1972, he arrived for the most important summit conference since the Big Three had met in Potsdam in 1945. His staff consisted of 36 persons, including Secretary Rogers and the ubiquitous, ready-smiling Dr. Kissinger. The accompanying press corps of 260 members duly noted the red carpets, the Red Square, the green felt table, the caviar, the champagne toasts, and the uncommonly cordial Communist boss, Chairman Leonid I. Brezhnev. Nixon was even granted the unprecedented privi-

---

[11] *Department of State Bulletin*, LXV (Sept. 27, 1971), 317–325.

[12] The signing or completion of earlier agreements augured well for success. These included the treaty on the Non-Proliferation of Nuclear Weapons, which became effective on March 5, 1970 (see p. 898); the banning of nuclear weapons from the ocean floor by more than sixty nations, including the U.S. and the USSR (February, 1971); agreements to fight cancer, heart disease, and environmental problems and also to ban biological warfare (February and April, 1972).

"SOMEWHERE IN BETWEEN SEEMS ABOUT RIGHT"

Reaction to the Nuclear Arms Pacts.

Courtesy of the San Francisco *Examiner*

lege of addressing the Russian people on radio and television from the Kremlin.[13]

But all this was minor when compared with the eight-day deliberations at the Moscow summit. Overshadowing all else were two pacts growing out of the earlier U.S.-USSR SALT conferences (Strategic Arms Limitation Talks), which had involved more than one hundred meetings during the previous two and one-half years, alternating between Vienna and Helsinki, Finland.

The first of the two agreements was the Treaty on Anti-Ballistic Missile [ABM] Systems, signed May 26, 1972.[14] Both nations had already spent billions in starting antimissile missile complexes, designed to shoot down "first strike" nuclear missiles and protect existing missile centers. One ABM defensive system, constructed by the Americans, shielded the "Minuteman" offensive missile establishment at Grand Forks, North Dakota, aimed northward over the globe at Russia. The one existing Soviet system protected Moscow. The new treaty limited each nation to two clusters of antiballistic missiles (ABM's), one protecting each nation's capital, each with a maximum of 100 ABM nuclear missiles and missile launchers. Specifically, the Americans were required

[13] For toasts and the Nixon address, see *Weekly Compilation of Presidential Documents*, VIII (June 5, 1972), 915 ff.

[14] *Department of State Bulletin*, LXVI (June 26, 1972), 918–920.

to locate their second defensive complex near Washington, while the Soviets would use their second, as the Americans were using their first, to protect an Intercontinental Ballistic Missile (ICBM) system.

In effect, the ABM treaty, which required Senate approval, bound both nations to abandon any further attempt to defend their cities against a nuclear attack. Each power thus handed over to the other its major population centers as hostages.

The second SALT pact, also signed May 26, 1972, was an executive agreement.[15] As such, it took effect immediately upon signature, although Nixon subsequently submitted it to both houses of Congress for approval by a simple majority. Entitled "Interim Agreement on Limitation of Strategic Offensive Arms," it sought to establish a rough temporary parity by limiting for five years the number of long-range offensive missiles to those already deployed or building. The Russians, then enjoying the momentum of an enormous nuclear build-up, supposedly had some 2,300 offensive missiles to about 1,700 for the Americans. But the United States had already equipped its warheads with three to ten independently targeted reentry missiles. Hence the superiority of the Americans in deliverable missiles (counting submarines and bombers) was about 5,700 to 2,300. Yet the biggest Soviet warheads were about ten times more powerful than those of the United States, and within several years they would almost certainly be changed to the most modern type, each carrying as many as twenty missiles.

In brief, the five-year Interim Agreement limiting the number of nuclear missiles on both sides assured the Russians of rough parity for the time being, and if they wished, they could cut down on their costly runaway program. They could and doubtless would modernize their warheads, thereby further assuring mutual annihilation in the event of war. The advantage to America was that the Interim Agreement reduced the risk of nuclear war, preserved American security temporarily, and might induce the Russians to throttle down the ruinous race.

Overshadowed by the two nuclear pacts at Moscow was the concurrent negotiation of five agreements of secondary importance. They were designed to: (1) protect environment, (2) avert dangerous "sea chicken" accidents involving warships, (3) promote cooperation in a space program, including a joint space flight, (4) provide cooperation in medical science and public health, and (5) improve cooperation in science and technology. The trend was definitely away from Cold War aloofness.

THE MOSCOW AFTERMATH

Vigorous objections to the two SALT agreements arose in America from a small conservative minority. Some assailed the "immorality" of

---

[15] *Ibid.,* pp. 920–921.

leaving all but one American city, inhabited by Washington "politicians," to nuclear incineration. Other critics pointed out that the pacts failed to insure even effective arms limitation, let alone disarmament. America merely froze her numerical superiority in offensive missiles for five years, while not freezing Russia's *temporary* qualitative inferiority. A frightfully costly new arms race could be expected to escalate into more fearsome weaponry, with Russia almost certain to win because her basic missiles, already more powerful, could be made immensely more sophisticated. In addition, there was no sure-fire way of knowing if the Russians would cheat, because spying from the heavens by satellites was by no means foolproof. New SALT II talks were scheduled to open in 1973, and the United States would have to spend billions on improving its nuclear weapons if it was to employ effective "bargaining chips" when another pact would have to be negotiated at the end of five years.

The strongest argument in favor of the two agreements was that they might head off an unbridgeable missile gap in favor of Russia. As journalist I. F. Stone observed, the two nations were descending "from the super-crazy to the plain crazy." In September, 1972, both houses of Congress, by overwhelming majorities, approved the five-year Executive Agreement. The Senators voiced some dissatisfaction by adding a reservation, quite acceptable to Nixon and concurred in by the House. It emphatically urged the President to seek a treaty near the end of the five years that "would not limit the United States to levels of intercontinental strategic forces inferior to the limits provided for the Soviet Union. . . ." [16] Meanwhile the Senate, by a vote of 88 to 2 (August 2, 1972), had approved the treaty limiting antiballistic missile complexes to the stipulated two of not more than 100 missiles each.

Impressively increased trade with Russia followed the signing of the two nuclear pacts in May, 1972. On July 8, 1972, Nixon announced a three-year agreement to sell at least $750 million worth of wheat, corn, and other grain to the food-short Soviets. On October 18, 1972, came the completion of a sweeping trade package. In it the Russians agreed, at long last, to pay their overdue lend-lease debt of World War II. The installments, to be spread out until the year 2001, would total some $722 million, counting principal and interest. For its part, the United States agreed to extend government-backed credit for large-scale sales to the Soviets.[17]

INDIA, PAKISTAN, AND BANGLADESH

The Asian subcontinent meanwhile was astir. On August 9, 1971, some three weeks after Nixon announced his visit to Peking, the Soviets

[16] *Public Law*, 92–418, 92 Cong., H.J. Res. 1227 (Sept. 3, 1972).
[17] For texts of the two agreements and related documents, see *Department of State Bulletin*, XLVII (Nov. 20, 1972), 595–604.

signed a twenty-year treaty of friendship (and quasi-alliance) with India. The Indians feared another crushing onslaught from the bordering Chinese (as in 1962), while the Russians were evidently eager to clasp hands with India against an increasingly menacing China. Although India and Pakistan had been enemies since the partition of British India in 1947, the United States had been supplying arms to the Pakistanis. Pakistan was an American ally in the Southeast Asia Treaty Organization (SEATO), and associated with the United States in CENTO (Central Treaty Organization), which was designed to "contain" the Soviet Union (see p. 851).

This unpromising Asiatic pot came to a furious boil in March, 1971. Populous East Pakistan, separated by more than a thousand miles from West Pakistan, formally rebelled against alleged mistreatment by West Pakistan overlords. The secessionists officially proclaimed the independent state of Bangladesh. The West Pakistan army, with alleged genocidal intent, undertook to crush the uprising with wholesale butchery, rape, and pillage. An estimated nine million destitute refugees began to pour across the border into already overpopulated and underfed India. In November, 1971, responding to protests from India, Washington cancelled further shipments of arms to the Pakistanis. Then, early in December, India, after declaring war on Pakistan, proceeded to invade and free Bangladesh in a mercifully short clash of fifteen days.

Uncle Sam, with his money on the losing horse, emerged from this episode looking rather foolish. Evidently seeking to counter a reported Russian naval presence in the Indian Ocean and to display sympathy for its Pakistani ally, Washington had hastily dispatched a powerful naval task force to the Indian Ocean. The transparent explanation given at the time was the necessity of evacuating a handful of American citizens, most or all of whom had already left Bangladesh. This futile exhibition of old-fashioned "show the flag" gunboat diplomacy, with its "tilt toward Pakistan" probably gratified pro-Pakistan China but pleased neither the Russians, the Indians, nor even the Pakistanis. Relations with India became frigid, especially after Washington suspended $87.6 million in development loans, charging that India, already the beneficiary of some $9 billion in American aid, was the "main aggressor" in the conflict. Nearly a year later, in November, 1972, Pakistan withdrew from the American-sponsored SEATO alliance, and in other ways indicated alienation from the United States.

JAPAN AND THE DROOPING DOLLAR

Intercourse with Japan, America's most potent ally in East Asia, became increasingly strained during the early Nixon years. The hard-working, ingenious Japanese had pulled themselves up by their sandal straps from the radioactive rubble of World War II to become an industrial giant. By the end of the 1960's, Japan ranked in productivity only below the United States and the Soviet Union.

Strident demands by the Japanese for the return of Okinawa, occupied by the Americans since World War II, rose to a crescendo in 1969, when mobs raged through the streets of Tokyo. Prime Minister Sato flew to Washington for consultation, and on November 21, 1969, he and President Nixon agreed on a joint communique looking to the return of Okinawa and other American-held Ryukyus.[18] After a formal agreement was subsequently drafted and ratified by both sides, the official transfer of administration occurred on May 15, 1972, thereby removing the last significant diplomatic carryover from World War II.

Ominous new economic problems had meanwhile risen to pollute the more relaxed diplomatic atmosphere. America was struggling with unemployment and inflation, both presumably a direct result of the multibillion dollar burden of the Viet Nam War. The national budget was running enormous deficits and the international balance of payments was increasingly adverse, owing in part to costly American military establishments from Germany to Korea. The distressing imbalance of payments roughly paralleled the adverse balance of trade. Increasingly, the United States, having ravaged its own natural resources, was being forced to import supplies from abroad, conspicuously oil. In 1971, for the first time since 1888, the value of imports exceeded that of exports, all told by some $2 billion. Trade with Japan, next to Canada, America's largest two-way customer, accounted for a trade deficit of some $3 billion, largely in inexpensive radios, television sets, and compact cars.

By the spring of 1971 the old expression "sound as a dollar" had a hollow ring. Once king of currencies, the Almighty Dollar was buckling abroad, where it either passed at a discount or was spurned outright. Yielding to this extreme pressure, President Nixon, on August 15, 1971, resorted to drastic measures ("Nixonomics"). Among various expedients, he severed the link between the dollar and gold in an effort to ease foreign pressures on the dollar and reduce the balance of payments deficit. A dollar thus devalued about eight percent would have the effect of enabling Americans to sell abroad cheaper and thus enlarge their export market. Concurrently, Nixon imposed a temporary 10 per cent tariff surcharge on imports, partly in response to pressure from textile manufacturers and others who were demanding protection against foreign imports, especially Japan's.

The industrious Japanese, with their huge export market in America, were especially hard hit by the devalued dollar and the 10 per cent surtax. Keenly aware of the problem, President Nixon staged a two-day conference in Hawaii with Premier Tanaka (August 31–September 1,

[18] *Ibid.*, LXI (Dec. 15, 1969), 555–558; text of final agreement in *ibid.*, LXV (July 12, 1971), 35–39.

1972). The outcome was an announcement that Japan would buy $1.1 billion worth of American goods to reduce the expected 1972 imbalance with Japan of $3.8 billion. In return, Nixon gave Tanaka assurances that the 10 per cent surcharge on imported commodities would be lifted, and this was done on December 20, 1971.

THE NEW ISOLATIONISM

Uncle Sam's back-breaking role of World Policeman and Chief Humanitarian gradually swung many Americans in the 1960's and early 1970's to what critics called neo-isolationism. Overall hung the somber shadow of the Viet Nam War, from which the United States was desperately trying to extricate itself with face-saving "honor." Congress was increasingly disposed to meat-ax the President's foreign aid recommendations, and in this respect proved relatively less generous than several other less wealthy foreign nations.

Clearly the fifteen-nation NATO alliance was becoming seriously frayed. Countless American taxpayers were wondering why, a quarter of a century after World War II, Uncle Sam should be forced to keep some 300,000 men in Europe (210,000 in Germany) to provide protection that the now-recovered European nations should be fully providing for themselves. In 1971, two serious efforts were made in the Senate to secure a unilateral withdrawal of troops, and in the presidential campaign of 1972, candidate Senator McGovern won considerable applause (and much criticism) when he advocated reducing America's army in Europe by 170,000 men.

President de Gaulle of France had undercut NATO by his go-it-alone nationalism, and America's defensive requirements had forced the Sixth Fleet in the Mediterranean to pull up anchor and establish its main forward base near Athens. The resulting need to support the Greek government, now an iron-fisted military dictatorship, evoked bitter complaints from American liberals who bemoaned the loss of democracy in the Athenian cradle of *dēmokratía*.

Disillusionment with the United Nations, which boasted 132 nations at the beginning of 1973, was growing with every passing year. The unseating of Chiang's China and the seating of Red China in 1971, to say nothing of the admission of dozens of mini-states that helped to swell the Communist and African blocs, added increasingly to the disenchantment. In November, 1971, the Gallup pollsters found for the first time in their canvassing that more American voters thought the U.N. was doing a poor job rather than a good one.[19]

The six-nation Common Market (European Economic Community),

[19] The vote was 35% good, 43% poor, 22% without opinion. Gallup Release, Nov. 12, 1971.

with its common tariff wall, posed an ominous threat. President de Gaulle of France, who had repeatedly blocked Britain's entrance, lost face and resigned in April, 1969, and this formidable Gallic roadblock disappeared. On January 1, 1973, Britain, Denmark, and Ireland formally entered the Common Market, thereby increasing its membership to nine countries and creating a potential economic colossus comparable in strength to a United States that ironically had served as a midwife.[20] A political union was thus foreshadowed—perhaps the United States of Europe—whose concentrated economic power created the nightmare of a formidable barrier to American exports. Protectionist-isolationist elements in the United States, already disturbed by the flood of goods from Japan, girded themselves for a battle of the tariff walls.

ISRAEL AND THE MIDDLE EAST

America's New Isolation was less conspicuous in the trigger-taut Middle East, largely because of the deep interest in Israel displayed by some 6,000,000 Jewish-Americans. Since 1948, the tiny new state had precariously survived three wars, and following the Six Day War of June, 1967 (see p. 907) had enormously expanded its territory, at least temporarily. The Soviet Union, evidently with an eye to the enormous oil reserves of the Middle East and strategic bases in the Mediterranean, continued to support Egypt financially and with billion-ruble outlays of tanks, aircraft, and other modern equipment. Washington's basic policy, strongly backed by many Jewish voters, was to supply Israel with enough modern airplanes and other weapons to insure peace by preserving the Middle Eastern balance of power.

In the absence of a treaty, the Six Day War continued for many more than a thousand days. The Israelis dug in on the east bank of the blocked Suez Canal and clung to the rest of their recently captured territory, pending guarantees of satisfactory defensive frontiers. Betrayed before, embattled Israel defied resolutions of the U.N. to withdraw, as well as pressures from the United States. Secretary of State Rogers, collaborating closely with the U.N. in a "stop shooting, start talking initiative," arranged for a cease-fire in 1970, and it continued uneasily despite recurrent Egyptian threats of renewed warfare.[21]

Rumbles from the Middle Eastern volcano probably posed the gravest threat of World War III during the first Nixon term, not excluding Viet Nam. If a blow-up came and Russia actively backed the Arabs, the United States would almost inevitably become involved. In September,

[20] The original members were Belgium, France, Italy, Luxembourg, the Netherlands, and West Germany, with Greece, Morocco, Tunisia, and Turkey associate members.
[21] *United States Foreign Policy, 1971: A Report of the Secretary of State* (Washington, D.C., 1972), pp. 94–98.

1970, Syrians and Palestinian rebels, operating from Syria and equipped with Russian tanks, burst into neighboring Jordan in an effort to establish an anti-Israel government. Secretary Rogers released to the press a strong condemnation of this incursion which stressed "the danger of a broadened conflict." [22] President Nixon alerted American airborne troops in Europe, while rushing a reinforced Sixth Fleet to the Eastern Mediterranean. (Jewish voters in America did not forget this welcome brandishing of the Big Stick when Nixon ran for reelection in 1972.) Fortunately for world peace, the Jordanian defenders managed to turn back the invading tanks from Syria, and normally troubled relations returned, highlighted by Arab terrorism.

Crisis tensions in the Middle East further eased on July 18, 1972, significantly the month after Nixon's Moscow visit. Egypt summarily expelled thousands of Russian advisers and technicians who were arming the Egyptians with sophisticated weapons. Informed observers concluded that this kick in the teeth was a protest against Moscow's refusal to send enough assistance to insure a reconquest of Egypt's lost territory. In addition, the reception accorded Nixon in Moscow indicated that the Kremlin was willing to abandon Egypt in order to insure more tolerable co-existence with the United States.

STORM OVER SOUTH AMERICA

Under Nixon, relations with Latin America on the whole remained embittered. The snail-paced Alliance for Progress (see p. 870) continued to be a costly disappointment, largely because of a refusal by the ruling elite to make the sacrifices that would insure progress. Latin America's population growth for some time had been the most explosive in the world, with a consequent increase in poverty and discontent. The drift was definitely away from democracy, as military dictators rose on the right and Communist regimes on the left. President Nixon, retreating considerably from the Alliance (Misalliance?) for Progress, delivered a speech (October 31, 1969) in which he stressed "Action for Progress for the Americas." But he made clear that the main impetus to social and economic reform would have to come from within, not from without.[23]

Early in his first administration, Nixon "honored" one of his recent rivals for the nomination, Governor Nelson Rockefeller of New York, with an invitation to make four scheduled "fact finding" trips to Latin America (May to July, 1969). The Yankee millionaire's overall reception

---

[22] *Department of State Bulletin*, LXIII (Oct. 12, 1970), p. 412.
[23] *Ibid.*, LXI (November 17, 1969), 409–414. Delivered before the Inter-American Press Association at Washington, D.C.

proved to be unpleasantly warm. "Rockefeller riots" and other un-friendly demonstrations, punctuated by shouts of *"Fuera, yanqui"* (Go home, Yankee) marred many of these "good will" visits. Venezuela, Chile, and Peru, fearing uncontrollable disorders, postponed or can-celled their invitations. The outbursts were frightening in Uruguay and especially Argentina, where tear gas was used and one labor leader was fatally shot. Not surprisingly, Rockefeller's lengthy report to Nixon underscored the need for more cooperative relationships, especially concessions by the United States aimed at economic improvement.[24]

Turbulence in Latin America continued to manifest itself in various ways. In Brazil, terrorists kidnapped and subsequently released the United States ambassador (1969); United States and other foreign of-ficials were kidnapped elsewhere, sometimes with death to the victim. Embittered nationalism prompted increasing expropriations of Yankee holdings, including oil and copper, in Peru, Bolivia, and Chile. Usually the investors were unable to secure satisfactory compensation.

Leftist trends in Chile, once a foremost democracy, were especially worrisome to Washington. A left-wing coalition, accusing American copper-mining and other interests of "milking" the country, won control in 1970 by electing to the Presidency Salvador Allende, a home-grown Marxist. This startling upheaval was regarded as the first time in history, certainly in the Americas, that a pro-Communist regime had triumphed in a fair and democratic election. The subsequent seizure of some $800 million in Yankee holdings, notably Anaconda and Kennecott copper interests, occurred without proper compensation—at least as viewed from Wall Street. An uproar occurred in 1972 with the revelation that a powerful American holding company (International Telephone and Telegraph Company) had earlier schemed to undermine Allende. Not surprisingly, he began to flirt more openly with Moscow.

Several of the South American nations, notably Peru and Ecuador, had for some years claimed jurisdiction over their coastal waters 200 miles out to sea, far beyond the traditional three miles and occasional twelve miles recognized by international law. Scores of Yankee tuna boats, long accustomed to fish these waters, suffered arrest. They were then routinely released after the operators paid fines that totaled nearly $2,500,000 for 51 seizures in 1971 alone.[25] Washington adopted the policy of reimbursing the owners and subtracting the fines from the foreign aid appropriations customarily granted to the offending countries. Peru and Ecuador were especially unhappy over this practice.

---

[24] *Ibid.,* LXI (Dec. 8, 1969), 493–540.
[25] *United States Foreign Policy, 1971: A Report of the Secretary of State* (Wash-ington, D.C., 1972), p. 221. By 1971, Chile and Brazil were also claiming 200-miles jurisdiction, bringing the total to ten Latin American countries.

CARIBBEAN DISQUIETUDE

The Caribbean banana-belt presented smaller scale but hardly less vexatious problems than South America. In the strategic isthmus, where conditions demanded a new or greatly enlarged canal, Panama was desperately determined to secure possession of the waterway and regain control of the Canal Zone ("a country within a country") leased "in perpetuity" to the United States in 1903. Washington was in no mood to surrender the operation and defense of the canal, with consequent deadlock and bitterness over draft treaties. A favorable omen came in July, 1970, when Nicaragua and the United States signed a pact ending the Bryan-Chamorro Convention of 1914 (pp. 551–552), which had given the United States exclusive rights for ninety-nine years in connection with a possible transisthmian canal across Nicaragua. The United States Senate approved the treaty of revocation in February, 1971, by a vote of 66 to 5.[26]

Communized and "Castroated" Cuba, still under Prime Minister Castro's rigid dictatorship, continued to soak up costly economic and military assistance from Russia. The highjacking ("skyjacking") of scores of airplanes in recent years had become a worldwide phenomenon, and increasingly involved the United States with Cuba. Castro did permit the victimized planes to return to Yankeeland, but he refused to hand over the highjackers, many of whom were criminals rather than honest citizens seeking "political asylum." His most telling argument was that the United States would not return Cubans who highjacked boats and fled to Florida.

The impasse was finally broken on February 15, 1973, when the two governments, negotiating through third-party countries, concluded a five-year executive agreement that was not retroactive.[27] It provided for the extradition or maximum prosecution of all persons guilty of major crimes in connection with highjacking airplanes or ships. Legitimate political refugees, involved only in "minor offenses," were protected, and all passengers, crews, planes, ships, and money were to be returned. The United States also agreed to suppress conspiracies to attack Cuba or even attacks on Cuban shores by American-based Cuban exiles. Although the agreement in no way implied eventual diplomatic recognition, it was a step forward and an almost certain guarantee of reduced highjacking.

[26] Text of treaty in *Department of State Bulletin*, LXIII (Aug. 10, 1970), 183–184. The U.S. thus yielded its leasehold on Great and Little Corn Islands in the Caribbean.

[27] Text in *The New York Times*, February 16, 1973, p. 4.

CANADA—UNEASY PARTNER

Canadian-American relations continued to betray the historic uneasiness that a weak neighbor usually shows toward an overshadowingly powerful one. A perennial fear of the Canadians was that they were in danger of being gobbled up by the huge capital investment of the Yankees. Yet they would have been displeased if such capital had been withheld or mutual trade cut off. By 1970, this commerce amounted to about $10 billion for each country each way, for an unprecedented total of $20 billion.

Neighboring Yankees were further disturbed by Canada's weakening commitment to NATO, by some new restraints on fishing in international waters, by Canada's opening of diplomatic relations with Red China (1970), and by Canadian criticism of America's entrapment in the Viet Nam morass. The Ottawa government further offended America by granting asylum to tens of thousands of conscientious objectors, draft dodgers, and deserters from the armed services. "Gone to Canada," the phrase once used to explain the absence of absconding bank tellers, was revived.

A happier note was sounded when, in April, 1970, President Nixon flew to Canada for a three-day visit with Prime Minister Trudeau. The most noteworthy fruit was the signing of a joint agreement to clear up the badly polluted Great Lakes.

"FOUR MORE YEARS" FOR NIXON

The entrenched Republicans, voicing the slogan, "President Nixon, Now More than Ever," were certain to renominate the President in 1972 and endorse his "no surrender" policy in Viet Nam. The left-wing element of the Democratic party tapped Senator George McGovern of South Dakota, the earnest "Prairie Populist," at Miami Beach, in July, 1972. He had long been championing a pull-out of American troops from Viet Nam within ninety days, and the clarion call of his acceptance speech was "Come Home, America." Unfortunately for him, his views were so liberal, leftist, and dovish as to antagonize the powerful conservative wing of his own party, as well as many independent voters.

In crowning Nixon anew at Miami Beach, in August, 1972, the Republicans chanted "Four more years, four more years" as they acclaimed their leader's triumphs for peace in China and Russia. They condemned the "New Isolationism" of the McGovernites, decried McGovern's proposed slashing of defense funds as threatening to reduce America to a "second class power," insisted on maintaining the nation's credibility as an ally by supporting the authoritarian government of President Thieu in South Viet Nam, and demanded "peace with honor" rather than "peace with surrender in Indochina." They pointed out, with spectacular charts, that Nixon had wound down "the Democratic war" from some 550,000 troops to about 30,000, with more scheduled to come home.

In the ensuing campaign, the McGovernites assailed Nixon's Viet Nam "flimflam." Far from ending the war, they insisted, he had spread it into Laos and Cambodia. While winding down troop strength with one hand, with the other he had conspicuously wound up the naval and aerial participation with some of the heaviest bombing in history. Far from securing the release of some 500 American prisoners of war (POWs), he was merely increasing their number. After "four long years," where was the peace that he had so earnestly promised as a candidate in 1968?

On October 26, 1972, twelve days before the election, McGovern was substantially robbed of the Viet Nam peace issue. After marathon negotiations with the North Vietnamese in Paris, Dr. Kissinger, Nixon's adviser, returned home to state to the press, "We believe that peace is at hand." Almost simultaneously, the North Vietnamese had published the terms tentatively agreed upon and demanded that the United States sign by October 31, 1972, a week before the election. They evidently expected Nixon, facing the voters, to be stampeded into acceptance. Among other provisions, American prisoners of war were to be released and American troops were to come home.[28] Dr. Kissinger explained that only a few relatively minor clarifications remained to be threshed out. The McGovernites, suddenly deflated, rather lamely replied that if peace was "at hand," it should have come four years earlier and thousands of casualties sooner. But, refusing to be railroaded, Nixon pledged, on November 2, 1972, that he would sign the accord "only when the agreement is right." He wanted a "lasting" peace, not a "temporary" peace. As a result, North Viet Nam's deadline of October 31 came and passed.

With peace seemingly—but only seemingly—in the bag, Nixon swept to victory in a landslide (521 to 17 electoral votes) that carried every state except one (Massachusetts), plus the District of Columbia. His percentage of the popular vote was 61 per cent to 38 per cent. The opinion polls had predicted the outcome with uncanny accuracy.

Though overwhelming, the Republican victory could hardly be interpreted as an endorsement of any one of Nixon's policies, including his having brought "peace" to Viet Nam.[29] Many voters, misled into believ-

[28] Text in *The New York Times*, Oct. 27, 1972, p. 19.
[29] Yet it is probable that a majority of those who voted for Nixon favored his wind-down approach to Viet Nam over that of pull-out McGovern. A Gallup Poll (Release, October 13, 1972) asked respondents who could deal better with Viet Nam. The response was 58% Nixon, 26% McGovern, and 16% undecided.

ing that the shooting had really ended, regarded the candidates as a choice of evils. McGovern, backed by assorted minorities, radicals, long-haired "peaceniks," and "liberated" women, was far too far to the left for conservative Democrats to swallow. Many of these bolted to Nixon and salved their "guilt" by voting for Democratic members of Congress.

If the result was a spectacular triumph for Nixon, it was not for his party. The Republicans lost seats in the Senate, gained only a scattering in the House, and failed to win either house of Congress—an unprecedented rebuke to a candidate winning such an epochal victory. The vote was possibly as much one of no-confidence in McGovern as confidence in Nixon, whose promised peace unhappily was far from being "at hand."

THE SO-CALLED VIET NAM CEASE-FIRE

The dove of "peace" that was "at hand" rapidly took flight shortly after Nixon's election. Both adversaries were moving frantically to gain as much advantage as they could before "a cease-fire in place." The United States airlifted an immense amount of war matériel to South Viet Nam, while the North Vietnamese and Viet Cong launched drives to seize as much more territory in South Viet Nam as possible. With President Thieu of South Viet Nam crying "sellout," both sides were stepping up their demands.

Serious negotiations in Paris came to a halt when the chief North Vietnamese negotiator, Le Duc Tho, left for Hanoi, December 15, 1972. Three days later, President Nixon unleashed massive bombing attacks on North Vietnamese military installations and chief urban centers in what appeared to be an angry effort to force the enemy back to the negotiating table. This "Christmas blitz" inflicted severe damage, including considerable loss of civilian life, while the defenders shot down an alarming number of attacking U.S. aircraft. World opinion expressed outrage, while the "doves" at home were hardly less vehement. After the furious "Christmas bombing" had continued for eleven days (one day off for Christmas), Hanoi signaled its willingness to negotiate seriously, and the massive attacks ceased, December 30, 1972.

The cease-fire agreements, signed on January 27, 1973, in the old Hotel Majestic in Paris, were lengthy, complicated, and purposely ambiguous.[30] Signatories represented the United States and South Viet Nam on one side, and North Viet Nam and the National Liberation Front (Viet Cong) on the other. Within sixty days, the United States would withdraw the remainder of its troops (some 27,000 men) from South Viet Nam, and would be permitted to support the Saigon regime with

[30] There were, in addition to the basic cease-fire agreement, seven detailed protocols. *Weekly Compilation of Presidential Documents*, IX (Jan. 29, 1973), pp. 45–64.

replacements for but not additions to worn-out military equipment. Arrangements were made for an election in South Viet Nam that presumably would permit the Thieu regime to outvote the Communist Viet Cong and hence survive (with American military supplies and continuing financial support).[31] At Paris the North Vietnamese had for many months insisted on a halt to all bombing and other aggressive acts by the United States, a complete pull-out of U.S. troops, and a coalition government in Saigon that would insure rather rapid Communist domination. Hanoi conceded a great deal when it yielded on this last point, although in fact it could hope to take over ultimately, by political or military means or both. North Viet Nam also agreed to a reciprocal exchange of prisoners of war within sixty days, and this meant releasing the imprisoned Americans.

In achieving this nominal cease-fire, Nixon had cleverly used both the stick and the carrot. The stick was the devastating "Christmas bombing," with the threat of more to come. The carrot was the promise that America would aid financially in the rebuilding of Indochina, as vaguely stipulated in the cease-fire (Article 21). A grand total of $7.5 billion over a five-year period was most commonly mentioned, of which North Viet Nam would presumably receive $2.5 billion, in the hope of preserving the "peace." Some right-wing critics, desiring a genuine victory, referred to this sum as "reparations from the losers." It was in effect the ransom to be paid for the 500 or so American prisoners. Otherwise the United States could have continued its withdrawal and left these Pawns of War to their fate. Even so, much hostility developed in Congress to appropriating one cent for the unrepentant and jubilant enemy.

PEACE WITH SHOOTING IN VIET NAM

Who won the war? In a sense all were losers, because all sides had suffered severely. There was little rejoicing in South Viet Nam but much in North Viet Nam, a tiny nation which claimed that it had beaten the biggest of the imperialist bullies. The United States had entered the war to halt Communism, but the Communists (Viet Cong and North Vietnamese) still occupied about one-third of Viet Nam, actually somewhat more than when the United States entered the conflict in 1964–1965. North Viet Nam lost no territory. Indeed, in some respects America was no farther ahead than in 1954, when Washington declined to support the Geneva Agreements. Surprisingly, these were reaffirmed in the first article of the new cease-fire pact and in three

[31] The Geneva Agreements of 1954 had scheduled a unification election for 1956, but it had never been held, owing in part to U.S. opposition. The new elections presumably would afford the anti-Communists a better chance of winning.

other places.[32] The United States had been fighting for self-determination of the Vietnamese under a free government. But Viet Nam was still divided, as in 1954, and President Thieu of South Viet Nam, who was authoritarian by American standards, openly declared that his country was not "ready" for democracy. Worse yet, the North Vietnamese were privileged to leave behind in South Viet Nam some unmentioned 145,000 soldiers, who were not to be replaced. The argument was that, unable to receive further supplies, they would wither on the vine. But pessimists predicted that they would don black pajamas, mingle with the shadowy Viet Cong, and pursue guerrilla warfare until the Saigon regime collapsed.

The cease-fire, though duly proclaimed, was openly violated hundreds or thousands of times in subsequent weeks, with thousands of Vietnamese casualties. Heavy American bombings of Communist centers in Laos and Cambodia, unprotected by the new agreements, continued intermittently. The first contingents of American prisoners of war came home, blessing President Nixon for having bombed his way to a nominal cease-fire—and their release. A handful of neutrals, by prearrangement limited to a scant 1,160 men, began to arrive to police the so-called peace for the four-nation International Commission of Control and Supervision. American heavy bombers remained poised on Guam, in Thailand, and on navy carriers, ready to attack North Viet Nam anew should continuing violations of the cease-fire become intolerable.

President Nixon rejoiced over the "peace with honor," despite many complaints that he had won neither "peace" nor "honor." He evidently believed that America would retrieve her prisoners of war and would not have to strong-arm President Thieu into accepting terms that would guarantee an immediate Communist takeover. In securing a negotiated settlement, the United States won the assent of President Thieu, preserved its credibility with its allies, averted a McGovernite "bug out," and saved more face than many critics thought possible or even desirable. Yet the truce was, as Nixon admitted, "fragile," and, unlike the situation in Korea, the enemy still occupied a large part of the country that America had attempted to rescue. Cynics said that about all the United States got out of Viet Nam, after the longest war in its history, was its troops and prisoners of war, after some 46,000 Americans had been killed, 300,000 had been wounded, and $130 billion had gone down the drain.

Dr. Kissinger observed that the cease-fire might hold if "good will" prevailed on both sides. But good will was in short supply. So bitter was the feeling between the South Vietnamese and the Viet Cong that neither side in Paris would affix its signatures to the same piece of paper. The immediate reaction of most Americans with opinions (many

[32] Articles 5, 8, 20.

contradictory) revealed that the cease-fire was most welcome, that it was actually "peace with honor," that South Viet Nam got better terms than North Viet Nam, that the truce would probably not last, and that the Communists would eventually take over. When the showdown came, the pollees believed, the United States should not renew the bombing and certainly not send in more war matériel and ground troops.[33]

A somewhat chastened United States thus embarked upon an uncertain course that was acceptable to much of world opinion, especially in Communist countries. The Russians and the Chinese, both of whom may have applied pressure to North Viet Nam, were evidently pleased. On February 22, 1973, Washington and Peking each announced the forthcoming establishment of a liaison office in the other's capital—that is, virtual diplomatic recognition. A few days later, on March 2, 1973, a twelve-nation conference in Paris, including the United States, China, Russia, Britain, and France, agreed to underwrite the new cease-fire.[34] At long last, officially and on paper at least, America had shouldered its peace commitment off onto an international body.

SELECTED BIBLIOGRAPHY

Most of what has been written thus far on the Nixon administration is biased contemporary journalism. Among the better received books on the President are Garry Wills, *Nixon Agonistes: The Crisis of the Self-Made Man* (Boston, 1970); John Osborne, *The Nixon Watch* (New York, 1970); and Ralph de Toledano, *One Man Alone: Richard Nixon* (New York, 1969). See also David Landau, *Kissinger: The Uses of Power* (Boston, 1972). High-quality journalism may be found in Henry Brandon, *The Retreat of American Power* (New York, 1973) and Rowland Evans, Jr. and Robert D. Novak, *Nixon in the White House: The Frustration of Power* (New York, 1971). Concerned with the American "empire" are Merlo J. Pusey, *The U.S.A. Astride the Globe* (Boston, 1971) and Ronald Steel, *Imperialists and other Heroes: A Chronicle of the American Empire* (New York, 1971). The respected series of the Council on Foreign Affairs, discontinued in the late 1960's, has started afresh with William P. Lineberry, *The United States in World Affairs, 1970* (New York, 1972).

[33] Gallup Release, January 30, 1973. It should be noted, however, that this survey was hastily conducted by telephone and represented a smaller cross section of respondents than usual.

[34] In addition to the five nations mentioned, there were the three Viet Nam belligerents, plus the four countries manning the International Commission of Control and Supervision: Canada, Poland, Hungary, and Indonesia. *The New York Times*, March 2, 1973, pp. 1, 3.

Epilogue:
From Colonies to Colossus

> *We are participants, whether we would or not, in the life of the world. The interests of all nations are our own also. We are partners with the rest. What affects mankind is inevitably our affair as well as the affair of Europe and of Asia.*
>
> Woodrow Wilson, 1916.

THE END OF THE AGE OF OSTRICHISM

The United States came into existence as a group of thinly populated colonies perched on the eastern seaboard of the North American continent. It entered upon the 20th Century as a gigantic world power, stretching magnificently from Maine to Manila, from Panama to the Pole. It emerged from two world wars as the richest and most powerful nation on the globe, supplanting Great Britain as the object of universal envy.

The world has changed, and the basic factors shaping American foreign policy, as outlined in the first chapter of this book, have changed with it. The United States is no longer geographically isolated: the Atlantic Ocean is now much smaller than was the Aegean Sea in the days of Socrates. The republic no longer has weak neighbors: the miracles of modern communication and transportation have made all nations neighbors. It no longer has room on this continent for territorial expansion: all contiguous lands have been staked out by others. It is no longer agitated to the extent that it once was by huge and undigested bodies of "hyphenates." The famed melting pot, immigration quotas, and the undertaker's hearse have all done their work, although certain noisy but diminishing groups remain.

Nor have the changes ended here. The nation can no longer count on Europe's distresses as its first line of defense: the world's distresses are now its distresses. The globe is like a huge drum; thump it anywhere, and it reverberates everywhere. Finally, the United States can no longer enjoy the luxury of subordinating foreign affairs to domestic affairs. With the nation's very life at stake, its citizens dare not thrust their heads into isolationist sands while the rest of the earth is in convulsion.

POLICIES ARE MADE FOR NATIONS

As fundamental conditions have changed, basic American foreign policies have changed with them, though sometimes with dangerous slowness. What, for example, has been the fate of the six traditional foreign policies described briefly in the first chapter of this book?

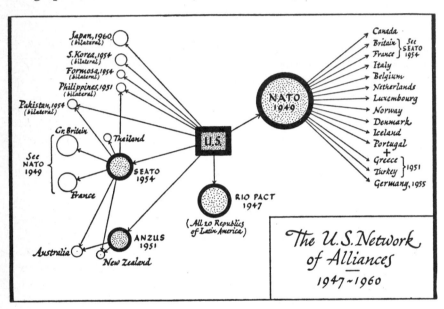

The U.S. Network of Alliances 1947–1960

Freedom of the seas, once the first line of defense of weak-navy nations like adolescent America, is no longer a burning issue. The United States, a great naval power, has no more use for this shackle than big-navy Britain had in the 19th Century.

The Open Door, though still a desirable objective, is sagging on rusted hinges. This is notably true in those vast areas of the world where the Iron Curtain of Soviet communism and the Bamboo Curtain of Chinese communism have descended.

The Monroe Doctrine, originally a unilateral policy of the United States, has become a multilateral possession of all the co-operating republics of the Western Hemisphere—a kind of Pan-Americanized defense doctrine. The threat of Nazism, followed by the menace of communism, induced the United States to share its precious dogma with its hemispheric neighbors.

Pan-Americanism, except notably for Castro's Cuba, has sporadically grown stronger in the face of rumblings from overseas. By the Rio Pact of 1947 the United States became united with its twenty southern neighbors in what amounted to a hemispheric defensive alliance.

Isolationism likewise has gone the way of the horse and buggy. The policy of no-entangling alliances has been spectacularly reversed, in response to outside dangers, to the point where the United States is involved in more than forty entangling alliances. Nonintervention has become wholesale intervention, whether in World War I, World War II, the Korean War, or the Viet Nam War. The republic is no longer content to drift at the mercy of events; it is determined to use its enormous power to control those events in the interests of its own peace and security. Noninvolvement has become involvement in the affairs of several score of nations, whether through economic or military programs. The United States cannot afford to leave the world alone because the world will not leave it alone.

The peaceful settlement of disputes, in general, has taken deeper root. Wars had lost their glamor even before the ill-starred Viet Nam blood bath. Modern conflicts can be so catastrophic that men must, at almost any price, avoid a global conflagration. The contrast between America's support of the UN and her rejection of the League of Nations provides abundant proof of this changed attitude.

Most of the shifts or reversals in these basic foreign policies were not freely willed by the American public. They were forced upon the nation by outside menaces, whether Axis or Communist. The objectives of the old ideals—peace, security, freedom—were not being achieved. New policies, or new twists to old policies, had to be adopted to cope with changed conditions. Just as the Sabbath is made for man and not man for the Sabbath, so policies are made for nations, and not nations for policies. When policies fail to attain their objectives, they should be scrapped, no matter how hallowed their associations, in favor of new ones that promise to be successful.

THE CHALLENGE TO EDUCATION

Ignorance is still perhaps the most formidable roadblock in the path of far-visioned foreign policies. The statesmen in Washington, as well as the great mass of better-informed citizens, know that America is no longer living in the era of William McKinley. But a dangerous minority of the voters do not know this. Many do not realize that rigid isolationism is both dead and dangerous; that the workaday American must learn to put himself in the sandals of other people and view their problems through their colored spectacles; that he must cultivate understanding and tolerance; that he must sublimate suspicion and ill will; that he must meet the other fellow at least halfway; and that he must continue to invest some of his precious sovereignty in what mankind hopes will be an effective world organization.

But the confused citizen cannot see all these basic truths clearly. All too often he is indifferent, ignorant, or misled by ill-informed, biased, and sometimes unscrupulous editors, columnists, radio commentators, and politicians. If the American people, through their Congress, insist on economic nonco-operation, ruinous tariff barriers, and other impediments to international intercourse, they will have their way—with the risk of disaster. America cannot exist forever as an island of prosperity in a world of poverty.

The level of American foreign policy, which sooner or later feels the impact of public opinion, cannot rise substantially higher than the masses will let it. Various polls have consistently shown that the lower one goes down the educational scale into the sub-eighth-grade group, one finds more provincialism, more isolationism, more militarism, more jingoism, more indifference to foreign affairs, more preoccupation with the World Series and other domestic trivia, more race prejudice, more distrust of foreigners, more desire for superpatriotic text books, more demand for high tariff barriers and other instruments of economic nonco-operation, more insistence on harsh terms for international debtors, more reluctance to pay foreign service officers and other public servants adequate salaries, more shortsightedness in foreign affairs, more unwillingness to see that there are at least two sides to most complicated disputes, more blind attachment to the concept of sovereignty, and more opposition to even a moderate amount of international co-operation.

A tremendous job in public education needs to be done. Narrowness, intolerance, bigotry, witch-hunting, and demagoguery fatten on ignorance. American educational institutions must receive more generous support from the taxpayers, because the proper kind of education is a relatively cheap form of international life insurance. If the people control foreign policy, as broadly they do, they should know something about the complicated mechanism they are controlling. The schools and colleges must offer more and better work in foreign languages, history, geography, foreign affairs, comparative government, international economics, international law, and international organization. The press, the radio, the public forums, and other informational agencies must rise to their responsibilities to present sound and enlightening information about the outside world. Events in strange and faraway places may hatch troubles that will come to roost in the United States.

Upon every citizen in this democracy rests a solemn obligation to inform himself, so that he may shape American foreign policy—*his foreign policy*—along constructive and far-visioned lines.

FROM ADOLESCENCE TO ADULTHOOD

The American people, on the whole, have shown a surprising maturity in dealing with foreign affairs since the end of World War II. In 1919 they were forced by events onto the global stage, but they fled like children from their new responsibilities, and left the still-born League of Nations in the laps of the other powers. But today the American people are locked on the world stage; there is no place to hide. The question is not whether they will play a role; the question is whether they will play a role that is irresponsible or one that is commensurate with their proliferating power and responsibilities. As the world grows smaller, their obligations grow bigger.

Who would have predicted before World War II that in the two decades thereafter the American taxpayer would spend about $100 billion abroad in various projects of defense and foreign aid? These expenditures were not prompted primarily by humanitarian motives. They were based generally on the assumption that the defense of certain foreign countries was essential for the defense of the United States. An acceptance of this fundamental but financially costly truth has been perhaps the most striking proof of the new maturity of the American people. Most citizens have evidently come to realize that they can have only the foreign policy that they are willing to pay for.

The United States has thus been thrust into the unwanted position of leader of the free nations. If it goes down, they may all go down like a row of falling dominoes. Walt Whitman wrote with curiously prophetic vision in 1865:

> Have the elder races halted?
> Do they droop and end their lesson, wearied over there beyond the Seas?
> We take up the task eternal, and the burden and the lesson,
>   Pioneers! O pioneers!

The elder races have faltered, and the American people have taken up the burden, which at times seems "eternal." But America can no more return to the relatively carefree days of 1789 than an adult with a large family can return to the carefree days of his childhood. Tiny nations like Switzerland, which cannot control world events and therefore have no responsibility for them, are in some degree to be envied by the great powers that must carry the heavy end of the log.

Not all Americans are bearing their new burdens cheerfully and responsibly. Not all of them are prepared to recognize that their very way of life is jeopardized by outside menaces. Many are grumbling over defense expenditures, not realizing that to Communists the most eloquent language is that of force. Many are in a mood to be taken in by Marxist smiles and wiles. Many would gladly cut off all foreign aid from certain countries whose continued freedom would further safeguard the freedom of the United States. Many do not perceive that liberty is more precious than dollars, and that when freedom is lost all is lost.

Many shortsighted Americans, unaware that some of the most important battles of the Cold War are being fought on the ideological front, are determined to choke the Voice of America and other propaganda weapons of the United States Information Agency. Many naïvely believe that America's democracy is so perfect that it speaks for itself in stentorian tones the world over. But the Cold War is also a war of words, and the Communists have put so much money and effort into this phase of it that they have achieved spectacular success. The American propaganda campaign, when compared with the Soviet sound truck, has at times seemed like a tin whistle.

Many complacent Americans do not know that ideas are more potent than tanks—and a good deal less costly; and that one cannot kill ideas with bayonets, only with better ideas, properly conveyed. What America needs is not so much A bombs or H bombs as I bombs—Idea Bombs.

THE PRICE OF FREEDOM

Eternal vigilance is traditionally the price that one has to pay for one's liberties. Yet many Americans, unfamiliar with the iron discipline of communism, are reluctant to sacrifice their luxuries for their priceless freedoms. Many are blindly determined to have business as usual, profits as usual, pleasures as usual, Cadillacs as usual. They refuse to concede that politics should stop at the water's edge, and that the United States, so far as possible under a bipartisan program, should present a united front to its diplomatic adversaries. A nation can have only one set of foreign policies at a time.

Some impatient Americans—a tiny minority—are eager to withdraw from the United Nations or to campaign for utterly visionary substitutes. The United Nations, although in some respects a disappointment, has proved more successful than the old League of Nations. Nations want to get into it rather than out of it.

Many Americans do not have the patience to sustain a long-range program in foreign affairs, and the Communists are counting on this weakness. The ordinary American wearies quickly of well doing; he is too willing to appease or to postpone the evil day. The American people must gird themselves for a long campaign and learn to live with chronic crisis.

Many Americans, especially those of the sub-eighth-grade group, are too ready to follow the leadership of headline-hogging demagogues. These gentry, in their search for scapegoats rather than solutions, have been conspicuously successful in diverting attention from the dangers of communism abroad to the lesser or imagined dangers of communism at home. Many are prone to smear with the label of communism all those who disagree with them or even have forward-looking views. Nonconformism and communism are not the same thing. America was founded by nonconformists, and one of her most cherished rights is the right to be wrong.

Some misguided Americans are prepared to strangle their basic freedoms in their own hands in an effort to protect them. What shall it profit a nation if, to find security, it adopts the methods of the dictators, whether Fascist or Communist? Truth should not become a captive in the land of the free. If Americans give up some of their basic freedoms in order to buy security, they may soon find themselves without either freedom or security. If they tear themselves asunder with internal dissensions, whether ideological or racial, they cannot live up to their high responsibility as torchbearer of the free world. A nation divided against itself cannot lead.

DEMOCRACY ON THE DEFENSIVE

When the American colonies declared their independence in 1776, democracy was on trial. Despotism, absolutism, monarchism, and illiberalism were its sworn foes. But the American people cherished a faith in freedom that was not to be denied, and they wrought the miracle known as America in the face of foreign frowns.

As in 1776, the American democracy is again on trial. Most of its people (excepting the one-sixth below the poverty line) are fat, sated, contented, "gone soft." With only 6 per cent of the world's population, they enjoy about 40 per cent of the world's wealth. The war is on to the knife with the Communists for the support of the uncommitted one-third of the world. And the spokesmen for world communism, with their illusory appeal to downtrodden humanity, have seized the ideological offensive.

The United States was once a revolutionary force in a world of conservatism. It is now a conservative force in a world of revolutionism. The republic cannot contend on equal terms with its ideological foes unless it can recapture the dynamic faith that it had in democracy in the 19th Century. Then the most feared "isms" were American constitutionalism, republicanism, and liberalism. The world is in the throes of a revolution, and if the United States is to hold its ground it must launch a counter-revolution of its own.

Most Americans evidently do not realize that the best way to promote democracy abroad is to practice it at home—to live it. Imperfect products are difficult to export, and American democracy is less than perfect. Every exhibition of bigotry, intolerance, discrimination, or violence that provides fuel for the Communist propaganda machine discredits the very democracy which the United States is striving to uphold.

"Peaceful coexistence" with Communism seems impossible. But "competitive coexistence" has been going on since 1917, when the Moscow

Communists launched their ideological war against capitalism, and it can presumably continue for a long time. The alternative seems to be World War III, in which there will be no winners. Coexistence of a sort is better than no existence at all.

The world crisis is formidable—but so is the United States. The American people, relative to their existing strength, have confronted and surmounted crises of comparable magnitude before. There is no need for defeatism; the republic is immensely strong. The American people should pray not so much for problems to disappear as for the resolution to grapple with problems in a manner befitting their vast strength. And above all they should elevate to high place men to match their mountains —men of strength and vision—for where there is no vision the nation stagnates and ultimately perishes.

SELECTED BIBLIOGRAPHY

General accounts are H. J. Morgenthau, *In Defense of the National Interest* (New York, 1951); R. E. Osgood, *Ideals and Self-Interest in America's Foreign Relations* (Chicago, 1953); F. S. C. Northrop, *European Union and United States Foreign Policy* (New York, 1954); J. J. McCloy, *The Challenge to American Foreign Policy* (Cambridge, Mass., 1953); C. B. Marshall, *The Limits of Foreign Policy* (New York, 1954); G. F. Kennan, *Realities of American Foreign Policy* (Princeton, N.J., 1954); Dexter Perkins, *The American Approach to Foreign Policy* (Cambridge, Mass., 1952); T. A. Bailey, *The Man in the Street* (New York, 1948); Gabriel Almond, *The American People and Foreign Policy* (New York, 1950); Frank Tannenbaum, *The American Tradition in Foreign Policy* (Norman, Okla., 1955).

7TH ED. REFS. General accounts are W. A. Williams, *The Tragedy of American Diplomacy* (Cleveland, 1959) [by an economic determinist]; K. W. Thompson, *Political Realism and the Crisis of World Politics: An American Approach to Foreign Policy* (Princeton, 1960) and *American Diplomacy and Emergent Patterns* (New York, 1962); L. J. Halle, *Dream and Reality: Aspects of American Foreign Policy* (New York, 1959) [by a former State Department planner]; T. K. Finletter, *Foreign Policy: The Next Phase* (New York, 1958) [by a U.S. Ambassador to NATO]; C. L. Sulzberger, *What's Wrong With U.S. Foreign Policy?* (New York, 1959) [by a New York *Times* correspondent]; Andrew Berding, *Foreign Affairs and You! How American Foreign Policy is Made and What it Means to You* (Garden City, N.Y., 1962) [by a former Assistant Secretary of State]; G. G. Van Deusen and R. C. Wade, eds., *Foreign Policy and the American Spirit: Essays by Dexter Perkins* (Ithaca, N.Y., 1957); E. McN. Burns, *The American Idea of Mission: Concepts of National Purpose and Destiny* (New Brunswick, N.J., 1957); Sister Dorothy Jane Van Hoogstrate, *American Foreign Policy; Realists and Idealists: A Catholic Interpretation* (St. Louis, 1960); S. D. Kertesz, ed., *American Diplomacy in a New Era* (Notre Dame, Ind., 1961); Stuart Chase, *American Credos* (New York, 1962). Among the numerous books on high strategy note Bernard Brodie, *Strategy in the Missile Age* (Princeton, 1959); H. A. Kissinger, *The Necessity for Choice: Prospects of American Foreign Policy* (New York, 1961); R. E. Osgood, *Limited War: The Challenge to American Strategy* (Chicago, 1957) and C. E. Osgood, *An Alternative to War or Surrender* (Urbana, Ill., 1962).

8TH ED. REFS. Harlan Cleveland, *The Obligations of Power: American Diplomacy in Search for Peace* (New York, 1966); Dexter Perkins, *The Diplomacy of a New Age: Major Issues in U.S. Policy Since 1945* (Bloomington, Ind., 1967); James Reston, *The Artillery of the Press: Its Influence on American Foreign Policy* (New York, 1967). Technical but intelligible to the layman are Bernard Brodie, *Escalation and the Nuclear Option* (Princeton, N.J., 1966), and Klaus Knorr, *On the Uses of Military Power in the Nuclear Age* (Princeton, N.J., 1966). See also SELECTED BIBLIOGRAPHY for Chapter 1 herein.

9TH ED. REFS. Charles E. Bohlen, *The Transformation of American Foreign Policy* (New York, 1969), by a veteran diplomatist; Gabriel Kolko, *Roots of American Foreign Policy* (Boston, 1969), a New Left polemic; and Eugene V. Rostow, *The Future of American Foreign Policy* (New York, 1972).

APPENDIX

A

Glossary of Diplomatic Terms *

[ABBREVIATIONS: cf. (compare); e.g. (for example); Fr. (French); Lat. (Latin).]
The page references are to examples in this book.

abrogate. Formally to annul, as of agreements.

ad hoc (Lat.). Pertaining to this case alone, as an *ad-hoc* committee.

ad interim (Lat.). Temporary, as an *ad-interim* agreement.

admiralty court. A court having jurisdiction over maritime questions.

aide-mémoire (Fr.). Written outline or summary of a document.

ambassador. A diplomatic agent of the highest rank.

Anglophile. A great admirer of England or things English. Cf. Francophile, etc.

Anglophobe. One strongly averse to England. Cf. Japanophobe, etc.

appeasement. Giving in to the demands of a dangerous power in the hope of
averting further trouble.

armistice. A suspension of military operations by mutual agreement.

asylum. Extension of protection to political refugees by a foreign government or
its representatives.

attaché (Fr.). An official attached to a diplomatic staff, as a military attaché.

autarky. A state of economic self-sufficiency.

autonomy. The power or right of self-government.

balance of power. Such an equilibrium in the power of neighboring states to
wage war on one another as to deter or preclude hostilities.

belligerency, recognition of. Recognition (as by a proclamation of neutrality)
that a state of war exists between two or more governments.

belligerent. A nation engaged in waging war.

benevolent neutrality. Technical neutrality that favors one belligerent.

bilateral. Affecting reciprocally two parties, as a bilateral treaty.

blacklist. In wartime a list of enemy-connected firms, at home or in a neutral
country, with which a belligerent forbids its nationals to trade. P. 586.

blockade. The interdiction of communication by armed force; traditionally the
patrolling of an enemy's ports so closely by warships as to make ingress or
egress hazardous.

broken voyage. See continuous voyage.

buffer state. A small independent state between two larger rival states.

capital ship. Defined in 1922 as a warship (except aircraft carriers) of more
than 10,000 tons, or carrying larger than 8 inch guns.

---

* The working definitions that follow are confined largely to American experience
and are necessarily reduced to brief compass. Consult unabridged dictionaries and
treatises for fuller explanations. Omitted are familiar or obvious terms, some terms
defined in the text, and highly technical terms.

capitulation. A surrender on stipulated terms; an agreement (usually in Near East) granting extraterritorial rights. *See* extraterritoriality.

career diplomat (or man). Professional diplomat, in contrast to political appointee.

cartel. An agreement between contending belligerents regulating their intercourse; a combination of trusts to promote monopolistic practices.

casus belli (Lat.). An alleged justification for war.

casus foederis (Lat.). A case within the provisions of a treaty.

chancellery. The office of an embassy or legation.

chargé d'affaires (Fr.). Commonly *chargé*. A temporary substitute for the regular diplomatic representative; a regular diplomat of inferior grade.

closed incident. A settled diplomatic question.

Cold War. An international struggle waged by means short of armed combat.

collective security. Maintenance of world peace by concerted action of the powers, or an organization of the powers, against an aggressor or potential aggressor.

Colossus of the North. Approbrious synonym for U.S.A. in Latin America.

Cominform. Communist Information Bureau, established 1947. P. 748.

Comintern. Communist International, established in Moscow, 1919. P. 800.

comity of nations. The consideration and good understanding among nations that lead each to respect the laws and institutions of the others. Hence an act of comity.

communiqué (Fr.). A piece of information given out officially.

condominium. A joint administration by several powers. P. 426.

consortium. An international business or banking combination.

consul general; consul; vice-consul; consular agent. Officials, usually ranked in the order given, appointed by a foreign country to serve the commercial interests of that country abroad; also to protect seamen.

consulate. Office of a consul.

consulate general. Office of a consul general.

containment. The restriction of communism to fixed territorial limits.

continuous voyage. A voyage which, in view of its obvious purposes, is regarded as continuous, even though interrupted. P. 324.

contraband of war. That which may be seized by a belligerent when being sent to its enemy. Before "total war" made such distinctions illusory, exports to a belligerent were classified as absolute contraband (e.g., explosives); conditional contraband (depending on their use for warlike or peaceful purposes, e.g., horses); and noncontraband (e.g., soap).

convention. A treaty, often multi-power and specific in nature, such as one relating to postage or copyright.

convoy. To protect merchantmen with armed escort; a group of ships so convoyed.

counselor. A high career officer assigned to an embassy or legation.

coup d'état (Fr.). Sudden forcible overthrow of a government.

credentials. Documents issued by a government to its diplomatic agent showing that he is entitled to exercise the official power of representation.

dean; doyen. Senior member in service of a given group of diplomats.

de facto (Lat.). A *de facto* government is one actually functioning, usually after an armed upheaval, but not yet permanently established or recognized.

de jure (Lat.). A *de jure* government is one deemed lawful, though it may or may not be *de facto*.

démarche (Fr.) A diplomatic step or representation.

denounce. To give formal notice of the termination of a treaty or agreement.

détente (Fr.). A relaxation of international tension.

diplomatic agent. A diplomatic representative of a nation. In order of conventional rank: ambassador; minister (full title: envoy extraordinary and minister plenipotentiary); minister resident; *chargé d'affaires.*

diplomatic immunity. See immunity, diplomatic.

dispatch. A written report, commonly sent to home office by agent in field.

Dollar Diplomacy. Governmental use of private investors to promote foreign policy (p. 530); also conducting foreign policy to help private investors.

Downing Street. Location in London of British Foreign Office and other offices; hence synonym for Foreign Office or British government.

doyen. See dean.

Drago Doctrine. Forbidding the use of force in the collection of international public debts. P. 502.

embassy. The ambassador and his suite; his residence or office.

entente (Fr.). An understanding or agreement between two or more nations.

envoy. General term for an official on a diplomatic mission.

envoy extraordinary and minister plenipotentiary. Full title of a diplomatic agent ranking between an ambassador and a minister resident.

executive agent. Personal envoy of President, not subject to Senate approval. P. 7.

Executive agreement. One made by or on behalf of the President, and not subject to Senate approval. P. 7.

exequatur. Written recognition of his authority given to a consular officer by the government to which he is accredited.

expatriation, right of. Right of a person to change his citizenship.

expropriation. Confiscation of property by a national government.

extradition. The surrender of a person charged with crime by one nation to another.

extraterritoriality. Exemption from the jurisdiction of local laws, as in China, where foreigners were long tried in their own special courts.

face. Dignity; prestige, as in the Oriental term, "lose face."

fait accompli (Fr.). Something accomplished and presumably irrevocable.

faux pas (Fr.). A false step; a mistake.

filibuster. To lead an unauthorized armed force against a friendly nation. Participants in filibusterism are filibusters or filibusterers. P. 277.

free ships, free goods. Immunity of noncontraband enemy goods from capture while being carried on neutral ships.

freedom of the seas. Right of merchantmen to traverse the high seas.

freezing. Impounding the assets of a foreign nation or foreign nationals. P. 717.

full powers. Written authority given a diplomatic agent or other representative by his government.

genocide. Mass extermination of whole groups of people; e.g., Jews.

gentlemen's agreement. Agreement based on mutual honor. P. 523.

good offices. Services of a third party in bringing disputing parties together. Usually a prelude to mediation. *See* mediation.

hegemony. The preponderant authority of a government or state.

"hyphenated" Americans; "hyphenates." Immigrants attached to "Old Country." P. 4.

identic. Identical, as an "identic" note.

imbroglio. Complicated or embarrassing state of affairs; embroilment.

immunity, diplomatic. Immunity of foreign envoys from local jurisdiction.

impasse (Fr.). A predicament permitting no escape.

imperialism. Policy of seeking to extend the domain or control of a nation in or over foreign territory.

indefeasible allegiance. Citizenship which a nation asserts is incapable of being changed.

instructions. Directions or orders by the home foreign office to an envoy in the field.

insurgency. State of revolt short of an organized revolutionary government, not recognized as amounting to belligerency.

intern. To hold or detain persons or ships in wartime, whether enemy or neutral.

international law; law of nations. Body of principles which civilized nations regard as binding on them in their dealings with one another.

Iron Curtain. An artificial barrier created by a government against international communication.

jingo. A supporter of a bellicose policy in foreign affairs; a chauvinist.

justiciable. Recognized as being suitable for adjudication.

Kremlin. Seat of Soviet government; hence synonym for that government.

legation. Official residence of a diplomatic minister.

letter of marque and reprisal. Written authorization from a government permitting the recipient to engage in privateering. *See* privateer.

Logan Act. U.S. statute forbidding unauthorized private negotiations. P. 96.

mandate. Territory administered by a mandatory nation under a commission granted, for example, by the League of Nations. P. 605.

mediation. Intercession of a third party in a dispute on the initiative or with the consent of the disputants. *See* good offices.

minister. *See* envoy extraordinary and minister plenipotentiary.

mission. An envoy or body of special envoys; permanent foreign embassy or legation.

modus vivendi (Lat.). Temporary arrangement of affairs pending a final settlement.

most-favored-nation clause. Treaty clause by which one nation grants to another nation such privileges as it may grant to third nations.

multilateral. Participated in by more than two nations, as an agreement.

note. A formal communication from one government to another.

nuncio. Ambassador of the Pope at a foreign capital.

Open Door. Equal opportunity for commercial intercourse. P. 2.

order in council. In British government, an executive act by the sovereign and privy council which in the 19th Century was in fact an executive order by the cabinet alone. P. 122 n.

Pan-Americanism. Policy of co-operation among the American Republics.

paper blockade. A blockade not effectively enforced; hence no penalties should be attached to ignoring it. *See* blockade.

persona grata (Lat.). A person acceptable as an envoy; opposite of *persona non grata.*

plebicite. Vote of the people in a given region, usually on sovereignty.

plenary. Full; entire, as a plenary session.

plenipotentiary. Diplomatic agent with full power to negotiate as instructed.

Porte. Government of the former Turkish Empire; also known as Sublime Porte.

pourparler (Fr.). Informal conference to discuss a diplomatic issue.

power politics. International politics by which a nation advances its interests through superior coercive power.

precedence. Right of diplomats to precede others at public functions.

privateer. An armed private ship authorized by its government to prey on enemy shipping, subject to restrictions. Practice abolished by European powers at Paris in 1856; not used by the U.S. since 1815.

prize court. A court authorized to judge upon captures at sea in wartime.

protectorate. Dependent nation over which another nation assumes protection.

protocol. Preliminary memorandum of discussions; rules of diplomatic etiquette.

Quai d'Orsay. French foreign office or government (from its location).

quid pro quo (Lat.). Something in return; an equivalent.

rapprochement (Fr.). An establishment of cordial relations between powers.

ratify. To make valid. In U.S. the Senate does not *ratify* treaties; it *approves* a treaty by a ⅔ vote. The President then *ratifies* the treaty, and ratifications are normally exchanged with the other government or governments.

reciprocity. Granting commercial privileges to another nation (usually lowering of tariff rates) in exchange for reciprocal concessions.

recognition. Recognizing a new government as exercising the powers of a state by entering into formal relations with it; often a recognition of independence. Also recognition of insurgency or belligerency.

reparations. Payments in money or goods by a power for damage inflicted.

reprisal. Retaliatory action by one nation against another.

reservation. Limiting conditions attached to a treaty or other instrument.

right of visit and search. Right of a belligerent to search merchantmen on high seas to determine nationality or cargo.

St. James's (Court). The British court (after St. James's Palace).

sanctions. Penalties, usually economic or military, established for a breach of an international obligation.

self-determination. Asserted right of a people (usually homogeneous) in a territorial unit to determine their political status.

shirt-sleeve diplomacy. Direct, informal, unconventional diplomacy.

sine qua non (Lat.). An indispensable thing or condition. P. 151.

sovereignty. Supremacy in rule or power; sovereign power.

sphere of interest. Also sphere of action or zone of influence. An area in which one power is permitted by others to exercise more or less exclusive influence. P. 479.

state. In diplomacy, a sovereign nation or power.

status quo (Lat.). State of affairs now existing.

status quo ante bellum (Lat.). State of affairs existing before the war. P. 153.

suzerain. A state exercising political control (sovereignty) over another state.

territorial waters. Marginal belt included within a state's boundaries.

three-mile limit. Extent to which a nation's marginal belt has traditionally (though not invariably) extended over adjacent seas.

trial balloon. A proposal put forward tentatively to test public reactions.

trusteeship. Commission granted to a trustee nation by the United Nations. P. 770.

two-thirds rule. Constitutional provision by which Senate approval of treaties requires a two-thirds vote of those Senators present.

ultimate destination. Final destination of goods, especially contraband, under doctrine of continuous voyage. *See* continuous voyage.

ultimatum. Final terms. Their rejection usually ends negotiations.

unilateral. One sided; said of single-handed action by one member of a group.

Vatican. The papal government (after Pope's palace).

visa. Endorsement made on a passport permitting bearer to proceed.

visit and search. See right of visit and search.

Whitehall. British government (after thoroughfare of that name).

Wilhelmstrasse. Imperial German Foreign Office (after street on which located).

B

Territorial Acquisitions of the United States

Date (if treaty, date of signing)	Acquisition	Area (sq. mi.)	How Acquired	Price
1783	Original Territory	892,135	Treaty—Gt. Br.	
1803	Louisiana	827,987	Purchase from France	$15 million in cash and assumed claims
1819	Floridas	72,101	Treaty with Spain	$5 million in assumed claims and relinquishment of Texas claim
1845	Texas	389,166	Independent Republic Annexed	
1846	Oregon	286,541	Treaty with Gt. Br.	
1848	Mexican Cession	529,189	Conquest from Mexico	$15 million plus maximum claims of $3.25 million
1853	Gadsden Purchase	29,670	Purchase from Mexico	$10 million
1867	Alaska	586,400	Purchase from Russia	$7.2 million
1867	Midway Islands	1½	Occupation	
1898	Hawaiian Islands	6,407	Independent Republic Annexed	
1898	Philippine Islands	114,400	Conquest from Spain	$20 million
1898	Puerto Rico	3,435	Conquest from Spain	
1898	Guam	206	Conquest from Spain	
1899	Wake Island	3	Occupation	
1899	American Samoa	76	Division with Germany and Gt. Br.	
1903	Panama Canal Zone (perpetual lease)	549	Treaty with Panama	$10 million; annual payment of $250,000 beginning 9 years after ratification
1916	Virgin Islands	133	Purchase from Denmark	$25 million

C

Previous Diplomatic Experience of Presidents

President	Date	Party		Diplomatic Experience
George Washington	Apr. 30, 1789– Mar. 4, 1797	Fed.		
John Adams	Mar. 4, 1797– Mar. 4, 1801	Fed.	1778 1780 1779–83 1785–87	France Netherlands Peace Commissioner Great Britain
Thomas Jefferson	Mar. 4, 1801– Mar. 4, 1809	Rep.[1]	1785–89 1790–93	France Secretary of State
James Madison	Mar. 4, 1809– Mar. 4, 1817	Rep.	1801–09	Secretary of State
James Monroe	Mar. 4, 1817– Mar. 4, 1825	Rep.	1794–96 1803–04 1803–06 1804 1811–14	France France Great Britain Spain Secretary of State
John Quincy Adams	Mar. 4, 1825– Mar. 4, 1829	Rep.	1794–97 1797–01 1809–14 1814 1815–17 1817–25	Netherlands Prussia Russia Peace Commissioner Great Britain Secretary of State
Andrew Jackson	Mar. 4, 1829– Mar. 4, 1837	Dem.		
Martin Van Buren	Mar. 4, 1837– Mar. 4, 1841	Dem.	1829–31 1831–32	Secretary of State Great Britain (uncon- firmed)
William Henry Harrison	Mar. 4, 1841– Apr. 4, 1841	Whig	1828–29	Colombia
John Tyler	Apr. 6, 1841– Mar. 4, 1845	Whig		
James Knox Polk	Mar. 4, 1845– Mar. 4, 1849	Dem.		
Zachary Taylor	Mar. 5, 1849– July 9, 1850	Whig		
Millard Fillmore	July 10, 1850– Mar. 4, 1853	Whig		
Franklin Pierce	Mar. 4, 1853– Mar. 4, 1857	Dem.		

[1] The Republican Party of Jefferson's time is not to be confused with the present Republican Party, which was organized in 1854.

President	Date	Party	Diplomatic Experience
James Buchanan	Mar. 4, 1857– Mar. 4, 1861	Dem.	1832–33 Russia 1845–49 Secretary of State 1853–56 Great Britain
Abraham Lincoln	Mar. 4, 1861– Apr. 15, 1865	Rep.	
Andrew Johnson	Apr. 15, 1865– Mar. 4, 1869	Union	
Ulysses Simpson Grant	Mar. 4, 1869– Mar. 4, 1877	Rep.	
Rutherford Birchard Hayes	Mar. 5, 1877– Mar. 4, 1881	Rep.	
James Abram Garfield	Mar. 4, 1881– Sept. 19, 1881	Rep.	
Chester Alan Arthur	Sept. 20, 1881– Mar. 4, 1885	Rep.	
Grover Cleveland	Mar. 4, 1885– Mar. 4, 1889	Dem.	
Benjamin Harrison	Mar. 4, 1889– Mar. 4, 1893	Rep.	
Grover Cleveland	Mar. 4, 1893– Mar. 4, 1897	Dem.	
William McKinley	Mar. 4, 1897– Sept. 14, 1901	Rep.	
Theodore Roosevelt	Sept. 14, 1901– Mar. 4, 1909	Rep.	
William Howard Taft	Mar. 4, 1909– Mar. 4, 1913	Rep.	1902 Special envoy to Pope
Woodrow Wilson	Mar. 4, 1913– Mar. 4, 1921	Dem.	
Warren Gamaliel Harding	Mar. 4, 1921– Aug. 2, 1923	Rep.	
Calvin Coolidge	Aug. 3, 1923– Mar. 4, 1929	Rep.	
Herbert Clark Hoover	Mar. 4, 1929– Mar. 4, 1933	Rep.	Food Relief experience
Franklin Delano Roosevelt	Mar. 4, 1933– Apr. 12, 1945	Dem.	
Harry S. Truman	Apr. 12, 1945– Jan. 20, 1953	Dem.	
Dwight D. Eisenhower	Jan. 20, 1953–	Rep.	Military-Diplomatic experience
John F. Kennedy	Jan. 20, 1961– Nov. 22, 1963	Dem.	London Embassy; Senate Foreign Relations Committee
Lyndon B. Johnson	Nov. 22, 1963– Jan. 20, 1969	Dem.	Various diplomatic missions abroad as Vice President: Viet Nam, Berlin, etc.
Richard M. Nixon	Jan. 20, 1969–	Rep.	Numerous diplomatic missions abroad as Vice President: Latin America (1958), Russia (1959), etc.

D

Previous Diplomatic Experience
of Secretaries of State

President	Party	Secretary of State	Dates of Service	Diplomatic Experience	
Washington	Fed.	Thomas Jefferson	Mar. 22, 1790– Dec. 31, 1793	1785–89	France
		Edmund Randolph	Jan. 2, 1794– Aug. 20, 1795		
		Timothy Pickering	Dec. 10, 1795–		
Adams	Fed.	Timothy Pickering	May 12, 1800		
		John Marshall	June 6, 1800– Feb. 4, 1801	1797–98	France
Jefferson	Rep.[1]	James Madison	May 2, 1801– Mar. 3, 1809		
Madison	Rep.	Robert Smith	Mar. 6, 1809– Apr. 1, 1811		
		James Monroe	Apr. 6, 1811– Mar. 3, 1817	1794–96 1803–04 1803–06 1804	France France Great Britain Spain
Monroe	Rep.	John Quincy Adams	Sept. 22, 1817– Mar. 3, 1825	1794–97 1797–01 1809–14 1814 1815–17	Netherlands Prussia Russia Peace Commis- sioner Great Britain
Adams	Rep.	Henry Clay	Mar. 7, 1825– Mar. 3, 1829	1814	Peace Commis- sioner
Jackson	Dem.	Martin Van Buren	Mar. 28, 1829– May 23, 1831	1831–32	Great Britain (not con- firmed by Senate)
		Edward Livingston	May 24, 1831– May 29, 1833		
		Louis McLane	May 29, 1833– June 30, 1834	1829–31	Great Britain
		John Forsyth	July 1, 1834–	1819–22	Spain
Van Buren	Dem.	John Forsyth	Mar. 3, 1841		
Harrison	Whig	Daniel Webster	Mar. 6, 1841–		
Tyler	Whig	Daniel Webster	May 8, 1843		

[1] The Republican Party of Jefferson's time is not to be confused with the present Republican Party, which was organized in 1854.

President	Party	Secretary of State	Dates of Service	Diplomatic Experience	
Tyler (cont.)		*Abel P. Upshur*	July 24, 1843– Feb. 28, 1844		
		John C. Calhoun	Apr. 1, 1844– Mar. 10, 1845		
Polk	Dem.	*James Buchanan*	Mar. 10, 1845– Mar. 7, 1849	1832–33	Russia
Taylor	Whig	*John M. Clayton*	Mar. 8, 1849– July 22, 1850		
Fillmore	Whig	*Daniel Webster*	July 23, 1850– Oct. 24, 1852		
		Edward Everett	Nov. 6, 1852– Mar. 3, 1853	1841–45	Great Britain
Pierce	Dem.	*William L. Marcy*	Mar. 8, 1853– Mar. 6, 1857		
Buchanan	Dem.	*Lewis Cass*	Mar. 6, 1857– Dec. 14, 1860	1836–42	France
		Jeremiah S. Black	Dec. 17, 1860– Mar. 5, 1861		
Lincoln	Rep.	*William H. Seward*	Mar. 6, 1861–		
Johnson	Union	*William H. Seward*	Mar. 4, 1869		
Grant	Rep.	*Elihu B. Washburne*	Mar. 5, 1869– Mar. 16, 1869		
		Hamilton Fish	Mar. 17, 1869– Mar. 12, 1877		
Hayes	Rep.	*William M. Evarts*	Mar. 12, 1877– Mar. 7, 1881		
Garfield	Rep.	*James G. Blaine*	Mar. 7, 1881–		
Arthur	Rep.	*James G. Blaine*	Dec. 19, 1881		
		Frederick T. Frelinghuysen	Dec. 19, 1881– Mar. 6, 1885		
Cleveland	Dem.	*Thomas F. Bayard*	Mar. 7, 1885– Mar. 6, 1889		
Harrison	Rep.	*James G. Blaine*	Mar. 7, 1889– June 4, 1892		
		John W. Foster	June 29, 1892– Feb. 23, 1893	1873–80 1880–81 1883–85 1890–91	Mexico Russia Spain Special Envoy at Large
Cleveland	Dem.	*Walter Q. Gresham*	Mar. 7, 1893– May 28, 1895		
		Richard Olney	June 10, 1895– Mar. 5, 1897		
McKinley	Rep.	*John Sherman*	Mar. 6, 1897– Apr. 27, 1898		
		William R. Day	Apr. 28, 1898– Sept. 16, 1898	1897–98	Asst. Sec. of State
		John Hay	Sept. 30, 1898–	1865	Sec. of Leg., Paris
Roosevelt	Rep.	*John Hay*	July 1, 1905	1867–69 1879–81	Sec. of Leg., Madrid, Vienna First Asst. S. of S.
		Elihu Root	July 19, 1905– Jan. 27, 1909		
		Robert Bacon	Jan. 27, 1909– Mar. 5, 1909		

President	Party	Secretary of State	Dates of Service	Diplomatic Experience	
Taft	Rep.	Philander C. Knox	Mar. 6, 1909– Mar. 5, 1913		
Wilson	Dem.	William Jennings Bryan	Mar. 5, 1913– June 9, 1915		
		Robert Lansing	June 24, 1915– Feb. 13, 1920	1914–15	Counselor, State Dept.
		Bainbridge Colby	Mar. 23, 1920– Mar. 4, 1921		
Harding	Rep.	Charles E. Hughes	Mar. 5, 1921–		
Coolidge	Rep.	Charles E. Hughes	Mar. 4, 1925		
		Frank B. Kellogg	Mar. 5, 1925– Mar. 28, 1929	1924–25	Great Britain
Hoover	Rep.	Henry L. Stimson	Mar. 28, 1929– Mar. 4, 1933	1927	Special representative to Nicaragua
Roosevelt	Dem.	Cordell Hull	Mar. 4, 1933– Nov. 27, 1944		
		Edward R. Stettinius, Jr.	Dec. 1, 1944–	1943–44	Under Sec. of State
Truman	Dem.	Edward R. Stettinius, Jr.	June 27, 1945		
		James F. Byrnes	July 2, 1945– Jan. 20, 1947	1945	At Yalta
		George C. Marshall	Jan. 21, 1947– Jan. 20, 1949	1945–47	China mission
		Dean G. Acheson	Jan. 21, 1949– Jan. 20, 1953	1941–45 1945–47	Asst. S. of S. Under S. of S.
Eisenhower	Rep.	John F. Dulles	Jan. 21, 1953– Apr. 15, 1959	1945–50 1951	del. San Fran. Conf.; UN Assembly; adviser to S. of S. *re* Japan treaty
		Christian A. Herter	Apr. 21, 1959– Jan. 20, 1961	1916–17 1917–18 1918–19 1920–21 1957–59	Attaché, Berlin Spl. Assist., State Dept. Sec. to U.S. delegation, Paris Conf. European Relief Council Under Sec. of State
Kennedy	Dem.	Dean Rusk	Jan. 21, 1961–	1946–51	Various offices in State Dept.
Johnson	Dem.	Dean Rusk	Jan. 20, 1969		
Nixon	Rep.	William P. Rogers	Jan. 22, 1969– Sept. 3, 1973	1967	U.S. rep. to UN General Assembly
		Henry A. Kissinger	Sept. 22, 1973–	1969–73	National Security Adviser to Nixon

APPENDIX

————————— E —————————

General Bibliography

THE INDISPENSABLE bibliographical work is S. F. Bemis and G. G. Griffin, *Guide to the Diplomatic History of the United States, 1775–1921* (Washington, 1935). It should be brought more up to date by Oscar Handlin, *et al.*, eds., *Harvard Guide to American History* (Cambridge, Mass., 1954). The most valuable treaty compilation is D. H. Miller, ed., *Treaties and other International Acts of the United States of America* (8 vols., Washington, 1931–1948), which unfortunately comes only through 1863. It may be supplemented by W. M. Malloy, comp., *Treaties, Conventions, International Acts, Protocols and Agreements between the United States of America and other Powers, 1776–1923* (3 vols., Washington, 1910–1923). The official *Foreign Relations of the United States* began the annual publication of selected documents in 1862, and is now about twenty years in arrears. The unofficial *Documents on American Foreign Relations* was published annually from 1938 through 1951 by the World Peace Foundation; since 1951, by the Council on Foreign Relations. A useful compilation is R. J. Bartlett, ed., *The Record of American Diplomacy* (4th ed., New York, 1964). A classic pertaining to American diplomacy is J. B. Moore, *A Digest of International Law* (8 vols., Washington, 1906). This work has been brought more up to date by G. H. Hackworth, in *Digest of International Law* (8 vols., Washington, 1940–1944) and by Marjorie M. Whiteman in *Digest of International Law* (14 vols., Washington, 1963–1970). See also J. B. Moore, *History and Digest of International Arbitrations* (6 vols., Washington, 1898).

There are about a dozen meritorious textbook accounts but in general they develop American diplomatic history with about the same depth as the present volume. Surveys relating to the twentieth century are David F. Trask, *Victory without Peace* (New York, 1968); Jules Davids, *America and the World of Our Time* (New York, 1960); Jean-Baptiste Duroselle, *From Wilson to Roosevelt: Foreign Policy of the United States, 1913–1945*, trans. by Nancy L. Roelker (Cambridge, Mass., 1963); John Spanier, *American Foreign Policy since World War II* (3rd. ed., New York, 1968); and two volumes in the American Diplomatic History Series, General Editor, Armin Rappaport: Julius W. Pratt, *Challenge and Rejection: The United States and World Leadership, 1900–1921* (New York, 1967); and Selig Adler, *The Uncertain Giant, 1921–1941: American Foreign Policy between the Wars* (New York, 1965). Somewhat the same ground is covered in L. Ethan Ellis, *Republican Foreign Policy, 1921–1933* (New Brunswick, N.J., 1968).

Special acounts are John Braeman *et al.*, eds., *Twentieth-Century American Foreign Policy* (Columbus, 1971), largely historiographical; Ernest R. May, "The Decline of Diplomatic History," in George A. Billias and G. N. Grob, *American History: Retrospect and Prospect* (New York, 1971), 399–

430 (the subject is becoming "international history"); and Alexander De Conde and Armin Rappaport, eds., *Essays Diplomatic and Undiplomatic of Thomas A. Bailey* (New York, 1969).

Useful general studies on specific topics, arranged alphabetically, are herewith listed on a highly selective basis and without derogation of other praiseworthy works. Emphasis is placed on books not previously cited.

AFRICA. Charles F. Gallagher, *The United States and North Africa: Morocco, Algeria and Tunisia* (Cambridge, Mass., 1963).

ALLIANCE FOR PROGRESS. Lincoln Gordon, *A New Deal for Latin America: The Alliance for Progress* (Cambridge, Mass., 1963); William D. Rogers, *The Twilight Struggle: The Alliance for Progress and the Politics of Development in Latin America* (New York, 1967).

AMBASSADORS. E. W. Spaulding, *Ambassadors Ordinary and Extraordinary* (Washington, D.C., 1961).

ANZUS. J. G. Starke, *The Anzus Treaty Alliance* (New York, 1965). *See* AUSTRALIA.

ARABS. *See* NEAR EAST.

ARBITRATION. *See* PEACE.

ARGENTINA. A. P. Whitaker, *The United States and Argentina* (Cambridge, Mass., 1954); T. F. McGann, *Argentina, the United States, and the Inter-American System, 1880–1914* (Cambridge, Mass., 1957); Harold F. Peterson, *Argentina and the United States, 1810–1960* (New York, 1964).

ASIA. Tyler Dennett, *Americans in Eastern Asia* (New York, 1922); L. H. Battistini, *The United States and Asia* (New York, 1955) and *The Rise of American Influence in Asia and the Pacific* (East Lansing, Mich., 1960); Russell H. Fifield, *Southeast Asia in United States Policy* (New York, 1963); Norman D. Palmer, *South Asia and United States Policy* (Boston, 1966). *See* CHINA; FAR EAST; INDIA; JAPAN.

AUSTRALIA. Werner Levi, *American-Australian Relations* (Minneapolis, Minn., 1947); C. H. Grattan, *The United States in the Southwest Pacific* (Cambridge, Mass., 1961); Raymond A. Esthus, *From Enmity to Alliance: U.S.-Australian Relations, 1931–1941* (Seattle, 1964). *See* ANZUS.

BELGIUM. John W. Rooney, Jr., *Belgian-American Diplomatic and Consular Relations, 1830–1850* (Louvain, 1969).

BIPARTISANSHIP. C. V. Crabb, Jr., *Bipartisan Foreign Policy: Myth or Reality?* (Evanston, Ill., 1957).

BRAZIL. L. F. Hill, *Diplomatic Relations between the United States and Brazil* (Durham, N.C., 1932); E. Bradford Burns, *The Unwritten Alliance: Rio Branco and Brazilian-American Relations* (New York, 1966).

CANADA. H. L. Keenleyside and G. S. Brown, *Canada and the United States* (rev. ed., New York, 1952); E. W. McInnis, *The Unguarded Frontier* (Garden City, N.Y., 1942); D. F. Warner, *The Idea of Continental Union* (Lexington, Ky., 1960); Gerald M. Craig, *The United States and Canada* (Cambridge, Mass., 1968); Robert R. Wilson, *et al.*, *Canada-United States Treaty Relations* (Durham, N.C., 1963); Alvin C. Gluek, Jr., *Minnesota and the Manifest Destiny of the Canadian Northwest: A Study in Canadian-American Relations* (Toronto, 1965); S. F. Wise and R. C. Brown, *Canada Views the United States* (Seattle, 1967); John S. Dickey, ed., *The United States and Canada* (Englewood Cliffs, N.J., 1964).

CARIBBEAN. Dexter Perkins, *The United States and the Caribbean* (rev. ed., Cambridge, Mass., 1966); J. F. Rippy, *The Caribbean Danger Zone* (New York, 1940). *See* LATIN AMERICA.

CHILE. F. B. Pike, *Chile and the United States, 1880–1962* (Notre Dame, Ind., 1963); H. C. Evans, Jr., *Chile and Its Relations with the United States* (Durham, N.C., 1927); W. R. Sherman, *The Diplomatic and Commercial Relations of the United States and Chile, 1820–1914* (Boston, 1926).

CHINA. F. R. Dulles, *China and America* (Princeton, N.J., 1946); J. K. Fairbank, *The United States and China* (2nd ed., Cambridge, Mass., 1958); Kwang-Ching Liu, *Americans and Chinese: A Historical Essay and a Bibliography* (Cambridge, Mass., 1963); A. T. Steele, *The American People and China* (New York, 1966); Foster R. Dulles, *American Policy toward Communist China: The Historical Record, 1949–1969* (New York, 1972); Warren I. Cohen, *America's Response to China: An Interpretative History of Sino-American Relations* (New York, 1971); Kenneth T. Young, *Negotiating with the Chinese Communists: The United States Experience, 1953–1967* (New York, 1968); Russell D. Buhite, *Nelson T. Johnson and American Policy toward China, 1925–1941* (East Lansing, 1968); Robert McClellan, *The Heathen Chinee: A Study of American Attitudes toward China, 1890–1905* (Columbus, 1971); John P. Davies, Jr., *Dragon by the Tail* (New York, 1972). See ASIA; INDIA; MISSIONARIES.

COLD WAR. Desmond Donnelly, *Struggle for the World: The Cold War, 1917–1965* (New York, 1965); Louis J. Halle, *The Cold War as History* (New York, 1967). *See also* references for Chs. 50 and 51, herein.

COLOMBIA. E. T. Parks, *Colombia and the United States, 1765–1934* (Durham, N.C., 1935).

COMMUNICATION. Howard B. Schonberger, *Transportation to the Seaboard: The "Communication Revolution" and American Foreign Policy, 1860–1900* (Westport, Conn., 1971).

CONGRESS. *See* Selected Bibliography of Chapter 1.

CUBA. P. S. Foner, *A History of Cuba in Its Relations with the United States, 1492–1845* (New York, 1962), vol. I; vol. II [1845–1895] (New York, 1963); R. H. Fitzgibbon, *Cuba and the United States, 1900–1935* (Menasha, Wis., 1935); Lester D. Langley, *The Cuban Policy of the United States: A Brief History* (New York, 1968); John Plank, ed., *Cuba and the United States* (Washington, D.C., 1967); Hugh Thomas, *Cuba: The Pursuit of Freedom* (New York, 1971)

DENMARK. S. J. M. P. Fogdall, *Danish-American Diplomacy, 1776–1920* (Iowa City, Ia., 1922). *See* SCANDINAVIA.

DEPARTMENT OF STATE. G. H. Stuart, *The Department of State* (New York, 1949).

DIPLOMATIC MACHINERY. *See* Selected Bibliography of Chapter 1.

DISARMAMENT. Merze Tate, *The United States and Armaments* (Cambridge, Mass., 1948).

DOLLAR DIPLOMACY. Dana G. Munro, *Intervention and Dollar Diplomacy in the Caribbean, 1900–1921* (Princeton, N.J., 1964).

DOMINICAN REPUBLIC. G. Pope Atkins and L. C. Wilson, *The United States and the Trujillo Regime* (New Brunswick, N.J., 1972). *See* SANTO DOMINGO.

EAST ASIA. *See* FAR EAST.

ECONOMICS. B. H. Williams, *Economic Foreign Policy of the United States* (New York, 1929).

ENGLAND. *See* GREAT BRITAIN.

EXECUTIVE AGENTS. H. M. Wriston, *Executive Agents in American Foreign Relations* (Baltimore, 1929).

FAR EAST. A. W. Griswold, *The Far Eastern Policy of the United States* (New York, 1938); K. S. Latourette, *The American Record in the Far East, 1945–1951* (New York, 1952); Akira Iriye, *After Imperialism: The Search for a New Order in the Far East, 1921–1931* (Cambridge, Mass., 1965) and *Across the Pacific: An Inner History of American-East Asian Relations* (New York, 1967). *See* ASIA.

FRANCE. E. B. White, *American Opinion of France from Lafayette to Poincaré* (New York, 1927); D. C. McKay, *The United States and France* (Cambridge, Mass., 1951); Henry Blumenthal, *A Reappraisal of Franco-American Relations, 1830–1871* (Chapel Hill, N.C., 1959); Crane Brinton, *The Americans and the French* (Cambridge, Mass., 1968); René Rémond, *Les États-Unis devant l'opinion Française, 1815–1852*, 2 vols. (Paris, 1962); Henry Blumenthal, *France and the United States: Their Diplomatic Relations, 1789–1914* (Chapel Hill, 1970).

FREEDOM OF THE SEAS. Henry Reiff, *The United States and the Treaty Law of the Sea* (Minneapolis, 1959).

FULBRIGHT. Walter Johnson and F. J. Colligan, *The Fulbright Program: A History* (Chicago, 1965).

GERMANY. Alfred Vagts, *Deutschland und die Vereinigten Staaten in der Weltpolitik*, 2 vols. (New York, 1935); C. E. Schieber, *The Transformation of American Sentiment toward Germany, 1870–1914* (Boston, 1923); H. M. Adams, *Prussian-American Relations, 1775–1871* (Cleveland, 1960).

GOOD NEIGHBOR. D. M. Dozer, *Are We Good Neighbors? Three Decades of Inter-American Relations, 1930–1960* (Gainesville, Fla., 1961); Bryce Wood, *The Making of the Good Neighbor Policy* (New York, 1961).

GREAT BRITAIN. H. C. Allen, *Great Britain and the United States* (New York, 1955); Crane Brinton, *The United States and Britain* (Cambridge, Mass., 1945); Frank Thistlethwaite, *The Anglo-American Connection in the Early Nineteenth Century* (Philadelphia, 1959); Herbert Nicholas, *Britain and the U.S.A.* (Baltimore, 1963); Bradford Perkins, *The Great Rapprochement: England and the United States, 1895–1914* (New York, 1968).

GREECE. S. A. Larrabee, *Hellas Observed: The American Experience of Greece, 1775–1865* (New York, 1957).

HAITI. R. W. Logan, *The Diplomatic Relations of the United States with Haiti, 1776–1891* (Chapel Hill, N.C., 1941); L. L. Montague, *Haiti and the United States, 1714–1938* (Durham, N.C., 1940); Hans Schmidt, *The United States Occupation of Haiti, 1915–1934* (New Brunswick, 1971).

HAWAII. *See* Selected Bibliography at end of Chapter 29.

HISTORIANS. F. L. Loewenheim, ed., *The Historian and the Diplomat: The Role of History and Historians in American Foreign Policy* (New York, 1067).

HYPHENATES. Louis L. Gerson, *The Hyphenate in Recent American Politics and Diplomacy* (Lawrence, Kans., 1964).

IMPERIALISM. Ernest R. May, *American Imperialism: A Speculative Essay* (New York, 1968). *See also* MANIFEST DESTINY.

INDIA. L. K. Rosinger, *India and the United States* (New York, 1950); W. N. Brown, *The United States and India and Pakistan* (rev. ed., Cambridge, Mass., 1963); H. R. Isaacs, *Scratches on our Minds: The American Image of China and India* (New York, 1958); Selig Harrison, ed., *India and the United States* (New York, 1961); Phillips Talbot and S. L. Poplai, *India and America* (New York, 1958); Gary R. Hess, *America Encounters India, 1941–1947* (New York, 1971).

INDOCHINA. *See* references for Ch. 56.

INTERVENTION. D. A. Graber, *Crisis Diplomacy: A History of U.S. Intervention Policies and Practices* (Washington, D.C., 1959).

IRAN. L. V. Thomas and R. N. Frye, *The United States and Turkey and Iran* (Cambridge, Mass., 1951); Abraham Yeselson, *United States-Persian Diplomatic Relations, 1883–1921* (New Brunswick, N.J., 1956).

IRAQ. *See* NEAR EAST.

IRELAND. Carl Wittke, *The Irish in America* (Baton Rouge, La., 1956); C. C. Tansill, *America and the Fight for Irish Freedom, 1866–1922* (New York, 1957); Thomas N. Brown, *Irish-American Nationalism, 1870–1890* (Philadelphia, 1966); Alan J. Ward, *Ireland and Anglo-American Relations, 1899–1921* (Toronto, 1969).

ISOLATION. Selig Adler, *The Isolationist Impulse* (New York, 1957); Alexander DeConde, ed., *Isolation and Security* (Durham, N.C., 1957); Manfred Jonas, *Isolationism in America, 1935–1941* (Ithaca, N.Y., 1966); L. N. Rieselbach, *The Roots of Isolationism: Congressional Voting and Presidential Leadership in Foreign Policy* (Indianapolis, Ind., 1966).

ISRAEL. F. E. Manuel, *The Realities of American-Palestine Relations* (Washington, D.C., 1949); Nadav Safran, *The United States and Israel* (Cambridge, Mass., 1963).

ITALY. H. S. Hughes, *The United States and Italy* (rev. ed., Cambridge, Mass., 1965); Sister Mary P. Trauth, *Italo-American Diplomatic Relations, 1861–1882* (Washington, D.C., 1958); Alexander DeConde, *Half Bitter, Half Sweet: An Excursion into Italian-American History* (New York, 1971); John P. Diggins, *Mussolini and Fascism: The View from America* (Princeton, 1972).

JAPAN. E. O. Reischauer, *The United States and Japan* (rev. ed., Cambridge, Mass., 1965); L. H. Battistini, *Japan and America* (New York, 1953); Foster R. Dulles, *Yankees and Samurai: America's Role in the Emergence of Modern Japan, 1791–1900* (New York, 1965); William L. Neumann, *America Encounters Japan: From Perry to MacArthur* (Baltimore, 1963).

KOREA. Yur-Bok Lee, *Diplomatic Relations between the United States and Korea, 1866–1887* (New York, 1970).

LABOR. Ronald Radosh, *American Labor and United States Foreign Policy* (New York, 1969).

LAOS. Charles A. Stevenson, *The End of Nowhere: American Policy toward Laos since 1954* (Boston, 1972). *See* INDOCHINA.

LATIN AMERICA. S. F. Bemis, *The Latin American Policy of the United States* (New York, 1943); Dexter Perkins, *The United States and Latin America* (Baton Rouge, La., 1961); G. H. Stuart, *Latin America and the United States* (5th ed., New York, 1955); M. S. Eisenhower, *The Wine is Bitter* (New York, 1963); Edwin Lieuwen, *U.S. Policy in Latin America: A Short History* (New York, 1965); J. Lloyd Mecham, *A Sur-*

vey of United States-Latin-American Relations (Boston, 1965); Gordon Connell-Smith, *The Inter-American System* (New York, 1966); D. F. Trask *et al., A Bibliography of United States-Latin American Relations since 1810* (Lincoln, Nebr., 1968); Wilfrid H. Callcott, *The Western Hemisphere: Its Influence on United States Policies to the End of World War II* (Austin, 1968); R. Harrison Wagner, *United States Policy toward Latin America: A Study in Domestic and International Politics* (Stanford, 1970). *See* ALLIANCE FOR PROGRESS; CARIBBEAN; GOOD NEIGHBOR; ORGANIZATION OF AMERICAN STATES; PAN-AMERICANISM; SOUTH AMERICA; and individual countries.

LIBERIA. R. W. Bixler, *The Foreign Policy of the United States in Liberia* (New York, 1957).

MALAYSIA. James W. Gould, *The United States and Malaysia* (Cambridge, Mass., 1969).

MANIFEST DESTINY. A. K. Weinberg, *Manifest Destiny* (Baltimore, 1935); Frederick Merk, *Manifest Destiny and Mission in American History* (New York, 1963).

MEDITERRANEAN. James A. Field, Jr., *America and the Mediterranean World, 1776–1882* (Princeton, N.J., 1969).

MEXICO. J. F. Rippy, *The United States and Mexico* (rev. ed., New York, 1931); H. F. Cline, *The United States and Mexico* (rev. ed., Cambridge, Mass., 1963); T. E. Cotner and C. E. Castañeda, *Essays in Mexican History* (Austin, Tex., 1958); Norris Hundley, *Dividing the Waters: A Century of Controversy between the United States and Mexico* (Berkeley, Calif., 1966); Robert F. Smith, *The United States and Revolutionary Nationalism in Mexico, 1916–1932* (Chicago, 1972).

MIDDLE EAST. *See* NEAR EAST.

MILITARY. Walter Millis, *Arms and the State* (New York, 1958); W. D. Puleston, *The Influence of Force in Foreign Relations* (New York, 1955); S. P. Huntington, *The Soldier and the State* (Cambridge, Mass., 1957); Burton M. Sapin and Richard C. Snyder, *The Role of the Military in American Foreign Policy* (Garden City, N.Y., 1954); Raymond G. O'Connor, *Force & Diplomacy: Essays Military and Diplomatic* (Coral Gables, 1972).

MINISTERS. *See* AMBASSADORS.

MISSIONARIES. P. A. Varg, *Missionaries, Chinese, and Diplomats: The American Protestant Missionary Movement in China, 1890–1952* (Princeton, 1958); Joseph L. Grabill, *Protestant Diplomacy and the Near East: Missionary Influence on American Policy, 1810–1927* (Minneapolis, 1971).

MONROE DOCTRINE. Dexter Perkins, *A History of the Monroe Doctrine* (rev. ed., Boston, 1955). See also the same author's three previous monographs on the Doctrine.

MOROCCO. Luella J. Hall, *The United States and Morocco, 1776–1956* (Metuchen, N.J., 1971).

NARCOTICS. Arnold H. Taylor, *American Diplomacy and the Narcotics Traffic, 1900–1939* (Durham, 1969).

NAVY. G. T. Davis, *A Navy Second to None* (New York, 1940); Harold and Margaret Sprout, *The Rise of American Naval Power, 1776–1918* (Princeton, N.J., 1030) and *Toward a New Order of Sea Power* (Princeton, N.J., 1940); D. W. Mitchell, *History of the Modern American Navy from 1883 through Pearl Harbor* (New York, 1946); Armin Rappaport, *The*

Navy League of the United States (Detroit, 1962); E. B. Potter, ed., *Sea Power: A Naval History* (Englewood Cliffs, N.J., 1960); W. R. Braisted, *The United States Navy in the Pacific, 1897–1909* (Austin, Tex., 1958); G. E. Wheeler, *Prelude to Pearl Harbor: The United States Navy and the Far East, 1921–1931* (Columbia, Mo., 1963); William R. Braisted, *The United States Navy in the Pacific, 1909–1922* (Austin, 1971).

NEAR EAST. E. A. Speiser, *The United States and the Near East* (2nd. ed., Cambridge, Mass., 1950); J. C. Campbell, *Defense of the Middle East: Problems of American Policy* (New York, 1958); John A. DeNovo, *American Interests and Policies in the Middle East, 1900–1939* (Minneapolis, 1963); William R. Polk, *The United States and the Arab World* (Cambridge, Mass., 1965); David H. Finnie, *Pioneers East: The Early American Experience in the Middle East* (Cambridge, Mass., 1967); John S. Badeau, *The American Approach to the Arab World* (New York, 1968).

NICARAGUA. I. J. Cox, *Nicaragua and the United States, 1909–1927* (Boston, 1927); William Kamman, *A Search for Stability: United States Diplomacy toward Nicaragua, 1925–1933* (Notre Dame, Ind., 1968).

NONINTERVENTION. *See* INTERVENTION; ISOLATION.

NORWAY. F. D. Scott, *The United States and Scandinavia* (Cambridge, Mass., 1950).

NO TRANSFER. J. A. Logan, Jr., *No Transfer: An American Security Principle* (New Haven, 1961).

OPEN DOOR. R. W. Bixler, *The Open Door on the Old Barbary Coast* (New York, 1959); Jerry Israel, *Progressivism and the Open Door: America and China, 1905–1921* (Pittsburgh, 1971). *See* ASIA.

ORGANIZATION OF AMERICAN STATES. Jerome Slater, *The OAS and United States Foreign Policy* (Columbus, Ohio, 1967); Ann Van Wynen Thomas and A. J. Thomas, Jr., *The Organization of American States* (Dallas, Tex., 1963). *See* LATIN AMERICA.

PAKISTAN. W. N. Brown, *The United States and India and Pakistan* (Cambridge, Mass., 1953). *See* INDIA.

PANAMA. W. D. McCain, *The United States and the Republic of Panama* (Durham, N.C., 1937).

PAN-AMERICANISM. J. B. Lockey, *Pan-Americanism: Its Beginnings* (New York, 1920); A. P. Whitaker, *The Western Hemisphere Idea* (Ithaca, N.Y., 1954); J. L. Mecham, *The United States and Inter-American Security, 1889–1960* (Austin, Tex., 1961). *See* LATIN AMERICA.

PEACE. M. E. Curti, *Peace or War: The American Struggle, 1636–1936* (New York, 1936); Dexter Perkins, *America's Quest for Peace* (Bloomington, Ind., 1962); Peter Brock, *Pacifism in the United States from the Colonial Era to the First World War* (Princeton, 1968); Charles Chatfield, *For Peace and Justice: Pacifism in America, 1914–1941* (Knoxville, 1971); Sondra R. Herman, *Eleven Against War: Studies in American Internationalist Thought, 1898–1921* (Stanford, 1969); Lawrence S. Wittner, *Rebels Against War: The American Peace Movement, 1941–1960* (New York, 1969).

PERSIA. *See* IRAN.

PERU. James C. Carey, *Peru and the United States, 1900–1962* (Notre Dame, Ind., 1964).

PHILANTHROPY. Merle Curti, *American Philanthropy Abroad: A History* (New Brunswick, N.J., 1963).

PHILIPPINES. G. A. Grunder and W. E. Livezey, *The Philippines and the United States* (Norman, Okla., 1951); Milton W. Meyer, *A Diplomatic History of the Philippine Republic* (Honolulu, 1965); George E. Taylor, *The Philippines and the United States: Problems of Partnership* (New York, 1964); Sung Yong Kim, *United States-Philippine Relations, 1946–1956* (Washington, 1968).

PRESIDENT. *See* Selected Bibliography at the end of Chapter 1.

PRESS. Bernard C. Cohen, *The Press and Foreign Policy* (Princeton, 1963); James Reston, *The Artillery of the Press: Its Influence on American Foreign Policy* (New York, 1967).

PROTESTS. Joseph C. McKenna, *Diplomatic Protest in Foreign Policy, Analysis and Case Studies* (Chicago, 1962).

PRUSSIA. *See* GERMANY.

PUBLIC OPINION. T. A. Bailey, *The Man in the Street* (New York, 1948); Gabriel Almond, *The American People and Foreign Policy* (New York, 1950); Manfred Landecker, *The President and Public Opinion: Leadership in Foreign Affairs* (1968). *See also* Selected Bibliography of Chapter 1.

RACE. Rubin F. Weston, *Racism in U.S. Imperialism: The Influence of Racial Assumptions on American Foreign Policy, 1893–1946* (Columbia, S.C., 1972).

RUSSIA. T. A. Bailey, *America Faces Russia* (Ithaca, N.Y., 1950); F. R. Dulles, *The Road to Teheran* (Princeton, 1944); W. A. Williams, *American-Russian Relations, 1781–1947* (New York, 1952); Alexander Tarsaïdzé, *Czars and Presidents* (New York, 1958); Oliver Jensen, ed., *America and Russia* (New York, 1962); Adam B. Ulam, *The Rivals: America and Russia since World War II* (New York, 1971); Anatol Rapoport, *The Big Two: Soviet-American Perceptions of Foreign Policy* (Indianapolis, 1971).

SANTO DOMINGO. C. C. Tansill, *The United States and Santo Domingo, 1798–1873* (Baltimore, 1938); M. M. Knight, *The Americans in Santo Domingo* (New York, 1928). *See* DOMINICAN REPUBLIC.

SCANDINAVIA. F. D. Scott, *The United States and Scandinavia* (Cambridge, Mass., 1950). *See* DENMARK; SWEDEN.

SECRETARY OF STATE. S. F. Bemis and R. H. Ferrell, eds., *The American Secretaries of State and Their Diplomacy*, 18 vols. (New York, 1927–1972); N. A. Graebner, ed., *An Uncertain Tradition: American Secretaries of State in the Twentieth Century* (New York, 1961); Alexander DeConde, *The American Secretary of State: An Interpretation* (New York, 1962); D. K. Price, ed., *The Secretary of State* (Englewood Cliffs, N.J., 1960); N. L. Hill, *Mr. Secretary of State* (New York, 1963).

SENATE. *See* Selected Bibliography of Chapter 1.

SOUTH. Charles O. Lerche, Jr., *The Uncertain South: Its Changing Patterns of Politics in Foreign Policy* (Chicago, 1964); Alfred O. Hero, Jr., *The Southerner and World Affairs* (Baton Rouge, La., 1965).

SOUTH AMERICA. A. P. Whitaker, *The United States and South America: The Northern Republics* (Cambridge, Mass., 1948). *See* CARIBBEAN; LATIN AMERICA.

SOVIET UNION. *See* RUSSIA.

SUMMITRY. Keith Eubank, *The Summit Conferences, 1919–1960* (Norman, Okla., 1966).

SWEDEN. *See* SCANDINAVIA.

SWITZERLAND. Heinz K. Meier, *The United States and Switzerland in the Nineteenth Century* (The Hague, 1963) and *Friendship Under Stress: U.S.-Swiss Relations, 1900–1950* (Bern, 1970).

TRANSPORTATION. *See* COMMUNICATION.

TURKEY. L. V. Thomas and R. N. Frye, *The United States and Turkey and Iran* (Cambridge, Mass., 1951); L. J. Gordon, American Relations with *Turkey, 1830–1930* (Philadelphia, 1932); Roger R. Trask, *The United States Response to Turkish Nationalism and Reform, 1914–1939* (Minneapolis, 1971); George S. Harris, *Troubled Alliance: Turkish-American Problems in Historical Perspective, 1945–1971* (Stanford, 1972).

UNITED NATIONS. Clark M. Eichelberger, *UN: The First Twenty-Five Years* (New York, 1970); Ruth B. Russell, *A History of the United Nations Charter: The Role of the United States, 1940–1945* (Washington, D.C., 1958) and *The United Nations and United States Security Policy* (Washington, D.C., 1968).

VIET NAM. *See* references for Ch. 56.

F

Bibliographical Addendum

Ch. 1. FACTORS, FORCES, AND FUNCTIONS

See new references on p. 18.

An able treatment by a political scientist, ranging widely over various episodes and stressing diplomatic machinery, is H. B. Westerfield, *The Instruments of America's Foreign Policy* (New York, 1963).

On Congressional machinery note H. N. Carroll, *The House of Representatives and Foreign Affairs* (Pittsburgh, 1958) and D. N. Farnsworth, *The Senate Committee on Foreign Relations* (Urbana, Ill., 1961). The story is carried to 1816 in J. W. Gould, "The Origins of the Senate Committee on Foreign Relations," *Western Pol. Quar.*, XII (1959), 670–682.

On hyphenates, consult L. L. Gerson, "Immigrant Groups and American Foreign Policy," in G. L. Anderson, ed., *Issues and Conflicts* (Lawrence, Kans., 1959); L. H. Fuchs, "Minority Groups and Foreign Policy," *Pol. Sci. Quar.*, LXXIV (1959), 161–175.

8TH ED. REFS. Arthur A. Ekirch, Jr., *Ideas, Ideals and American Diplomacy: A History of Their Growth and Interaction* (New York, 1966), is a sophisticated approach by an American intellectual historian.

Donald Brandon, *American Foreign Policy: Beyond Utopianism and Realism* (New York, 1966), provides a critique of U.S. foreign policies and attitudes in the 20th Century which emphasizes the clash between the realist and utopian approaches.

James N. Rosenau, ed., *Domestic Sources of Foreign Policy* (New York, 1967), is a series of interdisciplinary contributions by representatives of political science, sociology, and psychology.

Sidney Warren, *The President as World Leader* (Philadelphia, 1964), deals perceptively with the role of the Chief Executive in foreign affairs from Theodore Roosevelt to Kennedy.

Elmer E. Cornwell, Jr., *Presidential Leadership of Public Opinion* (Bloomington, Ind., 1965), analyzes the techniques by which the Presidents from Theodore Roosevelt to Kennedy have sought to control public opinion. Taft and Hoover are regarded as unusually inept.

Bernard C. Cohen, *The Press and Foreign Policy* (Princeton, N.J., 1963), is especially critical of the shortcomings of the newspapers in their efforts to interact with the government and to shape public opinion.

Lloyd A. Free and Hadley Cantril, *The Political Beliefs of Americans: A Study of Public Opinion* (New Brunswick, N.J., 1967), analyze public opinion polls on a number of key questions, including foreign policy.

Lee Benson, "An Approach to the Scientific Study of Past Public Opinion," *Public Opinion Quar.*, XXXI (Winter, 1967–68), 522–567, makes detailed suggestions for a scientific analysis, which historians have thus far failed to achieve.

Thomas A. Bailey, *The Art of Diplomacy: The American Experience* (New York, 1968), presents more than 250 maxims for the conduct of diplomacy, which are derived from American history, and illustrates them with numerous examples.

Ellis Briggs, *Anatomy of Diplomacy* (New York, 1968), by a witty veteran diplomat, neatly dissects the machinery that causes American diplomacy to function or malfunction.

Revealing and often critical observations on the foreign service by retired veterans appear in Ellis Briggs, *Farewell to Foggy Bottom* (New York, 1964); Henry S. Villard, *Affairs at State* (New York, 1965); Robert Murphy, *Diplomat Among Warriors* (Garden City, N.Y., 1964); Lawrence E. Gelfand, ed., *A Diplomat Looks Back: Lewis Einstein* (New Haven, 1968).

9TH ED. REFS. Among the more useful general works are W. Wendell Blancké, *The Foreign Service of the United States* (New York, 1969), by a retired Foreign Service officer; Richard A. Johnson, *The Administration of United States Foreign Policy* (Austin, 1971), by a career administrator; Manfred Landecker, *The President and Public Opinion: Leadership in Foreign Affairs* (Washington, 1968), which discusses how FDR and Truman dealt with public opinion; Edgar E. Robinson, *et al.*, *Powers of the President in Foreign Affairs, 1945–1965* (San Francisco, 1966), consisting of four essays by recognized scholars; and Francis O. Wilcox, *Congress, the Executive and Foreign Policy* (New York, 1971), which stresses the separation of powers. Eleanor Lansing Dulles, *American Foreign Policy in the Making* (New York, 1968); I. M. Destler, *Presidents, Bureaucrats, and Foreign Policy* (Princeton, 1972).

Among the more revealing memoirs one should note James B. Conant, *My Several Lives: Memoirs of a Social Inventor* (New York, 1970), by the ambassador to West Germany, 1955–1957; John K. Galbraith [ambassador to India], *Ambassador's Journal: A Personal Account of the Kennedy Years* (Boston, 1969); W. Averell Harriman [ambassador to Russia], *America and Russia in a Changing World* (Garden City, N.Y., 1971); and Orville H. Bullitt, ed., *For the President, Personal and Secret: Correspondence Between Franklin D. Roosevelt and William C. Bullitt* [ambassador to Russia and France] (Boston, 1972).

See also SELECTED BIBLIOGRAPHY in the EPILOGUE of this book.

Ch. 3. THE DIPLOMACY OF THE FRENCH ALLIANCE, 1775–1778

The works by Van Alstyne and Gilbert, added as new references on p. 25, are relevant. Gilbert analyzes American ideas about entanglements, pro and con.

R. R. Palmer, *The Age of the Democratic Revolution: A Political History of Europe and America, 1760–1800* (Princeton, 1959) is a masterly analysis of reciprocal impacts.

H. M. Adams, *Prussian-American Relations, 1775–1871* (Cleveland, 1960) shows how Frederick the Great's strict neutrality interfered with the movements of the Hessians, to the advantage of the United States.

Durand Echeverria, *Mirage in the West: A History of the French Image of American Society to 1815* (Princeton, 1957) describes the rise of sentimental French attachment to America.

A detailed and heavily documented study is J. P. Boyd, "Silas Deane: Death by a Kindly Teacher of Treason?" *William and Mary Quar.*, Ser. 3, XVI (1959), 165–187, 319–342, 515–550. Deane is portrayed as knowingly entering into treasonable correspondence with the secret British agent, Bancroft, to promote the private speculations of both; the circumstantial evidence indicates that Bancroft poisoned Deane to silence him.

T. A. Bailey, "America's Emergence as a World Power: The Myth and the Verity," *Pacific Hist. Rev.*, XXX (1961), 1–16 contends that the United States, by injecting a significant new element into the world balance of power, "emerged" as a world power with the declaring of independence in 1776.

8TH ED. REFS. Richard W. Van Alstyne, *Empire and Independence: The International History of the American Revolution* (New York, 1965), views the story in its European setting, with a pro-British slant and with the highly questionable thesis that Burgoyne's surrender had no important relationship to France's decision to intervene.

9TH ED. REFS. William C. Stinchcombe, *The American Revolution and the French Alliance* (Syracuse, N.Y., 1969) supplements but does not seriously challenge other standard accounts. There is stress on pro- and anti-Alliance feeling, especially the propaganda of French agents.

Ch. 4. THE DIPLOMACY OF PEACE WITH BRITAIN, 1778–1783

Note the added references to Chapter 3 (above), particularly the books by Gilbert, Palmer, Adams, and Echeverria.

R. W. Van Alstyne, *The Rising American Empire* (New York, 1960) concludes that Britain lost the war but won the peace by keeping America within her orbit through generous concessions.

Page Smith, *John Adams* (New York, 1962), Vol. I describes Adams as a prickly negotiator in Paris and in Holland.

Isabel de Madariaga, *Britain, Russia, and the Armed Neutrality of 1780* (New Haven, 1962), though exhaustive on the European side, shows that this group benefited the United States by further predisposing Britain to a favorable peace.

M. L. Brown, Jr., ed., *American Independence through Prussian Eyes* (Durham, N.C., 1959), stresses Frederick's interest in the effect of America's independence on the European balance of power, and his astonishment at Britain's favorable peace terms.

George Dangerfield, *Chancellor Robert R. Livingston of New York, 1746–1813* (New York, 1960) notes that America's first Secretary for Foreign Affairs did not exercise much influence on the peace treaty; but he would not accept a boundary line short of the Mississippi River.

J. A. Logan, Jr., *No Transfer: An American Security Principle* (New Haven, 1961) stresses Washington's objections to a proposed Franco-American expedition against Canada; he feared that the French, as powerful neighbors, would wind up in possession.

H. E. Klingelhofer, ed., "Matthew Ridley's Diary during the Peace Negotiations of 1782," *William and Mary Quar.*, Ser. 3, XX (1963), 95–133 reveals that Ridley shared Adams' and Jay's distrust of Vergennes, while shedding supplementary light on the negotiations.

8TH ED. REFS. Richard B. Morris, *The Peacemakers: The Great Powers and American Independence* (New York, 1965), is now the most detailed and exhaustively researched book on the subject. The main thrust is that

Jay and his colleagues were more fully justified than scholars had previously thought in meeting guile with guile and in making what amounted to a separate peace.

Richard B. Morris, *The American Revolution Reconsidered* (New York, 1967), Chapter III, encapsules some of the conclusions of his larger book (above), and stresses the point that the French alliance (though not French aid) was "at least as much a liability as it was an asset" in achieving victory. It stiffened British resistance and involved the Americans in generally futile French global strategy.

Richard B. Morris, *John Jay, the Nation and the Court* (Boston, 1967), outlines the foreign affairs background of Jay's constitutional thought.

Piers Mackesy, *The War for America, 1775–1783* (London, 1964), treats the conflict in its global setting, in which it became substantially submerged after 1778.

Roger Burlingame, *Benjamin Franklin: Envoy Extraordinary* (New York, 1967), presents the essentials in popularized form.

Claude Anne Lopez, *Mon Cher Papa: Franklin and the Ladies of Paris* (New Haven, 1966), describes with much charm how diplomacy and femininity can be successfully mixed.

H. A. Barton, "Sweden and the War of American Independence," *William and Mary Quar.*, XXIII (1966), 408–430, shows that the Swedish monarch disliked American republicanism, and that any aid he rendered was indirect, in pursuit of Sweden's maritime interests, especially under the Armed Neutrality.

Orville T. Murphy, "The Comte de Vergennes, the Newfoundland Fisheries, and the Peace Negotiation of 1783: A Reconsideration," *Canadian Hist. Rev.*, XLVI (1965), 32–46, demonstrates that, contrary to Jay's suspicions, Vergennes had no real objection to America's securing a share of the fisheries, provided that this was not done at France's expense.

9TH ED. REFS. David M. Griffiths, "American Commercial Diplomacy in Russia, 1780 to 1783," *William and Mary Quar.*, XXVII (1970), 379–410, deals largely with the failure of Dana's mission.

Ch. 5. FOREIGN AFFAIRS UNDER THE ARTICLES OF CONFEDERATION

R. W. Van Alstyne, *The Rising American Empire* (New York, 1960) deals briefly with Franco-American relations, and notes Vergennes' lack of enthusiasm for a British abandonment of the frontier posts.

Background material appears in Durand Echeverria, *Mirage in the West: A History of the French Image of American Society to 1815* (Princeton, 1957).

Page Smith presents colorful details of John Adams' difficult ministry in London in *John Adams* (New York, 1962), Vol. II.

J. P. Boyd, "Two Diplomats between Revolutions: John Jay and Thomas Jefferson," *Virginia Magazine of Hist. and Biog.*, LXVI (1958), 131–146 is concerned largely with the French consular convention as viewed by the pro-French minister in France (Jefferson) and the pro-British Secretary for Foreign Affairs (Jay).

R. W. Bixler, *The Open Door on the Old Barbary Coast* (New York, 1959) is sketchy but useful.

Joel Barlow's skilful negotiations (1796–1797) for the release of seamen imprisoned in Algiers are described in James Woodress, *A Yankee's Odyssey:*

The Life of Joel Barlow (Philadelphia, 1958); in Milton Cantor, ed., "A Connecticut Yankee in a Barbary Court: Joel Barlow's Algerian Letters to His Wife," *William and Mary Quar.*, Ser. 3, XIX (1962), 86–109; and in Milton Cantor, "Joel Barlow's Mission to Algiers," *The Historian*, XXV (1963), 172–194.

8TH ED. REFS. H. G. Barnby, *The Prisoners of Algiers: An Account of the Forgotten American-Algerian War, 1785–1797* (New York, 1966), demonstrates, despite the subtitle, that there was no war: America was too poor to pay, too weak to fight. After fumblingly protracted negotiations, about one hundred captive seamen were released under the ransom treaty of 1795.

9TH ED. REFS. Charles A. Jellison, *Ethan Allen: Frontier Rebel* (Syracuse, N.Y., 1969) is a standard work that shows Allen to have been disloyal to both the U.S. and Vermont, though moved by a genuine concern for Vermont's future.

F. W. Marks III, "Foreign Affairs: A Winning Issue in the Campaign for Ratification of the United States Constitution," *Pol. Sci. Quar.*, LXXXVI (1971), 444–469, details both federalist and anti-federalist desires for a stronger posture abroad.

Ch. 6. EMBROILMENTS WITH BRITAIN, 1789–1795

8TH ED. REFS. Paul A. Varg, *Foreign Policies of the Founding Fathers* (East Lansing, Mich., 1963), treats broadly the period from 1776 to 1812, with emphasis on nationalism and the interaction of domestic and foreign affairs. The author views the Federalists as realists, the Jeffersonians as moralists.

Julian P. Boyd, *Number 7: Alexander Hamilton's Secret Attempts to Control American Foreign Policy* (Princeton, N.J., 1964), convicts Hamilton (known to the British as Agent Number 7) of near treason when, in an attempt to head off Jefferson's plan of commercial warfare against Britain, Hamilton betrayed Cabinet secrets to the British agent Beckwith in 1789–1790, and in turn allegedly misrepresented Beckwith's views. The essence of this story was earlier revealed in S. F. Bemis' *Jay's Treaty* (1923), which is less harsh on Hamilton. This sort of thing was widely done in Europe in that age; Jefferson himself entered into secret correspondence with the French in 1793; and President Washington adopted Hamilton's policies, which resulted in peace with Britain, and rejected Jefferson's, which might well have resulted in war. The British probably perceived that George Washington was in control of foreign policy, and that public opposition in America to harsh measures against Britain insured neutrality.

Merrill D. Peterson, "Thomas Jefferson and Commercial Policy, 1783–1793," *William and Mary Quar.*, XXII (1965), 584–610, describes Jefferson's unsuccessful efforts to establish a pro-French commercial policy.

Raymond A. Young, "Pinckney's Treaty—A New Perspective," *Hispanic Amer. Hist. Rev.*, XLIII (1963), 526–535, notes that Spain sought a protective alliance with America. The United States rejected the proposal and held out stubbornly and successfully for the right of deposit at New Orleans.

Gerard H. Clarfield, "Postscript to the Jay Treaty: Timothy Pickering and Anglo-American Relations, 1795–1797," *William and Mary Quar.*, XXIII (1966), 106–120, shows how Washington's pro-British Secretary of State successfully preserved the peace, despite British impressment of seamen and other outrages.

Gerard H. Clarfield, "Victory in the West: A Study of the Role of Timothy Pickering in the Successful Consummation of Pinckney's Treaty," *Essex Institute Historical Collections*, CI (1965), 333–353, gives considerable credit to a forgotten Secretary of State.

9TH ED. REFS. Jerald A. Combs, *The Jay Treaty: Political Battleground of the Founding Fathers* (Berkeley, Calif., 1970) analyzes the conflicting views of Federalists and Republicans on foreign policy.

Charles R. Ritcheson, *Aftermath of Revolution: British Policy toward the United States, 1783–1795* (Dallas, Texas, 1969) strongly challenges the traditional belief that British policy was largely motivated by antipathy to the U.S.

Joanne L. Neel, *Phineas Bond: A Study in Anglo-American Relations, 1786–1812* (Philadelphia, 1968) deals with the professional activities of an important British consul in the U.S.

Jack L. Cross, *London Mission: The First Critical Years* (East Lansing, Mich., 1968) reveals that Minister Pinckney's efforts were handicapped by his not having had a primary hand in the key negotiations.

Robert Ernst, *Rufus King: American Federalist* (Chapel Hill, N.C., 1968) assesses this second-drawer diplomatist who twice served as minister to Britain, 1796–1803 and 1825–1826.

Gilbert L. Lycan, *Alexander Hamilton and American Foreign Policy: A Design for Greatness* (Norman, Okla., 1970) is a vigorous defense of Hamilton against his pro-Jefferson critics.

Helene J. Looze, *Alexander Hamilton and the British Orientation of American Foreign Policy, 1783–1803* (The Hague, 1969), strongly pro-Hamilton, concludes that the Secretary of the Treasury betrayed little to the British that they did not already know.

Ch. 7. FRICTION WITH FRANCE, 1789–1800

See new references on p. 99.

L. M. Sears, *George Washington and the French Revolution* (Detroit, 1960) is an admiring year-by-year account of Washington's shift from cool acceptance to active opposition.

S. G. Kurtz, *The Presidency of John Adams* (Philadelphia, 1957) concludes that the real struggle was between Hamilton and Adams, not Jefferson and Adams, and that Adams was supported in his peace bid by Washington, who was alarmed by the Virginia and Kentucky Resolutions.

Durand Echeverria, *Mirage in the West: A History of the French Image of American Society to 1815* (Princeton, 1957) shows how the American dream dissolved after Thermidor, 1794.

Felix Gilbert, *To the Farewell Address* (Princeton, 1961), develops the evolution of the Address, with attention to the ideas and influence of Hamilton.

S. G. Brown, ed., *The Autobiography of James Monroe* (Syracuse, 1959) reveals Monroe, in his mellow old age, attempting to vindicate his controversial French mission.

G. G. Shackelford, "William Short: Diplomat in Revolutionary France, 1785–1793," *Proceedings of the American Philosophical Soc.*, CII (1958), 596–612 points out that this able chargé, though disillusioned by the French Revolution, served the United States well as a fiscal agent and in elaborating Jefferson's commercial policy.

E. F. Kramer, "Some New Light on the XYZ Affair: Elbridge Gerry's

Reasons for Opposing War with France," *New England Quar.*, XXIX (1956), 509–513 reveals that Gerry stayed on, not because he was pro-French or anti-British, but because he felt that the United States could not sustain a war with France, especially economically.

A. A. Richmond, "Napoleon and the Armed Neutrality of 1800: A Diplomatic Challenge to British Sea Power," *Jour. of the Royal United Service Institution*, CIV (1959), 186–194 concludes that Napoleon accepted the Convention of 1800 so as to take over Louisiana and inveigle the Americans into the abortive Armed Neutrality of the North European powers aimed at Britain.

R. L. Ketcham, "France and American Politics, 1763–1793," *Pol. Sci. Quar.*, LXXVIII (1963), 198–223 considers the Republican-Federalist espousal of France and Britain less an ideological attachment than a jockeying for political advantage.

8TH ED. REFS. Alexander DeConde, *The Quasi-War: The Politics and Diplomacy of the Undeclared War with France, 1797–1801* (New York, 1966), a monumental piece of research, is now the standard work on the subject. A surprised Talleyrand, who overestimated pro-French feeling in America, appears more pacifically inclined (for realistic reasons) than in the previous accounts, and Adams less so, at least in the early stages. Adams turned against Hamilton and toward peace for reasons not altogether worthy, including jealousy of Hamilton. The British navy, which destroyed the French fleet in Egypt in 1798 and further disposed Paris to peace, co-operated to an unusual degree with the United States navy, though impressing some American sailors.

S. G. Kurtz, "The French Mission of 1799–1800: Concluding Chapter in the Statecraft of John Adams," *Pol. Sci. Quar.*, LXXX (1965), 543–557, reasons that this peacemaking venture was Adams' greatest contribution to the public service, and that it was largely prompted by his concern over internal unrest.

Ralph L. Ketcham, "France and American Politics, 1763–1793," *Pol. Sci. Quar.*, LXXVIII (1963), 198–223, argues that American attitudes and biases were shaped more by the American Revolution than by philosophical differences over the French Revolution.

Harry Ammon, "The Genêt Mission and the Development of American Political Parties," *Jour. of Amer. Hist.*, LII (1966), 725–741, spells out the extraordinary role that the Genêt impact had in crystallizing the differences between Federalists and Republicans.

Lawrence S. Kaplan, *Jefferson and France: An Essay on Politics and Political Ideas* (New Haven, 1967), portrays Jefferson as a Francophile from the time of the Franco-American alliance of 1778, and as one who had fallen to some extent under the spell of the French Revolution.

Marvin R. Zahniser, "The First Pinckney Mission to France [1795]," *South Carolina Hist. Mag.*, LXVI (1965), 205–217, demonstrates that the mission, though unsuccessful, was important in rallying political support behind Washington and Adams. The story was subsequently presented in fuller detail in the same author's *Charles Cotesworth Pinckney: Founding Father* (Chapel Hill, N.C., 1967).

Detlev F. Vagts, "The Logan Act: Paper Tiger or Sleeping Giant?" *Amer. Jour. of International Law*, XL (1966), 268–302, traces the origins and subsequent applications of the act, which has resulted in no prosecutions and only one indictment. If a case is ever appealed, the act may be declared unconstitutional, in part because of conflict with the First Amendment (free speech). The author doubts the utility of the law, and urges a narrowing of it.

James A. Carr, "John Adams and the Barbary Problem: The Myth and the Record," *American Neptune*, XXVI (1966), 231–257, contends that Adams' presumed lack of concern was due primarily to the lack of American naval strength.

9TH ED. REFS. Harry Ammon, *James Monroe: The Quest for National Identity* (New York, 1971), now the standard biography, describes sympathetically Monroe's mission to France.

Peter P. Hill, *William Vans Murray, Federalist Diplomat: The Shaping of Peace with France, 1797–1801* (Syracuse, N.Y., 1971) adds detail to Murray's key role in smoothing over the XYZ affair and helping to negotiate the Convention of 1800.

Gerald H. Clarfield, *Timothy Pickering and American Diplomacy, 1795–1800* (Columbia, Mo., 1969) is a conventional treatment of this double-dealing, Anglophile Secretary of State under Washington and Adams.

Ch. 8. JEFFERSON AND THE LOUISIANA PURCHASE, 1801–1803

9TH ED. REFS. Dumas Malone, *Jefferson the President: First Term, 1801–1805* (Boston, 1970) makes out a good case for the importance of Jefferson in inducing Napoleon to sell Louisiana.

Merrill D. Peterson, *Thomas Jefferson and the New Nation: A Biography* (New York, 1970), now the best one-volume treatment, is generally defensive of Jefferson and critical of his opponents. The role of Jefferson in the Louisiana Purchase is stressed.

Harry Ammon, *James Monroe: The Quest for National Identity* (New York, 1971) details Monroe's part in the Louisiana Purchase, without claiming too much credit (as Monroe did not) for his subject's role.

Ch. 9. JEFFERSON AND NEUTRAL WOES, 1803–1809

8TH ED. REFS. Lawrence S. Kaplan, *Jefferson and France: An Essay on Politics and Political Ideas* (New Haven, 1967), describes Jefferson as a proponent of the balance of power, determined to throw America's weight into the scales against Britain on the side of France. See also the two articles by Kaplan, above, p. 130, under 7TH ED. REFS.

Alfred W. Crosby, Jr., *America, Russia, Hemp, and Napoleon: American Trade with Russia and the Baltic, 1783–1812* (Columbus, Ohio, 1965), demonstrates how America's large-scale trade with Russia, often under British convoy from 1807 to 1812, helped to undermine Napoleon's Continental System blockade of Britain. In 1811 some 225 American ships reached Russia, carrying back hemp, flax, and iron.

Merrill D. Peterson, "Henry Adams on Jefferson the President," *Va. Quar. Rev.*, XXXIX (1963), 187–201, challenges Adams' evaluation of Jefferson as a failure and a doctrinaire, and argues that he should be studied in the light of his pragmatism.

9TH ED. REFS. Merrill D. Peterson, *Thomas Jefferson and the New Nation: A Biography* (New York, 1970) is generally sympathetic toward Jefferson's neutrality policies.

Harry Ammon, *James Monroe: The Quest for National Identity* (New York, 1971) presents a rather favorable view of Monroe's soundness of judgment in connection with the rejected Monroe-Pinkney Treaty.

Ch. 10. BLUNDERING INTO WAR WITH BRITAIN, 1809–1812

See new references on p. 145.

Bradford Perkins' *Prologue to War* (Berkeley, Calif., 1961), in discussing immediate causes, stresses orders in council (which squeezed Americans out of European markets retained by the British), impressment, and national honor. He downgrades the Indian menace, the desire for Florida (the Americans were nibbling there successfully), the desire for Canada (the Western militia went home six weeks after the Battle of the Thames), and sectionalism in general, especially the West. His meaningful map on the war vote (p. 409), based on the residence of Congressmen, reveals that support of the declaration was partisan rather than sectional. A popular majority may even have opposed war.

Reginald Horsman, in *The Causes of the War of 1812* (Philadelphia, 1962) has essentially the same maritime emphasis as Perkins and comes to about the same general conclusions. He belittles the Indian menace, though traders and unauthorized British officials doubtless encouraged the red men, and concludes that America probably would have gone to war without this issue. "The conquest of Canada was primarily a means of waging war, not a reason for starting it. America in 1812 was acting essentially in reaction to British maritime policy" (p. 267). Horsman, like Perkins, emphasizes the interest of the South and West in a free-sea export market, and notes that Britain's orders in council infuriated Americans partly because they were inspired by commercial jealousy.

Irving Brant, *James Madison: The President, 1809–1812* (Indianapolis, 1956) notes that Federalist partisanship contributed to British obduracy; that Prime Minister Perceval seemed more fearful of American commercial rivalry than of Bonaparte; and that Clay and Madison agreed that war would have been declared even if Britain's concession on orders in council had been known.

Irving Brant's *James Madison: Commander in Chief* (Indianapolis, 1961) examines the President's rather devious secret diplomacy, and concludes that without his support there would have been no war. He was most concerned with British "piracy" (seizing of American ships) and "monopoly" (the squeeze-out from the markets of Europe by the British orders in council).

A. Z. Carr, *The Coming of War* (Garden City, N.Y., 1960) is a semi-popular account through the Peace of Ghent which discounts the inevitability of the war.

A. B. Sears, *Thomas Worthington* (Columbus, Ohio, 1958) demonstrates that this Senator from Ohio voted against war because he deemed the country unprepared and feared Indian attacks on the Northwest frontier. Sears thinks that a popular majority in both Ohio and the nation opposed hostilities.

James Woodress, *A Yankee's Odyssey: The Life of Joel Barlow* (1958) deals with Barlow's unsuccessful mission to secure commercial concessions from Napoleon (1811–1812). A letter that he wrote may have averted a declaration of war on both France and England.

Irving Brant, in "Joel Barlow, Madison's Stubborn Minister," *William and Mary Quar.*, Ser. 3, XV (1958), 438–451 concludes that Barlow was more resolute in dealing with the French regime than unfriendly Federalist propaganda would concede.

N. K. Risjord, "1812: Conservatives, War Hawks, and the Nation's Honor," *ibid.*, XVIII (1961), 196–210 stresses national honor and its effective use by the War Hawk minority. The alternatives seemed to be war or submission to Britain's monopolistic commercial system. The author doubts that British orders in council really hurt prices in the South and West, but the people living there thought so.

Bradford Perkins, "George Joy, American Propagandist at London, 1805–1815," *New Eng. Quar.*, XXXIV (1961), 191–210 reveals that this self-appointed American agent exercised some influence in getting the orders in council suspended.

Reginald Horsman's *The Causes of the War of 1812* embodies much of the material in two previously published articles: "Western War Aims, 1811–1812," *Indiana Mag. of Hist.*, LIII (1957), 1–18; "British Indian Policy in the Northwest, 1807–1812," *Miss. Valley Hist. Rev.*, XLV (1958), 51–66. The latter article concludes that in any event American encroachments would have aggravated the Indians. British agents tried to line the Indians up for purely defensive purposes but the red men had offensive ideas of their own; hence trouble.

8TH ED. REFS. Roger H. Brown, *The Republic in Peril: 1812* (New York, 1964), downgrades or dismisses all conventional "causes" of the War of 1812 and argues that, in the face of British humiliations, the ruling Republican party believed that war was necessary if the republic and its republican form of government were to survive. The author states that the sharpest division in Congress was partisan (Republican versus Federalist), rather than sectional, and that the role of the War Hawks, who privately were less bellicose, has been overrated. Clay and Calhoun did not openly advocate hostilities until late in 1811, some months after Madison's decision for war.

Reginald Horsman, *Matthew Elliott, British Indian Agent* (Detroit, Mich., 1964), makes clear that this zealous British agent encouraged the Indians to resist the advancing American pioneers.

Lawrence S. Kaplan, "France and Madison's Decision for War, 1812," *Miss. Valley Hist. Rev.*, L (1964), 652–671, shows that Jeffersonian Republicans were counting on French diversionary support, though not desiring an alliance. Rather indifferent to the fate of Napoleon, they were more isolationist than the Federalists, who were deeply concerned about Britain.

Richard Glover, "The French Fleet, 1807–1814; Britain's Problem; and Madison's Opportunity," *Jour. of Modern Hist.*, XXXIX (1967), 233–252, reveals that Napoleon in 1812 was rapidly building a more powerful navy than Britain's, and this common knowledge may have helped to prompt Madison to attack Canada while Britain was in grave danger and before Napoleon could seize Canada for France. The collapse of Napoleon's Russian invasion changed the picture dramatically.

Indiana Magazine of History, LX (1964), 119–158, contains a symposium consisting of two papers and two commentaries, under the general title, "The War Hawks of the War of 1812." Roger H. Brown, using private letters and other data, argued that there was no identifiable body of War Hawks in Congress, and that the opprobrious term had been fastened on them by the

Federalists. Reginald Horsman, using voting statistics, discerned a body of War Hawks. Alexander DeConde and Norman K. Risjord sought to resolve the seeming contradictions by placing the interpretations of the first two papers in the larger mosaic of causation.

William R. Barlow, "Ohio's Congressmen and the War of 1812," *Ohio History*, LXXII (1963), 175–194, notes that two of the three Ohio members of Congress (two senators and one representative) opposed war because of the defenseless condition of the frontier and the unreadiness of the nation for war. They supported the attack on Canada for strategic rather than expansionist reasons.

Irving Brant, "Madison and the War of 1812," *Virginia Magazine of Hist. and Biog.*, LXXIV (1966), 51–67, is a spirited defense of Madison as a decisive President by his ablest apologist, who seeks to demolish Federalist stereotypes of weakness.

9TH ED. REFS. Irving Brant, *The Fourth President: A Life of James Madison* (Indianapolis, 1970) is a compression of the author's multi-volume biography which retains a militantly pro-Madison bias.

Ralph Ketcham, *James Madison: A Biography* (New York, 1971) is a well-documented volume judiciously critical of Madison's Presidential leadership; he felt that national honor demanded war.

Harold S. Schultz, *James Madison* (New York, 1970) is a brief biography for the general reader which stresses how Madison's attachment to strict construction hampered his executive leadership.

Victor A. Sapio, *Pennsylvania and the War of 1812* (Lexington, Ky., 1970) reveals that this state did not support the war declaration because of expansionist desires, fear of Indians, or economic depression. Pennsylvanians were more concerned about national honor (maritime grievances), independence (including independence of British manufacturers), and the welfare of the Republican Party.

Lawrence S. Kaplan, "France and the War of 1812," *Jour. of Amer. Hist.*, LVII (1970), 36–47, notes that France, though a co-belligerent (not an ally) extended some limited privileges to the U.S. but refused to make desired concessions, owing to preoccupation with the larger war.

Ronald L. Hatzenbuehler, "Party Unity and the Decision for War in the House of Representatives in 1812," *William and Mary Quar.*, XXIX (1972), 367–390, after an elaborate analysis of voting records, stresses the need for party unity as a major factor in the war declaration.

Leland R. Johnson, "The Suspense was Hell: The Senate Vote for the War in 1812," *Indiana Mag. of Hist.*, LV (1969), 247–267, concludes that fear of a Republican defeat at the polls motivated a requisite number of Republican Senators.

William Barlow, "The Coming of the War of 1812 in Michigan Territory," *Mich. Hist.*, LIII (1969), 91–107, reverses the old "remove the Indian menace theory" by demonstrating that the exposed settlers feared that war would result in massacres by the Indians.

Ch. 11. THE TRUCE OF GHENT AND AFTER, 1812–1818

8TH ED. REFS. Bradford Perkins, *Castlereagh and Adams: England and the United States, 1812–1823* (Berkeley, Calif., 1964), is now the most authoritative account of the negotiations at Ghent, and the nine years of repercussions to the treaty, including the Rush-Bagot Agreement and the Convention of 1818. The Congress of Vienna did not always overshadow the proceedings at Ghent, and Ghent sometimes affected Vienna. Foreign Secretary Castlereagh emerges as a key figure; vigorously seeking an accommodation, he was the first in his office to treat America as a truly sovereign nation and a diplomatic equal.

Four books, primarily sketchy syntheses, have recently appeared on the War of 1812: Harry L. Coles, *The War of 1812* (Chicago, 1965), which is fullest on the military aspects from the American viewpoint; J. M. Hitsman, *The Incredible War of 1812* (Toronto, 1965), which is most detailed on the military aspects from the Canadian viewpoint; P. P. Mason, ed., *After Tippecanoe: Some Aspects of the War of 1812* (East Lansing, Mich., 1963), which is a series of lectures by both Canadian and American scholars; and P. C. T. White, *A Nation on Trial: America and the War of 1812* (New York, 1965), which is primarily concerned with the diplomacy preceding the war and the negotiation of the peace. The author presents in brief form conclusions similar to those of Bradford Perkins and his predecessors.

9TH ED. REFS. For the new biographies of Madison by Brant, Ketcham, and Schultz, consult the 9th Edition references at the end of the previous chapter.

Reginald Horsman, *The War of 1812* (New York, 1969) is a balanced account with a useful summary of causes.

Samuel E. Morison, Frederick Merk, and Frank Freidel, *Dissent in Three American Wars* (Cambridge, Mass., 1970) discusses the War of 1812 (Morison), the Mexican War (Merk), and the Spanish-American War (Freidel). Morison questionably concludes that the War of 1812 was the "most unpopular" in American experience, not excluding the Vietnam War.

Ch. 13. AMERICA AND THE MONROE DOCTRINE, 1815–1825

J. A. Logan, Jr., *No Transfer* (New Haven, 1961) regards the no-transfer of territory in the Americas from one European power to another as a fundamental American foreign policy. Though related to the Monroe Doctrine, it did not have its origins in that doctrine and was not an extension of it. The no-transfer principle, as a fundamental bulwark of national security, had been present since independence. Not until 1869 and 1870 did President Grant and Secretary Fish associate it specifically with the Monroe Doctrine. The Monroe administration, fearing that Spain might transfer Cuba to Britain or France for help of various kinds, had already invoked the no-transfer principle in London, Madrid, and St. Petersburg, and there was no need to repeat it in Monroe's message, which was concerned primarily with the revolted Spanish colonies. The author's arguments are persuasive, but broadly speaking, the no-transfer principle was implicit in the Monroe Doctrine.

Irving Brant, *James Madison: Commander in Chief, 1812–1836* (Indianapolis, 1961) observes that Madison advised Monroe in 1823 to go further in co-operation with Britain than Monroe and Adams were willing to go. Madison also favored a declaration in behalf of Greece and one in behalf of Spain, recently invaded by France.

Bradford Perkins, "The Suppressed Dispatch of H. U. Addington, Washington, November 3, 1823," *Hispanic Amer. Hist. Rev.*, XXXVII (1957), 480–485 reveals that Canning suppressed the report of the conversation between the British chargé in Washington and Secretary Adams regarding Canning's original proposal to Rush. The reasons are conjectural.

8TH ED. REFS. Bradford Perkins, *Castlereagh and Adams: England and the United States, 1812–1823* (Berkeley, Calif., 1964), has two chapters outlining the birth of the Monroe Doctrine in the larger context of Anglo-American relations.

Irby C. Nichols, Jr., "The Russian Ukase and the Monroe Doctrine: A Re-evaluation," *Pacific Hist. Rev.*, XXXVI (1967), 13–26, demolishes assorted myths (some of them now straw men) about the famous ukase of 1821. Its issuance and withdrawal (the author contends) were motivated primarily if not solely by Russian internal problems, and not by Russian imperialism or the Monroe Doctrine.

9TH ED. REFS. Harry Ammon, *James Monroe: The Quest for National Identity* (New York, 1971) emphasizes Monroe the nationalist, and shows that he was in command, though Secretary Adams worked well in tandem with him, especially on the Monroe Doctrine.

Irby C. Nichols, Jr. and Richard A. Ward, "Anglo-American Relations and the Russian Ukase: A Reassessment," *Pacific Hist. Rev.*, XLI (1972), 444–459, concludes that the ukase partly inspired the Monroe Doctrine, which in turn helped prompt Britain to conclude the Treaty of 1825 with Russia. This pact paralleled the Russo-American treaty of 1824.

Ch. 14. THE AWKWARD AGE OF DIPLOMACY, 1825–1840

9TH ED. REFS. James C. Curtis, *The Fox at Bay: Martin Van Buren and the Presidency, 1837–1841* (Lexington, Ky., 1970) has a brief discussion of foreign affairs, especially Canadian-American relations, which Van Buren handled creditably.

Ch. 15. BRITAIN AND THE WEBSTER-ASHBURTON TREATY

9TH ED. REFS. Frederick Merk, *Fruits of Propaganda in the Tyler Administration* (Cambridge, Mass., 1971) describes in detail how Secretary Webster (and Lord Ashburton) used many thousands of dollars for lobbyists, propagandists, and other agents to induce Maine to accept the boundary compromise.

George J. Gill, "Edward Everett and the Northeastern Boundary Controversy," *New England Quar.*, XLII (1969), 201–213, provides detail on the "battle of the maps" which further show that the extreme U.S. claim to Maine was justified.

Ch. 16. THE OREGON DISPUTE AND ITS SETTLEMENT

8TH ED. REFS. Frederick Merk, *The Oregon Question: Essays in Anglo-American Diplomacy and Politics* (Cambridge, Mass., 1967), presents a series of studies, most of them previously published. One of the new essays shows that America rejected arbitration in 1846 primarily because the arbiters would presumably have split the difference in the disputed triangle, thus leaving the U.S. without an adequate seaport in the Northwest. In another new essay, Merk sharply rebuts the thesis that French seapower, as a threat to Britain's flank, had a significant bearing on the Oregon settlement, which was brought about by diplomacy and internal politics in both countries. There was a strong sentiment for peaceful settlement in Congress.

Charles Sellers, *James K. Polk: Continentalist, 1843–1846* (Princeton, N.J., 1966), is the second volume of the near-definitive three-volume biography. The author makes it clear that although Polk's slippery policy of bluff and bluster finally succeeded, he ran the grave risk of involving the republic in a two-front war, which might well have thwarted all prospective territorial gains. The final British offer of compromise on Oregon left London only ten days before the news of the outbreak of war on the Rio Grande reached England; had there been a further delay of ten days, the offer might not have been sent.

Frederick Merk, *The Monroe Doctrine and American Expansionism, 1843–1849* (New York, 1966), relates Polk's concern over a British "intrusion" in Oregon, contrary to the Monroe Doctrine, to his demands for the whole of Oregon. Worried also about California, Polk was disingenuous in his application of the Doctrine. Supposed European threats served as pretexts for expansion in the name of security, especially in the mouths of Democrats.

Richard S. Cramer, "British Magazines and the Oregon Question," *Pacific Hist. Rev.*, XXXII (1963), 369–382, shows that the leading British magazines, from 1820 to 1846, consistently supported Britain's claim to the triangle north of the Columbia River.

Ch. 17. THE ANNEXATION OF TEXAS

8TH ED. REFS. Charles Sellers, *James K. Polk: Continentalist, 1843–1846* (Princeton, N.J., 1966), describes President-elect Polk's successful work in getting the Texas annexation resolution through Congress; his "gratuitous" supporting of the Texans' extreme claim to the Rio Grande; and his determination to achieve annexation speedily and "as offensively to Mexico as possible" (p. 224).

Frederick Merk, *The Monroe Doctrine and American Expansionism, 1843–1849* (New York, 1966), relates America's preclusive designs on Texas (with its extreme boundary) to the Monroe Doctrine and a desire to head off a balance of power in the Americas. A careful contemporary study by a State Department expert (Greenhow) demolishing the claim to the Rio Grande was evidently suppressed (pp. 144–145).

J. M. Nance, *After San Jacinto: The Texas-Mexican Frontier, 1836–1841* (Austin, Tex., 1963) and *Attack and Counterattack: The Texas-Mexican Frontier, 1842* (Austin, Tex., 1964) both connect these disturbances with the growth of annexation sentiment in Texas and the U.S.

Kinley J. Brauer, "The Massachusetts State Texas Committee: A Last Stand against the Annexation of Texas," *Jour. of Amer. Hist.*, LI (1964), 214–231, describes a final effort to thwart implementation of the joint resolution of annexation.

P. H. Laurent, "Belgium's Relations with Texas and the United States, 1839–1844," *Southwestern Hist. Quar.*, LXVIII (1964), 220–236, reveals that Belgium, anxious to stimulate commerce, encouraged the U.S. to annex Texas to protect the Texans from foreign colonization.

9TH ED. REFS. Frederick Merk, *Fruits of Propaganda in the Tyler Administration* (Cambridge, Mass., 1971) describes (with documents) how the Tyler administration used slavery propaganda, both abolitionist and anti-abolitionist, to promote sentiment for the annexation of Texas.

Ch. 18. WAR AND PEACE WITH MEXICO

Frederick Merk, *Manifest Destiny and Mission in American History* (New York, 1963) attributes the failure of Manifest Destiny to secure all of Mexico partly to America's freedom-loving sense of mission, which required a good example to the rest of the world.

Charles Vevier, "American Continentalism: An Idea of Expansion, 1845–1910," *Amer. Hist. Rev.*, LXV (1960), 323–335 is a study of geographical or geopolitical determinism as embraced by many Americans from early days.

G. M. Brooke, Jr., "The Vest Pocket War of Commodore Jones," *Pac. Hist. Rev.*, XXXI (1962), 217–233 shows that when Jones seized Monterey in 1842 he was acting on flimsy evidence and was spurred on by the proximity of superior British and French naval units. He had specifically in mind Monroe's message of 1823. The Mexican government was so angry that the Tyler administration was forced to suspend negotiations for the purchase of California; Jones was never officially censured and was given a more important command.

F. A. Knapp, Jr., "The Mexican Fear of Manifest Destiny in California," in T. E. Cotner and C. E. Castañeda, eds., *Essays in Mexican History* (Austin, Tex., 1958), pp. 192–208 concludes that Mexico opposed a peaceful settlement with Texas on the Rio Grande because she knew of the Yankee desire for California; she feared that appeasement might cause her to lose her entire northern frontier and jeopardize her national existence.

C. A. Hutchinson, "Valentín Goméz Farías and the Movement for the Return of General Santa Anna to Mexico in 1846," in *ibid.*, pp. 169–191 tells of Santa Anna's return, with Polk's connivance, with attention to the factions that invited the general. He later betrayed them, after having first shown signs of wanting to negotiate a peace.

J. A. Hawgood, "The Pattern of Yankee Infiltration in Mexican Alta California, 1821–1846," *Pacific Hist. Rev.*, XXVII (1958), 27–37 notes that infiltration before the 1840's has been exaggerated; T. O. Larkin, the United States consul and secret agent, regretted the forcible intervention of Frémont and the Bear Flag rebels. Polk's suspicions of a possible foreign acquisition are supported by the author's revelation that in 1841 Mexico actively negotiated for the sale of California to Prussia for $6 million. The Prussian Foreign Office finally backed off (perhaps remembering the Monroe Doctrine).

W. H. Marti, *Messenger of Destiny: The California Adventures, 1846–1847, of Archibald H. Gillespie, U.S. Marine Corps* (San Francisco, 1960) deals with this officer, who was supposed to have brought secret orders to Frémont in 1846.

P. S. Klein, *President James Buchanan* (University Park, Pa., 1962) shows that Secretary Buchanan, whom Polk distrusted, was less anxious than the President to provoke war with Mexico, but he increased his demands for Mexican territory with the success of American arms, evidently wanting to ride into the Presidency on this popular demand.

I. D. Spencer, *The Victor and the Spoils: A Life of William L. Marcy* (Providence, R.I., 1959), has a brief chapter on Secretary Marcy's connection with the Gadsden purchase treaty.

E. K. Chamberlin, "Nicholas Trist and Baja California," *Pacific Hist. Rev.*, XXXII (1963), 49–63 proves that Trist cannot be blamed (as he often is) for a failure to secure this territory: the attempted American conquest was stalemated and Polk at no time demanded it in the treaty.

8TH ED. REFS. Charles Sellers, *James K. Polk: Continentalist, 1843–1846*

(Princeton, N.J., 1966), deals with the causes and early phases of the Mexican War, concluding that while Polk preferred peaceful coercion to war, he would accept war, particularly if he could place the blame on Mexico.

Frederick Merk, *The Monroe Doctrine and American Expansionism, 1843–1849* (New York, 1966), discusses the Monroe Doctrine in relation to presumed British designs on California, as well as to foreign designs on Texas.

W. H. Goetzmann, *When the Eagle Screamed: The Romantic Horizon in American Diplomacy, 1800–1860* (New York, 1966), is a sketchy overview of expansionism.

P. T. Harstad and R. W. Resh, "The Causes of the Mexican War: A Note on Changing Interpretations," *Arizona and the West*, VI (1964), 289–302, is a survey of historiography since 1848; it stresses the need for more work on nationalism and cultural tensions.

Glenn W. Price, *Origins of the War with Mexico: The Polk-Stockton Intrigue* (Austin, Tex., 1967) revives suspicions, without convincing proof, that Polk deliberately sought to provoke hostilities with Mexico months before the clash finally occurred.

Charles A. Lofgren, "Force and Diplomacy, 1846–1848: The View from Washington," *Military Affairs*, XXXI (Summer 1967), 57–64, argues that Polk carefully coordinated American military action against Mexico with diplomatic overtures to the Mexican government.

9TH ED. REFS. Seymour V. Connor and Odie B. Faulk, *North America Divided: The Mexican War, 1846–1848* (New York, 1971) echoes Justin H. Smith by blaming Mexico as well as America for the "guilt" of starting the war.

Shomer S. Zwelling, *Expansion and Imperialism* (Chicago, 1970) is a prize-winning master's essay which criticizes the Norman A. Graebner thesis regarding Polk's commercial-territorial expansionism.

Ch. 19. THE FERMENT OF THE FIFTIES

D. F. Warner, *The Idea of Continental Union: Agitation for the Annexation of Canada to the United States, 1849–1893* (Lexington, Ky., 1960), describes the forces, especially economic, that led to the annexation flurry in Canada in 1849, and associates the Reciprocity Treaty of 1854 with the prosperity that quieted annexation agitation north of the border.

P. S. Klein, *President James Buchanan* (University Park, Pa., 1962) deals with Buchanan as minister in London and as President in connection with the Crampton and Central American crises. Buchanan condemned the Clayton-Bulwer Treaty as reversing the Monroe Doctrine by aiming it at the United States rather than Europe, and concluded that the British were looking for a fight at the time of the Crampton affair.

Kenneth Bourne, "The Clayton-Bulwer Treaty and the Decline of British Opposition to the Territorial Expansion of the United States, 1857–60," *Jour. of Modern Hist.*, XXXIII (1961), 287–291 shows that because the treaty "had failed in every way," London yielded to American demands in Central America.

T. L. Karnes, *The Failure of Union: Central America, 1824–1960* (Chapel Hill, N.C., 1961) concludes that Britain was not opposed to union as such but seemed to be pursuing such a policy primarily to thwart the United States.

R. A. Naylor, "The British Role in Central America Prior to the Clayton-Bulwer Treaty of 1850," *Hispanic Amer. Hist. Rev.*, XL (1960), 361–382 covers in more detail the same ground as Karnes, above, and demonstrates that the British did not oppose federation as such; their policies were dictated more by commercial than political considerations.

E. W. Richards, "Louis Napoleon and Central America," *Jour. of Modern History,* XXXIV (1962), 178–184 sees in Louis Napoleon's interest in a trans-Nicaraguan canal in the 1840's one of the roots of his later involvement in Mexico with Maximilian.

Cyril Allen, "Félix Belly: Nicaraguan Canal Promoter," *Hispanic Amer. Hist. Rev.,* XXXVII (1957), 46–59 reveals that this French promoter secured a grant in 1858 from Costa Rica and Nicaragua to construct a canal but the hostility of the United States contributed to his failure.

H. E. Landry, "Slavery and the Slave Trade in Atlantic Diplomacy, 1850–1861," *Jour. of Southern Hist.,* XXVII (1961), 184–207 demonstrates that friction with Britain over this issue had brought unity to America; a relaxation of such tensions on the eve of the Civil War promoted disunion. The author consequently sees some merit in Seward's scheme for promoting unity by provoking the great powers.

8TH ED. REFS. Frederick Merk, *The Monroe Doctrine and American Expansionism, 1843–1849* (New York, 1966), has an informative chapter (VIII) on Polk's purposefully ambiguous reinvocation of the Doctrine in connection with Yucatan's alleged scheme for annexation to Britain.

Mario Rodríguez, *A Palmerstonian Diplomat in Central America: Frederick Chatfield, Esq.* (Tucson, Ariz., 1964), is a detailed treatment of the aggressive British envoy who stirred up much trouble for the U.S. before and after the Clayton-Bulwer Treaty of 1850.

Mario Rodríguez, "The 'Prometheus' and the Clayton-Bulwer Treaty," *Jour. of Modern Hist.,* XXXVI (1964), 260–278, relates how a British warship fired on the U.S. steamer *Prometheus* in 1851, to enforce the collection of disputed port dues at the free port of Greytown, in violation of the Clayton-Bulwer Treaty. The resulting uproar resulted in a formal British apology and hastened the liquidation of the Central American problem.

A. H. Carr, *The World and William Walker* (New York, 1963), is a popular attempt at psychologizing which adds little to W. O. Scroggs' classic study of Walker.

Irene W. D. Hecht, "Israel D. Andrews and the Reciprocity Treaty of 1854: A Reappraisal," *Canadian Hist. Rev.,* XLIV (1963), 313–329, argues that Andrews was a key man in the story: he helped to lobby the treaty through in Washington and to lobby and bribe it through in British North America. He was striving for Manifest Destiny in the form of a commercial empire embracing the U.S. and British North America.

Walter G. Sharrow, "William Henry Seward and the Basis for American Empire, 1850–1860," *Pacific Hist. Rev.,* XXXVI (1967), 325–342, concludes that Seward, though frustrated as a Senator in seeking territorial gains, helped to shape both the ideology and the actual progress of American expansion.

R. R. Davis, Jr., "Diplomatic Plumage: American Court Dress in the National Period," *American Quarterly,* XX (1968), 164–179, shows that Secretary Marcy's dress order of 1853 enjoyed only "limited success"; diplomats rather freely exercised the options given them. In 1867 Congress laid down more rigid rules of simplicity.

9TH ED. REFS. Lawrence H. Officer and Lawrence B. Smith, "The Canadian-American Reciprocity Treaty of 1855 to 1866," *Jour. of Econ. Hist.,* XXVIII (1968), 598–623, disputes the "classic" interpretation that reciprocity gave a great impetus to Canadian prosperity.

Ch. 20. AMERICA AND CUBA TO 1860

8TH ED. REFS. P. S. Foner, *A History of Cuba and Its Relations with the United States,* vol. II [1845–1895] (New York, 1963), is a part of a multi-volumed series which concludes that the primary goal of most Cuban insurgents in the 1850's was annexation to the U.S.

Irving Katz, "August Belmont's Cuban Acquisition Scheme," *Mid-America,* L (1968), 52–63, shows that the Ostend Manifesto owed much to the pressures brought by this German-born Wall Street banker.

9TH ED. REFS. Hugh Thomas, *Cuba: The Pursuit of Freedom* (New York, 1971) is a magisterial history of Cuba by an English scholar, with considerable attention to relations with the U.S., especially in the twentieth century.

Ch. 21. THE DAWN OF ASIATIC INTERESTS

8TH ED. REFS. William L. Neumann, *America Encounters Japan: From Perry to MacArthur* (Baltimore, 1963), recounts in broad terms the story of the opening.

Jeannette C. van der Corput and Robert A. Wilson, translators and eds., *Japan Journal: 1855–1861* [of Henry C. J. Heusken] (New Brunswick, N.J., 1964) presents the observations of Townsend Harris' Dutch interpreter, who adds luster to the diplomatic record of his chief.

Samuel E. Morison, *"Old Bruin": Commodore Matthew C. Perry, 1794–1858* (Boston, 1967), now the standard biography, contains a fascinatingly written account of Perry's great adventure; it vividly portrays the ticklish nature of the enterprise and Perry's skill as a diplomat.

Foster R. Dulles, *Yankees and Samurai: America's Role in the Emergence of Modern Japan, 1791–1900* (New York, 1965), uses broad strokes, with emphasis more on culture and personalities than on diplomacy.

Te-kong Tong, *United States Diplomacy in China, 1844–1860* (Seattle, 1964), based on both Chinese and Western sources, shows that while Peking's attitude toward the Western "barbarians" vacillated between firmness and appeasement, U.S. policy at an early date came to be based on preserving equal commercial opportunity and China's territorial integrity.

Marlene J. Mayo, "A Catechism of Western Diplomacy: The Japanese and Hamilton Fish, 1872," *Jour. of Asian Studies,* XXVI (1967), 389–410, reveals that the Japanese embassy, which came to Washington, failed to secure a revision of the treaty of 1858 but learned some lessons in Western diplomacy from Secretary Fish.

Paul H. Clyde, "Historical Reflections on American Relations with the Far East," *South Atlantic Quar.,* LXI (1962), 437–449, disposes of a number of popular myths, including the one that the Chinese loved the Americans better than the other "barbarians."

9TH ED. REFS. Roger Pineau, ed., *The Japan Expedition, 1852–1854: The Personal Journal of Commodore Matthew C. Perry* (Washington, D.C., 1968), hitherto unpublished, adds some detail, especially testy comments, excluded from the official *Narrative.*

John K. Fairbank, "'American China Policy' to 1898: A Misconception," *Pacific Hist. Rev.,* XXXIX (1970), 409–420, notes that America's policy was a part of European policy (especially British) and that the Chinese lumped all foreign "barbarians" together.

Ch. 22. THE EARLY CRISES OF THE CIVIL WAR

8TH ED. REFS. Glyndon G. Van Deusen, *William Henry Seward* (New York, 1967), now the standard biography, gives a generally favorable picture of the Secretary of State, who worked on friendly terms with Lincoln. Seward's memorandum of April 1, 1861, does not seem quite so foolish in the light of Spain's return to Santo Domingo and France's alleged help to Spain in attempting to secure Haiti.

Philip Van Doren Stern, *When the Guns Roared: World Aspects of the American Civil War* (Garden City, N.Y., 1965), is a popularized account by a non-academic author–publisher. He adds little essential to the standard works, except for some new light on the British intrigues at Liverpool regarding the construction of the Confederate commerce destroyers.

Kenneth Bourne, *Britain and the Balance of Power in North America, 1815–1908* (Berkeley, 1967), relates British naval power to diplomacy during the Civil War crises, when Canada was largely defenseless. At the end of 1864, there were 71 ironclads in America's navy of 671 vessels (building and afloat), compared with thirty in Britain's steam navy of 417 (p. 275). These figures do not take into account the disparity in types. The U.S. navy was allowed to deteriorate sharply after the war.

Patrick Sowle, "A Reappraisal of Seward's Memorandum of April 1, 1861, to Lincoln," *Jour. of Southern Hist.*, XXXIII (1967), 234–239, presents evidence that Seward's arrogant and warlike memorandum was deliberately designed for publication after Lincoln's anticipated acquiescence.

Henry Blumenthal, "Confederate Diplomacy: Popular Notions and International Realities," *Jour. of Southern Hist.*, XXXII (1966), 151–171, concludes that the South, too confident of success, did not press for foreign intervention soon enough or skillfully enough. Much resentment developed in the Confederacy over the nonintervention of the British, who had more money invested in Northern enterprises than in the English cotton industry.

Joseph M. Hernon, Jr., "British Sympathies in the American Civil War: A Reconsideration," *Jour. of Southern Hist.*, XXXIII (1967), 356–367, argues that the British workingmen, often hostile to and fearful of the Yankees, revealed much pro-South feeling, contrary to a common stereotype. The upper classes hated Northern democracy more than they loved Southern aristocracy; the Emancipation Proclamation, the author argues, effected no great change in British opinion.

Joseph M. Hernon, Jr., "The Irish Nationalists and Southern Secession," *Civil War History*, XII (1966), 43–53, shows that kinship with Irish immigrants in the North was largely offset by sympathy for the Confederates, who, like the Irish, were struggling to be free of a presumed overlord.

R. H. Jones, "Anglo-American Relations, 1861–1865, Reconsidered," *Mid-America*, XLV (1963), 36–49, provides further evidence that the British deliberately pursued a policy of neutrality because it was to their best interests, economic and otherwise.

Amos Khasigian, "Economic Factors and British Neutrality, 1861–1865," *Historian*, XXV (1963), 451–465, concludes that war profits were not the primary objective of British neutrality; they were somewhat incidental to larger purposes.

John Kutolowski, "The Effect of the Polish Insurrection of 1863 on American Civil War Diplomacy," *Historian*, XXVII, 560–577, shows that the diversionary effect of the insurrection diminished the possibility of recognition of the Confederacy by England and France.

9TH ED. REFS. Lynn M. Case and Warren F. Spencer, *The United States and France: Civil War Diplomacy* (Philadelphia, 1970), a work of rich scholarship, is now the "definitive" treatment. At first Napoleon favored an unbroken Union as an offset to Britain; later he favored a broken Union because of his Mexican venture.

Daniel B. Carroll, *Henry Mercier and the American Civil War* (Princeton, 1971) represents the French Minister in Washington as so pro-South that his zeal on occasion outran his instructions.

Serge Gavronsky, *The French Liberal Opposition and the American Civil War* (New York, 1968) demonstrates that the liberal press supported the North, partly as an indirect way of attacking the authoritarian regime of Napoleon, whose journals supported the South.

Charles P. Cullop, *Confederate Propaganda in Europe: 1861–1865* (Coral Gables, Fla., 1969) concludes that the effort failed primarily because it had to uphold inept Southern diplomacy.

Harold Hyman, ed., *Heard Round the World: The Impact Abroad of the Civil War* (New York, 1969) describes various repercussions, from Latin America to Russia. One conclusion is that the outcome of the war actually did influence the passage of the British Reform Bill of 1867.

Joseph M. Hernon, Jr., *Celts, Catholics and Copperheads: Ireland Views the American Civil War* (Columbus, Ohio, 1968) finds much sentiment for the Confederacy, despite immigrant ties with the North, because the Irish were, at heart, secessionists from Britain.

Frank J. Merli, *Great Britain and the Confederate Navy: 1861–1865* (Bloomington, Ind., 1970) shows that the Confederate raiders had little more than nuisance value and doubts that the Laird rams would have raised the Union blockade.

Alice O'Rourke, "The Law Officers of the Crown and the *Trent* Affair," *Mid-America*, LIV (1972), 157–171, details how the legal experts shifted to a harder line following British outrage.

Ch. 23. THE COLLAPSE OF KING COTTON DIPLOMACY

See new references on p. 347.

F. A. Logan, "India—Britain's Substitute for American Cotton, 1861–1865," *Jour. of Southern Hist.*, XXIV (1958), 472–480, notes that India provided over 55 per cent of Britain's supply during the four years; the cotton famine was thus relieved, and the pressures for intervention were reduced.

E. A. Brady, "A Reconsideration of the Lancashire 'Cotton Famine,'" *Agricultural Hist.*, XXXVII (1963), 156–162, with accompanying note by M. B. Sherwood, argues that the famine was really brought on by overproduction of textiles, 1858–1861, and that many mills would have had to shut down in any event.

J. A. Boromé, "Henry Adams Silenced by the Cotton Famine," *New England Quar.*, XXXIII [New Ser. XXVII] (1960), 237–240 presents an unpublished letter of Adams analyzing the groups in England for and against intervention.

R. J. Zorn, "John Bright and the British Attitude to the American Civil War," *Mid-America*, XXXVIII (1956), 131–145 presents Bright as the most influential of the pro-Union voices in England.

Douglas Maynard, "Civil War 'Care': The Mission of the *George Griswold*,"

New England Quar., XXXIV (1961), 291–310 tells how this ship, loaded with food gifts from America, reached the hungry cotton operatives in time to build up goodwill for the United States.

T. H. O'Connor, "Lincoln and the Cotton Trade," *Civil War Hist.*, VII (1961), 20–35 reveals that Lincoln permitted the export of cotton under license from occupied territory, owing to the needs of Northern, British, and French mills. When the Southerners found that King Cotton had failed, they engaged in a vast illicit trade with their conquerors, with attendant scandals.

Claude Fohlen, "La Guerre de Sécession et le Commerce Franco-Américain," *Revue d'Histoire Moderne et Contemporaine*, VIII (1961), 259–270, concludes that although the cotton trade was disrupted, the high Morrill tariff was more damaging to French markets in America than the war.

R. W. Winks, "The Creation of a Myth: 'Canadian' Enlistments in the Northern Armies during the American Civil War," *Canadian Hist. Rev.*, XXXIX (1958), 24–40 demonstrates that they fell far short of the 40,000 figure often quoted.

Guy MacLean, "The *Georgian* Affair: An Incident of the American Civil War," *ibid.*, XLII (1961), 133–144 describes how this vessel, suspected of being an intended Confederate privateer, was seized by the Canadian government, though owned by a British subject. It was successfully claimed by Washington after the war.

N. A. Graebner, "Northern Diplomacy and European Neutrality," in David Donald, ed., *Why the North Won the Civil War* (Baton Rouge, La., 1960), pp. 49–75, praises the masterly diplomacy of Seward, who took full advantage of the European tradition of not intervening until the success of a revolution was assured.

F. A. Logan, "Activities of the *Alabama* in Asian Waters," *Pacific Hist. Rev.*, XXXI (1962), 143–150 shows that this vessel at best got a lukewarm, sometimes a hostile, reception in Asiatic waters, including British ports. Partly for this reason, she may have sought other waters.

Sister Mary P. Trauth, *Italo-American Diplomatic Relations, 1861–1882* (Washington, 1958) deals with the successful efforts of the United States to prevent Italy from recognizing the Confederacy and succoring Confederate ships.

S. E. Humphreys, "United States Recognition of the Kingdom of Italy," *The Historian*, XXI (1959), 296–312, describes the negotiations leading to the accrediting of America's first minister to newly united Italy; the United States favored unity abroad since it was struggling for unity at home.

8TH ED. REFS. Paul Pecquet Du Bellet, *The Diplomacy of the Confederate Cabinet of Richmond and Its Agents Abroad: Being Memorandum Notes Taken in Paris during the Rebellion of the Southern States from 1861 to 1865*, ed. by William S. Hoole (Tuscaloosa, Ala., 1963), is a condemnation by a former New Orleans attorney of the stubbornness, stupidity, and venality of the Confederate authorities. It was written in 1865, after Appomattox.

Robert H. Jones, "Long Live the King?" *Agricultural Hist.*, XXXVII (1963), 166–169, shows that U.S. wheat exceeded cotton as a British import during only three of the four years of the war. America was never the near-exclusive supplier of wheat to the extent that she had been of cotton.

Stuart L. Bernath, "Squall Across the Atlantic: The *Peterhoff* Episode," *Jour. of Southern Hist.*, XXXIV (1968), 382–401, shows that the seizure of this Mexico-bound British steamer, in line with "ultimate destination," led to "contradictory actions" which could be best explained on grounds of national self-interest.

9TH ED. REFS. See also references for the previous chapter.

Stuart L. Bernath, *Squall Across the Atlantic: American Civil War Prize Cases and Diplomacy* (Berkeley, Calif., 1970) considers in depth the legalistic controversies growing out of the U.S. seizure of British merchant ships trying to run the Union blockade.

Kinley J. Brauer, "British Mediation and the American Civil War: A Reconsideration," *Jour. of Southern Hist.*, XXXVIII (1972), 49–64, argues that various other factors besides Antietam chilled British mediation.

Conway W. Henderson, "The Anglo-American Treaty of 1862 in Civil War Diplomacy," *Civil War History*, XV (1969), 308–319, regards the easily negotiated slave-search pact as a factor in preserving amity during the Civil War.

Richard A. Heckman, "British Press Reaction to the Emancipation Proclamation," *Lincoln Herald*, LXXI (1969), 150–153, reports that some seventy Irish, English, and Scottish newspapers were overwhelmingly unfavorable.

Howard I. Kushner, "The Russian Fleet and the American Civil War: Another View," *Historian*, XXXIV (1972), 633–649, concludes, without convincing proof, that the Lincoln administration correctly guessed the main reason for sending the fleets.

Robert L. Reid, ed., "William E. Gladstone's 'Insincere Neutrality' during the Civil War," *Civil War History*, XV (1969), 293–307, publishes documents which show that Gladstone really did not favor disunion when he blundered into hailing the South as a nation in his Newcastle speech, Oct. 7, 1862.

Ch. 24. NAPOLEON III AND MEXICO

Henry Blumenthal, *A Reappraisal of Franco-American Relations, 1830–1871* (Chapel Hill, N.C., 1959) shows that Southerners turned against Maximilian when they saw that he could not help them. The author concludes that the pressure of the Austro-Prussian conflict, combined with fear of a war with the United States, contributed heavily to Napoleon's withdrawal. France was grievously offended by pro-German sentiment in America during the Franco-Prussian War. Yet there was much pro-French sympathy in the South, which had also tasted invasion and which distrusted Prussian monarchy and militarism. Protestant Germany was generally favored in the United States over Catholic, dictatorial France.

H. M. Adams, *Prussian-American Relations, 1775–1871* (Cleveland, 1960) stresses enthusiasm for enlistments and other manifestations of pro-Northern sentiment during the Civil War, while noting the sympathy of conservative and aristocratic Prussian elements for the South. The ideals of unity and abolition were strong in Germany, and partly offset the cotton famine there, as did a heavy trade in arms and other supplies with the North.

W. M. Armstrong, *E. L. Godkin and American Foreign Policy, 1865–1900* (New York, 1957) relates how the influential but erratic editor of the New York *Nation* opposed the Maximilian venture, but was critical of the Juárez regime; he finally objected to the summary execution of so decent an aristocrat as Maximilian.

E. J. Berbusse, "The Origins of the McLane-Ocampo Treaty of 1859," *The Americas*, XIV (1958), 223–245 shows that the United States, seeking Lower California and transit rights across the Isthmus of Tehuantepec, established friendly relations with the Mexican liberals, but the resulting treaty, which conceded only transit rights, was rejected by the Senate.

R. R. Miller, "The American Legion of Honor in Mexico," *Pacific Hist. Rev.*,

XXX (1961), 229–241 notes that some 3000 Union veterans joined Juárez's forces after the war, attracted by bonuses (never fully paid) and aroused by the Monroe Doctrine (there were numerous Monroe Doctrine Committees whipping up enthusiasm throughout the country). [Secretary Seward may not have mentioned the Monroe Doctrine but the public certainly did.] The Yankee Legion fought gallantly, but its total contribution to the entire seven-year war was not great.

8TH ED. REFS. Glyndon G. Van Deusen, *William Henry Seward* (New York, 1967), has an appreciative summation (Chapter 33) of Seward's contribution to the solution of the Maximilian difficulty. It emphasizes how Seward forced Napoleon out without appearing to do so.

Carl H. Bock, *Prelude to Tragedy: The Negotiation and Breakdown of the Tripartite Convention of London, October 31, 1861* (Philadelphia, 1966), presents in great depth the larger ambitions of Napoleon, and shows that the French deliberately presented excessive demands to Mexico in the hope they would not be met. There are some details on U.S. reactions and tangential involvement.

Robert R. Miller, "Matías Romero: Mexican Minister to the United States during the Juárez-Maximilian Era," *Hispanic Amer. Hist. Rev.*, XLV (1965), 228–245, shows that this ailing and youthful envoy revealed great skill in procuring arms, promoting propaganda, and making the proper contacts.

9TH ED. REFS. Alfred J. Hanna and Kathryn A. Hanna, *Napoleon III and Mexico: American Triumph over Monarchy* (Chapel Hill, 1971) is a well-documented monograph which holds that Napoleon's scheme failed largely because of the U.S. commitment to a republican government.

Ch. 25. THE CARIBBEAN AND ALASKA, 1865–1867

Glyndon G. Van Deusen, *William Henry Seward* (New York, 1967) develops fully the genesis and partial fruition of Seward's dreams of an American territorial empire.

Hector Chevigny, *Russian America: The Great Alaskan Venture, 1741–1867* (New York, 1965), downgrades Russia's fears of a British takeover and reveals that there was no real desire among Russians to sell Alaska (much opposition was voiced at the time). He concludes that a major motive in the sale was Russia's desire to preserve cordial relations, which, ironically, were hurt by friction over the approval of the treaty and the transfer of sovereignty. "A nation having small desire to sell did so to a nation that was not eager to buy, their motives the belief that they would please each other" (p. 245).

C. Ian Jackson, "The Stikine Territory Lease and Its Relevance to the Alaska Purchase," *Pacific Hist. Rev.*, XXXVI (1967), 289–306, shows that the Hudson's Bay Company, having found its trade declining in this part of the panhandle of present Alaska, was not interested in renewing its lease there. The company was no threat to Russian sovereignty; the British were not interested in buying Alaska; only the U.S. had any interest in doing so.

9TH ED. REFS. David Donald, *Charles Sumner and the Rights of Man* (New York, 1970) presents interesting details on Sumner's key role in purchasing Alaska.

Henry R. Huttenbach, "Sale of Alaska: A Reply to a Soviet Commentary," *Alaska Review*, IV (1970), 33–45, corrects a Communist interpretation that "aggressive . . . American capitalism" "compelled" a Russia weakened by the Crimean War to cede Alaska for a pittance.

Ch. 26. GREAT BRITAIN AND THE GRANT ERA, 1865–1877

See new references on p. 390.

J. A. Logan, Jr., *No Transfer* (New Haven, 1961) shows that this fundamental policy was not officially joined to the Monroe Doctrine until the days of President Grant (1869–70), in connection with the Dominican annexation scheme. The retrocession of the West Indian island of St. Bartholomew by Norway and Sweden to France in 1877 stands as the only violation of no-transfer; Washington did not protest, partly because France had originally owned it and continued to hold other nearby islands.

D. G. Creighton, "The United States and Canadian Confederation," *Canadian Hist. Rev.*, XXXIX (1958), 209–222 downgrades the Civil War as inspiring Confederation; the conflict merely gave urgency to drives for constitutional reform and retrenchment.

Maureen M. Robson, "The *Alabama* Claims and the Anglo-American Reconciliation, 1865–71," *Canadian Hist. Rev.*, XLII (1961), 1–22 plays up the European crisis growing out of the Franco-German War as accelerating the settlement.

Samuel Shapiro, "Problems of International Arbitration: The Halifax Fisheries Commission of 1877," *Essex Institute Historical Collections*, XCV (1959), 21–31 concludes that the United States was badly gouged by the three arbitrators: the American was sleepily inept; the "neutral" Belgian was notoriously pro-British; the Canadian was intimately in contact with the British government.

J. A. Field, Jr., "A Scheme in Regard to Cyrenaica," *Miss. Valley Hist. Rev.*, XLIV (1957), 445–468 deals with the efforts of the U.S. Consul in Tripoli to secure a naval base in that area; the scheme was not followed up and American naval strength was reduced in the Mediterranean late in 1875 because of the Cuban crisis.

8TH ED. REFS. James O. McCabe, *The San Juan Water Boundary Question* (Toronto, 1965), is a detailed monograph which argues that the British officials (indifferent as usual to Canadian interests) needlessly gave away a good claim. They foolishly consented to exclude from arbitration by the German Emperor the "Middle Channel," which might have been considered under the ambiguous Oregon Boundary treaty of 1846.

Thomas N. Brown, *Irish-American Nationalism, 1870–1890* (Philadelphia, 1966), provides a chapter in British history and American social history, while analyzing the activities of the Fenians and other Irish agitators active in the U.S.

Hereward Senior, "Quebec and the Fenians," *Canadian Hist. Rev.*, XLVIII (1967), 26–44, and Arthur H. DeRosier, Jr., "Importance in Failure: The Fenian Raids of 1866–1871," *Southern Quar.*, III (1965), 181–197, both add some details to the familiar story. The DeRosier article notes that these fiascos strengthened Canadian nationalism and hence helped to defeat the Fenian aim of destroying British rule in Canada.

Arthur H. DeRosier, Jr., "The Settlement of the San Juan Controversy," *Southern Quar.*, IV (1965), 74–88, outlines the dispute and points out that this was the only part of the U.S. boundary ever settled by reference to a disinterested arbitrator.

9TH ED. REFS. David Donald, *Charles Sumner and the Rights of Man* (New York, 1970), the second volume of a masterly biography, causes Sumner to appear to better advantage than usual in his encounters with Grant and Fish. Sumner long dreamed of annexing Canada.

Brian Jenkins, *Fenians and Anglo-American Relations during Reconstruction* (Ithaca, N.Y., 1969) adds considerable detail on diplomacy to older accounts, particularly on the Irish impact on the negotiation of the Naturalization Treaty of 1870 with Britain.

Mabel G. Walker, *The Fenian Movement* (Colorado Springs, Colo., 1969) largely retraces in briefer form the same ground as the older monograph of William D'Arcy.

Henry A. Kmen, "Remember the Virginius: New Orleans and Cuba in 1873," *Louisiana History*, XI (1970), 313–331, describes the pre-Hearstian atrocity propaganda in Louisiana, with its demand from ex-Confederates to reunite the sections by warring on Spain for honor, justice, humanity, Manifest Destiny, and commercial advantage.

Barry M. Gough, "British Policy in the San Juan Boundary Dispute, 1854–72," *Pacific Northwest Quar.*, LXII (1971), 59–68, gives credit to British forbearance and preponderant naval power for the amicable settlement.

Jackson Crowell, "The United States and a Central American Canal, 1869–1877," *Hispanic Amer. Hist. Rev.*, XLIX (1969), 27–52, describes President Grant's real interest in a waterway and the breakdown of negotiations with Nicaragua over a route.

Ch. 27. DIPLOMACY A FOOTBALL OF POLITICS, 1877–1889

See new references on p. 406.

R. H. Bastert, "A New Approach to the Origins of Blaine's Pan American Policy," *Hispanic Amer. Hist. Rev.*, XXXIX (1959), 375–412 shows that Blaine, though about to leave office, issued the invitations for the conference in 1882 largely as a grandstand play to divert attention from his diplomatic blunderings. Anti-Blaine feeling being what it was in Latin America, the Conference probably would have failed if it had been held.

C. S. Campbell, Jr., "The Dismissal of Lord Sackville," *Miss. Valley Hist. Rev.*, XLIV (1958), 635–648 concludes that the British were not given a proper chance to recall Sackville-West; in the light of international law the hasty dismissal seems to have been discreditable. The American minister in London misled the State Department.

T. C. Hinckley, "George Osgoodby and the Murchison Letter, *Pacific Hist. Rev.*, XXVII (1958), 359–370 reveals that Osgoodby, born in America of British parents, was not induced by Republican managers to write the letter; he sent it on his own initative in an excess of partisan zeal. He held it back, fearing Democratic reprisals, but was finally persuaded by Republicans to turn it over to the Los Angeles *Times*, on October 18, 1888. It was published three days later.

Sister Mary P. Trauth, *Italo-American Diplomatic Relations, 1861–1882* (Washington, 1958), focuses on the twenty-one year mission of the distinguished pro-Italian philologist George P. Marsh. Highly regarded in Italy, he dealt capably with such secondary problems as arose, including commerce and navigation, immigration and naturalization.

Milton Plesur, "America Looking Outward: The Years from Hayes to Harrison," *The Historian*, XXII (1960), 280–295 sees this period not as a "low point" in American diplomacy but as a time of preparation for the later Large Policy. The same general theme is applied to the Far East in the same author's, "Across the Wide Pacific," *Pacific Hist. Rev.*, XXVIII (1959), 73–80.

8TH ED. REFS. John A. S. Grenville and George B. Young, in *Politics,*

Strategy and American Diplomacy: Studies in Foreign Policy, 1873–1917 (New Haven, 1966), Chapter II, reveals that President Cleveland, despite a capacity for righteous self-delusion, shamelessly played politics with foreign affairs, as did the rival Republicans. This was notably true in connection with Canadian fishing rights and Chinese immigration.

Robert C. Brown, *Canada's National Policy, 1883–1900: A Study in Canadian-American Relations* (Princeton, N.J., 1964), focuses on four disputes: fisheries, seals, reciprocity, and the Alaska boundary. He emphasizes how they affected Canada's domestic policy and contributed importantly to her will to become a nation.

Charles S. Campbell, Jr., "American Tariff Interests and the Northeastern Fisheries, 1883–1888," *Canadian Hist. Rev.*, XLV (1964), 212–218, concludes that President Cleveland, although unsuccessful in getting the new fisheries treaty approved, worked out a modus vivendi which kept the peace until the final settlement of 1912.

Daniel Cosío Villegas, *The United States versus Porfirio Díaz*, trans. by Nettie Lee Benson (Lincoln, Nebr., 1963), shows that the Hayes administration recognized the Díaz government in 1878 without extorting a satisfactory settlement of the problems growing out of Indian raids, smuggling, and other disputes. The Mexicans outwaited and outwitted the Yankees.

Owen D. Edwards, "American Diplomats and Irish Coercion, 1880–1883," *Jour. of American Studies*, I (1967), 213–232, notes that Secretaries Blaine and Frelinghuysen supported Irish-Americans arrested by the British authorities; Minister Lowell was less warm in his support.

G. E. Paulsen, "The Gresham-Yang Treaty [1894]," *Pacific Hist. Rev.*, XXXVII (1968), 281–297, notes that the pact regularized existing arrangements by authorizing the exclusion of Chinese laborers for ten years.

9TH ED. REFS. Milton Plesur, *America's Outward Thrust: Approaches to Foreign Affairs, 1865–1890* (De Kalb, Ill., 1971) analyzes America's outside contacts during the Gilded Age, whether political, economic, naval, commercial, cultural, technological, or diplomatic. The era is seen not as "a low point" in diplomacy but as a harbinger of the New Imperialism.

Stuart C. Miller, *The Unwelcome Immigrant: The American Image of the Chinese, 1785–1882* (Berkeley, Calif., 1969) traces the growing antipathy toward the Chinese that found vent in the Exclusion Act of 1882.

Ch. 28. BLAINE AND SPIRITED DIPLOMACY, 1889–1893

H. U. Faulkner, *Politics, Reform and Expansion, 1890–1900* (New York, 1959) deals sketchily with foreign affairs against the background of domestic development.

F. B. Pike, *Chile and the United States, 1880–1962* (Notre Dame, Ind., 1963) discusses in detail the *Baltimore* crisis. European warnings did much to impress Chile with the seriousness of the situation; Blaine was thought by Chileans to have shown a friendly attitude and to have been forced to act by a bellicose President Harrison, who ignored the progress being made by diplomacy.

J. L. Mecham, *The United States and Inter-American Security, 1889–1960* (Austin, Tex., 1961) treats at length the "new" Pan-Americanism inaugurated in 1889 under Blaine.

D. F. Warner, *The Idea of Continental Union* (Lexington, Ky., 1960) shows that Irish-descended Blaine, who disliked the British, was one of the few American leaders who urged the annexation of Canada. This movement of the late 1880's and early 1890's, never that of a majority and stronger in Canada than in the United States, was largely inspired by economic motives; the American panic of 1893 gave it a chill, as did Cleveland's pugnacious handling of the Venezuela boundary crisis.

W. M. Armstrong, *E. L. Godkin and American Foreign Policy, 1865–1900* (New York, 1957) portrays this censorious *Nation* editor as critical of Secretary Blaine, especially in connection with the Chilean crisis.

C. S. Campbell, Jr., "The Anglo-American Crisis in the Bering Sea, 1890–1891," *Miss. Valley Hist. Rev.*, XLVIII (1961), 393–414 reveals that Secretary Blaine did not push for the seizure of more Canadian pelagic sealers because the British had ordered four ironclad warships into the area.

Bingham Duncan, "Protectionism and Pork: Whitelaw Reid as Diplomat, 1889–1891," *Agricultural Hist.*, XXXIII (1959), 190–195 shows how the American Minister in France negotiated for the removal of disease-based restrictions on pork; but the French, in retaliation for the American tariff of 1890, levied excessively high duties on pork.

J. L. Gignilliat, "Pigs, Politics, and Protection: The European Boycott of American Pork, 1879–1891," *ibid.*, XXXV (1961), 3–12 notes that many European nations in the 1870's and 1880's, alleging trichinosis, boycotted American pork; but in some cases the sanitary restrictions were covert protective tariffs, more easily justified to poor people than outright tariffs.

Mary P. Chapman, "The Mission of Lansing Bond Mizner to Central America," *The Historian*, XIX (1957), 385–401 concludes that Blaine's inexperienced Minister in Central America complicated the Secretary's problems by becoming involved in the unfortunate affair of General Barrundia (1890), who was shot by Guatemalan officials on an American ship.

8TH ED. REFS. John A. S. Grenville and George B. Young, *Politics, Strategy, and American Diplomacy: Studies in Foreign Policy, 1873–1917* (New Haven, 1966), Chapter III, credits both Secretary Blaine and President Harrison with being devotees of Manifest Destiny and with having a hemispheric outlook, which the succeeding Cleveland administration lacked. Surprisingly, Harrison is regarded as a "strong" President, with a good grasp of foreign affairs.

Robert C. Brown, *Canada's National Policy, 1883–1900: A Study in Canadian-American Relations* (Princeton, N.J., 1964), shows how the disputes of the Harrison-Blaine era promoted Canadian nationalism. (See also references for the previous chapter.)

Charles S. Campbell, Jr., "The Bering Sea Settlements of 1892," *Pacific Hist. Rev.*, XXXII (1963), 347–367, reveals the difficulties of negotiating the arbitration agreement of 1892, while Canadian sealing interests were pressing Britain in the tripartite negotiations. The reluctance of the British to continue temporary suspension of pelagic sealing during the proposed arbitration angered President Harrison, who at times seemed bent on war with Britain, partly because of his desire for re-election.

Harry J. Sievers, *Benjamin Harrison: Hoosier President* (Indianapolis, 1968), is quite general on foreign affairs and further reveals Harrison's distrust of Blaine's aggressiveness.

9TH ED. REFS. Allan Spetter, "Harrison and Blaine: Foreign Policy, 1889–1893," *Indiana Mag. of Hist.*, LXV (1969), 215–227 further demonstrates that Harrison was often more active than Blaine in directing foreign policy.

Ch. 29. SAMOA AND HAWAII: AN IMPERIALISTIC PREVIEW

W. A. Russ, Jr., *The Hawaiian Revolution, 1893–94* (Selinsgrove, Pa., 1959) is now the standard monograph on the subject. Conceding that the royal government was bad, the author finds Stevens guilty of grave irregularities, the Harrison administration of undue haste, and Cleveland of ineptitude in dumping the issue on a partisan Congress. It was better for annexation to have come in 1898 rather than in 1893; the United States in 1893 looked like a receiver of "stolen goods."

W. A. Russ, Jr., *The Hawaiian Republic, 1894–98* (Selinsgrove, Pa., 1961) is a sequel to the above volume, and likewise a standard authority on the subject. Although it deals largely with the political affairs of the Hawaiian Republic, the pressures for and against annexation are explored fully, including the Japanese bogey and the need for Hawaii during the Spanish-American War.

Ethel M. Damon, *Sanford Ballard Dole and His Hawaii* (Palo Alto, Calif., 1957) publishes some interesting sidelights on this prominent figure in the Hawaii revolution and its aftermath. There is some evidence that Minister Stevens decided to raise the American flag partly to forestall a rumored takeover by the Japanese.

W. R. Braisted, *The United States Navy in the Pacific, 1897–1909* (Austin, Tex., 1958) includes a brief account of preparations by the Navy for a possible clash with Japan over disputes connected with the annexation of Hawaii.

E. R. May, *Imperial Democracy* (New York, 1961) presents some sidelights on popular agitation for and against Hawaiian annexation.

I. D. Spencer, *The Victor and the Spoils: A Life of William L. Marcy* (Providence, R.I., 1959) has a brief chapter on early American interest in Hawaii.

Merze Tate, "Slavery and Racism as Deterrents to the Annexation of Hawaii, 1854–1855," *Jour. of Negro History*, XLVII (1962), 1–18 stresses American opposition to slavery as a factor in shelving the abortive annexation treaty.

Merze Tate, "British Opposition to the Cession of Pearl Harbor," *Pacific Hist. Rev.*, XXIX (1960), 381–394 shows that at first the British were unfavorable to exclusive American rights at Pearl Harbor in the treaty of 1887, but acquiesced when they discovered that access to Honolulu harbor was all they needed.

Merze Tate, "Great Britain and the Sovereignty of Hawaii," *ibid.*, XXXI (1962), 327–348 notes that Britain showed little interest in acquiring Hawaii; up to 1840 she might have taken it without "serious opposition from any great power." In line with the end-century Anglo-American cordiality, she did not protest against annexation by the United States in 1893 and especially 1898; "the liberal press acquiesced in it; and some statesmen unofficially and secretly encouraged it."

Merze Tate, "Canada's Interest in the Trade and the Sovereignty of Hawaii," *Canadian Hist. Rev.*, XLIV (1963), 20–42 traces the evolution of opinion to the point of complete acquiescence in the 1898 annexation.

W. P. Strauss, "Pioneer American Diplomats in Polynesia, 1820–1840," *Pacific Hist. Rev.*, XXXI (1962), 21–30 reveals that early consular and other agents in Hawaii, Samoa, Fiji, Tahiti, and New Zealand were generally ineffective and damaging to America's position.

W. D. McIntyre, "Anglo-American Rivalry in the Pacific: The British Annexation of the Fiji Islands in 1874," *ibid.*, XXIX (1960), 361–380 concludes that there was no real quarrel over these islands; the United States was willing that Britain should take them, but the British were spurred into annexation by somewhat groundless imaginings of growing American power in Samoa, Hawaii, and even Borneo.

Jeannette P. Nichols, "The United States Congress and Imperialism, 1861–1897," *Jour. of Economic Hist.*, XXI (1961), 526–538 shows that by 1898 "Imperialism had become attractive psychologically, economically, strategically."

Walter LaFeber, "A Note on the 'Mercantilistic Imperialism' of Alfred Thayer Mahan," *Miss. Valley Hist. Rev.*, XLVIII (1962), 674–685 contends that it is misleading to call Mahan a "mercantilist"; though advocating some mercantilist concepts, he favored an "open-door commercial empire secured by naval bases and a battleship fleet."

8TH ED. REFS. Walter LaFeber, *The New Empire: An Interpretation of American Expansion, 1860–1898* (Ithaca, 1963), is an important synthesis which attributes a global vision to American statesmen after the Civil War. Prompted by recurring depressions and the enormous productivity of the postwar industrial revolution, they were moving toward a commercial (not a colonial) empire. The emphasis throughout is on economic motivations, which the author believes to have been paramount, although conceding that there were other factors. As regards Hawaii, President Harrison appears as a consistent expansionist. LaFeber believes that the islands were annexed not so much as potential markets as because they were a strategic link (with the projected Isthmian Canal) in establishing America's commercial empire in the Pacific. (The market-motivation thesis does not fit Alaska and Samoa so well.)

Merze Tate, *The United States and the Hawaiian Kingdom: A Political History* (New Haven, 1965), despite the title, devotes more pages to the Republic. Although well researched, the book adds little that is significantly new to earlier works, and further proves that the revolution and annexation were brought off by American or American-descended propertied interests.

Ralph S. Kuykendall, *The Hawaiian Kingdom, 1874–1893: The Kalakaua Dynasty* (Honolulu, 1967), is the third and final volume of a classic, the last chapter of which (with additional apparatus) was prepared by Dr. Charles H. Hunter. Evidence is presented regarding the political bias of Secretary Gresham and "Paramount" Blount; and the "sugarites" are further absolved of providing the primary motivation for the 1893 revolution.

John A. S. Grenville and George B. Young, in *Politics, Strategy, and American Diplomacy: Studies in Foreign Policy, 1873–1917* (New Haven, 1966), argue that Cleveland (who as President-elect had used his influence with the Senate to block Hawaiian annexation) shortsightedly and deliberately stirred up a partisan debate which identified the Democratic party with anti-imperialism and ruined any hope of evolving a bipartisan foreign policy.

George W. Baker, Jr., "Benjamin Harrison and Hawaiian Annexation: A Reinterpretation," *Pacific Hist. Rev.*, XXXIII (1964), 295–309, contends that Harrison, far from being an expansionist regarding Hawaii, refused to encourage annexation before the revolution, and then he supported it cautiously and lukewarmly. If he had thrown himself strongly behind it, argues the author, it might have secured Senate approval in 1893.

Merze Tate, "The Myth of Hawaii's Swing toward Australasia and Canada," *Pacific Hist. Rev.*, XXXIII (1964), 273–293, shows that in the 1870's and 1880's there was no danger of Hawaii's moving from the U.S. sphere of influence to any part of the British Empire.

Merze Tate, "Twisting the Lion's Tail over Hawaii," *Pacific Hist. Rev.*, XXXVI (1967), 27–46, reveals that Britain did not oppose annexation even though, in 1893, the American press decried presumed British opposition; London was determined to work toward a general understanding with the U.S.

Merze Tate, "Hawaii: A Symbol of Anglo-American Rapprochement," *Pol. Sci. Quar.*, LXXIX (1964), 555–575, demonstrates that in the four decades before annexation the British moved from active opposition to pleased acquiescence, thus paralleling their retreat from an aggressive Isthmian policy and providing further evidence of a desire for a *rapprochement*.

Dorothea R. Muller, "Josiah Strong and American Nationalism: A Reevaluation," *Jour. of Amer. Hist.*, LIII (1966), 487–503, holds that Strong was not "a prophet of imperialism" in 1885 nor an advocate of the "large policy" at the turn of the century but a Christian philosopher who would use "nationalism as an instrument for serving internationalism."

9TH ED. REFS. Merze Tate, *Hawaii: Reciprocity or Annexation* (East Lansing, Mich., 1968) traces U.S.-Hawaiian relations with some new details and emphases, while focusing on commerical reciprocity in bringing about annexation.

Thomas J. Osborne, "The Main Reason for Hawaiian Annexation in July, 1898," *Oregon Hist. Quar.*, LXXI (1970), 161–178, gives the need for Far Eastern markets as the "main reason," although this has conventionally been regarded as one of many reasons, and although the Spanish War is conceded to have been the needed catalyst.

Ch. 30. ANGLO-AMERICAN TENSIONS AND THE VENEZUELA CRISIS

Walter LaFeber, *The New Empire: An Interpretation of American Expansion, 1860–1898* (Ithaca, 1963), points out that Cleveland, myth to the contrary, received considerable support from the business world for his bellicose stand, and contends that Cleveland and Olney were both acting because America's larger commercial interests were in jeopardy. As the author concedes, other motives were also involved.

John A. S. Grenville and George B. Young, in *Politics, Strategy, and American Diplomacy: Studies in Foreign Policy, 1873–1917* (New Haven, 1966), develop fully the important role of William L. Scruggs (he conferred with Cleveland) as a propagandist for Venezuela. Britain, pressed in various theaters by Germany, France, and Russia, did not want war. Cleveland, who had "no consistent foreign policy," had no intention of going to war and hence was bluffing. Secretary Olney, with no love for Venezuela, was determined to uphold the Monroe Doctrine and assert America's primacy in the Western Hemisphere. Commercial motivations were evidently not the determining ones, according to these authors.

Joseph J. Mathews, "Informal Diplomacy in the Venezuela Crisis of 1896," *Miss. Valley Hist. Rev.*, L (1963), 195–212, demonstrates that both adversaries used a number of unofficial emissaries (including newspaper men), who sometimes complicated negotiations but who on the whole helped to lessen the danger of war. Lord Salisbury, as both Prime Minister and Foreign Secretary, appears as the most unyielding member of the Cabinet.

Bradford Perkins, *The Great Rapprochement: England and the United States, 1895–1914* (New York, 1968), has a brief but perceptive treatment of the Venezuela "crisis" and its aftermath. He downgrades the possibilities of war.

Ch. 31. THE COMING OF THE WAR WITH SPAIN, 1895–1898

Walter LaFeber, *The New Empire: An Interpretation of American Expansion, 1860–1898* (Ithaca, 1963), argues that the business world (despite a prevalent misconception) was not "monolithic" in its opposition to war; that McKinley kept control of policy despite the yellow press (he was able to head off a recognition of the Cuban insurgents by Congress); that commercial aims were a motivating force in the White House and in Congress; and that McKinley did not want war but only what war would provide—a free Cuba. LaFeber contends that the stereotype of a spineless President must be discarded.

H. Wayne Morgan has contributed two books: *William McKinley and His America* (Syracuse, 1963) and *America's Road to Empire: The War with Spain and Overseas Expansion* (1965). The first is a full-length biography; the second, a rather sketchy overview. McKinley appears as an effective President, neither intimidated by public opinion nor cowed by Congress: he took the course that he regarded as inevitable in view of Spain's stubbornness.

John A. S. Grenville and George B. Young, in *Politics, Strategy, and American Diplomacy: Studies in Foreign Policy, 1873–1917* (New Haven, 1966), Chapter IX, praise McKinley's patient and consistent diplomacy, and his skill in handling Congress. War came because the Spanish government could not grant independence to Cuba, and McKinley (and the public) would not settle for less in their efforts to bring peace to the island.

Philip S. Foner, *A History of Cuba and Its Relations with the United States,* vol. II [1845–1895] (New York, 1963), stresses U.S. policy and the internal conflicts among the Cuban leaders.

R. G. Neale, *Great Britain and United States Expansion: 1898–1900* (East Lansing, Mich., 1966), contends that the influence of British friendship during this period has been greatly exaggerated. The *rapprochement* began in 1896 (if not before), and was not of significance in heading off intervention by the powers in 1898: their jealousies and rivalries were enough. The British ambassador in Washington, quite without authorization, was more active for intervention than was traditionally believed.

Bradford Perkins, *The Great Rapprochement: England and the United States, 1895–1914* (New York, 1968), deals trenchantly with the period of the Spanish War and concludes that, whatever Ambassador Pauncefote's indiscretions, the British navy in the last analysis prevented any effective intervention by the powers.

Richard Hofstadter, *The Paranoid Style in American Politics and Other Essays* (New York, 1966), contains a revised essay ("Cuba, the Philippines, and Manifest Destiny") which holds that the impulse for war came largely from a "psychic crisis" among frustrated elements in the depression-cursed population, including the silverites. The urge to keep the insular fruits came largely from the more contented economic interests and active nationalists.

Paul S. Holbo, "Presidential Leadership in Foreign Affairs: William McKinley and the Turpie-Foraker Amendment," *Amer. Hist. Rev.*, LXXII (1967), 1321–1335, presents impressive evidence that McKinley led Congress, rather than the reverse, particularly in blocking an attempt to include in the war resolution a recognition of the insurgent Cuban government. (Yet the Teller Amendment, adopted in the same resolution, tied the President's hands.)

Gerald G. Eggert, "Our Man in Havana: Fitzhugh Lee," *Hispanic Amer. Hist. Rev.*, XLVII (1967), 463–485, reveals that Consul General Lee, a rash and impetuous ex-Confederate cavalry officer, pressed for intervention and annexation, partly to promote private speculations in Cuba. His personal interests colored his recommendations, which may have contributed to the *impasse* with Spain. In response to his urgings, the *Maine* was sent to Havana, although sooner than he really wanted it.

H. Wayne Morgan, "The DeLome Letter: A New Appraisal," *Historian*, XXVI (1963), 36–49, concludes that the letter's "real importance lay in its destruction of official and popular confidence in Spain's honesty and its ability either to devise or to implement a solution to the Cuban problem."

John A. S. Grenville, "American Naval Preparations for War with Spain, 1896–1898," *Jour. of American Studies*, II (1968), 33–47, reproduces official documents relative to plans for descending on the Philippines.

Paul S. Holbo, "The Convergence of Moods and the Cuban-Bond 'Conspiracy' of 1898," *Jour. of Amer. Hist.*, LV (1968), 54–72, demonstrates that much of the popular pressure to free Cuba stemmed from a fear that the holders of Spanish bonds (including some American interests) would continue to milk Cuban revenues or transfer the liability to the United States. Teller may have been motivated by such fears when he pressed his amendment.

9TH ED. REFS. William A. Williams, *The Roots of the Modern American Empire: A Study of the Growth and Shaping of Social Consciousness in a Marketplace Society* (New York, 1969) amasses quotations from presumed farm spokesmen to argue unconvincingly that pressures from the agricultural element for foreign markets played "the primary causal role" in bringing on the war. Little or no weight is given to the Cuban insurrection and its impact.

P. S. Foner, "Why the United States Went to War with Spain in 1898," *Science and Society*, XXXII (1968), 39–65, cites the "predominance" of economic factors in bringing on the war, although conceding the presence of political, social, and psychological forces.

Harold J. Sylwester, "The Kansas Press and the Coming of the Spanish-American War," *Historian*, XXXI (1969), 251–267, examines eighteen newspapers and finds only two outspokenly jingoistic.

Ronald Spector, "Who Planned the Attack on Manila Bay?" *Mid-America*, LIII (1971), 94–102, plays down any Roosevelt intrigue by noting that U.S. Navy officers drew up plans as early as June, 1896.

Ch. 32. AMERICA AS A GREAT POWER, 1898–1900

See new references on p. 485.

Paolo E. Coletta, "McKinley, the Peace Negotiations, and the Acquisition of the Philippines," *Pacific Hist. Rev.*, XXX (1961), 341–350 concludes that the President, far from being a drifter, took a series of affirmative actions that resulted in acquiring the Philippines.

Thomas McCormick, "Insular Imperialism and the Open Door: The China Market and the Spanish-American War," *ibid.*, XXXII (1963), 155–169 concludes that the United States annexed Pacific possessions primarily to acquire a large part of the China market on an Open Door basis.

Charles Vevier, "American Continentalism: An Idea of Expansion, 1845–1910," *Amer. Hist. Rev.*, LXV (1960), 323–335 regards overseas expansion as a logical extension of the long-held ideal that the Republic would spread itself over the continent.

Christopher Lasch, "The Anti-Imperialists, the Philippines, and the Inequality of Man," *Jour. of Southern Hist.*, XXIV (1958), 319–331 holds that the anti-imperialists were on no higher moral ground than the imperialists:

many of them believed that the Filipinos were an inferior breed, but, unlike the imperialists, were willing to turn them adrift. The South wanted no more race problems, complicated by coolie labor.

J. A. S. Grenville, "Diplomacy and War Plans in the United States, 1890–1917," *Transactions of the Royal Historical Society*, Ser. V, vol. XI (London, 1961), 1–21 describes how American military power caught up with the Monroe Doctrine but not with the Open Door; the Navy was much more eager than the State Department for bases in Asia.

D. L. McKee, "Samuel Gompers, the A.F. of L., and Imperialism, 1895–1900," *The Historian*, XXI (1959), 187–199 demonstrates that this organization favored a free Cuba in the interests of free labor; it fought overseas annexations in opposition to cheap immigrant labor.

P. C. Kennedy, "La Follette's Imperialist Flirtation," *Pacific Hist. Rev.*, XXIX (1960), 131–144 shows that while campaigning for governor in 1900, La Follette vigorously supported the war and imperialism, possibly for political expediency. Later he turned against imperialism and dollar diplomacy as instruments of exploitation by the trusts.

Geoffrey Seed, "British Reactions to American Imperialism Reflected in Journals of Opinion, 1898–1900," *Pol. Sci. Quar.*, LXXIII (1958), 254–272 reveals that British opinion favored American imperialism, for such reasons as racial affinity, the white man's burden, and possible support for British policies in China.

R. C. Brown, "Goldwin Smith and Anti-Imperialism," *Canadian Hist. Rev.*, XLIII (1962), 93–105 notes that while Canada generally applauded the Spanish-American and Boer Wars, Smith (a Briton moved to Canada) bitterly opposed both and aided the American anti-imperialists.

Harold Baron, "Anti-Imperialism and the Democrats," *Science and Society*, XXI (1957), 222–239 contends that the Democrats showed little interest in imperialism during the Congressional elections of 1898, and that even in the campaign of 1900 Bryan was inclined to soft-pedal it, especially in silverite areas.

8TH ED. REFS. Walter LaFeber, *The New Empire: An Interpretation of American Expansion, 1860–1898* (Ithaca, 1963), argues that the Spanish War did not open the eyes of the U.S. to commercial opportunities in the Far East; many businessmen were already aware of them. McKinley, fully in control of policy, was quite aware of the existence of the Philippines before the war, and he took them, not primarily for direct economic returns, but as a staging area for hoped-for commerce in Asia. The image of a wishy-washy and drifting leader must be abandoned, the author believes.

H. Wayne Morgan, in *William McKinley and His America* (Syracuse, 1963), and in the much sketchier *America's Road to Empire: The War with Spain and Overseas Expansion* (New York, 1965), concludes that McKinley, at an early date after Dewey's victory, decided on all of the Philippines, but gave the impression that he was following public opinion rather than leading it. He flattered men by letting them think they had influenced him. See also the same author's, "William McKinley as a Political Leader," *Review of Politics*, XXVIII (1966), 417–432.

John A. S. Grenville and George B. Young, in *Politics, Strategy, and American Diplomacy: Studies in Foreign Policy, 1873–1917* (New Haven, 1966), show that the high strategy of destroying the Spanish fleet at Manila, worked out in the Navy Department in 1896, imprisoned foreign policy. Before Dewey's victory neither McKinley nor other prominent officials in Washington sought to secure the Philippines as such.

H. Wayne Morgan, ed., *Making Peace with Spain: The Diary of Whitelaw Reid, September–December, 1898* (Austin, Tex., 1965), is especially valuable in depicting the clashes within the five-man peace commission in Paris over expansion into the Philippines. Their differences prefigured the upcoming debate at home on imperialism.

David F. Healy, *The United States in Cuba, 1898–1902* (Madison, Wis., 1963), details the development of a policy for Cuba (largely by the War Department), which led to the Platt Amendment and the reciprocity treaty of 1902, and which, the author believes, set a pattern for U.S. overseas policy in the years ahead. Economic concerns, he holds, were not over-shadowing.

R. G. Neale, *Great Britain and United States Expansion: 1898–1900* (East Lansing, Mich., 1966), concludes that Anglo-American friendship, brought to fruition by the Spanish War, did not cause either nation to put sentiment above hard-headed realism in pursuing its own policies. Britain did not urge the United States to enter the Far Eastern arena (with the Philippines), and did not push for the Open Door, which was somewhat out of line with British policy. American nonco-operation with the British in Asia impelled Downing Street toward the Anglo-Japanese Alliance of 1902. Britain realized that a too-open courting of America would be self-defeating by arousing the Anglophobes in the United States.

Bradford Perkins, *The Great Rapprochement: England and the United States, 1895–1914* (New York, 1968), describes in broad terms how and why Britain welcomed America as a participant in imperialism.

Thomas J. McCormick, *China Market: America's Quest for Informal Empire, 1893–1901* (Chicago, 1967), considers America's interest in a non-colonial commercial empire in the Far East in terms of a desire to cure the current socio-economic malaise, which had grown in large part out of in-dustrial overproduction.

Paul A. Varg, "The Myth of the China Market, 1890–1914," *Amer. Hist. Rev.*, LXXIII (1968), 742–758, explains in detail why the wildly extravagant hopes of American exporters for a huge China market were foredoomed to disappointment.

Marilyn B. Young, "American Expansion, 1870–1900: The Far East," in Barton J. Bernstein, ed., *Towards a New Past: Dissenting Essays in American History* (New York, 1968), pp. 176–201, sharply challenges the view of the "Wisconsin school" that the drive for markets is the primary explanation of expansionism at the turn of the century. Both business and government failed to pursue economic opportunities in China, while Washington energetically defended the rights of missionaries. Expansion, the author holds, must be viewed in the light of many factors, including the imperialism of other powers and social tensions at home.

Ernest R. May, *American Imperialism: A Speculative Essay* (New York, 1968), examines the various elements in the impulse toward imperialism, showing how it unexpectedly rose and suddenly died. There is emphasis on the impact of the discussion of imperialism abroad on the small and sophisti-cated American Establishment that provided the essential leadership of public opinion in the United States.

Robert L. Beisner, *Twelve Against Empire: The Anti-Imperialists, 1898–1900* (New York, 1968), deals with a group of Republicans who failed in their battle against imperialism largely because they were too divided, too old (average age 69), and too deeply rooted in the past.

Richard E. Welch, Jr., "Senator George Frisbie Hoar and the Defeat of Anti-Imperialism, 1898–1900," *Historian,* XXVI (1964), 362–380, shows that the Hoar–Schurz plan of a protectorate over the Philippines, as an alternative to annexation, held promise but failed partly because of divisions among the anti-imperialist leaders.

E. Berkeley Tompkins, "The Old Guard: A Study of the Anti-Imperialist Leadership," *Historian,* XXX (1968), 366–388, analyzes in terms of age, profession, etc., the high-principled members of this elite group.

E. Berkeley Tompkins, "Scylla and Charybdis: The Anti-Imperialist Dilemma in the Election of 1900," *Pacific Hist. Rev.,* XXXVI (1967), 143–161, notes that the anti-imperialists, unhappy over their forced association with the financial heresies of Bryan, did not regard the outcome of the election as a defeat for their cause. Relieved of Bryan, they pressed on toward their goal.

Philip W. Kennedy, "The Racial Overtones of Imperialism as a Campaign Issue, 1900," *Mid-America,* XLVIII (1966), 196–205, concludes that the Democrats (racists in the South) opposed taking on a new race problem in the Philippines. The Republicans, who had "freed" the black man, were seeking to "enslave" the brown man.

D. J. Tweton, "Imperialism versus Prosperity in the Election of 1900," *North Dakota Quarterly,* XXX (1962), 50–55, provides further evidence that prosperity was the crucial factor.

Richard E. Welch, Jr., "Opponents and Colleagues: George Frisbie Hoar and Henry Cabot Lodge, 1898–1904," *New England Quar.,* XXXIX (1966), 182–209, concludes that while the two Senators were at odds on the great issues of imperialism, they managed to avoid a rupture in their personal relations.

Robert L. Beisner, "Thirty Years before Manila: E. L. Godkin, Carl Schurz, and Anti-Imperialism in the Gilded Age," *Historian,* XXX (1968), 561–577, shows that these two men waged verbal war against expansion for a third of a century before 1898.

Geoffrey Seed, "British Views of American Policy in the Philippines Reflected in Journals of Opinion, 1898–1907," *Jour. of American Studies,* II (1968), 49–64, notes that British periodicals approved the takeover but became increasingly critical of U.S. mismanagement.

N. Ray Gilmore, "Mexico and the Spanish-American War," *Hispanic Amer. Hist. Rev.,* XLIII (1963), 511–525, reveals that the Mexican government, for realistic reasons, remained formally neutral; yet there was much public sympathy for Spain. The resulting anti-Yankee feeling gave impetus to Pan-Hispanism.

Paul S. Holbo, "Perspectives on American Foreign Policy, 1890–1916: Expansion and World Power," *Social Studies,* LVIII (1967), 246–256, is a useful bibliographical survey.

9TH ED. REFS. David Healy, *US Expansionism: The Imperialist Urge in the 1890's* (Madison, Wis., 1970) assesses all factors, including economic, without going overboard for any one.

E. Berkeley Tompkins, *Anti-Imperialism in the United States: The Great Debate, 1890–1920* (Philadelphia, 1970) complements Healy (above) by describing fully the rise and demise of this protest group.

Marilyn B. Young, *The Rhetoric of Empire: American China Policy, 1895–1901* (Cambridge, Mass., 1968) shows that many factors were involved, aside from the presumed pressure for more markets.

Paul A. Varg, *The Making of a Myth: The United States and China, 1897–*

1912 (East Lansing, Mich., 1868) consists of ten essays which examine various myths, including the exaggerated role given John Hay's Open Door and the presumed predominance of American business influences.

James H. Hitchman, *Leonard Wood and Cuban Independence, 1898–1902* (The Hague, 1971) analyzes the military occupation.

Paul S. Holbo, "Economics, Emotion, and Expansion: An Emerging Foreign Policy," in H. Wayne Morgan, ed., *The Gilded Age* (rev. ed., 1970), 199–221, downgrades the pressure for foreign markets in turning America into a reluctant imperialist after 1865; the author stresses political, psychological, and other factors as well.

Richard E. Welch, Jr., "Motives and Policy Objectives of Anti-Imperialists, 1898," *Mid-America*, LI (1969), 117–129, shows that only a minority of the anti-imperialists placed "any great emphasis" on economic factors.

Jerry Israel, " 'For God, for China and for Yale'—The Open Door in Action," *Amer. Hist. Rev.*, LXXV (1970), 796–807, demonstrates that the Open Door involved a broad-front interrelationship among American mercantile, industrial, financial, and missionary endeavors.

Ch. 33. CANAL ZONE DIPLOMACY, 1900–1921

Useful background accounts are G. E. Mowry, *The Era of Theodore Roosevelt* (New York, 1958); W. H. Harbaugh, *Power and Responsibility: The Life and Times of Theodore Roosevelt* (New York, 1961); and E. C. Wagenknecht, *The Seven Worlds of Theodore Roosevelt* (New York, 1958). The last-named book advances the interesting thesis that Roosevelt's intervention in Panama may have headed off a French intervention, with serious complications.

A. E. Campbell, *Great Britain and the United States, 1895–1903* (London, 1960) shows that an American owned and fortified Isthmian canal would put Britain at a military disadvantage, assuming the United States to be a potential enemy; hence London held out for nonfortification in the first Hay-Pauncefote Treaty. But predicating continuing American friendship, the British finally surrendered every major point. Except for an Anglo-American war, the stronger the grip of the United States on the canal, the better for Britain. The British thus got all the commercial and military advantages they sought, plus American friendship.

J. A. S. Grenville, "Great Britain and the Isthmian Canal, 1898–1901," *Amer. Hist. Rev.*, LXI (1955), 48–69 covers somewhat the same ground, and concludes that, by removing current and future friction, the British in the second Hay-Pauncefote Treaty recognized the eventual supremacy of the United States in the Western Hemisphere. Britain's distresses in Europe and the Far East promoted this decision, although there is no truth in the myth that the British yielded the Caribbean in return for American support against Russia in the Far East.

C. D. Ameringer, "The Panama Canal Lobby of Philippe Bunau-Varilla and William Nelson Cromwell," *Amer. Hist. Rev.*, LXVIII (1963), 346–363 proves that these two men worked closely together (contrary to some accounts) and with Mark Hanna and the Colombian Minister in Washington (also to some extent with the State Department) in achieving the brilliant coup that caused Congress to abandon Nicaragua in favor of the Panama route.

R. A. Friedlander, "A Reassessment of Roosevelt's Role in the Panamanian

Revolution of 1903," *Western Political Quar.*, XIV (1961), 535–543 is a one-sided defense which questionably concludes that T.R.'s actions "were morally straightforward and legally justified."

D. H. Burton, "Theodore Roosevelt: Confident Imperialist," *Review of Politics*, XXIII (1961), 356–377 exhibits T.R.'s lifelong enthusiasm for the white man's burden and the mission of superior peoples.

8TH ED. REFS. Charles D. Ameringer, "Philippe Bunau-Varilla: New Light on the Panama Canal Treaty," *Hispanic Amer. Hist. Rev.*, XLVI (1966), 28–52, concludes that Bunau-Varilla, though technically authorized to make a treaty, violated "the letter and spirit" of his instructions. He gave away too much, misrepresented the need for haste to Panama (which he had not seen since 1887), and conspired in questionable dealings with Secretary Hay, who was fully aware of the grossly one-sided nature of the bargain.

Allan R. Millett, *The Politics of Intervention: The Military Occupation of Cuba, 1906–1909* (Columbus, O., 1967), raises the question as to whether temporary occupation, unaccompanied by intensive reform, can solve persistent problems.

9TH ED. REFS. G. A. Mellander, *The United States in Panamanian Politics: The Intriguing Formative Years* (Danville, Ill., 1971) argues that the United States from 1903 to 1908 was more acted upon than acting, more the seduced than the seducer, especially in the revolution of 1903.

Ch. 34. BIG STICK DIPLOMACY

8TH ED. REFS. Bradford Perkins, *The Great Rapprochement: England and the United States, 1895–1914* (New York, 1968), deals in broad terms, and with due regard for British backgrounds, with the Hay-Pauncefote Treaty, the Alaska Boundary, Japanese-American relations, and the Roosevelt Corollary, to which "Britain reacted favorably" (p. 194).

Nicholas Roosevelt, *Theodore Roosevelt: The Man as I Knew Him* (New York, 1957), is by a cousin. He relies largely on his memory of many conversations to support the Rooseveltian version of the controversial issues in foreign affairs (Chapter 13).

F. Bradford Burns, *The Unwritten Alliance: Rio-Branco and Brazilian-American Relations* (New York, 1966), deals with the Brazilian Foreign Minister (1902–1912) who achieved a *rapprochement* by shifting the diplomatic axis from London to Washington. He approved Roosevelt's Panama coup and the Roosevelt Corollary to the Monroe Doctrine.

Lejeune Cummins, "The Formulation of the 'Platt' Amendment," *The Americas*, XXIII (1967), 370–389, concludes that the evidence overwhelmingly supports the view that "its sole purpose was strategic."

James H. Hitchman, "The Platt Amendment Revisited: A Bibliographical Survey," *The Americas*, XXIII (1967), 343–369, is especially valuable in presenting Cuban views, which were largely unfavorable.

9TH ED. REFS. David H. Burton, *Theodore Roosevelt, Confident Imperialist* (Philadelphia, 1968) argues that T.R.'s imperialism was shaped largely by his pre-Presidential experiences and not by bookish Darwinism. The author is more concerned with ideology than diplomacy.

Raymond A. Esthus, *Theodore Roosevelt and the International Rivalries* (Waltham, Mass., 1970) outlines T. R.'s concern over developments in Europe, Africa, and East Asia, where he largely lost interest after 1905.

Allan R. Millett, *The Politics of Intervention: The Military Occupation of*

Cuba, 1906–1909 (Columbus, Ohio, 1968) points out that although numerous reforms were introduced, conditions reverted to near normal after the U.S. left, as elsewhere in the Caribbean.

Edward B. Parsons, "The German-American Crisis of 1902–1903," *The Historian,* XXXIII (1971), 436–452, uses fresh documents to show that T.R. advanced war preparations and brought pressure on the Kaiser through various indirect means. The ultimate story about Venezuela sounds less preposterous.

Paul S. Holbo, "Perilous Obscurity: Public Diplomacy and the Press in the Venezuelan Crisis, 1902–1903," *Historian,* XXXII (1970), 428–448, concludes that an examination of the domestic and foreign press does not disprove (or prove) Roosevelt's story of an ultimatum; the deployment of the fleet was ultimatum enough.

Douglas Cole, "Allen Aylesworth on the Alaska Boundary Award," *Canadian Hist. Rev.,* LII (1971), 472–477 presents some scant evidence that Lord Alverstone was not "consciously" influenced by T.R.'s threats.

Tom T. Lewis, "Franco-American Relations during the First Moroccan Crisis," *Mid-America,* LV (1937), 21–36, concludes that T.R. gave only "very limited support" to France; his primary goal was to prevent a general war, and secondarily to promote the Open Door.

Ch. 35. THEODORE ROOSEVELT AND THE FAR EAST

See new references on p. 528.

Roger Daniels, *The Politics of Prejudice: The Anti-Japanese Movement in California and the Struggle for Japanese Exclusion* (Berkeley, 1962) deals with the problem from the standpoint of domestic pressures, particularly the illiberalism of the Progressives.

W. R. Braisted, "The United States Navy's Dilemma in the Pacific, 1906–1909," *Pacific Hist. Rev.,* XXVI (1957), 235–244 describes the difficulties of protecting America's two-ocean interests with a one-ocean navy. Before 1905 the Russian fleet had indirectly protected the Philippines by holding Japan in balance; after that date Japan ceased to be a sure friend and became a probable enemy. By November, 1909, Germany had passed America as the second naval power, and some American experts were sure that she would challenge the Monroe Doctrine in South America even at the risk of war. Rather than have two relatively weak fleets, Washington concentrated the Navy in the Atlantic and relied on a holding operation in the Far East.

W. E. Snowbarger, "Pearl Harbor in Pacific Strategy, 1898–1908," *The Historian,* XIX (1957), 361–384 shows that not until the Japanese war scare of 1907 was the decision taken to make Pearl Harbor the major naval base in the Pacific. A holding operation was envisaged for the Philippines, with later recovery, as in 1941–1945. The world cruise of the fleet demonstrated the indefensibility of the islands: the Navy was dependent on foreign colliers and far-distant repair yards.

D. C. Gordon, "Roosevelt's 'Smart Yankee Trick,'" *Pacific Hist. Rev.,* XXX (1961), 351–358 deals with T.R.'s behind-the-scenes attempt to bypass London and deal directly with Canada and Australia in an effort to establish a common front against Japanese immigration. He may have hastened their independence in naval and foreign affairs.

Fred Greene, "The Military View of American National Policy, 1904–1940," *Amer. Hist. Rev.,* LXVI (1961), 354–377 discusses the views of the military planners on foreign policies and their efforts to devise measures to implement them.

R. A. Esthus, "The Taft-Katsura Agreement—Reality or Myth?" *Jour. of Mod. Hist.*, XXXI (1959), 46–51 concludes that the so-called "agreed memorandum" was not a highly secret bargain: it merely recorded a conversation which did not involve a guarantee of the Philippines by Japan in exchange for America's recognizing Japanese suzerainty in Korea. Even though these two issues were discussed, they were not quid pro quos. Some four months earlier T.R. had informally advised the Japanese leaders that he favored their taking Korea. The "agreement" was that the "agreed memorandum" reflected the views of Taft and Katsura.

R. A. Esthus, "The Changing Concept of the Open Door, 1899–1910," *Miss. Valley Hist. Rev.*, XLVI (1959), 435–454 contends that Willard Straight and F. M. Huntington Wilson, two official underlings, perverted Hay's original concept into something that had no reasonable chance of success. They expanded the idea of commercial equality into equality of investment opportunity and an aggressive anti-Japanese policy in behalf of China. Both the Japanese and historians, thinking in terms of the original Open Door, have been confused by this perversion.

R. E. Minger, "Taft's Missions to Japan: A Study in Personal Diplomacy," *Pacific Hist. Rev.*, XXX (1961), 279–294 demonstrates that the two visits, in 1905 and 1907, went off well, but Taft was somewhat naïve regarding Japan's expansionist designs, especially on Korea. Apparently he saw no conflict between the Taft-Katsura understanding and the future of the Open Door in China.

S. W. Livermore, "The American Navy as a Factor in World Politics, 1903–1913," *Amer. Hist. Rev.*, LXIII (1958), 863–879 discloses that United States naval cruises during these years were used to demonstrate friendliness toward France and Britain, while snubbing the Germans and consequently increasing illwill.

Warren Schiff, "German Military Penetration into Mexico during the late Díaz Period," *Hispanic Amer. Hist. Rev.*, XXXIX (1959), 568–579 observes that the Germans, with scant success, tried to displace French influence and weapons in the army from about 1900 to 1910, and also to build up the Mexican army as a counterweight against the United States. Germany did not go all-out for fear of provoking the Americans unduly.

8TH ED. REFS. Raymond A. Esthus, *Theodore Roosevelt and Japan* (Seattle, 1966), carries the story in detail from 1904 to 1909, adding more depth to the older works of Dennett, Bailey, and Beale, and using Japanese microfilms. Roosevelt's support of Japan against various Asian adversaries is regarded as good power politics, in view of America's weakness in the Far East. Esthus believes that the subsequent worsening of the immigration and Manchurian problems was the responsibility of later Presidents. The battleship cruise was designed to quiet Japan, but Roosevelt's statements to this effect were much more emphatic after he announced the decision. The Root-Takahira Agreement did not give America a "free hand" in Manchuria; it merely recognized the rights already established by Japan.

Charles E. Neu, *An Uncertain Friendship: Theodore Roosevelt and Japan, 1906–1909* (Cambridge, Mass., 1967), covers essentially the same ground as Esthus (above), except for the Russo-Japanese War, but with somewhat different emphasis. Facing the realities of power politics, T.R. placed a low value on U.S. interests in China and Manchuria. His consistent pro-Japanese policy was "shrewd, skillful, and responsible." If the battleship cruise was designed as a menace, it left Japan cold. China was deliberately slighted by Roosevelt's sending only a detachment of the fleet to Amoy.

Charles E. Neu, "Theodore Roosevelt and American Involvement in the Far East, 1901–1909," *Pacific Hist. Rev.*, XXXV (1966), 433–449, in broader terms than the book (above), treats T.R. as one who regarded Japan as upholding American interests in the Far East, and who therefore was deeply concerned about establishing American military power in that area.

Robert A. Hart, *The Great White Fleet: Its Voyage Around the World, 1907–1909* (Boston, 1965), reveals in lurid detail the magnitude of Roosevelt's gamble. The sixteen obsolescent battleships displayed grave technical defects: two had to be replaced at San Francisco. The ships and their quarrelling officers were too old. The fleet was fatally dependent on foreign colliers, which would have been withdrawn in the event of war in the Far East. The Japanese were not overawed (British experts were betting on them). Shortly after the American fleet left Japan, the Japanese paraded 123 warships of all classes in a line 20 miles long. Roosevelt's deliberate snub of China (with a partial fleet) ended what scant hope there was of a *rapprochement* with both the Chinese and the Germans.

John A. White, *The Diplomacy of the Russo-Japanese War* (Princeton, N.J., 1964), is not so strong on the American side as the Esthus book (cited above), which used more of the relevant Japanese and other manuscripts. White shows that the Japanese leaders, at the very beginning of the war, envisaged Roosevelt as a possible mediator (after they had won what they wanted).

Jongsuk Chay, "The Taft-Katsura Memorandum Reconsidered," *Pacific Hist. Rev.*, XXXVII (1968), 321–326, concludes that the document was "at least an understanding—not quite an agreement, but more than a mere exchange of views."

9TH ED. REFS. Eugene P. Trani, *The Treaty of Portsmouth* (Lexington, Ky., 1969) uses the Japanese archives and some Russian materials to add details to previous accounts.

Edward B. Parsons, "Roosevelt's Containment of the Russo-Japanese War," *Pacific Hist. Rev.*, XXXVIII (1969), 21–43, presents some suggestive but not completely convincing evidence that T.R. may have forcefully warned Germany and Japan to keep hands off.

Ch. 36. TAFT AND DOLLAR DIPLOMACY

Dana G. Munro, *Intervention and Dollar Diplomacy in the Caribbean, 1900–1921* (Princeton, N.J., 1964), reveals that the interventions were primarily for political and strategic, rather than economic, reasons.

Robert F. Smith, "Cuba: Laboratory for Dollar Diplomacy, 1898–1917," *Historian*, XXVIII (1966), 586–609, argues that U.S. Dollar Diplomacy in Cuba, whatever its short-run effect, in the long run produced instability.

John P. Campbell, "Taft, Roosevelt, and the Arbitration Treaties of 1911," *Jour. of Amer. Hist.*, LIII (1966), 279–298, looks upon Roosevelt's opposition to the abortive Taft arbitration treaties, which commanded widespread popular support, as contributing importantly to T.R.'s decision to challenge Taft for the presidential nomination in 1912.

Naomi W. Cohen, "The Abrogation of the Russo-American Treaty of 1832," *Jewish Social Studies* (1963), XXV, 3–41, credits the pressure campaign of the American Jewish Committee with having had a large hand in achieving abrogation by Congress.

Alvin C. Gluek, Jr., "The Passamaquoddy Bay Treaty, 1910: A Diplomatic

Sideshow in Canadian-American Relations," *Canadian Hist. Rev.*, XLVII (1966), 1–21, details the difficulties of negotiating a treaty with Britain making a minor rectification of the northeastern boundary and ending the last of the Canadian boundary disputes.

9TH ED. REFS. Walter V. and Marie V. Scholes, in *The Foreign Policies of the Taft Administration* (Columbia, Mo., 1970) throw additional light on aggressive Dollar Diplomacy in Latin America and China. In China it was especially unsuccessful because of impingement on the interests of the other great powers.

Nemai S. Bose, *American Attitude and Policy to the Nationalist Movement in China, 1911–1921* (Bombay, 1970) argues that the U.S. failed to support or even understand Chinese nationalism during this critical period.

W. M. Baker, "A Case Study of Anti-Americanism in English-Speaking Canada: The Election Campaign of 1911," *Canadian Hist. Rev.*, LI (1970), 426–449, concludes that the outcome was largely the result of imperial considerations, not bitter hatred for the U.S.

K. A. Clements, "Manifest Destiny and Canadian Reciprocity in 1911," *Pacific Hist. Rev.*, XLII (1973), 32–52, demonstrates that outright annexation was a bogey, raised chiefly in Canada; the real issue was the Americanization of Canada.

Clifford L. Egan, "Pressure Groups, the Department of State, and the Abrogation of the Russian-American Treaty of 1832," *Procs. of the Amer. Philosophical Soc.*, CXV (1971), 328–334, shows how Jewish-Americans forced Taft to the futility of ending the pact in response to alleged passport discrimination against Jewish-Americans.

Ch. 37. WILSON AND THE "NEW" DIPLOMACY, 1913–1917

A. S. Link, *Wilson: The Struggle for Neutrality, 1914–1915* (Princeton, 1960) is the third volume in a valuable biographical study by the foremost Wilson scholar. Troubled relations with Mexico are dealt with in depth, as are the interventions in Haiti and Santo Domingo.

Arthur Walworth, *Woodrow Wilson* (2 vols., New York, 1958) covers essentially the same ground in more general terms. "Among the White House family, Huerta's name could not be mentioned without a grimace and a scorching adjective . . . (p. 358)."

Earl Latham, ed., *The Philosophy and Policies of Woodrow Wilson* (Chicago, 1958) provides interesting insights, some personal, in sixteen chapters; the four chapters on foreign policy by four different experts have all been published elsewhere.

E. H. Buehrig, ed., *Wilson's Foreign Policy in Perspective* (Bloomington, Ind., 1957) is a series of lectures on subjects ranging from Colonel House, through collective security, Wilson's Far Eastern policy, and his Latin American policy to a British view of Wilson.

R. E. Quirk, *An Affair of Honor: Woodrow Wilson and the Occupation of Veracruz* (Lexington, Ky., 1962) concludes that Wilson, in pursuance of his vendetta with Huerta, acted precipitately and self-righteously, without proper information and without realizing that there would be considerable bloodshed. The Mexican press, reviling the "pigs of *Yanquilandia*" (p. 107), especially resented Wilson's attitude of moral superiority.

C. C. Clendenen, *The United States and Pancho Villa* (Ithaca, N.Y., 1961), reveals that relations with Villa were friendly until Wilson recognized Carranza. Villa's raiders at Columbus suffered heavy losses; the Pershing expedition was not a mortifying failure. Its orders were to disperse the outlaw band (not bring Villa back dead or alive); in this it was completely successful. Villa never again seriously threatened the American border.

T. L. Karnes, *The Failure of Union: Central America, 1824–1960* (Chapel Hill, N.C., 1961) emphasizes the undermining of the Central American Court of Justice by the refusal of the United States and Nicaragua to abide by its decision regarding the Bryan-Chamorro Treaty.

P. E. Coletta, ed., "Bryan Briefs Lansing," *Pacific Hist. Rev.*, XXVII (1958), 383–396 presents a lengthy memorandum that Bryan drew up in 1915 summarizing the state of negotiations with individual countries. It reveals the Secretary's preoccupation with the "cooling-off" treaties and relations with Latin America, especially the problems growing out of the pending Nicaraguan treaty.

T. C. Hinckley, "Wilson, Huerta, and the Twenty-one Gun Salute," *The Historian*, XXII (1960), 197–206 covers essentially the same ground as the Quirk book, listed above.

G. R. Donnell, "The United States Military Government at Veracruz, Mexico," in T. E. Cotner and C. E. Castañeda, eds., *Essays in Mexican History* (Austin, Tex., 1958), 229–247 notes that the regime of General Funston, though cleaning up the city and governing benevolently under Mexican law, was highly unpopular, and probably strengthened Huerta in his quarrel with President Wilson.

L. G. Kahle, "Robert Lansing and the Recognition of Venustiano Carranza," *Hispanic Amer. Hist. Rev.*, XXXVIII (1958), 353–372 describes how Washington, unsuccessfully exerting pressure to secure safeguards for American financial interests, delayed *de jure* recognition nearly two years after the *de facto* recognition of October, 1915. Recognition was finally extended because American national interests demanded a quick solution of the Mexican problem so as to free Wilson's hands to deal with the European crisis.

G. J. Rausch, Jr., "The Exile and Death of Victoriano Huerta," *ibid.*, XLII (1962), 133–151 relates how Huerta, after fleeing to Europe, came to the United States (1915), where he received German money with which to foment a new revolution in Mexico and embarrass Wilson. Arrested in Texas, he died before he could be tried. Had he reached Mexico, he might well have stirred up a dangerous diversion.

8TH ED. REFS. E. David Cronon, ed., in *The Cabinet Diaries of Josephus Daniels, 1913–1921* (Lincoln, Nebr., 1963), presents interesting details on the bankers' consortium, Mexico, and the crisis with Japan over California's alien land legislation. The latter brought serious discussion in Cabinet meetings of a possible Japanese attack.

Barton J. Bernstein and F. A. Leib, "Progressive Republican Senators and American Imperialism, 1898–1916: A Reappraisal," *Mid-America*, L (1968), 163–205, questions an earlier thesis of William E. Leuchtenburg by concluding that there was no "intimate connection" between progressivism and imperialism, including the dollar imperialism of the Taft and Wilson years.

Paolo E. Coletta, "Secretary of State William Jennings Bryan and 'Deserving Democrats,'" *Mid-America*, XLVIII (1966), 75–98, demonstrates that Bryan, concerned with merit as well as partisanship, was no worse a spoilsman than some other Cabinet members.

Paolo E. Coletta, "Bryan, Anti-Imperialism and Missionary Diplomacy,"

Nebraska History, XLIV (1963), 167–187, shows that Bryan's early anti-imperialism gave way to Dollar Imperialism when he became a "do-gooder" Secretary of State.

Paolo E. Coletta, "William Jennings Bryan and the United States–Colombia Impasse, 1903–1921," *Hispanic Amer. Hist. Rev.*, XLVII (1967), 486–501, causes Bryan to appear to good advantage as a pioneer Good Neighborite in his unsuccessful efforts to shepherd a Colombia indemnity treaty through the Senate.

Paolo E. Coletta, " 'The Most Thankless Task': Bryan and the California Alien Land Legislation," *Pacific Hist. Rev.*, XXXVI (1967), 163–187, portrays Bryan's "Jovian patience" in soothing Japan but not preventing the offensive legislation.

Spencer C. Olin, Jr., "European Immigrant and Oriental Alien: Acceptance and Rejection by the California Legislature of 1913," *Pacific Hist. Rev.*, XXXV (1966), 303–315, concludes that Bryan's mission to California was hopeless, and that Governor Johnson rather disingenuously supported the Alien Land Law to promote his own political fortunes.

William S. Coker, "United States-British Diplomacy over Mexico, 1913," unpublished doctoral dissertation (University of Oklahoma, 1965), exploits recently available British manuscripts to deny that Wilson espoused the tolls repeal as a part of a deal with the British to win their support for his Mexican policy. But the British did ratify the pending arbitration treaty shortly after Wilson came out for repeal. The author associates the tolls repeal in a significant way with the proposed renewal of the Arbitration Treaty of 1908. See W. S. Coker, "The Panama Canal Tolls Controversy: A Different Perspective," *Jour. of Amer. Hist.*, LV (1968), 555–564.

Bradford Perkins, *The Great Rapprochement: England and the United States, 1895–1914* (New York, 1968), makes it clear that there was no "deal" about tolls repeal because the British had never developed (contrary to American suspicions) any hostility to Wilson's Mexican policy.

Walter V. Scholes and Marie V. Scholes in "Wilson, Grey, and Huerta," *Pacific Hist. Rev.*, XXXVII (1968), 151–162, conclude that while Britain deemed Wilson's Mexican policy unwise and made some little effort to change it, Foreign Secretary Grey nevertheless tried to cooperate with the U.S., even though there was no demonstrable "deal" on the canal tolls issue.

Peter A. R. Calvert, "The Murray Contract: An Episode in International Finance and Diplomacy," *Pacific Hist. Rev.*, XXXV (1966), 203–224, shows how U.S. diplomacy thwarted a British attempt to secure an oil concession in Colombia in 1913.

George W. Baker has several articles showing that Wilson's idealistic policies were made more realistic by his three secretaries of state: "The Wilson Administration and Cuba, 1913–1921," *Mid-America*, XLVI (1964), 48–63; "The Woodrow Wilson Administration and El Salvadorean Relations, 1913–1921," *Social Studies*, LVI (1965), 97–103; "The Woodrow Wilson Administration and Guatemalan Relations," *Historian*, XXVII (1965), 155–169; "Ideals and Realities in the Wilson Administration's Relations with Honduras," *The Americas*, XXI (1964), 3–19. The same author's "Woodrow Wilson's Use of the Non-Recognition Policy in Costa Rica," *The Americas*, XXII (1965), 3–21, describes the bitter fruits of a policy that was also applied without signal success in Mexico.

9TH ED. REFS. Paolo E. Coletta, *William Jennings Bryan: Progressive Poli-*

tician and Moral Statesman, 1909–1915 (Lincoln, Nebr., 1969) [vol. II], the most exhaustive biography, gives Bryan higher marks as Secretary of State than did contemporaries.

Louis W. Koenig, *Bryan: A Political Biography of William Jennings Bryan* (New York, 1971) is a first-rate, one-volume biography that sympathetically presents the familiar story of Bryan's diplomacy.

Kenneth J. Grieb, *The United States and Huerta* (Lincoln, Nebr., 1969) is rather favorable to Huerta and critical of Wilson's moralistic, blundering intervention.

P. Edward Haley, *Revolution and Intervention: The Diplomacy of Taft and Wilson with Mexico, 1910–1917* (Cambridge, Mass., 1970) adds new details to the main outlines of the conventional accounts.

Seward W. Livermore, " 'Deserving Democrats': The Foreign Service under Woodrow Wilson," *South Atlantic Quar.*, LXIX (1970), 144–160, demonstrates that Wilson worked hand in glove with Bryan and Lansing in his zeal to reward Democratic hacks with offices.

Noel Pugach, "Making the Open Door Work: Paul S. Reinsch in China, 1913–1919," *Pacific Hist. Rev.*, XXXVIII (1969), 157–175, describes the largely unsuccessful efforts of President Wilson's minister to keep the Open Door ajar and induce businessmen to enter.

C. W. Trow, "Woodrow Wilson and the Mexican Interventionist Movement of 1919," *Jour. of Amer. Hist.*, LVIII (1971), 46–72, describes how a recovering Wilson thwarted a serious attempt by Senate Republicans (responding to oil interests) to force a protectorate on Mexico.

Ch. 38. WAGING NEUTRALITY, 1914–1915

See the new books on Wilson listed above for the previous chapter.

A. S. Link, *Wilson: The Struggle for Neutrality, 1914–1915* (Princeton, 1960) concludes that Wilson remained commendably neutral, though such neutrality worked against Germany. His policy was based on expediency and realism, not idealism. The author surprisingly argues that German propaganda, contrary to an accepted view, was not bungling, inept, or inadequate. Secretary Bryan is somewhat downgraded, Lansing upgraded. Wilson appears patient, cautious, canny, detached, and understanding.

E. R. May, *The World War and American Isolation, 1914–1917* (Cambridge, Mass., 1959) is the most significant over-all synthesis in recent years. It stresses the interaction of domestic pressures with diplomacy in America, Britain, and especially Germany. Wilson is portrayed as working not so much for neutrality as for the best interests of the United States.

F. T. Epstein, "Germany and the United States: Basic Patterns of Conflict and Understanding," in G. L. Anderson, ed., *Issues and Conflicts* (Lawrence, Kans., 1959), pp. 284–314 shows how antipathy toward America grew in Germany, especially among intellectuals, before, during, and after World War I.

Marion C. Siney, "British Official Histories of the Blockade of the Central Powers during the First World War," *Amer. Hist. Rev.*, LXVIII (1963), 392–401 reviews these publications, chiefly a once-confidential analysis, and concludes that the British were determined not to push the United States to the breaking point, but that they sought to guard British export trade then and after the war, even against American competition.

R. P. Wilkins, "Middle Western Isolationism: A Re-Examination," *North Dakota Quar.*, XXV (1957), 69–76 contends that the virulent isolationism of

North Dakota sprang not so much from German and other foreign groups as from the suspicion in this frontier state of war-mongering Wall Street.

8TH ED. REFS. Daniel M. Smith, *The Great Departure: The United States and World War I, 1914–1920* (New York, 1965), is an excellent brief survey, generally sympathetic to Wilson and stressing Lansing's perspicacity, which was not always appreciated by Wilson.

Gaddis Smith, *Britain's Clandestine Submarines, 1914–1915* (New Haven, 1964), reveals how an American manufacturer (Bethlehem) fabricated ten submarines in Canada for the British navy, using United States materials and technicians, in a successful effort to evade American neutrality laws.

Ross Gregory, "A New Look at the Case of the *Dacia*," *Jour. of Amer. Hist.*, LV (1968), 292–296, reveals that the *Dacia*, a German merchantman taken over by the U.S., was intercepted routinely by the French and not as the result of a clever scheme suggested to the British by Ambassador Page.

G. A. Dobbert, "German-Americans between New and Old Fatherland, 1870–1914," *Amer. Quarterly*, XIX (1967), 663–680, demonstrates that not until the 1890's did a strident German nationalism emerge and it continued highly vocal well into World War I.

9TH ED. REFS. Ross Gregory, *Walter Hines Page: Ambassador to the Court of St. James'* (Lexington, Ky., 1970) fleshes out the picture of an envoy so pro-British that he rapidly lost influence with his superiors and his hosts. His significance has been overestimated.

John M. Cooper, Jr., *The Vanity of Power: American Isolationism and the First World War, 1914–1917* (Westport, Conn., 1969) makes a distinction between the ultranationalists and the idealists, rather than between the isolationists and the internationalists. Among the ultranationalists were internationalists and isolationists; among the idealists were internationalists and isolationists.

Sidney Bell, *Righteous Conquest: Woodrow Wilson and the Evolution of the New Diplomacy* (Port Washington, N.Y., 1972) discusses the impact of the Wilsonian dream, which envisaged a world empire of righteousness and trade based on recognition of the innate goodness of America.

Mary R. Kihl, "A Failure of Ambassadorial Diplomacy," *Jour. of Amer. Hist.*, LVII (1970), 636–653, shows that Ambassador Page in London and the British Ambassador Spring Rice in Washington both forfeited the confidence of the Wilson administration.

Ch. 39. THE ROAD TO WORLD WAR I, 1915–1917

See new references on p. 595.

D. M. Smith, *Robert Lansing and American Neutrality, 1914–1917* (Berkeley, Calif., 1958) portrays Lansing as one of the principal architects of the pro-Ally policy oriented toward war; he was more influential in shaping Wilson's decisions than was formerly thought. More consistent than Wilson in viewing the cause of the Allies as that of America, he was primarily concerned with the national interest (balance of power).

A. P. Dudden, ed., *Woodrow Wilson and the World of Today* (Philadelphia, 1957) is a collection of perceptive lectures on Wilson's neutrality and peacemaking policies.

Barbara W. Tuchman, *The Zimmermann Telegram* (New York, 1958), though overlurid and overstressing the importance of the incident, is the fullest account. Zimmermann sent a follow-up telegram (February 5) instructing the German Minister in Mexico not to wait for war but to act "even now." Zimmermann blundered by admitting the authenticity of the telegram; Wilson was indignant that the Germans should have been plotting and using State Department cable facilities while still talking peace.

Charles Seymour, "The House-Bernstorff Conversations in Perspective," A. O. Sarkissian, ed., *Studies in Diplomatic History and Historiography* (London, 1961), pp. 90–106 describes the failure of these two-year conversations in Washington; but they are here credited with postponing America's entrance into the war by a number of months.

T. J. Kerr, IV, "German-Americans and Neutrality in the 1916 Election," *Mid-America*, XLIII (1961), 95–105 notes that German pressures increased Wilson's distrust of Berlin and facilitated the final break.

F. A. Bonadio, "The Failure of German Propaganda in the United States, 1914–17," *ibid.*, XLI (1959), 40–57 shows that the major failure was in not recognizing that the melting pot had changed the Europeanism of the immigrant population.

D. M. Smith, "President Wilson and the German 'Overt Act' of 1917—A Reappraisal," *University of Colorado Studies Series in History*, No. 2, November, 1961, pp. 129–139 refutes the claim that the sinking of the British *Laconia* rather than the four American ships in mid-March was the "overt act" for which Wilson was waiting.

J. A. S. Grenville, "Diplomacy and War Plans in the United States, 1890–1917," *Transactions of the Royal Historical Society*, Ser. 5, vol. XI (London, 1961), 1–21 reveals that the possibility of involvement in World War I on the side of the Allies was not properly anticipated.

James Weinstein, "Anti-War Sentiment and the Socialist Party, 1917–1918," *Pol. Sci. Quar.*, LXXIV (1959), 215–239 shows that there was much more opposition to the declaration and prosecution of the war, not alone among Socialists, than previously thought. Many Americans felt that "American democracy had nothing at stake in the European war."

8TH ED. REFS. Arthur S. Link, *Wilson: Confusions and Crises, 1915–1916* (Princeton, N.J., 1964) [vol. IV], has revealing chapters on Mexico and World War I, notably those on the *Sussex* crisis and the House-Grey memorandum. Using secret French materials, the author concludes that in connection with the latter episode House misrepresented, misinformed, and misled Wilson (p. 141). Europe did not take the memorandum seriously.

Arthur S. Link, *Wilson: Campaigns for Progressivism and Peace, 1916–1917* (Princeton, N.J., 1965) [vol. V], shows that Wilson was in firm control of foreign policy; that he distrusted Allied war aims and hence was not strongly pro-British; that he preferred some kind of stalemate peace that would check Germany in a balance of power; that he was not pressured by public opinion, advisers, or the business world into asking Congress for a declaration of war; that, in April, 1917, he was not worried about any immediate German threat to the U.S.; that he did not then know that the Allies were collapsing (he learned that later); and that (in the author's opinion) he was convinced that "American belligerency now offered the surest hope for early peace and the reconstruction of the international community."

Daniel M. Smith, "National Interest and American Intervention, 1917: An Historiographical Appraisal," *Jour. of Amer. Hist.*, LII (1965), 5–24, reviews the most recent writings and reaches many of Link's conclusions (see above). Smith shows that, aside from the submarine precipitant, American national interests (economy, security, national honor, and a world organization for peace) entered to some extent into the thinking of Wilson's advisers, if not into that of Wilson himself, when he asked for war.

Daniel M. Smith, *The Great Departure: The United States and World War I, 1914–1920* (New York, 1965), elaborates on the conclusions presented in the article above.

Warren I. Cohen, *The American Revisionists: The Lessons of Intervention in World War I* (Chicago, 1967), analyzes the historians who in the 1920's and 1930's questioned the "guilt" of the Central Powers in precipitating World War I, as well as the wisdom of U.S. participation in the war. The emphasis is on Barnes, Grattan, Beard, Millis, and Tansill. They reflected the changing climate of opinion but differed among themselves as to the impact of pro-interventionist forces.

Richard Lowitt, "The Armed-Ship Bill Controversy: A Legislative View," *Mid-America*, XLVI (1964), 38–47, points out that the eleven "willful men" in the Senate did not consume half as much time in their so-called filibuster as the proponents of the bill. It seems evident that many members of Congress, of all persuasions, were eager to force Wilson to call a special session of Congress so that they might keep a more careful eye on his foreign policy.

Gerald H. Davis, "The *Ancona* Affair: A Case of Preventive Diplomacy," *Jour. of Modern Hist.*, XXXVIII (1966), 267–277, reveals that a German submarine, showing Austro-Hungarian colors, sank the Italian passenger liner *Ancona*, November 7, 1915, with a loss of nine American lives. A *Sussex*-type crisis was averted when Austria falsely assumed full responsibility.

Edward Cuddy, "Irish-American Propagandists and American Neutrality, 1914–1917," *Mid-America*, XLIX (1967), 252–275, concludes that the leaders of the Irish-German neutrality coalition were far more anti-British than the rank and file. The Irish and Germans did contribute to "the diplomacy of neutrality" by keeping the nation so divided that war was averted until April, 1917.

Dean R. Esslinger, "American, German and Irish Attitudes toward Neutrality, 1914–1917: A Study of Catholic Minorities," *Catholic Hist. Rev.*, LIII (1967), 194–216, concludes that although the Italian and Polish Catholics were pro-Ally, the Irish and Germans were pro-German. Of the prominent Catholic journals examined, one was "distinctly" anti-German while at least nine were "openly or subtly" hostile to the Allied cause.

William M. Leary, Jr., "Woodrow Wilson, Irish-Americans, and the Election of 1916," *Jour. of Amer. Hist.*, LIV (1967), 57–72, demonstrates that the Irish-Americans, despite the exhortation of many of their leaders, supported Wilson fully as well as they had any other Democratic presidential candidate in the immediate past, partly because he had "kept us out of war" on the side of Britain.

Ross Gregory, "The Superfluous Ambassador: Walter Hines Page's Return to Washington, 1916," *Historian*, XXVIII (1966), 389–404, concludes that Page was largely ignored because the administration was tired of his repeated pro-British complaints and feared more of the same.

George W. Baker, Jr., "Robert Lansing and the Purchase of the Danish West Indies," *Social Studies*, LVII (1966), 64–71, demonstrates that Secretary Lansing was the prime pusher of the purchase; he convinced Wilson of its defense advantages.

Walter I. Trattner, "Progressivism and World War I: A Reappraisal," *Mid-America*, XLIV (1962), 131–145, shows that the attitudes of the Progressives were not clearly distinguishable from those of most Americans regarding involvement in the war.

9TH ED. REFS. Ross Gregory, *The Origins of American Intervention in the First World War* (New York, 1971) is a broad treatment, directed toward a student audience, which finds American, rather than German, policies primarily responsible for the clash.

W. B. Fowler, *British-American Relations, 1917–1918: The Role of Sir William Wiseman* (Princeton, 1969) reveals how the youthful head of the British secret service in the U.S. served usefully as an intermediary between British and American policy makers by establishing a confidential relationship with Wilson's Colonel House. There are revelations on the Siberian intervention.

Edward Cuddy, "Pro-Germanism and American Catholicism, 1914–1917," *Catholic Hist. Rev.*, LIV (1968), 427–454, concludes that pro-German were stronger than pro-Ally pressures but the Church, in keeping with its international character, generally occupied a position of neutrality.

David S. Patterson, "Woodrow Wilson and the Mediation Movement, 1914–1917," *Historian*, XXXIII (1971), 535–556, reveals how Wilson adroitly withstood pressures from the peace groups and pursued his independent policies.

Sterling Kernek, "The British Government's Reactions to President Wilson's 'Peace' Note of December, 1916," *Historical Journal*, XIII (1970), 721–766, demonstrates that London deeply resented this "threat" of peace. The note gave impetus to the campaign of Allied propagandists against "Peace without Victory."

Raymond Weitekamp, "The Virgin Islands Purchase and the Coercion Myth," *Mid-America*, LIV (1972), 75–93, plays up the role of the U.S. Minister Egan in Denmark and plays down the so-called "threat" of Secretary Lansing to seize the islands if not sold.

Ch. 40. NEGOTIATING THE TREATY OF VERSAILLES

Observations of a general nature appear in Arthur Walworth, *Woodrow Wilson* (2 vols., New York, 1958); E. H. Buehrig, ed., *Wilson's Foreign Policy in Perspective* (Bloomington, Ind., 1957); A. P. Dudden, ed., *Woodrow Wilson and the World of Today* (Philadelphia, 1957).

Herbert Hoover, *The Ordeal of Woodrow Wilson* (New York, 1958) sheds light not so much on Wilson as on Hoover's reactions to Wilson. The most revealing material describes Hoover's contribution to the economic rehabilitation of Europe after the Armistice, especially the food program. He makes clear his distrust of European machinations that contributed to his later isolationist outlook. Although glorifying Wilson, he concedes that the latter made mistakes.

D. F. Trask, *The United States in the Supreme War Council: American War Aims and Inter-Allied Strategy, 1917–1918* (Middletown, Conn., 1961) concludes that the Council proved less significant than hoped, largely because Wilson excluded political decisions that might tie his hands at the peace table.

L. W. Martin, *Peace Without Victory: Woodrow Wilson and the British Liberals* (New Haven, 1958) deals with the influence of this small group on Wilson, and vice versa, in connection with the Fourteen Points and the Treaty. He finally came around to endorsing many of the views held by the British radicals.

A. J. Mayer, *Political Origins of the New Diplomacy, 1917–1918* (New Haven, 1959) focuses on European war aims, with attention to the impact of Wilson's idealism on them.

S. P. Tillman, *Anglo-American Relations at the Paris Peace Conference of 1919* (Princeton, 1961) observes that England and America enjoyed a basic community of interest, and that they largely contributed the "moral" parts of the treaty.

B. F. Beers, *Vain Endeavor: Robert Lansing's Attempts to End the Ameri-can-Japanese Rivalry* (Durham, N.C., 1962) analyzes Lansing's differences with Wilson at Paris, especially his opposition to the Shantung settlement. Though disagreements had appeared much earlier, Lansing rarely argued with Wilson until 1919, preferring to work by indirection.

V. S. Mamatey, *The United States and East Central Europe, 1914–1918: A Study in Wilsonian Diplomacy and Propaganda* (Princeton, 1957) contends that these new nations were not created at Paris: "they created themselves by their own efforts," although stimulated by American and Russian propaganda.

G. F. Kennan, *Russia and the West under Lenin and Stalin* (Boston, 1960) has two chapters on the Paris conference and the unsuccessful efforts made there to bring Bolshevik Russia into the community of nations.

G. F. Kennan, *Russia Leaves the War* (Princeton, 1956) covers in scholarly detail some of the material sketchily presented in the book just cited, and is especially concerned with American reactions to the Bolshevik Revolution and Allied efforts to keep Russia in the war. The author concludes that these had no chance of success. High-level decisions in Washington were based on ignorance and misinformation, while American agents worked at cross-purposes, especially the nonprofessionals. See also the same author's *The Decision to Intervene* (Princeton, 1958), discussed at the end of the next chapter.

L. I. Strakhovsky, *American Opinion about Russia, 1917–1920* (Toronto, 1961) reveals that popular views were based largely on ignorance and misinformation. The only real interest of the public, which favored a strong intervention policy, was in using Russia as an ally against Germany. But Washington pursued a policy of nonrecognition, nonintervention, and nondismemberment.

Christopher Lasch, *The American Liberals and the Russian Revolution* (New York, 1962) is a study of clashing interpretations: one group of liberals regarded the Bolsheviks as democrats; another, as mere tools of the German Kaiser.

George Curry, "Woodrow Wilson, Jan Smuts, and the Versailles Settlement," *Amer. Hist. Rev.*, LXVI (1961), 968–986 spells out Smuts' influence on Wilson's decisions, especially regarding the League and reparations. A fellow idealist who objected to the final treaty, Smuts suggested compromises which Wilson readily accepted.

R. H. Ferrell, "Woodrow Wilson and Open Diplomacy," in G. L. Anderson, *Issues and Conflicts* (Lawrence, Kans., 1959), pp. 193–209 provides further evidence that Wilson believed in private negotiations but published results. He accepted lying as an instrument of public policy.

C. E. Fike, "The Influence of the Creel Committee and the American Red Cross on Russian-American Relations, 1917–1919," *Jour. of Modern Hist.*, XXXI (1959), 93–109 demonstrates that these agencies meddled scandalously in Russia's internal affairs, arousing the suspicions of the Bolsheviks and influencing Wilson's decision to intervene.

C. E. Fike, "The United States and Russian Territorial Problems, 1917–1920," *The Historian*, XXIV (1962), 331–346 describes how the Wilson administration exercised its considerable influence to safeguard the territory of Russia.

See also references on the interventions in Russia in the new references of Chapter 42.

8TH ED. REFS. Seward W. Livermore, *Politics is Adjourned: Woodrow Wilson and the War Congress, 1916–1918* (Middletown, Conn., 1966), builds up to the "October Appeal" and concludes that at no time during the war was Democratic-Republican partisanship truly "adjourned."

Lawrence E. Gelfand, *The Inquiry: American Preparations for Peace, 1917–1919* (New Haven, 1963), is the only detailed study of the group of some 150 experts, operating in New York and elsewhere, who turned out hundreds of reports on the imminent problems of peacemaking. The influence of the Inquiry on the Versailles Treaty was not commensurate with this effort, though the experts did prepare a memorandum which Wilson used as a basis for his Fourteen Points address.

Charles Seymour, *Letters from the Paris Peace Conference*, Harold B. Whiteman, Jr., ed. (New Haven, 1965), presents a collection by the chief American adviser on Austria-Hungary. The letters, though generally favorable to Wilson are not particularly revealing, in part because of fear of censorship.

Arno J. Mayer, *Politics and Diplomacy of Peacemaking: Containment and Counterrevolution at Versailles, 1918–1919* (New York, 1967), is an impressive multidimensional, multinational study of the Paris negotiations, with special attention to the domestic political pressures on the negotiators and the impact of the Bolshevik-inspired revolution (and counterrevolution), especially in countries like Austria-Hungary.

Beatrice Farnsworth, *William C. Bullitt and the Soviet Union* (Bloomington, Ind., 1967), describes in detail how young Bullitt, attached to the American delegation in Paris, went to Russia and returned with the draft of an extraordinary treaty with Lenin. When Wilson chose not to accept it, Bullitt turned bitterly against him.

Harry N. Howard, *The King-Crane Commission: An American Inquiry in the Middle East* (Beirut, 1963), describes the American commission that was dispatched to report on conditions (including the ill-starred Turkish mandate) and make recommendations.

N. Gordon Levin, Jr., *Woodrow Wilson and World Politics: America's Response to War and Revolution* (New York, 1968), elaborates the thesis that U.S. policy from 1917 to 1919 represented an effort by Wilson to steer a realistic middle course between the new revolutionary socialism of Russia and the outdated nationalism-imperialism of the old order.

Ivo J. Lederer, *Yugoslavia at the Paris Peace Conference: A Study in Frontier-Making* (New Haven, 1963), reveals in detail why the Yugoslavs did not realize full self-determination, despite Wilson's efforts on their behalf.

John M. Thompson, *Russia, Bolshevism, and the Versailles Peace* (Princeton, N.J., 1966), shows that Wilson wavered between an idealistic and a realistic treatment of Russia. Fear of Bolshevism led him to accept compromises in the hope of more quickly solving the problem of Russia.

Joseph P. O'Grady, ed., *The Immigrants' Influence on Wilson's Peace Policies* (Lexington, Ky., 1967), contains eleven essays describing the considerable pressures from ethnic groups such as the Poles, Czechs, and Italians.

J. B. Duff, "The Versailles Treaty and the Irish-Americans," *Jour. of Amer. Hist.*, LV (1968), 582–598, demonstrates that Wilson deliberately and needlessly alienated the Irish-Americans by flatly refusing to push for the cause of Ireland at Paris, thereby contributing to the defeat of the treaty in America.

9TH ED. REFS. Keith L. Nelson, "What Colonel House Overlooked in the Armistice," *Mid-America*, LI (1969), 75–91, reveals that House inadvertently compromised Wilson's position at the coming peace conference; House accepted Allied military demands which in effect recognized the validity of Allied policies.

James D. Startt, "Wilson's Mission to Paris: The Making of a Decision," *Historian*, XXX (1968), 599–616, concludes that Wilson primarily went because of his regard for the "stricken" people of Europe and belief in a moral obligation to undertake a mission which he alone could discharge.

James D. Startt, "The Uneasy Partnership: Wilson and the Press at Paris," *Mid-America*, LII (1970), 55–69, describes how Wilson failed to establish satisfactory relations with the newsmen.

Leon E. Boothe, "Anglo-American Pro-League Groups Lead Wilson, 1915–1918," *Mid-America*, LI (1969), 92–107, notes that Wilson's early support of a league was "limited and inhibiting."

Roland N. Stromberg, "Uncertainties and Obscurities About the League of Nations," *Jour. of the History of Ideas*, XXXIII (1972), 139–154, observes that arguments as to the nature of the League resulted in compromises and enmities among its original sponsors; consequently the League, especially through lack of effective teeth, was doomed to failure.

John B. Duff, "The Versailles Treaty and the Irish-Americans," *Jour. of Amer. Hist.*, LV (1968), 582–598, describes Wilson's refusal partially to quiet Irish fears by making public a strong statement regarding the future relationship of Ireland to the League of Nations.

Ch. 41. THE RETREAT TO ISOLATIONISM, 1919–1935

Herbert Hoover, *The Ordeal of Woodrow Wilson* (New York, 1958) relates that Hoover and his staff at Paris believed that the League Covenant would be more effective without Article X; there were already built-in economic sanctions. Hoover concludes that the Lodge reservations did not destroy the major functions of the League, and that the anxious European leaders would have accepted the reservations.

W. F. Kuehl, *Hamilton Holt* (Gainesville, Fla., 1960) shows that this internationalist supported the League enthusiastically, and at the time blamed Wilson more than the Senate for the deadlock over reservations. Ultimately he blamed the Senate more than Wilson.

S. P. Tillman, *Anglo-American Relations at the Paris Peace Conference of 1919* (Princeton, 1961) deals with Wilson and the Senate deadlock, and rather questionably concludes that the British would have rejected the Lodge reservations if Wilson had accepted them.

G. F. Sparks, ed., *A Many-Colored Toga: The Diary of Henry Fountain Ashurst* (Tucson, Ariz., 1962) reveals that this Democratic Senator, though basically friendly to Wilson, severely criticized the President for failing to compromise with the Senate and for having condemned the League to certain defeat by forcing it to run in the campaign of 1920.

Alden Hatch, *Edith Bolling Wilson* (New York, 1961) is laudatory and adds little to Mrs. Wilson's memoirs except some later observations. She regarded the October appeal as Wilson's "greatest mistake," and Senator Lodge as a "snake."

Arthur Walworth, *Woodrow Wilson* (2 vols., New York, 1958) is a general account, strongly pro-Wilson and anti-Lodge.

C. T. Grayson, *Woodrow Wilson: An Intimate Memoir* (New York, 1960), by Wilson's personal physician, adds only a few details to what was already known.

M. C. McKenna, *Borah* (Ann Arbor, Mich., 1961) deals briefly with the League fight, the sponsorship of the Kellogg-Briand Pact, and the Senator's campaign for better relations with Russia.

W. M. Bagby, *The Road to Normalcy: The Presidential Campaign and*

Election of 1920 (Baltimore, 1962) concludes that the tale of "the smoke-filled room" nomination is grossly exaggerated; that Wilson was bitterly disappointed in not getting a third nomination; and that the election of 1920 was not a clear-cut rejection of the League.

K. G. Redmond, "Henry L. Stimson and the Question of League Membership," *The Historian*, XXV (1963), 200–212 shows that Stimson was favorable to the League, though critical of certain of its weaknesses and also of both Wilson and the irreconcilable Senators.

D. M. Smith, "Robert Lansing and the Wilson Interregnum, 1919–1920," *The Historian*, XXI (1959), 135–161 notes that Lansing's dismissal resulted from long standing friction between the idealist-moralist and the legalist-realist; Lansing had stayed on only through a sense of duty.

Kurt Wimer, "Woodrow Wilson's Plans to Enter the League of Nations through an Executive Agreement," *Western Pol. Quar.*, XI (1958), 800–812 discusses Wilson's abortive plan to include the League in a preliminary peace; the scheme was dropped following House's alleged bungling while Wilson was absent from Paris.

Kurt Wimer, "Woodrow Wilson's Plan for a Vote of Confidence," *Pennsylvania History*, XXVIII (1961), 279–293 demonstrates that the "solemn referendum" stemmed from an abortive secret scheme to have a special election in which the voters would choose between Wilson and the opposition Senators.

Kurt Wimer, "Woodrow Wilson and a Third Nomination," *Pennsylvania History*, XXIX (1962), 193–211 describes Wilson's abortive efforts to secure renomination and hence ratification of the League; his friends turned from him on account of his ill health and certain defeat.

D. D. Burks, "The United States and the Geneva Protocol of 1924: 'A New Holy Alliance'?" *Amer. Hist. Rev.*, LXIV (1959), 891–905 describes how this attempt to strengthen the League of Nations, by imposing sanctions on non-members like the United States, threatened to challenge the Monroe Doctrine; it was abandoned in the face of American and British opposition.

R. L. Daniel, "The Armenian Question and American-Turkish Relations, 1914–1927," *Miss. Valley Hist. Rev.*, XLVI (1959), 252–275 shows how the stereotype of the "terrible Turk," who massacred Armenians, complicated relations with Turkey and contributed to the defeat of the Treaty of Lausanne in 1927 by the United States Senate.

John C. Vinson, *Referendum for Isolation* (Athens, Ga., 1961), deals in detail with the defeat in the Senate of Article X of the League Covenant.

8TH ED. REFS. E. David Cronon, ed., in *The Cabinet Diaries of Josephus Daniels, 1913–1921* (Lincoln, Nebr., 1963), makes clear that Wilson was in touch with some affairs of state (or appeared to be) less than a week after the stroke; that he was much better some days than others; and that his strategy of putting the onus on the Lodge-led Republicans was not completely irrational but had the support of a majority of the Cabinet.

Sigmund Freud and William C. Bullitt, *Thomas Woodrow Wilson: A Psychological Study* (Boston, 1967), is thoroughly untrustworthy either as history or psychology. The thesis is that Wilson subconsciously hated his domineering father (while loving him), and took out his resentment on Senator Lodge. For a refutation see Arthur S. Link, "The Case for Woodrow Wilson," *Harper's Magazine*, CCXXXIV (April, 1967), 85–93.

Gene Smith, *When the Cheering Stopped: The Last Years of Woodrow Wilson* (New York, 1964), is a racily written, highly popularized, and generally sympathetic account of Wilson's fight for the League. It contains so many factual errors as to be unreliable.

Raymond B. Fosdick, *Letters on the League of Nations: From the Files of Raymond B. Fosdick* (Princeton, N.J., 1966), reveals the passionate loyalty to Wilson of this Undersecretary General of the League of Nations (1919–1920). He fought hard for the League and was shocked by Secretary Lansing's excessive timidity toward it.

Andrew Sinclair, *The Available Man: The Life Behind the Masks of Warren Gamaliel Harding* (New York, 1965), concludes that Harding, while relying heavily on Secretary Hughes, showed unexpected resolution in standing up to the Senate on the World Court and other issues.

Donald R. McCoy, *Calvin Coolidge: The Quiet President* (New York, 1967), notes that Coolidge, while cautiously supporting the World Court, was not willing to fight the Senate for it.

Albert N. Tarulis, *American-Baltic Relations, 1918–1922: The Struggle over Recognition* (Washington, D.C., 1965), by a Lithuanian expatriate, condemns Wilson for not pressing for the recognition of Lithuania, Estonia, and Latvia. The author praises the Harding administration for extending recognition in 1922.

Laurence Evans, *United States Policy and the Partition of Turkey, 1914–1924* (Baltimore, 1965), points out that U.S. policy moved from noninvolvement to intense concern (under Wilson), and then back to noninvolvement.

Kurt Wimer, "Woodrow Wilson Tries Conciliation: An Effort that Failed," *Historian*, XXV (1963), 419–438, contends that Wilson strove harder to work out acceptable reservations with the moderate senators before his trip West than is generally known.

Kurt Wimer, "Senator Hitchcock and the League of Nations," *Nebraska History*, XLIV (1963), 189–204, reveals that this Senate minority leader tried vainly to persuade Wilson, a secluded and misinformed man, to compromise effectively after his collapse. Wilson was determined to pigeonhole the Lodge reservations and to put the onus for rejecting the treaty on the Republican Senate rather than on himself.

Kurt and Sarah Wimer, "The Harding Administration, the League of Nations, and the Separate Peace Treaty," *Review of Politics*, XXIX (1967), 13–24, describes the success of the Senate "irreconcilables" in keeping Harding in line and Wilson's unsuccessful behind-the-scenes effort to defeat approval of the separate treaty with Germany.

Ralph A. Stone, "The Irreconcilables' Alternatives to the League of Nations," *Mid-America*, XLIX (1967), 163–173, finds that there were sixteen irreconcilables (two of them Democrats) who were badly divided among themselves. Three groups are recognizable: the isolationists; the realists (the League was "unworkable"); and the idealists, including La Follette and Norris, both of whom were sympathetic toward a League. Norris wanted one that would go much further than Wilson's.

Ralph A. Stone, "Two Illinois Senators among the Irreconcilables," *Miss. Valley Hist. Rev.*, L (1963), 443–465, deals with Sherman and McCormick among the "irreconcilables." They were moved by such emotions as anti-Wilsonism, anti-collective security convictions, Anglophobia, and extreme nationalism.

Richard L. Merritt, "Woodrow Wilson and the 'Great and Solemn Referendum,' 1920," *Review of Politics*, XXVII (1965), 78–104, adduces further evidence that Wilson, in asking for a referendum, not only blundered but asked the impossible.

Public Opinion Quarterly, XXXI (Winter, 1967–68), 521 ff., contains an important symposium organized by Arthur S. Link. Lee Benson, in "An Approach to the Scientific Study of Past Public Opinion" concludes that the subject has not been studied scientifically because historians have not tried to work out techniques for doing so. He offers suggestions for such an approach. Wolfgang J. Helbich, in "American Liberals in the League of Nations Controversy," notes that while there were extreme rejectionists, the majority of liberals were probably willing to accept a compromise. James L. Lancaster, "The Protestant Churches and the Fight for Ratification of the Versailles Treaty," reveals that most of the leaders, alienated by Wilson's stubbornness, were willing to compromise on any terms after the second defeat of the treaty. Kenneth R. Maxwell, "Irish-Americans and the Fight for Treaty Ratification," shows that the Irish opposed the Versailles pact even while it was being framed, and exerted strong pressure on the Senate for rejection.

9TH ED. REFS. Warren F. Kuehl, *Seeking World Order: The United States and International Organization to 1920* (Nashville, Tenn., 1969) portrays the weakness and diversity of those seeking world order; their qualified approval of the League helped to defeat it.

Ralph Stone, *The Irreconcilables: The Fight against the League of Nations* (Lexington, Ky., 1970) concludes that only three among the sixteen were authentic isolationists; four probably would have voted for a treaty implementing the Fourteen Points.

Daniel M. Smith, *Aftermath of War: Bainbridge Colby and Wilsonian Diplomacy, 1920–1921* (Philadelphia, 1970) is the fullest account of Wilson's Secretary of State; Wilson had already set the main course, especially regarding Mexico and Russian recognition.

Robert K. Murray, *The Harding Era: Warren G. Harding and His Administration* (Minneapolis, 1969) rehabilitates Harding, on the basis of his recently opened papers, and pronounces his administration a "success."

Francis Russell, *The Shadow of Blooming Grove: Warren G. Harding in His Times* (New York, 1968), using the newly available papers, is a generally unfriendly biography.

Robert J. Maddox, *William E. Borah and American Foreign Policy* (Baton Rouge, La., 1969) examines particularly the League fight, the Washington Conference, peace plans, and Russian recognition.

Jerome E. Edwards, *The Foreign Policy of Col. McCormick's Tribune: 1929–1941* (Reno, Nevada, 1971) presents this journal's extravagantly isolationist views.

Edwin A. Weinstein, "Woodrow Wilson's Neurological Illness," *Jour. of Amer. Hist.*, LVII (1970), 324–351, suggests that Wilson's irrational, uncompromising behavior may have been related to recorded episodes of brain damage in 1896, 1906, 1908, and culminating in 1919. The author is a neurologist.

Lloyd E. Ambrosius, "Wilson, the Republicans, and French Security after World War I," *Jour. of Amer. Hist.*, LIX (1972), 341–352, demonstrates that many of the so-called isolationist Senators were favorable to a security treaty with France but spurned one tied to Wilson's League.

Robert J. Maddox, "Another Look at the Legend of Isolationism in the 1920's," *Mid-America*, LIII (1971), 35–43, sharply challenges the well-known article by William A. Williams; the U.S. was deeply involved economically (if not politically) in the outside world.

James E. Hewes, Jr., "Henry Cabot Lodge and the League of Nations," *Proceedings of the American Philosophical Society*, CXIV (1970), 245–255, shows that Lodge had consistently battled against abridging sovereignty, even in amending the Taft (Republican) arbitration treaties of 1911.

David Mervin, "Henry Cabot Lodge and the League of Nations," *Jour. of Amer. Studies*, IV (1971), 201–214, emphasizes Lodge's "overwhelming concern" for the Republican Party and the Senate.

Richard C. Lower, "Hiram Johnson: The Making of an Irreconcilable," *Pacific Hist. Rev.*, XLI (1972), 505–526, shows that this flaming Progressive turned against Wilsonian internationalism largely because of the threat to American democracy posed by World War I and the prospective League involvement.

Peter G. Boyle, "The Roots of Isolationism: A Case Study," *Jour. of Amer. Studies*, VI (1972), 41–54, deals with the isolationist Senator Hiram Johnson, whose attitude was determined by progressivism, negativism, provincialism, and other factors.

John H. Flannagan, Jr., "The Disillusionment of a Progressive: U.S. Senator David I. Walsh and the League of Nations Issue, 1918–1920," *New England Quar.*, XLI (1968), 483–504, reveals how this loyal Wilsonian turned against the Treaty because Wilson did not more fully carry out his principles, especially self-determination (which aroused Walsh's Irish-American constituency).

Ch. 42. THE FAR EAST AND DISARMAMENT, 1917–1938

There are two important new works by G. F. Kennan: *The Decision to Intervene: The Prelude to Allied Intervention in the Bolshevik Revolution* (Princeton, 1958) and the briefer and more popularized *Russia and the West under Lenin and Stalin* (Boston, 1960). The author contends that Wilson, in deciding on the Siberian intervention, had no thought of strangling Bolshevism. He proposed to save the immense military supplies at Vladivostok and particularly to rescue the Czechs. Nothing, Kennan concludes, could have kept the Bolsheviks from dropping out of the war; the half-hearted Allied interventions probably united them and contributed to their ultimate success.

B. F. Beers, *Vain Endeavor: Robert Lansing's Attempts to End the American-Japanese Rivalry* (Durham, N.C., 1962) shows that Lansing was for protecting the dollar in China; Wilson was for promoting the welfare and independence of China; hence he restricted the Lansing-Ishii negotiations. The author states that in regard to Siberia the President was "primarily" interested in keeping "the Japanese straight" (p. 128), and also in rescuing the Czechs; Lansing was more interested in halting Bolshevism.

J. W. Morley, *The Japanese Thrust into Siberia, 1918* (New York, 1957) discloses that while there were strong imperialist elements in Japan, the government intervened in Siberia with great reluctance, fearful of the spread of Bolshevism and of German power in the Far East. Japanese motives were diverse and often conflicting. The American decision to intervene on behalf of the Czechs triggered the Japanese decision to intervene. "There is little substantial, direct evidence" that fears of Japan played a leading role in the American intervention (p. 262). Major considerations were an unwillingness to hurt Allied morale by not co-operating and a concern for the Czech contingent.

R. H. Ullman, *Anglo-Soviet Relations, 1917–1921* (Princeton, 1961) reveals that Britain's chief aim before the Armistice was to keep Russia in the war; London had to mislead Wilson to get his approval of the Siberian intervention.

L. E. Ellis, *Frank B. Kellogg and American Foreign Relations, 1925–1929* (New Brunswick, N.J., 1961) portrays Kellogg as a mediocre, overworked, irascible Secretary ("Nervous Nellie"), who showed considerable vigor in regard to China and the Kellogg-Briand Pact, which he belatedly clasped to his bosom.

R. H. Ferrell, *Frank B. Kellogg; Henry L. Stimson* (vol. XI in *The American Secretaries of State and Their Diplomacy*, New York, 1963) takes sharp issue with the detractors of Kellogg, who is here regarded as a "worthy successor" to Hughes, and "in some ways" a "more able individual" than the "well-known" Stimson.

Armin Rappaport, *The Navy League of the United States* (Detroit, 1962) demolishes the legend that this group was effective in promoting a big navy in the 1920's and 1930's; it was active but not effective.

E. E. Morison, *Turmoil and Tradition: A Study of the Life and Times of Henry L. Stimson* (Boston, 1960) views Secretary of State Stimson as a key figure in the London Naval Conference, and concludes that it was a failure, even though both Hoover and Stimson tried to puff it up as a success.

R. G. O'Connor, *Perilous Equilibrium: The United States and the London Naval Conference of 1930* (Lawrence, Kans., 1962) regards the conference as a "formal repudiation" of imperialism by the three major naval powers, and a kind of implementation of the Kellogg-Briand Pact. As the culmination of the disarmament movement after World War I, it was a victory for the civil authorities over the naval experts. Hoover did not build up to blueprint quotas because he regarded economic recovery as more important.

G. E. Wheeler, *Prelude to Pearl Harbor: The United States Navy and the Far East, 1921–1931* (Columbia, Mo., 1963) reveals that during the decade before 1931 the navy planners regarded war with Japan as inevitable, but were handicapped in their preparations by public indifference and "miserly" Congressional support.

G. F. Kennan, "Soviet Historiography and America's Role in the Intervention," *Amer. Hist. Rev.*, LXV (1960), 302–322 makes it plain that these writers grossly misrepresented the motives and actual participation of the United States.

Betty M. Unterberger, "The Russian Revolution and Wilson's Far-Eastern Policy," *Russian Review*, XVI (1957), 35–46 shows that once American troops were in Siberia, Washington's concern shifted from a rescue of the Czechs to protection of the railroad; hence American policy unwittingly became anti-Bolshevik.

Christopher Lasch, "American Intervention in Siberia: A Reinterpretation," *Pol. Sci. Quar.*, LXXVII (1962), 205–223 argues that the United States intervened to rescue the Czechs and at the same time to bolster the Allies against the Germans—not to restrain the Japanese. The conclusions are controversial and weakened by the erroneous assumption that the anti-Japanese theory did not appear until *after* the hates generated by World War II.

Gaddis Smith, "Canada and the Siberian Intervention, 1918–1919," *Amer. Hist. Rev.*, LXIV (1959), 866–877 reveals that Canada sent some 4000 men largely in the hope of economic advantages in Siberia after the war: she acted as a buffer between America and Britain.

J. C. Vinson, "The Imperial Conference of 1921 and the Anglo-Japanese Alliance," *Pacific Hist. Rev.*, XXXI (1962), 257–266 demolishes the myth that at this conference the Canadian Prime Minister singlehandedly forced the other dominions to accept an abrogation of the Alliance; in the interests of preserving American friendship, this step had essentially been agreed upon in advance.

Merze Tate and Fidele Foy, "More Light on the Abrogation of the Anglo-Japanese Alliance," *Pol. Sci. Quar.*, LXXIV (1959), 532–554 concludes that by the time the Washington Conference met, all the Dominion representatives seemed opposed to exclusive alliances and favorable to collaboration with the United States.

Sadao Asada, "Japan's 'Special Interests' and the Washington Conference, 1921–22," *Amer. Hist. Rev.*, LXVII (1961), 62–70 demonstrates that Japan, unlike the United States, interpreted the Nine Power Treaty as giving her a free hand to pursue her "security" in Manchuria and Outer Mongolia and hence reviving the "special interests" concept of the old Lansing-Ishii agreement. To Japan, "Open Door" meant an open door for Japanese exploitation of Asia.

J. C. Vinson, "The Annulment of the Lansing-Ishii Agreement," *Pacific Hist. Rev.*, XXVII (1958), 57–69 likewise contends that the substitution at Washington of the Nine Power Pact for the Lansing-Ishii agreement did not effectively restrain Japan's designs on the Open Door.

R. N. Current, "Consequences of the Kellogg Pact," in G. L. Anderson, *Issues and Conflicts* (Lawrence, Kans., 1959) argues that later statesmen like Stimson stretched the Pact to mean joint responsibility for enforcing it; hence America drew closer to the League and became more directly involved in collective security.

G. E. Wheeler, "Isolated Japan: Anglo-American Diplomatic Co-operation, 1927–1936," *Pacific Hist. Rev.*, XXX (1961), 165–178 shows America drawing closer to Britain because of the need for containing Japan; America was not strong enough to go it alone.

8TH ED. REFS. Dorothy Borg, *The United States and the Far Eastern Crisis of 1933–1938* (Cambridge, Mass., 1964), concludes that the F.D.R.-Hull policy was to encourage the Chinese without unduly offending the Japanese, at whom moral preachments were aimed. The main goal of the administration, in line with public opinion, was to avert war with Japan. Hull in 1937 rebuffed British and League proposals for intervention.

Betty Glad, *Charles Evans Hughes and the Illusions of Innocence: A Study in American Diplomacy* (Urbana, Ill., 1966), is a study in many respects more psychological than historical. It shows how a somewhat puritanical figure with 19th-Century idealism attempted to adjust, without complete success, to the harsh realities of a changing 20th Century.

Donald R. McCoy, *Calvin Coolidge: The Quiet President* (New York, 1967), demonstrates that Coolidge stumbled badly in connection with the Geneva Conference. As for the Kellogg-Briand Pact, he was "shoved" into it. Belatedly, and with misgivings, he supported the "swordless sheath."

M. G. Fry, "The North Atlantic Triangle and the Abrogation of the Anglo-Japanese Alliance," *Jour. of Mod. Hist.*, XXXIX (1967), 46–64, presents further evidence that the Canadians (in the face of opposition from Australia and New Zealand) managed to push London toward abrogation at the Washington Conference of 1921–1922.

Russell D. Buhite, "Nelson Johnson and American Policy toward China, 1925–1928," *Pacific Hist. Rev.*, XXXV (1966), 451–465, demonstrates that this State Department official helped shape a patient policy in regard to China's treaty obligations.

William A. Williams, "American Intervention in Russia, 1917–1920," *Studies on the Left*, III (1963), 24–48; IV (1964), 39–57, argues that Wilson's anti-Bolshevism (despite his espousal of self-determination) was the most important factor in the intervention decision, and that the U.S. rejected all opportunities to cooperate with the Bolsheviks.

Claude E. Fike, "Aspects of the New American Recognition Policy toward

Russia following World War I," *Southern Quar.*, IV (1965), 1–16, describes
the rebuff given to the Bolshevik attempt (ending in 1921) to establish a
diplomatic representative in the U.S., and the departure of the Kerensky representative in 1922.

9TH ED. REFS. Thomas H. Buckley, *The United States and the Washington
Conference, 1921–1922* (Knoxville, Tenn., 1970), now the most thorough-
going account, concludes that the national interest was served by trading unfinished battleships and bases for (temporary) security.

L. Ethan Ellis, *Republican Foreign Policy, 1921–1933* (New Brunswick,
N.J., 1968) details the fitful progress toward "involvement without commitment" in attaining a fairly high level of international cooperation.

Russell D. Buhite, *Nelson T. Johnson and American Policy toward China,
1925–1941* (East Lansing, Mich., 1968) sketches policy while attempting to
build up this little-known U.S. minister-ambassador in China.

Robert J. Maddox, "Woodrow Wilson, the Russian Embassy and Siberian
Intervention," *Pacific Hist. Rev.*, XXXVI (1967), 435–448, reveals that Wilson, behind a pose of hands-off, actively supported financial and other measures designed to help anti-Bolshevik elements.

Ira Klein, "Whitehall, Washington, and the Anglo-Japanese Alliance, 1919–
1921, *Pacific Hist. Rev.*, XLI (1972), 460–483, further supports the thesis that
Britain's decision to abandon the alliance with Japan for the Four Power
Pact was reached in advance of the Washington Conference, and not primarily as a result of American or Dominion pressures.

David Carlton, "Great Britain and the Coolidge Naval Disarmament Conference of 1927," *Pol. Sci. Quar.*, LXXXIII (1968), 573–598, concludes that
the conference failed because the Americans and the British regarded each
other as potential enemies.

Ch. 43. ECONOMIC FOREIGN POLICY BETWEEN WARS, 1919–1939

Peter G. Filene, *Americans and the Soviet Experiment, 1917–1933: American Attitudes toward Russia from the February Revolution until Diplomatic
Recognition* (Cambridge, Mass., 1967), shows that public opinion changed
from a strong anti-recognition stance, in March, 1931, to a strong recognition
stance in 1933, largely because of the depression and the menace of Japan.
(There was little mention of Hitler.) The major grievances had become
Soviet propaganda and revolutionary activity, while debts and expropriated
property had become secondary.

Beatrice Farnsworth, *William C. Bullitt and the Soviet Union* (Bloomington, Ind., 1967), demonstrates that Bullitt, enthusiastically pro-Soviet, had a
large hand in bringing about recognition and was rewarded with the ambas-
sadorship in Moscow in 1933. By mid-1935 he had become furiously anti-
Soviet, primarily because the Russians violated their recognition pledge not
to permit anti-American Communist activity in the U.S.S.R. Other misunder-
standings about the terms of recognition in 1933 arose from vagueness of
language, especially the promised "loan," about which the Soviets may have
been technically right. Transferred to the Paris Embassy, Bullitt influenced
Roosevelt's foreign policy, but his bitter anti-Russian bias partially blinded
him to the danger of Hitler.

Donald G. Bishop, *The Roosevelt-Litvinov Agreements: The American
View* (Syracuse, 1965), discusses the implementation of Russian promises,
most of which were in some degree broken (in the view of the U.S.). The

result was largely due to imprecision in the negotiations, yet recognition itself is praised as having made possible the alliance with Russia in World War II.

Richard N. Kottman, *Reciprocity and the North Atlantic Triangle, 1932–1938* (Ithaca, N.Y., 1968), analyzes the diplomatic and political aspects of the economic *rapprochement* in three major trade agreements involving the U.S., the U.K., and Canada.

Lloyd C. Gardner, *Economic Aspects of New Deal Diplomacy* (Madison, 1964), argues that Rooseveltian policy, by continuing to encourage economic expansion and involvement abroad, did not mark a sharp break with the past. Secretary Hull appears as highly influential in shaping F.D.R.'s trade (and other) policies.

George F. Kennan, *Memoirs, 1925–1950* (Boston, 1967), is a distinguished book by a top-flight foreign service officer who initially was highly distrustful of the Bolsheviks. He joined Ambassador Bullitt in 1933 as third secretary in Moscow, thought highly of his chief as a diplomatist (except for his impatience), and held Ambassador Davies, Bullitt's successor, in low esteem. This volume may be supplemented by the same author's *From Prague after Munich: Diplomatic Papers, 1938–1940* (Princeton, N.J., 1968), largely related to the Nazi occupation of Prague.

Julius W. Pratt, *Cordell Hull*, 2 vols. (New York, 1964), vols. XII, XIII in S. F. Bemis and Robert H. Ferrell, eds., *The American Secretaries of State and Their Diplomacy*, 17 vols. (New York, 1927–1967), is the best general treatment available, critical yet respectful. F.D.R. was not always his "own" Secretary of State; he kept certain matters in his own hands but consistently gave Hull a relatively free rein with others.

Robert E. Bowers, "Hull, Russian Subversion in Cuba, and Recognition of the U.S.S.R.," *Jour. of Amer. Hist.*, LIII (1966), 542–554, suggests (without conclusively proving) that Communist activity in Cuba caused Secretary Hull, who was somewhat sidetracked by F.D.R., to oppose recognition clandestinely.

Elliot A. Rosen, "Intranationalism vs. Internationalism: The Interregnum Struggle for the Sanctity of the New Deal," *Pol. Sci. Quar.*, LXXXI (1966), 274–297, points out that Roosevelt made the decision, 1932–1933, to give national recovery a higher priority than international economic adjustment.

J. C. Vinson, in "War Debts and Peace Legislation: The Johnson Act of 1934," *Mid-America*, L (1968), 206–222, regards the Johnson anti-banker debt default act, initially aimed at South American defaulters, as the first of the neutrality laws. It reflected public opinion, and was accepted by F.D.R. to insure passage of the Reciprocal Trade Agreements Act of 1934.

9TH ED. REFS. Carl P. Parrini, *Heir to Empire: United States Economic Diplomacy, 1916–1923* (Pittsburgh, 1969) demonstrates that the U.S., heir to Britain as an exporter of capital, fought hard and farsightedly for a worldwide commercial open door (as it was to again after World War II). The era was not one of economic isolationism.

Joan H. Wilson, *American Business and Foreign Policy, 1920–1933* (Lexington, Ky., 1971) shows that business opinion was widely diversified and did not dominate foreign policy.

Melvyn Leffler, "The Origins of Republican War Debt Policy, 1921–1923: A Case Study in the Applicability of the Open Door Interpretation," *Jour. of Amer. Hist.*, LIX (1972), 585–601, concludes that other important influences besides foreign markets were operative, including domestic fiscal problems and public opinion.

Bernard V. Burke, "American Economic Diplomacy and the Weimar Republic," *Mid-America*, LIV (1972), 211–233, reveals that the U.S. government, interventionist in economic policy but isolationist in politics, shortsightedly failed to support a liberal government in Germany.

B. D. Rhodes, "Reassessing 'Uncle Shylock': The United States and the French War Debt, 1917–1929," *Jour. of Amer. Hist.*, LV (1969), 787–803, explains that the U.S. was not "grasping" and that the French, seeking complete cancellation, were dilatory and evasive.

B. D. Rhodes, "The Origins of Finnish-American Friendship, 1919–1941," *Mid-America*, LIV (1972), 3–19, stresses fiscal fidelity, plus the heroic resistance to Russia. The "war debt" was for postwar relief, involved no great burden, and was made lighter because the balance of trade with America favored Finland.

Arthur W. Schatz, "The Anglo-American Trade Agreement and Cordell Hull's Search for Peace, 1936–1938," *Jour. of Amer. Hist.*, LVII (1970), 85–103, attributes the non-success of Hull's program to his inability to perceive that economic problems also involved political factors.

Roger R. Trask, "The 'Terrible Turk' and Turkish-American Relations in the Interwar Period," *Historian*, XXXIII (1970), 40–53, shows how both countries worked together to protect American commercial and missionary activity in Turkey.

Ch. 44. GOOD NEIGHBORS SOUTH AND NORTH, 1917–1941

See new references on p. 691.

D. M. Smith, "Bainbridge Colby and the Good Neighbor Policy, 1920–1921," *Miss. Valley Hist. Rev.*, L (1963), 56–78 credits Secretary Colby with unusual success in softening the imperialism of the earlier Wilson years by foreshadowing withdrawals from Haiti and Santo Domingo, and by a highly successful goodwill tour of South America.

J. R. Juárez, "United States Withdrawal from Santo Domingo," *Hispanic Amer. Hist. Rev.*, XLII (1962), 152–190 explains the troop withdrawal in 1924 in terms of such factors as lessened strategic value, financial unprofitableness, and charges of illegality.

D. B. Cooper, "The Withdrawal of the United States from Haiti, 1928–1934," *Jour. of Inter-American Studies*, V (1963), 83–101 concludes that the occupation was "beneficial" to neither the United States nor Haiti.

S. R. Ross, "Dwight Morrow and the Mexican Revolution," *Hispanic Amer. Hist. Rev.*, XXXVIII (1958), 506–528 shows that Morrow, by strengthening the central government in the interests of all concerned, temporarily slowed down the revolution. He strengthened it by normalizing Mexican-United States relations.

L. E. Ellis, "Dwight Morrow and the Church-State Controversy in Mexico," *ibid.*, 482–505 relates how Morrow, given virtually a free hand by Washington, exercised great skill in persuading church and state to compromise their differences; the church got relatively modest concessions but set great store by them.

E. D. Cronon, "Interpreting the New Good Neighbor Policy: The Cuban Crisis of 1933," *ibid.*, XXXIX (1959), 538–567 reveals how the Cuban crisis forced Washington to sharpen and clarify the Good Neighbor policy. Despite pressure to land troops, F.D.R. used only naval patrols and employed nonrecognition to topple the government of Grau San Martín.

R. N. Kottman, "Volstead Violated: Prohibition as a Factor in Canadian-

American Relations," *Canadian Hist. Rev.*, XLIII (1962), 106–126 discusses the diplomatic embarrassment to 1933 caused by rum-running from Canada.

8TH ED. REFS. Bryce Wood, *The United States and Latin American Wars, 1932–1942* (New York, 1966), shows that with respect to three unimportant South American wars Washington pursued a policy of nonintervention that amounted to indifference, though U.S. diplomats made some overtures toward mediation.

Donald R. McCoy, *Calvin Coolidge: The Quiet President* (New York, 1967), has a brief discussion of Coolidge's Mexican and Nicaraguan policies, and emphasizes the highly favorable impression that he made in going to Havana.

Robert H. Ferrell, "Repudiation of a Repudiation" [J. Reuben Clark Memorandum], *Jour. of Amer. Hist.*, LI (1965), 669–673, discloses that although the Clark Memorandum repudiated the T.R. corollary to the Monroe Doctrine and was approved by Secretary Stimson, President Hoover and State Department officials really repudiated the Memorandum, which was a private and unofficial document, by virtually ignoring it.

Lester D. Langley, "Negotiating New Treaties with Panama: 1936," *Hispanic Amer. Hist. Rev.*, XLVIII (1968), 220–233, presents as a phase of the Good Neighbor the negotiation of two pacts, one of which (Hull-Alfara) softened the treaty of 1903 by ending the protectorate, increasing the annuity to $436,000, and including other concessions.

M. Paul Holsinger, "The 'I'm Alone' Controversy: A Study in Inter-American Diplomacy, 1929–1935," *Mid-America*, L (1968), 305–313, notes that the two arbiters (American and Canadian) concluded that the U.S. had no right to sink a vessel about 200 miles off the coast, but greatly reduced the asked-for indemnity of $400,000, partly because the ship was American-owned. The settlement improved Canadian-American amity.

Richard N. Kottman, "The Canadian-American Trade Agreement of 1935," *Jour. of Amer. Hist.*, LII (1965), 275–296, notes that the pact marked a "return to economic sanity" after several years of Smoot-Hawleyism, and presaged the growing *rapprochement* of the prewar and war years.

9TH ED. REFS. Richard N. Kottman, *Reciprocity and the North Atlantic Triangle, 1932–1938* (Ithaca, N.Y., 1968) details the three-way negotiations among Britain, Canada, and the U.S., in response to Hull's trade-agreements obsession. The two pacts with Canada and the one with Britain came hard; London had strong commitments to imperial preference.

Joseph S. Tulchin, *The Aftermath of War: World War I and U.S. Policy toward Latin America* (New York, 1971) develops U.S. attitudes until 1925, principally economic foreign policy; the end of the European threat decreased military and diplomatic intervention.

William Kamman, *A Search for Stability: United States Diplomacy toward Nicaragua, 1925–1933* (Notre Dame, Ind., 1968) is a detailed account of the interventionism which was supplanted by the Good Neighbor Policy.

Kenneth J. Grieb, "Warren G. Harding and the Dominican Republic: U.S. Withdrawal, 1921–1923, *Jour. of Inter-Amer. Studies* XI (1969), 425–440, credits Harding with having determinedly fulfilled his campaign pledge, particularly through the appointment of Sumner Welles as his personal envoy.

Dana C. Munro, "The American Withdrawal from Haiti, 1929–1934," *Hispanic Amer. Hist. Rev.*, XLIX (1969), 1–26, reviews the last years of the U.S. occupation, especially 1930–1932, when the author was minister to Haiti.

Ch. 45. JAPAN, NEUTRALTY, AND THE DICTATORS, 1923–1939

See new references on p. 710.

Roger Daniels, *The Politics of Prejudice: The Anti-Japanese Movement in California and the Struggle for Japanese Exclusion* (Berkeley, 1962) stresses the domestic backgrounds of the movement, concludes that complete exclusion reflected majority sentiment, and criticizes Secretary Hughes' inept handling of the problem.

J. M. Blum, *From the Morgenthau Diaries: Years of Crisis, 1928–1938* (Boston, 1959) notes that F.D.R.'s Secretary of the Treasury, taking a more vigorous line against the dictators than Secretary Hull, meddled in foreign affairs by using financial pressures.

George Kennan, *Russia and the West under Lenin and Stalin* (Boston, 1960) outlines the background of the Russo-German nonaggression pact of 1939. Kennan doubts that the Russians would have supported the Czechs with troops at the time of Munich. Hitler was determined to attack Poland even before the nonaggression pact was negotiated; Stalin cynically got the Allies and the Germans to bid against each other.

Allen Guttmann, *The Wound in the Heart: America and the Spanish Civil War* (New York, 1962), analyzes the reactions of various groups, especially the dilemmas confronting democracy-loving Catholics and fascist-hating isolationists.

E. E. Morison, *Turmoil and Tradition: A Study of the Life and Times of Henry L. Stimson* (Boston, 1960) shows that Hoover, distrusting F.D.R. and scheming to bind him to a conservative course regarding the war debts and other matters, resented Secretary Stimson's postelection confabulations with Roosevelt.

F. I. Israel, *Nevada's Key Pittman* (Lincoln, Neb., 1963) shows how this Senator, though often under the influence of alcohol and obsessed with the parochial interests of the least populous state, by the rule of seniority became chairman of the powerful Senate Committee on Foreign Relations. His fanatical dedication to silver produced an international silver agreement at London in 1933. In connection with neutrality legislation, he was a problem to F.D.R., who could not easily bypass him.

D. M. Dozer, *Are We Good Neighbors?* (Gainesville, Fla., 1961) demonstrates that the doctrine of the two spheres received new emphasis with the rise of the European dictators. Franklin Roosevelt's policy of pro-Franco neutrality was unpopular in Latin America, especially in leftist circles.

Nicholas Halasz, *Roosevelt through Foreign Eyes* (Princeton, 1961) is a collection from printed sources showing that abroad Roosevelt was regarded as a great man from the beginning; a superman by 1945. Even Mussolini admired him as late as 1937 as something of a fellow dictator.

Nancy H. Hooker, ed., *The Moffat Papers: Selections from the Diplomatic Journals of Jay Pierrepont Moffat* (Cambridge, Mass., 1956) contains inside observations by one of the more able American foreign service officers.

Bernard Sternsher, "The Stimson Doctrine: F.D.R. versus Moley and Tugwell," *Pacific Hist. Rev.*, XXXI (1962), 281–289 points out that Roosevelt, thinking it now too late to build up Japanese liberals against the military, accepted Stimson's policy of a strong position against Japan, contrary to the advice of Moley and Tugwell.

J. E. Wiltz, "The Nye Committee Revisited," *The Historian*, XXIII (1961) 211–233 concludes that neutrality legislation would have come without Nye;

he was one of the mildest members of the Committee, but his intemperate speeches on the outside gave the Committee a bad name.

W. S. Cole, "Senator Key Pittman and American Neutrality Policies, 1933–1940," *Miss. Valley Hist. Rev.*, XLVI (1960), 644–662 makes clear that the powerful Senator had a large hand in the mandatory arms embargo of 1935, though generally a middle-of-the-roader between isolationists and interventionists.

H. B. Braddick, "A New Look at American Policy during the Italo-Ethiopian Crisis, 1935–1936," *Jour. of Mod. Hist.*, XXXIV (1962), 64–73 contends that the moral embargo did not work well; American exports rose. Washington was anxious not to see Britain involved in this war; involvement would weaken her naval strength in the Far East and encourage the Japanese to launch new attacks on China, as they soon did.

J. McV. Haight, Jr., "France, the United States, and the Munich Crisis," *ibid.*, XXXII (1960), 340–358 reveals that the failure of Roosevelt to support the French contributed to their diplomatic capitulation.

T. B. Jacobs, "Roosevelt's 'Quarantine Speech,'" *The Historian*, XXIV (1962), 483–502 argues that, despite the isolationist outcry, the reaction was surprisingly favorable; Roosevelt retreated largely because he was caught without a specific plan.

8TH ED. REFS. John E. Wiltz, *In Search of Peace: The Senate Munitions Inquiry, 1934–1936* (Baton Rouge, La., 1963), concludes that the Nye Committee conducted a fair inquiry; that it failed to convict the arms merchants of conspiring to cause wars; that it did not have major responsibility for the neutrality legislation; and that on balance it did more good than harm. (Yet the exaggerated emphasis by the press on the work of the committee did contribute heavily to the head-in-the-sands psychosis.) See also the same author's brief *From Isolation to War, 1931–1941* (New York, 1968).

Brice Harris, Jr., *The United States and the Italo-Ethiopian Crisis* (Stanford, Calif., 1964), focuses on the problem in its larger setting, with attention to the precarious balance both with regard to Hitler and Japan. The U.S., while not officially supporting sanctions, unofficially indicated that it would not undercut them.

Armin Rappaport, *Henry L. Stimson and Japan, 1931–1933* (Chicago, 1963), is a scholarly monograph which concludes that Secretary Stimson's policy, though meeting with some temporary and minor successes, merely angered the Japanese without halting them.

Takehiko Yoshihashi, *Conspiracy at Mukden: The Rise of the Japanese Military* (New Haven, 1963), explains in detail how the headstrong militarists defied the civilian authorities in Tokyo.

Thaddeus V. Tuleja, *Statesmen and Admirals* (New York, 1963), surveys the interplay between naval policy and diplomacy in the two decades after World War I, and stresses the weakness of repeatedly taking positions in the Far East not realistically backed by power.

Manny T. Koginos, *The Panay Incident: Prelude to War* (Lafayette, Ind., 1967), is a detailed treatment, including U.S. public opinion. Probably an "elite inner group" of Japanese military extremists provoked the attack but there is considerable evidence that the vessel could have been mistaken for a fleeing Chinese craft (p. 129). The incident gave impetus to F.D.R.'s naval program.

James B. Crowley, *Japan's Quest for Autonomy: National Security and For-*

eign Policy, 1930–1938 (Princeton, N.J., 1966), throws light on the interaction between the military and the civilian officials in shaping policy.

Warren I. Cohen, *The American Revisionists: The Lessons of Intervention in World War I* (Chicago, 1967), shows how the historians who questioned Germany's "war guilt" of 1914 contributed to the isolationist spirit of the 1930's.

Manfred Jonas, *Isolationism in America, 1935–1941* (Ithaca, N.Y., 1966), is a richly detailed study which explains isolation in terms of go-it-alone unilateralism and fear of war.

Finis H. Capps, *From Isolationism to Involvement: The Swedish Immigrant Press in America, 1914–1945* (Chicago, 1966), demonstrates that while most of the editors endorsed the League of Nations and the United Nations, they retained strong suspicions of Germany and Russia, especially the latter.

John P. Diggins, "The Italo-American Anti-Fascist Opposition," *Jour. of Amer. Hist.*, LIV (1967), 579–598, shows that the opposition, though supported by the radical elements in the U.S., commanded little popular support; Mussolini appealed to Italian nationalistic sentiments.

Robert A. Friedlander, "New Light on the Anglo-American Reaction to the Ethiopian War, 1935–1936," *Mid-America*, XLV (1963), 115–125, discloses that U.S. Ambassador Long, strongly pro-Italian, played an important role in opposing effective sanctions.

J. David Valaik, "Catholics, Neutrality, and the Spanish Embargo, 1937–1939," *Jour. of Amer. Hist.*, LIV (1967), 73–85, concludes that about two-thirds of the Catholic laymen did not follow their leaders in supporting Franco, and suggests that Roosevelt mistook the voice of the leaders in following a policy favorable to Franco.

R. D. Burns and W. A. Dixon, "Foreign Policy and the 'Democratic Myth': The Debate on the Ludlow Amendment [1937–38]," *Mid-America*, XLVII (1965), 288–306, reveals that while the newspaper press seems to have overwhelmingly opposed this war-declaring referendum, it commanded impressive popular support.

Robert Dallek, *Democrat and Diplomat: The Life of William E. Dodd* (New York, 1968), describes a tactless and anti-fascist liberal (F.D.R. wanted him as an example) who tried to awaken America to the Hitlerian menace. He made himself *persona non grata*, though he perceived the upcoming dangers more clearly than did his British and French ambassadorial colleagues.

Robert Dallek, "Beyond Tradition: The Diplomatic Careers of William E. Dodd and George S. Messersmith, 1933–1938," *South Atlantic Quar.*, LXVI (1967), 233–244, concludes that the undiplomatic and non-professional Ambassador Dodd in Germany foresaw the menace of Hilter as clearly as did the professional Messersmith, Consul General in Berlin and later minister to Austria.

John P. Diggins, "Flirtation with Fascism: American Pragmatic Liberals and Mussolini's Italy," *Amer. Hist. Rev.*, LXXI (1966), 487–506, reveals that the liberals were fascinated by the theory of Fascism and its innovative character; they failed to consider its workability. Democratic America was more friendly to Fascism than "any other Western nation."

John P. Diggins, "Mussolini and America: Hero-Worship, Charisma, and the 'Vulgar Talent,' " *Historian*, XXVIII (1966), 559–585, examines the reasons for the dictator's surprising popularity and concludes that Americans were attracted by "the cult of personality" rather than by admiration for Fascist ideology.

9TH ED. REFS. Akira Iriye, *After Imperialism: The Search for a New Order in the Far East, 1921–1931* (Cambridge, Mass., 1965) focuses on the clashing rivalries of Japan, China, and Russia, with primary attention to Japan and somewhat incidental reference to the U.S. A handful of Japanese subordinates in Manchuria did not precipitate the crisis of 1931: the military officers there kept in close touch with their military superiors in Tokyo (p. 300).

Arnold A. Offner, *American Appeasement: United States Foreign Policy and Germany, 1933–1938* (Cambridge, Mass., 1969) is critical of the repeated failure of the Roosevelt administration to take a strong stand against Nazi Germany.

Richard P. Traina, *American Diplomacy and the Spanish Civil War* (Bloomington, Ind., 1968) details FDR's cautious approach, which was urged by Secretary Hull and motivated in part by a desire not to forfeit Congressional support for New Deal legislation.

Hamilton D. Perry, *The Panay Incident: Prelude to Pearl Harbor* (New York, 1969) is a journalistic recapitulation from the U.S. side.

Edgar B. Nixon, ed., *Franklin D. Roosevelt and Foreign Affairs*, 3 vols., (Cambridge, Mass., 1969) is a valuable collection of official documents and personal reports (which FDR encouraged from men in the field).

Robert A. Hecht, "Great Britain and the Stimson Note of January 7, 1932," *Pacific Hist. Rev.*, XXXVIII (1969), 177–191, reveals that the British declined to go along with non-recognition because they could not afford to offend Japan for political, strategic, and economic reasons.

John M. Haight, Jr., "Franklin D. Roosevelt and a Naval Quarantine of Japan," *Pacific Hist. Rev.*, XL (1971), 203–226, presents evidence that FDR was initially thinking of a naval quarantine but was discouraged by American isolationism and British non-cooperation.

Ch. 46. WORLD WAR II: THROUGH LEND LEASE, 1939–1941

J. A. Logan, Jr., *No Transfer* (New Haven, 1961) deals with this principle during World War II, especially preclusive occupations like those of Iceland and Greenland by the United States. An abortive plan to take over the Azores greatly distressed the Portuguese. Washington had to go slowly for fear of providing a precedent for the Japanese in the Dutch East Indies.

R. A. Divine, *The Illusion of Neutrality* (Chicago, 1962) describes Roosevelt's protracted efforts to secure a repeal of the arms embargo; uncertainty as to his third-term aspirations clouded the issue. He uncandidly emphasized the theme of keeping America out of war while actually seeking to help the democracies.

Robert Sobel, *The Origins of Interventionism: The United States and the Russo-Finnish War* (New York, 1960) notes that since the isolationists wanted to help Finland, the debate served as a half-way house toward ultimate interventionism. Ill-informed newsmen exaggerated Finnish victories. The modification of the American arms embargo to a cash-and-carry basis, though designed to help the British, hurt the Finns: they did not have enough "cash" or "carry."

Max Jakobson, *The Diplomacy of the Winter War, 1939–1940* (Cambridge, Mass., 1961), by a then Finnish official, points out the reluctance of the Roosevelt administration to help the Finns with arms lest it hinder the repeal of the arms embargo and involve America in the war. The Russian attack was preemptively strategic; Moscow had no confidence that Finland could hold back Hitler.

Andrew J. Schwartz, *America and the Russo-Finnish War* (Washington, D.C., 1960), is based heavily on State Department records, with relatively little attention to American public opinion.

Joachim Remak, " 'Friends of the New Germany': The Bund and German-American Relations," *Jour. of Mod. Hist.*, XXXIX (1957), 38–41 shows that Berlin was forced to disavow this offshoot of the Nazi Party, for by extravagant Hitlerian antics the Bund did great harm to the Nazi cause in the United States.

Alexander DeConde, "The South and Isolationism," *Jour. of Southern Hist.*, XXIV (1958), 332–346 challenges the assumption that the South was less isolationist than the rest of the country in the months before Pearl Harbor, despite the circumstances that made it conspicuously interventionist.

8TH ED. REFS. John M. Blum, *From the Morgenthau Diaries: Years of Urgency, 1938–1941* (Boston, 1965), describes how Secretary of the Treasury Morgenthau, in his enthusiasm for the Allied cause, took advantage of his friendship with F.D.R. to involve himself heavily in the bailiwick of Secretary Hull, who resented such interference.

T. R. Fehrenbach, *F.D.R.'s Undeclared War, 1939 to 1941* (New York, 1967), is a popularized version of the relation between a reluctant American public opinion and Roosevelt's somewhat clandestine leadership toward intervention in World War II.

Philip Goodhart, *Fifty Ships that Saved the World: The Foundation of the Anglo-American Alliance* (New York, 1965), by a British Member of Parliament, interprets the most significant aspect of the destroyers-for-bases transaction as a giant step toward lend-lease and massive aid to Britain. The immediate significance of both the destroyers and the bases was oversold, the author holds.

Richard J. Whalen, *The Founding Father: The Story of Joseph P. Kennedy* (New York, 1964) shows how Kennedy's vehemently isolationist stance as Ambassador in London (1937–40) caused F.D.R. great embarrassment and brought about his replacement.

Julius W. Pratt, "The Ordeal of Cordell Hull," *Review of Politics*, XXVIII (1966), 76–98, concludes that "competitive" administration worked out well when other Cabinet members (Ickes, Morgenthau) and subordinates undercut the slow-moving Hull to accelerate a policy of halting the aggressors.

9TH ED. REFS. Theodore A. Wilson, *The First Summit: Roosevelt and Churchill at Placentia Bay 1941* (Boston, 1969) describes the discussions and discussants in scholarly detail, emphasizing the military exhaustion of the British and the unpreparedness of the U.S.

The Wartime Journals of Charles A. Lindbergh (New York, 1970) throw much light on the rather naive and pro-Fascist leanings of the famed aviator who achieved oratorical leadership of the isolationist America Firsters.

Mark L. Chadwin, *The Hawks of World War II* (Chapel Hill, N.C., 1968) deals with the small group of extremists (to the right of the White group) who emerged in 1940 and helped create the pro-interventionist sentiment that led to the destroyer deal.

John M. Haight, Jr., *American Aid to France, 1938–1940* (New York, 1970) recounts the desperate attempts of France to buy planes in the U.S.; few were delivered but these orders ultimately helped America to build up air superiority against Hitler.

Warren F. Kimball, *The Most Unsordid Act: Lend-Lease, 1939–1941* (Baltimore, 1969) describes in depth the most significant step leading to war; while FDR was uncandid, he was not obligated (it is argued) to harp on the dangers of Lend-Lease. The opposition did that.

James M. Burns, *Roosevelt: The Soldier of Freedom* (New York, 1970) is the second and concluding volume of a superior biography. FDR is portrayed as a great leader with high ideals who all too often felt obliged to bow to expediency.

David S. Wyman, *Paper Walls: America and the Refugee Crisis, 1938–1941* (Amherst, Mass., 1968) reveals that at a time when Hitler's policy was one of expulsion rather than extermination, the executive and legislative branches in Washington, responding to depression-ridden public opinion, refused to lower the immigration bars.

Klaus Kipphan, *Deutsche Propaganda in den Vereinigten Staaten, 1933–1941* (Heidelberg, 1971) reveals that German propaganda in the U.S. was ineffective and the Bund was an embarrassment to Berlin.

S. E. Hilton, "The Welles Mission to Europe, February-March 1940: Illusion or Realism?" *Jour. of Amer. Hist.*, LVIII (1971), 93–120, demonstrates that Welles' mission was primarily designed to weaken the Axis by delaying Hitler's expected spring offensive.

W. M. Tuttle, Jr., "Aid-to-the-Allies Short-of-War versus American Intervention, 1940: A Reappraisal of William Allen White's Leadership," *Jour. of Amer. Hist.*, LVI (1970), 840–858, relates how an aging White was forced out of leadership when the other leaders became more interventionist than he desired.

See also references for the next chapter.

Ch. 47. THE ROAD TO PEARL HARBOR

See new references on p. 742.

P. W. Schroeder, *The Axis Alliance and Japanese-American Relations, 1941* (Ithaca, N.Y., 1958) concludes that Washington, backed by a public opinion that was strongly anti-appeasement, pursued a "hard" policy in behalf of China which drove Japan into a corner, made war inevitable, and brought disaster to the Chinese. The moralists opposed compromise, which might have averted hostilities.

E. L. Presseisen, *Germany and Japan: A Study in Totalitarian Diplomacy, 1933–1941* (The Hague, 1958) portrays two faithless allies, each ready to exploit the other if possible and betray the other if necessary. Each expected the other to pull its chestnuts out of the fire; neither obliged.

F. W. Iklé, *German-Japanese Relations, 1936–1940* (New York, 1956) likewise stresses the cross-purposes.

R. J. C. Butow, *Tojo and the Coming of the War* (Princeton, 1961) is a major contribution utilizing Japanese sources. The Hawley-Smoot Tariff accelerated the expansionism of the war lords, who thought that any nation trying to curb them was not "sincere." The proposed meeting of Prime Minister Konoye with F.D.R. would have failed; both were determined not to back down. Tokyo spurned a modus vivendi from its Washington Embassy to ease the war in China. The Japanese note of November 20 (not the Hull note of November 26) was the true ultimatum: American acceptance would lead to further demands; nonacceptance meant war. There was a third choice between surrender and war for Tokyo: that was compromise. Without concessions, the war lords were bent on fighting; and they felt that they would lose if they did not begin by December 1. Every day of delay cost some 12,000 tons of oil and also favorable weather. Tokyo feared that the Western powers might strike first; and Japan dreaded abasement to a third-rate status.

Tōgō Shigenori, *The Cause of Japan* (New York, 1956) is a book by the then Foreign Minister which declares that the Hull note of November 26 forced Japan to choose between war and surrender; it delighted the militarists, who wanted war.

Louis Morton, "Japan's Decision for War," in K. R. Greenfield, ed., *Command Decisions* (New York, 1959), 63–87 is an able summary stressing dwindling oil supplies, weather conditions, the need to prepare for a Russian attack in the spring, and the desirability of striking before the Western powers were ready. Japan did not seek the total defeat of the United States; merely retention of her gains and dominance in the Far East.

Roberta Wohlstetter, *Pearl Harbor: Warning and Decision* (Stanford, Calif., 1962) is an important work which does not pinpoint the blame; there was so much undigested information pouring into Washington about so many different areas that the net result was uncertainty, confusion, and cross-purposes. When Hull presented his so-called ultimatum of November 26, the attacking Japanese task force had been under way twenty-four hours, although it could have been recalled twenty-four hours before the attack. Some of these facts were earlier revealed in T. B. Kittredge, "United States Defense Policy and Strategy, 1941," *U.S. News and World Report*, XXXVII, 53–63 (Dec. 3, 1954).

Useful collections of pertinent documents are H. L. Trefousse, ed., *What Happened at Pearl Harbor?* (New York, 1958) and P. S. Burtness and W. U. Ober, eds., *The Puzzle of Pearl Harbor* (Evanston, Ill., 1962).

D. J. Lu, *From the Marco Polo Bridge to Pearl Harbor: Japan's Entry into World War II* (Washington, 1961) focuses on Tokyo's reluctance to back down in China. The Japanese navy, less keen for war with America than the army, was so disturbed by the oil embargo as to demand a definite decision for peace or war while there was yet time. The author believes that Roosevelt would have been well advised to have invoked the Neutrality Act in 1937 and to have met with Prime Minister Konoye.

B. K. Wheeler, *Yankee from the West* (Garden City, N.Y., 1962) recapitulates the antiwar views of a leading "America First" Senator; he confesses that he "leaked" the secret war plans of the Administration to the press three days before Pearl Harbor.

R. J. C. Butow, "The Hull-Nomura Conversations: A Fundamental Misconception," *Amer. Hist. Rev.*, LXV (1960), 822–836 discloses that Ambassador Nomura, inexperienced and understanding English imperfectly, incorrectly represented to Tokyo that Hull was prepared to make certain concessions. When such were not forthcoming, Washington seemed to be falling back to a "hard" position, and the break was facilitated.

R. A. Esthus, "President Roosevelt's Commitment to Britain to Intervene in a Pacific War," *Miss. Valley Hist. Rev.*, L (1963), 28–38 hypothesizes that F.D.R., after rejecting earlier pressures, definitely assured the British (December 1–3) of armed support in the event of "a Japanese attack on British or Dutch territory or on Thailand." The evidence suggests that he would seek the backing of Congress.

8TH ED. REFS. James V. Compton, *The Swastika and the Eagle: Hitler, the United States and the Origins of World War II* (Boston, 1967), reveals Hitler's ambivalence: he did not regard the U.S. as a great power yet he ordered his submarine commanders not to provoke the Americans. Simultaneously he urged Japan to pursue a course in the Far East that was bound to involve Germany in war with the U.S. In the short run, at least, his ambitions seem to have been continental rather than global; hence he had no immediate plans to attack the U.S. when he invaded Poland.

Saul Friedländer, *Prelude to Downfall: Hitler and the United States, 1939–1941* (New York, 1967), arrives at somewhat the same conclusions as Compton (above). Hitler was counting on a short war when he attacked Poland; Berlin was astonished by the mild reaction in the U.S. to the sinking of the *Robin Moor;* fear of possible U.S. intervention caused Hitler to opt for a blitz strategy in Russia which, with poor communications, invited disaster; according to the German documents, the *Greer* first fired upon the German submarine; the *Kearny* was attacked in a convoy battle as a British ship; Roosevelt's secret German map dividing South America into five vassal states has never been found.

Alton Frye, *Nazi Germany and the American Hemisphere, 1933–1941* (New Haven, 1967), marshals impressive evidence that Hitler, through Nazi infiltration in the U.S. and Latin America, posed such a menace for the future that F.D.R. was justified in supporting the embattled Allies. The absence of any detailed plan in 1940 to attack the U.S. does not mean that Germany could not have devised one. Many signs pointed in that direction.

Johanna M. Meskill, *Hitler and Japan: The Hollow Alliance* (New York, 1966), shows how each ally tried to interpret the tripartite alliance of 1940 to suit its selfish ends, with a resultant lack of coordination. Secret addenda (unknown to the Berlin Foreign Office) gave Japan leeway in deciding when to fight under the alliance, but bound Germany to render Japan military help in a Japanese-American war.

Nobutaka Ike, ed., *Japan's Decision for War* (Stanford, Calif., 1967), consists of translations, with introductions, of the deliberations of the Imperial and Liaison Conferences. There was little reference to the consequences of defeat. The navy (less eager for war than the army) thought that Japan could put up a good fight for two years; then there might be hope of a negotiated peace with a war-weary U.S. Remembrance of the defeat of Russia in 1904–1905, combined with fatalism and reliance on good luck and clever strategy, helped to shape the decision for war. Germany constantly pressured Japan in vain to attack Russia from the rear.

Ladislas Farago, *The Broken Seal: The Story of "Operation Magic" and the Pearl Harbor Disaster* (New York, 1967), tells the story of the "cracking" of the top Japanese "Purple" Code; the Americans were aware that the Japanese were negotiating in bad faith. The so-called U.S. ultimatum of November 26 was marked "Tentative," but Ambassador Nomura, who did not understand English well and who constantly misreported, failed to send this key word to Tokyo (p. 315). F.D.R. did not see all of the "magic" intercepts.

William L. Neumann, *America Encounters Japan* (Baltimore, 1963), surveys, with considerable sympathy for Japan, the events antecedent to Pearl Harbor, and raises questions as to whether America's stake in the Far East was worth a war with the Japanese.

Robert A. Divine, *The Reluctant Belligerent: American Entry into World War II* (New York, 1965), is a brief overview, designed as a textbook supplement, which holds that American policy was largely reaction to the action of the aggressors, and that Roosevelt was timid rather than resolute in providing leadership commensurate with the peril.

Waldo H. Heinrichs, Jr., *American Ambassador: Joseph C. Grew and the Development of the United States Diplomatic Tradition* (Boston, 1966), describes the 40-year career of a professional diplomatist who was stationed in Japan (1932–1941) and who vainly sought, with perhaps undue optimism, to use negotiations to head off an explosion.

Gerhard L. Weinberg, "Hitler's Image of the United States," *Amer. Hist. Rev.*, LXIX (1964), 1006–1021, reveals that Hitler vacillated between a view of the U.S. as a degenerate nation and one that was an industrial colossus—between dreaming of ultimately attacking the U.S. and avoiding a provocation of the U.S.

Warren F. Kimball, "Dieckhoff and America: A German's View of German-American Relations, 1937–1941," *Historian*, XXVII (1965), 218–243, recounts the unsuccessful efforts of the German ambassador in Washington to improve relationships and the reasons for his ill success.

James H. Herzog, "Influence of the United States Navy in the Embargo of Oil to Japan, 1940–1941," *Pacific Hist. Rev.*, XXXV (1966), 317–328, concludes that the navy officials were divided on the embargo issue. Admiral Stark, Chief of Naval Operations, did not want to divert naval strength from the Atlantic to combat a possible Japanese reaction. Roosevelt froze Japanese assets on July 25, 1941, thinking that the Japanese would not choose to fight both the British and the Americans.

John H. Boyle, "The Drought-Walsh Mission to Japan," *Pacific Hist. Rev.*, XXXIV (1965), 141–161, tells how two Catholic priests, as self-appointed negotiators of peace (contrary to the spirit of the Logan Act) became involved in unsuccessful negotiations with Tokyo officials which, by confusing the issues, may have "gone far toward producing the final debacle of December 7."

9TH ED. REFS. Robert H. Jones, *The Roads to Russia: United States Lend-Lease to the Soviet Union* (Norman, Okla., 1969) recounts in detail the magnitude of the shipments and the friction which foreshadowed the Cold War. FDR insisted on not attaching political or economic strings.

Donald J. Friedman, *The Road from Isolation: The Campaign of the American Committee for Non-Participation in Japanese Aggression, 1938–1941* (Cambridge, Mass., 1968) is a slender book describing the considerable efforts of this small pressure group to stop the flow of war materials to Japan.

John Toland, *The Rising Sun: The Decline and Fall of the Japanese Empire, 1936–1945* (New York, 1970), based heavily on Japanese interviews and documents, relates how American diplomacy and ineptitude led to the attack on Pearl Harbor.

David Bergamini, *Japan's Imperial Conspiracy* (New York, 1971) contains a massive but thoroughly unreliable indictment of the Emperor as a warmonger.

F. C. Adams, "The Road to Pearl Harbor: A Reexamination of American Far Eastern Policy, July 1937–December 1938," *Jour. of Amer. Hist.*, LVIII (1971), 73–92, sees the U.S. policy of tough economic sanctions against Japan beginning as early as late 1938, with the $25 million loan to China for war materials.

R. J. C. Butow, "Backdoor Diplomacy in the Pacific: The Proposal for a Konoye-Roosevelt Meeting, 1941," *Jour. Amer. Hist.*, LIX (1972), 48–72, concludes that the meeting would have been better than none at all. The negotiations were complicated by the intrusion of several amateurs.

Hilary Conroy, "The Strange Diplomacy of Admiral Nomura," *Proceedings of the American Philosophical Society*, CXIV (1970), 205–216, notes that not only was Nomura's English faulty, thereby confusing Tokyo, but he pursued an anti-Axis policy that brought on conflict with his Foreign Minister.

R. T. Ruetten, "Harry Elmer Barnes and the 'Historical Blackout,'" *His-*

torian, XXXIII (1971), 202–214, shows how the historian Barnes misused evidence to support the "higher truth" that FDR was a devil who wanted war. Barnes believed that on December 4, 1941, the President had learned from the British of the impending Japanese attack.

See also references for previous chapter.

Ch. 48. DIPLOMACY FOR VICTORY, 1941–1945

Adrienne D. Hytier, *Two Years of French Foreign Policy, Vichy, 1940–1942* (Geneva, 1958) concludes that Washington's Vichy policy as such was not influential, but it did bolster French morale and it made possible needed intelligence.

Wartime relations with Latin America are treated broadly in J. L. Mecham, *The United States and Inter-American Security, 1889–1960* (Austin, Tex., 1961) and in Donald Dozer, *Are We Good Neighbors?* (Gainesville, Fla., 1961). The latter shows how the war brought richer economic ties and further adoration of Roosevelt, but there was much uneasiness over the dollar deluge, Yankee "cultural aggression," and the diplomatic crackdown on Argentina and Chile.

Bryce Wood, *The Making of the Good Neighbor Policy* (New York, 1961) covers essentially the same ground as Dozer, and is especially useful in analyzing reactions to Senator Butler's unfavorable report.

Claude G. Bowers, *Chile Through Embassy Windows: 1939–1953* (New York, 1958) has affectionately personal glimpses of Chile during these years by the then American ambassador.

Annette B. Fox, *The Power of Small States: Diplomacy in World War II* (Chicago, 1959) describes how the small nations, chiefly by virtue of their peripheral position, managed to stay out of the war by playing the great powers (including the United States) off against one another.

8TH ED. REFS. Gaddis Smith, *American Diplomacy during the Second World War, 1941–1945* (New York, 1965), is a broad but perceptive survey. It represents American policy as viewing Russia as a maligned giant who would behave under sympathetic treatment, and Britain as a misguided friend whose policies ought to be changed for her own and the general welfare. In the light of subsequent events, the author regards such an approach as unrealistic and unjustified.

Kent R. Greenfield, *American Strategy in World War II: A Reconsideration* (Baltimore, 1963), stresses the difficulties of coalition warfare, with Stalin ruthlessly looking after his own interests, with Britain most reluctant to launch a cross-channel invasion, and with Roosevelt overruling his military advisers (often for the best) in at least twenty instances. American military men were bitter over the decision to go into North Africa instead of France.

The Earl of Birkenhead, *Halifax: The Life of Lord Halifax* (Boston, 1966) shows that Halifax, the British Ambassador in Washington, 1941–1946, did much to promote coordination between the two allies. There are eight chapters (XXIX–XXXVI) relevant to his career in the United States.

Robert Murphy, *Diplomat Among Warriors* (Garden City, N.Y., 1964), describes F.D.R.'s rather jaunty participation in the Casablanca Conference, his eagerness to liquidate the French empire (despite de Gaulle), and the cleverness of the British in committing the U.S. to a diversionary invasion of Sicily. He dwells on the unfortunate effect of "unconditional surrender" in promoting German propaganda.

Fred L. Israel, ed., *The War Diary of Breckinridge Long: Selections from the Years 1939–1944* (Lincoln, Nebr., 1966), presents the frank thoughts of the Assistant Secretary of State, who agreed with Secretary Hull in resenting interference with the Department by outsiders, and who had a large hand in restricting the emigration of refugees (chiefly Jews ultimately destined for gas chambers).

Arthur D. Morse, *While Six Million Died: A Chronicle of American Apathy* (New York, 1968), presents shocking evidence that the Washington government, though largely aware of Hitler's genocide, failed to take energetic steps to provide a sanctuary. There were, however, strong diplomatic reasons for noninvolvement.

Lord Moran, *Churchill: Taken from the Diaries of Lord Moran* (Boston, 1966), by Churchill's personal physician, throws considerable light on the F.D.R. relationship, which was not as cordial as appeared on the surface.

Douglas G. Anglin, *The St. Pierre and Miquelon Affaire of 1941: A Study in Diplomacy in the North Atlantic Quadrangle* (Toronto, 1966), relates in detail how de Gaulle's unexpected seizure of these two tiny islands in the St. Lawrence River for the Free French (December 24, 1941) angered Hull out of all proportion to their significance and further turned the Roosevelt administration against the difficult Frenchman.

Milton Viorst, *Hostile Allies: F.D.R. and Charles de Gaulle* (New York, 1965), presents a brief for the single-track-minded de Gaulle, and sees in F.D.R.'s lack of understanding some of the continuing animosity shown toward America.

Allen Dulles, *The Secret Surrender* (New York, 1966), recounts how Dulles, then an agent of the OSS, negotiated (contrary to express instructions) the surrender of nearly one million German and Italian troops in Italy. This coup infuriated Stalin, who feared that the prisoners would be released for the Russian front.

John M. Blum, *From the Morgenthau Diaries: Years of War, 1941–1945* (Boston, 1967), is especially full on the Morgenthau plan for de-industrializing Germany. Although Roosevelt was forced to back down, the scheme had more support in high places than is generally believed.

Richard M. Leighton, "Overlord Revisited: An Interpretation of American Strategy in the European War, 1942–1944," *Amer. Hist. Rev.*, LXVIII (1963), 919–937, argues that, contrary to a common belief, the British were prepared to support the cross-channel invasion whenever it had a reasonable chance of success.

Robert H. McNeal, "Roosevelt through Stalin's Spectacles," *International Journal*, XVIII (1963), 194–206, argues that Stalin's Marxism caused him to view F.D.R. as a bourgeois reformer who was promoting American postwar imperialism under the guise of friendship for the U.S.S.R. Both men grievously misunderstood each other.

9TH ED. REFS. James M. Burns, *Roosevelt: The Soldier of Freedom* (New York, 1970) is a sympathetic yet critical interweaving of wartime grand strategy with domestic problems; there is considerable attention to the complexity of FDR's character and his inability to hold firmly to announced principle.

Gabriel Kolko, *The Politics of War: The World and United States Foreign Policy, 1943–1945* (New York, 1968) is a heavily documented effort by a leading New Left "revisionist." The Western Allies are blamed for laying the foundations of the Cold War by pressing for an open-door economy in Eastern Europe, to the detriment of Communist interests.

Robert A. Divine, *Roosevelt and World War II* (Baltimore, 1969) is a slender book embracing four interpretive lectures stressing the development of FDR's foreign policies, which were less successful than his domestic policies; the former did not insure peace.

William H. McNeill, *America, Britain, and Russia: Their Cooperation and Conflict, 1941–1946* (New York, 1970) is a reissue of an admirably balanced account, first published in 1953. In the new introduction the author states that he retains his original views, despite the subsequent publication of much material by "revisionists" and others.

Robert Beitzell, *The Uneasy Alliance: America, Britain, and Russia, 1941–1943* (New York, 1972), solidly based on published documents, is largely concerned with the clashing aims and objectives of Roosevelt, Churchill, and Stalin.

Raymond G. O'Connor, *Diplomacy for Victory: FDR and Unconditional Surrender* (New York, 1971) argues that "unconditional surrender," by further insuring Allied unity, was helpful if not indispensable in the pursuit of victory.

Barbara W. Tuchman, *Stilwell and the American Experience in China, 1911–1945* (New York, 1971) recounts General Stilwell's futile and frustrating efforts to collaborate with Chiang Kai-shek.

Russell D. Buhite, *Patrick J. Hurley and American Foreign Policy* (Ithaca, 1973) casts light on this flamboyant and controversial ambassador's mission in China, 1944–1945.

Orville H. Bullitt, ed., *For the President, Personal and Secret: Correspondence between Franklin D. Roosevelt and William C. Bullitt* (Boston, 1972) contains the reflections of the first ambassador to the USSR (1933–1936) and later the pro-French ambassador to France (1936–1941) when World War II erupted.

Henry L. Feingold, *The Politics of Rescue: The Roosevelt Administration and the Holocaust, 1938–1945* (New Brunswick, N.J., 1970) criticizes the failure of Washington to do all it could to rescue at least some of the millions of doomed Jews.

Warren F. Kimball, "Lend-Lease and the Open Door: The Temptation of British Opulence, 1937–1942," *Pol. Sci. Quar.*, LXXVI (1971), 232–259, relates how Washington attempted to secure economic concessions by using lend-lease as leverage.

Ch. 49. FOUNDING THE UNITED NATIONS, 1941–1945

See new references on p. 775.

Herbert Feis, *Churchill, Roosevelt, Stalin: The War They Waged and the Peace They Sought* (Princeton, 1957) has a full and well-buttressed account of Yalta, which contends that F.D.R. did not "sell out" to the Russians. Feis concludes that unconditional surrender was a maturely considered policy, that Churchill was forewarned of it, and that it did not demonstrably prolong the war.

G. F. Kennan, *Russia and the West under Lenin and Stalin* (Boston, 1960) argues that unconditional surrender was a blunder; it discouraged the German underground. He blames F.D.R. for not throttling down lend-lease when Russia's plans of conquest became evident and for naively counting on his ability to charm away Stalin's nasty beliefs. The only way to have prevented Stalin from taking over Poland and the rest of Central Europe was to have launched the second front earlier and to have made a deeper penetration. Yalta restricted Stalin in the Far East; Chiang fared better than he could have alone;

the Soviets in the long run gained little in the Far East from the Yalta agreements.

E. J. Rozek, *Allied Wartime Diplomacy: A Pattern in Poland* (New York, 1958), by an embittered Polish scholar in exile, blames Churchill and F.D.R. for having betrayed Poland and trusted Stalin's promises at Yalta. The author thinks that the United States, backed by the atomic bomb and leagued with Britain, should have insisted on Stalin's carrying out his pledges.

G. N. Crocker, *Roosevelt's Road to Russia* (Chicago, 1959), by a right-wing attorney, is a viciously one-sided indictment which claims that Roosevelt deliberately set out to aggrandize Russia at the expense of his own country and its allies. The book is unworthy of scholarly attention except that it cleverly embalms many popular myths.

E. E. Morison, *Turmoil and Tradition: A Study of the Life and Times of Henry L. Stimson* (Boston, 1960) analyzes the reluctant decision of the Secretary of War to use the atomic bomb against Japan.

Herbert Feis, *Between War and Peace: The Potsdam Conference* (Princeton, 1960) demonstrates that Stalin, while not getting all he wanted, came off the best; the United States was so intent on Soviet armed co-operation in the Far East that it proved amenable. Increasingly the Soviets were resenting the attempts of the West to deprive them of the fruits of victory.

Herbert Feis, *Japan Subdued: The Atomic Bomb and the End of the War in the Pacific* (Princeton, 1961) justifies with scholarly thoroughness the use of the atomic bomb, and concludes that the "only score" on which the United States could be "fairly criticized" was the failure to spell out frankly the nature of the weapon that would be used if the Potsdam ultimatum was spurned.

Louis Morton, "The Decision to Use the Atomic Bomb, 1945," in K. R. Greenfield, ed., *Command Decisions* (New York, 1959), pp. 388–410 reasons that the bomb, together with Russia's intervention, tipped the scales for surrender.

R. C. Batchelder, *The Irreversible Decision, 1939–1950* (Boston, 1962), largely concerned with ethics, concludes that the bombing of Hiroshima was defensible, but that of Nagasaki could have been avoided. Fears of a prior German breakthrough (groundless, it developed) hastened America's atomic project.

H. S. Truman, *Mr. Citizen* (New York, 1960) and *Truman Speaks* (New York, 1960) contain some off-the-cuff remarks about the atomic bomb and other decisions which are treated with more detail and greater sobriety in the ex-President's *Memoirs*.

Ruth B. Russell, *A History of the United Nations Charter: The Role of the United States, 1940–1945* (Washington, D.C., 1958) is a heavily detailed and massively documented piece of scholarship.

8TH ED. REFS. Gar Alperovitz, *Atomic Diplomacy: Hiroshima and Potsdam: The Use of the Atomic Bomb and the American Confrontation with Soviet Power* (New York, 1965), by a political economist, strongly suggests, without convincing proof, that the bomb was dropped not primarily to subdue Japan but to impress Russia with America's military muscle and bend Moscow to Washington's policy goals after the war. There can be no doubt that concern about Russia played some role, but its significance can easily be overplayed.

Herbert Feis, *The Atomic Bomb and the End of World War II* (Princeton, N.J., 1966), is a substantial revision of the author's *Japan Subdued* (Princeton, 1961). Feis discounts the "atomic blackmail" thesis regarding the Soviet Union, and notes that the U.S. exercised commendable restraint toward the

Russians after the war ended (recognizing, of course, that the Russians would one day have atomic weapons). Victory no doubt could have been won without the A-bomb, but, the author concludes, the goal of a speedy and complete victory, with a saving on balance of both Japanese and Allied lives, was the controlling motivation.

Len Giovannitti and Fred Freed, in *The Decision to Drop the Bomb* (New York, 1965), argue that the decision was "taken in good faith not to unleash a weapon in vengeance against a ruthless enemy, but primarily to bring a quick end to a barbaric war and secondarily to derive the benefits of a timely victory" (p. 319).

Robert Murphy, *Diplomat Among Warriors* (Garden City, N.Y., 1964), contains illuminating reflections by a veteran diplomat who believes that the Russians outscored the West at Potsdam with persistence. Truman was greatly annoyed by Stalin's stubbornness and was too impatient.

Robert A. Divine, *Second Chance: The Triumph of Internationalism in America during World War II* (New York, 1967), is an important study of public opinion which describes how the internationalists, defeated in 1919–1920, overcame the isolationists and helped build up a tremendous tidal wave of support for the new United Nations organization.

William L. Neumann, *After Victory: Churchill, Roosevelt, Stalin and the Making of the Peace* (New York, 1967), is a balanced appraisal which concludes that the Big Three were fallible men striving as best they could to achieve their goals within the limitations set by "the international state system."

Richard L. Walker, "E. R. Stettinius, Jr.," in S. F. Bemis and R. H. Ferrell, eds., *The American Secretaries of State and Their Diplomacy*, 17 vols. (New York, 1927–1967), vol. XIV (1967), 1–83, presents in detail the handsome and gifted administrator who was poorly versed in foreign affairs but who was chosen Secretary of State by Franklin Roosevelt to serve primarily as an imposing front and to handle details. Stettinius showed considerable skill in helping to midwife the United Nations.

Athan Theoharis, "James F. Byrnes: Unwitting Yalta Myth-Maker," *Pol. Sci. Quar.*, LXXXI (1966), 581–592, shows that Byrnes, an adviser at Yalta, later (as Secretary of State) denied knowing of the secret Far Eastern agreements before they were released. His attitude threw more of the onus on Roosevelt and further overplayed the alleged conspiratorial nature of the conference.

Michael J. Francis, "The United States and the Act of Chapultepec," *Southwestern Soc. Sci. Quar.*, XLV (1964), 249–257, traces the stand of the U.S. on proposals concerning aggression, and shows that the Act of Chapultepec was in several sections notably weakened as a result of the insistence of the U.S.

Warren I. Cohen, "American Observers and the Sino-Soviet Friendship Treaty of August, 1945," *Pacific Hist. Rev.*, XXXV (1966), 347–349, adduces further evidence from a Chinese document to show that American observers were correct in their view that the Chinese Communist party "was bewildered and dismayed" by the treaty growing out of the deal made at Yalta.

Herbert A. Fine, "The Liquidation of World War II in Thailand," *Pacific Hist. Rev.*, XXXIV (1965), 65–82, describes how the U.S. exerted influence on Britain to insure a lenient peace treaty for Thailand, which had declared war on Britain under Japanese pressure.

Donald R. McCoy, "Republican Opposition during Wartime, 1941–1945,"

Mid-America, XLIX (1967), 174–189, reveals how bipartisanship in foreign affairs was achieved without restrictions on a tolerable amount of partisanship.

9TH ED. REFS. Dorothy B. Robins, *Experiment in Democracy: The Story of U.S. Citizen Organizations in Forging the Charter of the United Nations* (New York, 1971) is a prime example of the power of public opinion.

Diane S. Clemens, *Yalta* (New York, 1970) challenges the traditional interpretation by arguing that Stalin was commendably cooperative with the West and did most of the compromising on key issues at Yalta.

Lisle A. Rose, *After Yalta* (New York, 1973) revises the "revisionists" on a number of points and suggests the inevitability of much of what happened.

Athan Theoharis, "Roosevelt and Truman on Yalta: The Origins of the Cold War," *Pol. Sci. Quar.,* LXXXVII (1972), 210–241 concludes that the inexperienced Truman took a tougher line, specifically in manipulating the Yalta agreements to the advantage of the U.S.

Gary R. Hess, "Franklin Roosevelt and Indochina," *Jour. of Amer. Hist.,* LIX (1972), 353–368, reveals that FDR, enthusiastic about a postwar trusteeship for French Indochina, encountered strong opposition from Britain and especially from De Gaulle's France. The scheme died with Roosevelt.

Howard G. Bruenn, "Clinical Notes on the Illness and Death of President Franklin D. Roosevelt," *Annals of Internal Medicine,* LXXII (1970), 579–591, by FDR's attending physician, presents evidence that the President's mind was unclouded at Yalta.

George C. Herring, Jr., "The United States and British Bankruptcy, 1944–1945: Responsibilities Deferred," *Pol. Sci. Quar.,* LXXXVI (1971), 260–280, portrays the U.S. as laggard and ungenerous in helping the British out of financial difficulties.

Robert J. Maddox, "Atomic Diplomacy: A Study in Creative Writing," *Jour. of Amer. Hist.,* LIX (1973), 925–934, attacks Gar Alperovitz's well-known New Left book for grossly misusing the evidence.

Ch. 50. THE RIFT WITH THE SOVIETS, 1945–1947

8TH ED. REFS. Walter LaFeber, *America, Russia, and the Cold War, 1945–1966* (New York, 1967), is a perceptive and well-balanced overview, with a minimum of detail.

Herbert Druks, *Harry S. Truman and the Russians, 1945–1953* (New York, 1967), provides an incisive survey and analysis of Truman's most serious confrontations with the Soviets.

David S. McLellan and John W. Reuss, "Foreign and Military Policies," in Richard S. Kirkendall, ed., *The Truman Period as a Research Field* (Columbia, Mo., 1967), 15–85, is an invaluable bibliographical essay. The authors downgrade the concept of "atomic blackmail" in regard to Russia, and doubt if an acquiescent approach would have produced better results or that F.D.R. would have followed such an approach.

Cabell Phillips, *The Truman Presidency: The History of a Triumphant Succession* (New York, 1966), is a lively and unscholarly journalistic account which questionably rates Truman as a "great" President and which provides a useful general introduction with a minimum of thoughtful analysis.

George Curry, "James F. Byrnes," in S. F. Bemis and R. H. Ferrell, eds., *The American Secretaries of State and Their Diplomacy,* 17 vols. (New York, 1927–1967), vol. XIV (1965), 87–317, plus notes, is a favorable appraisal, based on personal papers. It credits Byrnes with helping to hold together the Potsdam Conference, negotiating peace treaties with the lesser powers, and foreshadowing the Truman Doctrine. The independent-minded Secretary, here acquitted of "babying the Russians," got along better with the President than Truman indicates in his *Memoirs*.

Herbert Feis, *Contest over Japan* (New York, 1967), details the struggle between the U.S. and the U.S.S.R. to direct the policies of Japan during the occupation (1945–1952). A victorious U.S. sat in the driver's seat and overrode a protesting but impotent Russia.

Richard P. Stevens, *American Zionism and U.S. Foreign Policy, 1942–1947* (New York, 1962), assesses the important influence of the Zionists (one of many forces or counterforces) in the creation of Israel.

Arthur Schlesinger, Jr., "Origins of the Cold War," *Foreign Affairs*, XLVI (1967), 22–52, is a balanced analysis which does not assign to the U.S. the lion's share of the blame.

Stephen G. Xydis, "America, Britain, and the U.S.S.R. in the Greek Arena, 1944–1947," *Pol. Sci. Quar.*, LXXVIII (1963), 581–596, shows how the U.S., through what to it was a series of insignificant and marginal developments, moved imperceptibly but inevitably into the Truman Doctrine intervention.

9TH ED. REFS. Walter LaFeber, *America, Russia, and the Cold War, 1945–1971* (2nd ed., New York, 1972) is an enlarged edition of the excellent survey first published in 1967.

Herbert Feis, *From Trust to Terror: The Onset of the Cold War, 1945–50* (New York, 1970), by a former State Department official, is a scholarly and well-balanced treatment of the widening rift.

Adam B. Ulam, *The Rivals: America and Russia Since World War II* (New York, 1971), by a leading scholar, is a hard-headed treatment of the major myths and realities; there is little sympathy for pro-Soviet "revisionism." The book covers much of the same ground as the author's *Expansion and Coexistence: The History of Soviet Foreign Policy, 1917–1967* (New York, 1968).

John L. Gaddis, *The United States and the Origins of the Cold War, 1941–1947* (New York, 1972) is a scholarly antidote to the overemphasis of New Left "revisionists" on open-door economics. The author considers political, psychological, and bureaucratic limitations; he concludes that public opinion left U.S. leaders with fewer options for conciliation than were afforded Stalin.

Lloyd C. Gardner, Arthur Schlesinger, Jr., and Hans J. Morgenthau, *The Origins of the Cold War* (Waltham, Mass., 1970) has Gardner blaming the U.S.; Schlesinger blaming Russia; Morgenthau blaming both.

William J. Bosch, *Judgment on Nuremberg: American Attitudes Toward the Major German War-Crime Trials* (Chapel Hill, 1970) shows that U.S. public opinion generally favored prosecution; exceptions were found among historians and experts on international law.

Bruce Kuklick, *American Policy and the Division of Germany: The Clash with Russia over Reparations* (Ithaca, 1972) is a "revisionist" treatment which blames the "hostile," "belligerent" and "unrealistic" American attitude for the partition of Germany and the hardening of European differences.

Gaddis Smith, *Dean Acheson* (New York, 1972), vol. XVI in *The American Secretaries of State and Their Diplomacy*, deals sympathetically with this powerful figure, one of the leading architects of the policy of "containment."

George C. Herring, Jr., "Lend-Lease to Russia and the Origins of the Cold War, 1944–1945," *Jour. of Amer. Hist.*, LVI (1969) 93–114, concludes that

Truman's abrupt and temporary cutoff (which also hurt Britain) was not coercive, only maladroit.

Thomas G. Paterson, "The Abortive American Loan to Russia and the Origins of the Cold War, 1943–1946," *Jour. of Amer. Hist.*, LVI (1969), 70–92, argues that the U.S. failure to extend generous credits contributed measurably to the Cold War. (Yet American opinion was unfavorable to a loan on terms acceptable to Russia.)

Alfred E. Eckes, Jr., "Open Door Expansionism Reconsidered: The World War II Experience," *Jour. of Amer. Hist.*, LIX (1973), 909–924, presents evidence (challenging the "radical" New Left) that U.S. postwar policy was not primarily self-seeking anti-Sovietism but a design for peaceful relationships through "economic internationalism."

Robert J. Maddox, "Atomic Diplomacy: A Study in Creative Writing," *Jour. of Amer. Hist.*, LIX (1973), 925–934, attacks Gar Alperovitz's well-known New Left book (*Atomic Diplomacy*, 1965) for grossly misusing the evidence. The author's reply is in the same issue, pp. 1062–1067.

Useful bibliographical studies are Norman A. Graebner, "Cold War Origins and the Continuing Debate: A Review of Recent Literature," *The Journal of Conflict Resolution*, XIII (1969), 123–132; Charles S. Maier, "Revisionism and the Interpretation of Cold War Origins," in *Perspectives in American History*, IV (1970), 313–347; and Robert W. Sellen, "Origins of the Cold War: An Historiographical Survey," *West Georgia College Studies in the Social Sciences*, IX (1970), 57–98.

See also the references for the next chapter.

Ch. 51. THE COLD WAR, 1947–1949

See new references on p. 795.

An excellent summary overview, with supporting documents, is N. A. Graebner, *Cold War Diplomacy: American Foreign Policy, 1945–1960* (Princeton, 1962).

Dean Acheson, *Sketches from Life of Men I Have Known* (New York, 1961), by the former Secretary of State, provides pen portraits of a number of contemporaries, notably General Marshall, who is credited with vigor, decisiveness, and vision in implementing the Marshall Plan.

W. P. Davison, *The Berlin Blockade* (Princeton, 1958) contends that the Soviet strategy was well conceived. It failed by the narrowest of margins, primarily because of the tenacity of the Berliners and the pertinacity of the Allies. The Soviet objectives were to prevent the economic recovery of Germany and the formation of a West German government; failure had an opposite effect.

R. E. Osgood, *NATO: The Entangling Alliance* (Chicago, 1962), though dealing briefly with the origins of the Alliance, is primarily concerned with later and current problems.

Arnold Wolfers, ed., *Alliance Policy in the Cold War* (Baltimore, 1959) is a symposium of ten essays which stresses American policy toward the more important Allies and the difficulties of operating an alliance composed of members of varying economic and political maturity.

D. F. Nuechterlein, *Iceland: Reluctant Ally* (Ithaca, N.Y., 1961) notes that there was strong opposition to the presence of American troops from 1946 to 1956, after which the atmosphere improved. The cause of friction was not so much Communist agitation or misbehaving troops as internal political struggles.

Washington Platt, *National Character in Action: Intelligence Factors in Foreign Relations* (New Brunswick, N.J., 1961) has revealing case studies on American propaganda operations in Italy during and after World War II, as well as through Radio Free Europe.

Donald Dozer, *Are We Good Neighbors?* (Gainesville, Fla., 1961) stresses the dislocations of Latin America's economy by the wartime outpouring of dollars and the resentment over the postwar diversion of dollars to Europe.

J. F. Rippy, *Globe and Hemisphere: Latin America's Place in the Postwar Foreign Relations of the United States* (Chicago, 1958) is primarily economic and to a considerable degree concerned with the vast waste of United States money.

A. P. Whitaker, *Spain and the Defense of the West: Ally and Liability* (New York, 1961) believes that the military bases granted in 1953 were an asset to America, but by bolstering the prestige and economy of the Franco regime Washington received something of a black eye.

K. M. Schmidt, *Henry A. Wallace: Quixotic Crusade, 1948* (Syracuse, N.Y., 1960) describes Wallace's "fight for peace" through an accommodation with Moscow; his Progressive Party was "Communist-influenced but *not* Communist-dominated . . . (p. 278)."

W. C. Mallalieu, "The Origin of the Marshall Plan," *Pol. Sci. Quar.*, LXXIII (1958), 481–504, based on unpublished records, notes the good effects of the Soviet refusal to participate and the influence of the Czechoslovak coup in overcoming American opposition or indifference.

8TH ED. REFS. See also references for previous chapter.

Martin F. Herz, *Beginnings of the Cold War* (Bloomington, Ind., 1966), is a careful analysis by a U.S. foreign service officer, who emphasizes the falling out over Poland and Stalin's breaking of alleged promises. Stalin had genuine grievances over the abrupt cutback of lend-lease, and the unwillingness of the U.S. to grant a $6 billion loan on Russian terms. Yet the U.S. had even greater reason to distrust Stalin, who was determined to have friendly satellite neighbors, whatever the cost.

Louis J. Halle, *The Cold War as History* (New York, 1967), is a sophisticated analysis by a former member of the Policy Planning Staff in the State Department who views the contestants not as good and evil incarnate but as nations pursuing what was from their viewpoint the national interest.

Robert H. Ferrell, *George C. Marshall* (New York, 1966), vol. XV, in S. F. Bemis and R. H. Ferrell, eds., *The American Secretaries of State and Their Diplomacy*, 17 vols. (New York, 1927–1967), provides a favorable picture of the Secretary, who operated on unfamiliar ground. He was universally respected and stood firm for policies, notably the Truman Doctrine and the Marshall Plan, which in a number of cases were originated by associates.

George F. Kennan's *Memoirs, 1925–1950* (Boston, 1967), brilliantly reveal the career of a distinguished foreign service officer who had a large hand in shaping the Truman Doctrine and the Marshall Plan. Widely regarded as the real architect of Truman's containment policy, he regretted its emphasis on military rather than political containment and its extension all over the world. Criticized in the 1930's and 1940's for his "hard line" on the U.S.S.R., he was later criticized for his "softer line."

Herbert Druks, *Harry S. Truman and the Russians, 1945–1953* (New York, 1967), supplies a heavily factual account which is highly favorable to Truman.

Robert Murphy, *Diplomat Among Warriors* (Garden City, N.Y., 1964), is by a professional participant who believes that the Soviet bluff at the time of the Berlin blockade should have been called, that the presumed Allied victory in Berlin was illusory, and that it may have helped inspire the Korean invasion of 1950.

Stephen G. Xydis, *Greece and the Great Powers, 1944–1947: Prelude to the "Truman Doctrine"* (Thessaloniki, 1963), uses materials in at least four different languages (including Greek) to provide an exhaustive background treatment of the Greek civil war and the contemporary international situation.

Anthony Kubek, *How the Far East Was Lost* (Chicago, 1963), provides an unscholarly, highly prejudiced, right-wing indictment of the alleged treason of responsible American officials, including General Marshall.

Harold L. Hitchens, "Influences on the Congressional Decision to Pass the Marshall Plan," *Western Pol. Quar.*, XXI (1968), 51–68, gives high marks to Truman's leadership in bringing various pressures to bear on Congress.

Lyman P. Van Slyke, ed., *The China White Paper, August 1949* (Stanford, Calif., 1967), is a reissue, with a new introduction, of the original so-called White Paper for the years 1944–1949. First issued to justify Truman's washing his hands of Chiang, it presents a reasonably fair picture of the hopeless state of the Nationalist regime. It was condemned more by the Chinese Communists than by the Nationalists, and helped ruin, through McCarthyism, the careers of U.S. specialists on China who had reported objectively.

Russell D. Buhite, "Patrick J. Hurley and the Yalta Far Eastern Agreement," *Pacific Hist. Rev.*, XXXVII (1968), 343–353, shows that this ambassador to China, though at the time favoring the Yalta terms, later condemned them, presumably in seeking scapegoats to excuse his own failure to unite China.

Barton J. Bernstein and Allen J. Matusow, eds., *The Truman Administration: A Documentary History* (New York, 1966), presents interesting insights on the decision to drop the A-bomb, the Cold War, China policy, and the Korean War. Truman appears as somewhat less than a "great" President.

9TH ED. REFS. Lloyd C. Gardner, *Architects of Illusion: Men and Ideas in American Foreign Policy, 1941–1949* (Chicago, 1970) presents biographical sketches of the leading American statesmen to demonstrate that each side in the Cold War overreacted to illusions it had about the other. The U.S. is judged the more responsible for the *way* in which the contest developed. Economic motivation rather than anti-communism is heavily stressed.

Joyce and Gabriel Kolko, *The Limits of Power: The World and United States Foreign Policy, 1945–1954* (New York, 1972), although based on impressive research by two New Left historians, is marred by the simplistic view that the Cold War was not basically a clash between Russia and the U.S. but a campaign by American capitalism to dominate the world.

Richard M. Freeland, *The Truman Doctrine and the Origins of McCarthyism: Foreign Policy, Domestic Politics, and Internal Security, 1946–1948* (New York, 1972) argues that Truman, in order to secure appropriations for the Marshall Plan that would insure American political and economic domination in Europe, deliberately overstressed the Communist menace and thus played into the hands of McCarthy.

Dean Acheson, *Present at the Creation: My Years in the State Department* (New York, 1969), the rather unrevealing memoirs of the hawkish and self-assured Secretary of State, presents in great detail his containment-of-Communism diplomacy which found its logical continuation in the Vietnam War. His regard for Truman is undisguised.

Barton J. Bernstein, ed., *Politics and Policies of the Truman Administration* (Chicago, 1970) contains seven essays which contend that Truman over-reacted to unfounded fears of Russian aggression by pushing economic and other policies that helped to shape the Cold War.

Thomas G. Paterson, ed., *Cold War Critics: Alternatives to American Foreign Policy in the Truman Years* (Chicago, 1971) has essays on various commentators whose pro-New Left criticism is sympathetically presented.

David Green, *The Containment of Latin America: A History of the Myths and Realities of the Good Neighbor Policy* (Chicago, 1971) holds that Roosevelt's policy devolved under Truman into one of containing Latin America against hostile regimes and ideologies, especially Communism.

Robert W. Tucker, *The Radical Left and American Foreign Policy* (Baltimore, 1971) is a sharp and sophisticated essay which basically attacks the views of extreme New Left "revisionists" on responsibility for the Cold War.

Bert Cochran, *Harry Truman and the Crisis Presidency* (New York, 1973) is a highly critical assessment of these troubled years by an economist.

Harold L. Hitchens, "Influences on the Congressional Decision to Pass the Marshall Plan," *Western Pol. Quar.*, XXI (1968), 51–68, analyzes the growth of favorable public pressures.

Robert A. Divine, "The Cold War and the Election of 1948," *Jour. of Amer. Hist.*, LIX (1972), 90–110, plausibly contends that Dewey's failure to attack Truman's containment policies may have cost him the election.

Alonzo L. Hamby, "Henry A. Wallace, the Liberals, and Soviet-American Relations," *Rev. of Politics*, XXX (1968), 153–169, describes how Wallace took so rigidly doctrinaire a stance for Russia that he lost much of his liberal following.

L. K. Adler and T. G. Paterson, "Red Fascism: The Merger of Nazi Germany and Soviet Russia in the American Image of Totalitarianism, 1930's–1950's," *Amer. Hist, Rev.*, LXXV (1970), 1046–1064, concludes that many leading Americans, noting the similarities between Nazi and Soviet policies and practices, transferred their hatred of Germany to Russia after 1945, with a consequent worsening of the Cold War.

Ch. 52. COMMUNISM AND THE KOREAN CONFLICT

The interrelation of domestic and foreign affairs is treated broadly in E. F. Goldman, *The Crucial Decade: America, 1945–55* (New York, 1956). Also general is J. A. Lukacs, *A History of the Cold War* (Garden City, N.Y., 1961), which praises Truman for the Korean intervention; and D. J. Dallin, *Soviet Foreign Policy After Stalin* (Philadelphia, 1961), which shows how Stalin plotted and directed the Korean War and used it for propaganda.

The new literature on the Korean War is voluminous. A. S. Whiting, *China Crosses the Yalu: The Decision to Enter the Korean War* (New York, 1960) involves the United States rather tangentially.

J. W. Spanier, *The Truman-MacArthur Controversy and the Korean War* (Cambridge, Mass., 1959) is a scholarly monograph which explores the problem of a headstrong general fighting a limited war with shackles; MacArthur deserved to be removed, but less brutally.

Trumbull Higgins, *Korea and the Fall of MacArthur* (New York, 1960) presents both sides and concludes that the General's arrogance and disregard of directives brought his downfall, even though subsequent events in some measure justified his demands.

Courtney Whitney, *MacArthur: His Rendezvous with History* (New York, 1956), by an aide of the General, is strongly pro-MacArthur.

W. H. Vatcher, Jr., *Panmunjom: The Story of the Korean Military Armistice Negotiations* (New York, 1958) reveals how the Communists almost sabotaged the negotiations several times, and how difficult it is to negotiate in good faith with men whose main aim is to make propaganda rather than peace.

Admiral C. T. Joy, *How Communists Negotiate* (New York, 1955), by the chief United Nations representative at Panmunjom, exposes Communist tactics and condemns the final terms as being much less than could have been obtained had General MacArthur's views been heeded.

F. S. Dunn, *Peace-Making and the Settlement with Japan* (Princeton, 1963) traces the story from 1941, with emphasis on decision-making. The role of Dulles has evidently been overrated; the treaty grew out of years of planning in Washington.

M. H. Halperin, "The Limiting Process in the Korean War," *Pol. Sci. Quar.*, LXXVIII (1963), 13–39 explains why both sides deliberately chose not to widen the conflict.

W. R. Willoughby, *The St. Lawrence Waterway* (Madison, Wis., 1961) analyzes the multifarious conflicting interests. The log jam was broken primarily by the separation of the power issue from navigation, thereby making it possible for the Canadians to threaten a go-it-alone policy.

8TH ED. REFS. Douglas MacArthur, *Reminiscences* (New York, 1964), although revealing the general's attitude toward the Korean War, is so filled with self-justification as to be of limited value.

David Rees, *Korea: The Limited War* (New York, 1964), is an objective account by a British free-lance writer describing the difficulties of waging a limited war in the teeth of the American tradition of crusading for complete victory.

Glenn D. Paige, *The Korean Decision, June 24–30, 1950* (New York, 1968), presents in great detail the hour-by-hour discussions that led to the intervention, which was designed to honor previous commitments and to preserve the viability of collective action under the United Nations.

Matthew B. Ridgway, *The Korean War* (Garden City, N.Y., 1967), by the general who succeeded MacArthur in Korea, is outspokenly critical of his predecessor's bad judgment in the drive toward the Yalu River, including disregard of the order to use only South Korean troops in approaching China's border. Ridgway is confident that he himself could have reached the Yalu in the spring of 1951 but the cost would have been "far too high" in casualties for what might have been gained (pp. 150–151). He believes that MacArthur had sought a preventive war with China so as to destroy her warmaking potential (pp. 143–144).

Richard H. Rovere and Arthur Schlesinger, Jr., *The MacArthur Controversy and American Foreign Policy* (New York, 1965), is a revised and expanded edition of the authors' 1951 book (*The General and the President*) which examines the continuing effects of Truman's "firing" of MacArthur.

David S. McLellan, "Dean Acheson and the Korean War," *Pol. Sci. Quar.*, LXXXIII (1968), 16–39, argues that the Secretary of State grievously misjudged Chinese sensitivity and revealed incredible acquiescence (as did the Joint Chiefs of Staff) in MacArthur's arrogant disregard of orders.

9TH ED. REFS. Athan G. Theoharis, *The Yalta Myths: An Issue in U.S. Politics, 1945–1955* (Columbia, Mo., 1970) discusses the political capital that the Republicans made of Hiss's alleged influence, FDR's presumed mental collapse, and the subsequent Communization of Eastern Europe and China. Eisenhower, although pledged in 1952 to repudiate Yalta, declined to do so.

Ronald J. Caridi, *The Korean War and American Politics: The Republican*

Party as a Case Study (Philadelphia, 1969) shows how critical spokesmen for the party, failing to offer a viable alternative, rode to victory in 1952 on their opposition to the war.

Athan Theoharis, *Seeds of Repression: Harry S. Truman and the Origins of McCarthyism* (Chicago, 1971) is a New Left condemnation of Truman for having taken a hard line toward Russia, with resulting hysteria against alleged subversion.

John E. Mueller, "Trends in Popular Support for the Wars in Korea and Vietnam," *Amer. Pol. Sci. Rev.*, LXV (1971), 358–375, demonstrates that opposition to both conflicts followed a similar pattern, with concerted opposition coming more slowly in Vietnam.

Charles A. Lofgren, "Mr. Truman's War: A Debate and Its Aftermath," *Review of Politics*, XXXI (1969), 223–241, concludes that Congressional approval probably would not have guaranteed continuing support.

Max Gordon, "A Case History of U.S. Subversion: Guatemala, 1954," *Science and Society*, XXXV (1971), 129–155, is a pro-Communist treatment of the overthrow of the pro-Communist Guatemalan regime.

For works relating to President Eisenhower and Secretary Dulles, see next chapter.

Ch. 53. WORLD TENSIONS AND THE MIDDLE EAST CRISIS

See new references on p. 847.

J. E. Dougherty, "The Aswan Decision in Perspective," *Pol. Sci. Quar.*, LXXIV (1959), 21–45 concludes that the British and the Americans, who did not consult closely enough in advance, blundered in not anticipating the canal seizure.

O. E. Clubb, "Formosa and the Offshore Islands in American Policy, 1950–1955," *ibid.*, pp. 517–531 argues that the United States worked itself into a dangerous corner by defending useless islands for a rump regime that was most unlikely to return to power.

8TH ED. REFS. Dwight D. Eisenhower, *The White House Years: Mandate for Change, 1953–1956* (Garden City, N.Y., 1963), is a presidential reminiscence that is generally bland and not too revealing. Eisenhower thinks that hints about using the atomic bomb may have induced the Korean settlement (p. 181). The picture here presented indicates that the President had the decisive voice in critical decisions, notably in avoiding war in Indo-China in 1954 and in the Formosa Straits in 1955.

Dwight D. Eisenhower, *The White House Years: Waging Peace, 1956–1961* (Garden City, N.Y., 1965), like the preceding volume, is bland and defensive of disputed policies, notably the Suez stance and the Lebanon landing.

Elmer Plischke, "Eisenhower's 'Correspondence Diplomacy' with the Kremlin—Case Study in Summit Diplomatics," *Jour. of Politics*, XXX (1968), 137–159, concludes that these public interchanges, heavily polemical, tended to result in frozen positions and were consequently by standard tests a "dismal failure."

Louis L. Gerson, *John Foster Dulles* (New York, 1967), vol. XVII, in S. F. Bemis and R. H. Ferrell, eds., *The American Secretaries of State and Their Diplomacy*, 17 vols. (New York, 1927–1967), is a balanced, documented, and generally favorable appraisal of the controversial Secretary of State. Gerson argues that Dulles' withdrawal of the Egyptian dam offer was not really "abrupt," and that Nasser had long planned nationalization of the canal.

Eleanor Lansing Dulles, *John Foster Dulles: The Last Year* (New York, 1963), is an appreciative and defensive appraisal by a sister who presents the Secretary as a man of principle who sought respect rather than popularity. The account ranges over far more than the year 1958, and gives the inside story of the famous *Life* "brinkmanship" interview (pp. 50–52).

Herman Finer, *Dulles over Suez: The Theory and Practice of His Diplomacy* (Chicago, 1964), contains much useful information but is badly marred by a strong pro-Israel and a bitter anti-Dulles bias.

Leon D. Epstein, *British Politics in the Suez Crisis* (Urbana, Ill., 1964), is a solid monograph which reveals that many direct-actionist Britons believed that the U.S. was determined to rob Britain of her place in the sun.

Andrew H. Berding, *Dulles on Diplomacy* (Princeton, N.J., 1965), records the presumed remarks of the Secretary, taken down in shorthand by Berding, who, as Assistant Secretary of State for Public Affairs, traveled extensively with him. Dulles claims that he "never" was in any disagreement "whatsoever" with Eisenhower (p. 15) and vigorously defends his own handling of the Egyptian dam offer (pp. 106–107).

Gordon A. Craig, *War, Politics, and Diplomacy: Selected Essays* (New York, 1966), has a perceptive chapter on Secretary Dulles (Chapter 15) which balances his assets against serious shortcomings and emerges with a generally favorable estimate.

O. M. Smolansky, "Moscow and the Suez Crisis, 1956: A Reappraisal," *Pol. Sci. Quar.*, LXXX (1965), 581–605, notes that when it became clear that U.S. opposition in the UN to the Israeli-British-French attack on Egypt insured its failure, Moscow came to the support of Nasser with threats of nuclear obliteration, but only after eight days of delay. U.S. counterthreats of nuclear retaliation reduced the Moscow threat to a bluff, from which the Kremlin squeezed much effective propaganda.

9TH ED. REFS. Richard E. Neustadt, *Alliance Politics* (New York, 1970) emphasizes Suez in 1956 and Kennedy's cancellation of the Skybolt contract with the British in 1962. Secretary Dulles appears dependent on Eisenhower and careful to consult him.

Nikita S. Khrushchev, *Khrushchev Remembers* (Boston, 1970), the presumed memoirs of the deposed Russian leader, presents the Soviet view on such problems as the Korean War, the Geneva Summit, the Berlin crises, the Suez crisis, and the Cuban missile crisis.

Herbert S. Parmet, *Eisenhower and the American Crusades* (New York, 1972) is the most substantial general biography to date.

Michael Guhin, *John Foster Dulles: A Statesman and His Times* (New York, 1972) presents a more favorable picture of the so-called moralistic cold warrior than is conventional.

Ch. 54. THE END OF THE EISENHOWER ERA

9TH ED. REFS. See also references for preceding chapter.

G. Bernard Noble, *Christian A. Herter* (New York, 1970), vol. XVIII in *The American Secretaries of State and Their Diplomacy*, deals with Eisenhower's last Secretary of State, a patrician without flamboyance who inherited and continued Dulles' overextended policies. In virtually every case the problems were more vexatious in 1961 than in 1959.

Philip W. Bonsal, *Cuba, Castro, and the United States* (Pittsburgh, 1971), by the last U.S. ambassador to Cuba, generally supports American policy but is critical of both the U.S. and Castro.

Jack M. Schick, *The Berlin Crisis, 1958–1962* (Philadelphia, 1971) demonstrates that the crises worsened because the Kremlin misread Washington's determination to stand fast.

Ch. 55. NEW FRONTIER DIPLOMACY

9TH ED. REFS. Richard J. Walton, *Cold War and Counterrevolution: The Foreign Policy of John F. Kennedy* (New York, 1972) is documented journalism, highly critical of virtually every major phase of Kennedy's foreign policy. JFK is condemned as an "entirely conventional" cold warrior and counterrevolutionary.

Louise FitzSimmons, *The Kennedy Doctrine* (New York, 1972) is a remarkably similar book which strongly criticizes Kennedy for further heating up the Cold War.

Henry Fairlie, *The Kennedy Promise: The Politics of Expectation* (New York, 1973) is a critical dissection by an English journalist of the "imperial politician."

Graham T. Allison, *Essence of Decision: Explaining the Cuban Missile Crisis* (Boston, 1971) is a monograph by a political scientist who uses the jargon of the behavioralist in demonstrating that since irrationality is the inevitable result of bureaucratic processes, the U.S. was supremely lucky to emerge unscathed.

Hugh Thomas, *Cuba: The Pursuit of Freedom* (New York, 1971), by an English scholar with many personal contacts in Cuba, contains excellent chapters on the Bay of Pigs and the missile crisis. The author is critical of Kennedy and sympathetic toward Castro.

Nikita S. Khrushchev, *Khrushchev Remembers* (Boston, 1970) unreliably presents the Soviet view of the Cuban missile crisis.

George F. Kennan, *Memoirs, 1950–1962*, vol. II (Boston, 1972) deals with the author's short and unhappy ambassadorial missions in Russia and Yugoslavia.

Ch. 56. THE ORDEAL OF LYNDON JOHNSON

9TH ED. REFS. Lyndon B. Johnson, *The Vantage Point: Perspectives of the Presidency, 1963–1969* (New York, 1971) is a favorable assessment of his administration, including Vietnam policies, by the President himself.

Eric F. Goldman, *The Tragedy of Lyndon Johnson* (New York, 1969) is a critical and somewhat limited assessment by a professional historian temporarily stationed in the White House as an "Intellectual-in-Residence."

Jerome Slater, *Intervention and Negotiation: The United States and the Dominican Revolution* (New York, 1970), while regarding the Communist menace as overplayed, is temperate, judicious, and soundly based.

Theodore Draper, *The Dominican Revolt: A Case Study in American Policy* (New York, 1968) is contemporary journalism unfavorable to U.S. policies and intervention.

Abraham F. Lowenthal, *The Dominican Intervention* (Cambridge, Mass., 1972) is a scholarly analysis of the vexatious episode.

Henry F. Graff, *The Tuesday Cabinet: Deliberation and Decision on Peace and War under Lyndon B. Johnson* (Englewood Cliffs, N.J., 1971) presents the author's personal observations and interviews in 1965–1968.

Townsend Hoopes, *The Limits of Intervention: An Inside Account of How the Johnson Policy of Escalation in Vietnam Was Reversed* (New York, 1969), by Johnson's last Undersecretary of the Air Force, describes the steps leading to the decision in March, 1968, to limit bombing.

Charles A. Stevenson, *The End of Nowhere: American Policy Toward Laos Since 1954* (Boston, 1972) is a scholarly exposé; the unannounced bombing began on December 14, 1964.

Joseph C. Goulden, *Truth is the First Casualty: The Gulf of Tonkin Affair— Illusion and Reality* (Chicago, 1969); Anthony Austin, *The President's War* (Philadelphia, 1971); and Eugene G. Windchy, *Tonkin Gulf* (Garden City, N.Y., 1971) all doubt that the two reported attacks by the North Vietnamese (August 2, 4) occurred as officially reported and all expose the dissimulation and trigger-happiness of the administration.

Of the spate of books on the Viet Nam intervention, one may mention the following: Chester L. Cooper, *The Lost Crusade: America in Vietnam* (New York, 1970), which is a constructive assessment by a governmental insider; W. W. Rostow, *The Diffusion of Power: An Essay in Recent History* (New York, 1972), which is an apologia for U.S. intervention in Southeast Asia; and three high-quality journalistic efforts: David Halberstam, *The Best and the Brightest* (New York, 1972), which describes how the bright advisers of two Presidents deepened the involvement; Frances FitzGerald, *Fire in the Lake: The Vietnamese and the Americans in Vietnam* (Boston, 1972); and Robert Shaplen, *The Road from War: Vietnam, 1965–1970* (New York, 1970).

A highly useful series continued with Richard P. Stebbins, *The United States in World Affairs, 1967* (New York, 1968).

Top-secret information was clandestinely revealed in *The Pentagon Papers as Published by The New York Times* (New York, 1971), both paperback and hardcover editions, and much more completely in *The Senator Gravel Edition, The Pentagon Papers: The Defense Department History of United States Decisionmaking on Vietnam* (5 vols., Boston, 1971–1972). Much of the significant information in these secret documents was already known or strongly suspected. Among the various revelations one should note that (1) The U.S., despite contrary assurances, undertook to sabotage the 1954 Geneva Accords from the outset (2) the Kennedy administration was deeply involved in the plot that resulted in the murder of President Diem (3) plans for large-scale bombing were tentatively adopted some two months *before* Johnson's election in 1964 (4) the Johnson administration had prepared a draft of the Tonkin Gulf resolution and had selected possible targets for air strikes more than two months *before* the (provoked?) incidents occurred (5) Johnson, despite existing contingency plans, did not order heavy bombing of the North until more than three months after his election (6) not until April 1, 1965, some five months after his pledge of no American boys for Asia's wars, did he decide to use American troops offensively.

A useful bibliographical study is Thomas A. Bryson, "United States Involvement in Vietnam: A Survey of Conflicting Interpretations," *West Georgia College Studies in the Social Sciences*, IX (1970), 40–56.

INDEX

ABC powers, mediate, 559-60
Aberdeen, Lord, 195, 211, 217; and Oregon, 227 ff., 230, 232-3; and Texas, 246-7; and California, 253
Acheson, Secy. of State Dean, 815, 817, 819, 855
Adams, Charles F., 318, 326; and *Trent*, 331; and Butler incident, 336; and British raiders, 342-5; end of mission, 346, 377; on Motley, 379; and Geneva Tribunal, 385, 387
Adams, Henry, 150, 156, 318; and Civil War, 329-30, 341-2, 345; on Sumner, 378
Adams, Pres. John, and Revolution, 28-9, 41-2; and peace, 44, 45, 48; in England, 53-4; on peace, 75, 87; French crisis, 93-4, 96-8; and Louisiana, 114; quoted, 118, 149
Adams, Pres. John Q., 148-50; at Ghent, 149-50, 154; and disarmament, 158; and Florida, 165-6, 167; and Latin America, 167-8; and Jackson's raid, 171-2, 174; and Russian threat, 178-9, 180-1; and Monroe Doctrine, 182-5, 188; Administration, 191-4; and Texas, 237; quoted, 198, 286, 302
Adams, William, 150
Adams-Onís Treaty (1819), 172-5
Adee, A. A., 9
Adenauer, Chancellor, 854, 887
Adet, Pierre, 90-1
Afro-Asian bloc, 860, 876
Agreements. See specific agreements; Executive agreements; Treaties
Aguinaldo, Emilio, 478
Aix-la-Chapelle Conference (1854), 295
Alabama (cruiser), 307, 342-3; claims from, 376-9, 383, 385-9
Alamo, 239
Alaska, 188; purchased, 363-71; boundary dispute over, 507-10, 527
Albania, 916 n.
Albert, Dr. Heinrich, 582
Albert, Prince (England), 330
Alcan Highway, 744
Aleutians, 641
Alexander I, 147-9, 177
Alexandra (warship), 343

Alexis, Grand Duke (Russia), 364
Algeciras Conference (1906), 512-3, 527, 529
Algiers, 64-5, 101
Allen, Ethan, 58
Allende, Pres. Salvador, 939
Alliance for Progress, 850, 870, 938
Alverstone, Lord, 509-10
Ambassador, rank of, 10
Ambrister, Robert, 169
Amelia Island, 166, 169
America First Committee, 711, 722, 739-40
Ames, Fisher, 80
Amiens, Peace of (1801), 103
Andrews, Israel D., 280
Anglo-Chinese War (1839–42), 302-3, 310
Anglo-Japanese Alliance, 515, 634, 638, 644
Anglo-Russian Treaty (1825), 188, 507-8
Antietam, Battle of, 337, 339
ANZUS (Australia, New Zealand), U.S. Pact (1951), 817
Aoki, Viscount (Japan), 525-6
Apia, Samoa, 423, 424, 425
Arabic (liner), sunk, 580-1
Arabs, 793, 843, 907-8
Aranjuez Convention (1779), 38
Arbitration, 2, 77; (post-1814), 155, 207-8; and Geneva Tribunal, 387-9; (post-1872), 408, 413-4; and Venezuela boundary, 439, 446-9; (post-1896), 448-9, 497, 502-3; (post-1902), 508, 527, 540-1; (post-1908), 540-1, 549, 651. See also Treaties
Arbuthnot, Alexander, 169
Archangel, 636
Argentina, 533, 684, 686, 690; refractory, 753-5; (post-1944), 769, 806
Armed Neutrality, 39-40
Armenia, 444, 455
"Aroostook War," 208
Arthur, Pres. Chester A., 395-6, 400
Articles of Confederation, 52
Ashburton, Lord, 211-7, 224, 248
Ashurst, Sen. Henry F., 561, 623-4
Astoria, 221-2

Washington
Adams
Jefferson
Madison
Monroe
Adams
Jackson
Van Buren
Harrison
Tyler
Polk
Taylor
Fillmore
Pierce
Buchanan
Lincoln
Johnson
Grant
Hayes
Garfield
Arthur
Cleveland
Harrison
Cleveland
McKinley
Roosevelt
Taft
Wilson
Harding
Coolidge
Hoover
Roosevelt
Truman
Eisenhower
Kennedy
Johnson
Nixon
Ford
Carter
Reagan

The United States and Its P

☆ Guam   **United States Possessions**

★ Trinidad   **Base sites leased from Gt. Britain, 1940**

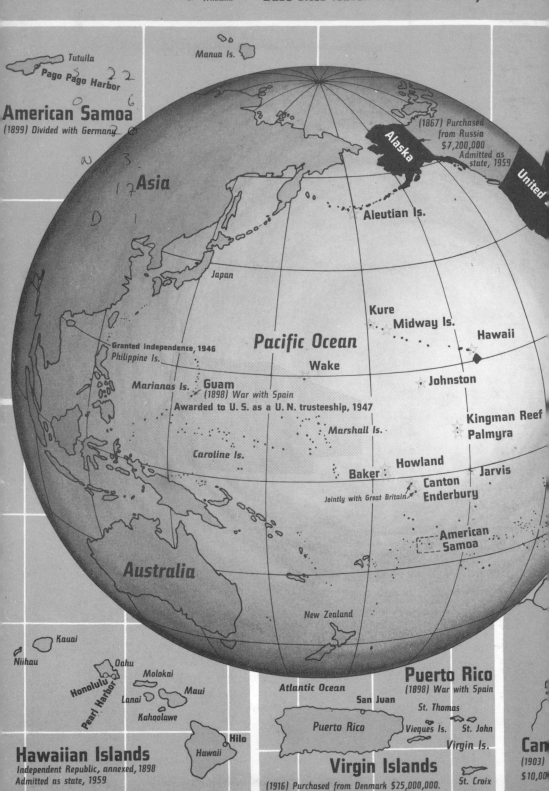

Manua Is.

Tutuila
Pago Pago Harbor

American Samoa
(1899) Divided with Germany

Alaska
(1867) Purchased from Russia $7,200,000 Admitted as state, 1959

United

Asia

Aleutian Is.

Japan

Kure
Midway Is.
Hawaii

Pacific Ocean

Granted Independence, 1946
Philippine Is.

Wake

Johnston

Marianas Is. **Guam**
(1898) War with Spain
Awarded to U.S. as a U.N. trusteeship, 1947

Kingman Reef
Palmyra

Marshall Is.

Caroline Is.

Howland
Baker   Jarvis

Canton
Jointly with Great Britain   Enderbury

Australia

American
Samoa

New Zealand

Kauai
Niihau
Oahu
Honolulu
Pearl Harbor
Lanai
Molokai
Maui
Kahoolawe
Hilo
Hawaii

Puerto Rico
(1898) War with Spain

Atlantic Ocean
San Juan
St. Thomas
St. John
Puerto Rico
Vieques Is.
Virgin Is.

Hawaiian Islands
Independent Republic, annexed, 1898
Admitted as state, 1959

Virgin Islands
(1916) Purchased from Denmark $25,000,000.

St. Croix

Can
(1903)
$10,00